NATIONAL GALLERY OF ART

KRESS FOUNDATION STUDIES

IN THE HISTORY OF EUROPEAN ART

NUMBER TWO

FRENCH PAINTING IN THE TIME OF JEAN DE BERRY

THE LATE FOURTEENTH CENTURY AND THE PATRONAGE OF THE DUKE

BY MILLARD MEISS

PHAIDON

Parement Master and Workshop: *Annunciation*. Paris, Bibl. nat., nouv. acq. lat. 3093, p.2

FRENCH PAINTING IN THE TIME OF JEAN DE BERRY

BY MILLARD MEISS

THE LATE FOURTEENTH CENTURY
AND THE PATRONAGE OF THE DUKE

TEXT VOLUME

PHAIDON

PHAIDON PRESS LTD · 5 CROMWELL PLACE · LONDON SW7

PHAIDON PUBLISHERS INC · 111 FOURTH AVENUE · NEW YORK · NY 10003

1967

TO MY WIFE

GB STANDARD BOOK NUMBER: 7148 1309 5

US LIBRARY OF CONGRESS CATALOG CARD NUMBER: 67-29885

US DISTRIBUTORS: FREDERICK A PRAEGER INC · 111 FOURTH AVENUE · NEW YORK · NY 10003

PRINTED BY R. & R. CLARK LTD · EDINBURGH

MADE IN GREAT BRITAIN

Contents

PREFACE   VII

I. INTRODUCTION   3
Painters and Workshops [3]   New Texts and Images [13]   The French Forerunners [18]   Italian Painters and Paintings in France [23]

II. THE LIFE OF JEAN DE BERRY   30

III. JEAN DE BERRY AS PATRON   36
The Buildings [36]   The Inventories [40]   Artists in the Duke's Service [43]   Agents and Dealers [45]   Gifts [48]   Precious Stones and *Joyaux* [50]   Cameos, Coins, and Medals [52]   Tapestries, Wall Hangings, and Embroideries [58]   Panel Paintings [61]   Pierre de Vérone, Librarian [63]   Appendix – Documents on Petrus de Sacco de Verona [66]

IV. THE PORTRAITS OF JEAN DE BERRY   68
The Varied Representations [68]   The Styles of the Portraits [77]   Features and Dress [79]   Appendix A. Iconographic Table of Jean de Berry [82]   Appendix B. Catalogue of Portraits; Possible Representations; Problematic and Rejected Representations [82]

V. THE ARMS AND EMBLEMS OF JEAN DE BERRY   95
Table of the Arms of Jean de Berry [98]

VI. THE PAREMENT MASTER   99
The *Parement de Narbonne* [99]   Early History of the *Très Belles Heures de Notre-Dame* [107]   Authorship [112]   Tradition and Innovation [119]   The Nude Figure [125]   Connections with Bohemia [130]   Table of Works of the Painters [134]

VII. BEAUNEVEU AND THE DUKE'S PSALTER   135
The Prophets and Apostles [135]   The New Color [140]   Beauneveu and his Circle [147]   The Role of Jacquemart and Pseudo-Jacquemart [151]

VIII. *PETITES HEURES*   155
Early History and Recent Opinions [155]   The Passion Master [160]   Jacquemart de Hesdin [169]   The Trinity Master [176]   Pseudo-Jacquemart [179]   Collation of the Manuscript [192]   Table of Painters of the *Petites Heures* [192]

IX. THE VATICAN BIBLE AND THE BRUSSELS HOURS   194

The *Vatican Bible* [194]   The *Brussels Hours*—Early History [198]   The Initial Diptych [202]   The Miniatures by Jacquemart [209]   Landscape and Interior [218] The Career of Jacquemart [223]

X. THE MASTER OF THE BRUSSELS INITIALS   229

The Problem of Identification [229]   The Illuminator and His Collaborators [230] Chronology in France and Italy [242]

XI. THE SECOND CAMPAIGN ON THE *TRÈS BELLES HEURES DE NOTRE-DAME*   247

The Flemish Episode [247]   The Holy Ghost Master [253]

XII. *GRANDES HEURES*   256

The Surviving Manuscript [256]   The Original Manuscript [265]   The Problem of Jacquemart's Late Work [270]   Appendix A. Table of Painters of the *Grandes Heures* [281]   Appendix B. Gatherings, Inserted Sheets, and Missing Miniatures [282]

XIII. THE LIBRARY OF JEAN DE BERRY   287

The Texts [287]   The Duke as Bibliophile [290]   The Duke's Taste [298] Appendix. List of the Extant Illuminated Manuscripts; Doubtful and Erroneous Ascriptions [309]

XIV. CATALOGUE OF MANUSCRIPTS   319

XV. TABLES   345

Historical Events; Genealogy; Jean de Berry's Children

XVI. THE VALOIS AND VISCONTI INVENTORIES   352

XVII. SOME REINTEGRATED FRENCH WORKSHOPS OF THE EARLY FIFTEENTH CENTURY   354

NOTES TO THE TEXT   362

BIBLIOGRAPHY   408

INDEX   435

Preface

THREE decades ago I turned to French manuscripts after several years of exclusive concern with Italian panel and mural painting. I was attracted by the relative spontaneity of illumination, by its fresh color, and its freedom from the alterations, losses and repair that mar most paintings of larger size. Paintings in books more consistently give one a better notion of what their creators wanted. They are often also far more varied in subject, and, given the almost complete loss of large-scale secular painting, they preserve for us something of this rather novel and increasingly important branch of the art of the late Middle Ages.

I confess that from time to time, when peering at these minute masterpieces, only three or four inches high, I have felt like an architect trying to get on with a watchmaker's job, and I have thought wistfully of the days when I was regularly concerned with frescoes forty feet long. Still, scale is not everything – the monument of Victor Emmanuel II in Rome proves that. And paintings in books offer the scholar certain simple, practical advantages. He can study them while he is seated comfortably in a chair. After long hours standing in galleries or in high, narrow, poorly-lit chapels one comes to value greatly this form of *Sitzkritik*.

Three decades is a long time even for intermittent concern with a subject, but in certain respects it is probably not long enough. A much shorter version of this history was approaching completion in 1956. When a friend told a French colleague of the present larger plan he exclaimed: 'Mais c'est impossible. Il ne finira jamais!' This estimate was probably not wrong. Difficulties there have been and will be. For one thing, access to surviving objects is far less easily gained by the historian of illumination than by students of painting, drawing, or other arts. Miniatures that will modify in one way or another the conclusions of this book remain to be discovered. If specialists were occasionally given the privilege of inspecting manuscripts on the shelves of libraries progress in the history of illumination would be greatly quickened.

The study of paintings in books is inherently intricate. A mural painting has – or at least had until the recent technical advances in detachment – only one face. A panel normally has in addition a back. When you have seen one or both you have seen what is to be seen. The immediate context of a miniature is a very different thing. The script and the parchment, the text or the texts, the Calendar and the saints, the gatherings, the colophon – all may contain vital information about the painting. Late medieval French illumination, furthermore, presents special difficulties. The number of extant manuscripts is great, and most of them have been little studied in the past. The situation is paradoxical: there is almost too much evidence, too many ascertainable facts.

In these circumstances monographs might seem to be preferable to a general history. Paul Durrieu followed this course in his great work on the Boucicaut Master, and Adelheid Heimann in her pioneering article on the Rohan Master. I soon observed, however, that the paintings of the major artists around 1400 were interrelated to an exceptional degree, partly because of the very rapid changes of style at this time and partly because of the common practice of collaboration. In a period notorious for scanty documentation many of the more refractory problems might, it seemed, be solved by comprehensive study, despite all its risks. Such study seemed to provide, furthermore, a better opportunity for the development of a method, or rather for the accumulation of sufficient knowledge of such matters as the range of a painter or a workshop and of the conventions of collaboration to permit a more valid reading of the evidence. In the study of this art as of others the use of the 'eye' alone, while fundamental, is not enough.

Comprehensive approach was indicated also by my recognition soon after beginning these studies that the library formed by Jean de Berry was itself an institution. The manuscripts contained in it had an effect upon the manuscripts that the Duke subsequently commissioned. Still more important appeared to be the general influence upon painting of this remarkable patron, 'der erste moderne Kunstfreund in grossem Stile', in the words of Julius von Schlosser. His taste, clear in his choice of artists as well as in his purchases and commissions, seemed unusually consistent over a period of nearly forty years. No patron of his time, and few before or after him, had a comparable effect upon the arts. I believe no-one will contest the statement – though it has not I think previously been made – that between about 1380 and 1400 every great cycle of miniatures in France was commissioned by the Duke of Berry. After 1400 the works he bought or ordered were not quite so unique, but he remained an unrivalled connoisseur until his death in 1416.

The thirty-six years of Jean de Berry's most active patronage coincide with what Jean Porcher (Paris, Bibl. nat. [Porcher], 1955, p. 51) has called '. . . la période la plus confuse, et aussi peut-être la plus riche de la peinture médiévale française'. Only one outstanding illuminator, the Rohan Master, came to maturity shortly after the Duke's death. The name Jean de Berry therefore appears in the title of this publication – a name far more significant for the arts than that of his nephew King Charles VI, whose reign from 1380 to 1422 had similar chronological limits. The primacy of the Duke did not extend to all the arts. His buildings in Bourges, Mehun-sur-Yèvre, Poitiers and Riom were outstanding. On the other hand his brother, Philippe le Hardi, certainly employed the greatest sculptor of the time, Claus Sluter, and as far as we can nowadays judge, the succession of Jean de Beaumetz and Jean Malouel as painters of panels and other large-scale works at the Court of Burgundy was not matched at the Court of Berry. For these reasons, and also perhaps because of the efflorescence of panel painting under Philippe le Bon after 1419, the art of the late fourteenth and early fifteenth centuries is often identified with Burgundy. Since illumination was then not a minor but a major art, and in it Berry was supreme, the present work aims to redress the balance. Paris too emerges further from the shadow of Dijon as an important artistic center.

While there was normally a relation throughout the Middle Ages between large- and small-scale painting, the Duke of Berry broke down the barriers in an unusual way. He gave commissions for miniatures to painters and to at least one artist who normally worked in other media and on a different scale. The title of this publication refers to French painting rather than illumination, and though it is perforce largely concerned with miniatures, the few surviving panels, the fragments of murals, and the relevant stained glass are introduced at appropriate places. Apart from the monographs on a few manuscripts only a portion of even the best miniatures has been reproduced before, and then often from negatives made from 1933 on for this publication but deposited in the photographic archives of the Bibliothèque nationale, the British Museum or elsewhere, and thus available over the years to other historians. The book has therefore been useful to the discipline a long time before its publication. It contains reproductions of all the miniatures in the important manuscripts. They appear on the plates in their original sequence. The comparative illustrations follow.

The state of our knowledge of this art indicated also the usefulness – as I saw it the necessity – of a comprehensive effort to establish the 'text', to distinguish the styles and determine their sequence. Basic contributions in this realm were made a century ago by the incomparable Léopold Delisle, who initiated scholarly study of this period. He was followed a generation later by Paul Durrieu and Georges Hulin de Loo, and more recently by several historians, above all Erwin Panofsky who laid down, I think definitively, some of the main lines of the development. Still, we know less about this art than we knew about Italian Trecento painting half a century ago.

Historians have on the whole given more attention to the artistic conventions of the period than to the departures from them. The diffusion of these conventions throughout most of Europe has been the subject of well-known studies, beginning with Courajod around 1890. The concepts of an International Style, of a Courtly Style, or of the *Weiche Stil*, while well founded, have nevertheless tended to mask regional and personal distinctiveness. As late as 1962 the impressive exhibition in Vienna of *Europäische Kunst um 1400* suggested the limiting power of these broad historical concepts. The great artists of the time – the Boucicaut Master, the Limbourgs, and Claus Sluter – were either inadequately represented or inadequately displayed. The present publication is much concerned with the uniqueness of the major works, but of course individuality can be distinguished only against the background of convention and tradition, iconographic as well as formal.

Given the nature of the book, questions of date and authorship are discussed in the main text, along with interpretations of other kinds. Though historians may thus find parts of the book especially intricate, the titles given to the sections of each chapter will facilitate selective reading. The entries in the *catalogue raisonné*, furthermore, contain summaries of the argument about time and 'place'. Each catalogue entry normally contains also a list of all the miniatures in the manuscript, exclusive of small initials, Calendar pictures in Books of Hours, and the like.

Ideally the content of this study of French painting would see the light all at once and between two – or at most four – covers. Even the huge, unwieldy tomes frequent nowadays would still, however, not be large enough, and for such a monster readers would need the muscles of Michelangelo's sibyls. Given such limitations – not to mention the stamina of the author – it has seemed better to effect more or less arbitrary fractures of what is clearly continuous and unified. We are, however, accustomed to such mistreatment of history in large-scale publications. Some compensation may be found in the fact that each volume has a certain unity, or at least a distinctive profile. The Duke of Berry hovers over this first volume of text and the second of plates. While these volumes are devoted primarily to the period 1380–1400, they include the late work, in the following decade, of Jacquemart de Hesdin and other painters who first appeared around 1380. The bibliography printed in this volume is comprehensive; in subsequent volumes the essential relevant works will be listed again, together with some additions. The next two volumes will be devoted respectively to the Boucicaut Master and his workshop and to the numerous Parisian workshops that became active around 1400, many of which I reintegrated and listed in 1956. The final volume will be reserved for the Limbourgs and the Rohan Master. It will also bring together the comments on some larger questions broached in the preceding volumes.

This publication has had the advantage of the interest and generous help of many persons and institutions. Long ago Miss Helen Clay Frick gave me the privilege of commissioning photographs, which were added to the great library of photographs of illuminated manuscripts that she has built. The staff of the library, especially Mrs. Henry Howell, the librarian, and Miss Mildred Steinbach have for many years facilitated my work. The subtleties of small miniatures painted on uneven surfaces are notoriously difficult to capture in photographs. Since 1959, when this publication took final shape, some of the best miniatures in Parisian libraries have been expressly photographed with exceptional skill and care by M. Georges Routhier. All negatives made by him for this history will eventually be deposited in the archive of the Bibliothèque nationale. This arrangement is only one of the ways in which the late Jean Porcher, Conservateur of the Département des Manuscrits, and now his successor, Marcel Thomas, have helped to make this book useful.

Many directors of libraries or keepers of manuscripts, and several friends, have generously participated in the collecting of more or less elusive photographs: Frederick B. Adams, Diego Angulo-Iñiguez, Jean-Pierre Babelon, Janet Backhouse, Germain Bazin, Pedro Bohigas, William H. Bond, Comte Raoul de Broglie, Julian Brown, the late Walter W. S. Cook, Paul Cravayat, Jean Favière, Margaret Freeman, Carmen Gomez-Moreno, José Gudiol, W. O. Hassall, Michèle Hébert, R. W. Hunt, Peter Kidson, Anne-Marie Pfister, John Plummer, C. Poupardin, Nicole Reynaud, Gerhard Schmidt, Ernst Schuselka, Ellen Shaffer, Erich Steingraeber, and George Zarnecki.

Everywhere private owners of manuscripts have responded to my requests for study or for photographs. I am grateful to L. V. Randall, Otto H. Ranschburg, and Lessing Rosenwald. Only Martin Bodmer, who informs me as he has other historians that his library on principle gives photographs to no-one, has made it necessary to reproduce miniatures of a splendid manuscript in his possession from old reproductions printed before he acquired it.

To list the colleagues who have contributed to this work in one way or another leads me to reminisce about many friendships and years of pleasant professional associations: Marie-Thérèse d'Alverny was unfailingly helpful both in and outside the Bibliothèque nationale. Catherine Gauchery Grodecki guided me through the mazes leading to the seals of Jean de Berry. I feel grateful also to Andrew Alföldi, Sylvie Béguin, Hugo Buchthal, Marthe Dulong, Helen M. Franc, Marie-Madeleine Gauthier, Rosalie Green, William Heckscher, Ernst Kitzinger, Françoise Isaac, Y. Jenny, Victor Lasareff, R. P. Marichal, M. Pecqueur, Ugo Procacci, Jean-Yves Ribault, Willibald Sauerlaender, Henri Seyrig, Eleanor Spencer, Charles Sterling, Vittorio Viale, J. Vielliard, Marie-Louise Vollenweider, Francis Wormald, and above all to Erwin Panofsky, in whose seminar this study really began. Dorothy Miner read half of the book with the wonderful curiosity and disinterestedness that are characteristic of her, and I am thankful to her for several good suggestions.

By a surprising and very agreeable coincidence these volumes will be published only a few months after the appearance of the first biography of the Duke of Berry. Early in 1965 its author, Mlle Françoise Lehoux, and I exchanged a few thoughts, and during an exciting week in Paris she permitted me to read the typescript of her brilliantly detailed and lucid biography, *Jean de France, duc de Berri. Sa vie. Son action politique. 1340–1416*. Since Mlle Lehoux touches only in passing on the Duke's patronage of art, our respective publications are complementary. My numerous references to her biography are perforce limited to citations of the relevant chapters.

I owe much to those persons who at various times contributed to the preparation of this text: Fritzie P. Manuel, Deirdre Roskill, Mary Schaefer, and Gerda Soergel Panofsky. Gertrude Coor, Kathleen Morand and Sharon Off Katić worked with me for longer periods; they gave the book, and especially the catalogue, the benefit of their scholarly experience, Mrs. Coor with Italian painting, Mrs. Katić and Mrs. Morand with French. I recall with deep sadness that Mrs. Coor, though still a young woman, died while engaged in this work.

I would not know how to thank Edith W. Kirsch, whose contribution to the book has been indispensable. From the beginning my wife has acted as critic and associate, particularly during our journeys in Europe and the United States. She has done this cheerfully even though she has, for interesting reasons, consistently been opposed to the whole affair. Now that the job is mostly done I hope she will become reconciled to the result.

The Institute for Advanced Study, Princeton   M. M.
New Year, 1966

FRENCH PAINTING
IN THE TIME
OF JEAN DE BERRY

I

Introduction

1 · PAINTERS AND WORKSHOPS

L ong before the late fourteenth century Paris excelled in illumination. We know it from surviving manuscripts – the *Psalter of St. Louis*, the miniatures of Honoré – and we are told it
by contemporary judges. Dante paid tribute to its eminence in the well-known lines referring
to 'quell'arte ch'alluminar chiamata è in Parisi'.[1] Around 1400 when a certain Alcherius, of whom
we shall speak later, was compiling a treatise on technique, he consulted two masters in Paris who
devoted themselves in part at least to painting in books. In 1406 Christine de Pisan, an author who
regularly commissioned illustrated copies of her many writings, heaped praise on the Parisian
masters, then for a century predominantly secular rather than monastic, but she accompanied it
with a call for reform of their mode of life. This remarkable but little-known passage, the forerunner of innumerable later attacks on artists as Bohemians, is worth quoting in its entirety:

> Among these masters . . . some who are very skillful – more skillful I think than those commonly found
> elsewhere – are in Paris, and this is a very fine and remarkable thing. . . . But, to speak briefly of their
> way of life, would that it pleased God and especially the artists themselves (for surely it would please God)
> that their lives were more temperate and not so lenient as they are now: for the excesses and luxuries in
> which they habitually indulge in Paris may bring many illnesses and misfortunes upon them . . .[2]

A year or so earlier, in chapter 41 of the first book of the *Cité des dames*, Christine referred to
Parisian painters and illuminators – the best in the world, she said – as a prelude to a eulogy of an
eminent female representative of the art. Hoping, like contemporary humanists, to advance a
cause dear to her heart by adducing ancient precedents, Christine persuades *Raison* to recount the
contribution of women to the arts and culture of antiquity. *Raison* cites, among other accomplished ladies, several painters. Thus, speaking as a sort of 'end man' – or perhaps I should say 'end
woman' – she sets the stage for Christine, who at once forcefully replies that things were better
then than now. But, she adds,

> with regard to painting at the present time I know a woman called Anastaise, who is so skillful and
> experienced in painting the borders of manuscripts and the backgrounds of miniatures that no one can cite
> a craftsman in the city of Paris, the center of the best illuminators on earth, who in these endeavors
> surpasses her in any way. . . . And this I know by my own experience, for she has produced some things
> for me which are held to be outstanding among the ornamental borders of the great masters.[3]

Though the significance of Christine's definition of the specialty of Anastaise is not immediately
clear – we shall return to it later – the poet obviously thought very well of the illuminator. Now
painters and illuminators of the feminine sex must have been rare in the Middle Ages, and any
woman who made bold to practice these crafts certainly knew what to expect. Even in the sixteenth century, when Albrecht Dürer decided to buy a leaf illuminated by a young woman, he
carefully recorded in his diary a payment of one florin for it, and added: 'Ist ein gross Wunder

dass ein Weibsbild also viel machen soll'.[4] Occasionally nevertheless a woman did take up the brush, particularly in families where there was a man practising the same art. Thus Jean le Noir, perhaps identical, as we shall see, with the Passion Master, had a daughter who was an 'enlumineresse'.[5] While Christine was not aware of this rather recent example, she did know – so dependent is the reputation of painters upon writers – of their predecessors in remote antiquity. She had learned of three female painters – Thamar, Marcia, and Irene – from Boccaccio's treatise on famous ladies in history, *De mulieribus claris*. Though he nowhere says so Boccaccio in turn had become aware of these three women from a passage on female artists in Pliny's *Natural History*.[6] It was clearly Pliny who launched them on their long journey into the Trecento and the modern world. It was, however, in the 'Gothic' North that they first assumed visible form. In manuscripts of a French translation of Boccaccio's text completed by 1402 we see them plying their craft.

The best miniatures in this unprecedented series of representations of painters at work are in copies of *Cleres et nobles femmes* received by Philippe le Hardi in 1403 and Jean de Berry early in 1404. One of the women described by Pliny was Marcia (*recte* Iaia), who 'painted a portrait of herself with a looking glass. No-one else had a quicker hand in painting, while her artistic skill was such that in the prices she obtained she far outdid the most celebrated portrait painters of the time.' In the two early French manuscripts we see Marcia engaged in painting her own portrait, working with the aid of a small mirror (Figs. 287, 289). These are the first easel portraits showing sitters in frontal position that have come down to us. In the Duke of Berry's manuscript (Fig. 289) the mirror is affixed to the wall, and the sculptor's chisels on the bench near Marcia evidently allude to her versatility.

Pliny had presented Marcia simply as a painteress, but in Boccaccio's text she becomes notable for a second commitment: to perpetual virginity. Pliny had remarked in passing simply that Marcia never married. Boccaccio heaped praise on her for this, and then, not wishing anyone to infer that chastity was a boon to art, he conjured up a serious conflict. Marcia, he states, often portrayed women but never men. 'Modesty was the cause of this, because the ancients mostly figured people nude, so that Marcia would either have had to render men imperfect, or if perfect, she would have been obliged to abandon the modesty of a virgin.' In a woodcut in a German translation of Boccaccio's book published at Ulm in 1473 Marcia has become a nun, and she paints a picture of, perhaps, the Madonna (Fig. 288).

A second painter of this group, Thamar (*recte* Timarete) painted according to Pliny and Boccaccio a number of public images, among them a *Diana* venerated in Ephesus. In Burgundy's fine manuscript, however, Thamar paints a Madonna (Fig. 290)![7] She is given an almost Vasarian introduction: 'en son temps et en son aage fut tres noble paintreresse'. Beautifully gowned, she has a good stock of colors and brushes, an escalloped palette and a young assistant who grinds colors. In the illustration of the same text made for Jean de Berry by a related master, the panel of the half-length Madonna has a round arch, Thamar is alone, and she no longer works in an interior (without walls) but in a walled garden under a canopy (Fig. 291).

According to Boccaccio Irene was, like Thamar, the daughter of a painter. She even surpassed her father in his craft, which is usually 'rimossa da ingeno di femmina'. Especially notable were her portrayals of a gladiator and a jumper. In the miniature in Burgundy's *Boccace*, however, she too becomes a Christian painter and puts the finishing touches of color on a statue of the Madonna, while on the table behind there is a completed image of the *Sacra Facies* (Fig. 292). In the Duke of Berry's manuscript she completes the Holy Face, which composes one leaf of a diptych (Fig. 294). In all these miniatures as in the relief of *Painting* in the Florentine Campanile[8] and other medieval representations the painters are intently occupied with the execution of a picture. In the Renaissance, when the idea of the craftsman had been replaced by that of the cultivated artist, the ancient *peinteresses* assume a very different form. In a copy of Boccaccio's text printed in Venice in 1506, for instance, Irene is given a formal posture; she faces us, declaiming like an orator (Fig. 293).

It is a pungent fact that a Roman natural history should have provided the main reason for an unprecedented series of pictures of painters fourteen hundred years later. Since the ladies are presented as heroines of the brush their workshops are no doubt tidier than those of contemporary painters, but the instruments and materials, like the subjects that engage them, must correspond. The use of the mirror was inspired by the text of Boccaccio and ultimately by Pliny; it was indeed Pliny who gave rise to the story – perhaps even the fact – of the self-portrait Giotto made with the help of a mirror.[9]

One kind of optical equipment we might have expected to see in the miniatures is lacking: a magnifying glass or a pair of spectacles. The former was known in antiquity and Roger Bacon refers to it in the mid thirteenth century, while spectacles, invented around 1300, were manufactured by the Venetians on a rapidly expanding scale during the fourteenth century.[10] One of the Dominicans, Hugh of Provence, in Tommaso da Modena's Treviso frescoes of 1352 wears spectacles, another uses a magnifying glass (Fig. 295). Not long afterward in French illumination the great Christian writers of the past begin to depend upon such equipment. Spectacles rest comfortably on the nose of St. Luke in a Missal around 1400, whereas in a later Book of Hours St. Matthew has to hold them in place, like lorgnettes (Figs. 296, 297). When not in use the 'lunettes' of Philippe le Hardi reposed, from 1403 on, in a silver case attached to his lectern.[11] A year earlier his sculptor, Claus Sluter, had a pair of copper spectacles put on the nose of one of the stone prophets in the 'Puits de Moïse'.[12] Mercury too reads better with them (Fig. 826).

These instruments, a great boon to readers and writers, would have been still more useful to painters of small panels and above all to illuminators. What we see in miniatures of the time as areas of rich, vibrant color often turn out to be, under magnification, a network of tiny strokes of different hues, laid neatly and with obvious control side by side. Youthful eyes can be trained for this kind of fine work, but they do not remain young. Spectacles and magnifying glasses would have been enormously helpful, and the availability of them probably facilitated the development in this period of an art of exquisite finish and microscopic form. They may even have contributed to the high favor bestowed on the miniature in books and on the very small panel. Surely these instruments enabled aging patrons such as Jean de Berry, Philippe le Hardi or his grandson Philippe le Bon to respond with greater excitement to the marvelous microcosms of the Limbourgs or of Jan van Eyck.

A history that aims in part to place a large group of paintings in time and space, to ascertain their authors and to re-establish the sequence of pictorial events, is bound to omit a very high percentage of the evidence upon which its conclusions are based. To include much more would be an intolerable bore for the reader (not to mention the writer), and yet even then too little would be offered for connoisseurs, not to mention historians who lack experience in these particular methods. Scholars thus have a tacit agreement to limit their 'proof' to a few indicative signs, and assume or at least hope that interested and qualified readers will discover the rest. Their work in this domain resembles an iceberg; only a small part of it comes into view. Still, the problems of rediscovering the main threads of pictorial history vary somewhat from age to age; they are bound up with the extent of our knowledge about artists and with the changing modes of production. Something therefore must be said about these matters at the outset.

Though the degree of difference between the stronger styles increased in the later fourteenth century in France and the pace of stylistic change quickened, painters rarely took occasion to identify themselves and to proclaim their individuality by signing their works. Not one extant panel bears a painter's name, and signatures in books are very rare. In this respect French masters did not follow Italian example, for Trecento panels are not infrequently signed; and while even in Italy illumination preserved during this period a more traditional, collective character, at least one master, Niccolò da Bologna, often put his name on his full-page miniatures. Dante's famous lines about Franco and Oderisi bear witness to the awareness of individual accomplishment in this art,[13] and if similar observations were not recorded later in the century, that was largely due to the fact that Italian illumination, unlike French, was overshadowed by panel and mural painting.

Two outstanding masters working in France did introduce a *me pinxit* into books on which they had worked. It is not surprising that the first of these should have been Jean Pucelle, the first great student of Trecento art in Northern Europe. A colophon in minuscule red script at the end of the *Bible de Robert de Billyng* reads: 'Jehan Pucelle, Anciau de Cens, Jaquet Maci, il hont en-luminé ce livre ci'.[14] The date, 1327, follows. The next instance is not properly described as a signature. It is an inscription in large gold letters on the first verso of a Bible (the recto is blank); it thus faces a miniature of the presentation of the book to King Charles V (Fig. 382).[15] The inscription informs us that the manuscript was illuminated for the King, and that John of Bruges – and only John of Bruges – painted the picture opposite: 'fecit hanc picturam propria manu'. In content, scale and place the inscription is unprecedented, even in Trecento art, with which the painter was familiar though he did not share Pucelle's great enthusiasm for it. Probably the bold-ness of the statement owed much to the serious intellectual interests of the King and the sense of the importance of books with which he no doubt imbued their producers.[16]

Curiously the example of neither Pucelle nor Bondol was followed in the great period of French illumination from 1380 to 1425. Documentation of other kinds about the persons responsible for the works is not plentiful but we do possess some, thanks mostly to the Duke of Berry and his remarkable 'registrar', Robinet d'Estampes. Robinet's inventories name a few painters – Beau-neveu, Jacquemart de Hesdin, Paul de Limbourg and his brothers, even Pucelle – and the entries give us sufficient details to link them with the miniatures in certain extant manuscripts. In addi-tion, documents of payment by Philippe le Hardi to two of the Limbourg brothers probably but not certainly refer to a *Bible moralisée* in the Bibliothèque nationale (Fig. 781).[17] For the authors of extant manuscripts that is all we have. Identification of some of the very few extant panel paintings has progressed in the last few years. Thanks to Charles Sterling we now know two panels by the painter of Philippe le Hardi, Jean de Beaumetz (Fig. 831);[18] Madame Nichole Reynaud has provided documentary proof for the view, already advanced by the writer for stylistic reasons, that Henri Bellechose alone painted the *Martyrdom of St. Denis* in the Louvre;[19] and the writer and Colin Eisler together have offered 'external' evidence for the ascription of the newly discovered *Madonna* in Berlin to the successor of Beaumetz, Jean Malouel.[20]

By a curious turn of fate most of the inscriptions and the written records, whether documents of payment or inventories, identify only *one* work by each of the above artists. Probably a second cycle is documented for two of the Limbourgs, and we may possess a fragment of a second documented cycle by Jacquemart de Hesdin. The connection (established by records) of Pucelle and Bondol with additional works is clouded by the documented – and quite visible – participation of collaborators. Certainties about the range of a painter's style in this period are therefore exceedingly scanty, and since the degree of transformation of an artist's manner is in part a historical phenomenon the difficulties of reintegrating the major œuvres are greatly increased. In such circumstances historians bear special burdens but they are not without resources. They can proceed, as indeed they must always to some extent do, by inference from analogous instances in other, more adequately documented arts. The writer has drawn upon his experience with approximately contemporary Italian painting – not Italian illumination, about which our knowledge is still limited, but panel and mural painting, about which we are relatively well informed.

The nature of creativity in Italian monumental painting was not so different as one might at first suppose from that in French illumination because the two arts were historically linked; the painters of French miniatures in this period studied Italian panels and murals with increasing interest and knowledge. Painting in books was not, moreover, a decisively secondary art in France as it was, with the exception of Visconti Milan, in Italy. Of course the Revolution destroyed a large part of France's heritage of medieval panel and mural painting, but the records that survive, the documents and the inventories of the kings and princes, do not suggest a production similar to the Italian. In any event quantity is not crucial; what counted was the enthusiasm for the art, and it seems abundantly proved that Jean de Berry and Philippe le Hardi loved pictures in books, and the former at least thought the task worthy of the efforts of the best painters. Under the stimulus of such an evaluation the kind of individuality called forth by the evolution of Trecento panel and mural painting emerged in France in the book.

From the Duke of Berry's inventories we learn that certain manuscripts, or sections of manuscripts, were considered to be the work of one painter. Apart from the Book of Hours called the *Heures de Pucelle* the inventories state that the prophets and apostles at the beginning of the Duke's *Psalter* are 'de la main maistre André Beaunepveu', and the miniatures in a Book of Hours, now in Brussels, 'de la main Jaquemart de Odin'. On the other hand the *Grandes Heures* are declared to be the work of 'Jacquemart et autres ouvriers' and the *Très Riches Heures* by 'Pol (de Limbourg) et ses frères'. All these statements conform well enough, as we shall see, with the visual evidence, and Robinet d'Estampes, the compiler of the inventories, was so remarkably well-informed and scrupulous about all other matters that it would be surprising if he were less so about the authorship of the major manuscripts. Thus occasionally one painter was exclusively or largely responsible for miniatures in part or in all of an important manuscript for the Duke[21] but two or more painters might work together. We possess records of two instances of a similar association for the illumination of manuscripts commissioned by Philippe le Hardi. In the last two years before his death three painters (Jacques Coene, Imbert Stanier, and Haincelin de Haguenau) were working for him on one large Bible while another was entrusted to two of the Limbourg brothers, Jean and Paul.[22]

In Italy two or three painters frequently formed an association. Numerous Trecento altarpieces are signed by two or occasionally three collaborators. Companies were not uncommon even in the fifteenth century, and, as Procacci has shown, they were usually based on agreements for a three-year period.[23] Often the associates continued to work in separate shops. The major painters in France who obtained appointments at the courts had much less need of the mutual economic protection provided by such companies. When they collaborated with other masters on large enterprises they acted as directors. Thus in 1388 Jean de Beaumetz was directing two ateliers, each of three or more painters,[24] and while much of the work they were doing was decorative, the use of associates or assistants for more demanding enterprises is clearly indicated.

We possess little information about individual illuminators beyond the statements and records mentioned above. The best ones who worked for the market or on commission had shops in Paris, and, like the scribes, they were licensed by the university. A few apparently belonged to the general guild of the painters, sculptors, and writers, established in the thirteenth century, but they never formed a company of their own.[25] The painters, however, joined with the sculptors in 1391 to form a Company of St. Luke.[26] Another possibility was open to painters and illuminators of this period. As early as 1304 we hear of the special position of 'peintre du roi', and later in the century the queen and each of the Valois dukes had one or more *peintres* with official titles, salaries, and what we would call fringe benefits, such as a place in which to live and work.[27] A few painters and illuminators, Paul de Limbourg for instance, achieved the position at court of *valet de chambre*, a position that could be overestimated unless one recalls that tailors, butchers, and other craftsmen were sometimes elevated to the same rank.[28] We know, however, from the exchange of gifts that the relationship between Paul and his patron was exceptionally close.

On the whole these salaried masters enjoyed privileges not obtained by those painters who were dependent on the vagaries of commissions or sales. They had a certain security – at the court of Berry it often seemed to amount to life tenure – and especially the illuminators were given the time to produce more thoughtful, finished work. Jean Porcher has made the very interesting proposal that the difference between the magnificent painting of the Rohan Master in the *Heures de Rohan* or similar manuscripts and earlier, slighter miniatures in a related style may be explained in part by the contrast between production for the market and production for a wealthy, highly cultivated employer.[29]

The relationship of the great patrons with the illuminators varied considerably. Jean de Berry was closest to them, as we shall see, and his best manuscripts were painted by his own employees. The Dukes of Burgundy, Philippe le Hardi and Jean sans Peur, relied more on commissions, and then often through agents, especially the great banker and merchant Jacques Raponde.[30] All the princes, Berry included, acquired manuscripts from the *stationnaires* ('publishers') and the *libraires* (booksellers). Sometimes they gave commissions to these dealers instead of taking what was in stock. On the whole the best and most richly illuminated manuscripts were not acquired in this way.

The kinds of collaboration between illuminators indicated by the records is confirmed by the extant manuscripts, which disclose forms of association ranging from the participation of an assistant or two of the chief master in the execution but not the designing of the miniatures – as in the case of the *Brussels Hours* – to the joint endeavors of two or three diverse masters who worked independently of one another. Even the favorite painters of the Duke of Berry, the Limbourg brothers, allocated several initials in the *Très Riches Heures* to another master, presumably in order to give all their time to the miniatures themselves.[31] The relationship between illuminators was especially complex in manuscripts painted for Jean de Berry; frequently two masters worked on the same folio, as we shall see, or even on the same small miniature.

Some kinds of association are of course more readily recognizable than others. The execution of initials in the *Très Riches Heures* by the Master of the Bréviaire de Jean sans Peur is apparent, but the borderlines between the contributions of the three Limbourg brothers to the miniatures of this manuscript are notoriously difficult to define. We can usually see that assistants executed the Calendar of a manuscript or the drolleries, normally considered subordinate parts. Much more difficult is of course the definition of the role of assistants when they shared the execution with a leading master – when for instance they laid in the ground colors and the *chef* then completed the forms. It is a moot question whether this kind of collaboration was more normal in illumination than in panel or mural painting.

The varied practice of the Boucicaut Master is instructive in many respects. The greatest illuminator in Paris in the first years of the fifteenth century, he received commissions from the Duke of Burgundy,[32] the Dauphin, Louis duc de Guyenne,[33] the Duke of Berry,[34] the counsellor of Charles VI for the King,[35] and the Marshal of France.[36] He never, however, seems to have been continuously employed by one patron and this odd fact was certainly responsible in part for the character of his work. His shadow is common, his presence rare. Several illuminators were more or less continuously associated with him, sometimes following his drawings or directions, often working largely on their own. The nature and degree of his participation in most manuscripts are unpredictable, and indeed, as we shall see,[37] not always easy to define. He collaborated with good illuminators, such as the Bedford Master, the Egerton Master, and the Cité des Dames Master. Not infrequently his choice of associates is surprising. For a *Trésor des histoires*, which was to receive 224 miniatures, the Boucicaut Master, who was clearly in charge of the enterprise though he painted little himself, engaged three amazingly inept collaborators.[38]

The appearance of three poor painters in this manuscript is only one of the all too frequent instances around 1400 of bad workmanship in otherwise excellent cycles. Apparently the number of assistants upon whom a *chef* could rely was insufficient during periods of high activity, and there must often have been a general shortage of well-trained illuminators in Paris. Looking at some larger cycles of miniatures one occasionally has the impression that the master must have gone out into the street and thrust a brush into the hand of the first person he encountered. Probably the varying rate of sales and commissions was a basic reason for the rather continuous collaboration of masters and ateliers; the peaks and hollows of production were leveled off by the participation of a larger number of painters. The apparent existence of these 'companies' of illuminators helps to explain why two distinct styles are often visible even in small cycles, as in Books of Hours.

In one important respect collaboration to produce a series of miniatures in a manuscript is different from collaboration on the leaves of an altarpiece or on a mural cycle. The latter are seen together whereas the miniatures are seen separately in sequence. There is therefore less need for uniformity in a series of miniatures, and indeed in manuscripts the styles of the painters are usually little affected by the occasion of collaboration. This maintenance of idiosyncrasy is bound up with another aspect of the work on books. Though during the period of the Duke of Berry, and particularly in manuscripts made for him, miniatures imitated panel paintings ever more closely, much of the illumination retained a distinctive character – less finished than painting on a larger scale, less studied, and more spontaneous. The brushwork was often more open, and grisaille far more common.

In manuscripts painted by two or three masters the styles normally remain relatively unadapted to one another. The *Grandes Heures* shows us that even the Duke of Berry's painters, when working together on one manuscript, did not believe that they needed to adjust their respective styles to give the miniatures a more uniform character. In the *Psalter* of the Duke, on the other hand, a greater effort of this kind was made, under the direction of Beauneveu. Indeed adaptation of diverse styles was sometimes effected by the authority of one of the participating masters. Such appears to have been the case in the production of the famous *Térence des ducs*, which was painted by masters trained in, or deeply influenced by, three main stylistic traditions, the 1402-Bedford group, the Cité des Dames Master, and – most extensively – the Luçon Master.[39] Though the first-named master, who painted the *Adelphoe*, was more refractory, an impressive continuity of color, pantomime, costume, and even composition was attained in the illustration of the other plays. Curiously a principal source of this continuity, manifested by conventions such as the two frontal interiors set side by side, was in my opinion a painter whose art appears only in diluted form in the *Térence des ducs*.[40] It is reflected to a degree also in the Terence acquired by the Duke of Berry in 1408, though there the influence of Jacquemart de Hesdin is more considerable also.[41] The full beauty of this style may be seen in a third, unpublished Terence begun by this excellent master but left incomplete. He himself finished only two miniatures, employing delicately modulated gray, blue, rose, and brown (Fig. 299). In other spaces left for the miniatures there are more or less faint drawings, some of them very beautiful and certainly by the same master (Fig. 300). Since no other miniatures by him, or by close followers, seem to survive, was he perhaps a *peintre*? He presumably was given in any event a special task – to undertake himself, or at least to supervise, the illustrations of the comedies of Terence, for which the much earlier medieval cycles were unavailable as models or judged unsuitable.

The quick, deft lines in the Terence, disclosing conspicuously the movement and varying pressure of the hand, are excellent examples of a kind of drawing that was widely practiced in France and elsewhere at the time. The function of these drawings was to locate the main figures within the pictorial space, characterize them in an elementary way, and indicate their posture. As such they were not new. Earlier uncompleted manuscripts often show drawings of this kind, the *Bible de Jean de Sy*, for instance, begun around 1355, or the *Planisio Bible*, illuminated in 1362 (Figs. 298, 302). Compared with these drawings, however, those in the Terence seem relatively free and spontaneous. They are more closely related to later efforts of this kind; they look, in fact, like modern drawings.

It is true that the notations in the Terence should not be regarded as typical of all early fifteenth-century compositional drawings in the fields of the miniatures. Other such drawings show more precise definition.[42] The sketches – they are that – in the Terence were made by a very good artist, and, equally important, they served as very quick indications for miniatures that he presumably intended to paint himself. They thus resemble in mode but not in function the compositional notations in the margins of manuscripts that served to guide other painters, especially when faced with large cycles and unfamiliar subjects. It was common practice in the Middle Ages to insert drawings for initials and for miniatures in the margins of manuscripts, but the number of them, at least for miniatures, increased in the late fourteenth century.[43] Normally these drawings were erased or they were removed when the codex was trimmed. Some specimens, however, have survived. Enough remains of the tiny but beautiful sketch of Abraham and the Three Angels at the lower margin of a folio in the *Bible of Jean de Sy* to show that the wings of the angel at the right in the splendid final drawing do not conform with it (Fig. 301). This sketch, like others in the Bible (folios 12 verso, 19), served to establish the relationship of the main figures only, and many later sketches in the margins, as well as some within the miniatures (the Terence), had the same important but limited function.

An exceptional number of marginal drawings is still visible in manuscripts or at least sections of manuscripts painted by the Boucicaut workshop, either because they were more frequently employed by this atelier or because less attention was paid to their removal.[44] Rarely they occur in a vertical margin, as the Fool (originally no doubt mocked by two men as in the miniature) in a Bible in London (Fig. 317). The drawing provides a complete outline of all the chief forms, and the only considerable change in the miniature is the shortening of the dog's tail. It is worth noting that there are very few, if any, earlier portrayals of smiling faces than in this miniature. The numerous drawings and instructions for the illuminators in the Boucicaut gatherings of a *Chroniques de France* in the British Museum are in the lower margins. The sketch of the scene of the desperately ill Louis, son of King Philippe, praying to the reliquary of St. Denis, is the work of a highly skilled professional hand, as are all the drawings in this codex (Fig. 309). But like many of the other drawings it shows forms largely parallel to the picture plane rather than oblique to it as in the miniature (Fig. 308).[45] The relationship between the partly obliterated drawing and the miniature is similar on folio 36 of Volume II, which represents King Louis VII before a reliquary (Figs. 310, 311). Here the drawing is a little more scanty and the illuminator might have referred for the setting to patterns of this rather frequently illustrated text, or to an earlier manuscript.[46] Sometimes such reference was necessary because the drawing defined so little that it could have served only as a key to the composition.[47] On folio 45 one of the two messengers before King Louis offers something or holds his hat in his hand while in the miniature the gesture has been altered (Figs. 306, 307). Here the draughtsman uses a hieroglyph for a king, indicating the crown by an arc below three equally spaced verticals. For the *Marriage of Philippe le Hardi and Marguerite de Flandre* the draughtsman supplied only the three principal figures; the illuminator added the rest (Figs. 304, 305).

In the *Chroniques de France* the space of the illuminator was normally more advanced than that of the draughtsman. The latter did not necessarily therefore bear the chief responsibility for the illustration; he was perhaps a specialist in drawings, a *paginator* as he was called in the Middle Ages. The relationship is the opposite in certain sections of a *Bible historiale* written in 1411 and now in the British Museum. In the scene of Abraham and the Three Angels, for instance, the drawing in the right margin is excellent, showing Abraham seated before a fine round tent while the angels approach him along a spatial diagonal (Fig. 312). The weak illuminator flattened the entire composition (Fig. 313). Similarly in a drawing in what is probably the earliest illustrated French translation of the *Meditationes Vitae Christi* the men bearing the litter of the Widow's Son strain under its weight whereas in the miniature, which is distinctly inferior, the men merely shuffle along (Fig. 316).

The drawings in these manuscripts seem sufficiently full notations of the compositions to have served as models for the miniatures, though the colors are lacking. In this respect they resemble the Italian *sinopie,* or preparatory drawings in sinoper for frescoes, though the *sinopie,* unlike the *portraits d'encre,* were obliterated before the painting was carried out.[48] Occasionally brief color notes are visible in the unpainted or damaged backgrounds of miniatures, as they are on the intonaco of Italian mural paintings.[49] Sometimes illuminators possessed as models for their miniatures an entire cycle of illustrations of the same texts. This might be an older cycle, and thus more useful iconographically than for composition, as in the case of Bondol's model for the designs of the Apocalypse tapestries, or it might serve for style as well, as did the Vatican *Décaméron* for the masters producing another copy some twenty years later (Figs. 319, 320), or several miniatures in the *Très Belles Heures de Notre-Dame* for the Pseudo-Jacquemart in the *Grandes Heures* (Figs. 14, 235). A cycle of this sort might even be a series of drawings made by the *chef* and retained in the workshop, or finally a series of miniatures painted a little earlier in the same atelier.

At this period illuminators turned increasingly too to drawings they had made earlier of figures or groups in other works of art that interested them. They accumulated these *exempla,* as a squirrel does nuts, for future use, and they often drew them in little books of parchment or box-wood. One outstanding example of these model books will be discussed below (Figs. 279, 281–285).

When painting miniatures illuminators were guided not only by what we nowadays call visual aids but by spoken and written instructions. In the illustration of Temperance in an early manuscript of the *Épître d'Othéa* a clock was represented, though there is no reference to one in the text. It must have been requested by the poet, or perhaps proposed by the illuminator. The clock appeared in copies of the text that were made shortly afterward, not only in the illustrations but incorporated into the text itself.[50] Usually instructions were placed in the lower margins,[51] and like drawings some of them escaped erasure or trimming. Near a battle scene on folio 433 of a *Roman de Lancelot* in the Yale University Library, written in 1357, there is a note saying simply 'une bataille cruelle'. Both the note and the miniature alongside imply that any vigorous scene of battle in the repertory of the workshop would do. This inscription stands at one pole in the category of written instructions for illuminators. At the other would be the lengthy instructions given by Jean Lebègue *ca.* 1417 for the illustration of Sallust. Lebègue carefully lists all the figures, defines their place, and describes the details of their costume as well as the setting. His account includes preferable colors and even, occasionally, an interpretation of a figure.[52] Similarly full and specific are the instructions for the illustration of Bouvet's *Somnium super materia scismatis*, instructions written *circa* 1395 by none other it seems than Jean Gerson. The following are descriptions of three miniatures representing respectively the Dukes of Berry and Burgundy and the King of France, the beautiful *joyaux* of the first-named singled out for particular mention.

> (Folio 279). Hic depingatur dux Bituricensis in quodam oratorio audiens missam in sua capella pulcherrimis iocalibus ornata, et in eadem celebrat missam unus prelatus cum copia cantorum; et actor depingatur loquens cum quodam scutifero.
>
> (Folio 279 verso). Hic depingatur dux Burgundie in quadam pulchra aula, et cum eo duces Aurelianensis et Bolbonii, et sit actor coram eis inclinatus.
>
> (Folio 280 verso). Hic depingatur rex Francie in sua pulcherrima capella et nobilissime adornata, et sit magna multitudo prelatorum, militum et cantorum, et depingatur actor inclinatus, flexis genibus, coram rege.[53]

The illuminators of the *Chroniques de France*, who were often guided by drawings, sometimes followed written descriptions. Thus in the lower margin below the miniature of a king receiving a message from a cardinal is still legible: 'l roy assis en sa m . . . ung cardinal qui du pape. . . .' (Figs. 314, 315). When the subject of a miniature was more familiar a short description sufficed, as in a *Bible historiale* in Brussels for a representation of Job: 'Job assis et tout nu'.[54] Thus the problem of getting the right composition in the right place, especially acute in the sphere of illumination, was accomplished in different ways. Mistakes of one kind or another are not, as we shall see, uncommon. 'Anneau' differs from 'agneau' by only one letter, but the visual consequences are enormous. Illuminators were not normally widely read, they knew little Latin, and most of the French texts were new. The special nature of their task around 1400 in this respect requires further discussion.

2 · NEW TEXTS AND IMAGES

The kinds of problems with which painters had to deal changed from generation to generation throughout the Middle Ages. In the latter half of the fourteenth century the number of new subjects they wished or were obliged to represent increased greatly. French illuminators and painters on larger scale both contributed to the innovations in religious iconography. Among surviving objects the new French image of the Man of Sorrows, for instance, appeared first in a book (Fig. 15), but one of the panels of which we have records was painted sometime before 1383.[55]

It was the illuminators, nevertheless, who were faced with an extraordinary number of iconographic challenges.

During the late fourteenth and early fifteenth centuries illuminators were occupied more and more with the illustration of a text that had begun to develop out of the Psalter a hundred years earlier. The Book of Hours, 'un bréviaire à l'usage des laïques', as Leroquais described it, contained prayers for the eight canonical Hours that supplemented the regular offices of the church. It constituted a major manifestation of that trend towards private devotion that characterized the late Middle Ages, and as a phenomenon it is linked with the popularity of the private chapel and with the wide diffusion, especially in Tuscany, of the small painted tabernacle. The new form of piety led, at the same time, to the creation of the devotional images. These new images, in fact, were frequently chosen to illustrate sections of the Book of Hours: the Man of Sorrows, for instance, for the Penitential Psalms and the *Sept Requêtes*, or the Madonna of Humility for the prayers to the Virgin. There were no long-established iconographic traditions for the Book of Hours, especially for these prayers and for others to the Virgin (O Intemerata and Obsecro Te) or the Office of the Dead. New subjects and designs were often introduced for the illustration of these sections, and the chief cycle, the Hours of the Virgin, as well as the frequent Hours of the Cross – these two concerned with the beginning and the end of Christ's life on earth – underwent constant development.

Until about 1420 the Book of Hours was a French phenomenon *par excellence*, and the most splendid examples were commissioned by members of the ruling Valois family. They too were responsible for the vogue of the illustrated manuscripts of the *Cité de Dieu*. The most remarkable innovation of the period was, however, the group of illustrated secular texts. The religious poem of Dante apart, the first great period of secular painting occurred in France, in the first quarter of the fifteenth century, half a century before the efflorescence of ancient mythology in Italy. The more favored texts ranged from Roman authors in the original Latin – such as Terence (Figs. 299, 300) – or in French translation, especially Livy or Valerius Maximus, to the contemporary Christine de Pisan. This indefatigable lady, as a professional author a novelty herself, turned out at least one work every year, and almost all of them were illustrated (Figs. 324, 834). Then there were vernacular historical compilations, such as the *Trésor des histoires*[56] or the *Chroniques de France* (Figs. 304–311, 565), and books of travel, Hayton's *Fleur des histoires* (Fig. 438) or the famous *Merveilles du monde* in the Bibliothèque nationale.

Most remarkable of all perhaps was the enthusiasm for a 'modern' Italian writer, Boccaccio. Three of his texts were translated and paraphrased in the early fifteenth century: the *Des cleres femmes* in 1401, the *Cas des nobles hommes et femmes* in 1409, and the *Décaméron* in 1414. The earliest fully illustrated copies of these writings by Boccaccio were produced not in Italy but in France (Figs. 289, 291, 294, 503, 561). Italian manuscripts of these texts sometimes contained frontispieces or even relatively small cycles of miniatures but these manuscripts were not known, it seems, in France, and the illuminators were faced with the production of a large series of paintings for which there was no representative tradition. Though such circumstances occurred at all times they were exceptionally frequent in the period of Charles VI and Jean de Berry. How did the illuminators proceed? Sometimes, as we have seen, they were given rather full written instructions, or a draughtsman versed in the matter might provide a series of drawings. We may exemplify some of the possibilities by closer examination of two manuscripts of this kind.

The earliest fully illustrated *Decameron* is a little-known manuscript in the Vatican, illuminated by the Cité des Dames Master for Jean sans Peur between 1414, the date of the translation, and 1419, the year of the Duke's death.[57] It served as a model for the famous manuscript in Paris, illuminated around 1440 by the French (?) Master of the Mansel and the Flemish Master of Guillebert de Mets.[58] The designer of the illustrations in the Vatican manuscript, an illuminator active in Paris, apparently read his text; that at least seems the most likely deduction from one miniature, rather naïve theologically though effective pictorially (Fig. 318). In the fifty-sixth *nouvelle* Michel Fallace (*recte* Scalzo) tells his companions a tall tale about the antiquity of the Baronci family and their ugliness. 'Les baroncionnois comencerent estre au monde des que dieu comenca a prendre art de painture . . . [ils] ont les visages bien [*sic!* – an error for *mal*] proportionnes ainsi telz comme ont acoustume de faire les enfans quand de nouvel apprennent art de painture. . . .'[59] The illuminator transformed the comparison of God learning to paint with children at the same stage of development into a representation of the youthful Lord producing (with effort) the malformed Baronci on his panel while the adult Lord displays a specimen of the well proportioned human kind that he has learned to design.

The less specific the instructions given to the illustrator the more he tended to tell the new stories with groups of figures from his repertory that seemed to suit.[60] The *nouvelle* numbered thirty-six, the sixth story on the fourth day, tells of the tragic end of the love of Androlla (*recte* Andreuola) and Gabriel (*recte* Gabriotto). On one of the many occasions when they were secretly enjoying each other's company in her father's garden Gabriel fell to the grass gravely ill. Androlla drew him into her lap and there he died.[61] The image suggested by these lines is realized in a drawing in the first fully illustrated Italian manuscript of the *Decameron*, dated 1427 (Fig. 303). The French painter of the Vatican miniature, on the other hand, has given to this sad farewell the much more formal composition, widely diffused in the North, of the *Vesperbild* (Fig. 319). The illustrator of the Arsenal manuscript copied this composition (Fig. 320). He copied also the subsequent episode of the intervention of the police as Androlla and a servant carry off the body.

Nouvelle number 26, the sixth story on the third day, is devoted to a highly successful though improbable ruse (Fig. 321). A Neapolitan nobleman, Richard Minutile (*recte* Minutolo), who has fallen in love with Catelle, the wife of another nobleman, has finally contrived to have a few words alone with her by joining a gay group that has foregathered at the seashore on a hot day. He persuades her to go to a certain bath,[62] where she will discover that her husband has been meeting another woman. Richard of course goes there first, rents from the bath-woman an absolutely dark room and, pretending to be Catelle's husband, shortly receives her there. The illuminator managed to show both important episodes in the story by placing the house at the seashore. To describe the setting of the second meeting as clearly as possible he has put the bath, which Boccaccio locates simply in the house, in the dark room itself.

The corresponding miniatures in the Arsenal codex, by a different illuminator than the author of the story of Androlla, are clearly related in general but very different in detail (Fig. 322). The sea and the strand described in both the Italian and French texts have been replaced by a meadow and a river. The view of the town has been shrunk to the room itself, still dark and with a tub, but now very much reduced in size. A woman bearing two containers of water, presumably for the bath, enters the room; all very practical but destructive of the privacy of the lovers. Wrong, too, is the evident connection of the room with the street. Whereas the master who painted the miniature of Androlla in the Arsenal manuscript followed the Vatican composition exactly the illuminator of the Neapolitan story – the Master of Guillebert de Mets[63] – produced something different. This relative independence is puzzling. By good luck we can come close in this instance to what actually happened.

The visual evidence is rather startling. For the tryst in the *étuve* the Master of Guillebert de Mets borrowed from a Breviary nothing other than the scene of the Birth of the Virgin, making of course the minor modifications that were needed (Fig. 323). These included the moderate enlargement of the infant's tub. There is no doubt whatever that the Master of Guillebert de Mets knew the miniature of the Birth of the Virgin. First of all, it is in the beautiful Breviary illuminated for Jean sans Peur and his wife Marguerite de Bavière, so that it formed part of the Burgundian library.[64] The *Birth of the Virgin* is one of several miniatures in the Breviary that were painted either by the Egerton Master or an assistant, under the influence of the *chef d'atelier* whom I have named, after this manuscript, the Master of the Breviary of Jean sans Peur.[65] The building is a stage prop of the Egerton Master that appeared in his earlier work – in, for example, miniatures he contributed between *circa* 1404 and 1409 to the Duke of Berry's copy of the writings of Christine de Pisan (Fig. 324).[66] The Master of Guillebert de Mets knew the Breviary very well because he himself early in his career added many miniatures in it. Thus the line of communication is completely re-established. It does not, however, tell us unequivocally *why* the choice was made. The new interior no doubt looked more modern, but the narrative was, we must admit, not improved.

We have already observed that the setting of the episode at the left failed to conform with the text. It does, however, follow exactly a note in Flemish in the lower margin of the folio that by chance escaped the usual erasure: '. j. mann enn . j. wijf, . j. man enn . j. wijf, staende neven . j. riviere' (a man and a woman, a man and a woman, standing near a river).[67] Now this description differs in two respects from both Boccaccio's Italian and Laurent's French. Boccaccio wrote that 'molte brigate di donne e di cavalieri . . . andassero a diportarsi a' liti del mare. . . .'[68] By way of the Latin this became in Laurent '. . . sur le rivage de la mer Catelle estoit en deduyt avecques plusieurs aultres femmes. . . .'[69] The note omits Laurent's decisive 'de la mer' and substitutes for *rivage*, which could refer to the shore of a sea as well as of a river, the word *rivière*, which refers to the bank of a river only.[70] Laurent's text had already been written of course on the folios of the Arsenal manuscript before the note was added in the margin, so that the substitution was either inadvertent or the consequence of a misunderstanding of the corresponding miniature in the Vatican manuscript.

Who was responsible for the content of the note? Clearly the bilingual adviser of an illuminator who knew only Flemish. It is certain that this adviser was familiar with the Vatican manuscript, because his instruction 'two men and two women' follows the miniature in that manuscript and not the words of Laurent, who speaks only of 'Catelle . . . avecques plusieurs aultres *femmes.*' Perhaps then he mistook the sea or bay of Naples in the Vatican miniature for a river.

Below the scene in the bath-house there is a legible inscription also. '. j. man en . j. wyf deen neven dand in een bedde neven . j. badecupe' (a man and a woman, the one near the other in a bed near a tub of water). This is indeed what the illuminator represented, adding however the woman carrying water, who was not mentioned by the text either. Again he apparently did not see, or at least did not follow, the miniature in the Vatican manuscript, and, as we have observed, he omitted the town visible in that work.

Similar inscriptions are still preserved on three other folios, though I have been unable to study them.[71] It has not been noticed that all of them appear on folios painted by the Master of Guillebert de Mets or an assistant. Now the style of this illuminator is Flemish, he worked in Flanders, and he undoubtedly was a Fleming.[72] The miniatures by him that I have been able to compare with corresponding illustrations in the Vatican manuscript are closely copied from the latter.[73] Either, then, he followed the pictorial model or the instructions of the adviser. The one thing he did not do was read the French text.

The performance of his chief collaborator in the manuscript, the so-called Master of the Mansel, was quite different.[74] The style of this illuminator derives from the French tradition, and particularly from the Bedford Master. Several miniatures by him, while following even in small details the designs of the corresponding scenes in the Vatican manuscript, introduce one or two differences, and in every instance these changes make his miniatures more effective – and sometimes even more correct – illustrations of the text.[75] Unlike his associate he could read French, and undertook to correct or enlarge upon his pictorial model.

At first sight the remarkable conjunction of subject and scene in the miniature of the *étuve* might look like the relatively innocent handiwork of an illuminator given scanty instructions and lacking, for whatever reason, his usual model (Fig. 322). He knew quite well, however, that he was illustrating a racy secular text, with which an episode in the life of the Virgin was not compatible. Could a half-hidden sacrilegious joke have been intended? The mode is not different from parts of the *Decameron*, and Boccaccio himself would probably have been amused.

The embodiment of the new secular subjects in more familiar religious images is only one of the common methods of iconographic innovation of the period. There was at the same time a migration of forms from one religious subject to another, and religious imagery was in turn nourished by secular. New religious subjects appeared – sometimes the inventions of artists – and old subjects were represented in a novel way. In an exquisite onyx carved *circa* 1400 an angel holds the body of Christ much as God holds the newly created Adam in an illustration of a Bible (Figs. 325, 326). The *Vesperbild* by the Rohan Master was based on a mother mourning her child who was killed as one of the Innocents (Figs. 327, 328).[76]

In the work of certain painters of the time – the Passion Master, for instance, and later the Rohan Master – the story of Christ's death was given a new intensity by the assimilation of figures from more secular marginal decoration.[77] Around 1370 the scene of the Nativity acquired a new, specifically wintry character by the coalescence of the traditional St. Joseph with the man in the Calendar picture for February (Figs. 91, 360).[78] Later miniatures develop the connection of the

Nativity and February by representing Joseph warming his hands at a fire (Fig. 329). In the *Petites Heures* he warms a cloth for the Child (Fig. 131). The figure of the old man, heavily wrapped against the cold and protected by his big round chair or by the fire, lends a new informality to the scene. Other kinds of domestic requirements are signified by the pot, in which the water for the Child's bath is warmed or perhaps food cooked. In Byzantine and earlier Northern representations of the Nativity the bath is prepared and tested by one or two midwives, and they sometimes immerse the Child in it (Fig. 330).[79] In the bourgeois culture of Trecento Italy the Virgin and Joseph themselves become active in the bathing. In a fresco by Vitale da Bologna originally in Mezzaratta the Madonna tests the temperature of the water while Joseph, with a wonderfully elaborate movement, fills the tub (Fig. 331). This new image of a more domestic Virgin was transmitted to the North, appearing in the painting, for instance, of the Rohan Master (Fig. 332), and it assumed a related form in the well-known panel by the Master of Flémalle in Leningrad (Fig. 333) which shows the Madonna with her nude Infant testing the warmth of a nearby fire.[80] In a miniature by the Luçon Master dated 1401 the Virgin accompanied by a midwife (?) holding the Child puts her hand into a tub that represents not the usual bath but the 'fontaine de tous biens' mentioned in the prayer written below it (Fig. 334).

3 · THE FRENCH FORERUNNERS

The chief pictorial events in France in the last twenty years of the fourteenth century occurred in Paris and in the developing centers of the duchies of Burgundy, Berry, Anjou, and Orléans that were closely linked with the capital. The reigning princes traveled frequently between, say, Dijon or Bourges or Angers and Paris; with quicker means of transportation they would have become commuters.[81] Though we are much less well informed about the artists than about the princes all the signs point toward frequent trips of those resident in the provinces into Paris, sometimes for extended visits. They often simply followed their patrons. Thus all the painters participated to some extent in a common enterprise, and it seems justifiable to characterize the products as the accomplishments of metropolitan France. A certain degree of uniformity was similarly visible in all the arts, but it was controlled by practical differences between them. Manuscripts and *orfèvrerie* were easily movable; they could be distributed from the capital. Indeed it clearly became the one great center for illumination,[82] and also, I suspect, for the work of goldsmiths.[83] Architectural sculpture, on the other hand, naturally tended to become a more local art, more highly differentiated, especially under the impact of a great artist such as Claus Sluter. Probably too the painters Jean de Beaumetz, Jean Malouel, and Henri Bellechose created a distinctive Burgundian trend,[84] but we are so ignorant of the course of monumental painting in Paris, Bourges, and Angers that it is difficult to be certain.

The painters and illuminators who were forming their styles in this central region of France around 1370–1380 were well aware, no doubt, of the distinctive qualities of the earlier Parisian tradition: exceptional refinement, sometimes leading to austere sparseness, moderation, usually productive of a marvelous poise but sometimes becoming sterile restraint, an inclination toward linearity, resulting in superb patterns but occasionally descending to empty diagrams. While the masters in the late fourteenth century responded to this tradition two styles seemed to them especially meaningful. One was still very alive though it had been created half a century earlier by Jean Pucelle: the other was developed in the 'fifties by a painter who can probably be identified with the documented Jean Bondol of Bruges.

Pucelle, the older and the greater of these artists, came in a sense ahead of his time. Early in his career, in the tiny but marvelous *Heures de Jeanne d'Évreux* of 1325–1328, he captured the revolutionary innovations of Duccio.[85] Having taken this tremendous step he did not, however, like Duccio or Giotto, continue on the same course. He drew back in his later work, and though he attracted some followers a continuous dialogue with Trecento art was initiated only in the period beginning about 1375.

Two miniatures in the minute book will serve to remind us of the main aspects of Pucelle's art. For the first time in Northern painting the Annunciation is enacted in a little three-dimensional house, with walls, ceiling, and floor convincingly receding into space (Fig. 335). This space is occupied by substantial figures whose modeling is all the more effective because it is monochromatic, that is, grisaille. The monumental *Crucifixion* breaks the bonds of the normal limiting frame, which Pucelle indeed abandoned so that the composition could occupy the entire folio (Fig. 336). The conquest of space enabled Pucelle, just as it had enabled Duccio and Giotto, to enrich the narrative (Fig. 339). He utilized the newly won concept of a ground plane to represent the grief-stricken Virgin swooning toward it and a terrified man already fallen upon it. In the *Entombment* a woman crouches before the sarcophagus (Fig. 342), and a tired old shepherd reclines across the foreground of the *Annunciation to the Shepherds*, supporting himself on his staff (Fig. 338). This figure, like many others introduced by Pucelle, proved paradigmatic for a century, and descendants of it may be seen as late as the Rohan Master.[86]

In the *Heures de Jeanne d'Évreux* appears, all at once, the highly varied Sienese pantomime. In the *Crucifixion*, as in Duccio's (Figs. 336, 339), we see the enlightened man, the scoffers, the terrified Jew who clutches his beard.[87] Another looks anxiously away from the event into the world beyond, and this description implies that Pucelle had acquired a new control of the glance of the eyes and of the expression of the face, and that the continuity of space implied by the random cutting-off of the forms, as though they disappeared behind a frame, served to enlarge the mental 'horizons' of the figures themselves. They take possession of an implied but unrepresented space.[88]

The depth of Pucelle's understanding of Sienese painting probably presupposes a journey to the source, but many Italian panels were visible in France, and nothing in the *Heures de Jeanne d'Évreux* makes us absolutely sure.[89] A miniature of a siege near Orléans in the *Miracles de la Vierge* painted in the workshop a little later, however, contains observations of Italian forms that were almost certainly recorded in Tuscany (Fig. 340). The castle is a Tuscan *castello*, with a slender, graceful, Sienese tower; and most telling of all, the image of the Virgin set upon the ramparts incorporates

Italian motives and terminates in a round Ducciesque or Lorenzettian arch, not a pointed French one. Even the *Glikophilousa* seems a recollection of a Sienese Madonna (Fig. 698).[90]

Though manuscripts illuminated in the style of Pucelle after the *Heures de Jeanne d'Évreux* contain beautiful miniatures and notable innovations – such as the scale of the space in the *Siege near Orléans* (Fig. 340) – the illuminator's performance in that tiny book was never equaled. Never again did he achieve the rich interlace, the superb swinging lines and the silken, gliding planes of the Book of Hours in New York. The *Bréviaire de Belleville* has an astonishing study of a flower, but most of the rest, while often bold and agitated, is relatively thin and dry (Figs. 344, 374). The same must be said of the *Bréviaire de Jeanne d'Évreux* (Fig. 343) and the *Heures de Jeanne de Navarre* (Figs. 341, 345–348 350, 544, 601), though the *Annunction* in the latter, for instance, has an imposing building and the search in *All Saints* for individuality of posture and physiognomy is impressive (Figs. 341, 345). The Psalter of Bonne of Luxembourg, Jean de Berry's mother, is exceptionally strong, and it is hard to believe that anyone but Pucelle designed and painted the *Three Quick and the Three Dead*, with its shying, maniacal horses and open-mouthed, screeching, decayed bodies (Figs. 354, 355).[91] The hideous caricature of a Jew in the *Dixit Insipiens*, a unique figure in the illustration of this Psalm, is no doubt his also (Fig. 353).

One very important illuminator emerged in Pucelle's workshop during the late 'forties: the Passion master, perhaps identical with Jean le Noir. Certain miniatures in the Psalter of Bonne, such as the *Quick and the Dead* (Fig. 354–355), represent the style from which he departed, and we see his hand clearly in the mid 'fifties in the *Heures de Yolande de Flandre*, of which we shall speak below (Figs. 364, 365). Much less close to Pucelle, but certainly inspired by him, was the fiery master of a magnificent Missal in Oxford, Bodleian Library, Douce 313 (Figs. 536, 663, 677). Active probably in North France or Flanders,[92] he understood both Pucelle's narrative intensity and his enthusiasm for Trecento art. He was not satisfied with the adoption of Pucelle's Italianate types but returned to the source for new ideas, as we shall see. The composition of his extraordinary *Crucifixion* is, as I have proposed on an earlier occasion, largely derived from a monumental Sienese model (Fig. 372).[93]

Around the middle of the century we have observed a revitalization of narrative art, effected initially it seems by Pucelle himself in the Psalter of Bonne, and then carried on by the Passion Master and the Master of the Douce Missal. In 1355 we encounter for the first time another great storyteller, whose style became dominant in Paris for three decades at least. He painted some miniatures and a few *portraits d'encre* in the *bas-de-page* of a Bible with commentary by Jean de Sy (Figs. 376, 377). The manuscript was begun for King Jean le Bon, work was interrupted when the King was captured at Poitiers, and though the illumination was resumed toward 1380 (Fig. 583) it was never completed.[94] The original illuminator cared above all else for the dramatic situation. He portrayed unforgettably the tiny exiled Ishmael under a large umbrella-like tree quenching his thirst from a flask his mother has just given him (Fig. 376). The pantomime here or in other episodes, such as Abraham accusing Abimelech's servants of capturing a well (Fig. 377),[95] is economical and telling.

The same pungent narrative, the small squat figures, and similar luminous drapery may be seen again in a Bible written in 1357 now in the British Museum, especially in the large miniatures at the beginning of the two parts (Figs. 383, 384).[96] The symbols of the Evangelists add to the vehemence of the act of composition by tugging vigorously at the curtains. The painter is not identical with the chief master of the Bible of Sy but the latter seems the source of his forms. The same must be said of the softer figures in a Bible in Berlin dated 1368 (Fig. 603)[97] and of the four scenes of the Infancy cycle in the Bible presented to Charles V in March, 1372 (Fig. 386). The miniatures in this Bible, now in the Hague, probably give us the key to the painter's identity, for the manuscript has at the beginning the double leaf mentioned above. One folio bears a large miniature, unfortunately damaged, of an official of the court, Jean de Vaudetar, presenting the manuscript to Charles V (Fig. 382). Facing it the inscription states that 'in . . . 1371 this manuscript (istud opus) was painted (pictum) by order . . . of Charles King of France . . . and John of Bruges, painter of the said King, has made this picture with his own hand (fecit hanc picturam propria manu)'. The form of the statement seems to assure us that it proceeds from the painting of the manuscript as a whole to the picture at the beginning,[98] and while it does not inform us *who* was responsible for the illustration of the Bible, the insistence upon John of Bruges as the *sole* author of the frontispiece seems to imply that other masters shared with him the execution of the Biblical cycle. The fact that there was one *chef* for the illumination of the manuscript is suggested also by a long and very unusual jingle written at the end of the text by one of the King's favorite scribes, Raoulet d'Orléans.[99] The good-humored poem was obviously written after the completion of the manuscript, when the exact date of its presentation to Charles V by Jean de Vaudetar – March 28, 1372 – was known. The relevant passage is as follows:

A vous, Charles, roy plain d'onnour,
Qui de sapience la flour
Estes sur tous les roys du monde,
Pour le grant bien qu'en vous habonde,
Presente et donne cestui livre,
Et à genolz cy le vous livre,
Jehan Vaudetar, votre servant,
Qui est cy figuré devant.

C'onques je ne vi en ma vie
Bible d'ystoires si garnie,
D'une main pourtraites et faites,
Pour lesquelles il en a faites
Pluseurs alées et venues,
Soir et matin, par my les rues,
Et mainte pluye sus son chief . . . .[100]

Raoulet thus ascribes the miniatures to one master, emphasizing the phrase 'd'une main.' This phrase contrasts, furthermore, with the many comings and goings of Jean de Vaudetar in his efforts to obtain them. Raoulet's 'une main' follows his reference to the frontispiece, which bears the statement mentioned above that Jean Bondol painted it with his own hand. Inasmuch as the 'ystoires' in the Bible were not in fact all executed by Bondol we may perhaps understand Raoulet's remark as a reference to the fact that he was the *chef d'atelier*. It must be admitted that though the verse is informative, neither it nor the inscription at the beginning of the Bible tells a modern historian all that he wants to know.

And the paintings themselves? The author of the large presentation miniature clearly felt his task was not like that of executing an illustration of a passage in the Bible. He gave more thought to the design and more finish to the surface. Still, the whole is pervaded by the kind of electric animation we have seen in other miniatures of this group, including the Infancy cycle in this very manuscript (Fig. 386). The glances are lively, the response of figure to figure warm, and there are

c

present also such characteristic details as the gesturing hand of Charles V, so much like that of Solomon or Herod in other miniatures (Figs. 384, 386). The shape of the 'umbrella' over Charles V is like that of the peculiar, omnipresent trees (Figs. 376, 382, 386). Thus while it is not possible to identify Jean Bondol absolutely with any illustrations of the Hague Bible, it is not possible to separate them – or at least the better ones (Fig. 386) – from him either.

This conclusion is tantamount to associating with Bondol the best miniatures in the large group brought together by Henry Martin under the name of Master of the Umbrella-Trees (Maître aux Boqueteaux).[101] These miniatures from 1355 into the 'seventies show an adherence to fundamental conceptions of form despite a certain range in character and in artistic strength. The most plausible inference is that Bondol, as *pictor regis*, directed the work of several illuminators as well as painters. In estimating the nature of these relationships we must take into account also the factor of time and of evolution. The *Baptism* in the Bible of 1357, for instance (one of the more conservative miniatures in this manuscript), still resembles an example of this scene in the *Bréviaire de Belleville* painted a quarter century earlier (Figs. 374, 375). In the Hague Bible of 1371 Christ is deep in the river and the Baptist, bursting with the energy so characteristic of Bondol's mature style, dances as he performs the rite (Fig. 378). In the later *Horae* of Philippe le Hardi the landscape widens but all the forms are at the same time flatter (Fig. 379). The alternatives that these works pose are either the impact of one great painter on his associates and colleagues (as we have preferred to believe), or, on the other hand, the more or less simultaneous arrival of three or four illuminators at the same stylistic station. It seems improbable here, as at other times, that a new art is created by a committee.

The hypothesis that Jean Bondol was the major painter who began to work for Jean le Bon *circa* 1355 and remained under Charles V is not free of problems. One other work is extant to which we know he made a contribution. In 1378 he was paid for full-scale models on cloth for the tapestries of the Apocalypse commissioned by Louis d'Anjou.[102] The tapestries were woven by Nicolas Bataille in Paris (Figs. 380, 381, 387). They are related in many ways to both the 'Boqueteaux' paintings and the miniature signed by Bondol, as Panofsky has demonstrated, but there are also disconcerting differences. In general the figures are taller and flatter, with a far more flaccid outline and pattern of drapery. The style of the tapestries is, however, by no means uniform. The understanding men who count in section I of the cycle, for example, show much of the vitality of the best miniatures (Fig. 380) while one of the large figures from section V belongs to another world (Fig. 381). Much, evidently, depended on the weaver himself; the problem of master and associates arises here also. The nature of the relationship of the tapestries with the cartoons is complex. We cannot control the Angers cycle by reference to any other by Bataille because no other work definitely by him has survived.[103]

We first hear of Jean Bondol in 1368, when he was, and for a certain time had been, in the service of Charles V. In that year the King gave him a house in rather far-off Saint-Quentin. Thereafter he received, with short interruptions, a high annual salary, and he disappeared after 1381. The salary payments for 1374 and 1378 included amounts for 'famulus suus', who may, as Durrieu thought, have been an assistant.[104] Though we know nothing about him before 1368 the span of Bondol's career corresponds well otherwise with what we know of the leading artist of Jean le Bon and Charles V. The portrait of King Jean in the Louvre, sometimes adduced for or against the identification of Bondol as the spiritual leader of the Boqueteaux workshop, offers no significant evidence because, in addition to being undocumented, it is in poor condition (Fig. 507). Severely damaged, it has been retouched especially along the profile; part of the plastic, Italianate effect of the face has been produced by this intervention.

Though the miniatures we have been discussing show a notable family relationship, stemming, as we have suggested, from one chief source, numerous painters participated, perhaps as many as a dozen. The style of each changed over the years. Thus in one of the two marvelously subtle grisailles at the beginning of a manuscript of the poems of Guillaume de Machaut, we recognize, after a period of ten or fifteen years, the painter of the *Majesty of Christ* in the Bible of 1357 in London (Figs. 383, 385). There is the same silken touch, but the vigor has diminished, the figures are slimmer, and the gray pigment, with here and there a little blue or pink, seems dusted onto the parchment. While the landscape spreads out extensively and is full of denizens of the countryside, all eager to be seen, it too is rather flat. The miniature, difficult to date precisely, represents that trend toward pallid, exquisite two-dimensionality that gathered momentum within the Bondol tradition in the 'seventies.[105] Though this style survived into the 'nineties, becoming ever more mannered, the major artists whom we are to study gave an entirely new direction to Parisian painting.

4·ITALIAN PAINTERS AND PAINTINGS IN FRANCE

Most of Europe became aware by 1325 that painters in Italy had recently created a new, strange, and expressive manner of painting.[106] Around this time artists in widely separate regions independently paid tribute to its significance by emulating one or another of its innovations. While Pucelle was executing the *Heures de Jeanne d'Évreux* the East Anglian illuminator of the *Gorleston Psalter* similarly adopted the new receding terrain and the freshly explicit Sienese pantomime for the figures that stand on it.[107] At this moment far to the east the author of the Klosterneuburg panels gave Austria an inkling of the innovations of Giotto, and somewhat later nearby Hungary discovered them also.[108] In all these countries the dialogue with Italian painting was, however, sporadic; in England, for instance, most painters judged it irrelevant to the vigorous local tradition.

Three regions, however, made a more constant effort to assimilate the new Italian mode. Emperor Charles IV imported panels by Tommaso da Modena into Bohemia,[109] and an Italian fresco painter himself may, I think, have made the journey.[110] From the middle of the century on, Bohemian masters continued to study Trecento painting, but its most enthusiastic admirers were in the Western Mediterranean, in Catalonia. Catalonia's chief city-states, Barcelona and Valencia, were peculiarly prepared for the new art because the techniques with which it was associated –

panel and mural painting – were firmly established there. In fact an outstanding Catalan master, Ferrer Bassa, had acquired such a familiarity with Tuscan forms and types that by 1345–1346 he could readily compose, indeed improvise with them (Fig. 390, 710). Years ago I said that Bassa must have visited Siena in the late 'thirties,[111] and recently there have come to light in Urbino, through the good efforts of Professor Giuseppe Marchini, large fragments of frescoes that resemble his work (Figs. 388, 391). It is certain at least that they were painted by the Catalan author of the now destroyed *Coronation* in Bellpuig (Figs. 389, 392), and if this altarpiece is Bassa's ten or fifteen years before Pedralbes, as I then proposed, the Urbino frescoes must be his also.[112] The painter was, as far as I can see, the first from the Iberian peninsula to have received large commissions in Italy. In the fifteenth century he was followed by the Master of the Bambino Vispo (who at least had been in Valencia), Alvaro Portogallo, and the Master of the Chiostro degli Aranci.

Ferrer Bassa and his chief successor in Barcelona, the Master of St. Mark, whom we may now probably identify with Ferrer's son Arnau (Fig. 559),[113] became students of Italian painting in the narrower sense. The Catalan masters in general could almost be described as provincial Italian, though later in the century they – and especially Pere Serra – turned their eyes more toward France. In Northern France itself the response to Trecento painting was no less fundamental, but nevertheless different. Instead of imitation we witness selective assimilation. The Gothic style was more deep-rooted, the creative power of the painters greater. Nevertheless several leading masters seem to have made the Italian journey. The Italophile King Philippe le Bel, of whom we shall speak shortly, sent his painter Étienne d'Auxerre to Rome in 1298.[114] We know that Jean d'Arbois was in Milan in 1373 and Jacques Coene in 1398. We may infer, with more or less assurance, a trip to Tuscany by Pucelle, by the closely related Master of the Miracles de la Vierge, by the Master of Douce 313, and by Jacquemart de Hesdin. The journey was certainly made by the Master of the Cité des Dames (Figs. 393, 394)[115] as well as by one or more of the Limbourgs.

For painters who did not travel as far as Bologna, Florence, or Siena major examples of Trecento paintings were visible in France – more, indeed, than anywhere else outside the peninsula. The new art was carried there in the very first years of its inception. Five angels and a male saint on the wall of the Chapel of the Holy Ghost in St. Nazaire, Béziers, constituting a sort of mural polyptych, belong among the earliest incunables of the *stil nuovo* (Figs. 398, 399). They were no doubt painted *circa* 1307 on commission of Bérenger III, Bishop of Béziers until 1305 and then a cardinal residing in Avignon.[116] Defaced during the Protestant revolt, they are still glowing specimens of Cavallinesque art, by a painter who was close to the master himself. Four scenes of the Legend of St. Stephen in the nave of the church were also executed by an Italian painter, again probably a Roman who was familiar with the innovations at Assisi (Fig. 395). The first of these remarkable pictorial events, and perhaps also the second, is very probably related to the no less remarkable entry of three Roman painters in 1309 into the service of King Philippe le Bel, who was in touch with Bérenger III.[117] Already in 1308, only some months after the painting of the Chapel of the Holy Ghost, one of them, Filippo Rusuti, was working for the King in his palace at Poitiers.[118] Since this building later belonged to Jean de Berry,[119] his painters might well have had excellent examples of Roman frescoes before their eyes. The three Roman masters, Filippo Rusuti (no doubt the signer of the mosaic on the façade of S. M. Maggiore, Rome, and the painter of the first scene of Creation at Assisi), his son Giovanni, and a certain Nicolas Desmarz ('de Rome'), received salaries as 'peintres du Roi' in 1309, and they are again named in 1317 as possessors of this title. In 1322 Giovanni alone is mentioned, and at an uncertain date Desmarz may have worked at St. Denis.[120] Inasmuch as some of their work is still extant today, how much more was visible towards 1400!

In 1316 two other Italian painters were working at Gentilly, near Paris, and in 1328, just after Pucelle completed the *Heures de Jeanne d'Évreux*, a painter, Jean de Gand, sold in Paris some panels 'de l'ouvraige de Rome'.[121] These records, which have by chance survived, suggest the extent of the interest in Trecento painting early in the century. As visual evidence there should be added to the important paintings in Béziers a little-known miniature in a manuscript written in Lavaur, near Toulouse, in 1319 (Fig. 396).[122] The miniature would appear to have been painted by an itinerant Sienese master. Meanwhile, in 1309, the Curia had been established at Avignon, transforming this South French city into an Italian outpost. Major Italian artists migrated there later, under Pope Benedict XII (1334–1341), when Simone Martini arrived,[123] and under Clement VI (1342–1352), for whom Matteo Giovanetti painted most of the still extant frescoes in the Papal Palace and at nearby Villeneuve (Figs. 405, 406). Of Simone's mural paintings there remain a *Christ Blessing* and a *Madonna of Humility*, both recently detached from their original places in Notre-Dame des Doms (Fig. 397).[124] A seventeenth-century drawing in the Vatican may preserve for us the main elements of Simone's large fresco in the atrium of St. George battling the dragon (Fig. 401).[125] While in Avignon Simone painted the panel of Christ with the Virgin and Joseph in Liverpool, dated 1342, the famous miniature in Petrarch's Virgil, and, I believe, the panels of the Annunciation and of the Passion in Antwerp, Berlin, and Paris (Figs. 674, 675, 676, 692, 693).[126]

The Master of the Codex of St. George, who was influenced by Simone, may have worked for a time in Avignon. The career of this illuminator and painter of small panels has not yet been convincingly traced, but his *St. George and the Dragon* seems to reflect Simone's composition in Avignon recorded in the drawing, though the unusual binding of the horse's feet by the tail of the dragon is lacking (Fig. 400). The inscription that originally was written alongside Simone's fresco appears at the end of the *Codex of St. George*, which was composed by Cardinal Stefaneschi.[127] A fine drawing in the margin of a thirteenth-century Pliny that belonged to Petrarch seems related to the art of the St. George Master (Fig. 402). It represents Vaucluse, described in Petrarch's hand as 'transalpina solitudo mea iocundissima'. Long ago De Nolhac, who thought the drawing was not good, ascribed it to Petrarch himself,[128] but it is much superior to other drawings in this and other manuscripts that may reasonably be attributed to the poet.[129] Petrarch bought the Pliny in Mantua on July 6, 1350, and when he returned to France in June 1351, he left it and other manuscripts in Verona, so that the drawing was apparently not made in Avignon.

During the period of Simone's residence in Avignon and in the years following his death there in 1344 numerous Italian painters – mostly Sienese or Florentine – were working in Southern France.[130] Of their painting little survives except the cycles of Matteo da Viterbo in the Papal Palace (Fig. 405) and at Villeneuve.[131] Only his prophets in the Salle de l'Audience are firmly dated, 1353 (Fig. 406). The two chapels were painted earlier and the frescoes at Villeneuve a little later. The independence of this master from the canons of the chief Italian centers is at once his strength and his weakness. It left untrammeled an engaging freshness and spontaneity. He saw, sometimes naively like a primitive, a wide range of personalities, and he caught the differences in their capacity for engagement and response. He possessed a delicate taste for color, and he liked to open wide, intricate spaces. His art was, for an Italian, exceptionally personal and variable. He never mastered the means developed earlier in Siena and Florence for the orderly projection of space and the organic movement of the figure. His limitations in these respects, described recently for instance by Toesca,[132] were probably recognized by the leading French painters, and scholars have not been able to show that his art had any significant effect upon them.[133]

Thus to say that Matteo was a good painter – as he was – does not assure his historical importance.[134] The great patrons of Northern France, who visited the Curia frequently, were no doubt impressed by his works, but they must have responded far more to the frescoes and panels of Simone Martini. Much that was visible then has been lost; we are reminded of this fact once again by the recent discovery of frescoes in St. Didier, Avignon, by a minor Florentine near Niccolo di Tommaso, in my opinion (Fig. 404).[135] Tuscan paintings, especially altarpieces, were not only produced in the region; many were imported, as we know by the lucky survival of the records of the Datini house.[136] Sometimes the orders of the Avignon branch of this firm to the Florentine left open the precise subject – either a Madonna or a Christ on the Cross would do – but stressed artistic quality, requesting a painting 'tutto di ghran vista e di bella forma'. These works were usually small panels, diptychs, or tabernacles for private devotion, of the kind we have mentioned above. Normally they were the work of Florentine painters; Jacopo di Cione was the author of four panels that arrived in 1386.[137] One document refers to a 'dossale d'altare molto bello', an embroidery of the kind described in the Duke of Berry's inventories as 'l'ouvraige de Florence'.[138] This piece, ordered in Florence by Charles VI but not paid for, was sent on to Paris for quiet sale. Similarly many of the panels brought to Avignon by the Datini and other firms – from other centers – found their way, as did apparently Simone's panels, into the great North French collections.

Of journeys to Avignon by major North French painters we know nothing. Some of them no doubt made the trip, if only on the way to the great centers in Italy. It is worth noting at this point that French examples of the Madonna of Humility do not follow the composition of Simone's prominent fresco in Avignon but an earlier design by him (Figs. 269, 270, 274, 397, 634).[139] Of course these generalizations anticipate the content of the present publication, and they are made here only because the description that follows of the great changes in French painting during the later years of the century will require very few references to the papal capital. While the Italian culture of this center facilitated and in general promoted these changes, as the preceding account was intended to suggest, it was not the fundamental cause of them, nor the source, apparently, of specific forms.[140] If the Byzantine Emperor rather than the Pope had moved to Avignon in 1309 it seems likely that the evolution of painting in metropolitan France would not have been greatly altered. The broad estimate of Panofsky seems to me quite right. Evaluating the effect of the new seat of the Papacy in the light of the response of the whole of Europe to Italian Trecento painting he concluded: 'We are faced with an infiltration too simultaneous and ubiquitous to be accounted for by an historical accident'.[141]

The establishment of the Curia at Avignon was the most important, but nevertheless only one of several 'accidents' that linked French and Italian painting during the fourteenth century. Later in the century the powerful Duke of Milan, Gian Galeazzo Visconti, married the sister of Charles V and the Dukes of Berry and Burgundy, and in 1389 his daughter Valentina became the wife of the influential brother of Charles VI, Louis d'Orléans.[142] During the last quarter of the century, when Lombard painting – especially illumination – broke new ground an exchange with Northern masters occurred that enriched the art of both regions. Perhaps the most remarkable evidence of the contribution of metropolitan French to Lombard painting is provided by the hitherto un-published illustrations of a *Commedia* of Dante, written at Piacenza in 1386.[143] In the beautiful miniature of *Inferno* hills of brown, gray, and light green succeed one another against a background half maroon and half blue, while the soft, flickering flames are an exquisite bluish-red (Fig. 403). The ivy borders and diapered backgrounds are only the obvious signs of French influence; it has rendered the colors more delicate, the linear pattern finer. Even the figures are a beautiful blend of Lombard and French style.

The most durable political connection between France and Italy was provided by the house of Anjou. From 1309 Robert d'Anjou reigned as King of Naples and since he was also Count of Provence it is not surprising that a panel painted in Naples such as the *St. Louis of Toulouse adored by King Robert and his Wife* should have been presented by them in 1340 to a convent in Aix (Fig. 407).[144] Robert, who died in 1343, was succeeded by his granddaughter Joanna I, a fiery queen who was said to have murdered her first husband; she then married thrice thereafter. She seemed to require ferocity even in her prayers, for the manuscript made for her and now in Vienna, to which we shall return shortly, contains subjects of unprecedented and horrifying aggressiveness, usually aimed at men and children (Figs. 416-418).[145] Shortly after 1352, when the French Duke Louis I of Anjou founded the famous Ordre du St. Esprit, he had the statutes illumi-nated by a good Neapolitan master.[146] Either this Duke, who died in Italy in 1384 after a vain attempt to gain control of Naples, or his son Louis II, who ruled there from 1390 to 1399, bought or commissioned an extraordinary *Bible moralisée*, which provided several models for the Rohan Master when he was painting for the Anjou.[147] Like many specimens of this enormous text, the Anjou manuscript is incomplete. It extends from Genesis through the third chapter of Judges, and contains miniatures arranged in two rows, both set between a passage from the Bible above and the moralization below (Fig. 408). This section is followed (on folio 113) by a series of New Testament scenes beginning with the Expulsion of Joachim from the Temple and extending through the Passion, each miniature on a separate leaf. Except for a small strip at the bottom of the folio reserved for a succinct description of the scene, the miniatures are full-page, so that the whole composes a picture Bible.

Most of these paintings, though mediocre in style, offer examples of very infrequently repre-sented scenes, and they tell us where the manuscript was illuminated, or at least where the painters were trained. The miniatures are similar in style, in details of ornament and even in the design and color of their frames to miniatures in a Missal we know was painted in Naples (Figs. 408, 409).[148] Eighteen of the New Testament scenes were designed and mostly executed by one of the most interesting Italian illuminators of the fourteenth century. He appears first on folio 132 verso, portraying the arrival of Joseph and Mary in Bethlehem, each guided by a blithe, fluttering angel (Fig. 410). In the foreground, indeed partly standing outside the picture space, Joseph points out to Mary the cave and the manger within it. She carries a book, Joseph their scanty belongings. Behind them, Bethlehem and the daily life of its inhabitants – including, it seems, a religious service at an altar – are described in a novelistic manner reminiscent of Ambrogio Lorenzetti's frescoes of Good Government (Fig. 703). As in all the miniatures in this style the colors are very pale – blue, pink, a little green, buff, and gray-brown. The highest value, whether in the landscape, the architecture, or the figures, is provided by the bare surface of the parchment. The colors are so light and the touch of the brush so delicate that the miniatures almost give the impression of silver-point.

The scene of the appearance of the angel to recommend flight into Egypt (folio 139 verso – Fig. 412) shows Joseph and the Virgin with her Child lying symmetrically at opposite sides of a large 'double bed'. The interior is as circumstantial as the town of Bethlehem (Fig. 410). It includes even a dog crowded close to the fire. The display of food, utensils, and domestic pets recalls the Lorenzettian *Last Supper* in the Lower Church at Assisi.[149] The delight in the portrayal of domestic and courtly life enlivens another exceedingly rare scene, Joseph of Arimathea on his knees before Pilate, requesting the body of Christ (Fig. 411).[150] The event takes place in a very spacious setting, a sort of court created by an architectural triptych that is set at considerable depth. The walls of the downstairs rooms – the center one a throne-room – are removed to permit intriguing views into them and their inhabitants, falcons perched on convenient tie-rods and a stag wearing a golden collar. Pilate is accompanied by two dogs, one on each side like diminutive bodyguards. One of them seems to snarl at Joseph. Pilate himself is an exceptional figure who has stimulated the interest and imagination of the painter. Tall, powerful, now in advanced age rather soft and stout, he is a commanding personality, his face individualized in an extraordinary way. The ornamental patterns in his tunic, like those in the clothes of the other figures, have the sparkle of highly burnished gold. A similar polished gold, with punched crosses, is employed also in the backgrounds of all these miniatures, and the vaults are normally studded with golden stars.

We have observed that the lesser illuminators of the *Bible moralisée* were in the workshop, definitely Neapolitan, that produced a Missal now in Avignon (Fig. 409). The major artist is also linked with Naples, particularly with the frescoes in the Barresi Chapel of S. Lorenzo (Fig. 413). The landscape of the damaged fresco of the Nativity resembles that in the miniature of the angel appearing to Joseph (Fig. 412). Even the peculiarities of proportion and the odd facial types of the miniatures recur in the frescoes. The long narrow head of the Virgin, for instance, has an inadequately full and rounded back, and it lacks a proper indication of a neck. The chief master of the Bible was thus familiar with Giottesque style in Naples and also no doubt with the paintings by both Giotto and a follower who may be Maso di Banco. The Bible was illuminated, however, in the third quarter of the century, and several of its compositions seem to presuppose a knowledge of the frescoes by Andrea Bonaiuti in the Spanish Chapel in Florence, painted in 1366–1368, or of related paintings of the time.[151] In style also the miniatures are related to these frescoes, as well as to the painting of Orcagna.

These miniatures throw some light on three enigmatic panels that have never found a satisfactory place in the history of fourteenth-century painting. The panels have usually been attributed to a Sienese painter, working either at home or, since the panels are now in Aix, in Avignon.[152] As I remarked a decade ago, however, they resemble the miniatures in the Bible with regard to large aspects of design and also details of delineation.[153] The cave and the animals in the Aix *Nativity* (Fig. 414) are the same as those pointed out by Joseph on arrival in Bethlehem (Fig. 410), and the reclining Virgin in the panel could be interchanged with the Virgin asleep in her house (Fig. 412). The extensive landscape above the chamber in this miniature is remarkably like the one in the *Nativity*, and in both grasses and similar vegetation are evoked by the same curling, crossed, sketchy strokes. The cave and the landscape with animals, neither common in representations of the Nativity at this date, were to be seen in the fresco in S. Lorenzo (Fig. 413), and the cave as well as related figures – especially St. Joseph – appear in the Prayer Book of Queen Joanna (Fig. 415). The connections with Naples are pervasive.

Though the panels are deeply linked with the Bible they are much more Sienese, and they appear to be earlier. Either we are confronted with one master at two successive phases of his career or, as I now prefer to believe, two masters who had worked together at one period.[154] Two of the panels are in Aix, a city that has a special connection with the Anjou. It was in that town that *le bon roi* René established himself permanently around 1470 after leaving Angers. René was the successor to Louis II d'Anjou, who possessed the Bible. It is difficult to avoid the hypothesis that the manuscript and possibly the panels were acquired by Louis I d'Anjou sometime before his death in 1384, that they passed to Louis II, and that the panels were transmitted to René, who took them, with the rest of his collection, to Aix. The Bible and perhaps the panels provide us with a precious fragment of the Angevin collection, and they suggest that the Italianate taste of Jean de Berry was to some extent shared by his brother and his nephew of Anjou.

II

The Life of Jean de Berry

THE painters who sat at their tables producing the little pictures that are the subject of this publication normally managed, we assume, to keep their minds on their work despite the trouble in the world around them. Trouble, of course, there was – first of all the unending sequence of conflicts between princes and states produced by personal ambition and the hope, often vain, of profit. A case that is not atypical is the claim of the King of England to the throne of France. The claim was pressed by Edward III in 1336, and was followed by war, which for a century passed through cold and hot phases, causing distress in both countries. After a hundred years of intermittent strife there came the glorious moment for England and for Henry V when he was accepted as the heir of King Charles VI of France, who in 1420 gave him his daughter in marriage. Just as the great prize seemed to be his, however, Fate – as so often – snatched it away, for Henry did not meet one seemingly simple but basic requirement. He failed to outlive his father-in-law, dying two years later, a few weeks before him.

Before many years had passed the English were driven from France, and the chief beneficiaries of this long struggle were the Dukes – I do not say the people – of Burgundy. For his own advantage Philippe le Hardi and after him Jean sans Peur promoted the Anglo-French conflict by playing one off against the other, meanwhile enlarging and consolidating their domains. Gaining by astute intermarriage the great cloth-manufacturing cities of Flanders they emerged during this period as a new great power in Europe. Like other rulers they usually preferred to make their way by well-calculated purchases or marriages rather than by battles, and they strove constantly to maintain the support of the two highest rulers – in theory at least – the Emperor and the Pope. From 1378 on they had to keep in mind one more power, for that year marked the beginning of the Great Papal Schism.

Despite sacrifices inferior social groups gained advantages from the conflcts of their betters. The burghers, whose wealth was growing steadily from trade and manufacture, increased their political strength, and for short intervals even the workers and the peasants tasted power. The patrons of the outstanding painters were almost all noblemen, and indeed mostly great princes, many of whom appeared at different moments in their lives with different titles, not to mention different wives. The maze of family and dynastic relationships during this period might be presented to the reader by a narrative account such as may be found in the *Cambridge Medieval History*.[1] For the purpose of the present work two tables seem preferable: one gives a series of selected events in chronological order, and the other is a stemma of the French royal house, including of course the great princely patrons of Anjou, Berry, and Burgundy. These tables begin on page 345.

Some at least of the major events of the time become more vivid if we consider their relationship to one man, whose passion for illumination necessitates in any event a brief account of his life. For the full history of his political career the reader will be able to consult the excellent monograph by Mademoiselle Françoise Lehoux, which I have had the privilege of reading rapidly in typescript. Jean Duke of Berry was born on St. Andrew's day in 1340, the son of Jean le Bon, King of France from 1350 till his death in 1364. His mother, Bonne of Luxembourg, died of the plague when her son was nine years old. The King and Queen liked the company of cultivated men: the poet Guillaume de Machaut lived at the court and Petrarch accepted an invitation to visit. Both parents of Jean de Berry possessed beautiful illuminated books. His father commissioned the wonderful *Bible de Jean de Sy* (Figs. 376, 377), which was left incomplete when he was captured by the English at Poitiers in 1356, and his mother owned the no less wonderful Psalter illuminated by Pucelle (Figs. 352-355, 361), a painter for whom Jean de Berry later showed a special affection. Jean's parents apparently set an example, for every one of his brothers later formed exceptional collections of books as well as tapestries, *joyaux*, and other works of art. Indeed Jean's older brothers Charles, from 1364 Charles V of France, and Louis, from 1356 Duke of Anjou, as well as his younger brother Philippe, later Duke of Burgundy, compose the most remarkable fraternal group of collectors in history.

During his youth the Count of Poitou – Jean had received Poitou from his father – witnessed the English invasion of parts of France and two major French defeats, first at Crécy in 1346 and then at Poitiers in 1356. His father, captured at Poitiers, was taken to England, and released in 1360 only in return for the presence there of three of his sons, including Jean. By the Treaty of Brétigny signed in that year Poitou was ceded to the English, and to replace it King Jean le Bon in 1360 gave his son Auvergne and Berry 'en apanage'.[2] He also appointed him lieutenant for much of the territory south of the Loire. Philippe received Burgundy at this time, and Louis had earlier been given Anjou. From 1360 to 1367 the Duke of Berry remained a hostage, but from time to time he was paroled to France. At the beginning of this period – precisely on June 24, 1360 – he married Jeanne d'Armagnac, the daughter of Jean I, Count of Armagnac. They probably had seven children, who are listed with their spouses in the table on p. 349. The three sons all predeceased their father by many years.

From 1368 on the Duke of Berry lived continuously in France. Until 1380 the country was governed strongly and well by Charles V, who did not hold the Duke in high favor. Berry lived mostly outside of Paris, in Bourges, the Auvergne, and Poitiers after its recovery from the English in 1372. Those documents that have survived fire and sale as waste parchment give us a glimpse into the Duke's personal life and the growth of his interest in the arts.

Apart from records of the employment of artists, which we shall discuss below, we know that in 1370 and 1371 the Duke of Berry had several organs rebuilt, and that he was one of the first to introduce into France the new Flemish models with pedals. Contemporaries spoke of his enjoyment of church ceremonies and of secular as well as religious music.[3] He liked to read romances.[4] Quite sensibly he turned to dice only on the days when he was bled.

We first hear at this time of the Duke's interest in animals, and especially in dogs. Noblemen in the fourteenth century usually kept large numbers of hunting dogs, and not infrequently they possessed small menageries of less common animals. Jean's brother Charles kept lions in his Hôtel St. Pol, and we hear that a bear tore one of his tapestries in 1352.[5] Jean's enthusiasm during the 'seventies for *mâtins*, a breed of mastiff in the Auvergne, was exceptional, and his kennels for these large mountain dogs at the castle of Nonette became famous.[6] He owned fifteen hundred dogs in

1388, and when at that time he negotiated for the hand of Jeanne de Boulogne with the Comte de Foix, the latter requested six of the Duke's best hunting dogs as part of the bargain.[7] Jean de Berry was fond of small dogs as well; one bore the affectionate name of Lion.[8] In many portraits, beginning with the *Petites Heures*, the Duke is accompanied by one or two little white dogs (Figs. 34, 114). By chance there survives in a manual of domestic economy of about 1393 a vivid record of his love for these creatures. In 1373 he and his retinue went to Niort to see a dog that remained, day and night, by the ditch in which lay the body of its master, killed by the English. The Duke was so touched he endowed the dog, so to speak, for life. 'Et lui fit Monseigneur de Berry donner 10 francs qui furent baillés à un voisin pour lui quérir à manger toute sa vie.'[9]

After dogs the favorite animals of the Duke were bears, of which there are records from 1377 on.[10] The bears had their special *gardien*, who at times attained the position of *varlet*.[11] They traveled with the Duke in special wagons, moving from château to château along with tapestries, plate, jewels, and countless other possessions with which the Duke, like other princes, temporarily furnished one or another of his residences. The bear was a common emblem of Jean de Berry, and in a rather late miniature a small one, like the little dogs, seems to appear at his side (Fig. 34). The swan, the second common emblem, was also present in the Duke's entourage. Two of the large birds swim in the moat around the château of Mehun in the 'portrait' of it by the Limbourgs (Fig. 424). On one occasion the Duke bought fifty of the birds.[12] In 1401 his menagerie contained in addition a monkey, a wolf, a camel, and an ostrich. Each of the latter was, not surprisingly, provided with a *gardien*.[13]

There may well have been contemporaries of Jean de Berry who maintained that he cared more for animals and for art than for men. As early as 1359, when he was serving as deputy of the King in Languedoc, the Comte de Foix spoke out against the severity of his taxation.[14] From 1384 on we hear again of excessive taxation by the Duke in the same region. Popular resentment burst forth in riots. Charles VI, who in 1388 had assumed the royal power previously exercised by his uncles, soon went to Languedoc. There he tried and executed the Duke's agent, Bétisac, and relieved the Duke of his powers in the region. Froissart wrote vividly of the trial, of the Duke's alleged greed, of his generosity to his *valets de chambre* and of his vast expenditures on châteaux and precious stones. Parts of the description are worth quoting:

> . . . Béthisach n'avoit nul tort en ses deffenses et excusations; car le duc de Berry fut le plus convoitteux homme du monde et n'avoit cure où il fuist prins, mais qu'il l'eust; . . . Béthisach . . . fut . . . examiné pour sçavoir que toutes ces finances povoient estre devenues, car l'en trouvoit la somme de trente cens mille frans. Il respondi . . .

> 'Messeigneurs, je ne le puis bonnement scavoir. Il en a mis grant foison en ouvrages et réparations de chasteaulx et d'ostels et en achata de terres au conte de Boulongne et au conte d'Estampes et en pierrie, ainsi que vous scavés que tels choses il a achatté légièrement, et s'en a estoffé son estat très-grant que il a tousjours tenu, et si en a donné à Thiebaut et à Morinot et à ses vallets autour de luy tant que ils sont tous riches.'[15]

Another side of the Duke's personality may be disclosed by views ascribed to him in a debate on love that probably was held in Avignon in 1389, during the presence there of the King and his uncles of Anjou, Berry, and Burgundy. Where women are concerned, he allegedly said in substance, the more the merrier, and never tell the truth.[16]

During the reign of Charles V Jean de Berry played only a secondary role in national affairs. At the death of this great sovereign in 1380 Charles VI was only a boy of twelve years, and in the regency formed to govern until his majority the Dukes of Burgundy and Berry had a leading part. Their brother Louis I, Duke of Anjou, was preoccupied with his quest for the Kingdom of Naples, and he died in Italy in 1384. In 1381 Charles VI gave Berry a large house in Paris – the Hôtel de Nesle – and thenceforth he spent much more time in the capital.[17] A new metropolitan life and national power coincide with an expansion of the Duke's program of building and his patronage of the arts. He was active in the government of France but his brother Philippe of Burgundy proved to possess far more political acumen and ambition. Philippe became the real ruler of France, though he used his position mostly to strengthen his own duchy. For this reason and others the strain between him and Jean increased, and in 1386 Berry's procrastination contributed to the failure of Philippe's projected invasion of England.[18] The control of the two brothers over the country continued, however, until 1388, when the young King, counselled by the old advisers of his father – the Marmousets – assumed power. One of his first acts, as we have seen, was to correct the injustices of his uncle in Languedoc. In 1389 he visited Pope Clement VII in Avignon. We are told that the Pope proudly displayed his treasures.[19]

In 1388 Jeanne d'Armagnac died. The Duke decided he wanted a youthful spouse, and he sought the hand of Jeanne de Boulogne, a girl of twelve years who was living with her guardian Gaston de Foix. The Duke's proposal astonished everyone, including the King of France. Froissart records an exchange between Charles VI and the Duke:

(Charles VI) 'Beaulx oncles, que ferés-vous de une si jeune femme? Elle n'a que douze ans, et vous en avés soixante. Par ma foy, c'est grant folie pour vous de penser à telle besoigne.' . . .

(Berry) 'Se la fille est jeune, je la espargneray trois ou quatre ans, voire si longuement qu'elle sera femme parfaitte et fourmée.'

(Charles VI) 'Voire, . . . beaulx oncles; mais elle ne vous espargnera pas.'[20]

This flash of wit is all the more refreshing because it comes from a man always described as 'mad'. Even years later, in moments free of illness, Charles VI demonstrated an impressive curiosity and penetration, if we may trust his intimate counsellor, Pierre Salmon. According to the *Dialogues* of the two recorded in 1409, the first question Charles addressed to Salmon was: if Adam and Eve had not yielded to temptation, how would human beings have multiplied? At the end of a long, circuitous discourse Salmon concluded that nothing more would have been required of Adam and Eve and their successors than the holding of hands. The King's second question was: how long did the rebel angels remain in heaven? Salmon, undaunted, decided in favor of one hour.[21]

The King did not really oppose the marriage of his uncle to Jeanne de Boulogne, but the Comte de Foix, no admirer of Jean de Berry as we have seen, did his best to prevent it. After a year's delay he induced the Duke to accept his ward not only without dowry but against payment of 30,000 francs and the best *chiens berrichons*.[22] The marriage was celebrated in 1389. There were no children.

A new phase in the political life of the Duke, and indeed a new and tragic era for France, began in 1392. King Charles was stricken with the first of the fits that were to incapacitate him for much of the remainder of his life. Burgundy and Berry dismissed the King's counsellors and recaptured his authority. They were soon faced, however, with a new contender, the King's brother, Louis Duke of Orléans. Since marrying Valentina Visconti in 1389 Louis had been allied with the Milanese Duchy, and by 1400 he was the leader of a strong anti-Burgundian faction, the so-called Armagnacs.[23] The rivalry of Armagnacs and Burgundians became ever more intense, with Jean de Berry for many reasons among the former. In 1407 the assassination of Louis d'Orléans by Jean sans Peur, who had succeeded Philippe le Hardi in 1404, carried France to the verge of civil war.

The bitter struggle brought grief especially to Jean de Berry, who was a major target of the Burgundian party. In the early fifteenth century one of the Burgundians painted an unflattering image of the Duke of Berry in *Le Songe Véritable*:

De Jehan aussi, duc de Berry,	Tant que bien ly devoit souffire,
Par cas pareil, autel vous dy;	Car haultement s'en povoit vivre.
Il doit bien estre mis en compte,	Maiz s'Oultrecuidance et Convoitise,
Car sans mesure et sans compte	Ou au moins Foleur et Sotise,
En il a pris par grant oultrage,	Qui maintesfoiz le conseillerent,
Dont a maint homme a fait dommage.	En ce chemin sy le bouterent.[24]

. . . .

King Charles VI fell increasingly under the influence of the aggressive Jean sans Peur, who was admired furthermore by the masses in Paris. For his own safety Berry had to remain outside Paris for over two years, beginning in April 1410. A developing Parisian hatred of the Duke deprived posterity of his major works of art. In 1411 his Hôtel de Nesle was looted, and Bicêtre, full of splendid paintings and works of art of all kinds, was destroyed by fire (Fig. 423). Though Jean did not pose a threat to the crown equal to that of the Duke of Burgundy,[25] in the following year he found the latter and the King united against him. Along with his fellow Armagnacs he was besieged in Bourges. Hard pressed for funds he withdrew books and *joyaux* from the Sainte-Chapelle, and he was constrained to melt down some of his gold objects for coins to pay the troops.[26] The siege, which lasted only a month, ended with a dramatic meeting of Jean de Berry and his nephew Jean sans Peur, which was described by a contemporary chronicler. After the usual greetings and compliments the Duke of Berry, with tears in his eyes, addressed these words to Jean sans Peur: 'My dearly beloved nephew I admit that I have made great errors but you assuredly have made still greater ones. We must now renounce our divisions, to assure henceforth the peace of the realm.'[27]

After the defeat at Bourges the Duke of Berry lived almost continuously in Paris, in his Hôtel de Nesle. His last years were not tranquil, for the anti-Armagnac sentiment that was so strong among the Parisians and that had erupted in the looting and destruction of his houses in 1411 continued to plague him. On May 25, 1416, he dictated his will and the next day he bequeathed all his *joyaux*, books, and liturgical vestments in the Hôtel de Nesle to the Sainte-Chapelle in Bourges. He fell ill on June 6, 1416, and died on the fifteenth.[28] His heart was removed for St. Denis, his entrails for his parish church, Saint-André-des-Arcs, Paris.[29] His body lay for a time in the monastery of the Grands Augustins in Paris, under a *chapelle ardente* decorated by the painter Jean d'Orléans.[30] Then it was slowly carried on the long road to Bourges in a great procession, formed by members of the mendicant orders, the Augustinians and the Carmelites, and dozens of familiars at his court, including the *valet des petits chiens* and the *valet des oiseaux*. In the Sainte-Chapelle at Bourges, which the Duke had built as a mortuary chapel, the 'chapelle de bois' for his casket was lined with black cloth inside and blue without. The blue cloth bore his coat of arms, and the whole must have resembled the *chapelle ardente* in the *Brussels Hours* (Fig. 198). So many torches burned along the nave – more than two hundred – that some of the stained glass was removed to admit fresh air. A chronicler of the time took note of the death, and referred to the passion for which the Duke had become famous.

> Cette année, le quinziesme de juin, mourut le duc de Berry oncle du Roy, qui fut grand dommage pour le royaume: car il avoit esté en son temps vaillant prince, et honorable. Et se delectoit fort en pierres precieuses. Festoyoit tresvolontiers les estrangers, et leur donnoit du sien largement.[31]

During his last years Jean de Berry saw a steep decline in the fortunes of his party and his country, but he was spared the worst. Jean sans Peur was assassinated in 1419, and in 1420 the English occupied Paris and the North of France. Patronage of the arts diminished, and craftsmen migrated elsewhere.[32] For them the departure of the French court was a disaster. Those who remained 'riens ne font', said Eustache Deschamps.[33] The sick King Charles VI died in 1422. His son Charles VII lived in Bourges and in Tours. By a strange turn of fate it was King Charles VII who to a degree carried on the work of Jean de Berry in the Sainte-Chapelle of Bourges. He provided a large sum in 1447 for a *chasse* for the relic of the cross, and around 1450 he ordered the completion of Jean de Berry's tomb.[34] In 1461 the King died where Jean de Berry would no doubt have wished to die – in the château at Mehun-sur-Yèvre (Fig. 424).

III

Jean de Berry as Patron

1 · THE BUILDINGS

THE manuscripts of the Duke of Berry, which have so large a place in the first part at least of this history, represented in their time only a small part of his vast possessions. He was an avid and discriminating collector of objects as small as rubies and as large as castles. Even among the Valois princes, famous for their constructions, he earned a reputation as a great builder. He enriched his chapels and his châteaux with sculpture and stained glass. The Sainte-Chapelle in Bourges and the Château de Mehun were envied by all the princes of Europe. We know that the walls of the palaces of Bicêtre, Riom, and Poitiers bore mural paintings and decorations of many kinds. The inventories record paintings on panel. The Duke assembled dozens of tapestries and hundreds of *joyaux* or goldsmith's work and precious stones.

Most of these countless possessions have been destroyed. Several prophets, presumably from the Sainte-Chapelle, are in the Musée Jacques-Cœur at Bourges and one is in the Hutinel collection in Paris (Figs. 593–595). A head from Mehun now in the Louvre is one of the most impressive sculptures of the period apart from the work of Sluter (Fig. 596). A few battered heads in the Musée Jacques Cœur have been connected with the Duke's buildings.[1] Many of the rubies, emeralds, pearls, and diamonds no doubt survive, but often in a different setting and they have not been identified. One large altarpiece of bone, ordered from the Embriachi in Venice for his great-niece Marie at the Abbey of Poissy, is preserved in the Louvre (Fig. 427).[2] It is an imposing but monotonous work. On the other hand the enamelled cup and the reliquary preserved in the British Museum are very beautiful; the latter indeed is one of the most splendid surviving *joyaux* of the period (Figs. 471, 473, 571). A handsome yellow agate cup, presumably once the Duke's, is in the Musée de Berry at Bourges (Fig. 472). Two of his marvelous golden medals of Roman emperors are preserved in copies (Figs. 462–465).

Of all the Duke's possessions only the manuscripts are still well represented today. We possess perhaps a third of the books that passed through his hands. Certainly the Duke or his courtiers, looking at their massive castles, would not have doubted that they rather than the fragile books would prove to possess the greater durability. The books have outlived the jewels, the tapestries, the paintings, and even the castles not so much because they were highly valued in subsequent periods but because they were not. Unlike the precious stones and goldsmith's work, they had no considerable intrinsic worth. They did not contain enough gold to make an *écu*. And unlike sculptures, which were exposed to violence at times like the Revolution, they were easily transported and sequestered.

The stoutest of the Duke's possessions, on the other hand – his buildings – have succumbed more readily. Some slowly crumbled; others, like the Château de Nonette, were razed for political reasons;[3] most were pillaged for stone. The castle of Lusignan, which the English surrendered to

Du Guesclin and the Duke of Berry in 1374 and which the Duke remodeled, has all but disappeared (Fig. 419). The great hall still stands in two palaces, Bourges and Poitiers (Figs. 429, 431, 432). At Riom one may still see the Sainte-Chapelle (Fig. 426), and at Mehun part of the north tower (Fig. 425).[4]

The Duke was directing work on several residences in the 'seventies. During the last years of the reign of Charles V he was transforming for his purposes the old royal palace in Bourges.[5] Guy de Dammartin served as his architect there and also, from around 1379 on, for the palace in Riom.[6] It may appear in the background of *May* in the *Très Riches Heures*.

With the assumption of a leading role in the regency after the death of Charles V in 1380 the Duke quickly increased his program of building and acquisition. In 1381 he received from the young King Charles VI, no doubt in response to a request, the Hôtel de Nesle in Paris. This building, on the site now occupied by the Institut de France, served as one of his principal residences for the rest of his life. A massive structure, it later became the bastion of the Armagnac faction in Paris. It was sacked by the Burgundians in January 1412 but restored, and the Duke died there in 1416. He acquired and transformed a second house in the Parisian region, the Château de Bicêtre, on the site of the existing hospital of the same name. It may have been represented by the Limbourgs in *September* in the *Très Riches Heures* (Fig. 423).[7] The Duke made it one of the richest houses in France, covering its walls with tapestries, mural paintings, and works of art of many kinds. When the Burgundians set fire to it in 1411 the chroniclers lamented its loss, and alluded particularly to a series of portraits of historic figures, of the emperors, popes, and kings of France.[8] In 1408 a 'paintre alemant' was working there, perhaps to be identified with Paul de Limbourg.[9]

The Duke obtained also the châteaux at Dourdan and Étampes. Dourdan, not far from Paris on the river Orge, is represented in the Calendar picture for *April* in the *Très Riches Heures* (Fig. 420).[10] Étampes, acquired in 1385 from Louis II d'Anjou, appears in *August*, showing the great *donjon* that still exists (Fig. 422). From 1382 to 1388 Berry undertook a major reconstruction of the Palais de Poitiers, building a large hall terminating in a great *cheminée* (Figs. 429, 434, 435). High on it – higher than any photographer has yet ascended – he placed large statues of himself and Jeanne de Boulogne, accompanied by Charles VI and Isabeau de Bavière (Figs. 436, 437). Guy Dammartin acted as his *maître des oeuvres* for the Palais and for the châteaux of Poitiers and of Lusignan in Poitou.[11] The château of Poitiers may be represented in *July* in the *Très Riches Heures* (Fig. 421) and Lusignan is clearly identifiable in *March* by the golden dragon that soars over the great structure (Fig. 419). According to a current legend the fairy Mélusine, protectress of the castle, assumed the form of a dragon.[12]

In the region of Bourges the Duke rebuilt the old château at Mehun-sur-Yèvre, which became one of his favorite residences. The construction, begun around 1367, was far advanced by 1385,[13] and in the early 'nineties the Duke was enriching it with sculpture and painting, entrusted we are told by Froissart, to the 'maistre de ses euvres de taille et de peinture . . . à faire nouvelles ymages et pointures'.[14] This *maître*, Froissart says, was the unrivalled André Beauneveu, first recorded in the Duke's service as 'ymagier' in 1386.[15] The beauty of the *nouvelles ymages* moved Philippe le Hardi, then engaged in the embellishment of Champmol, to send his own masters to Mehun to see what was going on. A builder-mason and a carpenter went in 1392, and the following year

D

Philippe despatched his painter, Jean de Beaumetz (Figs. 830, 831), and his sculptor, Claus Sluter.[16] The Limbourgs have preserved for us the appearance of the exterior of the château in the *Très Riches Heures* (Fig. 424). In the scene of the Devil's endeavor to corrupt Christ with worldly riches he stands on a hill behind the château, which presumably appears as the symbol of the greatest imaginable temptation. The château, occupied in the mid-fifteenth century by Charles VII, was represented again in the background of a miniature of the *Annunciation* dated 1465 now in the Metropolitan Museum, New York (Fig. 430). The 'high-fidelity' of the Limbourg portrait is proved by an engraving of 1737 showing what was left of the building (Fig. 425).

Around 1390, as Mehun was nearing completion, Jean de Berry turned his attention to his tomb. A bull of Pope Clement VII in 1391 referring to the Cathedral of Bourges stated that the Duke had chosen to be buried there.[17] Indeed he wanted a monument in a prominent place in the choir, and when the canons objected he obtained permission from the Pope in 1392 to construct a large chapel adjoining his palace in Bourges.[18] Inasmuch as the Pope gave him the right to control the appointments of the officers of the chapel, he obtained a certain independence of the canons of the cathedral and the archbishop.[19] He was no doubt moved by the example of his brother's mortuary chapel at Champmol, consecrated in 1388, and he adopted for his own the plan of introducing statues of the donor and his wife into the building. The chief relic destined for the chapel was a piece of the cross, which Charles V had given him early in 1372 (Fig. 475). This was a piece cut, according to the charter of the chapel, by the King's own hand from the famous royal relic that King Louis had deposited in the Sainte-Chapelle in Paris. For a similar relic Charles V began the construction of his own Sainte-Chapelle in 1379 at his castle at Vincennes. By building large palace chapels at Bourges as well as at Riom (begun in 1395) the Duke of Berry was following a royal convention.

The chapel at Bourges was begun by Guy de Dammartin and completed by his brother Drouet in 1405. It was consecrated on April 18 (Figs. 431, 432). Already in 1404 the Duke began to give to the Sainte-Chapelle a considerable part of his vast treasure and his library. Apart from a few objects such as a copy of Virgil's *Bucolics*[20] the gifts possessed a religious significance, but the size and richness of the collection indicate that the Duke had in mind their aesthetic effect also. In this respect his donation anticipated the 'museums' created later by individuals such as Pope Sixtus IV, who in 1471 installed a collection of antiquities in the Capitol, or Julius II, who established a similar collection in the Belvedere. Of course in these instances a religious personage put on exhibition a group of secular works, whereas the case of Jean de Berry was just the reverse.

The Duke did not relinquish immediately all control over the splendid collection. He obtained from Pope John XXIII the right to withdraw objects whenever he should wish or need to do so.[21] This provision, which strikes us perhaps as odd, conformed with the economic realities of a time when a prince's working capital lay largely in his *joyaux*. The Duke indeed occasionally availed himself of this privilege, especially during the siege of Bourges in the summer of 1412, when many objects were melted down for gold coins to pay the Armagnac troops.[22]

The Sainte-Chapelle in Bourges, similar to its model in Paris but larger, consisted of one great nave. It was composed of six bays, and, according to a sixteenth-century historian, a colored statue of an apostle or an evangelist, larger than life-size, stood on each pier.[23] For the apse the

Duke commissioned the statue of *Notre-Dame-la-Blanche* worshipped by effigies of his wife and himself, parts of which are still extant (Fig. 501). He ordered his tomb from the same sculptor, Jean de Cambrai. Like the tomb of Philippe le Hardi it consisted of the *gisant* and of *pleurants*, though Jean de Cambrai executed only a few of the latter, presumably before the Duke's death (Fig. 502).[24] The large windows of the chapel were filled with stained glass, some panes of which were removed, as we have seen, during the ceremony of burial.[25] They were praised in the sixteenth century by Geoffroy Tory, but a bad storm in 1756 broke four of them and damaged the chapel, which had already been seared by fire in 1693. Because of a conflict between the chapter of the Cathedral and the clergy of the Sainte-Chapelle, the building was abandoned to the weather.[26] Little remains today but the scattered sculptures mentioned above, some of the stained glass rearranged in the crypt of the Cathedral (Figs. 597-599), and a wooden *sedilia* for celebrants of the mass in the church at Morogues. The chapel at Riom still stands, but its glass belongs to the later fifteenth century (Fig. 426). It should be mentioned that in the Burgundian church at Champmol there stood a 'chappelle et autel de Monseigneur de Berry',[27] which, to be sure, was established by Philippe le Hardi before the intensification of the Burgundian-Armagnac conflict.

These chapels were understood in their time as proper demonstrations of piety, and the anonymous chronicler of the reign of Charles VI speaks in one breath of the Duke's passion for precious stones and of his gifts to the Church:

> He was distinguished among all the princes of the blood by his munificence, and he endowed several churches of the realm with relics and with *joyaux* enriched by gems. The royal monastery of St. Denis and the chapter of Notre-Dame-de-Paris must especially acknowledge this if they are not to incur the reproach of ingratitude. He enjoyed continually importing rubies, sapphires, and emeralds from the Orient. He also liked craftsmen who worked with pearls and precious stones, and from them he often ordered chasubles, copes, and other ecclesiastical ornaments enriched by gold fringes and of almost inestimable value. These were so numerous that he could have clothed with equal splendor the canons of three cathedrals. Animated always by an ardent devotion to the service of God, he maintained in his home many chaplains who day and night sang the praises of God and celebrated mass, and he took care to compliment them whenever the service lasted longer or was more elaborate than usual.[28]

Like almost all other resourceful men in the late Middle Ages, in or outside the church, Berry collected relics avidly. Given the fervor that they evoked, it was quite natural that the high point of the visit of the crippled Emperor Charles IV to Paris in 1377–1378 should be the display of the famous relics in the Sainte-Chapelle, the piece of the cross, the crown of thorns, and the head of St. Louis.[29] In a miniature representing the Sainte-Chapelle the Boucicaut Master removed one wall of the church to show them (Fig. 428).

The chapter of the Cathedral of Chartres, to which the Duke presented a splendid *parement d'autel*,[30] gave him in 1406 a reliquary of the cross, 'de si ancien temps en ladicte eglise qu'il n'en estoit memoire à homme vivant'.[31] Fragments of nails used in the Crucifixion were given to the Duke in 1384 by Pope Clement VII.[32] Jean de Berry owned already in 1401 the chalice from which Christ drank at the Last Supper; at his death the appraisers put a low price on it.[33] The yellow agate cup preserved in the Musée Jacques Cœur at Bourges is probably identical with one that, according to the inventory of 1402, bore a golden head of the Baptist and was set in a jewelled base (Fig. 472).[34] The Doge of Venice gave him a relic of the body of one of the Innocents.[35] An enamelled gold reliquary of a thorn now in the British Museum bears the Duke's arms (Fig. 571).[36] We shall discuss this rare and beautiful object shortly.

2 · THE INVENTORIES

Of Jean de Berry's vast collection the manuscripts alone survive in considerable number. We know about the other objects only from the inventories and from scattered records of payment or purchase, still not fully published. These inventories, which give us a glimpse into a lost world of dazzling splendor, are remarkable documents in themselves. They represent another exceptional accomplishment of an unrivaled connoisseur. Inventories of the possessions of the great collectors of the time were normally made immediately after their death. The records, ordered by the executors, were needed for the testamentary bequests and for the attempt to satisfy the creditors. Testamentary inventories have survived of the collections of Charles V (1380),[37] Philippe le Hardi (1404),[38] Louis d'Orléans (1408),[39] Jean sans Peur (1420),[40] and Marguerite de Bavière (1424).[41]

The great exceptions were Louis I d'Anjou and Jean de Berry. Towards 1380 the former produced, apparently himself, a remarkably detailed inventory of his fabulous collection of *joyaux*.[42] Jean de Berry too, wanted to take stock during his lifetime. To be sure, his brother Charles V had asked his librarian Gilles Malet to make a catalogue in 1373, but only of his books.[43] Jean de Berry undertook his first general inventory shortly after his sixtieth birthday. It was begun in December 1401 at the Château de Dourdan by Guillaume de Ruilly, *garde des joyaux*, and continued at the Hôtel de Nesle in Paris. In May 1402 Ruilly was succeeded by Robinet d'Étampes for the work at Mehun and Bourges. Robinet remained as keeper with Jean de Berry until the latter's death. The Duke chose his man well, for his skill and diligence combined to produce the most informative inventories of the time. The length of his entries is less proportionate to the costliness than to the complexity and exceptional nature of the objects. Famous rubies are described briefly, whereas the accounts of rare objects such as medals of the Emperors Constantine, Heraclius, Tiberius, and Augustus, include a precise transcription or translation of the inscriptions on them (Figs. 462-465).[44] When Robinet possessed the information he regularly recorded the sources of acquisitions and the dates. When the Duke disposed of an object, Robinet recorded the recipient (but unfortunately not often the date) in a marginal note. Thus he dutifully indicated in the inventory of 1401–1403 all the objects withdrawn from the Duke's collection and given to the Sainte-Chapelle. For this gift we possess also the record of receipt of Arnoul Belin, the first treasurer of the chapel.

In the fullness of their descriptions and the variety of their facts Robinet's inventories are unmatched. His descriptions of the Duke's manuscripts surpass even those of the exceptional Gilles Malet.[45] He might, however, have found a good model in the catalogue of 1338 of an exceptional scholarly collection, the library of the Sorbonne.[46] Robinet's entries are much fuller than those of the Medici inventories in the second half of the fifteenth century. Piero de' Medici did, to be sure, order an inventory of his objects in 1456 and again in 1465, a year after his father's death, but the entries are only brief identifications.[47] Lorenzo's possessions were inventoried, and again summarily, only after his death in 1492. In this inventory, as well as in Piero's second, each item is priced.[48] Unfortunately for historians of art even the *inventario generale della guardaroba* of the Medici from 1553 to 1568 is not as rich in information as Robinet's accounts.[49]

Jean de Berry's inventories are thus exceptional in character as well as number. The Duke rewarded his counsellor and 'garde des joyaux' by ennobling him and his wife.[50] After compiling the list of 1413–1414 Robinet continued to record acquisitions, with their dates, up to the Duke's death. He thus reached the stage of current documentation of accessions, a practice that became normal only in later museums. Though Robinet was present when the Duke made and signed his will on May 25, 1416,[51] and remained during the compilation of the inventory after the Duke's death several weeks later, authority for the commission was given by the executors to Jean Lebourne. All the items were appraised, usually at levels below their purchase prices. The many creditors, bankers, and dealers at first attempted to attach the estate. It was not unusual for princes of the time to die insolvent. After the death of Philippe le Hardi in June 1404 his sons could not find enough money in the ducal treasury to buy mourning clothes. The sixty torchbearers in the funeral procession were paid in gold plate.[52] The noteworthy aspect of Jean de Berry's financial position was not the existence of a swarm of creditors, but the fact that these creditors were almost all purveyors of precious objects and works of art.[53] The claim which they filed thus gives us further information about the purchases of the Duke in his last years.

The most exceptional aspect of Robinet's inventories is that his descriptions often go beyond the materials and the subjects represented to the classification of the techniques and the styles. To accomplish this he employed a group of concepts, one of which at least has haunted modern writing on European art of this period. 'Ouvraige de Lombardie' has symbolized for a long time that close relationship between France and Italy, especially France and Lombardy, that characterized the painting of this period. Fifty years ago the term was thought to be vague but perhaps signifying French paintings that were exceptionally Italianate in character.[54] Some recent historians, while still expressing uncertainty, have noticed related concepts in the Duke of Berry's inventories, and are inclined to identify 'ouvraige de Lombardie' with North Italian illumination.[55]

No study of the concepts employed by Robinet has yet been made. They were probably current in the Duke's circle, and some of them, with more or less the same content, were used elsewhere during this period. A comprehensive exploration of fourteenth- and early fifteenth-century terminology, which would provide the fullest clarification, is beyond the scope of this publication. What follows, limited to Robinet's usage, represents only a beginning, though his inventories are by far the richest source of the time.

'Tableaux de l'ouvrage de Rome', as we have seen, were sold in Paris in 1328.[56] On the other hand terms of this kind were not used by Nicolas Viaut and Arnoul Belin when they began the first inventory for Jean de Berry in December 1401. A crucifix, for instance, that the Emperor Manuel II Paleologus gave to the Duke[57] was not characterized, as it very probably would have been by Robinet, as 'ouvrage de Grèce'; indeed he later used precisely this formula for a textile that the same Emperor gave the Duke.[58] The very second item that Robinet described when he took charge in May 1402 was a gold and enamelled *Madonna* 'de l'ovrage d'Angleterre'.[59] From then on similar phrases recur in his inventories and, under his influence, in the testamentary inventory of 1416.

A phrase very similar to the one Robinet applied to the *Madonna* – 'ovrage d'Angleterre' – he employed several times to characterize the famous embroideries of the kind generally known as *opus anglicanum*, which served for ecclesiastical vestments, for altar frontals ('frontiers') and dossals ('doussiers').[60] From these instances we learn that the concepts of Robinet, though they may most frequently refer to one kind of object, were not inherently limited to them. 'Ouvrage de Grèce' was applied to panel paintings as well as to *joyaux* and textiles.[61] Two golden chandeliers were described as 'à la façon d'Alemaigne',[62] and a *houppelande* as 'à la façon de Hongrie'.[63] 'Ouvraige de Venise' seems to have been applied only to *orfèvrerie*, especially to objects of chalcedony or crystal.[64] The one painting that was, I believe, produced there is not identified in this way.[65]

As far as I can see every object characterized as 'ouvraige de Florance' was an embroidery.[66] 'Sienne' is lacking entirely, and the great interest of the Duke and his painters in Tuscan painting is not reflected in Robinet's classifications. It is possible to understand why this was so. Robinet's distinctions were based primarily on materials and techniques, and in his time certain centers were identified with certain ways of working. Since the Duke, like other princes of the time, received examples of local handicrafts as gifts from rulers as remote as Constantinople, Cyprus, Hungary, Venice, and Spain, he and his registrar had at hand 'documented works' for their connoisseurship. No Sienese or Florentines gave gifts to the Duke, and the Doge of Venice did not offer a painting. There were, furthermore, no large technical or material differences between the paintings of the several Italian centers. Even today scholars are not quite sure about all of them.

Despite the difficulties presented by paintings of unknown provenance Robinet occasionally introduced classifications. He may of course have had facts lost to us, such as information offered by the seller or donor. He said that three manuscripts had miniatures 'de l'ouvraige de Lombardie'.[67] The grounds for Robinet's ascriptions are not evident, but that he often, at least, intended to refer to a regional style, and that his statements could be correct, is indicated by another entry. He said that an *Epistles* of Seneca was written 'de lettre lombarde', and he noted later that it had actually come into the collection from the Duke of Milan.[68] In these instances Robinet had in mind the style of the script, and in the realm of paleography there is other evidence to prove the soundness of his judgments. The beautiful French Bible of *circa* 1400, Bibliothèque nationale, fr. 159 (Fig. 822), for instance, is said to be 'de lettre françoise',[69] and the Bolognese Missal in the Staatsbibliothek in Munich is correctly and more subtly described as 'de lettre boulonnoise'.[70] Robinet did not, on the other hand, similarly classify the miniatures in this Missal (Figs. 716, 717, 751), and he did not mention the fact that one of them is signed by Niccolò da Bologna. He did, however, characterize the 'hystoires' in four of the several other manuscripts said to be written in Bolognese script: in one, a Psalter, they were 'en l'ovrage de Lombardie',[71] and three others, a Decretal, a Missal, and a Book of hours, had 'imaiges romains' or 'de la manière romainne'.[72]

Robinet seems to have had no concept of peculiarly Bolognese illumination, just as he had no idea of Tuscan painting. This is surprising, because even though the 'Lombard' domain of Gian Galeazzo Visconti was vast, and Italians themselves sometimes identified all of North Italy with Lombardy,[73] illumination flourished in the *city* of Bologna, and one may suspect that the Decretal originated there. Rome, on the other hand, was quite unproductive during the Trecento, and the miniatures ascribed to this center might actually have been executed in Tuscany, or even Bologna, not to mention Naples. In fact a Bible 'enluminée d'ouvrage roumain' that Jean de Berry kept at Mehun had belonged to Robert d'Anjou, King of Naples.[74]

In the arts of illumination and painting, where technique and material yielded much less evidence for classification, Robinet's attributions were less precise and reliable. We are probably safe, however, in interpreting Lombardy as North Italy, and Rome as Rome, Naples and perhaps Tuscany, with Bologna lying uncertainly between. This classification conforms with the convention of calling Italians from Tuscany or north of Tuscany 'Lombards'.[75] Robinet's ideas, however, apply only to 'modern' painting. He possessed some sense of time and history. He characterized the panels of one altarpiece as 'tous neufs'.[76] Other paintings he described as 'ancien' or 'bien ancien' or 'très ancien'. When he coupled these temporal concepts with a spatial one, say, Rome, the latter acquired a very different connotation. One 'très ancien Psautier . . . ystorié d'ovrage romain' happens to be preserved. This well-known manuscript is no older than the eleventh century, it is English, and the Duke may have purchased it while he was a hostage on the island.[77] This is the only instance of the connection of 'ancien et romain' with Romanesque.

Robinet classified many panel paintings as 'd'ancienne façon'. One, he reported, was said to have come from Rome,[78] another was given to the Duke by the Queen of Cyprus.[79] The origin of the rest is obscure,[80] but they were not ancient in our sense. The same probably should be said about two golden goblets, full of scrolls with Latin inscriptions, and described as 'd'ancienne façon'.[81] Robinet apparently did not, in fact, employ the term *ancien* for objects of Greco-Roman antiquity. Those items in the inventories that might seem the more likely candidates for this category are not classified at all. The medal of Julius Caesar, for instance, is not described in this way, though his face is said to be 'contrefait au vif'.[82] None of the cameos is identified as *ancien*, though some of them surely were antique (Fig. 458).[83] Whereas in France around 1400 the idea of pagan antiquity was clear enough in literature,[84] it seems not yet to have come into sharp focus in the visual arts.

3 · ARTISTS IN THE DUKE'S SERVICE

Before considering the main categories of the Duke's work of the art we may ask when and how so huge a collection was actually formed. We have referred earlier to the Duke's increased building activities in the 'eighties, after he assumed greater power in the government of France. Of course he constructed or remodeled residences even in the 'seventies, and from this decade come references to the employment of painters and illuminators as well as sculptors and weavers of tapestries. Employment at a salary is normally more of a commitment than the purchase of an object, and it is therefore worth while to give a brief account of these artists even when none of their work for the Duke has been identified.

As early as 1369 Étienne Lannelier served as 'peintre du duc', and in 1371 he was described as 'peintre et vallet de chambre'.[85] Thus he already held the position at court filled by his famous successors, Paul, Jean, and Herman de Limbourg. The Duke gave the honorific title to crafts-men as well as noblemen, and tailors along with painters and illuminators were eligible. In 1398 there were twenty-three *valets de chambre* at the court.[86] Records of Lannelier in subsequent years are lacking, but in 1391 he was in Bourges, active still (or again) as the Duke's painter, and in that year he was one of the small group of painters who served as 'charter members' of the new craft corporation in Paris.[87]

In 1369 and 1371, around the time when Étienne Lannelier began to work for him, the Duke bought some *tableaux* from the King's painter, Jean d'Orléans.[88] A master of the same name, though probably not identical, was active in Bourges as the Duke's painter from 1410 on. In 1379 Jean de Berry paid another painter and *valet de chambre* of the King for 'certaines pourtrai-tures'.[89] This master we know: the famous 'Jehan de Bruges', author of a signed miniature for the King (Fig. 382), designer of the Angers tapestries (Figs. 380, 381, 387), and a leading painter during the reign of Charles V. Bondol and his followers are not extensively represented in the Duke's books;[90] the Duke quickly outgrew his interest in their style.

While Étienne Lannelier bore the titles of *peintre du duc* and *valet de chambre* in 1369–1371 as well as in 1391, Jacquemart de Hesdin was receiving a salary in 1384 as *peintre du duc*, though we know his work only as *enlumineur*. He remained in the employ of the Duke through 1409, at least.[91] Jacquemart is not described as *valet* in extant documents, but contrary to the usual assumption it seems probable that at many periods the Duke had more than one major painter at his court, retained on a salary. He was clearly much attached to the painter and *valet* Michelet Saumon, to whom he gave gifts, and of whom we hear from 1401 to 1415.[92] Of course there were always at the châteaux one or more painters busy with decorative work of one kind or another,[93] but they were not recipients of gifts from the Duke, and probably not of much attention either.

The illuminator Jean le Noir, who had worked for King Charles, received payments from Jean de Berry in 1372 and 1375; he may be identical with the so-called Master of the Passion (Figs. 107-113).[94] Paul de Limbourg worked for Philippe le Hardi early in his career, but he served as *valet de chambre* of Jean de Berry from 1413 on, according to extant documents. There is in fact good reason to believe he and his brothers entered the service of Jean de Berry earlier, very probably by 1408, when the *Belles Heures* seem to me to have been begun, and in fact already in 1405.[95] Indeed we learn that in 1408 the Duke was holding captive a girl of eight years for his 'paintre alemant' in Bicêtre, who wanted to marry her,[96] and the following year he gave a house in Bourges to 'ung sien paintre nommé Pol, natif du païs dallemaigne'.[97] Usually Paul and his brothers are said to have been engaged by the Duke only after Jacquemart de Hesdin completed the *Grandes Heures* in 1409 and disappeared from view, but study of the Duke's manuscripts shows that he had more than one major artist working on books at the same time.[98] The Duke seems not to have felt constrained by any fear of competition; indeed, he rather liked it, as we shall see. And there have survived occasional records of payment to other, presumably minor, illumina-tors whose presence would in any event have to be inferred from the nature of the existing manuscripts.[99]

In addition to painters of panels, murals, and miniatures, specialists in other kinds of painting were employed by the Duke. He needed, especially for his chapels, *verriers* such as Milet le Cavelier, to whom he gave a diamond ring after 1402, and to whom he lent, perhaps as a model, a manuscript of the *Seven Planets*.[100] Shortly after 1408 the Duke probably engaged a Sienese painter in wood, in other words an *intarsiatore* (Fig. 553),[101] and he employed several tapestry weavers, including Nicolas Bataille, maker of the Angers *Apocalypse*.[102]

André Beauneveu is recorded in the service of Jean de Berry as a sculptor and painter in 1386,[103] and Jean de Rupy de Cambrai, as *imagier* or sculptor, the following year.[104] Beauneveu died around 1402, and in the last ten or fifteen years of the Duke's life Jean de Cambrai executed the effigy of the Duke for his tomb (Fig. 502) and also the figures of the Duke and Duchess kneeling before Notre-Dame-la-Blanche (Figs. 501, 510, 511). He was to the much greater sculptor Beauneveu at the court of Berry what Jacques de Liège was to Sluter at the court of Burgundy.

Records of the Duke's employment of goldsmiths go back to the 'sixties.[105] Members of this craft were much in demand at a time when the table service was silver and gold (Fig. 489), forks crystal,[106] spoons serpentine and cornelian.[107] Even the toothpicks were refulgent.[108] Strawberries came to the table in specially designed 'broches de cristal montées en or ou en argent'.[109] The Duke played chess with men of gilded silver or jasper and crystal.[110] Of all this, and of the splendid reliquaries the goldsmiths made of enamelled gold and precious stones – their major works – very little remains. Quite commonly the objects were melted down within a few years of their completion. The life of the goldsmiths was thus somewhat like that of cooks: a relatively long period of preparation and a relatively short one of enjoyment. But the goldsmiths, of course, sometimes cooked an object for years, and we learn from Lorenzo Ghiberti that the greatest of them, a certain Gusmin, was so saddened by the melting of one of his major works that he retired to a monastery, abandoning his craft forever.[111]

These men had to face a special kind of occupational frustration, but in the service of Jean de Berry they suffered less than with many other employers, at least until the intensification of the Armagnac-Burgundian conflict and the English war in the last six years of the Duke's life. During the siege of Bourges in 1412 the Duke withdrew precious objects from the Sainte-Chapelle, as we have observed. The greatest of his golden crosses, which he gave to Charles VI shortly before his death, was melted down by the King within a year to pay the soldiers who were battling the English.[112] Among the goldsmiths who served the Duke, three deserve mention. Jean de Morselles left the service of the King for that of the Duke of Berry, and remained with him from 1369 until, apparently, his death in 1400.[113] As godfather the Duke attended the baptism of Morselle's son. Jean Chenu is recorded as 'orfèvre du duc' and 'valet de chambre' from 1402 to 1413,[114] and Herman Rince held this title at the end of the Duke's life. He acted as appraiser of the *ioyaux* for the executors.[115]

4 · AGENTS AND DEALERS

The extant manuscripts and sculptures prove that an important part of the Duke's collection was produced by artists in his service. Another large section was accumulated by purchase. The Duke, like the early collectors of ancient texts, was served by scouts. We happen to learn of one, Pierre

Salmon, who during his travels watched out for artists as well as objects that he thought would please the Duke. Pierre Salmon was the scholarly counsellor of King Charles VI. Given the Duke's taste, it is no accident that we should hear of him writing his patron from Italy and recommending an Italian artist. In a letter sent from Florence in January 1408 Salmon said: 'Et d'autre part . . . je say que vous désirez veoir et avoir choses propres et plaisans et ouvriers souverains et parfais en leur art et science. . . .'[116] Salmon then referred to an outstanding artist not of Florence but of Siena, an *intarsiatore* and sculptor who was probably Domenico dei Cori, author of the intarsia in the Cappella del Popolo of the Palazzo Pubblico, Siena (Fig. 553). Salmon asked the Duke, if interested, to arrange with Jean Sac (Giovanni Sacco) in Genoa for funds to bring the artist to France. The Duke replied to Salmon in April, addressing him in Genoa, and asking him to invite the artist to come to France. 'Et avecques ce avez trouvé un ouvrier très solemnel de musayque et de faire ymages de merqueterie, auquel, pource que vous savez que nous prenons plaisir en choses estranges, vous traicteriez voulentiers qu'il venist devers nous. . . .'[117] If the *ouvrier solemnel* was Domenico dei Cori, he might have gone to France, because references to him in Siena are lacking between June and October 1408.[118] Furthermore, the Duke's inventory of 1413 lists several specimens of Domenico's specialty, wood marqueterie with 'images', a kind of object not mentioned in the earlier inventory of 1401–1403.[119]

If Domenico dei Cori did go to Bourges or Paris he would not, as we shall see, have found himself the only Italian artist in the Duke's service. But by far the greatest number of Italians in the circle of Berry were the so-called Lombards. These were the Italian bankers, money-changers, and merchants who not only served the Duke's financial needs but sold him objects of many kinds. They were in fact vendors of everything under the sun and of some things really not, such as the horns of unicorns. They specialized, however, in precious stones and *joyaux*. These objects, readily convertible into cash, they frequently took back again as security against loans. A few of these great merchants were French,[120] but the Italians are more prominent in the inventories and they compose a strikingly high proportion of the creditors at the time of the Duke's death.[121] They possessed greater capital, their businesses were more highly organized, and some, like the Rapondi and the Spifami, had branches in several cities, Bruges, Dijon, Avignon, as well as Paris and Italy.

Most of these dealers were Tuscan. In 1378 Bernardo di Cino of Florence or du Cigne (Bernard de Chinon) helped the Duke sell some valuable objects that he had given in pawn to Jewish money-lenders,[122] and in 1389 Cino raised money for a payment to the Comte de Foix in return for his release of Jeanne de Boulogne. Bernard du Cigne (the same man?) was for a time *maître d'hôtel* of the Duke.[123] The Duke bought three of his famous gold medals from Florentine 'marchants' living in Paris. Michele de' Pazzi ('de Paxi' or 'de Passy') supplied the medals of Tiberius and of Augustus,[124] the former in 1402, while Antonio Mancini (Manchin) sold to the Duke the medal of Constantine (Figs. 462, 463).[125] In 1402 Mancini found for the Duke a valuable golden panel with reliefs on both sides, containing Latin and Greek inscriptions.[126] Whereas the panel may have been an Italian object, perhaps Venetian, the medals, or at least the surviving Constantine and Heraclius (Figs. 462-465), probably were not, as we shall see. Another Florentine merchant, known as Baude de Guy, was *valet de chambre* of the Duke in 1385–1388,[127] and to judge from the gifts the two exchanged, their close relationship lasted throughout the Duke's life.[128] At one time he obtained many manuscripts for his client.[129] One of the merchants from the Arno, Constantin de Nicolas, is also described as 'orfèvre'. He sold the Duke, along with precious stones, a small enamelled gold bear.[130]

The records do not tell us that these Florentine merchants, apart from Baude, procured panels or manuscripts for the Duke, although we know that the great house of Francesco Datini in Prato imported panels from Florence into Avignon.[131] In the inventories the only objects designated as Florentine – 'ouvrages de Florence' – are the embroidered frontals, dossals, copes and other vestments which the city did in fact produce. Florentine merchants facilitated the import of them to France.[132] The Duke possessed numerous specimens, many of which contained stories and scenes.[133] The significance of these embroideries for French painters will de discussed shortly.

No less prominent in Paris than the Florentine merchants were the Lucchese. Representatives of all the great Lucchese houses appeared among the creditors of the Duke at his death: Gauvin Trente (Galvano Trenta), Dino, Jacques, Jean and André Raponde, Guillaume Cenami, Pierre de l'Esclat (Schiatta), Giovanni, Bernardo, and Bartolommeo Spifame.[134] The Rapondi served the house of Burgundy far more extensively than that of Berry. Dino was a counsellor and the principal banker of Philippe le Hardi, and it was he who ransomed the Duke's son, later Jean sans Peur, from the Turks at Nicopolis in 1397–1398.[135] Jean sans Peur even placed a statue of him, kneeling in prayer, in a church.[136] Dino's brother Jacques procured many manuscripts for the two Burgundian dukes, and served, in fact, as an important artistic adviser. Jean de Berry gave no one comparable influence in shaping his collections; he wanted to do the job himself. Jacques Rapondi engaged outstanding illuminators, mostly from his patrons' Netherlandish territories. He was involved in the early employment of the Limbourgs, and also of Jacques Coene, Haincelin de Haguenau, and Imbert Stanier. Among the identifiable Rapondi manuscripts some, like the Boccaccio he gave to Philippe le Hardi in 1403 (Bibliothèque nationale, fr. 12420) and a *Fleur des histoires* that Philippe gave to Berry in the same year (Bibliothèque nationale, fr. 12201), are advanced in style, introducing into metropolitan France the so-called style of 1402 (Figs. 287, 290, 292, 438).[137] In 1413 he obtained a book, not further specified, for Jean de Berry.[138]

Several merchants and bankers from a third Italian city, Genoa, were conspicuous in the service of Jean de Berry. Christophe and Jean de la Mer (de' Mari), Jean Sac (Sacco), and Pierre Fatinant (Fatinelli) were all large creditors of the Duke at his death.[139] Along with Janus de Grimault (Grimaldi)[140] and Nicolas Pigace,[141] likewise Genoese, these merchants sold Jean de Berry a high proportion of his rubies, emeralds, pearls, and diamonds.[142] Apart from the Genoese, Lucchese, and Florentine merchants only one other Italian city provided the Duke with an active dealer. Loys Gradenigo of Venice sold Jean de Berry two famous rubies in 1412, and presented him with one more as a gift.[143] The most highly prized rubies, the pale *balais*, came from the Orient.

5 · GIFTS

While the Duke acquired much of his collection by purchase a very sizeable part of it came to him by gift. The inventories of Robinet and other records show that he was presented with 350 objects. Of these objects 177 *joyaux* and eighty manuscripts were given to him at *étrennes*, the beginning of the new year.[144] In accordance with a well-established French custom the Duke exchanged New Year's gifts with his family, members of his household, including artists, officers of the realm, French and foreign princes, and highly placed members of the Church. The Duke in turn distributed 231 gifts, a hundred less than he received. Many of these he already possessed, so that his collection constantly changed through withdrawals as well as acquisitions.

Persons possessing great resources of course presented expensive gifts, mainly golden objects and precious stones, whereas officials of the Duke's household often gave simpler utensils or manuscripts. In one instance he even received a simulated manuscript. In 1411 Paul de Limbourg and his brothers offered an object described by Robinet with his usual care: 'un livre contrefait d'une pièce de bois paincte en semblance d'un livre où il n'a nuls fueillets ne riens escript'.[145] This gift was both a joke and a show of virtuosity. One of the most expensive gifts the Duke received was an exceptionally large and fine pale ruby of the kind known as 'balay', and the transfer of this highly prized stone from Charles VI to him shows that the custom of giving at *étrennes* was so firmly established that it even permitted banking operations. The ruby was valued at 1800 *écus*, and the King gave it to the Duke against payment of 400 *écus*, the remaining 1400 to be considered the King's New Year's gifts for three years, 1402–1404.[146] The Duke had the ruby set in a great cross, which he gave the King shortly before his death. The latter melted it down and sold the gold and the stones a few months later to help pay the costs of the war against the English.[147]

All the available records suggest that Jean de Berry's marriage to the young Jeanne de Boulogne was not very happy, and the Duchess does not appear as a large donor in the inventories. She did give her husband a ruby carved in the shape of a rose, and another that took the form of a cross,[148] but it is difficult to know how to characterize the acquisition of the sapphire that, according to Robinet, 'Monseigneur a prins de la belle couronne de madame la Duchesse'.[149] Queen Isabeau de Bavière gave the Duke six objects of jasper and crystal in 1408,[150] and the oldest son of Charles VI, the Duc de Guyenne, an avid collector from early youth, gave his great-uncle many objects during his short life; he bequeathed others at his death in 1415.[151] In 1407 Louis II d'Anjou, the Duke's nephew, gave him a Book of Hours in which his grandfather Jean le Bon, Berry's father, 'apprist à lire'.[152] This family treasure was important; the Duke kept it with him in Paris during his last years. Its text, and probably also to a degree its illustrations, had served Jean de Berry earlier as the model for his *Petites Heures* and *Très Belles Heures de Notre-Dame*, as we shall see.[153]

Despite the rivalry of Jean de Berry and Philippe le Hardi the two exchanged gifts regularly, and even when this rivalry sharpened into bitter conflict after the accession of Jean sans Peur the exchanges at New Year continued. The gifts consisted mostly of *joyaux*, especially in the case of those offered to Berry, which were often golden statues of Berry's patron, St. Andrew.[154] Occasionally, however, the Dukes of Burgundy presented a panel or a splendid manuscript. In March 1403 Philippe le Hardi gave Berry one of the three copies of the *Fleur des histoires* that he had recently ordered from Jacques Raponde;[155] the manuscript is preserved in the Bibliothèque nationale (Fig. 438). This gift was perhaps made in response to an extraordinary one of Jean de Berry, for he may have given the *Brussels Hours* to Philippe around this time, though it did not appear in the inventory of 1404 at the latter's death.[156] The exchange would hardly have been quite equal, for though the illumination of the *Fleur des histoires* is beautiful, it is not comparable to that of the *Brussels Hours*. Furthermore, only the clasps of the *Fleur* bore the arms of Burgundy, whereas the pages of the *Brussels Hours* contain many emblems and shields of Jean de Berry, and even two portraits. Jean sans Peur received the *Hours* by bequest or by direct gift, and by 1407 he had given his uncle a splendid Bible that his father had commissioned for the great collector.[157]

Often, of course, the gifts were prompted by specific political motives, which are no longer readily grasped. One may surmise, however, that there was an element of appeasement in Berry's gift of a ruby to Jean sans Peur in May 1412, near the climax of the Burgundian-Armagnac strife.[158] And in January 1413, after the siege and the great reconciliation at Bourges, Jean sans Peur gave Berry the magnificent *Merveilles du monde* illuminated by the Boucicaut Master and associates.[159] A month later Jean de Berry replied, giving his nephew a splendid three-volume *Mirouer historial* of Vincent de Beauvais.[160]

The collection of Jean de Berry was enriched with exotic objects by gifts from distant cities or countries. No full notice need be given here of relics, sent by rulers such as the Byzantine Emperor[161] or the Doge of Venice,[162] nor of such objects as the horn of a unicorn given by Pope John XXII,[163] or a stone ('bauzar') as an antidote for poison offered by the Maréchal de Boucicaut – in 1404, and thus presumably sent from Genoa.[164] Charles le Noble, King of Navarre, gave presents regularly from 1404 to 1409,[165] and we shall see that around the beginning of this period he employed the Master of the Brussels Initials, an illuminator who had worked for Jean de Berry.[166] Pope Clement VII (*fl.* 1378–1394) gave the Duke a huge Bible in ten volumes, and the inventory of 1402 records a second Bible written in 'lettre boulonnoise' and richly illuminated.[167] Like the Bible now in the Vatican (Figs. 177, 178) it bore the arms of both the Pope and the Duke. Notwithstanding, the Duke gave the manuscript to Louis d'Orléans, and then retrieved it after the latter was murdered in 1407.[168] For many years Jean de Berry kept in close touch with Lubert Hautschild, the Abbot of the Augustinian house of Eeckhout near Bruges from 1394 (Fig. 480). The two exchanged gifts, and an astrological manuscript that the Abbot sent the Duke in 1403 is of such significance that the relationship of the two men is discussed at length in Chapter XI.[169]

Two other members of the Church responded to the Duke's enthusiasm for manuscripts by presenting them at *étrennes*. One of the gifts of Guillaume Boisratier, Archbishop of Bourges, can be identified with an extant manuscript, though it is not illuminated.[170] Martin Gouge, treasurer of Jean de Berry at the time of the compilation of the first inventory and then Bishop of Chartres, gave the Duke an important Terence in 1408 (Fig. 440), among other manuscripts not today identifiable.[171] The Duke in turn gave to the Cathedral of Chartres the great embroidered retable that will be discussed below (Figs. 450, 451).

Scholars and writers normally of course chose to give books. Gontier Col, learned secretary of the Duke, gave him 'une bien grant mappamonde, bien historiée', rolled up in a long wooden box.[172] Pierre Salmon, another counsellor of the King, gave the Duke an 'historiated' *Cité de Dieu*.[173] Simon Alegret, the Duke's physician, appropriately gave his patient a sort of *Tacuinum Sanitatis*.[174] The relationship of Christine de Pisan to the Duke was unusual. A prolific writer, she depended upon the Valois princes for her livelihood, and she presented to one or more of them copies of each of her works as she completed them. Jean de Berry received a manuscript from her in 1403, 1404, 1405, 1410, 1413, and 1414.[175] Robinet's entries specify miniatures in all of these manuscripts but two.[176] The Duke presumably made a gift, cash or the equivalent, in return. One of her works, however – a collection of her early poems – is described by Robinet as purchased by the Duke from the author (Fig. 833).[177]

Among the producers of manuscripts, the privilege of giving specimens to princes was reserved to writers and translators. Illuminators, though professionally occupied with another aspect of bookmaking, did not make gifts of their handiwork. The Limbourg brothers, however, perpetrated a joke about their craft; they gave the Duke, as we have seen, a fake book.[178] On another occasion they offered their patron a specimen of goldsmith's work.[179] In 1408 the painter Jean d'Orléans gave the Duke a fine perfume-container, which he had decorated with pictures.[180] Goldsmiths themselves sometimes made a gift of their own work.

6 · PRECIOUS STONES AND *JOYAUX*

In several portraits Jean de Berry wears a golden chain bearing a great ruby; in one miniature he is preoccupied with a ruby worn by Jean sans Peur, and even at the gate of Paradise, facing St. Peter, he fingers a sapphire (Figs. 231, 478). In Chapter IV we shall discuss these representations in relation to the religious connotations of precious stones in the Middle Ages, when they were understood as symbols of the beauty of God and therefore as guides to the contemplation of metaphysical mysteries. They therefore adorned objects used in the cult and the persons of pious Christians rich enough to own them. At the same time they served, in the era before capitalism, as a prime repository for wealth, readily convertible at all times into cash. These various values of precious stones and *orfèvrerie* were reflected in contemporary linguistic usage. Robinet d'Étampes tended to employ *joyaux* as a generic term for objects containing precious metals and precious stones, whether religious or secular in character – or both. They might be enamelled, or contain medals, or be used primarily as inkholders or portable altars.[181] These objects were too precious to have survived very long. The greatest of the crucifixes, three and a half feet high and laden with stones and golden figures, including the Duke and the Duchess, was taken from the *garde* in 1415 by the Duke himself and, doubtless deprived of its stones, it was melted for its gold.[182] In a miniature of the *Elevation of the Cross* in the *Très Riches Heures* the Limbourgs have preserved for us a crucifix similar to the *croix au serpent* described in the inventory of 1413 (Fig. 442).[183] The base with a rock and a great lizard correspond, but the *croix au serpent* showed a crucifix on one side and the Virgin above a crescent moon on the other, while the cross in the miniature bears a string of coins or medals, perhaps representing the Christian emperors or those who, like Augustus, foresaw the Savior. Other medals lie mysteriously on the altar. A similar partial correspondence exists between the great gold *nef* on the table in the picture for January (Fig. 489) and the splendid container that was given a special name, the *salière du pavillon*.[184] The latter however bore precious stones, its bear wore a helmet, and its swan an escutcheon, all lacking in the miniature.

The early possessors of the few surviving reliquaries and *joyaux* can seldom be identified. We know that the reliquary in the Louvre belonged to the *Ordre du Saint Esprit*, founded by Louis d'Anjou in 1352 (Fig. 574), and that the *Goldenes Rössl*, a New Year's gift of 1404 from Queen Isabeau to Charles VI, was pawned by him to his brother-in-law Ludwig of Bavaria (Fig. 573). Two objects belonged to Jean de Berry, apart from the agate cup in Bourges for which there is no binding evidence (Fig. 472).[185] Both are in the British Museum. One is the *Royal Cup* of the Kings of France and England, with translucent red, sapphire blue, yellow, dark brown, and gray enamel (Figs. 471, 473). The enamel, as usual in this technique, has been let into shallow troughs carved in the gold, and the amount of light reflected back from the gold through it is controlled by the depth of the trough. By this means the goldsmith can produce subtle variations of luminosity. The cup has been unfortunately altered by the addition of two bands to its stem, one bearing Tudor roses, the other an inscription. It has furthermore lost its finial and its crown of pearls around the cover. It appears to be identical with a splendid cup (*hanap*) given by Jean de Berry to Charles VI in 1391.[186] The Duke was not necessarily the first owner; he did not especially venerate St. Agnes, whose legend is related on the enamels, whereas Charles V was born on St. Agnes' day. In style the enamels resemble conservative illumination of around 1380 or even 1390. The *Reliquary of the Thorn* bears the arms of Jean de Berry, though it was oddly connected until recently with Louis d'Orléans.[187] Made around 1400, it is one of the most beautiful surviving specimens of the fully developed art that combines qualities of the work of the goldsmith, sculptor, jeweler, and painter (Figs. 571, 842). Those aspects of the reliquary that are related to painting will be discussed below.[188]

Countless other small objects in the Duke's collection that would enrich our understanding of painting have been lost. Our image of what has disappeared is broadened by the chance survival of a few curious boxes – rare specimens of a forgotten art (Figs. 454, 455). The largest, used to contain relics or liturgical objects, was not in the collection of the Duke; we happen, in fact, to know that it originally belonged to Alderigo Antelminelli, one of the many Lucchese merchants who lived in Northern Europe, and who died in Bruges in 1401.[189] The box is covered inside as well as out with leather that is raised into low relief to compose a cycle of scenes of the Infancy and Passion of Christ. Some surfaces are colored or gilded.[190] Working in what seems an unpromising medium the artist has nevertheless achieved a remarkably beautiful result. The style indicates that the box was not made long before the death of Antelminelli. Some motifs, such as the Virgin sinking into the bosom of St. John, are unusual and surprisingly advanced. Equally exceptional is the procession of lay figures traveling from one town to another across the foreground of the *Crucifixion*. The scenes have the homely vivacity of Netherlandish art, and since the first owner of the box resided in Bruges it seems very probable that the art was cultivated there.

7 · CAMEOS, COINS, AND MEDALS

By forming a collection of carved gems Jean de Berry manifested an interest that had been transmitted by Rome to Christianity. The Middle Ages appreciated these little objects not only for their admirable combination of delicacy and durability but for magical powers that linked them with the stars. These properties were described in the lapidaries and in innumerable other medieval texts.[191] The cameo of Jupiter that King Charles V gave to the Cathedral of Chartres in 1367 contained an inscription enumerating the worldly perils against which it offered protection.[192] For Christians, furthermore, cameos and intaglios, like precious stones, exemplified the glory of God, as the Apocalypse said;[193] they therefore were inserted into liturgical objects and even simulated on tombs.[194] The very word *camaeus* or *camaïeu* is high medieval, providing a special term for a relief that utilizes two or three differently colored layers of a stone;[195] antiquity employed only the generic term *gemma* or *imago ectypa*, which referred also to intaglios. The Middle Ages valued antique cameos for their subjects as well as their form, giving a Christian interpretation of pagan figures, so that Poseidon and Athena became Adam and Eve.[196] The demand for genuine Roman specimens outran the supply, and therefore copies were produced from time to time in certain centers.

When in 1363 the Duke of Berry's father, King Jean le Bon, wanted a seal he ordered an intaglio copied from an ancient bust.[197] A son-in-law of the Duke and a friend gave him rings set with cameos 'à la semblance du visaige de Monseigneur'.[198] Both these stones, perhaps inspired by Imperial coinage, are apparently lost. We still have a similar ring of Jean sans Peur, though the style of the portrait is not in the least antique (Fig. 512). The Duke of Berry may frequently have worn a ring set with a cameo; he possessed five in addition to the two showing his portrait.[199] Many of the cameos were set with pearls and precious or semi-precious stones, comprising *joyaux* without a stated function. Others were affixed to reliquaries (Fig. 509) and especially to splendid golden crosses, of which the Duke had a number.[200]

Robinet's entries often identify, albeit briefly, the subjects of the cameos. On the reliquary of St. Ursin, first Archbishop of Bourges, a clasp on the cope contained a cameo representing a nude man.[201] One cameo bore 'une teste de Sarrasin';[202] another showed two horses pulling a chariot,[203] suggesting a subject similar to the famous Medici cameo of the chariot driven by a winged genius.[204] Other specimens showed 'idols' or heads of emperors.[205] Robinet identified certain representations as Christian: the Annunciation,[206] the head of a bishop,[207] and two Madonnas.[208]

Many of the Duke's cameos are probably preserved today in museums and in the treasuries of churches; lacking arms or other marks they are very difficult to identify, though close study of the inventories of the Duke and of the Sainte-Chapelle might be fruitful. A few beautiful extant cameos have been connected with the collection, though the historical evidence is not always explicit or complete. Among the surviving precious objects of the Sainte-Chapelle in Bourges that were transferred to the Cathedral in 1762 there was a 'croix aux camées'. This cross, which had appeared in inventories of the Sainte-Chapelle from 1564 on, passed to the state during the revolution, and some cameos now in the Louvre belonged to it.[209] Several are Roman (Figs. 456, 458, 459, 461).

The splendid sardonyx of Christ bearing a globe and a scepter and crowned by two angels seems to me definitely identifiable in the inventory of 1762 (Fig. 457). Professor Wentzel has demonstrated that it was made in the thirteenth century, perhaps in Italy.[210] The most likely center is Venice, where sculpture at this time drew from Early Christian models.

The bust of a man in the Louvre also seems to be identifiable in the Revolutionary inventories (Fig. 460), and its beauty naturally tempts me to accept the common view that it belonged to Jean de Berry and Wentzel's opinion that it may even have been produced, all'antica, for him (if not a century earlier). The cameo is certainly not antique. Though the model was a bust of the period of Augustus or Tiberius, the three rows of oak-leaves in the fillet do not conform with the antique convention. But is this relief, with its exquisitely graduated planes, its well-articulated ear and its soft flesh and drapery really a work of around 1400 or earlier? It seems to me rather an outstanding Renaissance gem, carved perhaps in Venice.[211]

Jean de Berry's fame as a collector of precious stones, gems, and cameos reached Quattrocento Italy. In his treatise Sforzinda Filarete praised the Duke's judgment and passion, citing as evidence one of the most magnificent of surviving Roman cameos, the Gemma Augustea now in Vienna.[212] He owned a cast of this work. He had been informed that the original belonged to the Cathedral of Toulouse, where indeed it was, as we know from inventories beginning in 1453. 'Dicesi', Filarete added, 'che fu sua' (i.e., Berry's). Modern scholarship has discarded this ascription to the Duke, because the cameo described as 'lapis preciosus qui vocatur commaheü' in the inventory of the sacristy of St. Sernin in 1246 has been assumed to be identical with the Gemma Augustea.[213] The connection is however not binding. Furthermore the fact that the Duke was the governor of the region of Toulouse has been overlooked. If Filarete was right Jean de Berry did not personally possess the famous cameo for very long because it was not listed in any of his inventories.

The cameos of Jean de Berry are impressive for their number.[214] He owned around thirty-three, whereas in 1456 Piero de' Medici possessed only nineteen.[215] Of course the proportion of the Duke's authentic ancient cameos to those all'antica cannot be determined. Notable is the proportion among surviving specimens of carvings of high quality (Figs. 456, 457, 459-461). They prove that, as Filarete said, the Duke's extraordinary connoisseurship extended to glyptography also.

The reputation of Jean de Berry is even greater as a collector of some related small objects. Robinet's inventory of 1413 informs us that in November 1402 the Duke, then in Bourges, bought a 'joyau d'or roont', in fact a medal representing the Emperor Constantine; the seller was Antoine Manchin (Mancini), a Florentine merchant living in Paris.[216] The next item in the inventory describes, in similar terms, a medal of Heraclius; neither the date of purchase nor the seller is

E

mentioned, but presumably this medal was acquired at the same time as the Constantine.[217] The next two entries describe copies in gold of these two medals, executed at the order of the Duke, and similar in all respects except that, unlike the originals, they were not set with pearls, rubies, and sapphires and they had no golden chain for suspension.[218] The two originals and these two copies in gold are lost but others in silver or less precious metal are extant, and they conform closely with Robinet's descriptions (Figs. 462-465).

These extraordinary objects, about nine centimeters in diameter,[219] resemble seals rather than coins in size, and they were apparently cast and chased by a goldsmith, not struck like coins or like the Carrara medals made a decade earlier. They are in fact the earliest medals of this kind that have come down to us, the predecessors and probably the models of Pisanello's. Objects of great beauty, they remain in many respects problematic. Robinet said nothing about their *façon*. Since they are unique and dependent no doubt in ways not yet clarified upon much earlier models, it is not surprising that divergent opinions have been held about their time and place of origin.[220] Believed in the sixteenth century to be antique, they were ascribed towards 1900 and subsequently to Italy or to Franco-Flemish circles, particularly Burgundian. Actually the closest surviving work is a bronze roundel of the same size which very probably belonged to Jean de Berry also (Fig. 466).[221] It represents the Madonna under a canopy held by four angels, and this is precisely the subject of the obverse of a *joyau d'or rond* described in the inventory of 1416.[222] This medallion, which the Duke bought from his painter Michelet Saulmon,[223] apparently between 1413 and 1416, showed on the reverse a portrait of 'Monseigneur de Berry'. These medallions share many qualities, but the relief of the Madonna is generally less subtle in its linear pattern and modulation of plane. Differences between what are only copies make it very difficult to decide whether the originals could have been made in the same workshop, but the place, in any event, would seem to be Paris.

The iconographic resemblance between these medallions is no less interesting than the stylistic. First, a word about the portrait of the Duke. It is true that he had already been represented in half-length on one of his seals (Fig. 477), and indeed in it the architectural supporting members below the figures resemble those on the medallion of the *Madonna* (Fig. 466). There is every reason to believe, however, that the medal acquired by the Duke in his last years showed a portrait in the new sense rather than a more conventional effigy, and that indeed the head enjoyed a prominence approximating that of Heraclius (Fig. 464). The inventory notice encourages us in this belief, because while the *Madonna*, actually about three-quarter length, is described as 'un image', the other side is said to show 'un demi ymage, fait à la semblance de Monseigneur, tenant en sa main un tableau d'or'. The Duke, holding the golden panel – probably with a religious subject – would thus have attained half length, but not much more.

In this medal, then, the Duke of Berry joined the company of the great Christian princes of the past. The series of these princes celebrated in medals included, as we have said, at least two more. Several months before the purchase of *Constantine* and *Heraclius* the Duke acquired medals of Augustus and Tiberius.[224] We know them only from Robinet's account. They were smaller, 'petit joyau d'or roont' as the first one was described. They were also somewhat less richly set and in 1416 they were appraised at half of the value of the larger medals.[225] The obverse of each, like the medal of Heraclius, showed the 'visaige' of the Emperor. The Duke bought these smaller medals from a Florentine living in Paris – not Mancini this time but Michiel de Paxi (*recte* Pazzi). The inventories record no copies of these objects, and the failure to make a mold probably explains why no replicas survive. These medals too were no doubt medieval creations more or less specifically *all'antica*; their inscriptions cannot be paralleled in authentic Roman coins.[226]

It is a striking fact that the four emperors represented on the Duke's medals ruled at crucial moments in the early history of Christianity: Augustus when Christ was born, Tiberius when he died, Constantine when the Church was established, and Heraclius at the recovery of the cross.[227] Since the four medals, furthermore, came to light within a short period of time it is all the more tempting to conclude that they form part of a specific program of celebration. The significance for Christianity of Constantine and Heraclius is communicated by inscriptions and the representations themselves. Clearest is the content of the medal of Heraclius (Figs. 464, 465). The obverse shows a bust of the Emperor above the moon and below the rays of the divine sun. In the field before the upturned countenance is written: ILLUMINA VULTUM TUUM DEUS. The moon, traditionally a Christian symbol of mundane temporaneity[228] but here perhaps alluding specifically to imperial conquests, is inscribed: SUPER TENEBRAS NOSTRAS MILITABOR IN GENTIBUS. The words around the perimeter refer to Heraclius as a Christian emperor; written in Greek, they were translated in Robinet's entry as 'Eracle en Jhesu Crist Dieu, féal empereur et moderateur des Romains, victeur et triumphateur toujours Auguste'.

The reverse of the medal illustrates an important moment in the medieval legend of the cross. The Greek inscription in the background, appearing below four symbolical 'lights', was translated in the inventory: 'Gloire soit es cieulx à Jhesu Crist Dieu qui a rompu les portes d'enfer et rachatée la croix saincte, imperant Eracle'. The Emperor, riding in a *carpentum* or *pilentum*,[229] approaches the gate of Jerusalem, proudly bearing the cross captured from Chosroes. One horse and the jockey turn questioningly toward him because, as we know from the legend, the gate swung closed to bar his entry. Only when he forsook pride, descended from his car, doffed his clothes, and himself shouldered the cross did the gate open for him. Both these moments were painted by the Limbourgs in the *Belles Heures*; the first miniature indeed gives a more comprehensible version of the event by representing the barrier of the closed gate.[230]

The triumphant Constantine (Fig. 462) is accompanied by the legend: CONSTANTINUS IN CHRISTO DEO FIDELIS IMPERATOR ET MODERATOR ROMANORUM ET SEMPER AUGUSTUS. The reverse contains a justly famous allegory, the precise significance of which has not yet been demonstrated (Fig. 463). Robinet described it as 'une fontainne ou il a un arbre, et dedens ledit arbre une croix . . .' The central form is indeed a cross, and the inscription refers to it: MIHI ABSIT GLORIARI NISI IN CRUCE DOMINI JHESU CHRISTI. The cross rises from a schematized plant, and from spouts at the top of it issues water. The life-giving water moistens the thriving plant as it falls into a basin, whence it presumably supplies the roots. Water appears again in the representation (a relief?) below the plant. It issues from the mouths of two serpentine creatures which are steadied, so to speak, by a nude infant.

This central form combines then the *lignum vitae* and the *fons vitae*. What Robinet identified as 'un arbre' is actually a recollection of the pine-cone that became identified in Christian symbolism with the Fountain of Life. The most famous of these fountains was the *pigna* known to have been within a tabernacle in the atrium of Old St. Peter's from the twelfth century on. In some Byzantine representations of the *Annunciation to Anna* a pine-cone fountain appears at her side, and the representation on the medal resembles especially the fountain in the eleventh-century miniature in the *Homilies of the Monk Jacobus* (Fig. 470). Below the cone here as in the medal there is a circular basin and also a pair of heads on eel-like bodies that spout water. In the *pigna* in St. Peter's as well as in the similar object at the Cathedral of Aachen water spurted from the tips of the scales of the cone, and the miniature shows similar jets of water. The flower-like projections in the medal might be a misunderstanding of these streams. It should be mentioned, however, that shapes resembling these projections on the medal appear in other representations as leaves or flowers growing near the pine fountain.[231]

Everyone recognizes that the two figures seated on benches at the sides of the cross and the fountain symbolize some kind of a typical medieval dualism, but there is no agreement about what precisely is at stake. Is it a dialogue between Christianity and Paganism or the Church and the Synagogue or, as Erwin Panofsky has proposed, Nature and Grace?[232] The older, clothed woman at the left – she wears even a wimple – responds to the cross, keeping it in view while gesturing toward it. While one of her hands rests on a scale or 'flower', the corresponding hand of the younger, largely nude woman seems a little further from the plant, grasping a form that is equally difficult to identify. She conspicuously turns her head away from the cross. She places her foot, furthermore, on a small animal, probably a weasel and thus, as the bestiaries say, a symbol of worldly pleasure. That this zone is in fact the realm of the devil is proved by what appears to be the tail of a serpent in the opening of the 'well' at the center. A snake often entwines the base of the cross in early medieval Crucifixions.[233]

In confrontations of Church and Synagogue, Synagogue sometimes is partly nude, but the weasel (?) and other aspects of the allegory suggest rather a representation of Grace and Nature. Each of the women is accompanied by a bird that flaps its wings. The bird at the right is tethered, the string held in the right hand of the nude. The opposite bird seems free – symbolically so? If these birds are eagles their presence near the fountain – but not the difference between them – might be explained by an allegory in the bestiaries. 'When the eagle grows old and his wings become heavy and his eyes become darkened with a mist he goes in search of a fountain . . . then (after a flight near the sun) he dips himself three times (in the fountain), and instantly he is renewed with a great vigor of plumage and splendor of vision.'[234] Eagles may properly appear, therefore, near a Fountain of Grace.

Oddly there is much less Christian reference in the medals of Augustus and Tiberius, which the Duke bought some months earlier. The head of the emperor on the obverse was encircled by an inscription giving the date according to imperial chronology (40 for Augustus and 16 for Tiberius). The verso of Tiberius bore an enigmatic figure of 'Phaustina' – the spelling indicative of Greek influence. On the verso of Augustus appears a woman holding a star and a sheaf of grain; she was labelled Lilia, perhaps for Livia, the Emperor's wife. Both women are accompanied by dates given 'ab urbe condita', an extremely rare form on Roman coins, and probably inspired more by medieval papal conventions.

So far, however, the content of the medals is not specifically Christian. A 'tableau' above the head of Augustus, on the other hand, was inscribed with a line from the Fourth Eclogue of Virgil that from Augustine on was understood as a prophecy of the era under Grace: 'MAGNUS AB INTEGRO SECULORUM NASCITUR ORDO'. The Emperor Augustus interested the Duke of Berry greatly, in part because of his connection with the birth of Christ. The subject of the Ara Coeli, rare in earlier art, was introduced in one of his manuscripts around 1400 (Fig. 203), and it was repeated, no doubt in conformity with his wishes, frequently thereafter.[235] The absence of any reference to this event in the medal is therefore noteworthy. If all four medals were programmatically linked the two earlier acquisitions, only in small part Christian, failed to correspond fully to what followed.

When considering the content of these medals and the significance of their appearance in 1402 we should keep in mind several additional objects in the collection. One, a relief in gold, was sold to the Duke at the same time, in the same place, and by the same dealer (Manchin) as the medals of Constantine and Heraclius. It likewise contained Greek as well as Latin inscriptions, and it represented a scene of the early Christian martyr Eugenia.[236] She was saved from her corrupt accuser, Melanthia, by the sudden descent of divine fire, which probably looked like the rays visible before Heraclius (Fig. 464). The next item in the inventory, perhaps acquired shortly after this plaquette, similarly represented an early Christian figure, Philip, often held to be the first Christian emperor. Philip was shown on his knees, looking at the 'face de Dieu' that appeared in the sky. The object, a small golden relief like the one held by the Duke in the lost medallion containing his portrait, was probably late medieval.[237]

The inventory of 1402 informs us that the Duke owned several dozen coins and medals, some of them no doubt antique.[238] In conformity with medieval practice his seals bore effigies of himself, at first his entire figure and later half-length (Figs. 474, 477). The idea, however, that a modern prince might possess a medal bearing his bust or head was conveyed to him by his cast of the remarkable medal, all'antica, of Francesco Carrara (Fig. 468). This was fully described in the inventory of 1402. Somewhat later the Duke acquired 'un grant denier d'or bien pesant' of Julius Caesar. Robinet distinguished this piece from all the other representations of emperors by calling it a denarius and adding 'le visaige contrefait au vif'.[239] He apparently wished to stress at least its approximation to ancient coins. The description suggests, however, a medieval imitation.

We have observed that within a short period around 1402 the Duke acquired – or was able to acquire – a number of objects with antique or Early Christian subjects. Four were medals, and two plaquettes. Some light may be shed on these unusual accessions by a stirring recent observation of Professor Roberto Weiss. He has pointed out that the triumphal titles on the medals of Constantine and Heraclius imply a knowledge of the imperial formulae of the Byzantine chancery.[240] Believing that this specialized knowledge was not possessed by anyone resident in France, Weiss advances the very interesting proposal that it was supplied by an official in the entourage of the Emperor Manuel II, who was in Paris from 1400 to 1402. Jean de Berry saw much of the Emperor himself; he went out to meet him, he had the pleasure of entertaining him at Bourges, and the honor of his company at the marriage of his daughter Marie.[241] We know of at least one object that Manuel brought to Paris: a manuscript of Dionysius, which he presented to the King when he departed.[242] The King in turn gave Manuel gems, *joyaux* and tapestries; on one of the tapestries, indeed, Manuel wrote an ekphrasis which is still preserved.[243]

The visit of Manuel's son, John VIII, to Ferrara and Florence in 1438–1439 made a deep impression upon Italian artists and patrons, and it seems probable that the Parisian sojourn of Manuel did not leave the French indifferent. The Limbourgs, who were in the capital at the time, showed thereafter a penchant for long flowing beards on all historical worthies (Fig. 442). We do not know that in Paris the Emperor wore his richest state dress, shining with gold and precious stones (Fig. 441), but the raiment of the Easterners must have delighted the French court, and above all Jean de Berry. Probably too these exotic men evoked a sense of earlier Christianity, and their presence may have influenced the development of the Duke of Berry's iconographic program. We may indeed speak of a program, for just as the medal with his portrait, though purchased, was produced for him, so the medals of the emperors were probably made either on commission or with him in mind. The Byzantines may well have supplied ideas about representations as well as formulae for imperial titles. Manuel would certainly have been interested in representations of Constantine, who founded his capital, and Heraclius, who recovered the cross. Constantine provided a link between East and West, and Manuel might well have conceived of him as a powerful symbol in his appeal to Europe for aid.

The Byzantine vistors no doubt brought as gifts many manuscripts and small objects in precious metals. Did works of art in their possession influence the Duke's only surviving objects of this kind, the medals of Constantine and Heraclius? This is a moot question; the sources of the medals still remain mysterious. The posture and the sensuousness of the nude on the verso of the *Constantine* lead one to inquire whether the designer had seen and partly understood some late antique or early Christian relief such as the Venus at her toilet in the Petit Palais (Figs. 463, 467).[244] The similarities however are not decisive, and the Synagogue seems conceivable as an advanced example of those nude figures to be discussed in Chapter VI.

8 · TAPESTRIES, WALL HANGINGS, AND EMBROIDERIES

Though some walls in the palaces of the Duke bore murals most of them had movable coverings. These coverings were of different kinds: they were embroidered, or woven like tapestries, or painted, like the objects called 'lymandes' in the Burgundian (but not the Berry) inventories.[245] Many of them composed cycles, and some were sets that covered the ceilings as well as the walls of a room. Inasmuch as the Duke, like other great lords of the time, was not short of helping hands, he could quickly surround himself at any moment with the subjects and designs that caught his fancy. The flexibility of the scheme had obvious advantages.

Practically all of the textiles bore designs, normally provided by painters, and these designs ranged from the arms and devices of the Duke to elaborate scenes, especially in tapestry, so that their almost complete disappearance deprives us of knowledge of another kind of monumental 'painting'. It is true, however, that the one extant set of tapestries that bear the arms of Jean de Berry, now in the Cloisters of the Metropolitan Museum, New York,[246] contributes little to what the manuscripts show of pictorial style (Figs. 445, 446). The surviving pieces, which belonged to a set of the *Neuf Preux*,[247] reflect the manner of the painters of Charles V and its development in the late fourteenth century in northeast France and Flanders. As rare early examples of a great art and of a widely diffused iconography the large fragments in the Cloisters are, however, of the greatest interest.

Many of the tapestries of Jean de Berry, as of other princes, represented hunting scenes, and probably resembled the miniatures in the *Livre de la Chasse de Gaston Phébus* (Fig. 439).[248] Others showed the great worthies of the past, such as Charlemagne, in action,[249] and occasionally they celebrated the feats of even so recent a hero as Bertrand du Guesclin.[250] Jean de Berry possessed a cycle setting forth 'l'histoire du Grand Khan',[251] a theme illustrated again in the miniatures of the splendid manuscript of the *Merveilles du monde* that he received from Jean sans Peur in 1413. Three of the Duke's tapestries were devoted to the frequent Petrarchan and Renaissance theme of *Fama*.[252] In *January* in the *Très Riches Heures* the Duke is seated before a tapestry representing a battle (Fig. 489). We learn that he was not always attentive to the subjects of his wall-coverings from an event that occurred in 1387, when several princes of France and England met in a chapel to attempt to negotiate an armistice between their respective countries. Jean de Berry had had the walls of the building hung with tapestries representing great battles of antiquity.[253] Upon entering the room the Duke of Lancaster demanded that scenes of war be removed from the chapel, and tapestries representing the symbols of the Passion were hung instead.

The Dukes of Burgundy and Orléans possessed tapestries of ancient literary and mythological figures, such as Juno, Venus, Athena, Hector, Jason, and Theseus.[254] While such figures were visible in Jean de Berry's manuscripts and *joyaux*[255] they appeared rarely in his wall-coverings. Illustrations of the *Roman de la rose* were of course not lacking,[256] and if the Duke looked attentively around his rooms he would have seen 'l'histoire d'Espérance et de Confusion'[257] as well as grimmer subjects, such as the Seven Deadly Sins.[258] The common themes of the Duke's embroideries and *joyaux* as well as of his manuscripts – the Trinity and the Coronation of the Virgin – appeared also in tapestries,[259] and stories, too, of his patron saints Andrew and John.[260]

Though most of the large hangings were of woven wool many consisted of embroidered silk and satin.[261] Jean de Berry possessed sets of many pieces intended to clothe an entire room, the ceiling included. One, known as the 'Chambre aux cynes', contained the Duke's emblem gliding along a pond, or, appropriately on the ceiling, in flight.[262] Another, characterized as the 'Chambre aux enfans', may have been a predecessor of the rampant Renaissance putti, though the precise subject is not stated in the inventory.[263] A number of pieces were decorated with animals, birds, gardens, like the secular murals of the time in the *Tour de la Garderobe* in Avignon or the Datini house in Prato. The Duke possessed a Byzantine textile with such subjects; it was described as 'ouvrage de Grèce', a gift of the Emperor Manuel Paleologus.[264] Most of the leather hangings seem to have come from Spain, for many bore the arms of Aragon and Castille.[265]

In addition to these hangings the Duke's collection included textiles for a different purpose, which were of special historical significance. Called in the inventories 'ornements de chapelle', they consisted of a series of altar hangings, both frontals and retables, embroidered in woolen, golden and silver threads and enriched with pearls and precious stones. Consistently characterized as 'ouvrage de Florance'[266] they composed the largest collection of these objects of which we possess a record. Among the few specimens of this *opus florentinum* that have come down to us one, an antependium in the Bargello, Florence, is dated 1325,[267] while the others, to judge from their style, were made in the second and third quarters of the century. The largest, in the Cathedral of Manresa, is signed by Geri di Lapo of Florence (Fig. 449). Its iconographical design – a *Crucifixion* accompanied by scenes from the life of Christ[268] – resembles that of an embroidered *dossier* in Jean de Berry's earliest inventory.[269] Other surviving fragments showing single scenes of the Passion were doubtless cut out from similar altar hangings, and they too reflect the style of the Florentine painters of the second quarter of the century, especially that of Bernardo Daddi (Fig. 452).

One of the extant embroideries is exceptional because its model was clearly not a Florentine but a Sienese painting (Fig. 447). The composition of the Nativity combined with the appearance of the Shepherds resembles closely an altarpiece in the Fogg Art Museum of Harvard University by the so-called Ugolino Lorenzetti, who is probably identical with the painter Bartolommeo Bulgarini (Fig. 448).[270] The composition of the panel has clearly been reduced: the disembodied arm of the shepherd at the right demonstrates that. The combination of cave and shed in the Nativity is characteristic of Sienese Trecento painting, and the Fogg altarpiece may have been the source of the embroidery, which translates the figures into the Florentine dialect. Perhaps the Fogg panel stood upon an altar in Florence, and if so it would have been the second work by the master for a Florentine church, because a relatively early polyptych by him is still preserved in the Opera of S. Croce.[271] 'Ugolino Lorenzetti' may on the other hand have made a drawing for the embroiderer.

Most of the 'ouvrages de Florence' listed in the Duke's first inventory were given in 1405 to the Sainte-Chapelle. The most splendid of all the pieces, however, he presented to the Cathedral of Chartres. Described as 'une très grant table de brodeure pour un autel . . . dudit ouvrage de Florance', it represented the Coronation of the Virgin midst a heavenly host. The event was witnessed by Charles V, his wife, and four children, all sponsored by saints.[272] The embroidery, originally commissioned it would appear by Charles V, hung in the choir of the Cathedral, and in 1731 Montfaucon published a drawing of the donor and his family (Figs. 450, 451).[273] The work has been lost.

The Duke's large collection of 'ouvrages de Florance' provided a series of diagrams of Tuscan ideas of composition and inscenation. Like engravings at a later period they served to transmit Italian pictorial conceptions to the North.[274] French painters remained, of course, quite free to take what they wanted, and until 1400 they far preferred Sienese to Florentine designs.

9 · PANEL PAINTINGS

Jean de Berry possessed a couple of dozen panel paintings, most of them acquired late in his life, for the inventory of 1402 lists only three.[275] One example is generally believed to be extant, for the very good reason that it bears his arms (Fig. 443). Because of the Duke's well-known interest in Italian painting some historians have not hesitated to ascribe this very Italianate *Crucifixion* to an Italian master, active to be sure in Avignon.[276] Others have maintained that the panel was painted in Northern France, within the circle – geographically a sizeable one – of the Duke.[277] His arms appear, however, in a most unusual place: on a book thrust toward the beholder by St. John. From the time I first saw the panel in the Renders collection the representation puzzled me, and inasmuch as the painting seemed damaged and rather extensively retouched I was not surprised when a technical examination kindly undertaken in 1956 at my suggestion by my much lamented friend Paul Coremans and his colleagues, proved that the arms were added within the last fifty years.[278] The panel was generally much repainted at that time.

Since the *Crucifixion* is interesting and important despite its bad condition the main conclusions of the technical study are worth recording. Three characteristics of the work point to a Northern rather than an Italian origin: the wood is oak, the ground for the color is chalk instead of gypsum, and, surprisingly, the vehicle contains oil.[279] I would add that the rather crude tooling also detaches the painting from the Italian models that it approximates. These models are Ducciesque rather than Simonesque; a Ducciesque *Crucifixion* in the New York Historical Society contains most of the figures, and even forms such as the skull, that the painter of the Brussels panel had in mind (Fig. 444).

Deeply Sienese though it is, the Brussels *Crucifixion* seems distinguishable stylistically from works of that school. The faces of the women at the left are consistently fleshy, not firm and compact in the Italian manner. In this respect they resemble the corresponding figures in the *Crucifixion* by the Passion Master in the *Petites Heures* (Fig. 111). Curiously the old man at the extreme right in this miniature presses his sword against his body in the manner of the man in the same place in the panel. The analogies extend even to the gray-blue color of the cornea of the women's eyes. Already, however, we move into quicksand, because the panel has been so extensively retouched that only careful cleaning, or at least microscopic examination, would enable us to ascertain what precisely is original. A large area such as the hillock, originally light green it seems, has been entirely gone over in a dark blue-green. Uncertainty surrounds even the arm of St. John and the book. Laboratory examination indicates that the arm moved in this direction, but the folds of the drapery over and around it certainly cannot be trusted and the book is a strange object, strangely placed. Occasionally in other representations of the Crucifixion St. John holds a book (Fig. 812), but how differently!

In size, 303 × 207 millimeters, the Brussels *Crucifixion* resembles most of the paintings described in the Duke's inventories. The great majority were small and contained subjects then judged suitable for private devotion. Notable are three paintings of the relatively new subject of the Man of Sorrows. In one instance the image appeared, as it sometimes did in Italy, with the Madonna as part of a diptych. Another example was introduced in the non-Italian context of a quadriptych with the Virgin and Saints Peter and Paul.[280] Two panels showed the Holy Face on a cloth – 'l'imaige de la Veronique'.[281] Since most of these subjects were common on small panels painted in many centers in the second half of the fourteenth century, and Robinet does not give us a hint of origin, the question of the provenance of the paintings must remain open. In one item, however, the subject does provide a definite clue. 'Un ymaige de Nostre Dame tenant son enffant dormant entre ses braz, fait de paincture'[282] was no doubt painted in Venice, where the sleeping Child originated in the late fourteenth century.[283] Northern imitations at this date are unknown, and it is notable that the panel is one of the very few characterized as 'grant'.

Other descriptions by Robinet are less readily related to contemporary or earlier iconographic conventions. Though the range of Trecento subjects includes *Vesperbilder* (Figs. 635, 638, 640, 641), the Virgin supporting the Man of Sorrows (Fig. 546), and the bust of the Virgin,[284] a panel described by Robinet as 'une Pitié de Nostre Dame tenant une couronne d'espines tachée de sanc' seems to be unprecedented in Italy or indeed anywhere else.[285] The panel, like some others, was covered with a curtain, no doubt of the kind preserved in a stone relief of the *Man of Sorrows* in the Musée Jacques Cœur (Fig. 433). Robinet's description of the painting may be misleading – possibly he intended a *Vesperbild* or a Man of Sorrows. Another panel is puzzling also, though Robinet's distinction between what he knows and what is merely 'said' proves again his unusual seriousness. The description – 'un Dieu de Pitié' – seems at first to refer to the new French theme of God the Father holding his dead son (Fig. 832), but the entry adds that it was 'un tableau d'ancienne façon, semblablement venu de Romme, comme on dit. . . .'[286] In Trecento Italy the type was, to our knowledge, unknown, so the subject more probably was God the Father with the crucifix, the so-called *Gnadenstuhl* type of the Trinity. Uncertain also is another description: 'Dieu lié à un pillier'.[287] The representation, appearing alongside a *Crucifixion* and composing with it a diptych, may have been a *Flagellation*, but we must also entertain the possibility that it was a devotional image created by isolating the figure of Christ from the historical scene.[288]

The number of multi-leaved paintings in the collection is noteworthy. The Duke owned three quadriptychs, one work of six pieces, and one of seven. These aggregations belonged no doubt to the type produced by Simone Martini in France (Figs. 674–676, 692, 693), and a few similar Northern examples have survived.[289] Several of the Duke's polyptychs are described as hinged or folding,[290] including a six-leaved work that is said to be the length of an altar.[291] The painting of seven pieces represented the Crucifixion at the center and three scenes of the legend of St. Lawrence at each side.[292] One extraordinary quadriptych bore four portraits, of Kings Jean le Bon and Charles, an Emperor (Charles IV?), and Edward III of England.[293] We can be certain that this was painted in the North; and one diptych was formed of two roundels, a favored French form.[294]

The portraits were the only secular subjects. The roundels and most of the other paintings were intended for private devotion. Only three paintings might have been large enough to serve in the cult: the six-leaved polyptych which was as long as an altar, the Venetian *Madonna* and a diptych representing the Crucifixion and the Last Judgment, which were both described as 'grans'.[295] Of course large paintings standing on the altars of the Duke's chapels, like monumental sculptures, were not included in the inventories.

Some of the pictorial techniques were unusual. A panel representing the Man of Sorrows and the Madonna and Child was painted in grisaille – 'de noir et de blanc'.²⁹⁶ Though contemporary illuminators frequently employed this technique it was exceptional on panel until the time of the Master of Flémalle and Jan van Eyck, when, however, it was applied to simulated statues. Another of the Duke's panels, apparently a diptych, combined some painted figures with others made of marquetry.²⁹⁷ A Madonna with two saints was painted in gold on a background of clear red. Robinet described the work as a square panel, but the figures were covered with glass, suggesting the possibility that the technique was not painting on wood but on glass – a kind of 'verre églomisé'.²⁹⁸

The few surviving French paintings from the time of Jean de Berry constitute a group similar in many respects to the one he assembled. They include portraits (Fig. 507), a *Man of Sorrows* (Fig. 694), a *Trinity with the Man of Sorrows* (Fig. 832), a *Lamentation* related in design to the type of Man of Sorrows (Louvre), an *Entombment* (Fig. 695), and one large altarpiece, the *Martyrdom of St. Denis*.²⁹⁹ Most of the panels are comparatively small, but when estimating what was to be seen around 1400 we must remember that altarpieces in churches were more subject to destruction during the Revolution.³⁰⁰ The *Parement de Narbonne* is in grisaille but on cloth (Figs. 1–5), and the same support was used for the large *Madonna* in Berlin, probably by Malouel. This unusual work was, however, painted in color, and formed part of a diptych.³⁰¹

Though few French panel paintings from around 1400 have come down to us we possess even fewer significant murals – in part because of the destruction of examples in secular buildings. Outstanding is a *Last Judgment* dated 1405 in the church at Ennezat (Fig. 405a).³⁰¹ᵃ It is especially relevant because Ennezat is near Riom, one of Jean de Berry's residences. The style of the painting is not clearly Parisian nor does it show the Italianate character of most of the work done for the Duke. It recalls somewhat more the Franco-Flemish masters patronized by the Duke at this very time (Figs. 29–33).

10 · PIERRE DE VÉRONE, LIBRARIAN

Unlike the Duke of Burgundy and most other princes Jean de Berry himself directed the growth of his library, at least until his later years, when he was distracted by the bitter factional struggle in France and the overwhelming power of England. In this period he employed Pietro da Verona, giving him some of the responsibilities of a librarian. Pietro held this position in 1415, but we do not know when he entered the Duke's service. In 1415 he was also a curate of Mongistral in the diocese of Toulouse, a benefice he owed no doubt to his patron. The presence of this Italian in the Duke's entourage has always attracted the attention of historians, and indeed overstimulated the imagination of some of them, resulting in statements that are quite unwarranted by the known facts. He was, however, a person of some consequence, and what we actually can learn about him should be fully recorded.

We first hear of Pierre de Vérone in France in 1397, when Louis d'Orléans ordered a payment to him for a Livy and a Boethius, both in French, that the Duke had just bought from him; acknowledgment for the sum is made by 'maistre Pierre de Varoune estudiant à Paris'.[302] The connection between Pierre and the Duke may perhaps be traced to the fact that the wife of Louis was Valentina Visconti, and he was in close touch with Lombardy. Pierre is not heard of again until 1410, when he was mentioned by Iohannes Alcherius or Archerius (Alcherio or Aucher), a remarkable figure who collected technical information about painting with the zeal that his contemporary, Cyriac of Ancona, devoted to Greek and Roman inscriptions. It required, however, a second person of similar interests to preserve part at least of Alcherius' treatise, for we know it only in the technical manual compiled in 1431 by Jean Lebègue.[303] Alcherius was at work already in 1382, when he left Milan for Paris, taking along, as he tells us, a formula for ink given him by the scribe Porzello.[304] He informs us that in Paris in July 1398 the painter Jacobus Cona (Coene) dictated to him a treatise on various colors,[305] and in early August the illuminator Antonius de Compendio ('illuminator librorum') performed a similar service for him.[306]

In Paris again, but on February 2, 1412, Alcherius obtained a formula for ultramarine from 'magister Iohannes de . . . [sic], Normanus, commorans in domo magistri Petri de Verona, qui sit afinare vel facere azurrum . . . dixit mihi. . . .'[307] The Latin syntax permits uncertainty as to who knew how to refine ultramarine, and although the context seems to indicate Iohannes the excellent Mrs. Merrifield in her translation favored Petrus. Since John and Peter were both called master by Alcherius, and the former was living in the house of the latter she concluded that 'Pietro da Verona was probably a painter'.[308] We are not informed explicitly by the document that Iohannes Normanus himself was a painter, but he may well be the same person who was invited, on the recommendation of Alcherius, to the Cathedral of Milan in 1399. The invitation was extended to 'Iohannes Companiosus nationis Normaniae';[309] he is not described as a painter but the two masters invited with him, for the same purposes, Jacobus Cova (Jacques Coene) and Iohannes Mignotus, were definitely practitioners of this art. It is possible, but far from certain, that Pietro da Verona was a painter also. Still, he came to life in modern literature on the history of art as an illuminator, a visitor to Padua,[310] and even as a friend of Altichiero.[311]

Shortly afterwards, when Jean de Berry's inventory of 1413 was being drawn up, 'maistre Pierre de Vérone' had on loan the first volume of the *Bréviaire de Belleville*.[312] On September 14, 1415, 'maistre Pierre de Vérone', brought before the magistrates of Paris on a charge of political intelligence with the English, spoke about his career.[313] He said that he was approximately thirty-six years old – 'XXXVI ans ou environ'. Perhaps he had forgotten a few years, because this age would imply that he was born as late as 1379, and that he was only eighteen when, as a 'maître', he was selling manuscripts to the Duke of Orléans and to King Richard II of England. He added that he had been in Paris for twenty-four years;[314] thus he arrived there in 1391 – at the age of only twelve, if we accept his own estimate. He said furthermore that he was born in Verona in Lombardy, that he had 'gone' to study (among the books of Berry?) and was administering this prince's library – '. . . se mesle de aler à l'estude et de gouverner la librairye de Monseigneur de Berry. . . .'[315] He was living, however, in a house on the Rue St. Jacques, apparently the same house in which Aucher found him in 1412. The Duke's librarian had been seized by the Parisian royalists and Burgundians together with 'maistre Regnault du Montet', *stationnaire* and one of the chief purveyors of books to Jean de Berry.[316] Probably the two men, who were released shortly afterward, were charged with treason because of their professional association with Jean de Berry.

Both masters freely admitted carrying on a lively but often unrewarding trade in books and related articles with Englishmen. Pierre said that he had gone to England during the reign of Richard II to arrange either for the sale to the King of a Bible he had sent him, or for the recovery of it. To his dismay he discovered on arrival in 1399 that Richard had been imprisoned in Ireland by the Duke of Lancaster; he therefore fled to 'Alemagne', and arrived in Bruges. There some burghers, having heard of the Bible, asked Pierre to show it to them, for purchase perhaps by the Duke of Burgundy. Pierre managed after some delay to obtain the shipment of the manuscript from England, but by the time it arrived in Bruges the Duke had gone elsewhere. Pierre returned to Paris, this time *with* his Bible, and he sold it to Jean de Berry. The sale may well have occurred in 1400 or shortly thereafter.

In 1415 and perhaps earlier Pierre was in touch with the English ambassadors, especially the Bishop of Norwich, an avid collector. The Bishop went to Pierre's *hôtel* to see a 'mappemonde et aultres livres', though he decided to buy nothing. The Bishop, in fact, habitually drove a hard bargain. On two occasions he asked Pierre to send manuscripts on approval to England, but the seller, remembering as he said his trouble with the Bible, refused to do so. In his deposition Regnault du Montet described a similar stalemate, when he asked six *escus* for a Boethius and the Bishop was unwilling to give more than four. Regnault said that he had visited the Paris house of the Bishop, the Hôtel de Bourbon, ten or twelve times, and that he saw there the 'enlumineur Haincelin',[317] who may actually have been the Bedford Master.[318] Regnault also said that Pierre de Vérone had sold the English more than twenty manuscripts.

In these documents Pierre de Vérone was always entitled *maître* and not *enlumineur*, and one must infer that if he had indeed ever practiced the art it constituted around 1415 the less important part of his career. The last records of him in France, dating from 1421–1423, again show him as a bookseller, having sold eleven manuscripts to the monastery of St. Victor. In them he wrote his name in Latin, significantly his full name: 'Petrus de Saco de Verona, rector Montis Giscardi, commorans Parisius'.[319]

Thanks to the generous collaboration of Professor Raffaello Brenzoni, Petrus de Sacco can be traced in Veronese records from 1388 to 1430. In 1388 Pietro, member of a noble family, was already a canon of the Cathedral and an inhabitant of the *contrada* of S. Eufemia.[320] In 1409 he was listed in the *estimo* of this *contrado*,[321] and again in 1418, but then his brother was said to be responsible for the payment, and Pietro was presumably away.[322] Indeed, a note added to the entry of 1418 reads 'Non, et vendidit bona'. In 1411 Pietro, qualified as 'teologo baccilier', took his share in a family financial settlement.[323] 'Petrus Sacre Theologie Professor' was named an heir in the will of his brother in 1415,[324] and in 1430 he was appointed an executor of the will of his sister.[325]

Though it cannot be proved absolutely that the records in Verona and in France refer to the same man, the correspondences are so numerous that a mere coincidence seems improbable. In Veronese

notarial acts he was consistently qualified as professor or bachelor of theology, while in the *estimi*
he is called simply *magister*, the title he customarily bore in France. The theological training of the
Veronese Pietro Sacchi would have qualified him, no doubt, for service as the Duke of Berry's
librarian; it was normal for canons to supervise cathedral libraries.[326] Pietro Sacchi added to
this ecclesiastical experience the career of a *stationnaire*, producing as well as selling manuscripts.[327]
This indeed was very probably Pietro Sacchi's profession, demonstrated by the fact that John the
Norman, apparently an illuminator, lived in his house. Pietro may in addition have learned and
practiced the craft of illumination. We have no evidence that he did, and painting of this kind
was evidently not an important activity when he made his deposition in 1415. On the other hand
neither his bachelor's degree in theology nor his position as canon of the Cathedral of Verona –
not to mention his activity as a bookseller – would exclude the possibility that he was a miniaturist. Canons and scholars occasionally practiced the craft.[328] It is barely possible that Pietro can
be identified with a well-known illuminator, as we shall see.

By choosing Pietro da Verona for the administration of his library Jean de Berry once again
manifested his predilection for Italian culture. For though Pietro had settled in Paris he came from
the peninsula, his first schooling was there, and he was in touch with Verona throughout his life.

APPENDIX

DOCUMENTS ON PETRUS DE SACCO DE VERONA

Document 1.   1397

'Loys fils de roy de France, duc d'Orléans, comte de
Valois et de Beaumont, à notre amé et féal conseiller
Jehan le Flament, salut et dilection. Nous voulons et
vous mandons que des deniers de nos finances vous par
Jean Poulain nostre trésorier général faisiez paier baillier
et delivrer a Pierre de Vérone ou à son certain commande-
ment, la somme de trois cens escuz dor que nous avons
ordonnee luy estre baillée pour cause dun Tite-Live et
dun Boece de Consolation, translatez et escripz en
francais, que deluy avons achetez au pris de ladiste
somme. . . . Lan de grace mil CCCIIIIXX et dix sept.'
(Champeaux and Gauchery, *Travaux*, 1894, p. 125;
Leroux de Lincy, *Paris*, 1867, pp. 40 f.)

Document 2.   1397

'. . . maistre Pierre de Varoune estudiant à Paris, con-
fesse avoir eu et receu de Jehan Poulain, trésorier de
Mgr le duc d'Orléans, la somme de trois cens trente sept
livres et dix solz t., qui deue luy estoit pour la vente de

deux volumes de livres, l'un nommé Titus Luvyus et
lautre Boece de consolacion, naguère achetez de luy par
mond. Sgr le duc. . . .' (Champeaux and Gauchery,
Travaux, 1894, p. 125)

Document 3.   1412 (n.s.)

'Anno circoncisionis 1411, die ij Februarii, post quam
magister Johannes de . . . (*sic*), Normanus, commorans
in domo magistri Petri de Verona, qui sit afinare vel
facere azurrum ultramarinum, et afinat diatim, seu facit,
cum expedit, dixit mihi Johanni Alcherio, in Parisiis,
modum quo utitur afiniando, seu faciendo ipsum azurrum, notavi, et feci presentem scripturam, secundum
avisum meum, et juxta eaque ab ipso audivi, et juxta
eaque per diversas scripturas vidi de hoc, et a diversis
aliis personis audivi.' (Merrifield, *Treatises*, 1849, I, p.
105)

Document 4.   1413

'Item maistre Pierre de Vérone, le premier volume
dun bréviaire en deux volumes appelé les Brevières de

Belleville, lequel volume lui a esté baillé en garde, pour ce icy ledit premier volume. [Arch. nat., K. K. 256]' (Champeaux and Gauchery, *Travaux*, 1894, p. 125)

Document 5.   1388

Verona, Archivio di Stato, Archivio da Sacco, no. 645. 'Dominus Petrus Augustinus filius Domini Isnardi de Sacho de Euphomia Canonicus Majoris Ecclesie Verone.'

Document 6.   1409

Verona, Archivio di Stato, Estimo anno 1409, Contrada di S. Eufemia. 'Magister Petrus de Saco filius quondam suprascripti Isnardini; Libre 1.'

Document 7.   1418

Verona, Archivio di Stato, Estimo anno 1418, Contrada di S. Eufemia. 'M. Petrus quondam D. Isnardi de Sacho pro bonis suis proprijs. . . . M. Franciscus de Sacho ejus Responsabilis; Libre 1.'

Document 8.   1411, 9 March

Verona, Bibl. Comunale, Ms. Carinelli. Divisione fra Francesco Sacco Medico e Pietro Teologo Baccilier, Agostino, Nicolo, Ravanin – e Isnardo padre – eredi tutti del quondam Nobile Pietro quondam Andrea, con Giacomo Benedetto Paolo Nicola Ravanin fratelli quondam Antonio quondam suddetto Isnardo.

Document 9.   1415

Verona, Archivio di Stato (Archivio Antico Ufficio del Registro). Anno 1415, no. 221. 'TESTAMENTUM SER AUGUSTINI DE SACCO QUONDAM D. ISNARDI DE PONTE PETRE VERONE. . . . Dominam Benevenutam Domini testatoris matrem, M. Franciscum Phisicum et M. Petrum Sacre Theologie Professorem fratres ejusdem testatoris sibi heredes universales equaliter instituit.'

Document 10.   1430

Verona, Archivio di Stato (Archivio Antico Ufficio del Registro). Anno 1430, no. 5. 'TESTAMENTUM DOMINE HELENE UXORIS QUONDAM M. FRANCISCI DE PASSIONIBUS DE S. FIRMO. . . . Commissarios autem suos et ejus sui testamenti, ultime voluntatis executores elegit et esse voluit venerandum atque Egregium Virum Dominum M. Petrum de Sacco Sacrae Theologie Professorem, fratrem ipse testatricis.'

IV

The Portraits of Jean de Berry

1 · THE VARIED REPRESENTATIONS

IMAGES of the Roman emperors and some of their medieval successors were multiplied in statuary and on coins, but few lesser rulers before Jean de Berry were represented so often, and certainly not in paintings. Quite apart from the effigies on the Duke's seals some thirty-five certain 'portraits', and a couple of dozen nearly certain, have come down to us. Records refer to fifteen or twenty more, all of course made during his life. Of the extant examples, three are in marble, one is a drawing after a lost easel portrait, and the rest are in manuscripts. All of them are listed and described in the catalogue appended to this chapter, and most of them are reproduced. Their number is so great that long ago Jules Guiffrey exclaimed, rather in despair: 'Qu'il se fît illusion sur ses avantages physiques, c'est une hypothèse difficile à comprendre. . . .'[1]

The Duke must have been seized with a mania, Guiffrey concludes, but we should add that an enthusiasm for portraits was shared more or less by his brothers. Indeed the Valois family more than any other in Europe favored the evolving new pictorial genre. None of Jean's close relatives was handsome, but he seems to have been something of a sport among them, at least among those whose faces we know rather well from surviving portraits. His father, Jean le Bon (Fig. 507), his brothers Charles V (Fig. 1) and Philippe le Hardi (Fig. 508), and his nephews Jean sans Peur (Figs. 506, 512) and Louis II d'Anjou (Fig. 505), all possessed narrow faces and long, aquiline noses. Only Jean de Berry departed greatly from the Valois norm by presenting to the world a round head and a pug nose (Figs. 487, 489, 502).

Most of the representations of the Duke conform, as types, with medieval convention. They are either funerary, like the marble by Jean de Cambrai (Fig. 502), or they are pious, showing the Duke in prayer. The latter range in scale from the tiny portraits in his Books of Hours to the large marble figure originally kneeling before Notre-Dame-la-Blanche in the apse of the Sainte-Chapelle (Figs. 501, 511). The Duke appeared in stained glass once in a window of the Cathedral of Bourges,[2] in orfèvrerie,[3] in the enamel of a paten,[4] and in a panel, together with his father Jean le Bon, before the Madonna.[5] In another panel he knelt with the Duchess below the Man of Sorrows.[6] We can judge from extant portraits that the degree of likeness varied greatly, and we may suppose that the ouvriers in Florence who embroidered the ducal features did not trouble to obtain a good model for them.[7] Certainly the Venetian workshop of the Embriachi, carving a large altarpiece in bone, did not (Fig. 494).

In addition to these conventional types of representation there are a few of remarkable originality. The illustration of sext in the Hours of the Holy Ghost in the *Grandes Heures*, painted by the Bedford Master, shows the Duke before St. Peter at the Gates of Paradise (Fig. 231). The scene is novel. There existed, of course, a tradition for the representation of St. Peter receiving souls into Paradise, normally as part of a Last Judgment (Fig. 515). Examples, rare in the twelfth and thirteenth centuries, multiply in the fourteenth.[8] The subject was furthermore introduced at the same place – sext in the Hours of the Holy Ghost – in an earlier Book of Hours of the Duke, the *Petites Heures* (Fig. 103), and again in a manuscript illuminated around 1415 by followers of the Bedford and Boucicaut Masters (Fig. 516). In these earlier scenes, however, and also in the later Book of Hours, the saint welcomes a group of figures. Their stations in life – as kings, bishops, friars – may be stipulated, but not their individual identity. Peter, furthermore, often grasps the arm of the nearest figure, but the others press closely behind. In our miniature, on the other hand, he singles out one man. He undertakes an individual, not a collective admission. As such it is reminiscent of an equally novel form of the Last Judgment that appeared around 1340 in a fresco by Maso di Banco in S. Croce, Florence (Fig. 513). Here, the angels blow their trumpets and Christ extends his arms in gestures of welcome and rejection, all for the benefit of one man, a member of the Bardi family that owned the chapel.

One other aspect of the action in the miniature in the *Grandes Heures* is unusual also. Peter often welcomes the elect with his left hand, his right being occupied with the keys. This allocation is true already in the twelfth-century tympanum of the Cathedral of Autun.[9] The leader of the elect, on the other hand, naturally extends to St. Peter his right hand, or, as at Autun, both hands. Jean de Berry's right hand, however, is busy with his jewel, so that St. Peter must accept his left.[10] The jewel, suspended from a golden collar, is a large blue stone, probably a sapphire, set amidst six huge pearls. It is especially prominent because the Duke's mantle is orange. When, therefore, Peter presents his keys as his *qualités*, Jean offers a prize from his collection.

Only an enemy would interpret Jean de Berry's action at the pearly gate as an attempt to bribe its keeper. He would have to disregard the fact that in the Middle Ages jewels and precious stones had religious meanings. Pearls often referred to Christ,[11] and sapphires, possessing the color of the sky, to the celestial sphere.[12] The Book of Revelations is studded, so to speak, with gems. The clarity of God is exemplified by 'a stone most precious, even like a jasper stone, clear as crystal',[13] and the Heavenly Jerusalem displays walls of sapphire, chalcedony, emerald, sardonyx, and pearl.[14] The limpid beauty of many-colored stones transported the mind to the contemplation of a purer, immaterial realm, as Suger says in a famous passage written over two centuries earlier.[15]

Of course Jean de Berry was no abbot and no Suger, but ideas of this kind were current in his time, and they were familiar to him and his entourage. Their importance was assumed in the *Songe du vieil pèlerin*, completed in 1393 by Philippe de Mézières, former counsellor of Charles V. In this allegory the young King Charles VI is identified with Moses, and he is advised to wear a breastplate set with stones, in the manner of Aaron and the High Priests of the Old Testament. The ruby signifies truth, the *balais* justice, the emerald mercy and the sapphire peace. The Queen Truth says to him:

> Beau filz, il te doit souvenir que le saint aaron, frère de ton grant père, en figure moyse l'ami de dieu, par le commandement divin portoit à sa poictrine une table d'or quarrée richement aornée, qui estoit appellée le racional. . . . tu porteras tousiours a ta poictrine en esperit cestui petit eschéquier quarré, affin que tu ayes tousiours fresche mémoire dudit eschéquier et du mistère, toutes les foiz que tes subgiez ou autres vouldront jouer aux eschez a ta royale magesté. Moralisant doncques et parlant par figure la forme du petit eschéquier estoit telle: C'est assavoir des quatre poins principaulx des cornières: le pr[e]mer si

F

estoit tout de un fin rubis d'orient, et représentoit en esperit la riche précieuse vérité la royne. Le second point de la seconde cornière estoit tout d'un fin balais, et représentoit iustice bonne adventure appellée. Le tiers point de la t[ier]ce cornière estoit tout d'une fine èsmeraude, et représentoit miséricorde l'amoreuse appellée. Mais le quart point de la dernière cornière estoit tout d'un fin saphir oriental et représentoit vraye paix, allégresse appellée.[16]

The wearing of precious stones and jewels by secular persons, common throughout history, reached a high level in the period of Charles VI, and Jean de Berry was the most fervid practitioner of all. His passion for *pierrerie* became legendary in France, as we have seen, and was still recalled in Italy a half century after his death.[17] Fourteen great rubies were so rare and splendid that they bore distinctive names, such as 'le roi des rubis' or 'le rubis de la vue'. We are told by a contemporary, Thomas de Saluces in his *Chevalier errant*, that the Duke did not permit affairs of state to interfere with collecting. Thomas, indeed, describes an incident when Berry, in a large gathering at court, was discussing the problem of the regency of Languedoc. Two Venetian vendors of precious stones appeared, offering him 'rubiz et balaiz et autres pierres précieuses, car ilz savoyent que moult amoit telles choses. . . .' The Duke immediately excused himself to talk with them. 'Alors il ne songea plus qu'aux pierres,' Thomas tells us. 'Et quand je vy ce . . . je n'y attendi plus, ainz passay oultre.'[18]

Froissart recorded a dialogue between Charles VI and Jean de Berry, in which the King teases the Duke about his love of rubies.

> The King asked the Duke of Berry: 'Good uncle, if the Sultan Bajazet, or any other pagan king, were to send you a rich and sparkling ruby, would you accept it?' 'My lord,' replied the Duke, 'I would consider it.' The King reminded him that it was not ten years since the Sultan had sent him a ruby that had cost twenty thousand francs.[19]

The Duke's greatest stone was a *balai*, the kind of clear pale ruby recalled by Dante:

> L'altra letizia, che m'era già nota
> per cara cosa, mi si fece in vista
> qual fin balasso in che lo sol percuota.
> (The other joy, which was already known to me as precious,
> became in my sight like a fine ruby on which the sun is striking . . .[20])

The Duke's splendid ruby was set amidst five diamonds to compose a jewel similar to the one he wears in several portraits (Figs. 231, 498). For this object the Duke spent the enormous sum of about 90,000 *livres tournois*.[21]

We see no reason to believe that Jean de Berry made such an expenditure and contemplated his purchase only to save his soul. It would be wrong, on the other hand, to insist exclusively on beauty and prestige. The kinds of stones with which the Duke decorated himself he placed in his reliquaries and altarpieces. At least one surviving French bust of a saint from this period wears a *joyau* of this sort (Fig. 509). Not uncommonly the very same rubies or sapphires were transferred from a reliquary to the 'corps de Monseigneur', or vice versa. They served God and man indiscriminately. Certainly the miniature of Jean de Berry before St. Peter (Fig. 231) seems to demonstrate that his beloved objects, far from diverting him to merely worldly and therefore passing delights, helped to save his soul. The miniature held out to him also the promise of eternal con-noisseurship in heaven.

Presumably out of deference to St. Peter the Duke is bareheaded, without one of the big hats he commonly wore during these later years, even when he was indoors. Two of the men behind him wear them. Of these heads the one at the right, in perfect profile, is strikingly individualized. He is, indeed, no other than Philippe le Hardi, Duke of Burgundy, whose appearance we know well from several nearly identical copies of a lost portrait (Fig. 508).[22] Despite the minuteness of the head in the miniature, it shows the unmistakable hooked nose, the protruding, determined mouth and chin, and the exceptionally arched brow, not to mention the same hat (though not worn quite so low on the ear) and brown fur collar. The hat bears a jewel, probably a ruby, in the miniature also. So close is the resemblance that we should ask, not whether the two paintings represent the same person but whether they derive from the same lost model.

Though we might expect to discover the Duke of Burgundy among the witnesses of Jean de Berry's entrance into heaven, we may be surprised to recognize that this Duke is Philippe, his brother. Philippe died in 1404, and when the manuscript was completed in 1409 the reigning Duke was Jean sans Peur, whose features were quite unlike his father's (Figs. 506, 508). There is every reason to believe that the miniature was not painted more than a year or two before 1409. Evidently the meeting at the gate was not conceived as an actual event. Jean de Berry, though seventy years old in 1409, was very much alive, and St. Peter's welcome was still in the realm of delightful prophecy. In the initial below this scene the Duke appears again, enraptured, naturally enough, with the vision of his own acceptance in heaven.

No less novel than the encounter with St. Peter is the appearance of Jean de Berry in miniatures illustrating a prayer for a safe journey. The prayer itself was not a common part of a Book of Hours; indeed after studying 315 manuscripts of this kind in the Bibliothèque nationale, Leroquais recorded only two examples, both of the seventeenth century, in addition to the *Petites Heures*.[23] The Itinerary was added to both the *Petites Heures* (Fig. 498) and the *Très Belles Heures de Notre-Dame* (Fig. 497); it was incorporated in the original text of the *Belles Heures* (Fig. 496). It seems never to have been included in the *Grandes Heures*, finished in 1409. The Duke apparently became interested in the prayer toward 1408–1410. At this time he was actually traveling less than formerly but the struggle between the Armagnacs and the Burgundians had become more bitter, and after Jean sans Peur had perpetrated the incredibly audacious murder of Louis d'Orléans in 1407 no-one in France could feel safe, least of all a leading Armagnac.

All three miniatures were painted by the Limbourgs, and they are alike in one respect: the Duke himself is a central figure. The illustration (but not the prayer) has thus a very personal character, like the miniature for sext in the Hours of the Holy Ghost. Otherwise the narrative in the three miniatures varies considerably, demonstrating that there was no representational tradition. The scene in the *Belles Heures* is probably the earliest (Fig. 496). Although the prayer is entitled 'Ad accipiendam viam suam in exitu domus, ville vel loci', the Duke and his party seem to be return-ing to, rather than leaving, a château. The painter was so eager for immediacy of effect, for an impression of the emergence of the riders from afar onto the pictorial stage, that even the Duke is only partly visible. He can be identified, however, by his jewels, his high black hat, and the deferential behavior of the others.[24]

The miniature in the *Très Belles Heures de Notre-Dame* has been lost, but its design is preserved in a lithograph made for Bastard d'Estang (Fig. 497). The text below the miniature does not begin with the title of the prayer but with the first line of it, 'In viam pacis salutis et prosperitatis dirigat dominus. . . .' The Duke and his company stand outside the gate of a town, through which emerges a group of monks or friars. Preceded by acolytes bearing banners they sing as they proceed, and the two foremost monks prominently display heavy bound books. The Duke's mace-bearer holds open his purse and looks inquiringly at his prince, as though he were expecting him to make a gift (hardly a payment for the purchase of the books). The Duke seems to acknowledge the appearance of the monks by lowering his head. He also lays a hand on his breast, touching his splendid jeweled band in a gesture that we shall discuss shortly. Perhaps this miniature was intended to commemorate an actual donation made after a return from a risky journey.

Instead of conveying travel this composition presents a more formal confrontation of two groups. The proportion of figure to architecture is more advanced than in the *Belles Heures*, and the space is deep. The setting of the miniature was frequently used by the Limbourgs. Its gate, moat, low wall or fence, and distant hills crowned by castles seem to have been inspired by Altichiero; a fresco by a follower in the Santo in Padua is especially close (Fig. 514). There is other evidence to show that the Limbourgs studied in this town.

The setting was used again for the Itinerary in the *Petites Heures*, though here the gate is proportionately smaller (Fig. 498). On the other hand the receding plane of the landscape is more highly articulated (if we can trust Bastard's copy of the miniature in the *Très Belles Heures de Notre-Dame*), and the narrative seems the most appropriate of all three scenes. Whereas the miniatures in the *Belles Heures* and the *Très Belles Heures de Notre-Dame* showed the travelers moving into the picture, in the *Petites Heures* they walk out of it. The hand of the mace-bearer extends into the invisible space, suggesting still more clearly the uncertainties and risks of travel. Overhead a guardian angel soars in the same direction. The Duke is at the center, on the little bridge that spans the moat. Close by is a cleric, perhaps his confessor; he seems to appear also at the Duke's side in the *Très Belles Heures de Notre-Dame* but not in the *Belles Heures* (Figs. 496, 497).

The prayer of the Itinerary of course contains no reference to the Duke, and its illustrations therefore must be accounted another instance of the emergence of Jean de Berry as an individual in contexts that had previously been anonymous and collective. There are still other representations of this kind. In the Pontifical perhaps commissioned for him by the Bishop of Luçon he seems to join the procession alongside the host (Fig. 483). He makes a similar appearance, but in a subject that is more secular than religious, in the famous picture for January in the *Très Riches Heures* (Fig. 489). In French Calendars the scene for this month normally showed feasting, and one might have surmised that if the Duke were to make his entry into the Calendar sequence this would be the right place – and not only because it is the first month. The connoisseur of art is more often than not a gourmet, and the Duke was, in fact, credited with the fateful introduction to French tables of the lowly but noble truffle.[25] Eating in January, one of the two traditional 'occupations of the months' that took place indoors, offered an opportunity also for the display of pieces of the Duke's golden table service as well as the wonderful raiment of his retinue and servants. We have already referred to the great golden *nef* at the right.[26] Colorful enamelled bottles from Venice or the Near East stand on the side-board. The setting of the table seems to make clear that though the Duke possessed splendid knives and forks,[27] they did not always interfere with the fingers in the final stage of the journey of the food, from table to mouth.

All but one of the unprecedented representations that we have discussed appear in manuscripts commissioned by the Duke, and moreover in religious manuscripts. He was so highly esteemed in his time as a connoisseur, especially of jewels, that contemporary writers and illuminators introduced him in secular scenes where there was no reference whatever to him in the text. It would seem safe to assume that the mind of Jean de Berry was not always full of visions of heaven as he contemplated his jewels. We catch a glimpse of him in a more worldly mood in a miniature by the Boucicaut Master in the *Dialogues de Pierre Salmon* of 1409 (Fig. 487). In this little painting Berry turns away from the formal ceremony of the presentation of the book to King Charles VI to inspect a jewel worn by a companion (possibly his nephew Jean sans Peur).[28] The Duke, it seems clear, is not lost in thought but gesticulating with surprise or delight as he touches the precious object.

This kind of action, unprecedented so far as I know, is hardly consistent with court protocol. The conspicuous inattentiveness to the King is very bold. When probing for reasons for its appearance in this miniature we should recall that the author of the text, Pierre le Fruitier called Salmon, knew Jean de Berry very well, and indeed even served him by watching out for objects or craftsmen that would please him. When Salmon was in Italy in 1408 seeking a cure for the King's illness he wrote to Berry from Florence, as we have mentioned above, about the virtues of a Sienese *intarsiatore*. This letter and the Duke's reply compose, in fact, part of the text of this very manuscript.[29]

The Duke's love of precious stones and jewels was so well known in his time that he could be presented as a paradigm of the connoisseur. When the Boucicaut Master, together perhaps with a learned adviser, decided to illustrate Book XVI of the *Livre de la propriété des choses* on precious stones, colors, and metals with a scene of a prince inspecting rings and precious stones, the prince seems to have acquired the features of Jean de Berry (Fig. 504).[30]

In addition to the exceptional appearances of the Duke of Berry in secular scenes there is a group of traditional representations. In them he is the patron of a text or a translation, receiving a copy from the author (Figs. 486, 500, 503). The number of portraits of this type is comparatively small, especially in relation to those of his brother Charles V, the great instigator of translations from Latin into French. King Charles appeared in many presentation miniatures – great, we may say, in quantity but rather uniform in style (Fig. 382).[31] A miniature at the beginning of Oresme's translation of Aristotle's *Ethics* shows a king listening to a lecture, crowned but seated at a desk along with other students and scholars (Fig. 517).[32] Unlike Charles V he is bearded, but the allusion is clear.

Jean de Berry did not lag behind his relatives in the practice of wearing rings bearing their portraits. He owned one that showed the head of King Jean, presumably his father, in silver.[33] He had three bearing his own 'visaige' in gold or cameo.[34] Though they are apparently lost we can gain some impression of their appearance from a fascinating extant example that contains a portrait of Jean sans Peur (Fig. 512).[35] The face, remarkably realistic, is cameo, the high hat and cloak are enamel. Late in his life Jean de Berry acquired also a more exceptional kind of portrait *joyau* – a gold medal, the obverse of which represented the Madonna under a canopy held by angels (Fig. 466).[36]

While Vasari regarded the appearance of the portrait as a sign of the creation of the *ars nova* in Italy, and he claimed many specimens for Giotto,[37] this view oversimplifies and distorts an exceedingly complex process, as the reference to the Valois portrait rings shows. The borderline between an effigy and a portrait is often difficult to draw, and the single specimens of one or the other type vary greatly in accordance with the diverse purposes they fulfill. In France in the fourteenth century effigies could, for instance, serve as 'stand-ins' for the person. They could in a sense pray, like the wax bust of himself that Charles VI placed near an image of St. Peter of Luxembourg during an illness in 1389.[38] Effigies could also make pilgrimages: in 1341 Jeanne de Bretagne and her daughter Yolande de Bar sent silver statues of themselves to St. James of Compostella, probably to avoid making the long journey.[39] Portraits aided diplomacy; Jean sans Peur, for instance, sent a panel by Malouel to King John I of Portugal, probably in 1413.[40] Transported on long journeys by a man to a woman (or vice versa) they aided – or sometimes hindered – matrimony.[41] They commonly served as public symbols of rulers. In the later fourteenth century, and only in Italy, they began to celebrate great writers, Dante and Petrarch.

Singly or in dynastic succession rulers were often represented during the Middle Ages in churches as well as in public and private buildings.[42] They appeared in sculpture or in mural painting.[43] Charles V included the Duke of Berry with his two other brothers on a monumental *vis* or staircase of the Louvre; the statue, made by Jacques de Chartres in 1365, is the earliest recorded portrait of the Duke of Berry.[44] In his castle at Bicêtre the Duke had a cycle of portraits of contemporaries and predecessors. The paintings, which were destroyed by a mob in 1411, represented the kings and princes of France, the Eastern and Western emperors, and Pope Clement VII as well as his cardinals. 'Facies eciam et effigies corporales Clementis pape defuncti, cardinalium sibi assistencium, dum vivebat, regum eciam Francorum et principum, nec non et imperatorum Romanorum et Grecie proprie representabant. . . .'[45] The Duke's gallery of historic personnages was followed by comparable groups in Italy, but unlike these Renaissance series, such as Flavio Biondo's, or even the *uomini famosi* of the Quattrocento, the Bicêtre cycle seems to have been devoted to men memorable more for their position than for their accomplishments.

Jean de Berry, who chose the motto 'le temps venra', lacked the political ambitions of most members of his family. Unlike Philippe le Hardi and Jean sans Peur, he did not devote himself tenaciously to the construction of a stronger and larger state, and he had no dreams of foreign empire, such as those that haunted – and exhausted – Louis I and Louis II d'Anjou. Nor of course did he bear the political responsibilities of the King. These facts throw some light on the relative scarcity of portraits of him as a ruler. He did commission statues of himself and the Duchess as well as of Charles VI and the Queen for the great *cheminée* of his palace at Poitiers. The figures still survive, though the statue of the Duke has a modern head (Figs. 436, 437).[46] In 1566 the historian Chaumeau mentioned a cycle of statues in the porch at Bourges between the palace and the Sainte-Chapelle. He said that they represented the Duchess as well as the Duke, and also the latter's 'progeniteurs et parens avec leur . . . espouses'.[47] In the crypt of the Cathedral of Bourges there are now statues of the kneeling Jean de Berry and Jeanne de Boulogne which might have belonged to the group described by Chaumeau.[48] They are crude and lifeless works, no earlier than the sixteenth century, and they certainly could not have been commissioned by the Duke for the portal of his chapel, as is sometimes asserted.[49]

Perhaps Jean de Berry's relatively moderate political ambitions account in part for the lack of a portrait on panel. None survives – though we shall discuss a probability shortly – and there is no record of one in the inventories. This is all the more notable because the earliest extant examples, and most of the records of lost works, represent the Valois or rulers closely connected with them. A portrait of the Duke's father, now in the Louvre (Fig. 507), may have come from the collection of Charles V, as one panel of a quadriptych representing, in addition to Jean le Bon, Charles V (then Duke of Normandy), Edward III of England, and Emperor Charles IV.[50] In any event the quadriptych, made before the death of Jean le Bon in 1364, passed to Charles V and before 1416 to Jean de Berry.[51] For a time the Duke thus possessed a model of easel portraiture representing his father and his brother. He surely knew, too, a portrait of his brother Philippe le Hardi (Fig. 508), portraits of his nephew Jean sans Peur (Figs. 506, 512),[52] and one of his nephew Louis II d'Anjou (Fig. 505). The Emperor Charles IV, who was raised in France, had his portrait painted in 1354, in Feltre near Aquileia.[53] The extant portrait of Rudolph of Hapsburg, Archduke of Austria (1358–1365), was executed within the next decade.[54]

The early easel portraits in the North, mostly French, are state portraits. The relatively large scale of the head of the famous Jean le Bon – large compared to the first Italian examples – seems to suggest essentially a political meaning. Jean sans Peur displays the ring that is the symbol of his power (Fig. 506). The early independent Italian portraits were commissioned by the Carrara in Padua (see the medal, Fig. 468) and by the ferociously ambitious tyrant of Milan, Gian Galeazzo Visconti, who was furthermore closely related to the Valois. The humanist Pietro Candido Decembrio tells us that Michelino da Besozzo painted a portrait of him,[55] and busts appear in the prayer book that Gian Galeazzo commissioned from Giovannino de' Grassi.[56] In the second quarter of the Quattrocento in North Italy the panel portraits of Pisanello depicted Lionello d'Este and, probably, his wife Margherita Gonzaga. It was on the other hand in the bourgeois circles of the Tuscan and Flemish towns that the easel portrait was adopted by – or in a sense became accessible to – merchants and bankers and men of military or cultural distinction.

Though no panel portrait of Jean de Berry survives, and no painted copy on panel,[57] an unusual drawing reflects an independent easel portrait of him. Among the copies after portraits of historic persons commissioned by Roger de Gaignières sometime before his death in 1715, one represent-ing the Duke is of exceptional interest (Fig. 490).[58] The draughtsman sought to preserve the styl-istic mode and the quality of his model, and he clearly possessed the capacity to do so. Such sympathy for a medieval work of art is unusual among the copies that Gaignières acquired. The half-length drawing of the Duke seems an extraordinary facsimile of a painting of about 1410–1415. Its outlines, its flow of planes, its light and shade, and its details of costume are all consis-tently of this period. Only the face contains conspicuously alien qualities. The reproduction is of such fidelity that the style of the original is easily recognized: that of the Limbourgs. The appearance of the Duke and his costume – the hat of light brown fur, *houppelande* with high collar, great golden band over his shoulder – date the painting in the last six or seven years of the Duke's life. The large features resemble most closely those in the famous portrait in the January miniature in the *Très Riches Heures* (Fig. 489). In the May miniature of that manuscript two figures, a man and a woman, wear similar golden bands over their shoulders, and indeed, the Duke himself again wears it in the portrait in the *Très Belles Heures de Notre-Dame* (Fig. 497).

The half-length portrait of the Duke is drawn primarily in black; the gold band is rendered in yellow and the fur in brown. On the drawing is written: 'Pris sur un Pastel original'. The meaning of this inscription is not immediately evident because the technique that we have called pastel since the eighteenth century did not exist in the time of Jean de Berry. The same inscription, however, appears below a copy in the Gaignières Collection of a fragmentary portrait of Louis II d'Anjou,[59] and here we possess the original (Fig. 505). It is actually watercolor on paper, and its technique was quite familiar to Gaignières because he owned it.[60] The copies in the Gaignières Collection of both this portrait and that of Jean de Berry give no information about the model that the draughtsmen used. There is every reason, then, to believe that the original portrait of Jean de Berry, like that of Louis d'Anjou, belonged to Gaignières and that it too was a drawing or painting of the early fifteenth century.

The posture of the Duke – head in profile, body towards three-quarters and extending down to the waist – conforms to a design represented by an extant panel (Fig. 506). The portrait of Jean sans Peur in the Louvre also includes the two hands, and indeed the stylistic character of the hand at rest is remarkably like the lower one in the drawing. One hand in the Louvre panel displays the ring that, as Mme Adhémar has shown, was the symbol of ducal investiture in Burgundy.[61] In view of the similarities between the drawing and the panel, it is interesting that the latter has been judged a copy of a painting by the Limbourg brother who painted the April miniature in the *Très Riches Heures*.[62] It is not easy to decide how much of the flattened surfaces, stringy drapery folds, and mannered outlines in this mediocre painting should be ascribed to the copyist and how much to the original.[63]

The placing of the hands of Jean de Berry in the drawing is not paralleled in any of the few surviving independent portraits of the time. We have observed the similar gesture of one hand, however, in the miniature in the *Très Belles Heures de Notre-Dame*, though it is placed higher on the body (Fig. 497). The motif of touching the splendid *joyau* links the two portraits. The Gaignières drawing certainly cannot be based on the miniature because it is included in the collection of 'Costumes de France' and the draughtsman would not have altered the *houppelande* of the Duke and still less discarded the moustache and beard, rendering the Duke as he was to appear later, from 1410 to his death. And just as he *would* not have modified the iconography he *could* not have readjusted the hands, making the lower one more parallel to the frame, without losing altogether their early fifteenth-century style.

What is the significance of the Duke's interest in the *joyau*? Similar bands are worn by other figures of the time,[64] but since the design is identical in the two representations of Jean de Berry the object may be a badge of honor of which he was especially proud. Or is this just one more instance of an altogether unprecedented representation of a love of precious objects, such as we have seen in the *Grandes Heures* (Fig. 231) and in the *Dialogues de Pierre Salmon* (Fig. 487)? I do not have the answer, but to put the question is a proper and necessary beginning.

Portraits of the fifteenth century and later not infrequently refer to a man's business or profession. Massys represented a money-changer, Botticelli a medallist, Bronzino a sculptor. Rarer are references to an avocation, and the representations of Jean de Berry as a collector and an amateur are unique.

2 · THE STYLES OF THE PORTRAITS

The representations of the Duke of Berry are much more varied in style than those of the most comparable group, of Charles V. They were painted over a longer period of time, and among them there are more paintings by major artists. They belong, furthermore, to a later period, and as we have seen, the Duke is engaged in entirely unconventional actions. We may see in the portraits, too, a new kind of physical and spiritual likeness. The earlier representations are more closely related to the medieval conception of a typical and timeless image – in this case of a middle-aged or elderly man – individualized by a unique feature or two (Figs. 474, 476, 491). The later portrayals on the other hand, especially those from *circa* 1410 to 1416 (Figs. 487, 489, 498, 499) are shaped from the very beginning by the idea of uniqueness. In the best of them we see a man whom we would recognize immediately if he were to pass us on the street.

Within our group of thirty-five or more representations the emergence of the realistic portrait is not consistent, gradual, and regular. The new form is an accomplishment of artists of stature, and even among them of some more than others, while lesser masters altered their conventions very little (Figs. 480, 493). It would thus be wrong to employ the degree of likeness, without qualification, as a criterion of the date of a portrait. The ubiquitous but rather limited illuminator whom we call the Pseudo-Jacquemart envisaged the Duke after 1400 (Fig. 219) in much the same way as he or other artists had seen him around 1385 (Fig. 491). On the other hand towards 1390 an outstanding painter, probably not by craft an illuminator, gave us an individualized portrayal that could be the result only of fresh, intent scrutiny (Fig. 179). The result resembles in kind the portraits in paintings and sculpture in the last years of the Duke's life (Figs. 487, 489).

This first great portrait of the Duke, which appears at the beginning of the *Brussels Hours*, shows us a balding middle-aged man whose countenance seems all the more fleshy by comparison with his two saintly companions.[65] His nose is bulbous, his lower lip loose and protruding, and altogether he gives an impression of determination blended with humorousness and sensuality. These qualities were not altered much by advancing age; they are more or less apparent in the numerous good portraits made from 1410 on, after the Duke had passed his seventieth birthday (Figs. 489, 499).

In these portraits as in those of later periods the character given a sitter is a function of the painter's style as well as of his understanding of the personality before him. There is much of the former and almost nothing of the latter in a miniature in a charter associating the Duke with an abbey in Bruges (Fig. 480). Instead of representing the robust, energetic person who appears in many other portraits the Flemish illuminator, probably uninformed, simply invoked local conventions. As a consequence Jean, small of feature and demure of countenance, sits modestly or even timidly on his throne. Wrapped in a great red cloak, his head protected by a heavy red muffler and a high black Flemish hat, he nestles into his clothing as though the ceremony were outdoors and December 13, 1402, a bitter winter's day.

In two portraits made between *circa* 1405 and 1409, in the *Heures de Turin* (Fig. 34) and the *Grandes Heures* (Fig. 231), the Duke looks older, softer, and much less vigorous than in other late representations. In one of these at least he also looks more pious (Fig. 231). Now the authors of both these paintings, the Baptist Master[66] and the Bedford Master, were less influenced than the painters of other portraits by the Parisian and Italian traditions, and one of them at least was a Netherlander. Age and piety were two conditions they valued, as did later masters from this region – Roger van der Weyden, for instance. Dignity and force, on the other hand, were the ideals of the French, and especially the Italo-French, traditions. We may see them in the portrait in the Lectionary in Bourges by the Boucicaut atelier, the poor state of which does not conceal the fact that the puffiness of age is transformed and ennobled in an Italianate manner (Fig. 499). The excellent portrait in *January* in the *Très Riches Heures* by the Limbourgs, the closest students of Italian style, is all force and will (Fig. 489). Despite the imminence of culinary delights the mouth and jaw are firmly set, and there is no pleasure even in the eyes. It is a striking fact that the Duke is more realistically depicted than all members of his household except the *maître d'hôtel* at his left. All the others have idealized features, mostly of youth. The Duke's face sags, and his ugliness is not concealed. The delineation is far from being – to use the words written by the draughtsman on an Italian portrait drawing of the same date[67] – 'caro e fresco e gentile'. Our conceptions of the International Style in painting must be broad enough to include images of this kind – visible elsewhere in the *Très Riches Heures* and in other works of the period.

The realistic trend in sculpture has been given its due since the time of Courajod, who based upon it his theory of the rise of the Renaissance in France.[68] How far the movement had carried in the circle of Jean de Berry is manifested by the *gisant* made by Jean de Cambrai for his tomb (Fig. 502). The figure was probably carved during his life, but we cannot be entirely certain.[69] The face is similar to the portrait in *January*, with the same fleshy cheeks and stubborn chin, but the lips protrude even more, the eyes are more deeply set and the head rounder.

Holbein's superb drawing gives us our most engaging portrait of Jean de Berry (Fig. 511). Its very beauty and its psychological subtlety raise, however, a fundamental question. What in this remarkable portrayal is Holbein's and what the original sculptor's? It may be said, first, that the drawings of the Duke and Duchesss have been judged careful copies, and as such exceptional in Holbein's œuvre.[70] It is true, furthermore, that Holbein's sitters are normally grave. He tends to 'freeze' his clients whereas in the Basel drawing the face of Jean de Berry is stirred in a sly, fleeting gaiety. Did Holbein introduce these qualities in his drawing, though they were lacking in the sculpture, just as he increased the vibrancy of light and shade in the flesh?

Though the head of the statue is preserved, now in the museum at Bourges (Fig. 501), it is largely deprived of its original paint and so damaged by its mistreatment during the Revolution that it provides no very precise answer to our question. One can say, however, that the sculpture in its present state suggests a face less lively than in Holbein's drawing and more like the sculpture of the tomb (Fig. 502). A man with a radiant countenance during prayer would be a rarity in the art of the time. It is true that the faces of Gothic statues, such as the angels at Reims,[71] not infrequently melt into an expression of divine bliss, and occasionally, especially in Germany, they are wreathed in broad, serene smiles – the blessed in Abraham's bosom at Bamberg, for instance, Queen Regilindis at Naumburg, or the Wise Virgins at Magdeburg.[72] Perhaps the face of the statue of the Duke when colored came somewhat closer to a smile and thus gave Holbein his cue.

It is clear, in any event, that of all the extant portraits, only Holbein's presents so warm and strangely glowing a countenance. By some odd working of history he has enabled us to see in Jean de Berry not the greedy prince who could overtax his subjects but the man who loved beautiful creatures and beautiful things, who 'endowed' for life a lonely, masterless mastiff, and precipitately abandoned affairs of state for the sight of an imported diptych or even a new little golden bear.

3 · FEATURES AND DRESS

The costume in which Jean de Berry chose to present himself in his paintings changed considerably over the years. During the fourteenth century he wore most frequently a robe of state, a *manteau d'apparat*, usually red velvet with a broad ermine collar. He appeared in the *manteau* at prayer as well as on official occasions. Occasionally, as in the first portrait in the *Brussels Hours* (Fig. 179), this robe was lined with ermine also. It is, indeed, the kind of robe that the Dukes of Berry and Burgundy ordered of their tailors in 1389 for the marriage of Isabeau de Bavière and Charles VI: 'veloux vermeil . . . pour faire . . . manteaulx fourréz d'ermines par dedens et par dehors, si comme a ducs appartient'.[73]

Jean de Berry appeared in this ducal *manteau* as early as the great seal of 1370 (Fig. 474), in the *Petites Heures* (Fig. 94), again in the *Brussels Hours* (Figs. 179, 181), and as late as the charter of 1405 (Fig. 481). Its use in the scene of the presentation of a book in Bibl. nat., fr. 1023, of 1410 must be regarded as one more sign of the conservative or indeed retrospective character of the painting (Fig. 486), for by this time the Duke had acquired other habits. During the last eight or ten years of his life he, like his brothers and the King, preferred to be painted in the great cloak or *houppelande* (Figs. 487, 489, 497, 498, 499). This he wore whether outdoors or in, the collar rising ever higher on his neck. Normally he liked a fur hat on his head. The *houppelande* was often embroidered with a gold pattern, occasionally taking the form of the Duke's device of swans (Figs. 487, 500). The splendor of his appearance was commonly enhanced by a golden collar bearing a great stone (Figs. 231, 498, 499), a jewel pinned to his hat (Fig. 504), and in two portraits an enormous gold band across his shoulders (Figs. 490, 497).

The portraits of Jean de Berry extend over a period of approximately forty-five years, and the physical appearance of the Duke in them naturally varies considerably. This variation was produced not only by nature but by the hand of the Duke himself. The process of aging was beyond his control, but he could and did determine whether to present to the world a face that was clean-shaven or adorned with different kinds of hirsute appendages. Of course the choices in this respect of a prince, as of any other man, are not entirely asocial; fashion plays its part. The short beard divided into two points, which we may call the double goatee, became fashionable within the French aristocracy about 1350, and then began to be abandoned in the 'sixties.[74] Around this period it may even be seen sprouting on the chin of Christ and of John the Evangelist in the *Crucifixion* in a Missal very probably made *circa* 1375 for a princely patron (Fig. 519). The Duke lagged somewhat behind this trend, as we shall see. In the later fourteenth century a man wore his hair long, but around 1400 the nape was shaved. The difference between the first and second portrait in the *Brussels Hours* (Figs. 179, 181) seems to conform to this trend.

The hirsute vagaries of the Duke were bound to tempt scholars to extract from them some chronological profit. Hulin de Loo first established a pattern,[75] and then Paul Durrieu.[76] Hulin utilized only a few of the surviving portraits. Durrieu introduced more, though by no means all. Both historians rightly observed that portraits from the last five or six years of the Duke's life all show him beardless. Indeed, an additional dated portrait that must be put in this period – in a *Cas des nobles hommes et femmes* – only further proves the rule (Fig. 500).[77]

Difficulties arise, however, with the conclusions of Hulin and Durrieu about earlier portraits. Hulin maintained that the Duke was clean-shaven from *circa* 1380–1390 (some portraits in the *Petites Heures*, the two in the *Brussels Hours*), that he began to wear a short beard *circa* 1390 (*Heures de Milan*, folio 87, later portraits in the *Petites Heures*), and that this beard was still in evidence as late as *circa* 1410 in the *Livre des bonnes mœurs* (Fig. 486). This scheme is partly incomplete and partly incorrect because Hulin based it upon a small number of miniatures, and because he overlooked the seals and the marriage contract of 1389. Durrieu pointed to the omission of the contract, in which the Duke is clean-shaven, and he also introduced as evidence some seals, specifying only one, however, in which the Duke wears a double goatee. Now he dated this seal 1384, following Roman;[78] but Roman himself places it *circa* 1380, and actually it is identical with the great seal, no. 1 in our catalogue, which was first employed in 1370 (Fig. 474). This seal, which remained in use during most of the Duke's life, is affixed to a document of May 13, 1401,[79] and again Durrieu read it as evidence of the Duke's appearance at this time.

Durrieu's scheme is: period 1, to 1384 (supposed date of the great seal), bearded; period 2, 1384 or 1386 to after 1390, clean-shaven; period 3, 1401 to 1410, beard or moustache; period 4, 1410–1416, clean-shaven. Durrieu tends to support this scheme by placing undated paintings in periods that seem to me incorrect: for instance, the bearded portrait in the Parement style in the *Heures de Milan* in the first decade of the fifteenth century (Fig. 491).[80]

Durrieu's scheme requires fundamental modifications. The iconography of the Duke must of course be based on all the available evidence, including the seals. But the seals have to be used with great caution because the date of a document cannot be taken to be the date of the design of the seal or the counter-seal affixed to it.[81] Though the Great Seal, no. 1 in our catalogue, shows the Duke wearing long moustaches and a beard, it was still used as late as 1410 and 1415, when Berry was certainly clean-shaven. Evidence has not yet been adduced for the date of the matrix of any of the known seals. The one exception is the seal of the treasurer of the Sainte-Chapelle, our Cat. no. 11, which can be connected with the consecration in 1405 (Fig. 482). The evidence offered by all the other seals is only ancillary.

APPENDIX A

ICONOGRAPHIC TABLE OF JEAN DE BERRY

Period 1. *Ca.* 1370–1388 (probably only to mid-'eighties).

The evidence is least decisive for this period, but our nos. 1-4 (Figs. 474, 475) show the Duke with a moustache and with a beard. In two instances the beard assumes the form of a double goatee. The rather long hair stands out from his head.

Period 2. 1389 (or a few years earlier) – 1405.

The Duke was clean-shaven; see our nos. 5-11 (Figs. 476–482). His hair, at first standing out (no. 5 – Fig. 476), soon afterward is combed flat and is cut shorter.

The Duke favors a mantle with a broad ermine collar that does not rise onto his neck (nos. 7, 8, 10 – Figs. 478, 479, 481).

Period 3. 1406–1410.

Contrary to convention at the court the Duke again wore a short beard (nos. 14, 19 – Figs. 234, 486) or a goatee (no. 13 – Fig. 484). In nos. 13 and 19 he has a moustache. In three small initials in the *Grandes Heures*, finished in 1409, he appears to be clean-shaven (nos. 16–18 – Figs. 243, 244, 485).

The Duke begins to prefer to wear a gold collar and a jewel (nos. 12, 16 – Figs. 483, 485).

Period 4. 1409/1410–1416.

The Duke was clean-shaven (nos. 20–22 – Figs. 34, 487, 489). He almost always wears a richly ornamented coat or *houppelande*, even indoors (*Très Riches Heures*, no. 22). The collar of the *houppelande* rises high on his neck. A pendant jewel is seldom absent.

APPENDIX B

CATALOGUE OF PORTRAITS OF JEAN DE BERRY

A. Examples dated, more or less narrowly, by 'external' evidence.

1. Great Seal (Fig. 474). Employed in 1370 (Gaignières, fols. 17, 18), 1379, 1401, 1410 (Gandilhon, no. 5) and 1415 (Gaignières, fol. 27).

The Duke stands under a canopy, flanked by a helmeted bear and a swan bearing a shield *semé de 8 fleurs-de-lys*. The Duke's beard has two rather long tufts, and his moustaches are long and drooping. His hair stands out from his head, below a headband set with stones. He holds a scepter in his right hand; a glove is attached to his left wrist. He wears a mantle with a wide collar, very open at the neck.

Gandilhon (pp. XXVII, L n. 4, LV) says that the matrix of this seal is the one paid for in 1374, when Jean de Nogent received a considerable sum for such a work. Gandilhon offers no particular proof of the connection of this document with this seal, and the connection seems disproved by the evidence provided by Gaignières of the use of the seal as early as 1370. It should be added that the value of Gandilhon's comprehensive

work on the seals is reduced by his failure to utilize the drawings of Gaignières.

Specimens:

Bourges, Arch. du Département du Cher, G, Ste-Chapelle de Bourges, liasse 1(4), (Title 776)

Paris, Arch. nat. J185(B), no. 45 (act of May, 1379).

Paris, Arch. nat., J382, no. 17 (act of 13 May, 1401).

Bibl. nat., Cabinet des Médailles, Coll. Bastard d'Estang, nos. 45a and 45b.

Paris, Arch. nat., cast (Douët d'Arcq, no. 421).

Bibliography:

Delisle, *Coll. Bastard d'Estang*, 1885, nos. 45a and 45b.

Douët d'Arcq, *Sceaux*, no. 421.

Gaignières, Bibl. nat., fr. 20368, fols. 17, 18: drawing of a seal affixed to an act of Aug. 15, 1370; fol. 27 . . . act of Nov. 25, 1415.

Gandilhon, *Sceaux*, 1933, no. 5, pl. IX.

Roman, *Sigillographie*, 1912, p. 99 and pl. XIII.

2. Initial K of a certificate of January 1372 (Fig. 475).

Paris, Arch. nat., AE II 393. It attests the authenticity

of a piece of the True Cross that Charles V gave to Jean de Berry. The King had himself cut the fragment from the relic preserved in the Ste-Chapelle in Paris. He is clean-shaven whereas the Duke wears a long beard.

Bibliography:
Paris, Arch. nat., Babelon, 1960, p. 28.

3. Copies of a miniature in a ms. of 1378–1379. The ms., *Registre des hommages du comté de Clermont en Beauvaisis*, was burnt in a fire in the Chambres des Comptes in 1737. The miniature had already been engraved by Jollain in 1683 and drawn by Gaignières. These copies, which must be used with caution, show the Duke with a short beard and a moustache.
Engraving: by Jollain in Le Labourer and Ménestrier, *Tableaux généalogiques, ou les seize quartiers de nos rois*, Paris, 1683 (not accessible to me); Montfaucon, *Les Monumens de la monarchie françoise*, Paris, III, 1731, pl. XI, p. 49; Bastard, *Librairie*, 1834, p. 12.
Drawing: by Gaignières, Bibl. nat., Cabinet des Estampes, Oa¹² fol. 8. Reproduced by: Couderc, *Portraits*, [1910], pp. 11-13, pl. XXIX; Gandilhon, *Sceaux*, 1933, pl. VII.

4. Seal. Employed in 1383 (Gaignières, fol. 19) and 1387 (Gandilhon, no. 8). The representation of the Duke resembles that on the seal of 1370. He wears a two-pointed beard, a moustache, and his hair stands out similarly from his head. He stands behind his shield, *semé de 8 fleurs-de-lys*. A swan (standing in water) and a bear appear at the sides.
Specimens:
Bibl. nat., fr. 20412, no. 43.
Paris, Arch. nat., J187, no. 11 (incomplete).
Bibl. nat., Cabinet des Médailles, Coll. Bastard d'Estang, no. 47 (incomplete).
Paris, Arch. nat., cast (Douët d'Arcq, no. 427, incomplete).
Bibliography:
Bosredon, *Sigillographie*, 1895, nos. 151, 152.
Delisle, *Coll. Bastard d'Estang*, 1885, no. 47.
Douët d'Arcq, *Sceaux*, no. 427.
Gaignières, Bibl. nat., fr. 20368, fol. 19: drawing after a seal affixed to an act of Nov. 5, 1383.
Gandilhon, *Sceaux*, 1933, no. 8, pl. XII (typographical error in caption).

5. Drawing. Contract of Marriage with Jeanne de Boulogne, June 5, 1389.

Paris, Arch. nat., AE II 411 (Fig. 476).
The Duke is beardless. His hair stands out from his head, as in earlier representations. The shield is *France ancien*.
The coiffure of the Duchess resembles that of the Duke. Alongside her is a shield with Berry and the red emblem of Auvergne. The draughtsman was mediocre, and no-one could possibly judge from his well-matched couple that the Duke was forty-nine years old, the Duchess twelve.
Bibliography:
Paris, Arch. nat., Babelon, 1960, p. 35.

6. Seal (Fig. 477). Employed in 1397.
The figure of the Duke emerges from a tower. He wears a headband set with stones. He is clean-shaven, and his hair hangs straight down, approximately to the lobes of the ears. The Duke's mantle has a high collar, and he wears a necklace with two circles of pearls. He holds a sword in his right hand and rests his left on the shield, which shows three *fleurs-de-lys*. At the left an old, bearded man holds the Duke's mace and helmet. A man at the right likewise brandishes a mace.
Specimens:
Bourges, Arch. du Département du Cher, G, Ste-Chapelle de Bourges, *liasse* 140, Title 306.
Paris, Arch. nat., cast (Douët d'Arcq, no. 422).
Bibliography:
Bosredon, *Sigillographie*, 1895, no. 156.
Douët d'Arcq, *Sceaux*, no. 422.
Gandilhon, *Sceaux*, 1933, no. 4, pls. VI, XIV.
   Though this seal shows *France moderne* (three *fleurs-de-lys*), the counter-seal used with it shows *France ancien* (*fleurs-de-lys semés*). See Grandilhon, *op. cit.*, no. 4 bis, pl. XV.

7. Miniature, *Brussels Hours*, p. 10 (Fig. 478). *Ca.* 1390 (definitely before 1402).
The Duke is clean-shaven. His hair, which has receded high on his forehead, is combed close to his head and ends in curls. He wears a robe lined in ermine and fitted with a deep ermine collar, which fits snugly around his neck. The shields show nine *fleurs-de-lys*.

8. Miniature, *Brussels Hours*, p. 14 (Fig. 479). Before 1402.
Generally similar to the preceding portrait, upon

which it depends. It is, however, a less faithful likeness. The hairline, furthermore, is still higher, and the
hair shorter, without the terminal curls of the preceding portrait. In this respect the portrait resembles
the seal of 1397.

The shields show three *fleurs-de-lys*, but the banner
waved by the bear shows six.

9. Miniature on act of December 13, 1402, associating
Jean de Berry with St. Barthélemy de Bruges (Fig.
480). Paris, Arch. nat., J1105, no. 8; AE II 422.

The Duke and the Abbot Lubert Hautschild are holding the charter, from which a seal and a counter-seal
dangle. The Duke is clean-shaven, as in other portraits of this period.

10. Copy of a miniature in the original charter of the
Ste-Chapelle, dated April 18, 1405 (Fig. 481). The
copy was published by Bastard, *Peintures*. The document itself, preserved in the Archives du Cher, was
destroyed by fire in 1858. In the account of the losses
published shortly thereafter the document was described as the original charter (Société du Berri,
Compte rendu des travaux, VI, 1858-1859, p. 193).

It is impossible to decide whether the light patches on
the upper lip and chin of the Duke represent highlights or a very light beard and moustache. There may
be stubble on his jowls. The Duke, wearing his
familiar ermine-lined and ermine-collared mantle, is
giving a black vestment lined in white to the cleric of
the chapel, dressed in pink, who kneels before him.
The page, dressed in blue, holds an article of clothing,
presumably for the cleric also. The Duke's canopy is
largely orange, the ceiling yellow, the curtain at the
left blue, and the floor black, gray, and maroon.

Between the frame of the miniature and a series of
acanthus leaves there is a section of a diapered ground.
Against this is set the Duke's shield, *France moderne*,
flanked by a swan and a bear. The seals affixed to this
document still show *France ancien*.

This important miniature has not attracted much
attention. Porcher (*Belles Heures*, 1953, p.7 n.10)
said that it cannot have been made in 1405, because
the Duke used the device of 3 *fleurs-de-lys* only in the
last years of his life and that it therefore is a later copy
of the act. He also says that, though the miniature has
been connected with the Limbourgs, the copy does
not permit us to judge. The authorship of the Limbourgs does, however, seem clear to me even in the
copy (*Burl. Mag.*, 1963, p. 51). Three *fleur-de-lys* were

furthermore quite proper in 1405. They appear, for
one thing, on the seal of the Ste-Chapelle of 1405 to
be discussed immediately below, not to mention the
seal of 1397 (Figs. 482, 477). Additional evidence for a
date in 1405 is the apparent age of the Duke, younger
than in the portraits dated from 1409 on, and the
mantle, which he wore commonly before 1405 but
not after.

This little miniature shows, then, that the Limbourgs
worked for Jean de Berry in April 1405, only a few
months after the death of their patron Philippe le
Hardi. It has been generally believed that they
entered Berry's service only in 1409-1410. A recon-
sideration of the chronology of the works of the Limbourgs is, in other words, involved.

11. Seal (Fig. 482). The Baptist presenting the Duke, and
St. Catherine the Duchess, to Christ. Employed in
October 1405, a few months after the consecration
of the Ste-Chapelle. It was the seal of the treasurer
of this chapel: S: THESAUR(ARII C)APPITULI:
SANCTE: CAPPELLE: SCI: SALVATORIS: PALA-
CII: BITURIS.

The Duke is clean-shaven. The arms are *France
moderne*. This seal is notable for its composition. The
presentation takes place in a framed space, and the
ceremony is watched by spectators in two-storey
arcades, as though it occurred in the portico of a
building. The wing of an angel who leans through
an opening at the left projects from another opening
behind. The matrix of this seal was evidently the
work of an excellent goldsmith.

Specimens:

Bourges, Arch. du Département du Cher, G, Ste-
Chapelle de Bourges, *liasse* 7⁷, (Title 780).

Musée de Bourges, B 1693.

Bibl. nat., Cabinet des Médailles, Coll. Bastard d'Estang,
no. 230.

Paris, Arch. nat., cast (Douët d'Arcq, no. 7840).

Bibliography:

Delisle, *Coll. Bastard d'Estang*, 1885, no. 230.

Douët d'Arcq, *Sceaux*, no. 7840.

Gandilhon, *Sceaux*, 1933, no. 583, pl. XXXVII.

Roman, *Sigillographie*, 1912, p. 176.

12. Miniature, Pontifical of Étienne Loypeau, Bishop
of Luçon. Bibl. nat., lat. 8886, fol. 318v. (Fig. 483).
In the miniature the host is carried in a procession.
Among the clerics and standard-bearers appears a
nobleman who is probably Jean de Berry. The identi-

fication rests on circumstantial evidence, which is not absolutely conclusive. The elderly man, who may be considered to resemble the Duke to some degree, wears a blue mantle and a gray fur hat with a very high crown. In his later years, beginning with the miniature of 1405 (Fig. 481), the Duke sports hats of this type (Figs. 487, 489, 497, 498, 499, 500), but the one in lat. 8886 has a proportionately lower brim and higher crown than any other. On the other hand the chain bearing a jewel, which appears in several late portraits, has a spiral design very much like the one in the miniature of 1409 by the Bedford Master (Fig. 485). The Duke's hair was gray in the miniature of 1405 (Fig. 481), but whereas in the representations of 1405 and the immediately preceding years he was clean-shaven, in lat. 8886 he wears a goatee and a closely trimmed moustache.

The ms. bears the arms of Jean de Berry on fol. 1. It is generally agreed, however, that it was written on order of Étienne Loypeau, Bishop of Luçon, a protégé of the Duke. He died in 1407, and the ms. was very probably completed by that date, though, for reasons of style, not much earlier. It may well have been made for presentation to Jean de Berry. Contrary to an old and persistent opinion, it cannot be definitely identified with any of the Pontificals mentioned in the inventories (see the catalogue entry for this ms. in a subsequent volume, *Paris 1400–1420*).

13. Portrait adjoining an initial, *Grandes Heures*, Bibl. nat., lat. 919, fol. 8 (Fig. 484). The ms. was completed in 1409. The miniature is on the first folio of the Hours of the Virgin.

The Duke is kneeling at a prie-dieu, praying to the Madonna, who appears in the adjacent initial. As in the Pontifical (Fig. 483), the Duke has a goatee and a closely trimmed moustache. The portrait, including the small crown,[82] is a rather close copy of a much earlier one in the Parement style in the *Très Belles Heures de Notre-Dame*, though the brown hair in that portrait (Fig. 491) has now appropriately become white. The painter of this miniature, Pseudo-Jacquemart, is the author of the related portraits in the *Petites Heures*.

14. Portrait in an initial, *Grandes Heures*, fol. 34 in None of the Hours of the Virgin (Fig. 234).

The Duke, kneeling at a prie-dieu, prays to the Virgin in the temple in the miniature above. He wears a pink, fur-lined cloak. He has a white, square beard, not a

G

goatee as on fol. 8 of this ms. (Fig. 484) and in the Pontifical (Fig. 483).

15. *Grandes Heures*, fol. 53. The man in an initial who prays to the Crucifixion with joined hands may be the Duke. He wears a red tunic and has a gray beard.

16. Jean de Berry received by St. Peter at the Gates of Paradise; in the initial below, Jean de Berry praying. *Grandes Heures*, fol. 96 (Fig. 485). Sext, the Hours of the Holy Ghost. The Ghost descends upon St. Peter in the larger scene. Miniature by the Bedford Master, initial by a much weaker painter (reworking the original?).

In this remarkable portrait by the Bedford atelier, one of the liveliest that has survived, the appearance of the Duke is exceptional: for once he really looks his age. His low gray-brown fur collar is unusual. He seems to have worn a small goatee, though damage and the minute scale make a certain judgment impossible (Hulin de Loo, *Heures de Milan*, 1911, p. 5, asserts he is beardless). There is a gray down on his chin, cheek and upper lip. The conventional face in the initial, on the other hand, is clean-shaven.

17. The Duke at a prie-dieu, in prayer before the Holy Ghost. Initial at None of the Hours of the Holy Ghost, *Grandes Heures*, fol. 97 (Fig. 243). Above, a miniature representing SS. Peter and Paul baptizing.

The cloth over the prie-dieu bears the arms of the Duke. He is represented as a clean-shaven man of great girth and heavy jowls.

18. The Duke at prayer before Christ, who appears in a cloud. Initial at Vespers of the Hours of the Holy Ghost, *Grandes Heures*, fol. 98 (Fig. 244). Above, a miniature representing St. Peter at an altar worshipped by the faithful, toward whom the Holy Ghost descends.

The Duke is leaner than in the preceding representation (fol. 97), but otherwise similar. He is again clean-shaven. The initial is by a follower of the Boucicaut Master.

19. Jean de Berry receiving the *Livre des bonnes mœurs* from its author, the Augustinian friar Jaques Legrand, Bibl. nat., fr. 1023, fol. 2 (Fig. 486). The author gave this copy of his treatise to the Duke on March 4, 1410. The recognizable round head of the Duke bears an

unusual escalloped crown set with pearls. The Duke's hair is white and he wears a white beard and a small drooping moustache, as in several representations during the preceding years. Here, however, the beard is divided into two points – a double goatee. One of the courtiers has a brown beard of the same type.

The miniature, which may be attributed to the atelier of the Luçon Master, was executed very indifferently. The design of the Duke's gold faldstool implies a more steeply sloping ground plane than is actually represented (and a floor rather than greensward?). The gold leaf for the chair was laid before the painting. Then by mistake the illuminator carried the mantles of the attendants too far downward behind it, so that it is left suspended in the air.

20. Jean de Berry and companions in a room in which Pierre Salmon presents his *Lamentations* to King Charles VI. Bibl. nat., fr. 23279, fol. 53 (Fig. 487). The text does not specify the presence of the Duke of Berry. It was written for the King, completed in 1409, and this ms. was probably presented to him in that year or early in the next. The miniature is by the workshop of the Boucicaut Master.

The Duke, clean-shaven, wears a brown fur hat and a black *houppelande*, ornamented with yellow swans. Around his neck there is a spiral gold chain from which is suspended a small golden animal, probably a bear. The Duke is engrossed with a similar specimen of goldsmith's work worn by his companion (dressed in red with a green collar and a white hat). His left hand fingers it and his right is raised in delight or surprise. He pays no attention whatever to the ceremony in front of him.

21. Jean de Berry praying to the enthroned Madonna (Fig. 488). *Très Belles Heures de Notre-Dame*, section *Heures de Turin*, fol. 78v. (burnt in 1904). Before 1409. By the Baptist Master.

The Duke, clean-shaven and with white hair, wears an ermine-lined *houppelande* ornamented with a pomegranate motif. He looks very old and pasty, qualities emphasized in this realistic style. The arms of the Duke are on the cloth that covers the prie-dieu. A tiny white dog, its tail over its back, looks up at the Duke. Toward the right are an undersized bear and another small animal, perhaps a dog.

22. The Duke at table in the Calendar picture for *January*. Chantilly, *Très Riches Heures* of Jean de

Berry, fol. 1v. (Fig. 489). Before 1416, by the Limbourgs.

This portrait, similar to the one in the *Dialogues de Pierre Salmon*, is very probably an excellent likeness. In profile the bulbous nose and protruding lower lip are especially conspicuous. These features, as well as the puffy cheek, are strikingly similar to the two sculptured heads (Figs. 501, 502). The Duke, clean-shaven, again wears a high fur hat and a velvety *houppelande*, blue in this instance and bearing a stylized flower pattern rather than golden swans. He wears not a chain but a gold collar with a round golden pendant.

23. Copy of a lost portrait of Jean de Berry by the Limbourgs. Bibl. nat., Cabinet des Estampes, Gaignières Collection Oa 13 Rés., fol. 15 (Fig. 490). The drawing is on 17th-century paper, bearing a watermark of a cross, monogram of Christ, and three nails (I owe this difficult identification to the kindness of Mlle Michèle Hébert). The half-length portrait of the Duke is drawn primarily in black; the gold band is rendered in yellow and the fur in brown. The 'pastel original' which, according to the inscription, the drawing copies probably belonged to Gaignières. The composition has been discussed in the text of this chapter and earlier by the writer in *Burl. Mag.*, 1963.

B. Portraits not narrowly dated

24. The Duke kneeling at a prie-dieu, a swan and his arms behind him, border of fol. 87, *Heures de Milan*, Turin, Museo Civico (Figs. 49, 491). *Ca.* 1380–1385. The Duke is praying to the Trinity, represented in the miniature. The shield shows *fleurs-de-lys-semés*.

The Duke's brown moustache and beard place this portrait in the period before 1388 or earlier. The mantle conforms with this date: the Duke wears the blue robe with a broad ermine collar set low on the shoulders in which he was frequently represented before the turn of the century: seal of 1370 (Fig. 474); *Brussels Hours* (Figs. 478, 479). The portrait by the Pseudo-Jacquemart on fol. 8 of the *Grandes Heures* is based on this portrait, and preserves near 1409 the outmoded mantle, but the illuminator has, on the other hand, changed the color of the Duke's hair from brown to white to conform with his appearance at this date and with the representative conventions (Fig. 484). The Duke's beautiful crown in the *Très Belles Heures de Notre-Dame*, set with white, red, and blue stones, is unusual.

Almost the entire folio, including the angels in the borders, and the script was retouched at a later date. God Father and Christ have been especially altered. Their mantles are now muddy in color and flattened, and their flesh orange-red. The deep blue bands of the left side of the mandorla are not original, nor is the dark blue central band of the right side. The dove, very similar to the one in the later miniature *Pentecost* (Fig. 46), must be regarded with suspicion. The portrait, on the other hand, is freer of repaint. The scarlet prie-dieu and the curtain are undisturbed, and much of the figure and the swan also, though the face and hands of the prince are lightly retouched. The red border of the shield has been carelessly repainted in brown. Delaissé has recently (1963, p. 135) remarked that the brown script on this page has been gone over in black. (I should add that the script on other folios, such as 30v., 48v., 90, has been retouched also.) He says too that the shield and swan are painted over a parchment roughened by erasure. If he is correct, we still cannot be certain that the arms replace those of an earlier donor. The Berry arms and device might simply have been altered. Delaissé's argument for an earlier donor rests upon the physiognomic dissimilarity between this portrait and the much later one (*circa* 1405) in the same manuscript (Fig. 34), but he does not take into account changing artistic styles and the changing appearance of the Duke.

Just before completing this book I had an opportunity to re-examine the folio in the light of Delaissé's conclusion. I have no competence in matters of parchment and erasure and I therefore record the following observations with some diffidence. The rough patch of parchment to which Delaissé referred is not limited to the area of the swan and the shield but extends diagonally down to the edge of the folio. Just what kind of form would have been painted to the edge and occasioned an erasure of this kind is hard to say. Examining the rest of the codex under seven-power magnification I found several identical troughs where there were certainly never any paintings and thus presumably no erasures. These troughs are all soft spots in the parchment, uneven in surface, creased a little, and thin. They occur at similar places in the outer margin on folios 48 (and verso), 90, and 100 verso. The flaw is so considerable on folio 90 that it has a small hole. Similar troughs occur on folios 106 and 113.

A portrait at this place was planned from the very beginning; the vines provide a space for it. The design of the figure and the swan is clearly in the style of the Parement Master. This is proved – if proof be needed – by comparison with the portrait of Charles V in the *Parement* (Fig. 1). The figure of the King is better preserved and grander, but the hands, for instance, are remarkably similar, and the prie-dieu nearly identical in the two paintings. Only the workshop of the Parement Master could have produced the design of the swan, also endowing this common Berry symbol with a most uncommon animation. The wings flap and curl, and the neck of the swan is tautly bent so that the beak is turned back toward the wound in its breast. Its movement recalls that of the pelican, and indeed the pelican atop the cross in the *Parement* is similar in action and in its linear design (Fig. 1).

One of the Duke's painters thought this portrait represented his patron. The Pseudo-Jacquemart used it as a model for his portrait of Jean de Berry on folio 8 of the *Grandes Heures* (Fig. 484), though he quite properly changed the hair from brown to white. If, then, as seems certain, the portrait in the *Heures de Milan* represents Berry, its place in the border would be another indication of its early date. In the Duke's later manuscripts he normally appears within a miniature, or at least in an initial. For both these positions there are earlier precedents, notably in Pucelle's *Heures de Jeanne d'Évreux* (fols. 16, 102v.), though earlier the donor is less intimately connected with the sacred figures in the same field. The earlier convention of a praying donor in the margins, exemplified by Jeanne de Navarre poised on a vine of the folio of the *Coronation of the Virgin* in her *Horae* (London, Thompson Collection, *Hours of Joan II*, pl. XIX), was not maintained in manuscripts illuminated for Jean de Berry. Jean de Berry seems to have shown a special devotion to the Trinity. One of the most precious objects in his Sainte-Chapelle was a great gold object, a 'grant tableau d'or, de haulte taille', in which the Trinity appeared at the top (Guiffrey, *Inventaires*, II, p. 309, no. 143). The Trinity was in the center of a silver gilt relief (*ibid.*, I, p. 24, no. 40), and the Hours of the Trinity were normally included in the Duke's Books of Hours.

For further discussion of the portrait in the *Très Belles Heures de Notre-Dame* see the entry in the catalogue for this manuscript.

25. Leaf from the *Très Belles Heures de Notre-Dame*. Louvre, Cabinet des Dessins, RF 2024 (Fig. 37). A prince, probably Jean de Berry, kneeling in prayer

before Christ, the Virgin, and St. John the Evangelist who appear within a mandorla (Fig. 492). The Virgin and St. John intercede for the prince, turning and pointing vigorously. Toward 1385? The text is the beginning of the prayer to the Virgin, O Intemerata, in which the Evangelist is mentioned, and the two figures appear again, enthroned side by side, in the main miniature above (the face and eyes of the Virgin retouched). It is notable that the iconography of the Evangelist varies in the two representations.

The illuminator who painted the kneeling prince is more conservative than the author of the portrait alongside the *Trinity* (Figs. 49, 491), but the style is related, and he was subject to the same general supervision. The prince again wears a mantle with a wide ermine collar, but it is brought somewhat higher on the neck and it lacks the dark marks of the tails of the animal that show in the *Trinity* portrait. The crown furthermore, is a straight band. The prince kneels nearest St. John the Evangelist. Jean de Berry's saint was the Baptist, and indeed this figure has been frequently identified as the great Precursor by those who believed the prince must be Jean de Berry (Durrieu, *Très Belles Heures de Notre-Dame*, 1922, p. 111, and apparently Hulin, *Heures de Milan*, 1911, p. 6). Unfortunately the facts are, as so often, complex as well as irreducible, and this saint cannot be the Baptist. The fact that the prince in the *bas-de-page* is beardless is not conclusive evidence against his identification with the Duke of Berry. At this time, in the 'eighties, fidelity in such details may not have been sought or required, especially in so small a portrait. The *bas-de-page* may, on the other hand, have been painted as much as a year or two later than the *Trinity* portrait, despite the more youthful appearance of the prince. Between 1378 and 1389, exactly when we do not know, Jean de Berry shaved off his moustache and beard, and the little portrait in the *bas-de-page* may have been executed after that event. The identity is evidently not certain, but the arguments for the definite exclusion of Jean de Berry (advanced most recently by Delaissé, 1963, p. 145, n. 43) do not seem adequate.

The *Petites Heures*

In the *Petites Heures* of Jean de Berry (Bibl. nat., lat. 18014) there are no less than twenty-two representations of a prince. There is general agreement that some, identified in the following list, represent the Duke of Berry. The outlines of some of the heads, all but one by Pseudo-Jacquemart, have been more or less altered – 106, 115v., 119, 122, 172, 173v., 196v., 198. The other representations vary considerably with regard to costume, the apparent age of the sitter, and the presence or absence of moustache and beard. The problem of identification is complicated by the fact that while the Duke wore a beard from about 1370 on, in 1389 he was clean-shaven, and he may have removed his beard while the manuscript was being illuminated. In some of the representations the Duke appears more aged than one would expect if, as we believe, the illumination was carried out in the 'eighties. On the other hand the concept of likeness to the sitter had certainly not yet become what it was in the early fifteenth century, and we can in fact observe a great difference in this regard between the more advanced and more conservative painters in the ms. In the chapter on the *Petites Heures*, p. 157, the portraits have been considered as products of the five artists who painted them and in relation to other aspects of the ms. It is perhaps worth adding that no more plausible candidate for these representations has ever been brought forward. Because of a later inscription on a fly-leaf of the ms. some scholars believed that the codex belonged in 1390 to Louis d'Anjou, and that it was originally made for him, but apart from the general flimsiness of this hypothesis (see the chapter on this ms.), it offers no advantage in the identification of the portraits. The difficulty that Jean de Berry, forty-five years old in 1385, would not have looked so old as the man in many of the portraits in the ms. is not alleviated by introducing Louis I d'Anjou, who was born only one year earlier. He died, furthermore, in 1384. Louis II, on the other hand, became the reigning duke only then, and in 1385 was exactly eight years old. Charles V, who might otherwise seem to be a candidate for the role of original patron, was clean-shaven. Almost all the miniatures that might conceivably refer to him show bearded portraits.

26. Portrait in the initial on fol. 22, at the beginning of the Hours of the Virgin in the *Petites Heures* (Fig. 94). The prince, here certainly Jean de Berry, shows even in this minute portrayal his characteristic round head, and he wears the familiar mantle with ermine collar. He is clean-shaven. On his head there is a very narrow gold crown – a simple band. He kneels at a prie-dieu, praying to a golden statue of the Madonna and Child standing on an altar close by. An attendant bearing a mace watches, partly concealed by a curtain or canopy. This portrait, as well as the figures in the architec-

tural frame around the page and the setting of the Annunciation in the main miniature, are by the most advanced painter in the ms. There is every reason to believe that the painting of this portrait was contemporary with the illumination of the ms. The purple of the background behind the tiny statue, for instance, is identical with the purple used outside the initial. The black line around the inside of the initial passes *over* parts of the portrait group.

27. *Petites Heures*, fol. 97v. (Fig. 114). Jean de Berry kneeling at a prie-dieu before the standing Virgin who holds the Christ Child on her right arm and a white flower in two fingers of her left hand. The miniature appears at the beginning of a Latin prayer to Christ and the Virgin. By the same advanced painter as the portrait on fol. 22 (Fig. 94).
Fleurs-de-lys are scattered over the drapery on the prie-dieu. The prince has the round head of Jean de Berry, and he is accompanied by two tiny white dogs of different species. Many later representations of the Duke show one or two small, white dogs. His affection for them is proverbial, but he was by no means the only nobleman of his time who liked them and wished them included in 'portraits' (see, for example, Queen Isabeau de Bavière in Brit. Mus., Harley 4431, fol. 3). The white collar of the mantle on fol. 97v. is much smaller than the one frequently worn by the Duke. The figure is clean-shaven.

28. *Petites Heures*, fol. 100v. (Fig. 115). A prince reading a ms., which is laid on a support that is lower than a prie-dieu and looks more like a couch. The prince seems curiously relaxed in the presence of *Deus Pater* (cross-nimbed), to whom the prayer is addressed. Perhaps the prince was held low in the pictorial field to make room for the large symbol of the universe held by God. Angels (or cherubs) are in the outer red circle, human beings in the inner white one.
There is less evidence to identify this prince with Jean de Berry than in the preceding instances. The face is clean-shaven. The style is related to that of the two preceding portraits, but the execution is by the Trinity Master.

29. *Petites Heures*, fol. 103v. (Fig. 116). Berry, clean shaven, in a blue tunic at a prie-dieu before the standing Virgin, who holds the Child. The composition resembles that of fol. 97v. (Fig. 114), and was probably influenced by it, but the illuminator of this second version is less advanced and less competent. The prince is clean-shaven and his hair, trimmed rather short, hangs straight down on his head. Altogether, the resemblance to the portraits of Berry is decisive. By the Trinity Master; the Madonna by Pseudo-Jacquemart.
The prince and the Madonna each are allotted an architectural compartment, which the painter has not bothered to unify in any structural way. The rear walls are covered with a rich drapery. The three windows behind the Virgin's head might conceivably be a reference to her in the prayer as 'nobile Trinitatis trichinium'.

30. *Petites Heures*, fol. 106 (Fig. 117). A prince, probably Jean de Berry, kneels at a prie-dieu in prayer before an altar on which reposes a figure of the Lord, not a golden statue as on fol. 22 (Fig. 94). A larger outline is visible around the head.
The prince wears a blue-gray mantle lined in ermine and with a wide ermine collar. His hair is gray while his moustache and goatee are white. This is the first of a series of similar representations in this section of the ms., which contains miscellaneous prayers to God, Christ, and the Virgin. The donor or prince is always bearded and mustachioed. It is notable that all these portraits are in the same style, that of the Pseudo-Jacquemart, different from the preceding portraits that represent a clean-shaven prince. Possibly this second series of portraits was painted some months earlier, when the Duke actually wore moustache and beard. Or the painter, not very observant in any respect, may simply have failed to revise an established convention in the light of new facts.

31. *Petites Heures*, fol. 106v. In this miniature a man with white moustache and beard very similar to the prince on the preceding folio (Fig. 117) kneels in prayer before an altar that bears a retable representing the Crucifixion. Here, however, the mantle is blue and lacks an ermine collar, while the tunic is orange. By the Pseudo-Jacquemart.

32. *Petites Heures*, fol. 115v. (Fig. 118). A similar figure, wearing a blue-gray mantle, kneels before Christ who holds a white globe. The man again has a white beard. A larger outline around the head is visible. By the Pseudo-Jacquemart.

33. *Petites Heures*, fol. 117v. (Fig. 119). A similar prince, with white moustache and beard, is presented to

Christ by a Dominican who is very probably St. Thomas Aquinas. The prince wears a blue mantle with gold ornament. The resemblance of the head to fol. 106 (Fig. 117) is especially close. By the Pseudo-Jacquemart.

34. *Petites Heures*, fol. 119 (Fig. 120). A similar prince prays to the Lord, but here he wears a gold crown (a band) and a collar with a pendant jewel. Here again traces of a different profile are visible. By the Pseudo-Jacquemart.

35. *Petites Heures*, fol. 119v. A similar kneeling prince praying to the Lord. His mantle is blue. By the Pseudo-Jacquemart.

36. *Petites Heures*, fol. 120 (Fig. 121). The prayer *O Intemerata* is illustrated, as often, with figures of the Virgin and St. John. Unusual, however, are the huge palm carried by the youthful saint and the complete nudity of the Child.[83] Unusual, too, is the symmetrical design chosen by the illuminator with the Virgin and St. John at the margins and the prince in the center, frontal. Normally the privacy of prayer suggests a figure turned away from the beholder, in one direction or another. By the Pseudo-Jacquemart. The prince, crowned, wears the broad ermine collar favored in these years by Jean de Berry, and visible in fol. 106 (Fig. 117) of this ms. as well as in the *Brussels Hours*.

37. *Petites Heures*, fol. 121v. (Fig. 122). A prince kneels in prayer before a prie-dieu. A small golden crown is on his head. His moustache and beard are white. By the Pseudo-Jacquemart.

38. *Petites Heures*, fol. 122 (Fig. 123). The prince, in prayer before the standing Madonna, appears much as in fol. 120 (Fig. 121). There are small differences in the features and in the pattern on the crown, which is again a narrow gold band. Traces of a somewhat different profile are visible. In the style of the Pseudo-Jacquemart.

39. *Petites Heures*, fol. 139 (Fig. 128). The donor, wearing an orange mantle, kneels during the elevation of the host. He wears no crown, but a gray double goatee. His face is round, very much like that of Jean de Berry. By the Pseudo-Jacquemart.

40. *Petites Heures*, fol. 144v. The prince, beardless, kneels in prayer below the Coronation of the Virgin. By the Pseudo-Jacquemart.

41. *Petites Heures*, fol. 145v. (Fig. 137). A prince in prayer before Christ.
Delaissé, who believes that this miniature is on a folio that was added at a later date for a second owner (Jean de Berry), described the portrait of the prince as unfinished (1963, p. 131). But it is badly damaged, and the losses extend to parts of the figure and also to the face of Christ. There are furthermore stains above and below the miniature, probably produced by a solvent. By the Pseudo-Jacquemart (?).

42. *Petites Heures*, fol. 167v. (Fig. 146). An old man, in an exceptionally plain mantle, and without a crown, kneels in prayer. He wears a white moustache and beard. White hair characterizes the following portraits through fol. 176v. By the Pseudo-Jacquemart.

43. *Petites Heures*, fol. 169v. The prince, who resembles closely the figure on fols. 120 and 122 (Figs. 121, 123), kneels between a choir and a celebrant at an altar. By the Pseudo-Jacquemart.

44. *Petites Heures*, fol. 170v. The prince, standing, gestures to two clerics engaged in a service. One of them, facing inward toward his lectern, is seen from the rear. The prince wears a crown, and his moustache and beard are white. By the Pseudo-Jacquemart.

45. *Petites Heures*, fol. 171. The prince, who receives the sacrament of wine, resembles, except for his patterned robe, the figure on fol. 169v. In the style of the Pseudo-Jacquemart.

46. *Petites Heures*, fol. 172 (Fig. 147). A man, with white moustache and double goatee, kneels during the elevation of the host. His head is not narrow, as in the immediately preceding portraits, but round and his face is broad, as on fol. 139 (Fig. 128). He might be described as a translation into the style of the Pseudo-Jacquemart of the portrait on fol. 97v. (Fig. 114). It is notable, too, that the three white stripes on the sleeve in fol. 97v. appear in fol. 172. Traces of a higher outline are visible above the head. By the Pseudo-Jacquemart.

47. *Petites Heures*, fol. 173v. (Fig. 148). The prince, of the narrow-headed type, receives the wafer during mass. He wears a crown, an ornamented robe, and his

moustache and beard are white. By the Pseudo-Jacquemart.

48. *Petites Heures*, fol. 174v. (Fig. 149). Two youths (possibly children of Jean de Berry) accompanied by a woman (the Duchess? though without a crown) receive the sacrament. The second youth (a girl?) wears a mantle with three horizontal stripes quite similar to that of the youth instructed by a Dominican friar on fol. 9v. (Fig. 87). By the Pseudo-Jacquemart.

49. *Petites Heures*, fol. 176. A prince, similar in all respects except the pattern on his blue robe to the figure on fol. 171, kneels during mass. In the style of the Pseudo-Jacquemart.

50. *Petites Heures*, fol. 176v. (Fig. 150). A prince, quite like the one on fols. 176 and 171, prays before an altar. He has a goatee and he wears a red mantle. On the altar there is a panel representing the Crucifixion, and at its side a crucifix. In the style of the Pseudo-Jacquemart.

51. *Petites Heures*, fol. 196v. (Fig. 159). A prince kneels before a prie-dieu on Golgotha before Christ on the cross. He wears the mantle with broad ermine collar visible on fol. 120 and in other miniatures (Figs. 94, 121), but here, unlike the representations in the preceding section of the ms., he is clean-shaven. By the Pseudo-Jacquemart.

52. *Petites Heures*, fol. 198 (Fig. 161). A layman at a prie-dieu kneels before the Trinity. The man is clean-shaven, as in the preceding miniature, but appears younger. By the Pseudo-Jacquemart.

53. *Petites Heures*, fol. 198v. (Fig. 162). Berry, in a light green mantle, kneels before the Madonna enthroned. The style of this painting, very different from that of the preceding miniatures, resembles that of the initial and the saints on fol. 22 (Fig. 94). It is significant that the round head of the suppliant and his features, including lack of moustache and beard, are very similar to the prince in the initial on fol. 22. By the Trinity Master.

54. *Petites Heures*, fol. 199v. (Fig. 163). An angel leads the prince to a sanctuary, illustrating *De manu angeli*. The prince wears an ermine collar, and is clean-shaven, as on fols. 22 and 97v. (Figs. 94, 114). It is notable that this miniature is not in the style of the Pseudo-Jacquemart but by the Fifth Master.

55. Statue of Jean de Berry on the *cheminée* of the great hall of the palace at Poitiers. The original head was lost during the Revolution; it has been replaced by a copy. The Duke holds a sword, as in the seal of 1397 (cat. no. 5). He is accompanied by the Duchess (Jeanne de Boulogne; not as Champeaux and Gauchery, *Travaux*, 1894, p. 19, say, Jeanne d'Armagnac), and by Charles VI and the Queen. There are casts of these three figures in the Trocadéro, Paris, and all existing photographs have been made from them, not from the statues themselves (Figs. 436, 437). The Duke has been photographed from below in Marburg no. 161673.

56. Evangeliary, Bourges, Bibl. municipale, ms. 48, fol. 181 (Fig. 493). Jean de Berry kneels at a prie-dieu (covered with a drapery bearing *fleurs-de-lys*) before his patron, St. Andrew. The Baptist is of course the Duke's namesake, but the latter was born on November 30, St. Andrew's day. The chariot that carried the Duke's body after his death from Paris to Bourges bore the red cross of St. Andrew.[84] In the miniature both the Duke, who for some reason is on the saint's left rather than right, and Andrew are honored by a setting of rich textiles. Two angels hold a cloth behind the saint while a canopy, partly opened by courtiers, rises behind the Duke.

The style of this miniature is clearly that of the Pseudo-Jacquemart, but at a later period of his career than the miniatures in the *Petites Heures* (see p. 93). This later date is proved also by the portrait of the Duke which, though still preserving the narrow head characteristic of this master, is more naturalistic. Furthermore the Duke wears the *houppelande* with high collar that appears in the portraits from about 1406 on, beginning with the Pontifical of Loypeau (Fig. 483), the *Grandes Heures* (Bedford Master, Fig. 485), and *Dialogues de Pierre Salmon* (Fig. 487). In the miniature in Bourges as in these portraits he wears a golden necklace or collar, from which a jewel hangs. Here the stone is pear-shaped, and set with several pearls. The portrait might be placed about 1405 but other aspects of the manuscript, which are related to the *Grandes Heures*, suggest the possibility of about 1410.

57. Jean de Berry, presented by the Baptist, kneels in prayer between an angel and St. Andrew (Fig. 494). Extreme left panel of the predella of a large altarpiece in bone by the workshop of the Embriachi in Venice. The altarpiece, which shows scenes of the life of

Christ, the Baptist, and St. John the Evangelist, was commissioned by the Duke for the Abbey of Poissy and is now in the Louvre. In a corresponding panel at the right the Duchess appears between an angel, St. John Evangelist, and St. Catherine. In 1393 Philippe le Hardi bought two similar altarpieces from the same workshop for Champmol; they are now in the Musée de Cluny, Paris.[85]

The Duke looks like a man of thirty, probably because the Venetian sculptors did not have a detailed model. He is clean-shaven. It is a commentary on the contemporary artistic scene that the North Italian angel looks more like a French High Gothic figure than any figure produced by one of the leading French pictorial ateliers of the time.

58. Jean de Berry in prayer, illustration of a prayer to the Virgin on the day of her Assumption, New York, The Cloisters, *Belles Heures*, fol. 91 (Fig. 495). The green cloth over the prie-dieu bears *fleurs-de-lys*. The representation of the mace-bearer is novel; only his right arm and a foot appear from behind the red curtain. Though both the floor and the 'ceiling' of the canopy are subdivided geometrically, no doubt to serve as indices of the space, the orthogonals of each vanish in a different region. The spatial effect is confused also by the fact that the nearer curtain, though attached above to a pole that seems to be in or close to the picture plane, hangs down into the rear of the space below. The two visible parts of the mace-bearer seem to exist at different depths.

The Duke wears the mantle with large ermine collar that he favored in the 'eighties and 'nineties, but here it rises higher on his neck, in accordance with the new fashion that was established from about 1405–1406 (Figs. 487, 493, 499). The high collar is used in these paintings, however, on the *houppelande* whereas in the *Belles Heures* it constitutes a new version of the old ermine collar.

The Duke is clean-shaven. He wears an exceptional chaplet, composed of golden disks. An area of discoloration around his head indicates that originally he wore an object of a different kind.[86] Though stout, he appears remarkably youthful, as a consequence no doubt of the illuminator's wish to idealize his features.[87] The Duchess, represented on folio 91 verso in prayer before the Trinity (Fig. 518), is remarkably slender and girlish, but during the first decade of the century she was in fact only in her twenties.

59. Jean de Berry and his entourage arriving at a

château, New York, The Cloisters, *Belles Heures*, fol. 223v. (Fig. 496). This is one of three illustrations of the Itinerary, or prayer for a safe journey, painted by the Limbourgs. The other two prayers and their illustrations (our nos. 60, 61) were added to mss. illuminated earlier by other painters. The development of the composition around a specific person is an innovation comparable to that in *January* (Fig. 489) and in the *Gates of Paradise* (Fig. 231). The Duke wears a high black hat bearing a gold pin, a red coat, and a golden necklace with a round gold pendant. Again he appears comparatively young, but here unlike the portrait on fol. 91 of this ms. (Fig. 495), he almost certainly has a moustache and beard. It is true that all the faces in the miniature are shaded in brown but the number and darkness of the strokes on the upper lip and jowls of the Duke are exceptional. The blue and gold banners on the château may refer to Burgundy.

60. Illustration of the Itinerary, a lost miniature of the *Très Belles Heures de Notre-Dame*, preserved in a lithograph of Bastard d'Estang (Fig. 497).[88] The Duke of Berry and his companions, including a mace-bearer who displays a purse which is held open conspicuously, are welcomed at the gate of a city or a monastery by chanting clerics. The clerics march onto a bridge over a stream or a moat.

The Duke has a moustache and a pointed beard, of the kind visible in the *Grandes Heures* (Fig. 484), the Pontifical of Loypeau (Fig. 483), and the *Livre des bonnes mœurs* (Fig. 486), all from around 1406–1410. He wears the familiar fur hat of the *Petites Heures* and other representations (Fig. 498), but his travel garb is still more resplendent. The great fur-lined travel coat with high fur collar is richly ornamented, bells or baubles hang from his girdle, and over his shoulder is slung a spectacular band displaying large stones and a series of pendant tear-shaped objects, lapidary or metallic. His thin necklace supports a series of small round forms and the usual large stone set between six pearls.

How reliable are lithographs by Bastard? Those that can be controlled, such as the plates of the *Grandes Heures*, are exact copies of the miniatures and the initials. Sometimes a border belongs to another folio, a confusion produced by a fire in the workshop.

61. The Duke setting out on a journey, *Petites Heures*, Bibl. nat., lat. 18014, fol. 288v. (Fig. 498). This

prayer and its miniature were added to the ms. many years after it had originally been illuminated. The border of the painting does not conform with the convention earlier established for this ms. The Duke and his retinue emerge from a city gate. In the background, among other buildings, is a church with a high spire, to the nave of which are joined, without great architectural understanding, aisles and an apse or subsidiary chapel. The roof of the nave is blue, of the aisle, choir(?) and chapel red.

The Duke is gorgeously dressed, in scarlet gaiters, black coat ornamented in gold, a high fur collar and a gold belt. His necklace of pearls and rubies is exceptionally rich, and it bears a large pendant ruby surrounded by six pearls. His hat, with its three or four pieces of brown fur, is similar to the one he wears in other portraits of his later years (Figs. 487, 489, 490, 497, 499).

The Duke appears much older and heavier than in the corresponding miniature in the *Belles Heures* (Fig. 496). His hair is white. He is clean-shaven, but his chin is covered with a white stubble.

62. Jean de Berry in prayer before St. Andrew, Lectionary, Bourges, Bibl. municipale, ms. 35, fol. 17v. (Fig. 499). The canopy bears the arms of the Duke. Contrary to a widely held opinion this ms. (including its other parts, mss. 33, 34, 36) cannot be definitely identified with any item known to have been given to the Sainte-Chapelle by 1405 (see the discussion in a subsequent volume). The subject of this scene is similar to that in Bourges, ms. 48 (our no. 56), but here the only figures are the saint and the Duke. This miniature is by the Boucicaut workshop.

Comparison with Bourges, Bibl. municipale, ms. 48 (no. 56 – Fig. 493) is instructive. The space is much more unified, the perspective is superior, the figures placed diagonal to the picture plane rather than frontal or in profile. There is now an interval between them and the frame. Instead of standing erect with a cross in his hands St. Andrew looks down meditatively towards the Duke while he steadies with one hand the large cross that is set on the floor. The saint's cross had earlier been set on the floor, as in the *Légende dorée*, Brit. Mus., Royal 19 B XVII, fol. 9v. (Fig. 610), but in the Bourges miniature its capacity to measure space has been much more fully exploited. Bourges ms. 35 is in all these respects much more advanced than Bourges 48, but not necessarily later therefore in actual time, because the painter of

Bourges 48 – the Pseudo-Jacquemart – is very conservative.

The Duke looks older in this miniature; his face, much fuller, sags. It is perhaps a consequence of age that he wears indoors the big fur hat in which he appears, indoors as well as out, so regularly from about 1407–1408 on. Because, furthermore, the Duke is clean-shaven, this miniature was very probably painted about 1410, and this date conforms with the evidence of style.

63. Jean de Berry receiving from Laurent de Premierfait his text of Boccaccio, *Cas des nobles hommes et femmes*. Paris, Bibl. nat., fr. 131, fol. 1 (Fig. 500). This French version of Boccaccio's *De Casibus virorum illustrium* was finished in April 1409, but this ms. contains no evidence of the Duke's ownership though his portrait as patron of the translation appears in the frontispiece. The miniature is from the atelier of the Master of the Cité des Dames.

The Duke is dressed very much as in the *Dialogues de Pierre Salmon* (Fig. 487). He does not wear a chain, and the pale pink swans on the *houppelande* appear within lozenges. He is again clean-shaven.

64. Jean de Berry receiving the *Cas des nobles hommes et femmes* from the translator, Laurent de Premierfait; Bibl. nat., fr. 226, fol. 1. (Fig. 503). The text was finished in 1409, but this miniature was painted later by an exceedingly lively Parisian illuminator. The arms of Berry are on the throne and the canopy. The Duke, dressed as in other late portraits and again wearing his fur hat indoors, is accompanied by a little brown dog. A large ruby hangs from his gold collar.

65. Altar of Notre-Dame-la-Blanche, Ste-Chapelle, Bourges. Statue of Jean de Berry kneeling, together with the Duchess, before the Madonna. The statues, damaged during the Revolution, were reconstructed for the Cathedral by Dumartel in 1840, with frightening results. The original head of the Duke, battered but still preserving traces of color, is now in the Museum at Bourges (Fig. 501). The sculpture is commonly ascribed to Jean de Cambrai. The Duke, clean-shaven, wears a mantle with a high collar.

The statues of the Duke and Duchess were drawn by Hans Holbein the Younger (Figs. 510, 511). These superb drawings, usually dated about 1525, are in the Öffentliche Kunstsammlung, Basel.[89]

The kneeling statues of the Duke and Duchess now in the crypt of the Cathedral of Bourges, related in type to the donors before Notre-Dame-la-Blanche, were made long after the Duke's death, probably in the early 16th century. See above, p. 75.

66. *Gisant* of the tomb of Jean de Berry for the Ste-Chapelle, Bourges (Fig. 502). It was moved to the Cathedral in 1756 by the Archbishop of Bourges, and is now in the crypt. The nose was broken during the Revolution, and the statue has been defaced by the imbecilic scrawls of visitors. The round face and protruding lower lip are very similar to the portraits in the *Dialogues* (Fig. 487) and the *Très Riches Heures* (Fig. 489). The Duke wears a crown in the form of a band set with stones.

It is commonly said that this *gisant*, some *pleurants* and a relief of the sleeping apostles were carved by Jean de Cambrai before the death of the Duke and his burial in the Ste-Chapelle in June, 1416 (see, for instance, Aubert, *Sculpture française*, 1946, p. 353). The only known fact, however, is disclosed by a record of 1450, which informs us that King Charles VII, who had undertaken the completion of the tomb, ordered a payment to the heirs of Jean de Cambrai (who had died in 1438) for the 'imaige d'albastre de ladite sepulture . . .' (Champeaux and Gauchery, *Travaux*, 1894, p. 35). Though the image actually is fashioned of marble, it is no doubt the one to which the document refers. Jean de Cambrai must, then, be regarded as its author, and it is plausible, but not certain, that he produced it before the death of the Duke and the subsequent cessation of his enterprises. See the recent paper by Pradel, 1957, pp. 141 ff.

POSSIBLE REPRESENTATIONS

In addition to the representations already discussed, which certainly or probably portray Jean de Berry, there are a few figures that may at least allude to him. The physiognomic or other evidence is much less decisive, however, than in the preceding instances.

1. Illustration of Book XVI, *Livre de la propriété des choses*, on the properties of precious stones, colors, and metals. Bibl. nat., fr. 9141, fol. 235v. (Fig. 504). By the Boucicaut Master and his workshop.

   There are no identifying arms, but the prince looks rather like Jean de Berry and he is dressed in similar fashion (though the fur cuffs would be exceptional).[90] None of the several other princely figures in this ms. (fols. 25, 43, 138v., 207) resembles Jean de Berry so much as this one. That a prince engaged in the inspection of rings and stones should be identified with the greatest collector of such things on earth is not surprising, even though such an allusion in illustrations of this text is novel.

2. Presentation miniature, *Trésor des histoires*, Paris, Bibl. de l'Arsenal, ms. 5077, fol. 1. Of the three princes present, the one fingering a pendant jewel might well represent Jean de Berry. He wears a dark green mantle, with brown fur at the neck and wrists. There is a ruby at the center of the jewel on his breast and on his hat. The man at the right, with the ruby pinned to his hat, might be Jean sans Peur. The recipient of the book would then be Charles V or possibly Charles VI.

PROBLEMATIC AND REJECTED REPRESENTATIONS

1. Geneva, Bibl. publique et universitaire, ms. fr. 77, fol. 46v. The features of Quintus Fabius in this miniature have been identified as those of Jean de Berry by Gagnebin, 1959, p. 203. The ms. belonged to the Duke, but the dress of the figure is not his, and the portrait not sufficiently like him.

2. London, Brit. Mus., Royal 20 C VIII, fol. 2. The prince who receives the book from the author may well be Jean de Berry. The miniature is so poor that it does not merit discussion. The ms. belonged to the Duke.

3. Paris, Bibl. nat., nouv. acq. lat. 3093, p. 173 (Fig. 19).

The foremost figure among the Faithful was tentatively identified as the Duke by Delisle (*Gaz. B.-A.*, 1884, pp. 291 f.), and the proposal was accepted by Durrieu (*Très Belles Heures de Notre-Dame*, 1922, p. 11) and Kreuter-Eggemann (*Daliwe*, Munich, 1964, I, p. 63). There is no decisive evidence. A beard is possible at this date (*ca.* 1405–1407) but hardly such a large one.

4. Paris, Louvre, *Entombment* (Fig. 695). In Paris, Musée du Louvre (Sterling and Adhémar), 1965, p. 4, Charles Sterling has suggested that the man at the left may be the Duke. The facial resemblance is notable, but the cap and the dress would be unique.

V

The Arms and Emblems of Jean de Berry

THE Duke of Berry, we have seen, kept bears as pets throughout his life, and he arranged that even in death he would not be separated from one of these beloved creatures. A bear instead of the usual lion lies curled at his feet in the *gisant* carved for his tomb by Jean de Cambrai. The normal connotation of the bear in the Middle Ages is not positive, but Pierre Bersuire did at least characterize it as 'bestia tenacis naturae'.[1] The Duke had adopted this animal as an emblem by 1365,[2] and in the Great Seal of 1370 the bear was accompanied by a swan (Fig. 474). Thereafter these two creatures (the swan usually wounded) flanked the Duke's shield commonly in his seals but in the religious manuscripts they appeared frequently only from the 'eighties on. The introduction of the emblems in the manuscripts parallels that of the portraits, which similarly did not appear before this period. An early example of an emblem in a manuscript is the swan holding the shield alongside the portrait of the Duke in the *Très Belles Heures de Notre-Dame* (Fig. 49), and then both creatures appear in the borders of the initial diptych of the *Brussels Hours* (Figs. 179, 180).

In the borders of the successive Books of Hours, the *Brussels Hours* and the *Grandes Heures*, the bears become increasingly active, though still within small subsidiary spaces (Figs. 181, 223). Finally, in one of the latest miniatures painted for the Duke, both creatures escaped, so to speak, from the borders and invaded the main field. In the *Temptation of Christ* in the *Très Riches Heures*, a swan floats on the water near the château of Mehun-sur-Yèvre and a bear stands on the bank (Fig. 424). The emblems have been naturalized, and this change in their mode of representation conforms with the contemporary change in religious symbols. For though the depiction of the swan and the bear in the space around the Duke's castle may be understood simply as a portrayal of an actual event, from the viewpoint of the representative tradition it is a rather early instance of that mode of conveying 'spiritualia sub metaphoris corporalium' that characterizes late medieval art, and especially Netherlandish painting, as Panofsky has demonstrated.[3]

The emblems and favorite creatures of the Duke were celebrated in works of art of every medium,[4] and it is not surprising that speculation about the reasons for his interest in them began not long after his death. In his *Livre du cuer d'amour espris* King René d'Anjou described a representation of the shield and emblems of Jean de Berry, below which was written:

> Jehan, duc de Berry suis, ce de verité scay-je,
> Qui en tenant prison et pour mon pere ostage,
> Le roy Jehan, qui estoit es mains des Anglois pris,
> Je fus si ardamment du feu amoureux espris
> Dune dame anglesche, servante au Dieu d'amours,
> Que vaincu me senty par ses gracieux tours.
> Pour elle prins ung mot et mis soubz mon escu
> Le cigne blanc navré; autre mot plus n'y fu.

En ces lectres me tins, dont je ne me peuz partir;
Et lors me commanda le Dieu d'amours venir
Moy rendre son subgect, avec ceulx qui y sont,
Aportant mon blason, comme les autres font.[5]

This tale was later embroidered by attributing to the English lady the name Oursine, for which the emblems chosen by Jean de Berry were a memorial rebus (*ours – cygne*). Less sentimental modern historians have observed that St. Ursin is the patron of Berry,[6] and also that the combination of bear and swan occurs much earlier, so that an old symbolism may be involved.[7] The swan figures frequently in knightly romances, and in one of them the knight of the swan encounters a maiden Beatrix – the name the Duke gave to one of his daughters.[8]

The shield of Jean de Berry, always *a bordure engrelée gule*, sometimes showed *France ancien*, that is, *fleurs-de-lys-semés* (Figs. 49, 476), and sometimes *France moderne*, with only three *fleurs-de-lys* (Figs. 481, 482 523,). Given this variation, some historians of art have believed it possible to fix chronological limits for the use of the two forms and thus to establish criteria for the dating of works of art on which they appear. Part of the evidence however – especially that provided by seals – has not been taken into account. When all the relevant documents, or at least those known to the writer, are put together the story becomes more complex, as usual, but one large trend does clearly emerge.

The use of three *fleurs-de-lys* rather than an undetermined number (normally more than three) was inaugurated on French royal shields in the late thirteenth century.[9] The three flowers in *France moderne* were said to have a religious significance; according to an obvious explanation repeated by Raoul de Praesles in the prologue to his translation of the *Cité de Dieu* (between 1364 and 1372) they referred to the Trinity. *France moderne* was quite frequently chosen by Raoul's patron, Charles V[10] and it became normal for Charles VI and his successors. For a century, however, *France ancien* was not entirely displaced.[11]

Jean de Berry was much slower than his brother Charles V to adopt *France moderne*. A glance at the chart that accompanies this discussion shows that, apart from three exceptions that will be examined, the Duke's seals and manuscripts up until the last decade of the century regularly showed *France ancien*. The evidence provided by the seals is of course limited by the fact that usually we know only the dates when impressions were attached to documents and not when the matrices were made. Some of them, furthermore, such as the Great Seal, employed as early as 1370, continued in use throughout the Duke's life (Fig. 474).[12] On the other hand the matrix of the seal of the treasurer of the Sainte-Chapelle (Fig. 482), used late in 1405, was no doubt made within a few months of this time.[13]

The one exception to the prevalence of *France ancien* among the early seals is the secret seal, the seal used for orders to pay, and kept by one of the *chambellans*.[14] Possibly the employment of three *fleurs-de-lys* on this seal was governed by a special convention (Fig. 523). Certainly the two exceptional instances in the Duke's manuscripts can easily be explained. The shields on the *chapelle ardente* in the *Très Belles Heures de Notre-Dame* seem, for technical and stylistic reasons, to have been added later (Fig. 14).[15] The shield on the altar in the *Annunciation* in the *Petites Heures* was added after the painting of the miniature (Fig. 94),[16] and it is in any event so small that the size of the field may have affected the number of *fleurs-de-lys* represented. A reduction in the number of units in very small fields is normal.

Three *fleurs-de-lys* were introduced in the main part of the Brussels Hours, finished before 1402, in the seal employed in 1397 (Fig. 477),[17] and in the *cheminée* of the palace at Poitiers, after 1389 (Figs. 520, 521).[18] From the 'nineties the Duke's painters used *France moderne* frequently,[19] but *ancien* persisted to the end of his life. Not only did he continue to use the Great Seal (Fig. 474) but the reverse of the seal of 1397 – the so-called counter-seal – showed, in contrast to the seal itself, *ancien* (Fig. 522). While the larger shields in the corners of the borders of the *Brussels Hours* and those on the *chapelle ardente* show *moderne*, the smaller pennons waved by the bears show *ancien* (Figs. 197, 198). Similarly both forms were used in the *Belles Heures* and in the latest of the great manuscripts, the *Très Riches Heures*.

From all these instances we may conclude that a shield showing *France moderne* is very unlikely to have been painted for Jean de Berry before about 1395. The chronological implications of *ancien* are far less definite. A Berry manuscript on the other hand without a coat of arms is clearly early; of all the important manuscripts of the Duke only the *Psalter* lacks arms, emblems, and portrait.

TABLE OF THE ARMS OF JEAN DE BERRY

The seals are listed at the date of their earliest known use; later instances are given in parentheses.*

	Fleurs-de-lys semés (France ancien) (as many as eight or nine, and early as few as one in small shields)	Three fleurs-de-lys (France moderne)
1358	Seal (Clairambault no. 7253)	
1359	Seal (Douët d'Arcq no. 1081)	
1365	Scel secret (Gandilhon no. 10; Douët d'Arcq no. 423)	
1370	(1410, 1415) Great Seal (Fig. 474; Portrait Cat. no. 1)	
1372		Scel secret (Fig. 523; Gandilhon no. 11)
Early 80's	Très Belles Heures de Notre-Dame, fol. 87 – Hulin de Loo erroneously gives 87v. (Fig. 49)	Très Belles Heures de Notre-Dame, Obsequies (Fig. 14; arms repainted at later date)
1383	Seal (Portrait Cat. no. 4)	
1384	Seal (Gandilhon no. 12; also p. LV n. 17)	
1386	Seal (Gandilhon no. 7)	
Mid 80's	Petites Heures (except fol. 22)	Petites Heures, fol. 22 (Fig. 94)
Towards 1390	Brussels Hours, initial diptych (Fig. 179; Portrait Cat. no. 7) Oxford, Bodl., Rawl. C.538, fol. 3v. (Fig. 654)	
1389	Marriage contract of Duke (Fig. 476; Portrait Cat. no. 5)	
After 1389		Poitiers, Palais, Cheminée (Fig. 520)
1389-94	Rome, Vat., lat. 50-51 (Figs. 177, 178)	
1397	Counter-seal of Special Seal (Fig. 522; Gandilhon no. 5 bis)	Special Seal (Fig. 477; Portrait Cat. no. 6)
Towards 1400	Brussels Hours, pennons of bears	Brussels Hours, quatrefoils in corners of borders and p. 202 (Fig. 198)
1405		Charter of Ste-Chapelle (Fig. 481; Portrait Cat. no. 10) Seal of the Ste-Chapelle (Fig. 482; Portrait Cat. no. 11)
Before 1407	Bib. nat., lat. 8886, fol. 1 (Portrait Cat. no. 12)	
Ca. 1407	Bourges, Bibl. mun., ms. 48, fol. 1 (Fig. 253)	
1408		Scel secret (Gandilhon no. 13)
1409	Grandes Heures, borders	Grandes Heures, Service for Dead (Fig. 232)
Ca. 1410	Lectionary, Bourges, Bibl. mun., ms. 33, fol. 1 Bibl. mun., ms. 34, fol. 1 Bibl. mun., ms. 35, fol. 17v. (Fig. 499)	
Ca. 1409-1411	Belles Heures, fols. 30, 215	Belles Heures, fols. 2, 13, 181
Ca. 1413-1416	Très Riches Heures, fols. 1v., 60v., 116v.	Très Riches Heures, fols. 14v., 26, 150, 161v., 195

For the inventory of the Clairambault seals see Demay, Sceaux, 1885-1886.
For the seals copied for Gaignières see Bibl. nat., fr. 20368.

* The author is aware that further exploration would yield additional examples, but probably would not alter the general conclusions.

VI

The Parement Master

1 · THE *PAREMENT DE NARBONNE*

IT is significant that the first French paintings outside books we know, apart from rather ruinous or provincial mural fragments, were royal commissions. The portrait of Jean le Bon (Fig. 507) and the *Parement de Narbonne* (Figs. 1-5) are, to be sure, only a tiny surviving remnant of a great manufacture, but the leading patrons of art during the reigns of Jean le Bon and Charles V were these monarchs themselves. The royal library grew rapidly, especially under the enthusiastic administration of Charles V. During the latter years of his reign this king, exceptional for his literary interests, devoted considerable attention to the other arts as well. He had provided more favorable conditions for them by drawing France back from the brink of disaster after the defeat by the English at Poitiers. By administrative and fiscal reforms he succeeded in re-establishing order, political as well as economic. With a greatly strengthened army, often under the skilful leadership of Bertrand du Guesclin, he reconquered most of the territory that had been taken by the English, including both Brittany and Poitou. When Edward III died suddenly in 1377 the great threat from the north was eliminated, for a time at least; the new king, Richard II, was only ten years old. The first phase of the Hundred Years War ended, leaving France scarred but still largely intact.

Charles V – 'le sage roi', as Christine de Pisan spoke of him – undertook much building and rebuilding at the Louvre and at the Château de Vincennes. His Hôtel de St. Pol in Paris was renowned for its luxury and its beauty. On his order Jean de Liège carved the tombs of Charles le Bel (+ 1328) and Jeanne d'Évreux (+ 1371), now in the Louvre.[1] The same sculptor, with associates, made the statues of the royal family for the great stairway or *vis* of the Louvre that had been built in 1365 by Raymond du Temple.[2] To this time belong also the statues of the King and Queen for the portal of the Célestins in Paris, and the most impressive extant sculptures of the period, the statues of St. Louis and St. Margaret of Provence bearing the features of King Charles and his Queen, Jeanne de Bourbon, now in the Louvre (Fig. 524).[3]

These remarkable figures carry into new spheres the realism of the famous tomb statue of the King commissioned to Beauneveu in 1364 (Fig. 591). Though they are large and monumental they possess an unprecedented informality and warmth; the King and Queen are presented to their subjects as benign, homely rulers accessible to all. They are endowed with a more personal, spontaneous movement. What persists of the conventional sway of earlier sculptures has been limited to the draperies; the stir of the bodies reflects a unique, individual impulse. While the statues still retain one principal aspect they invite the beholder, as earlier figures do not, to move around to the sides for varying effects.[4] These are the most beautiful French sculptures that have survived from the period between the tomb of Beauneveu at St. Denis and the work of Sluter at the Chartreuse of Champmol.

Though we possess today only a few major sculptures from the reign of Charles V, even less of the monumental painting survives. In 1352 Charles' father had taken a painter, Girard d'Orléans, into his service; in 1355 he was described as *valet de chambre*, and the King found his work so satisfactory that he took him to England when he was exiled there in 1356.[5] The painter Jean d'Arbois was employed in the same capacity in 1373 by Philippe le Hardi, who called him from 'Lombardie'.[6] He was succeeded in 1375 by Jean de Beaumetz (Figs. 830, 831). Showered with commissions, Beaumetz established a large workshop, and by 1388 he was employing nineteen assistants.[7] Jean d'Orléans entered the service of Charles V as *valet de chambre* in 1364,[8] and Jean Bondol was similarly employed in 1368. Bondol soon received an annual wage and assurance of a pension for life.[9] In 1371 he signed the famous frontispiece of the King's Bible in The Hague as 'pictor regis' (Fig. 382). While associated closely with the King, Bondol occasionally worked for one of his brothers, in 1376 undertaking for Louis I d'Anjou the cartoons for the great Angers tapestries (Figs. 380, 381, 387). The relationship of his art to the dominant and ubiquitous '*Boqueteaux*' style of illumination current during the period of Charles V has been discussed in Chapter I. Apart from the many manuscripts illuminated in this style, which was probably created by Bondol, little of importance remains from the pictorial enterprises of the 'seventies. Perhaps at this time Louis d'Anjou commissioned or acquired the beautiful *Bible historiée* painted by a master who was trained in Naples (Figs. 410-412).[10] Alongside the Angers tapestries it represents one of the two poles – Italian and Netherlandish – between which painting in metropolitan France tended to oscillate for nearly half a century.

The capital painting of French origin during this period is the *Parement de Narbonne* (Figs. 1-5), one of those silks painted in gray of which we hear in the inventories of Charles V and his brothers. Groups of these works, including copes, orphreys, mitres, and other liturgical vestments as well as hangings, were called *chapelles*, usually 'de satin blanc, painturé de noir', intended, as the inventories occasionally state, 'pour servir en Karesme'.[11] Though they had a particular religious purpose these *chapelles* were executed in a technique that was widely used in illuminated manuscripts of the time. Grisaille paintings, of the type introduced by Pucelle in the *Heures de Jeanne d'Évreux*, were especially popular in the manuscripts of the late fourteenth century; often their blondness was thrown into relief by patches of color in the buildings or the background. This was the period, too, of the wide diffusion of light-colored stained glass, especially of the yellowish glass produced by silver stain.[12]

A very few of these exquisite paintings on cloth have come down to us. One, a mitre that was brought out from the abbey church of St. Sixt in Haute-Savoie for the exhibition *Notre-Dame de Paris* in the Sainte-Chapelle, Paris, in 1963, shows impressive representations of the *Annunciation* (Fig. 525) and the *Coronation*. The style contains so much of Jean Pucelle that the designs might even have been provided by his workshop towards 1340. A second mitre, in the Musée de Cluny, Paris, has the main field on one side filled with the *Resurrection*, on the other with the *Entombment* (Fig. 526).[13] The *Entombment* shows the Magdalen flinging her arms over her head in a gesture of grief transplanted from Italian painting into French by Jean Pucelle (*Heures de Jeanne d'Évreux*).[14] The style is not unrelated to that of the *Parement*, but the figures are slighter and on the whole it is a much more conservative work.

The *Parement* now in the Louvre has taken its name from the city in which it was found early in the nineteenth century. It represents five scenes of the Passion, followed by the *Descent into Limbo* and the *Noli Me Tangere*. At the sides of the central and largest scene, the *Crucifixion* (Fig. 1), stand the triumphant Church with Isaiah and the defeated Synagogue with King David. Below them kneel the King and Queen of France, Charles V and Jeanne de Bourbon. The King's initial is repeated in the borders, and the painting was clearly commissioned for him. It is generally agreed that since Charles, who was born in 1337, appears to be around thirty-five years old, and the Queen, born in 1338, seems about the same age, the *Parement* was very probably painted between 1370 and 1375.[15] In any event, it should be before 1378, when Jeanne de Bourbon died, or at most 1380, the date of the death of the King.

As long ago as 1911 Hulin de Loo called the Master of the Parement 'un grand artiste'. Later scholars have not always seen as clearly, but the painter's mastery even of the more traditional aspects of his forms is exceptional. Despite the effectiveness of his mass and space he maintained a rich interweaving of lobed frame and figure. The latter, indeed, almost appear to be a continuation of the former, most strikingly in the *Flagellation* (Fig. 3). The figures and frame, both of the same gray color, constitute a traceried, diaphanous plane similar to an architectural triforium – a plane that is repeated deeper in space in the upper rear wall of the room. Designing his scenes mostly in a continuous band, the painter has given them an impressive rhythmical unity. Figures extend from one arcuated space to the next. The strong horizontal pattern in the *Betrayal* (Fig. 2) of the arms of Judas and a soldier is continued in the *Flagellation* (Fig. 3) and in the cross-bar of the *Way to Calvary* (Fig. 4), ascending to the higher *Crucifixion* (Fig. 1). The *Entombment* (Fig. 5) laps over, in a studied way, into the area of Limbo. The remarkable two-faced devil at the right is another manifestation of the painter's concern with continuity, because he looks towards Christ and Adam while fleeing into the freer air of the *Noli Me Tangere*.

These qualities represent, however, only one side of the Parement Master's art. Rich and compelling as the pattern of interlace is, it does not exclude depth from the scenes or mass and density from the figures. The painter accomplishes, in other words, that combination of the planar and the tri-dimensional that had been introduced into French painting by Jean Pucelle, drawing from Ducciesque sources (Figs. 335, 336). Much of north European painting had been affected by Pucelle's innovations, but a comparison of the *Parement* with the major surviving works of its decade reveals how much more it owes to Pucelle than they. Bondol's frontispiece of 1371 for the Hague Bible shows slight, delicate figures, one moving nimbly but disjointedly through an ample space. The Apocalypse tapestries of 1376–1379, which represent a translation of Bondol's pictorial ideas into another medium, diffuse the compact forms and rather simple, orderly rhythms of the miniature into expansive, flowery shapes (Figs. 380, 381, 387). The tall tottering figures are spongy manikins for loosely wrapped drapery that spills over the blue and red backgrounds and cascades to the ground. Closer to the *Parement* are certain miniatures by followers of Bondol. The Virgin in the *Crucifixion* in the Hague Bible falls forward, arms dangling, as in the *Parement* and Stephaton approaches Christ similarly in both works, only one leg visible as he brandishes his sponge. Here and in the scene of the *Way to Calvary* there is more interest in landscape in the Bible,[16] whereas the painter of the *Parement* concentrates on the drama of the event.

H

In one respect the *Parement* has no rival among these earlier or contemporary French paintings. The figures are not only more solid; they exhibit a far more highly developed structure, nowhere more beautifully telling than in the St. John of the *Entombment*, from whose supporting arms the Virgin has just escaped to fling herself on the body of Christ, and who continues to lean, anxious, sad, and uncertain, over her (Fig. 5). St. John's shoulder, arm, wrist, and hand combine in a complex expressive action that was unprecedented in Northern painting up to this time. Unprecedented also, as we can see by referring to paintings by Pucelle or the associates of Bondol (Figs. 336, 519), is the controlled tension of Christ on the Cross, his arms stretched taut as a bow, his beautifully modelled legs parted in great strain. All of this implies a new, organic articulation of the figure, and this as well as the straight fall of Christ's body that identifies it with the cross is derived from Italian models.

What new expressive possibilities are offered by this great advance in articulation may be seen even in portraits by comparing Charles V in the *Parement* (Fig. 4) with the same figure in Bondol's miniature in the Hague (Fig. 382). Though the King was portrayed many times, only in the *Parement* did he acquire determination and a commanding presence – qualities with which many far less powerful Italians had been endowed for half a century (Fig. 513). The representation of Charles in the *Parement* lacks, on the other hand, that large measure of physiognomic individuality that Beauneveu gave to his tomb statue in St. Denis carved some ten years earlier (Fig. 591). Indeed in the *Parement* Charles and his Queen look like brother and sister, though he has not been subjected to that slenderizing process which seems to be the explanation of the *pentimenti* to the left and right of her figure.

The new conquests of the Parement Master with regard to the figure are frequently applied to rather un-Italian ends. The thrust of his solid bodies is most highly developed for aggressive, even brutal action, and the novel structure and articulation often serve violent behavior. The physicality of the figures, which is most crude in the case of the soldiers but visible everywhere in the description of bone and flesh, recalls the Netherlands or Bohemia rather than Italy. We shall return below to these resemblances with north European painting outside France.

The immediate origins of the art of the *Parement* in French painting of the mid-century remain undiscoverable today. It is not surprising to recognize that its style cannot be matched in the earlier or contemporary illuminated book. We should expect rather to find precursors in more monumental painting, but almost all of that has been destroyed. The one extant royal commission of real importance, the portrait of Jean le Bon, has suffered so much from losses and retouching that it is a highly unreliable guide (Fig. 507).

Among surviving paintings the strongest affinities of the Master of the Parement are with Pucelle and his followers. His style, like theirs, is a blend of Italian and French forms. In the *Way to Calvary* in the *Parement* the Virgin helps to reduce the weight of the cross by supporting the cross-bar (Fig. 4). This action does not appear in Byzantine or indeed in Italian representations, where a soldier normally separates Christ from his mother, and it is not described in the influential late thirteenth-century text, the *Meditationes Vitae Christi*. On the other hand it is frequently represented in French and German art, as early as the *Horae* from the atelier of Honoré in the Stadtbibliothek, Nuremberg,[17] and as close in time to the *Parement* as the *Heures de Yolande de*

Flandre, illuminated in, or just after, 1353 (Fig. 364). The Parement Master has, to be sure, transformed the action, for the Virgin seems to caress the cross, as though it were a part of Christ himself.

This change in the behavior of the Virgin is accompanied by another to the right, where a man next to Christ brandishes a hammer and a companion shows three large nails. The painter has thus greatly heightened the contrast of emotion and of morality at the two sides of Christ. This polarization is anticipated in the *Heures de Yolande de Flandre*, where a man with an upright claw-hammer is pulling Christ toward the hill, on top of which stands the old woman holding the three nails which, according to the legend, she forged after her husband refused to make them (Fig. 364).[18] The gruesome juxtaposition of the claw-hammer and the head of Christ is a feature of the tense *Way to Calvary* by Barna in the Collegiata, S. Gimignano, painted perhaps twenty years before the *Parement* (Fig. 538).

Comparison with Barna's fresco indicates immediately the source of a figure in the scene in the *Parement* that is apparently unprecedented in the French representation of this scene. A soldier, seen from the back, tugs on a rope bound around Christ. The ultimate origins of this figure are twofold. A soldier pulling Christ along (the rope usually around his neck) may be seen in the school of Duccio – in Ugolino's panel in the National Gallery, London, for instance[19] – and in numerous later Sienese paintings. This soldier, however, faces the beholder while the one between Christ and the Virgin, beginning with Simone Martini and the Lorenzetti, turns his back. An averted man just to the right of Christ, however, appears in Giotto's *Way to Calvary* in the Arena Chapel. In the *Parement* the two traditions coalesce, perhaps under the influence of an Italian model. But it seems highly improbable that any Italian painting approximated the tight alternation of postures in the *Parement*, or the corresponding drama of the collision of good and bad persons, of love and brutal hate, anticipating Bosch.

The soldier in the *Way to Calvary* is only one of three figures in the *Parement* seen from the back. The averted figure, a legacy of ancient art used occasionally in earlier medieval sculpture for one or more of the resurrected in the Last Judgment,[20] was first generally exploited in painting by Giotto in the Arena Chapel. In the shallow but vivid space of these scenes in Padua figures of all kinds are seen from the back: apostles at the *Last Supper* as well as a henchman in the *Massacre of the Innocents*, mourning women in the *Lamentation* and Judas (almost) in the *Betrayal*. Giotto's innovation had an immediate effect upon his followers, and, beginning with Simone and the Lorenzetti, upon the Sienese. The first example in French painting appears to be one of the Maries in the *Entombment* in the *Heures de Pucelle* around 1325 (Fig. 342). In the *Parement* a second averted figure is a scourger in the *Flagellation*, and here, as in the *Way to Calvary*, it serves to confront reversed images at the sides of a salient main axis. Another instance of the averted scourger, absent from earlier French painting, may be seen in the *Flagellation* in the extraordinary Missal in the Bodleian Library, Oxford (Fig. 373). These figures were inspired, no doubt, by Italian models, such as the scourger in the Giottesque glass in the Lower Church at Assisi.[21]

It is notable that both of these averted figures in the *Parement* are soldiers. Aversion, in other words, is often associated with inferiority, or even downright evil; this is a medieval view still prevalent in the fourteenth century.[22] The third figure seen from the back conforms with this convention. He is the centurion in the *Crucifixion*, pigtailed in this instance, and as he announces his recognition of Christ he turns from what we might call tergality (Fig. 1). He flings up the scroll towards Christ while casting his head back demonstratively toward a companion in arms, a complex movement for which an Italian model, not yet discovered, seems probable.

The origins of the figures at the other side of the cross are clearer. The representation of the grief-stricken Virgin at the Crucifixion, so central a theme in Italian art from the time of Nicola Pisano's Pisa pulpit,[23] was introduced in France by Jean Pucelle in the Hours now in the Cloisters, New York (Fig. 336). Pucelle's design derives ultimately from Duccio's *Crucifixion* in the *Maestà*, with its two groups of figures rolled back from the center to reveal the cross fixed in a hillock (Fig. 339). The faces and gestures of the old men at the right come from Duccio, and the man fallen to the ground may be seen in the *Maestà*. Other figures, however, presuppose other models: the arms of the thieves are bent over the cross as in Ducciesque (or later) paintings, such as the *Maestà* in Massa Marittima.[24] Similarly St. John comes to the support of the Virgin, whereas in early Sienese painting she is held by the Maries alone, and the Virgin in Pucelle's miniature collapses frontally, rather than in profile.

In all these respects the corresponding group in the *Parement de Narbonne* represents a return to early Sienese models, but a return, so to speak, at a new altitude. Pucelle approximated Italian forms unevenly, adopting some of the drapery folds of a figure, for instance, but weaving them into his own French pattern (Fig. 336). This was true even in the *Heures de Jeanne d'Évreux*, when he felt closest to Italian painting, and it is much more true of his followers (Figs. 341, 345), including the remarkable chief illuminator of the Douce Missal in Oxford (Figs. 372, 677). The Parement Master, on the other hand, has a deeper understanding of the principles of early Sienese painting, and his group of the grief-stricken Virgin tenderly supported by two Maries shows a remarkable resemblance to the corresponding group in the *Crucifixion* in the collection of the Earl of Craw-ford, Balcarres, by the Master of Città di Castello (Fig. 528). Only the dangling arms of the Virgin and the spread fingers, adumbrated by Pucelle, are lacking in the Ducciesque model, and they may be seen in a panel by a follower of Ambrogio Lorenzetti in the Vatican (Fig. 527). The French painter's conquest of the structure of the figure has permitted him to capture the beautiful move-ment of the women in the Crawford *Crucifixion*, and to differentiate with equal effectiveness between the live and the limp bodies. The folds of the drapery, more consistently functional than in earlier French painting, are similar likewise to Sienese conventions, even with regard to their suppleness and weight. One has the impression that the Parement Master possesses sufficient knowledge and sympathy even to improvise *all'italiana*.

Where, indeed, we cannot cite models for the innovations of the Parement Master we are not always certain whether this lack is to be ascribed to the loss of originals, to our ignorance, or simply to the painter's own inventiveness. In the scene of *Limbo*, for instance, Christ glides down towards the jaws of the monster, gracefully and convincingly suspended in air while grasping Adam's arm and spearing a devil with his lance-like cross. This unusual levitation was probably motivated in part by the narrowness of the available space. In any event, comparable representations do not appear in Italy until the end of the century, when they emerge as one manifestation of a general interest in floating figures.[25] It is true that earlier, however, *circa* 1367, the Christ in the *Descent into Limbo* by Andrea da Firenze in the Spanish Chapel of S. M. Novella, Florence, scarcely touches the fallen door as he soars towards Adam.[26]

We have already referred to the extraordinary tension of the figure of Christ on the cross, to the outstretched arms, the taut bend of the leg, and the heaving chest. This characterizes only one aspect of the figure, for the painter has combined a maximum of tension with a very high degree of geometric stability. He has identified the figure with the cross by the nearly straight extension of the arms and the right leg, and he has even raised the head towards verticality from its usual pathetic inclination. The painter has abandoned, in other words, the agonized posture characteristic of Gothic painting in France and, in a more restrained version, of painting in Siena as well (Figs. 339, 674). His figure is rather like that of Giotto and his followers, but even Florentine representations show legs more bent and a more fallen head. The posture of Christ in the *Crucifixion* of the *Parement* is, in fact, closer to those representations of the early fifteenth century that tend increasingly to show a simpler, geometric, cruciform figure. This trend, which culminates in paintings of Jan van Eyck (Fig. 537) and Masaccio (Naples), involves of course not merely a change of posture but a different conception of Christ on the cross. In a kind of reversion to Romanesque ideas, painters convey his triumph as well as his suffering. They also present his physical vitality as well as his distress. It is this much later image that the figure in the *Parement* foreshadows.

The geometrical principle that informs the figure of Christ, exceptional in French painting of the time, is effective in another aspect of the *Crucifixion*. The prominent diagonals of the Virgin's arms are repeated on the right side of the composition by the arms of St. John and of the centurion. On the left, however, the diagonal movement is downward, on the right, up. Furthermore, the falling motion of the Virgin is absorbed, so to speak, by the firmly planted, seated figure of St. John. The lowliness of St. John also allows us to see, unobstructed, the complex torsion of the centurion. Although the figure of St. John fulfills admirably several functions in the scene, it is the source of a major difficulty in the design. Occupying the foreground opposite the group of the Virgin it pushes the soldiers to a deeper plane, and they are slightly reduced, accordingly, in scale. But the unrepentant thief behind them seems no more – perhaps even less – distant than the repentent thief at the left, so that the spatial relations of the figures left and right of the cross are confusing. Furthermore, the figure of St. John, 'functional' in some respects though it be, is not perfectly integrated in the design.

The St. John is one of the figures in the *Crucifixion* by which the painter evidently set great store. It is, indeed, an early example in France of a type that played a fundamental role in the *stil nuovo* of Trecento Italy. During the first thirty years of the fourteenth century many figures that in earlier art had been represented standing or enthroned were shown seated or kneeling on the floor or the ground. These new postures were assumed especially by the Virgin Mary, in the Crucifixion (Fig. 530), the Adoration of the Magi, the Annunciation, and the Madonna of Humility (Figs. 397, 634), but numerous other sacred figures took them as well (Figs. 530, 532).[27] The origins of these novel postures were twofold. Their emergence was conditioned, and no doubt stimulated, by the transformation of the ground *line* of earlier medieval painting into a ground *plane*. They responded, at the same time, to the desire of the period to bring the sacred figures 'down to earth', a desire manifested by other aspects of the art of the time. The saints become earthy in the figurative as well as the literal sense. In the context of late medieval art, in which elevation still symbolized hierarchical superiority, lowliness signified humility, homeliness, accessibility. Thus these images convey the new religious qualities fostered by Franciscanism and the values of bourgeois, as opposed to feudal, society.

Though the new postures were developed mostly in Tuscan painting, the earliest extant example of the lowly St. John in the Crucifixion is to be seen in a fresco by a Roman painter *circa* 1300 in S. Maria in Vescovio (Fig. 529).[28] In an unpublished miniature from the same general region, and executed only a few years later, the Virgin as well as St. John is seated on the ground.[29] It is conceivable that this innovation in the Crucifixion was actually made in the Roman region, in the circle of Pietro Cavallini, and this hypothesis must certainly be weighed in relation to another proposed by Dorothy Shorr some years ago.[30] The 'grounded' Virgin and St. John were inspired, Mrs. Shorr suggested, by the mourning captives seated at the sides of a *tropaeum* in ancient Roman reliefs (Fig. 531). The type was used on coins for images of *Germania* or *Judaea capta*.[31] It is notable that in the fresco at S. Maria in Vescovio St. John, like a captive, is perched on a small mound, while in early Sienese examples he rests his weary head, again like a captive, on the palm of his hand. The very least that must be concluded, then, is that several elements of an ancient type reappear, combined in the new late medieval theme.

Though a spectator, overcome with emotion, falls to the ground in the Pucelle *Crucifixion* as in Duccio's, the seated St. John appeared in French painting only toward 1340 in the *Heures de Jeanne de Navarre* (Fig. 544)[32] and around 1353 in the *Heures de Yolande de Flandre*. It is noteworthy that the latter manuscript was in the library of the patron of the Parement Master; Charles V had it, perhaps as early as 1372 and certainly a few years later.[33] In the *bas-de-page* in the *Heures de Yolande*, executed in the late workshop of Pucelle, partly by an illuminator who may be called the Passion Master,[34] St. John clasps an upraised knee, as in the fresco at S. Maria in Vescovio (Figs. 365, 529) and many other Italian paintings. Instead of interlocking his fingers, however, one hand grasps the back of the other. This gesture, uncommon in early Tuscan painting but occasionally employed even by St. John in the Crucifixion,[35] may be seen again in two French miniatures, one showing a standing St. John in a late Pucellesque Bible in Leningrad,[36] the other a seated figure in the Missal in the Bodleian Library, Oxford (Fig. 536).

The best miniatures in the Bodleian Missal were painted by one of the most powerful illuminators of the century. He learned much from Pucelle, including an attentiveness to Italian painting that almost equalled Pucelle's at the height of his enthusiasm around 1325. The more drastic emotionalism of the painter of the Missal, however, his uncouth figures, and his strong chiaroscuro point to activity outside the Parisian environment. Probably he worked, as the writer has earlier proposed,[37] in northeastern France or even in Flanders, and this hypothesis is supported by the similarities of his work with a Missal of St. Vaast, Arras (Fig. 534).[38] One of the striking and beautiful aspects of the Douce manuscript is the execution of the miniatures in washes of gray, pale green, violet or brown, and similar colors were employed in the Arras Missal. The bold drapery patterns of the Arras Missal are reminiscent of the Oxford manuscript, and so too are the enormous indented rocks (Figs. 372, 677). In view of the normally close connections of England with the Artois and neighboring regions, it is significant that the Douce *Crucifixion* (Fig. 536) apparently influenced an English manuscript of around 1365.[39]

The seated St. John in the Douce *Crucifixion*, probably painted somewhat earlier than the corresponding figure in the *Parement*, shares with it one striking feature. In both figures one leg is crossed under the other in such a manner that the bare sole of the foot is exposed to the beholder. This posture, which originated in antique art, was preserved in Byzantine painting, especially in representations of the apostles in the Agony in the Garden (Fig. 543). It was resisted by early Italian painting, perhaps because it seemed undignified.[40] French painters, as early as the thirteenth century, had no such scruples,[41] and the workshop of Pucelle adopted it in its most common French and Byzantine form (Fig. 541).

The miniature in the Douce Missal appears to be the earliest example of the attribution of this folded leg to the seated Evangelist in the Crucifixion. The figure in the miniature demonstrates his grief by clasping one hand in the other, as we have observed above. This combination of gesture and posture was effected earlier in a large and accessible monument, the famous relief – famous no doubt already in the fourteenth century – of the *Death of the Virgin* in the south portal of the Cathedral of Strasbourg (Fig. 542). The illuminator may well have taken his figure from this relief.

In its union of geometry and Gothic interlace, its combination of ideal Sienese imagery with a raw Northern naturalism, the *Parement de Narbonne* is a remarkable and fateful work. Nothing at once so strong and so exquisite had been created in France since the *Heures de Pucelle*. The *Parement* carries to a novel depth the French engagement with the two great foreign pictorial traditions of the century, the Netherlandish and the Italian. It seems probable, indeed, that if the date of execution of the painting had not been fixed by the representation of Charles V and his Queen, scholars would have placed it a decade or two later. The only paintings that are close to it in style – miniatures in the *Très Belles Heures de Notre-Dame* – have in fact often been, and still frequently are, dated in the early fifteenth century.

2 · EARLY HISTORY OF THE
TRÈS BELLES HEURES DE NOTRE-DAME

The new phase of French painting represented by the *Parement de Narbonne* includes a group of miniatures in a famous, perhaps we should say notorious, Book of Hours. This book contains a greater variety of major styles than any other of the period that has come down to us, and the identity of these styles as well as their date have been the subject of controversy during the half century since the book became known to modern scholarship. Unique also is the history of the execution of the manuscript. Successive campaigns were conducted, I believe, over a period of some thirty-five years, and these campaigns were ordered, furthermore, by several patrons, two of whom were active during the period covered by the present book. Because conclusions about chronology and authorship are bound up with the early history of the manuscript I shall tell this intricate story, as I see it, in the following paragraphs. Readers who would be content with a summary of the account, which differs at certain important points from any hitherto given, may find it in the catalogue entry for the manuscript. This entry contains also a selective bibliography of the manuscript.

Around 1900 the first eminent historians ever to devote themselves to the history of pictorial style in the late medieval French and Netherlandish book – Paul Durrieu and Georges Hulin de Loo – were fascinated by three extraordinary manuscripts. During the following two decades they published monographic studies of all of them. The *Heures de Turin* of Durrieu appeared in 1902, just two years before the manuscript was destroyed by a fire in the National Library in that city. Hulin de Loo followed in 1911 with a volume on the *Heures de Milan*, then in the Trivulzio Collection, and Durrieu completed the series in 1922 with an edition of the section in the Rothschild Collection in Paris.

In 1910 Durrieu demonstrated that the three manuscripts just mentioned, together with some single folios in the Louvre, originally comprised an exceptionally rich Book of Hours, and in the *Très Belles Heures de Notre-Dame* of 1922 he reconstructed the sequence of the folios.[42] The section in Paris came first, he showed, followed by the *Heures de Turin*, which included the folios now in the Louvre. Then followed the *Heures de Milan*, consisting actually of masses, and finally the lost miniature copied by Bastard (Fig. 497). He connected the manuscript with a Book of Hours described in the inventory of 1413:

> Item, d'unes très belles Heures de Nostre-Dame, escriptes de grosse lettre de fourme, declairees ou IIe XLIIIe fueillet du livre desdiz comptes precedens, est deschargié et acquictié ledit Robinet d'Estampes des dictes Heures, sanz la pipe d'icelles, pour les causes contenues en la correction faicte sur la partie desdictes Heures; pour ce icy seulement une pipe faicte d'un fermail d'or, garnie d'un fin balay ou milieu, pesant XX carazs et IIII perles fines roondes entour, pesant chascune un caraz; lequel fermail mondit Seigneur retint pour mectre esdictes Heures de plusieurs joyaulx et autres choses que Barthelemy Rust, marchant, demourant à Paris, lui vendi et delivra, tant pour la feste et joustes faictes à Bourges le XXI et le XXII[e] jours d'avril l'an mil CCCC et cinq après Pasques, que autrement; et cousta la somme de III[c] XXXVII frans X sous t.(ournois).[43]

Before 1413 the Duke gave the manuscript to Robinet in exchange for another Book of Hours, 'lesquelles Heures a prinses mondit Seigneur dudit Robinet d'Estampes en lieu d'unes autres Heures qui lui a données . . .'; and then the latter is identified precisely as the manuscript described above.[44] The *Horae* the Duke received from Robinet he gave to his treasurer, Martin Gouge, in 1416; it has not been identified among extant manuscripts.

Durrieu's identification of the several surviving parts of an elaborate Book of Hours with the 'très belles Heures de Nostre-Dame' has been accepted as a fact by subsequent scholarship. The case for the identification, curiously never presented in full, is strong if not absolutely conclusive. It rests on four facts. (1) All the parts listed above belonged originally to one Book of Hours, a fact that is shown not only by internal evidence but by the great similarity of this whole to the

Petites Heures of Jean de Berry. (2) The extant manuscript was for a long time in the collection of Jean de Berry, because it contains two certain portraits of him, one painted in the 'eighties, the other *circa* 1405, and the Duke's arms are on the *chapelle ardente* in the *Funeral Service*. (3) The 'très belles Heures de Nostre-Dame' is the only major Book of Hours, 'escriptes de grosse lettre de fourme', which is described in the inventories but is not identifiable with another existing manuscript. (4) One part of the manuscript was, as we shall see, in the possession of Robinet's family, the Estampes, from the third quarter of the fifteenth century to the early eighteenth.

When the Duke gave the manuscript to his keeper of *joyaux* and books he retained the jewelled *pipe*, with its book marks.[45] The purchase of the material for it in 1405 proves that the manuscript was attracting the attention of the Duke at that time. This is an interesting fact, the significance of which has not hitherto been recognized. There is other evidence, as we shall see, that work on the book was begun again around that date.

The section of the manuscript now in Paris seems to have remained in the Estampes family into the eighteenth century. The female donor on pages 2 and 155, added in the third quarter of the fifteenth century, has the shield of the Beauvillier family, one member of whom Robertet d'Estampes married in 1438. Furthermore, the arms on the present binding are Du Plessis-Châtillon, and Philippe-Charles d'Estampes married into this family in 1707. This section of the manuscript was acquired in the mid-nineteenth century by Baron Adolphe de Rothschild.

The second part of the manuscript became the property of a prince of the house of Holland and Bavaria, William IV or, as Châtelet has argued, Jean.[46] It in turn was later divided into two parts. One went to the house of Savoy and, in 1720, into the University Library in Turin, where it was burnt in 1904, shortly after the publication of Durrieu's facsimile. The other passed into the Trivulzio collection in Milan. The two parts became known, from their whereabouts, as the *Heures de Milan* and the *Heures de Turin*, and the most recent stage, almost unimaginable, in the intricate history of this manuscript occurred when the *Heures de Milan* was transferred to Turin.

The original manuscript contained, in addition to characteristic elements of a Book of Hours, a series of masses that were less common in a book of this kind. Many of them appeared earlier in the *Heures de Savoie*,[47] to which Charles V had made extensive additions, and in the *Horae* of Philippe le Hardi in the Fitzwilliam Museum (Fig. 564).[48] All of them were included in the *Petites Heures* of Jean de Berry, and many in the *Très Riches Heures*. The text of the *Petites Heures* is in fact exceptionally similar, and it was employed by Durrieu as a model for the reconstruction of the *Très Belles Heures de Notre-Dame*. Durrieu, who dated the latter after 1404, of course thought that it had been based on the *Petites Heures*, but the reverse is more likely to be correct.

The composition of the manuscript facilitated its eventual division, as Durrieu pointed out. The first section, now in Paris, has basic parts of a Book of Hours: the Hours of the Virgin, the Hours of the Holy Ghost and of the Passion, and the Office of the Dead. The *Heures de Turin* contained a series of prayers while the *Heures de Milan* consists largely of masses. It should be pointed out also that the 'Book of Hours', the part presumably retained by Robinet d'Estampes, was almost fully illustrated when the Duke gave the manuscript to him, whereas there were gaps in the remaining folios, especially with regard to the large miniatures. In the *Heures de Turin* only two folios were completely illuminated.

When the *Très Belles Heures de Notre-Dame* was mentioned in the Duke's inventory of 1413 it was, so to speak, in one piece. The early history of the manuscript points to the strong probability that Robinet d'Estampes divided it, keeping one part and disposing of the rest. But where was the manuscript before 1413, or rather before 1405, when the Duke bought a *pipe* for it? For whom was it originally written? The evidence, of various kinds, does not all seem to point in the same direction, but it leads us in the end to a high degree of probability. We shall present the several elements in what seems to us an ascending order of importance.

The Calendar of the manuscript now in Paris contains entries of the anniversaries of the death of Jean de Berry's wife, father, and other relatives, the latest being Philippe le Hardi, who died in 1404. Inasmuch as these notices are integral with the Calendar Durrieu concluded that the original manuscript was written after 1404, and he held this position in 1922,[49] long after Hulin had pointed out that this Calendar differed from the rest of the manuscript with regard to script and lack of the border decoration that is visible in the other folios. Hulin suggested that this Calendar was added by Robinet d'Estampes, but it seems more probably an addition of Jean de Berry.

The *Heures de Turin* contained a Calendar also, and it resembles the other early folios not only with regard to script but also in the decoration of its borders. Hulin, therefore, contrary to Durrieu, believed that this was the original Calendar. It is difficult, however, to be certain of its contemporaneity, because there are at least two styles of script as well as some slight variation in border design in the main body of the manuscript, and of the Calendar only a reproduction remains. The initials and of course the miniatures are of a much later date. Chatelet, indeed, has proposed that this Calendar was produced in imitation of a style of script and decoration current nearly forty years earlier. The saints are characteristic of the Hainaut and of the dioceses of Liège and Arras, as Hulin observed, and Chatelet concluded that the Calendar was made for John of Bavaria before 1419, while he was Bishop of Liège.

In 1884 Delisle remarked that two prayers in the *Heures de Turin*, beginning on folio 58 verso and 77 verso respectively, were written for a King of France.[50] He believed that the manuscript might, therefore, have been commissioned by Charles V. It is true that the second prayer is quite explicit in its reference: 'Servo tuo auxilium et consilium Francorum regi tribue . . .' and it is illustrated, in post-Eyckian style, by the representation of a King of France praying before a panel of the Crucifixion (Durrieu, *Heures de Turin*, pl. XLIII). The miniature for the first prayer, on the other hand, is the famous Eyckian representation of a mounted prince of Holland and Bavaria praying to God while he and his miliatry aides are foregathered at the seashore. It is true however that both prayers are included in the *Petites Heures* (folios 106 and 121 verso), and there the prince in the miniatures is not distinguishable from the other figures in this sequence of prayers who are probably intended to represent Jean de Berry (Figs. 117, 122). He wears a moustache and a goatee, and cannot therefore be identified with Charles V. These prayers seem to be appropriate, then, to a duke or a count as well as to a king. The evidence that they were not *originally* written for a king is not, however, quite as decisive as one would wish, because the head of the prince on folio 106 (but not on 121 verso) of the *Petites Heures* was reworked (see pp. 89, 90), and the loss of the *Heures de Turin* prevents us from excluding the possibility that the great Eyckian miniature was painted over an earlier one representing a French king. Durrieu's belief, however, that the prayer on folio 77 verso of the *Heures de Turin*, which refers to the King of France, was an interpolation is incorrect because the same prayer appears, as we have said, in the *Petites Heures* (folio 121 verso).

In the *Très Belles Heures de Notre-Dame*, as in the *Petites Heures*, one of the patrons of the Duke of Berry, John the Baptist, appears first among the saints in the suffrages (folio 104 in the latter and *Turin* folio 57). The text of these two exceptional manuscripts is, indeed, so similar that they were very probably written for the same prince (see also the catalogue entry for the *Petites Heures*). The *Petites Heures* carries the celebration of the Baptist a step further by devoting to him, near the end, a complete Hours. Inasmuch as this is a development of the text of the *Très Belles Heures de Notre-Dame* it tends to strengthen our view, which is contrary to that of Durrieu, that the *Très Belles Heures* is earlier. Another link with Jean de Berry would seem to be provided by the representation of the *Marriage at Cana*, an exceptional subject in the Hours of the Virgin that reappears in the *Grandes Heures* (Figs. 12, 235). No less significant is the presence of Dominicans in the *Funeral Service* (Fig. 14). They reappear in the corresponding miniature in the *Brussels Hours* (Fig. 198) and in the *Grandes Heures* (Fig. 232), both manuscripts indubitably made for Jean de Berry. Furthmore, the Duke's confessor who fell ill in 1373 was a Dominican, and he was succeeded by another member of this order.[50a]

The arms of Jean de Berry embellish the *chapelle ardente* in the *Funeral Service*, which belongs to the first campaign of illustration (Fig. 14). They prove that the manuscript was at one time in the possession of the Duke. Since they take the form of *France moderne*, used regularly by the Duke only in the fifteenth century, these coats of arms have often been judged decisive evidence of the rather late date of the first campaign of illumination. The fleurs-de-lys are not painted, however, in the good style of the ornament executed by the Parement workshop, and the shield in the gable on the right side of the *chapelle* seems too large for its space. The axis of all three shields on this side, futhermore, does not conform with that of the structure. By holding the folio against the light one may see that the dark gray of the *chapelle ardente* underlies these shields. Normally, when elements of this kind are foreseen from the beginning, dark colors are not run under them.[51] It seems probable, then, that these coats of arms were added by the Duke, perhaps around 1405-1408. This supposition accords with the growing tendency of the Duke in the later years of his life to identify paintings with himself in one way or another. The arms in the *Annunciation* in the early *Petites Heures* were added after the completion of the painting.[52]

Additional evidence of the Duke's early ownership of the *Très Belles Heures de Notre-Dame* is provided by the portrait in the margin of folio 87 of the *Heures de Milan* (Fig. 49). This portrait is fully discussed in Chapter IV, catalogue no. 24. The identity of the person represented has sometimes been questioned, but all the facts point toward the Duke. If it is he the portrait was painted, for iconographic reasons, before 1389. Some later retouching makes it difficult to be certain that it was executed by the Parement Master himself, but it was clearly designed by him. Very probably, then, it was painted by 1385, if not a few years earlier.

If we weigh all the evidence, of text as well as illumination, we must conclude that the illumination of the *Très Belles Heures de Notre-Dame* was being carried forward by Jean de Berry around 1382, and that in all probability he commissioned the manuscript originally. After this first campaign, however, the folios, far from complete, were abandoned for about twenty years. This is an unusual though not unique case.[53] In evaluating it we must remember that the later history of the manuscript was exceptional also. The most likely explanation of the initial cessation of work is that the Parement Master disappeared – we know no later work by him. The Duke, concerned with the illumination of a series of exceptionally rich manuscripts – the *Psalter*, the *Petites Heures*, and later the *Brussels Hours* – apparently found no painter to whom he wished to assign the completion of the work.

Around 1405 the Duke became interested in the manuscript again. In that year he bought material to make a *pipe* for it, and not far from this date he asked three painters to carry the illumination forward. Because of the influence of their painting (and that of the Parement campaign also) upon the *Grandes Heures*, which was completed in 1409, we can judge rather accurately the span of years within which this second campaign fell. Toward the end of this period the second certain portrait of the Duke in the manuscript was painted (Fig. 34 – see Chapter IV, catalogue no. 21).

Once again, however, the fate of this Book of Hours was unique among the Duke's manuscripts. First of all, the new campaign, like the first, was entrusted to painters otherwise unknown in the illuminated book, except for the Limbourgs, who painted only three miniatures. More important, these masters too failed to finish the job, probably because the Duke was not satisfied with their work. On the other hand he doubtless cared too much about the painting of the Limbourgs to assign to them the completion of a manuscript begun years earlier, in an outmoded style. One little fact, hitherto unnoticed, suggests what may have happened. The *pipe* made for the *Très Belles Heures de Notre-Dame* but retained by the Duke when he gave the book to Robinet was attached to the *Belles Heures*. It was described precisely in the testamentary inventory of 1416,[54] but not yet in the inventory of 1413. Since the *Belles Heures* was far advanced or completed in 1412 the Duke may have found it so preferable to the still unfinished *Très Belles Heures de Notre-Dame* that he decided to be rid of the latter, but to retain the jewelled *pipe* for the *Belles Heures*. In any event, not long after the campaign of around 1405, and certainly before early 1413, the Duke ended his thirty years of concern with the *Très Belles Heures de Notre-Dame*. Presumably in a mood of final frustration he gave the incomplete and heterogeneous work to his keeper, Robinet d'Estampes. Robinet then proceeded to divide the book into two parts, as we have seen, but no further painting in it seems to have been undertaken during the Duke's lifetime or, in other words, until the Eyckian miniatures were added by yet another owner.

3 · AUTHORSHIP

In the preceding account of the painting of the *Très Belles Heures de Notre-Dame* we have attempted to garner as many facts as possible from documents and from other kinds of 'external' evidence but, caught by the usual dilemma of historical method, we have been constrained to assume some fundamental judgments of the *art* of the manuscript. These now remain to be justified. The earliest miniatures, with which quite naturally we shall begin, were correctly evaluated as long ago as 1911, when Hulin de Loo, in a brilliant, succinct essay, connected them with the *Parement de Narbonne*.[55] The miniatures were, he argued, made by the same painter between 1380–1390, that is to say perhaps a decade after the *Parement*.

This view was rejected by Hulin's colleague, Paul Durrieu, who concluded that the resemblance of the miniatures with several in the *Grandes Heures* and the first two in the *Brussels Hours* of the Duke proved that Jacquemart de Hesdin must have been responsible for them.[56] So great was Durrieu's authority and so magnetic the name of Jacquemart that this hypothesis, rather than Hulin's, has prevailed for a quarter century, up to the present time.[57] Hulin himself contributed to the eclipse of his own view in 1925, late in his career, when he took a surprising new tack, giving both the *Parement* and the miniatures in the *Très Belles Heures de Notre-Dame* to André Beauneveu.[58] A tendency to revert to Hulin's theory of 1911 is observable in brief references to the miniatures during the past ten years,[59] and in 1956 the present writer endorsed it emphatically.[60]

Any attempt to evaluate nicely the relationship between miniatures and more monumental painting must face the difficulty of viewing the relationship through the screen of differences of size, of technique, and probably also of function. The *Parement* was painted in grisaille, the miniatures in full color. It seems probable, furthermore, that painters of the late fourteenth century – and the Parement Master was, it seems to me, not an illuminator – might well have taken a different attitude toward the production of a long series of very small paintings on the page of a book than toward their normal tasks on panel, plaster, or cloth. If such a difference of viewpoint did in fact exist, it was probably shared by patrons. The question is, to be sure, very subtle, and it can be answered, even tentatively, only by inference from several instances. These will be discussed later in the present book.[61]

Most of the miniatures that Hulin attributed to the Parement Master are in the section of the manuscript now in Paris. Among them are two subjects that we have already considered in the *Parement*, the *Betrayal*, and the *Flagellation* (Figs. 22, 25). Comparison of these two pairs of scenes discloses immediately obvious differences within a context of close, pervasive similarities. In the miniature of the *Flagellation* the building as well as the frame lacks the delicate tracery of the *Parement* (Fig. 3), but this may have been inspired in the latter by a wish for conformity with the architecture of the chapel in which it was to hang. Less easily interpreted is the difference of format and of figure canon. The painter of the *Parement* consistently preferred vertical axes and tall figures. They seem fundamental to his rhythmical designs, at that moment at least, and if the miniatures were painted, as I believe, only eight or ten years later, so considerable a change would be surprising. Still, these new proportions are accompanied by corresponding innovations in other aspects of the style: especially significant is a diminution of the strength of the surface pattern and a greater development of the extension into space. A striking symptom of that is the introduction in the miniature of the tessellated floor, a device originally exploited by the Lorenzetti to serve as a spatial index, and adopted first in France, it seems, by Jean Bondol in his miniature of 1371 in the

Hague Bible (Fig. 382). Both Bondol and the painter of the *Flagellation* employ the vanishing axis system for the orthogonals; in the *Flagellation* it is applied not only to the tessellated floor but to a similar ceiling. Pucelle and his followers had earlier taken the geometric, coffered ceiling from Duccio; an approximation of it appears in the *Flagellation* in the *Parement*. In the miniature the perspective accomplishments of Pucelle and Bondol are combined, or, to describe the historical process more correctly, the complete interior as conceived by the Lorenzetti is introduced into French painting.

Along with these advances in the representation of perspective space the building has acquired a greater actuality, with its decorated frieze and articulated moldings, and its doors opening onto exterior and other interior spaces. This more substantial room is filled by the figures, who appear in two layers, so to speak, rather than one. Now that their spatial aspect has increased at the expense of their planar, they are rounder and shorter. One of them, Pilate, can even assume a blunt shape that compromises little with the linear surface pattern. The figures share the greater actuality of the architecture. The scourger at the right rear has a corpulence unmatched in the *Parement*, and the scourger in front of him has become Negroid. The Negro is certainly not novel in fourteenth-century painting; he had appeared in the Arena Chapel (the *Mockery*), and, in France, in the *Betrayal* in Pucelle's *Psalter of Bonne de Luxembourg*, illuminated before 1349 (Fig. 352).[62] His appearance in the *Très Belles Heures de Notre-Dame* seems consistent, at the same time, with its realistic trend. This consistency is certainly proved by the unprecedented rendering of the thick Negroid lips and the general fleshiness of the head.

The differences between the two scenes of the *Betrayal* are the same as those between the paintings of the *Flagellation* (Figs. 2, 22). Once again the elaborate interlace of the design of the *Parement* has been altered to a more rectilinear pattern. The arabesque of Malchus is resolved into a horizontal and a vertical, and the complex interweave of two soldiers and Christ has given way to a greater plastic individuality of the figures. Though the figures in the miniature are again closer to the lower frame, they extend deeper into space and their extension is marked in this instance not by the geometry of floor and ceiling but by the distribution of the lances and clubs at varying depths rather than merely behind the figures, as in the *Parement*. The variety of the persons portrayed has been increased by the prominence given to a woman, a most unusual figure in this scene.[63] Her head alone is visible in the *Parement*, and there too she seems to bear the lantern. Just beyond her in the miniature we may follow the receding terrain to a tree-crowned hillock deep in space.

The relationships between these two pairs of scenes are typical of those between the *Parement* and the manuscript generally. Although the advances in space and perspective point toward the major developments of the 'nineties in the work of Jacquemart de Hesdin, other innovations of the miniatures – the physicality and the uncanonical faces especially – were rejected by the painter's successors, so far as I can see. The prominence of these qualities makes it difficult to understand the widespread attribution of the miniatures to one or another of the painters of the *Petites Heures*, the *Brussels Hours*, or the *Grandes Heures*.

It is not at all clear, however, that in the miniatures we are confronted with a designer distinct from the author of the *Parement*. The greater refinement of the *Parement* should not, we have suggested, be interpreted simply as the usual difference between creator and imitator, but as a quality of style valued more highly in one work than another. There remains, it is true, a certain relative dullness in some parts of the miniature of the *Flagellation* – the painting of the mantle of Pilate, for instance. Perhaps this is the consequence of more rapid and less careful execution, but it may be due also to the intervention of an assistant. This interpretation is strengthened by the fact that the miniatures are more uneven in quality than the scenes in the *Parement*, which are, indeed, quite uniform. In the manuscript the first miniatures in the Hours of the Virgin are superior, while the illustrations of the Hours of the Passion, to which the *Flagellation* belongs, are more uneven.

Perhaps, then, such specific inconsistencies in the miniatures as the spatial position of the scourger at the right may be ascribed to execution by an assistant. It is important to observe, however, that the miniaturist only maintains a confusion that is apparent in the *Parement*, where the scourger's arm overlaps a side wall that is cut back as if to accommodate him, but which nevertheless springs forward because of its identity above with the arch that, at the center, exists in the forward plane. It seems improbable that the Parement Master himself would have committed the curious blunder of giving a wrong foot to Christ in the *Betrayal* (Fig. 22). The pattern of his drapery in the miniature resembles that in the *Parement*, but whereas he has a left foot in the latter, the illuminator has given him a right foot. This right foot implies an extraordinary, almost impossible bodily torsion, but the illuminator seems not to have been unaware of these implications because he has given the foot a proper knee above, in profile as if the figure were twisting on its axis.

It must be said, on the other hand, that the painter of the miniature has eliminated a highly confusing passage in the *Parement* (Fig. 2). Though the soldier in the *Betrayal* who tugs at Christ's garment from the right has his own odd but visible body, his head and shoulders tend to merge with the body of the soldier behind him. The back and rump of this soldier deeper in space jut out toward the right while his head, covered with a scale helmet, is at an unexpected distance, even though the body inclines sharply inward. Only a close examination succeeds in extricating these two figures.

While we have up to this point attempted to describe the characteristic differences between the *Parement* and the miniatures, we have assumed the existence of profound similarities. The miniatures clearly exploit certain possibilities of the style of the larger work. We have referred to the advances in the representation of space, of architectural actuality, and of a more diversified cast of characters. When impressed by the physicality of figures in the miniatures, we must not overlook similar qualities in the *Parement*. The features of the Virgin in the *Entombment* in the latter are heavy, and the cheeks of the *Church* and the *Synagogue* are very fleshy. The soldiers in the *Betrayal* and the *Way to Calvary* of the *Parement* resemble the gross doctors in the miniature of *Christ in the Temple* (Fig. 11). The miniatures always preserve even the minutiae of the *Parement* mode of representation. The imperial double eagle, for instance, visible on the house of the *Flagellation* in the *Parement* but not in the miniature of the same subject, may be seen in another miniature representing Pilate's house, less delicately rendered but quite appropriate iconographically (Fig. 24). The crowns of Christ and the Virgin in the *Coronation* (Fig. 13) are almost identical with those in the *Parement*. The design of the belt of the Virgin in the *Visitation* (Fig. 7) is that of the tiny orthogonal beams in the ceiling of the *Flagellation* in the *Parement* (Fig. 3). The peak of the turban of Isaiah in the *Parement* (Fig. 1) is that of Joseph in the *Adoration of the Magi* (Fig. 9). The angels on escalloped clouds in the *Crucifixion* in the *Parement* reappear, with a similar girdle, in the left border of the *Presentation in the Temple* (Fig. 10). This catalogue of nearly identical details might be continued almost *ad infinitum*.

Details are, of course, imitable, but very rarely are *all* a painter's small forms and mannerisms repeated. The relationship we are considering does not, furthermore, involve mere repetition but composition or improvisation in the manner of the *Parement*. The music-making angels just below the *Coronation*, their postures so beautiful that they 'make music' with them also (Fig. 13), are seated with a crossed leg like St. John in the *Parement Crucifixion*, but they are not derived from him. There is a deep aesthetic affinity between the two works even when they are superficially quite dissimilar.

One more fact bears on the resolution of this difficult problem. The master responsible for the *Parement* was presumably a painter rather than an illuminator. The author of the miniatures was apparently not an illuminator either. For this judgment there are two kinds of evidence. Though the figures or compositions of the early miniatures in the *Très Belles Heures de Notre-Dame* were occasionally imitated many years later, as we shall see, there are no known miniatures really close to them in style; in this sense the master had no followers.[64] There are no school pieces among monumental works either, but the extent of the destruction of these objects makes this fact insignificant. In the second place, the technique employed in these miniatures is more characteristic of work on panel than on vellum. The layer of paint is thick. It includes a green earth underpainting in the flesh areas, heavy in the first miniatures in the Hours of the Virgin and lighter thereafter. The surfaces are built of superimposed layers: in the head of Simeon in the *Presentation in the Temple*, for instance, a layer of carmine was spread over most of the green underpainting, and then the carmine was brought up in places to white, but there are also strokes of gray and, on the lips, of a bright red (Fig. 10). A film of this dimension, common in Italian panel painting, was suitable for a stable ground. It was not employed in Italy on cloth, and pliable parchment did not provide an adequate support. It has, inevitably, cracked and peeled in the *Très Belles Heures de Notre-Dame*. It is the improper technique that accounts for the numerous small losses in these miniatures. Of course these difficulties might possibly be ascribed to an experienced illuminator who was making technical experiments, but this hypothesis seems farfetched in general and even more in the present case.

The miniatures were executed as well as designed, then, in the workshop of a painter. The head of this shop was, in our opinion, the author of the *Parement*. He provided drawings for the miniatures, either made expressly for the purpose or furnished out of the 'stock' of the workshop. He participated in the execution of some of the miniatures, working on this small scale in a manner different from his normal one, exemplified by the *Parement*.[65] Some difference in style is apparent as the work proceeded; the colors are less strident in the Passion cycle than in the Hours of the Virgin, and the delineation softer. Miniatures such as *Christ among the Doctors* are cruder, and the *chef* seems to have utilized for much of the execution an assistant who had worked with him for many years, and who possessed a capacity for assimilation and mimicry superior to that of Van Megeren.

Hitherto our discussion of the *Très Belles Heures de Notre-Dame* has been limited to miniatures; we have referred to the borders and the *bas-de-page* only when required by the argument. Any consideration of the procedures adopted in the painting of this manuscript must begin with the design and the iconography of the folio. On all those folios containing miniatures in the Parement style, and in many others that follow this pattern, the subjects of the miniature, of the initial, and of the *bas-de-page* are closely interrelated, and the angels in the borders are deeply involved in the main story. For Matins of the Hours of the Virgin the large miniature is the *Annunciation*, the initial 'D' encloses the Virgin weaving in the temple, the *bas-de-page* shows her marriage, and four angels in the margins bear symbolic flowers, the one at the center above, the lily (Fig. 6). On the folio of the *Nativity* the archangel bringing the tidings to the shepherds, who are in the *bas-de-page*, stands in the initial, while the spaces in the margins are filled with angels bearing scrolls inscribed 'Gloria in excelsis' and similar phrases (Fig. 8).

Integration of the content of a folio is not novel. It was developed at the very beginning of the fourteenth century, especially in the Artois. In a Book of Hours, use of Amiens, in the Walters Art Gallery, Baltimore, executed around 1325, two monks officiate over a coffin in the initial of the Vigils of the Dead. In the border above an angel holds a soul, while devils carry one to hell in the *bas-de-page* (Fig. 563). In the left border there is a miser with a devil, in the right a Knight Templar with a coffin under his arm. In illustrations of this service in other manuscripts of the region the margins may contain bones and skulls,[66] or the *bas-de-page* may show a funeral procession.[67] Pucelle began to unify the folio similarly in his early Book of Hours in the Vatican, where the zodiacal signs and the activities of the months in the Calendar are echoed, often playfully, in the borders.[68] The principle is greatly developed in the Calendar of the *Bréviaire de Belleville* and in several, but not all, the folios illustrating the Hours of the Virgin in the *Heures de Jeanne d'Évreux*.[69] The folio of the *Annunciation to the Shepherds*, for instance, is entirely unified, the main theme extending into the initial, the *bas-de-page*, and the margins (Fig. 338).

The layout of the *Très Belles Heures de Notre-Dame* follows, then, the principle exemplified by the design of certain folios in the *Heures de Jeanne d'Évreux*, a manuscript which belonged to Charles V and then to Jean de Berry.[70] Its designer, unlike Pucelle, applied this principle consistently to all the illumination of the Hours of the Virgin and of other Hours in the manuscript as well. A program of this kind implies a *chef d'atelier*, and there is much evidence to show that the most plausible candidate – the author of the main miniatures – was actually responsible for it.

The *chef* had no part, as Hulin saw, in the actual execution of the initials and the *bas-de-page*. When the text was written the sheets first were given to assistants for the painting of the bars, the vines, and the initials. This task was completed for the entire manuscript, so that ornamental forms of the early 'eighties surround even the famous miniatures in Eyckian style. The next stage was the selection of the subjects for the main miniatures, the corresponding initials and *bas-de-page*, and the margins. The painting of these several areas was carried forward more or less simultaneously, although in the last Hours of the Passion the miniatures lagged so much behind the rest that they were completed by a later master. The most conservative assistant, working in a

I

style derived from the Bondol tradition, had a large share in the execution of the *bas-de-page*, while the assistant responsible for the figures in the initials and for the angels in the borders approximated the style of the *chef* most closely.

Though the enterprise was clearly collaborative, unity of conception is apparent not only in the iconographic program but in the pattern of color on the folios, and frequently the style of the painter of the miniatures affected that of his more conservative collaborators. Gray, blue, light yellow, and hard vermilion are equally distributed throughout the folios, including the miniatures. When the palette is altered in the miniature it is altered correspondingly in the other areas of the folio. The coloristic unity is especially striking on the folio of the *Vigils of the Dead* (Fig. 14). Exactly the same beautiful, transparent gray-black used in the miniature was employed for the mourners in the *bas-de-page*. The other colors of the miniature – blue, white, rose – are repeated similarly. The cloth over the bier – red pattern on a gold ground – is identical in both places. Only the opaque owl disturbs the unity of the folio, and indeed the birds in the border seem to have been added by an illuminator who was not controlled by the main master. Perhaps they were painted a little later. On pages 46 and 56 they seem squeezed into inadequate spaces, and on page 76 the drawing of the bird was never painted.

The angels in the borders around the *Vigils of the Dead* show the usual close stylistic relationship to the miniature. The movement of the uppermost one is especially impressive: the figure bends forward to swing the bell free of the body with a gesture that is affected by the weight of the large object. A beautiful balance is restored to the inclined and burdened figure by the sustaining effect of the opposite arm, which is locked to the girdle, and by the rising beat of a wing. The dynamism and the poise of this little figure reveal the ideas of a major artist, one who had mastered the Italian concepts of bodily structure and statics. Few of the angels in the manuscript reach so high a level, but most of them are similarly articulated and attain through movement a similar equilibrium. In a few instances the angels seem to have been painted by the illuminator who executed the *bas-de-page* (Fig. 17).

The more conservative initials and *bas-de-page* tend to vary between a style much influenced by the Parement Master, as on the folio of the *Annunciation* (Fig. 6), to one more related to the Bondol tradition, as on the folios of the *Visitation* (Fig. 7) or the *Nativity* (Fig. 8). On the *Nativity* folio the landscape in both the miniature and the *bas-de-page* is constructed of a similar series of terraces, and in both it is sprinkled with little plants of similar shape and spacing. These likenesses do not, however, conceal very perceptible differences. The figures in the *bas-de-page* are shorter and squatter, the drapery twists around them in a different way, the gestures are livelier, and the trees are grouped in the characteristic little *boqueteaux*. Not infrequently a figure in a miniature is repeated in the initial or the *bas-de-page* below. The tunic of Christ as he stands before Caiaphas contains the same loops and swirls as Christ's garment in the *bas-de-page* below (Fig. 23). Such precise reflections of the Parement style may also be seen on folios where the miniature has not been painted in this style; for instance, the figures of the Virgin in the initials in the Hours of the Holy Ghost (Figs. 16-21).

4 · TRADITION AND INNOVATION

Most of the miniatures by the Parement Master and his assistant are enclosed by rectangular frames, each painted in slightly variegated shades of gray or pink or green.[71] In the Hours of the Virgin the rectilinear moldings are shaded to simulate stone. Like the similar forms employed by Giotto in the Arena Chapel or Simone Martini in his *Maestà* of 1315, they give the impression of actual window-frames through which one looks at a view beyond. Frames of this kind were adopted in Bohemian illumination, in, for instance, the *Laus Mariae* (Figs. 566, 567) or the *Evangeliary of Johann von Troppau*, of 1368.[72] Earlier French Gothic frames were intended to mediate between the depth of the miniature and the flatness of the page; they fulfilled this function especially well when, as in the *Heures de Jeanne d'Évreux* (Fig. 338), they were drawn in the same color as the script and were left unpainted. The stone frames of the *Très Belles Heures de Notre-Dame*, possessing visible depth themselves, prefigure the illusory space of the miniatures and separate it decisively from the relatively flat expanse of the folio.

The spatial extension announced by the frames is continued immediately inside them, very often by a building that, like structures in Italian paintings, fills, or very nearly fills, the entire area. The progression inward from the lower frame is frequently measured by a tessellated floor, and above by characteristic red bands with white dots that support the boards of the ceiling, as in the *Flagellation* (Fig. 25) or the *Annunciation* (Fig. 6). The perspective of these planes sometimes follows the vanishing axis system; sometimes the orthogonals converge towards a small area, but sometimes also they diverge, as in *Christ before Pilate* (Fig. 24). The buildings are usually placed parallel to the picture plane, so that one sees the inner surface of both side walls, but occasionally (*Christ before Caiaphas* – Fig. 23) one outside wall is visible along with one inside. And in the *Nativity* (Fig. 8) the shed along with several large forms is set oblique to the picture plane. Here, where indices of space such as banded floors or ceilings are lacking, an even deeper extension has been accomplished by a careful overlapping of large forms along a diagonal axis. There is a progression through the wicker fence, the animals, the lively Child, Mary, Joseph, and finally into the landscape. The fence provides a *repoussoir* below, very much like the little crenellations in *Christ before Pilate* (Fig. 24).

The painter owes much to Pucelle and his followers. He frequently uses the form of background filled with heads or busts of angels that was in vogue among painters in that tradition.[73] He exploits a spectacular motif that Pucelle introduced in the borders of his manuscripts at the time of his greatest enthusiasm for Italian painting. In the *Heures de Jeanne d'Évreux*, for instance, figures whose backs are turned to the beholder twist their heads up and back towards the picture plane, so that their faces are strongly foreshortened.[74]

Pucelle adopted here an old stock device, current in Italian manuscripts as early as 1300,[75] and not uncommon in early fourteenth-century Bolognese illumination.[76] In the *Très Belles Heures de Notre-Dame* the formula is applied to an angel below the *Visitation* (Fig. 7). The halo is foreshortened also. Such playful forms are not permitted in the main fields, but in the frieze below the *Nativity* one of the shepherds turns his head into the same impossible position (Fig. 8).[77] On the folio of the *Trinity* an angel in the upper border flies down head foremost towards the large miniature below (Fig. 46). Its head and face are greatly foreshortened, and to avoid concealing them the halo has been omitted. Apparently for consistency haloes are omitted also from the heads of four of the five other angels in the margins. On the folio showing *Christ before Pilate*, however, an angel flying in a rather similar way has been given a partial halo, a sort of metallic circlet around the head, and in the lower margin an angel seen from above wears a similar form around its fluffy hair (Fig. 24).

The *Annunciation*, with Gabriel behind a column in an antechamber and a large lily in front of him, resembles the scene in the *Heures de Jeanne de Navarre*, about 1340 (Figs. 6, 345). The heterogeneous building of the latter, however, has been rationalized; the superstructure has been omitted, and the interior unified. Both side walls of the room are visible, as they were in the *Heures de Jeanne d'Évreux* (Fig. 335). In the miniature by the Parement Master God appears directly opposite the Virgin; it is now possible to place him in a receding plane. Like Duccio and Pucelle the Parement Master permits minor perspective inconsistencies so as to show prominent forms, such as Gabriel's wing, in their entirety. Otherwise his control of the space is firm and, together with the gliding withdrawal of the anxious Virgin, suggests a renewed study of Italian paintings, probably Simonesque. Her gesture – both hands raised, with fingers spread – seems to have been created by the Parement Master, and resembles the similar gesture of one of the Maries in the *Entombment*, though there it communicates grief (Fig. 5).

In one respect the *Annunciation* by the Parement Master differs from its Pucellesque predecessors, and from the usual Italian representation of this scene as well. The building is 'fait en manière de maçonnerie', as simulated tabernacles in embroideries were called at the time.[78] The stone is light pink; there are traceried windows and a small though elaborate façade at the left. All of this gives the building a novel ecclesiastical character. It may be a mere coincidence that a related structure appears in a beautiful panel now in the museum at Aix-en-Provence, but if a suggestion made by the writer several years ago is correct, the painting was in the collection of Louis I d'Anjou at the very time when the *Très Belles Heures de Notre-Dame* was begun.[79] The two works have in common also a drapery spread behind the Virgin, rhomboid units in the moldings and figures in medallions, though in the panel the bust, probably of a prophet, is enclosed by a six-pointed Hebraic star set within the roundel, whereas in the miniature each of the roundels encloses a head seen down to the base of the neck, as in paintings by Giotto and later Italian masters.[80]

It need not be said that, though the miniature and the panel are related in some respects, they are very different in others; one may only point in the panel to the remarkable vaulted space behind the Virgin's chamber or to the figure, perhaps God Father, who seems to soar down from the radiance at the upper left to the Virgin's room.[81] In the Aix panel, as in earlier paintings of the Annunciation in Italy as well as France, the windows are normally dark. Indeed a bright space lying outside an interior was rarely envisaged during the earlier fourteenth century in subjects of any kind, though already in the Arena Chapel Giotto had opened the windows of a simulated chapel – especially the one at the left of the great arch by the master himself – onto a luminous blue sky. The very light blue windows of the miniature of the *Annunciation* herald a new era.

Glass of similar luminosity may be seen in the *Visitation* (Fig. 7) and the *Presentation* (Fig. 10), but not, significantly, in later miniatures such as *Christ among the Doctors* that show, as we have already mentioned, an inferior execution. The brightness of the windows varies in accordance with their relation to the light: the window at the left in the *Presentation* is more greenish than the others, while the one at the right in the *Vigils of the Dead* (Fig. 14), with less green preparation, is more luminous. Attentiveness to light is apparent in the description of the figures and, in the *Visitation* as well as the *Annunciation*, in the conspicuous gradation of the values in the ceiling. The painter has a nascent sense of a light-filled room. The waxen lily glistens, a more luminous version of Pucelle's iris in the *Bréviaire de Belleville* (Fig. 344). And in the *Agony in the Garden* in the initial below the *Betrayal* the terrain and the trees are a gray-green, suggesting dusk if not night (Fig. 22).

In several miniatures in the *Parement* style the figures seem to presuppose, as we have suggested, a study of post-Ducciesque Italian painting. In the *Presentation* the Parement Master, for the first time in France so far as we can nowadays judge, constructs an interior of the kind introduced by Simone Martini in a painting such as the *Obsequies of St. Martin* in Assisi, where the pictorial space is seen through an arcade extending across the picture plane (Figs. 10, 540). His perspective is not as consistent as Simone's (witness the altar!), and he or an assistant permits minor irregularities, as in the placement of the bases of the columns of the arcade. The proportion of figures to building is less naturalistic, not to mention the diameter of the spindly columns, but the general effect of a shallow but vivid space seen through a sort of window has been captured successfully.

The excited recoil of the Child from the bearded priest and the contrapposto that it involves are both developed early in Trecento painting as one of the many infusions of ordinary human behavior into an ostensibly formal ritual. The miniatures of the Parement Master are replete with such less ceremonial, often impulsive actions taken from Italian models.

Elizabeth greets Mary in an interior, an unusual setting for the *Visitation* (Fig. 7). St. Luke, to be sure, said Mary entered into the house of Zacharias (I, 40), but until the mid-fourteenth century the encounter was almost always represented outdoors.[82] Thereafter the house appeared in a very few instances, the most important of which is the miniature in the *Très Belles Heures de Notre-Dame*.[83] The new domestic setting conformed not only with the Gospel but with the *Meditationes Vitae Christi*, of which the Duke, as we shall see, commissioned a French translation that was completed in 1380. An Italian manuscript of this text, with illustrations – probably Pisan – of the second quarter of the century shows the embrace of Mary and Elizabeth in an interior,[84] and immediately thereafter the two, engaged in conversation, sit humbly on the floor of the room (Fig. 532). The Parement Master welcomed the opportunity of measuring the space through use of a tessellated floor, a ribbed wood ceiling, and side walls with doors. He delighted also in the description of luminous windows, which contrasted with adjacent dark openings, and he added a domestic warmth to the chamber by hanging a drapery on the wall and offering a glimpse of a clothes chest in an adjoining room.

The *Coronation of the Virgin* follows neither of the earlier French methods of representing this act: the crown is not lowered on the Virgin's head by a descending angel (Fig. 535), nor does Christ deposit it with his right hand while he holds a globe or scepter in his left.[85] Rather, like Christ in Tuscan (not North Italian) paintings [86] he gives his mother his full attention, abandoning the globe – to a precarious place! – and turning towards her as he fits the crown on her head with both hands (Fig. 13). This scene follows Italian precedent in another respect also. The throne is suspended within an aureole in the heavens, and it follows thus a form of the Coronation that had appeared in Torriti's mosaic of 1296 in S. Maria Maggiore, Rome, and was revived by Florentine and Sienese painters in the 'sixties (Fig. 539).[87] In Italian representations the witnesses below the two main actors stand on what is more or less explicitly described as a ground plane. In the miniature we are clearly confronted with heaven alone; even the two lower angels, who may seem to rest on the frame, are seated on clouds. The celestial Coronation seen through a ring of clouds appeared as early as the *Bréviaire de Belleville* (II, folio 290 verso). In a more naturalistic form and with the throne included, as in the *Très Belles Heures de Notre-Dame*, it may be seen in a miniature of about 1380 by an illuminator who emerged clearly in the 'seventies from the Bondol tradition (Fig. 535).[88] The manuscript, a *Cité de Dieu*, belonged to the Duke of Berry.[89] Related compositions in the *Très Belles Heures de Notre-Dame*, which, like the *Coronation*, show a divine inner realm surrounded by a cloudy heaven, recur in the image of the Savior in the *Heures de Turin* and the *Trinity* in the *Heures de Milan* (Figs. 38, 49).[90] These compositions anticipate the kind of celestial Coronation that appeared in the early fifteenth century, in the *Très Riches Heures*, for instance.[91]

The second *Nativity* in the *Très Belles Heures de Notre-Dame*, illustrating a midnight mass in the *Heures de Milan*, is radically different from the more traditional one in the Hours of the Virgin (Figs. 8, 41), and it reflects very modern Italian ideas.[92] First, however, a word is necessary about the date and authorship of the miniature itself. Though it was ascribed to a later hand by Hulin, it very probably was designed, as Panofsky has observed,[93] by the Parement Master. The pattern of the four angels above is his, not to mention the blue angels in the background and the terraced rocks. The gesture of St. Joseph is like that of the Virgin in the *Annunciation* (Fig. 6). Much of the present surface, however, must be ascribed to the second campaign around 1405. The blue of the Virgin's mantle and the pink of St. Joseph belong to this period. The trees and the landscape at the right as well as the head of the ox seem to be post-Eyckian.[94]

Even more clearly than the *Coronation of the Virgin* the *Nativity* reflects very recent Tuscan innovations. The conception of the Virgin kneeling in adoration, which had appeared in Florentine painting of the beginning of the century, was described in the late thirteenth century in the text of the *Meditations on the Life of Christ* and – what has not been observed – still earlier in the poetry of Jacopone da Todi.[95] The representation of these figures within a cave reflects the vision of the Nativity that St. Bridget had in Rome in 1370. This vision was first embodied in art, probably during the 'seventies, in panels of Niccolò di Tommaso (Fig. 690).[96] Another miniature in the *Très Belles Heures de Notre-Dame* may testify to the same attentiveness to recent Italian conceptions.

At the beginning of the prayers for the Passion of Christ there is a miniature of the *Man of Sorrows* (Fig. 15), an example of one of the great devotional types that was created in Italy in the later thirteenth century and adopted during the fourteenth by the whole of Europe. Its popularity reflected the increasing concern with Christ as a man and with his pain in the world. By the end of the century the image had become so central that it could appear in a Bible at the beginning of a Gospel, replacing a story or the figure of the evangelist.[97] Even a collector of beautiful, precious, and on the whole not very disturbing images such as Jean de Berry possessed numerous representations of the subject on panel and in other media.[98]

In Italian paintings of the Man of Sorrows the vitality of Christ is scarcely impaired by physical death. His body is well preserved, without the scars and wounds visible in the miniature, which derive no doubt from German representations. In Italian paintings Christ frequently appears alone, but he is quite erect in the tomb, sustaining himself by his own strength. This paradoxical image of the independent, erect, but dead Christ was adopted in France soon after the middle of the century; indeed it appears on the altar in miniatures depicting the coronation of King Charles V, painted in 1365.[99] In French paintings of a slightly later date signs of suffering and imminent collapse begin to undermine the noble poise of the Italian prototypes (Fig. 545). In Italy itself there was a second type of representation in which Christ is given more support. In Tuscany the Virgin and St. John, or more rarely two angels, hold Christ's arms,[100] but it was, characteristically, in North Italy that the conception of a dignified Christ, independent and strong in death, gave way to a more pathetic image in which he is sustained by the embrace of the Virgin Mary. The earliest extant example of this type is a panel in the Longhi collection, Florence, painted by Vitale da Bologna around the middle of the century (Fig. 546). Later the image appeared in the circle of Altichiero (Fig. 547),[101] and around 1400 in a miniature by a North Italian illuminator working in France (Fig. 809). The Parement miniature, with an angel at both sides, stands between the older Italian and the fully developed French type, in which an angel, rather than the Virgin, supports Christ from behind. This French form, known from a document as early as 1383,[102] may be seen again in the beautiful enamel in the Rijksmuseum, Amsterdam (Fig. 572). It becomes standard in France and was, indeed, transmitted back to Spain and Italy.[103]

The miniature by the Parement Master is one of his most imposing. The large figures that incline their heads to one side or another appear before a rigid pattern of verticals and horizontals. More solid and articulated than the figures of Vitale, Christ and the angels are placed in a shallow space that is measured by the cross behind them and the drapery slung from one side frame to the other. The drapery is a novel form that enhances the impression of the continuity of space beyond what is actually represented, the figures continuing downward while the cross passes behind the lateral frames. The impact of the work is greatly heightened by extending Christ's free, waving arms before the drapery into, it seems, the real space occupied by the observer. The kind of vivid illusionism of which the stone frames are elements here reaches its most daring level. The painter might have seen a drapery pinned to the frame in one of those Tuscan Coronations that gave him ideas of other kinds, although there the stuff moves back into a plane behind the figures (Fig. 539). The effect of the cloth in the *Très Belles Heures de Notre-Dame* is more like that of the low parapets in early fifteenth-century painting (Jan van Eyck or Gentile da Fabriano),[104] or Mantegna's festoons that swing across the surface in the picture plane. In any event it proved a fruitful idea for subsequent French painting, as we shall see.[105]

The drapery spread across the lower space of the *Man of Sorrows* represents a significant technical innovation also. The ground of this form is gold leaf. A dark green paint was laid over the gold, reserving the shapes of the vine and the flowers. Over the four-petalled flowers the painter then laid a light red glaze, perhaps in a vehicle of oil, and quite transparent. This technique was employed earlier in France and especially in Italy for small details. It began to be exploited on a larger scale in the last quarter of the century, in France as we see here, and in Lombardy (Figs. 578, 579). Its wide use was only one consequence of the growing fascination of the period with the phenomena of reflection, transparency, and translucency. To this we shall return in the following chapter.

In still another subject the Parement Master, even when close to Italian models, did not fail to introduce novel forms of his own. The group of the Virgin, Christ, and St. John in the *bas-de-page* below the *Deposition* has often been discussed, especially by Panofsky,[106] as the earliest example in France of a new form of Lamentation (Fig. 28). Though the *bas-de-page* was executed by an assistant, the ideas and perhaps a summary drawing must be ascribed to the Parement Master. The mantle of the first Mary to the right of the group almost repeats that of the Virgin in the *Deposition* above, presumably designed by the original *chef d'atelier*. Insofar as the Virgin is seated on the ground with Christ in her lap, the group resembles the Italian type of *Vesperbild*. This resemblance, and the novel aspects of the French composition, will be discussed in Chapter VIII.[107]

Nothing tells us more about the depth of the Parement Master's understanding of Tuscan art than the *Adoration of the Magi* (Fig. 9). The initial decision to portray the Virgin at the glorious moment of the Epiphany in the humble position and in the simple setting of the Nativity had been made early in the Trecento in Tuscany.[108] The significance of the innovation is conveyed by the words of the *Meditations on the Life of Christ*: 'You see how great was their [i.e., the Kings'] faith, which asked them to believe that this Child, so scantily clothed and found with his poor mother in so wretched a place, with no attendants or family, and lacking all furnishings, was King and true God.'[109] The new iconography, showing the Virgin on her mattress and often under a shed, was adopted by French illuminators in, for instance, the *Bible of Charles V* (Fig. 386) and the *Douce Missal*.[110]

The Parement Master, taking this homely scene, has imposed on it an almost Tuscan geometry, arranging the figures along the sides of an inverted triangle, the kneeling King at its apex. In earlier French representations of the Adoration, furthermore, while the oldest Magus knelt before the Child either to kiss his foot or to offer him a gift, the second usually pointed to him or to the star, and the third gestured in response. In the *Très Belles Heures de Notre-Dame* the action of the three Kings has been rationalized in a deeply Tuscan sense. The oldest has already given his chalice to the Child; Joseph, in fact, now more active as *pater familiae*, carefully stows it away in a box.[111] This King, on his knees, holds his crown with one hand[112] and the hand of the Child with the other, while he prepares to kiss it. The next King, still standing, begins to doff his crown and bends forward eagerly, extending his gift toward the Child. The youngest, holding his gift, stands quietly by awaiting his turn. The action unfolds in successive stages, exhibiting a regular cinematic progression of the sort that, introduced in the Trecento, became prominent in early Renaissance art from Masaccio onward.[113]

In the miniature the oldest King is about to kiss the hand of Christ, and this show of humble affection calls for some comment. The idea of signalizing this first great moment of public homage in the life of Christ by the bestowal of a kiss may be found in the *Meditations*.[114] Representations of a Magus kissing Christ's feet began to appear in the later thirteenth century, rarely in France[115] but commonly in Italy after Nicola Pisano's pulpit of 1265–1268 in the Cathedral of Siena. This action was adopted by Pucelle, beginning with the *Bréviaire de Belleville*, and by his followers, including the Passion Master (Fig. 367).[116] There was, on the other hand, another tradition in which the Magus kissed a hand rather than a foot. This may be encountered as early as the twelfth century in France,[117] and the famous *Meditations* describes the two actions, one succeeding the other: '. . . with reverence and devotion they [the Magi] kissed his feet. Perhaps at this the judicious Child gave them his hand to kiss and blessed them.'[118] It was in Bohemian painting around the middle of the fourteenth century that this second, less humble action of the oldest King was especially favored (Fig. 568).[119] Once again, then, we encounter a relationship of the Parement Master with Bohemia.

5 · THE NUDE FIGURE

The connection observed above of miniatures by the Parement Master with Bohemian painting extends to the decision to allow the Child to appear quite nude at the ceremonial occasion of the homage of the Magi (Figs. 551, 568). In some French examples of the Adoration before the *Très Belles Heures de Notre-Dame* the Child was, to be sure, technically nude, that is he wore no clothing, but he was more or less wrapped in the Virgin's mantle. This initial stage in the French trend toward nudity may be seen in that great nexus of innovations, the *Heures de Pucelle*.[120] The unclothed, uncovered Child in the Adoration of the Magi that appeared relatively early in Bohemian painting was soon adopted in other schools. Meister Bertram carried it, along with other Bohemian innovations, to northwest Germany. The nude Infant appeared in his altarpiece of 1379 in Hamburg and in other paintings of the region,[121] and around this time it became popular also in Lombardy.[122] In France, after the *Très Belles Heures de Notre-Dame*, the figure was adopted by most of the leading illuminators, beginning with the approximately contemporary *Petites Heures* (Fig. 93).

It was not only the Christ Child when adored by the Magi whom certain centers in the later fourteenth century wished to see nude. Traditionally Christ was of course always nude in the Baptism, often in the Nativity and the Presentation in the Temple, but rarely in the Flight into Egypt[123] and in the cult image of the Madonna. These innovations seem in large part inspired by a desire for the visualization of Christ as a baby, but there are a few other very unusual nude figures that suggest a broader concern with the unclothed body. In the impressive Catalan altarpiece in the Morgan Library, New York, painted about 1355–1360 by the Master of St. Mark (very probably Arnau Bassa) Christ hangs on the cross completely nude (Fig. 559).[124] This nakedness is, to be sure, inspired by the text of the *Meditations*; the veil in the Virgin's hands proves that. When Christ is stripped of his garments before ascending the cross, the Virgin 'is saddened and shamed beyond measure when she sees Him entirely nude; they did not leave Him even His loincloth. Therefore she hurries and approaches the Son, embraces Him, and girds Him with the veil from her head.'[125] At the birth of Christ she had wrapped him in her veil,[126] so that once again – as in the Madonna of Humility and the Man of Sorrows or *Vesperbild* and many other subjects – events at the beginning and the end of Christ's life are paralleled.

Though the text of the *Meditations* was written in Italy in the late thirteenth century, and though many of its images had an almost immediate effect upon Italian art, the nude Christ in the Cruci-fixion began to be represented, so far as I can see, only towards the middle of the fourteenth century, and outside Italy. In an English picture Bible in London the Virgin wraps her kerchief around Christ's loins,[127] and in an early fifteenth-century Parisian miniature Christ is naked on the cross. In this manuscript he is naked in the *Entombment* also.[128]

In the 'seventies and 'eighties there are more startling instances of nudity, unprepared, it seems, by religious texts, but reflecting the habit of sleeping without clothes. At the moment of parturi-tion in the superb altarpiece from Schloss Tirol, painted between 1370 and 1372, only the lower half of the Virgin's body is covered, while the upper is rendered with the tender sensuousness of a Renaissance Venus (Fig. 557).[129] In the scene of the *Birth of the Virgin*, on the other hand, in a Lombard miniature of the 'eighties, it is a remarkably youthful St. Anne who is represented in a similar way (Fig. 558).[130]

The nude Child in the cult image of the Madonna is the most widely diffused of these new forms, in sculpture as well as in painting. Though I cannot claim to have made a thorough survey of the countless representations, it seems possible to detect a pattern in the history of the appearance and diffusion of the nude infant. In the cult image of the Madonna, as in the Adoration of the Magi, the Child appeared without any clothes of his own with increasing frequency from the beginning of the fourteenth century, both south and north of the Alps. For about half a century, however, this technically naked Child was partly covered by the Madonna's mantle or veil.[131] Examples of the completely exposed Child were much rarer; perhaps the earliest, if we may trust a seventeenth-century drawing, was the *Madonna* of about 1250 on the screen of the Cathedral of Strasbourg.[132] In painting the figure appeared at the very beginning of the fourteenth century in a manuscript formerly in the Dyson-Perrins collection, illuminated in Metz, not far from Strasbourg (Fig. 548).[133] It was in Metz also, just after the middle of the century, that the naked Child was intro-duced into the theme of the Madonna of Humility (Figs. 549, 550).[134] The examples of this particular manifestation of nudism are especially conspicuous because in this version of the Madonna the new figure did not become very popular.

In view of the special predilection for the nude Child in Lorraine and perhaps also in neighboring Alsace (Strasbourg), it is interesting to recall that Metz possessed a venerated image of the 'Madonna' holding on one arm an unclothed child (Fig. 453). This monumental relief, now in the collection of Raymond Pitcairn in Bryn Athyn, Pennsylvania, was once in the church of St. Gangolf or Gengoulf, and later in a courtyard at no. 28, Rue St. Gengoulf.[135] Some recent scholars have suggested, probably correctly, that it originally was a twelfth-century tomb-relief of a mother and a child,[136] but in the late Middle Ages, and indeed until the end of the nineteenth century, it was regarded without question as a Madonna and Child.[137] The motif of the bared breast must have made this image seem all the more strange and impressive around 1300. It is worth noting, in any event, that the novel Metz version of the Madonna of Humility combines nudity with the act of suckling (Figs. 549, 550).

In the third quarter of the century the nude Child began to appear in Madonnas painted in a great center rather far to the east of Metz. One of the earliest examples, the famous panel commissioned just after 1370 by the Archbishop of Prague, shows a resemblance with the Metz relief, perhaps fortuitous but worth mentioning (Fig. 552).[138] The Virgin holds a piece of fruit in the panel just as she holds her breast in the relief, and the posture of the Child is rather similar. In both works the Virgin wears a rope-like girdle. There would seem, on the whole, sufficient evidence to warrant an investigation of the Metz relief as the object of a special cult. At most, however, this sculpture would have given a religious impulse to what was a growing interest during the course of the fourteenth century in the portrayal of an infant Christ. In this broader context infancy is associated, on naturalistic grounds, with both nudity and nursing.

The nude child in the lap of a mother with bared breast appears in the *Très Belles Heures de Notre-Dame* (Fig. 50). Around the same time, or a few years later, the figure was adopted by Lombard illuminators. One instance is in the Missal in Paris, illuminated before 1395 (Fig. 560), which, as we have seen, introduced a nude St. Catherine and a semi-nude St. Anne (Fig. 558).[139] The nude infant Christ, then, seems to have become popular early in Lorraine and Alsace, later in Bohemia, and in the last quarter of the century in Lombardy and in metropolitan France.

Conspicuously absent from this development are the great Tuscan centers. There the figure appeared much later, in Masaccio's Madonnas of about 1424 in the Uffizi and 1426 in London, as well as in the paintings of masters influenced by him.[140] Thus it is associated in Florentine painting with the new art. It is a striking fact that the first Florentine nude Child, in the Uffizi *Madonna*, resembles closely an Etruscan bronze, and was probably based upon it (Figs. 555, 556).[141] Evidently the nudity of the Christ Child was acceptable to the Florentines only when it assumed a classical, indeed pagan form – a rather paradoxical situation. As everyone knows, Florentine artists at this time, chiefly Florentine sculptors, were endowing the nude figure once again with the highest values. If we apply Kenneth Clark's distinction to the early history of the unclothed Child, we will say that Masaccio's figure was the first *nude* Christ; all the earlier figures were simply naked.[142] But such a distinction, while it sheds much light on the course of the development, at the same time tends to blur some aspects of it. For when designing a nude Child Masaccio, like almost all early Renaissance artists, did not really seek to emulate the poise and noble detachment of antiquity, and the Child of the Parement Master, on the other hand, could not have been conceived without the heritage of Greece and Rome – transmitted, of course, through Byzantium and Trecento Italy. Perhaps, then, these two stages in the evolution of an important new form were not really as distinct as we often suppose. We know that the delicately sensuous nudes of the Limbourgs – the Zodiacal Man, Eve in the Garden, St. Catherine in the *Belles Heures* – impressed Pisanello and other North Italian masters. Nature or the Synagogue on the Duke's medal may have been known to them also (Fig. 463). The Florentines were undoubtedly familiar with these advances. If the now famous *Madonna* dated 1422 with a Child wrapped in a filmy veil is Masaccio's, as the writer believes it must be (Fig. 554), he approached the new form without the sanction of

Greece and Rome or the benefit of their exalting patterns. This is not to say that antiquity was not vital to Florence. Indeed, if it had not existed the Florentines would have had to invent it, or remain barren in the visual arts.

In the *Très Belles Heures de Notre-Dame* (Fig. 50) the Child, lying on the Virgin's leg and arm, is large in the Italian manner and he puts a finger to his lips like the Infant in Ambrogio Lorenzetti's *Presentation in the Temple*.[143] In the miniature a jet of milk streams from the Virgin's breast, but it is not entirely clear for whom it is intended. The Child does not prepare to suckle, and the milk seems directed more at the kneeling donor than at the Child. There are many medieval legends of such supernatural or symbolic occurrences, in which the Virgin gives milk to various persons, especially monks, including St. Bernard.[144] In such cases she enacts one of the roles – *nutrix omnium* – which is ascribed to her in the Madonna of Humility. These miracles are visually and in some other respects related to the *Caritas Romana* which, described by Boccaccio in his *De Mulieribus Claris*, began to be represented at the turn of the century when this text was fully illustrated – for the first time – in France (Fig. 561). The *Caritas Romana* became a familiar Renaissance subject, but the miracles of the Virgin giving milk, nowhere frequently represented, seem to be especially scarce in Italy and Tuscany, and we may perhaps once again see a sequence in which a highly physical subject first became acceptable to central Italian culture in an antique guise.

There are several fourteenth-century representations of the *Virgo lactifera*, the most beautiful being two miniatures in the *Miracles de la Vierge* by Pucelle and his workshop (Fig. 562).[145] The healing, conversion, or intermediation effected in these miracles were more frequently accomplished in late medieval art without lactation. The Virgin merely displays her uncovered breast, often when accompanied by Christ displaying his wounds, both of them thus demonstrating their power as intercessors before God.[146] It is in this capacity that the Virgin appears to a Burgundian prince in Philip the Bold's Book of Hours in the Fitzwilliam Museum, Cambridge (Fig. 564). This miniature was not painted much earlier than the one in the *Très Belles Heures de Notre-Dame*. The prayer written below the latter reads '. . . dei genetrix intercede pro nobis. . . .' One of the women in the group in the *bas-de-page* holds a scroll reading 'beatus venter qui te portavit', and Christ says 'beati qui audiunt. . . .'

The iconography of the miniature in the *Très Belles Heures de Notre-Dame* is quite complex, including lactation on the one hand and on the other the 'coronation' of both the Virgin and Christ, who receives a triple tiara. The identity of the figure in the red garment toward whom the Virgin looks is not clear. The most plausible candidate would of course be Jean de Berry, and we should recall that the Duke, who owned relics of his patron saints Andrew and John the Baptist, also had two cruets of the Virgin's milk.[147] There are, however, iconographic difficulties; this clean-shaven man with brown hair does not look like the Duke, and no arms are visible. The great stone throne with its multi-colored inlay is a characteristic innovation of the Parement Master. It is reminiscent of the furniture of the Cosmati in Italy, and also of the Bohemian painters of the third quarter of the century.

A special devotion of Jean de Berry probably accounts for the very unusual introduction of the Marriage at Cana at Vespers in the Hours of the Virgin (Fig. 12). The Marriage together with the

Multiplication of the Loaves and Fishes that appears below normally symbolizes the Eucharist. It therefore was rarely chosen for the Hours of the Virgin,[148] but it appears again (at Compline) in the *Grandes Heures* (Fig. 235). Possibly in these miniatures the scene refers to the marriage of Christ with the Church, the water of the Old Testament transformed into the wine of the Gospels and the Synagogue replaced by *Ecclesia*. In the nineteenth century a yellow agate cup from the Duke's Sainte-Chapelle was said to be a relic of the Marriage at Cana (Fig. 472), but its shape does not resemble other goblets that were associated with this scene.[149] No such object, moreover, is identifiable in either miniature; the three wine glasses are all alike. In the *bas-de-page* below the Parement miniature, however, a youth drinks from a conspicuously large gilt goblet. This cup, not traditional in this scene of eating rather than drinking, is on the other hand lacking in a later representation of the subject included in a Book of Hours for the Duke, the *Très Riches Heures*.[150]

The story is told in the Byzantine manner, with the Virgin alongside Christ interceding for the wine-less party, and the bride in the middle.[151] In the usual Byzantine composition, and in later Italian representations that derive from it, such as the frescoes in the Upper Church, Assisi, and in the Arena Chapel, Christ is seated at the left. In the miniature, however, the figures are reversed. It is notable that the window behind Christ is not only larger and more elaborate than the others, but much brighter. The building, with its tiled floor and triple arch, resembles that of the *Annunciation*, and, as in that miniature, the spatial construction, though advanced, contains some confused passages. The table top at the left overlaps the shaft of the building while the table legs are set rather deep in the space, and one leg of the kneeling servant extends over an improbable distance, the foot seemingly ending – like the hands of Christ in the *Imago Pietatis* (Fig. 15) – in actual space before the picture plane.

In addition to the miniatures by the Parement Master and his assistant there are in the *Très Belles Heures de Notre-Dame* several that were begun by him but completed some twenty years later. Hulin recognized that the last three scenes in the Hours of the Passion were begun by the Parement Master (Figs. 26-28), although he overlooked his role in the *Adoration of the Child* (Fig. 41). These scenes, as we have observed, show the compositions of the Parement Master and even tiny characteristic details such as the little plants sprouting from the rocks, yet they attain to a luminosity that is foreign to his art. In the *Deposition* (Fig. 28) the deep blue of the angel background and the gray of the foreground rocks are colors constantly employed by the Parement Master; the more distant rocks show his typical shapes also, but the green finish must be ascribed to a later illuminator, whom we shall recognize in several miniatures in the manuscript, including two notable representations of the Baptist (Figs. 16, 29). He may therefore be designated 'the Baptist Master'. His luminous, slightly bluish green hues with yellow shades recur throughout these Passion scenes.[152] Concerned with pictorial qualities, he had little interest in the great accomplishments of the Parement Master in constructing the figure, and where the painting or drawing by this master was not crystal clear he allowed contradictions to appear. The falling body of the Virgin in the *Crucifixion*, for example, is not adequately supported either aesthetically, in the design, or naturalistically, by the figure of the Mary who hovers over her.

Two figures in the *Crucifixion* demonstrate with great clarity the relationship of this group of miniatures to the Parement Master. The seated St. John resembles the corresponding figure in the *Parement* (Fig. 1), and differences such as the lowered position of the hands and the drapery wrapped around the arm seem in keeping with the later style of the Parement Master. The same figure – except for the lack of bare sole – appeared in the *Crucifixion* by Pseudo-Jacquemart in the *Petites Heures* (Fig. 97) and again around 1400 in a miniature by a master who was in touch with the Duke's illuminators (Fig. 533). Pseudo-Jacquemart either drew from another, lost work of the Parement Master or he knew the drawing for the *Crucifixion* in the *Très Belles Heures de Notre-Dame*. The latter alternative is preferable because the swooning Virgin in another Crucifixion by him is completely dependent on the Parement Master – the tubular folds prove that – and identical with the figure in the *Très Belles Heures de Notre-Dame* (Figs. 27, 172). The preparation of this miniature by the Parement Master must therefore have been the source.

The *Lord Enthroned*, originally in the *Heures de Turin* and now in the Louvre, was, like the group of miniatures just discussed, begun by the Parement Master and completed by another hand, though not by the same illuminator (Fig. 36).[153] One need only compare the design of the stones inlaid in the throne with the corresponding patterns in the *Virgin Enthroned* (Fig. 50) or *Christ in Heaven* (Fig. 38) to recognize the inferiority of the Louvre miniature. Two of the three music-making angels in the *bas-de-page* of this folio are virtually identical with those below Christ in Heaven, but much stronger. It should be added that this folio has been even more retouched than the *Virgin and St. John*, likewise in the Louvre (Fig. 37). These sheets, detached from the book, have been subjected to the normal fate of panels and other independent paintings. The contrast in the state of preservation reminds us of one of the rewards of the study of illumination.

6 · CONNECTIONS WITH BOHEMIA

The attempt to define the uniqueness of the illumination of the *Très Belles Heures de Notre-Dame* has led us to refer not only to Pucelle and his followers in France and to Trecento panels or murals but to painting in Bohemia as well. Indeed it is the relationship with this last art that tends to differentiate the miniatures from the *Parement* itself. Apart from iconographic and architectural similarities the kinship is subtle and not easily defined. It resides partly in the somewhat greater fleshiness of the figures and in the physiognomic variety (Figs. 566, 567). The greater suppleness of the bodies in the *Très Belles Heures de Notre-Dame*, responding to the curvatures of the composition at the sacrifice of their own structure, similarly connects them with Bohemian conventions. The predilection for the nude Christ Child, apparent in the miniatures of the *Adoration of the Magi* (Fig. 9) and the *Madonna Enthroned* (Fig. 50), joins the two arts. The Magus kissing the hand rather than the foot of the Child is common to both. Bohemian illuminators, twenty years earlier than the *Très Belles Heures de Notre-Dame*, employed frames simulating stone. Their elaborate architecture contained numerous details that appear in the miniatures of the Parement Master: lozenges and disks as units of ornament, *cosmati* inlay, and round projections as at the front of the base of the Virgin's throne (Figs. 566, 567).

The observation of these relationships is important for two reasons. In the first place it helps to define the differences between the *Parement* and the miniatures in the *Très Belles Heures de Notre-Dame*. In no case does the influence of Bohemian painting seem to have reshaped the art of the Parement Master fundamentally; rather it led to the development of qualities already present. In the second place it confirms the early date of the miniatures, at the beginning of the 'eighties. For the Bohemian style that the Parement Master admired was formed just after the middle of the century, and by the 'seventies it had been overshadowed by another style, best exemplified by the murals of Master Theodoric in Karlštejn.[154] With this next, ectoplastic Bohemian phase the *Très Belles Heures de Notre-Dame* seems to have little or no connection. If the manuscript had actually been illuminated as late as the early fifteenth century, could one so easily account for an interest in Bohemian art of about 1360?

The fact that a major French master of the 'seventies and 'eighties should have studied Bohemian painting of a decade or two earlier is not surprising, because just after the middle of the century the style created in Prague was the most advanced in northern Europe. To be advanced in this part of Europe around 1350 meant in large part to have approximated Italian pictorial principles, and this the painters of Prague did more than their fellow craftsmen elsewhere north of the Alps. They were stimulated in this endeavor by the great patrons of painting, Charles IV, King of Bohemia and Holy Roman Emperor, and his chancellor Johann von Neumarkt. The city of Prague was transformed by Charles from a rather provincial center into one of the liveliest and most cosmopolitan capitals in Europe. The King brought architects from France, where he had spent his early years, and the great architect and sculptor Parler from Schwäbisch Gmünd (Fig. 592). He modeled his new palace on the Louvre, and he built Karlštejn as a French burg. He and his chancellor were deeply impressed by the writing of Petrarch. Johann von Neumarkt corresponded with him, and he and the Emperor met him when they were in Italy in 1354. They wished to bring him to Prague. They recognized the primacy of Italy in painting as well as in Latin literature, they acquired altarpieces by Tommaso da Modena, and, as we observed above, they brought one Italian master to their capital.

The new forms created in Prague around 1350 were unequalled in northern Europe for their approximation to Trecento painting. The *Madonna* in Boston,[155] the Morgan and Vyšši Brod panels (Fig. 568),[156] and the miniatures of the *Laus Mariae* (before 1364) are unique in their period. The miniatures, with their simulated stone frames, look like transpositions of a diptych to the pages of a book (Figs. 566, 567). They are exceptional even in Bohemia, and they may well be the work of the painter responsible for the Boston and Morgan panels. Other manuscripts, however, such as the *Liber Viaticus* of Johann von Neumarkt, are scarcely less Italianate.[157]

Given the advanced nature and the distinction of this school of Bohemian painting, it is understandable that a major French master should have studied it with profit. It offered, among other things, a continentalized version, and therefore a more comprehensible one, of peninsular style. In the *Parement de Narbonne*, however, the painter had demonstrated his capacity to come to terms with Italian originals. From this point of view the miniatures in the *Très Belles Heures de*

Notre-Dame might seem more explicable if they were dated earlier than the *Parement* and considered a first step in the Italianization of the master's style, but our analysis of the relationship of the two works makes this chronology very improbable. It was thus the Northern, indeed the Bohemian, ingredient in the Prague amalgam that attracted the Parement Master, and it was precisely the more realistic version of Italian style, as we have described it, that he wished to emulate. Perhaps an historical event promoted the artistic impulse. In 1378 Charles IV visited Paris, where he was received by the Dukes of Berry and Burgundy.[158] As usual on such occasions, gifts were exchanged (Fig. 565); we know he was offered two manuscripts, and he no doubt gave some in return.

In the light of the relationship with Bohemian painting of the miniatures in the *Très Belles Heures de Notre-Dame* it is interesting to consider a drawing of an archer in Christ Church, Oxford. This drawing, often vaguely called Sienese, has recently been attributed to the Parement Master by Otto Pächt (Fig. 569).[159] At first glance the resemblance of this archer with a figure by the Parement Master such as the averted scourger may seem decisive (Fig. 3). The two figures have much in common: tubular drapery folds, finely graduated chiaroscuro, spindly legs, a sharp profile. On closer scrutiny, however, the archer proves lacking in that degree of bodily articulation which is so fundamental to the art of the Parement Master. The mass of the figure has an impressive fluency, but not an equally impressive structure. The features, unlike those of the Parement Master, are applied to the head rather than built into it. The crown of the hat has neither the roundness nor the vigorous outlines of the *Parement* headgear.

The huge locks of hair that sprout unbelievably from the head are so voluminous and so animated that they would seem more appropriate to Samson than to an anonymous archer. Though the hair of the figures in the *Parement* frequently falls into circlets and curling locks, it never approaches the archer's in weight and mass. In one European center, however, the rendition of such hirsute abundance was not simply the obsession of one painter but of an entire culture. In Bohemian painting innumerable figures, female as well as male, wear bushy manes like the archer's (Fig. 568).[160] The tradition was firmly established by the middle of the century, and was maintained in many workshops for several decades. It was in one of these that the archer, which in all other respects shows Bohemian qualities also, was drawn.

The painter Jean d'Orléans has sometimes been proposed as the author of the *Parement* because he served as *pictor regis* during the period when it was executed. He was apparently an outstanding master; as early as 1364 he was called by Charles V 'nostre amé paintre et vallet de chambre'.[161] He remained in the royal service for many years, and in 1391 his name appeared at the top of the list of painters, sculptors and illuminators who formed a new craft society distinct from the guild of saddlers to which the painters belonged.[162] In 1371 the Duke of Berry visited the workshop of Jean d'Orléans to see some paintings, and left large gratuities for his 'valets'.[163] Dufour, Champeaux and Gauchery, and others believed that this painter, whose career had begun before 1364, entered the employ of the Duke in the early fifteenth century, but the documents on which they based this view probably refer to another master of the same name, sometimes called Jean Grancher d'Orléans.[164] It is true, however, that the Duke was interested in the King's painter in 1371, and in the early 'eighties he may have persuaded Charles VI, a new and not very demanding patron, to free his painter for the task of illuminating the *Très Belles Heures de Notre-Dame*.

This identification is merely speculative. It is, however, certain that the Parement Master was the foremost painter of his day. It is clear also that the *chef d'atelier* of the first campaign to embellish the *Très Belles Heures de Notre-Dame* was a painter rather than an illuminator.[165] He had no followers, in the narrow sense of the term, in the art of illumination. The imitation of his work in later miniatures of the *Très Belles Heures de Notre-Dame* and of the *Grandes Heures*, which will be discussed in subsequent chapters, constitutes a very different case. The technique of the Parement Master in the miniatures was more characteristic of a panel painter than of an illuminator. He employed a much thicker film of paint than the Limbourgs in this same manuscript.

Though the Parement Master trained no illuminators his work nevertheless had a deep effect upon the art and no doubt upon more monumental painting as well. He did for French painting in the 'seventies what Jean Pucelle had done in the 'twenties: he enriched it by importing the accomplishments of the Italian Trecento in the representation of tri-dimensional space and of an organic figure – a figure self-motivated and endowed with an emotional as well as intellectual 'personality'. Unlike Pucelle, the Parement Master was not alone in his time as a close student of Italian painting. The Passion Master, as we shall see, shared his interest though not his understanding. The Parement Master, again unlike Pucelle, was followed at brief intervals by other major painters who were equally oriented towards Italy: Jacquemart de Hesdin and the Limbourgs. He was thus the initiator of a movement in the last quarter of the century that carried the assimilation of Italian forms to a progressively higher level. These later masters did not, however, seek only to acquire a greater mastery of Italian pictorial principles; they were equally concerned with the development of the non-Italian aspects of the style of the Parement Master. In the *Adoration of the Magi* (Fig. 9), for instance, they were impressed not only by the geometry of the design, the repertory of postures, and the rationality of the narrative, but also by the distant trees rising just above the shed. The painting of the Parement Master contained, in other words, provocative ideas about the representation of landscape. His portrayal of openings into these spaces, his luminous windows especially, revealed the new dimension provided by light. These were two of the realms in which French painting was destined shortly to take the lead in Europe.

K

'TRÈS BELLES HEURES DE NOTRE-DAME'
TABLE OF THE WORKS OF THE PAINTERS DISCUSSED IN THE TEXT

First Campaign. Early 'eighties. (Hulin: Hand A, 1380–1390).

1. Master A. The Master of the *Parement de Narbonne.*

The first director of the illumination. He established the design of the folios, fixed the subjects, and probably provided indications for the marginal figures as well as the miniatures, the initials and the *bas-de-pages.* The vines in almost all the borders of the manuscript were executed at the outset under his direction. He probably painted the first miniatures in the Paris section. For the later miniatures especially he had an excellent assistant who had previously worked with him for many years. The style of the angels in the borders is close to that of the miniatures. The initials and the friezes are generally more conservative. Many are still connected with the Bondol tradition while some resemble the early work of the Pseudo-Jacquemart. A few reflect the Parement style, for instance the initial on p. 162 and the frieze on p. 62 in the Paris section. Hulin ascribed all this work to his hand A bis, but at least two illuminators seem to have been responsible for it.

These assistants worked on the following folios (the Paris section only is paginated):

Paris Section: 2 (except for portrait of lady), 28, 42, 50, 56, 62, 68, 76, 104, 155 (except the initial), 162, 166, 169, 173, 176, 178, 181, 189, 194, 197, 203, 209, 216.
Heures de Milan: 4v., 87, 120, and the vines only on many folios.
Heures de Turin: 39v. and the vines only on many folios.
Louvre: *The Lord Enthroned* and the *Virgin and St. John the Evangelist,* both damaged and retouched.

A with assistants executed the following miniatures:

Paris Section: 2, 28, 42, 50, 56, 62, 68, 76, 104, 155, 181, 189, 194, 203.
Heures de Milan: 87v. (*Trinity*) – retouched, 120 (*Madonna Enthroned*).
Heures de Turin: 39v. (*Christ Enthroned*).

A also drew in and partly painted the following miniatures:

Paris Section: 203 (*Way to Calvary*), 209 (*Crucifixion*) 216 (*Deposition*), all finished by B.
Heures de Milan: 4v. (*Adoration of the Child*) – finished by B and a post-Eyckian illuminator.

Second Campaign. Probably beginning 1405, but certainly before 1409.

2. Master B. 'The Baptist Master.' Flemish. Before 1409. (Hulin: Hand B, 1402–1405, and Hand C, 1410–1412).
Paris Section: 162 (*Baptism*) – figures of Christ and upper part of Baptist only; the rest by C; 203 (*Way to Calvary*), 209 (*Crucifixion*) but center of terrain by A, 216 (*Deposition*); all three over a drawing and partial painting by A.
Heures de Milan: 1v. (*Annunciation*), 4v. (*Adoration of the Child*) – over a miniature partly executed by A, 20v. (*Entry into Jerusalem*), 84v. (*Pentecost*) – begun by A, 90 (*Last Supper*), 122 (*Martyrdom of St. Andrew*) – begun by A – omitted by Hulin.
Heures de Turin: 57 (*St. John the Baptist in the Desert*), 57v. (*Prophets and Apostles*), 58 (*Christ in House of Simon*), 78v. (*Madonna Enthroned*), 80v. (*St. Jerome in his Study*).
Louvre: *Martyrdom of Saints, Holy Confessors.*

3. Master C. The Master of the Hours of the Holy Ghost. A follower of André Beauneveu. Before 1409 (Hulin: Hand D, after 1412).
Paris Section: Hours of the Holy Ghost: 162 (*Baptism*) – but Christ and upper part of the Baptist by B, 166 (*Pentecost*), 169 (*Resurrection of the Dead*), 173 (*The Faithful before the Holy Ghost*), 176 (*The Unbelievers*), 178 (*Dispersion of the Apostles*).

4. Master D. Later imitator of A, and reworking his designs.
Heures de Milan: 13v. (*Adoration of the Magi*), 16v. (*Presentation in the Temple*), 80v. (*Ascension*), 100v. (*Coronation of the Virgin*) – probably begun by A, 103 (*Birth of the Virgin*), 106 (*St. Michael*).

5. The Limbourgs.
Paris Section: p. 225 (*Adoration of the Trinity.* Initial: *Creation of Eve.* Bas-de-page: *Creation of the World*). p. 240 (*Faithful praying to Angels and God.* Initial: *Anthony and Lion.* Bas-de-page: *Anthony visiting Paul*). At end of ms. (?): Illustration of Itinerary (Fig. 497 – after lithograph of Bastard).
The Eyckian and later Netherlandish miniatures lie outside the scope of this book.

VII

Beauneveu and the Duke's Psalter

1·THE PROPHETS AND APOSTLES

OVER half a century ago Leopold Delisle identified a beautiful Psalter in the Bibliothèque nationale that belonged to Jean de Berry with an entry in the Duke's inventory of 1402 describing a Psalter written in Latin and French, richly illuminated, and containing at the beginning 'pluseurs histoires' by André Beauneveu.[1] The proof of the connection is not as complete as one would wish: in this instance Robinet recorded neither the first words on the second folio nor the subjects of the 'histoires' (or miniatures with figures as opposed to borders and decorative initials). Still, richly illuminated Psalters written in both languages were of course rare, and altogether the circumstantial evidence is so great that the identification has been accepted without question by subsequent scholarship. In stating our agreement we emphasize the fact that the 'histoires' at the beginning of the manuscript in the Bibliothèque nationale do indeed seem to be the work of an artist who was not normally an illuminator, and there is good reason to ascribe them to André Beauneveu. To that question we shall return later.

The twenty-four miniatures at the beginning of the manuscript lie on twelve pairs of facing folios; the back of the folio bearing a miniature is always blank. Twelve prophets confront twelve apostles. The apostles hold books and individual attributes, the prophets scrolls. The scrolls however are blank, and the sayings of the prophets as well as of the apostles are written below the miniatures, first in Latin and alongside in French – though sometimes the latter is slightly abbreviated. The arrangement conforms to a scheme of concordance of the Old and New Testaments established in the thirteenth century, in which statements of the prophets are revealed as prophecies of Articles of the Faith.[2] The *Psalter* is, so far as we can judge today, one of the two earliest appearances of the iconography in a work commissioned by Jean de Berry. It was a subject for which he had a pronounced predilection, partly perhaps because one of his two patron saints was the apostle Andrew.[3] He chose it for the windows of his own chapel, fragments of which survive in the Cathedral of Bourges (Figs. 597-599).[4] As in the Sainte-Chapelle in Paris, which was the model for his building, the piers of the interior contained life-size statues of the apostles,[5] and some part of the chapel seems to have held smaller figures of prophets, a few of which are extant in the museum at Bourges and in the Hutinel Collection in Paris (Figs. 593-595).[6] It would be too much to say, with Mâle, that Jean de Berry was responsible for the diffusion of the theme in the fifteenth century on a monumental scale,[7] but his special interest in it is undeniable.

Jean de Berry's enthusiasm for this form of concordance was displayed in the realm of the illuminated book also. In or after 1399 he acquired – certainly not only for iconographic reasons – the *Bréviaire de Belleville*, which around 1325 had first introduced the theme in the Calendar. The innovation made so great an impression generally that the Calendar of the Breviary was copied no less than seven times.[8] Indeed, long before he possessed the original the Duke commissioned a version of it in the *Petites Heures*, which was illuminated about the same time as the *Psalter* (Figs. 83-85). He had it repeated towards 1409 in the *Grandes Heures* (Figs. 217, 218, 249). The popularity of the subject might lead us to expect an identity in the cast of characters. The truth is, however, that some of the prophets in the *Psalter* have been variously identified, and one scholar has even claimed that the present sequence of folios is not the original one. We shall return to these questions later; let us assume for the present that the order has not been altered.

Some historians have inferred the intervention of assistants in the series of prophets and apostles, and Henry Martin has even claimed that only one figure, *David*, is by Beauneveu himself.[9] Most scholars have, however, judged that all the miniatures are very largely the work of this master, as the inventory states. More significant than differences of quality, it seems to me, are differences of artistic experience and intention, which have not previously been observed. Even the borders vary, and the differences correspond to those within the miniatures. One border appears on the first five pairs of folios except 10 and 15 verso (Figs. 51-60). It is the older of the two, with broader vines, larger leaves, and more unfilled space. The newer style takes over on 17 verso and appears around all the following miniatures[10] except folios 31, 63, and 85. These three, which are in the earlier manner (Figs. 75–77), comprise the first three illuminated folios in the *Psalter* itself. It appears that the two sections of the manuscript were begun at approximately the same time. The vines and leaves in the second style are more delicate, they are lighter in color, and they compose not so much a group of forms waving in space as a continuous, more densely filled frame around miniature and text.

The frames of the twenty-four miniatures show a similar evolution, again not quite continuous. Up through the first five pairs of folios most of the frames have, inside a narrow strip of gold, a band painted with frets, guilloches, or lancets. There are, however, three exceptions, folio 8 (*St. Peter*), which shows moldings simulating stone like those of the Parement Master (Figs. 52, 6-8), and folios 10 and 15 verso (Figs. 54, 59), which have only a very narrow painted band smaller in fact than the gold. From 17 verso, this type of narrow painted band prevails. The change is significant. The linear pattern of the broader frames of the first type shows an affinity for the linear details of the thrones, and tends, therefore, to draw all forms into a plane. The second type promotes recession into space, though less, to be sure, than the stone frame of St. Peter. The newer type is not, however, adopted for the miniatures in the *Psalter* itself. Indeed, the frames in this main section of the book are even broader than those at the beginning of the prophets and apostles. These miniatures were, of course, painted by other masters, and the frames as well as the borders prove that they began on Beauneveu's indications and then went ahead independently, probably at the same time.

These progressive alterations of the borders and frames in the first twenty-four folios are more significant because they are accompanied by corresponding changes within the miniatures themselves. These folios were clearly illuminated under the eye of one master, and the execution of the miniatures as well as the decorative parts was not routinized in the usual way. The haloes of the apostles for instance, while generally similar, differ with respect to size or pattern; in the case of the cusped haloes, the line forming the cusps varies. The last apostle, Mathias, is bareheaded, probably for artistic reasons that we shall describe. Curiously, the result of the aesthetic evolution is to render the last and most evolved apostle in one respect exactly like the prophets: he lacks a halo.

The artist's inclination to approach each miniature freshly is implied also by the variety of postures and of thrones. The twenty-four thrones, each of a distinctive design, constitute a splendid display of ecclesiastical furniture. They were designed by an artist possessed of both enthusiasm for such objects and experience in designing them, though he was not equally at home with the problem of projecting them on a two-dimensional surface. The figures are as individual as the thrones; no two of them sit or act in the same way. In differentiating them the painter has taken advantage of traditional attributes. Many of the apostles show bare feet while all the prophets are shod. The latter, lacking the diversified haloes of their successors, are compensated with interesting headgear: turbans, flat hats and peaked ones. Since St. Thomas was to be given a scroll, Hoseah, facing him, carries an abnormally large one (Figs. 59, 60).

This process of individualization of the miniatures, which encompasses their color also, has entailed a sacrifice of their relationship to one another, at least in the initial paintings. The first prophets and apostles show, in any event, a high degree of discreteness. While the prophet turns towards the apostle, expressing thereby his role as precursor, the latter scarcely acknowledges the movement. The thrones on facing folios may show some similarity, as do the four high finials crowning those of Jeremiah and Peter (Figs. 51, 52), but then the frames and the patterns in the floor differ. David's throne, very different from Andrew's, is placed on a russet and yellow tessellated floor while his companion's is on greensward (Figs. 53, 54).

The separateness of prophet and apostle in the first pairs is accompanied by a discreteness of elements within each miniature. The perspective of the thrones, often internally inconsistent, implies a level of sight very different from that of the floor. Sometimes the floor is not presented in perspective at all; its tiles, as on folio 13 verso (Fig. 57), are defined by parallel orthogonals and rise up in the picture plane to strike the lower edges of the throne. Consequently the thrones have no ground plane upon which to rest. The figures, no less voluminous and solid than the thrones, likewise do not sit down on the large seats provided for them. Even parts of one figure are not convincingly joined. The right foot of St. Peter is not where it ought to be (Fig. 52), and the artist seldom gives us any sense of the whereabouts of the legs beneath the drapery. The feet of St. John and other figures, showing a peculiarly high arch, are carefully articulated, but similarly unattached to a leg.

The qualities of the first miniatures of the *Psalter* seem to imply that the artist was not highly skilled in perspective projection and in design within a field limited by a frame. This inference is confirmed by the demonstration in the later miniatures of a better grasp of these aspects of design. On folios 10 and 15 verso, exceptional for their borders, the ground plane is extended beneath and beyond the throne (Figs. 54, 59), and the painter invariably adopted this design from folio 17 verso on (Fig. 61). This folio, indeed, marks a turning point in the design of the miniatures. From here on the ground plane, with the sole exception of folio 26 (Fig. 70), is grassy rather than tessellated. This may seem a strange decision, because it puts the thrones outdoors, but it becomes artistically intelligible when related to the simultaneous abandonment of the diapered background for the arabesque. Both these changes unify the figure and his environment. The monochrome of the figures is repeated – though the hue is different – in the terrain, while the flowery lines of the figures are echoed by the large curling leaves of the background.

Other changes assure us that the painter was seeking a greater unity between figure and setting as well as a greater general harmony in the pictorial field. The thrones, which had been so massive and elaborately plastic, become quieter. Their framework is simpler, and the narrow bands of light that had accented the edges of planes have been dimmed or eliminated. Orthogonal members have been reduced in favor of surfaces parallel to the picture plane. In the first miniatures the figures too tended to be conceived in the round; from folio 17 verso they expand laterally, presenting a broad front, so to speak, to the beholder. The backs of the thrones, which had in some miniatures (*St. Peter*, for instance) risen only to about the breast of the figure, now more consistently reach its shoulders or even head. The figure is thus more enclosed by the throne, and rises before one 'foil' rather than two. A compensatory enlivenment is introduced by 'opening' the front face of the throne base, exposing the plane of the platform gliding inward (Figs. 68, 71-73).

The progressive unification is shown also by the development of a form that is introduced in the first two miniatures (Figs. 51, 52). The arches in the back of each throne are filled with a network of black lines that resemble the mullions of a glass window.[11] These minuscule '*vitraux*', which appear again on the two exceptional folios 10 and 15 verso, become large and radiant, glowing with a yellow-green light. They do much to transform the masonry of the thrones, so massive in the earlier miniatures, into flat, diaphanous planes. In one of the first miniatures a narrow glass window rises on both sides of the head of David, framing it (Fig. 53). This pattern is employed in the last pair of figures (Figs. 73, 74). The windows, now broad and grand in scale, rise above the heads, leaving only a narrow slot for them. The painter, stimulated no doubt by a wish to refrain from concealing the enframing architecture, decided to leave St. Mathias without a halo. When taking this bold step at the very end of the series, he may have judged that the function of the halo was at least partially fulfilled by the yellow light of the windows.

These last two miniatures, representing Micah and Mathias, are the most completely harmonized of the series, in color as well as in shape. Both thrones are pink, and contain yellow 'lights'. In both miniatures the terrain is graded from pale blue to pale green. The backgrounds are darker blue and red, though varied in pattern. The outlines of the two figures, furthermore, have been related in the most sophisticated way. The idea of the prophet 'qui baille à l'apostre une prophécie envelopée' is of course retained. While the apostle holds to the central vertical axis of his miniature, the prophet is shifted on his throne toward him. To balance this shift of the body, and to serve at the same time as an introductory motive, a long fold of the prophet's mantle is flung out to the left. There is a corresponding but smaller fold in the miniature of the apostle; otherwise, however, his outlines are more compact and closed.

Some similarities between juxtaposed miniatures were of course sought from the very beginning. The tessellated floors and diapered backgrounds of folios 7 verso and 8 are related (Figs.

51, 52), but the violet throne of the latter breaks away from the correspondences. A decisive step forward in unity of color was taken on 17 verso, the folio that marked innovations of other kinds. In both it and 18 the throne is salmon pink, the background deep blue, the ground plane pale blue (Figs. 61, 62). Folios 19 verso and 20 share an orange background and a light green throne, though in the former the ground is gray while green in the latter. These likenesses continue to folios 29 verso–30, where the colors are almost identical: pink thrones with yellow-green 'lights', blue and red backgrounds (though of different designs), green grounds, bluish nearby and yellowish deeper in space (Figs. 73, 74).

Folios 10 and 15 verso fall out of the series of early miniatures with regard to borders, frame, throne, and terrain, as we have seen (Figs. 54, 59). Their pale colors resemble the last miniatures, and they are unique in possessing '*vitraux*' in the wings as well as in the backs of the thrones. These two miniatures induce us to ask whether the diversity of style in the two groups of paintings is to be ascribed to the presence of two painters rather than to successive phases of one. For several reasons, especially the extent of the progressive refinements in the later miniatures, the more probable hypothesis is that the entire series was designed and largely executed by one artist, while the two exceptional miniatures on folios 10 and 15 verso were not completed at their allotted times but painted later, along with the others of similar style.

These observations are of course predicated on the fact that the original sequence of the miniatures has been preserved. In 1894, however, Durrieu suggested that six of the prophets are now in the wrong places.[12] This view, which has since been neither accepted nor indeed even discussed, is based upon two unmentioned premises: a particular identification of the prophets, and a concept of a canonical sequence. The former is questionable and the latter cannot be shown to have existed. There was, on the contrary, a bewildering variety of sequences, and, as Mâle has pointed out, the order of even the apostles was not absolutely fixed.[13] It is not surprising, then, that modern writers have not always identified the prophets in the same manner.

The identity of the prophets is indeed not obvious. They are named in the Calendar of the approximately contemporary *Petites Heures*, almost certainly written for the Duke also, and comparison with this series would therefore appear to provide a reliable key (Figs. 83-85).[14] Caution is suggested immediately, however, by the fact that the prophets in the *Petites Heures* differ somewhat with regard both to identity and sequence from earlier versions of the same type of concordance in the *Heures de Jeanne II de Navarre* and the *Heures de Yolande de Flandre*.[15] In each month of these Calendars, as in the *Petites Heures*, a prophet removes a stone from a progressively ruinous building and gives it to an apostle – a scheme first introduced in the *Bréviaire de Belleville*, where it is accompanied by a lengthy explanation. This manuscript, the Calendar of which has come down to us incomplete, was acquired in 1399 by the Duke of Berry, as we have mentioned. The later *Grandes Heures* was provided with a Calendar and a sequence of prophets like the *Petites Heures*.

Durrieu seems to have identified the prophets in the *Psalter* by reliance upon the texts of the prophets in the *Petites Heures*, who bear their names. This method gave him a sequence different in six instances from that of the *Petites Heures*, and he therefore proposed that three pairs of prophets must have been inadvertently switched during a rebinding.[16] Leroquais was not more informative than Durrieu about the grounds for his identifications. Presumably he depended upon the texts exclusively, and he ended up with identities and a sequence rather different from that of Durrieu and the *Petites Heures*.[17] Where his identifications differ, they can be supported by passages in the books of the prophets. In the case of each prophet a phrase in the book proposed by Leroquais comes closer than any passage in the book proposed by Durrieu to what is actually written in the *Psalter*.[18]

This superior correspondence of Leroquais' scheme with the text of the Bible would seem to prove wrong not only Durrieu but the *Petites Heures* and the *Grandes Heures* themselves. The difficulties, moreover, do not end at this point. For one thing, the sayings of some pairs of prophets and apostles are hardly clear demonstrations of the fact asserted in the *Bréviaire de Belleville* that 'le Nouvel Testament est tout figuré et baillié en figures en l'Ancien'.[19] The concordance, in other words, is scarcely perfect.

Two facts, hitherto unobserved, seem to point toward a satisfactory solution. The word 'malachias', written in an early hand and no doubt in the original workshop, is still legible on folio 29 verso, though it was greatly reduced when the lower margin was trimmed. Similarly at the bottom of folio 21 verso a word in the same brown script may still be seen, clearly legible as 'sophonias'.[20] The sayings on the scrolls of these two prophets are those of Malachi and Zephaniah in the *Petites Heures* or the *Grandes Heures*. There is excellent reason, then, to believe that the sayings were connected with the same prophets in the three manuscripts, and, much more relevant to our concerns, that the present order of the prophets in the *Psalter* was the original one.

It becomes much easier to choose, therefore, between the more 'correct' connections of texts and prophets proposed by Leroquais and the 'historical' connections provided by contemporary manuscripts. When preferring the latter we must resign ourselves to the fact that no-one in the entourage of Jean de Berry corrected, in any one of three manuscripts, the assignment of texts to the prophets. Where the confusion began is not clear, but nothing is commoner in history than the perpetuation of error. Durrieu was right in his identifications and wrong in his sequence. Certainly the reordering of the sequence that he proposed is destructive of those compositional correspondences that are so basic to the later pairs in the cycle. The exchange that he proposed of the present folios 29 verso with 25 verso is, from a visual point of view, well nigh impossible. His other alternatives are scarcely less improbable.

2 · THE NEW COLOR

One of the most memorable aspects of the miniatures of the prophets and apostles is their color. This may seem at first an odd statement, for they are the work of an artist who was primarily a sculptor, and, strictly speaking, the figures themselves have scarcely any color at all. The prophets and apostles are painted in only a soft, pale gray, with touches of red in the cheeks and blue or brown in the eyes. Grisaille technique was highly valued, as we have observed, in the fourteenth century. Pucelle had used it masterfully in the *Heures de Jeanne d'Évreux*, pitching the figures generally at a medium gray, and setting them off by touches of thin blue, red or brown in the buildings and landscapes (Fig. 335). Frequently he filled the background with one of these colors. The gray of the figures resembles the brown ink of the text, and inasmuch as some parchment was left uncovered within the miniatures, a beautiful overall balance of tone was attained on each folio. This was maintained by leaving the frames unpainted, and by distributing grisaille figures through the borders.

Grisaille painting was practiced by the illuminators of Charles V in the third quarter of the century, and in their best works, such as the *Œuvres de Guillaume de Machaut, ca.* 1375 (Fig. 385), the gray, blue, green, and russet are so delicately laid that they seem to be powdered onto the parchment rather than brushed. The gray of the figures is somewhat lighter than in Pucelle, and in manuscripts of the late 'seventies, such as the *Cité de Dieu* in Paris and the *Grandes Chroniques* (Fig. 565),[21] it becomes whitish while the color of the background is more saturated.

The general effect, then, approximates the *Psalter*, but there is an important difference. The colors around the prophets and apostles are more delicate, more varied, and more subtly combined. The throne of St. Philip is apple green, the background red-brown, and the terrain straw strewn with small plants (Fig. 64). Joel has a similar environment, except that the sward is dark gray, with blue and yellow grasses (Fig. 63). Isaiah sits on a violet throne, placed on a dull orange and green tiled floor and before a blue background (Fig. 55). This diapered background contains, as often in these miniatures, exceptionally small units, and the effect, especially when tiny squares of gold alternate with color, is that of a shining mosaic or of stained glass. Gold is used for the text and for some of the bars, vines, and leaves; it is interspersed there with red and blue. This luminosity is sustained by the tessellated floors and light-struck thrones, the tracery of which sometimes glows with a yellowish radiance. The very blond figures are thus suspended in a scintillating, exotic sea of color.

The pale, mixed hues of Beauneveu's miniatures may be found in other manuscripts, coloristically advanced, of the period around 1380, especially the late miniatures in the *Bible of Jean de Sy* (Fig. 583) and a *Bible historiale* that belonged to the Duke of Berry, perhaps already in 1383 (Fig. 611). But Beauneveu's luminous gray-white forms surrounded by bouquets of color remind us less of the illumination of the time than of the reliquaries and other enamelled and jewelled objects called, in the inventories of the period, *joyaux*. Around the luminous figures of Zachariah and David, reminiscent of white enamel, the throne of one appears as a pale ruby, the other a sapphire (Figs. 57, 53).

The works in 'émail en ronde bosse', or *Goldemailplastik*, though usually small in scale, constitute one of the major arts of the time.[22] Until recently they were either appreciated merely for their gorgeous display of gold and gems or they were dismissed for lack of moderation and an implied immorality. 'Time the destroyer,' said Huizinga, 'has made it easy for us to separate pure art from all these gewgaws and bizarre trappings. . . . This separation . . . our aesthetic sense insists upon. . . .'[23] What makes these objects so enchanting and at the same time significant in the history of art is not chiefly the richness of their components – there was nothing new about that in a Europe that had seen for centuries the incredibly showy crown and *Reichsapfel* of the Holy Roman Empire. It was the exquisite combination of translucent enamel, gems, and gold that made these delicate, sparkling little objects one of the greatest accomplishments of the European goldsmith.

The reliquaries and *joyaux* presupposed the creation, or at least refinement, of new methods and techniques. Superposition of a film of translucent enamel over silver was developed in France, probably primarily in Paris, during the course of the fourteenth century (Fig. 572),[24] and an exceptional mastery of *champlevé* on gold was acquired during the same period. Enamelled gold objects, still very scarce during the reign of Charles V, became numerous in the reign of his son.[25] This new art was combined with an equally novel arrangement of stones. In earlier *orfèvrerie* pearls and precious stones were normally set side by side, embedded in one plane. They composed, so to speak, a mosaic of color. During the fourteenth century the gems began to rise from the 'setting-bed', projected upward by small filaments or tendrils. In the fourteenth-century additions to the *Pala d'Oro* in S. Marco, Venice, many small pearls rise on stems, but they all attain the same height (Fig. 575). They frame the larger, embedded stones in a regular way. Later, in French jewels, these small spots of concentrated color became free in space, and at the same time the 'background' itself tended to dissolve (Figs. 571, 573).

Thus the *joyaux* display color in three dimensions, and the designs take full advantage of the opportunities provided by the distribution of objects at different levels. Surfaces catch the light in an endlessly varied manner; some are even partly or wholly in shade. The objects were designed to be seen from one point of view, and in them sculpture in relief and in the round drew very close to painting. Small wonder that the *joyaux* were often described in the inventories as *tableaux*. Painting in turn showed a related taste and was in addition stimulated by the effects achieved in enamel. In the late fourteenth century line yielded its function of defining form to color – to color increasingly conceived in interaction with light. The luminosity of enamel began to be simulated in paint, and even its techniques were approximated in order to produce similar effects. Illuminators such as the Boucicaut Master and the Egerton Master delighted in transparent glazes of red, green or blue over gold and silver. Chafing at the limitation of earth pigments, the Boucicaut Master and the Limbourgs utilized metallic emulsions or foil to produce their great radiances and sun-bursts. The painters and the goldsmiths shared a delight in the interaction of color and light. Though the illuminators could not quite equal the sparkle of enamel and the depth of color of the gems, they nevertheless came remarkably close.

Like contemporary paintings the little sculptures consist of a peculiar blend of naturalistic and fanciful forms. 'Naturalism' in art is of course a relative concept, and indeed in the context of the *joyaux* the objects that are in fact natural – chalcedony, pearls, rubies, emeralds, and sapphires – appear fanciful, whereas the artificial forms – that is, the simulated animals, flowers, and human beings – are the more 'naturalistic'. The quality of the style demanded that these two categories of forms be held in intimate relationship (we may see a similar combination in the recent sculpture-painting of artists such as Marisol). The Madonna of the *Goldenes Rössl*, her body and flesh described with a lively sense of actuality, wears a brooch as large as her head, formed by a pale ruby or *balai* and six pearls. The enormous jewel serves to qualify her worldliness and even her substance, transmuting it into the mode of pure light and color (Fig. 573). Such quite deliberate disproportions are common in the *joyaux* of the time, only one of which, incidentally, is dated – the *Goldenes Rössl* at Altötting, which was given by Queen Isabeau de Bavière to her husband Charles VI as a present for the new year 1404 (Fig. 573). In another piece made for the royal pair, now preserved only in a painted copy, the Madonna wears a huge pearl-set halo, and again a disproportionately large brooch (Fig. 576). And the pearls and gems in the frame of Jean de Berry's *Reliquary of the Thorn* are sometimes larger than the heads of God, Christ, and the apostles (Fig. 571).

The naturalistic forms in the *joyaux* are not only the figures and the animals but the white, rose, or gray-blue flowers and the exquisite vines in modulated translucent green. In this respect the painting that approaches them most closely is not French at all, but Lombard. The folios of Giovannino dei Grassi's prayer book for Gian Galeazzo Visconti, the supreme masterpiece, it seems to me, of Italian Trecento illumination, contain an unprecedented display of gold lacquered in rose or pale green. The glaze gives the color a novel depth and sparkle, remarkably similar to the translucent enamel of the *joyaux*. The shapes, too, are similar (Figs. 578, 579).[26] Indeed, like the gems, the flowers or leaves often wave into space, each on its stem. On some folios they radiate into circular sprays, like the mandorlas in the reliquaries (Fig. 576). Their rose and pale blue or green hues, sometimes set off with a little burnt-orange, resemble the *balais*, sapphires, and carnelians of the *joyaux*. And because the paint is laid in small bars or dots it acquires some of the luminosity of the stones. Around each spray of flowers the painter sets an arc of small gold rectangles, as if to portray the light reflected from the petals. If this interpretation is correct he has rendered phenomena of both translucency and reflection, one in a more naturalistic, the other in a more stylized way. Such a combination, involving both analytical study and imaginative recreation, is characteristic of the best styles of the time.

The 'real' and the fanciful are held in a perfect amalgam by Giovannino's exquisite taste. The borders introduce the most colorful of natural objects – peacock feathers (folio 22). Often they contain small patches of landscape, rendered in color as fluid and atmospheric as Broederlam's, though more monochromatic. Alongside these segments of nature, inhabited by rabbits, grazing deer, hoopoes, or brilliant opalescent beetles – little masterpieces of realistic still-life – there rise in the margins lacquered golden trees (Fig. 578). These surprising, formalized arboreal specimens bear not only flowers or leaves but diminutive oratories, and in the crotches little hermits crouch, comfortably reading. If in some miniatures a small patch of orange would enliven the spectrum of color the painter did not scruple to spread it on grapes.[27] The unflagging vitality, the vibrancy of repeated small shapes, the profusion of powdery rose, violet, gray, and buff remind one of an orchard suddenly bursting into bloom on the spring's first warm day.

The chief illuminator of the prayer book of Gian Galeazzo Visconti was no doubt Giovannino dei Grassi, the artist who signed one sheet in the famous pattern book in Bergamo.[28] Giovannino died in 1398, Gian Galeazzo followed him to the grave in 1402, and the Book of Hours was left unfinished at that time, to be completed later by Belbello da Pavia for Filippo Maria Visconti. We do not know when it was begun: a date that is difficult to read (1370, 1380, or 1320?) is inscribed on the base of the building in the *Expulsion of Joachim* in the part of the manuscript that belongs to Count Visconti di Modrone,[29] but this cycle of Anna and Joachim is unusually full, and the date may refer to some event associated with it rather than to the execution of the miniature. In 1396 Giovannino was commissioned by the *Fabbrica* of the Cathedral to illuminate a Beroaldo, and after his death in 1398 payments for it were given to his son Salomone, who worked with him.[30] The Beroaldo is less lively than the prayer book, and even further from the latter is the heavy-handed relief usually identified as Giovannino's in the Cathedral.[31]

Good manuscripts from this extraordinary phase of Lombard illumination are very rare, and it is therefore useful to point to a beautiful reflection of it in Spain (Figs. 580, 581). A Book of Hours recently given by Apeles Mestres to the Archivo Histórico in Barcelona was originally written, to judge from the rubrics, in the region, but the genial illuminator must have been in the workshop of Giovannino in Milan or Pavia. Only there could he have had an opportunity to see the rare colors he spreads on the folios – dusty blue, gray, pale green, matte gilt, violet, and orange. His exquisite combination of pallid tones with a scattered sparkle of metallic emulsion derives from the same source. In Lombardy he acquired his mastery of lacquer. Transparent pale rose, yellow, and green are spread over silver in the backgrounds. The borders capture much of the animation of the Visconti Hours (Figs. 578, 579); the spray of color can mount, as there, to an explosive climax, like the last rockets in a display of fireworks.

The naturalistic vignettes, portraying with exceptional perceptiveness a lioness with her cubs or a faithful little white dog looking up at his wandering master (Fig. 580), rival the work of Giovannino. Like many of Giovannino's forms the dragon, lightly overlaid with gilt, resembles a jewel. The grim skeleton at the beginning of the Office of the Dead (Fig. 581) derives from a Lombard convention of illustration of this text (Fig. 584), but in the Barcelona Hours the figure no longer appears upright within a sarcophagus, a sort of mundane Man of Sorrows, but stands alongside his grave, which he has just dug or rather from which he has just exhumed himself. He disposes his hoe with the bravura of a knight wielding his lance. The terrain, bare of vegetation and strewn with bones, is an ominous dull green and brown touched at places with gilt. From it rise the stumps of very dead trees.

The Barcelona *Horae* is certainly a decade or more later than the related Lombard manuscripts. The Calendar gives the year, 1405, of the 'Translatio Sancti Severi', but no-one would be tempted to place the work this early. The illumination has been ascribed to Bernardo Martorell, a Catalan master documented from 1427 to his death in 1453/4.[32] While primarily a panel painter, one miniature by him is known, and that, of 1448, is utterly different in style.[33] Some of his earlier panels resemble to a degree the illumination of the Barcelona Book of Hours, but they are permeated by the conventions of Borassà and of Catalan panel painting, which are conspicuously absent from the manuscript. If the illumination is by Martorell, we must suppose him to have been in Lombardy as a very young man, and the Book of Hours to have been painted immediately upon his return to Barcelona. Whatever the truth about its author, the manuscript is, along with the earlier *Missal of St. Eulalia* in the Cathedral of Barcelona,[34] the finest flower of Catalan late medieval illumination.

Lombard illumination in the last quarter of the Trecento was distinguished by a second major trend very different from that guided by Giovannino. The style of the *Giron* (Fig. 585) and the

Lancelot, both now in Paris,[35] is much closer to that of Trecento panel and mural painting, especially Giovanni da Milano's (Fig. 635), though it shows nevertheless relationships with the art of Giovannino. Whereas in the latter's miniatures even God is subjected to a novel foreshortening (Fig. 578), the *Giron* boldly creates an architectural space behind the columns of the text, partially transforming the latter into simulated sheets that hang down in front of the building (Fig. 585). This device marks the beginning of the kind of illusionism of the book that was to reach a higher consistency in Paduan and Ferrarese illumination, largely under the impetus of Andrea Mantegna.

The color in both of these beautiful manuscripts owes its richness and its *sfumatura* to Giovanni da Milano, but it is thinly spread, as in Giovannino, and the illuminators similarly favor a luminous pale violet, green, gray, and buff. The other surviving Lombard manuscripts, such as the *Tacuinum* in Paris[36] and several Books of Hours, show a harder enamel, less modulated color, and more rigid forms.[37] This is true of the interesting, imposing, but nowadays overrated Missal and Book of Hours in Paris, finished definitely by 1395 (Figs. 558, 560, 584).[38] Among artists who appeared somewhat later than Giovannino, Michelino da Besozzo, documented from 1388 to 1445, was outstanding,[39] and local praise of him as *pictor supremus* (1420) and *pictor excellentissimus inter omnes pictores mundi* (1431) is perhaps understandable.[40] Deeply influenced, like almost all other Lombard masters of the late fourteenth century, by Giovannino, he tended to perpetuate the luminous color of that painter, but he moved toward a more linear style, developing enchanting flame-like patterns (Fig. 582). His art, while enormously influential, did not touch what was to be most vital in the painting of the fifteenth century in Italy and France. Similar observations might be made about his excellent Lombard successors, the Master of the *De Natura Deorum*[41] and Belbello da Pavia.

We have referred above to the close ties between the Visconti and the Valois in the late fourteenth century. The first wife of Gian Galeazzo was French, and his only daughter, Valentina, in 1389 married her cousin Louis d'Orléans. When Valentina came to France she brought, as part of her dowry, jewels and manuscripts.[42] The mother of Isabeau de Bavière, wife of Charles VI, was a Visconti. Still more important is the fact that in Milan as in France the court was the chief patron, whereas the middle class, which acquired so important a role in central Italy and the Low Countries, was relatively unimportant. Tuscany and, later, the Netherlands patronized panel painting while the Valois and the Visconti showed a special preference for the illuminated book.

Jean de Berry as well as other French collectors possessed Milanese manuscripts.[43] At the same time French artists, including the painter Coene, were employed at the Cathedral of Milan,[44] and there were French manuscripts in the Visconti library in the *castello* at Pavia.[45] In view of all these exchanges a similarity of the illumination of Giovannino with the *joyaux* is scarcely surprising. In one respect, however, Giovannino's color is conspicuously unlike that of the sculptures. He made little use of white, whereas it is the most prominent of all colors in the *joyaux*. It was certainly not only a desire to stress the Virgin's chastity that led goldsmiths around 1400 to give her a white mantle. She wears one in the *Rössl* (Fig. 573), in the similar object made for Charles VI and known in a copy (Fig. 576), in the superb little figure in the Victoria and Albert

Museum, in the reliquary of the *Ordre du St. Esprit* in the Louvre (Fig. 574), and in the Duke of Berry's *Reliquary of the Thorn* (Fig. 571). It is evident that the central figure of a *joyaux* normally was white, and many other figures also. Even the Baptist wore a white mantle over his tunic of hair in the *Reliquary of the Thorn* and in a small pin in the Bargello (Figs. 571, 577). In the spectacular sculpture at Altötting the horse, like the Virgin and the angels, is white, while the Christ Child and the King are red and blue respectively, though their faces are white (Fig. 573).

The delight with a luminous, central area of white set against brown or gray may be seen in a related form of sculpture, the cameo (Figs. 456-458, 460, 461). While antique cameos were valued throughout the Middle Ages, the princes around 1400 showed a quickened interest in them. Jean de Berry possessed dozens of specimens, as we have seen, and the inventories inform us that he commissioned at least one large new one.[46]

Enthusiasm for subtle variations of pale colors, especially white, was not limited to cameos, goldsmiths' work, stained glass, and painting. It extended to monumental sculpture. The central statue in the apse of Jean de Berry's Sainte-Chapelle was Notre-Dame-la-Blanche – all in gleaming white marble, touched with gold in the hair. Unpainted white marble statues, known earlier, enjoyed a special vogue in the late fourteenth and early fifteenth centuries.[47] The high estimation of this 'color' is suggested by the emblem of the order created in 1399 by the Maréchal de Boucicaut and twelve companions. For aesthetic as well as symbolical reasons they chose 'la Dame Blanche'.[48]

The *joyaux* reflect with remarkable consistency a new ideal of color. The basic counterpoint of shining white and radiant yellow (gold), the intermittent *basso* of deep blue, red, or even black, and the chords of sharps and flats – bluish rose, yellow- or gray-green, violet – compose a distinctive phase in the development of Western color. This phase is significant not only for its pattern of hues but for its effects of transparency, translucency, and reflection. It surpasses all earlier periods in the rendering of the interaction of color and light. While it drew, of course, upon the traditions of Gothic art, its quality was novel, and it contributed much to the patterns of color in fifteenth-century painting in France and, I believe, Italy also.

If dun browns and dusty grays are added to the pattern as foils – and we have seen them in the related painting of Giovannino – we recognize the formation of a 'style' of color that affected not only the painters of North Italy, in Milan, Verona, and Venice in the first third of the century, but later central Italians, guided by Domenico of Venice. It is not after all surprising that a century of painting preoccupied with light should have been inspired by the art we have been considering. The researches in color undertaken primarily by Gothic France laid the foundations for the color of Renaissance Tuscany. A sign of this fundamental continuity is the fascination of later fifteenth-century masters with jewels. No other painters in history took such delight in the depiction of *joyaux*. The panels of Jan van Eyck and his Netherlandish successors, and of Domenico Veneziano, Piero della Francesca, and later Quattrocento masters abound in jewels radiant with opalescent pearls and glistening gems and metals. And stones become common forms in the borders of Italian manuscripts in the second half of the fifteenth century.

3·BEAUNEVEU AND HIS CIRCLE

We have observed some aspects of the prophets and apostles in the Duke's *Psalter* that suggest an artist whose medium was not primarily paint but stone or metal, and the painstaking care with which the forms are modeled would seem likewise to point to a sculptor or goldsmith. The grisaille is laid in tiny parallel strokes that follow the planes, curling around the cheek of an apostle or the hollow of a concave molding. In the larger surfaces of the thrones the strokes are generally parallel to the bounding lines, and in receding planes they conform with the orthogonals. Thus in the platform of *Zephaniah* the strokes that darken the plane as it recedes meet along a central axis in accordance with the 'vanishing axis' system of perspective (Fig. 61). On the facing folio the axis is shifted toward the right so that the awkward areas along it can take cover under St. James's mantle, which serves as what Panofsky has called a 'perspective fig-leaf' (Fig. 62).[49]

The prophets and apostles are men of character and will. Their heavy-lidded eyes peer out intently beneath knitted brows; the first figures seem even aggressive. When they do not, like Zachariah, thrust their chins forward (Fig. 57), their great aquiline noses serve as surrogates to convey a similar force. And their postures, endlessly varied, seem the consequence of great vitality and a considerable restlessness. These crusty figures resemble to some degree the tomb statues in St. Denis carved in 1364 and the years immediately following under the direction of André Beauneveu. Inasmuch as the statues were commissioned by King Charles V – at the very beginning of his reign – it seems almost certain that Beauneveu carved part of the effigy of the King himself (Fig. 591), and he would seem to be responsible for the design at least of the figures of Charles's father, King Jean le Bon (Fig. 589), and his grandfather, King Philippe VI (Fig. 590).[50] Although only Charles V was living, each king shows a degree of individuality of character as well as physiognomy that was novel in French sculpture, and that was paralleled only by the busts of Peter Parler in the triforium of the Cathedral of Prague (Fig. 592). They are in this respect perfectly plausible predecessors of the apostles and the prophets of the *Psalter*. The drapery style of the statues is of course quite dissimilar, and other differences, such as the greater placidity, could well be ascribed to a difference of purpose and to the span of nearly twenty years between the two groups of works.

Our first certain notices of André Beauneveu come from Valenciennes, 1363-1364, but the Master Andrew who was already active there in 1361 and at the Château de Nieppe (Nord) in 1360 is usually, with much reason, believed to be Beauneveu. In 1364 he went to Paris, where Charles V appointed him 'ymager' and supervisor of the execution of a group of tombs in St. Denis. From 1372 until at least 1381 Beauneveu was acting, in Courtrai or in Valenciennes, as 'faseur de thombes' for Louis de Mâle, Count of Flanders. In 1377 he made a statue of the Virgin for the Belfry of Ypres, and he was paid in 1383-1384 for a crucifix he had made in Malines.[51] Sometime between 1383-1384 and 1386, probably in 1384 when Louis de Mâle died, Beauneveu began to work for Jean de Berry. The earliest record of him in this service, of 1386, informs us that he already had three assistants, and describes him as 'ymagier'.[52] This is the title he bore when acting as sculptor for Charles V. In 1390 Froissart, speaking of the Duke of Berry at Mehun, said '[il] se devisoit au maistre de ses euvres de taille et de pointure, maistre Adryen Beau-Nepveu, à faire nouvelles ymages et pointures . . . et il estoit bien adreschié, car dessus ce maistre Adryen dont je parle, n'avoit pour lors meilleur, ne le pareil en nulles terres, ne de qui tant de bons ouvrages fuissent demourés en France ou en Haynnau dont il estoit de nation, ne ou royaulme d'Angleterre'.[53]

Though we are informed that in 1374 Beauneveu was paid for some painting in the Halle des Jurés, Valenciennes,[54] and he was *in charge of* both painting and sculpture for the Duke of Berry, he worked principally as a sculptor.[55] This tallies with the impression we have formed of him from the miniatures in the *Psalter*. These miniatures are explicitly ascribed to him by the inventory begun December 2, 1401, and finished February 23, 1403. This inventory lists, further-more, a 'livre *Cur Deus homo*, qui fu de feu maistre André Beaunepveu . . .', a reference apparently to prior ownership by the artist, and not, as has been said, to a book painted by him.[56] The entry informs us that by this date Beauneveu had died.[57]

The prophets and apostles in the *Psalter* are unique in style among surviving paintings. The rarity of a named work, and the great reputation of the artist in his time have combined to tempt historians to ascribe many paintings to Beauneveu, including the *Parement de Narbonne* and the early part of the *Très Belles Heures de Notre-Dame*, as we have seen.[58] None has stood the test of time. Only a drawing in the Louvre, two miniatures in the *Brussels Hours* and six later miniatures reflect, as we shall see, one or another aspect of his style. Among sculptures, on the other hand, a group of prophets presumably from the Sainte-Chapelle and long associated with Beauneveu, are indeed closely related to the miniatures of the *Psalter* (Figs. 593-595). The resemblance of the head of the best statue to *Ezekiel* is striking (Figs. 71, 594), and the crossed, overlapping, loosely wrapped mantle of another may be found again in *Zephaniah* (Figs. 61, 595). The statues, which vary in style and were probably not all carved at one time nor by one hand, show a simpler, more assured arrangement of the drapery than the painted figures.[59] They might well have been made a few years later than the paintings. Realization, however, of the same subjects in the two arts naturally led to differences between them, and it is difficult therefore to infer the relative dates of the two cycles. The miniatures were, it is generally agreed, not painted later than 1387 nor before 1384. The statues should not, therefore, be dated in the early fifteenth century[60] but in the late 'eighties or early 'nineties, as Troescher proposed and Bober tentatively agreed.[61]

More difficult is the relationship to these works of a figure and some heads in the Musée Jacques Cœur in Bourges, one of which resembles closely a head from Mehun-sur-Yèvre, now in the Louvre (Fig. 596).[62] The last-named, the best preserved of the group, differs from the prophets by exhibiting broad, frontal planes, on which the features are inscribed in delicate, ornamental lines. The alertness and vitality of the prophets are replaced by great sensitiveness and a quiet, solemn inner life. Any attempt to ascertain the late work of Beauneveu will have to define the relation of some members of this group to it.[63]

Beauneveu's figure style had an impact upon painting, as we shall see, but he was not an illuminator and he had no real followers in this art. Apart from the stained glass of the Sainte-Chapelle in Bourges, which we shall consider shortly, the paintings that are most closely related are exceptional in one way or another. The miniatures in the Hours of the Holy Ghost in the *Très Belles Heures de Notre-Dame*, which will be discussed in Chapter XI, are, I believe, not the work of an illuminator nor perhaps even a painter. The first two folios of the *Brussels Hours*, often ascribed to Beauneveu, remain, as we shall see, isolated works. Nor can one precisely classify the pen and wash drawing of the *Death, Assumption and Coronation of the Virgin* in the Louvre, likewise frequently given to Beauneveu (Fig. 587).[64] This drawing, so exquisite in finish and yet so dull, is not the work of a great artist, but it must be at least a copy of such a work. Though beautiful and bold in design, its smooth gradations of value are monotonously regular. The patterns of the hair and beards of the apostles, including plaited locks and perfectly spiral beards, are varied and interesting but stale in finish. None of the arms and hands function very well, but St. Peter's left arm does not function at all. The hand seems to rest on the book of the neigh-boring apostle, but the arm of which it is a part is unimaginable. The draughtsman, indeed, remained quite unaware of it, and although description of the body and its movements is not highly advanced in this art, the failure in Peter's arm is disagreeably conspicuous.

The great height of the composition in proportion to its width indicates that it was probably not made for a panel or an altarpiece but for a mural of unusual shape, or, as Grete Ring suggested, a glass window.[65] The presence of the Baptist and St. Stephen, who kneel on a cloud just below the chief event, may connect the work with the Cathedral of Bourges and Jean de Berry. The features of the apostles are conventionalized versions of those of the *Psalter*. The figures, however, are more compact, and the drapery lighter in weight and less varied in disposition. The angels seem to imply Lombard influence.

The successive episodes of the death, bodily assumption, and coronation of the Virgin were represented on French ivories of the fourteenth century, but aspects of the last act in the drawing are novel in France and derive from the Italian tradition. We have already observed the introduction, in the *Coronation* of the *Très Belles Heures de Notre-Dame*, of the heavenly throne suspended above the ground plane (Fig. 13).[66] In the drawing the Virgin kneels, in conformity with a genial Italian conception of the period that, from the late thirteenth century, sought thus to express her humility and to dramatize the moment from a human point of view.[67] The mother and the Sponsa, and now also the rather youthful daughter, kneels before the Son.

In French painting the earliest instances of this figure are in the *Coronation* by the Luçon Master in the Barcelona Hours of 1401 and in the *Brussels Hours* (Figs. 705, 189). In the latter the Virgin bows her head and clasps her hands before her as in the drawing. The two works have in common also a curved throne (the back only in the miniature) and the representation of a fold of drapery falling over the platform of the throne and hanging free in space. In the miniature a fold of Christ's mantle as well as of the Virgin's is disposed in this way, whereas the fall into space is more extensive in the drawing. So vivid is it, indeed, that it arouses in the beholder a little vertigo. Still bolder is the portrayal of the body of the Virgin, not in profile as in Brussels, but turned a little inward toward God Father. The spatial relations, to be sure, are not entirely clear, because the Virgin's mantle hangs over the angels that frame the scene. In the *Brussels Hours* the folds clearly overlap the platform. Despite these differences, and one other still to be discussed,

L

the two works are interrelated, and the hypothesis of a connection of the drawing with Bourges and Jean de Berry is strengthened.

The relation between drawing and miniature suggests also that the former, or at least its model, was made around the time of the latter, that is, the 'nineties and certainly before 1402. This is supported by the absence in both works of the angels who hold the train of the Virgin in advanced French paintings of the Coronation from the early years of the new century.[68] For reasons of style the drawing or its model might well have been made a little earlier than the miniature.

The boldness of these spatial conceptions suggests an Italian model, though none with all these particular features seems to be extant. The likelihood of such a source, and indeed one in Tuscan painting, is increased by the curvature of the throne. Curved benches, representing the *scholae* in ancient art, persisted in certain scenes, such as Christ Teaching, in Byzantine painting, and were adopted in Tuscan and Roman painting from the late thirteenth century on.[69] The curved throne in some Tuscan Trecento Madonnas[70] may derive from Byzantine examples of this form, known in the late thirteenth century.[71] Especially close to the throne of the Brussels miniature, with its low back, is the throne in Ambrogio Lorenzetti's *Annunciation* in the Pinacoteca, Siena (Fig. 628).[72] All these relationships seem to point to a Tuscan model of around 1330 for the novel form of the Coronation in France. In the Brussels miniature, furthermore, as in Tuscan painting (Fig. 539), Christ holds the crown with both hands as he lowers it onto the head of the Virgin.

Two aspects of the composition in the Louvre drawing are, however, foreign to the Italian tradition. Though representation of the reception of the Virgin in heaven, a stage between her death and her coronation, became popular in France, it was, as we have said, rare in Italy. In the second place, when in Italian representations God the Father joins Christ in the ceremony of the Coronation, as he does in Venetian painting of the fifteenth century, he appears above and between the enthroned Christ and the Virgin.[73] In the drawing the kneeling Virgin is crowned by the enthroned God and Christ, while the dove hovers between them. The Coronation of the Virgin is here merged with the Trinity, and more precisely with the form, showing God and Christ enthroned, that served as the illustration of Psalm 109 (110) from the thirteenth century on. The representation of the crowning of Mary by the three separate members of the Trinity rather than the triune God seems to begin around 1400, in Spain and Germany as well as France.[74] A related Coronation, however, may be seen in an earlier representation of about 1365 and probably by a Nuremberg painter, in the Germanisches Nationalmuseum, Nuremberg (Fig. 588).[75] In it Christ and the Virgin, seated in heaven, crown a kneeling St. Clare, and the form given to this ceremony is so like that of the Brussels miniature and the Louvre drawing that it would seem to presuppose an earlier example of the Coronation of the Virgin of this type.

The drawing in the Louvre may be a design for a large window, and specimens of this art have come down to us in which the influence of Beauneveu is generally recognized. This glass, from no less important a place than the Duke's Sainte-Chapelle at Bourges, consists of fragments of the extensive cycle of apostles and prophets which we have referred to above (Figs. 597-599). The windows were in place, we know, by 1408.[76] After the destruction of the chapel in the eighteenth century they were installed in the crypt of the Cathedral, where they remained until the recent World War. The figures appear below towering canopies, rendered in luminous grisaille. The style and even the date of execution seem to vary somewhat from pane to pane. The animated, yet exquisitely balanced figure of David recalls the best of the stone prophets, though the drapery is softer and the surfaces more suffused with light. At the opposite pole are Daniel or the much weaker and later Isaiah.

While we are considering the diffusion of Beauneveu's style in spheres other than the mainstream of French illumination – which will be dealt with in its proper place – a word should be said about a remarkable embroidered antependium preserved in the Diocesan Museum at Vich (Fig. 586). The work, apparently commissioned in 1393,[77] represents Christ enthroned between the four Evangelists. The figures are not, however, uniform in style. The drapery of Christ and St. John shows florid Spanish patterns whereas Matthew and especially Luke, with his mantle wrapped broadly across his body and under his arm, recalls Beauneveu (Fig. 61).[78] The design of Matthew's turban and even his features would seem to derive from the same source. These resemblances are difficult to explain; for many reasons this impressive embroidery warrants further study.

4 · THE ROLE OF JACQUEMART AND PSEUDO-JACQUEMART

The description of the *Psalter* in the inventory attributes to André Beauneveu 'pluseurs histoires au commencement', and remains silent about the illustration of the text of the Psalter itself. Certainly no-one would ever have been tempted to ascribe these subsequent miniatures to the same hand. Some years ago I divided them into two main groups,[79] the second consisting of two beautiful and advanced paintings that will be discussed further in the chapters on the *Petites Heures* and the *Brussels Hours*. Their author was probably Jacquemart de Hesdin. All but one of the miniatures in the first group were executed for the most part by an illuminator who continued to work for Jean de Berry at least until 1409, when the *Grandes Heures* was completed. His paintings in the *Petites Heures* and the *Grandes Heures* have normally been included in the œuvre of Jacquemart de Hesdin, and I therefore dubbed him the Pseudo-Jacquemart.

The *Psalter* is the second manuscript illuminated for Jean de Berry in which we encounter complexities uncommon even in an era of considerable division of labor in the workshops. Apart from the prophets and apostles most of the miniatures show a collaboration within one field, and in this respect they resemble the *Petites Heures* more than the *Très Belles Heures de Notre-Dame*. It is interesting that the division is made according to hierarchic categories, as sometimes in the *Petites Heures*. All figures in heaven or in the air – figures of God on folios 63, 85, 177 and an angel on folio 201 – are by one illuminator, or at least in one style, because God on folio 63 seems less strongly painted (Figs. 76, 77, 81, 82). When God the Father and Christ are on the ground, as on folio 201, they were painted by the 'terrestrial' master (Fig. 82). The 'celestial' style is superior, and very close to the style of the two advanced miniatures. The God Father who appears in one of these (folio 127) is very probably by the same hand as the figure of David, so that this miniature is uniquely uniform (Fig. 79). The God Father who is rendered in black lines on gilt in the first miniature in the Psalter section is very old-fashioned and unique in the manuscript (Fig. 75).

The figure of David in this first miniature – which has a very beautiful border – is rather old-fashioned also (Fig. 75). The style, which appears in this figure alone in the manuscript, is very close to the later style (around 1375-1380) in the *Bible de Jean de Sy* (Fig. 583). The building, however, with its great depth measured by a double arcade, is disconnected from the figure, disproportionate and pretentious. The illuminator was desperately vying with Beauneveu, and probably serving him also; for the presence of similar broad, weighty structures in the following miniatures implies that the chief master gave indications to his associates. The graduation of the floor from light to dark, which appears in subsequent miniatures in the manuscript but not in those by Beauneveu, may perhaps be ascribed to the influence of Jacquemart.

Pseudo-Jacquemart first appears in the miniature for *Dominus illuminatio mea* (folio 63, Fig. 76). The diapered background formed of small units, however, derives from Beauneveu, and the tubular folds of David's mantle, similarly not characteristic of Pseudo-Jacquemart, imply some other source in sculpture. The fine pink canopies with pale green vaults on folio 85 (Fig. 77) were certainly taken from Beauneveu, and from him too must have come the throne and the great scale of the frame for the bells on folio 153 (Fig. 80). The rust-colored background of the latter is a rather coarse copy of Beauneveu's design on folio 15 verso (Fig. 59). Folio 177 by Pseudo-Jacquemart and an associate adopts Beauneveu's grassy terrain (Fig. 81), but in all these three miniatures the flowing drapery conforms with the illuminator's conventions.

The *Trinity* follows in many respects the conventional illustration of Psalm 109 (110) that had become established in the thirteenth century. Christ and God the Father, identical figures, are enthroned side-by-side, while the dove hovers between and above them (Fig. 82). This type appears in a miniature by the workshop of Jean Pucelle in Chantilly, illuminated about 1330 (Fig. 600).[80] Both figures hold books and bless similarly, though Christ has a cruciform halo. In a later miniature from the Pucelle shop in the *Heures de Jeanne de Navarre* rays pass from the mouths of Christ and God to the dove, making more explicit the concept of the spiration of the Holy Ghost from the other two members of the Trinity.[81] Sometimes this idea is expressed by placing a foot of the dove on the shoulder of each of the two other persons,[82] or by allowing its wings to touch their cheeks.[83] The tips of the wings touch the lips in a beautiful miniature in a Bible dated 1368 (Fig. 603). This design is approximated in another French Bible of around 1380–1385 (Fig. 602). In the *Psalter* the wings come close to their mouths. A complication of meaning, however, appears with the introduction of a descending angel who seems almost to steer or steady the dove, and the same puzzling notion is more vividly conveyed in a miniature in the *Petites Heures*, which in almost every respect is very closely related (Fig. 127).

In all four miniatures Christ and God Father, who had often remained identical in the earlier tradition (Fig. 601), are given distinctive attributes. Christ holds the book of the Gospels and the

Lord the orb. The cross surmounting the orb in the *Petites Heures* and the later Bible was omitted in the *Psalter*, one of the bits of evidence that this miniature is not the original. As we shall see, Pseudo-Jacquemart is never an innovator. It is notable that Christ, seated on God's right, has the position that was for centuries understood to be the more important. Christ always took this place in the Coronation, while God has it in the early *Trinity* in Chantilly (Fig. 600). In our three later examples, however, God remains more frontally placed while Christ turns toward him. The hierarchy of position has yielded to one of behavior.

The miniatures in the *Psalter* of the Duke, the *Petites Heures*, and the Bible are obviously inter-related. The Bible, it should now be said, belonged to Jean de Berry; his signature appears in an unusual place, at the end of the Book of Esdras on folio 218 verso. Delisle said that the manu-script was loaned to the Duke by Charles VI on November 6, 1383,[84] a view that has been generally accepted[85] but for which no binding evidence has hitherto been offered. Ideologically the *Trinity* in this Bible might seem to have been created first because the relationships of the three members are not encumbered with an angel (Fig. 602). The idea of spiration, however, is more clearly expressed in the other two miniatures, and especially in the *Petites Heures*, where the postures of Christ and God Father are more appropriate, and the angel more gracefully guides the dove (Fig. 127). The miniature in the Bible shows, furthermore, other misadventures that clearly indicate a copy. The drapery of the two figures is very nearly identical with that in the *Petites Heures*, but a fold of God's mantle could not be contained within the pictorial field and was simply allowed to lap over the frame. The miniature in the *Psalter*, which resembles that in the Bible with respect to the position of Christ's left hand and the existence of a throne-back, ran into similar trouble with the drapery. In this instance Christ's 'train' overlaps, irrationally, the wing of the throne at the left. This miniature does preserve, however, the head-on view of the dove of the *Petites Heures*, whereas the head is turned into profile in the Bible.

The *Trinity* in the *Petites Heures*, by an illuminator whom I have called the Trinity Master after this cycle in the Duke's *Horae*, is much the strongest of the three miniatures and, except for the presence of the angel, it has the best claim to be the original of this composition. The evidence however, is not decisive, and there hangs over the problem the usual specter of a lost model, perhaps on a larger scale. Unfortunately one cannot therefore deduce any definite sequence for the *Psalter*, the *Petites Heures*, and the Bible.

The most impressive miniatures in the latter section of the *Psalter* are the *Fool* (Fig. 78) and *David in the Water* (Fig. 79). Though the most advanced, the figures follow Pucellian models very closely. The *Trinity* in the *Psalter* also depends to a degree upon Pucelle, and the three clerics singing (Fig. 81) are related to the corresponding figures in the *Bréviaire de Jeanne d'Évreux* in Chantilly from his workshop (Fig. 606). The disposition of draperies is similar, and the Pseudo-Jacquemart adopts the motif of a hand holding a large fold that is wrapped more or less across the body – a motif of classical origin that was enthusiastically revived by Italian painters around 1300.[86] The space around the clerics in the *Psalter* has been widened and deepened, and a similar extension was worked in the *Fool* and *David in the Water*.

The figures in the *Salvum me fac* resemble closely those in the *Bréviaire de Jeanne d'Évreux* (Fig. 604)[87] and also those in the corresponding miniature in the *Psalter of Bonne of Luxembourg*, which contains in addition a boat, though on the opposite side of David.[88] The gray-brown landscape in the *Psalter* still recalls Pucelle, but the bushy, high-lighted green and yellow trees, and the luminous white flesh are novel. The Fool is even closer to a Pucelle model; this complex figure cannot have been conceived by the illuminator without an opportunity to study the corresponding figure in the *Bréviaire de Jeanne d'Évreux* (Fig. 605) or an identical Pucellian drawing.[89] In both a partly naked man – the Fool is sometimes entirely naked, a sign of his evil nature[90] – brandishes in his right hand a jester's stick surmounted by a puppet. In his left he holds a round, yellowish object, upon which he munches. This object is often said to be a stone but it must actually be the bread described in the Psalm 52 (53) that this miniature illustrates: '. . . the workers of iniquity, who eat up my people as they eat bread'.

Though the painter of the Fool in the *Psalter* selected a wonderfully animated model he was not greatly interested in preserving its vigor and excitement. On the contrary, he eliminated the flying locks of hair and the drapery swirling across the left thigh. The Fool has stopped biting into the bread.[91] He is quiet and reflective. Instead of dominating the pictorial field he stands between two hillocks in a wide grassy meadow that gradually darkens.[92] His mood, not his body, fills the space. This spiritual subtlety is bound up with a novel mode of painting – suffused light on subtly variegated planes, rather than modelled masses with salient edges. This miniature is evidently the work of a major painter, still youthful it seems and trying to find his way. We shall see more of him in the *Petites Heures*.

VIII

Petites Heures

1 · EARLY HISTORY AND RECENT OPINIONS

Although the *Petites Heures* of the Duke of Berry has for a half century figured prominently in accounts of Northern painting at the end of the Middle Ages, it is the least
well known of all the major manuscripts made for this collector. It is the only one of the
Duke's Books of Hours that remains in large part unpublished. It is the smallest but certainly
not the least beautiful of this wonderful series, measuring only about 21 × 14 cm.,[1] whereas the
Très Belles Heures de Notre-Dame comes to about 28 × 20 cm., and the elephant of the group,
the *Grandes Heures*, attains nearly 40 × 30 cm. It is no less richly illuminated than these larger
manuscripts, however, for while the original layout of the *Très Belles Heures de Notre-Dame*
called for about ninety-five painted pages, there are in the *Petites Heures* more than one hundred.
With the exception of one miniature in the style of the Limbourgs, these were all probably
executed, as we shall see, within a period of five years or less. The paintings are thus far more
homogeneous than those of the *Très Belles Heures de Notre-Dame*, but whereas the latter was
undertaken by one master who for a time dominated the entire work and who himself executed
some of the large miniatures, the *Petites Heures* is the product of at least five illuminators, two
of whom were major artists. They exchanged ideas with one another, and two painters not
infrequently worked on one miniature, small though it be, so that the determination of their
respective roles is an even more subtle task than that presented by the *Très Belles Heures de Notre-
Dame*.

The manuscript that we call the *Petites Heures* is described in the Duke of Berry's inventory of
1402 as:

> Item, unes très belles Heures, contenant pluseurs heures et commémoracions de Dieu et de ses sains, ou
> commencement desquelles est le kalendrier très richement historié des épistres de saint Paul, de l'ancien
> et nouvel Testament, et après sont pluseurs enseignements escrips en françois de bien et honnestement
> vivre selon Dieu, lesquelles heures sont très richement historiées en pluseurs lieux, et mesmement, au
> commencement des heures de Nostre Dame, d'une annonciacion et de pluseurs apostres à l'entour, et en
> la fin a une oroison en latin qui se commence Sancta crux. Et sont couvertes d'un sathin bleu doublé d'un
> tercelin vermeil, garnies de deux fermouers d'or à deux ors, tenens les armes de Monseigneur, assis sur
> tixuz noire, semez de trefles d'or. Et est la pipe des dictes heures esmaillée aux armes de mon dit seigneur,
> garnie de deux perles; et a ou milieu un balay longuet.

This notice describes three of the most unusual features of the *Petites Heures*: the Calendar,
which belongs to a small group deriving from the *Bréviaire de Belleville*; instructions on the
conduct of life, directed primarily to princes; and the *Annunciation* surrounded by the figures
of apostles. No other item in the Berry inventories can be identified with the *Petites Heures*, and
although the final prayer beginning *Sancta crux* does not form part of the book in its present
state, the identification would seem to be conclusive.

While the book was in the possession of the Duke of Berry prayers for travellers were added at the end and embellished around 1412 with a miniature by the Limbourgs. The miniature, which contains a portrait of the Duke setting out on a journey, is discussed in Chapter IV, p. 72 and no. 61. The description in the inventory of 1413 contains no recognition of this alteration, but it does refer to a new binding: 'Et a present sont couvertes de drap de damas violet'. This re-binding was presumably necessitated by the above-mentioned addition, and it was probably at this time that the prayer beginning *Sancta crux* was either removed or mislaid. Shortly before the Duke's death the *Petites Heures* was given to the wife of Robinet d'Estampes; the gift is mentioned in the final inventory:

> Date fuerunt per dominum ducem Bitturicensem, et per ejus litteras data xxviii die maii mccccxvi, uxori Robineti de Stampis.

Although ownership of the *Petites Heures* by the Duke of Berry is an incontrovertible fact, some scholars (Couderc, and in 1963 Delaissé) have maintained that it was not he who originally commissioned the manuscript. They point to a note on folio A:

> Ces heures ont esté reliées en l'estat qu'elles sont en l'an 1606, par ordre de Charles, par la grace de Dieu duc de Lorraine et de Bar. Auparavant, elles estoient couvertes d'argent, mais les pièces estoient fort gastées et rompues, et paraissoit y avoir eu des pierreries sur l'argent. Et estoit escrit dessus: Louys, roy d'Hierusalem et de Sicile, duc d'Anjou, 1390.

A date of 1390 for the manuscript is plausible, and the inscription was accepted by Gaignières, who engraved the back of the book with the title *Heures de Louis, duc d'Anjou, roy de Jérusalem,* while it was in his possession.[2] A nearly identical inscription was, however, observed by Leroquais, stamped in gold on the inside of the cover of a book which is definitely of a much later period.[3] This Book of Hours (Bibl. nat., lat. 1156B) was made for Marguerite d'Orléans, who married Richard, comte d'Étampes, in 1426; her Hours seem to have been executed shortly after this date. Since in this case the inscription has obviously nothing to do with either Louis d'Anjou or 1390, one must conclude that both inscriptions were written at a time when the original owners were no longer known. The name 'Louys' has been altered in the *Petites Heures* but speculation about what it might originally have been does not seem profitable.

We are left, thus, with no particular reason to believe that the *Petites Heures* was ever connected with Louis d'Anjou, whether Louis I, who died in 1384, or Louis II, who became Duke at the age of seven.[4] The Calendar entry for August 19 shows the comparatively unknown St. Grant rather than that memorable member of the Anjou family, St. Louis of Toulouse. It is true that St. Louis appears twice in the Litanies, but the representation of him among other saints confessors on folio 105 verso – a fact that is emphasized by the Angevin party – does not seem significant because of the popularity of this new Franciscan saint. The appearance of the arms of Anjou on his cope conforms with tradition, which may here be exemplified by a representation in a slightly earlier manuscript that has Burgundian, not Angevin connections (Fig. 608).[5]

More weighty is the argument based on the portraits, which Delaissé has presented recently in careful and refined form.[6] Noting the use on certain folios of a grayer ink for the script instead of the more common brown, and relating these observations to the make-up of the folios, he proposed that folios 96-97, 145-154, and 196-199 were added to the original volume. These additions, together with the Calendar, the Hours of the Baptist, and perhaps other sections were, he said, added by Jean de Berry to a book he had obtained from someone else – probably one of the Anjou. The portraits, he claims, fall into two groups, one representing the original lean-faced owner and the other the pudgy Jean de Berry, and all the latter appear on folios he allegedly added.[7] Delaissé's study of the composition of the book, though incomplete, is valuable, but his proposals about patrons raise serious difficulties.

First of all, a beardless man with round face similar to the one that appears in many portraits of Jean de Berry may be found on folios of the *Petites Heures* that Delaissé has not said were added – folios 22, 100 verso, 103 verso (Figs. 94, 115, 116). The last looks like a copy of the portrait on the inserted folio 97 verso (Fig. 114). Furthermore, a round face, but bearded, may be seen on folios 139 and 172 (Figs. 128, 147).

The portraits in this manuscript, which are all described in Chapter IV, do indeed vary with respect to physiognomy, color of the hair, and the presence or absence of a beard and moustache. With regard to style (not considered by Delaissé) they fall into two large classes, one by the conservative Pseudo-Jacquemart, who painted most of them, and the other by the advanced Jacquemart or his very close associate in this enterprise, the Trinity Master (see table of the illuminators of the *Petites Heures*). In most of his 'portraits' Pseudo-Jacquemart made little attempt at likeness, and to anyone seeking the identity of the 'sitter' he presented a bewildering variety of faces (Figs. 117-123, 128, 147, 148, 150, 159, 161). This is no less true of the three figures selected by Delaissé as representations of the first patron (Figs. 121, 128, 150). Though they all sport beards and moustaches, the appendages of one are white, of the others gray; one has a round face like that of Berry, the others a narrow head, but very different in precise shape. All the portraits by Jacquemart and the Trinity Master, on the contrary, beginning on folio 22 and continuing through the book, seem to represent one man, and the arms that accompany him or the close resemblance with other identifiable portraits prove that that man was Jean de Berry (Figs. 94, 114, 116, 162).[8] Style, always relevant to the identification of portraits, is an especially important criterion in the late fourteenth century, when the concept of portraiture was undergoing a fundamental change.

The problem is still more complex. There are other factors. We must recall that by 1389, and quite possibly several years earlier, the Duke abandoned his beard and moustache. This change in his appearance could very well be reflected in the portraits, but we cannot be certain that a minor, conservative illuminator would respond to it as quickly as an *avant-garde* colleague. Thus the different heads in the *Petites Heures* might as well be ascribed to a changing patron and to diverse artists as to a change of ownership. The catalogue of portraits demonstrates, furthermore, that most of the pentimenti appear in portraits that represent the lean, bearded 'first patron', and that therefore physiognomic alterations are not necessarily indicative of a new patron.

The study that follows of the pictorial styles of the *Petites Heures*, based on an outline I published in 1956, shows that the painters who collaborated on its production contributed to many parts of the book. A comparison of the gatherings of the manuscript with the table of contributions by the five painters – both tables published as appendices to this chapter – discloses the nature of the distribution. Apart from the gathering added at the end that contains the *Itinerary* by the Limbourgs only the *last* part of the book, folios 217-286, is exclusively illuminated by the weakest painter, Pseudo-Jacquemart. Even if this is all that remains of the manuscript that the Duke presumably acquired – a most unlikely hypothesis – he would have taken over the illuminator as well as the book, because the style is evident on preceding folios. The same conclusion is true *a fortiori* of other parts of the book.

It should be said, on the other hand, that the arms of Berry on the altar within the important miniature of the *Annunciation* (Fig. 94) overlap the drapery and were not included initially. The arms in the initials, containing a different kind of pigment than was employed elsewhere, may have been an afterthought also. All of this, however, must be interpreted in relation to the fact that the Duke did not see fit to intrude into his early manuscripts to the degree that he did later. The arms on the *chapelle ardente* in the early *Très Belles Heures de Notre-Dame* were probably added later, as we have seen, and in the Duke's manuscripts we can watch the portraits moving from the margins into the initials, then into subordinate miniatures, and finally into the main fields.

Long ago Paul Durrieu observed the extensive relationship of the text of the *Petites Heures* to that of the *Très Belles Heures de Notre-Dame*.[9] The two manuscripts include even those prayers containing a specific reference to a King of France that were mentioned in the discussion of the latter work.[10] Because of these prayers we allowed for the possibility that the *Très Belles Heures de Notre-Dame* was begun for Charles V, although the evidence against an initial royal commission is very considerable. The same may be said of the *Petites Heures*. It is true that in this manuscript the text describing the instructions of St. Louis to his sons is illustrated by a beautiful miniature (Fig. 89), and we know that Charles V was devoted to St. Louis. On the other hand Jean de Berry too had sons, Charles and Jean, who died before 1383 and in 1397 respectively. Much more damaging to the hypothesis of Charles V as the initial patron is the fact that the portraits of the supposed 'first campaign' in the *Petites Heures* show a prince with beard and moustache, whereas Charles was clean-shaven.

Though the hypothesis of an initial patron other than the Duke of Berry cannot be absolutely disproved the evidence that he was the initiator is very nearly compelling. His saint, the Baptist, has unique prominence in both the text and the illumination. He appears twice in gold letters in the Calendar, a prayer to him precedes those of the prophets, patriarchs, and apostles, and he is called *Monseigneur saint Jehan Baptiste* in a communion prayer. There is furthermore an entire office in his honor with a special *Te Deum*. Though this office appears near the end of the manuscript and has sometimes been considered a later addition, the beautiful miniatures in it offer evidence, as we shall see, to the contrary. On folio 22 the Baptist appears at the left of Christ, replacing the more usual John Evangelist, and on folio 104 he has been singled out from other saints and given a separate composition. If the manuscript was begun for a patron other than Jean de Berry the work cannot have been carried very far, and the book must have been completely transformed before leaving the workshop to fit the requirements of the Duke of Berry. Styles interpenetrate throughout the book, indicating not only completion within the same workshop but also continuity, or near-continuity, in execution. More will be said of this matter below.

The first significant attempt to deal historically with the miniatures of the *Petites Heures* was made by Durrieu in 1894, when he followed an opinion already expressed by Gonse and attributed the majority of the miniatures to Beauneveu or his atelier. Some of the miniatures grouped together in this pioneer study are obviously not by the same hand. He regarded the *Trinity* (Fig. 154) and the apostles around the *Annunciation* (Fig. 94) as particularly characteristic of Beauneveu's style, and he ascribed to this painter the Calendar and all miniatures in the Hours of the Virgin, with the exception of the *Annunciation to the Shepherds* (Fig. 92). He recognized the hand of the sculptor also in the *Grandes Heures*, the Evangeliary and the Lectionary in Bourges, the *Très Belles Heures de Notre-Dame*, and two earlier manuscripts. While the attribution to Beauneveu was never very widely accepted, it continues to find advocates, as recently indeed as the Vienna Catalogue of 1962.

Lasteyrie took a step forward in 1896, when he recognized similarities of style between certain miniatures in the *Grandes Heures* and in the *Petites Heures*. Since the *Grandes Heures* was executed some years after Beauneveu's death and the only painter associated with it in the inventory is that of Jacquemart de Hesdin, he concluded that this artist also played a major part in the execution of the *Petites Heures*. Lasteyrie, who like Durrieu had an unwarranted impression of a uniform manuscript, similarly attributed the miniatures to a single leading master. He found the most striking resemblances to the *Grandes Heures* in the Calendar, which seemed to him especially characteristic of the style of Jacquemart de Hesdin. Since this time the *Petites Heures* and the *Grandes Heures* have tended to be linked as works of Jacquemart and recently the early miniatures in the *Très Belles Heures de Notre-Dame* have been included in the group by Panofsky and Porcher.[11]

The miniatures illustrating the main cycle of the Passion and the Penitential Psalms, which Durrieu had excluded from his group of Beauneveu's works, attracted the attention of Bouchot in 1904.[12] He concluded that these miniatures were by the painter of the *Parement de Narbonne*, who might be identified with Jean d'Orléans. The individuality and the power of the painter of the Passion cycle in the *Petites Heures* were recognized by Panofsky in 1953, and in 1955 Porcher noted the connection of this artist with the *Bréviaire de Charles V*.[13] In 1956 and in 1961 I identified an earlier stage of the same style in the *Heures de Yolande de Flandre* as well as in the *Bréviaire de Charles V*,[14] and in 1962 Dr. Kathleen Morand suggested that this artist maintained Jean Pucelle's workshop after Pucelle's own death.[15]

In 1956 the writer distinguished five styles in the *Petites Heures*, and outlined the share of these illuminators in other manuscripts produced for the Duke. Inasmuch as these conclusions are developed without change in the text that follows they need not be set forth here.

2 · THE PASSION MASTER

In general layout the folios of the *Petites Heures* resemble the *Très Belles Heures de Notre-Dame* (Figs. 7, 86, 90). The margins in the *Petites Heures* are proportionately wider, but the vines are more than correspondingly large, and active. They tend to fill more completely the space outside the bars and frames. In design and content they resemble the *Psalter of Bonne de Luxembourg* (Figs. 353, 361). The folios with miniatures look as though they had been planned, like the *Très Belles Heures de Notre-Dame* and numerous *Horae* of the Bondol and late Pucelle traditions, for *bas-de-page* with scenes or drolleries. Most of these spaces, however, have remained quite blank. It is significant that they were filled only by the most retrospective of the illuminators who worked on the manuscript, below the miniature for the Penitential Psalms (Fig. 99) and at the beginning of the Hours of the Passion (Fig. 106). This painter, who may be called the Master of the Passion after his cycle in this manuscript, painted two episodes of the Pact of Judas below the miniature of the *Betrayal*. In the initial he portrayed the Agony in the Garden, thus presenting a system and a choice of subjects precisely like the *Très Belles Heures de Notre-Dame* (Fig. 22). We may infer that the Passion Master was responsible for the design of the folios of the *Petites Heures*. The decision of his collaborators to abandon the friezes and the historiated initials was momentous: it implied a desire to give the main picture uniqueness and a much greater importance.

Whereas in this aspect of their design the *Petites Heures* seem more advanced than the *Très Belles Heures de Notre-Dame*, in another respect they are not. The frames of most of the miniatures are delicate and fanciful; they show the kind of quatrefoil that was favored by followers of Pucelle and Bondol but with the cusps more flattened than before. These beautifully curved bounding lines are more suitable to the compositions of the Passion Master than to those of his more or less progressive associates, and this fact strengthens our belief that it was he who designed the folios. His most advanced associate, in fact, felt that these quatrefoils were undesirable, and in a few miniatures in the Hours of the Virgin he substituted for them a simple rectangular frame, similar to that used by the Master of the Parement de Narbonne (Figs. 90, 93, 94).

The Hours of the Virgin, the most important part of a Book of Hours, indeed the one indispensable section of the text, was usually illustrated by the *chef d'atelier*; he normally painted at least the first miniature in the cycle. In this part of the *Petites Heures*, however, the master whom we have supposed to be the designer of the *vignetures* and the quatrefoils had only a very secondary role. On the other hand he did paint all of the next most important sequence in the manuscript, the Hours of the Passion, and whether or not the decision to do this was his it was precisely this sequence that offered the greatest scope for his extraordinary narrative and dramatic gifts. He provided in this cycle the most impassioned French paintings of the late fourteenth century. He appears almost as Pucelle reincarnate, an even more fervent if less profound and noble Pucelle. Actually he emerged in the workshop of his great predecessor. He becomes recognizable first in the *Heures de Yolande de Flandre*, executed after her marriage in 1353,[16] and in the *Bréviaire de*

Charles V, illuminated certainly before 1380, when it appeared in the King's inventory.[17] The *Bréviaire* came into the possession of Jean de Berry, but only in 1407 or 1408.

The *Heures de Yolande de Flandre* was seriously damaged in a flood of the Thames River in the nineteenth century, but enough has been preserved to disclose the agitated, almost explosive narrative art of the Passion Master. The *Entombment*, which has been largely spared from damp, shows a distraught Virgin giving Christ a last embrace, her straw-colored hair streaming out from her head and her eyes rolling wildly (Fig. 366). Over her the high emotion of the crowd that presses forward culminates in one of the Maries, who in both the *Heures de Yolande de Flandre* and the *Petites Heures* flings her arms into the air (Figs. 113, 366).[18] Some of the figures in the Hours in London are very short, but their faces as well as their bodies possess the kind of fleshiness that is so conspicuous in the *Petites Heures*. Forms in both manuscripts are defined by a red line that shows an exceptional vibration. The resemblances of compositions or figures in the two Books of Hours are innumerable. As he hangs from the cross, Christ's legs are tightly twisted in agony, and his head is bent into horizontality, as though his neck were broken (Figs. 111, 365.)

Given the difference of subjects, the correspondences of the miniatures in the *Bréviaire* with the Passion cycle in the *Petites Heures* are less numerous, but we shall observe a connection with other scenes in the Duke's manuscript. There are indeed telling similarities, such as the appearance in the *Bréviaire* of the genial conception of David's little dog, which stands before its master and snarls at the giant Goliath (Figs. 99, 362). Landscape is painted in the pearly blue-green favored by the Passion Master, and his rather dusty colors – violet, pink, buff, pale blue – abound in the *Bréviaire*. In both manuscripts the illuminator creates a weird emotionality by modelling flesh in red-brown and occasionally rendering the corneas of the eyes in blue.[19]

Though the continuity of style from the *Heures de Yolande de Flandre* through the *Bréviaire* to the *Petites Heures* cannot be doubted, the designs of the Passion Master in the *Petites Heures* often reflect miniatures known only in other manuscripts from the Pucelle circle. *Christ in Majesty* (Fig. 99) is almost identical with the corresponding figure in the much earlier and stylistically rather different *Bible historiale* in Geneva (Fig. 349).[20] While the little dog in the *bas-de-page* appeared earlier in the *Bréviaire*, as we have mentioned (Fig. 362), the figure of David is nearly identical with the corresponding figure in the *Psalter of Bonne de Luxembourg* (Fig. 361).[21] The background of seraphim in the *Majesty* of the *Petites Heures* occurs in red as well as blue in the *Psalter of Bonne* and in the *Heures de Jeanne de Navarre*. Since neither of these manuscripts is known to have belonged to Jean de Berry or indeed to the royal collection, the Passion Master would seem to have possessed numerous drawings of Pucelle's compositions and motifs, and Dr. Morand's proposal that he inherited workshop patterns seems entirely acceptable.[22] The influence of Pucelle in the *Petites Heures* extends, as we shall see, beyond the Passion Master to his collaborators and successors.

The first miniature in the *Petites Heures* painted entirely by the Passion Master is the *Majesty of Christ* at the beginning of the Penitential Psalms (Fig. 99). While the swirling lines of Christ's drapery derive from a Pucellesque model (Fig. 349) the bench on which he is seated, with its vigorously curling scrolls, is a favorite of the Passion Master; it had appeared earlier in the

Bréviaire de Charles V (Fig. 351). The four evangelists squirm in the tension of composition, and their symbols are caught up in the excitement. These figures imply the influence of the *Boqueteaux* style (Fig. 383), a reminder of which may also be seen in the umbrella-like trees in the *bas-de-page*. In the borders brightly colored birds and a rabbit perch on the vines while a large crane fastens his bill on a solid but not very nourishing formalized leaf. In the right margin several figures parody the main events. The grotesque two-headed warrior reduces to absurdity the battle of David and Goliath by fighting, it seems, with himself. The ill-clad old men waving scrolls while they try to stabilize themselves with the tails and legs of animals poke fun at the solemn enthusiasm evoked by books in the miniature nearby. The cardinal turns his back, his position the opposite of the frontal Christ, and he stares at his book unmindful of the giddy rooster on which he is seated and which is wrapped in his mantle. The rooster, like the symbols of the evangelists, has a message: he bears a scroll in his beak. The only attentive witness of the exaltation of Christ and of the composition of the gospels is a snail, who holds up his head with what seems to be self-conscious solemnity.

Such mockery of major themes was not new in medieval art. It had a long history insubordinate fields of representation, such as choir stalls and capitals. The juxtaposition of theme and counter-theme in the *Petites Heures* is striking, but it may be seen earlier in the circle of Pucelle. Below the *Nativity* in the *Heures de Jeanne de Navarre*, illuminated around 1340, a kind of centaur hugs an infant and nearby a woman seated on the 'ground' nurses a child – a secular Madonna of Humility (Fig. 346).

In the *Betrayal* a sly and serpentine Judas winds himself around Christ, at the same time looking out at us like the knowing villain in a play who greets with professional pride the hisses of his audience (Fig. 106). He thrusts against Christ's cheek a sinister profile. Most of the soldiers at the right have ape-like features, and one is a Negro. In accordance with a medieval convention the illuminator is employing ugly and dark countenances to express evil. Deep brown skin characterizes malefactors in the *Légende de St. Denis* of 1317,[23] and black is the color of the devil and sometimes of the synagogue.[24] Pucelle and his associates sometimes give Negroid faces to the enemies of Christ, and a Negro appears in the *Betrayal* in the *Psalter of Bonne de Luxembourg* shortly before 1349 (Fig. 352). The painter had living models for these figures. We know that in 1354 King Jean le Bon received as a gift from Peter of Aragon a handsome Negro ironically named Charles Blanc.[25]

It is the *Psalter of Bonne* that gave the strongest impetus towards the use of ugliness to convey evil and to create a powerful contrast between the believers and the unbelievers. The amazing Fool in the *Psalter* is an anti-Semitic caricature, unprecedented in the tradition of the illustration of this psalm (Fig. 353). The self-conscious Judas in the *Betrayal* (Fig. 352) anticipates the figure in the *Petites Heures*.[26]

The antecedents of such figures are, as we mentioned in Chapter I, the creatures in the margins of manuscripts, and in the *Petites Heures* we witness a new invasion of the main fields. In the *Mockery* Christ sits erect and still amid a mad Bosch-like throng, his tormentors' arms waving wildly about him like the tentacles of an octopus (Fig. 108). In sadistic excitement they twist into impossible postures. As in the *Heures de Jeanne de Navarre* (Fig. 348) Christ's head is entirely shrouded in an orange cloth, which heightens the contrast, as Panofsky described it, between 'depraved cruelty and supreme patience'.[27] Contrary to convention in the later fourteenth century this scene, as well as *Christ before Pilate* (Fig. 107) and the *Flagellation* (Fig. 109), is set out of doors. The painter finds the flickering forms of a green-blue terrain (ultimately Ducciesque) and of a lively arabesque in the backgrounds more expressive than the stable geometry of buildings. The *Flagellation* is performed as though it were a sort of vehement ritualistic dance. The scourger at the right, wearing one yellow stocking and one scarlet, displays from head to toe a fantastic and flickering profile. His drooping nose and pointed chin, the features of evil, seem to anticipate the so-called 'nutcracker' type of Leonardo da Vinci.[28] A pantomime of similar vehemence, and with equally beautiful postures, may be seen in the *Flagellation* in the Douce Missal (Fig. 373).

In the *Way to Calvary* Christ tries to lighten the weight of the cross on his neck by extending his hand under the cross-bar, a most unusual gesture (Fig. 110). The cross seems almost to sever his head from his shoulders in a remarkably pathetic design. For the *Crucifixion* the Passion Master adopted the dramatic composition created by Duccio and introduced into France by Pucelle in the *Heures de Jeanne d'Évreux* (Figs. 111, 336). He increased to two the men who fall to the ground, and he heightened the contrast between believers and unbelievers. Two of the latter, at the left, smirk; at the right there is a pug-nosed, square-headed man, red of face, and alongside him a yellow-skinned rascal, long-nosed, and squawking. While the neck and body of Christ are twisted with violent pain in this scene, in the *Deposition* he is limp in the arms of Joseph of Arimathea and a voraciously affectionate Mary (Fig. 112). Before a rocky terrain strewn with skulls and bones stands a sort of pink platform that probably represents the red stone of unction on which Christ was said to have been laid after the Crucifixion, and which appears in later paintings, such as the *Lamentation* of Roger van der Weyden or the *Entombment* by Caravaggio.[29] The *Entombment* in the *Petites Heures* has an exceptionally broad and firm geometric structure, the diagonals of which, even in space, are concentrated above in the despairing arms of one of the Maries (Fig. 113).

The Master of the Passion may be found, as I proposed in 1956, in the *Petites Heures* outside the Hours of the Passion. His participation in several sections of the manuscript gives us important insight into its production. We may recognize him, first of all, in the border of the first folio bearing a miniature after the Hours of the Passion. The miniature, which will be discussed later as a work of the most advanced painter in the manuscript, represents the Duke of Berry in prayer before the standing *Madonna* (Fig. 114). In the border, now abraded, a poor old fellow in a scarlet shirt hopefully extends a bowl, and above him a grotesque creature, part man and part beast, exploits for similar purposes a young child in his arms. The group is a transformation of the real beggars to whom the queen gives alms in the *Heures de Jeanne de Navarre* (Fig. 347). The compound creatures in the *Petites Heures* all tactfully look away from the Duke. But, as on the folio of the *Majesty* (Fig. 99), these marginal figures are sardonic commentaries on the inhabitants of the main field. It is difficult here to avoid associating the infant in the arms of his hooded 'parent' with the Christ Child in the arms of Mary. Nor can one fail to link the begging creatures with the beseeching prince, equated as they are back to back. Such mockeries of Christian subjects even so central a one as the Crucifixion, are not uncommon in earlier Gothic art; they become rarer in the later fourteenth and early fifteenth centuries (Fig. 623).

These paintings are on what appears to be an added folio, but the presence of figures by the Passion Master, in the style of his preceding miniatures, proves that the addition was not made after the lapse of any considerable period of time.[30] This extraordinary illuminator may be seen again further along in the book, in what may seem a surprising place. He had a share in the Hours of the Baptist, that part of the *Petites Heures* that is often said to be the latest, and to contain miniatures that belong to a new phase.[31] There he painted a charming miniature at Tierce showing the youthful Baptist seated at the mouth of a cave in the desert (Fig. 167). The iconography seems to be unique. The *Protoevangelium of James* said that Elizabeth and her son hid in a mountain, and the two are frequently represented in a cave in Byzantine and Near-Eastern art.[32] John alone, however, was not shown in such an environment, though other hermits frequently were,[33] and even St. Francis is given a cave in one of Pucelle's earliest works (Fig. 356). An earlier image by the Passion Master himself in the *Bréviaire de Charles V* may be regarded as a rehearsal for the miniature in the *Petites Heures*. St. Theobald, an eleventh-century hermit who lived near Provins in the Champagne, sits in a cave in a flamboyant landscape – basically Ducciesque in character (Fig. 369). The decision to portray the Baptist in this manner was no doubt given impetus by the concluding lines of the prayer in the office on the preceding folio, which speak of penitence in the 'antra deserti'. The prayer may have suggested also the most extraordinary aspect of the miniature, the trustfulness and affection of the animals in this Peaceable Kingdom, because God is addressed as the 'innocentis amator etatis'. It seems probable at the same time, as Mrs. Marilyn Lavin proposed, that the illuminator drew from a fourteenth-century life of the Baptist which states that the youthful saint 's'abbraciava coi lioni e colle bestie grandi salvatiche che trovava nel diserto'.[34]

Beginning with these earlier ideas and representations the Passion Master has created a unique scene. The saint fondles a lion, as the text said, but the visible eye of the 'great wild beast' stares out at us with the sly, self-conscious expression of many of the painter's human actors. The panther, too, crouching like a big domestic cat at the saint's foot, presents the strange, loose-jawed profile familiar from the scenes of the Passion.

The *St. John* exemplifies another aspect of the migration from the borders into the main pictorial field that we discussed above. We recognize in the trees and on the rocks many of the creatures that inhabited the vines around the Passion scenes and the *Majesty*. A hoopoe perches on the rock behind the saint, and an inquisitive snail bends down to inspect his face. The rabbits darting in and out of holes, their noses quivering or the white patch of their tails just disappearing in darkness, are presented with the affection for animals and the humor that we have already recognized in the Hours of the Passion. The painter could not refrain from further populating this desert with a boar, a bear, a mountain goat, and a heavily antlered buck. There are even two apes, normally creatures of evil but here, it seems, in the era after St. Francis, also representatives of the 'etas innocens'; one of them is even honored by the glance of the Baptist. Weaving all this wild-life together, and binding the violet-robed saint to it is a flickering, straw-colored landscape, narrow strips of which were visible in the Hours of the Passion.

The Baptist in this miniature seems a more substantial figure than we have seen in the preceding miniatures by the Passion Master, and this painting, probably made somewhat later than the others, shows in this respect the influence of the master's associates,[35] whose more plastic art we have yet to consider. The relationship of styles is more complex in the two other miniatures of this cycle in which the Passion Master participated. He was certainly responsible for the design of the *Birth of the Baptist* at Lauds, with its brown Pucellesque building, its blue ceiling with red ribs, and its agitated drapery (Fig. 166). Characteristic too are the women at the left, the puckish man in the doorway, and the pale blue, violet, and ocher colors. But the solid Zacharias and the head of the man whom he addresses are not simply influenced by a second master but painted by him. This same kind of collaboration, despite the small size of the miniature, produced the *Dance of Salome* at Vespers (Fig. 170). The Passion Master again designed the composition and the figures and determined the colors. Salome wears a violet dress darkened to deep bluish-purple, and the rocks in the foreground, which the illuminator is loath to abandon even when he represents an interior, are blue-green. The cool, dusky palette of the Passion Master is still dominant, and the little dogs belong to the breed we have seen below the *Majesty* (Fig. 99) and in the *Bréviaire de Charles V* (Fig. 362). The painting of the heads, and perhaps also of parts of the torsos, must be ascribed to an associate, the illuminator to be designated below as the Trinity Master.

Unprecedented in the work of the Passion Master are the perspective and the depth of the space. The orthogonals in his earlier interiors were drawn more or less parallel and oblique to the picture plane (Fig. 368), in the manner of the Pucelle tradition. The ceiling of the *Birth of the Baptist* shows a vanishing axis system, which had been introduced into French painting, however, half a century earlier by Pucelle himself in the *Annunciation* in the *Heures de Jeanne d'Évreux* though its use had lagged afterwards (Fig. 335). It is all the more surprising that the orthogonals in the ceiling of the *Dance of Salome* should focus in one small region (Fig. 170). What was the illuminator's model for this? A one-point system was introduced by Jean Bondol in the frontis-piece of the *Bible de Charles V* of 1371 (Fig. 382), which of course the Passion Master saw while working for the King. In the library of Jean de Berry the illuminator could have studied approximations to it in some miniatures of the Parement Master (Figs. 14, 25). A ceiling very similar to that of the *Dance* appears a few folios further on in the *Petites Heures* (Fig. 176). This second interior contains evidence, as we shall see, that both ceilings reflect an advanced model that is either lost or not yet identified.

The Passion Master had a share in the first *Horae* in the manuscript as well as the last. He worked indeed at the very beginning, in the *Annunciation* (Fig. 94). Since he was the master who designed the pages one might have expected him to embellish the margins, as he did for the *Majesty* (Fig. 99) and the first folio of the Hours of the Passion (Fig. 106). This, however, he failed to do. He left to his collaborator, identifiable with Jacquemart de Hesdin, the border with its apostles and the choice of a rectangular rather than a cusped frame. His collaborator certainly painted the elaborate pink stone church and the small bust of God the Father who peers over it, almost squeezed out of the space. The Gothic shapes as well as the light color of the building are not characteristic of the Passion Master. The tessellated floor furthermore contains units

M

with a longer dimension oblique to the picture plane, as in the following miniature of the *Visitation* (Fig. 90). While, however, most of the orthogonals in the floor of the *Annunciation* focus on one point as in the *Birth*, those in the *Visitation* focus on two, located near one another. Perhaps the Passion Master and Jacquemart both contributed to the design of this composition, but the latter was clearly responsible for the execution of the church.[36]

There can be no doubt, however, who designed and painted the figures of Gabriel and Mary.[37] The animated postures, the strongly coursing rhythms, the pointed narrative, are familiar from other paintings of the Passion Master. His St. Michael in the Breviary is a prototype (Fig. 839). The drawing in the *Petites Heures* is the characteristic red-brown, the shading is similar, and the violet of Gabriel's mantle typical. Of course the figures seem rather slight in volume and rather unsteady in the great stone church; they lack the statuesque poise that the setting requires. But the great innovation in this miniature, the angel pointing spontaneously to heaven, would seem to have been conceived by the author of the Magus pointing to the star in the *Bréviaire de Charles V* (Fig. 367), of the wonderful gesture of one of the Maries in the *Entombment* (Fig. 113) or the waving arms of Christ's tormentors in the *Mockery* (Fig. 108). The idea seems consistent with his genius rather than with that of the master who painted a similar angel in an *Annunciation* deeper in the book (folio 141 verso – Fig. 130). Though the painter of this miniature, often said to be Jacquemart[38] but in my opinion the Trinity Master, has been credited with the invention, he normally prefers gravity to animation. It is true that Gabriel's gesture is more vehement in this miniature than on folio 22, but it is at the same time much less subtle, and the composition on folio 141 verso is remarkably Pucellesque, as Panofsky has observed. Indeed it is in many respects similar to the *Annunciation* in the *Bréviaire de Charles V* (Fig. 368). We are thus brought back even for the design of this miniature to the Passion Master himself.

The figure of the pointing Gabriel did not appear in the *Petites Heures* as a wholly unprecedented form. One of the most intellectual masters of the century, Ambrogio Lorenzetti, showed the archangel conspicuously gesturing toward heaven, though he used only the thumb of his right hand (Fig. 628). Once again the germ at least of the new pantomime turns out to have been Italian. The pointing Gabriel of the *Petites Heures* proved attractive to many later artists. It reappeared first in a manuscript of about 1390 that is very close generally to the *Petites Heures* and that repeats several of its figures and compositions (Fig. 618).[39] The demonstrative Gabriel appeared again in a second manuscript that must be dated around 1390, the Bible in the Vatican that will be discussed in the following chapter (Fig. 658). The figure was employed soon afterward in a Book of Hours of more conservative style (Fig. 620),[40] and then in numerous paintings of the fifteenth and sixteenth centuries, as far afield as Germany and Italy.[41] The miniature mentioned first (Fig. 618) is a copy of folio 141 verso rather than of folio 22, and in conformity with the current trend in painting, the pantomime is made quieter by abandonment of the raised right arm of the Virgin. Dr. Dorothy Miner has given convincing textual evidence for dating this Book of Hours between 1387 and 1394,[42] and we have thus a *terminus ante quem* for the latest style in the *Petites Heures*.

The compelling art of the Passion Master is visible once again in the Hours of the Virgin. Here he appeared in a role opposite to the one he assumed in the *Annunciation*. Again selecting a subject congenial to his talent, he must have drawn and partly painted the *Annunciation to the Shepherds* (Fig. 92). The yellow-brown landscape, in design much like the Baptist's desert (Fig. 167), is certainly his invention, and his too are the lively, howling dogs as well as the impish shepherds with bagpipes. The ocher and violet colors are characteristic. The placement of two shepherds (one with red hair and beard) deep in clefts in the rock is also consistent with his interests. This largely subterranean placement, which had a later history in France and in the Italian early Renaissance,[43] was anticipated in the same scene in the Master's earlier *Heures de Yolande de Flandre* (Fig. 364) as well as in the *Heures de Jeanne de Navarre*.[44] The miniature in the *Heures de Yolande* contains, in fact, almost all the figures that appear in the *Petites Heures*: angels bearing scrolls in similar postures, the shepherd with a crook attentive to them, a man bent over his bagpipe, the hunched shepherd at the right,[45] and the little dog sprawled on the ground. The hunched shepherd is one of those eccentric beings that looks as though it had moved in from the borders. Some of the figures in this miniature in the *Petites Heures* – the shepherd leaning on his crook and the six graceful and symmetrically arranged angels above – show the brighter color and the suffused light of the major collaborator of the master.

The relationship of the Passion Master to fourteenth-century painting in France was exceptional. He emerges clearly first, so far as we can see, around 1355, intimately aware of Pucelle's art of the period of the *Psalter of Bonne*, painted only a few years earlier. Over the years Pucelle had modified his style, giving the forms greater volume and reducing lines for luminous planes, but the basic principles remained largely unchanged. The Passion Master did not alter them either. Rather he gave to the style of Pucelle personal accents, especially of heightened and often bizarre emotionality. He increased the volume of his forms and their luminosity, learning no doubt from Bondol and his associates, with whom, indeed, he collaborated in the *Bréviaire de Charles V*.

In the *Heures de Yolande de Flandre*, illuminated shortly after 1353, the Passion Master is closest to Pucelle, and he probably worked on that manuscript with the great old master himself. In the *Bréviaire de Charles V*, painted ten or fifteen years later, his individuality is much more evident. Soldiers perform their brutal tasks with unprecedented vehemence, and the affection of the 'family' of Christ or the mothers in the *Massacre of the Innocents* has become desperate (Fig. 370). In this phase the figures are short, and they crouch, huddle, or tumble. About a decade later the illuminator accepted an important commission from the prince who was emerging as the most perceptive patron in France. Stimulated by the occasion he began to adopt some – but not many – of the innovations he saw around him. The figures are taller, related in proportion to those of the Parement Master (Figs. 25, 109) or of the illuminator of the Bible, Bibl. nat., fr. 20090 (Fig. 611). Working as a mature if not old master side by side with young, experimental painters of the day he showed a new interest in architecture and in focus perspective, particularly in his designs for the Hours of the Baptist (Figs. 166, 170).

The illuminator who was employed by patrons of such distinction as Yolande de Flandre, Charles V (probably),[46] and Jean de Berry must have enjoyed an exceptional reputation from the mid-'fifties to the mid-'eighties. A long time ago Léopold Delisle suggested that the *Heures de Yolande de Flandre* was illuminated by Jean Le Noir, who was in the employ of Yolande at the time when the manuscript was painted.[47] Shortly afterward Le Noir, together with his daughter Bourgot, 'enlumineresse', left the service of Yolande for that of the King; they were working for him in December 1358. In 1372 Jean de Berry made gifts of cloth to him, clearly in return for – or expectation of – illumination, and in 1375 Le Noir, living in Bourges, was again the recipient of payments from Berry. The document describes him as 'enlumineur du roy et de mon dit seigneur'.[48] Delisle confused the issue by attributing to the painter of the *Heures de Yolande de Flandre* the *Bible de Jean de Sy* (Figs. 301, 377), which belongs to quite a different stylistic trend. Dr. Morand has recently revived the hypothesis,[49] which gains greatly in probability from the reconstruction of a part at least of the painter's œuvre, for the Passion Master did indeed pass from the service of Yolande to that of Charles V and to Jean de Berry. It is noteworthy too that the *Heures de Yolande de Flandre* had entered the collection of Charles V by 1380,[50] so that the King acquired not only the painter but an earlier work from his hand.

If the Passion Master was Jean Le Noir, could the *Petites Heures* have been entrusted to him as early as 1372–1375, when we know that Le Noir was working for Berry? To answer this question affirmatively we should have to suppose, for one thing, that ten years elapsed between the work done by Le Noir and a second campaign by the more advanced painters in the manuscript, for their contribution could scarcely have been made in the early or mid-'seventies. Such an interval would be possible, furthermore, only if we assume that the Passion Master laid out the architecture of the *Annunciation*, which must have been designed before he painted the figures. This premise raises difficulties. Furthermore the assumption of an early date would imply that the Passion Master, in this event Le Noir, began to execute the Hours of the Virgin, jumping from the *Annunciation* to the *Annunciation to the Shepherds*, then jumping again to the *Majesty* (Penitential Psalms) and on to the Hours of the Passion. Finally he would have worked on two miniatures in the Hours of the Baptist near the end of the book. Not a very plausible course of work, and in the border of folio 97 verso (Fig. 114) he would have parodied the main miniature before it was painted, though of course he could have known what its subject was to be. The alternative hypothesis of simultaneous collaboration in this sequence of paintings with other illuminators is not free of difficulties because of the episodic appearance of the Passion Master, but it seems to me far preferable.

The Passion Master, perhaps Jean Le Noir, was a great artist and deserves an important place in the history of European painting of the fourteenth century. Formed in the workshop of Pucelle, he carried into an age increasingly concerned with problems such as the realization of volume and space through linear and aerial perspective Pucelle's deep concern with the quality of human feeling as it was stirred by tragic events. In vigorous narrative he resembled Bondol and the best painters of his circle; in intensity of emotion he surpassed them all. In dramatic art he had no immediate followers; he was the last of a line, and his interests were revived only in the fifteenth century, by the Bedford and the Rohan Masters.

In his last years the Passion Master saw painting take a radically new turn. His values no longer seemed important to the gifted younger artists who were working around him – André Beauneveu and Jacquemart. Still, an associate of the latter paid him the compliment of adopting one of his novel motifs, the pointing angel in the *Annunciation* (Fig. 130). Such borrowing was a tribute to the narrative strength of his art, a strength that the new style did not otherwise seek to maintain. The lesser talents among the young, such as Pseudo-Jacquemart, leaned to a greater extent on their predecessor, as minor artists always do.

After the disappearance of the Passion Master in the period 1375-1385 Jean de Berry did not again employ a great painter with a similar bent. For a generation, indeed, none was available. He had to content himself with Pseudo-Jacquemart, scarcely more than a reminder of the past. The Duke did, on the other hand, continue to acquire manuscripts by Pucelle and his associates, building the greatest collection of them that was ever formed.[51] This group of manuscripts from the circle of the outstanding illuminator of the fourteenth century bears eloquent testimony to the taste of this extraordinary patron. He continued to appreciate vivid expressiveness when it was no longer *à la mode*. Of course the art must have proved much more congenial to him because of its unique Italianate strain, touching thus one of the greatest passions of the Duke's career.

3 · JACQUEMART DE HESDIN

In the *Annunciation* at the very beginning of the Hours of the Virgin (Fig. 94) we have already encountered a collaborator of the Passion Master to whom we shall attach, provisionally, the resonant name of Jacquemart de Hesdin. It was probably he who designed the folio, giving it the character of a façade. He seems to have translated into architecture a design like that of the Passion Master in the *Heures de Yolande de Flandre*, which shows superimposed saints at the sides of the miniature (Figs. 363, 364).[52] It was Jacquemart who painted, and in part at least designed, the impressive interior for the *Annunciation*, making much more explicit than the Parement Master its ecclesiastical character (Fig. 6). Though the perspective of the side walls of the church is conspicuously incorrect, the beautiful vaults create a majestic space, and the orthogonal lines of the deep floor, except at the extremities, meet approximately in one point. Between the figures, below a glass window and just at the vanishing point, appears an altar, bearing a shield with the Duke's arms – a bold intrusion which was not, as we have seen, initially contemplated. Over the left 'side aisle', in a rather inconspicuous place, peeps God the Father, likewise painted by Jacquemart. Outside the miniature, underneath heavy stone arches he painted figures greatly favored by the Duke in every medium – the twelve apostles, quiet, poised, statuesque. The central figure below, the only one without a halo, is a prophet, probably Jeremiah.[53] He sits frontally. The painter's concern with symmetry goes beyond placing the two apostles at his sides in profile: they are both given vermilion mantles.

The corresponding group above the miniature is a much modified form of the Italian triptych of the Man of Sorrows. The Duke's saint, the Baptist, replaces the usual John Evangelist, as we have mentioned above, and the Virgin at the left holds the child – an addition that never was made in Italy. However, the Man of Sorrows alone and the Madonna had been coupled in Trecento painting; they occasionally appear alongside one another in diptychs as combined images of intercession (Fig. 631). In the *Petites Heures* the Virgin presses the infant to her with crossed arms, repeating those of Christ. Her gesture seems to be specifically proleptic, containing an allusion that is not clearly present in its rare antecedents nor in the numerous subsequent examples (Figs. 221, 633). The crossed wrists appeared in early Italian representations of the Man of Sorrows; in this image they reflect the ancient type of the bound prisoner. The transfer to the Madonna in the painting of Jacquemart and his contemporaries is consistent with the remarkable passivity they gave generally to their figures.[54] Indeed the choice of this gesture rather than a more active one for Christ himself is significant. The arms of the Man of Sorrows by the older Parement Master wave in the air (Fig. 15).

With an Italianate sense of propriety, the painter has represented the figures above the miniature in half-length and those below seated on the ground. The central figure of David, massively conceived and with a mantle showing exceptionally lively and prominent tubular folds, resembles the seated St. Joseph in the Parement Master's *Nativity* (Fig. 8). The Man of Sorrows recalls the Parement Master also because he along with the attendant figures appears behind a golden cloth stretched across the lower part of the picture space (Fig. 15).[55] As in the Parement Master's painting Christ's hands are extended in front of the cloth. The painter of the figure in the *Petites Heures* has, however, clung to the Italian form of Christ alone, rejecting the new type including an angel that appeared in the *Très Belles Heures de Notre-Dame* and that became canonical in France.

While some of the figures in the frame of the *Annunciation* recall the Parement Master most of them owe far more to Beauneveu. That is apparent even in the architecture, with its broad, heavy arches, similar to those in the *Psalter* (Figs. 77, 78). The smooth, rounded forms of the apostles resemble their counterparts in the *Psalter*; in both the complex patterns of drapery in earlier painting has been greatly simplified. The long uninterrupted curves of the mantle of John the Evangelist in the *Petites Heures* are like those of St. Andrew in the *Psalter* (Fig. 54). Occasionally, for variety, the outline is broken by a small flying fold: compare in this respect John the Baptist in the *Petites Heures* with Matthias in the *Psalter* (Fig. 74). The colors of the apostles in the *Petites Heures* are similar, too – not grisaille, of course, but a related blondness, again often set off, as in the *Psalter*, by a deep blue or orange ground. The figures in the *Petites Heures* are less structured and more delicate than those in the *Psalter*, and their chiaroscuro is even more exquisitely graduated. The portrait of Jean de Berry in the initial, which was discussed in Chapter IV, is in this new style.

Reminiscences of the Parement Master are more extensive in the *Visitation* (Figs. 7, 90). The painter followed that master in locating the event indoors and in employing a little stone building that completely fills the picture space. He makes the pregnancy of Mary equally explicit, and he wraps Elizabeth in an ample mantle that shows very similar folds, especially over the legs. All these likenesses, however, illuminate for us the individuality of Jacquemart's style. He diminishes the momentariness of the event, the excitement of Elizabeth's approach to Mary. The two become meditative. The painter suppresses also the central shaft of the building, the scroll, and other linear aspects of the design. He reduces the size of the two figures and sets them deeper in the room, casting upon them a soft light that also plays over the ceiling, walls, and floor. The result is that the space not only provides a vivid tri-dimensional setting but also echoes the sentiment of its inhabitants. For this the painter had little precedent in France or Italy. This luminism is largely his own creation, and his greatest contribution to the history of painting.

The *Nativity* (Fig. 91), unlike the *Visitation* or the *Annunciation*, is framed in the elaborate quatrefoil that is familiar to us in the Hours of the Passion, and it is not unlikely that the Passion Master himself played a role in its design. We sense his taste in the flickering landscape behind. The composition follows very closely his design for this scene in the *Heures de Yolande de Flandre* and in the *Bréviaire de Charles V* (Fig. 359). The *Nativity* in the *Petites Heures* may in fact be regarded as the third stage in the development of this design. The large elements common to all three are the shed, the left end and one side of which are visible, the thatched roof with a 'dormer', and the Virgin seated or lying in a bed. In all Joseph has an arctic look, his heavily bearded face visible between a large snug hat and a heavily wrapped body. Leaning on a stick, he is huddled in a wicker chair, and, as we have observed above, the painter again altered and enriched religious iconography by borrowing from secular. He chose to represent Joseph in the *Nativity* under the guise of Jean Pucelle's old man who, frozen to the marrow in *February*, tries to warm himself before the fire (Fig. 360). In the earliest of the Passion Master's paintings of the Nativity Joseph sits in front of the bed; in the second miniature he is partly behind it, and in the *Petites Heures* altogether on its far side.

The Virgin holds the swaddled infant before her in the *Heures de Yolande*, looking affectionately at him.[56] She turns about in the *Bréviaire* and he nurses eagerly, an action that is repeated in the *Petites Heures*, but with Jacquemart's characteristic diminution of the involvement of his figures, so that the Child looks out at the audience like the infant in the Simonesque type of the Madonna of Humility (Fig. 634).

The *Meditations on the Life of Christ* tells us that at the time of the Nativity 'Joseph remained seated, downcast perhaps because he could not prepare what was necessary'. When, however, he and Mary arrived in Bethlehem and were forced to take shelter in a cave that was ordinarily used by people caught in the rain, we may suppose, the *Meditations* says, that 'Joseph, who was a master carpenter, possibly closed it in some way'.[57] Perhaps it was this notion of Joseph's solicitude and skill that led the painter of the *Nativity* in the *Bréviaire* to enclose the animals within a wattled fence. In the *Très Belles Heures de Notre-Dame* and in the *Petites Heures* a similar fence extends between the posts of the shed, giving privacy to the entire company.

The *Nativity* in the *Petites Heures* probably owes to the *Très Belles Heures de Notre-Dame* also the idea of two hills rising behind the shed. But what a landscape this has now become! Adopting the Passion Master's lace-like forms Jacquemart – for it was surely he who executed the miniature – transformed the stylized and studio-like forms of his predecessors into masses that extend up above the roof of the shed. For the first time in French painting they give the impression of the great scale of mountains. They are relatively irregular in shape and they are lighted rather than modelled. Slate-green in color, they are struck by a white light, producing a glacial effect that is unique in the entire manuscript. When we recall Joseph's origin in the Calendar picture for February, we cannot help wondering whether the painter extended these wintry qualities into the landscape. Did he intend to suggest (not actually to realize) snow? The first unmistakable snow landscapes appear some twenty-five years later, in a Calendar picture for January at the Torre dell'Aquila in Trento, datable, it seems, before 1407 and then in the famous February miniature in the *Très Riches Heures*.[58] Some snow, however, is visible in the *Brussels Hours* (Figs. 184, 185).

The painting of the roof of the shed in the *Petites Heures* shows a delight in the movement of light and the variety of form in the world. The thatch, punctured in a Flemish *Nativity* of 1366 (Fig. 619),[59] appears still more decrepit in Jacquemart's miniature, worn by the weather and open in two places. This is the beginning of the era of joy in the picturesque. Despite the incorrect linear perspective the slope of the roof creates an effect of recession, all the more powerful because it parallels the diagonal arrangement of the figures rather than, as in the Parement Master's composition, running counter to them (Fig. 8).

The Passion Master, present at least as a ghost in the *Nativity*, very probably designed the next miniature, the *Annunciation to the Shepherds* (Fig. 92), leaving only a small share, as we have seen, to Jacquemart, but he had nothing whatever to do with the *Adoration of the Magi* (Fig. 93). This is from the beginning the work of a great innovator. The frame is rectangular, and within it a world of distinctive color bursts forth. The palette of the Passion Master is cool and sombre – violet, yellow-brown, pale blue, pink. The flesh areas are reddish-brown, and the hair often mustard. The surface has a dusty look, and in conformity with this quality gold and silver are applied in emulsion, not in leaf, and they are not burnished. Jacquemart introduced a wider range of colors, light pale ones intermixed with more intense, developing those employed by the second master in the *Bible de Jean de Sy* (Fig. 583). The paint film in the *Adoration of the Magi* is unusually thick, and in places it has cracked and peeled. The range of the rich red, used for the kneeling man at the left, the retainer holding a mace, and the sleeping dog, is an exciting innovation in book illumination, and it ushers in a new era that culminates in the painting of the Limbourgs. The broad areas of color are varied subtly; the thatch is sprinkled with small plants, and white, blue, and green are laid into the rocks behind. Red rays, glazed, issue from the head of the Virgin, and a red glaze appears on the crowns and in the cup of the second Magus. The Virgin, clothed in deep blue, is seated on a scarlet mattress, and these stronger hues are relieved against the grayish roof and the gray-green mountain behind. The painter's sensitiveness to relations of color is especially evident in the faces of the three shepherds, which become progressively more reddish as they approach the red ground behind them.

The illuminator has given the *Adoration* the same setting as the *Nativity*. The thatched roof, now seen from a different point of view, is even more delapidated; the rafters are visible through three gaping holes. Joseph's wattled fence has become a substantial accomplishment, reaching up almost head-high on two sides of the shed. Along with the jug that the painter introduced first into the *Nativity* it creates a cozy, domestic environment for the nomadic couple. This atmosphere is enhanced by the preoccupation of the ass with his food. In earlier art he eats hay but the hay of the crib in the scene of the Nativity.[60] His concern with food is a sign of his inferiority to the ox, who refrains from eating or even venerates the child. In the *Petites Heures* the ass, quiet in the *Nativity*, satisfies his appetite during the visit of the Magi, and it is not clear that the painter had the old symbolic connotation in mind, for the ox, while abstaining, is given a subordinate position and its head is overlapped by a post. What the ass munches, moreover, seems not to be what Joseph provided for him in the manger but rather the hay that, according to the *Meditations*, the old man spread at Mary's feet just before the birth. 'Then he rose and, taking some hay from the manger, placed it at the Lady's feet and turned away. Then the Son of the eternal God came out of the womb of the mother without a murmur or lesion, in a moment; as He had been in the womb so He was now outside, on the hay at His mother's feet.'[61]

The rural setting is further developed by the portrayal in the foreground of two dogs, one sitting on his haunches, the other stretched out in deep sleep, his head between his paws. On the terraced hill graze three groups of sheep – one it would seem, for each of the shepherds who stand under the shed behind St. Joseph, on the 'humble' side of the scene. Indeed it is the presence of these three men, for the shepherds had not before been

gi. One or more of them had stood by – usually held apart – in early Tuscan representations of the Nativity, such as then been introduced to the Nativity in the North in the an their appearance in the *Adoration* in the *Petites Heures*. *es Heures* simply as normal inhabitants of the countryside, mind the thought recorded by the *Meditations*, that while les or pagans through the Kings, the shepherds made him

spired by an Italian text he was deeply impressed by Italian by the presence of the shepherds but by their form. Only a g could have conceived these heads, high-browed, square-t throughout. They are different, in fact, from the painter's re were following specific Italian models.

otation from Italian art in this painting, but its principles gning it the illuminator probably had in mind the Parement action of the three Kings – he may even have appropriated eir gifts (Fig. 9). He has, however, come much closer to the d pantomime by simplifying the outlines of the Kings – at action. And even more, he has added a spatial dimension to tical plane that he probably took from the Parement Master. 'hapel (Fig. 653) the kneeling Magus is the apex of triangles rough the two younger Magi on the one side, and through shepherd) on the other. The shed, given more volume than ctive, is set oblique to the picture plane and roughly parallel y of the design extends even to the Virgin and Child. She turns and leans to the left, while he inclines slightly towards the right, so that the two are dynamically interrelated, as in many fifteenth-century Italian Madonnas. Her greater inclination gives the Child a special prominence, which is enhanced by the portrayal of his white flesh against her blue mantle. He is entirely nude, as in the Parement Master's *Adoration* (Fig. 9), and even more exposed.

Compared with the *Adoration of the Magi* the next miniature, the *Flight into Egypt*, looks downright old-fashioned (Fig. 95). Within a quatrefoil frame the figures move along parallel to the picture plane on a small strip of dark green ground. The composition conforms to the Pucelle tradition: the Virgin enfolds the Child, as in representations beginning with the early *Heures de Jeanne d'Évreux*. Behind her the golden statues that Romulus had erected in his palace and which, according to the oracles, would not fall till a virgin should give birth, tumble to the ground, as in the *Heures de Jeanne de Navarre* or the *Heures de Yolande de Flandre* (Figs. 350, 366). The canopy, too, is present in the former miniature. The only significant differences from this earlier representation are that Joseph turns back to look at the riders, involved in a sort of contrapposto that Jacquemart could have found in innumerable Tuscan examples of the Flight,[64] and that the statues drop from a tabernacle rather than from a wooden cross or platform.

Is the *Flight* a copy from a drawing provided, or left behind, by the Passion Master, or did this master actually lay in the miniature? The quatrefoil frame is perhaps indicative, and the strip of terrain seems to have been begun with the wavy shapes of the Passion Master and then painted over in a quieter pale green. The exquisite execution resembles that of the *Adoration of the Magi* – it must be ascribed to the same hand or a close assistant. The exterior of the tabernacle is delicately shaded in yellow-green while the interior glows in a soft violet.

The *Coronation*, the last miniature in the Hours of the Virgin, again has a cusped frame and a generally conservative character. The delicate painting in light and shade, however, resembles the new style of the preceding miniatures. The illuminator who may be called the Trinity Master participated in the execution.[65] The composition is related to the Parement Master's miniature (Fig. 13), though Christ's use of one hand only for the coronation reverts to the older, non-Italianate tradition. As in the *Très Belles Heures de Notre-Dame* the Virgin and Christ are suspended before a multitude of golden angels, but now this splendid area is revealed through an opening in a blue, cloud-like ground of angels that has no bands or defining borders. An even more naturalistic sky, with wispy clouds, had been introduced just a few years earlier in the *Cité de Dieu* that was perhaps made for Charles V but certainly belonged to Jean de Berry (Fig. 535).[66] Whereas in this miniature and in the *Très Belles Heures de Notre-Dame* Christ and the Virgin are seated on a throne, this heavy furniture is replaced in the *Petites Heures* by an inconspicuous cushion. Most important of all, the painter has had the audacity to overturn a basic principle of the medieval tradition that equates the size of a figure with his place in the religious hierarchy. He has reduced the scale of Christ and the Virgin to that of the angels, or even less, so that the two figures seem to recede in space, to a more distant, resplendent heavenly region. This recession is enhanced by a differentiation in color: the angels are bright and variegated, but Christ and the Virgin appear in pale pink and gray.[67]

Only a few other miniatures among the hundred in the *Petites Heures* can, it seems to me, be attributed with assurance to the painter who worked on the Hours of the Virgin and whom we have agreed for the present to call Jacquemart de Hesdin. He had a share in that unusual early part of the manuscript that contains 'enseignemens . . . de bien et honnestement vivre selon Dieu'. These lessons were compiled for 'les nobles et de haut lieu', and the most impressive miniature (Fig. 89) shows St. Louis on his deathbed handing a piece of parchment to his eldest son on which is written: 'Tres chier filz tout premierement ie tenseigne que' (which may then be completed by the text below) 'tu aimes Dieu. . .' Unfortunately the miniature has been rubbed considerably and damaged by a later reinforcement in ink of the outlines of the figures, especially the arm of St. Louis, the mantle of his son, and the bed cover. The scene remains nevertheless impressive, with the solemn father and the almost over-eager son beneath a canopy that helps to create an intimate and vivid enclosure. The courtiers are gathered around the bed in such a convenient order of height that the head of one does not overlap that of another.

The first miniature in this section of the manuscript, which is well preserved, was in part the work of our illuminator (Fig. 86). The young prince, with scarcely sufficient ground on which to kneel, and the figure of God above show his hand most clearly. The rest was painted largely by the Pseudo-Jacquemart, who executed all of the next miniature except perhaps the small figure of God (Fig. 87), and also most of the subsequent scene of Eli and his undisciplined sons (Fig. 88).

In this first section of the text, then, we witness the emergence of Jacquemart, still using the cusped frame, the very narrow ground plane, and the diapered background of his predecessors. His exceptional capacities seem already to have been recognized, for he painted much of the first miniature in the section and all of the most important scene, the testament of St. Louis. He had the largest share in the cycle of the Hours of the Virgin, and thereafter he undertook only one large miniature of the Duke before the Virgin and three near the end of the book in the series devoted to the Duke's patron. The first of these subsequent miniatures by Jacquemart appears after the Hours of the Passion and at the beginning of prayers to the Virgin and to God. It contains an imposing image of the Madonna, who looms up before the small kneeling Duke, accompanied by his favorite little white dogs (Fig. 114). In her right arm the Virgin holds the Child, in her left hand, marvelously modelled, a white flower. In the border nearby the beggars by the Passion Master turn their backs on the scene.

The compositional scheme, showing two suspended curtains that provide enclosure and privacy, is very similar to that employed *circa* 1380 for numerous miniatures in the *Heures de Philippe le Hardi* in the Fitzwilliam Museum in Cambridge (Figs. 564, 609). The curtains, which in the Cambridge manuscript hang at either side of the suppliant, are enlarged in the *Petites Heures*, and spaced more widely. One of them serves as a cloth of honor for the standing Virgin. Like the drapery near the Duke it is a beautiful rich cloth, showing a red pattern on gold; the glazed colors on both hangings are bright and strong, as in the textiles in the *Annunciation* (Fig. 94). The darkening of the blue in the Madonna's mantle has dimmed the beauty of this exquisite and majestic figure. The outlines, the wrapping of the mantle, and her features imply the same stylistic source as many of the apostles around the *Annunciation*. These forms do not derive from the Passion Master or the Pucelle tradition, nor from Bondol or the Parement

Master, nor even from Italian Trecento painting. They were inspired by contemporary sculpture, and above all by André Beauneveu, who had arrived at the court of the Duke of Berry between *circa* 1384 and 1386.

4 · THE TRINITY MASTER

Three styles may be distinguished in the *Petites Heures* in addition to those of the Passion Master and Jacquemart de Hesdin. All three resemble the art of the latter more than that of the Passion Master, and one is so closely related that it can be extricated only with great difficulty. This is a puzzling fact, because if Jacquemart was a young master, as we have inferred, one would not expect him to have already trained so good an assistant. Troubled by this question, and by the apparent conjunction of the styles in a few miniatures, I have several times tested the hypothesis that the two groups represent only two phases of the same painter. Such a solution would seem to gain some support from the fact that I can find the style of the Trinity Master in only a few paintings later than the *Petites Heures,* and even then not with great assurance. But the same methods that were employed to reintegrate Pseudo-Jacquemart and other illuminators of the period[68] have been applied to the problem of the Trinity group, and they point towards a second personality.

The contribution of this alter ego of Jacquemart may be found chiefly in the Hours of the Holy Ghost and in the Hours of the Trinity. He painted four of the seven miniatures in the former: folio 67, *The Baptism* (Fig. 98); folio 70, *The Trinity* (Fig. 101); folio 72, *St. Peter introducing a young man into the Church* (Fig. 103); folio 74, *Peter celebrating mass.* He was responsible for six of the nine miniatures in the Hours of the Trinity, and because of this large group I have given him his name: folio 183, *The Trinity* (Fig. 154); folio 188, *Abraham and the Trinity* (Fig. 152); folio 189, *The Lord with two seraphim* (Fig. 153); folio 192, *Christ on Mount Tabor with Moses and Elijah* (Fig. 156); folio 194 verso, *Christ adored by Kings*; folio 196, *The Trinity* (Fig. 158). The latter is exceptional in so far as it is based on a drawing by the Passion Master, which had earlier served for his miniature in the *Bréviaire de Charles V* (Fig. 351).

Though very close to Jacquemart's forms, the Trinity Master's are much rounder, compact, even neat, and they give the effect of sculpture. The hair is so strongly modelled as a mass that it seems carved. Even the Holy Ghost becomes a solid monument (Fig. 154). Flesh surfaces have a distinctive chalky pallor, the effect of which is heightened by the surrounding mixed colors, blue-green, red-blue, yellow-green. The hues of the drapery, as of Christ on Mount Tabor, are sometimes changeable, shifting from yellow to pink (Fig. 156). Altogether the palette of the painter seems remarkably cool and almost over-refined. When first examining the manuscript years ago I had already associated these miniatures before observing that the landscape in all of them was painted in a quite distinctive dry, blue-green color.

This painter contributed also to the Hours of St. John the Baptist. In the miniature at Matins he painted Zacharias, while the illuminator whom we shall consider shortly, Pseudo-Jacquemart, painted the angel and the church (Fig. 164). The church is light green-blue, with a blue roof and an orange door, colors that, while typical of Pseudo, reveal a very different taste from that of the Trinity Master. The second miniature, the *Visitation*, is entirely the work of Pseudo-Jacquemart (Fig. 165); the third, the *Birth of the Baptist* (Fig. 166), is largely by the hand of the Passion Master, as we have seen, but the Trinity Master painted Zacharias and the man addressing him. A similar combination of styles is apparent in the *Dance of Salome* (Fig. 170), where the aggressive little dogs, the violet dress of the dancer, the architecture of the room, and the general liveliness recall the Passion Master, while the surface of the Trinity Master is visible in such areas as the head of Herod and the blue-green rocks in the foreground.

Three of the last miniatures in this cycle, the *Baptism*, the *Baptist before Herod*, and *Salome receiving the head* (Figs. 168, 169, 171), were all executed in part by the Trinity Master. They are the closest in style, however, to the most advanced miniatures in the Hours of the Virgin. These great resemblances accord with a development that may be discerned in the work of the Trinity Master in the *Petites Heures*. The miniatures in the Hours of the Holy Ghost are the most traditional and no doubt the earliest (Figs. 98, 101). One work by the Trinity Master that follows this cycle in the manuscript is the *Trinity* that, as we have seen,[69] resembles the representation of this subject in the *Psalter* and the Bible (Fig. 127). It is probably not the source of these two miniatures but rather closest to the model that is reflected in all three (Figs. 82, 602).

The development from this *Trinity* and from the Hours of the Holy Ghost to the Hours of the Trinity is thrown into relief by comparison of the similar representations of the Trinity in the two cycles (Figs. 101, 127, 154). The second one, which has pentimenti clearly visible even in the reproduction, is less linear, more sculpturesque, and more luminous. At the same time movement has been diminished. The dove no longer flies, as in the first representation and still in the *Trinity* with seated figures on folio 137 verso in this second cycle (Fig. 101, 127), but perches on the globe. Iconographically, the miniature on folio 183 represents the last stage in the equation of God Father and Christ, and in the expression of simultaneous spiration (Fig. 154). The wings of the dove had already touched the lips of both on folio 137 verso but only on folio 183 are the postures and gestures of the two persons indistinguishable and only there do they share the globe.

Another opportunity to grasp the unity of the style and its successive phases is provided by the virtual repetition in the Hours of the Baptist of the *Baptism* in the Hours of the Holy Ghost (Figs. 155, 168). The angel is, except for the position of the wings, almost identical. The figures in the miniature in the Hours of the Baptist are denser and yet more luminous. The water is transparent and liquid, the space deeper although partly denied by the placing of the lamb. The traditional lacy terrain is replaced by less conventional rocks. The dove, strangely enough, is omitted. The ideas if not the hand of Jacquemart have greatly affected this miniature.

The same impression of relative lateness and still greater approximation to Jacquemart is conveyed by the painting at None, which shows the Baptist brought before Herod (Fig. 169). Laid in an 'interior' that is still like Jean Bondol's title page of 1371 (Fig. 382) – a floor, a throne, a conical canopy, but no walls or ceiling – its comparatively free placing of the figures along diagonals in a rather deep space suggests again the imagination of Jacquemart de Hesdin. Once more, however, the actual surface seems duller than his and the facial types as well as the drapery recall the Trinity Master. The soldier at the right shows the same kind of spatial confusion as the Lamb in a preceding miniature in this cycle (Fig. 168): his head and shoulders are behind Christ, his feet way in front. Herod seems structurally weaker than typical figures by either master.[70] In the last miniature (Fig. 171) the lithe, poised Salome looks like the Virgin in the *Visitation* by Jacquemart (Fig. 90), and the heavy-browed face of the executioner recalls heads in the *Death of St. Louis* (Fig. 89). Still, the dusky green of the executioner and the blue-green of the terrain are characteristic colors of the Trinity Master.[71]

Outside the Hours of the Trinity, the Holy Ghost and the Baptist, the Trinity Master painted several miniatures in the *Petites Heures*, including the *Trinity* on folio 137 verso already discussed (Fig. 127). The miniatures by this illuminator are normally painted in greenish or bluish tones, but the beautiful *Agony in the Garden* is especially cool and dark (Fig. 139). The landscape is deep blue-green, the mantles of the figures are blue or bluish-pink, and the background is dark blue – a 'midnight blue'. It seems quite possible that the painter intended to create the impression of dusk or night. This would be one of the early night scenes in the North. It was preceded in Italy by the Lorenzettian *Nativity* in Frankfurt and by Taddeo Gaddi's fresco of the *Annunciation to the Shepherds* in S. Croce (Fig. 651).[72] In France night is suggested by lowered values in a miniature by Pucelle's workshop in the *Miracles de Notre-Dame*, and the darkness of the *Agony* in the *Petites Heures* was followed twenty odd years later at a new level by the *Crucifixion* in the *Belles Heures* by the Limbourgs.[73] The *Agony* in the *Petites Heures* would seem to reflect an intention like that perhaps conveyed by the frosty landscape in a preceding miniature in the *Petites Heures*, the *Nativity* (Fig. 91). One specifies the time of day, the other the time of year.

There are in the *Petites Heures* a few miniatures that may be distinguished as the fourth style in the manuscript and that are related, especially in color, to the paintings of the Trinity Master. There are only four miniatures in this style: folio 160, *The Way to Calvary* (Fig. 140); folio 161, the unusual scene of the making fast of the Cross, while Christ and the Virgin stand by, a subject suggested by the text of the Office of the Compassion in which the miniature occurs (Fig. 141); folio 186 verso, *The Creation of Adam*; folio 199 verso, *The Duke* (?) *with his guardian angel* (Fig. 163). Like the Trinity Master, this painter sharply contrasts warm and cool colors, the latter predominating. On the other hand his style is conservative, and the lively postures of the man with a hammer in the *Way to Calvary* and the workmen around the Cross recall the Passion Master. Generally his art has much in common with the later style in the *Bible de Jean de Sy* (Fig. 583).

5 · PSEUDO-JACQUEMART

Throughout the preceding discussion we have referred to another illuminator, who was in fact responsible for more of the paintings in the *Petites Heures* than any of his colleagues. A respectable but not a major artist, he was employed as a sort of workhorse and given such sections as the Calendar and numerous small miniatures in the latter part of the manuscript that often do not extend the width of the column of the text. Such illumination was usually executed in a more routine way. Still, it would be incorrect to overemphasize his subordination, for he did have a share in the miniatures illustrating the first section of the text, and many of the small miniatures by him contain portraits of the patron. While possessing a distinctive style, he was neither imaginative nor self-assured, and he frequently relied upon the compositions of other masters. Thus the figures in his *Visitation* in the Hours of the Baptist resemble closely their counterparts in the same scene in the Hours of the Virgin (Figs. 90, 165). This and numerous similar relationships with Jacquemart evident throughout his œuvre seem to have prevented scholars from disentangling his work from that of his much greater collaborator.

Not that the task is simple. While the Pseudo-Jacquemart eschews the chamber used in the preceding *Visitation* in favor of an intense blue background and a rather fancy but old-fashioned terrain, the interlocking of his figures composes a design superior to that in the Hours of the Virgin. Mary responds to Elizabeth more warmly in the later miniature, putting her arm on the latter's shoulder, as in the *Visitation* in the *Heures de Jeanne de Navarre*. On the other hand the nearer knee of Elizabeth in Pseudo's figure is basically misunderstood. How then shall we interpret these complex relationships? That both the miniatures imperfectly reflect a model, or that Jacquemart, so tentative in the Hours of the Virgin, had increased his command of narrative and provided a better design for the figures in the Hours of the Baptist?

The *Visitation* more than most other miniatures by Pseudo-Jacquemart captures, at least in the figure of Mary, the soft luminous surfaces and the quiet flow of the draperies of his great collaborator. The quality, indeed, is so high and the posture so superior that the suspicion of participation by the Trinity Master, who worked with Pseudo on the neighboring folio 203 (Fig. 164), cannot be allayed. In Elizabeth, on the other hand, we recognize Pseudo's more linear art, his predilection for more spontaneous movement, a lively narrative and a wholly different taste in color. The *Visitation* in the Hours of the Virgin is painted in pastel colors (Fig. 90). The architecture is blue-green, the beams of the ceiling yellow-brown, the floor blue and buff. The Virgin wears salmon-pink, Elizabeth's mantle is white. The faces are modelled in white, the eyes are blue and the Virgin's hair a straw yellow. Into this pallid shimmering field the painter, with exquisite taste, has immersed two small spots of intense scarlet, on Elizabeth's tunic and the small lean-to over the door. Pseudo-Jacquemart, on the other hand, while preserving pink (though intensified) for Mary's mantle, has added orange in her hair and has chosen scarlet for the broad surface of the mantle of Elizabeth. Then behind all this he has spread an intense blue background.

Pseudo's color lacks Jacquemart's subtle modulations. He is fond of scarlet and blue in combination. Lemon yellow is almost a signature. His taste recalls that of the painters of the *bas-de-page* in the *Très Belles Heures de Notre-Dame*, or of the most advanced illuminator in the Bible, Bibl. nat., fr. 20090 (Fig. 611). His style as a whole, in fact, is related to this earlier moment in French painting. The liveliness of his narrative resembles Jean Bondol or the Parement Master. His landscape forms in the *Petites Heures* are essentially those that were current in the 'seventies, and the fundamental linearity of his style indicates that it was formed at that time. His hair is normally composed of wriggly strands, utterly different from the quiet, luminous masses of Jacquemart. His radical difference from that painter is manifest also in the painting of eyes. Instead of employing blue and gray and pink, he defines the upper lid by a strong black line, encircles the iris with another, and paints the pupil jet black.

His *Baptism* (Fig. 155), a small miniature in the Hours of the Trinity, is dependent upon the representation of this scene in both the Hours of the Holy Ghost (Fig. 98) and the Hours of the Baptist (Fig. 168). Its derivative character is declared immediately by the anomaly of a river flowing above its banks, the consequence of course of retaining the level of the water in the other miniatures, especially the one in the Hours of the Baptist, while lowering the rocks at either side. The result recalls a representation of the subject painted half a century earlier – the *Baptism* in the *Bréviaire de Belleville* (Fig. 374), though this miniature lacks the *Christus pudicus* common to all the Baptisms of the *Petites Heures*. Some elements of Pseudo's composition, such as the Baptist's hair-shirt and the placement of his feet, are taken from the miniature in the Hours of the Baptist – which occurs a little further on in the manuscript and must have been under way at the time. On the other hand the painter could not resist the splendid blue mantle of St. John in the Hours of the Holy Ghost (Fig. 98) and he unblushingly wrapped him in it, leaving exposed a small kilt-like part of the hair-tunic as a reminder of more austere days.

The sources of Pseudo-Jacquemart were not limited to Jacquemart himself nor to the *Petites Heures*. He found compositions, first of all, in the paintings by the Parement Master in the *Très Belles Heures de Notre-Dame*, as we have observed in Chapter VI. For his *Crucifixion* on folio 63 verso (Fig. 97) he took the comparatively straight figure of Christ and the seated St. John from the *Crucifixion* by the Parement Master (Fig. 27), which he must have known before the Master of the Baptism reworked it. The St. John is in almost every respect an exact copy. Pseudo-Jacquemart even followed the Parement Master in representing the bottom face of the cross-bar as if seen from below – from the level of the figures seated on the ground. He used the figure of the Madonna in the Parement Master's miniature for another representation of the Crucifixion (Fig. 172). He has arranged her hands and legs similarly, and adopted for the latter even the peculiar drapery folds of his source. He has given the swooning Virgin a supporting hand that she needs but does not receive in the *Très Belles Heures de Notre-Dame*, although this hand was very probably included in the original design. It is in any event certain that the narrow wrist and spidery fingers of the hand now visible of the Mary who hovers over the Virgin do not belong to the Parement Master's canon.

This folio of the *Crucifixion* in the *Très Belles Heures de Notre-Dame* that Pseudo-Jacquemart studied so closely served him also for his portrayal of the nailing of Christ to the Cross (Fig. 142).

Indeed the *bas-de-page* in the *Très Belles Heures de Notre-Dame* rather than the miniature in the *Petites Heures*, which is usually cited,[74] is the earliest surviving example of this scene in France. The scene, which became so prominent in later painting, was not common anywhere earlier, though it does appear in exceptionally extensive cycles of illustration, such as *Queen Mary's Psalter*,[75] as well as in an approximately contemporary English picture Bible,[76] and, in the third quarter of the century, the *Bible moralisée* which was illuminated in Neapolitan style and perhaps already by 1380 in the possession of Louis d'Anjou.[77] Thus the subject was known in the North as well as in Italy, and Mâle's thesis of an origin of the French examples in Italian art of the Trecento is somewhat weakened. Lombard representations, indeed, seem to increase in number only around 1375,[78] and in some instances one cannot exclude the hypothesis of a reverse relationship. A miniature in a Lombard Book of Hours of about 1390, for instance, includes even the two groups of spectators that appear in the *Très Belles Heures de Notre-Dame*, peering over the hill (Fig. 614).

Pseudo-Jacquemart borrowed from the scene in the *Très Belles Heures de Notre-Dame* the posture of the henchman in the foreground, but as so often he lost sight of the purpose of the action, and in his own version the fellow has become a bungler who could not possibly strike the spike at which he is aiming. Pseudo borrowed also the terraced terrain and the skulls and bones strewn over it. He adopted even a novel aspect of his model, the figures standing on the far side of the knoll and visible therefore only in part. The representation of a figure or two, usually iconographically subordinate, beyond a hill and only partly visible had been retained in Byzantine painting as a heritage from antique art,[79] and by the late thirteenth century it was transmitted to Italian painting.[80] It was at home in the Italian Trecento, as exemplified by the Lombard miniature just cited (Fig. 614). French painters in the earlier fourteenth century had gradually developed a conception of the existence of space within interiors and also in front of (or at the sides of) the larger represented forms. They had not, however, realized with equal vividness the continuation of space *beyond* and *behind* these forms. It was Jean Pucelle who began to visualize the existence of this space in his early work in the 'twenties, putting into it a shepherd in the scene of the appearance of the angel[81] or the tips of steeples and towers in the distance behind a hill (Fig. 357). In the *Boqueteaux* style figures occasionally are overlapped by rocks.[82] The *bas-de-page* by the assistant of the Parement Master represents a more decisive conquest for painting of this dimension. The white parchment now becomes more definitely a symbol of tri-dimensional space. Into this space Pseudo-Jacquemart has put the Maries and St. John rather than mere spectators, and over at the left, just beyond and below the brow of the hill (as if to demonstrate his grasp of a continuum), a castle.

Pseudo-Jacquemart was on the whole attracted less by the power of the large miniatures in the *Très Belles Heures de Notre-Dame* than by the lively narrative of the *bas-de-page*, and to them he may have turned again for his *Death of the Virgin* (Figs. 13, 132). The figure of Mary is a close replica, similar in the disposition of the tubular folds of the mantle and the curvature of the body. Pseudo-Jacquemart again makes us aware of lapses in detail, which impoverish his own compositions. Christ no longer addresses the Virgin and blesses her, as in the *bas-de-page*, but looks off aimlessly toward the right. The Virgin's hands do not lie quietly crossed on her body, relaxed

N

in death, but are suspended in a curiously strained fashion. This design is not adequately characterized, however, only by its shortcomings compared to its model. It shows attractive figures not present in the *bas-de-page* nor indeed in the Pucelle tradition (Fig. 343). We must assume they were taken from an unknown model or, less likely, that they were Pseudo-Jacquemart's invention. The sentimental angels that incline with intimate affection on the Madonna's cushion remind us vividly of the mood and action of the angels in Sienese Nativities or around the throne in Sienese Madonnas beginning with Duccio's *Maestà*.[83] Pseudo-Jacquemart did not, however, adopt the touching action of the closing of the Virgin's lips that was introduced in the *Très Belles Heures de Notre-Dame*. The two apostles crouching in the foreground had appeared around the middle of the century in a few French ivories.[84] They are seated before the bier like the huddled Magdalen or other mourning women that Pucelle and the Passion Master, following Italian precedent, had introduced into the foreground of the Entombment (Figs. 342, 113). The enthusiasm, almost ferocity, with which the apostle at the left buries himself in his book reminds us of the Passion Master, or perhaps of that art that consistently defied the French canon of poised and circumspect behavior – the Netherlandish, and its representatives in France, Jean Bondol and his followers.

We are reminded once again of Netherlandish art by Pseudo-Jacquemart's *Nativity* (Fig. 131). The composition, very old-fashioned in certain respects, resembles Jacquemart's only with respect to the diagonal placement of the shed (Fig. 91), while the single domestic allusion in that miniature has been developed. The jug has become a group of utensils conveniently set out on a little table together with Joseph's golden canteen. That solicitous old man sits in the foreground before a small fire in a brazier, warming a cloth for the infant. At the right a woman, presumably a midwife, is about to pick up the Child. Homely activity in the Nativity began to be cultivated earlier in the *Bible de Charles V* (Fig. 386), where great prominence is given the Child's bath, but the actual forms that it assumes in the *Petites Heures* do not seem to appear in the Low Countries or the Lower Rhine until the early years of the fifteenth century. The 'picnic table' and the midwife reaching for the Child both enliven a panel painted perhaps in Guelders soon after 1400; St. Joseph studiously splits one of his stockings to clothe the Child (Fig. 629).[85] In a *Nativity* by a follower of Broederlam in Antwerp Joseph holds a cloth before the fire,[86] but this action had already appeared in a *Nativity* by Giovannino dei Grassi, approximately contemporary with the one in the *Petites Heures* (Fig. 630). Such themes were in the air at the time, and a few years later domestic activities of all kinds proliferate in the Nativity.

The 'Lamentation' by Pseudo-Jacquemart on folio 286 is a very unusual subject (Fig. 175); I know, in fact, only one earlier example of it in Northern art. There is, to be sure, a related image of a Madonna alone with the dead Christ in her lap in an English Book of Hours (1330-1340?), where it is labeled 'Cy en bracea nre dame douz ihu de posee de la croyz' (Fig. 644).[87] The more complete prototype is in a *bas-de-page* of the *Très Belles Heures de Notre-Dame* (Fig. 28). The rarity of the theme and the similarity of the compositions prove that the two miniatures are connected. The subjects may be defined as representations mid-way between the Lamentation and the *Vesperbild*. To understand their nature and their historical significance we must turn to related developments in Italy. There the growing desire in the later thirteenth century to portray

the impact upon Christ's friends and relatives of his suffering and death had given a new prominence to the scene of lamentation after Christ was removed from the cross. Following Byzantine
precedent the Virgin frequently threw herself upon the body, which was laid on a cloth stretched
out on the ground.[88] Later in the century the Madonna often held her dead son across her lap,
so that the two figures were somewhat isolated from the group of mourners (Fig. 645). 'This
tragic group', to quote the words of Erwin Panofsky, 'appears surrounded by compassion
without being relieved of its loneliness.'[89]

This novel form of the Lamentation reflected a wish to pause amidst the progress of the fateful
story and to dwell upon the human response to it; in short, to transform a historical scene into
a devotional picture. This impulse, which lay behind the creation in the later thirteenth century
of the Man of Sorrows, led, a generation later, to the development of both the Madonna of
Humility and the Italian form of the *Vesperbild*. At least eight Trecento examples of it have been
preserved: a panel in the David Museum, Angers (Fig. 641) and one of two wings of a triptych
in the Detroit Institute of Arts (Fig. 640), both by a Sienese painter active in the third quarter
of the Trecento whom I have called the Master of the Pietà;[90] the central panel of an altarpiece
dated 1377 in the Museo Civico of Pisa, by the Pisan painter Cecco di Pietro (Fig. 638); a fragmentary and badly damaged fresco by a Neapolitan painter of the late Trecento in S. Chiara,
Naples;[91] a beautiful small panel by Giovanni da Milano (Fig. 635); a panel in the Museum at
Trapani, by Roberto di Oderisio; a Tuscan panel of *circa* 1365 in the Palazzo dei Priori, Volterra
(Fig. 639) and a somewhat later Tuscan panel, unpublished so far as I know, number 169 in
the Museo Civico, Pavia.[92]

This group of images reflects two different sources, which are most clearly represented by the
paintings of the Master of the Pietà. The figures in the Detroit panel resemble the group of the
Virgin with the dead Christ lying across her lap that appeared in Dugento representations of
the Lamentation (Fig. 645). This composition is much less common in our group. Though the
fresco in Naples and the panel by Cecco di Pietro (Fig. 638) also recall the Lamentation, the
Detroit composition is closest to it for, beyond the horizontal posture of Christ, it has a landscape, a cross rising behind the Virgin, and, alone among these works, a white cloth under the
limp figure of the dead Savior. There is in fact a Florentine panel in the Boymans Museum,
Rotterdam (Fig. 642) that demonstrates the simplicity of creating this image from the Lamentation. This painting, which seems at first glance to be similar to the early fifteenth-century German
type of *Vesperbild*, is probably only a fragment of a *Lamentation*, Florentine and around 1400,
which was at some later time pruned down to the central figures.

In the panel at Angers (Fig. 641), on the other hand, Christ is seated in the lap of the Virgin.
Like a Madonna with the Child, she presses her cheek against his (Fig. 698). The resemblance
with the composition of the Madonna is increased by the upright position of his torso and by
the fact that his figure, with very short legs, is almost entirely contained within her outline. In
this painting as well as the one in Volterra (Fig. 639) the Virgin's posture proves that we
are confronted with a Madonna of Humility in which the Infant has been replaced by the relatively small adult Christ. In Giovanni da Milano's panel Christ is similarly reduced in scale;
the Virgin, overcome with emotion, faints away as she often does in the Trecento Crucifixion

(Fig. 528). This drastic portrayal in a devotional picture may be connected with the North Italian origins of the painter. On the other hand the ties with the Lamentation in this group of images are numerous. From it came the horizontal position of Christ in the painting in Detroit. The cross is absent only from Cecco's panel, and Oderisio's has a sarcophagus. The Italian group of images thus has a dual origin whereas the German *Vesperbild*, which appeared only in sculpture during the fourteenth century, derives from the Madonna enthroned, as Panofsky has shown. Since however, most paintings in the Italian group derive also from the Madonna, though the 'Humility version', it seems to me appropriate to designate them *Vesperbilder* also, of the Humility type.[93] The differences between the Italian and German images, furthermore, can disappear, for in fifteenth-century German sculptures the Virgin sometimes is seated lowly, as in the Italian paintings,[94] and earlier, around 1405 in France, the Italian Virgin seated on the ground takes onto her lap the horizontal Christ with head twisted back as in German *Vesperbilder* (Figs. 637, 650).

The Italian *Vesperbild* as a type has the informality and intimacy of the Madonna of Humility, and it is not surprising that many of the examples of it as of the Madonna are quite small, evidently intended for private ownership and prayer. As I have remarked on another occasion,[95] the Madonna of Humility and the *Vesperbild* are complementary or polar themes, since they represent Christ in the lap of the Virgin at the beginning and the end of his life on earth. This complementarity of content is conveyed by the similar forms assumed by the two types. The Italian images were in fact products of the same region and the same historical moment.

The Virgin holds Christ in the same way in the Angers, Pisa, and Trapani panels: one hand behind his head, the other reaching across his body and grasping his hip or midriff. It would be difficult to believe that similarities of this kind, appearing in the work of minor painters who are not very inventive, are accidental, just as it is unlikely that this new image should have appeared simultaneously and independently in Pisa, Naples, and Siena. The painting in Trapani shows the influence of Simone Martini; the curling borders of the Madonna's mantle, the shape of the panel, the soaring angels at the sides, all resemble the Madonna of Humility in S. Domenico Maggiore, Naples, likewise painted around 1350 by Roberto di Oderisio.[96] The panel in Angers by the Master of the Pietà (Fig. 641) shows a striking approximation to Simone's style, unparalleled in any of this painter's other works.[97] On the other hand, the triangulation of the group of the Virgin and Christ and the resilient volume of the Virgin recall Ambrogio Lorenzetti. These extraordinary similarities with the great styles of the first half of the Trecento are due in part to the relatively early date of the Angers panel among the works of the Master of the Pietà, but they also suggest, together with the Simonesque character of the paintings by Roberto di Oderisio and of Giovanni da Milano, the probability of the existence of the image in Siena in the second quarter of the Trecento. Painted at that time by Simone Martini and perhaps Ambrogio Lorenzetti, the Italian *Vesperbild* would have appeared at the same time and in the same artistic circles as the closely related Madonna of Humility.

Though no Sienese *Vesperbild* of this period seems to have been preserved, the wing of a Florentine triptych of 1336 (Fig. 647) proves that the theme was in the air at that time. Christ is seated in the lap of the Virgin – perhaps we should say on her legs – and the representation differs from the normal, fully developed type only in the presence of two mourners. This panel also shows us how the Giottesque conception of the group, with both figures erect and relatively detached from each other, differs from the Sienese, and therefore confirms our hypothesis of the Sienese origin of the Italian paintings of the theme.

In these Italian paintings Christ is quiet and still possesses a certain vital force. His body and head do not fall back into the drastic position of the German figures. The Virgin supports his head or his neck except in the Detroit panel, and there she puts her arm around his body while his head falls gently onto his shoulder. In both the Italian and German images the Virgin is moved by two emotions, love and sorrow. The German works emphasize her sorrow, the Italian her love. The German sculptures represent a final separation of mother and son; the Virgin is distraught by Christ's human pain and death. This sense of separation and loss is transcended in the Italian paintings (except the one by Giovanni da Milano) by the Virgin's surpassing love and, it seems, by an awareness of her son's mission as God. Similarly the suffering of Christ throughout the Passion in Italian art is mitigated by a constant sense of the orderly and necessary progress of the drama of sacrifice and redemption, and by the warmth of human feeling evoked among those who participate in these sad events. These works show a wonderful balance between pain and love, between Christ's lonely fulfillment of his purpose and the steady affection and understanding of the relatives and followers who surround him. To attain an equilibrium of this sort, the growth around 1300 of the human character of Christ and of his capacity to suffer was accompanied by the development of affectionate actions such as the Virgin reaching for Christ on the Way to Calvary or embracing him in the Deposition and Lamentation. At the same time the Magdalen was introduced into the Crucifixion, clinging passionately to the foot of the cross.[98] This new Italian 'humanism' and this new religious understanding proved to be a revelation to the North, and nowhere did it have a greater effect than in France.

In both the *Très Belles Heures de Notre-Dame* and the *Petites Heures* (Figs. 28, 175) the Virgin bearing her son in her lap is seated on a little knoll. The relationship with the Italian *Vesperbilder* is evident, even though both the manuscripts still include mourners. In one important respect the painting from the circle of the Parement Master approximates the Italian panels much more closely. The Virgin places one hand behind the head of Christ, holding it near her and preventing it from falling backward. Thus, like his Italian predecessors, the Parement Master avoids the limp and broken body that was favored by the German sculptors and then by the Pseudo-Jacquemart. Both illuminators made a beautiful and highly expressive addition to the theme. St. John, seated or kneeling just behind the Virgin, is caught in a sad conflict. Wanting to offer consolation, he puts an arm around her, but wanting also to respect her privacy, he turns his face in the opposite direction. This remarkable presentation of an ambivalent figure, though entirely characteristic of the Tuscan Trecento,[99] is not to be found in any of the surviving Tuscan Lamentations or *Vesperbilder* themselves. It was incorporated at a later date in the most moving of all Italian renditions of the closely related subject of the Man of Sorrows—Giovanni Bellini's painting in the Brera in Milan. Inasmuch as a similar St. John tending the Virgin appeared early in Bohemian Crucifixions[100] the Parement Master, who was familiar with this art, might have found the motive there.

In a Book of Hours illuminated in Metz there is a modest representation that resembles to some extent the two we have just considered (Fig. 646).[101] Though the cross and the proximity of numerous mourners are characteristic of the usual composition of the Lamentation, it shares with our two French miniatures the peculiar feature of the Madonna seated on a natural eminence.[102] The eminence, it is true, is higher here, and in that respect the group recalls the enthroned Madonna in the German *Vesperbild*. Surprisingly this provincial manuscript contains a second miniature of exceptional design that shows an even closer resemblance to a miniature by Pseudo-Jacquemart in the *Petites Heures* – the exceedingly rare representation of the kneeling Virgin nursing the Christ Child (Figs. 136, 625). In the *Petites Heures* the Virgin kneels on a tiled floor alongside her canopied bed and the Child's crib – she is a sort of Madonna with the Cradle.[103] In the Metz *Horae* on the other hand she resembles a Madonna of Humility who has risen to kneel on her cushion. In the former she wears a crown, in the latter two flying angels place it on her head.

In which manuscript did these novel forms first appear? The miniatures themselves do not provide a definite answer, and the dates of the manuscripts concerned are somewhat uncertain. If the Metz *Horae* can actually be dated about 1383,[104] it would have been made around the time of the miniatures by the Parement Master, including the *Vesperbild*, and a little earlier than the paintings in the *Petites Heures*. Normally we would be inclined to assume that the provincial manuscript was the dependent one, but it was precisely in manuscripts made in Metz, and closely related to Bibl. nat., lat. 1403, that the Italian image of the Madonna of Humility may first be found in the painting of Northwest Europe. One peculiarity of the Metz Madonnas of Humility, the naked Child, seems furthermore to conform with a local predilection, as we have suggested above.[105] We cannot therefore exclude the possibility that the Metz *Lamentation* had an influence upon the early French *Vesperbild*.

The Italianate image of Mary mourning her dead son on her lap, rare in France (Fig. 650) and not common in Italy itself, may be found again in a charming little Book of Hours painted around 1400 in Tournai (Fig. 648).[106] John kneels beside the Virgin, as in the *Petites Heures* (Fig. 175), though he now comes to her assistance without emotional conflict. In two respects, however, the miniature suggests a direct relationship with Italian examples: the cross rising behind the group, and the more frontal position of Christ, his head falling limply onto his shoulder as in the Detroit panel by the Master of the Pietà (Fig. 640). Several elements of the little Netherlandish miniature reappear in a panel made later by another, and greater, painter of Tournai, Roger van der Weyden (Fig. 636).[107]

In the last section of the *Petites Heures*, not far from the *Vesperbild*, Pseudo-Jacquemart painted three other miniatures that are unusual in one way or another. The *Funeral Service* on folio 217 is performed in a conventional way, but the space behind the figures is surprising (Fig. 176). The building is elaborate, and the extension of the turrets behind and above the frame, while not novel, is very vivid. We have already referred to the exceptional perspective of the coffered ceiling, which is very similar to that in the nearby *Dance of Salome* (Fig. 170). Here it is accompanied by an extraordinary luminary phenomenon. The upper part of the left and rear walls is in shadow – a shadow that is graduated uniformly from pale yellow-orange near the ceiling to deep orange-brown below.[108] The lowered faces of the two clerics at the lectern are in similar shadow from the brow to the chin. These innovations appear in the miniature side by side with spatial and luminary inconsistencies: the shaft at the right disappears behind the clerics, and the braziers have no plane on which to stand. Pseudo-Jacquemart once again followed an advanced model, the same one used by the Passion Master for the *Dance of Salome*, which in addition to an impressive ceiling apparently contained, we now see, an even more remarkable shadow, a form not to be matched in French painting for many years.[109]

The Pseudo-Jacquemart was, as we have seen, not unmindful of the stylistic transformations taking place around him, but it was mostly narrative diagrams that he took from his major contemporaries. Other miniatures by him draw for such purposes from the Passion Master and the circle of Jean Pucelle. Two exceptional subjects that appear in sequence in the last section of the *Petites Heures* may be seen in similar order in the Psalter and prayer-book of Bonne of Luxembourg, illuminated in the atelier of Pucelle before her death in 1349. The first illustrates the 'VI degrez de charité selon la figure du trone de salemon' according to the rubric above the miniature in the *Petites Heures* (Fig. 173). 'Oroyson' kneels on the top step, 'Esperance' stands with elevated hands in the next, then 'Charité', a youth, addresses two children. Penitence, Judgment and Faith follow in sequence.[110]

The second unusual subject is the *Three Quick and the Three Dead* (Fig. 174). The marvellous encounter in the *Psalter of Bonne* is divided into two miniatures on facing folios (Figs. 354, 355). The three noblemen are not standing, as in the French example of this rare subject from the end of the thirteenth century, but on horse – and what horses! – in accordance with an Italian tradition firmly established in the early Trecento[111]. Pseudo-Jacquemart reverted to the early French form by putting the quick on their feet and greatly reducing the evidences of progressive decomposition in the dead. Probably this less gruesome show reflects not only the mental simplicity of Pseudo but the taste of the time. Jean de Berry himself, to be sure, had no aversion to the theme of death. In 1408 he was said to have commissioned a sculpture of the Three Quick and the Three Dead for the portal of the Church of the Innocents in Paris.[112] Personifications of death appeared in several of Berry's manuscripts, but the grim reaper always performed his task with elegance and sophistication (Fig. 643).

The compositions by Pseudo-Jacquemart that derive from the Pucelle tradition include the *Funeral Service* on folio 134 verso, which is much closer to the representation in the *Heures de Jeanne de Savoie* in the Musée Jacquemart-André, Paris (Fig. 613) than to the miniature by the Parement Master (Fig. 14). The *Resurrection* (Fig. 134) shows at the left a soldier in an elaborate posture of sleep who appears, reversed, in the *Bréviaire de Charles V* (Fig. 371), but in the same sense in the *Bréviaire de Belleville*.[113]

By well-established custom the *chef d'atelier* left the painting of the Calendar to an assistant, and it was Pseudo-Jacquemart who was given this task for the *Petites Heures* (Figs. 83-85). He fulfilled it by adopting, doubtless on instructions, the scheme introduced by the *Bréviaire de Belleville* and followed by the *Heures de Yolande de Flandre* as well as the *Heures de Jeanne de Navarre*.[114] The Duke apparently liked the iconography so well that he had it included in the Calendar of the *Grandes Heures*, again executed by Pseudo-Jacquemart. For the most part in the *Petites Heures* Pseudo-Jacquemart followed his model.

Pseudo-Jacquemart executed most of two miniatures in the initial section of the manuscript that presents moral precepts for princes. Jacquemart painted the fourth of this cycle, as we have seen (Fig. 89), and he finished the main figures and God in the first of the series (Fig. 86). In the second miniature all the figures except Christ were painted by Pseudo-Jacquemart (Fig. 87). It presents the same chief protagonists as the first, but the problem of moral choice and kingly destiny is made more vivid for the young man. The Dominican friar can now point not only to Christ and the heavens but also to a sort of hell that undoubtedly held – and would still hold – special terrors for a Frenchman: amidst goats and pigs and a bull the naked ex-king Nebuchadnezzar must forage on all fours for an execrable leguminous dinner.

The fourth miniature, likewise painted mostly by Pseudo-Jacquemart, tells a very rare story, so rare that even the Abbé Leroquais did not identify it, though the rubric is an adequate guide (Fig. 88). Eli, a good priest in the temple, had two bad sons, whose chief sin against the Lord was demanding and eating part of the meat brought to the temple for sacrifice. Eventually the angry Lord declared that he would 'judge his [Eli's] house forever for the iniquity which he knoweth; because his sons made themselves vile, and he restrained them not'.[115] Above Christ addresses Eli. Below, alongside his sons who gorge on meat, the lax father falls. The tumbling priest is similar to the falling man before Obadiah in the manuscript that contains several compositions adopted by the Duke's illuminators at this time, the *Bréviaire de Jeanne d'Évreux* (Fig. 358).[116]

Pseudo-Jacquemart painted the larger part of another cycle in the *Petites Heures* – a series of representations of Jean de Berry and other figures in prayer before the Madonna, a crucifix, or a saint. We have discussed these many small miniatures above and in the chapter on portraits of the Duke. There remains to be recalled again that the precedents for so extensive a cycle of princes (or any other figure) at prayer were to be found in the miniatures added to the *Heures de Savoie* by Charles V and in the Book of Hours of Philippe le Hardi in Cambridge (Figs. 564, 609). These manuscripts were illuminated by followers of Bondol, and the portraits, like those in the *Petites Heures*, were not executed by the strongest hand. The painters of Jean de Berry were seldom interested in the style of Bondol or his followers but here they adopted an iconographic program.

The style that has been the subject of the preceding paragraphs can be traced from the *Petites Heures* to the *Grandes Heures* of 1409 – a period of around twenty-five years. It originated in the *bas-de-page* of the *Très Belles Heures de Notre-Dame*; Pseudo-Jacquemart may have participated in the execution of these friezes or he may have worked earlier with these illuminators. A discussion of the later career of the illuminator is better postponed to Chapter XII, but at this point reference to some closely related manuscripts would seem to be profitable, especially one that bears a date. The text of a *Légende dorée* in London is dated 1382 by a colophon (see the Catalogue). The miniatures at the beginning, including the largest painting in the book, were executed in the style of Pseudo-Jacquemart, and they would seem approximately contemporary with the *Petites Heures* (Figs. 610, 612, 615). Over a period of twenty-five years the art of Pseudo-Jacquemart changed remarkably little, so that his paintings are in this respect a poor guide to actual date. The miniatures in the *Légende dorée* seem less vigorous than those in the *Petites Heures*; perhaps

Pseudo-Jacquemart employed an assistant for the execution, or more likely he worked under better conditions in the *Petites Heures* for his great patron. The figures in the manuscript in London are taller, and they resemble those in the *bas-de-page* of the *Très Belles Heures de Notre-Dame*. This relationship is quite in accord with our view that his share in the *Petites Heures* was undertaken after 1382. If he participated in the execution of the *bas-de-page* of the *Très Belles Heures de Notre-Dame*, that work would have been done first of all.

The relationship of Pseudo's work in the *Petites Heures* with the *Légende dorée* is indicative of actual date; the connection with the *Très Belles Heures de Notre-Dame* is binding with regard to the sequence of the two manuscripts. The *Crucifixion* (Fig. 97), *Nailing to the Cross* (Fig. 142), and *Lamentation* (Fig. 175) by Pseudo-Jacquemart all derive from corresponding miniatures in that manuscript. Pseudo-Jacquemart's character as an illuminator thus serves the historian well because his eagerness to adopt new paradigms of action, coupled with a neglect of the function of the figures in them, provides precious clues to the correct sequence of the manuscripts. This evidence is confirmed by that of style, because, as we have said, the *bas-de-page* in the *Très Belles Heures de Notre-Dame* seem to be the major source of Pseudo-Jacquemart's art. He very probably participated in the execution of such friezes as the *Burial Procession* (Fig. 14), the *Baptism* (Fig. 17), or the *Pact of Judas* (Fig. 24), more or less following designs provided by his *chef*. And the style of these *bas-de-page*, like their iconography, is earlier than that of the *Petites Heures*.

The *Petites Heures* was not begun before about 1384 and it must have been completed, for many reasons, before 1390. When discussing the pointing angel in the miniature of the *Annunciation* on folio 141 (Fig. 130) we observed that it was copied in a Book of Hours (Baltimore, Walters Art Gallery, ms. 96) that may be dated between 1388 and 1394 (Fig. 618). The chief illuminator of that manuscript was, so to speak, steeped in the *Petites Heures*; he adopted its borders, its birds, and several additional figures, such as the oldest Magus in the *Adoration*, the Virgin in the *Visitation*, a seated shepherd in the *Annunciation to the Shepherds*, or Joseph in the *Nativity* (Fig. 616). The church in the *Vigils of the Dead* has a similar source (Figs. 621). Since the manuscript ends with a prayer for Clement VII, with whom Jean de Berry exchanged manuscripts,[117] the little Book of Hours may well have been a gift to him, like the Vatican Bible, from the Duke, or, because coats of arms are lacking, from someone in the Duke's circle to a friend in Avignon.[118]

A style very close to that of Walters 96 may be seen in a Bible in the British Museum that belonged to Jean de Berry (Figs. 617, 622).[119] Most of the miniatures in this Bible were painted by the Virgil Master, whose career began in the 'nineties and continued on into the early fifteenth century (Fig. 841). His work, listed on p. 360, will be considered in a subsequent volume. The paintings by the followers of Jacquemart are closest to the miniatures by the second hand in Walters 96 rather than to the *Annunciation* or the *Nativity*. The two manuscripts were probably illuminated around the same time, but the Bible lacks the naturalistic flowers in the borders that are so delightful an addition to the pattern of the *Petites Heures*.

The style quickly passed into secular illustration. It was employed by the illuminators of a *Roman de la rose* that Jean de Berry received in 1403 as a gift from his treasurer Martin Gouge (Fig. 624).[120] An inscription by Flamel informs us that the Duke gave the manuscript away after a decade. He may have been bored with it for the miniatures, which never reach the level of the best master of Walters 96, are not very impressive.

A second Book of Hours in the Walters Gallery, ms. 94, depends to a degree upon the *Petites Heures* also.[121] It is a smaller, simpler book, and the illuminator followed only Pseudo-Jacquemart. His style is indeed so close to the latter that he must have worked with him, and we cannot exclude the possibility that Pseudo directed the illumination of this manuscript. The *Trinity* (Fig. 627) is a nearly exact copy of the monumental representation of this subject by the Trinity Master in the *Petites Heures* (Fig. 154). Without such models the illumination descends to a duller level (Fig. 626).

Our conclusions in this chapter about the relationship of the *Très Belles Heures de Notre-Dame*, the *Psalter*, and the *Petites Heures* coincide fully with those reached in Chapters VI and VII, in the study of the manuscripts from other points of view. We will not, I hope, be accused of having unduly labored a point of chronology, at least not by those who have in mind the late date given to the *Très Belles Heures de Notre-Dame* since the time of Paul Durrieu. Some scholars still place the work of the Parement Master in it as late as 1405–1407,[122] while others believe that it should be dated after the *Petites Heures*.[123] There are periods of rapid development in the history of painting when a few years are crucial, and knowledge of the priority of the Parement Master contributes to recognition of his artistic stature. Indeed, the problem of chronology is intimately bound up, as usual, with the problem of authorship. The participation of the Parement Master in the design, at least, of the illumination of the *Très Belles Heures de Notre-Dame* will be questioned less if we recognize that this participation occurred in the very first years of the 'eighties rather than five, ten, or twenty years later.

The first campaign in the *Très Belles Heures de Notre-Dame* constituted the most important pictorial enterprise in France around 1380 – the most important, indeed, since the *Heures de Pucelle*, illuminated half a century earlier. Part of the power and novelty of these paintings derived from a study of Trecento painting. This interest was shared by the leading painter in the *Petites Heures*, who learned much from the Parement Master but who turned also to Italian panels themselves. In the *Adoration of the Magi* (Fig. 93) he went beyond the Parement Master's assumption of Italian structure to approximate Italian surface. The shepherds in this scene even seem based on specific Italian models.

This miniature represents the height of Italianism in the *Petites Heures*, but it reflects only one aspect of the painter's interests at that time. In other miniatures he is more concerned with an analysis of color and light, striving to dissolve both Tuscan modelled plasticity and French linearity in a new luminary style. His efforts resemble those put forth by Giovannino dei Grassi in Milan-Pavia at the same time; probably the two worked quite independently of each other. The master of the *Petites Heures* probed in so many diverse directions – light and color, linear perspective, geometric composition – that problems of the unity of the style and of singleness of authorship become exceedingly complex. With the benefit of some hindsight we may judge that the paintings in question were the work of a young master in a new and stimulating environment.

In the preceding chapter we encountered this style and that of the Pseudo-Jacquemart in the

Duke's *Psalter*. The former was, characteristically, visible in a somewhat different vein. The figures in the two relevant miniatures, like those in the *Nativity* and the *Flight* in the *Petites Heures*, are based on models found in the Pucelle tradition (Figs. 78, 79). The figure of *David in the Water* is certainly by the painter of the *Nativity* and the *Adoration of the Magi* in the *Petites Heures*; even the features, the large nose and narrow mouth are similar. The escalloped terrain, however, remains more attached to earlier conventions. What this painter could do with the same form at approximately the same time is demonstrated by the adjoining miniature of the *Fool* (Fig. 78). Here the terrain is composed of delicately modulated and freely painted reeds and grasses, moving sporadically into pockets of shade. The supple mantle of the figure falls naturally, lying in flat plaits or curling gently into space and responding everywhere to the movement of the figure. The surfaces of the white mantle and the grayish flesh are very subtly varied in value. Exquisite in texture, they glow in the extensive enveloping atmosphere.

A determination of sequence within two such closely related groups of paintings, and by such a variable artist, would be risky. Comparison of the contributions of Pseudo-Jacquemart to the two manuscripts leads to scarcely more decisive results. On the whole the miniatures by him in the *Psalter* look a little earlier, but we have already seen that his *Trinity* (Fig. 82) depends upon the representation of this subject in the *Petites Heures* (Fig. 127), or possibly on a common model now lost. The two manuscripts are linked even by minor technical details: the green rays in the haloes of the *Psalter* are used in the *Petites Heures*. More important is the deep influence of Beauneveu upon the painter of the frame of the *Annunciation* (Fig. 94) and other miniatures. Beauneveu was in Bourges in 1386, and may have arrived a year or two earlier, possibly even with Jacquemart, who was established there in 1384. Probably work on both the *Psalter* and the *Petites Heures* was going forward in the same period. For the *Petites Heures* the latter limit of this period, we should recall, is firmly fixed around 1390 by the copies of several of its miniatures in a Book of Hours datable between 1387 and 1394. All other evidence seems to point towards the mid 'eighties.

The nature of the collaboration in the *Petites Heures* is unusual even in an art in which collective activity was normal. Especially rare is the allocation in the *Petites Heures* of the *completion* of surfaces within a small pictorial field to two illuminators. The manuscript shares this peculiarity with the body of the *Psalter* of the Duke. Two of the same painters participated in both instances, so that a particular association was involved. Jacquemart, the stronger and more advanced, took the lion's share of the heavens. The collaboration in the *Petites Heures* extended, however, to other painters and to diverse divisions of the work. Perhaps the unusual role of the Passion Master was affected by the emergence of a new style that began to overshadow his. If furthermore the bearer of this new style was not a professional illuminator, as we shall suggest below, his relationship to the book might well have been exceptional. Nor can we ignore the wishes of the Duke, who even at this earlier moment in his career as a patron did not lack either critical judgment or the intention to apply it to the work he commissioned. For all these reasons the circumstances surrounding the illumination of the *Très Belles Heures de Notre-Dame*, the *Psalter*, and the *Petites Heures* were as exceptional as the results.

PETITES HEURES – COLLATION

(from Delaissé, 1963, p. 142 n. 21)

FOLIOS

1–6   Calendar.

7   Blank with a stub that probably appears before the Calendar.

8–15   Precepts for a prince.

16–21   Teachings of St. Louis.

22–52   Hours of the Virgin. Four quaternions. Fols. 51v. and 52 blank. Third quaternion incomplete; between fols. 43-34 the miniature of None has been removed but the stub is glued to fol. 39.

53–154   Thirteen quaternions. Penitential psalms, Hours of the Holy Ghost, Hours of the

FOLIOS   Passion, prayers. Change of ink suggests that fols. 96-97 and 145-154 were added.

155–182   Hours of the Cross, prayers. One ternion (significance unclear), two quaternions, and one ternion.

183–202   Hours of the Trinity. Two quaternions and one binion. Fols. 196-199 added.

203–216   Hours of St. John. One quaternion and one ternion.

217–238   Office of the Dead. Two quaternions and one ternion.

239–286   Prayers of the Passion and others.

287–290   A gathering added. Lamentation of the Cross and the Itinerary.

TABLE OF PAINTERS OF THE *PETITES HEURES*

I. PASSION MASTER

Probably design for the folios

22, Annunciation, Virgin and Gabriel only

40v., design of Annunciation to Shepherds (?)

53, Christ with the four Evangelists, *bas-de-page*, drolleries

76, Betrayal, initial, *bas-de-page*

79v., Christ before Caiaphas

82, Mockery

83v., Flagellation

86v., Way to Calvary

89v., Crucifixion

92v., Deposition

94v., Entombment

97v., drolleries only

207, Birth of Baptist, in large part

208, Youthful Baptist in Desert

212v., Dance of Salomé, in large part

II. JACQUEMART DE HESDIN

8, Prince, God and some angels

17, St. Louis on his death bed (color retouched a little and outlines reinforced in ink)

22, Annunciation, everything but the angel and the Virgin

32v., Visitation

38, Nativity, though possibly begun by Passion Master

40v., Annunciation to Shepherds, part of execution

42v., Adoration of Magi

45v., Flight into Egypt, but with assistance of Trinity Master

48v., Coronation, with assistance of Trinity Master

97v., Madonna and donor

209v., Baptism, with Trinity Master

211, Baptist before Herod, with Trinity Master

214, Salomé and the Executioner, with Trinity Master

III. TRINITY MASTER

45v. and 48v., part of execution

67, Baptism

70, Trinity

72, St. Peter leading youth into church

74, St. Peter celebrating mass

100v., Lord Enthroned with a prince in prayer

103v., Madonna and donor (Madonna by Pseudo-Jacquemart)

137v., Trinity (outlines reinforced in ink)

140v., Betrayal (outlines strengthened with pen)

141v., Annunciation
158, Agony in Garden
163, Three Maries at the Tomb
183, Trinity
188, Abraham and the Trinity
189, The Lord with two seraphs
192, Christ on Mount Tabor
194v., Christ adored by Kings
196, Trinity
198v., A prince before the Madonna
203, Annunciation to Zacharias (Zacharias only)
207, Birth of Baptist, two heads only
209v., Baptism (with Jacquemart)
211, Baptist before Herod (with Jacquemart)
212v., Dance of Salomé, part of the execution only
214, Salomé and the Executioner (with Jacquemart and Pseudo-Jacquemart)

IV. Pseudo-Jacquemart and Workshop

1–6v., Calendar
8, Dominican instructing young prince, with Jacquemart
9v., Dominican instructing young prince
12, The story of Eli and his sons
48v., Angel in border
63v., Crucifixion
69, Pentecost
71, Peter preaching
73, Peter and Paul baptizing
75, St. Ambrose
103v., Madonna and donor (with Trinity Master)
104, Baptist and angels
104v., Prophets and Apostles; Magdalene
105, Holy Martyrs (damaged)
105v., Confessors and Holy Virgins

106
106v.
115v.
117v.
119   } A series of miniatures showing a prince
119v.   in prayer before Christ or the Virgin
120
121v.
122

123v., A bearded monk in brown habit praying
132v., Trinity
134v., Funeral Service

136, Christ, the Virgin, and saints in heaven
139, A prince attending mass
141, Deposition and Resurrection
142v., Virgin and her parents entering temple; Virgin in prayer
143, Nativity
143v., Virgin nursing Child; angel appearing to her
144, Death of Virgin
144v., A prince praying to Christ and the Virgin
145v., A prince praying to Christ (damaged) (?)
155, Entombment of Christ
162, Nailing Christ to Cross
164, Crucifixion
166, Limbo

167v.
169v.
170v. } Series of representations of a prince at
171   mass
172
173v.

174v., A communion
176, A prince at mass
176v., A prince in prayer before crucifix
181v., St. Julien and St. Martha
191, Baptism
193, Christ preaching
196v., Prince before crucifix
197v., Pentecost
198, Prince before the Trinity
203, Zacharias at the Temple, except Zacharias
206, Visitation
214, A King (Herod?) in the border
217, Funeral Service
239, Crucifixion
267, Holy women and faithful in prayer
278v., Throne of Solomon
282, Three living and three dead
286, Lamentation

V. The Fifth Master

160, Way to Calvary
161, Making the cross fast
186v., Creation of Adam
199v., The Duke (?) with his guardian angel

VI. The Limbourgs

288v., Jean de Berry setting out on a journey

IX

The Vatican Bible and the Brussels Hours

1 · THE VATICAN BIBLE

THE two major advanced styles in the *Petites Heures*, that of the Trinity Master and of the presumed Jacquemart, cannot be found again in similar phases during the years immediately after the completion of the manuscript. There is, in other words, a caesura in the sequence of style, and it greatly complicates our understanding of the chief painters in the service of the Duke during the 'eighties and 'nineties. One miniature in a French translation of the pseudo-Aristotelian *Secreta Secretorum* is a partial exception (Fig. 654).[1] The manuscript, which bears the arms of Jean de Berry, resembles the *Petites Heures* in the design of the folio, including the *bas-de-page*, though here it is perfunctorily filled with hound and hare, as in Walters ms. 96 (Fig. 618). Even the subject of the manuscript, the 'gouvernement des princes', recalls the content of the first section of the *Petites Heures*. The one miniature has much in common with the *Baptist before Herod* in the *Petites Heures* (Fig. 169). The colors, pink, gray-green, blue, violet, are like those commonly employed in this style in the *Petites Heures*, and they are similarly softened by a suffused light. Alexander is almost identical with Herod, and indeed one might be led to question which composition was designed first. Certainly the composition in the *Petites Heures* is artistically superior; alongside it the other looks cramped and ill-adjusted in its field. It is also less vigorous. This dull existentialism may, however, be connected with an increasing interest in volume and the definition of form by color and light rather than line – an interest to which Otto Pächt, who published the miniature, pointed, and which led him, rightly I think, to regard it as a little later than the *Petites Heures*.[2] A small but not insignificant symptom of the concern with radiance is visible in the background, where the center of each tiny gold square is punched so as to vary the quality of the light and increase the kinds of reflection.

Of far greater significance is a Bible in the Vatican Library in two volumes, each containing the signature of Jean de Berry. Although scholars have given it little attention, it provides a key to the understanding of the major innovations in French painting. Not that the normal Biblical illumination in it is exceptional. This still follows Bondol's canon, though it has been affected also by newer trends, and especially by the *Petites Heures*. *Daniel in the lion's den* (Fig. 661) seems to reflect the eremitic Baptist in the *Petites Heures* (Fig. 167), although the latter offered no model for Daniel's nudity. A second prophet is nude also: Nehemiah, when riding a camel presumably to inspect the walls of Jerusalem.[3] The angel in the *Annunciation* points heavenward, in the manner of the figures in the *Petites Heures*, though here Gabriel raises his left hand (Figs. 94, 130, 658). The gesture, especially motivated by the appearance of the Trinity immediately above the scene, is quite like that of Gabriel in the *Annunciation* in a Book of Hours in the British Museum, of which we have already spoken (Fig. 620). Indeed we are confronted here not simply with very similar figures but identity of workshop. The members of the Trinity in the Bible reappear, so to speak, as St. Matthew in one of the more animated miniatures in the Book of Hours (Fig. 660). The *Horae* in London, which does not preserve an original coat of arms,[4] is therefore linked also with the circle of Jean de Berry.

Even more notable in the *Vatican Bible* is the *Madonna of Humility* (Fig. 662), the earliest surviving example of the subject in metropolitan France.[5] The design of the figures resembles a *Madonna* of the early fifteenth century (Fig. 269), which approaches still more closely an Italian model, no doubt from the circle of Ambrogio Lorenzetti (Fig. 698).[6] We must, in fact, infer that by about 1390 there was visible in Bourges or Paris either the Italian model or a good French copy of it. Both manuscripts in which the copies appear, the Vatican Bible and Yates Thompson 37 in the British Museum, were connected with the painters of Jean de Berry and with Bourges.

The great interest of the *Vatican Bible* lies in the paintings of a very different style that were added to the first folio of each volume (Figs. 177-178). These paintings are definitely dated within a limited period – a rare distinction among outstanding French paintings of the time. In the margin below the lower bar on the first folio of the first volume the tiara and escutcheon of Clement VII – *cinq points d'or equipollés à quatre d'azur* – are flanked by those of Jean de Berry and his wife Jeanne de Boulogne, *d'or au gonfanon de gueules frangé de sinople*. On the first folio of the second volume a larger field was available for a similar display, and the papal arms are set above those of the Duke and Duchess. Since the Duke married Jeanne de Boulogne, his second wife, in 1389, and Clement VII died in 1394, these fields were painted within that period. The dependence of some miniatures in the older style upon the *Petites Heures* proves that the manuscript as a whole was not produced much earlier.

These two initial folios display the emblems not only of the Pope and the Duke but also of the Duke's physician, Simon Alegret. He appears modestly in the guise of a little white dog bearing in his mouth a scroll inscribed 'Alegret'. Paul Durrieu explained these arms and emblems as a record of a gift by Alegret to the Duke for presentation to the Pope.[7] There can be no doubt about the last stage, because of the prominence of the papal arms and the fact that the manuscript did go into the papal library. It was listed in the earliest extant inventory, that of Nicholas V of 1455.[8] One wonders, however, about the relationship of Alegret. It is true that in the first volume he is closer, so to speak, than the Duke to the Pope. If, however, Durrieu's hypothesis is correct, why and when did the Duke inscribe both volumes as part of his collection? If the manuscript was destined for the Pope why should he have inserted his arms in the initial on the first folio of the first volume? Inasmuch as the Duke seems to have had the books in his library, for however short a time, a more plausible explanation would be that when he decided to present them to the Pope he included Alegret because his physician had reason to be grateful to the Pontiff. Perhaps he had treated Clement – during, say, Berry's visit to Avignon in 1391 – and been rewarded for his success.

Both Jean de Berry and his new wife of 1389 were very devoted to Clement VII. The two men frequently exchanged presents, especially on New Year's day. Berry's inventory of 1401-1403 identifies objects as gifts of 'feu pape Clement de Genève'. These gifts include an early fourteenth-century manuscript of Priscian, now British Museum, Burney 275, and a Bible in ten volumes.[9]

Another Bible, 'escripte de lettre boulonnoise', bore the arms of both Clement and Jean de Berry; the Duke gave this manuscript to Louis d'Orléans.[10] Berry visited the Pope at Avignon several times. The Duke exchanged gifts with his physician too through the long period of their relationship. Entries in the inventory of 1401–1403 state that he gave Alegret numerous objects, a jewel of gilded silver containing two angels that held a round crystal (for a relic), some ivory boxes decorated in relief, and embroidered cushions bearing the Duke's motto, 'le temps venra'.[11] Alegret in turn was inclined to combine in his gifts pleasure and instruction. For though he gave the Duke an emerald ring for New Year's 1411, and a sapphire ring in 1413, he presented him with a Psalter in 1414, a medical treatise of Avicenna in 1404, and, in 1412, a book of medicinal recipes describing the 'vertu des herbes et des bestes . . . ouquel sont les dictes herbes et bestes contrefaictes de painture. . . .'[12]

The dog was sometimes connected with the *Ars Medica* in the Middle Ages.[13] Whether or not the little creature has this connotation in the *Vatican Bible* it is clearly a symbol of fidelity, and Alegret is associated also with one of the little high-bred creatures resembling Pomeranians so beloved by the Duke. He cared as much for them as for his bears, and he bestowed on one of them the fond name of 'lion'. The Duke's peers and friends vied with one another in offering him images of his pets in all conceivable media, and on New Year's day 1407 'monseigneur de Bourbon' gave him what seems in part a goldsmith's version of the Vatican 'terrace' and 'chiennet': '. . . . un chandellier d'argent doré, fait en manière d'une terrace esmailliée de vert, . . . ouquel a par dessus un arbre esmaillié de vert et un chiennet d'argent blanc . . .'[14] Among surviving objects a small brooch with a camel now in Florence shows some resemblance to the dog on the mound (Fig. 664).[15]

The emblematic paintings in the *Vatican Bible*, simple in subject, are of an astonishing beauty. The strip of terrain in the first volume, which must have been painted at the same time as the dog and the coats of arms, is a tender blue-green from which rise trees with very deep crowns and wonderfully pale, luminous vines bearing dark blue grapes. The painter knew even more about birds than about plants. The variegated browns of the wren, the red cheek, white head, black cap, and gold bar of the goldfinch are deliciously rendered. The freedom and openness of the brushstrokes have no precedents; leaves, rocks, grasses, butterflies and birds, shimmering in a pale light, are evoked with the simplest means. The deftness and assurance of the painter's touch cannot be matched anywhere in the late fourteenth century. The closest approximation is the *Fool* in the Duke's *Psalter*, with its exquisite tonal variations, its deep green foliage brought up to yellow in light (Fig. 78). That miniature could conceivably have come from the same brush, but several years earlier.

When I called attention to the beauty and importance of these paintings in 1956 I confessed to anxiety that my attribution of the two pairs of angels in the second volume to two quite different painters would lead my colleagues to question my sanity. I had forgotten that in 1909 Paul Durrieu had briefly recorded exactly the same observation. One master, the lesser of the two, I believe, was responsible for the two angels at the left; the second master painted everything else on this folio and also the entire border in Volume I. The difference between the two is readily suggested by their use of color. The clouds at the left are executed in two shades of crimson;

the parchment itself serves as the highest value. The painter working at the right added two reds higher in the scale, a rose-white and a white just tinged with rose. He too allows the parchment to show in places, but it is the third value, and therefore looks grayish. The little dog below shows a similar range of high values and is equally luminous. He and his *terrace* provide the key to the authorship of the landscape in the first volume, which is all in the same style.

There are of course more obvious differences between the two pairs of angels. The two at the left were executed in grisaille, those at the right in color. In one pair each wears a flowing mantle, in the other a tunic tucked in over a girdle at the waist. One pair kneels on clouds, the other flies, trailing them. These differences arise in part from the unequal fields allotted to the two pairs, which suggested the employment of two different traditional designs. But whereas the flying angels are in perfect accord with the colors and shapes around them the kneeling figures are heavy and obtrusive. The energy of the flying angels, with their lithe wings and broken outlines – even at the clouds – radiates through the entire field. The tense, curling tail of the dog seems to be galvanized by it. The kneeling angels are more inert.

Whereas the angels at the left are projected forward from the plane of the escutcheon and the parchment and give us a sense that their opposite sides are flat or only dimly conceived, those at the right move in a space that extends back from the shield. With what a beautifully simple pantomime they unite the shield and the tiara, composing a design that is almost, but not quite, geometric! Each angel places a hand on the further, invisible plane of the tiara, so that through their action it and the escutcheon acquire weight and volume. Yet the energy of the angels is applied so perfectly that, with the help of the mound and the tree, they effortlessly sustain the two forms in space.

The two angels at the left, much more traditional in character, were no doubt painted first. The second master tended to follow them when he began on the angel at the extreme right. He employed the same red in the hair of this angel, and the conspicuous drawing resembles that in the hair of the two angels at the left. His second angel lacks these curling red lines; the hair is a fluffy yellowish mass. Furthermore, the initial drawing for the angel at the extreme right shows an angular cloud, similar to the two clouds at the left. This angular form was altered in the painting to a simpler mass like that of his companion. In this last-named angel there is a full conformity of drawing and painting. This figure was clearly executed last by the second master, and it is indeed the latest of all four.

The painter at the right is the greater and the more advanced. He visualized forms in a light-filled space so vividly that he introduced a transparent shadow below the brow of each of the angels, and also in their cupped upper hands. It was certainly he who conceived the graduated rose shadows that transform all the tiaras into billowing conical balloons. His too must be the pale yellow-green twigs on which the birds perch, oriental in their linear delicacy. The identity of these two painters is of crucial importance for our knowledge of the course of French painting. The more advanced master resembles, as we have said, the author of the *Fool* in the *Psalter*, and his Italianism connects him with the painter of the *Adoration of the Magi* and similar miniatures in the *Petites Heures*. The angels at the left show the relatively heavy, rounded forms of the Trinity Master, and this relationship is supported by the details of the faces and the hair. These

o

angels are also related, in another way, to the diptych at the beginning of the *Brussels Hours*. Since the rest of the painting in the *Brussels Hours* is still more profoundly connected with the Bible, an estimate of the identities must be postponed until it has been discussed.

At this point we may at least ask why two leading painters should have joined forces to produce a bit of heraldry in a Bible? The possibility that the author of the angels at the left failed for some reason to complete the figures at the right cannot be excluded. This interpretation is not, however, really convincing. Were the painters engaged in a little competition, set by the Duke? Could this have been inspired by tales of ancient competitions such as Apelles and Protogenes, transmitted by Pliny? Competitions, though not within such close quarters, occurred later, as that of Clement VII for his pectoral, ultimately commissioned to Cellini.[16] And much closer to the *Vatican Bible* in time, Charles d'Orléans suggested the initial line of a poem to half a dozen poets.[17]

2 · THE BRUSSELS HOURS – EARLY HISTORY

Modern research on the *Très Belles Heures* of Jean de Berry, as on countless other manuscripts, was initiated by Leopold Delisle when, in 1868 and 1880,[18] he identified the splendid manuscript in the Royal Library in Brussels with a Book of Hours described in the Berry inventory of 1402:

> Item, unes très belles heures, richement enluminées et ystoriées de la main Jaquemart de Odin, et par les quarrefors des fueillez en pluseurs lieux faictes des armes et devises de Monseigneur; couvertes d'un sathin bleu, doublé d'un tercelin vermeil, à deux fremouers d'or esmaillez ausdictes armes, en l'un un saphir, deux grosses perles, et en l'autre un balay et deux grosses perles; et en la pipe deux grosses perles et un rubi. (Guiffrey, *Inventaires*, II, pp. 132-133, no. 1050.)

The item was followed by a note to the effect that the book had been given to the Duke of Burgundy:

> Date domino duci Burgondie, ut constat per compotum dicti Robineti

Delisle found that the same book could be traced in the Burgundian inventory drawn up in 1420 after the death of Jean sans Peur, where the following item occurs:

> Item, unes Heures de Nostre Dame, fermans à II fermouers d'or, armoyées des armes de feu Monseigneur de Berry en deux lieux, et sont les tissuz semez de triffeille d'or; et ou milieu de l'un des fermouers a un balay à jour, accompaigné de II grosses perles, et en l'autre fermouer I saphir à jour et une grosse perle et une perle perdue; et y sert une pipe d'or armoyée desdites armes esmaillées, et a ou milieu ung ruby accompaigné de deux perles rondes; couvertes de satin azuré. (Doutrepont, *Inventaires*, 1906, p. 5, no. 6.)

Once again there was a marginal note to help with the further tracing of the manuscript, saying that this and another book had been requested by the widow of Jean sans Peur:

> Madame mère de Monseigneur a demandé à Bouloigne ces II paires de Heures de Notre-Dame et les a par devers elle.

An item in the inventory of her effects made after her death in 1424 shows that it remained in her possession.

> Les Belles Heures de ma dicte dame, à deux fermaulx d'or armoyez aux armes de Monseigneur de Berry, à tixu de soye semé de fueilles de treffle; l'un des diz fermaulx garny de deux grosses perles rondes et ung balay plat ou milieu, et l'autre fermail garny d'une perle et d'un saphir plat; en ycellui fermail fault une perle. Es dites heures a ung tuyau d'or à tourner les fueillez, garny de deux perles et ung petit ruby ou milieu; lesquelles heures sont couvertes d'une chemise de satin noir. (Barrois, *Bibl. protypographique*, 1830, p. 115, no. 668.)

Although only the Duke of Berry's inventory gives any information regarding illustration, the close correspondence of the minutely described clasps and *pipe* in the three inventories makes it obvious that the same Book of Hours is referred to in each case. Only two changes in the condition of the manuscript are discernible: between 1402 and 1420 a pearl from the clasp had been lost and is recorded as such; and between 1420 and 1424 there is the possibility that the silk cover had been changed, since the *satin bleu* or *azuré* of the first two descriptions is now given as *satin noir*. It is therefore certain that Jean de Berry presented the Duke of Burgundy (probably his brother, Philip le Hardi, who died in 1404, or possibly his nephew, Jean sans Peur) with one of his most richly adorned and most personal Books of Hours, and an examination of both the Berry and Burgundian inventories proves that a gift of this kind was made on this one occasion only.

It is true that Berry regularly gave gifts to the Dukes of Burgundy and they similarly to him. Usually the objects were more expensive than manuscripts.[19] In March 1403, however, Philippe le Hardi gave a *Fleur des histoires* to his brother (Fig. 438), and in January 1413 Jean sans Peur presented his uncle with the *Merveilles du monde*.[20] Though these are both splendid manuscripts they have none of the personal qualities of the *Très Belles Heures*.

The contents of the Book of Hours in Brussels that Delisle identified with these notices are unusual insofar as the Calendar, which normally precedes a Book of Hours, is lacking, and the book opens instead with a devotional diptych in which the Duke of Berry, presented by St. John the Baptist and St. Andrew, kneels to the Virgin and Child. This diptych, originally larger than the manuscript to which it is now attached and possessing borders of a significantly different kind, was not designed as an integral part of the book. The Duke's original ownership of the diptych as well as the Book of Hours is, however, proved by the presence of his arms in the 'quarrefors des feuillez'. The six quatrefoils between those in the corners or quarrefors show his devices: the wounded swan, the bear, and the enigmatic VE monogram. Both sections likewise contain a portrait of the Duke.

Under these circumstances, it would seem that the mere existence of a fine Book of Hours, which could be shown to have passed from the Berry to the Burgundian collection, would be sufficient to clinch an identification with all three inventory items. The only weak link in Delisle's identification of the Brussels manuscript lay in his failure to see the necessity of establishing an early connection between it and the house of Burgundy, for, contrary to his expressed opinion of 1880, the splendid Book of Hours did not follow the fate of those Burgundian manuscripts which can be traced in direct descent from the early collections to the time of entry into the Bibliothèque Royale in Brussels. Instead, the manuscript that passed from the Berry to the Burgundian collection and then belonged to Margaret of Bavaria is no longer recorded after 1424, while the manuscript now in Brussels entered the collection of the Chevalier J. Marchal in 1840 without a clear provenance[20a].

Despite this cloudy history Delisle's identification remained without serious challenge until recently. Van den Gheyn, in his catalogue of the Brussels manuscripts of 1901, prefaced his acceptance of the identification with the word 'probably'. In 1937 Lyna took a firmly negative position, and he was later followed by Delaissé, Pächt, Porcher, and others, whereas Panofsky and the writer upheld Delisle's position. The divergent conclusions based on this 'external' evidence reflect, as they always do, judgments in the realm of style; the case of the *Brussels Hours*, in fact, demonstrates vividly the interrelationship of the two kinds of evidence, one just as 'historical' as the other. Before discussing the documentation further, therefore, it will be useful to give a brief account of the most influential estimates of style.

Until 1937, when Lyna's article was published in the Brussels Catalogue, the participation of Jacquemart de Hesdin in the *Brussels Hours* was regarded by all authorities as an *a priori* fact. In 1880 Delisle drew the logical conclusion that 'unes très belles heures très richement enluminées et ystoriées de la main Jaquemart de Odin' applied to the section actually comprising the Book of Hours and, since he saw a resemblance in the diptych to the style of André Beauneveu, he attributed the latter to this artist. This attribution was contested by Lasteyrie, who in 1896 made the first attempt to define the style of Jacquemart de Hesdin. It was in the diptych rather than in the remainder of the volume that he found the best analogies with the illustration of the Calendar and Hours of the Virgin of the *Grandes Heures*, the only other work connected by documents with the name of Jacquemart de Hesdin. With this attribution we have the only possible alternative to Delisle's original interpretation of the inventory item of 1402, and among those who accept the identification of the *Brussels Hours* with this item opinion continued to be divided.

The most significant elaboration of Lasteyrie's theory was made by Durrieu, who in 1906 attributed the main section of the manuscript to the Boucicaut Master (or Jacques Coene) and gave the diptych to Jacquemart. These conclusions were the only two serious errors committed by Durrieu in his long and productive career. His opinion is perpetuated in Thieme-Becker in articles on Coene and Hesdin written, respectively, by Leo Baer in 1912 and Winkler in 1923. Its most recent adherent was Grete Ring (1949). In the meantime, however, an attempt had been made by Fierens-Gevaert in his publication of the facsimile in 1924 to return to Delisle's original judgment.

The possibilities for disagreement about the *Brussels Hours* were increased by Lyna in 1937, when he emphasized the unknown provenance of the manuscript and refused to accept the identification of it with the fifteenth-century inventory items. The manuscript was consequently freed from documentary restrictions regarding artist or date. Lyna's concept of Jacquemart de Hesdin's style was similar to that of Lasteyrie, but since he could not reconcile the style of the *Grandes Heures* with either of the main styles in the *Brussels Hours* he chose to reject the inventory identification.

In recent publications three scholars have firmly adhered to the identification with the inventory items. In 1953 Panofsky pronounced in favor of the attribution of the main cycles to Jacquemart de Hesdin, suggesting a date of *circa* 1390–1395. At the same time he modified his own earlier view that the diptych could be regarded as the work of André Beauneveu, and dated it earlier, *circa* 1380.[21] An attribution of the main cycles to Jacquemart de Hesdin has also been favored by Carl Nordenfalk and consistently by the writer in articles of 1956, 1960, 1961, and 1963, which adduced the *Vatican Bible* as proof of the existence of the style of the main Brussels cycles as early as 1390, and pointed to the leather Veronica as evidence that the Brussels manuscript had actually belonged to the Burgundian collection.

In 1953 Jean Porcher concluded that the *Madonna and the Writing Christ Child* was copied from Bibliothèque nationale, fr. 926, written for Jean de Berry's daughter in 1406 (Fig. 667), and that it must therefore have been executed after this date. He thus associated himself with the opinion of Lyna and Delaissé that the *Brussels Hours* was not the *Très Belles Heures* of the inventories and that the main section of the manuscript must have been painted *circa* 1409.[22] In 1955, however, he admitted the possibility that this section might have been painted before 1402 by Jacquemart de Hesdin. This hypothesis, based on partial identification with the inventory item of 1402, assumes a later date for the diptych and necessitates a combination of parts after the manuscript had left the possession of Jean de Berry.

An alternative view, also implying partial rejection of the inventory identification, was expressed in 1956 by Otto Pächt. Characterizing the main cycles in the *Brussels Hours* as derivative, he argued that they were executed after the *Grandes Heures* (i.e. after 1409) by an artist of the generation of the Boucicaut Master, who may have been a pupil of the most Italianate artist in the *Petites Heures*. The Louvre *Way to Calvary* exemplified for him the authentic late style of Jacquemart de Hesdin, and the diptych in the *Brussels Hours* rather than the main cycles seemed an early work by the same hand. Thus only the diptych would remain from the richly illuminated *Horae* described in the inventories, and this fragment would have been combined after 1402 at the Burgundian court with a second rich *Horae* illuminated for Berry and likewise presented by him to Burgundy. The mere statement of this hypothesis discloses its implausibility.

There is, however, sufficient evidence to prove beyond the shadow of a doubt that the manuscript in Brussels, which accords well with the inventory notices, was actually in the Burgundian collection in the early fifteenth century. To begin with, in 1924 Fierens-Gevaert drew attention to Marchal's description of the binding of the manuscript that he acquired in 1840. It was black satin, and so old that Marchal suggested for it the period of Charles V. Black satin, Fierens remarked, covered the manuscript when it was inventoried in 1424. In 1960 Eisler and the writer pointed to the fact that the Veronica painted on leather glued to page 8 indicates that the manuscript was at the Burgundian court around 1420.[23] It was curiously Lyna, who denied the connection of the manuscript with the inventory notices, who pointed in 1937 to the devotion of the house of Burgundy to the Holy Face, and to the cult, fostered by Margaret of Bavaria, of St. Veronica, who was customarily invoked against sudden death.[24] Margaret, in whose possession the Hours given by the Duke of Berry to the Duke of Burgundy were last recorded, had lost her husband in 1419 by assassination, and her practice of adding Veronicas to her manuscripts seems appropriate (Fig. 666). These were of an unusual type, painted on leather, and glued or fastened by threads into the manuscript. In the *Brussels Hours* the leather is attached to a page that precedes the diptych, which must therefore already have formed part of the manuscript.

One additional fact, not hitherto cited, points to the presence of the *Brussels Hours* at the court of Burgundy in the early fifteenth century. The miniature of the *Crucifixion* (Fig. 195) was copied in the Breviary illuminated for Jean sans Peur in the second decade of the century (Fig. 678). The copyist left the pole of the banner at the left unsupported and he did not understand the structure of the figure with upraised arm; on the other hand he corrected an ambiguity of the Brussels miniature by showing the arms of the thieves. It is true, as Porcher has observed,[25] that three miniatures in the Breviary are nearly identical with compositions of corresponding subjects in the *Belles Heures* of Jean de Berry, but these relationships do not diminish the significance of the copy of the *Crucifixion*. The fact is that the illuminator, whom I have called the Master of the Bréviaire de Jean sans Peur, maintained a close connection with the Limbourgs (Figs. 780, 781), and even painted some of the initials in the *Très Riches Heures*.[26] He did not, however, have a similar relationship with other painters of the Duke, and naturally not with earlier ones. His copy of the Brussels *Crucifixion* is exceptional among his works, and strongly suggests that his model was available where he worked. The presence of the *Brussels Hours* in the Burgundian collection early in the fifteenth century is indicated also by the influence of the Child in the initial diptych upon the Child in the *Madonna* added about 1415 to the prayerbook of Philippe le Hardi (Fig. 668).

The identity of the *Brussels Hours* with the manuscript ascribed to Jacquemart de Hesdin in the inventory of 1402 can, I believe, no longer be questioned. The form of Robinet's reference, 'richement enluminées et ystoriées de la main Jaquemart de Odin', assures us that this master did the bulk of the miniatures and not the initial diptych. This is a solid fact with which all stylistic interpretations of the period must conform. The seventeen historiated initials, which we have not hitherto mentioned, constitute a third style in the manuscript. They were painted by a North Italian illuminator. The initials and other work of this master will be discussed in the following chapter.

The title *Très Belles Heures de Jean de Berry* derives, as do the other current names of his manuscripts, from the original inventory descriptions. Unfortunately this title resembles the *Très Belles Heures de Notre-Dame*, and the two have in fact been confused in several important recent books.[27] Since the title of the manuscript in Brussels could also be confused with the *Belles Heures*, the Book of Hours is referred to consistently in the present publication as the *Brussels Hours*.

3 · THE INITIAL DIPTYCH

The first two miniatures in the *Brussels Hours* impress us as marking in some respects a turning point in the history of French illumination (Figs. 179, 180). The figures have the scale and the detail of panel painting and indeed Panofsky and Delaissé have suggested that these two folios were not originally intended for a book but to be hung on a wall.[28] In any event they were no doubt bound in a book not long after they were painted, for the second dedication miniature in the *Brussels Hours* is inspired by them and the illuminator was probably asked by the Duke to incorporate the diptych in his *Horae* at the outset of his work.

The illusion of substance and space in these miniatures approximates that of Trecento panels, which are actually the source of their author's style, but the transfer of such an illusion to the pages of a book created certain problems of taste and design. These problems were posed by the tradition of book illumination and that in turn was affected by the nature of a book itself – a collection of pages, the thinness and insubstantiality of which are constantly impressed upon the reader as he turns them. Weight and space in paintings on pages thus tend to be denied by the tactile and visual impression of the pages themselves. They are denied also by the two-dimensionality of the text written across the page. French illumination of the thirteenth and fourteenth centuries had taken account of these peculiarities of painting on parchment and had sought to maintain a certain unity of text and illustration. In Italy and also in Bohemia this kind of unity was less highly valued; the illuminators were less willing to sacrifice any of the illusory qualities of their paintings.

In France the painted forms were closely connected with the script; they were either tied to it or surrounded by it or even penetrated by it. Inscriptions on scrolls or on the backgrounds are more numerous in Gothic art than any other. In pursuit of the harmony of the folio as a whole the ornamental forms in the borders echoed the shapes of the script. In an Evangeliary made about 1280 for the Sainte-Chapelle in Paris, for instance, the 'vines' that begin to move out from the initials around this time have lobes, kinks, and spikes like the letters (Fig. 659). Their red, blue, and gold colors are repeated in the line-endings, rubrics, and other parts of the text. The larger expanses of color within the miniatures themselves detach them from the text, but this detachment was compensated by unifying qualities of other kinds. Compositions in the miniatures were given the same basic rhythmical structures as the vines; in the *Crowning with Thorns* in the Evangeliary the arms of Christ's tormentors form a sort of vase exactly like the vines below, but inverted (Fig. 659). The diapered backgrounds that now commonly replace gold in initials and miniatures spread behind the figures a sparkling screen of small, variously accented units much like the letters on the page.

The awareness of potential conflicts on painted pages was most vivid and enduring in Paris, or at least in the Ile-de-France. It was there that painters showed not only an enthusiasm for naturalistic scenes but also an unflagging sense of the peculiarities and special limitations of pictures in books. Thus Parisian illuminators resisted for a while the attractions of the *bas-de-page*, which had become firmly established in the course of the thirteenth century in England and in Picardy and the Artois. They could not fail, however, eventually to succumb to it. They finally accepted the idea of a more elaborate border that provided a habitat for *drôleries*, thus offering illuminators opportunities for wit and satire similar to those that sculptors had enjoyed for a long time. The *bas-de-page* seems to appear in Paris in the early years of the fourteenth century and then, with the *drôleries*, it was adopted by Jean Pucelle and disseminated throughout the rest of France.

As the forms in the miniatures and the *bas-de-page* acquired mass and weight and began to move in space, so did the vines. On folios illuminated by Pucelle the leaves wrinkle and curl up from the flat vellum and the vines cross over one another, so that a shallow layer of space is created that extends just before and just behind the plane of the script (Figs. 336-338). The whole *vigneture* becomes a sort of filigree just substantial enough to support the birds, insects, and grotesques that begin to inhabit it. At the same time, the connection of the miniature with the text and the page is maintained by more prominent initials and line-endings, and leaves like those in the border are inserted in interstices of the text. Arabesques, more akin to the vines, often replace geometric forms in the backgrounds, and Pucelle admits into them the birds, animals, and grotesques of the borders, only somewhat reduced in scale (Figs. 353-355). Pucelle as well as many later Parisian illuminators even denied the figures color, preferring to execute them in a monochrome similar to the surface of the page (Figs. 335, 336).

Gradually during the course of the century the vines in the borders become longer, and if one glances in succession at the *Heures de Jeanne de Navarre* (Fig. 345), the *Bible de Charles V* (Fig. 386), the *Très Belles Heures de Notre-Dame* (Fig. 6), and the *Petites Heures* (Fig. 91), one recognizes that they tend to curl ever more actively and to occupy the border more completely, especially on folios containing miniatures. Thus all of the page except the area of text has a certain limited depth, and the rather dense vine around the miniature acts as a sort of frame. Within the vines appear birds, insects, and flowers, so that the borders acquire a variety of colors corresponding to the richer, more varied colors in the miniature. The shallow space of the border, moreover, mediates between the flatness of the text and the depth of the picture.

Throughout this long development the formalized vines normally preserved their free, meandering nature, though it was increasingly threatened. The cursive patterns were partly abandoned in one of the earliest manuscripts in the style of Bondol, a Bible written in 1357. On the first folio the painter, influenced by English and Italian borders and perhaps also by earlier book covers, introduced a more systematic, axial structure (Fig. 383). In the lower and outer borders he employed a series of quatrefoils, regularly spaced within each border and connected by straight stems. In the quatrefoils he placed lively, individualized busts of prophets, somewhat influenced in type and posture by Pucelle. The painter of the Brussels diptych completed this structure and made it more regular (Figs. 179, 180). Into each corner he put a quatrefoil,[29] and others at approximately equal distances. The quatrefoils are connected by stems from which issue at regular intervals not the traditional red, blue, and gold vines but light yellow-green tendrils. These tendrils curve in a rather regular manner and at their tips they bear flowers. The flowers between any two quatrefoils are all alike, and different from all the other flowers on the page. Even the exquisitely painted birds and butterflies, normally the freest forms of all, are subjected to a principle of rhythmical regularity.

In this way the painter provided a novel frame, firmer and tighter, for miniatures that create an unprecedented illusion of mass and space. And, in keeping with the dialectic of the folio, the greater illusion within the miniature was countered by figures executed in grisaille and by backgrounds composed of curling leaves and grotesques, or of bevies of small angels.

The painter, an artist of great sophistication, used blue, a more recessive color, for the miniature at the left in which the space is relatively deep, and orange, a color that tends to come forward, for the Madonna, whose throne hovers close to the picture plane. Her scrolls and parts of her throne overlap the gold border around the painting, and the recession of the deepest part of the throne is minimized by the gold and red cloth thrown over it. The tiled floor is not continued on the far side of the throne, but in the representation of the Duke and his saints, where the painter wished to suggest a more real world, the red and yellow tiles extend deep behind the figures. And whereas the floor of the *Madonna* is laid out on the 'vanishing axis' system[30] the Duke's floor exhibits the kind of convergence in one small area that was introduced in the last miniatures in the *Petites Heures* (Fig. 170, 176). Exceedingly effective as a spatial device, this tessellated floor entirely lacks a superstructure, like the miniature of Charles V by Jean Bondol, who first introduced this kind of partial interior and this kind of perspective into French painting (Fig. 382).

The spatial differences implied by the diverse treatment of the floor in the two miniatures are developed consistently by the painter. While in the *Madonna* some forms overlap the gold frame, in the other miniature the frame very pointedly overlaps the figures, producing the most vivid sense of spatial contingency in Northern painting up to this time. Both miniatures are enlivened by curling and cascading drapery, and in both the light moves with a new subtlety across these beautifully turned surfaces. It gives, especially to the faces, unprecedented nuance and animation, and the exquisite head of the Duke of Berry attains a new degree of individuality, with regard to both physiognomy and personality. In these respects it decisively surpasses the portrait by the Parement Master (Fig. 49) and even its Italian models (Fig. 513). It strikes us as the first of a series of Northern accomplishments that ultimately made Jan van Eyck's portraits possible. It also tells us that the art of Simone Martini was finally understood fully in the North, and that a painter had appeared there who could render Simone's surfaces even more luminous while losing none of his refinement and not much of his bodily structure. These miniatures resemble the equally Simonesque French panels of the late fourteenth century (Figs. 694, 695).

The painter of the miniatures presented the Duke on the same scale as the accompanying saints, a departure from the medieval tradition that began in Italy with Giotto's Enrico Scrovegni and in France before 1346 in the *Bréviaire de Catherine de Valois* (Figs. 656-657).[31] The kind of equality implied in this uniformity of size is audaciously developed in the Brussels miniature into intimacy: the saints, who as patrons normally stand, drop down to their knees alongside the kneeling Duke. This device of kneeling figures was essential to the design of the whole diptych, for only it would have allowed so large a scale.

The simultaneous involvement of the Child in two actions reflects one of the major accomplishments of early Trecento art as it strove to extend the range of human behavior and the depth of the life of the mind. The creator of this image undoubtedly had in mind a Madonna of Humility by Simone Martini or one of his followers in which the Child, while nursing, turns his glance outward to look at the beholder.[32] Here, however, the Infant performs an additional act for which there was no Italian precedent. He writes while drawing sustenance from the Virgin, spiritual as well as physical – for, as Panofsky has observed, she is understood here not only as the mother but the *Sedes Sapientiae*.[33]

This complex Madonna is a special version of the image of the Madonna with the writing Christ Child that appeared in Northwestern Europe in the third quarter of the century.[34] The early examples differ from one another in design, but those made by artists in the circle of Jean de Berry, which are by far the most beautiful, fall into two groups. The first consists of the Brussels *Madonna* and an ivory in the Louvre, which is remarkably similar except for the absence of the large throne, the turn of the Child's head inward and the lower position of the Madonna's right hand (Fig. 669). Nothing is known of the early history of the work. A third example, however, brings us back definitely to the ambient of Jean de Berry. It appears in the initial miniature in a collection of moral treatises, Bibl. nat., fr. 926, made between November 1405 and May 1406 for Marie, daughter of Jean de Berry, who is shown kneeling before the Madonna (Fig. 667).

This *Madonna* and the one in Brussels are so nearly identical that either they have a common source or one must have been copied from the other. Recently Jean Porcher argued for the priority of fr. 926, stressing the fact that in it the scroll is not left dangling but passes to the donor.[35] It bears moreover an inscription containing a prayer to *Maria Mediatrix* and the response of Christ, 'fiat'. A similar inscription, Porcher pointed out, was written by the Child on a scroll extending to Cardinal Pierre de Luxembourg in a miniature in his book of prayers of 1386 (Fig. 655). Here the posture of the Child is very different, but these two miniatures of 1386 and 1406 do indicate that the *Madonna* in Brussels did not initiate a tradition but reflects an earlier prototype of the image. On the other hand the Brussels *Madonna* cannot, I believe, have been painted after 1406. The details of drapery and physiognomy that it shares with fr. 926 are characteristic of the former, not the latter. The drapery folds of the two Madonnas may be found again, for instance, in the mantles of the Duke and the two saints but not in the dresses of Marie de Berry and her companion. These dresses show the long, sweeping patterns that are typical of the Master of Luçon, in whose workshop the miniature was painted.[36]

Though the *Madonna* in Marie de Berry's manuscript owes much to the *Madonna* in the *Brussels Hours*, both seem to show an awareness of a lost model. This model need not have been a painting; indeed, the large thrones and the odd, suspended scroll in Brussels suggest a sculpture with a metallic scroll. We have lost so high a proportion of the sculpture, the panel paintings, and the goldsmith's work of the time that we can only grope for solutions to problems posed by the few surviving objects. The truth of this statement is indicated no less clearly by the second type of writing Child that was current in Berry's milieu. Two examples of it have survived, first a well-known and beautiful drawing in a boxwood pattern-book in the Morgan Library, New York (Fig. 279). A second is a little known miniature, perhaps grisaille, in a manuscript that was in S. María del Mar in Barcelona, unfortunately destroyed or lost during the Civil War (Fig. 280).[37] The style is related to that of the drawing, but weaker. Perhaps, like the script, it is not French but Catalan, or a mixture. The Child reaches for flowers (roses?) proffered by a soaring angel, while another flies in with an inkwell. The Madonna sits within a tabernacle, an architectural form that began to be employed frequently for scenes and for saints in the early fifteenth century by the Limbourgs and the Boucicaut Master.[38] This miniature, or rather its model, seems somewhat earlier. No similar Madonna in a tabernacle has come down to us.

The miniature and the Morgan drawing must reflect a lost Madonna, because the miniature is scarcely strong enough to be the source of this design. The drawing, on the other hand, shows only part of a composition. The suspension of the scroll at the left is explicable only by the arm of the throne, which is lacking in it. Lacking in the drawing too are the letters on the scroll of the miniature. The style of the miniature seems to reflect that of the main group of miniatures in the *Brussels Hours*, which will be discussed shortly. One unusual detail supports this identification: the halo of the Child is behind the body of the Virgin in both the miniature and the drawing. We shall see that Jacquemart de Hesdin used a similar halo in his Brussels *Madonna*. Except for the flying angels one might have supposed that the *Urbild* was a sculpture or perhaps a *joyau*, especially because of the charming little wicker fence, which probably refers to the *hortus conclusus*.

The use of grisaille in the Barcelona miniature and the Brussels *Madonna* may be related to the symbolic value of white, to the veneration of Notre-Dame-la-Blanche, and also to the general preference for white that was so marked toward the end of the century, as we have remarked in Chapter VII. Here there remain to be added only proofs of the high estimation of the *Madonna* in the *Brussels Hours*. In the early fifteenth century, perhaps around 1415, a master very close to the Limbourgs and yet not really identifiable with any of them, painted a haunting image of an effete Madonna on the Crescent Moon, and in it he put an Infant that must reflect the Child in the Brussels diptych (Fig. 668).[39] The curious eye, nearly frontal, looks of course even more archaic than in the model. A second work, known only by a document, may have been a copy of the entire diptych. The inventory of 1483 of the collection of the Duke of Savoy lists a diptych in embroidery, one 'tabulla' of which represented the Madonna, the other the Duke of Berry between the Baptist and St. Andrew.[40] The *tabulle* probably passed into the Savoy collection when Bonne, a daughter of Jean de Berry, married the Count of Savoy, an event that occurred in 1379. He died in 1391.

Who was the remarkable author of the Brussels diptych and when did he paint it? The countenance of Jean de Berry, so attentively observed and subtly rendered, leads us to infer 1390 as the approximate date, for the Duke, born in 1340, would probably have been in his forties when this painting was made. 1390, or at most, 1395 would be the *terminus ante* as far as portraiture and armorial bearings are concerned, for the shields contain *fleurs-de-lys semés*. The second portrait in the manuscript, definitely a later image, must have been made before 1402.[41] As for the painter, Delisle's old attribution to Beauneveu has something to recommend it. In the *Psalter* the figures likewise are in grisaille (Figs. 51–74), and there too one may find a throne like the Madonna's, with two squat supporting columns (Fig. 62). In several backgrounds there are large curling leaves, though in none the angels that appear behind the Madonna (they are, in fact, by a different, more conventional painter).[42] The Madonna is poised on the front edge of the throne rather than seated, just like the prophets and apostles in the *Psalter*, and the awkward foreshortening of her left arm and knee – the consequence of insufficient study of Italian prototypes – is readily matched in several miniatures of the *Psalter* (Figs. 51, 56).

These similarities acquire still more meaning when we recognize the numerous likenesses of details. The hand of the Baptist that supports the Lamb – rather lifeless, it must be admitted – conforms to a formula for a hand in profile that recurs several times in the *Psalter* (Figs. 56, 58,

62). The pleats of the folds over the visible leg of the Baptist are duplicated by those over the leg of Zachariah (Fig. 57). The Baptist's foot has that attenuated, high-arched shape that we have already remarked in John the Evangelist in the *Psalter* (Fig. 58). The hair of both figures just above the forehead falls into a peculiar, swastika-like pattern. The complex folding of the Virgin's mantle on the seat of the throne recurs in several paintings of the *Psalter*, and with remarkable similarity of detail in John the Evangelist (Fig. 58).

These resemblances taken together are impressive, but not conclusive. For there are, after all, obvious differences between the style of the *Psalter* and of these two miniatures. St. Andrew in Brussels is not the brother of Andrew in the *Psalter* (Fig. 54). While the high forehead and fleshy cheeks of the Madonna recall Flemish sculpture, such as the St. Catherine related in style to Beauneveu (Fig. 672), the bony structure of the head of each of the saints implies a study of Italian models, a study that is completely absent from Beauneveu's paintings in the *Psalter*. The painter of these saints learned much from Simone Martini or from followers of Simone, including perhaps Giovanni da Milano (Figs. 635, 671, 674, 692, 693). The drapery folds of the paintings in Brussels consist mostly of long, smooth, curling tubular folds that recall the Parement Master but are rare in the *Psalter*.

The Brussels miniatures, on the other hand, surpass all their sources in the depiction of soft texture and in luminosity. In this respect they are strikingly similar to the two angels at the left in the *Vatican Bible* (Fig. 178), and the fact that this resemblance is not casual is shown by the similar dispostion of drapery. Even the wrapping of the cloth over the lower foot of the Christ Child, and the odd flatness of the foot, are to be seen in the Bible. The painter of the angels, very probably the Trinity Master, was in close touch with the painter of the diptych. The connection between the two supports a date towards 1390 for the latter, since the Bible can be fixed at that time. This was the period when the Duke was especially active in inducing *maîtres de taille et de peinture* to turn from sculpture and from panel or mural painting to parchment. The author of the diptych was probably a master of this kind, who may never have painted again on parchment. Nothing else, in any event, seems to have come down to us from this remarkable artist.

The scarcity of large-scale paintings in France at this time is so extreme that it seems worth while to refer at this point to one that resembles the Brussels diptych in certain respects, though it is later. Of the original glass that still survives in the chapel of Simon Alegret in the Cathedral of Bourges one pane shows the Duke's physician with his two nephews Simon and Denis Faverot kneeling in prayer as they are presented to the Madonna by a saint, probably St. Simon (Fig. 670).[43] The arms of Alegret are visible below him – the shield is charged with swans.[44] The glass was probably made between about 1412 and 1415, for the chapel was completed shortly before the former year and Alegret died in the latter.[45] Despite the much earlier date of the diptych in the *Brussels Hours* the subtle undulations of the planes of the face of the Baptist are similar to those in Alegret's saint (Figs. 181, 670). The profile of the physician, less sensitive than that of Jean de Berry, shows an eye that is inadequately foreshortened, though better than the Child's in the Brussels miniature. The long, smooth, flowing folds of drapery, while conventionalized in the manner of the early fifteenth century, still show a relationship with the drapery of the saints and the Duke in the miniature.

4·THE MINIATURES BY JACQUEMART

The presentation of Jean de Berry to the Madonna, enacted on pages 10 and 11 of the *Brussels Hours* (the manuscript is paginated), is re-enacted on page 14 (Fig. 181).[46] The actors, now brought together into the deeper space of one pictorial field, are painted by the master who, with assistants, was responsible for the rest of the book. The subject of these two miniatures is itself rare at the beginning of a Book of Hours; the repetition is unique. And even though the first representation was not made for this book it was apparently there when the second was painted. The relationship between these two works is thus strikingly like that between the two pairs of angels in the *Vatican Bible* (Fig. 178). Only the Duke's wishes, his delight with novel styles, and, one senses, his pleasure in pitting one leading painter against another, adequately account for these exceptional occurrences.

The painter of the second version, who must be, as the inventory states, Jacquemart de Hesdin, certainly had at hand the work of his predecessor. He adopted not only the iconography but many details such as the cross of Andrew, the spindly legs of the Lamb, the pleats of the Baptist's mantle over his leg, and the peculiar shape of his foot. He omitted the banner that, in the first version, the Lamb manages to bear in its hoof, and he reset the Lamb's halo, putting it behind the Baptist rather than allowing it to cover part of his shoulder. Perhaps the most telling indication of Jacquemart's awareness of the diptych is his use here of haloes with similar cusped patterns; they are absent from all the subsequent miniatures by him.

Jacquemart also adopted for this and the following miniatures the revolutionary borders of the diptych. Into the quatrefoils of the corners he put the arms of the Duke, now *France moderne* rather than *ancien*, and into two others the initials V E interlaced. Each of the remaining four is filled, as in the model, with a swan or a bear. The bear in Jacquemart's borders no longer always sits hunched as in the diptych but stands up and waves a banner with the ducal arms – here *ancien* rather than *moderne*. His greater activity is facilitated by a larger quatrefoil. The entire border itself is wider and it is more decisively adjusted than its model to its place in the codex. Jacquemart's presentation miniature, like all the miniatures after it in the book, is on a left-hand page.[47] The border nearest the binding is much narrower than the other three. The perspective point of sight is not central to the miniature, as in earlier illumination, but to the entire surface of the open book, falling thus along the line of the binding. Jacquemart's borders are not only wider than those of his model but also somewhat more densely filled with stems and flowers, so that they create a larger, more solid frame around the miniature. This frame accompanies a greater depth in the painted space, a depth that is foreshadowed in the framework itself by the passage of the tips of the quatrefoils over the gold border of the miniature. And though in the presentation miniature Jacquemart retained the angels in the background – they all now clasp their hands in prayer – in the rest he introduced a background of uniform blue, thus abandoning the last convention that distinguished miniature from panel and fresco painting. This step had, however, been taken almost a generation earlier in Bohemia, in the manuscript of the *Laus Mariae* (Fig. 566, 567).

The proportions of Jacquemart's miniatures follow those of the diptych. The height of the diptych was greater than that of the miniatures in the *Très Belles Heures de Notre-Dame* and the *Petites Heures*. The ratios of height to width are: *Très Belles Heures de Notre-Dame* 1·19; *Petites Heures* (*Nativity*) 1·27; diptych 1·55; main miniatures, *Brussels Hours* 1·55. The greater height in the *Brussels Hours* provides space for higher buildings and landscapes, which are so distinctive an innovation in these paintings. Probably the format was determined by the master with the new kind of composition in mind.

Jacquemart's scene of presentation is more intimate than his predecessor's. He brought the Duke into the same space and close to the throne, his mantle even falling upon it. The glances are now more precisely controlled, and the Duke as well as St. Andrew looks directly up at the Madonna. She returns his glance and moves the Child towards him. The Infant seems almost eager to touch him as he blesses. This presentation picture was presumably the only composition in which Jacquemart contended with a model immediately at hand, and among all his miniatures this one is exceptional for the power of its spatial recession. The foreground is almost empty, exposing fully the diagonal inward movement of the light green base of the throne and the russet and green tiles of the floor. The rapidity of the recession is increased by the magnetism of the brilliant scarlet robe of the Duke, the strongest color in the painting. Even the Madonna is placed oblique to the picture plane and somewhat foreshortened, a bold innovation in a scene of formal presentation, though it, too, has precedents in Italy. A fresco by Altichiero in S. Anastasia, Verona, recalls Jacquemart's composition in this respect and also with regard to the movement of the Virgin and Child (Fig. 696).

Though these similarities suggest the possibility of a study by Jacquemart of Altichiero and other North Italian painters, the comparison shows us at the same time that he would have looked elsewhere for principles of figural structure. For this only Tuscan painting could have provided adequate models, and only Sienese painting offered the sort of nimble, flexible figures that made possible the response of the Virgin and Child to Jean de Berry, and the rhythmical, marvellously graceful stir of the angels around her. The recently uncovered fresco of a similar subject by Pietro Lorenzetti in S. Domenico, Siena, makes the importance of Sienese painting very clear (Fig. 697). Jacquemart's similar Child in the *Adoration of the Magi* comes still closer to Pietro's (Fig. 186). A glance at the diptych in the *Brussels Hours* or the paintings of the Parement Master quickly discloses how much more Jacquemart had learned about the human figure from the great Sienese masters.

Jacquemart delights in describing the movement of light over the wings of the angels, the mantle of the Virgin, and the curved planes and molding of the throne. Each of his enchanting little angels moves in a different way, and their fluttering individuality is heightened by wings of a distinctive color – light blue, yellow and olive green, orange, light green, russet, and violet. Whereas the painter of the diptych created volumes by modelling in exquisitely graduated values, Jacquemart tended rather to define planes by variations of color and by contrasts of relatively large lighted and shaded areas. In the diptych all hair, for instance, including the eyebrow of St. Andrew, was rendered by fine strokes, each quite visible. Similarly the shaded areas were defined by tiny parallel brush strokes. Jacquemart abandoned such linear rendering.

The scrolls of wool on his Lamb are not actually described, as in the diptych; their presence is suggested by a few rather large strokes of gray. Jacquemart could evoke an eye by a curved line over a patch of brown. As Ghiberti said of Maso di Banco, Jacquemart 'abbreviated' the mode of painting.[48] In or very near the eyes of the angels above the throne there are small but intense highlights – perhaps the earliest observation in painting of reflected light.

The faces of the saints and of the Dukes are less individualized than their postures. Jacquemart was not greatly interested in personality; his portrait of Berry is far less penetrating than his predecessor's. His subsequent miniatures show that he was not much more concerned with the portrayal of deep and varied emotion. Endowed with a lyric rather than a dramatic gift, he promoted in French painting an era of restrained, composed behavior, while greatly enriching the pantomime that he inherited from his predecessors.

This first miniature by Jacquemart points clearly to the sources that enabled him to increase his repertory of posture and gesture. Though the little angels hovering above the Madonna have the sprightliness and spontaneity of Jean Pucelle's, it was in Sienese painting, from the time of Duccio's early *Madonna* on, that they performed in exemplary fashion the role of honoring the Madonna by holding a rich cloth behind her. A cloth of gold, escalloped like that in the *Brussels Hours*, became common in Tuscany in the third quarter of the century (Fig. 699). Bearing a painted pattern, it was often spread quite flat, and there was in this art an ambivalence about naturalism that might have suggested to Jacquemart the seating of a heavenly figure on a cushion that has little visible support.[49] The throne has, to be sure, a narrow seat at the left, but it is inconspicuous, and there is none whatever on the far side of the Child.[50] The earliest forbears of the angels kneeling on the base of Jacquemart's throne are Tuscan also. First there appeared in this place little figures of virtues seated below the Madonna, as in the *Maestà* by Ambrogio Lorenzetti at Massa Marittima[51] and in a panel by the Stefaneschi Master belonging to Wildenstein and Company.[52] Angels on the base of the throne playing music were introduced into the Coronation of the Virgin in the second quarter of the century.[53]

In his first miniature Jacquemart made some small changes in his design as he passed from the drawing to the painting. Similar alterations, but on a larger scale, are visible in the *Annunciation* (Fig. 182). The series of quatrefoils drawn in the uppermost molding or cornice of the building were not painted, leaving the building quieter and the action of the figures without distraction. This is a fascinating alteration, anti-Gothic in tendency, and it shows vividly how the painter strove for simplicity, concentration, and monumentality. The wall at the left was originally topped by a lintel. The preparatory drawings give no hint, furthermore, of an arch or a window, and they suggest that this side of the building was to be left open. Possibly the angel was to fly through it, approaching more directly in the line of the Virgin's glance, and avoiding the anomalous space in which it now moves.

The little stone house is reminiscent of the structure in the *Très Belles Heures de Notre-Dame* (Fig. 6), but like still earlier 'interiors' it does not fill the field and it is seen from the side. The peaked roof has a gable twisted into a frontal plane exactly as in several compositions of Pucelle (Fig. 335). The prie-dieu, however, faces a small vaulted space resembling a chapel that continues the ecclesiastical suggestions inherent in the *Très Belles Heures de Notre-Dame* (Fig. 6).

The tiles in the floor have a pattern of hexagons with six-pointed stars that show a fresh study of Tuscan Trecento frescoes.[54]

The event had never been enacted this way before in the North nor indeed, in some respects, in Italy itself. The representation of the Virgin kneeling humbly at the moment of the Annunciation, though common in Italian painting from the time of Giotto's fresco in the Arena Chapel, did not begin to be diffused in Northwestern Europe until the third quarter of the century. The earliest example of which I am aware is a miniature by the remarkable follower of Pucelle to whom I have referred above; in it, furthermore, the Virgin turns about to face the angel as in Jacquemart's miniature (Fig. 663).[55] A mediocre but still notable instance of this type of the Virgin appeared in an *Annunciation of the Virgin's Death* in the *Petites Heures* by the workshop of Pseudo-Jacquemart, where, in addition, above the Virgin Gabriel flies horizontally (Fig. 136). Jacquemart's figure shows once again that his deepest admiration is reserved for the Sienese masters, above all Simone Martini. We learn this not only from the supple outline and the ineffable grace of the Virgin but from the specific defensive gesture of her hand, traditional in Siena from the thirteenth century on but strikingly similar to Simone's Virgin of 1333 (Fig. 708).[56]

The flying Gabriel, too, is a creation of the Sienese. Though in his S. Croce frescoes Taddeo Gaddi had represented a half-length angel diving head-foremost down towards the Virgin, it seems to have been Ambrogio Lorenzetti who first introduced a Gabriel who soars toward the Virgin. Ambrogio's painting is lost, but its design, with Gabriel similar to his floating *Securitas* in the fresco of Good Government, Siena, is preserved for us in two free copies, a fresco by a follower in S. Michele, Paganico, and a fresco in Pedralbes by Ferrer Bassa, a Catalan master who had certainly studied in Siena (Fig. 710).[57] In Ambrogio's painting Gabriel extended his hand toward the Virgin and his legs dangled, but in the enamel of 1338 by Ugolini di Vieri, profoundly influenced by the Lorenzetti, Gabriel or possibly a second archangel flies with his arms crossed on his breast much as in the *Brussels Hours* (Fig. 709).[58] Gabriel assumed a similar posture in a later, very Simonesque *Annunciation* by Giovanni da Milano (Fig. 707).[59]

Close as Jacquemart was in the *Annunciation* to Sienese models, he made something fresh and original of them. He equalled Simone himself in endowing the moment with poetic sentiment, drawing the two figures closer together than ever before. They are linked by patches of lemon yellow, which appear on her mantle and his wings, and his white dalmatic bears blue shades, almost as a reflection of the Virgin's mantle. Jacquemart gave the two a unique kinship, within their enclosing rectangles, by a wholly unprecedented arrangement of parallel diagonals. Only rarely had the Virgin in earlier art knelt with her back toward the angel (Fig. 663), and she therefore could not confront him with that gentle, spontaneous turn that, though generically Italian, had apparently not even there been introduced into the Annunciation. She and Gabriel exchange meaningful glances, and the solemn privacy of their encounter is enhanced by the golden curtain that is withdrawn to disclose her chamber.

The beautiful posture of the Virgin, as she turns to face the angel and sustains her weight by resting her hand on the open book, is so masterful that one suspects a Simonesque model, though none exists. Certainly Jacquemart's *Annunciation* strikes human depths scarcely adumbrated in the approximately contemporary painting by Melchior Broederlam (1394–1399), though it contains none of Broederlam's elaborate symbolism (Fig. 711).[60] Jacquemart's simple building lacks for one thing the statues of Moses and Isaiah that adorn the spandrels of Mary's chamber, but he did place Moses and another prophet on the capitals of the temple in his *Presentation* (Fig. 187). There they follow the great model of such symbolic statuary, Ambrogio Lorenzetti's *Presentation* of 1342 (Fig. 712). Broederlam, on the other hand, having used them in the *Annunciation*, omitted them from his *Presentation*, though in other respects his composition derives from Ambrogio's. Whereas Broederlam diminished the space around the figures and the scale of the architecture Jacquemart increased them. He dealt more freely than Broederlam with Ambrogio's composition, though his control of linear perspective was inferior.[61] By adding to the quite grand portico of the temple a sort of cloisters that winds at another angle into space he made the most spacious construction yet seen in Northern painting. He succeeded, at the same time, in achieving the effect of looking from outside into a darker interior. The painter of the extraordinary *Annunciation* again shows his capacity for telling action in the gentle solicitude of the oddly episcopal High Priest as he bends over the recoiling Child and gives the Virgin a look of full understanding.[62]

The three miniatures in the *Brussels Hours* by Jacquemart that we have discussed raise typical questions, which recur in most of the other paintings. His dialogue with Trecento painting continues throughout the manuscript. In some instances what Jacquemart took and what he invented is clearer than in others. Despite the great losses of paintings of the time, which normally prevent a precise estimate, it is in general perfectly clear that Jacquemart, like every other major artist, was discriminating in his choices despite his great enthusiasm for another art, and he did not hesitate at any time to strike out on his own. In the *Visitation* (Fig. 183) he turned away from the interiors of the *Très Belles Heures de Notre-Dame* (Fig. 7) and of the Hours of the Virgin in the *Petites Heures* (Fig. 90) and placed the figures, as Pseudo-Jacquemart had done in the *Petites Heures* (Fig. 165), out of doors. This decision is symptomatic of the painter's fascination at this time with landscape. While Mary and Elizabeth are normally placed amidst rocks and before a little house in Italian paintings, in none of them, not even Sienese, would Jacquemart have found so vivid a sense of the arrival of the visitors. This is suggested by the flow of the mantle of the majestic Mary, by the posture of Joseph, and by the continuation of this forward movement in the landscape. The road over which the figures have just walked winds forward from the city.

Joseph rarely accompanies Mary on her visit to Elizabeth in earlier art. There are, however, a few Italian precedents, beginning as early as *circa* 1300 (Fig. 704),[63] and his participation in the journey is explicitly mentioned by the author of the *Meditationes Vitae Christi*.[64] His appearance at the side of the Virgin conforms with the great interest manifested by the *Meditations* and by Italian art from the late thirteenth century on in the family of Christ and in domestic affairs. In the beautiful *Bible moralisée* of blended Florentine and Neapolitan style that may well have been in the possession of the Anjou before the *Brussels Hours* was painted,[65] Joseph bears personal articles on his stick, in the rare scene of the arrival at the site of the Nativity in Bethlehem (Fig. 410). Though Joseph is prominent in the *Brussels Hours*, in the *Visitation* and other scenes, he has no halo.

The *Nativity* in the *Brussels Hours* shows the Madonna kneeling in prayer before the nude

P

Infant (Fig. 184), an action that we have encountered in the *Très Belles Heures de Notre-Dame*, in a miniature that may have been designed by the Parement Master but was painted later (Fig. 41). Jacquemart, however, made the relationship more intimate by placing the figures on the mattress rather than on the floor of a cave.[66] The large animals are active in the foreground, as in the *Nativity* painted by the Parement Master in the *Très Belles Heures de Notre-Dame* (Fig. 8), while the diagonal arrangement and dilapidated roof of the shed and the high mountains behind resemble the *Nativity* in the *Petites Heures* (Fig. 91). The enclosing wicker fence, present in both the representations just mentioned, attains a great height on the far side of the shed, as in the *Adoration of the Magi* in the *Petites Heures* (Fig. 93).

While the strange whitish color of the rocks in the *Nativity* in the *Petites Heures* raised suspicions of snow, small but conspicuous amounts of the stuff are definitely present in the Brussels *Nativity* and again in the *Annunciation to the Shepherds* (Figs. 184, 185). In both miniatures snow-capped peaks rise in the distance, the first of their kind, so far as I know, in Western painting. Jacquemart extended his characterization of a winter landscape in the *Annunciation to the Shepherds* by introducing only trees that are bare of leaves. Such seasonal variations had been depicted in the Calendar paintings of Pucelle and his circle but not in the religious stories.[67] These are realms into which the Italian painters of the fourteenth century did not venture, but in the sphere of human engagement we suspect once again that they might have given Jacquemart a cue. In a Riminese panel that combines the Adoration of the Magi with the bathing of the Child, Joseph offers the lower part of his mantle as a towel in a gesture similar to the *Brussels Hours* (Fig. 701).

The relationship with the Riminese panel is probably casual rather than causal, but it should be said that here and there Jacquemart's miniatures bring to mind painting of the Val padana. Apart from his landscapes, which will be discussed shortly, the arcade joined to the apse in the *Presentation in the Temple* (Fig. 187) might reflect something like the still more elaborate church in Altichiero's *St. James Preaching* (Fig. 713). Jacquemart employed a somewhat related structure for the scene of Christ before Pilate (Fig. 192), and in this miniature the bulky figures of two soldiers do approach Altichiero's canon. The squat, ugly figure of Malchus in the *Betrayal* (Fig. 191) suggests Bolognese illumination of the third quarter of the century, but I have not found there nor indeed anywhere else a similar Malchus tugging on the mantle of Judas.[68] The scourger at the left in the *Flagellation* (Fig. 193) might have had a similar origin.

Jacquemart's relative lack of interest in North Italian figures proves as clearly as anything could that good artists have minds of their own, and that while chance does of course play a real role in history human purpose must be accorded a place also. When painting the *Brussels Hours* Jacquemart paid little attention to specimens of peninsular art that were right under his nose, for all the initials in the manuscript were painted by a North Italian illuminator who, as we shall see, had an intimate knowledge of Paduan as well as Bolognese painting, including the monumental art of Altichiero.

This Italian illuminator must have possessed a stock of drawings, and what was not down on paper he would have been able to describe. Jacquemart may have been impressed by the action of the Magdalen and the solicitous St. John in his *Entombment*, but the figures are of a very different character and Jacquemart was not dissuaded from his attachment to Tuscan, and above all

Sienese art (Figs. 197, 199). He introduced into the *Betrayal*, following a Ducciesque or later Sienese model, apostles who begin to flee as Judas kisses Christ (Fig. 191). In the foreground of a *Crucifixion* that is compounded largely of Duccio and Simone he placed a remarkably fat man, unprecedented in this scene (Fig. 195). He wears a wide head-kerchief, and rests his thumb on his belt. He recalls the very few corpulent figures of this kind in Trecento painting, in Giotto's *Miracle of Cana* in Padua, and in the fresco by Ambrogio Lorenzetti in the Palazzo Pubblico, Siena (Fig. 703). Ambrogio's man, one of the *Ventiquattro* of Siena, is in profile, wears a white cap under his hat, and places his feet similarly. His thumb is again hooked over his clothing, though his mantle rather than his belt. If this figure was Jacquemart's model how would he have known it? From a drawing, a copy in a painting of some other subject, or from the original in Siena? The resemblance is not complete enough to provide an unequivocal reply. The probability of a journey to Italy is increased, however, by Jacquemart's apparent knowledge of other paintings by Ambrogio, including the great landscape in this very room. The question will be discussed shortly.

Jacquemart's miniature of the *Coronation* carried still further that Italianization of this subject that the Parement Master had begun (Fig. 189). In the *Très Belles Heures de Notre-Dame* (Fig. 13) and again in the drawing in the Louvre (Fig. 587) the throne was suspended within a mandorla, as in the late thirteenth-century mosaic in S. Maria Maggiore, Rome. Jacquemart eliminated the symbol of the supernatural, allowing the throne and its base to hover before the background. Below it a group of angels witness the ceremony while kneeling on greensward. The painter has thus divided the scene into the two zones that characterize the new form of the Coronation introduced by Tuscan painters around 1360 (Fig. 702).[69]

The curved throne-back in the *Coronation* was adopted by early Tuscan painters from Byzantine models, as we have seen (Fig. 628), and it was brought into Jacquemart's environment by his collaborator on this manuscript (Fig. 727). The kneeling Virgin is ultimately Tuscan in origin also. We have observed above that the motive appeared more or less simultaneously in France in the drawing in the Louvre, where the posture with folded hands recurs, and a miniature by the Luçon Master dated 1401 (Figs. 587, 705).[70] In accordance with the Tuscan convention, too (though the Veronese Turone adopted it in 1360), Christ lowers the crown with two hands. Among surviving panels the Giottesque *Coronation* in the Museum of Fine Arts, Budapest, shows the greatest resemblance to certain aspects of the Brussels miniature (Fig. 700). The comparison illuminates at the same time the Sienese qualities of Jacquemart's style, and it is the art of Simone that, as we have observed, he found most congenial. Whether or not he became familiar with it in Italy or in Avignon he may have had access to magnificent examples in Northern France, for there is some reason to believe that the famous series of small panels that, I believe, Simone painted in France was in Dijon around the time of the painting of the *Brussels Hours* (Figs. 674, 675, 676, 692, 693).[71] The folded arms and the modest gesture of Jacquemart's *Annunciation* may be seen in Simone's. But it is two or three of Simone's Passion scenes that, as has often been observed,[72] contain the most decisive evidence about Jacquemart's specific models.

The presence in the miniature of the *Way to Calvary* of children who follow the procession, of St. John hovering solicitously behind the Virgin in the same unusual manner, and a detail such as the polygonal building in the town, assure us that Jacquemart had studied this very painting by Simone (Figs. 194, 675). The very extensiveness of the relationship sharpens our awareness of the drama of this moment in Northern painting. After a half century of more or less knowing study of the revolutionary art of the early Trecento the comprehension and skill of a Northern illuminator are such that he can reproduce at will many of the essential qualities of that art. Were he a contemporary painter in Spain – the other region of Europe that was continually fascinated by Italian art – he would have been satisfied with his accomplishment. Even at the moment of triumphant assimilation, however, Jacquemart sought to 'improve' Simone's art, like the early Renaissance masters who, despite their enthusiasm for ancient art, transformed it for their own ends. Thus whereas Jacquemart did not equal, whether by design or incomprehension, Simone's figural structure or volume – how Mediterranean by comparison even the linear art of Simone looks! – he proceeded to deepen the space, to extend the crowd inward, and to transform the compact mass of the town (as he had the compact mass of Ambrogio's temple) into something more picturesque, more spacious, and in a sense more real.

Renouncing, as usual, emotional intensity, Jacquemart eliminated the brutal intervention of the soldier between mother and son, normal in Sienese representations, and he avoided the desperate colloquy between the two that Pucelle had adopted long ago. He preferred the silent pathos of inevitable separation, with Christ, unaided by Simon the Cyrene, bent by the weight of the cross. He eliminated the wild lament of Simone's Magdalen, and the outstretched, yearning arms of the Virgin. Not she but a youth looks into Christ's face, searchingly and with sympathy – an impressive innovation by Jacquemart in the iconography of this scene. In the design the youth serves, too, as a buttress to the bowed figure of Christ. Even the exciting criss-cross of Simone's flag and lances is omitted, in favor of a quiet view of the landscape behind. At the head of the procession Jacquemart added figures of the two thieves led by a soldier, a group he undoubtedly had seen in Lorenzettian or other Italian paintings of the scene (Fig. 689).[73] These curiously small, puppet-like figures replace Simone's children, and they have the same function in the design of propelling the procession toward the right. Simone, having introduced the long descending horizontal of the cross, countered the movement at the right by the postures of two powerful figures. Jacquemart however increased the flow along the road – the kind we have observed in the *Visitation* (Fig. 183) – by introducing both a *buysine* that reaches just beyond the frame and a soldier below it who tilts his sword forward.

The precise sources of Jacquemart's *Crucifixion* are much less clear, partly because he as usual dealt freely with his models, transferring gestures from one figure to another and combining figures inspired by varied models. It was in Siena, in paintings by Simone (Fig. 674) and Ambrogio that the Virgin first fell in a swoon to the ground.[74] The Parement Master had already designed a falling Virgin supported by one of the Maries (Fig. 1), and Jacquemart seems to have adopted this group, substituting, however, the solicitous St. John that was popular in German painting. We have already referred to Ambrogio the man with sagging paunch who is a rather detached spectator, unmoved by the event. The old man clutching his beard in Jacquemart's miniature, and the two men huddled close to him, are in physiognomy and behavior derived from Duccio or his immediate followers (Fig. 339).[75] Over the years, or during a trip to Italy,

Jacquemart had no doubt recorded in drawings many figures and groups that interested him. So far as we can judge today it was primarily in the circle of the Lorenzetti that a landscape began to rise behind the figures in the Crucifixion, though it is far less varied and less extensive than Jacquemart's (Fig. 673).

To provide a more complete view of this landscape Jacquemart introduced intervals between the figures, and in his *Deposition* he broadened and opened Simone's composition still more (Figs. 196, 676). He reduced the number of witnesses and rearranged the ladders on each side of the cross, without caring very much, it must be admitted, about their actual stability. By this re-arrangement he produced a quieter, more symmetrical design, less disturbed than Simone's by the vehemence of gesture and expression. He avoided also the torsion, difficult in any event to realize, of Simone's youth pulling the nail, and he reverted to the simpler profile of Duccio and his followers.[76] The design of the landscape, on the other hand, is broken and active, animated further by the rumpled mantle of the Madonna. This discarded mantle is laid in the place occupied by the episcopal donor in Simone's panel, while the figure of the donor is in a sense preserved by the boy pulling the nail. Jacquemart's sense of the desirability of these buttresses below the cross and below the limp, falling body of Christ reveals vividly the depth of his understanding of Tuscan art.

The similarities with Simone's *Deposition* are so pervasive that we learn not only the specific source of much of Jacquemart's miniature but also the extent of his revision of that source. He has shifted St. John to the place above the Virgin occupied by one of the Maries in Simone's panel, and the arms of this figure reaching up toward Christ have been transferred down to the Virgin, who is further from Christ's body and does not touch it. The two men at the far right again are drawn from the older, Ducciesque tradition while the mantle, a rare if not unique form, may have been inspired by a much more recent work. In the Nativity revealed to St. Bridget in 1370 the Virgin knelt in prayer before the nude Child, her discarded mantle lying on the ground nearby, and this scene was represented by Tuscan painters very shortly after the vision (Fig. 690).[77] Inasmuch as the Parement Master may already have been familiar with the Brigittine vision (Fig. 41), Jacquemart, who habitually varied the themes of his models, might have introduced into the Deposition the doffed mantle of the Brigittine Nativity.

The Passion cycle in the *Brussels Hours* contains another example of discarded clothes, unprecedented so far as I know. In the *Flagellation* Christ stands on his tunic, a strangely pale, insubstantial garment strewn on the floor (Fig. 193).[78] Though there seems to be no source for this specific representation, the text of the *Meditations on the Life of Christ* refers repeatedly to the doffed clothing and emphasizes the indignity of Christ's nakedness around the time of the Flagellation.[79]

The woman who passionately kisses Christ's hand in the *Entombment* may be another instance of transposition. She wears a vermilion mantle over a blue tunic, and although she has no halo she undoubtedly represents the Magdalen. Now in France the Magdalen was given a much smaller role in Passion scenes than in Italy, and Jacquemart did not include her in either the *Way to Calvary* or the *Crucifixion*, though she was prominent in Simone's two panels (Figs. 675, 674). Instead of hugging the Cross or kissing Christ's foot in the *Crucifixion* Jacquemart represented her desperately kissing his hand in the *Entombment*, a role she did not have in Simone's painting. In Pietro Lorenzetti's intense *Deposition* in Assisi, however, she flings herself on the ground in similar fashion to kiss the foot of Christ (Fig. 688), and in an *Lamentation* painted around the time of the *Brussels Hours* by Jacquemart's Italian collaborator in that manuscript she kisses his hand (Fig. 199).

Jacquemart preserved for his figures a certain reserve and detachment, even at the climactic moments of the Passion. They seem urbane and often dull alongside the passionate figures in his Italian models. Beginning with the *Way to Calvary* he consistently reduced the directness and intensity of the Virgin's relation to Christ. In the *Entombment* (Fig. 197) she does not bend to embrace him as in Simone's panel and generally in Italian representations. Though her hand touches the bloody wound in Christ's side, she falls fainting in the opposite direction, supported by St. John as in the *Crucifixion* (Fig. 195). A similar group was included in an *Entombment* in the Louvre, though the Virgin clasps her hands in grief (Fig. 695). This panel, which is French and close in time to the miniature, shares with it a diagonal sarcophagus, frequent in France but uncommon in Italy, and a similar disposition of all the figures. The placement of Nicodemus in front of the sarcophagus while holding the body of Christ, which seems suspended over it, betrays the same kind of uncertainty in spatial relations as in some of Jacquemart's miniatures. Still, the *Entombment* in the Louvre, like the painting most closely related in style, the Troyes *Man of Sorrows* (Fig. 694), shows that a panel painter approached Simonesque style more closely than Jacquemart did when he worked on parchment and on a relatively small scale. The miniatures are only about 15 cm. high by 12 cm. wide.

5 · LANDSCAPE AND INTERIOR

Jacquemart's miniatures, which share with the surviving North French panels a very advanced Italianism, possess one element lacking in them and in all other French paintings of this kind. The landscapes that appear so prominently in almost every scene are the great glory of the *Brussels Hours*. The outstanding earlier landscapes in French painting, particularly those by Bondol and his followers (Fig. 385), are of a different type. As in a few Italian examples,[80] the terrain is flat, and is projected regularly inward and upward. This is the form visible in the miniature of the Fool in the *Psalter*, very probably an earlier work by Jacquemart (Fig. 78), and it was employed around 1400 by the Coronation Master (Fig. 438), as well as in the somewhat later *Livre de la chasse* (Fig. 439) and in the *Belles Heures* by the Limbourgs.[81]

The landscapes in the *Brussels Hours*, however, are mountainous, and they derive from the Italian – ultimately Byzantine – tradition. Their context, however, is often unusual. In the *Nativity* the mountains rise above the ridge of the shed, and terminate with two snow-capped peaks in the distance. While the hills in the *Nativity* in the *Petites Heures* may predict such accomplishments they do not really prepare them. The closest parallels are to be found in Italy, but not in this case in Tuscany. On the contrary, it was those centers that lay at the maximum distance from Tuscany, Verona-Padua to the north and Naples to the south, that produced scenes of the birth of Christ with mountains rising above the shed (Fig. 691) or the cave (Figs. 412, 413). In both the angel brings the news to the shepherds in the hills above,[82] and Altichiero's fresco in Padua displays a castle also (Fig. 691). The Neapolitan type was brought to the Angevin court, probably before the painting of the *Brussels Hours*, in the beautiful *Bible moralisée* now in Paris (Fig. 410). Perhaps the very similar panel, by a closely related master, was visible in the Angevin collection also (Fig. 414).[83]

Though Jacquemart's mountains resemble Altichiero's in scale they are less massive, and they do not possess their rigid, stepped structure, ultimately Florentine in origin. They have rather the fluidity of the Sienese. Sometimes, as at the left in the *Entombment* (Fig. 197), the hills are lambent, like Duccio's (Fig. 339). Their planes wave and their edges flicker. More often the forms recall Simone's (Fig. 674). The strange overhanging rocks in the *Flight* (Fig. 188) and the *Adoration of the Magi* (Fig. 186) are anticipated in the St. Martin frescoes in Assisi or the S. Agostino polyptych (Fig. 680). The castles perched on mountain tops and approached by winding roads, as in the *Presentation* (Fig. 187), could scarcely have been created without a knowledge of Simone's works, notably the fresco of Guidoriccio dei Fogliani in Siena (Fig. 685). Jacquemart owes no less to Ambrogio Lorenzetti. He adopted for his *Adoration of the Magi* (Fig. 186) the round dune-like hills in regular succession that appear in Ambrogio's *Ager Senensis* (Figs. 686, 687); they are, indeed, characteristic of the Sienese countryside itself. Jacquemart's marine view in the *Flight* (Fig. 188) might have been inspired by Ambrogio's maritime *Miracle of St. Nicholas*, or a similar lost work.[84] But whereas Ambrogio masked the transition from foreground to the water Jacquemart tried, not very successfully, to describe it. Still, the repetition of similar trees to measure recession became a standard feature of the 'International Style', employed as late as Gentile da Fabriano.[85]

In the *Entombment* (Fig. 197) Jacquemart was the first Northern painter to adopt a Lorenzettian principle that had a fundamental effect upon subsequent French and Flemish painting. When in the late thirteenth century Italian masters wished to provide a more extended world for religious stories they first transformed the ground line to which figures and objects had formerly adhered into a ground plane, and then at the further edge of this plane, in scenes laid out of doors, they set hills.[86] It was the Sienese painters, beginning with Duccio, who took the lead in the development of landscape, accompanying their narratives, in which the flow of time is so vividly suggested, with an environment containing a fluent space (Figs. 339, 685). The mountains in their paintings, inspired by Byzantine models that in turn reflect late antique conventions, rose rather abruptly and steeply. Little foreshortening was therefore required, and recession in space coincided with elevation in the pictorial field. This was the principle that controlled the design of the most impressive landscape painted in Italy up to the late 'twenties, Simone Martini's fresco of Guidoriccio dei Fogliani, dated 1328 (Fig. 685). Simone's fresco contains, however, two innovations. First, the landscape passes behind and *below* the lower frame, a rare arrangement before the early fifteenth century, but to a degree it was adopted in Jacquemart's *Annunciation to the Shepherds*

(Fig. 185). Second, the protagonist is introduced in the foreground, or rather one should say in the lower picture plane, because the equestrian figure actually has no 'ground' and only hovers in space. Simone no doubt deliberately lowered the plane of the landscape in order to detach Guidoriccio decisively from it. Still, the lack around the figure of the kind of spatial continuum so carefully described in the landscape leaves Simone's solution of his problem less than satisfactory.

No more than ten years later Ambrogio Lorenzetti met a related problem far more success-fully. Wishing to join to a representation of the city of Siena a view of its *contado*, and at the same time to maintain a uniform scale for the figures, he represented a road leading through a gate and winding down into the country below (Figs. 686, 687). People move up and down the road, and are scattered in varied pursuits throughout the country. Ambrogio's design required that the countryside at the left, though *above* the road in the pictorial field, be understood to lie *below* it in the illusory space. This first great post-classical Western landscape is also the one that abandoned an established principle of pictorial projection. Nothing quite like it has come down to us from antiquity, though occasionally in Roman murals a mass of rock rises in one area just behind the picture-plane (Fig. 681).

Ambrogio's manner of representing near and more distant space by the use of a large fore-ground form that overlaps the middleground eliminated for him the problems of the gradual diminution of forms. The design therefore had an obvious technical advantage, and one of the two famous 'landscapes' in the Siena Pinacoteca, probably painted by Ambrogio, seems to exploit it (Fig. 684). I say 'seems' because these two panels still raise questions about their original purpose and shape that can be answered only by careful laboratory study, unfortunately never yet undertaken. Although traces of gold along the upper and lower edges were observed some years ago,[87] they do not dispel all the doubts raised by the uniqueness of the representations and the anomaly of the designs, which seem by Trecento standards incomplete. In the panel repro-duced the powerful curve of the shoreline into space, given further strength by the steady diminution of the row of trees, is not countered near the frame, as it would normally be in a completely preserved Tuscan design. The cutting of the hills and trees along the upper edge seems aesthetically arbitrary. Still, as the panel now stands, its basic compositional principle conforms with the *Ager Senensis* in the Palazzo Pubblico (Figs. 686, 687).

Ambrogio's principles remained undeveloped, or even unapplied, for at least half a century in both Italy and the North. From about 1350 Tuscan painters established quite different stylistic norms, and French masters beginning with Jean Pucelle were striving to learn the lessons of Duccio and Simone Martini. One impressive late follower of Pucelle, for instance, outdid these Sienese predecessors in the size of his mountain in the Passion cycle, but he still adhered to the principle of the plane rising and receding from the foreground (Fig. 677). In one respect his representation of the rare episode of the Bearing of the Body anticipates Jacquemart's *Entombment* (Fig. 197), because it is seen from a high and rather distant point of sight. Whereas the landscapes in the *Brussels Hours* normally follow the type of the Douce *Deposition and Bearing of the Body* (Fig. 677), the miniature of the *Entombment* decisively abandons it.

The lowering of the body into the tomb is enacted on a brown plane that begins at the lower frame, extends below the sarcophagus and the figures and then at the right rises, in conventional fashion, in a brown hill. In the center, however, behind St. John a flat green plane appears to be far below the figures; the trees, building and other objects at its distant limit are greatly reduced in size. Jacquemart has adopted the principle of the foreground plateau and the low-lying country beyond it that Ambrogio introduced in the *Ager Senensis* (Fig. 686, 687). He had trouble with his ambitious project at the left, where he failed to mask the transition from near to far and allowed the planes of the gray mountain to reach back uncertainly in space. At the same time he boldly extended the central plane straight back to a horizon more distant than Ambrogio's.

The possibilities of the plateau composition that Jacquemart introduced into France were only dimly perceived by his successors. The Boucicaut Master occasionally employed it rather timidly (Fig. 682). It was developed by Jacquemart himself in the early fifteenth century, for the composition of a *Crucifixion* of about 1405-1410 is no doubt based on his ideas (Fig. 264). The miniature appears in a Book of Hours that reflects other aspects of his art,[88] and the *Crucifixion* was probably executed by the Trinity Master, previously encountered with Jacquemart in the *Petites Heures*. The rolling, intersecting hills are portrayed with greater assurance than the landscape in the *Brussels Hours*. The forms show less resemblance to the *Entombment* or to the extant landscapes of Ambrogio than to the sequence of rounded hills receding in space in the remarkable Lorenzettian allegory of redemption in the Siena Pinacoteca (Fig. 679). Deep in the landscape of the miniature a man drives a laden ass along a road, away from the scene of the *Crucifixion*. Ambrogio's fresco is full of such figures and they occasionally emerge in French secular paintings of the later fourteenth century (Fig. 385) but they are novel in the Passion cycle. After Jacquemart they began to appear in miniatures of the Boucicaut Master, but their major development occurred in the painting of Jan van Eyck (Fig. 537). It was he, too, who made the most of Jacquemart's plateau landscape. For him it became a basic principle of composition.

Jacquemart would be assured an important place in the history of landscape painting simply as a transmitter of Lorenzettian principles. We have seen, however, that even at moments of great dependence he did not cease to be inventive. No Lorenzettian painting would have contained fanciful, overhanging crags such as those in the *Flight* (Fig. 188). It seems equally improbable that the snow on these crags, as on the peaks in the *Nativity* (Fig. 184) or the *Annunciation to the Shepherds* (Fig. 185), would have been visible in any Sienese work.[89] No extant Trecento landscape is characterized with respect to the season of the year, whereas the trees in miniatures by Jacquemart representing events that occurred in winter (*Annunciation, Annunciation to the Shepherds, Flight into Egypt*) or early spring (*Entombment*) are bare, while those in the *Visitation* (July) are in full leaf.[90] We cannot be entirely certain of Jacquemart's intentions, however, because three trees in the background of the *Betrayal* (March or April – in any event before the *Entombment*) bear leaves (Fig. 191), and so do several in the background of the *Entombment* itself, despite the leaflessness of those in the foreground (Fig. 197).

Precedents in Trecento painting are lacking also, so far as I know, for the low rocky masses set immediately behind the frame to serve as a *repoussoir*. In the *Flight* they compose the nearer wall of a small ravine (Fig. 188), whereas in the *Annunciation to the Shepherds* (Fig. 185) they loop across the lower part of the space, lapidary equivalents of the drapery introduced for a similar purpose by the Master of the Parement de Narbonne (Fig. 15) and by Jacquemart in the *Petites Heures* (Fig. 94). The *repoussoir* in one guise or another was adopted by the Boucicaut Master, and it became in fact one of the most frequently employed conventions in early fifteenth-century painting.

For one large miniature in the *Brussels Hours* (Fig. 198) no Tuscan model was available. Books of Hours were rare in Italy until the late fourteenth century, and the Office of the Dead was not usually illustrated by a service but by a skeleton (Fig. 584). Jacquemart therefore took the next best alternative. He adopted the most advanced rendering of the subject, which was furthermore at hand in the Duke's collection: the miniature by the workshop of the Parement Master (Fig. 14). The two versions are in some respects so close that one can understand why some scholars insisted that the miniature in Paris was the later. One detail alone would almost suffice to prove the opposite: the tubular folds in the habits of the three Dominicans in the foreground are characteristic of the Parement Master but not of Jacquemart, who has here merely imitated them.

Though the miniature in the *Très Belles Heures de Notre-Dame* was bold in its time as a representation of an interior filled with figures, it appears cramped and insignificant alongside Jacquemart's majestic new edition of it only about fifteen years later. Jacquemart's scene gains much from the additional height permitted by the format of his miniatures. The painter made the most of it, introducing a groin vault and closing the ecclesiastical interior in the picture plane with an impressive cusped arch. The three friars who are almost disconcertingly close in the *Très Belles Heures de Notre-Dame*, at least by Italianate standards, are moved back a little into the space, while the braziers are brought forward to measure the interval between the frame and the figures. The most salutary alteration of the composition, however, is the twisting of the sarcophagus and the *chapelle ardente* so that it is more nearly parallel to the picture plane and its opposite end becomes visible. The rhythm of the composition, especially as it affects the position of the reader and the entry of the nuns, is so greatly improved that one is almost tempted to speculate that the miniature in the *Très Belles Heures de Notre-Dame* is itself a corrupt copy of a lost original showing the alternate design.

By means of a better perspective and more ample intervals between the figures Jacquemart made a unified and imposing composition of his model. His revisions of its color are no less important. Most important, he darkened the very bright walls of the *Très Belles Heures de Notre-Dame*, covering them in varying shades of purple, which is much more appropriate for the subject.[91] He reduced the declamatory contrasts of the floor by painting it entirely in soft pink, and then overpainting every other tile in pale blue (most of which has peeled off). Overhead the rose ceiling of the *Très Belles Heures de Notre-Dame*, with red ribs, has been replaced by yellow vaults. Above the sombre purple walls these glowing stones appear even more luminous, and give the hall a wonderfully spacious look.

6 · THE CAREER OF JACQUEMART

In miniatures such as the *Presentation of the Duke to the Madonna* and the *Annunciation* we have observed some minor but significant differences between the painting and what is visible of Jacquemart's preparatory drawing (Figs. 181, 182). Two similar discrepancies may be seen in the *Annunciation to the Shepherds* (Fig. 185). Beneath the green ground of the enclosure a line is visible that seems to define a higher upper edge of the wicker fence than was eventually painted. Just above the head of the shepherd at the right there are lines that disclose a different design at this point. In the *Betrayal* (Fig. 191) a tree may have been originally contemplated above the head of the soldier immediately to the left of Christ. In all these miniatures the drawing has with the passage of time 'burned' through the rather thin film of paint.

Whereas these instances concern small changes within the compositions the general design of two miniatures underwent a metamorphosis, as Delaissé has observed recently.[92] In the *Majesty* Christ was originally contained within the traditional rhomboid (Fig. 190); the shape is still visible below the present film of paint. The two lowest seraphim at both sides were executed in a different color, traces of a wing are visible over the lion and the ox, and a scroll occupied the upper left corner of the field. A drawing for a Coronation of the Virgin on page 116 similarly shows Christ and the Virgin within the traditional mandorla, perhaps like that in the *Très Belles Heures de Notre-Dame*, with an angel in each corner (Fig. 189, 13). The painting of this subject on page 118 – an added page, as Delaissé has shown – introduced a new composition for this subject in the North, as we have pointed out.

Delaissé considers these two miniatures the work of a later and inferior hand, and he puts in this category also the presentation miniature, which is painted on an added double sheet (Fig. 181). His grouping of these three miniatures is supported by an aspect of their technique, which he did not mention. Green underpainting, which is so conspicuous in all the other miniatures, was not employed in these three, nor indeed in the *Funeral Service*, which he regarded as exceptional also though not inferior. I agree, then, that these miniatures were executed at a different moment, and their association on grounds of technique with the last large miniature in the manuscript provides a clue that they are later. But significantly later, as Delaissé argued? A decision is bound up, of course, with a conclusion about the painter or painters responsible. A distinctly inferior hand is visible in parts of the *Majesty*; although in the *Nativity* the ass and the ox – see his hindquarters! – inform us that Jacquemart possessed no exceptional zoological prowess, he still could not have painted the lumpy lion and ox in the *Majesty* nor the crude eagle. Both Christ, however, and the angel seem to me Jacquemart's own work, in large part at least, and the same must be said of the presentation miniature, the *Funeral Service*, and even of the *Coronation*, though it is less subtle in color and somewhat emptier than the others.

The iconographic innovations in these miniatures as well as the blonder colors and rosier flesh point to a subsequent moment. But they are not much later and they were not conceived, I think, by a different *chef d'atelier*. They show on a larger scale the changes in the course of work that we have observed in other miniatures, clear signs of the painter's constant searching study.

All these judgments presuppose at the same time that Jacquemart utilized help to a greater or less degree in the execution of the miniatures. The phrase in the inventory ascribing the miniatures to him – 'de la main Jacquemart' – cannot be taken literally to mean that the brush of no other painter touched these folios. While the presentation miniature, as one would expect, and the *Annunciation* seem entirely by the hand of the master, Joseph in the *Visitation* gives us the first intimations of an assistant, and the averted soldier in the *Way to Calvary* makes us quite sure (Fig. 194). Lest we be misled by this and other weaknesses into concluding that the entire miniature (and indeed the entire cycle) is the work of a copyist,[93] we should keep in mind such details as the purple shadow behind the head of Christ on his further shoulder and that of the youth in yellow near him. The miniature has overall a gloomy violet tone, while the interposition in the city of pale red roofs between blue ones is remarkably subtle in color and yet effective in defining volumes and space. In the *Betrayal* Jacquemart allowed the green underpainting to show to an exceptional degree, and this together with the rather gray town and prominent lantern suggests that he may have had dusk in mind. The painter of the *Agony in the Garden* in the *Petites Heures*, however, described nocturnal light far more explicitly (Fig. 139).

If we conclude, as I believe we must, that the largest group of miniatures in the *Brussels Hours* was painted by one master whose style was diluted in varying measure by assistants, this master can be identified earlier in the *Vatican Bible*. The style of the relevant figures in the Bible (Fig. 178) is not without differences, one of them surprising. The angels in the Bible do not show the tendency toward flatness of plane that is conspicuous in the Hours; they are rounder, the mass of their hair fuller. The painter's touch, especially in the description of the birds and butterflies, is more sensitive even than in the best passages in the Hours, in say the *Annunciation* or the *Funeral Service*. Some of the same birds – the wren, goldfinch, hoopoe – reappear in the borders of the Hours – and indeed a few do also in the diptych, but there their very quantity destined them for assistants. The soft light and pale, subtle color of the Bible – the rose, blue, violet – link the angels indissolubly, however, with the Hours. No two painters at the same moment could have mastered the palette of Simone Martini so completely and made the same delicate alterations, reducing somewhat the saturation of the colors for greater conformity with the pages of the book.

There are other signs of the unity of the styles. The orphrey of the angel in the *Annunciation* swings out with the rhythm of the lappets of the tiara in the Bible; the hair is blond, and the drawing of the hands is similar (Figs. 178, 182). The wings, plausibly attached to the torso, function effectively to sustain the figure. In both manuscripts the painted wings do not conform exactly with the preparatory drawings. The little, bluish-green trees of the Bible reappear, with their yellow highlights, in the *Brussels Hours*, but more perfunctorily executed.

More subtle than the relationship of the Bible with the *Brussels Hours* is its connection with the *Petites Heures*. The soft suffused light is not far from the *Nativity*, for example, in that manuscript (Fig. 91). The cut of the brow of the angels, the deep depression under it, and the delineation of the eye by a horizontal stroke above a pupil and a patch of shade all reappear in the head of St. Joseph, which like the angels is turned at three-quarters.

While the additions to the Bible, made around 1390, were painted only five to ten years before the *Brussels Hours* the *Petites Heures* preceded the latter by some fifteen years. This is a long span in the career of a major artist, and it is not surprising that an identity of authorship, if such there be, should prove difficult to ascertain. The paintings in the *Petites Heures* cannot of course be expected to resemble closely those in the *Brussels Hours* but to be capable of developing into them. To state fully the case for this development – a case that I have contemplated many years without reaching absolute certainty – would require long tedious pages of analysis. It should be remembered, furthermore, that not all the available evidence has yet been presented; the later phases of the style, which are not irrelevant, will be discussed in Chapter XII. At this point I shall allow the discussion of the three manuscripts to stand as evidence, and limit myself to a few observations that seem to me especially significant.

The remarkably graceful, animated little angels playing musical instruments on folio 8 of the *Petites Heures* (Fig. 86) anticipate those in the presentation miniature of the *Brussels Hours* (Fig. 181). The colors, too, are similar – lemon yellow, vermilion, lilac, rose shaded in bluish gray. The beautiful *Fool* in the *Psalter* seems a forerunner of Christ in the Brussels *Flagellation*, with a similar idiosyncratic disposition of the limbs and a dangling foot (Figs. 78, 193). The flat terrain in the *Psalter*, however, does not reappear later; the French form of landscape, stemming from the illuminators of Charles V (Fig. 385), gives way in the *Brussels Hours* to the Italian form. Probably the most telling likenesses between the 'Jacquemart group' in the *Petites Heures* and the *Brussels Hours* are in color and basic compositional patterns. Lemon yellow, rose, vermilion, and gray are combined in similar amounts in the figures, while the landscapes are often pale blue-green. Red angels – cherubim or seraphim – have unusual orange highlights in the *Man of Sorrows*, for instance, in the *Petites Heures* (Fig. 94) as well as in the background of Jacquemart's presentation scene in the *Brussels Hours* (Fig. 181). The mantle of the youngest Magus in the *Adoration of the Magi* in the *Petites Heures* (Fig. 93) is painted in a rich carmine not previously used in a miniature, and perhaps not, for all we know, on panel. This deep color appears again in the *Brussels Hours*, on the mattress in the *Adoration of the Magi*, for instance (Fig. 186).[94]

These two miniatures of the *Adoration* bring into focus perhaps better than any others the nature of the relationship of the two manuscripts. The structure of the composition is the same – triangles simultaneously in the picture plane and in depth, in the Italian (Florentine) manner. Identical likewise is the principle, again Italian, of a cinematic sequence in the action of the three Magi. The geometric design and the closure of the figural group are in one respect more elaborate in the *Petites Heures*. Under the shed, behind the brooding Joseph, three shepherds stand in a row. They compose a third diagonal plane, repeating and strengthening the similar planes of the Madonna and the Magi. Their function in the design is like that of the two old Jews at the right in the *Deposition* in the *Brussels Hours* (Fig. 196), and this application of the same compositional principle in very different scenes at widely separate dates is strong evidence for the single authorship of these miniatures. The shepherds and the Jews in the *Deposition* resemble each other, in fact, in one further respect. In both very similar but not identical figures are repeated and overlap. This exceptional arrangement is employed again in the *Brussels Hours* for the two acolytes behind the priest in the *Presentation in the Temple* (Fig. 187).

The three shepherds in the *Petites Heures* seem, as we have said, to be quotations from Italian art. Far more Italianate than the other heads they are also rather obtrusive, and they confirm the general impression of this style in the *Petites Heures* as unsure, variable, experimental. The miniatures of this group seem more easily understood as the work of a relatively young master in a stimulating new environment. The far greater uniformity of the *Brussels Hours*, on the other hand, implies a mature artist; and the partial understanding of Tuscan painting manifested in the *Petites Heures* has grown to mastery of its methods of composing in color as well as in shapes. Though the painter had in mind primarily the art of Simone Martini and particularly some of Simone's late panels, his knowledge of Tuscan painting was considerable. This knowledge could perhaps have been gained in metropolitan France, and there seems to be no Italian form that could not have been transmitted by a drawing or a copy, but a simpler explanation would be a trip to Italy. This trip may well have been made before the painting of the *Vatican Bible* around 1390.

How do these inferences from the paintings conform with the known facts of the career of Jacquemart? Contemporary records tell us little about him. We are somewhat uncertain where he was born because he is called variously Jacquemart from 'Esdin', 'Esdun', 'Oudain', 'Odin', and 'Hodin'. He might therefore have come from Hesdin in the Artois or Houdin near Calais, or, less likely, one of the two places called Houdeng in the Hainaut.[95] His birth date is unknown, but he was probably born not later than 1365 since in November 1384 he was 'peintre' of the Duke of Berry.

> A Jaquemart de Esdun, pintre de mons., pour autre don à luy fait par mon seigneur tant pour soy vestir en l'iver comme pour luy deffraier d'aucuns despens que luy et sa fême firent en la ville de Bourges avant qu'il preist aucuns gaiges ou salaire de mons., yci par mandement donné le 28ᵉ jour de novêbre MCCCIIII××IIII et quittance donné 11ᵉ jour du dit mois, tout rendu à court, 30 l.t.[96]

Inasmuch as the painter was reimbursed for expenses incurred by him and his wife in Bourges before he had received any wages or salary from the Duke, we may safely infer that Jacquemart had entered his service not long before November 1384. We are not constrained, however, to believe that the Duke made good on these arrears quickly, or even that he had given Jacquemart money for clothing his first winter of service. Furthermore, the phrase we have read as 'pour autre don'[97] implies a preceding payment, but how much earlier we cannot know. It seems improbable that Jacquemart had begun to work for the Duke more than a year earlier.

We hear of Jacquemart in Bourges again on April 10, 1399, when a courier was paid for delivering there to 'Jacquemart de Hodun' some letters from the Duke.[98] The year before he was working in the Duke's castle at Poitiers. We owe this information not to the painter's pictorial accomplishments but to his professional feud with another painter, a certain John of Holland. John filed a complaint with Jean Guerart, 'lieutenant du maistre des œuvres . . . du duc de Berry'. He alleged that Jacquemart, his valet Godefroy, and his brother-in-law Jean Petit had broken open his strong box in the Palais and had stolen 'certaines couleurs et patrons estant icelui'. The 'patrons' were preparatory drawings or patterns, perhaps bound into pattern books, very valuable property of a painter.[99] The bad feeling between the two parties erupted into violence a little later when Godefroy, accompanied by Jacquemart, met John of Holland's wife and his brother-in-law, and murdered the latter.[100] Charles VI later pardoned Godefroy and his master.

After the notices of 1398 in Poitiers and 1399 in Bourges we hear of Jacquemart only in the ducal inventories. There he was singled out for special mention in 1402 (for the *Brussels Hours*) and in 1413 (for the *Grandes Heures*). Only two other painters, Beauneveu and Paul de Limbourg, were so honored. Jacquemart was presumably still alive in 1413 because his name in the inventory of that year as one of the authors of the *Grandes Heures* is not accompanied by 'feu'.[101]

Jacquemart came to Bourges from the general region in which Beauneveu had worked. If Beauneveu entered the service of Jean de Berry shortly after the death of his patron Louis de Mâle in January 1384, he and Jacquemart might have arrived in Bourges at about the same time. Inasmuch as we cannot be certain of the precise place where Jacquemart was born, speculation about his early local training is not very profitable. Mahaut d'Artois had undertaken pictorial enterprises during the earlier part of the fourteenth century in Hesdin, and Philippe le Hardi had some painters there.[102] In the document of 1384 Jacquemart was described as 'peintre'. Nowhere else is his craft designated, except for the generic reference in 1413 to 'Jaquemart de Hodin et autres ouvriers de Monseigneur' as responsible for the illumination of the *Grandes Heures*.[103] Though the facts are not entirely clear, there does not seem to have been a strict corporate difference between the 'peintres' and the 'enlumineurs' at this time.[104] In one document of 1402–1403 Paul and Jean de Limbourg are called 'enlumineurs', in another 'peintres'.[105] Jean had two years earlier served an apprenticeship as a goldsmith. The Rohan Master, who worked regularly as an illuminator, did paint – we happen to know – a panel, but then he, like Jacquemart, may have been freed of guild and municipal regulations by his attachment to a prince.

Nothing decisive, then, can be gleaned about Jacquemart from the documents. We are not told what he and John of Holland were painting in the Palais at Poitiers, but we may surmise it was work on a sizeable scale. Does the evidence not suggest that Jacquemart had a career as a *peintre* as well as an *enlumineur*? He was called the former in the only reference to his craft. Though two important manuscripts are ascribed to him, at least in part, by the inventories, and we have given him a small share in two other manuscripts, he does not seem to have founded a tradition in the book. If he had worked continuously as an illuminator for Jean de Berry from 1384 to 1409 – a quarter century – one would expect more manuscripts by him or by immediate followers to have survived.

Of Jacquemart's two early associates one, the Trinity Master, developed his style in Jacquemart's workshop, but after the *Petites Heures* he can be found only in the *Vatican Bible* and in one miniature in Yates Thompson 37, as we shall see. So little of Jacquemart's style rubbed off on Pseudo-Jacquemart, despite their participation in common enterprises over a quarter of a century, that we are led to infer, in addition to a lack of understanding on Pseudo's part, a tendency to work in separate places. The one master who seems to have been trained by the mature Jacquemart painted only a few miniatures. His scenes in the *Antiquités judaïques* were, I believe, executed not long before the Duke of Berry's death, when the illumination of the manuscript was interrupted (Fig. 683). Earlier he had worked on the Duke's Terence (Fig. 440).[106] We may speak of the deep influence of Jacquemart also in the instance of several miniatures that probably can be dated 1401 and identified, I believe, as early works of the Cité des Dames Master (Fig. 706).[107]

Documents and general circumstances, then, leave us uncertain about the nature of Jacquemart's career. Though his technique does not indicate it, he may have been one of those artists, like the Parement Master and André Beauneveu, who were not normally illuminators and whom the Duke of Berry persuaded to try their hands in books. His first efforts in the *Petites Heures*, and the *Psalter* in fact, fall into the very same years when Berry had successfully elicited some illumination from those other masters. While they, for whatever reason, never returned to the book, Jacquemart did on three notable occasions – the *Vatican Bible*, the *Brussels Hours* and the *Grandes Heures*. In the last, however, he painted only miniatures of unprecedented size, quite as large as small panels. And only at the beginning of his career, in the *Petites Heures*, did he execute an initial. Otherwise he avoided initials and borders (except for the special case of the Bible for the Pope), and limited his painting to the larger fields of miniatures. It seems possible, indeed, that the miniatures of Jacquemart look so much like panels partly because he actually practiced as a panel painter. This fact, if true, does not diminish his achievement; it only helps us understand it.

X

The Master of the Brussels Initials

1 · THE PROBLEM OF IDENTIFICATION

ALL the initials in the *Brussels Hours* were, we have seen, painted by an Italian master. In recent years a large œuvre has been reconstructed for this interesting illuminator by Otto Pächt and the writer.[1] While recognizing the importance of Professor Pächt's contribution to the stylistic reintegration I must record a dissent from his conclusion about the actual identity of the painter. This negative word needs to be written at the outset because the illuminator has been given a place in numerous studies on late medieval painting, and almost everywhere he has appeared as the historical Zanobi da Firenze, the name that Pächt gave to him.[2] I expressed serious doubts about this identification shortly after it was published, and I have continued to call the illuminator by the name that appears at the head of this chapter. I must now show in detail why I believe the identification is without any substance.

The borders of the *Heures de Charles le Noble*, as of other manuscripts by the illuminator, abound in the fantastic hybrids beloved and feared in the Middle Ages. In the lower margin of page 414 there is a lively chimera, pink, four-footed and eagle-headed (Fig. 761). His open beak, elevated crest, and wild eye give him a fearsome look, but, like a domestic pet, he wears a gold bell around his neck. His front paws rest on an open book, the pages of which bear script. According to Pächt, this script is to be read: 'zebo da firenze dipintore'. Zebo was, he concluded, the nickname of the illuminator; his full name was Zanobi, and he was identical with the Zanobi da Firenze recorded in Malaguzzi Valeri's documents on illumination in Bologna.[3] This argument is unacceptable for several reasons. First, the only Zanobi from Florence recorded by Valeri or by other historians appeared in Bologna in the mid or late Quattrocento; he is sometimes specifically identified as the well-known follower of Fra Angelico, Zanobi Strozzi,[4] and elsewhere the context clearly suggests this later master.[5] Similarly, in Florence no illuminator corresponding to the supposed Zanobi (or Zebo) appears in published documents,[6] or in unpublished ones known to Professor Ugo Procacci.[7] In the second place, the form Zebo was not used as an abbreviation of, or substitute for, Zanobi.[8]

Most important of all, though the first word is difficult to read, specialists agree that it cannot be Zebo. It is very probably 'Checho', an abbreviation for Francesco.[9] A corresponding Francesco cannot be identified at present in published documents on Florentine illuminators.[10] Nor can we assume Checho's connection with Florence, for if the preposition is read *di* then Firenze could be a corruption of Fiorenzo, the name of Checho's father rather than of his city. Neither the style of the chief painter nor that of his assistants shows Florentine roots, and our Francesco might some day be discovered in Bologna or Padua.

Indeed it is time to ask how we are to understand this inscription. If an illuminator wished to record his name, why should he do so upside down in a book held by a monster? While the short word after *dipintore* is unclear,[11] *sino* is definitely the next. The last word is perhaps $\bar{vo}$ (the sign usually indicating an 'r'). Is this inverted inscription in a book held by an open-mouthed chimera a malicious joke: 'Checho di (*or* da) Firenze dipintore o un asino vero?'[12] Such an interpretation would conform perfectly with the naughty, satirical nature of these marginalia. But then at whom is the remark aimed? The chimera was not painted by the master himself, as has been assumed, but by an assistant who preferred to the more saturated, solid tones of the *chef* pale washes of pink and green. This assistant executed the drolleries from page 406 through page 414, on which the inscription occurs, and it gave him as well as his associates pleasure to mock the act of reading by putting books in the paws of fantastic creatures.[13] In only one of the other books by the workshop, however, can the 'writing' perhaps be made out.[14] If the inscription on page 414 was written by the painter of the chimera holding the book, as seems likely, who was the 'dipintore da firenze?' The assistant or the master? Since the artist cannot in any event be identified no further speculation seems warranted.[15]

2·THE ILLUMINATOR AND HIS COLLABORATORS

Though four of the Books of Hours on which our master worked bear coats of arms, only one series has so far proved identifiable, as that of Charles le Noble, and even it provides no exact chronological evidence.[16] For firmly fixed dates we have only the initials in the *Brussels Hours*, before 1402, and a *Madonna* in a Bolognese text of 1408 (Fig. 792). The style of one other manuscript, however, demonstrates that the career of the illuminator in France began about five to ten years before 1400, and precisely in the circle of Jean de Berry. Much of this information is conveyed by the work of his collaborators and these inferences are confirmed by the changes in the master's own art. It is probably useful to list at this point the chief products of the workshop – there were assistants – in the presumed order of their execution.

ca. 1390–1395	*Horae*, Parma, Biblioteca Palatina, ms. 159
before 1402	Initials in the *Brussels Hours*
ca. 1400	*Horae*, Madrid, Biblioteca del Palacio, ms. 2099
ca. 1402	*Horae*, Oxford, Bodleian Library, ms. Douce 62
	Calendar, Warsaw, Bibl. Narodowa, lat. Q.v.I.III
ca. 1405	*Heures de Charles le Noble*, Cleveland, Museum of Art
ca. 1407	*Horae*, British Museum, Additional 29433
1408	Miniature, *Statuti della Compagnia dello Spedale di S. Maria della Vita*, Bologna, Biblioteca del Archiginnasio
ca. 1409	Lactantius, Holkham, ms. 120
late works	Two initials, probably from the same manuscript:

St. Dominic, formerly London, Maggs Bros.
Prophet, Venice, Fondazione Giorgio Cini
St. Catherine, added to Gradual, Modena,
Biblioteca Estense, ms. 1021, folio 195.

In the beautiful little Book of Hours in Parma the role of the Master of the Brussels Initials was subordinate to that of a French illuminator whose art was shaped by the *Petites Heures*. The borders, throughout by this French painter, resemble the *Petites Heures*, though birds are lacking (Figs. 735-738). The Virgin in the *Visitation* and the figures in the *Adoration of the Magi* are copied from that manuscript (Figs. 737, 90; 738, 93). Even the long hair and the large brooch of the Virgin in Jacquemart's *Visitation* have been imitated. A similar figure has been introduced into the Parma *Annunciation*; the painter, however, ignored the Gothic architecture of the *Petites Heures* for a simpler, Pucellesque house (Figs. 735, 94).[17] He borrowed again from the *Petites Heures* for his *Annunciation to the Shepherds* (Figs. 736, 92), and what in his illumination was not taken from that manuscript is so early in character that it confirms a date around 1390.[18] The style, furthermore, resembles that of Walters 96, which is similarly dependent upon the *Petites Heures* and is definitely dated to approximately the same time.[19]

The master of the Brussels Initials was allotted the Calendar, the Evangelists, and the Funeral Service. The sequence of activities represented in the Calendar conforms with the usual Italian cycle rather than with the French. In *February* a man fishes (Fig. 714), a far less agreeable way of spending a deep winter month (even in Italy) than seated before a fire, which all French figures enjoy (Fig. 360). Indeed the seeming aberration in the Italian Calendars suggests that fishing did not appear as a 'labor of the month' but was inspired by the corresponding sign of the zodiac, Pisces.[20] In the Book of Hours in Parma the two conspicuous fish make this relationship clear. The fisherman, who appeared at *February* also in the Missal by Niccolò da Bologna that belonged to Jean de Berry (Fig. 716), was repeated in later Calendars by the Master of the Brussels Initials (Fig. 720). *January*, usually devoted in the North to a feast, is spent beside the fire in the Calendars of the Brussels Initials Master (Figs. 718, 719), again a normal Italian representation (Fig. 717). Characteristically Italian, too, are the figures for March and October: in the former a man blowing simultaneously on two horns (Figs. 715, 721),[21] and in the latter, sowing (Fig. 723).

The Calendar pictures to which we have referred are suggestive not only of the Italian origins of the illuminator but also of the transformation of his style in the North. The cycles in Parma and in the British Museum appear to represent approximately the poles of the development. In *January* in the Warsaw Calendar, some years later than Parma, the space includes, in addition to the man and the fire, a jug on a table – a reference to the eating and drinking normal in French representations of this month but absent in Italian (Fig. 717). The scene in the later Additional 29433, probably executed by another hand in the workshop, contains three tables and a conspicuous display of food (Fig. 718). *April* in the Warsaw Calendar shows a man culling flowers (Fig. 722 – an action more frequent in France than in Italy), while in the manuscript in Oxford, Douce 62, the man, reduced to his knees by a low format, is supplemented by a woman in the margin holding flowers (Fig. 724). The action of the month has moved out into the borders. A similar woman appears in the margin of *May* (Fig. 725), while the miniature shows a freshly conceived version of the falconer, who calls his bird from its prey. In the still later Book of Hours in London the galloping horse of the falconer seems to shy at the hunter's snarling dog (Fig. 726). The medieval subjects, typifying in purpose, are embroidered with casual incidents and become 'genre'.

The illuminator is clearly inventive, or at least alert, open-minded, and curious. He delighted in variety, and no other painters of the time, except the Limbourgs, borrowed forms and subjects from so wide a range of sources. He even seems sometimes to have read and reflected upon the text he was illustrating; that at least is suggested by the rare if not unique representation of the Virgin and Joseph seated beside a pool, in which the youthful Christ stands (Fig. 799). This miniature in the Book of Hours in London illustrates the prayer to the Virgin beginning 'Doulce dame de misericorde, fontaine de tous biens qui portates iesu Christ. . . .' Several years earlier, in 1401 to be precise, a Parisian illuminator had introduced water into the miniature illustrating this text, but it is much less relevant – indeed the 'fontaine' here seems a pretext for a domestic scene (Fig. 334). While a midwife (?) holds the naked child nearby the Virgin tests the tempera-ture of the water in a wooden tub, as if in preparation for a bath – an action that became popular in the representation of the Nativity soon thereafter.[22] In his manuscript in Madrid the Master of the Brussels Initials conveyed a different aspect of this text (Fig. 798). Mary is seated at the center of the Holy Family, and is distinguished by an enormous halo. She lays one hand, rather posses-sively, on Christ, and gestures demonstratively to Joseph with the other. He responds by address-ing her in prayer. Christ plucks the strings of the psaltery proffered him by two kneeling angels, and the heavens behind resound with the music made by a host of angels.

When designing the Evangelists, who normally appear at the beginning of the readings from the Gospels, our illuminator was not satisfied to establish types that would then be repeated over and over again. He continually experimented from the time we first meet him, in the manuscript in Parma. Partly because he wanted for St. Matthew a large, active figure in a necessarily small field he abolished the saint's angel and put the wings on the Evangelist himself (Fig. 728). Winged Evangelists are not common in medieval art, but they do occur, with or without symbols.[23] Our illuminator might have seen four of them in an altarpiece dated 1360 by Turone of Verona (Fig. 732), in the very region in which, as we shall see, he studied intently. The wings of Matthew in Parma emphasize the spirituality of the figure, conveyed already by the restless, heaving drapery, and they are particularly expressive as a foil to the exceptional massiveness and weight. Matthew does not write; he displays his great God-given book to his audience as Moses displayed the tablets of the Law. In the later *Heures de Charles le Noble* all four Evangelists, but none of their animals, wear wings; Matthew alone has no symbol (Fig. 729). In this manuscript Mark, eager to write on his scroll but possessing no desk, is well served by his lion, who poses patiently as a sort of living desk (Fig. 731). Luke's ox makes a similar contribution to the composition of the Gospel (Fig. 730).[24] Occasionally an Evangelist sits with one leg crossed over the other and the sole rather conspicuously turned to the observer, as in Caravaggio's famous first image of St. Matthew (Figs. 733, 734).

The Master of the Brussels Initials revived rare forms that were ultimately Byzantine or even antique in origin. The aged figure in the *Annunciation to the Shepherds* in the Madrid Book of Hours, bearded and tousled, looks less like a shepherd than an ancient philosopher or poet (Fig. 768). Raising a hand in recognition of the significance of the event he might be a pagan prophet of the coming of Christ. The throne of St. Luke in the Parma manuscript has a circular back that derives from Lorenzettian or Giottesque – and ultimately Byzantine – models (Fig. 727).[25] We have observed the appearance of the curved throne several years later than the Parma *Horae* in Jacquemart's *Coronation of the Virgin* in the *Brussels Hours* (Fig. 189).

One of the Brussels initials shows the Tiburtine Sibyl pointing out to the Emperor Augustus the Virgin and Child in the sun (Fig. 203). This seems to be with one crude exception the earliest surviving representation of the subject in France, and it is also of exceptional iconographic interest, though its existence has not been noticed by the authors of several valuable recent accounts of the early history of the theme.[26] The legend of the vision can be traced back to the sixth century, and it is described by Orosius, Pope Innocent III, and then the *Mirabilia Urbis Romae* in the twelfth century.[27] Drawing on these sources Jacobus de Voragine retold the story in the widely read Golden Legend. At the hour of Christ's birth the Sibyl of Tibur led the Emperor Augustus to the summit of the Campidoglio and pointed out to him in the sky, within a golden circle, 'virgo . . . puerum gestans in gremio'.[28] About half a century later the event was again described in the *Speculum Humanae Salvationis*, in connection with the birth of Christ.[29] These two texts were chiefly responsible for the growing interest in the representation of the subject from the late thirteenth century on.

Given the loss of a high percentage of medieval monuments, it is difficult to trace the early development of the representative tradition of so rare a subject. According to the texts an altar was placed on the site of the vision, and today presumably this very place – near the crossing of the church of Aracoeli built to commemorate the event – is occupied by an altar bearing an inscription: NOSCAS QUOD CESAR TUNC STRUXIT. OCTAVIANUS HANC ARA(M) CELI SACRA PROLES CUM PATET EI. The sides of the altar are covered with sculpture and mosaic, perhaps of the twelfth century, and in the spandrels of the arch one may see two little-known primitive figures of the Emperor and a frontal Virgin bearing on her arm a Child in profile (Fig. 814).[30]

The next extant representation of the subject is the well-known miniature in a manuscript in Modena dated 1285 (Fig. 815).[31] Here again the Virgin appears within a mandorla, but she is full length, enthroned, and she as well as the Child, who blesses with his right hand while holding a scroll with his left, conform generally with the traditional *Nikopoia* type. The Sibyl as well as the Emperor are represented, both of them standing below. Augustus points to the visionary figures. Muratori, in his *Antiquitates*, and numerous later writers regarded this miniature as a copy of the monumental mural painting in the apse of the church,[32] which Vasari ascribed to Pietro Cavallini. Vasari's attribution may of course have been incorrect, but the style of the miniature is much earlier than his, and recently Pico Cellini, pointing to the resemblance of the general outline of the miniature to the well-known panel of the *Last Judgment* in the Vatican, has made the interesting proposal that the miniature reflects a large panel then in the church of Aracoeli.[33]

The large painting in the apse was destroyed some time after Vasari had described it, when the semi-circular apse was replaced by a rectangular one. He said that it showed 'la Nostra Donna col

Figliuolo in braccio circondata da un cerchio di sole', below which appeared the Sibyl and the Emperor.[34] This monumental portrayal of the legend must have greatly influenced the representative tradition, and it is tempting to search for reflections of it among extant works. The present fresco on the vault, painted by Giuseppe Passeri in the late seventeenth century, offers no help; in it the Virgin stands and the Child is mostly nude with arm raised high. Recently Professor Vayer has proposed that a late fourteenth-century Venetian panel in the museum in Stuttgart was based on Cavallini's painting (Fig. 820).[35] This hypothesis, however, is not acceptable because the posture of the Virgin – she crouches within the mandorla with the Child on her knee – presupposes the Madonna of Humility, an image that did not appear in Italian painting until the third decade of the fourteenth century.[36] More suggestive of Cavallini's lost work is a mosaic in the tympanum over the south lateral door of the church, a mosaic made during the painter's lifetime and probably influenced by him (Fig. 819). Of course the informal, relaxed posture of the child would not be suitable for the apse. Still, the group is encircled by a mandorla and the blue sky bears stars.

Now it is precisely as a half-length figure within a mandorla that the Virgin appears normally in fourteenth- and early fifteenth-century representations of the celestial image, both in Italy and in the North. Scholars have agreed about the convention in the North (Fig. 816),[37] but it has recently been claimed that the early Italian examples showed the Virgin standing or at least full-length.[38] While one late Trecento miniature in an Italian *Speculum* does show a standing, full-length Madonna,[39] and in the miniature of 1285 the Virgin is enthroned (Fig. 815), two Italian miniatures of this period prove that there was also a tradition of the Virgin in half-length. One, on a folio devoted to scenes from the life of Christ and signed by Niccolò da Bologna, shows the mandorla supported by four angels, and below it the standing Sibyl points out the phenomenon to the kneeling Emperor (Fig. 818).[40] The Child puts an arm around the Virgin, who is half-length within a circular mandorla, as in the North. This type reappears in the initial in the *Brussels Hours* (Fig. 203), though as so often our illuminator has introduced exceptional motives and themes.

By means of an unusual lighting the mandorla in the Brussels initial becomes a shallow disk with an almost sculptural quality, like the concave form on the altar in the church of Aracoeli (Fig. 814). Equal importance, furthermore, is no longer given to the Virgin and the Child. The legend, it must be recalled, centers on the birth of Christ, and the Sibyl's proclamation to the Emperor – HIC PUER MAIOR TE E(ST) IDEO IP(SU)M ADORA – is written on her scroll. To convey this meaning the Virgin holds the Child forward, exhibiting him to the beholders. His legs hang, in fact, beyond the mandorla while she remains well within it. He is not nude or wrapped in his mother's mantle, nor responding to her in a childlike manner, as in other fourteenth- and fifteenth-century images (Figs. 816, 818).[41] He is fully dressed in a tunic, and the fact that the illuminator had in mind a past event, an historical image of some sort, seems proved by the extraordinary position of the Child's arms. He raises them in the old, formal orans gesture.

The initial in the *Brussels Hours*, painted around 1395–1400, is especially interesting because the miracle began to be more frequently represented in French painting in the early fifteenth century, and precisely in the circle of Jean de Berry. The Limbourgs introduced it into the

Belles Heures and the *Très Riches Heures*.[42] While the initial in the *Brussels Hours* is coupled with the Annunciation to the Shepherds as an additional instance of revelation of the coming of the *puer maior*, in the *Belles Heures* and the *Très Riches Heures* the subject replaces more traditional illustrations of the prayer O Intemerata. Perhaps it was suggested by one of the first epithets of the Madonna in this prayer, 'Janua regni celorum'. The image of the Aracoeli appeared also in a copy of the *Épître d'Othéa* by Christine de Pisan that was presented to the Duke of Berry;[43] the miniature was painted in the period 1404–1409 by the Egerton Master, who collaborated with the Master of the Brussels Initials during this period in the *Heures de Charles le Noble* and who was in touch also with the Limbourgs (Fig. 817). In the *Épître* rays emanate from the Madonna, their brightness enhanced by the dark disk behind them. In the *Très Riches Heures* there are rays without a disk, but in the earlier *Belles Heures* only a moon, the symbol of the Apocalyptic Woman that thus replaces the traditional golden circle.[44] In all these representations, as in the Brussels initial, the Emperor kneels, clasping his hands, while the Sibyl stands, pointing out the half-length Madonna. The strikingly formal, demonstrative posture of the Child in the Brussels initial was, however, not followed. It should be observed that two, at least, of the Limbourg brothers very probably saw the initial, because they were working for Philippe le Hardi from 1402 to his death in 1404,[45] and this prince probably received the *Brussels Hours* from Jean de Berry shortly after the inventory of 1402 was drawn, as we have seen.

We know that Jean de Berry possessed still another representation of the Aracoeli. It appeared just below an image of the Trinity in 'un grant tableau d'or' that he gave to the Sainte-Chapelle in 1405.[46] This object, long lost, has been considered a possible source for the Limbourgs by three recent writers,[47] who have, however, remarked on the difficulty of judging from Robinet's description alone, good though it is. He speaks of 'Nostre Dame tenant son enfant, et un ront à l'entour duquel a escript . . .', and then he records an inscription from Psalm xviii, 6, that is not prominent in the *Golden Legend*. Both the Sibyl and the Emperor were kneeling, she 'fait joindre les mains audit empereur et lui montre avec la main ladite Trinité [*sic!*]'. Above their heads were written two prophetic statements of Isaiah, so that the program was more complex and more interpretative than the surviving paintings.

We cannot be sure how long before 1405 this golden 'tableau' belonged to the Duke; it did not appear in the inventory of 1402. The Brussels miniature may have been earlier, but we do not in any event know whether the remarkable Madonna and Child in it were related to the corresponding figures in the lost 'grant tableau d'or'. Certainly the Sibyl and Augustus were not, for the joining of the Emperor's hands is not represented and in this respect the Brussels initial, small though it is, resembles more closely the early fifteenth-century paintings.[48] Jean de Berry clearly had a special fondness for the subject of the miraculous vision. Furthermore, Augustus was the subject of one of the four medals representing Roman emperors that he acquired in or around 1402.[49] The Duke might well have felt a special sympathy for this great ancient ruler, who learned in so dramatic a manner of the birth of Christ. He could easily have identified himself with one of the princes and kings described in the prophetic verse of Psalms that was written above the head of Augustus in the gold 'tableau': 'REGES VIDEBUNT, ET CONSURGENT PRINCIPES, ET ADORABUNT DOMINUM'.

Some paintings of the Nativity by our master are no less remarkable than the representations we have been discussing. They were inspired by two widely read religious texts, the *Meditations on the Life of Christ* and the *Revelations of St. Bridget*, but they draw upon passages that were rarely illustrated, at least until the second quarter of the fifteenth century. The *Meditations* tells that after the birth of Christ Joseph, eager to make Mary comfortable, brought the stuffing of the saddle of the ass as a cushion for her. In a translation made in 1380 for the Duke of Berry, which will be discussed below, this passage reads: 'Apres il prit le bas de lasne et destacha le coussi qui estoit de laine et de bourre et fist seoir notre dame dessus'. The Latin text is: 'Joseph . . . accipiens sellam asini, & extrahens de ea cussinellum de lana sive bora posuit juxta praesepe, ut Domina super eo sederet. Ipsa ergo se posuit ibi ad sedendum, & sellam posuit subtus cubitum, & sic stabat Domina mundi. . . .'[50] In the *Nativity* in the Book of Hours of around 1400 in Madrid, an extraordinary manuscript from many points of view, the Virgin sits not upon Joseph's cushion but upon the saddle itself – one of the rare references to this passage in Western painting, and perhaps the most unusual (Fig. 752). In the *Heures de Charles le Noble*, painted around five years later, Joseph rather than the Virgin makes use of the saddle (Fig. 758), and though this departs still further from the text, it was the more frequent version of the theme. It reappears in Quattro-cento painting, in for instance the famous panel by Piero della Francesca in London (Fig. 757).[51]

Northern painters were not attracted by the use of the saddle as a stool for Mary or Joseph, though scarcely because it produced so 'simple an array', as the early fifteenth-century English translation of the *Meditations* puts it. Other aspects of our illuminator's representation of the Nativity, however, anticipated innovations in Flemish painting by fifteen or twenty years. The miniature in Madrid presupposes a knowledge of St. Bridget's vision of the Nativity, one feature of which – the Virgin adoring the newborn child in the cave – had already been reflected in the *Très Belles Heures de Notre-Dame* (Fig. 41). St. Bridget told that Joseph brought a candle into the cave, producing a *splendor materialis* that was obfuscated after the birth by the *splendor divinus* that emanated from the child. Toward the end of the century one Italian representation of the Brigittine vision of the Nativity showed Joseph holding a candle (Fig. 756).[52] The miniature in Madrid, of about 1400, is the earliest example in the North (Fig. 752). Our illuminator repeated the figure about seven years later in the manuscript in London (Fig. 755),[53] and after a decade it was not infrequently chosen by Netherlandish illuminators and painters, including the Master of Flémalle.[54]

Perhaps it was the Brigittine text that inspired also the representation in both the Madrid and London miniatures of the Virgin adoring the Child with clasped hands. In the *Nativity* in the *Heures de Charles le Noble* she even kneels in adoration before the Child in the crib (Fig. 758), an action already represented in Tuscan painting in the second quarter of the Trecento[55] and popularized in France around 1407 by the Boucicaut Master. In the *Nativity* in London, Add. 29433, the Child lies in Mary's lap quite nude,[56] and the image thus anticipates the famous *Madonna* by Gentile da Fabriano (Figs. 755, 821). The London *Nativity* includes two midwives, whose presence was attested by apocryphal gospels, and one at least of whom had occasionally been represented in fourteenth-century art. Following Byzantine precedent she usually tested the temperature of the bath water,[57] whereas in our miniature one midwife warms a cloth at a fire while the other prepares a chicken for the pot that stands over it. Such domestic activities, already stressed in the *Meditations*, acquired equal prominence only a little later, in the Netherlandish or Lower Rhenish painting in Berlin.[58] Our illuminator gives them a special overtone by representing, three folios beyond and still in the office of Matins, a rooster carefully roasting a fox on a spit (Fig. 762).

The sequence suggested by the iconography of the three miniatures of the Nativity by our master – Madrid, Cleveland, London (Figs. 752, 758, 755) – is confirmed by their style. Even apart from the splendid landscape, the *Nativity* in London is the most 'Northern' and iconographically the most complex, whereas the earlier *Nativity* in Madrid lacks the dilapidated roof that, as we have seen, became so prominent a feature of French paintings of this subject (Figs. 91, 184). A similar sequence is indicated by the representation of the Visitation in the three manuscripts (Figs. 748-750). In the composition in Madrid, set outdoors in the normal Italian manner, Elizabeth kneels to pay homage to the Virgin, as in several Trecento representations beginning with Taddeo Gaddi (Fig. 748).[59] In Niccolò da Bologna's *Visitation* in the Duke's Missal both ladies kneel, partly because of the low format (Fig. 751). The encounter occurs indoors in the *Heures de Charles le Noble* (Fig. 749), an uncommon *décor* in Italy, as we have seen, but employed by the Parement Master in the *Très Belles Heures de Notre-Dame* (Fig. 7) and by Jacquemart in the *Petites Heures* (Fig. 90). The single chamber of these French manuscripts becomes more complex in the *Heures de Charles le Noble* and exceedingly elaborate in Additional 29433 (Fig. 750). The latter includes a view into Mary's bedchamber, a stair outside that is mounted by a man bearing a bucket, and the roofs and towers of an entire town, including the apse of a large Gothic church. The perspective is, for the period, remarkably consistent, and in scale the structures resemble those designed in just this same period by the Boucicaut Master and the Limbourgs (Figs. 487, 496, 498). While our illuminator was no doubt attentive to the accomplishments of his great contemporaries, they in turn seem to have responded to his work; indeed, we shall shortly offer more precise evidence of the interest of the Limbourgs.

The buildings in Additional 29433 are more Gothic, whereas those in the *Heures de Charles le Noble*, with their numerous round arches and small domes, are Italian (Figs. 776, 772). The changing character of the architecture thus parallels that of the iconography and of the style in general. The structure of the *Annunciation* in Additional 29433 (Fig. 747) might be viewed, iconographically, as a rather playful elaboration of the two houses that contain the angel and the Virgin – likewise both kneeling – in the Arena Chapel. Although a few forms in the conglomeration in Additional 29433 are Northern Gothic most of the elements are Italian, and the specific Italian source is demonstrated unequivocally by the compact, impressive structure in the *Annunciation* in the *Heures de Charles le Noble* (Fig. 745). This is a close reproduction of Altichiero's central building in a fresco of the martyrdom of St. Lucy in S. Giorgio, Padua (Fig. 744). We cannot doubt that our illuminator had studied in this very *oratorio*: the beautiful house of the apostles in *Pentecost* in Additional 29433 is the building in the fresco of St. George baptizing the King (Figs. 776, 778). Altichiero's splendid building impressed other Italian painters of the period also: a copy may be seen in the fragments of an excellent cycle of frescoes of the late Trecento in S. Antonio in Polesina, Ferrara (Fig. 777). Our illuminator even completed the building above, where in

Altichiero's fresco it disappears behind the frame; he added a dome, a form reminiscent of the neighboring Santo and visible in smaller scale in the *Annunciation* in this manuscript (Fig. 747) and elsewhere in the miniatures of our group. The large dome is especially appropriate to the representation of the Pentecost because it reflects the circular plan of the figures in this scene that is traditional in Byzantine art and adopted occasionally by the Trecento.[60] Indeed the Brussels Initials Master employed the dome for this subject earlier, in simpler but even more telling form, in the Madrid manuscript, where the arrangement of the apostles actually approximates a circle more closely (Fig. 775).

The Master of the Brussels Initials is usually not satisfied with a mere copy; he invariably adds to his models or rearranges them. From an interplay of the idea of a high exterior pulpit, appearing in Altichiero's scene of baptism (Fig. 778), with the idea of actors or spectators in a second storey, so prominent in Altichiero's painting (Fig. 744), he seems to have devised the prophets in the London *Annunciation*, gesticulating above the main action from their pulpits or small bays (Fig. 747). The chamber of the *Annunciation* in the *Heures de Charles le Noble* is significantly altered by the addition, on the central axis, of a small chapel containing an altar and a retable (Fig. 745). This little oratory may be the painter's response to the French preference, beginning with the Parement Master (Figs. 6, 94), for setting the Annunciation in an ecclesiastical interior, and indeed just around 1405, when the *Heures de Charles le Noble* was illuminated, the Boucicaut Master in his wonderful manuscript for the Maréchal represented a great nave behind the angel and the Virgin, though its lower part is hidden by a large hanging.[61] Whether or not the triple-arched interior with adjoining chapel was first designed by the Brussels Initials Master – as seems to be the case – it was employed again and again for meditating saints by the Limbourgs a few years later in the *Belles Heures* (Fig. 746).[62]

The throne in the *Coronation* in the Madrid *Horae* – like the architecture generally – is relatively simple, containing only a broad high back (Fig. 770); it becomes an imposing structure a couple of years later in Douce 62, rising without a containing frame (Fig. 771). The main model for this lofty building was again a design by Altichiero, the throne of the *Coronation* in the Eremitani in Padua (Fig. 774). Our illuminator preserved even the curved apse at the center, but at the top he improved upon his model by adding a circular drum and a hexagonal dome, of the kind that Altichiero employed in, for instance, his great *Coronation* in S. Giorgio, Padua (Fig. 773). Similar structures may be seen in a second, and somewhat later, *Coronation* by the Brussels Initials Master in the *Heures de Charles le Noble* (Fig. 772).

Even here, midst this really dazzling display in the North of rich and intricate Italian architecture, our illuminator maintains a certain independence. In none of his representations of the Coronation does Christ, as in the painting of Altichiero and of the Veneto, hold a scepter; he has an orb, in conformity with French convention (Fig. 535). Sometimes our master seems to have had no model at all. In the *Presentation in the Temple* in Madrid only the back of one figure (Joseph?) is seen entering the door of the building (Fig. 786). Many of the details in the *Annunciation* in London seem unprecedented also (Fig. 747). In this crowded miniature the painter let his fancy run more freely than ever before. Some of the small elements – the lilies and the roses growing just outside the Virgin's chamber, for instance – clearly have a symbolical meaning. Possibly the spider and the bug on Jeremiah's tower are not just bits of still life, but in estimating their significance we must bear in mind also the appearance of the same bug in the margin of the Oxford manuscript (fols. 28, 78, 182) and the disproportionately large fly on the flank of the ass in the *Flight* in the London manuscript (Fig. 765). The bird in the cage over the Virgin's head in the *Annunciation*, which appears in later Italian representations of the subject,[63] may refer to the incarnation,[64] and the peacock (?) on the doorstep beyond the Virgin to immortality.[65] While cats and dogs, on the other hand, occasionally enliven the margins of Trecento religious stories,[66] they were never, to my knowledge, admitted to the center of an Annunciation nor to a space immediately in front of an altar (Fig. 747).

Our illuminator's representations of the Man of Sorrows show a similar point of departure in North Italian painting followed by an assimilation of French ideas and some personal innovations. In the miniature in Madrid Christ, the Virgin and St. John appear before a background of uniform hue strewn with symbols of the Passion (Fig. 808). Christ, dead though quite erect, extends his unflexed arms to form a triangle, all in conformity with later Trecento convention.[67] He is embraced by the Virgin, as in the Bolognese and Veronese paintings discussed above (Figs. 546, 547),[68] and our illuminator thus brought to France that very type which had earlier, we surmised, influenced the creation of a new composition (Fig. 15). In the miniature in Cleveland the embrace of the Virgin is more passionate – she utters a cry – and Christ's head falls more limply toward hers. His arms are bent, his fingers spread, and his hands tend to dangle, as in French paintings of the theme (Fig. 809). The place of St. John is taken by the eerie white tunic of Christ, upright and, in a sense like him, empty. The space is deeper despite the use of the French diapered background. This gives way in the late miniature in London to a landscape with a rocky hill, which rises behind the figures. Christ, now simply a corpse, is held by an angel, in accordance with the recently developed French type (Fig. 806).[69] Indeed his head, narrow with delicate features, reflects the forms of a French collaborator from the workshop of the Master of Luçon (Fig. 741).

Unprecedented, as far as I know, is the reintroduction into the French *Christ de Pitié* of the Virgin and St. John, sorrowfully seated on the ground, as in the Crucifixion (Fig. 97). This unusual combination, like other innovations of the Master of the Brussels Initials, reappears in Flemish art, as Dr. Kreuter-Eggemann has observed.[70] In a drawing by Jacques Daliwe the seated Virgin and St. John accompany the Man of Sorrows who, however, is half-length, surrounded by cherubim, and suspended on clouds (Fig. 807). This version of the 'heavenly' Man of Sorrows, frequent in somewhat later Flemish illumination,[71] may be seen as early as 1401 in a miniature by the Luçon Master (Fig. 810). The Brussels Initials Master introduced into the manuscript in London a second unusual, if not entirely novel, representation of the dead Christ: a beautiful version of the *Vesperbild* in which four youthful angels appear alongside the Madonna, helping her to hold Christ's head and limbs (Fig. 811). Their natural sprightliness contrasts with the spent corpse, as in the Donatellesque relief in the Victoria and Albert Museum of the Man of Sorrows similarly attended by putti.[72]

In his paintings of the Flight into Egypt the Master of the Brussels Initials frequently represented the palm tree that bends toward Christ and the Virgin to offer its fruit. The miracle was described by the apocryphal gospels, and it appeared in fourteenth-century painting, for example in a miniature by an interesting Italianate (an itinerant Italian?) master who painted a Book of Hours of the use, apparently, of Clermont (Fig. 766).[73] When the Brussels Initials Master first represented the Flight, in the Madrid manuscript *circa* 1400 (Fig. 763), the landscape consists of characteristic Giottesque terraced rocks, though the flowers are unusually luxuriant and the repoussoir at the left resembles the one in the *Flight* which had been painted a few years earlier by Jacquemart in the *Brussels Hours* (Fig. 188) and which reappeared in several French miniatures of the first decade of the century. In the *Flight* in Douce 62 the landscape, now possessing the scale of Altichiero's, has become more luminous (Figs. 767, 691). In the *Heures de Charles le Noble* the space is as vast and open as in the *Brussels Hours* (Figs. 764, 188); our illuminator had clearly studied the main miniatures in that manuscript while executing the initials. Thus he adopted the landscape of Jacquemart around the same time as the Boucicaut Master, who disclosed his own deep understanding of the Brussels book in some miniatures in the *Boucicaut Hours.*

Symptomatic of the interest of the Brussels Initials Master in Jacquemart's landscape is his introduction of a windmill on a hillock in the distance, similar to the one in the *Betrayal* in the *Brussels Hours* (Fig. 191). In the *Heures de Charles le Noble* he abandoned, furthermore, the diapered ground for the blue sky so characteristic of the Brussels miniatures. Our illuminator's sky is, however, streaked with clouds, and thus it seems to imply a knowledge of a later stage of Jacquemart's style, a stage that is reflected also in the *Crucifixion* in Yates Thompson 37, datable *circa* 1405–1410 (Fig. 264). Most of these innovations reappear in the *Flight* in the *Horae* in London (Fig. 765). This late miniature is as usual more complex and less coherent. Departing from tradition it introduces shepherds and their sheep. The windmill appears again in the London *Horae* in the *Adoration of the Magi*, once more as part of a freely painted, extensive landscape (Fig. 760).

Three paintings of the *Adoration of the Magi* by the Brussels Initials Master bring to the North a Sienese version of this theme that adds to the act of veneration the representation of the retinue on the road, still traveling to the scene (Figs. 753, 754, 760). This extension of the narrative into the landscape was adopted by the Limbourgs, and it served as a point of departure for Eyckian compositions, such as the *Way to Calvary* and the *Crucifixion*, both known from copies (Fig. 537). In these compositions the religious episodes are no longer understood only as stages in the development of a divine plan; they tend to become historical events. Moments preceding the climax are represented and, more significantly, subsequent ones. In Jan van Eyck's *Crucifixion* the soldiers and their companions leave the site of the homicide and return to their normal daily activities (Fig. 537). In the second decade of the fifteenth century, as we shall see, the Boucicaut Master had already portrayed a similar but much less conspicuous movement of soldiers away from the cross. This historical conception of even the Passion gave rise to the appearance of incidental figures in the landscape, such as the peasant and his horse in the *Crucifixion* in Yates Thompson 37, to which we have already referred (Fig. 264).[74] Such figures may already be seen, indeed, in the *Adoration of the Magi* by the Brussels Initials Master in Douce 62, where a peasant on horseback as well as a disproportionately large companion travel in the opposite direction from the oncoming throng (Fig. 753). Here again Altichiero may have proved suggestive, as in the fresco of St. James led to martyrdom in the Santo, Padua, executed by an assistant (Fig. 514). This historical conception of the religious events was greatly developed in later art, especially in the sixteenth century in the painting of Peter Breughel.

The 'travelogue' appeared in what we have judged to be the earliest of the illuminator's miniatures of the Adoration of the Magi (Fig. 754) but not in one apparently later example, in the *Heures de Charles le Noble* (Fig. 759). The landscape in the Madrid manuscript, furthermore, is much more advanced than the conservative, Giottesque rocks in the *Heures de Charles le Noble*. Inasmuch as we shall shortly add further evidence in support of the sequence Madrid, Oxford, Cleveland, London that has emerged from our discussion so far, we must conclude from a comparison of the landscape in the paintings of the Adoration of the Magi that the changes from one manuscript to another were not always homogeneous, partly because of the intervention of assistants. Some details in the miniature in Cleveland do, on the other hand, betray its later date. The thatch of the shed is not intact, as in the miniatures in Madrid and Oxford, but dilapidated, as in London. The effect of French models is disclosed also by the greater size and prominence of the golden gifts. As in the *Adoration* in London, Joseph holds the large cup that was offered by the eldest Magus. In both these miniatures the youngest Magus wears a large golden necklace over a well-cut *houppelande*, and in Additional 29433 bells dangle from the waist of one member of the retinue (Fig. 760).

If we consider the illuminator's illustrations for the Penitential Psalms we arrive once again at the sequence Madrid, Oxford, Cleveland, and London (Figs. 787-790). He consistently chose for this point in his Books of Hours not the Last Judgment sometimes employed in France[75] but Hell only, for which there is no Northern precedent. Most of his characteristic inhabitants of this realm appear already in the manuscript in Madrid: the tub full of souls (a sort of wooden *bolgia*), Satan munching on one body, and another – actually a pope (in Oxford and London only a bishop) – turned on a spit (Fig. 787). Religious are already prominent in this miniature and their number rises to four-fifths of the population in the later manuscripts (Figs. 788-790). So as to be unmistakable most of them wear the attributes of their earthly offices. The miniatures in Oxford and Cleveland are unusually close; they were certainly based on the same design (Figs. 788-789). Cleveland, with its greater fluidity and its picturesque vegetation, seems later. London is, as usual, the most complex (Fig. 790). Satan devours his chosen victims in a nicely designed, perfectly functional building. The supply of bodies for his greedy maw has been mechanized by the provision of a barrow and a wagon. Logistics in general are improved. Some souls are now brought by air.

3·CHRONOLOGY IN FRANCE AND ITALY

We have concentrated in the preceding discussion on the sources of the compositions of the Master of the Brussels Initials, on his inventiveness, and his contributions to French and Netherlandish painting. In the course of the study the order of execution of the chief Books of Hours has slowly but surely emerged. It remains now to confirm this sequence with other kinds of evidence. We must correlate it with the work of the illuminator's French collaborators, with the style of the other manuscripts of the group, and especially with the two that can be more or less precisely dated, the initials in the *Brussels Hours* before 1402, and the *Madonna* in the manuscript of 1408. We have already discussed the style and the date *circa* 1390–1395 of the French illumination of the manuscript in Parma. Only the *Horae* in Madrid was executed by our master alone. One of his French collaborators in Douce 62, who painted in grisaille (Fig. 739) as well as in color (Fig. 740), still worked in the style of the late 'eighties, and especially of the *Petites Heures*, though he is not so close to that manuscript as the French painter of the Parma *Horae* (Figs. 735-738). His design for the entire folio resembles that of Walters 96, painted around 1390, and there too animals appear in the *bas-de-page*, though in Douce 62 they may be emblematic. A second French collaborator in this manuscript, author of the *Madonna Enthroned* (the head of Mary is repainted – Fig. 742) came from the workshop of the Master of Luçon, whose first dated work, similar in style, appeared in the Book of Hours of 1401 in the Biblioteca Central, Barcelona (Fig. 810). This fact tallies with others that, as we shall see, lead us to date the Douce manuscript around 1402.

An illuminator from the same Luçon workshop was invited to make a similar small contribution to another Book of Hours, British Museum, Additional 29433. He painted four miniatures near the end of the manuscript in a style similar to the miniatures in the *Pontifical of Luçon* of about 1407 (Fig. 268).[76] Another French illuminator painted one miniature only, the *Coronation of the Virgin* in a somewhat Italianate style that is as impressive as it is rare (Fig. 743).

The five miniatures in the *Heures de Charles le Noble* that were allocated by the Brussels Initials Master to a Northern collaborator – all of them in the Hours of the Passion – are of considerable historical importance, and they will be discussed in a subsequent volume of this publication. Three of them, the *Nailing of Christ to the Cross*, the *Deposition*, and the *Entombment*, are delicate yet deeply felt portrayals of the tragic events, with a remarkably pathetic, collapsed torso of Christ in the *Deposition* (Figs. 813, 805). The light shimmers and the atmospheric perspective is very advanced. These qualities as well as the pointillist technique, the color, and the physiognomic types point to the early Egerton Master. The miniatures are, to be sure, finer than most of the later miniatures by him and his workshop, including the slightly later ones in the Duke of Berry's copy of the collected works of Christine de Pisan (Fig. 817).[77] They owe much of their luminary quality to the styles, Netherlandish in origin, that appeared around 1400 in Paris (Figs. 824, 825, 829), and two other Passion scenes in the *Heures de Charles le Noble* show this relationship no less clearly. The *Way to Calvary* is an unusual fusion of these styles with what seems to be the early Egerton workshop (Fig. 804); the *Betrayal* shows even fewer Egerton elements.

They have the nimble figures and the fluid color of the Duke of Berry's Bible, Bibliothèque nationale, fr. 159 (Fig. 822), and his Boccaccio (Figs. 289, 291, 294). For these miniatures in the *Heures de Charles le Noble* a date around 1405 seems plausible.[78]

The initials by our master in the *Brussels Hours* were, we can be certain, completed before 1402, and the fact is that for many reasons they would appear to take a place near the beginning of our series, after the miniatures in Parma of about 1390–1395, and before the Book of Hours in Madrid of around 1400. The handsome, ample, loosely wrapped drapery of the Parma Evangelists survives, though with less movement, in Jeremiah in the *Brussels Hours* (Figs. 201, 728). The Madonna of the *Assumption*, seated and clasping her hands (Fig. 207), is an Italian (ultimately Tuscan) form unaffected by French versions of the subject. A comparison of the initial of Christ led into the pretorium (Fig. 209) with the miniature of Christ before Pilate in the *Heures de Charles le Noble*, which contains figures in similar postures, throws into relief the extent of the admission of Northern ideas of color and light, and the diminution of the Italian preoccupation with *rilievo*.

Of course our master had already responded to French painting in this respect when we first encounter him in the Calendar and the Evangelists in Parma (Figs. 714, 715, 727, 728). He had begun to temper the solid Italian colors, clothing St. Luke in pale blue and green, and giving St. John a beautiful, delicate orange mantle. In the *Brussels Hours* he was apparently attentive also to Northern compositions and iconography. In its diagonal design the *Lamentation* resembles the *Entombment* in the *Petites Heures* (Figs. 199, 113); perhaps indeed a model of this kind accounts for the fact that in the initial the mourners are grouped around the body as though it lay on a sarcophagus whereas it is actually on the ground.

All these considerations have confirmed the correctness – or at least approximate correctness – of the sequence of paintings by the Brussels Initials Master that was suggested above: Parma, Brussels, Madrid, Oxford, Cleveland, London. For these manuscripts we have only one firm date: the Brussels initials not long before 1402. The original owner of the Book of Hours in Cleveland was identified by Léopold Delisle as Charles III, called 'le Noble', King of Navarre from 1387 to 1425,[79] but we do not know precisely when he acquired the manuscript. This prince was in Paris, where he was born, in 1405 and 1408.[80] From 1404 to 1409 he made a series of gifts to his uncle, Jean de Berry, who employed the Brussels Initials Master *circa* 1400.[81] These facts conform well enough with our hypothetical date for the Cleveland manuscript of *circa* 1405, but of course they do not prove it.

While the *Brussels Hours* provides a firm point for the earlier work of our illuminator, the *Madonna* in a text of 1408 gives us a date for the later phase (Fig. 792). The Child extends his arm toward the *battuti* just as he does toward the Magi in the *Adoration* in Madrid (Fig. 754), but his soft luminous flesh resembles far more that of Christ in the late *Adoration* in Additional 29433 (Fig. 760). It is indeed with the manuscript in London that the *Madonna* of 1408 shows the closest relationship. The Virgin is similar to the figure in prayer in the initial of O Intemerata (fol. 164), and the disposition of her drapery is remarkably like that of God in the *Trinity* (Fig. 769). Even the form that seems foreign to the work of our illuminator – the heavy frame – is at least approximated by the frame around St. Mark in Additional 29433 (Fig. 733). The latter is equally broad, and it has similarly beveled studs in the corners, but between the studs there are wide flat bands of burnished gold. Frames simulating stone were of course not new to illumination in France; we have seen them in miniatures by the Parement Master (Figs. 6-10), and in earlier paintings by the Master of the Brussels Initials, such as the *St. John* in Cleveland (Fig. 734).

Still, the frame of the *Madonna* of 1408 is exceptionally heavy for our illuminator, and it is one of several signs of a determined effort to produce something more 'Bolognese' for Bolognese clients. Perhaps, too, a local painter intervened. The gold arabesque on a black background is a Bolognese convention that was used earlier by our painter, but in a much less insistent form (Figs. 728, 729). The border of the folio lacks not only our master's characteristic refinement and intricacy but also any trace of a French element. It consists only of 'paramecia' and of heavy leaves painted in the same stark red and blue that is used for the frame. Though all this shows a strong infusion of *la maniera bolognese*, the Virgin's canopy seems entirely French, and indeed a little pale and exotic in this context. Without an architectural definition adequate for so plastic a Madonna, the canopy consists of rose disks on gold, and a red and green fringe. Its design is precisely that used by the Boucicaut Master from at least 1407 on. Thus we must conclude either that the Brussels Initials Master sent someone from his atelier to Bologna or that he went himself. In the latter case, which seems more likely, he would have been accompanied by an assistant, for the initial on folio 63 of the *Statuti* is probably not by the *chef* himself. It appears at the beginning of the roll of the confraternity, which was written in 1410.[82]

This hypothesis of the continuation of the workshop in Bologna – or at least North Italy – after 1408 is greatly strengthened by a manuscript of Lactantius in the library of the Earl of Leicester at Holkham.[83] Here the late pictorial phase of the master may be seen at a declining level. French forms include not only the kind of canopy we have just discussed but also birds, butterflies, and flowers similar to those used by the Master from the time when he collaborated on the *Brussels Hours* (Figs. 791, 200). They approximate most closely, however, the corresponding forms in Additional 29433, although they are more densely distributed and more perfunctorily executed. The smooth gradations of value and the suffused light in the Lactantius resemble the late manuscripts also. The same period of execution is suggested by the similarity of the folds over the knees of Constantine with corresponding ones in the miniature of 1408 (Figs. 794, 792).

There are signs in the Lactantius not only of a declining vigor but of the collaboration of another illuminator. The massive, comparatively block-like figure of the priest celebrating mass seems more plausibly attributed to an Italian – probably Bolognese – illuminator adapting his style to that of the Brussels Initials Master than to the latter himself in a fundamentally new and rather decadent phase (Fig. 793). Some miniatures in the Douce manuscript (Figs. 782, 783) contain similar bulky figures, but not quite so broad and heavy as in the Lactantius. On the other hand the better strain in this late manuscript may be detected elsewhere, first of all in a miniature of St. Catherine added to a Gradual from Catajo, near Padua (Fig. 795).[84] The Gradual was illuminated originally in the early fourteenth century in a style of generally Bolognese character. The *St. Catherine* was added on folio 195, at the beginning of the fourth gathering.

Two initials cut from their books belong to this phase of the style: one, representing St. Dominic, was owned by Maggs Bros. in London (Fig. 797)[85] while the other, representing a prophet, is in the Fondazione Cini in Venice (Fig. 796).[86] The initials are so similar that they may have belonged to the same manuscript. Indeed, they also resemble so closely the initials in the Lactantius (Fig. 791) that one might suppose this manuscript to be the source, though only one initial (folio 158) seems to be missing from it.

The latest known work of the Brussels Initials Master is linked with Bologna, and there can be no doubt that this center provided the basic elements of the painter's vocabulary. One Book of Hours, which has been ascribed to him,[87] has a Calendar with Bolognese saints such as Petronius. The manuscript contains related borders, similar subjects, including Hell for the Penitential Psalms (Fig. 800), and even similar motifs, such as the attendant wringing a chicken's neck in a birth scene, here the *Birth of the Virgin* (Fig. 801). The differences in detail, such as the fact that Satan spears a soul in Additional 34247 whereas he invariably devours one in the scenes of the Master of the Brussels Initials, might be ascribed to an earlier stage of the same painter's development. The painting of Additional 34247 is, however, cruder than that of the Brussels Initials Master himself, and the cold, smoky colors – common in Bologna – are lacking even in the Master's earliest work (Figs. 727, 728). The *uffiziolo* in London would therefore seem to represent the work of an early associate. Such relationships cannot be defined more precisely until we know more about illumination in Emilia and indeed in the eastern part of the valley of the Po.[88] Some miniatures in a manuscript in Vienna, the text of which was written as early as 1356, are certainly related to the earlier work of the Brussels Initials Master, and this style was probably his point of departure (Fig. 802).[89]

Though the early style of our illuminator derives from Bologna, we must bear in mind that what we have identified as his earliest known paintings – the miniatures in the Parma and Brussels Books of Hours – seem in some respects less Bolognese than the Douce manuscript. We must recall also that Bolognese style radiated to Ferrara, Verona, and Padua,[90] and with the latter center the manuscripts of our group are linked in clear and precise ways. Copies of Altichiero's architecture such as we described above have not been identified in manuscripts painted in Bologna. Suggestive also, though not decisive, are indications of early ownership. The Gradual in Modena came from Catajo, near Padua,[91] and the Lactantius in Holkham Hall was given to S. Giovanni in Verdara in Padua by Pietro da Montagnana, a scholar and professor of law at the University who was buried in the church in 1476.[92] The color of the early miniatures by our Master, warmer, softer, and higher in value than Bolognese, suggest an awareness of Veronese manuscripts, particularly of the group connected with Turone (Fig. 803). He may have studied also the color of Giovannino dei Grassi and his Milanese contemporaries, pondering especially the golden suns that project long sparkling rays down the margins of the manuscripts.[93] In view of these relationships with Padua and Verona it is noteworthy that the Brussels Initials Master went to France around the same time as Pietro da Verona; the latter, however, was then apparently only twelve years old.[94]

Though the miniatures of the Brussels Initials Master could not have served the more venturesome French illuminators of the time as substitutes for the work of the major Trecento painters

R

they had no doubt an influence upon the course of French painting. The very presence in Paris and Bourges of so curious and alert a master from Italy must have had a stimulating effect. He often read carefully the texts that he was illustrating, and he drew with unusual frequency from the *Meditations on the Life of Christ* and the *Revelations of St. Bridget*. At the same time he (and his assistants) enjoyed satirizing the intellectual life by painting monsters reading texts and music. The main forms in his borders – the large curling leaves, 'paramecia', and nude putti – were certainly known to French masters from earlier specimens of Bolognese or Bohemian illumination, but the more delicate versions of the Brussels Initials Master may have stimulated the vogue for pseudo-acanthus that began in the first decade of the fifteenth century (Figs. 749, 750). It was adopted by the Limbourgs for an initial painted for the Duke of Berry in 1405 (Fig. 481), in 1406 by the Master of the Bréviaire de Jean sans Peur (Fig. 780), and by the Boucicaut Master for borders around the same time.[95] Our illuminator preceded the Boucicaut Master also in the representation of the Christ Child playing a psaltery (Fig. 798).[96] Another form used by the Brussels Initials Master, gilt arabesques on dark brown or black backgrounds,[97] was no doubt familiar also to French illuminators from earlier Bolognese manuscripts, but it was the Egerton Master, an associate of the Brussels Initials Master around 1405, who first exploited it in France. Even the Rohan Master may have been impressed by the work of our illuminator: at least he employed such characteristic elements as arcaded domes and Evangelist symbols serving as desks.[98]

Inasmuch as the Limbourgs turned directly to Italian monumental painting in the early years of their career it is difficult to know whether the work of the Brussels Initials Master played any role in the development of their Italianate taste. The great scale of the buildings that they introduced into their miniatures in the *Belles Heures* around 1409–1410, their love of pageants, their fondness for installing witnesses of these pageants in the pictorial space, all recall the similar but more modest efforts of the Brussels Initials Master, and indeed they were inspired by the same Italian sources. We cannot, however, exclude the possibility that the interest of the Limbourgs in these matters was aroused by the work of our illuminator. Perhaps this interest extended also to the borders in which putti frolic amid large curling leaves (Fig. 779), and to compositions such as the *Adoration of the Magi* in which figures move from the more distant into the nearer space. There is one specific form, furthermore, that in the light of our present knowledge does seem to have been taken by the Limbourgs from the Brussels Initials Master. As I have proposed on another occasion,[99] the chapel or oratory placed perpendicularly to a three-arched interior that is so common in the miniatures of the *Belles Heures* (Fig. 746) reflects the similar juxtaposition in the *Annunciation* of the *Heures de Charles le Noble*, painted presumably about five years earlier (Fig. 745). Similarly the exceptional representation of the nude Christ Child seen from the back in an image of the Madonna in the *Belles Heures* (Fig. 785)[100] was preceded by a similar figure in Additional 29433 (Fig. 784).

The Limbourgs, though employed by the Duke of Berry, did not to our knowledge collaborate with the Brussels Initials Master, whereas Jacquemart, who did, cannot be said to have learned much from him. We can point only to his round throne-back in the *Coronation of the Virgin* (Fig. 189) in relation to *St. Luke* in the Parma manuscript (Fig. 727), and to such non-Sienese figures as Malchus in the *Betrayal* (Fig. 191) or the scourger in the *Flagellation* (Fig. 193).

XI

The Second Campaign on the
Très Belles Heures de Notre-Dame

1·THE FLEMISH EPISODE

IN Chapter VI we left the *Très Belles Heures de Notre-Dame* around 1385, when work on it was abandoned by the Parement Master and his assistants. Hulin de Loo, in his masterly account of the manuscript written in 1911, proposed that the illumination begun in the first campaign was continued some twenty odd years later. The work was first taken up again, he said in 1410–1412, just before the Duke gave the manuscript to Robinet d'Estampes, and then carried on by the latter. Hulin's identification of the several styles that appear at this later date in the manuscript seem to me, with minor modifications, correct. I shall on the other hand offer evidence for a not insignificant revision of the chronology.

Before turning to the two important and more independent groups of later miniatures, it may be simpler to discuss briefly one group in the *Heures de Milan* that is connected with the painting of the Parement Master in two ways (our Hand D). The compositions were drawn and possibly partly painted in the first campaign, and the illuminator, though working in a later and different style, attempted to harmonize his painting with that of the Parement workshop.

The *Adoration of the Magi* appears at first glance to be the work only of a rather clumsy imitator of the Parement Master (Fig. 42). Closer inspection, however, suggests that the later illuminator was working on a miniature partly executed by the Parement workshop or at least from a model in this style. Some of the blue in the Virgin's mantle, her orange cushion, and the pink mantle of the kneeling Magus are characteristic of the Parement Master. In this miniature, as in the related *Presentation in the Temple* and the *Ascension* (Figs. 43, 45),[1] the faces show no traces of the Parement style, while such details as the cap of the priest in the *Presentation* or the rocks in the *Ascension* are inexplicable without it. The angel in the upper border flying down with a star in its hands is modelled on the similar figure above the earlier *Adoration* (Fig. 9). Of course the relationships are especially complex because the later illuminator imitated the Parement Master, so that it is not always possible to decide what was deliberate simulation and what was actual inheritance.

In the *Adoration of the Magi* the building, the pink and blue vaults, the tessellated floor, the active Infant, are all reminiscent of the Parement Master. In the architecture the failure of the central shaft to extend down into the correct plane would seem explicable on the grounds that the painter who carried out the design omitted the little parapet that normally appeared at the lower margin of the compositions of the Parement Master and failed, at the same time, to lengthen the column. Indeed with this hypothesis as guide one can discern, beneath the paint of the present floor, a line across the miniature at just the level where the upper edge of such a parapet would fall. Some evidence for the localization of this illuminator may be provided by a Book of Hours, use of Rome, in the Huntington Library, San Marino.[2] The prayers in the Langue d'Oc point to the region in which the book may have been made.

The first important group of paintings in this second campaign, by our Master B, is composed of miniatures in all three parts of the manuscript. The *chef* may be called the Baptist Master, because he painted Christ and the upper part of the Baptist in the *Baptism* in Paris (Fig. 16) and a wonderful *Baptist in the Desert* in the *Heures de Turin* (Fig. 29). This group consists first of the three last scenes in the Hours of the Passion in Paris, the *Way to Calvary*, *Crucifixion*, and *Deposition* (Figs. 26-28). These scenes, which we have already discussed, were completed by B over drawings and some painting by the Parement workshop.[3] The same must be said about three miniatures in the *Heures de Milan*: the *Adoration of the Child* (Fig. 41), *Pentecost* (Fig. 46), and the *Martyrdom of St. Andrew* (Fig. 48). Hulin coupled the first two of these miniatures as the work of a master active in 1402-1405, but he ascribed the *Martyrdom* (its earlier surfaces) to an illuminator working in the 'nineties. We have already proposed, however, that the Parement Master began the *Adoration*, and he seems very probably to have begun also the *Martyrdom* and perhaps the *Pentecost*. His design of the *Martyrdom* included only the landscape in the foreground, with its characteristic rocks and plants; the more distant terrain and the wood were added by his successor.[4]

The same style, but freed of Parement models, may be seen in the figures of Christ and the Baptist in the *Baptism* in Paris (Fig. 16), and in several miniatures in the *Heures de Turin*: *John the Baptist in the Desert* (Fig. 29), *Prophets and Apostles* (Fig. 30), *Christ in the House of Simon* (Fig. 31), *Madonna enthroned with Jean de Berry* (Fig. 34), *St. Jerome in his study* (Fig. 35). *The Martyrdom of Saints* and the *Holy Confessors*, now in the Louvre, originally belonged to this section (Figs. 32, 33).[5]

Three miniatures in the *Heures de Milan* – *Annunciation* (Fig. 39), *Entry into Jerusalem* (Fig. 44), and *Last Supper* (Fig. 47) – are closely related to this group, though they are in a rather different vein. After long vacillation I have grouped them, as did Hulin, with Master B (our Baptist Master). They do not themselves compose a homogeneous group; the *Last Supper*, for instance, is less luminous. Probably these miniatures were painted at somewhat different moments, or executed by different assistants. They are full of reminiscences of the Parement Master, which are lacking in other works of the group. The *Annunciation*, which follows the Italian 'portico type', employs a building that is remarkably like the one in the early *Christ among the Doctors* (Fig. 11). The tiled floor and wall hanging, lacking in the latter, are visible in other miniatures by the Parement Master, such as the *Annunciation* in Paris (Fig. 6). The doctors in this miniature – or possibly another, lost miniature by the Parement Master – reappear as apostles in the *Last Supper* (Fig. 47). Lest this seem an improbable transmigration we can point to the emergence as Judas in the *Last Supper* of the barefooted John the Evangelist from the *Crucifixion* of the *Parement* or the *Très Belles Heures de Notre-Dame* (Figs. 1, 27).

Two of the miniatures in this group have significant relationships with miniatures in the *Grandes Heures* of Jean de Berry. The connection between the two representations of the Entry into Jerusalem is striking, though it has not previously been observed (Figs. 44, 226). We can normally conclude that when two paintings show an almost identical action, it originated in the one where it is most rational, where it is most consistent with surrounding forms and most decisive in character. By these criteria the miniature of the *Entry* in the *Très Belles Heures de Notre-Dame* is certainly the model. Witness in it the posture of the man before the gate: the inclination of his body is governed by reverence and by the act of spreading his mantle, which he holds with both hands. The relaxed torso of the corresponding youth in the *Grandes Heures* is relatively unaffected by the spreading of the cloak, and well it might be because the boy scarcely grasps it. Similarly St. Peter in the *Très Belles Heures de Notre-Dame* actually draws his mantle together with his left hand, whereas in the *Grandes Heures* the corresponding hand appears indecisively before his chest. Most telling of all, in the *Très Belles Heures de Notre-Dame* Christ holds the bridle in the hand that grasps the book; in the other miniature the illuminator began to paint the bridle around the ass's head but, either because he was nodding or he misunderstood, he carried it only to the ass's neck, where it abruptly ends. The long slender arm of Christ, moreover, is characteristic of the painter of the miniature in the *Très Belles Heures de Notre-Dame*; it may be found again, with similar spidery fingers, in his *Annunciation* (Fig. 39).

A similar relationship may be observed between the two figures painted by the Baptist Master in the *Baptism* in Paris and the corresponding figures in the *Grandes Heures*, though there the saint has been raised to his feet (Figs. 16, 229).[6] In the *Très Belles Heures de Notre-Dame* the Baptist lays a hand gently upon Christ's shoulder; in the *Grandes Heures* the hand, overlapped by Christ's shoulder, has no clear function. Christ's left hand, accurately covering his crotch in the *Très Belles Heures de Notre-Dame*, is somewhat displaced in the *Grandes Heures*. And it should be said, finally, that putting the Baptist on his feet has not improved the credibility of his action. Indeed by elevating the arm holding the flask the illuminator of the *Grandes Heures* has introduced a difficult duality of motion – pouring, and striding forward. The remarkable length of his hair shirt does not increase his freedom of action.

Pseudo-Jacquemart was playing his usual role when he imitated miniatures painted recently by the Baptist Master in the second campaign on the *Très Belles Heures de Notre-Dame*. In the next chapter, indeed, we shall see that elsewhere in the *Grandes Heures* he even took over two miniatures by the Parement Master in that same manuscript. The miniatures by the Baptist Master must therefore have been executed in the years immediately preceding 1409, not later, as has generally been maintained. It was clearly the Duke of Berry, then, who turned the incomplete manuscript over to the Baptist Master, and in so doing he manifested a very different taste than had guided his choice of the first painter of this book as well as the illuminators of his *Psalter* and his other great Books of Hours. While a few of the miniatures by the Baptist Master, such as the *Annunciation* (Fig. 39) and the *Last Supper* (Fig. 47), reflect the early miniatures in the manuscript in one way or another, the style of the illuminator is utterly different from that of the Parement Master, not to mention the Italian Trecento. The Duke would have had to hunt hard to find an illuminator less suited stylistically to continue and complete the work of the Parement Master. By the same token the Baptist Master, though similar in his narrative liveliness to two illuminators of the *Petites Heures*, the Passion Master and the Pseudo-Jacquemart, was different from the leading masters employed by the Duke for that manuscript and for the *Brussels Hours*. How are we to understand this new tack?

The Baptist Master was not, for one thing, an inconsiderable artist. We have already observed how, in completing the unfinished Passion scenes of the Parement Master, he gave the action an impressive vehemence and zest (Figs. 26-28). Under his brush the figures acquired a beautiful opalescence. In the *Baptist in the Wilderness* he took up a theme earlier portrayed in the *Petites Heures* (Figs. 29, 167), and comparison with the work of the Passion Master is not to his disadvantage. His saint is more sentimental than his predecessor's. Older and bearded, he nevertheless seems youthful and small. He is innocent, wistful and helpless in the world, a true and worthy predecessor of Geertgen's touching image in Berlin.[7] In all these late medieval images of the Baptist in the desert, loneliness and silence, not the *vox in deserto clamans* described by the text, are the actual themes.

The Baptist Master will not, however, permit stillness in the entire space. Emerging from the rocks and the gloom, unseen by the saint, is a group of faithful who pray and gesticulate. Similarly, in the scene of the *Death of the Martyrs* one butcher works overzealously while the other, exhibiting the broken, predacious profile of Judas, scrambles towards his approving audience (Fig. 32). In another miniature the illuminator, instead of simply lining up the prophets and apostles, created an animated conversation piece (Fig. 30), and no painter ever accomplished a greater stir among the apostles as the Magdalen kisses Christ's feet (Fig. 31). In another miniature the Child almost dances in the arms of the Madonna (Fig. 34). Only the *Holy Confessors* in the Louvre, somewhat retouched, are quieter, weightier, and more orderly, and may well be the work of another moment though scarcely of another hand (Fig. 33).

The remarkable portrayal by the Baptist Master of St. Jerome in his study constitutes what is commonly described as early fifteenth-century realism (Fig. 35). Noisy naturalism might be more appropriate. The saint is sharpening his pen while two slightly sinister-looking associates compete for his attention. One glares balefully at the saint while standing with an armful of codices – like a modern *gardien* of whom a reader has requested a couple of oversize *Bibles historia-les*. The dour man faces a chest, but whether he is packing or unpacking books is not clear; the books within the chest are, in any event, arranged with maximum inefficiency. His companion peers impishly over the crowded lectern, only adding to the confusion in this room. The threat of quiet overhead is eliminated by the insertion of three grilles, one of which belongs to a bird-cage in which a parakeet, no doubt, vainly tries to be heard. How remote is this image of bustling disorder from the slightly later conception of the Limbourgs, both in the *Belles Heures* and in the composition that served as a model for the famous drawing in the *Bible moralisée*, Bibl. nat., fr. 166![8] The portrayal of scholarly paraphernalia brings the miniature closer, however, to the composition by Jan van Eyck and Petrus Christus in the Detroit Museum.[9]

The antecedents of this noisy naturalism are not to be found in metropolitan France, but further north. Indications of the correct route are given by the manuscript of the Apocalypse in Paris illuminated around 1400, perhaps, according to Panofsky, in Liège,[10] and we have the sense of coming near our destination when confronting the astrological treatise now in the Morgan Library. The homely dwarf who represents none other than the *Moon in Exaltation* in this manuscript (Fig. 827) is at least a cousin of the central executioner in the miniature of the *Martyrdom* in the Louvre (Fig. 32). *Mercury in Exaltation* has much of the misanthropy, not to mention the physique, of the inhabitants of St. Jerome's study (Fig. 826). These likenesses do not suggest an identity of author but of school or tradition, a tradition that in an earlier form, in the 'nineties, may probably be seen in the *Pèlerinage de l'âme* in Brussels (Fig. 828).[11]

The astrological treatise is the more interesting because it was given to the Duke of Berry on June 7, 1403, by the Abbot of the house of Augustinian Canons at Eeckhout near Bruges. The Abbot, Lubert Hautschild, had commissioned the illumination, presumably in Bruges.[12] In May of 1403 we know that this eminent man went to Paris as one of the ambassadors of Flanders to Charles VI,[13] and it was probably on this occasion that he presented the manuscript to Jean de Berry. Hautschild, furthermore, was the Abbot of the house with which Jean de Berry had associated himself in December 1402, as we learn from the document that contains the miniature representing the Duke and the Abbot, which we have discussed above (Fig. 480). The Duke became a *frater ad succurrendum,* one of a few leading figures of the period who associated themselves spiritually with the canons, and as such 'Iohannes, filius regis Francie, dux Bituricensis', appears in the necrology of the house, with an obit on June 6, 1416.

The interest of Jean de Berry in Hautschild is demonstrated also by gifts, of which we learn from the inventories. After 1413 the Duke gave to 'abbati de Bruges' a gold ring set with a half-length figure of the Baptist in chalcedony.[14] All the other gifts were made between 1401 and 1413. Two manuscripts went to Bruges, a *Vie des Pères* and an *Istoire des contes de Flandres*; likewise a crystal reliquary with a piece of the mantle of Christ.[15] The abbot received also objects for his table, a crystal goblet, an 'esvière' of the same material, and, no less impressive, some gold forks and knives, the latter possessing steel cutting edges.[16] In return Lubert sent the Duke vases, birds, and books.[17] He dedicated to the Duke his Latin translation of the *Pèlerinage de l'âme* of Guillaume Deguilleville, and the presentation copy contained beautiful miniatures.[18]

As one would infer from these records, Lubert Hautschild was an exceptional man. He was learned, especially in mathematics, and he constructed an instrument to show the movements of the planets and the zodiac. He was prominent in the Church as well as in political life. At the Council of Constance he was charged by Cardinal Pierre d'Ailly to review his proposal for the reform of the calendar that he had presented to Pope John XXIII in 1411.[19]

The Duke of Berry, like the Duke of Burgundy, appointed Lubert *consiliarius.* The Abbot was said to possess an exceptional gift of prophecy, and his presentation of an astrological treatise to Berry indicates one realm in which his counsel was valued. When we consider, however, the beauty of the illumination of this manuscript, the alleged beauty of the miniatures in the Latin *Pèlerinage*, and on the other hand the Duke's propensity to turn into scouts competent friends such as Pierre Salmon who were in more or less remote artistic centers,[20] we wonder whether the good Abbot did not serve as *consiliarius* in this realm also. Weale, indeed, pointed to the fact that the illuminators of Bruges held their meetings in Eeckhout, and that they established their chapel there when they formed a corporation. For these and other reasons Weale believed that Lubert recommended painters to Jean de Berry.[21]

This plausible hypothesis becomes fascinating in the light of the fact that in the first years of the fifteenth century Jean de Berry rapidly acquired a group of manuscripts for which a Flemish connection has been inferred in recent years.[22] In precisely what sense they are Flemish and exactly where the illuminators were trained we do not know, beause little produced in this region *ca.* 1400 has survived, and that little has not yet been closely studied. There is general agreement, however, that these manuscripts, though mostly produced in Metropolitan France, are related to what preceded and followed in Flanders.[23] We refer to the works of the Masters of the Coronation and of Berry's Cleres Femmes, a high proportion of which went directly or indirectly to the Duke of Berry between 1400 and 1405.[24] They consist of two copies of the *Bible historiale*, the earlier, Bibl. nat., fr. 159, in the Duke's collection in 1402 (Fig. 822);[25] the later, Paris Bibl. de l'Arsenal, ms. 5057-58, acquired by Jean de Berry probably around 1405 (Fig. 829).[26] The strongest miniatures of the later Bible approach the astrological paintings given by Hautschild in bold, earthy naturalism. The other manuscripts acquired by the Duke are more delicate and flowery, and they come closer to the French tradition of refined linearity. Still, in their subtle color, luminosity, and their use of bright contemporary costumes, they represent a real innovation in Paris, and it is highly significant that two of them contain Flemish, or at least Netherlandish, inscriptions.

One of these manuscripts with Teutonic words is the Duke's very beautiful earlier copy of the *Bible historiale* mentioned above (Fig. 822).[27] The chief illuminator of this Bible was responsible also for the magnificent *Coronation of the Virgin* in the *Légende dorée* of 1402 and for the direction of a *Fleur des histoires*, which Philippe le Hardi bought from the dealer Jacques Raponde at the beginning of 1403 and gave to Jean de Berry in March of that year (Fig. 438).[28] In February 1404 the Duke of Berry received as a gift from Jean de la Barre a *Cleres et nobles femmes* (Fig. 291), and one miniature in this manuscript, too, has a Netherlandish inscription.[29] The most vigorous illuminator of the Duke's *Bible historiale* of around 1405 seems to have worked also on this Boccaccio, as well as on a *Roman de Lancelot* that Berry purchased in 1405 (Fig. 824) and a French Livy now in Geneva (Fig. 825).[30]

These acquisitions constitute a distinctive period in the Duke's collecting. It is true that some of the manuscripts were given to him. The *Fleur des histoires* came from Philippe le Hardi, who in 1403 himself received from his administrator Jacques Raponde a closely related *Cleres et nobles femmes*.[31] As Duke of Burgundy Philippe would be expected to be in closer touch with Flemish painting – though as we have seen, all the major manuscripts of the time except this Boccaccio ended up in his brother's library. Berry's own *Cleres et nobles femmes* was a gift of Jean de la Barre, *receveur des finances* in Languedoc and Guienne, while Raoulet d'Auquetonville, master of the King's horse, gave him the earlier *Bible historiale* (Fig. 822). In view of the nature of these personal relationships, and of the remarkable homogeneity of Berry's major acquisitions at this period, it would seem probable that these donors gave Berry not what *they* liked but what they believed he wanted.

The years from 1400 to 1405 compose an exceptional period in the development of the Duke's taste, a moment of fascination with Flemish illumination, or at least illumination *à la dominante flamande*. Recognition of it explains the otherwise startling commission to Flemish painters around 1405 of the unfinished *Très Belles Heures de Notre-Dame*. Lubert Hautschild played a role in this episode. He gave the Duke an outstanding specimen of the Flemish art, he was a patron of books, and he was close to the illuminators of Bruges. It may have been he who recommended the Masters of the Coronation and of Berry's Cleres Femmes as well as the Baptist Master, the chief illuminator of the second campaign on the *Très Belles Heures de Notre-Dame*.[32] In the earlier manuscripts of the group are to be discerned the origins of the Boucicaut Master and of the Bedford Master, the heads of the two best workshops in Paris during the first twenty years of the fifteenth century.[33]

2·THE HOLY GHOST MASTER

One further group of miniatures in the *Très Belles Heures de Notre-Dame* remains to be discussed. They are the six surviving miniatures for the Hours of the Holy Ghost, and they are all by the same master, except for the figures of Christ and part of the Baptist in the *Baptism*, which are the work of the Flemish illuminator we have already discussed (Fig. 16). Though the two artists share this one miniature, their styles are utterly different; indeed the miniatures of the Hours of the Holy Ghost are unlike any other in the *Très Belles Heures de Notre-Dame*. The designs are bold and firm, with powerful, sweeping curves, often opposed to one another so as to quicken the pace and the tension. Reversals are carried from the plane into depth, and the figures often show a complex torsion, their bodies twisted one way, the heads another. The heads in fact are frequently tilted so far up or down that they create a very unnatural strain. The movements of the limbs, particularly in the *Resurrection of the Dead*, are similarly excited (Fig. 18). The vividness of this scene is not overestimated if it is described as a precursor of Roger's tremendous representation at Beaune. And in the miniature more than in the altarpiece the world itself responds to the drama of the moment, throwing up over the stir of figures and the strew of lids great masses of cracked rock. In the *Baptism* these fanciful crags rise over the figures like two giant waves (Fig. 16). In the *Dispersion of the Apostles* they curl toward each other, like the claw of a lobster (Fig. 21).

The agitation of the figures in the *Pentecost* and other scenes is heightened by a display of hands with sharp spidery fingers (Fig. 17). The forms are exceptionally solid, but they flatten at their extremities, so that the outlines have a thin, knife-like character. Within these cutting boundaries the planes are remarkably smooth. They are also taut – even the garment held by the angels in the *Baptism* (Fig. 16). It is not surprising that occasionally they crack open, as does the terrain behind the Baptist.

Why the master of the Baptist worked on only the two chief figures in the *Baptism*, leaving the rest to a bolder and more fanciful artist – or vice versa – we cannot know. We cannot even assume approximate contemporaneity, especially in the case of a manuscript with so checkered a history. Fortunately there is other evidence to prove that the painter of the landscape as well as the Master of the Baptist worked during the second campaign on the manuscript, and more precisely, before 1409. Once again Pseudo-Jacquemart has performed a valuable service for us.

Just as he took the figures of Christ and the Baptist for his *Baptism* in the *Grandes Heures* (Fig. 229), so he, or a member of his atelier, reproduced in the *Resurrection* the upheaval of stratified rocks common to several miniatures in the Hours of the Holy Ghost (Fig. 228). Furthermore the man visible through the arch in the scene of the *Faithful in Church* in the *Grandes Heures* (Fig. 244) is an exact replica of the apostle setting out into the landscape in the *Dispersion* by the Holy Ghost Master (Fig. 21).

Other miniatures in the *Grandes Heures* by associates of Pseudo presuppose a study of miniatures in the style of the author of the Hours of the Holy Ghost. Several figures who listen to St. Peter preaching in the *Grandes Heures* (Fig. 242) resemble apostles in the *Pentecost* in posture and even in physiognomy (Fig. 17). Peter's tunic, with its straight lower edge and two parallel folds, recalls the tunics of two apostles in the *Dispersion* (Fig. 21). In view of these resemblances it is not surprising that the figures in *Pentecost* on folio 56 in the *Grandes Heures* are copies of those in the miniature of the same subject by the Master of the Holy Ghost (Figs. 17, 237).[34] A second *Pentecost* in the *Grandes Heures* is a freer version of the same group (Fig. 241).

We conclude, then, that the impressive paintings in the Hours of the Holy Ghost were, like the Flemish miniatures discussed above, executed earlier than the period after 1412 to which they have hitherto been assigned; they must, indeed, have been completed by 1409. At this date the landscapes are advanced. The long, continuous extension in the *Resurrection of the Dead* (Fig. 18) resembles the extraordinary landscapes of the *Dialogues de Pierre Salmon* of 1409.[35] In depth and in the scale of their mountains the miniatures recall those added by the Limbourgs to the *Très Belles Heures de Notre-Dame* at the same time (Fig. 497).[36] Of course in other respects the style of the master of the Hours of the Holy Ghost is fundamentally different. He turned away from the poise and the serenity of the Limbourgs and of French style in the late fourteenth and early fifteenth century to a more animated narrative and a tumultuous design. He shares these values with the young Rohan Master and the Master of the Berry Apocalypse (Fig. 843),[37] and to an extent also, with the Bedford Master.

It would be desirable to demonstrate more precisely the place of so powerful a painter in French illumination. The truth is, however, that to my knowledge the painter had no pupils nor, it seems, any true predecessor in the realm of the book. Again, as in the instance of the first *chef* of this manuscript, the Duke seems to have engaged an artist who normally worked in other media. This hypothesis is supported by the peculiarities of the technique. The forms are built up in layers, and the film reaches an exceptional thickness. The paint as a consequence has cracked and flaked. In the miniature of the *Unbelievers* the several layers for the heads are superimposed on a blue background, complete with its arabesques (Fig. 20). The paint of the heads has not adhered well to the blue and has flaked in many places, exposing it.[38] The finish of these miniatures is exceptional in illumination. The gradations of value and hue are unusually subtle and there is so much fine detail, some executed with a pen or a tiny brush, that Durrieu called the painter 'le maître au travail minutieux'.[39]

If the painter was not by craft an illuminator, what was he? He worked very skillfully in paint, and he used successfully techniques that had been recently developed, such as transparent green and yellow glazes over silver for the river in the *Baptism* (Fig. 16).[40] His interest in the frames of the miniatures might indicate he was a painter: he abandoned the rather light colored bands inside the gold used in some contemporary and earlier miniatures for dull, narrow ones, so that the pictorial space drops back more easily. Works related to the illustrations of the Hours of the Holy Ghost are found, however, not in panel or mural painting but in miniatures painted by a sculptor. They descend in certain respects from the prophets and apostles executed by André Beauneveu at the beginning of the Duke's *Psalter* (Figs. 51-74). These figures by Beauneveu were painted twenty years earlier, but they contain the germs of the eccentricities of those in the *Très Belles Heures de Notre-Dame*: the discreteness of the figure in its space, the torsions, the bony heads, crabbed faces and big aquiline noses. The smoothness of plane is anticipated, the unusually deep blues and reds, and even the sparkling floor of the *Pentecost*, with its exceptionally small units.[41] The later miniatures show, of course, a great increase in intensity; their knife-edged forms and their strident scarlets and yellow-greens cannot be found in the *Psalter*.

The miniatures in the Hours of the Holy Ghost offer, then, something quite precious: apart from the earlier *Death and Assumption of the Virgin* in the Louvre (Fig. 587), they provide the only reflection after 1400 of the art of Beauneveu in drawing or painting. The Duke's sculptor is not himself of course a candidate for the authorship of them. He was dead by 1402, a few years before the miniatures were painted, and though his late style has not yet been firmly established, no surviving sculptures from his circle are so linear or so mannered.

Given the resemblance to Beauneveu, we may wonder whether the author of the miniatures was a sculptor too, or rather, because of the remarkable precision of definition, a goldsmith. The fact that the voluminousness of the single forms is vividly envisaged but not the intervals between them indicates that the designer was not accustomed to represent a three-dimensional realm on a two-dimensional surface. It would seem to have been not simply the subject that made the forms in the *Dispersion of the Apostles* so disconnected (Fig. 21). All of this remains, of course, only inference. What is certain is that the author of these miniatures deserves a not inconspicuous place in the history of late medieval French art.

XII

Grandes Heures

1 · THE SURVIVING MANUSCRIPT

THE manuscript generally called the *Grandes Heures* might more appropriately be known by the phrase that identifies it in the inventory of 1413: '*très grans moult belles et riches heures*'. It is still rich and originally was 'moult belles'. It is the largest of the Duke's Books of Hours, and an elephant among all manuscripts of this kind. Two of the Duke's earlier *Horae*, the *Très Belles Heures de Notre-Dame* and the *Brussels Hours*, are large for their class (the former measures 279 × 199 mm., the latter 275 × 185 mm.). The last of the Duke's prayer books, the *Très Riches Heures*, is a little larger, but the *Grandes Heures* swells to about four-thirds of its dimensions. No doubt during his later years the Duke wanted more imposing books, and during his sixties he would have been grateful for larger pictures – the writer can testify to the truth of that. Perhaps also the exceptional size reflects an inclination of the painter chosen for the commission. Jacquemart's miniatures in the *Brussels Hours* had the character of panel paintings. They lacked only the scale of panels, and that his miniatures in the *Grandes Heures* no doubt finally acquired.

Jacquemart certainly was the *chef d'atelier* for the *Grandes Heures*; this Robinet's notice in the inventory of 1413 states explicitly, and the identification of Bibliothèque nationale, lat. 919, with this notice has not been, and cannot be, doubted. Here then we seem once again to have documentary proof of the master's art, only to have fate snatch – or almost snatch – the prize from our grasp. The truth is that while the documentation is unusally full, the manuscript has come down to us in an altered state, deprived of all its largest and probably best miniatures.

Folio A of the *Grandes Heures* contains three statements. The first, and most important, was written by the Duke's secretary.[1]

> Ces belles et notables heures fist faire tres hault et tres puissant prince Jehan fils de Roy de France Duc de Berry et Dauvergne Conte de Poutou. . . . et furent parfaittes et complies en Lan de grace Mil Quatre cens et Neuf
>
> Flamel

The manuscript is definitely identifiable in the inventories of 1413 and 1416.

> Item, unes très grans moult belles et riches *Heures*, très notablement enluminées et historiées de grans histoires de la main Jaquemart de Hodin et autres ouvriers de Monseigneur, esquelles sont les Heures de Nostre Dame, les sept Pseaulmes, les Heures de la Croix et du Saint Esperit, de la Passion et du Saint Esperit encores, et l'Office des mors; et au commancement du second fueillet des Heures Nostre Dame a escript: *flamme*; couvertes de veluiau violet, et fermans à deux grans fermouers d'or, garniz chascun d'un balay, I saphir et VI grosses perles; et y a une pipe d'or, où sont atachiez les seignaulx, garnie d'un gros balay et IIII grosses perles; laquelle pierrerie est d'une chaienne en façon de paternostres et de certains culez qui furent de feu messire Jehan de Montagu, declairez lesdiz chastons en la IIIᵉ partie du IIIᵉ IIᵉ fueillet desdiz comptes precedens, et ladicte chaienne en la première partie du IIIᵉ IIIIᵉ fueillet ensuivant;

et ont lesdictes Heures une grant chemise de drap de damas violet, doublé de mesmes; lesquelles Heures mondit Seigneur a faictes faire ainsy et par la manière qu'elles sont dessus devisées.[2]

In 1416, after the Duke's death, the manuscript was appraised at 4000 *livres tournois*, an astonishingly high figure, over four times the price put on the *Belles Heures* and eight times that given to the unfinished *Très Riches Heures*.[3] The richness of the cover and its stones no doubt accounts in part for this price but the manuscript itself may have been highly valued. This possibility is relevant to the problem of the reconstruction of the original book.

Inasmuch as an inscription by the Duke's secretary records the date of completion of the *Grandes Heures*, and Robinet's inventory drawn up four years later names the chief master responsible for the illumination, one might have expected that the manuscript would be free of those intricate problems that hover over all the other great books of this prince except the *Psalter*. For a long time indeed historians believed the *Grandes Heures* spoke unequivocally; Lasteyrie and many others held that the illumination of the Calendar and the Hours of the Virgin gave us indisputable evidence of the art of Jacquemart de Hesdin.[4] More recently scholars became less enthusiastic about the quality of these works but the prestige of Jacquemart tended to cling to them. The painter of these miniatures is, however, none other than the Pseudo-Jacquemart whom we have encountered earlier in the *Psalter*, the *Petites Heures*, and other manuscripts.[5] What, then, was done by the painter whom Robinet named?

Over half a century ago Delisle published and elucidated with his usual skill an important record of a repair of a *Grans Heures* no doubt identical with our manuscript. The manuscript that is the subject of the document of 1488 possessed seventeen more miniatures than the *Grandes Heures*. Observing that the latter must have contained full-page miniatures at the beginning of each of the Hours of the Virgin and of the Passion, and noticing gaps in the series of original numbers still visible in the lower margins of certain folios, he concluded that the seventeen miniatures present in the manuscript in 1488 were indeed originally in the *Grandes Heures*. Delisle's hypothesis has been generally accepted in recent years. In section 2 of this chapter we shall prove absolutely that it was correct.

Jacquemart de Hesdin must then have been responsible for most if not all of the full-page pictures in the *Grandes Heures*. In the rest of the manuscript there is not a trace of his brush, not even in the early section, where alongside Pseudo-Jacquemart more advanced painters undertook small tasks. He apparently worked independently on his large miniatures. Here and there, however, one suspects his ideas and even directions, first of all in the borders, as we shall see. One of the large miniatures that were removed from the *Grandes Heures* may, however, be identifiable. It is a large painting on parchment of the Way to Calvary, now in the Louvre (Fig. 277). There is now general agreement that Jacquemart or a master very close to him painted this work, and though some scholars believe it was made for the *Grandes Heures* the hypothesis cannot yet, in my opinion, be proved. Discussion of the question, which involves a reconstruction of the original manuscript, will be deferred to sections 2 and 3 of this chapter and to Appendix B. The *Grandes Heures* as it exists today, a large and indisputable fact, will be considered first.

The borders of the *Grandes Heures* derive from those of the *Brussels Hours*; indeed comparison of the two discloses the kind of similarities and differences that suggest successive designs by one artist. The structure of the borders surrounding the large miniatures in the *Brussels Hours* was adopted in the *Grandes Heures* for borders on folios containing the beginning of an office and a miniature at the top of the upper left column (Figs. 181-198; 219, 221-225, 233-235). The *Grandes Heures* shows once again regularly spaced quatrefoils connected by stems, and the quatrefoils are similarly filled with coats of arms and devices of the Duke. While the shields (but not the banners) in the *Brussels Hours* show *France moderne* those in the *Grandes Heures* show *France ancien*.[6] In almost every other respect however the borders of the *Grandes Heures* are more modern, if not more beautiful.

The old gold ivy leaf, to be sure, employed in folios bearing initials in the *Brussels Hours* (Fig. 199) and still rampant on the corresponding folios of the *Grandes Heures*, had disappeared from the borders that surround large miniatures in the *Brussels Hours*. The borders of the Calendar (missing in the manuscript in Brussels) consist of ivy alone in the *Grandes Heures* (Figs. 217, 218), but in the subsequent historiated folios the ivy usually becomes subordinate to columbine, pinks, roses, daisies, and birds very similar to those in the main pages of the *Brussels Hours*. The flowers are more densely distributed in the *Grandes Heures*; the border has become a firmer unit, partly because the larger, more complex folio seemed to require it, and partly in conformity with the general trend to provide a more conspicuous frame for miniatures that project a much greater depth. Important, too, was the desire for more sparkle and richness.

For dazzling splendor the borders of the *Grandes Heures* could hardly be surpassed, and indeed they were not. They remained the last stage of this type of border. Their opulence as well as many details indicate that they were designed later than the borders of the *Brussels Hours*, a manuscript datable in the period 1395-1402. The bears again hold standards, but they are on longer poles and more vigorously waved. On many folios, beginning with 53, the swans take to water (Fig. 236) as they had much earlier on a seal.[7] From folio 56 this water is occasionally rendered by silver lacquered in green – a technique that was exploited in France in the first decade of the fifteenth century, especially by the workshop of the Egerton Master. On folio 53, along with the provision of water for the swans, scrolls bearing the motto of the Duke appear, winding around the stems that connect the quatrefoils.

The most important innovation of all is the angels, who may be seen as early as folio 8 in the four corners of the border (Fig. 219). They mark the main sections of the text: here the Hours of the Virgin, then on folio 61 the Hours of the Passion (Fig. 226), and on folio 86 the Hours of the Holy Ghost (Fig. 229). At the beginning of the Passion some of them grieve (Fig. 226). For the opening of the Hours of the Holy Ghost they provide instrumental music (Fig. 229). On folio 106, the Office of the Dead, their place is taken by four reading monks, who repeat the actions within the miniature itself (Fig. 232). On folio 8 the upper angels are seated, the lower ones kneel; both groups grasp the vines, which turn red at their ends as though they were roots (Fig. 219). Thus quatrefoils that served as anchors in the corners of the *Brussels Hours* have been displaced by mobile angels, whose action creates a more dynamic design. The new motive, appearing on folios illuminated by Pseudo-Jacquemart, was probably conceived by Jacquemart himself. In a Book of Hours illuminated around 1410 by the Boucicaut atelier (just after work on the *Grandes Heures*) its angels appear in the lower borders bearing vines in their hands or on their shoulders. [8]

After the initial appearance of the angels in the borders of the *Grandes Heures* their participation in the successive subjects increases. The borders vary in other respects also; changes are quite natural in a work that was carried out over a period of perhaps several years. Small alterations are visible as early as the gathering beginning on folio 16, others from folio 38 on. The birds fly ever more freely in the margins outside the vegetation. On folio 28, and more frequently from folio 65, they even head speedily for outer space.

The drolleries that enliven the folios without miniatures were painted by assistants of Pseudo-Jacquemart and of the Boucicaut Master. The execution in both instances differs from that characteristic of these masters or their assistants in miniatures. The drolleries in the style of Pseudo-Jacquemart are more drily and yet more freely painted than his 'framed' work. They satirize, as drolleries usually do, the religious above all: a monk eagerly drinking wine, a bishop wearing a bellows as a miter (folio 12), a monk blessing a dog which has caught a bird (folio 47 verso). On two folios the same ugly woman combs her hair while gazing intently into a mirror. These 'inventions gauloises' invade the secondary initials. In one a nude woman, a sort of medieval Leda, has an affair with a lion (folio 26). Very often these figures are copies of Pucelle's, as Dr. Morand has pointed out. [9] This dependence is characteristic only of Pseudo-Jacquemart, who in the *Petites Heures* collaborated with Pucelle's heir, the Passion Master, and who may well have kept some drawings in the possession of his associate at that period. While Pucelle's drolleries were widely imitated in the late fourteenth century, they were usually employed as figures in the margins, but the *Grandes Heures* frequently made use of them as line-endings, and thus restored them to their original context (Fig. 251). Very probably this restoration reflected study of the *Bréviaire de Belleville*, which the Duke received not long after the death of King Richard II of England in 1399. [10]

The arrival of the *Bréviaire de Belleville* in the Duke's collection perhaps quickened his interest in the sort of moralized Calendar taken from it that he already possessed in the *Petites Heures*. In any event the *Grandes Heures* was provided with a very similar sequence of scenes of the progressive destruction of the Synagogue without, as usual, any corresponding construction of the Church. In the margins above there are the teachings of St. Paul and the seasons of the year (Figs. 217, 218). The execution was entrusted to Pseudo-Jacquemart, who had painted the Calendar in the *Petites Heures* twenty years earlier, and indeed he often still preserved Pucellesque conventions, such as yellow-brown doors and black window openings. The narrow ground plane of the Calendar in the *Petites Heures* has, however, been deepened, and its execution was often allocated to more modern masters. Pseudo-Jacquemart turned from Pucelle's rather Italianate buildings to contemporary forms, including half-timber houses. A few prophets and apostles show quite clearly that the illuminator had studied the figures of the Limbourgs (Fig. 249).

It is surprising that the greatest connoisseur of illuminated manuscripts in Europe should have been content with the choice of Pseudo-Jacquemart around 1406 for so considerable a role in one of his great Books of Hours. The Boucicaut Master was apparently available. He designed two of the head pieces, but oddly his work was rather perfunctory, and his associates in the borders, initials, and elsewhere in the manuscript were not really distinguished. The Duke employed the Boucicaut Master, it seems, only for the small contribution to this manuscript and for a few miniatures in the Lectionary for the Sainte-Chapelle, a striking manifestation of lack of interest in a great painter. In the case of the *Grandes Heures* the preferences of Jacquemart perhaps carried some weight. He might have preferred collaboration with a weaker, conservative painter to full competition with the Boucicaut Master, the Bedford Master, or even the Egerton Master.

The prominence of Pseudo-Jacquemart on the surviving folios of the *Grandes Heures* is a guarantee of something less than artistic brilliance. If, however, his aesthetic contribution is modest his gift to history is considerable; indeed, as often happens, the latter depends on the former, for it was the Pseudo's lack of imagination and assurance that led him to take the compositions of others, as he had done in the *Petites Heures*, and thus to give us basic information about recent artistic events in Paris and Bourges. He drew from three main sources: (1) the paintings of Jacquemart de Hesdin in the *Brussels Hours* and perhaps also in the *Grandes Heures*, though about the latter of course we can only surmise; (2) the *Petites Heures*, on which he had worked extensively, and of which he perhaps possessed drawings, though the manuscript itself was available in the Duke's library; and (3) the *Très Belles Heures de Notre-Dame*.

The borrowings of Pseudo-Jacquemart from the *Petites Heures* include figures from the initial folio of the Hours of the Virgin: Jacquemart's *Man of Sorrows* (Fig. 94) reappears in the initial below the *Crucifixion* (Fig. 236), and the adjacent *Madonna* was employed in reverse for another initial (Fig. 219).[11] The dusky *Agony in the Garden* by the Trinity Master (Fig. 139) was adopted for the same scene in the *Grandes Heures* (Fig. 220). The terrain is rendered in a lower key than usual, even brown in its further reaches; the sky is darker, the trees without their usual highlights, all to suggest night. Pseudo-Jacquemart, who painted the hooded Christ in the *Mockery* in the *Grandes Heures* and who probably designed the entire composition, leaving the rest to an associate of the Boucicaut Master (Fig. 239), borrowed from the beautiful miniature by the Passion Master in the *Petites Heures* (Fig. 108). Another design by this master served as a partial source for the *Resurrection* in the *Grandes Heures*. (Fig. 228). Pseudo-Jacquemart was responsible for much of this miniature but the textures of the flesh and the drapery of Christ are not characteristic of his style. The composition is based on a representation of the subject in the *Bréviaire de Charles V* (Fig. 371),[12] which the Duke received from the Duchess of Orléans in the period following the death of her husband in 1407 and hers in 1408.[13] The miniature in the *Grandes Heures* is on folio 81, thus in the latter part of the manuscript; Pseudo-Jacquemart apparently inspected the new acquisition shortly after its arrival in the collection. The painting in the *Grandes Heures* preserves the red color of the tomb in the model and even the Pucellesque modelling of the legs of Christ. For the space and the landscape required in 1408–1409 Pseudo-Jacquemart had to turn to later paintings. The road behind Christ resembles similar forms in the *Brussels Hours* (Fig. 183), but here it has been elevated to a strange sort of viaduct. On the other hand the stratified rocks, especially at the right, were probably inspired by the landscapes by the Holy Ghost Master, especially in the *Baptism* (Fig. 16), – which, as we have seen, Pseudo-Jacquemart clearly had an opportunity to study.

Pseudo-Jacquemart took from the *Petites Heures* not only the compositions and figures of Jacquemart and the Passion Master but his own, now revised in accordance with developments since the 'eighties. The temple on folio 31 is a tripartite turreted structure like the church in the *Funeral Service* in the *Petites Heures* (Figs. 224, 176), but the coffered ceiling and other Italianate forms have been abandoned for a purely Gothic structure. The space is more clearly measured by a receding floor, and the shaft that passed behind the figures in the *Petites Heures* now extends across the Virgin's hands. The perspective of the ceiling, however, is not as complex nor as effective as in the *Petites Heures*, where in fact we have earlier suggested that Pseudo-Jacquemart was relying on a collaborator's model.[14]

Vestiges of the arabesques of the older form of background are visible at the right; in this composition, and still more in the *Marriage of the Virgin* (Fig. 225) we have the impression that the miniature has outgrown its frame. The main elements in the border now serve to contain the miniature, but the turrets inconsistently cross over them. In other scenes, such as the *Disrobing of Christ*, the *Fastening to the Cross*, or the *Lamentation* (Figs. 239, 240, 216) the upper frame loops around the uppermost objects so as to contain them. Generally in illumination around this time the upper areas of miniatures contain a lobe; in the work of the major painters, the Limbourgs or the Boucicaut Master,[15] this lobe is centrally placed. The introduction of such shapes would seem to be due in part at least to the wish to counter the increasing depth of the pictorial field by a form that would more tightly connect the miniature with the shapes of the borders and initials that lie flat on the page.

The *Lamentation* is a modernized version of the composition by Pseudo-Jacquemart in the *Petites Heures* (Figs. 216, 175), though the figures are dispersed more widely and set in a deep landscape, after the fashion of the preceding miniature of the *Fastening of Christ to the Cross*, painted in large part by an associate of the Boucicaut Master (Fig. 240). The Magdalen in the *Lamentation*, perhaps borrowed from the miniature of the *Entombment* by the Passion Master in the *Petites Heures* (Fig. 113), has now taken over the Virgin's role as chief mourner. The right arm of Christ is still placed as in the *Petites Heures*, but since no figure is there to clutch it, it dangles.

In the *Resurrection* we have seen a curving stone road similar to those used in the *Brussels Hours* (Figs. 228, 183); in the *Appearance of the Angel to Joachim and Anna* Pseudo-Jacquemart adopted an entire landscape by Jacquemart, drawing his elements especially from the very advanced *Entombment* (Figs. 222, 197).[16] He is on safer ground when taking a more measurable form such as a building: his temple in the *Rejection of Joachim's Offering* closely resembles Jacquemart's in the *Annunciation* (Figs. 219, 182). The building is broader in the *Grandes Heures*, the arch in the left wall is open, and the moldings of the base have been misunderstood. Those above the open space contain quatrefoils and, just in front of the ceiling, an arabesque of leaves appears where Jacquemart drew decorative forms but left them unpainted. What then was Pseudo-Jacquemart's model? Whereas the studded bands in the ceiling of the *Rejection* (instead of the coffers of the *Annunciation*) might point to the Parement Master, all the other elements indicate a drawing by Jacquemart or a miniature by him now missing from the *Grandes Heures*.

In another interior, the *Virgin in the Temple* (Fig. 234), Pseudo-Jacquemart abandoned the

s

coffered ceiling of his model for ribs, and this form appeared in several of his miniatures as a small token of his dependence upon miniatures by the Parement Master. Indeed the near identity of two miniatures by the latter in the *Très Belles Heures de Notre-Dame* with two by Pseudo-Jacquemart in the *Grandes Heures* was observed long ago by Durrieu. Durrieu concluded from these resemblances that the same master, for him Jacquemart, painted the two scenes in question, and this inference supported the date after 1404 that he gave to the beginning of the illumination of the *Très Belles Heures de Notre-Dame*.[17] So highly respected were the opinions of Durrieu and so readily transferable the prestige of Jacquemart that this view prevailed until recently, though in the past decade a number of scholars have recognized that the true relationships must be different. The case becomes fully clear only with the identification of the author of the miniatures in the *Grandes Heures* as a minor master entirely distinct from Jacquemart. He was, as I once characterized him, artistically a sponge. His interest in the *Très Belles Heures de Notre-Dame* was indeed indiscriminate; he took from it also designs by other painters, much more modern than the Parement Master, as we have seen.

The *Wedding at Cana*, which is represented at Compline in the the *Grandes Heures*, repeats the miniature at Vespers in the *Très Belles Heures de Notre-Dame* (Figs. 235, 12). The iconography of this scene, and its unusual appearance in the Hours of the Virgin, have been discussed above.[18] Though the painter of the miniature in the *Grandes Heures* avoids a spatial inconsistency of his predecessor by stopping the left corner of the table at the shaft rather than permitting it to overlap, he compensated for this correction with a whole new series of troubles by drastically reducing the space on the floor between the table and the lower frame. As a result two of the jars are pushed up onto the frame and the servant balances there precariously. Proof that it was the painting in the *Très Belles Heures de Notre-Dame* that served as the model rather than a drawing for or after it, is provided by a repetition of most of the colors. The building is altered from green to gray, the Virgin's tunic from gray to rose, and the rose bodice of the extreme left figure is different; otherwise the colors are the same.

In the *Funeral Service* Pseudo-Jacquemart departed from his model with similar consequences (Figs. 232, 14). It is true that by moving the nearer right post of the *chapelle ardente* to the far side of the bier he disengaged from it the face of the Dominican at the end of the bench, but the spatial inconsistency created thereby he compounded by moving forward in space, as compensation, the more distant post! In the process the brazier, a useful index of space, was lost. The hood of the nun in the doorway, worn low in the *Très Belles Heures de Notre-Dame*, has slid down over her eyes in the *Grandes Heures*, the book of the Dominican in front of her is impossibly wide, and his foot has got into the wrong place. Though the windows in the *Grandes Heures* are not as luminous as in the *Très Belles Heures de Notre-Dame* Pseudo-Jacquemart has preserved the colors of all objects in his model except one: the altar was changed from blue to greenish-gray, introducing a disastrous discordance. Otherwise, however, the color of this folio is very beautiful. The pink, blue, white, and gray-black are repeated in the flowers and scrolls in the borders, and in the corners sit two brown and two gray-black friars. The man in the initial wearing gray and black is in every respect an impressive figure. The shields of the Duke on the catafalque, discussed above, show *France moderne*[19] whereas *France ancien* appears in the borders.

When composing the group of the Trinity in the *Grandes Heures* (Fig. 230) Pseudo-Jacquemart and his assistants turned to a third miniature originally designed by the Parement Master (Fig. 49). Here only the main figures and the seraphim were utilized; behind them, in the widened space, a great cloth is spread by two angels (executed by still another hand). Since the miniature in the *Très Belles Heures de Notre-Dame* was repainted, as we have remarked above,[20] the copy in the *Grandes Heures* tells us how it originally looked. Pseudo-Jacquemart exploited this folio in the *Très Belles Heures de Notre-Dame* for another purpose. As we have seen, he used the portrait in the border for his own portrait of the Duke on folio 8 (Fig. 219).

Pseudo-Jacquemart's use of compositions and figures of the early 'eighties for miniatures in a manuscript of about 1406 to 1409 is ample proof of his conservatism, but it also tells us something about the nature of his association with Jacquemart. When adopting the Parement Master's scene of the obsequies Pseudo-Jacquemart ignored Jacquemart's more advanced version in the *Brussels Hours* (Fig. 198). This manuscript was, to be sure, no longer in Berry's possession, but one might have expected Jacquemart, as *chef*, to have provided drawings or models of some kind for his obviously limited collaborator. Only in two instances, the building and the landscape already cited (Figs. 221, 222), does Pseudo-Jacquemart seem to draw from Jacquemart's art at the stage of the *Brussels Hours*, not to mention the *Grandes Heures*. One is again led to conclude that the two artists worked independently, in different places.

Of course the Duke's decision to carry on the illumination of the *Très Belles Heures de Notre-Dame* probably gave to all the miniatures in it a certain topical interest and prestige. A unique attempt to imitate the technique and style of the Parement Master as well as his compositions was made by an illuminator around 1410, working in collaboration with a painter from the Berry circle and the Boucicaut Master.[21] The Boucicaut Master, who worked a little for the Duke in 1408–1409, was no doubt familiar with the *Très Belles Heures de Notre-Dame*, but the miniatures by the Parement Master could offer little or nothing to him. His limited contributions to the *Grandes Heures*[22] imply no special interest, either, in the later paintings in this manuscript by the Baptist Master and the Master of the Holy Ghost.

Before turning to other aspects of the *Grandes Heures* it seems appropriate to discuss briefly the late works of Pseudo-Jacquemart, whom we first encountered as early as 1382 in a *Légende dorée* (Fig. 615). In the last decades of the fourteenth century Pseudo-Jacquemart worked mainly for the Duke of Berry, participating in the execution of the *Psalter* and the *Petites Heures*, and his reappearance in the *Grandes Heures* toward 1409 is only one of the signs of his continuous employment by that prince. He illuminated the now battered Evangeliary in the Bibliothèque municipale in Bourges, which was certainly made for Jean de Berry and probably belonged to the Sainte-Chapelle (Fig. 253). The iconography of the Duke, which we discussed in Chapter IV, suggests a date of around 1405 or 1410 (Fig. 493), and the density of the borders as well as the active bears in them seem to draw the manuscript close to the *Grandes Heures* in time. The voluminous stone canopies, powerful as architectural forms, similarly suggest a late date in the career of this conservative painter. The Evangelists themselves, however, are still based on figures current thirty years earlier.

In a second manuscript illuminated for the Duke, a Lectionary that probably was likewise in the

Sainte-Chapelle, Pseudo-Jacquemart collaborated with the Boucicaut atelier, which painted Berry's portrait (Fig. 499). The proximity of this great artist did not leave Pseudo-Jacquemart untouched. In the Lectionary his compositions take on a spatial breadth and a scale quite uncommon to him (Fig. 254). His interiors reflect the ideas of the Boucicaut Master so completely that they will be discussed with the work of that painter in a following volume. Pseudo-Jacquemart's response to his collaborator seems to show that the Evangeliary, which lacks Boucicaut influence, was illuminated before the collaboration on the Lectionary, which probably occurred around 1410–1412.

The kneeling Virgin in the *Coronation* in the Lectionary resembles the corresponding figure in the drawing in the Louvre and in the *Brussels Hours* (Figs. 587, 189); the fall of her drapery is more like the latter, but she is more averted in the manner of the former. While she is crowned by the Trinity, as in the Louvre drawing, the dove does not hover between the first two Persons but issues rather pointedly – and awkwardly – from the Father's mouth.[23]

Though Pseudo-Jacquemart worked mainly for the Duke of Berry several manuscripts illuminated by him or by his assistants have no apparent connection with the prince, though one was produced for, and perhaps in, Bourges. We have cited above three early manuscripts, painted in the 'eighties or early 'nineties,[24] and there are several from the first two decades of the fifteenth century. In one, a Book of Hours of the use of Bourges in the British Museum, Pseudo-Jacquemart painted the *Annunciation*, adopting for it the posture, novel in France, of the Virgin sitting on a cushion on the floor (Fig. 276). As we shall observe in the course of the fuller discussion of this manuscript later in this chapter two illuminators from Northeastern France or even Flanders collaborated with Pseudo-Jacquemart in the execution of the book, and he may have owed to them his new posture in the *Annunciation*. Certainly it appeared rather early there, and it had a greater future in the Netherlands than in France.[25]

Pseudo-Jacquemart employed the lowly Virgin in the *Annunciation* again in a book of prayers that he probably painted around the same time, but the figure looks very different because he drew from another model (Fig. 245).[26] In this instance the round head and full cheeks of the Virgin as well as the curling folds of her drapery point clearly to the Low Countries and especially to the circle of Broederlam. The angel gesturing toward heaven, on the other hand, has descended from the *Petites Heures* (Figs. 94, 130). In this manuscript, which belongs to Count Jean Durrieu, Pseudo-Jacquemart seated another figure humbly on the ground: Anna outside the gate, waiting for Joachim (Fig. 246). The desire for a lively story, always characteristic of the illuminator, led him to represent a dog as well as Joachim responding to the angel. In another miniature, which is spatially advanced for the painter, the bathing of the newborn Virgin is unusually prominent (Fig. 247). Even Anna and her attendants are actors in a little drama, occasioned it seems by the birth pangs of the old woman.

Not far from the time when he was working on the *Grandes Heures* Pseudo-Jacquemart painted an initial in a Lactantius in the British Museum (Fig. 248),[27] and a few miniatures in a Book of Hours in the State Library in Leningrad.[28] In the *Annunciation* in Leningrad the kneeling angel has just disturbed a very elegant standing Virgin, who had been reading (Fig. 255). The halo of the Child in the miniature of the enthroned Madonna in this book shows the rays that began to be popular in French painting around the turn of the century (Fig. 256).[29] The miniature gives us still one more image of the writing Child in the circle of Jacquemart (Fig. 279). The collaborator who painted the *Nativity* in this manuscript, with its strangely hooded and averted Joseph, might have worked fifteen years earlier on one of the Duke of Berry's Bibles (Figs. 259, 617).

The style of the Pseudo-Jacquemart lingers on into the second decade of the century, and it seems probable that the illuminator himself, who began to paint no later than 1378–1380, was still at work in 1412 and even later. A Book of Hours in the British Museum that was illuminated later than the *Belles Heures*, on which one at least of its miniatures depends,[30] has two complex miniatures by the Pseudo-Jacquemart (Figs. 257, 258). The landscape of the *Visitation* derives ultimately from Jacquemart's *Entombment* in the *Brussels Hours*, which Pseudo-Jacequemart had already adapted for the *Annunciation to Joachim and Anna* in the *Grandes Heures* (Fig. 222). The *Annunciation to the Shepherds* has similar sources (Fig. 258). Some qualities of this style are still evident in a representation of the same subject in a Book of Hours in the Walters Gallery (Fig. 262). The miniatures in this manuscript are generally much influenced by the Boucicaut and the Bedford Masters, and the scene of the shepherds would seem to have been executed by a follower of Pseudo-Jacquemart who went on to work with these greater masters.

The style of Pseudo-Jacquemart appears to have radiated earlier into stained glass. A fine bust of an angel in the collection of Monsieur Jean Lafond in Paris clearly reflects his art, grown more robust on the larger scale (Fig. 840). It is noteworthy that the fragment was formerly in the Ponroy collection, Bourges.[31]

2 · THE ORIGINAL MANUSCRIPT

At the beginning of this chapter we spoke briefly of the losses suffered by the *Grandes Heures*. We must now discuss them more fully, to clarify as much as possible the relation to the manuscript of the *Way to Calvary* in the Louvre (Figs. 277, 278). My interest in this painting, which is executed on parchment, was aroused in the 'thirties, shortly after it had entered the Louvre, when I recognized its similarity with the main cycles in the *Brussels Hours* and supposed that it was one of the missing miniatures of the *Grandes Heures*. Often since then, as I explored the relationship, I believed that the proof was in sight – only to discover the contrary shortly thereafter. This account has been written four times (over several years), and it has ended at opposite positions on alternate occasions.

Thanks to the decision of M. Porcher three years ago to remove the *Grandes Heures* from its binding, it has been possible to explore the problem of the losses much more extensively. Some of the questions that this close examination raises are intricate, and even seven-power magnification does not seem to answer all of them. Perhaps microscopic study in a laboratory by a specialist in medieval manuscripts and in parchment would bring us nearer the truth than I have been able to go. Inasmuch as my work has not yielded decisive evidence only an outline is presented in what follows. These observations are supplemented by tables appended to this chapter, which show the manuscript in its present state and as it was originally.

A note on the fly-leaf of the *Grandes Heures* states that the manuscript belonged to King Louis XII. This fact adds to the relevance of some documents published by Delisle half a century ago that refer to payments made by the predecessor of Louis, Charles VIII, for the rebinding of a *Grans Heures* that once belonged to Jean de Berry. The identity of this manuscript with lat. 919 cannot be doubted because in the time of Delisle it still bore the cover given it by Charles VIII.[32] The document that refers to the content of the *Grans Heures* is the following:

> A lui (messire Robert Moreau, chappelain ordinaire du roy), la somme de soixante s. t., pour avoir, ledit jour (7 juillet 1488), couvert en aiz de bois et relyé unes Grans Heures en parchemin, en volume de deux fueilletz la peau, historiees d'environ quarante cinq grans histoires, appellées les HEURES DU FEU DUC JEHAN DE BERRY, et d'icelles Heures avoir timpané toutes les histoires, grandes et petites, et avoir fait environ IIII^{xx} couleures sur le fons d'icelles, et pour papier de Lombardie lysse qu'il a fourny et livré pour servir à mectre sur lesdites histoires, que aussi pour avoir couvert leasdites Heures d'une aulne de veloux cramoisi, cy devant comptée le IIIe jour dudit mois, sur Jehan Estienne, pour ce lad. somme de LX s. t.[33]

Observing that the record refers to 45 'grans histoires' while the only miniatures in the manuscript as it survives that could be called large are the 28, each one column wide, at the beginning of many offices, Delisle inferred that 17 had been lost. He could show where these missing miniatures had been by observing certain gaps in the series of small signatures for the folios that are still visible in some lower margins (see the accompanying chart). These gaps in the sequences of numeration occur before the beginning of each of the offices from Lauds through Compline in the Hours of the Passion, and just before Matins in the Hours of the Holy Ghost. Delisle concluded that if these gaps were produced by the excision of large miniatures, similar miniatures would have been cut from Matins in the Hours of the Passion and from each of the eight Hours of the Virgin, and that the loss of these also would account for precisely the seventeen missing miniatures.

The missing folios contained no text; the miniatures were full-page. The composition of the manuscript can be apprehended most readily by a glance at the chart of the reconstruction that accompanies this chapter. The original *Grandes Heures* was similar, therefore, to the *Brussels Hours*, the first manuscript of its kind and the product, in fact, of the same painter, as the inventories tell us. The versos of most of the large miniatures in the *Brussels Hours* were blank, and in this respect too the paintings in the *Grandes Heures* resembled the earlier book. The *Brussels Hours* is a much smaller manuscript, and the miniatures at the beginning of the offices are not a column wide as in the *Grandes Heures*, but only initials (Fig. 199). In the Hours of the Virgin these initials represent mostly Old Testament antetypes rather than the scenes from the life of the Virgin and her parents that were chosen for the *Grandes Heures*. The scenes in the headpieces of the Hours of the Passion in the *Grandes Heures* show a greater similarity with the subjects of the corresponding initials in the *Brussels Hours*.

Delisle left us with some small problems. He did not tell us what he understood the restorer had done when he had 'timpané toutes les histoires'. Nor did he comment on the eighty colors put on 'le fons d'icelles'. The reference is obscure; certainly the backgrounds of the surviving miniatures are all free of repainting.[34] Delisle's hypothesis of the excision of large miniatures is, however, quite correct. He observed that in place of these miniatures blank sheets of parchment had been inserted, 'à une époque relativement moderne' (Fig. 252). Decisive facts can be added.

Examination of the unbound *Grandes Heures* discloses cuts in many of the folios that faced the large miniatures (8, 18, 24, 28, 31, 34, 41, 65, 67, 81). These vertical cuts are 6 mm., more or less, from the inner edge of the folios. They are visible in Figs. 222 and 223. The knife responsible for these slashes sometimes cut through to a following folio (18-19, 24-25, 41-42). The knife travelled in all but one instance from the front to the back, that is from a recto to a verso and sometimes on to the next folio beyond. This fact would lead one to believe that the large miniatures were painted on rectos because normally a person would choose to cut out a miniature while watching how his knife traveled in relation to it. Since, however, the knife moved along deep in the gutter this argument is probably not binding. The thief, moreover, may have been left-handed. Thus there is no good reason to doubt that, as in the *Brussels Hours*, each large miniature faced a smaller picture and the beginning of an office just below it.

When long ago I concluded that the *Way to Calvary* was by the chief painter of the *Brussels Hours* – an opinion first published by Beenken and Panofsky[35] – I tested the hypothesis that it was one of the missing miniatures from the *Grandes Heures*. I reluctantly abandoned the idea, as I said in 1956, because of the size of the painting, relatively large even for a mammoth Book of Hours, and also because it contained two donors. The presence of donors in a miniature for one Hour of the Passion (Sext) seemed – and still seems – to imply similar figures in the illustrations for the other seven Hours, not to mention the preceding Hours of the Virgin. The inclusion of donors or their families in the historical scenes of Books of Hours is unparalleled in French illumination, and it is indeed uncommon anywhere till the second half of the fifteenth century. The presence of these figures and the size of the painting suggest some other original purpose, and we do know that large miniatures were sometimes hung on the wall.[36] Within a couple of months of the publication of my opinion the view that the *Way to Calvary* did belong to the *Grandes Heures* was expressed by both Carl Nordenfalk and Otto Pächt, who pointed to the rarity of miniatures of such size, the presence of emblems of the Duke (the dogs), and the general conformity of the style with the *Brussels Hours*.[37] Nordenfalk shared my belief that the *Way to Calvary* was painted by the author of the Brussels cycles, Jacquemart, whereas Pächt argued that the *Brussels Hours* was only an inferior reflection of the art of the master of the *Way to Calvary*, who therefore had the better claim to identification with Jacquemart. Pächt tentatively ascribed to this superior painter the initial diptych of the *Brussels Hours* and the drawings on boxwood in the Morgan Library, usually attributed to 'Jacquemart' (Figs. 279, 281-286).

What evidence does close examination of the *Grandes Heures* provide about the candidacy of the painting in the Louvre? We need first a more precise description of the *Way to Calvary* itself. It was executed on parchment and subsequently mounted on canvas, the texture of which detracts from the effectiveness of the painting.[38] The scene is bounded by a narrow gold bar about 2 mm. wide, which in turn is contained by thin black lines at both sides. The folio has been trimmed, and whereas the frame is visible at places along the sides it cannot be seen above, where a small strip of the painting itself has probably been lost. The laboratory of the Louvre reports small traces of the frame along the lower edge, but one would have supposed that here too the present edge running through the legs of a dog and the dress of the donor was not original. What kind of decorated border there may have been, if any, outside the gold frame we cannot ascertain; there is no trace of it.

Within its gold border the *Way to Calvary* measures approximately 379×278 mm. (the distances vary slightly at different points). The folios of the *Grandes Heures*, which differ somewhat from gathering to gathering, measure approximately 395 × 300 mm. They have, of course, been trimmed considerably. The outermost birds, for instance on folio 31, have been partially cut away, but it is difficult to determine precisely how much has been lost. The remains of the binding of 1488, which would help, have been misplaced. The relative size of the *Way to Calvary* would in any event have been exceptional; it would have dwarfed the two columns of text, the outside measurements of which are 258×189 mm. Only the extravagant Rohan Master a decade later introduced miniatures of similar relative size, such as the *Annunciation* in the *Heures de Rohan*.

The original presence in the *Grandes Heures* of miniatures like the *Way to Calvary* seems at first to be confirmed by the presence near the outer edge of five folios of traces of a pair of gray lines that might have rubbed off from the black lines bounding the gold border of a miniature. These five folios, 28, 65, 74, 77, 84, were all preceded by large miniatures, according to the reconstruction of the original manuscript (see table). The gray lines are visible in the reproductions of folios 28 and 65 (Figs. 223, 220). They always appear along the upper or outer edges of the folios, never near the lower or inner. On folio 28 the distance from the inner gray line along the outer edge to the knife-cuts is 290 mm., just about the width of the *Way to Calvary*. The similarity is striking. If the miniature were opposite this folio its inner gold border would have fallen just about opposite the inner side of the inner border of folio 28, that is to say, about 20 mm. from the line of the sewing.

So far all the facts seem, if not positive, at least permissive. Further examination of the manuscript brings only difficulties. On folio 28, for example (Fig. 223), a bird along the upper edge at the right, close to the gray lines, was clearly damaged by pressure. Along the upper and outer edges of numerous folios the parchment has been indented or crimped by pressure, the band that it produced being approximately the width of the gray lines. On folios 37, 61, 81 this indentation occurs opposite large original miniatures, but many folios that bear similar marks were not opposite large miniatures.[39] On a few folios the gray lines are within indentations, and there seems to be a connection between the two. Probably both were produced by the pressure of clamps or a press applied to the folios to flatten them before rebinding; M. Desbrosses, head of the bindery at the Bibliothèque nationale, is inclined to agree. The work was done, for reasons that follow, when the book contained the blank sheets.[40]

The hypothesis that the gray lines were produced by rubbing from the borders of large miniatures is not strengthened by the fact that one of the blank sheets inserted in place of a miniature bears the lines (folio 64 – Fig. 252), and three other such sheets, folios 60, 64, 102, are indented. These blank sheets are in themselves problematic. Some of them seem to me, and to helpful friends, to be pasted onto old stubs, but M. Desbrosses does not share this opinion. Certainly the gray turret that appears at the left margin of folio 64 was painted around the time of the *Grandes Heures*, and if it is on an old stub that constituted a verso it might have been a projection very close to the line of sewing of a building in one of the large miniatures. Jacquemart employed related architectural forms in the *Flagellation* in the *Brussels Hours* (Fig. 193).

Study of the original gatherings of the *Grandes Heures* shows that only in certain instances – folios 27 and 36 or 30 and 33, for instance – could two large miniatures have been painted on the halves of a single sheet ('deux feuillets la peau', as the document of 1488 stated). In almost all other cases the large miniature, painted on a single folio and provided with a small stub to hold the sewing, was inserted into the gathering. These physical findings make quite tenable our hypothesis that Jacquemart worked independently of the 'autres ouvriers' engaged on the manuscript.

Unfortunately the emblems and donors in the *Way to Calvary* do not at the present time seem to offer evidence more compelling than the make-up of the book. Small white dogs were not prized by Jean de Berry alone. The one at the right resembles closely the dog in the *Vatican Bible* (Fig. 178), but a rather similar breed appears also near Queen Isabeau de Bavière in a miniature by the Master of the Cité des Dames.[41] The small figures in the *Way to Calvary* are closely identified with one another, as though they were members of one family. The nearer one wears a golden diadem and a white dress ornamented with golden bands and the kind of stylized 'cufic' shapes that were *à la mode* in France at this time. The figure only partly visible wears a pale green dress decorated with plainer gold bands. In the hair there are traces of gold, perhaps again of a diadem. It is difficult to determine the ages of the women represented, but they are clearly youthful rather than middle-aged. They seem to me to be standing, not kneeling as Pächt said, and identification with either or both of the daughters of Jean de Berry, which that historian proposed, seems to me excluded.[42] In 1409 Bonne was no less than forty-two years old, and Marie was thirty-three or four. Already in 1406 Marie, married to her third husband, no longer allowed her hair to hang in tresses down her neck (Fig. 667). Jeanne de Boulogne, though thirty-two in 1409, would probably not have appeared in this way either. Just about this time the Limbourgs portrayed her as a young woman but with hair bound up and a full crown rather than a diadem (Fig. 518).

If this painting was actually the miniature for Sext the portraits would seem to imply preceding ones in the Hours of the Passion and in the Hours of the Virgin. If such a wholly unprecedented series existed it seems reasonable to suppose that the main members of the Duke's family appeared earlier, and that the two women in the *Way to Calvary*, if relatives, were less close, possibly grandchildren. All this, however, is still speculative.[43]

3 · THE PROBLEM OF JACQUEMART'S LATE WORK

The large miniature in the Louvre, an impressive composition, assumes special importance if it is a candidate for a place in the *Grandes Heures* (Fig. 277). Since we lack definite physical or documentary evidence we are thrown back on style. In this sphere some extrapolation is required. We must estimate the compatibility of the style of the painting with what seems predictable for Jacquemart de Hesdin around 1409. Unfortunately the work is in poor condition, damaged especially by damp. The colors have faded or changed, as in the case of azurite turning green, or even disappeared. Ultraviolet photography indicates markedly, and infrared only somewhat less, green patches on Christ and the Virgin that are the consequence of retouching (Fig. 278). Some of the faces and especially the eyes have been 'strengthened'; this repainting is most conspicuous in the head of Christ on Veronica's kerchief and in the heads of the men wearing pointed hats.

Originally blue was prominent, as it is in the *Brussels Hours*: this color in varying values covered the dress of Christ, the stout man above him, the 'bishop' alongside, St. John, the Virgin, the foremost soldier in the procession, the tunic of Veronica, the woman in the lower left corner, and – again as in the *Brussels Hours* – the sky. The reds, originally less numerous, have also suffered more than the blue. The three shields in the upper right were red, as were the dress of the woman holding the child's arm and of the three Jews near the gate, the tunic of Judas, part of the cuirass of the averted soldier, his stockings, and both the stockings and the mantle of the soldier to the right. The nearer masonry was gray, the roofs light gray, with a ridge and gable of blue – a color much used on the roofs of the *Brussels Hours*. The more distant buildings were brown and rose. The large tree, now gray, was green, and the hills show greenish and gray lights on brown. The oxidization of numerous areas of silver has further altered the appearance of the painting. Silver covered several helmets, as it did those in the *Betrayal* in the *Brussels Hours* (Fig. 191). It appeared also on some of the armor (notably of the mace-bearer), the tips of the three uppermost spears, and apparently also the sword and helmet of the soldier in the right foreground.

Despite losses and alteration the color of the painting in the Louvre is very similar to that of the *Way to Calvary* and other miniatures in the *Brussels Hours*. Some forms point to a later date. The haloes of the *Brussels Hours* are the disks normal in French painting up to about 1400; those of the *Way to Calvary* consist of golden rays, and they thus conform with the newer convention visible in panels and manuscripts in the early fifteenth century (Figs. 695, 832).[44] These 'radiant' haloes, which probably derive from Simonesque models,[45] began to be used also around 1409 by the Limbourgs, who were in touch with Jacquemart at this time and who began the *Belles Heures* just as he finished the *Grandes Heures*.[46] The rays of Christ in the Louvre miniature, in conformity with the new convention, form a cross.

Because of trimming and damage it is now difficult to see that several forms extend onto the narrow gold border. The shoulder of the mace-bearer, the sword of the foremost soldier, two banners at the right, a molding of the gate and even the entire battlement all lap onto the gold (Fig. 277). These forms occur at various depths in the perspective space. In a painting in which spatial extension is important, and in which the illusory space was bounded by a very narrow border, one would not have expected such inconsistencies. Whether these forms extended beyond the gold frame also we cannot know, because the miniature has been trimmed.

The *Way to Calvary* contains other inconsistencies, the consequence of the immaturity of certain ideas and perhaps of the exigencies of the production of a large cycle of paintings. The almost heraldic confrontation of the little white dogs does not harmonize with a composition in which all the figures are in motion, and the same is true a fortiori of the donors to the left of them, who likewise are set in the landscape. Their attitude of prayer is, to be sure, repeated (though more freely) by a woman in the group above them, but it is precisely the degree of their involvement in the composition that creates the problem. The hand of the child, just behind them and apparently a little deeper in space, nevertheless crosses over the tresses of the nearer donor. Yet these two donors, so closely related to surrounding forms, are in perfect profile and, even if very youthful, unnaturally small in scale. Possibly the donors and the two dogs, evidently emblems, were not envisaged at the beginning, but the infrared photograph gives no support to such a hypothesis.

The dynamics of the composition raise questions also about the original purpose of the painting. The group of figures, rather open at the left, becomes dense at the right, and the strong momentum that is generated strikes hard against the narrow gold frame. The impact is somewhat mediated, to be sure, by some soldiers above who face in the opposite direction, and the mace-bearer as well as three heads below him turn back toward the center of the group. One soldier just inside the frame, however, marches resolutely forward, and his sword, as we have observed, overlaps the border. The powerful, unbalanced impulses toward the right prove that the painting did not originally stand alone. It could have formed part of a diptych, though its subject would be unusual. It could have been on a left-hand folio, and indeed it would have occupied just this place if it belonged to the *Grandes Heures*. It is, however, proportionately so large for that book that the movement would have plunged deep into the binding.

These references to the original context of the *Way to Calvary* and to some of its artistic limitations are of course relevant to the question of its author. When we compare the *Way to Calvary* in the Louvre with the representation of the same subject in the *Brussels Hours* (Fig. 194) we recognize immediately that the latter contains figures such as the averted soldier or the thieves that are less well articulated than any figures in the Louvre composition. We have seen, however, that the miniatures in Brussels vary considerably in quality, presumably because of the participation of assistants. The strongest compositions and the better figures have given us a clear idea of the capacities of the *chef d'atelier*. Is the beauty of the tender, gracious Mary of the *Visitation* (Fig. 183) surpassed by any figure in the *Way to Calvary*? Are not the structure and complex movement of Christ in the *Flagellation* (Fig. 193) at least as impressive as the torsion of Christ in the Louvre painting? When evaluating the chief painter of the Brussels cycles we must keep in mind the superb soaring angel of the *Annunciation*, the touching response of the Virgin to the startling visitation, and the rare unification of the two diverse figures in a broad diagonal design (Fig. 182). And in the Brussels *Way to Calvary* itself there are subtleties that imply not only the inventiveness and the supervision of an outstanding artist but also his participation in the painting.

The *Way to Calvary* in Brussels as well as the one in the Louvre owes much to Simone's panel (Fig. 675) but the narrative differs from it in significant respects. Only in Brussels is Christ framed laterally by loving rather than by hateful people. In Simone's painting, in accordance with Sienese tradition, a soldier forcefully bars the Virgin from Christ (Fig. 675). The painter of the Brussels miniature has moved her directly behind her son, and in front of him Simone's rather brutal henchmen are replaced by a youth who turns sympathetically toward Christ. The two figures are joined also by the shadow that the head of Christ casts on the boy's shoulder. This fundamental change transforms into an elegy the tragic contrasts of emotion in Simone's painting. The different mood is maintained consistently throughout the Brussels miniature. The Virgin no longer flings her arms towards Christ but claps a restraining hand to her face. The tumult in the procession is diminished, and the strongest surge of forward movement is transferred to the three prancing boys introduced into the foreground.

It is true that this general relaxation in the Brussels *Way to Calvary* becomes, in figures such as the three in the right foreground, empty limpness. But the painting in the Louvre is not everywhere superior. Witness the same soldier, for instance, who appears in both miniatures holding his sword in front of him. In the Brussels miniature his hand grasps the hilt with the firmness required by the weight, in the Louvre only loosely. The relationship of the procession to the city is very different in the two paintings. In the work in Brussels, which is more open and panoramic, the buildings trace an ascending line as a kind of counterpoint to the descent of the figures. The city-gate in the Louvre miniature serves as an anchor for the falling lines and forms of the composition. Its massiveness is well calculated for this purpose but its position in space and its leftward turn disconnect it from the design of the figures.

Compared to the miniature in Brussels the one in the Louvre shows in some respects what one might have expected of a penetrating student of Sienese painting after further contemplation of his chosen models. He acquired a somewhat better control of organic movement. The animation of the procession has increased, yet the group is more unified. The cross, as in Simone's panel, serves as a sort of compositional spine, having attained approximately the fifteen feet ascribed to it in the *Meditationes Vitae Christi* and other texts.[47] The painter has indeed outdone Simone by giving each of the thieves a large cross also; perhaps here he was inspired by other Italian models such as a miniature by Niccolò da Bologna in a Missal that was acquired by Jean de Berry.[48] When adopting Simone's large cross the painter of the Louvre miniature also took from his great Sienese predecessor the gesture of Simon the Cyrenean supporting it.

This more developed articulation and geometric design are not achieved without sacrifices. While Christ is more athletic in the Louvre miniature his countenance is less dolorous and his posture less pathetic than in Brussels. The impressive effect in the painting in the Louvre of inexorable movement toward Golgotha is achieved partly by crowding the figures and piling them high in the space. When designing the *Way to Calvary* in Brussels the painter was more concerned with the sweep of landscape and the portrayal of a large part of Jerusalem, from which Christ and his captors had come. Even the restoration of the small strip lost at the bottom of the Louvre miniature would not produce a spatial interval between the figures and the frame comparable to that in Brussels.

Perhaps deliberately as a contrast to the closed, compact composition the painter of the miniature in the Louvre has opened the space at one point, placing over the hill at the horizon an unnaturally large tree with the figure of Judas pendant from a branch. Before the blue sky at the right a devil flies away with his soul. Still further away, but very conspicuous against the horizon, a man half-hidden by the hill looks up at the traitor, raising his right arm precisely as does one of the shepherds in the *Annunciation to the Shepherds* in the *Brussels Hours* (Fig. 185). The suicide of Judas was not infrequently represented in medieval art either independently or in relation to such scenes as his pact with the High Priests,[49] or in the Agony in the Garden. Indeed the pendant Judas had already appeared in the *Grandes Heures* in the initial below the *Agony* (Fig. 220), but the figure seems never before to have appeared in the scene of Christ bearing the cross. In the initial both arms of Judas are, as usual earlier, extended downwards. The painter of the Louvre miniature on the other hand found a more expressive model in the *Bréviaire de Belleville* that had only recently entered the Duke's collection (after 1399, in any event) and that had stirred the admiration of his illuminators in other respects, as we have observed (Fig. 260). This Judas, conceived by Pucelle as an image of Despair opposite Hope, is very expressive, clutching the rope with one hand while groping with the other.[50] And just as the figure in the Louvre *Way to Calvary* originated in a manuscript in the Duke's collection so the idea of putting the figure into a new context, the scene of the Way to Calvary, was transmitted to another manuscript in the collection, or at least to a manuscript that the Limbourgs were just about to begin for the Duke (Fig. 261).[51] In the *Belles Heures* Judas once again clutches the rope with his right hand. The transmission of this figure provides one more example of the significance for the art of the time of the patronage and the collection of the Duke.

The prominence of the distant Judas in the Louvre miniature is increased by the fact that the suicide becomes the focus of a second, subsidiary event. Numerous soldiers and bystanders in the uppermost row of figures turn to look at him. Some of these figures are very similar to men who gaze at Christ in the Brussels *Crucifixion* (Fig. 195). There one may find prototypes for the old man nearest the gate and his companion represented in lost profile. In the Brussels *Crucifixion* a spectator flings up his arm like the man over the hill in the Louvre miniature; we have already observed that this gesture is used elsewhere in the *Brussels Hours* (Fig. 185).[52]

In attempting to understand the nature of the relationship of the two paintings of the Way to Calvary we must remember that the Louvre example resembles Simone's composition with regard to the long cross supported by Simon, the turn of Christ's head, and the posture of the averted soldier,[53] whereas the miniature in Brussels preserves Simone's solicitous St. John and Simone's cityscape, including an octagonal church or baptistery. Some Italian motifs that are not Simonesque appeared first in Brussels, notably the thickset man above Christ; he is very similar to the stout figure in the Brussels *Crucifixion* whose origins we have discussed above.[54] On the other hand another Italian model is implied by the fine group, absent in Brussels, of the woman holding a child's arm in the left corner of the Louvre miniature.[55]

To those aspects of the painting in the Louvre that point to a somewhat later date should probably be added the lack of a green earth underpainting. This conspicuous feature of the Italianate technique of the *Brussels Hours* has been abandoned for a blonder palette. The change conforms with one trend of painting in the early fifteenth century, led by the Coronation Master, the Épître Master, and the Boucicaut Master. On the other hand the space and perspective of the painting in the Louvre do not represent a significant advance beyond the *Brussels Hours*; they might even be judged regressive. The lack of an interval in the foreground, the terraced figures, the steadily ascending plane, all disclose no further study of Trecento panels and certainly not of the works of the major new painters who were conspicuous in Paris by 1405, the Limbourgs and the Boucicaut Master. If, then, the *Way to Calvary* was made for the *Grandes Heures* we are driven to two alternatives. Either Jacquemart became conservative in the second lustrum of the century, a posture that for him would be novel and surprising, or he began work on this book immediately after completion of that earlier manuscript. It is even then not easy to suppose that the subject of Christ carrying the Cross would have been painted early in the enterprise.

The compositional conservatism of the *Way to Calvary* in the Louvre is dramatized by the chance survival of two other paintings that must be connected with the late style of Jacquemart. They appear in a small Book of Hours, use of Bourges, in the British Museum.[56] In the *Entry into Jerusalem*, the more important of the two miniatures, the similarities with the *Brussels Hours* are pervasive (Fig. 263). The two men at the right are placed like Pilate and his companion in the *Flagellation* (Fig. 193), the boy spreading the mantle resembles a shepherd (Fig. 185), and the mantles of the apostles recall those of the prophets in grisaille in the *Presentation in the Temple* (Fig. 187). In simplicity of outline and flatness of plane these small prophets are very similar to the figures in the *Entry*. The latter are only around three centimeters high, and we may therefore infer that their simplified character is bound up to a degree with their scale. The small scale may have affected the colors too, which are paler but still clearly related to those in the *Brussels Hours* – yellow, blue, pink, with a patch of strong red on the mantle of Christ. It seems very significant that the sides of the buildings in the city that do not catch the light are gray and dusky,[57] like the similar structures in miniatures in Brussels such as the *Way to Calvary* (Fig. 194). These buildings in both the *Entry* and the Brussels miniatures are rendered by an identical open brushwork, and the stippling in the landscape and the sky of the *Entry* may be found in the *Brussels Hours* also, for instance in the shaded wall in the *Flagellation* (Fig. 193). The touch of the painter is similar in both works.

In the *Entry* the lighting is more unified, and this is only one of the qualities that indicates a later stage in the development of Jacquemart's style. Though a repoussoir was introduced in the *Annunciation to the Shepherds* in Brussels (Fig. 185), in the *Entry* it overlaps some of the main figures. The concern of Jacquemart in the *Brussels Hours* with an architectural setting that would be at once more imposing and more natural in scale is manifested in the *Entry* by the great city, the upper part of which even continues behind the frame. The plane of the foreground rises rather steeply, in the manner of the *Brussels Hours*, but then the city, projected in a remarkable perspective, approximately two-point, continues inward on a plane parallel to that of the main figures. Beyond this impressive space rise two green hills, one overlapping the other and carrying the eye to the most distant horizon we have hitherto observed.

For a similar command of space and perspective one must turn to the paintings of the Limbourgs and the Boucicaut Master toward the end of the first decade of the century. A small hill in the foreground overlapping figures was commonly employed by the Boucicaut Master, and models for the radiant sun introduced into the *Entry* were visible in the miniatures by the same painter from around 1407 in the *Boucicaut Hours*. All this gives us an approximate date for the painting of the *Entry*. What does the rest of the book tell us? The miniature is the only work by this painter in the manuscript and we cannot be absolutely certain that it was not added somewhat later than the others. In the present state of the book it is the only miniature in the last section of the text, which consists of readings from the gospels and prayers to the Virgin and to the Saints.[58] This section is separated by three blank though ruled folios from what precedes it, but its borders, script, and ink are no different, and the other miniatures, though by different hands, come from the circle of Jacquemart. The remarkable *Crucifixion* is by his collaborator in the *Petites Heures*, the Trinity Master, and several miniatures were executed by Pseudo-Jacquemart and assistants. The locus of this constellation of illuminators is supported by the fact that the use of the text is Bourges.

The extraordinary composition of the *Crucifixion* has been discussed above (Fig. 264).[59] Its masterful control of hills receding to a distant horizon parallels in pure landscape the accomplishment in the cityscape of the *Entry*. The orderly succession of the intersecting planes is maintained by differentiation of hue: the plateau is pale green, the valley is tan, the further hill is gray-green, and the mountain at the right is brown. While the distant castle, trees, and figures are less distinctly rendered, the sense of atmospheric perspective is limited. The sky is a flat blue, but toward the right a luminous white cloud floats in front of it. This small cloud is apparently present not because of the requirements of the subject but simply as an incidental natural phenomenon, and as such it is one of the first in Western painting. The earliest dated appearance of phenomena of this kind seems to be in the *Dialogues of Pierre Salmon* of 1409.[60] The cloud in the *Crucifixion*, like the plateau composition, the perspective, and the incidental mule-driver in the distance, implies the thought of a major master, and he can be none other than Jacquemart de Hesdin.

The close relationship to Jacquemart is demonstrated also by the presence of Pseudo-Jacquemart and the sources from which he drew. The latter had, indeed, pride of place in the manuscript as the illuminator of the first miniature in the Hours of the Virgin (Fig. 276). He preserved the kind of design the Passion Master employed for the folios of the *Petites Heures*, and he introduced two music-making angels in the *bas-de-page*. The one playing the psaltery is an exact copy, except for the shift of a wing, of the very beautiful angel on the base of the Madonna's throne in the *Brussels Hours* (Fig. 181). The Virgin seated on a cushion on the floor in the *Annunciation* is a novelty in the early fifteenth century in France, and although Pseudo-Jacquemart employed the figure once again (Fig. 245) the conception was probably not his.[61] The motive was originally disseminated by Simone Martini, but the enclosure of the two figures in a simple interior was probably conceived in the later Trecento in North Italy and perhaps transmitted to Pseudo-Jacquemart by the *Annunciation* in the *Très Belles Heures de Notre-Dame*.[62] The *Brussels Hours* provided, indirectly through a drawing, still another figure for Pseudo-Jacquemart; Elizabeth in the *Visitation* was adopted, with some changes, for the corresponding miniature in Yates Thompson 37, executed by an assistant (Fig. 265).

The other miniatures in Pseudo's style, painted by equally inept hands, seem to disclose nothing significant,[63] and the three miniatures by the workshop of the Master of Luçon only show this style once again in the circle of Jean de Berry (Fig. 267). The *chef* himself worked for the Duke's daughter, Marie, in 1406 (Fig. 667), and around this time he produced a Pontifical for the Bishop of Luçon that passed to the Duke (Fig. 268).[64] Yates Thompson 37 contains, however, other miniatures of much greater interest. One is a *Madonna of Humility* of unprecedented design in the North, based on a Madonna by Ambrogio Lorenzetti, either a surviving work or a lost one perhaps then visible in France (Figs. 269, 698). So much of the imposing Italian group has been transmitted to the small miniature that the identity of the illuminator earlier escaped me.[65] Even now the reader, relying only on reproductions without color, may doubt the assertion that the same master painted, for All Saints, a group of figures huddled together on the floor (Fig. 272). The difference between these two miniatures is not of hand but of model, which for the saints was Flemish rather than Italian. The illuminator is more recognizable in a *Trinity*, which repeats the composition of this subject on folio 137 verso of the *Petites Heures* (Figs. 271, 127).[66] He paints swarthy faces, is fond of yellow-brown, and on the lining of the mantles in the *Trinity* as well as in the *Madonna* he uses a unique kind of green gold.

This master played a prominent part in the illumination because it was he who undertook the portrait of the donor. Shown in prayer before the Madonna, he wears a scarlet *houppelande* with high collar of the kind Jean de Berry preferred from around 1405, and indeed the figure has been tentatively identified as the Duke.[67] This hypothesis is incorrect but there is additional evidence to place the manuscript in the Duke's circle and to date it. Whereas *All Saints* is full of Flemish echoes (Fig. 272) *Pentecost* was actually painted by a Flemish illuminator from the atelier that worked on the *Très Belles Heures de Notre-Dame* between about 1405 and 1409 (Fig. 266). When I first saw this miniature, with its deep brown and blue colors, I suspected it had been added, just as Hulin de Loo dated the similar miniatures in the *Très Belles Heures de Notre-Dame* after 1413, as we have seen.[68] It appears, however, on a folio containing the same border as other folios in the manuscript, and the peculiar facial types affected *All Saints* and other miniatures (Fig. 272). It would in any event not be plausible to suppose that spaces for miniatures were left unfilled in this little Book of Hours, and that the owner asked each of the authors of new styles who appeared in Bourges to add a miniature.

Everything points to the fact that the Book of Hours was painted between 1405 and 1410 for a member of Jean de Berry's court. It holds a mirror to the kaleidoscopic sequence of artistic events in that circle. The painter of the *Madonna of Humility*, of *All Saints*, and of the *Trinity*, the chief newcomer among the illuminators of the Book of Hours, is such a chameleon that his hand is not easily recognized. Thus though I observed long ago that virtually an identical *Madonna of Humility* appeared in another Book of Hours in the British Museum[69] I did not see that it was painted by the same master, or at least by the same atelier (Fig. 270). The use of grisaille and of a star-strewn background, both frequent in this manuscript, threw me off the scent. Yates Thompson 37 was the earlier of the two miniatures of the Madonna because, for one thing, the tassel of the cushion at the right hangs down, as a tassel should, while the one at the left is raised to accommodate the lectern, whereas in Harley 2952 the same tassel is meaninglessly suspended in air.

The cushion itself, to be sure, cannot be said to be firmly supported in either miniature. Still, the borders in Harley 2952 appear to be later, and the representation of the Coronation in this manuscript is an abbreviated version of the *Coronation* in Yates Thompson 37.

Where color is used in Harley 2952 it is similar to that of the related miniatures in Yates Thompson 37, and the linings of mantles are golden. The haloes of both manuscripts show black lines and little crosses between the cusps, and the cross in Christ's halo folds over the bands at the outer rim (Figs. 270, 271, 273, 274). The compact pattern of folds over the knees of the Virgin in the *Flight* in Harley 2952 (Fig. 275) and the repoussoir in *St. Christopher* confirm what the stars suggested: that the painter had been impressed by the work of the Boucicaut Master. The wild drapery of St. Christopher, however, implies another source. Together with the grisaille it points toward a relationship with the Master of the Berry Apocalypse (Fig. 843), and it is a reflection of the more agitated style that rises in France in the second decade of the century.

Though the Madonna of Humility attained popularity in France in the early fifteenth century[70] our painter outdid all his contemporaries in devotion to the subject. He introduced it before prayers to the Virgin no less than three times in Harley 2952.[71] For this he earned, it seems to me, the title of Master of the Humility Madonnas. He was quite familiar with the original Simonesque type (Fig. 634), revising it, however, in one basic respect (Fig. 274). In conformity with the early paintings of the subject in Metz (Fig. 549, 550), and with the interest in nudity in the early fifteenth century, he represented the Child without clothes. He represented him nude again in the same manuscript in the more formal image of the Madonna enthroned. This group seems to reflect another aspect of a Lorenzettian original more closely than did the *Madonna of Humility*. The posture of the Child, and especially the juxtaposition of his cheek, is quite like Ambrogio's great Massa *Madonna* (Fig. 698). The Madonna's left hand grasps the rump of the Child as it does in Ambrogio's S. Francesco *Madonna*. It is a striking symptom of the time and of the Berry milieu that this minor painter should be so knowing about the great Sienese masters, and that he should transfer to miniatures only about three inches high figures and motives contrived for monumental altarpieces.

Study of Yates Thompson 37 and its relation to Harley 2952 has yielded much evidence to show that the *Entry into Jerusalem* and the *Crucifixion* were painted between about 1405 and 1409 or possibly even as late as 1412. The precise date is not so important as the fact that both disclose new ideas of landscape and perspective that are most convincingly traced to Jacquemart. They are entirely consistent with aspirations manifested in the *Brussels Hours*. The *Crucifixion* was, to be sure, executed by the Trinity Master, and the brush of Jacquemart himself cannot be detected with assurance in the *Entry*, but the latter especially is better understood as a reflection of his late work – he was, we recall, still alive in 1413 – than a development beyond it by an otherwise unknown follower. If this is true the difficulties of placing the *Way to Calvary* in 1408–1409 as part of the *Grandes Heures* are obvious. If the painting in the Louvre really belonged to that manuscript, which is indeed quite possible, some paths still remain open for the avoidance of contradictory evidence. The *Entry into Jerusalem* may be later than it has seemed, or it may be the work of a follower with new conceptions. The painting in the Louvre might conceivably have been one of the first miniatures Jacquemart painted for the *Grandes Heures*, which

T

could have been begun around 1403, when Jean de Berry gave the *Brussels Hours* to Philippe le Hardi.

Our hypothesis that Jacquemart was a painter and not an artist who specialized in the book seems strongly supported by the fact that when he needed a real illuminator as a collaborator, to do the initials for instance in the *Brussels Hours*, he or the Duke chose a man who had not learned to paint in his style and who was obviously not a member of his workshop. The borders and the smaller miniatures in the *Grandes Heures* were allocated similarly to Pseudo-Jacquemart, to the Boucicaut Master, and to other illuminators working in styles different from his and whom he evidently had not formed. On the other hand the painter or painters who helped to execute his own compositions in the *Brussels Hours* were assistants trained to the manner. This group probably included the Trinity Master and the author of the *Entry into Jerusalem*, both of whom rarely appeared in manuscripts. Perhaps they normally worked with Jacquemart on panels or on the wall.

Such hypotheses are also supported by the drawings in the Morgan Library, one of which was discussed in a preceding chapter (Fig. 279).[72] Most of these superb drawings, in silverpoint on six lightly sized boxwood panels, would seem to be what the first one, the *Madonna with the Writing Christ Child*, has been proved to be – a record of a work that interested the draftsman and that he copied for future use. The figures are exquisitely finished, and the artist may have intended them also as portable demonstrations to show future employers and others what he could do. The *patrons* that the painter John of Holland said Jacquemart's valet had stolen at Poitiers in 1398 may have been very similar in nature.[73] The Morgan drawings too seem to have been the property of a painter rather than an illuminator; the carnival figures on 2 verso, with two 'wild men', normally belong to the sphere of secular murals or tapestries rather than to the book.[74]

The three standing figures on 2 verso, like the enthroned *Madonna*, are well placed within their fields (Fig. 283). Most of the busts, on the other hand, are placed high, either because the artist intended to extend them at some time, or more probably to leave room for a second row of heads that he actually never added (Fig. 282). We may see such a second row on one of the panels in a comparable book by the contemporary Netherlandish painter Jaques Daliwe.[75] At least one of the six Morgan panels (back cover) bears drawings by a different hand; the youthful king at the right is in fact a mediocre copy of the head at the extreme left on 1 recto (Fig. 281). The retouching on other surfaces, conspicuous on 2 verso (Fig. 282), may be the work of this hand. It is difficult to be certain of the authorship of those panels (3 recto, 3 verso, 4 verso) that contain figures in an earlier style (Figs. 284–286). The artist may be the same, possessing the capacity to 'thin down' his style when copying works of a more linear character. Certainly two manners are apparent in such forms as the kneeling man and the tree at the side of the seated woman on folio 3 (Fig. 284). Whereas she is clearly a figure of the earlier fourteenth century the forms at the right belong to the advanced style on other folios (Figs. 279, 281-283). They might, of course, have been inserted on a surface that bore an earlier figure.

The drawing of the *Madonna* has hitherto always been connected with the *Madonna* of the Brussels diptych, and it as well as the other drawings have therefore been ascribed to the alleged author of the diptych, Beauneveu[76] or more recently Jacquemart.[77] They have consequently sometimes been dated, with the diptych, in the 'eighties.[78] Although the two figures of Mary do resemble one another in softness of texture, luminosity, and to a degree even in facial type the similarity is due in part to the accident that they are both grisailles and also to their common iconography. But even with regard to composition we have learned from the newly discovered miniature once in Barcelona (Fig. 280) that the model of the Morgan drawing was not the Brussels *Madonna* but another, lost one. Perhaps this work was conceived by Jacquemart; certainly the solid round head of the Child in the Morgan drawing shows a striking resemblance to the Child in Jacquemart's own revision of the diptych in the *Brussels Hours* (Fig. 181).

Two details indicate that the model of the drawing and the Barcelona miniature was a work of around 1400. The halo of the Child consists of a faintly outlined disk and more salient cruciform rays, a form we have observed in the *Way to Calvary* in the Louvre, and which became common in the early fifteenth century. In the second place the Virgin wears her mantle folded back on her head, uncovering much of her hair, in the manner of numerous Virgin Marys of the early fifteenth century, in for example the *Visitation, Hours of the Maréchal de Boucicaut*. The Morgan *Madonna* would therefore not be much earlier than around 1400, and the period 1400–1405 would appear to be the most likely date for the closely related drawings on folios 1-2 verso (Figs. 281-283).

This date is interesting in view of the fact that in volume and luminosity the figures in the drawings resemble the Louvre *Way to Calvary* more than the main miniatures in the *Brussels Hours*.[79] The drawings seem, however, rather less Italianate than Jacquemart's miniature, the strokes of the pencil seeking the subtlest nuances of light and texture and less penetrating in the analysis of structure. Of course judgment is rendered more difficult because the *Way to Calvary* is poorly preserved and not comparable with the exquisitely finished drawings. It seems clear to me, however, that the drawings were made in the circle of Jacquemart, or, more precisely formulated, that the similarity with his work is greater than with any other surviving miniature or panel painting. The drawings show no special resemblance with the few small extant French panels in the Louvre (Fig. 695), in Troyes (Fig. 694), and in Berlin.[80] They are somewhat closer to the large tondo in the Louvre, probably by Malouel around 1400 (Fig. 832).[81]

Apart from preparatory indications of compositions in manuscripts drawings by French artists of the period are exceedingly rare. It is very odd that the two most impressive that have survived should be the work of known painters. Scholars agree that the wonderful *Miracle of Bethesda* in Braunschweig is by the Rohan Master,[82] who painted at least one panel. An impressive drawing of three Madonnas in Basel seems to me identifiable with a known master also (Fig. 830).[83] It has been attributed to the circle of Jacquemart[84] and to Broederlam,[85] but the sweeping rhythms and the great attenuation of some forms are foreign to the work of those masters.[86] The long folds of the mantle in the two lateral Madonnas, the thin arms and spidery fingers are, however, encountered again in two panels of a series that Charles Sterling has recently proved, in a masterly study, was executed between 1390 and 1395 by Jean de Beaumetz, painter of Philippe le Hardi, and a collaborator (Fig. 831).[87] In the panels Beaumetz proves, moreover, that he commands more than one figural canon. While Christ in one panel is a lean, marvellously graceful figure, he is shorter and less rhetorical in the other. This same range may be seen even within the panel in the Cleveland Museum, where the head and body of the kneeling Carthusian are as broad as the Madonna and Child at the center of the drawing. The existence of this variability in one pictorial field supports the ascription of the drawing to the same master, for there the central figures, and indeed all three representations of the Child, are broad and heavy.

The heads wave in the panels as in the two lateral Madonnas; the problems of foreshortening presented by their turning and tilting are met in a similar fashion. The eyes are often rolled left or right and they are unusually small, covered by the same puffy lids. The flesh of the face and lips has a texture that is normally absent in the Italianate styles of Jacquemart and other masters in the circle of Jean de Berry. Not that Beaumetz himself had failed to study the painting of Simone and the Sienese; without such models as the *Crucifixion* in Antwerp, with its searching drawing of the body, the joints, and the kneecap, his Christ would surely have been different (Fig. 674).

Like Jacquemart, Beaumetz came from the region of Northeast France or the Low Countries. He developed his art in France through study of Italian painting, in which Philippe le Hardi had been interested already in 1373, when he called the painter Jean d'Arbois from Lombardy to his court.[88] Beaumetz was a parallel figure to Jacquemart, though he belonged to an earlier generation and his assimilation of Italian ideas was far more limited. He died in 1396 after twenty-one years of service with the Duke of Burgundy and his successor, Jean Malouel, much impressed by him, brought his style remarkably close to that of Simone Martini in the tondo (probably his) in the Louvre (Fig. 832). Still, even here there are traces of the physicality of Flemish painting that are scarcely visible in the art of Jacquemart. The ideals of what we may call Northeastern art were maintained at the court of Burgundy by the presence of Sluter; the painters as well as the sculptors were impressed by his wonderful statues. Malouel even had the experience of coloring some of them,[89] and the power and animation of his Berlin *Madonna* of around 1410 reflect his contemplation of the work of his great contemporary.[90]

APPENDIX A

TABLE OF PAINTERS OF THE 'GRANDES HEURES'

I. JACQUEMART DE HESDIN
perhaps originally between the present folios 71 and
72, *Way to Calvary* (Louvre).

II. PSEUDO-JACQUEMART AND ASSISTANTS
folios 1, 1v., 2, 2v., 3, 3v., 4, 4v., 5, 5v., 6, 6v., 8, 18,
24, 28, 31, 34, 37, 41, 45, 53, 56, 61, 65, 67, 70, 74,
77, 81, 86, 89, 93, 94, 97, 98, 106.

III. BOUCICAUT WORKSHOP AND FOLLOWERS
folio 1v. most of vegetation
2 bare trees
2v. most of vegetation
3 Virgin and most of vegetation
3v. figures in upper frieze and most of vegetation
4 figures in upper frieze and most of vegetation
5 vegetation lower left
5v. vegetation lower left
18v. secondary initial
19v. secondary initial
31 two secondary initials
37 initials
70 initials, in part
74 except Magdalen and a few other figures
81 main initial
84 Descent into Limbo (Boucicaut workshop)
and Noli Me Tangere
89 main initial
93 main initial
97 main initial
98 main initial
100 St. Gregory dictating to a scribe (Boucicaut
workshop) and St. Gregory reading

Assistants working in a style related to that of the
Boucicaut Master made minor contributions to other
folios, occasionally painting on a design that seems to
have been provided by the Pseudo-Jacquemart. The
drolleries on 8v. through 15v. were executed by an
assistant of Pseudo-Jacquemart. This style appears
occasionally on the following folios. From fol. 53 on
most of the drolleries were painted in a style more
closely related to that of the Boucicaut Master. The two
styles still intermingle to a degree, even on fols. 98-99
that are two halves of one sheet.

Marked changes in the design of the border frames occur
on fols. 53 and 86.

IV. BEDFORD MASTER
folio 96 St. Peter leading the Duke and others into
Paradise; initial (Duke praying)

V. EGERTON WORKSHOP
folio 1 tree at lower left
folio 6v. man killing pig and tree at lower left.

APPENDIX B

'GRANDES HEURES' *Gatherings, Inserted Sheets, and Missing Miniatures*

Missing full-page miniatures in italics. The single sheets, blank on both sides, that were inserted to replace them are indicated by ★.

		EXISTING MINIATURES IN TEXT-COLUMN	SIGNATURES OF FOLIOS
I-II	Flamel inscription on I (which is pasted onto stub of II)		
1-6	CALENDAR		
	HOURS OF THE VIRGIN, through 42		
	{*Annunciation* (Matins) ★7		
8-15		8. Rejection of Joachim's offering	
16-25			
	{*Visitation* (Lauds) ★17		
		18. Annunciation to Joachim and Anna	
	{*Nativity* (Prime) ★23		
		24. Meeting at Golden Gate	
26-37			
	{*Annunciation to Shepherds* (Tierce) ★27		
		28. Birth of Virgin	
	{*Adoration of Magi* (Sexte) ★30		
		31. Presentation of Virgin in Temple	
	{*Presentation of Christ in Temple* (None) ★33		
		34. Angel brings food to Virgin in Temple	
	{*Flight into Egypt* (Vespers) ★36		
		37. Marriage of Virgin	
38-44			
	{*Coronation of Virgin* (Compline) ★40		
		41. Marriage at Cana	

(43 and 44 are blank sheets, but not separate, and they were ruled. 44v. was ruled, but the lines were partly erased.)

45-52	PENITENTIAL PSALMS		
		45. David in prayer	
53-59			
	HOURS OF THE CROSS	53. Crucifixion	

	EXISTING MINIATURES IN TEXT-COLUMN	SIGNATURES OF FOLIOS

HOURS OF THE HOLY GHOST   56. Pentecost
(an original blank sheet between present 58 and 59 cut out and lost)
HOURS OF THE PASSION
(61-85)
{Betrayal (Matins)
{★60

61-70

                        61. Entry into Jerusalem

                                            62 b III
                                          63 b IIII
{Christ before Caiaphas (Lauds)   c I missing
{★Blank sheet missing

                        67. Judas receiving silver (Lauds   c II
                            incorrectly *follows* Prime in
                            manuscript at present. Fols. 67, 68
                            must precede 65, 66)

                                            68 c III
{Christ before Pilate (Prime)   c IIII missing
{★64

                        65. Agony in Garden   d I
                                            66 d II
{Flagellation (Tierce)   d III missing
{★69   70. Disrobing of Christ   d IIII

71-82

                                            71 e I
{Way to Calvary, now Louvre (?) (Sext)   e II missing
{★72
73 (paper) a late addition glued to 72
                        74. Christ fastened to Cross   e III
                                          75 e IIII
{Crucifixion (None)   f I missing
{★76
                        77. Lamentation   f II
                                          78 f III
                                          79 f IIII
{Deposition (Vespers)   g I missing
{★80
                        81. Resurrection   g II
                                          82 g III
{Entombment (Compline)   g IIII missing
83-91   {★83
                        84. Descent into Limbo   h I
                                          85 h II

HOURS OF THE HOLY GHOST
(86-101)
(a folio missing before 86 bearing a
miniature)   h III missing
                        86. Baptism (Matins)   h IIII
                                            87 i I
                                          88 i II
                        89. Pentecost (Lauds)   89 i III
                                          90 i IIII
                                          91 iz I

	EXISTING MINIATURES IN TEXT-COLUMN	SIGNATURES OF FOLIOS
92-99		92 iz II
	93. Trinity (Prime)	iz III
	94. Peter preaching (Tierce)	iz IIII
		95 l I (indistinct)
	96. Berry admitted to Paradise (Sext)	l II
	97. Peter and Paul baptizing (None)	l III
	98. Peter celebrating mass (Vespers)	l IIII
		99 m I
100-104	100. St. Gregory (Compline)	m II
		101 m III
Miniature?		m IIII missing
102		
		103 n I

OFFICE OF THE DEAD (106-113)

106-113	106. Funeral Service	
114-121		
122-125		
126 missing		
127		
128		

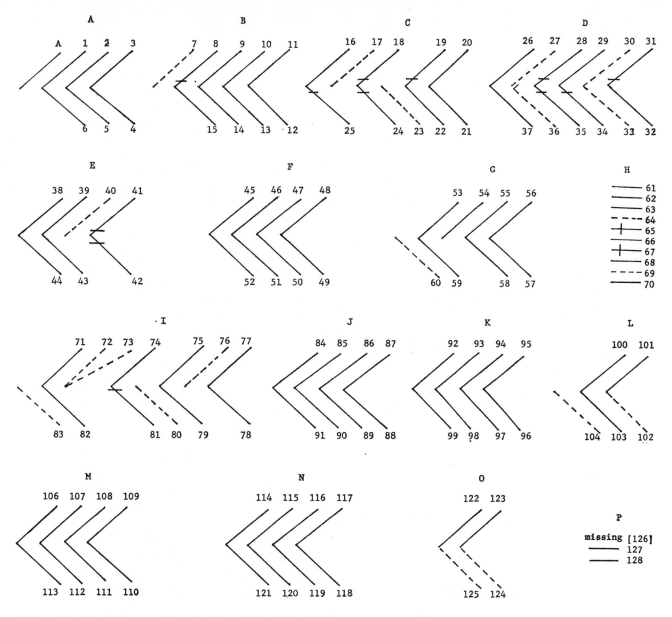

Sheets inserted after 1488 are indicated by dotted lines.

Short horizontal lines indicate cuts in folio near, and parallel to, inner edge of folio.

The sewing holes of the present fol. 7 correspond with those that follow but the original fol. 7 might have been the other half of fol. A.

Fol. 40 was probably half of a folded sheet; the latter, now lost, would have been ruled but blank like fols. 43 and 44.

The other half of fol. 54 was no doubt blank.

For the original sequence exchange fols. 65 and 67, 66 and 68 (evidence is supplied by the text and the original numbers).

The original numeration of gathering I proves that the three large miniatures originally within this gathering were on half sheets. Fol. 73 is paper.

The original numeration indicates a folio missing between present fols. 85 and 86.

There is no folio numbered 105.

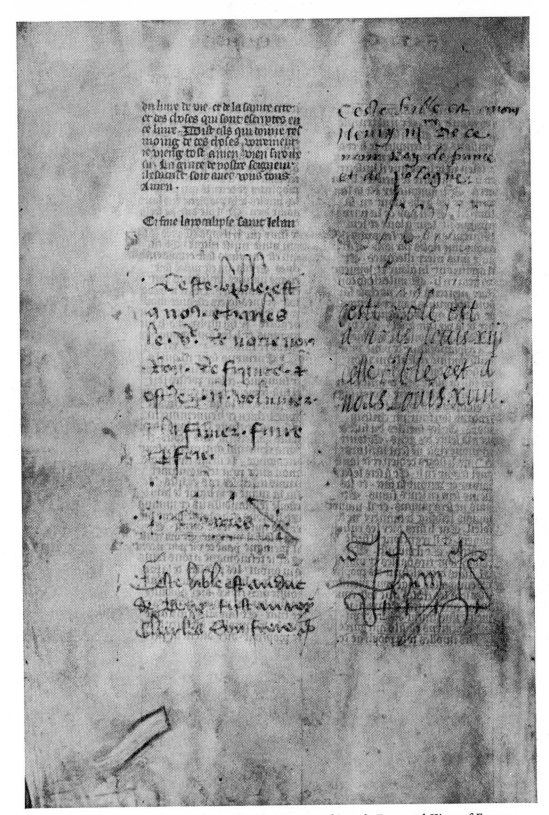

Last folio of Bible (Bibl. nat., fr. 5707) with signatures of Jean de Berry and Kings of France

XIII

The Library of Jean de Berry

1·THE TEXTS

THE library of Jean de Berry was large, but numbers did not make its fame. In his later years the Duke possessed about three hundred manuscripts, more to be sure than his wealthier brother, Philippe le Hardi of Burgundy, who had about two hundred,[1] but much less than another, still more powerful brother, King Charles V, who accumulated nearly a thousand.[2] Though she died young, a sister, Isabelle, wife of Gian Galeazzo Visconti, no doubt played a role in the building in Pavia and Milan of the Duke's great library of about a thousand manuscripts – exceptional in Italy.[3] The interest in books and illumination was transmitted to all members of this generation of the Valois – for Louis I d'Anjou was touched by it also.[4] It came from their parents, Jean le Bon and Bonne de Luxembourg. Bonne was a patroness of Pucelle, from whom she ordered the beautiful Psalter now in the Bodmer Library at Geneva (Figs. 353-355). Early in his career King Jean bought books and commissioned translations, and when he was captured at Poitiers he had an illuminated Bible and probably a *Miracles de Notre-Dame* in his baggage (Fig. 340). While a prisoner in England from 1356 to 1360 the unhappy King did not cease buying books.[5] A Book of Hours in which, we are told, he had learned to read belonged later to Louis II d'Anjou and then to Jean de Berry.[6]

The remarkable fondness of the Valois for this relatively new kind of devotional volume can be traced back to Jeanne d'Évreux, wife of Charles IV, who in 1325–1328 commissioned from Pucelle the superb Book of Hours now in the Cloisters (Figs. 335, 336).[7] The lines of the late fourteenth-century poet Eustache Deschamps are especially relevant to the members of this family:

> Heures me faut de Nostre Dame,
> Si comme il appartient a fame
> Venue de noble paraige,
> qui soient de soutil ouvraige,
> Bien ordonnees et bien paintes . . .[8]

Charles V collected on so much larger a scale than his father and other predecessors that he is rightly considered the founder of the French royal library. In 1367–1368, not content with the practice of distributing manuscripts in numerous residences and storing them there in chests, he had rooms specially prepared for them in a tower of the Louvre. He appointed a well-qualified *gardien des livres*, Gilles Malet, who remained in this position under Charles VI until his death in 1411. Though many of the manuscripts of Charles V were illuminated the style of the painting was remarkably uniform. One group of illuminators, working in the so-called Boqueteaux style that was probably formed by Bondol, possessed almost a monopoly in the royal library (Figs. 376, 377, 383, 384, 386).[9] The King was evidently quite satisfied with their accomplishments and with the addition to his collection of numerous manuscripts painted in limited variations of one style. He cared, in fact, mostly for the texts. He was an avid reader, a learned man who enjoyed the company of scholars at the university of Paris, and he even approved of allusions to himself as a student (Fig. 517). Devoted generally to the diffusion of knowledge and concerned especially with law, history, politics, and morals, all subjects important to a ruler, he commissioned a long series of translations from Latin into French. Among them were the *Propriétés des choses* (1372), the *Rational* of Durandus (1372), the *Remèdes* of Petrarch (1377), the *Politiques*, *Éthiques*, and *Économiques* of Aristotle (1371–1374), the *Cité de Dieu* (1371–1375), Valère Maxime (first four books, 1375), and the Bible, translated anew by Raoul de Presles.[10]

Charles VI added little to the great library of his father and indeed he was unable or unwilling to prevent raids on it by his uncles and brothers. After his death in 1422 the Duke of Bedford purchased what remained, and the manuscripts were removed from Paris. In the early 1380's, on the other hand, Jean de Berry began more actively to build his library. From the beginning he proved himself more deeply interested in illumination than Charles V or any other member of this family of great bibliophiles. He was not, however, simply a visual gourmet, as he is often considered. He liked to read. We learn of his purchases of four 'romans' in 1371.[11] Many of his later acquisitions had either mediocre illuminations or none at all,[12] and in one instance he borrowed a Livy from the royal library that was described in the inventory as 'escript de mauvaise lettre, mal enluminée et point historiée'.[13]

The Duke possessed many copies of the texts normal to all medieval religious libraries; he had, for example, fourteen Bibles, sixteen Psalters, eighteen Breviaries.[14] Most of the manuscripts of this kind were transferred to the Sainte-Chapelle in 1404 and in the following years. More personal in nature were the Books of Hours, fifteen in all, and in another sense the thirty-eight romances. He acquired also manuscripts of many Roman writers, Pliny,[15] Suetonius,[16] Vegetius, Frontinus,[17] and Priscian.[18] He owned French translations of Ovid's *Metamorphoses*[19] and of his *Ars Amatoria*,[20] and four copies of Livy in French.[21] A more exceptional initiative is implied by a manuscript of the *Bucolics* of Virgil,[22] and by two copies of the *Comedies* of Terence. Although both of the latter, which survive (Fig. 440), were given to the Duke, we must remember that he had a way of eliciting such gifts.[23] He even possessed 'un grand livre ancien, escript en grec',[24] its text unspecified because neither Robinet nor apparently anyone in his entourage could read it.

We shall discuss later the Duke's collection of Roman authors and also his patronage of Laurent de Premierfait, who devoted his later years to the translation of Boccaccio into French. Some copies of the second and better-known version by Laurent of Boccaccio's famous *De casibus virorum illustrium* bear a dedication to the Duke of Berry.[25] The Duke was a constant patron of another of Boccaccio's admirers in contemporary France, Christine de Pisan (Figs. 324, 817, 833, 834).[26] Though he did not nearly equal his learned older brother, Charles V, as an initiator of translations into French, he was nevertheless quite active in this sphere. The translation of Valerius Maximus, begun at the command of Charles V, was completed with his support.[27] Already in the early 'seventies he patronized the translation of Seneca, *Le livre des quatre vertus*.[28] Léopold Delisle, who was rarely wrong about anything, said that he had seen an incunable printed in Gothic containing a French translation of a life of the Virgin made for the Duke.[29]

This book has not been identified, but we do possess copies of a corresponding translation of the most widely read of all religious treatises of the fourteenth century. Though generally overlooked this was the most interesting of all these literary events, certainly from the viewpoint of the history of art and of religious iconography.

A French translation of the famous *Meditationes Vitae Christi*, ordered by Jean de Berry, was completed in Paris in 1380. Though a Provençal version was made around the same time the Duke's text was the earliest in the language of the painters and patrons of Northern France.[30] We learn of the translation from the first lines of an exceedingly rare little book, published by Guillaume Leroy at Lyons before 1480 under the title *Vie de nostre bénoit sauveur Jésus Christ*:

> Cy commēce une moult belle et moult notable devote matiere qui est moult proffitable a toute creature humayne Cest la vie de nrē benoit sauveur ihesuscrist ordonnée en brief langayge ou parolles Pource que le peuple dauiordui ayme & requiert avoir choses briefues comme cellui que est de courte duree & de petite devocion Et fut translatee a paris de latin en frācois a la rq̄ste de treshault & puissant prince jehan duc de berry duc dauvergne conte de poytou & de tampes lā de grace mil ccc lxxx.[31]

The emphasis in the introduction on brevity reminds us that lengthy texts were resisted by other periods than ours, though with less reason. We are told that the 'matière' is not only pious, beautiful, and important but also 'de courte duree' – a late medieval digest. The translator usually rendered in French the narrative chapters and omitted those devoted to meditation or to theological speculation.[32] Within the chapters he made a similar choice. In Chapter III, on the Nativity, he tells the story of the journey to Bethlehem, the finding of an abode, and the birth of Christ, up to the statement 'here ends the revelation'. After suppressing the long commentary on the Incarnation the translator continues with the Annunciation to the Shepherds. The commentary on that is similarly omitted. Only a part of the *Meditationes* is put into French; the translation, in this printed copy at least, ends with the *Last Supper*.

Just as the translator did not hesitate to exclude parts of his model he felt quite free to add to it, inserting details that were not apparently to be found in the early Latin and Italian texts. Thus the Latin text states that Joseph and the Virgin lodged themselves in a 'via coperta' or covered alley (a cave according to the Italian) where the people of Bethlehem were accustomed to take shelter when it rained.[33] The French, however, reads: 'une place commune ou les gens tenoient le marchié et la ou ils mectoyent leurs bestes ou temps de pluie. . . .' (page vi verso).

Many of the iconographic innovations in the manuscripts illuminated for Jean de Berry were inspired by the *Meditations*, and most of these features could have been found in the French translation prepared for the Duke. He certainly had a copy in his library, and its contents could have been revealed also to the painters in his entourage by the use of parts of the text in the mystery plays or in the chants of the confraternities that were increasing rapidly in number.[34] The relationship between the *Vie de nostre sauveur* and the miniatures is all the more striking because the text was completed in 1380 and the novel iconography was introduced in manuscripts begun around or shortly after this date. Thus the French text of the Nativity as well as its models stresses Joseph's skill as a carpenter and tells that he spread hay at the Virgin's feet, descriptions that seem to have influenced the illuminators of the *Petites Heures*.[35] The Parement Master gave the *Visitation* a novel domestic character (Fig. 7), in conformity with the text. When in the *Vie* the Magi arrive to pay homage, Christ and the Virgin are still in the humble setting of the Nativity, just as in the *Très Belles Heures de Notre-Dame*. There, too, as in the *Vie* the oldest Magus kisses the hand of Christ.[36] In the *Vie* Joseph accompanies Mary when she visits Elizabeth, as in the *Brussels Hours*.[37] If, however, the manuscript of the translation was as incomplete as the printed copy, all reflections of the *Meditations* in the Passion scenes of these manuscripts must of course have come from Latin or Italian versions.[38]

2 · THE DUKE AS BIBLIOPHILE

Jean de Berry regularly inscribed his name in his manuscripts. Both his brother Charles V and his father, Jean le Bon, identified their codices in a similar way, but they were less diligent than he. The Duke put his name in almost all his manuscripts and sometimes he signed at the beginning as well as at the end.[39] The *ex libris* of these princes seem to suggest something of the character of the collectors. In a few manuscripts that belonged to King Charles and then to his brother, such as the Bible, Bibl. nat., fr. 5707, we may see the successive inscriptions, supplemented in the Duke's case by a large and imposing signature at the right, in the second column (p. 286). This Bible later belonged to three French kings, Henry III, Louis XIII, and Louis XIV, and their signatures, in the upper part of the second column, provide ample evidence of the decline of handwriting. Jean's signature is almost a monogram containing two capitals of the kind charmingly termed at the time as *cadeaux*.[40] Elaborate as they seem, they are only pale shadows of those developed by a few great contemporary scribes. Characteristically, the Duke engaged the best of them, Jean Flamel, as his secretary. Flamel frequently embellished the flyleaf of a manuscript with a fantastic and quite marvelous inscription (Fig. 845). The trills, arpeggios, and cadences – one cannot avoid analogies with music – seem obviously related to the tracery of contemporary borders. They remind us also of the waving compositions of illuminators such as the Master of Luçon (Figs. 705, 810).

The rate of the Duke's acquisitions of manuscripts increased in the fifteenth century; in 1402 one hundred twenty-four manuscripts were inventoried, but in 1413 about three hundred. Seventy-eight of the three hundred came as gifts or exchanges; thirty-two were bought, and some of the rest were commissioned.[41] One hundred twenty-one, comprising nearly half of the collection, were illuminated – a very high proportion. And though the proportion of illuminated manuscripts was impressive their quality was still more so.

To assemble a collection of this kind required not only extraordinary taste but alertness and persistence. The Duke kept an eye on contemporary production and he also watched constantly for the availability of older manuscripts that interested him, such as those of Pucelle. He quickly acquired manuscripts from the libraries of deceased collectors – Charles V, Jean de Montaigu, Louis and Valentine d'Orléans, the duc de Guyenne. He often elicited the gift of a codex he liked, or if otherwise unsuccessful he borrowed it and developed an inseverable attachment. In 1383 King Charles VI lent him a Bible 'pour icelle veoir'. It found its way back into the royal collection only after Berry's death.[42] The Duke borrowed a copy of the *Chroniques de France* from St. Denis, wanting to show it to the Emperor (Charles IV or Manuel II?), and also to have it copied. The manuscript, still in Berry's possession at his death, was returned to the church by his executors, who were informed by his confessor that this was his expressed wish.[43] He gave a splendid three-volume copy of the *Mirouer historial* of Vincent de Beauvais to Jean de Montaigu, and after this keen collector was executed for political reasons in 1409 Berry, according to Robinet's phrase, 'l'a recouvré'.[44] To accomplish this recovery, however, he had to get the first volume from the Provost of Paris and the last two from the duc de Guyenne.[45] He managed to retrieve shortly after the murder of Louis d'Orléans a 'belle Bible' that he had given to him sometime earlier.[46] Where illuminated manuscripts were concerned Jean de Berry was a kind of ambulance-chaser.

We are not well informed about the way in which the Duke of Berry kept his books.[47] During the earlier years they were in Mehun; this was the 'librairie' at the time of the inventory of 1402, and after the gift to the Sainte-Chapelle it remained a principal repository of the books the Duke retained as his personal property. The larger part of the collection was still there at his death but many manuscripts, outstanding for their beauty or modernity or both, were in Paris. How long they had been there we do not know, but their presence in the capital leads us to raise interesting questions concerning the whereabouts of the Duke's illuminators. These questions bear upon the closeness of the Duke to his artisans and their works, and they touch the long-established concepts of the princely schools of illumination.

Like other princes of the blood Jean de Berry was a wealthy nomad, wandering from one château to another, visiting his brothers, or traveling further on political missions into the Languedoc or to the Pope at Avignon.[48] After he assumed a large role in the affairs of France in 1380 he spent much more time in Paris and less in his centers at Bourges, Mehun, Poitiers, or Riom. Indeed he was in the Berry far less than has been supposed. His successive duchesses resided there continuously, usually in Mehun, and during the life of Jeanne d'Armagnac the Duke returned regularly almost every year. He rarely remained, however, more than a month or two until 1389, when shortly after her death he lived in Bourges and Mehun from January through June. During this stay he might have enjoyed at leisure the recently completed Psalter, the *Petites Heures*, and the partially illuminated *Très Belles Heures de Notre-Dame*.

At the end of this period, on June 5–6, the Duke married Jeanne de Boulogne in the Sainte-Chapelle at Riom. From this time on his visits to Bourges were less frequent, partly because of the disappointment of this marriage and also because events required his presence elsewhere, chiefly in Paris. He seems not to have left the capital for the Berry in 1390, he paid a short visit in 1391, but he was there about five months in 1392, when he may have inspired the unusual, apparently competitive juxtaposition in the *Vatican Bible* (Fig. 178) – if indeed Jacquemart was then living in Bourges, as he had been in 1384. The Duke visited Mehun again in December 1393, but during the following four years he is not recorded there or in Bourges, though we know of two appearances at Poitiers (July 1396, and March 1397). During the latter stay he might have inaugurated the painting at the château in Poitiers on which Jacquemart was engaged in May 1398.[49] In August 1398 the Duke appeared in Bourges and Mehun, and he remained there, with trips to Riom, until January of the following year. During this relatively long visit he perhaps watched the progress of the illumination of the *Brussels Hours*. In April he was back in Paris, and addressed a letter to Jacquemart in Bourges.[50]

Of course these proposed connections between the presence of the Duke and the activities of his painters and illuminators are only hypotheses, but the unflagging interest of the great patron in his buildings and his collections is abundantly attested by documents. In 1384, for instance, his visit at Riom launched a new campaign of building, and in the same year after inspecting the construction at Poitiers he requested numerous changes, including the shape of the arch of the window in the chapel 'qui nestoit pas au plaisir de monseigneur'.[51] On his order a model of the new *donjon* was hastily prepared,[52] and he asked for specimens of the tiles that were to line the walls of a room in the palace.[53] The Duke visited his château at Dourdan in November, 1401;[54] a month later his *conseillers* began there the first of his great inventories. The visit and the inventory would appear to be related. Similarly in July, 1402, the Duke ordered the work continued in the library at Mehun, and we know that he was there or nearby in Bourges for several months beginning in August.[55]

During this long sojourn in his capital from August 1402 to January 1403, the Duke probably enjoyed at leisure the completed *Brussels Hours*. Soon, however, for reasons we can scarcely guess, the Duke decided to part with the manuscript and to give it to Philippe le Hardi.[56] Perhaps he made this difficult decision when he returned to Bourges in April 1403, or during another short visit in the fall. He apparently did not visit Bourges in 1404, but the death of Philippe le Hardi in April moved him to order the completion of his own burial monument, the Sainte-Chapelle in Bourges, and in April of the following year (1405) he had the satisfaction of participating in its consecration (Figs. 431, 432, 481, 482).

The assumption of power in Burgundy by Jean sans Peur in 1404 opened a new and critical era for France and the Duke of Berry. The Duke, preoccupied with the growing civil strife, rarely visited the Berry. He did not return until the spring of 1410, when he might have witnessed the Limbourgs at work on the *Belles Heures*, if they were in fact established in Bourges rather than in Paris. In the winter of 1410, after accomplishing a reconciliation of the Burgundians and the Armagnacs, signalized by the Peace of Bicêtre of November 2, the Duke retired to Bourges and Mehun and remained until June 1411. He took refuge there in November when the King turned against his party (Armagnacs), and in June and July he witnessed the disastrous siege of his capital by the King and Jeans sans Peur. Utterly defeated, and deprived of many of his most splendid golden *joyaux*, which were melted down to pay his troops, he left Bourges to sign a treaty of peace at Auxerre in August. Except for a few days at Poitiers in the fall of this year the Duke never saw the Berry or Poitou again.

From November 1412 to his death in June 1416, Jean de Berry lived exclusively in Paris or its environs. The great city in which he had spent most of his life now became his only home. This fact has a special significance because by common consent these were the years when the Limbourgs worked on the *Très Riches Heures* (Figs. 419-424, 442, 489, 844). If we accept the usual view that the illuminators lived in Bourges we must suppose either that the Duke never saw this marvelous and very personal manuscript, or, more probably, that Paul or one of his brothers journeyed to Paris from time to time with specimens of what had been done. To evaluate the possibilities it is useful to consider the circumstances of the other great contemporary patron of the arts, Philippe le Hardi, about whom we possess similar information.

The Duke of Burgundy, more ambitious politically than his brother, devoted even less time to his capital. According to the records he visited Dijon briefly seven years out of the ten during the decade 1386–1396.[57] Thus he had the pleasure of contemplating Broederlam's altarwings, which were delivered to Dijon from Ypres in 1389 (Fig. 711). He saw Sluter prosecute the work on the five famous sculptures for the portal, and he could admire *in situ* the central Virgin, installed in 1391, and the statue of the Duchess, put in place two years later.[58] He did not grant himself the privilege, however, of seeing any of Sluter's statues for the *Puits de Moïse*, nor a single work in Champmol by his great painter, Malouel (Fig. 832). Sluter received the commission for his most beautiful work in 1395; it was completed only after 1402.[59] Malouel, who had been working for the Queen in Paris in 1396, was appointed *peintre* of Duke Philippe in 1397, as successor to the recently deceased Jean de Beaumetz (Figs. 830, 831).[60] The last recorded visit of the Duke to Dijon was, however, on May 1, 1396. He lived thereafter mostly in Paris and he died in 1404, apparently without having laid eyes on the most impressive masterpieces that he – or indeed any other patron of that time except Jean de Berry – had commissioned.[61] The prophets of Sluter and the altarpieces of Malouel were not readily portable.

Philippe was not entirely out of touch with his artists during this period. Malouel, we know, was in Paris as well as Arras for a few weeks in 1402,[62] and he might well have stopped in the capital a year earlier, when he journeyed to Conflans, near Arras, to install some paintings for the Duchess.[63] In 1396–1397 he had worked for Queen Isabeau in Paris and he kept in touch with the capital; he was there again after the death of Philippe le Hardi for several months in 1406.[64] The Duke's personal library – distinct from the manuscripts he bought or commissioned for Champmol – seems to have been established in Paris.[65]

Philippe le Hardi allowed himself to miss the most important artistic events of his reign – the most important events, at least, for which he was partly responsible. There is no record either that his brother, Jean de Berry, though a more passionate lover of the arts, found time to journey to Dijon to see the marvelous new works. Nor did he return to his own capital after the summer of 1412. Probably therefore he did not see the effigy that Jean de Cambrai was carving for his tomb (Fig. 502)[66] – an omission that does, after all, seem understandable. Jean de Berry, like Philippe le Hardi, was caught up in the ceaseless conflicts of the realm, but an inclination to extricate himself from them was, as we have seen, well known to his contemporaries. Would he have failed to keep in touch with the work on his greatest manuscript, the *Très Riches Heures*, that was going forward during these years of residence in Paris, from 1412 to 1416?

It is normally assumed that the Limbourgs, like other painters and illuminators in the service of the Duke of Berry, were continuously resident in Bourges, or at least in the Berry and Poitou. For one of these painters – not to mention the sculptors and architects – there is substantial evidence. Jacquemart de Hesdin was living in Bourges in 1384, and the Duke addressed letters

U

to him there in 1399.[67] A year before he was working in the palace at Poitiers.[67] That is all we know about his habitat. Our information about the Limbourgs points more clearly to two centers. The Duke gave Paul – 'sien paintre, natif du païs dallemaigne' – a house in Bourges in 1409, after the death of its former occupant, his treasurer Christophe de Lamer.[68] In March of the preceding year 'ung paintre alemant' of the Duke was working for him in the famous *hôtel* of Bicêtre, on the periphery of Paris, and its seems probable for several reasons that this painter was Paul.[69] The brothers were certainly at home in the capital, for they were there when we first hear of them. In 1400 Herman and Jean had been serving as apprentices of a goldsmith in Paris,[70] and then Paul and Jean worked from early 1402 to 1404 on a Bible for Philippe le Hardi, residing in Paris in the house of the Duke's physician, Jean Durand.[71] The surviving records of payment by Jean de Berry from the year 1413,[72] and the gifts recorded in the inventories,[73] do not tell us where Paul or his brothers were.[74] That fact we cannot learn either from the gifts of the Limbourgs to the Duke in 1411 and 1414.[75] These records do disclose, however, the Duke's high estimation of his illuminators, and they suggest a rather close personal relationship.

An important bit of evidence is provided by the inventory of 1416. At the Duke's death the unfinished *Très Riches Heures* was not in Bourges but in Paris.[76] The manuscript could of course have been brought to the capital a short time earlier for the Duke's perusal, but the illuminators might very well have been working in Paris or nearby Bicêtre, where the aged Duke would have enjoyed watching their progress. Indeed the testamentary inventory shows that the Duke kept near himself many of his favorite manuscripts. The larger part of the library was still, to be sure at Mehun, and it included some books that the Duke must have admired very much, but their retention so far away was perhaps determined by the dire conditions in the capital. The Duke became a target of the Burgundian sympathizers. His château at Bicêtre was sacked in 1411, and even the massive Hôtel de Nesle was invaded. In 1413 the aged man himself had to take refuge for some weeks in the cloister of Notre-Dame.

Among the manuscripts that Jean de Berry had in Paris there were a few to which he was no doubt attached for reasons of sentiment: the Book of Hours of his father, for instance.[77] He probably valued the *Heures de Pucelle*, now in the Cloisters, New York (Figs. 335, 336),[78] not only for its superb illumination but also for its association with his mother, who had employed the same illuminator when he was a boy (Fig. 353). In addition to the *Très Riches Heures*, presumably being painted in Paris, the Duke had there the simulated book that the Limbourgs gave him as a New Years' present in 1411.[79] The *Belles Heures* by these illuminators, on the other hand, was in Mehun – the most surprising omission from the books in Paris (Figs. 746, 779).[80] The *Grandes Heures*, however, was in the capital – a spectacular book with its large paintings by Jacquemart de Hesdin, finished in 1409.[81] The Duke kept there also the three-volume *Mirouer historial* of Vincent, with nearly a thousand miniatures,[82] the *Comedies* of Terence now in the Bibliothèque nationale (Fig. 440), the *Mutacion de Fortune* by the workshop of the Épître Master now in the Hague. He had in Paris also an outstanding specimen of Flemish style around 1402, the *Livre d'astrologie* he received from the Abbot of St. Barthélemy and now in the Morgan Library, New York (Figs. 826, 827), as well as the somewhat related *Fleur des histoires* in the Bibliothèque nationale (Fig. 438).

The manuscripts at Mehun in 1416 that are outstanding for their illumination were, in addition to the *Belles Heures*, the *Psalter* now in the Bibliothèque nationale, the Duke's copy of the collected works of Christine de Pisan, containing the beautiful miniatures of the Épître Master (Figs. 833, 834), the excellent *Bible historiale* (Fig. 822), two French translations of Boccaccio (Figs. 289, 291, 294, and Geneva, fr. 190), the Pontifical by the Master of Luçon (Fig. 268), and the *Bréviaire de Charles V* by the Passion Master (Figs. 362, 367, 368).[83]

Of all the painters and illuminators represented in the Duke's library only those more or less permanently in his service would have resided for long periods of time in Bourges. Beauneveu, primarily a sculptor, and busy also at Mehun and Riom, was of course settled there. Much of the time he may have had as companion Jacquemart, who was recorded there in 1384 and again in 1399. Pseudo-Jacquemart, the workhorse for the collection, probably lived more in Bourges than elsewhere, whereas the evidence for the Limbourgs suggests a return to Paris in their last years. The Parement Master had been employed by Charles V, no doubt in Paris, before he initiated the *Très Belles Heures de Notre-Dame* for the Duke, probably in Bourges. Paris was the home, on the other hand, of all the illuminators of the manuscripts that came into the possession of Jean de Berry by gift or purchase. Since we do not know the real names of any of them we of course lack documents of residence. But the Luçon Master, the Épître Master, the Boucicaut Master, the Virgil Master, the Master of the Cité des Dames, were all resident mostly in the capital. Only there could they have engaged in the continuous collaboration during the first fifteen years of the fifteenth century of which the manuscripts provide abundant evidence.

The continuous association of these illuminators is one aspect of their activity that justifies the application to them of the concept 'school of Paris'. Variously trained and variously endowed, these painters all acquired in the metropolis certain common qualities that are difficult to define but nevertheless recognizably present. They shared to a degree the values established by the earlier Parisian tradition and they responded more or less to the contemporary artistic and intellectual climate. Alongside this great center of illumination the Duke of Berry created a second – more distinct and separate in the earlier decades, when his chief artists were active in Bourges, and much less after 1400, when the Duke resided mostly in Paris and when, in any event, artistic interchange with the capital, then in a brilliant phase, increased.

The patronage of the Duke had a profound effect upon painting. He brought together illuminators, painters, and craftsmen of other kinds, giving them opportunities to study each other's work and sometimes setting for them unusual tasks. He asked a major sculptor, Beauneveu, and a leading painter, the Parement Master, to execute some miniatures. It seems clear that the Master of the Holy Ghost was not a professional illuminator either. The Limbourgs – two of them trained as goldsmiths – adopted for their miniatures forms and figures of the Duke's two surviving medals. They took the chariot of the sun in the *Très Riches Heures* from the *carpentum* of Heraclius, and one of the Magi from Constantine (Figs. 462, 465).[84] The great cross in this manuscript certainly reflects one of the Duke's possessions, probably the *croix au serpent* (Fig. 442). Practically all the Duke's *joyaux* are lost, but given the connection with painting of the extant specimens we may safely surmise specific interchanges in other instances also. The little dog on a mound under a tree in the *Vatican Bible* strikingly resembles, as we have observed, a *joyau* described in an inventory (Fig. 178). Probably the image of the Madonna with the writing Child was realized in gold-enamel also (Fig. 669). Certainly the painted copy of a *joyau* of St. Michael that Queen Isabeau gave to her brother resembles St. Michael in the *Bréviaire de Charles V* (Figs. 838, 839). Here the miniature was clearly the earlier. Underlying all these similarities of design is the relationship of color and light. In this respect these jewelled *tableaux* must have incited in the painters wonder, and at the same time despair.

Jean de Berry promoted a distinctive trend in painting by his choice of artists and by imbuing them with his ideas and his taste. What the paintings imply Robinet seems to state explicitly. Describing the *Grandes Heures* – the splendid binding as well as the book itself – he said: '. . . lesquelles Heures mondit Seigneur a faictes faire ainsy et par la manière qu'elles sont dessus devisées'.[85] Futhermore, by bringing the painters together for periods of collaboration the Duke gave them unusual opportunities for mutual exchange. And last but not least he formed a uniquely rich library that extended the horizons of his *équipe*. The library offered to these masters what the collection of the Medici offered the artists of Quattrocento Florence.

We possess little written evidence about access to Jean de Berry's books. We know that princes of the time commonly lent manuscripts to 'peintres' who, like Jean Bondol when he designed the Angers tapestries,[86] needed iconographical guides for uncommon subjects.[87] Charles V commonly lent manuscripts from the royal library to noblemen and friends.[88] In 1413 the first volume of the *Bréviaire de Belleville* was 'charged out' of Jean de Berry's library to Pierre de Vérone.[89] This Italian, who was serving two years later as the librarian of the Duke, had long been in Paris as a producer of books or *stationnaire*. We have seen that certain manuscripts illuminated for Jean de Berry prove that his illuminators enjoyed access to some at least of his books. The most telling instance is the *Grandes Heures*, which contains nearly exact copies of miniatures in the *Très Belles Heures de Notre-Dame*.[90] These copies reflect miniatures executed in both campaigns on that manuscript, the first campaign of the early 'eighties and the second around 1405. The *Resurrection* in the *Grandes Heures* seems to be dependent upon the miniature of the same subject in the *Bréviaire de Charles V*, which the Duke acquired before the death of Valentine d'Orléans in December 1408 (Fig. 371). Some of the *drôleries* in the *Grandes Heures* were imitated from corresponding forms in the *Bréviaire de Belleville*.[91] Miniatures by Jacquemart and by Pseudo-Jacquemart in the *Petites Heures* derive from slightly earlier representations by the Parement Master and his associates in the *Très Belles Heures de Notre-Dame*.[92] The text itself of the *Petites Heures* is based upon the *Très Belles Heures de Notre-Dame*. Later, when painting the *Brussels Hours*, Jacquemart must again have studied the *Très Belles Heures de Notre-Dame*: his *Funeral Service* makes that abundantly clear (Figs. 198, 14).

It is usually not easy to learn whether a relationship between works made within rather short intervals of time involved a personal acquaintance also, which would have heightened the impact of one art upon another. The Duke of Berry's patronage, however, enables us often to be certain of personal exchanges, because the artists were working for him at the same moment or even collaborating upon one manuscript. Not infrequently, indeed, they shared the same folio or even the same miniature. Jacquemart de Hesdin, coming down to Bourges around 1384, encountered three major artistic forces. He might already have known André Beauneveu or his work in Courtrai, Valenciennes, Malines, or Ypres, where the sculptor had been active, but he probably had not seen any paintings by him. The prophets and apostles at the beginning of the *Psalter* were exceptional ventures by Beauneveu, clearly promoted by the wishes of his patron. In Bourges there began an association of the two masters that affected deeply the growth of Jacquemart's early style. We have pointed to these effects in Jacquemart's miniatures in the *Petites Heures*. When the painter undertook his share of the illumination of this manuscript the Parement Master was completing, or had recently completed, his work on the *Très Belles Heures de Notre-Dame*. Jacquemart had at hand also paintings that reflected later Trecento as well as Bohemian style. Certainly he knew the Passion Master, the extraordinary artist who was at first in charge of the execution of the *Petites Heures*. Here he came into the most intimate relationship with a style that stemmed partly from Duccio and the Duccieschi. Whereas the Parement Master was more concerned with the definition of space and with figure structure the Passion Master inherited Pucelle's fascination with the expressive aspects of early Trecento painting, its pantomime and its vivid description of the thought and feeling of the actors.

Sometimes the Duke of Berry seemed to delight in pitting one artist against another. This kind of competition occurred in the *Vatican Bible* (Fig. 178), and in another sense – because one work was painted a few years earlier – in the initial miniatures of the *Brussels Hours* (Figs. 179-181). In the latter manuscript the Duke – we may probably presume the decision was his – engaged an Italian illuminator for the initials. For the second campaign on the *Très Belles Heures de Notre-Dame* he employed, it seems simultaneously, painters as diverse as the Baptist Master with his assistants and the Master of the Holy Ghost. For the *Grandes Heures* the Duke added to Jacquemart and Pseudo-Jacquemart the Boucicaut Master and the Bedford Master. The Boucicaut Master had studied the art of Jacquemart a few years earlier – the *Boucicaut Hours* imply a serious contemplation of the *Brussels Hours*. But towards 1409 he was given an opportunity to see specimens of Jacquemart's late style. The Boucicaut Master was early, it seems, aware of the early accomplishments of the Limbourgs also, but his work on the *Grandes Heures* may well have facilitated his study of the *Belles Heures*, which the Limbourgs had very probably begun for the Duke at that time. Manuscripts from the Boucicaut atelier beginning in 1407 show also the influence of another of the Duke's illuminators, the Master of the Brussels Initials.[93]

These are only some of the more significant and fateful encounters occasioned by a remarkable patron. Nothing has been said here about Pseudo-Jacquemart, who was hardly more than a vane that veered with the prevailing wind of style. His constant presence in this brilliant entourage proves that Jean de Berry, whatever his motives, could on occasion accept less than the best. Detailed comparison in the future of the manuscripts acquired by the Duke with those he commissioned will certainly disclose other important derivations, stylistic as well as iconographic. We have, however, seen enough to tell us that Jean de Berry left his mark upon the course of painting in France, and that means also the whole of northern Europe.

3. THE DUKE'S TASTE

The range of styles in the great library was wide. The Duke had strong and durable preferences but he enjoyed variety, and his curiosity obviously was unlimited. In this period of exceptionally rapid change, marked by the regular and frequent appearances of gifted painters, the Duke acquired in one way or another impressive examples of every – or almost every – leading artist. He possessed three outstanding specimens of the style that prevailed in metropolitan France when he began to build his library, and which he in fact did more than any other patron to overthrow. Jean Bondol and the illuminators working in the Boqueteaux manner had given the French manuscript of the time a remarkable uniformity. Jean de Berry owned a codex containing beautiful early drawings and paintings in this style – the *Bible de Jean de Sy* (Figs. 376, 377). He acquired from Louis d'Anjou the *Bible de Charles V*, with the famous frontispiece signed by Bondol and dated 1371 (Fig. 382). He could enjoy a later, distinctive version of this style in one of three fine copies of the *Cité de Dieu*, now divided between the Bibliothèque municipale in Angers and the Hofer Collection of Harvard University (Fig. 535).

While other princes continued to favor these illuminators the Duke of Berry resolutely set out in the early 'eighties to transform the book. He invoked the assistance of Beauneveu, the sculptor, and of the painter we call the Parement Master. He engaged a great though aged perpetuator of the tradition of Pucelle and a young, still unformed but gifted painter from Hesdin. Only one of these artists seems to have been a professional illuminator. Within a decade they had initiated a new era in the history of the painted book.

To build his library the Duke turned also to lesser masters. He took Pseudo-Jacquemart into his service. Beginning around 1390 and for about fifteen years thereafter he patronized a conservative illuminator, the Virgil Master, acquiring first a *Bible historiale* now in London,[94] then a French Livy.[95] His copy of the works of Durand de Champagne also had miniatures by this master.[96] For New Year 1402, furthermore, he received a Valère Maxime in this style from his treasurer, Jacques Courau, for whom the same master illuminated in 1403 the impressive French translation of Virgil's *Bucolics* and *Aeneid* (Fig. 841).[97] More venturesome were the manuscripts of the Luçon Master; they showed much more linear flourish, brighter color and, because of patches of delicately tooled and burnished gold, a greater splendor. The three manuscripts, however, entirely in this style that belonged to the Duke came as gifts: a Pontifical from Étienne Loypeau, Bishop of Luçon (Fig. 268)[98]; the *Livre de bonnes mœurs* from its author, Jacques Legrand (Fig. 486);[99] the *Cas des nobles hommes et femmes* from the Archbishop of Chartres, Martin Gouge.[100] The famous *Térence des ducs*, partly in a related style, was similarly given to the Duke – though only a few months before his death – by the Bishop of Châlons.[101] Already at New Year 1408 he had received from Martin Gouge another Terence, with miniatures by a follower of Jacquemart de Hesdin (Fig. 440).[102]

When a new, more pictorial style was developed around 1400, clearly by Flemish illuminators, members of Jean de Berry's circle hastened to give him outstanding specimens of it, as we have pointed out above.[103] The gifts extended over a period of three or four years, and the givers were scattered and of different walks of life so that the approval of the Duke was probably generally known. There can be no doubt that he did approve, despite his usual taste for a different kind of painting, because he seems to have bought a manuscript or two in this style, and around 1405 he engaged a Flemish painter and his assistants to carry forward the illumination of the incomplete *Très Belles Heures de Notre-Dame*. Shortly thereafter the Duke's interest in this art flagged. He seems not to have acquired any important later examples, and more significant, he showed little interest in the greatest illuminators who emerged from this Flemish group. One, the Bedford Master, who adhered more closely to its principles, painted only one miniature in a commissioned manuscript – an important miniature, to be sure, showing the Duke of Berry welcomed by St. Peter at the gate of Paradise (Fig. 231). He may have been asked to execute this painting by his constant collaborator, the Boucicaut Master, or by the Duke himself because he had easier access to a portrait of Philippe le Hardi, who appears in Berry's company at the gate. The Bedford workshop had a larger share of the illumination – again with the Boucicaut Master – in the splendid *Merveilles du monde* that entered Berry's collection in 1413, a gift however from Jean sans Peur.

Jean de Berry's lack of enthusiasm for the works of the Bedford Master seems quite consistent with his taste – except for the brief period of the 'Flemish episode'. Less evident is the reason for his failure to give more work to the Boucicaut Master. He did, to be sure, employ this great atelier around 1408–1410 on two of his manuscripts, the *Grandes Heures* that has just been mentioned, and the Lectionary in Bourges (Fig. 499). And in January 1413, he received – or elicited? – from Jean sans Peur the *Merveilles du monde*, one of the splendid achievements of the Boucicaut workshop. It is striking, however, that we know of no major commission, or apparently even purchase, by Jean de Berry during that marvelously productive decade when the Boucicaut Master was working for the Maréchal, for Pierre Salmon and Charles VI (Fig. 487),[104] for the Duc de Guyenne (Breviary at Châteauroux), and for Jean sans Peur (*Merveilles du monde*).[105] It is true that the style of the Boucicaut Master was less superficially Italianate than that of Jean de Berry's favorite painters, but both his figures and his compositions presuppose a deep understanding of Trecento structure. And one would have supposed that the sheer greatness of the artist would have proved irresistible. Perhaps it almost did but the Duke was restrained by other considerations – an uncontrollable jealousy of the Limbourgs, for instance.

Three manuscripts by the Master of the Cité des Dames entered the Duke's collection – one certainly, and perhaps two, by purchase.[106] He received a fine copy of the *Cité des Dames* in this style, probably from Christine, the author.[107] Though this master could scarcely have been considered one of the great illuminators of the time he was, as we have seen, an admirer of Jacquemart and an Italophile. He shared to a degree the Duke's passion for order, geometry, and monumentality (Figs. 325, 706). Though the Duke possessed nothing exceptional by this painter he acquired the chef d'œuvre of a related illuminator, whom I shall call the Master of the Épître d'Othéa because his most beautiful surviving painting was the illustration of this poem in the manuscript of the collected writings of Christine in the Duke's collection (Figs. 833, 834). He and the Master of the Cité des Dames worked simultaneously for the poet and they learned much from each other. They also learned from Trecento painting, and it is in fact barely conceivable that one or the other of them came from Italy; but when we first meet them, the Master of the Cité des Dames in 1404 (Fig. 706)[108] and the Épître Master in 1403–1404, they had already become students of Jacquemart and of the Master of the Coronation. The Épître Master and his workshop completed early in 1404 two copies of Christine's *Mutacion de Fortune*, one for Jean de Berry and the other for Philippe le Hardi.[109] Around the same time he also produced two other copies, the miniatures of which have not previously been identified or published (Figs. 835, 836).[110]

The Épître Master is perhaps the most mysterious painter who appeared in Paris around 1400. At times, as in the miniatures of Atropos (Fig. 833), his figures and his compositions seem almost Tuscan. More often his soft, luminous colors recall Lombard illumination, especially that of Giovannino dei Grassi (Fig. 578). The fluid, open brushwork resembles the *Tacuina*. He owed much also to the Master of the Coronation and his associates: they helped him develop his remarkably nimble figures and compositional arabesques (Figs. 822, 825). These aspects of his art contributed to the formation of the bold style of the painter I have called the Master of the Berry Apocalypse; the book from which he takes his name, now in the Morgan Library, New York, was one of the most impressive manuscripts in the Duke's collection (Fig. 843).[111] The Épître Master is a major representative of the coloristic trend in Paris, Lombardy, and the Netherlands that we have discussed above.[112] He shares with Giovannino and the Master of the Coronation a fascination with high values and with the interplay of white, pale gray, gray-brown, and rose. In delicacy and sophistication he is a fifteenth-century Watteau.

In his copy of the *Œuvres* of Christine de Pisan, executed probably between about 1404 and 1409, the Duke possessed also a few miniatures by the one notable illuminator in Paris not hitherto mentioned – the Egerton Master (Fig. 324). The library presented therefore a full spectrum of contemporary illumination, at least in France and Flanders. Though as a young man the Duke lived in England for several years, and may have acquired at that time an early English manuscript, as we have seen, the sojourn appears to have had no lasting effect. The half of the Duke's library that we know assures us that he did not find the flowery International Style uncongenial. To a degree he accepted it, but at the same time he strove for something different. It was his more serious commitments – the manuscripts produced by painters in his service – that made him unique in his time.

Jean de Berry was obviously not, on the other hand, a mere hunter of novelty. He early conceived an enthusiasm for the illumination of Pucelle and his associates. Probably he was attracted by it already as a boy of eight or nine when he saw his mother's marvelous Psalter (Figs. 353–355), and although this style was very old hat by 1400 he continued to acquire specimens of it. It certainly cannot be an accident that so many Pucellesque manuscripts were put, so to speak, into the Duke's hands. They belonged to his relatives and they had to be acquired by gift or bequest. Many of them, in the royal collection at the death of Charles V, had to be won from his successor or from the members of the family to whom Charles V – no admirer of Jean de Berry – had bequeathed them. The tiny but marvelous *Heures de Jeanne d'Évreux* (Figs. 335, 336) entered the collection between 1380 and 1402; the Duke was quite aware of the name of the author, for Robinet described the book as the *Heures de Pucelle*.[113] The *Bible historiale* in the Bibliothèque de l'Arsenal, Paris, which has a fine miniature by the same master at the beginning,[114] came to Jean de Berry from Charles VI in 1403.[115] Shortly before the death of the Duchess of Orléans, Valentina Visconti, in 1408 the *Bréviaire de Charles V* by the Passion Master entered the Duke of Berry's library (Figs. 359, 368).[116] The *Bréviaire de Belleville*, in the possession of Charles V at his death in 1380, appeared in Berry's inventory of 1413, one volume being then out on loan to Pierre de Vérone (Figs. 344, 374).[117] The same inventory records the Duke's possession of the *Miracles de Notre-Dame* (Figs. 340, 562).[118] No such assemblage of paintings by Pucelle and his followers ever had been or ever will be effected again. Nor did the Duke's contemporaries share his enthusiasm. After his death the *Heures de Jeanne d'Évreux* was appraised at the very low figure of fifteen pounds.[119]

Much of Jean de Berry's love for Pucelle's work was inspired quite simply by its greatness. But the *character* of this style, and especially its Italian strain, no doubt was very attractive to him also. When the Duke began to commission illuminators to undertake impressive books, one of the first he chose was Pucelle's greatest successor, the Passion Master, perhaps identical with Jean le Noir. The Parement Master was already a close student of Sienese painting when the Duke engaged him for the *Très Belles Heures de Notre-Dame*, but the Italian tendencies of Jacquemart developed only after he entered the ducal service. Indeed Jacquemart presumably came to Bourges a Northern painter, trained in the Pas-de-Calais and the Netherlandish region; under his patron's stimulus he became the most Italianate painter in Northern Europe. The Limbourgs had certainly studied Trecento paintings in Paris, their eyes opened to it probably by their uncle Jean Malouel. The Duke of Berry quickly recognized both their strength and their Southern inclination in their miniatures in the Bible of his brother Philippe (Fig. 781). He no doubt engaged them as quickly as he could – they seem to have painted one miniature for him already in the year after Philippe's death (Fig. 481), and they may have been in his service when they (or Paul alone?) went to Italy.

Jacquemart may have gone to Italy too,[120] and it seems that even a lesser painter such as the Master of the Cité des Dames made the journey (Figs. 393, 394).[121] There is good reason to believe that, half a century earlier, Pucelle and his associate who worked on the *Miracles de Notre-Dame* had gone south also (Figs. 336, 340). Why did not the Duke make the trip himself? We cannot of course answer this question with any assurance, but that need not deter us from a little speculation. He led a very full life, but he probably could have disengaged himself from politics for a few weeks if he had been sufficiently eager. Beginning in 1358 he was often at Avignon, where he saw the panels imported by Italian merchants. The last of the frescoes of Matteo da Viterbo had not long been finished in Villeneuve (Figs. 405, 406). Was he not tempted to go further, to Lombardy and to Tuscany, to see what I still wish to call, despite a current critical fashion to exalt the painting of the periphery, the 'real thing'? Perhaps not. He could, for one thing, enjoy Trecento paintings in the great collections of Paris and particularly in his own. His *Madonna with a Sleeping Child*, for instance, was surely Venetian.[122] Two of his Italian manuscripts are still extant: the magnificent early Trecento Bolognese Bible in the Cathedral of Gerona (Fig. 837), and the Missal by Niccolò in Munich (Figs. 717, 751). Furthermore he may have employed for a short time a Sienese *intarsiatore*, probably Domenico dei Cori (Fig. 553).[123] He took into his service a North Italian illuminator; indeed he may have given him his first work in France.

On the other hand the Duke's great admiration for Tuscan painting did not lead him to bring a major Italian painter to his court, as Francis I was to do later. He might well have preferred the good French transformations of Tuscan and Lombard style, their softer, more luminous color, their more open space and more restrained pantomime. The world of Trecento painting probably appeared stark and bare, without the warm, inviting, populated landscape that was conjured up by his own artists. And the new styles of 1390–1400 that he might have encountered in the peninsula – the styles of Giovannino and Michelino in Milan, Niccolò di Pietro in Venice, Lorenzo Monaco in Florence – would have pleased but not deeply stirred him. He was ready for something different and, in many respects, more advanced. One can understand therefore that he did not feel impelled to make the trip.

We have had occasion to observe that the deep interest of Jean de Berry in Italian painting was not an isolated phenomenon in France. As early as 1373 Jean d'Arbois, painter of the Duke of Burgundy, was in Italy,[124] and the art of two of his successors, Jean de Beaumetz and Jean Malouel, presupposes the study of Trecento models. The Angevin Dukes, haunted by dreams of a southern empire, had special reasons – and special facilities – for admiring the art of the region. So far as we know, however, none of these princes equalled Jean de Berry in the intensity or constancy of their devotion to the principles of Trecento painting. Only the Emperor Charles IV and his chancellor Johann von Neumarkt should be cited. They brought paintings by Tommaso da Modena to Prague,[125] and they stirred local painters to emulate the achievements of their great predecessors to the south.

In a period when Jean de Berry and his chief illuminators held Trecento painting in high esteem several influential French scholars were devoting themselves to the study of Trecento writing. The Duke was close to four of these humanists. Gontier Col and Jean de Montreuil served him as secretaries, the former for a long time,[126] The Duke was a constant patron, as we have seen, of the indefatigable Christine de Pisan,[127] whose writing drew heavily upon Boccaccio. He supported Laurent de Premierfait during the years when he was working on his French version of Boccaccio's *De casibus virorum illustrium*.[128] These pioneering scholars, as well as Pierre Col and Nicolas de Clamanges, revered Boccaccio and Petrarch and shared their enthusiasm for ancient literature.[129] They insisted, however, on the richness of their own French tradition of classical study, beginning in the twelfth century, and they – except for Christine, more a poet and 'composer' than a scholar – held that a *translatio studii* led from Greece to Rome to France.[130] They disagreed with Petrarch's conviction that the Papacy should be re-established in Rome, and a jurist of the University of Paris, serving as ambassador of Charles V, asserted to the Pope: 'haec gloria Romanorum Parisius in Gallos est translata'.[131] However meritorious the French past, the present seemed full of promise to these writers, and Jean de Montreuil, exhorting others to study the ancient authors, spoke of a return of the *saecula aurea*.[132] And while the Italians had earlier described the new enlightenment as a reawakening or a return from the darkness of ignorance to the light of knowledge[133] Nicolas de Clamanges characterized the newly won eloquence, long buried, as reborn – *renata*.[134]

Although these scholars valued the ancient writers primarily as moralists they became increasingly impressed by their style. The favorite authors of Jean de Montreuil were Cicero, Virgil, and Terence. Nicolas de Clamanges could say: 'vultus est, ut ita dixerim, animi stilus'.[135] Montreuil even transposed such conceptions of the importance of form to the visual arts. Describing a statue of the Madonna at Chaalis, which he liked, he said that one might have thought it was made by Praxiteles or Lysippus.[136] Though he intended to convey nothing precise by this comparison his remark discloses the prestige acquired by ancient art and the view that medieval beauty was quite commensurable with ancient.

The convictions and the accomplishments of these humanists illuminate for us several less traditional aspects of the Duke of Berry's patronage. We understand how he happened to acquire certain texts, such as Virgil's *Bucolics* and Terence's *Comedies*, which were not present even in a library so rich in ancient authors as that of the Visconti at Pavia.[137] The Duke possessed also, often in French translation, most of the Roman writings that frequently appeared in late medieval libraries: Valerius Maximus, Lucan and Sallust, Seneca, Josephus. He acquired also French translations of Petrarch's *De Remediis*[138] and of Boccaccio's *De mulieribus claris* and *De casibus virorum illustrium*.[139]

We should observe, however, that these ancient or recent Italian texts were not matched with equally Italianate illustrations.[140] It was not the Duke's Boccaccios but his Books of Hours that came closest to Simone, the Lorenzetti, and the Giotteschi. And while all European painting towards 1400 was influenced to some degree by Italian art the illustrations of the Duke's secular texts were more purely Northern. The Duke evidently was most serious about his religious books. The illuminators whom he chose to retain at his court worked on Books of Hours, or occasionally on a Psalter, a Bible, or a Lectionary. They made these books personal in a special sense, often adding the ducal motto and emblems. Usually they included portraits too, not only in the frontispieces – where by tradition they appeared also in dedication scenes in secular manuscripts – but in subsequent margins or miniatures in the book. It is a striking fact that, so far as we know, neither the Parement Master, Jacquemart, or the Limbourgs ever touched a secular text.[141] The major artists were occupied with religious art. This was true also in Italy in the first half century of what we call the Renaissance. Thus it happened that Italian artists first came close to the ancient nude in representations of David, of putto-like angels, or, as we saw in the instance of Masaccio, even the Christ Child (Figs. 555, 556).

The values of the contemporary humanists no doubt had an effect upon another aspect of the Duke's collecting. While Roman coins and medals attracted some interest throughout the Middle Ages the Italian humanists, beginning with Petrarch and his follower Lombardo della Seta, valued them as relics of a great, vanished civilization. It has not been shown that their French followers emulated them in this respect but Jean de Berry apparently had many.[142] His collection of carved gems and cameos was so large and important that it would seem to presuppose an appreciation that transcended the common medieval interest in them as talismans or as seals. Even the Medici collection of these objects in the later Quattrocento was perhaps not richer. Only some of the Duke's cameos were Roman (Figs. 456, 458, 459); others were medieval but more or less *all'antica*, such as the 'Christ with two angels', originally inserted it seems in a great cross in the Sainte-Chapelle (Fig. 457).[143] It is significant that the late medieval origin of this object has only recently been demonstrated. Since the Duke himself commissioned the cutting of some cameos, including two showing his own portrait, he was aware that not all his examples that looked Roman were produced in Roman times. Of his five representations of the emperors, only Julius Caesar was described as a denarius and 'contrefait au vif'. Robinet is silent about the *façon* of the other four. The *semblance* of antiquity was valuable in itself.

To judge from Robinet's descriptions the Duke possessed many other objects that were either antique, Byzantine, or copies.[144] Since, as we have seen, he had no clear concept of the arts of antiquity it is usually difficult to be certain of their presence in the collection unless they survive. In 1407, however, he gave to the Sainte-Chapelle a gilt silver dish with a representation of what Robinet described as the first great Christian Emperor: 'un ymaige de Constantin assis sur un cheval volent, emprès lequel a un lion dormant. . . .' Schlosser thought that the subject must actually have been Bellerophon on Pegasus soaring over the Chimaera, but Robinet was probably right for we have large plates of this kind – Berry's weighed about seven and a half pounds – that show an emperor on horseback with a lion nearby. The border consisting of an arabesque of leaves and animals conforms with the type, all examples of which are datable before the seventh century.[145]

Some objects described in the inventories contained classical elements put together in a late medieval way. Notable is the splendid gold *hannap* that bore six figures (with names *alla Romana*) accompanied by mysterious Latin inscriptions, one of which refers to the 'cup of Athene.'[146] Gold reliefs celebrated early Christian figures such as the Emperor Philip the Arab[147] or the third-century martyr Eugenia,[148] but they were probably of medieval manufacture. Several objects containing Greek inscriptions were probably Byzantine. These included a cameo, a relief of the Madonna,[149] and a silver statuette of the Madonna whose throne bore enamels.[150] Seven panels ('tableaux') in the collection contained 'ymages d'ouvrage de Grèce'.[151] Any lingering doubt that these objects were Byzantine is removed by the entry that describes a wool altar-hanging 'fait à ouvrage de Grèce'; it was given to the Duke by the Emperor of Constantinople.[152] The Duke received three reliquaries from this city, brought back by his friend Jean de Chasteau-morant, who in 1396 took part in the disastrous crusade to save the capital and the Empire from the Turks. These silver reliquaries had 'ymaiges . . . de la façon de Grèce', and one of them was said by Robinet to have been taken from the tomb of St. Helena.[153]

The famous gold medals of Constantine and Heraclius, of which copies survive (Figs. 462-465), were probably influenced also by relationships with the Christian East. One of the inscriptions, we have seen, shows a familiarity with formulae of the Byzantine court, and in subject too the medals may have been affected by the Parisian sojourn of the Byzantine Emperor, Manuel II, from 1400 to 1402.[154] Little light has yet been thrown on the sources of their forms, but we have suggested that the Fountain of Life may be based on Byzantine models. What, however, is the origin of the curious projections from the crowns, which make the emperors look like Sioux chiefs? Crowns of this form, which are worn by the emperors in miniatures of the Limbourgs also, may be misunderstandings of the solar rays of the ancient Roman emperors that continue as spikes in medieval crowns. Both Constantine and his horse have, it seems to me, French medieval precedents, as on a remarkable seal of Renaud de Montfaucon (Fig. 469), but the antique reminiscences are more pervasive. If the medals were made in Paris around 1400 but based in part on earlier models, the Duke could have known the truth about their origin; indeed, it would scarcely have been possible to conceal it from him.[155] He would have been happy with objects that evoked in some way the features of the earlier emperors. He surely knew that his medal of Francesco Carrara was a lead copy, not an original. Even later, in the Renaissance, no sharp distinctions were made or sought between ancient originals and copies. No more relevant and piquant proof could be provided than the fact that our very medals were widely believed to be antique in Italy as elsewhere throughout most of the sixteenth century.

We can recognize with special clarity in these Byzantine or pseudo-Byzantine objects the blending of three of the Duke's major values: the religious, the historical, and the aesthetic. The first two were more traditional and their presence is also easier to demonstrate. The purchase of the medals of Constantine and Heraclius was evidently part of a larger program. Some months earlier in 1402 he had bought from another dealer – these professionals knew what the Duke wanted – two smaller gold medals of Tiberius and Augustus, and in the same year he acquired the gold relief of the Emperor Philip. These additions to the collection were certainly related to the famous gallery of portraits established by the Duke at his château of Bicêtre. There one could see not only the kings of France and the emperors of the Holy Roman Empire but the Eastern emperors as well.[156] We have observed that several princes of the fourteenth century created or continued pre-existing series of historic portraits. The genre was established; what was exceptional about the cycle formed by Jean de Berry was the comparative authenticity of the models that were employed and the quality of the result.

In the absence of written evidence it is difficult to be certain that the Duke took delight in the formal qualities of his early medieval and ancient objects also. Given, however, the great number of them, their varied subjects, and his wholly exceptional 'eye', it is safer to conclude that he valued many of his 'ouvrages d'ancienne façon' (early medieval objects), 'ouvrages de Grèce', and even ancient objects for their form as well as their meaning. If this is true he would have advanced beyond the notions of most of the fourteenth-century French humanists, who appreciated such objects for their historical and symbolical significance. He would have resembled a younger scholar such as Niccolo Niccoli in early Quattrocento Florence more than Jean de Montreuil, with his vague, bookish ideas of Praxiteles and Lysippus. There was nevertheless a real difference between the great Northern connoisseur and the Florentine humanists and sculptors. They were acquiring an understanding of ancient monumental relief and statuary, in which the Duke, so far as we know, had no interest. His appreciation was limited to small objects, often in precious materials. But this, we should add, tended to be a limitation of his taste in general. With certain notable exceptions – Sluter, Beauneveu – this was a period of *Kleinkunst*.

Jean de Berry's sculptors, Beauneveu and Jean de Cambrai, seem to have been innocent of even a rudimentary concern with Byzantine or ancient art. Among the painters, only the latest, the Limbourgs, seem to have studied and utilized a few of the non-Gothic images in the collection. One of the antique or Early Christian ones may have served as a model for Adam in the Garden of Eden. Twisting himself into an elaborate contrapposto as he reluctantly accepts the apple from his temptress Adam is an exceptional figure in the painting of the Limbourgs, not fully adapted to his new role.[157] The one certain instance of dependence upon such an object is the Magus in the scene of the Meeting of the Magi. This image of power and authority, conveyed by an absolutely masterful control of a prancing horse, is a copy of the medal of Constantine (Fig. 462).[158] If this medal is connected with the presence of the Byzantine emperor in Paris history would have been destined to repeat itself. The son and successor of Manuel II, John VIII, likewise journeyed to the West, and his visit similarly affected the representation of the mounted Magi, in this instance Benozzo Gozzoli's in the famous mural in the Medici Palace in Florence.

That Jean de Berry had an elementary appreciation of the form of his Byzantine and his ancient objects is suggested also by his enthusiasm for Trecento painting. Some of the Italian masters whom he apparently admired and whom his painters studied – Ambrogio Lorenzetti and Giotto – were themselves able to comprehend and even to utilize ancient models. The painting of the earlier Trecento probably served the Duke – without his awareness – as a first approach to antiquity, a stage in the process of understanding it. At best this was, we must repeat, an initial stage. Still, the patronage of Jean de Berry clearly promoted a major phase of the return of the North to the Mediterranean.

The Duke was nevertheless not antagonistic to an opposing trend that was fostered by all but the greatest masters, and accepted to a lesser degree even by them: a trend characterized by the rhythmical interplay of all elements of a composition, a salience of the borders of these elements, a delight in stylization and abstraction, so that the figures themselves would seem harmonious with the filigree and ornaments that enliven the designs. This trend is visible among the more earthy Netherlanders as well as the astonishingly sophisticated 'pure' Parisians. This is what we normally identify as the International Style.[159]

The strength of this *maniera parigina* checked the efforts of the more vigorous artists to assimilate the achievements of the great Trecento painters. It also compromised their intention to move beyond these achievements by fresh observations of the natural world and their wish to represent the world in a more 'direct' and less stylized manner. Jacquemart de Hesdin appears to have been less troubled by these problems, but the Boucicaut Master and the Limbourgs were unable or unwilling to make a radical decision to abandon the *maniera* – at least until the end of their careers. Whether the Limbourgs thought the Duke would not be pleased we cannot guess.

Though in this respect the Limbourgs were irresolute in others, we must recall, they were very venturesome. Their journey to Italy implies a deep concern with problems of form and representation. This they shared with Jacquemart and the Boucicaut Master as well as their patron. The period as a whole cared relatively little about drama, and most of the Duke's painters sacrificed emotionality to their concern for the structure of figures and space and for their fascination with light. Their study of Italian painting differed in this respect from Pucelle's. In general their estimate of their primary task – the synthesis of novel, more naturalistic forms with ideal, geometrical principles of representation – anticipated to a degree that of the second generation of Renaissance painters, Uccello, Domenico Veneziano, and Piero della Francesca.

The outlook of Jacquemart, the Boucicaut Master, and the Limbourgs did not persist in France. The hard-won positions were abruptly lost. France was moving deeper into civil war and then foreign occupation. Among the humanists there were signs of a reaction, provoked also by advancing age. Around 1418 Nicolas de Clamanges wrote to Gontier Col upon the receipt of some manuscripts of Jerome and Augustine: 'These authors satisfy my true inner preferences. I am sated with reading the pagans, who now arouse in me distaste rather than pleasure. . . . Neither the beautiful fronds of their verbal elegance nor the vernal blooms of their faultless eloquence now nourish my spirit, eager as it is for true fruits. . . . In our youth we were permitted to traverse the gardens of the oratorical art and gather blossoms for a while, but spring is transformed into summer, and summer into autumn. . . .'[160]

Nicolas de Clamanges was dead in 1420, and by a remarkable and solemn coincidence all our protagonists disappeared within a few years: Gontier Col in 1415; Pierre Col, Jean de Berry, all three Limbourgs in 1416; Jean de Montreuil in 1420. The Limbourgs, killed by the plague, were still young, artistically, at death. Their Calendar pages of the *Très Riches Heures* had only recently opened new pictorial horizons, and *October* was a portent (Fig. 844). Its basic conception of a spatial continuum, of which one part only is visible, the uninterrupted recession of the ground plane, the volumetric rather than linear structure, the cast shadows, all are harbingers of the Brancacci Chapel. Its intimate observation of the natural world, on the other hand, its description of the unique and accidental, and its analysis of the interaction of color and light point toward the van Eycks. The further conquests, in fact, were to be made outside of France, by the great masters in Italy and the Netherlands. There is a deep appropriateness in the fact that Jan van Eyck began, as far as we know, to paint in the spaces of a book left empty by the Duke of Berry.

The one great painter that was rising in France, the Rohan Master, and his vigorous colleague, the Master of the Berry Apocalypse, pursued very different ideals. They strove for bold, exciting, rushing designs and clamorous color. The Rohan Master restored narration to its old importance, and he dwelt on unrestrained, even extreme, emotional states. He was obsessed by the representation of death, and there he was most powerful. His art proved clearly that if there was a trend toward a Renaissance in France it was – to borrow a phrase from a historian of early French humanism – decisively 'avortée'.[161] In literature too after 1420 a note of deeper melancholy was sounded, particularly in the poetry of Alain Chartier.

October in the *Très Riches Heures* was perhaps the last painting Jean de Berry saw, and it may have been the last miniature that the Limbourgs painted, for the Duke died on June 15, 1416 and all three of the brothers followed him to the grave three or four months later. Let us assume, in any event, that the Duke did see the picture and let us hope that he had an inkling of his own considerable share in moving painting into a new realm. No-one else in his time sensed it, as far as we can see. Critical and historical literature did not emerge in France until much later, and its absence may indeed have contributed to the decline of the new art. The Duke enjoyed, to be sure, a great reputation in France for his passion for luminous *joyaux*. The King twitted him, as we have seen, for his readiness to accept gifts of rubies even from pagan rulers,[162] and already in the early 'nineties Thomas de Saluces said that Jean de Berry promptly deserted political gatherings when Venetian vendors of precious stones appeared on the scene.[163]

The Duke's reputation as a collector of gems spread to Italy, and he was still remembered there in the later fifteenth century. In the section on precious stones and gems in his *Trattato dell'archi-*

tettura Filarete wrote: '. . . si loda ancora il duca di Berri della sua tanta dilectatione di queste cose. . . .' Then, like a reporter for the *New York Times*, he proved his point by a reference to prices: '. . . dove avessi sentito, che fusse stata una cosa degnia, non guardava in danari; chè bisogniava che l' avesse, se possibile era'.[164] Only Christine de Pisan wrote a broader evaluation of her patron. Describing him briefly in an historical text she gave him at New Year 1405, she chose to refer to his collection of manuscripts, richly illuminated in the Berry, Paris, and elsewhere. She even remarked on his affection for his good craftsmen and his generosity in rewarding them. The sketch is well balanced, except that as a scholar and a woman and an evangelist she somewhat overstressed the educational and moral aspect of his library.

> . . . il est prince de grande bénignité envers tous ceux qui ont à lui parler . . . moult est débonnaire à ses serviteurs, les aime et porte, et enrichist, par especial, ceulx dont a singulière oppinion, ou a trouvé bons. Se délicte et aime gens soubtilz, soyent clercs, ou autres, beaulx livres des sciences morales et histoires notables des pollicies rommaines, ou d'autres louables enseignemens; moult aime et voulentiers en oit, tous ouvrages soubtilment fais et par maistrise beauls et polis, aornemens riches, beauls édifices dont a fait faire maint en son pays, à Paris, et alieurs. . . .[165]

Beyond this Christine could hardly go. Like all estimates of this sort it was partly conventional. Though she was closer to painting than any other writer of her time she found in France no tradition for discussing it. She probably knew Boccaccio's remarks in the *Decameron* about a certain famous Giotto, but other Italian approaches to the history of art, as in Filippo Villani's *Elogium*, had probably not yet come North. They took no account, in any event, of patrons and collectors – there were none, in fact, comparable to Jean de Berry. Christine was probably unaware of his predecessors in France, such as Abbot Suger; she did not speak of the larger role of secular art in the Duke's collections and the greater independence of aesthetic values in his judgments. That the Medici and the Renaissance popes were soon to appear not even an extraordinary woman could know.

APPENDIX

LIST OF BERRY'S EXTANT ILLUMINATED MANUSCRIPTS

The list contains ten additions to the lists of Delisle and Guiffrey, as well as some deletions. The only publications cited here are those relevant to ownership by the Duke. Studies of other kinds are cited in the catalogue or elsewhere in the publication.

ANGERS, Bibl. municipale, fr. 162 (154).
Cité de Dieu. First part of ms. (Books I-X) of which second part is in Cambridge (Mass.), Harvard College Library. French, *circa* 1380.
Laborde, *Cité de Dieu*, 1909, I, pp. 244-264 no. 8; Plates, pl. XIA.

BALTIMORE, Walters Art Gallery, ms. 1251-26 (formerly Ashburnham and Yates Thompson).
Bible historiale. French, end of the 14th century.
Signature of Jean de Berry and Flamel inscription. Not in 1402 inventory; given to Jean Harpedenne in 1410.
Guiffrey, *Inventaires*, I, p. CLXII no. 8; II, p. 316 no. 10; Delisle, *Charles V*, 1907, II, pp. 225 no. 10, 272.

BOURGES, Bibl. municipale, ms. 33-36. (Figs. 254, 499).
Lectionary of the Ste-Chapelle. Pseudo-Jacquemart and the Boucicaut Workshop. Portrait, arms and devices of Jean de Berry. The ms. belonged to the canons of the Ste-Chapelle, according to an early inscription on the last folio (not hitherto mentioned), and it may be the *Lectionnaire* that appears in the list of mss. given to the chapel by the Duke (Bibl. nat., lat. 17173, fol. 228).
Guiffrey, *Inventaires*, I, p. CLXIII no. 17; II, p. 317 no. 44; Delisle, *Charles V*, 1907, II, pp. 230 no. 44 bis, 277 f.

BOURGES, Bibl. municipale, ms. 48. (Figs. 253, 493).
Evangeliary. Pseudo-Jacquemart.
Portrait, arms and emblems of Jean de Berry. Contrary to assertions by Delisle and later historians, the ms. cannot be identified in the Duke's inventories (see Catalogue of mss., pp. 320 f.).

BRUSSELS, Bibl. Royale, ms. 9542.
Geoffroi de la Tour-Landry, *Livre pour l'enseignement de ses filles*. Written 1371-1372. One miniature, late 14th century.
Two signatures of Jean de Berry. Not inventoried.

Delisle, *Cabinet*, III, 1881, p. 389; Guiffrey, *Inventaires*, I, p. CLXXVIII no. 76; Brussels, Gaspar and Lyna, I, 1937, p. 336 no. 138 pl. LXXIC; Delisle, *Charles V*, 1907, II, pp. 251 no. 170 bis, 303.

BRUSSELS, Bibl. Royale, ms. 9555-8.
Durand de Champagne, *Œuvres*. The Virgil Master.
Signature of Jean de Berry.
Guiffrey, *Inventaires*, I, p. CLXXVI no. 65; II, p. 318; Delisle, *Charles V*, 1907, II, pp. 269 no. 285 bis, 316.

BRUSSELS, Bibl. Royale, ms. 11060-1. (Figs. 179-215, 478, 479, 665).
Très Belles Heures de Jean de Berry. Jacquemart de Hesdin (with assistants), the Master of the Brussels Initials, and an anonymous master.
Arms, devices, and portraits of the Duke. Acquired before 1402, and shortly thereafter given to the Duke of Burgundy (inv. of 1402).
Guiffrey, *Inventaires*, I, p. CLXVI no. 24; II, p. 132 no. 1050; Delisle, *Charles V*, 1907, II, pp. 238 no. 98, 282-283.

CAMBRIDGE (Mass.), Hofer Collection, Harvard College Library, ms. Typ. 201 H. (Fig. 535).
Cité de Dieu (second part, Books XI–XXII; for first part see Angers). A distinctive style in the Bondol tradition, very close to Bibl. nat., fr. 22912-3, and Brit. Mus., Add. 15245. Towards 1380.
Arms of Jean de Berry (but ms. perhaps originally made for Charles V).
Yates Thompson, Second Series, pp. 206-209 no. 80; Delisle, *Charles V*, 1907, I, pp. 223, 411; II, p. 317.

CHANTILLY, Musée Condé, ms. 65. (Figs. 419-424, 442, 489, 844).
Très Riches Heures de Jean de Berry. The Limbourg brothers.
Arms and a portrait of the Duke. Incomplete in 1416 (inv. of 1416).
Guiffrey, *Inventaires*, I, p. CLXV no. 22; II, p. 280 no. 1164; Delisle, *Charles V*, 1907, II, pp. 239 no. 101, 290.

CHANTILLY, Musée Condé, ms. 277 (formerly 1327).

Éthiques d'Aristote. Late Bondol tradition.

Given by Louis d'Orléans between 1402 and 1407 to Jean de Berry, whose signature appears on fol. 1. Bibl. nat., fr. 9106 is the first volume of these translations.

Guiffrey, *Inventaires*, I, p. 248 no. 947; Delisle, *Charles V*, 1907, II, pp. 248 no. 151, 303; Chantilly (Meurgey), *Manuscrits*, 1930, p. 48; A. D. Menut, *Maistre Nicole Oresme: Le Livre de Éthiques d'Aristote*, New York, 1940, p. 48, gives the signature incorrectly as no. 227.

DUBLIN, Coll. A. C. Beatty, ms. 75 (formerly Ashburnham and Yates Thompson).

Vincent of Beauvais, *Mirouer historial*, Vols. I and II (for Vol. III see London, Brit. Mus., Add. 6416). Related to Bondol style, *ca.* 1370.

Arms and signature of Jean de Berry, and inscription of Flamel. Owned by Jean de Berry before 1402. Given to Jehan de Montagu and recovered after his death. Given to the Duke of Burgundy February 9, 1413.

Guiffrey, *Inventaires*, I, p. CLXX no. 44; London, Thompson Coll., 1902, pp. 193–206 no. 79; Delisle, *Charles V*, 1907, II, pp. 255 no. 201, 306; Dublin, Beatty Coll., Millar, 1930, no. 75.

GENEVA, Bibl. publique et universitaire, fr. 77. (Fig. 825).

Tite-Live. Illuminated by the workshop of Berry's Cleres Femmes.

Signature of Jean de Berry and inscription of Flamel.

Delisle, *Charles V*, 1907, II, pp. 261 no. 236 bis, 311 f.

GENEVA, Bibl. publique et universitaire, fr. 190.

Boccaccio, *Cas des nobles hommes et femmes.* Luçon Master.

Given to Berry for New Year, 1411, by Martin Gouge, Archbishop of Chartres.

Guiffrey, *Inventaires*, I, p. 265 no. 993; Delisle, *Charles V*, 1907, II, pp. 256 no. 208, 333 f.

GERONA, Cathedral.

Bible. Bolognese, early 14th century (Fig. 837).

In an inscription (fol. 493v.) Charles V says he bought the Bible in Beauvais. A note added to the inventory item of the royal library states that the Bible passed to the Duke of Berry in November, 1383.

Brutails, 1886, p. 638; Delisle, *Charles V*, 1907, II, pp. 3 no. 2, 223 no. 1 bis.

THE HAGUE, Museum Meermanno-Westreenianum, ms. 10 B 23. (Figs. 378, 382, 386).

Bible de Charles V. Jean Bondol (1371) and related masters.

The Bible passed from Charles V, who received it March 28, 1372, to Louis d'Anjou, and then to Jean de Berry, at whose death it was returned to the royal library (royal inv. of 1424).

Douët d'Arcq, *Bibliothèque de Charles VI*, 1867, p. 64 no. 213; The Hague, Kon. Bibl., Byvanck, 1924, pp. 104 f.

THE HAGUE, Royal Library, ms. 78 D 42.

Christine de Pisan, *Mutacion de Fortune.* Atelier of the Master of the Épître d'Othéa.

Given by the author to the Duke in March 1404, according to an inscription of Flamel (fol. 170v.) and the inventories of 1413 and 1416. Signature of Jean de Berry.

Guiffrey, *Inventaires*, I, pp. CLXXVI no. 70, 250 no. 952; II, p. 277 no. 1116; Delisle, *Charles V*, II, 1907, p. 269 no. 287.

LONDON, Brit. Mus., Add. 6416.

Vincent of Beauvais, *Mirouer historial*, Vol. III (for Vols. I and II see Dublin, Coll. A. C. Beatty, ms. 75).

Guiffrey, *Inventaires*, I, p. CLXX, no. 44; Dublin, Beatty Coll., Millar, 1930, no. 75.

LONDON, Brit. Mus., Add. 29986.

Le miroir des dames. French, *ca.* 1405.

Acquired after 1402 and before 1413 (inv. of 1413). Folio 2 begins 'ter et reposer'.

Guiffrey, *Inventaires*, I, pp. CLXXV no. 64, 262 no. 983; Delisle, *Charles V*, 1907, II, p. 268 no. 285.

LONDON, Brit. Mus., Burney 275.

Works of Priscian. Early 14th century.

Arms and signature (fol. 560v.) of Jean de Berry; inscription of Flamel (fol. 2v.).

Ms. given by Pope Clement VII to the Duke in 1387 (colophon). The Duke gave it to the Duke of Orléans (note added to entry in the inv. of 1402), and then recovered it after the death of the latter in 1407 (inv. of 1413).

Guiffrey, *Inventaires*, I, pp. CLXXIV no. 57, 252 no. 957; II, p. 122 no. 954; Delisle, *Charles V*, 1907, II, pp. 264 no. 257, 314.

LONDON, Brit. Mus., Harley 4381-82. (Figs. 617, 622).

Bible historiale. Follower of Jacquemart, Virgil Master and collaborators.

Inscriptions by Berry and Flamel. Not inventoried.

Guiffrey, *Inventaires*, I, p. CLXII no. 7; II, p. 317 no. 12 bis; Delisle, *Charles V*, 1907, II, pp. 225 no. 11 bis, 273.

LONDON, Brit. Mus., Lansdowne 1175.
Bible, Vol. I. Miniatures in the Bondol tradition.
Inscription of Jean de Berry (fol. 414v.).
Guiffrey, *Inventaires*, I, p. CLXI no. 4; Delisle, *Charles V*, 1907, I, p. 147 no. V; II, p. 226 no. 14.

LONDON, Brit. Mus., Royal 19 E VI.
Les croniques de Burgues. Cité des Dames workshop.
Bought by Berry October 29, 1407 (inv. of 1413). Inscription on fol. 457v., erased but recorded in the *Catalogue of Royal Manuscripts* (London, Brit. Mus., Warner and Gilson, 1921).
Delisle, *Charles V*, 1907, II, p. 264 no. 254.

LONDON, Brit. Mus., Royal 20 C VIII.
Larbre des batailles. Ca. 1400.
Miniature on fol. 1 shows presentation to a prince, perhaps Jean de Berry; his arms are in the lower border. (Ms. does not correspond with the copy in the inv. of 1413).
Guiffrey, *Inventaires*, I, pp. CLXXVI no. 68, 262 no. 985; Delisle, *Charles V*, 1907, II, pp. 270 no. 294, 316.

LYONS, Bibl. municipale, ms. 742.
Ovid, *Métamorphoses*. Ca. 1390.
Inscription, largely effaced, of Jean de Berry.
Guiffrey, *Inventaires*, I, p. 237 no. 914; II, p. 127 no. 987; Delisle, *Charles V*, 1907, II, pp. 266 no. 264, 315; France, *Cat. général des manuscrits*, III, 1885, p. 641.

MUNICH, Bayr. Staatsbibliothek, lat. 10072. (Figs. 716, 717, 751).
Missal, written in 1374 and illuminated by Niccolò da Bologna (one miniature signed by him).
The arms of Jean de Berry were added on fol. 1 over those of Cardinal Pierre d'Estaing, Archbishop of Bourges, presumably the original owner. He died in 1377. The ms. appears in the Berry inv. of 1402; it was given to the Ste-Chapelle in 1404, but withdrawn in 1412.
Guiffrey, *Inventaires*, II, p. 123 no. 957; Durrieu, 1916, pp. 111 ff.

NEW YORK, The Cloisters.
Belles Heures de Jean de Berry. The Limbourg brothers. (Figs. 261, 495, 496, 518, 746, 779, 785).

Arms, devices, and portraits of the Duke. Illuminated for him before 1413 (inv. of 1413).
Guiffrey, *Inventaires*, I, pp. CLXVI no. 26, 253 no. 960; II, pp. 238 no. 507, 319; Delisle, *Charles V*, 1907, II, pp. 239 no. 100, 290.

NEW YORK, The Cloisters.
Heures de Jeanne d'Évreux. Illuminated by Jean Pucelle, 1325–1328. (Figs. 250, 335-338, 342, 360).
Entered Berry collection between 1380 and 1402 (all inventories).
Delisle, *Charles V*, 1907, II, pp. 241 no. 108, 299.

NEW YORK, Morgan Library, ms. 133. (Fig. 843).
Apocalypse. The Berry Apocalypse Master.
Signature of Jean de Berry. Not in the Duke's inventories.

NEW YORK, Morgan Library, ms. 785. (Figs. 826-827).
Livre d'astrologie. Flemish (Bruges), 1402–1403.
Given to the Duke by the Abbot of St. Barthélemé, Bruges, June 7, 1403 (inscription).
Guiffrey, *Inventaires*, I, p. 245 no. 935; II, p. 276; Delisle, *Charles V*, 1907, II, pp. 252 no. 177, 304.

OXFORD, Bodleian Library, Rawl. C. 538. (Fig. 654).
Secret des secrez. Workshop of Jacquemart de Hesdin.
Arms of the Duke. Probably identical with no. 1032 of the inv. of 1402, rather than with no. 1022 (as proposed by Pächt, *Burl. Mag.*, 1956, p. 146). No. 1022 gives a full title, including *Secret des secrez*, but only no. 1032 had a miniature at the beginning, representing a subject similar to that of the Oxford ms. Furthermore no. 1022 was appraised in 1416 at an almost negligible sum (10 *sous*), whereas a figure six times as much was fixed for no. 1032.
Guiffrey, *Inventaires*, I, pp. 232 f. nos. 890, 893; II, pp. 237 no. 476, 276 no. 1093.

PARIS, Bibl. de l'Arsenal, ms. 650.
Book of Hours. Egerton Master and follower of Boucicaut Master.
This ms. probably corresponds with a Book of Hours purchased by the Duke in 1415. The contents of the text are similar, though not now identical, and the *incipit* on the second folio of the Hours of the Virgin is, as in the inventory item, *quoniam*.
Guiffrey, *Inventaires*, I, p. 330 no. 1232; Delisle, *Charles V*, 1907, II, p. 241 no. 110.

PARIS, Bibl. de l'Arsenal, ms. 664.
Térence des ducs. The Terence Master, the Luçon workshop, the Master of the Cité des Dames, and the Adelphoe Master.
Given to the Duke by the Bishop of Châlons early in 1416 (late additions to inv. of 1413).
Guiffrey, *Inventaires*, I, p. 335 no. 1248; II, p. 301 (but not in Guiffrey's list of the Duke's mss.); Delisle, *Charles V*, 1907, II, pp. 265 no. 262, 314.

PARIS, Bibl. de l'Arsenal, ms. 5057-5058. (Fig. 829).
Bible historiale. Formerly in one volume. Master of Berry's Cleres Femmes, Master of the Cité des Dames, and other illuminators.
Inscription of Jean de Berry, but no longer readable.
Paris, Arsenal, Martin, *Catalogue des manuscrits*, v, 1889, p. 29; Delisle, *Charles V*, 1907, II, pp. 225 no. 8, 272.

PARIS, Bibl. de l'Arsenal, ms. 5107.
Les échecs moralisés. Late 14th century, in a style derived from the Bondol tradition.
In collection before 1402 (all inventories). Signature of Jean de Berry.
Delisle, *Charles V*, 1907, II, pp. 251 no. 172, 304.

PARIS, Bibl. de l'Arsenal, ms. 5212.
Bible historiale, Vol. I. Frontispiece late Pucelle; the rest influenced by Bondol.
Given to Jean de Berry by Charles VI on April 25, 1403.
Guiffrey, *Inventaires*, I, p. 244 no. 934; II, p. 276 no. 1106; Delisle, *Charles V*, 1907, II, pp. 255 no. 12, 273.

PARIS, Bibl. nat., fr. 117-120. (Fig. 824).
Lancelot du Lac. Early 15th century, Master of Berry's Cleres Femmes and associates (mostly repainted, later 15th century).
Arms and signature of Jean de Berry. Probably this was the ms. bought from the dealer Regnault du Montet in 1405 (inv. of 1413). The inventory refers to 'un grant livre' and not to four volumes.
Guiffrey, *Inventaires*, I, pp. CLXXIV no. 60, 239 no. 920; II, p. 237 no. 490; Delisle, *Charles V*, 1907, II, p. 266 no. 270.

PARIS, Bibl. nat., fr. 159. (Fig. 822).
Bible historiale. Master of the Coronation of the Virgin and related illuminators. Signatures of Jean de Berry and inscription by Flamel. Given to Berry by Raoulet d'Auquetonville before 1402 (inv. of 1402).
Guiffrey, *Inventaires*, I, pp. CLXI no. 6, 225 no. 854; II,
p. 236 no. 456; Delisle, *Charles V*, 1907, II, pp. 225 no. 9, 272.

PARIS, Bibl. nat., fr. 172-173.
Cité de Dieu. Mediocre follower of the Bedford Master. Given to Berry by Pierre Salmon before 1413. Not in lists of Berry mss. of Delisle or Guiffrey. Correctly identified by Laborde with an item in 1413 inv. Colophon in 173, fol. 304, erased and not legible.
Guiffrey, *Inventaires*, I, pp. 255 no. 964, 341; II, pp. 238, 301; Laborde, *Cité de Dieu*, 1909, I, p. 285.

PARIS, Bibl. nat., fr. 176.
Durand, *Rationale.* In style derived from the Bondol tradition.
Inscribed by Berry. Acquired before 1402 (inv. of 1402).
Guiffrey, *Inventaires*, I, pp. CLXIV no. 18, 226 no. 858; II, pp. 125 no. 970, 236 no. 459; Delisle, *Charles V*, 1907, II, p. 229 no. 43.

PARIS, Bibl. nat., fr. 246.
Livre de Suétoine. Written in 1346. French illumination of this period.
Signature of Jean de Berry. Acquired before 1402 (all inventories).
Delisle, *Cabinet*, I, 1868, p. 66; Guiffrey, *Inventaires*, I, pp. CLXX no. 42, 227 no. 861; II, pp. 125 no. 974, 236 no. 461; Delisle, *Charles V*, 1907, II, pp. 260 no. 232, 309 f.

PARIS, Bibl. nat., fr. 247. (Fig. 683).
Les antiquités judaïques. Two miniatures by a follower of Jacquemart de Hesdin, a third by a contemporary French illuminator, the rest by Fouquet later in the century.
Inscription of the late 15th century refers to three miniatures by the Duke of Berry's illuminator and nine others by Fouquet (some in the second volume, nouv. acq. fr. 21013). This ms. cannot be identified in the inventories.
Guiffrey, *Inventaires*, I, p. CLXVIII no. 37; II, pl. 137 nos. 1028, 1029; Delisle, *Charles V*, 1907, II, pp. 257 no. 210 ter, 308.

PARIS, Bibl. nat., fr. 256.
Histoire ancienne. Early 15th century.
Ms. now contains only an historiated initial on fol. 10. The appearance of 'pour troie restaurer' at the beginning of fol. 11 (the second folio of the text proper) proves that this was the ms. bought by the Duke *ca.* 1405. Inscription of Jean de Berry (fol. 198 v.).
Guiffrey, *Inventaires*, I, p. 241 no. 925.

PARIS, Bibl. nat., fr. 263.
Tite-Live. The Virgil Master.
Inscriptions of Jean de Berry and Flamel; acquired before 1402 (inv. of 1402).
Guiffrey, *Inventaires*, I, pp. CLXIX no. 40, 226 no. 856; Delisle, *Charles V*, 1907, II, p. 261 no. 233.

PARIS, Bibl. nat., fr. 282.
Valère Maxime. The Virgil Master.
Signature of Jean de Berry. Given to Berry in January 1402 by his treasurer Jacques Courau (inv. of 1402), and then transferred to the Ste-Chapelle.
Guiffrey, *Inventaires*, I, pp. CLXIX no. 39, 236 no. 911; II, p. 276 no. 1097; Delisle, *Charles V*, 1907, II, p. 256 no. 206.

PARIS, Bibl. nat., fr. 373.
Ovid, *Métamorphoses*. French, *ca.* 1400.
Signature of Jean de Berry. Acquired before 1402 (inv. of 1402).
Delisle, *Cabinet*, III, 1881, p. 192 no. 267; Guiffrey, *Inventaires*, I, pp. CLXXIV no. 56, 226 no. 859; II, pp. 125 no. 972, 236 no. 460; Delisle, *Charles V*, 1907, II, p. 266 no. 267.

PARIS, Bibl. nat., fr. 380. (Figs. 624, 845).
Roman de la rose. 1390-1400, influenced by Jacquemart.
Signature of Jean de Berry and inscription by Flamel. Acquired on July 7, 1403 (inv. of 1413), as a gift from Martin Gouge, and given by the Duke on March 3, 1414 to Guillaume Lurin (inscription of Flamel).
Guiffrey, *Inventaires*, I, pp. CLXXV no. 61, 245 no. 936; II, p. 238 no. 505; Delisle, *Charles V*, 1907, II, p. 267 no. 276.

PARIS, Bibl. nat., fr. 425.
Composition de la Sainte Écriture (*Le cy nous dit*). Mediocre miniatures of the end of the 14th century.
Signature of Jean de Berry. Bought by Berry in Paris in February 1404 (inv. of 1413).
Guiffrey, *Inventaires*, I, pp. CLXII no. 11, 238 no. 918; Delisle, *Charles V*, 1907, II, p. 229 nos. 40-41.

PARIS, Bibl. nat., fr. 565.
Aristotle, *Du ciel et du monde*.
Signature of Jean de Berry. This ms., containing illuminations of around 1410, cannot be identified, as has been proposed, with the ms. of this text in the inv. of 1402 (that ms. is Bibl. nat., fr. 1082).
Guiffrey, *Inventaires*, I, pp. CLXXIII no. 52, 230 no. 877; Delisle, *Charles V*, 1907, II, p. 248 no. 154.

PARIS, Bibl. nat., fr. 568.
Brunetto Latini, *Livre du trésor*. Derived from the Bondol tradition.
Acquired before 1402 (inv. of 1402).
Guiffrey, *Inventaires*, I, pp. CLXXII no. 51, 228 no. 870; II, pp. 127 no. 990, 236 no. 465; Delisle, *Charles V*, 1907, II, p. 247 no. 147.

PARIS, Bibl. nat., fr. 574.
Image du monde. Parisian, *ca.* 1325.
Acquired before 1402 (inv. of 1402).
Delisle, *Cabinet*, I, 1886, p. 66; Guiffrey, *Inventaires*, I, pp. CLXX no. 45, 235 no. 908; II, pp. 135 no. 1064, 237 no. 485; Delisle, *Charles V*, 1907, II, pp. 246 no. 141, 302.

PARIS, Bibl. nat., fr. 598. (Figs. 289, 291, 294, 561).
Des cleres et nobles femmes. Master of Berry's Cleres Femmes.
Signature of Jean de Berry and inscription of Flamel. Given to Berry in February 1404 by Jean de la Barre.
Guiffrey, *Inventaires*, I, pp. CLXXVI no. 72, 246 no. 940; II, p. 237 no. 500; Delisle, *Charles V*, 1907, II, p. 256 no. 209.

PARIS, Bibl. nat., fr. 606, 835-836. (Figs. 324, 817, 833, 834).
Œuvres de Christine de Pisan. Master of the Épître d'Othéa, and the Egerton Master. 1404-1409.
Fr. 835, the first part of this work, originally had a second folio beginning 'Tous mes bonjours', and thus conforms with item in the inv. of 1413.
Delisle, *Charles V*, 1907, II, pp. 269 no. 291, 316; M. Roy, *Œuvres poétiques de Christine de Pisan*, Paris, I, 1886, pp. v ff.

PARIS, Bibl. nat., fr. 607.
Cité des Dames. Master of the Cité des Dames.
Signature of Jean de Berry.
Guiffrey, *Inventaires*, I, p. CLXXV no. 63; II, p. 318 no. 293; Delisle, *Charles V*, 1907, II, p. 270 no. 293.

PARIS, Bibl. nat., fr. 829.
Pélerinage du corps et de l'âme. Bondol tradition, *ca.* 1390.
Signature of Jean de Berry. Acquired between 1402-1413 (inv. of 1413).
Delisle, *Cabinet*, III, 1881, p. 193; Guiffrey, *Inventaires*, I, pp. CLXXVI no. 66, 242 no. 928; II, p. 237 no. 496; Delisle, *Charles V*, 1907, II, p. 268 no. 280.

PARIS, Bibl. nat., fr. 835-836: see fr. 606.

PARIS, Bibl. nat., fr. 1023. (Figs. 486, 643).
Le livre de bonnes mœurs. Luçon Master.
Given to Berry March 4, 1410 by the author Jacques
Legrand (Flamel inscription and inv. of 1413).
Guiffrey, *Inventaires*, I, pp. CLXVIII no. 34, 264 no. 991;
II, p. 238 no. 522; Delisle, *Charles V*, 1907, II, p. 245
no. 134.

PARIS, Bibl. nat., fr. 1082.
Aristotle, *Du ciel et du monde.* Bondol tradition.
Signature of Jean de Berry. Acquired before 1402 (inv.
of 1402).
Guiffrey, *Inventaires*, I, pp. CLXXIII no. 53, 230 no. 877;
II, pp. 128 no. 1003, 236 no. 469; Delisle, *Charles V*,
1907, II, p. 248 no. 154.
Cf. Bibl. nat., fr. 565.

PARIS, Bibl. nat., fr. 1210.
Informacion des rois et des princes. Frontispiece only, in a
style derived from the Boucicaut and Bedford Masters.
Signature of Jean de Berry. Bought in February 1410
from the Parisian bookseller Regnault du Montet (inv.
of 1413).
Guiffrey, *Inventaires*, I, pp. CLXVIII no. 35, 263 no. 989;
II, p. 238 no. 521; Delisle, *Charles V*, 1907, II, pp. 250
no. 167.

PARIS, Bibl. nat., fr. 1229.
Le livre de Vegèce.
In collection before 1402 (all inventories).
Delisle, *Charles V*, 1907, II, pp. 253 no. 189, 305.

PARIS, Bibl. nat., fr. 1454.
Le brut d'Angleterre. Follower of the Berry Apocalypse
Master.
Partially erased signature of Jean de Berry. Purchased
from Jehan Colin, *escolier*, September 3, 1413 (inv. of
1413).
Guiffrey, *Inventaires*, I, pp. CLXXIV no. 59, 330 no. 1231;
II, p. 239 no. 527, 338; Delisle, *Charles V*, 1907, II, p.
266 no. 271.

PARIS, Bibl. nat., fr. 2608.
Chroniques de France. Ca. 1400, Lower Rhenish (?).
Signature of Jean de Berry. Acquired before 1402,
perhaps from executors of the estate of Aimeri de
Rochechouart, who died in 1397 (inv. of 1402). Ms.
bears arms of the latter.
Guiffrey, *Inventaires*, I, pp. CLXXI no. 47, 227 no. 863;
II, pp. 126 no. 980, 236 no. 863. Delisle includes this ms.

in his list but identifies it wrongly with another *Chronique* (*Charles V*, 1907, II, p. 262 no. 244).

PARIS, Bibl. nat., fr. 2810.
Merveilles du monde. Boucicaut Master and collabora-
tors.
Given to Jean de Berry by Jean sans Peur in January
1413 (inv. of 1413).
Guiffrey, *Inventaires*, I, pp. CLXXII no. 49, 270 no. 1005;
II, p. 242 no. 558; Delisle, *Charles V*, 1907, II, pp. 254
no. 196, 305.

PARIS, Bibl. nat., fr. 5631.
Marco Polo, *Le devisement du monde.* Bondol tradition.
Signature of Jean de Berry.
Guiffrey, *Inventaires*, I, pp. CLXXII no. 50, 262 no. 982
(contrary to the statement of Guiffrey, this ms. has two
miniatures). Delisle, *Charles V*, 1907, II, p. 254 no. 197.

PARIS, Bibl. nat., fr. 5707.
Bible, Vol. II. Illuminated no doubt immediately after
the writing in 1362–1363.
Given to Berry August 1407 by his maître d'hôtel,
Vidame de Laonnois (inv. of 1413).
Guiffrey, *Inventaires*, I, pp. CLXI no. 3, 256 no. 966;
Delisle, *Charles V*, 1907, I, pp. 153 ff.; II, p. 226 no. 13.

PARIS, Bibl. nat., fr. 6271.
Cité de Dieu, Book One. Illuminated about 1390.
Signature of Jean de Berry. Acquired before 1402, and
given to the Ste-Chapelle in 1404 (inv. of 1402 and list of
mss. given to the Ste-Chapelle).
Guiffrey, *Inventaires*, I, p. CLXVII no. 30; II, pp. 134 no.
1060, 169 no. 167; Delisle, *Charles V*, 1907, II, pp. 242
no. 114, 300. Laborde, *Cité de Dieu*, 1909, I, p. 253 does
not accept the identification with a ms. in the inventories.

PARIS, Bibl. nat., fr. 6446.
Antiquités judaïques. By the atelier of the Cité des Dames
Master.
Signature of Jean de Berry and inscription of Flamel.
Guiffrey, *Inventaires*, I, p. CLXIX no. 38; Delisle, *Charles
V*, 1907, II, p. 257 no. 210 bis.

PARIS, Bibl. nat., fr. 9106.
Aristotle, *Politiques et Yconomique.* Ca. 1400. For the
Éthiques, vol. II of this ms., see Chantilly, Musée Condé,
ms. 277.
Signature of Jean de Berry. Inscription on last folio says

copied for 'Louis, duc d'Orléans', in 1397, 'qui le donna au duc de Berry . . .' Given by the Duke of Orléans to Jean de Berry before 1407, when the former was killed (inv. of 1413).
Guiffrey, *Inventaires*, I, pp. CLXXIII no. 54, 248 no. 947; II, p. 237 no. 503; Delisle, *Charles V*, 1907, II, pp. 248 no. 151, 303 (text incorrectly given as *Éthiques et Politiques*).

PARIS, Bibl. nat., fr. 9221.
Poésies de Guillaume de Machaut. Illumination of *ca.* 1390.
Signature of Jean de Berry and inscription of Flamel. This ms., apparently identical with the poems of Machaut already in the inv. of 1402, was given to the Ste-Chapelle and then presumably withdrawn because it was presented to the Duke of Clarence before 1413 (inv. of 1413).
Delisle, *Cabinet*, I, 1868, pp. 58 notes 2 and 3, 66; III, 1881, p. 193 no. 283; Guiffrey, *Inventaires*, I, pp. CLXXVI no. 67, 226 no. 860, 339 f.; II, pp. 125 no. 973, 127 n. 4, 318; Delisle, *Charles V*, 1907, II, p. 268 nos. 282-283.

PARIS, Bibl. nat., fr. 12201. (Fig. 438).
Fleur des histoires de la terre d'orient. Workshop of Master of the Coronation of the Virgin.
Given by the Duke of Burgundy to Berry March 22, 1403 (inv. of 1413).
Guiffrey, *Inventaires*, I, p. 244 no. 933; Delisle, *Charles V*, 1907, II, pp. 264 no. 256, 313.

PARIS, Bibl. nat., fr. 12595.
Roman de la rose. Ca. 1408.
Signature of Jean de Berry.
Paris, Bibl. nat., *Catalogue manuscrits français*, II, 1896, p. 571.

PARIS, Bibl. nat., fr. 13091. (Figs. 51-82).
Psalter of Jean de Berry. Miniatures by Beauneveu, the Pseudo-Jacquemart, and Jacquemart. *Ca.* 1386.
In the collection before 1402 (inv. of 1402).
Guiffrey, *Inventaires*, I, pp. LXXIV, CLXII no. 11, 235 no. 906; II, pp. 132 no. 1049, 237 no. 483; Delisle, *Charles V*, 1907, II, pp. 228 no. 30, 275 ff.

PARIS, Bibl. nat., fr. 15397. (Figs. 298, 301, 376, 377, 583).
Bible de Jean de Sy. Miniatures and drawings probably by Bondol and his atelier, and by a later illuminator *ca.* 1380.

Signature of Jean de Berry (mostly erased).
Durrieu, *Le manuscrit*, 1894, p. 93. This Bible was not included in the list of Berry's mss. compiled by either Delisle or Guiffrey.

PARIS, Bibl. nat., fr. 20090. (Figs. 602, 611).
Bible historiale. French, *ca.* 1380-1385.
Signature of Jean de Berry. While it has often been said that this is the ms. loaned by Charles VI to Berry on November 6, 1383, and returned to the royal library after the death of Berry (inventories of 1402, 1413, 1416), proof is lacking.
Guiffrey, *Inventaires*, I, pp. CLXI no. 5, 224 no. 853; II, pp. 122 no. 950, 236 no. 455; Delisle, *Charles V*, 1907, II, pp. 224 no. 7, 272.

PARIS, Bibl. nat., lat. 248.
Bible de Philippe le Bel. Early 14th century.
Signature of Jean de Berry. Inscription by Flamel of 1403. Not inventoried.
Guiffrey, *Inventaires*, I, p. CLX no. 2; Delisle, *Charles V*, 1907, II, p. 224 no. 6.

PARIS, Bibl. nat., lat. 919. (Figs. 217-244, 249, 251, 252, 484, 485).
Grandes Heures de Jean de Berry. Jacquemart (?), Pseudo-Jacquemart, the Boucicaut and Bedford workshops, and others.
Arms and portraits of the Duke. Inscription by Flamel stating that the work was completed in 1409. Inv. of 1413.
Guiffrey, *Inventaires*, I, pp. CLXIV no. 21, 253 no. 961; II, p. 280 no. 1159; Delisle, *Charles V*, 1907, II, p. 238 no. 99.

PARIS, Bibl. nat., lat. 1052. (Figs. 351, 359, 362, 367-371, 839).
Bréviaire de Charles V. Master of the Passion and collaborators.
Given to Jean de Berry in 1407-1408 by the Duchess of Orléans, who died in 1408, after the death of her husband, Louis, in 1407. Ms. earlier belonged to Charles V.
Guiffrey, *Inventaires*, I, pp. CLXIV no. 19, 258 no. 971 (incorrectly as lat. 4052); II, pp. 238 no. 512, 298.

PARIS, Bibl. nat., lat. 7907A. (Fig. 440).
Terence, *Comedies* (in Latin). Follower of Jacquemart de Hesdin.
A New Year's gift to the Duke of Berry from his

treasurer Martin Gouge on January 1, 1408 (inv. of 1413).
Guiffrey, *Inventaires*, I, pp. CLXXIII no. 55, 257 no. 969; II, p. 277 no. 1122; Delisle, *Charles V*, 1907, II, pp. 265 no. 261, 314.

PARIS, Bibl. nat., lat. 8824.
Psalter. English, 11th century.
Acquired before 1402 (inv. of 1402). Given to the Ste-Chapelle in 1404. Signature of Jean de Berry.
Delisle, *Cabinet*, III, 1881, p. 172 no. 18; Guiffrey, *Inventaires*, I, p. CLXIII no. 13; II, p. 131 no. 1027; Delisle, *Charles V*, 1907, II, pp. 226 no. 18, 274.

PARIS, Bibl. nat., lat. 8885.
Missal, early 14th century.
The Duke gave the ms. to the Ste-Chapelle between 1404 and 1406–1407.
Delisle, 1856, pp. 156 f.; Guiffrey, *Inventaires*, II, p. 177 no. 176; Leroquais, *Sacramentaires et missels*, 1924, II, pp. 180 ff.

PARIS, Bibl. nat., lat. 8886 (Figs. 268, 483).
Pontifical of Étienne Loypeau. Master of Luçon.
Missal and Pontifical, probably written for Étienne Loypeau, Bishop of Luçon.
Arms of Jean de Berry.
Guiffrey, *Inventaires*, I, p. 229 no. 874; II, pp. 169 no. 156, 236 no. 466; Delisle, *Charles V*, 1907, II, pp. 236 no. 90, 281, identify this Pontifical with a ms. in the Duke's collection by 1402. The key words given in the inventory do not, however, coincide with those in this ms.

PARIS, Bibl. nat., lat. 9321.
Boethius, *De Consolatione*. One miniature remaining (fol. 157), by the Master of the Orosius, Bibl. nat., fr. 301.
Signature of Jean de Berry. Presented to the Duke in 1404 by Nicolas Viaut and then given by the Duke to the Ste-Chapelle (list of 1404).
Guiffrey, *Inventaires*, I, p. CLXVII no. 32; Delisle, *Charles V*, 1907, II, p. 249 no. 158.

PARIS, Bibl. nat., lat. 10426.
Bible de St. Louis. French, *ca.* 1270.
Inscription of Flamel. Given to the Duke in September 1414.
Guiffrey, *Inventaires*, I, pp. CLX no. 1, 333 no. 1242; Delisle, *Charles V*, 1907, II, p. 224 no. 5.

PARIS, Bibl. nat., lat. 10483-4. (Figs. 260, 344, 374).
Bréviaire de Belleville. Pucelle workshop, *ca.* 1325.
Given to the Duke by Henry IV of England after death of Richard II (1399). Flamel inscription. Berry gave the ms. to Marie de France, nun at Poissy, October 7, 1413 (inv. of 1413).
Guiffrey, *Inventaires*, I, pp. CLXIV no. 20, 254-255 no. 963; Delisle, *Charles V*, 1907, II, pp. 231 no. 55, 278.

PARIS, Bibl. nat., lat. 18014 (Figs. 83-176, 498).
Petites Heures de Jean de Berry. Jacquemart, the Trinity Master, Pseudo-Jacquemart, and other illuminators.
Arms and portraits of the Duke. In his collection before 1402 (inv. of 1402).
Guiffrey, *Inventaires*, I, pp. CLXV no. 23, 224 no. 851; II, p. 31 no. 172; Delisle, *Charles V*, 1907, II, p. 239 no. 102.

PARIS, Bibl. nat., nouv. acq. fr. 24541, formerly Grand Séminaire, Soissons. (Figs 340, 562).
Miracles de Notre-Dame. Associates of Pucelle.
Given to Jean de Berry by Charles VI between 1402 and 1413 (inv. of 1413).
Delisle, *Cabinet*, III, 1881, pp. 324 ff.; Guiffrey, *Inventaires*, I, pp. CLXXIV no. 58, 248 no. 946; II, p. 237 no. 502; Delisle, *Charles V*, 1907, II, p. 258 no. 214.

PARIS, Bibl. nat., nouv. acq. lat. 3093 (Figs. 6-28, 570).
A part of the *Très Belles Heures de Notre-Dame*. Master of the Parement de Narbonne and assistants, Holy Ghost Master and Baptist Master.
Arms and portraits of the Duke. Evidence of various kinds indicates that the illumination of the ms. was begun by the Duke around 1383. He initiated a second campaign around 1405, and then in 1412 gave the ms. to Robinet d'Estampes (inv. of 1413).
Guiffrey, *Inventaires*, I, p. CLXVI no. 25; Delisle, *Charles V*, 1907, II, pp. 240 no. 102 bis, 297 ff.

PARIS, Louvre, Cabinet des Dessins, RF2022-2024. (Figs. 32, 33, 36, 37, 492).
Four folios from the *Très Belles Heures de Notre-Dame*.
Guiffrey, *Inventaires*, I, p. CLXXVIII no. 78; II, p. 319; Delisle, *Charles V*, 1907, II pp. 240 no. 102 bis, 295 ff.

ROME, Bibl. Vaticana, lat. 50-51 (Figs. 177, 178, 658, 661, 662).
Bible in two volumes. A French illuminator *ca.* 1390, Jacquemart de Hesdin, and the Trinity Master.
Arms and signature of Jean de Berry. Arms of Clement VII and a device of Simon Alegret, physician and

counselor of the Duke. The arms were executed between 1389 and 1394. Ms. was apparently a gift of the Duke and his physician to Pope Clement VII.
Delisle, *Charles V*, 1907, II, p. 224 no. 2 bis.

TURIN, Museo Civico.
Heures de Milan, a part of the *Très Belles Heures de Notre-Dame*. (Figs. 39, 41-50, 491, 537).
Delisle, *Charles V*, 1907, II, pp. 240 no. 102 bis, 295 ff.

TURIN, Museo Storico.
Roi Modus. French, *ca.* 1395.
Signature of Jean de Berry. Acquired by the Duke after 1409.
Delisle, *Cabinet*, III, 1881 pp. 340, 389; Guiffrey, *Inventaires*, II, p. 318; Nordenfalk, *Kung praktiks*, 1955, p. 57.

TURIN, Royal Library, ms. EV.49.
Heures de Savoie (destroyed 1904). Begun in Pucelle workshop. Completed for Charles V by his illuminators. Given to the Duke by Charles VI, July 7, 1409 (Flamel inscription). Not inventoried.
Guiffrey, *Inventaires*, I, p. CLXVI no. 27; II, p. 318; Delisle, *Charles V*, 1907, I, pp. 208 ff. no. XXX; II, p. 240 no. 102 ter.
Cf. Winchester, fragment of this ms.

TURIN, Royal Library, ms. K.IV.29 (Figs. 29-31, 34, 35, 38).
Heures de Turin (destroyed 1904). A part of the *Très Belles Heures de Notre-Dame*.
Reproduced by Durrieu (*Heures de Turin*, 1902).
Guiffrey, *Inventaires*, I, p. CLXVII no. 28; Delisle, *Charles V*, 1907, II, pp. 240 no. 102 bis, 295 ff.

WINCHESTER, Library of the Bishop.
Fragment from the *Heures de Savoie*.
Blanchard, *Heures de Savoie*, 1910.
See Turin, University Library, ms. E.V.49.

Doubtful and Erroneous Ascriptions

CHANTILLY, Musée Condé, ms. 278 (575).
Livres d'Éthique et Yconomique. French, *ca.* 1415.
A. D. Menut, *Maistre Nicole Oresme: Le Livre de Éthiques d'Aristote*, New York, 1940, p. 49, incorrectly states that Jean de Berry was the initial owner of the ms., and refers to a non-existent portrait of Jean de Berry on fol. 4. For a description of this ms. see Chantilly (Meurgey), 1930, pp. 80 ff.

CHANTILLY, Musée Condé, ms. 279 (320).
Aristotle, *Politiques et Yconomiques*. No miniatures. Erroneously said to possess ex-libris of Jean de Berry by A. D. Menut, 1950, p. 58 n. 7.

GENEVA, Bibl. publique et universitaire, fr. 176.
Ovid, *Métamorphoses moralisées*. French, *ca.* 1385.
There seems to be no evidence to support the assertion of Panofsky, *Renaissance and Renascences*, 1960, p. 86, that this ms. belonged to Jean de Berry (statement deleted from second ed., p. 196). The only indication of ownership is an inscription on fol. IV. of Gilbert, Comte de Montpensier. For this collector see Delisle, *Cabinet*, I, 1868, p. 173.

LENINGRAD, State Library, ms. Fr.Q.v.XIV.3.
Gerbert de Montreuil, *Le rommant de la violette*, followed by the *Roman de la panthère*. Luçon Master.
It is possible that this ms. once belonged to Jean de Berry (Delisle, *Charles V*, 1907, II, pp. 267 no. 277, 315 f.). However, the copy of these two texts he owned contained also the *Roman de la rose*, and this ms. went to the Duchesse de Bourbonnais at his death. The ms. in Leningrad, on the other hand, was in the library of Philippe le Bon, Duke of Burgundy, in 1420 [Leningrad (Saint-Pétersbourg), Laborde, I, 1936, pp. 53-55; pl. XVI].

LONDON, Brit. Mus., Harley 2891.
Missal for the Use of Paris. French, *ca.* 1335.
Delisle, *Charles V*, 1907, II, pp. 234 no. 68, 278, citing Warner (London, Brit. Mus., *Manuscripts Exhibited*, 1906, p. 130). Warner put this ms. in the Berry collection, but evidence is lacking.

LONDON, Robinson Trust, ms. 832.
Œuvres de Jean de Mehun. Master of the Berry Apocalypse.
A *Débat sur le Roman de la rose* in the Collection of Sir Thomas Phillipps was noted by Delisle, *Cabinet*, III, 1881, p. 340, and Guiffrey, *Inventaires*, II, p. 319, but it cannot be identified with this ms. The inventories record the acquisition of a 'Trésor maistre Jean de Mehun' after 1413 (Guiffrey, *Inventaires*, I, p. 332 no. 1238) but the first words on the second folio do not correspond with those in this ms.

MADRID, Museo Lázaro Galdiano, ms. 505.
Propriétés des choses. French, *ca.* 1400.
Domínguez Bordona, *Manuscritos*, 1933, I, p. 165 no.

1202, connects this ms. with Jean de Berry, but there is no evidence to support this claim.

PARIS, Bibl. nat., fr. 129.
Boccaccio, *Décameron*, translated by Laurent de Premierfait.
Warner and Gilson (London, Brit. Mus., 1921, II, p. 347) must have inferred from the translator's prologue addressed to the Duke that the ms. was given to him, but this inference is erroneous. The illumination was executed during the third quarter of the 15th century and the script appears to be of this period also.

PARIS, Bibl. nat., fr. 131 (Fig. 500).
Boccaccio, *Cas des nobles hommes et femmes*. The Master of the Cité des Dames and others.
On fol. 311v. 'Cest' is followed by an effaced word and then 'Gontier', which was brought up by chemical treatment in the 19th century. The script is not that of Flamel or Jean de Berry. Gontier may well be Gontier de Col. Laborde, *Cité de Dieu*, 1909, I, p. 278 n. 4.

PARIS, Bibl. nat., fr. 226 (Fig. 503).
Boccaccio, *Cas des nobles hommes et femmes*, translated by Laurent de Premierfait. Bedford, Rohan, and Cité des Dames workshops.
Neither Laurent's dedication to Jean de Berry nor the portrait of him in the scene of presentation proves that the ms. belonged to him.

PARIS, Bibl. nat., fr. 290.
Valère Maxime. Rightly rejected by Delisle, *Cabinet*, III, 1881, p. 187 n. 4 and Guiffrey, *Inventaires*, I, p. CLXXX, but the statement of Porcher (*Belles Heures*, 1953, pp. 12 f.) might be understood to ascribe the ms. to the Berry collection.
The text, the same as that of Bibl. nat., fr. 282, was completed for Berry in 1401, but there is no evidence – no inscription, colophon, or arms – that this ms. belonged to the Duke.

PARIS, Bibl. nat., fr. 301.
Histoires d'Orose. Orosius Master.
Though this ms. was placed in the library of the Duke by Guiffrey (*Inventaires*, I, p. CLXX no. 43) and by Delisle (*Charles V*, 1907, II, p. 328), the ms. itself provides no cogent evidence.

PARIS, Bibl. nat., fr. 2813. (Fig 565).
Chronique de Saint-Denis. Style in the tradition of Bondol. (Formerly in two volumes?)

Delisle, *Cabinet*, I, 1868, p. 66 n. 1; III, 1881, p. 190 no. 241; *Charles V*, 1907, II, pp. 262 no. 241, 312. For the identification Delisle refers to Lacabane, 1840–1841, p. 71. Lacabane had seen an inventory in the possession of Bastard, now not traceable. The opening words reported by Lacabane would seem to coincide. Ms. bears the royal arms, but no marks of Berry ownership.

PARIS, Bibl. nat., fr. 15455.
Compilation d'histoire ancienne. French, ca. 1416–1420, completed ca. 1450.
Guiffrey (*Inventaires*, I, p. 62 no. 9; II, p. 317 no. 14) referred to a partly obliterated inscription of the Duke. This is now not verifiable.

PARIS, Bibl. nat., ital. 72.
Dante, *Divina Commedia*. Though the first initial contains the arms of the Berry family, the entire ms. is late 15th century.
Guiffrey, *Inventaires*, I, p. CLXXX no. 6, wrongly connects ms. with Jean de Berry.

PARIS, Bibl. nat., lat. 5762.
Sallust, *Catalina and Jugurtha*. Illumination in the Bedford style.
Arms identified as probably those of Jean de Berry by Porcher, *Mélanges Calot*, 1960, p. 36 n. 1. The shield, however, seems to be added, and the engrailed border is gold, not the red of Jean de Berry.

Manuscripts Listed here as Possessions of the Duke but not in Delisle's Last List (1907)

Angers, Bibl. municipale, fr. 162 (154)   *Cité de Dieu*

The Hague, Museum Meermanno-Westreenianum, ms. 10 B 23   *Bible de Charles V*

Munich, Bayr. Staatsbibliothek, lat. 10072   *Missal*

New York, Morgan Library, ms. 133   *Apocalypse*

Oxford, Bodleian Library, Rawl. C.538   *Secret des secrez*

Paris, Bibl. nat., fr. 172-173   *Cité de Dieu*

   Delisle erroneously said that fr. 172 (instead of fr. 176) is a *Rationale* of Durandus.

Paris, Bibl. nat., fr. 606, 836   *Œuvres de Christine de Pisan*

   Of the group – 606, 835, 836 – Delisle listed only 835.

Paris, Bibl. nat., fr. 12595   *Roman de la rose*

Paris, Bibl. nat., fr. 15397   *Bible de Jean de Sy*

Paris, Bibl. nat., lat. 1052   *Bréviaire de Charles V*

XIV

Catalogue of Manuscripts

Baltimore

WALTERS ART GALLERY, ms. 94
(p. 190; Figs. 626, 627)
Book of Hours; Paris Calendar. 186 fols.; 137×100 mm.

STYLE AND DATE: The style of the miniatures derives directly from the *Petites Heures*, and the *Trinity* is an almost exact copy of the representation of this subject by the Trinity Master on fol. 183 of that ms. Pseudo-Jacquemart probably directed the illumination of this book, around 1390.

BIBLIOGRAPHY: Ricci, *Census*, I, 1935, p. 784 no. 174; Baltimore, Walters (Miner) 1949, p. 29 no. 74; Meiss, *Art Bull.*, 1956, p. 192; Baltimore, Walters, *International Style* [1962] p. 45.

MINIATURES:

Folio 40v. Visitation
51v. Nativity
57v. Annunciation to Shepherds
60v. Adoration of Magi
65v. Presentation in Temple
69v. Flight into Egypt
80v. Crucifixion
84 Trinity
108 Office of the Dead
153v. Virgin and Child and donoress (repainted)
159 Last Judgment

Baltimore

WALTERS ART GALLERY, ms. 96
(p. 189; Figs. 616, 618, 621)
Book of Hours. Use of Paris. 348 fols.; 155×110 mm.

STYLE AND DATE: The last prayer in the book dates it around 1390, as Miss Miner (1962) has shown. The Virgin and the blessed Pierre de Luxembourg, who died in 1387, are invoked in aid of Clement VII, who died in 1394. Armorials are lacking but the ms. may have been a gift to the Pope from someone in Jean de Berry's circle.

This ms., like Walters 94, gives us full assurance about the date of the *Petites Heures*. It took from the Duke's ms. the design of the borders and many figures, which are mentioned in the text above (p. 189). The stronger painter in Walters 96, who executed the *Annunciation* and the *Nativity*, was very close to Jacquemart. He was probably responsible for the splendid birds and insects, represented on a comparatively large scale in the borders. The second illuminator worked also on a Bible that belonged to Jean de Berry, now Harley 4381-2 in the British Museum (Figs. 617, 622.)

BIBLIOGRAPHY: Ricci, *Census*, I, 1935, p. 785 no. 177; Baltimore, Walters (Miner) 1949, p. 31 no. 80; Panofsky, *Netherlandish Painting*, 1953, I, p. 34 n. 4; Los Angeles, Los Angeles County Museum, *Exhibition*, 1953, no. 48; D. Diringer, *The Illuminated Book*, London, 1958, p. 398; Oberlin, Oberlin College, 'Exhibition', 1960, p. 95 no. 4; Baltimore, Walters, *International Style* (Miner) 1962, p. 46.

MINIATURES:

Folio 30 Annunciation
50 Visitation
60 Nativity
65v. Annunciation to Shepherds
70 Adoration of Magi
74 Presentation in Temple
78v. Flight into Egypt
85v. Christ and Virgin enthroned
92 Christ and Four Evangelists
108v. Crucifixion
112 Pentecost
115v. Meeting at Golden Gate
123 The Five Wounds
138 Office of the Dead

Bologna

BIBL. DEL ARCHIGINNASIO, Deposito Amm. Ospedali No. 4
(p. 243; Fig. 792)
Statuti della Compagnia dello Spedale di S. Maria della Vita

STYLE AND DATE: The Madonna at the beginning of the *Statuti*, dated 1408, was painted by the Master of the Brussels Initials. The initial at the beginning of the roll of the members, dated 1410, is by a follower.

BIBLIOGRAPHY: Salmi, *Tesori*, 1932, fig. 8; Pächt, *Mary of Burgundy* [1948] p. 52 n. 19; Meiss, *Art Bull.*, 1956, pp. 193 ff.

MINIATURES:

Folio 23   Madonna enthroned with members of the Company (Master of the Brussels Initials)

63   Initial containing six *battuti* (by a follower)

Bourges

BIBL. MUNICIPALE, ms. 16 (p. 154 n. 91; Fig. 607)
Breviary of Saint-Ambroix, Bourges. 348 fols.; 156 × 112 mm.

EARLY HISTORY: There are references in the Calendar to the dedication of the church of Saint-Ambroix (Sept. 10) and to the feast of St. Ambrose (Oct. 16–23). On fol. 1: 'Breviarium ad usum canonicorum Sancti Ambrosii Bituricensis . . .'

STYLE AND DATE: This Breviary was illuminated in the early 'eighties by Pseudo-Jacquemart. The ms. has suffered from use and damp; several miniatures lack part or all of their paint.

BIBLIOGRAPHY: Leroquais, *Bréviaires*, 1934, I, pp. 151 f. no. 103; Meiss, *Art Bull.*, 1956, p. 191.

MINIATURES:

Folio 10   David playing harp
21   David pointing to his eyes
28v.   David pointing to his mouth
36   Fool
44   David saved from drowning
62v.   Monks at lectern
72v.   Trinity
105   Prophet Isaiah
128v.   Nativity
229   Resurrection
255   Ascension
267   Pentecost
277   Mass: Elevation of Host

Bourges

BIBL. MUNICIPALE, mss. 33-36
(p. 263; Figs. 253, 254, 499)
Lectionary of the Sainte-Chapelle, Bourges. 4 volumes. 183, 231, 221, 225 fols., 505 × 355 mm.

EARLY HISTORY: The first three volumes bear arms, emblems, and a portrait of Jean de Berry. The ms. belonged to the Ste-Chapelle in 1583 (see list of mss. of Duke). Though Delisle and subsequent historians have definitely identified this ms. with a Lectionary listed in the records of gifts to the Ste-Chapelle in 1404–1407, the evidence is insufficient.

STYLE AND DATE: The iconography of the Duke and aspects of style indicate that these volumes were illuminated around 1410 by Pseudo-Jacquemart, the Boucicaut Master, and their assistants. The compositions of Pseudo-Jacquemart were based on designs of the Boucicaut Master.

BIBLIOGRAPHY: Delisle, *Cabinet*, I, 1868, pp. 58 n. 4, 67; Guiffrey, *Inventaires*, I, p. CLXIII no. 17, II, p. 317 no. 44; Durrieu, *Rev. de l'art a. et m.*, 1906, pp. 413 f.; Delisle, *Charles V*, 1907, II, pp. 230 no. 44 bis, 277 f.; Durrieu, *Rev. de l'art chrét.*, 1913, p. 308; Bourges, *Musées* [1951] p. 37 nos. 14-16; Panofsky, *Netherlandish Painting*, 1953, I, pp. 59 f., 244; Paris, Bibl. nat. (Porcher) 1955, pp. 94 f. no. 193; Meiss, *Art Bull.*, 1956, p. 191; Bourges, *Mécènes berrichons*, 1956, p. 33.

MINIATURES:

Ms. 33
Folio   I   Four prophets (Boucicaut Workshop)
23v.   Nativity (French painter)
173   Ascension (Pseudo-Jacquemart)
178v.   Pentecost (Pseudo-Jacquemart)

Ms. 34
Folio   IV.   Coronation of Virgin (Pseudo-Jacquemart)
46v.   Birth of Virgin (Boucicaut workshop)
138v.   All Saints (Boucicaut workshop)

Ms. 35
Folio 10   Trinity (Pseudo-Jacquemart)
17v.   Duke of Berry adoring St. Andrew (Boucicaut workshop)

Bourges

BIBL. MUNICIPALE, ms. 48
(p. 263; Fig. 493)
Evangeliary. 220 fols.; 380 × 255 mm.

EARLY HISTORY: The frontispiece contains the arms and emblems of Berry. All historians but Guiffrey followed Delisle in identifying this ms. with an Evangeliary listed in the gift to the Ste-Chapelle, presumably in 1404. Guiffrey suggested the possibility that it may be a ms. given to the Duke in 1415 (n.s.) The first words, however, on fol. 2 of Bourges 48 are: IN ILLO TEMPORE, and the last words in the ms. are: ET VOCAVIT NOME(N) EIUS IHESUM. These words are different from those given in the document.

STYLE AND DATE: The two miniatures were painted by Pseudo-Jacquemart. His style and the iconography of the Duke suggest a date around 1410, but *ca.* 1405 is also possible.

BIBLIOGRAPHY: Hiver de Beauvoir, *Trésor*, 1857, p. 96 no. 3; Delisle, *Cabinet*, I, 1868, pp. 58 n. 4, 67; III, 1881, p. 177 no. 81; Guiffrey, *Inventaires*, I, pp. CLXIII no. 14, 334 no. 1244, II, p. 178 no. 180; Delisle, *Charles V*, 1907, II, pp. 235 no. 81, 280; Bourges, Musées [1951] pp. 37 f. no. 17; Paris, Bibl. nat. (Porcher) 1955, p. 95 no. 194; Meiss, *Art Bull.*, 1956, p. 191; Bourges, *Mécènes berrichons*, 1956, p. 34.

MINIATURES:

Folio   1   Four Evangelists with symbols
         181 Duke of Berry adoring St. Andrew

Brussels

BIBL. ROYALE, ms. 11060-61

(Chap. IX; Figs. 179-215, 665)

Book of Hours, so-called *Très Belles Heures de Jean de Berry*, 276 fols.; 275 × 185 mm.

EARLY HISTORY: This ms. came to light in 1840, when it entered the collection of J. Marchal without a clear provenience. In 1868 and 1880 Delisle identified it with the 'très belles Heures, richement enluminées et ystoriées de la main Jaquemart de Odin' listed in the inventory of 1402. The correspondence is not exact, because the inventory mentioned arms and devices in the corners of many folios, whereas in the ms. arms appear in the corners and devices in similar quatrefoils between them. Still, no other Book of Hours in the inventory is described in this way, and no other extant ms. could be identified with the item. A note added to the item states that the 'très belles Heures' was given to the Duke of Burgundy, and it can be identified in the inventory of the possessions of Jean sans Peur after his death in 1419 as well as in that of his widow Margaret of Bavaria after her death in 1424. After that the ms. disappeared from inventories of the Burgundian library.

The apparent lack of proof that Brussels 11060-61 was ever actually in the library of Burgundy has led several scholars, beginning with Lyna in 1937, to reject or at least doubt the identity of the ms. with the 'très belles heures'. Most of these scholars have held that the identification was dubious also because the style of the main section of the ms. seemed to indicate a date closer to 1410 than to 1402. The diptych at the beginning of the ms., which everyone now agrees was not made for this codex and is by a different hand, has been dated after 1406 by Porcher, for specific (but in my opinion untenable) reasons. For a fuller account of the hypotheses advanced in recent years the reader is referred to Chapter IX, section 2.

In recent articles and in the text above I have offered evidence to show that Brussels 11060-61 was actually in the Burgundian library in the early 15th century. First of all, when Marchal acquired the ms. in 1840 it was covered in black satin, precisely as in the inventory of 1424. Secondly, a Veronica painted on leather is glued to page 8, and we know that the house of Burgundy venerated the Holy Face and that Margaret, wife of Jean sans Peur, added Veronicas to her mss. In the third place, the *Crucifixion* was copied in a Breviary of Jean sans Peur (323, 678), by a master who otherwise was not interested in the style of the *Brussels Hours*. Finally the Child in a Madonna added to a prayer book of Philippe le Hardi around 1415 (Fig. 668) reflects to a degree the Child in the initial diptych of the *Brussels Hours*.

STYLE AND DATE: The facts set forth above seem to me to prove conclusively that the *Brussels Hours* is the ms. that Jean de Berry gave to the Duke of Burgundy after the summer of 1402. Jacquemart de Hesdin must therefore have had the main responsibility for the illustration of the Hours of the Virgin and of the Passion. Jacquemart utilized for his presentation miniature and for his borders the initial diptych, which was painted by a major master about 1385 and trimmed for use at the beginning of the *Brussels Hours*. The initials and borders on the folios opening an office were executed by an illuminator who was trained in Bologna and studied in Padua. He takes his name from this work, the Master of the Brussels Initials.

BIBLIOGRAPHY: Monographs: Brussels, Ms. 11060-11061 (de Mont) [1904]; Fierens-Gevaert, *Très Belles Heures*, 1924; Marchal, 1844, pp. 407-424; Delisle, *Cabinet*, I, 1868, pp. 63 n. 4, 67; III, 1881, p. 178 no. 98; *idem, Mélanges*, 1880, pp. 295-303; *idem, Gaz. B.-A.*, 1884, p. 400; Guiffrey, *Inventaires*, I, pp. LXXIV-LXXV, CLXVI no. 24; II, p. 132 no. 1050; Lasteyrie, 1896, pp. 71 ff.; Brussels, Bibl. Roy. (van den Gheyn) I, 1901, pp. 445 f. no. 719; Doutrepont, *Inventaire*, 1906, p. 5 no. 6; Durrieu, *Rev. de l'art a. et m.*, 1906, pp. 408-413, fig. p. 404; Fry, 1906–1907, p. 37; Durrieu, *Bulletin*, 1911, p. 87 no. III; *idem, Rev. de l'art chrét.*, 1913, p. 308; Winkler, in Thieme-Becker, XVI, 1923, pp. 571-573; Hulin de Loo, 1925, p. 125; [Barrois] *Bibl. protypographique*, 1930, p. 115 no. 668; Brussels, Gaspar and Lyna, I, 1937, pp. 399-409 no. 167, pls. XCIII-XCIV; Troescher, *Burgundische Plastik*, 1940, p. 42; Ring, *French Painting* [1949] p. 197 no. 46; Bourges, *Musées* [1951] no. 2; Baldass, *Jan van Eyck* [1952] p. 5 n. 2; Thomas, 1952, pp. 81 ff.; Panofsky, *Netherlandish Painting*, 1953, I, pp. 42 f.; Porcher, *Belles Heures*, 1953, pp. 7, 11, 25; *idem*, 1953, pp. 121-123; Paris, Bibl. nat. (Porcher) 1955, p. 90 no. 186; Meiss, *Art Bull.*, 1956, pp. 190, 192; Nordenfalk, 1956, pp. 185 f.; Pächt, *Burl. Mag.*, 1956, pp. 149 f.; *idem, Rev. des Arts*, 1956, pp. 149 ff.; Delaissé, *Medieval Illuminations*, 1958, pp. 90-92; Porcher, *Medieval Miniatures* [1959] pp. 60-62; Meiss and Eisler, 1960 pp. 236 f.; Meiss, *Gaz. B.-A.*, 1961, pp. 291 ff.; Vienna, Kunsthist. Mus., *Katalog*, 1962, p. 170 no. 108; Delaissé, 1963, pp. 124-129.

MINIATURES:

Page 8 Veronica (painted on leather, which is glued to the page)

10 Jean de Berry kneeling between SS. Andrew and John the Baptist (French painter, *ca.* 1390)

11 Virgin and Child (French painter, *ca.* 1390)

14 Jean de Berry with SS. Andrew and John the Baptist before the Virgin (Jacquemart de Hesdin)

Hours of the Virgin

18 Annunciation (Jacquemart de Hesdin)

19 Isaiah (Master of the Brussels Initials)

54 Visitation (Jacquemart de Hesdin)

55 Jeremiah (Master of the Brussels Initials)

72 Nativity (Jacquemart de Hesdin)

73 Moses and the Burning Bush (Master of the Brussels Initials)

82 Annunciation to the Shepherds (Jacquemart de Hesdin)

83 Augustus and Sibyl (Master of the Brussels Initials)

90 Adoration of the Magi (Jacquemart de Hesdin)

91 Solomon and Queen of Sheba (Master of the Brussels Initials)

98 Presentation in the Temple (Jacquemart de Hesdin)

99 Samuel brought to Eli (Master of the Brussels Initials)

106 Flight into Egypt (Jacquemart de Hesdin)

107 Daniel and the vision of the broken statue (Master of the Brussels Initials)

118 Coronation of the Virgin (Jacquemart de Hesdin and assistant)

119 Assumption of Virgin (Master of the Brussels Initials)

Penitential Psalms

130 Christ in Majesty (Jacquemart de Hesdin and assistant)

131 David repenting (Master of the Brussels Initials)

Hours of the Cross

164 Betrayal (Jacquemart de Hesdin and assistant)

165 Christ led into Pretorium (Master of the Brussels Initials)

168 Christ before Pilate (Jacquemart de Hesdin and assistant)

169 Mocking of Christ (Master of the Brussels Initials)

182 Flagellation (Jacquemart de Hesdin and assistant)

183 Christ crowned with thorns (Master of the Brussels Initials)

186 Christ carrying the Cross (Jacquemart de Hesdin and assistant)

187 Christ nailed to Cross (Master of the Brussels Initials)

190 Crucifixion (Jacquemart de Hesdin and assistant)

191 Two Jews before Pilate (Master of the Brussels Initials)

194 Deposition (Jacquemart de Hesdin and assistant)

195 Lamentation (Master of the Brussels Initials)

198 Entombment (Jacquemart de Hesdin and assistant)

199 Harrowing of Hell (Master of the Brussels Initials)

Office of the Dead

202 Office of the Dead (Jacquemart de Hesdin)

203 Office of the Dead (Master of the Brussels Initials)

Cleveland

MUSEUM OF ART

(Chap. X; Figs. 729-731, 734, 745, 749, 758, 759, 761, 764, 772, 789, 804, 805, 809, 812, 813)

Book of Hours. Use of Paris. 668 pages; 200 × 140 mm.

HISTORY: The arms on several folios were identified by Léopold Delisle as those of Charles III of Navarre (called *le Noble*). This prince, who was born in France, visited Paris at least twice in the early years of the 15th century, and from 1404 to 1409 he gave gifts to Jean de Berry, who had employed the Master of the Brussels Initials before 1402. When in 1936 the writer first studied the ms. it was in the collection of Baron Maurice de Rothschild.

STYLE AND DATE: The illumination was undertaken, probably around 1405, by the Master of the Brussels Initials and an assistant. A painter influenced by the Master of Berry's Cleres Femmes contributed two miniatures, the Egerton Master three. The exchange between the two styles was considerable; in particular the landscape and the sky of the *Way to Calvary* followed the conventions of the Egerton Master. A very minor role was played also by another French illuminator.

BIBLIOGRAPHY: Pächt, *Burl. Mag.*, 1956, p. 15; Meiss, *Art Bull.*, 1956, p. 195; Porcher, *Medieval French Miniatures*, New York [1959] p. 59; Meiss, *Gaz. B.-A.*, 1963, p. 159 and fig. 17; Wixom, 1965, pp. 50 ff.

MINIATURES:

This manuscript is paginated. All miniatures are by the Master of the Brussels Initials unless otherwise indicated.

Pages 1-24 Calendar pictures

25 *Obsecro Te.* Initial: Bust of the Virgin

33 *O Intemerata.* Initial: Virgin and Child

Pericopes

42 St. John

45 St. Luke

49 St. Matthew

53 St. Mark

Hours of the Virgin

57 Annunciation

109 Visitation

133 Nativity

148 Annunciation to the Shepherds

156 Adoration of the Magi

165 Presentation in the Temple

175 Flight into Egypt

191 Coronation of the Virgin

204 Initial: Bust of Virgin reading

Penitential Psalms

211 Hell

Hours of the Passion

255 Man of Sorrows

Hours of the Holy Ghost

274 Pentecost

Hours of the Cross

Page 287 Betrayal (Follower of Berry's Cleres Femmes)

322 Mockery of Christ (mixed style: Master of Brussels Initials influenced by French collaborator)

347 Christ before Pilate (mixed style)

355 Way to Calvary (Follower of Master of Berry's Cleres Femmes)

367 Christ nailed to the Cross (Egerton Master)

379 Crucifixion

395 Descent from the Cross (Egerton Master)

405 Entombment (Egerton Master)

Office of the Dead

415 Office of the Dead

Suffrages

The miniatures from p. 29 on are all initials.

529	Trinity
531	Holy Ghost
533	Virgin and Child
535	Instruments of the Passion
536	Two angels with scales
537	St. John Baptist
538	St. Peter
540	St. Paul
541	St. Andrew
542	St. John Evangelist
544	St. James
545	St. Bartholomew
546	St. Matthew
547	St. Thomas
549	SS. Philip and James
550	SS. Simon and Judas
552	St. Matthias
553	St. Barnabas
554	St. Mark
556	St. Luke
557	Four Evangelists
559	St. Stephen
560	St. Clement
562	St. Vincent
563	St. Lawrence
564	St. Denis
566	St. Christopher
567	St. George
569	St. Blaise
570	St. Sebastian
572	SS. Job and Eustace
573	SS. Cosmas and Damian
574	St. Valentine
575	St. Thomas à Becket
577	St. Lazarus
578	Martyrs: Unidentified saint, St. Stephen and St. Lawrence
580	Four Doctors of the Church
582	St. Martin
583	St. Nicholas
584	St. Marcel
586	St. Benedict
587	St. Anthony
588	St. Bernard
589	St. Germain
591	St. Francis
592	St. Dominic
594	St. Maur

595	St. Fiacre
596	St. Leonard
598	St. Ive
599	St. Louis
600	The Confessors
602	St. Anne
604	St. Mary Magdalene
605	St. Elizabeth
606	St. Catherine
608	St. Lucy
609	St. Margaret
610	St. Agnes
612	St. Agatha
613	St. Genevieve
614	St. Cecilia
616	St. Oportuna
617	St. Apollonia
619	The Virgin Martyrs
620	St. Martha
622	St. Barbara

Office of the Holy Spirit

625	Initial: Bust of Christ

Mass of Our Lady

638	Initial: Virgin and Child

Mass of the Dead

654	Bust of Death

Holkham Hall

LIBRARY OF THE EARL OF LEICESTER, ms. 120   (p. 244; Figs. 791, 793, 794)

Lactantius, *Divinae Institutiones* and *De Ira Dei*. 172 fols.; 320 × 230 mm.

HISTORY: The charge on the shield on fol. 2 is badly abraded and not readily identified. The black bird (eagle?) on the shield in the upper right corner of this folio may not be original. An inscription on fol. 172v. states that in 1479 the ms. was given by Pietro da Montagnana to the canons of S. Giovanni in Verdara, Padua.

STYLE AND DATE: The illumination was executed no doubt in Italy by the Master of the Brussels Initials or a close associate, together with a North Italian illuminator who strove to imitate his style. This associate painted the initial on fol. 103.

The miniatures are most closely related to the latest works of the Brussels Initials Master in France, and the border on fol. 2 contains elements introduced by the Master into his work there from the time of the painting of the initials in the *Brussels Hours*. Other borders are purely Bolognese in character. The ms. was probably illuminated shortly after the work on the *Statuti* of the Company of Santa Maria della Vita of 1408.

BIBLIOGRAPHY: Meiss, *Gaz. B.-A.*, 1963, p. 168 n. 36.

MINIATURES:

There is an initial with one or more figures at the beginning of each book of the *Divinae Institutiones* and at the beginning of the *De Ira Dei*. The miniatures appear on the following folios: 1, 2, 23, 31v., 84v., 103, 125v., 144 (*De Ira Dei*). An initial has been cut out from fol. 158.

Leningrad

STATE LIBRARY, ms. Q.v.I.8

                   (p. 264; Figs. 255, 256, 259)

Book of Hours (information incomplete)

STYLE AND DATE: Illumination by Pseudo-Jacquemart and associates around 1410.

MINIATURES:

Folio	
	Annunciation (Pseudo-Jacquemart)
	Nativity (French painter)
63v.	Annunciation to the Shepherds (French painter)
	Madonna with the writing Child (Pseudo-Jacquemart)
134	Office of the Dead (French painter)

London

BRIT. MUS., Add. 23145   (p. 194; Figs. 620, 660)
Book of Hours, Use of Rome. 254+6 fols.; 345×187 mm.

STYLE AND DATE: The arms of Andrault, seigneurs de Langeron, and Gencien on fol. 44 are later than the ms. itself. The illumination was executed around 1390 by a workshop that included the painter of many miniatures in the Bible, Vat. lat. 50-51.

BIBLIOGRAPHY: London, Brit. Mus., *Reproductions*, IV, 1928, p. 13; London, Brit. Mus., *Schools of Illumination*, VI, 1930, pp. 6 f.

Y

MINIATURES:

Folio	
Folio 15v.	Ecclesiastic before St. Anthony (retouched)
17	St. John
19	St. Mark
21	St. Matthew
23v.	St. Luke
25	St. Anthony
26	St. Michael
27	St. John the Baptist
28	St. John the Evangelist
29	St. Peter
30	St. Paul
31	St. Thomas
32	St. James the Greater
33v.	St. Nicholas
34v.	St. Sebastian
36	St. George
37v.	St. Maurice
39	St. Catherine
40	St. Margaret
41	St. Mary Magdalen
44	Annunciation
67	Visitation
82v.	Nativity
93v.	Annunciation to the Shepherds
100	Adoration of the Magi
106v.	Presentation in the Temple
123	Coronation of the Virgin
138	Christ enthroned
162	Betrayal
164	Christ before Pilate
166	Flagellation
168	Way to Calvary
170	Crucifixion
172	Deposition
174	Entombment
176	Pentecost
188	Office of the Dead
244	The Madonna
250v.	Last Judgment

London

BRIT. MUS., Add. 29433

       (Chap. x; Figs. 718, 726, 733, 741, 743, 747, 750, 755, 760, 762, 765, 769, 776, 784, 790, 799, 806, 811)

Book of Hours. Use of Paris. 219 fols. 223 × 160 mm.

HISTORY: The shield on fol. 71v. is quarterly, 1 and 4 gules, 2 and 3 azure. The colors have been scratched but none of the quarters seems ever to have borne charges. The surviving traces of color on the shield on fol. 76 suggest the same coat. Elsewhere in the ms. the numerous blank shields seem never to have been painted.

STYLE AND DATE: All but seven miniatures were painted by the Master of the Brussels Initials. These seven were executed by a follower of the Luçon Master, by an Italianate French illuminator, and by another minor French master. 1406–1407 seems the most probable date.

BIBLIOGRAPHY: London, Brit. Mus., *Reproductions*, I, 1910, p. 11, pl. XXVI; London, Brit. Mus., *Schools of Illumination*, VI, 1930, p. 8, pl. VIIa; London, Brit. Mus., Millar, 1933, p. 34; Pächt, *Mary of Burgundy* [1948] p. 52 n. 19; Baltimore, Walters (Miner) 1949, p. 32 no. 83; Pächt, *Burl. Mag.*, 1956, p. 115; Meiss, *Art Bull.*, 1956, pp. 193 ff.; Wixom, 1965, pp. 51 ff.

MINIATURES:

All miniatures are by the chief master and his assistants unless otherwise designated.
Calendar miniatures, fols. 1-12v.

Gospel readings

Folio 13   St. John on Patmos
     14v.   St. Luke
     16v.   St. Mark
     18   St. Matthew

Hours of the Virgin

     20   Annunciation; young male donor in initial
     43v.   Visitation
     56   Nativity
     62   Annunciation to the Shepherds
     67   Adoration of the Magi
     71v.   Presentation
     76   Flight into Egypt
     83   Coronation of the Virgin (Italianate French painter)

Penitential Psalms

     89   Hell; David kneels to God in initial

Hours of the Cross in conjunction with account of the Vision of St. Gregory

     107v.   Man of Sorrows with Virgin and St. John

Hours of the Holy Ghost

     111v.   Pentecost

Vigils of the Dead

     115v.   Last Judgment

Prayers and Masses

     161   *Obsecro Te*. Initial: Virgin and Child with male donor
     164   *O Intemerata*. Initial: Virgin in prayer
     168   *15 Joys*. Christ Child nude in water, and Virgin and St. Joseph in portico; donor in initial
     174   *Vesperbild* (Five Wounds)
     178   Trinity (*triciput*)
     184   Virgin and Child
     186   Veneration of the Cross
     188v.   Priest takes wafer in Mass for the Dead
     192   Trinity
     193   Virgin and Child enthroned
     193v.   Bishop and acolytes kneel before cross on altar

Commemorations of Saints

     194v.   St. Michael killing the dragon
     195   St. John the Baptist (Brussels Initials Master and French painter)
     196   St. Peter and St. Paul
     197v.   St. Andrew and St. James the Major
     198v.   St. Thomas and St. Bartholomew
     199v.   St. Simon and St. Jude
     200   St. James the Minor and St. Philip
     200v.   St. Matthias
     201v.   The Four Evangelists
     202v.   Stoning of St. Stephen (follower of Luçon Master)
     203   Martyrdom of St. Lawrence
     204   Martyrdom of St. Vincent and St. Blaise
     205   St. Christopher (follower of Luçon Master)
     206   Martyrdom of St. Denis and his companions
     207   St. George killing the dragon
     208   St. Job, St. Louis King, St. Eustace
     208v.   The four Church Doctors
     210   St. Martin and Pope Silvester
     210v.   St. Nicholas of Bari and St. Louis of Toulouse
     211v.   St. Fiacre, St. Bernard and St. Benedict (follower of Luçon Master)

212   St. Anthony enthroned (follower of Luçon Master)
213   St. Catherine
214   Noli me tangere (follower of Luçon Master)
214v. St. Margaret
215v. St. Lucy, St. Agatha, St. Agnes
216   St. Genevieve
217   St. Anne walking with the young Virgin
218   All Saints

London

BRIT. MUS., Add. 34247   (p. 245; Figs. 800, 801)

Uffiziolo. Bolognese Calendar. 189 fols.; 131 × 100 mm.

STYLE AND DATE: Pächt's attribution of the ms. to the Master of the Brussels Initials was accepted by the writer. It is linked closely with his work with respect to both style and iconography. The illumination is, however, unlike any other of his paintings. It is more purely Italian and indeed Bolognese. Its colors are hard, cool, and smoky, and the style in general cruder. If the Brussels Initials Master illuminated the ms. he must have done so early in his career. Perhaps it is the work of an early associate, and represents the master's point of departure.

BIBLIOGRAPHY: Pächt, *Mary of Burgundy* [1948] p. 52 n. 19; Meiss, *Art Bull.*, 1956, p. 194.

MINIATURES:

All the miniatures are in initials.
Calendar pictures

Folio 32   Annunciation to Joachim
      36v. Annunciation to Anna
      41   Meeting at the Golden Gate
      45v. Birth of the Virgin
      50   Presentation of the Virgin in the Temple
      57v. Marriage of the Virgin
      62   Madonna of Mercy
      63v. Virgin reading
      68   Virgin enthroned, adored by three monks
      85   Hell
      116 Flagellation
      120 Christ before Pilate
      122v. Mocking of Christ
      125 Christ nailed to the Cross

127   Christ on the Cross, and a monk with a chalice catching his blood on one side while a priest baptizes a baby on the other
129v. Lamentation
133v. Entombment
138   Man of Sorrows
172   Office of the Dead
      (Folios 13 and 108 were added later.)

London

BRIT. MUS., Harley 2952

(p. 276; Figs. 270, 273-275)

Book of Hours. 179 fols.; 176 × 125 mm.

STYLE AND DATE: The ms. was entirely illuminated by one master with assistants; I have called him the Master of the Humilities because of the exceptional number of representations of the Madonna of Humility. The painter was responsible also for many miniatures in Brit. Mus., Yates Thompson 37, including a remarkable Madonna of Humility of which a replica appears in Harley 2952.

Only the two pairs of full-page miniatures with donors and Madonna on fols. 18v.-20 are in full color. They are also the strongest miniatures in the ms. The subsequent miniatures show figures painted in grisaille, a light green terrain, and often a light blue, stellated sky. Some of the miniatures are influenced by the style of the Boucicaut Master. The illumination was probably carried out towards 1415.

BIBLIOGRAPHY: London, Brit. Mus., *Reproductions*, II, 1910, p. 12; London, Brit. Mus., Millar, 1933, no. 48; Meiss, *Florence and Siena*, 1951, p. 142; Pächt, *Burl. Mag.*, 1956, p. 115.

MINIATURES:

Folio 18v. Male portrait
      19   Madonna
      19v. Female portrait
      20   Madonna
      20v. St. Anthony in flames
      21   St. George
      22   Betrayal
      23   Christ before the High Priest
      23v. Flagellation
      24v. Way to Calvary
      25   Crucifixion
      26   Deposition

26v. Resurrection
27v. Crucifixion
32v. Trinity
39 The Lord enthroned
49 Crucifixion
61 Christ showing his wounds
62v. Charlemagne
67 Madonna
71v. Madonna of Humility
76v. Madonna
82 Madonna
86v. Madonna of Humility in garden (prayer authorized by Pope Benedict XII)
95 Madonna with the writing Child
102v. St. Jerome
115 Madonna of Humility
119v. St. Luke
121 St. John
122v. St. Matthew
124 St. Mark
126 Annunciation
134v. Visitation
142v. Nativity
146v. Annunciation to the Shepherds
150 Adoration of the Magi
153 Presentation in the Temple
156 Flight into Egypt
159 Coronation of the Virgin
163 St. Christopher
165 David before the Lord

London

BRIT. MUS., Harley 4947   (p. 264; Fig. 248)

Lactantius, *Institutiones, De Ira Dei, De Opificio Dei*

STYLE AND DATE: The single miniature in this ms., an initial on fol. 2, was painted by Pseudo-Jacquemart around the time of the *Grandes Heures*.

BIBLIOGRAPHY: London, Brit. Mus., *Harleian Manuscripts*, III, 1808, p. 231 no. 4947; Meiss, *Art Bull.*, 1956, p. 192.

London

BRIT. MUS., Roy. 19 B XVII.
                    (p. 188; Figs. 610, 612, 615)

Jacobus de Voragine, *La légende dorée*. Translation by Jean de Vignay. 1382. 355 fols., 306 × 216 mm.

EARLY HISTORY: On fol. 355 the ms. is inscribed in red: 'Ceste legende fut escripte lan mil .ccc. quatre vins et deus'. The form of the inscription suggests that it refers to this particular ms.

The arms on fol. IV. of Beaufort, together with the motto 'Me sovent sovant', refer to the Duke of Somerset, John (1443–1444), Edmund (1448–1455), Henry (1455–1464), or Edmund (1464–1471).

STYLE: Most of the miniatures in this ms. were painted by mediocre illuminators, followers more or less of Bondol and his associates. The first three folios, however, contain the earliest precisely dated paintings by Pseudo-Jacquemart.

BIBLIOGRAPHY: London, Brit. Mus., Warner and Gilson, 1921, II, pp. 330 f.; London, Brit. Mus., *Schools of Illumination*, VI, 1930, p. 6; Meiss, *Art Bull.*, 1956, p. 192.

MINIATURES:

Folio 2 St. Jerome (Pseudo-Jacquemart)
5 Coronation of the Virgin ⎫
   Male saints   ⎬ (Pseudo-Jacquemart)
   Female saints   ⎪
   Last Judgment   ⎭
9v. St. Andrew (Pseudo-Jacquemart)

For the list of the additional 76 miniatures, most of which represent saints, see the catalogue of 1921 cited in the bibliography.

London

BRIT. MUS., Yates Thompson 37.
          (p. 274; Figs. 263–267, 269, 271, 272, 276)

Book of Hours. Use of Bourges. 198 fols.; 190 × 140 mm.

STYLE AND DATE: The illumination of this ms. is exceptionally interesting because it provides a spectrum of the styles prevalent in the mss. of the Duke of Berry, with the notable exception of the Limbourgs. They range from Pseudo-Jacquemart and his followers to the workshops of the Luçon Master and of the Flemish Baptist Master. The painter of several Madonnas of Humility seems to make his first appearance here and, stimulated by the enthusiasm around him for Italian painting, he adopted a Lorenzettian design for one of his miniatures, a Simonesque for another. Two miniatures appear to reflect the latest phase of the style of Jacquemart. One, by his associate, the Trinity Master, has a remarkably advanced landscape, and another, very close in style to Jacquemart, an equally advanced cityscape. It is difficult to date the ms. precisely, but it would not have been painted before around 1405 and not much after 1410.

BIBLIOGRAPHY: London, Thompson Collection (Thompson) 1912, pp. 141-145 no. CVI; London, Thompson Collection, *Illustrations*, VII, 1918, pp. 5 f.; Meiss, 1936, p. 250; *idem, Florence and Siena*, 1951, p. 142; *idem, Art Bull.*, 1956, pp. 192, 193 n. 23; Pächt, *Burl. Mag.*, 1956, p. 150 n. 18; Meiss, *Gaz. B.-A.*, 1961, pp. 292 f.

MINIATURES:

Folio 19   Annunciation (Pseudo-Jacquemart)

36v.   Visitation (follower of Pseudo-Jacquemart)

47v.   Nativity (follower of Pseudo-Jacquemart)

53v.   Annunciation to Shepherds (Luçon workshop)

58   Adoration of Magi (Luçon workshop)

62   Presentation in Temple (Luçon workshop)

66   Flight into Egypt (follower of Luçon Master)

72   Coronation of Virgin (follower of Luçon Master)

79   Trinity (Master of Humilities)

83v.   Office of the Dead (follower of Pseudo-Jacquemart)

86   All Saints (Master of Humilities)

89   Mass: Elevation of Host (Master of Humilities)

92   Virgin of Humility (Master of Humilities)

103   Christ enthroned between symbols of New and Old Testaments (follower of Pseudo-Jacquemart)

118v.   Crucifixion (Trinity Master)

122   Pentecost (workshop of Baptist Master)

125v.   Office of the Dead (follower of Pseudo-Jacquemart)

159   Entry into Jerusalem (Jacquemart workshop)

Madrid

BIBLIOTECA DEL PALACIO, ms. 2099
(Chap. X; Figs. 748, 752, 754, 763, 768, 770, 775, 786, 787, 798, 808)
Book of Hours. Use of Paris. 205 fols.; 195 × 140 mm.

HISTORY: It has not yet proved possible to identify the several shields in this ms. The charge on fol. 95, 'd'azur à la bande de gueules accompagnée de deux amphittères d'or', appears to be that of the Parisian family Baillet. The same charge appears in quarter 4 on fols. 116 and 166v. On fol. 120, 'de sable à la croix d'argent cantonnée de 16 fleurs-de-lis d'or', may be the shield of the De Fresnes family.

STYLE AND DATE: All the miniatures and the borders surrounding them were painted by the Master of the Brussels Initials. The borders of the other folios in the ms. are French in character. The ms. was probably illuminated around 1402.

The appearance of busts or prophets in initials below the miniatures (Joel on fol. 81v., Isaiah on fol. 172v.) conforms with Lombard practice.

BIBLIOGRAPHY: Domínguez Bordona, *Manuscritos*, 1933, I, p. 459 no. 1194; Pächt, *Mary of Burgundy* [1948] p. 52 n. 19; Meiss, *Art Bull.*, 1956, p. 194.

MINIATURES:

Calendar miniatures

Pericopes

St. John

St. Luke

St. Mark

Obsecro Te. Initial: half-length Madonna and Child

O Intemerata. Initial: the Virgin in Prayer

Hours of the Virgin

Folio 27   Annunciation

51   Visitation

62   Nativity

68   Annunciation to the Shepherds

72v.   Adoration of the Magi

77   Presentation in the Temple

81v.   Flight into Egypt

88v.   Coronation of the Virgin

Penitential Psalms

95   Hell

Hours of the Holy Ghost

116   Pentecost

120   Office of the Dead

Fifteen Joys of the Virgin

166v.   Holy Family

Five Wounds

172v.   Man of Sorrows

Modena

BIBL. ESTENSE, lat. 1021, fol. 195

(p. 244; Fig. 795)

Initial with St. Catherine by the Master of the Brussels Initials (or an associate). This initial was added to a Gradual illuminated by Bolognese, Emilian or Paduan masters in the early 14th century.

New York

MORGAN LIBRARY, ms. 346

(p. 278; Figs. 279, 281-286)

Pattern book. 6 boxwood panels; *ca.* 130 × 70 mm. The panels have been sized, and the drawings are silver point.

STYLE AND DATE: These drawings are the most beautiful that have come down to us from the period around 1400. The best and most advanced are clearly closer to the painting of Jacquemart than to any other known works. For many reasons – including a special relationship with the *Way to Calvary*, probably by him – they would seem to have been executed in the early years of the 15th century, later therefore than the miniatures in the *Brussels Hours*. The *Madonna with the Writing Child* on the inside of the front cover of the Morgan book has, on the other hand, usually been connected with the Madonna in the initial diptych of the *Brussels Hours*, frequently (and rightly) dated around 1390, though wrongly, in my opinion, attributed to Jacquemart. These two Madonnas are, furthermore, related more in technique (grisaille) and in subject (writing Christ Child) than in personal style. In design the Morgan Madonna is not, moreover, narrowly connected with the Brussels Madonna but with the miniature formerly in Barcelona (Fig. 280) and a crude Suabian drawing in St. Gall. These Madonnas must derive, indeed, from a lost model, perhaps by Jacquemart himself.

The silver-point drawings are certainly not all by one master. Those on the back cover must be ascribed to a different, far inferior hand that may be responsible for the retouching on other panels, such as 2v. More difficult is the problem of the authorship of those panels (3, 3v., 4v.) that show figures or forms in an earlier manner, sometimes alongside contemporary ones. Either the drawings represent two campaigns, the first in the earlier 14th century, or the advanced master drew from earlier models, retaining their style.

BIBLIOGRAPHY: Fry, 1906–1907, pp. 31 ff.; Lavallée, *Dessin*, 1930, pp. 12 f., 61 f.; Dimier, 1928–1933, pp. 12 ff.; Stange, *Deutsche Malerei*, II, 1936, p. 201; Parkhurst, 1941, pp. 300-302; Ring, *French Painting* [1949] p. 197; Boon, 1950, p. 267; Squilbeck, 1950, pp. 127 ff.; Pächt, *Rev. des arts*, 1956, p. 160; Scheller, *Model Books*, 1963, pp. 104 ff.

Oxford

BODL. LIB., Douce 62

(Chap. X; Figs. 724, 725, 739, 740, 742, 753, 767, 771, 782, 783, 788)

Book of Hours. Use of Paris. 239 fols.; 193 × 138 mm.

HISTORY: The shields are charged with azure a bend lozengy argent and gules between two mullets of eight-points pierced or. Two confronted dogs, often with a small green tree between them, are probably heraldic. One is gray with black spots, the other, wearing gold bells around its neck, is white.

STYLE AND DATE: The Book of Hours was illuminated around 1402 by the Master of the Brussels Initials and an assistant in collaboration with three French masters, one of whom executed only many drolleries from fol. 20 on.

BIBLIOGRAPHY: Oxford, Madan, *Bodleian*, IV, 1897, p. 509 no. 21636; Pächt, *Mary of Burgundy* [1948] p. 52 n. 19; Meiss, *Art Bull.*, 1956, p. 194; D. W. Robertson, Jr., *A Preface to Chaucer*, Princeton, 1963, pp. 95, 129, 156, 251, 257. Wixom, 1965, pp. 70 f.

MINIATURES:

All miniatures are by the Master of the Brussels Initials and assistants unless otherwise indicated.

Calendar miniatures

Pericopes

Folio 15   St. John
     16   St. Luke
     17v.   St. Matthew
     19   St. Mark
     20   *Obsecro Te*. Initial: Virgin and Child

Hours of the Virgin

     28   Annunciation
     51v.   Visitation (French illuminator)
     63   Nativity (French illuminator)
     69v.   Annunciation to the Shepherds

73v. Adoration of the Magi
78 Presentation in the Temple
82v. Flight into Egypt
89v. Coronation of the Virgin

Penitential Psalms

95 Hell

Hours of the Holy Ghost

119 Pentecost
125 Vigil of the Dead
171v. *Doulce Dame.* Initial: Madonna enthroned (close to the Luçon Master – face of the Madonna repainted)

Hours of the Passion

182 Betrayal
188v. Mockery
194v. Christ before Pilate
198 Way to Calvary
203v. Christ nailed to the Cross
209 Crucifixion
215 Lamentation
218v. Entombment

Paris

BIBL. NAT., fr. 13091

(Chap. VII; Figs. 51-82)

Psalter in Latin and French of Jean de Berry. 272 fols.; 250 × 177 mm.

EARLY HISTORY: The ms. contains no Calendar, but the litany establishes that it was written for the use of Bourges (Leroquais). Its text is unusual. The opening folios are devoted not to a Calendar but to large miniatures. The Duke thus followed the precedent of the great 13th-century Psalters that begin with a cycle of miniatures not narrowly connected with the text. For this ms. he selected a favorite theme, the twelve articles of the Credo and a concordance of Old and New Testament, exemplified by pairs of confronted prophets and apostles. Both Berry's ownership and the unity of the ms. in his time are indicated by inscriptions at the beginning and end of the book. Berry himself signed 'Jehan' on fol. 272v. His secretary, Flamel, wrote on fol. 1:

Ce Psaultier, qui est en latin et en françois, est à Jehan, filz de Roy de France, duc de Berry et d'Auvergne, conte de Poitou, d'Estampes, de Bouloingne et d'Auvergne. Flamel.

An entry appearing in all three of the Berry inventories was first connected with this ms. in 1881 by Delisle, and the identification has been accepted by all authorities, although it cannot be proved absolutely. In 1402 this item reads:

Item, un Psaultier escript en latin et françoys, très richement enluminé, où il avoit pluseurs histoires au commancement de la main maistre André Beaunepveu, couvert d'un veluiau vermeil, à fermouers d'or, esmaillez aux armes de Monseigneur.

The 1413 and 1416 inventories vary only in so far as the artist is described as 'feu maistre André Beaunepveu'.

STYLE AND DATE: The 24 apostles and prophets at the beginning of the ms. have been generally accepted as the work of Beauneveu. The cycle of eight miniatures illustrating the divisions of the Psalter have been loosely associated with Jacquemart de Hesdin since Lasteyrie's attempt in 1896 to define the personality of this artist. Durrieu originally thought the *Fool* was by Beauneveu, and he found traces of the same style in other miniatures. Lasteyrie attributed both the *Fool* and *David in the Water* to Jacquemart de Hesdin, by analogy with a style present in the *Grandes Heures* and *Petites Heures*. Although he considered that these two miniatures best exemplified the style of Jacquemart, he saw only one master in the cycle.

In Chapter VII of this book, which develops ideas published by the writer in 1956, these two miniatures are ascribed to Jacquemart whereas Pseudo-Jacquemart is given responsibility for most of the execution of the other miniatures in the Psalter proper. The heavenly figures – God or an angel – were, however, painted by Jacquemart or at least in his style. The first miniature in this cycle is unique and conservative. The ms. was illuminated around 1386.

BIBLIOGRAPHY: Waagen, *Kunstwerke*, III, 1839, p. 335; Delisle, *Cabinet*, I, 1868, pp. 62 f.; III, 1881, p. 173; *idem, Gaz. B.-A.,* 1884, pp. 392 f.; Dehaisnes, *Histoire*, 1886, pp. 254-256; Durrieu, *Le manuscrit*, 1894, pp. 51-56, 83-95; *idem, Monuments et mémoires*, 1894, pp. 185-202; Champeaux and Gauchery, *Travaux*, 1894, p. 95; Guiffrey, *Inventaires*, I, pp. LXXIV, CLXII no. 11, 235 no. 906; II, pp. 132 no. 1049, 237 no. 483; Lasteyrie, 1896, pp. 71 ff.; Fry, 1906-1907, p. 37; Delisle, *Charles V*, II, 1907, pp. 228, 275 f.; Durrieu in Michel, *Histoire*, 1907, pp. 158-160; Mâle, *Fin du moyen âge*, 1908, pp. 259 ff.; Martin, *Peintres de*

manuscrits [1909?] pp. 67-69; *idem, Miniature française,*
1923, pp. 61 f., 97; Paris, Bibl. nat., Couderc, 1927,
pp. 33 f.; Fierens-Gevaert, *Très Belles Heures,* 1924,
pp. 35 ff.; Leroquais, *Psautiers,* II, 1941, pp. 144 ff.;
Ring, *French Painting* [1949] p. 196 no. 42; Panofsky,
Netherlandish Painting, 1953, I, pp. 40 f.; Paris, Bibl.
nat. (Porcher), 1955, no. 180; Meiss, *Art Bull.,* 1956, p.
191; Porcher, *Medieval Miniatures* [1959] p. 59; Meiss,
Gaz. B.-A., 1961, p. 285; Morand, *Pucelle,* 1962, p.
29; Vienna, Kunsthist. Mus., *Katalog,* 1962, no. 180.

MINIATURES:

Folio 7v. Jeremiah (Beauneveu)
      8   St. Peter (Beauneveu)
     9v. David (Beauneveu)
    10   St. Andrew (Beauneveu)
   11v. Isaiah (Beauneveu)
    12   St. James Major (Beauneveu)
   13v. Zachariah (Beauneveu)
    14   St. John the Evangelist (Beauneveu)
   15v. Hosea (Beauneveu)
    16   St. Thomas (Beauneveu)
   17v. Zephaniah (Beauneveu)
    18   St. James Minor (Beauneveu)
   19v. Joel (Beauneveu)
    20   St. Philip (Beauneveu)
   21v. Malachi (Beauneveu)
    22   St. Bartholomew (Beauneveu)
   23v. Amos (Beauneveu)
    24   St. Matthew (Beauneveu)
   25v. Daniel (Beauneveu)
    26   St. Simon (Beauneveu)
   27v. Ezekiel (Beauneveu)
    28   St. Jude (Thaddeus) (Beauneveu)
   29v. Micah (Beauneveu)
    30   St. Matthias (Beauneveu)
    31   David playing harp (French illuminator)
    63   David pointing to his eyes (Pseudo-Jacquemart and associate)
    85   David pointing to his mouth (Pseudo-Jacquemart and associate)
  106   Fool (Jacquemart de Hesdin)
  127   David saved from drowning (Jacquemart de Hesdin)
  153   David playing carillon (Pseudo-Jacquemart)
  177   Three monks singing (Pseudo-Jacquemart and associate)
  201   Trinity (Pseudo-Jacquemart and associate)

Paris

BIBL. NAT., lat. 919

(Chap. XII; Figs. 216-244, 249, 251)

Book of Hours, so-called *Grandes Heures* of Jean de
Berry. Use of Paris. 126 fols.; 400 × 300 mm.

EARLY HISTORY: The manuscript was executed for
Berry and completed in 1409. On fol. A Flamel
wrote: 'Ces belles et notables heures fist faire . . .
Jehan . . . duc de Berry . . . et furent parfaittes et
acomplies en l'an de grace mil quatre cent et neuf. J.
Flamel.' At the bottom of the same folio is written in
another hand: 'Les heures du feu duc de Berry appar-
tenant au roy Louis XIIme'. The ms. is listed in the
Berry inventories of 1413 and 1416. The inventory of
1413 includes a reference to the artists: 'Item, unes
très grans moult belles et riches Heures, très notable-
ment enluminées et historiées de grans histoires de la
main Jacquemart de Hodin et autres ouvriers de Monseigneur . . .' These records and those that follow are
printed in full in Chapter XII.

In 1488 the ms. was rebound for Charles VIII, acquiring a cover that remained on it until recently. The
payments to the binder refer to 'environ quarante
cinq grans histoires'. The ms. now contains only 28
miniatures that could be described as large; they
appear at the beginning of many offices and are each
the width of a column of text. In 1907 Delisle rightly
concluded that the additional 'histoires', approximately 17, in the book in 1488 were full-page miniatures in the Hours of the Virgin and of the Passion.
To the evidence he provided for this plausible hypothesis I can add the presence of cuts in numerous folios
adjacent to these presumed miniatures. The cuts were
made accidentally by the knife employed to excise the
large miniatures. These miniatures, like those in the
Brussels Hours, probably faced the beginning of an
office, and their versos were blank (see the table of the
reconstruction, p. 282).

STYLE: It is quite possible that the *Way to Calvary* in
the Louvre was originally at Sext of the Hours of the
Passion in the *Grandes Heures* (see the entry in the
Catalogue for this painting).

A large part of the illumination of the ms. in its
present, reduced condition was executed by Pseudo-
Jacquemart and his assistants. He was joined, however,
by the Boucicaut Master and his assistants, by the
Bedford Master, and by the Egerton Master. Perhaps
the Boucicaut Master painted a few of the missing
full-page miniatures, though the inventory named

only Jacquemart. Several miniatures by Pseudo-Jacquemart copied compositions or figures in the *Très Belles Heures de Notre-Dame* by the Parement workshop, the Baptist Master, and the Holy Ghost Master. We thus learn that the second campaign on that ms. (as well, of course, as the first) was completed well before 1409.

BIBLIOGRAPHY: Delisle, *Cabinet*, I, 1868, pp. 58 n. 3, 65; III, 1881, pp. 178 f. no. 99; Guiffrey, *Inventaires*, I, pp. CLXIV f. no. 21, 253 f. no. 961; II, p. 280 no. 1159; Durrieu, *Rev. de l'art a. et m.*, 1906, pp. 413 f.; Delisle, *Charles V*, 1907, II, pp. 283 ff.; Martin, *Miniature française*, 1923, p. 98; Leroquais, *Livres d'heures*, 1927, I, pp. 9-15; Bourges, Musées [1951] pp. 31 f. no. 6; Panofsky, *Netherlandish Painting*, 1953, I, pp. 42, 49 f., 55; Porcher, *Belles Heures*, 1953, pp. 15, 25; Paris, Bibl. nat. (Porcher) 1955, p. 89 no. 183; Pächt, *Burl. Mag.*, 1956, pp. 149 ff.; Meiss, *Art Bull.*, 1956, pp. 191, 194; Nordenfalk, 1956, p. 185; Pächt, *Rev. des Arts*, 1956, pp. 149 ff.; Porcher, *Medieval Miniatures* [1959] p. 60.

MINIATURES:

Folio 1   January. Conversion of St. Paul; Water Bearer; Jeremiah and St. Peter – Pseudo-Jacquemart; a tree by Egerton workshop

1v. February. St. Paul preaching; Fishes; David and St. Andrew – Pseudo-Jacquemart (but most of vegetation by follower of Boucicaut Master)

2   March. St. Paul preaching; Ram; Isaiah and St. James Major – Pseudo-Jacquemart (but bare trees by follower of Boucicaut Master)

2v. April. St. Paul preaching; Bull; Zachariah and St. John the Evangelist – Pseudo-Jacquemart (but most of vegetation by follower of Boucicaut Master)

3   May. St. Paul preaching; Twins; Hosea and St. Thomas – Pseudo-Jacquemart (but Virgin and vegetation by follower of Boucicaut Master)

3v. June. St. Paul preaching; Crab; Amos and St. James Minor – Pseudo-Jacquemart (but Virgin, Paul preaching and vegetation partly by follower of Boucicaut Master)

Folio 4   July. St. Paul preaching; Lion; Zephaniah and St. Philip – Pseudo-Jacquemart (but Virgin, Paul preaching and vegetation partly by follower of Boucicaut Master)

4v. August. St. Paul preaching; Virgin; Joel and St. Bartholomew – Pseudo-Jacquemart (but figures and landscape above and hill at lower left largely by follower of Boucicaut Master)

5   September. St. Paul preaching; Balance; Micah and St. Matthew – Pseudo-Jacquemart and assistant of Boucicaut Master

5v. October. St. Paul preaching; Scorpion; Malachi and St. Simon – Pseudo-Jacquemart and assistant of Boucicaut Master

6   November. St. Paul preaching; Archer; Ezekiel and St. Thaddeus (Jude) – Pseudo-Jacquemart

6v. December. St. Paul preaching; Goat; Daniel and St. Matthias – Pseudo-Jacquemart (but December scene and tree at lower left in Egerton style)

8   Joachim's offering rejected; Duke of Berry adoring Virgin and Child – Pseudo-Jacquemart

18   Annunciation to Joachim and Anna; Annunciation to Shepherds – Pseudo-Jacquemart

24   Meeting at Golden Gate; Joachim and Anna – Pseudo-Jacquemart

28   Birth of Virgin; Anna nursing Virgin – Pseudo-Jacquemart

31   Presentation of Virgin; Anna leading Virgin – Pseudo-Jacquemart; two secondary initials by follower of Boucicaut Master

34   Angel bringing food to Virgin; Duke of Berry at prayer – Pseudo-Jacquemart

37   Marriage of Virgin; Joachim, Anna, and Virgin – Pseudo-Jacquemart; initials by followers of Boucicaut Master

41   Wedding at Cana; distribution of remaining food among poor – Pseudo-Jacquemart

45   David at prayer; David playing harp – Pseudo-Jacquemart

53   Crucifixion; Man of Sorrows – Pseudo-Jacquemart

56   Pentecost; Trinity – assistant of Pseudo-Jacquemart

61   Entry into Jerusalem; Christ blessing people – Pseudo-Jacquemart

65   Agony in Garden; Judas hanging himself – Pseudo-Jacquemart

67   Judas receiving pieces of silver; Judas throwing away pieces of silver – assistant of Pseudo-Jacquemart

70   Spoliation; Mocking – Assistant of Pseudo-Jacquemart; initials in part by follower of Boucicaut Master

74   Christ attached to Cross; Soldiers casting lots for garments – follower of Boucicaut Master (but Magdalen and a few other figures partly by Pseudo-Jacquemart)

77   Lamentation; Soldiers guarding sepulcher – Pseudo-Jacquemart

81   Resurrection; Holy Women at Sepulcher – Pseudo-Jacquemart and assistants

84   Harrowing of Hell; Noli me Tangere – Boucicaut Master and assistants

86   Baptism; Lamb of God – Pseudo-Jacquemart and assistants

89   Pentecost; Angel giving food to Virgin – assistant of Pseudo-Jacquemart; initial by follower of Boucicaut Master

93   Trinity; St. Augustine and Christ Child – assistant of Pseudo-Jacquemart; initial by follower of Boucicaut Master

94   St. Peter preaching; Dove of Holy Ghost – assistant of Pseudo-Jacquemart

96   St. Peter leading Duke of Berry into Paradise; Duke of Berry at prayer – Bedford Master and follower of Boucicaut Master

97   SS. Peter and Paul baptizing; Duke of Berry at prayer – assistant of Pseudo-Jacquemart; initial by follower of Boucicaut Master

98   St. Peter celebrating mass; Duke of Berry at prayer – assistant of Pseudo-Jacquemart; initial by follower of Boucicaut Master

100 St. Gregory dictating to a scribe; St. Gregory reading – Boucicaut Master and assistant

106 Office of the Dead; Monk reading – Pseudo-Jacquemart

Paris

BIBL. NAT., lat. 18014   (Chap. VIII; Figs. 83-176)
Book of Hours, so-called *Petites Heures* of Jean de Berry. Use of Paris. 292 fols.; 215 × 145 mm.

EARLY HISTORY: The *Petites Heures* may be identified with an item in the inventory of 1402; the entire entry and other records mentioned in the following summary are quoted at the beginning of Chapter VIII. Shortly before his death the Duke gave the ms. to the wife of his registrar and keeper, Robinet d'Estampes. A note on fol. A, written in 1606, states that the cover replaced at that time bore the name of Louis II d'Anjou and the date 1390. This reference, together with the varied features of the prince represented in many miniatures, has led Couderc and recently Delaissé to argue that the ms. was begun for the Duke of Anjou and completed for the Duke of Berry. The reliability of the inscription is shaken, however, by the fact that it appears in the same form on the cover of Bibl. nat., lat. 1156B, which was not illuminated until after the death of Louis d'Anjou. The portraits, furthermore, differ more with respect to the painter than the sitter. A conservative painter such as Pseudo-Jacquemart had little conception of likeness to an actual person, and his 'portraits' vary considerably. The advanced painters, on the other hand, all seem to represent one man, the Duke of Berry. Inasmuch as the text, which resembles that of the *Très Belles Heures de Notre-Dame* and which contains an entire office in honor of the Baptist, is appropriate for Jean de Berry also, the ms. was no doubt commissioned by him.

STYLE AND DATE: The illumination of the *Petites Heures* probably extended over a period of two or more years, and for many reasons it was completed no later than about 1388. The prayer for travel was added around 1414 and the miniature executed by the Limbourgs. The degree of collaboration in the main part of the ms. was extraordinary even for a ms. of the Duke of Berry. Four painters made large contributions. Not infrequently two and in one instance even three masters worked on one miniature. The Passion Master, perhaps identical with the Jean le Noir who had been in the service of Yolande de Flandre and Charles V, probably designed the folios, began the Hours of the Virgin, and painted entirely the wonderful Hours of the Passion. Jacquemart took over the miniatures of the Hours of the Virgin and in them his style began to show the effects of a study of Italian principles that was shortly to make him the leading champion of Trecento painting in the North. A close associate painted, among other miniatures, most of those in the Hours of the Trinity, from which he takes his name. Pseudo-Jacquemart executed the Calendar and most of the smaller miniatures in the book, including a few of exceptional quality or iconographic interest.

BIBLIOGRAPHY: Delisle, *Gaz. B.-A.*, 1884, pp. 397-399; Guiffrey, *Inventaires*, I, pp. CLXV f. no. 23, 224 no. 851; II, p. 31 no. 172; Lasteyrie, 1896, pp. 98 ff., III ff.; Bouchot, 1904, pp. 12-16; Delisle, *Charles V*, 1907, II, p. 239 no. 102; Couderc, *Portraits* [1910] p. 15; Durrieu, *Rev. archéol.*, 1910, pp. 46, 48; Martin, *Miniature française*, 1923, pp. 63 f., 98; Leroquais, *Livres d'heures*, 1927, II, pp. 175-187; Panofsky, *Netherlandish Painting*, 1953, I, pp. 42-49; Bourges, Musées [1951] nos. 5, 13; Paris, Bibl. nat. (Porcher) 1955, pp. 88 f. no. 182; Meiss, *Art Bull.*, 1956, pp. 191-193; Pächt, *Burl. Mag.*, 1956, pp. 149 ff.; Porcher, *Medieval Miniatures* [1959] pp. 60 ff.; Meiss, *Gaz. B.-A.*, 1961, pp. 285 ff.; Baltimore, Walters, *International Style* [1962] no. 43; Morand, *Pucelle*, 1962, pp. 26 f.; Delaissé, 1963, pp. 129-133.

MINIATURES:

Folio 1   January. Conversion of St. Paul; Water Bearer; Jeremiah and St. Peter (Pseudo-Jacquemart)

1v. February. St. Paul preaching; Fishes; David and St. Andrew (Pseudo-Jacquemart)

2   March. St. Paul preaching; Ram; Isaiah and St. James Major (Pseudo-Jacquemart)

2v. April. St. Paul preaching; Bull; Zachariah and St. John the Evangelist (Pseudo-Jacquemart)

3   May. St. Paul preaching; Twins; Hosea and St. Thomas (Pseudo-Jacquemart)

Folio 3v. June. St. Paul preaching; Crab; Amos and St. James Minor (Pseudo-Jacquemart)

4   July. St. Paul preaching; Lion; Zephaniah and St. Philip (Pseudo-Jacquemart)

4v. August. St. Paul preaching; Virgin; Joel and St. Bartholomew (Pseudo-Jacquemart)

5   September. St. Paul preaching; Balance; Micah and St. Matthew (Pseudo-Jacquemart)

5v. October. St. Paul preaching; Scorpion; Malachi and St. Simon (Pseudo-Jacquemart)

6   November. St. Paul preaching; Archer; Ezekiel and St. Jude (Pseudo-Jacquemart)

6v. December. St. Paul preaching; Goat; Daniel and St. Matthias (Pseudo-Jacquemart)

8   Dominican friar instructing young prince (Jacquemart and Pseudo-Jacquemart)

9v. Dominican friar instructing young prince (Pseudo-Jacquemart)

12   Christ and High Priest Eli; death of Eli; Hophni and Phineas sinning (Pseudo-Jacquemart)

17   Saint Louis, King of France, on his deathbed (Jacquemart)

22   Annunciation; Man of Sorrows with Virgin and St. John the Baptist; Twelve Apostles and Jeremiah; Berry (Passion Master and Jacquemart)

32v. Visitation (Jacquemart)

38   Nativity (Jacquemart)

40v. Annunciation to Shepherds (Passion Master and Jacquemart)

42v. Adoration of Magi (Jacquemart)

45v. Flight into Egypt (Jacquemart and Trinity Master)

48v. Coronation of Virgin (Jacquemart and Trinity Master)

53   Christ enthroned and Four Evangelists (Passion Master)

63v. Crucifixion (Pseudo-Jacquemart)

67   Baptism (Trinity Master)

69   Pentecost (Pseudo-Jacquemart)

70   Trinity (Trinity Master)

71   St. Peter preaching (Pseudo-Jacquemart)

72   St. Peter leading man into church (Trinity Master)

73   SS. Peter and Paul baptizing (Pseudo-Jacquemart)

74   St. Peter celebrating mass (Trinity Master)

75   St. Ambrose (?) writing (Pseudo-Jacquemart)

76   Betrayal (Passion Master)

79v.   Christ before Pilate (Passion Master)

82   Mocking (Passion Master)

83v.   Flagellation (Passion Master)

86v.   Christ carrying Cross (Passion Master)

89v.   Crucifixion (Passion Master)

92v.   Deposition (Passion Master)

94v.   Entombment (Passion Master)

97v.   Virgin and Child adored by Berry (Jacquemart)

100v. Christ-Logos supporting the world adored by a prince (Berry?) (Trinity Master)

103v. Virgin and Child adored by Berry (Trinity Master)

104   Angels; St. John the Baptist (Pseudo-Jacquemart)

104v. Apostles; St. Mary Magdalen (Pseudo-Jacquemart)

105   Martyr saints (damaged) (Pseudo-Jacquemart)

105v. Holy confessors; female martyr saints (Pseudo-Jacquemart)

106   A prince (Berry?) praying before Christ (Pseudo-Jacquemart)

106v. A prince (Berry?) at prayer (Pseudo-Jacquemart)

115v. A prince (Berry?) at prayer (Pseudo-Jacquemart)

117v. A Dominican presenting a prince (Berry?) to Christ (Pseudo-Jacquemart)

119   A prince (Berry?) at prayer (Pseudo-Jacquemart)

119v. A prince (Berry?) at prayer (Pseudo-Jacquemart)

120   Virgin and Child, St. John the Evangelist, and a prince (Berry?) (Pseudo-Jacquemart)

121v. A prince (Berry?) at prayer (Pseudo-Jacquemart)

122   Virgin and Child adored by a prince (Berry?) (Pseudo-Jacquemart)

123v. Monk in prayer (Pseudo-Jacquemart)

132v. Trinity (Pseudo-Jacquemart)

134v. Office of the Dead (Pseudo-Jacquemart)

136   Christ, Virgin, and Saints enthroned in Paradise (Pseudo-Jacquemart)

137v. Trinity (Trinity Master)

139   Berry (?) attending mass (Pseudo-Jacquemart)

140v. Betrayal (retouched) (Trinity Master)

141   Deposition; Resurrection (Pseudo-Jacquemart)

141v. Annunciation (Trinity Master)

142v. Virgin and her parents entering Temple; Virgin at prayer (Pseudo-Jacquemart)

143   Nativity (Pseudo-Jacquemart)

143v. Virgin nursing Child; Annunciation of Virgin's death (Pseudo-Jacquemart)

144   Death of Virgin (Pseudo-Jacquemart)

144v. Coronation of Virgin; a prince (Berry?) at prayer (Pseudo-Jacquemart)

145v. Berry (?) praying to Christ (damaged) (Pseudo-Jacquemart)

155   Entombment of Christ (Pseudo-Jacquemart)

158   Agony in Garden (Trinity Master)

160   Way to Calvary (The Fifth Master)

161   Erection of Cross (The Fifth Master)

162   Christ nailed to Cross (Pseudo-Jacquemart)

163   Holy Women at Sepulcher (Trinity Master)

164   Crucifixion (Pseudo-Jacquemart)

166   Harrowing of Hell (Pseudo-Jacquemart)

167v. Berry (?) at mass (Beginning of Mass) (Pseudo-Jacquemart)

169v. A prince (Berry?) at mass (Chant of Gospel) (Pseudo-Jacquemart)

170v. A prince (Berry?) at mass (between First Prayer and Gospel) (Pseudo-Jacquemart)

171   A prince (Berry?) at mass (making offering and kissing hand of priest) (Pseudo-Jacquemart)

172   A prince (Berry?) at mass (Elevation of Host) (Pseudo-Jacquemart)

173v. A prince (Berry?) at mass (Kiss of Peace; Berry kissing paten) (Pseudo-Jacquemart)

174v. Communion (Pseudo-Jacquemart)

176 A prince (Berry?) at mass (after communion) (Pseudo-Jacquemart)

176v. A prince (Berry?) adoring crucified Christ (Pseudo-Jacquemart)

181v. Christ, St. Martha, and St. Julian on voyage (Pseudo-Jacquemart)

183 Trinity (Trinity Master)

186v. Creation of Adam (The Fifth Master)

188 Abraham adoring Trinity (Trinity Master)

189 Christ enthroned between seraphim (Trinity Master)

191 Baptism (Pseudo-Jacquemart)

192 Christ on Mount Tabor (Trinity Master)

193 Christ preaching (Pseudo-Jacquemart)

194v. Christ worshipped by kings (Trinity Master)

196 Trinity (Trinity Master)

196v. A prince (Berry?) adoring crucified Christ (Pseudo-Jacquemart)

197v. Pentecost (Pseudo-Jacquemart)

198 Berry (?) adoring Trinity (Pseudo-Jacquemart)

198v. A prince (Berry) adoring Virgin and Child (Trinity Master)

199v. A prince (Berry?) and guardian angel (The Fifth Master)

203 Annunciation to Zacharias (Trinity Master and Pseudo-Jacquemart)

206 Visitation (Pseudo-Jacquemart)

207 Birth of St. John the Baptist and Zacharias writing name (Passion Master and Trinity Master)

208 St. John the Baptist in Desert (Passion Master)

209v. Baptism of Christ (Jacquemart and Trinity Master)

211 St. John the Baptist before Herod (Jacquemart and Trinity Master)

212v. Salome's dance (Passion Master and Trinity Master)

214 Salome and the executioner (Jacquemart, Trinity Master and Pseudo-Jacquemart)

217 Office of the Dead (Pseudo-Jacquemart)

239 Crucifixion (Pseudo-Jacquemart)

267 Holy Women and faithful adoring Virgin (Pseudo-Jacquemart)

278v. Solomon's throne with personifications of Prayer, Hope, Charity, Penitence, Justice, and Faith (Pseudo-Jacquemart)

282 Three Living and Three Dead (Pseudo-Jacquemart)

286 'Vesperbild' (Pseudo-Jacquemart)

288v. Duke of Berry beginning a trip (Limbourgs)

Paris

BIBL. NAT., nouv. acq. lat. 3093 (Chap. VI)

Très Belles Heures de Notre-Dame of Jean de Berry. Of the original ms. the following parts are known, in some cases only from reproductions.

(1) Paris, Bibl. nat., nouv. acq. lat. 3093. 240 pp.; 279 × 199 mm. (Figs. 6-28, 570)

(2) Turin, Museo Civico, 'Heures de Milan'. 126 fols.; 284 × 205 mm. (Figs. 39, 41-50, 491)

(3) Turin, Bibl. Nazionale, 'Heures de Turin' (burnt in 1904). 280 × 190 mm. (Figs. 29-31, 34, 35, 38)

(4) Four folios in the Cabinet des Dessins, Musée du Louvre. RF 2022, RF 2023 r. and v., RF 2024. (Figs. 32, 33, 36, 37)

(5) Lithograph by Bastard of lost miniature of the Itinerary (Fig. 497)

DESCRIPTION AND EARLY HISTORY: The first owner of the ms. cannot be identified with absolute certainty, but there are almost no grounds for doubt that the text was written, and the illumination undertaken, for Jean de Berry. Even if another prince was responsible for the initiation of the work the ms. was being embellished for Jean de Berry no later than around 1384. The evidence for these conclusions is drawn from the iconography of the Duke, from the contents of the book, from its subsequent history, and from its relationship with other manuscripts. A full discussion of this intricate but compelling evidence, which cannot be briefly formulated, may be found in Chapters IV, VI, VIII.

The Master of the *Parement de Narbonne*, a painter rather than a professional miniaturist, directed the beginning of the illumination. He established the design of the folios, and allocated to three or more assistants the painting of the vines and the angels in the borders, the initials, and the *bas-de-page*. The styles of these assistants range from one close to the Bondol tradition (in many of the *bas-de-page*) to a few of the angels in the borders that are very close to the Parement Master himself. The borders were executed at this time for almost the entire ms., the one major exception being the Calendar in the Paris section, which indeed was added after 1404 by Jean de Berry. The Calendar in the *Heures de Turin* may have been written and illuminated at a still later date (around 1419?), in deliberate imitation of the original script and decoration, as Chatelet proposed. The initials are clearly of this time or still later.

At the outset the Parement Master apparently intended to provide drawings for many of the miniatures, and he furthermore undertook to paint some of them himself, particularly in the Hours of the Virgin, at the beginning of the ms. Others were executed by an assistant whose style, though inferior, was very close to that of the *chef* himself. When the work was interrupted around 1385, perhaps by the death of the Parement Master, some scenes, such as the last in the Hours of the Passion, were only drawn or partly painted.

For reasons about which we can only surmise, the ms. was left in its unfinished state until around 1405. In this year the Duke bought material to make a jewelled *pipe* for it, and from that time up to 1409 at least, a campaign to complete the book was undertaken. Almost all the miniatures in the Hours of the Holy Ghost were painted by a master who was influenced by André Beauneveu and who was perhaps a sculptor himself. An illuminator, probably trained in the Netherlands, worked on six miniatures in the *Heures de Milan*, and completed the unfinished scenes of the Passion in the Paris section. Working with associates he executed part of a miniature in the Paris section, two miniatures now in the Louvre, and five miniatures in the *Heures de Turin*. Some of the miniatures painted during this campaign are reflected in the *Grandes Heures*, finished in 1409. This entire campaign is discussed in Chapter XI. The Limbourgs, too, illuminated three folios during this period. One, containing the miniature of the Itinerary, is discussed in Chapter IV. All three will be dealt with in a later section of this publication devoted to the painting of these masters.

The second campaign of illumination, like the first, ended without completing the decoration of the ms.

We learn from the inventory of 1413 that the Duke had given the book to his keeper, Robinet d'Estampes. Shortly afterward Robinet divided the ms. into two parts, keeping the one in which the illumination had been completed and disposing of the other. This latter section became the property of a prince of the house of Holland and Bavaria, who added the famous Eyckian illuminations. This section was itself later divided into two parts, one of which, the so-called *Heures de Turin*, passed eventually into the Biblioteca Nazionale in Turin, only to be burnt in 1904. The other section, which was owned by the Trivulzio family in Milan and therefore became known as the *Heures de Milan*, was recently given to the Museo Civico, Turin.

BIBLIOGRAPHY: Monographs: Durrieu, *Heures de Turin*, 1902; Hulin de Loo, *Heures de Milan*, 1911; Durrieu, *Très Belles Heures de Notre-Dame*, 1922; Delisle, *Gaz. B.-A.*, 1884, pp. 290-292, 391 f.; *idem*, *Charles V*, 1907, II, pp. 240 no. 102 bis, 295 ff.; Durrieu, *Rev. archéol.*, 1910, pp. 30 ff., 246 ff.; Hulin de Loo, 1925, pp. 123 ff.; Winkler, *Flämische Buchmalerei*, 1925, p. 15; Martens, *Meister Francke*, 1929, fig. 94; Robb, 1936, p. 496; Bourges, *Musées*, 1951, pp. 32 f.; Schilling, 1952, p. 168; Bober, 1953, p. 744; Panofsky, *Netherlandish Painting*, 1953, I, pp. 45 f.; Paris, Bibl. nat. (Porcher) 1955, no. 181; Sterling, 1955, p. 80; Chatelet, 1956, pp. 199 ff.; Meiss, *Art Bull.*, 1956, p. 190; Pächt, *Burl. Mag.*, 1956, p. 153; Nordenfalk, in Stockholm, Nationalmuseum, 1958, p. 19; Porcher, *Medieval Miniatures* [1959] p. 60; Meiss, 1960, p. 235; Vienna, Kunsthist. Mus., *Katalog*, 1962, p. 169; Delaissé, 1963, pp. 133 ff.; Kreuter-Eggemann, *Daliwe*, 1964, I, pp. 69, 77; Paris, Louvre (Sterling and Adhémar) 1965, pp. 1 f.

MINIATURES:

Page 2   Annunciation; Virgin spinning, miraculously provided with food; Marriage of Virgin (kneeling donor repainted) (Parement Master and workshop)

28   Visitation; Joseph questioning Virgin; Angel assuring Joseph; Virgin and Joseph at Bethlehem (Parement Master and workshop)

42   Nativity; Annunciation to Shepherds (Parement Master and workshop)

50   Adoration of Magi; Annunciation to Magi; Magi before Herod (Parement Master and workshop)

56 Presentation in Temple; Virgin warned by Angel; Miracle of the Corn; Flight into Egypt (Parement Master and workshop)

62 Christ among Doctors; Herod ordering Massacre of Innocents; Massacre of Innocents (Parement Master and workshop)

68 Wedding at Cana; Christ blessing loaves and fishes; Eating of loaves and fishes (Parement Master and workshop)

76 Coronation of Virgin; Assumption; Death of Virgin (Parement Master and workshop)

104 Office of the Dead; Two monks; Funeral procession (Parement Master and workshop)

155 Man of Sorrows; Harrowing of Hell (Parement Master and workshop)

162 Baptism; Holy Ghost and Virgin; Baptismal procession (Workshop of Parement Master, Baptist Master, and Holy Ghost Master)

166 Pentecost; Holy Ghost and Virgin; Sacrament of Baptism (Workshop of Parement Master and Holy Ghost Master)

169 Resurrection of Dead; Holy Ghost and Virgin; Sacrament of Confirmation (Workshop of Parement Master and Holy Ghost Master)

173 Descent of Holy Ghost on Faithful; Holy Ghost and Virgin; Sacrament of Eucharist (Workshop of Parement Master and Holy Ghost Master)

176 Holy Ghost and Unbelievers; Holy Ghost and Virgin; Sacrament of Marriage (Workshop of Parement Master and Holy Ghost Master)

178 Apostles going forth to preach; Holy Ghost and Virgin; Sacrament of Extreme Unction (Workshop of Parement Master and Holy Ghost Master)

181 Betrayal; Agony in Garden; Judas receiving pieces of silver (Parement Master and workshop)

189 Christ before Caiaphas; Mocking; Christ before Annas (Parement Master and workshop)

194 Christ before Pilate; St. Peter and maid; Judas throwing away pieces of silver and hanging himself (Parement Master and workshop)

197 Flagellation; Christ before Pilate; Christ before Herod (Parement Master and workshop)

203 Christ carrying cross; Pilate washing hands; Ecce Homo (Workshop of Parement Master and Baptist Master)

209 Crucifixion; Soldiers casting lots for garments; Christ nailed to cross (Workshop of Parement Master and Baptist Master)

216 Deposition; Joseph of Arimathea and Nicodemus before Pilate; Lamentation (Workshop of Parement Master and Baptist Master)

225 Faithful adoring Trinity; Creation of Eve; Creation of world (the Limbourgs)

240 Faithful adoring God; St. Anthony Abbot; St. Anthony Abbot visiting St. Paul the Hermit and meeting a centaur (the Limbourgs)

Heures de Turin

Folio 39v. Christ in Glory; Two angel musicians; Three angel musicians (Parement Master and workshop)

57 St. John the Baptist in Desert (Baptist Master)

57v. Patriarchs, prophets and apostles (Baptist Master)

58 Mary Magdalene at Christ's feet in house of Simon (Baptist Master)

78v. Duke of Berry kneeling at prie-dieu before enthroned Virgin (Baptist Master)

80v. St. Jerome at work, aided by two clerks (Baptist Master)

Turin, Museo Civico, *Heures de Milan*

Folio 1v. Annunciation (Baptist Master)

4v. Nativity; Angel of Annunciation; Shepherds (Workshop of Parement Master and Baptist Master)

13v. Adoration of Magi (later imitator of Parement Master)

16v. Presentation in Temple (later imitator of Parement Master)

20v. Entry into Jerusalem (Baptist Master)

80v. Ascension (later imitator of Parement Master)

84v. Pentecost (Baptist Master)

87   Trinity with Duke of Berry in margin; marriage; ceremony of marriage (retouched) (Parement Master and workshop)

90   Institution of Eucharist (Baptist Master)

100v. Coronation of Virgin (later imitator of Parement Master)

103   Birth of Virgin (later imitator of Parement Master)

106   St. Michael (later imitator of Parement Master)

120   Madonna with kneeling male figure; Two angels; Christ preaching (Parement Master and workshop)

122   Martyrdom of St. Andrew (Baptist Master)

Paris, Musée du Louvre, Cabinet des Dessins

God the Father enthroned (damaged) (Workshop of the Parement Master and Flemish painter)

Martyrs (Baptist Master)

Confessors (Baptist Master)

St. John the Evangelist and Virgin; Crucifixion; Duke of Berry (?) presented by Baptist to Christ (Parement Master and workshop)

Lithograph by Bastard of miniature formerly in his collection: Duke of Berry at gate of city

Paris

MUSÉE DU LOUVRE   (Chap. VI; Figs. 1-5)

Parement de Narbonne. Grisaille on silk. 78 × 286 cm.

CONDITION: Generally good. There are creases and tears along a horizontal line running through the thighs of Christ on the cross, and less conspicuous, a horizontal line passing through the right shoulder of Christ. Numerous tears mar the border towards the left. The surface of the *Betrayal* has been more generally damaged than that of other scenes. The figure of the Queen shows pentimenti. (For a more negative view of the condition see Panofsky.)

EARLY HISTORY: The initials K and the iconography of the portraits demonstrate that the painting was executed for Charles V and Queen Jeanne. It was found in Narbonne in the early 19th century.

STYLE AND DATE: It is generally agreed that the appearance of Charles V and his Queen, Jeanne, fix the painting towards 1375. She died in 1378, he in 1380. The painter, who cannot definitely be identified with any master recorded in documents, directed around 1382 the first campaign in the illumination of the *Très Belles Heures de Notre-Dame.*

BIBLIOGRAPHY: Bouchot, 1904, pp. 5 ff.; Berthomieu, 1912, pp. 291 ff.; Hulin de Loo, 1925, pp. 125 f.; Sterling, *Peintres du moyen âge*, 1941, rép. no. 2, p. 4; E. Michel, *École flamande*, 1944, pp. 6, 38; Ring, *French Painting* [1949] p. 191; Panofsky, *Netherlandish Painting*, 1953, I, pp. 41 f.; Smith, 1959, pp. 43 ff.; Paris, Louvre (Sterling and Adhémar) 1965, p. 1.

Paris

MUSÉE DU LOUVRE

(Chap. XII; Figs. 277, 278)

Way to Calvary, very probably by Jacquemart de Hesdin. Perhaps originally at Sext in the Hours of the Passion, *Grandes Heures.* 379 × 283 mm. (largest dimensions)

The painting was executed on parchment, which was glued to cloth at a later date.

EARLY HISTORY, STYLE, AND DATE: Shortly after this painting entered the Louvre in 1930 Huyghe published it as Avignonese, an attribution that was accepted by many scholars. Soon thereafter Beenken, pointing to its connection with the *Brussels Hours,* proposed the circle of Jacquemart, and this opinion has prevailed in the literature of the past decade. In 1956 three historians simultaneously discussed its relationship with the *Grandes Heures.* Nordenfalk, ascribing the work to Jacquemart (i.e. the painter of the main cycles in the *Brussels Hours*), believed it was one of the lost miniatures of the *Grandes Heures.* The writer, proposing the same attribution and dating the *Way to Calvary* towards 1405, concluded that it did not belong to the *Grandes Heures* because of its size and the presence within the main field of two contemporary figures in prayer. Pächt took the third position, that the painting was indeed one of the lost miniatures and therefore probably by Jacquemart, but *not* by the painter of the main cycles of the *Brussels Hours*. His Jacquemart would be rather the author of the initial diptych in that ms. and also the pattern book in the Morgan Library.

In the past three years the writer has been able, through study of the unbound leaves of the *Grandes Heures*, to add evidence to that published by Delisle in 1907 about the original composition of the ms. Seven-power magnification has left unanswered one or two questions, which may be clarified by the microscope and analysis in a laboratory. I find now no compelling evidence to show that the *Way to Calvary* did or did not belong to the book. Nor do style and iconography seem decisive, though I am much more inclined than I was earlier to an affirmative judgment.

Inasmuch as the identity of Jacquemart is now established by what seem to me definitive proofs that the *Brussels Hours* is the ms. ascribed to him in the inventory, the stylistic relationship of the best miniatures in that ms. (exclusive of the diptych and the initials) with the *Way to Calvary* becomes crucial. The latter still seems to me very probably a later work of the Brussels painter, but not necessarily as late as towards 1409. Two miniatures in a Book of Hours in the British Museum, Yates Thompson 37, seem likewise to have come from the workshop or immediate circle of Jacquemart in the period 1405–1412, and they show basic compositional advances that are lacking in the *Way to Calvary*.

If the *Way to Calvary* did not belong to the *Grandes Heures*, for what purpose could it have been made? A Passion cycle in another, even larger ms., would still leave the iconographic problem of the 'donors'. If, like a few large paintings on vellum of which we know, it had been intended for the wall, it could not, in my opinion, have hung alone because of the imbalance in its design. It requires something – one or more Passion scenes? – at the right. Analogues for such a cycle on parchment are, to my knowledge, lacking.

BIBLIOGRAPHY: Huyghe, 1930, pp. 99 f.; Beenken, 1933–1934, p. 216 n. 41; Sterling, *Peintres du moyen âge*, 1942, pl. 42; Bazin, *École provençale XIV-XV siècles*, Geneva [1944]; Ring, *French Painting* [1949] p. 195; Bologna, 1953, no. 37, p. 50; Porcher, *Belles Heures*, 1953, p. 17; Panofsky, *Netherlandish Painting*, 1953, I, p. 82; Meiss, *Art Bull.*, 1956, p. 192; Nordenfalk, 1956, p. 185; Pächt, *Rev. des arts*, 1956, pp. 149 ff.; Porcher, *Medieval Miniatures* [1959] p. 60; Paris, Louvre (Sterling and Adhémar) 1965, p. 3.

z

Paris

COLL. JEAN DURRIEU (p. 264; Figs. 245-247)

Book of Prayers. 107 fols., but ms. is not foliated; 180 × 130 mm.

STYLE AND DATE: One group of miniatures in this ms., rightly ascribed by Porcher in 1955 to the chief painter of the *Grandes Heures*, was given by the writer in 1956 to the reconstructed Pseudo-Jacquemart. The second group was painted by the workshop of the Egerton Master, and this group includes the *Majesty* at the beginning, which Porcher attributed to the Bedford Master and I to the Boucicaut Master.

The illumination should be dated around 1410.

BIBLIOGRAPHY: Paris, Bibl. nat. (Porcher) 1955, pp. 89 f. no. 184; Meiss, *Art Bull.*, 1956, pp. 191 f., 195.

MINIATURES:

Christ enthroned and Four Evangelists (Egerton workshop)

Presentation in Temple (follower of Pseudo-Jacquemart)

Annunciation (Pseudo-Jacquemart)

Resurrection (follower of Pseudo-Jacquemart)

Ascension (Egerton workshop)

Pentecost (Egerton workshop)

Trinity (follower of Pseudo-Jacquemart)

Mass (Egerton workshop)

St. John the Baptist in Desert (follower of Pseudo-Jacquemart)

Assumption of Virgin (Egerton workshop)

Birth of Virgin and bathing of Christ Child (Pseudo-Jacquemart)

Martyrdom of St. Andrew (workshop of Pseudo-Jacquemart)

Meeting at the Golden Gate (workshop of Pseudo-Jacquemart)

Office of the Dead (Egerton workshop)

Office of the Cross (Egerton workshop)

Parma

BIBL. PALATINA, lat. 159

(Chap. X; Figs. 714, 715, 727, 728, 735-738)

Book of Hours. North French Calendar. 262 fols.; 165 × 120 mm.

HISTORY: The shield on fol. 22, 'd'argent au sautoir de sable cantonné de quatre perdrix au naturel, becquées et membrées de gueules', appears to be that of the Raguier family. The Palatine collection began with the mss. of Marie-Louise de Bourbon, who became Duchess of Lucca in 1817, and no. 159 may have been one of her possessions (see F. Odorici, *La nazionale biblioteca di Parma*, Turin, 1873, pp. 17 ff.).

STYLE AND DATE: The painter chiefly responsible for this ms. was French; he designed the borders and painted the important miniature of the *Annunciation* on fol. 22 as well as several others. A few miniatures were allocated to the Master of the Brussels Initials. The work was probably done around 1395. Some of the compositions by the French master, such as the *Adoration of the Magi*, reflect the *Petites Heures*, and his style is closely related to that manuscript.

BIBLIOGRAPHY: Meiss, *Art Bull.*, 1956, p. 194 n. 26.

MINIATURES:

Folios 2-13   *Calendar* (Master of the Brussels Initials)

Pericopes

14   St. John (Master of the Brussels Initials)

15v.   St. Luke (Master of the Brussels Initials)

17v.   St. Matthew (Master of the Brussels Initials)

19v.   St. Mark (Master of the Brussels Initials)

Hours of the Virgin

22   Annunciation (Follower of Jacquemart)

35   Visitation (Follower of Jacquemart)

56   Annunciation to the Shepherds (Follower of Jacquemart)

62   Adoration of the Magi (Follower of Jacquemart)

67v.   Presentation in the Temple (Follower of Jacquemart)

73   Flight into Egypt (Follower of Jacquemart)

82   Coronation of the Virgin (Follower of Jacquemart)

117   Office of the Dead (Master of the Brussels Initials)

Penitential Psalms

170   Christ in Majesty (French painter)

Rome

BIBL. VATICANA, lat. 50-51
(Chap. IX; Figs. 177, 178, 658, 661, 662)

Bible. 398 fols.; 484 × 324 mm.

EARLY HISTORY: The arms on the first folio of both volumes are those of Pope Clement VII, Jean de Berry, and his wife Jeanne de Boulogne. An emblem of Simon Alegret, physician and counsellor to the Duke, appears also. The Bible was for a time in the Duke's library, because his arms appear in the initial on fol. 1 of Vol. I, and he inscribed both volumes (lat. 50, fol. 397v.; lat. 51, fol. 437v.). The Pope and the Duke not infrequently exchanged mss. Probably the Duke and Duchess, with Alegret, gave the Bible to the Pope. The gift must have been made between 1389, when the Duke married Jeanne de Boulogne, and 1394, when Pope Clement died. Perhaps the Duke gave the ms. to the Pope when he visited him in Avignon in 1391.

The Bible was described in the earliest papal inventory, compiled in 1455 on the death of Nicholas V: 'Item duo volumina majora, forme regalis. Primum volumen in quo est *Biblia*, incipiens a prologo frater Ambrosius usque ad prologum exclusive Ysaie prophete. Et in dicto volumine etiam continetur *Glosa Nicolai de Lira*, in merginibus (*sic*) ad modum decretalium; in littera in principio cum ymagine beati Ieronimi cum leone et scuto cum tiara supra cum quadris V de auro et IIII^{or} de adzurro et armis regis Francie. A dextris et sinistris ducis Barensis, copertum de cetenino celesti et IIII^{or} serraturis largis argenti deaurati cum acuto et armis lilii. Explicit liber ecc^{cus} et finis primi voluminis Biblie.

'Item secundum volumen in quo est secunda pars voluminis *Biblie*, incipiens a prologo Ysaie prophete: Nemo cum prophetis etc., cum littera in principio cum ymagine Ysaie, leone, bove, angelo et aquila et armis sicut primum, excepto quod angeli habent tiaram in manu, ejus voluminis et forme; et in primo scuto claves cum angelis tenentibus in manu et supra tiaram. Cum *Glosa Nicolai de Lira*, ut primum. Volumen finit: gratia dñi nñ Ihesu Xñ, coopertum serico rubeo cum rosis diversorum colorum et serraturis de argento deaurato similibus primo volumini (fol. 3v°).'

STYLE AND DATE: The ms. was probably illuminated in two phases. First a rather modest master, with assistance, undertook the Bible itself, soon after about 1386. One or two of his miniatures derive from compositions in the *Petites Heures*. He was the author also of a Book of Hours, Brit. Mus., Add. 23145. The beautiful frieze in the lower margin of the first folio of lat. 50, and all the forms but the two angels at the left on the first folio of lat. 51, were painted by Jacquemart de Hesdin between 1389 and 1394. The two angels at the left in lat. 51 were executed slightly earlier (a day?) by a collaborator, probably the Trinity Master. Jacquemart began the further of his two angels under the influence of the Trinity Master; his preparatory drawing for the figure discloses this relationship clearly. Jacquemart's second angel was conceived quite independently.

BIBLIOGRAPHY: Müntz and Fabre, *Bibliothèque du Vatican*, 1887, pp. 48 f.; Rome, Vatican, *Codices Vaticani latini*, I, 1902, pp. 58-63; Delisle, *Charles V*, 1907, II, pp. 223 f. no. 2 bis, 271; Durrieu, *Comptes rendus*, 1909, pp. 868-875; idem, *Rev. de l'art a. et m.*, 1910, pp. 5-20; idem, *Bulletin*, 1911, p. 87 no. III; Winkler, in Thieme-Becker, XVI, 1923, p. 572 (s.v. Hesdin); Meiss, *Art Bull.*, 1956, p. 192.

MINIATURES:

All the illumination is by a French painter around 1390 except the lower borders of the first folios of both volumes.

Folio 1   Arms of Pope Clement VII, Jean de Berry and Jeanne de Boulogne; emblem of Simon Alegret. By Jacquemart de Hesdin
4v.   St. Jerome writing
5v.   Scenes of Creation. Annunciation; Crucifixion. (*Genesis*)
33v.   Moses receiving tablets. (*Exodus*)
38v.   Sacrificial offering. (*Leviticus*)
80   Lord addressing Moses. (*Numbers*)
102   Moses directs placing of tablets in Ark. (*Deuteronomy*)
122v.   Lord addresses Joshua. (*Joshua*)
133v.   Samson and the lion. (*Judges*)
145   Ruth reaping. (*Ruth*)
148   The Ark of the Covenant taken by the Philistines. (*Kings I*)
160v.   David: punishing a man. (*Kings II*)
170v.   Abishag brought before David. (*Kings III*)
183v.   Elijah appearing to Ahaziah. (*Kings IV*)
194v.   Creation of Adam. (*Paralipomena I*)
203v.   Solomon speaking to all Israel. (*Paralipomena II*)

213v.   Cyrus the Great: proclamation. (*Esdras I*)
214   Levites offer burnt offerings. (*Esdras I*)
218   Nude Nehemias inspecting the walls of Jerusalem. (*Nehemias*)
223   Josias asperging an altar
227   Tobias and two priests. (*Tobias*-Prologue)
227v.   Tobias lying under a tree. (*Tobias*)
231   Judith combing her hair. (*Judith*)
235v.   Feast of Ahasuerus. (*Esther*)
240   Job. (*Job*)
262v.   David and Goliath. (*Psalms*)
263v.   David playing the harp. (*Psalms*)
273v.   David pointing to eye. (*Psalms*)
278   David pointing to mouth. (*Psalms*)
282   Dixit Insipiens. (*Psalms*)
287   David in the water. (*Psalms*)
292v.   David plays on bells. (*Psalms*)
297v.   Clerics singing. (*Psalms*)
302v.   Trinity
317   Solomon addressing youths. (*Proverbs*)
328v.   Ecclesiastes the Preacher. (*Ecclesiastes*)
332v.   Virgin of Humility. (*Song of Songs*)
337v.   Three Judges. (*Wisdom*)
345v.   A theological discussion. (*Ecclesiastes*)

Vatican lat. 51

1   Arms of Pope Clement VIII, Jean de Berry and Jeanne de Boulogne; emblem of Simon Alegret. By Jacquemart de Hesdin and (?) the Trinity Master
4v.   Majesty and two seraphim
46   Jeremiah
95   Baruch
100   Ezekiel's Vision
142v.   Daniel
175v.   Habakkuk
212   Christ on Cross with Evangelists
214v.   Nativity
248v.   St. Mark

Turin

MUSEO CIVICO, *Heures de Milan*
(Chap. VI; Figs. 39, 41-50, 491, 537)
See Paris, Bibl. nat., nouv. acq. lat. 3093

Venice

FONDAZIONE CINI (p. 245; Fig. 796)

Initial: Prophet by the workshop of the Master of the Brussels Initials.

Warsaw

BIBLIOTECA NARODOWA, lat. Q.v.i.iii
(pp. 231; Figs. 719-723)

Paris Calendar. 8 fols.; 247 × 177 mm.

HISTORY: The Calendar, originally part probably of a Book of Hours, was in the Zaluski Collection in Warsaw. The folios were carried off to Russia, and Laborde published them in 1936 in his work on the Public Library in Leningrad. The Calendar entered the Biblioteca Narodowa in Warsaw before 1938.

STYLE AND DATE: The miniatures, all in quatrefoils and medallions, were painted by the Master of the Brussels Initials in the first years of the 15th century. Sawicka dated the Calendar before 1374 because it lacks the feast of the Presentation on November 21 (instituted in 1374 by Pope Gregory XI) and the Visitation on July 2 (instituted by Urban VI in 1389), but the illumination cannot be so early. These feasts were not immediately included in Calendars, at least of Books of Hours. The examples recorded by Leroquais are all of the 15th and 16th centuries (*Livres d'heures*, 1927, I, pp. 185, 293, 298, 334; II, 17, 200).

BIBLIOGRAPHY: Leningrad (Saint-Pétersbourg), Laborde, I, 1936, pp. 6 f. no. 8, pl. IV; Warsaw, Sawicka, 1938, pp. 60-66, pl. VIII; Meiss, *Art Bull.*, 1956, p. 194 (incorrectly as still in Leningrad).

MINIATURES:

The miniatures, on fols. 2 through 7v., represent the labors of the months and corresponding zodiacal signs.

Whereabouts Unknown

(formerly Milan, Antiquariato Libraio Radaeli and London, Maggs (p. 245; Fig. 797)

Initial: St. Dominic, by the workshop of the Master of the Brussels Initials.

XV

Tables

A CHRONOLOGY OF EVENTS IN FRANCE: 1328–1422

1328

Philippe VI, first of the Valois kings, comes to French throne after disputed succession.

1336

Philippe VI visits Pope in Avignon. Crusade planned to depart from Marseilles, but annulled by events elsewhere.
Popular rising in Flanders, and Philippe VI again supports Count of Flanders. England, which supplies wool to Flanders, supports insurgents against Count and France. Edward III presses claim to throne of France.

1337

Outbreak of Hundred Years' War.

1345

Murder of Jacques van Artevelde, leader of popular movement in Flanders, which was supported by England.

1346

English invasion of Northern France culminates in French defeat at Crécy.

1347

Siege of Calais, followed by truce with England lasting till 1351.

1348–1349

The Black Death.
Purchase by Philippe VI of Dauphiny; eldest son of King of France henceforth known as Dauphin.

1350

Death of Philippe VI and Accession of Jean II (Jean le Bon).

1355

Fresh outbreak of war. Black Prince, Commander-in-Chief for first time, lands at Bordeaux to ravage Languedoc. Edward III disembarks at Calais.
Need for funds results in convocation of States-General. Étienne Marcel emerges as leader of the Third Estate. Taxational measures approved, but supervision of expenditure by commissioners revolutionary.

1356

Defeat of French at Poitiers. Capture of Jean le Bon and detention in England till 1360.
The Dauphin (later Charles V) assumes control of government.

1356–1357

Country in state of unrest. Power of States-General and of Étienne Marcel as its leader greatly increased.

1357

Dauphin visits Emperor Charles IV at Metz in vain hope of obtaining effective alliance.

1358

Civil War. Étienne Marcel and rebels of Paris join forces with rising peasantry (*Jacquerie*) against Dauphin and followers. Treachery of Charles le Mauvais leads to fall of rebels and assassination of Marcel. Dauphin re-enters Paris to establish his authority.

1360

Treaty of Brétigny (or Treaty of Calais). Territory ceded

to England. Enormous ransom demanded for Jean le Bon. His brother and three sons held as hostages. His daughter married to Gian Galeazzo Visconti in return for large sum.
Jean le Bon returns to France.

1361–1362

Plague. Brigandage throughout the country, especially because mercenary companies no longer engaged in war.

1363

Duchy of Burgundy, newly fallen to French crown, given to Philip the Bold. Jean le Bon returns to England after defection of Louis d'Anjou as hostage.

1364

Death of Jean le Bon. Accession of Charles V.

1369

Repudiation by Charles V and States-General of Treaty of Brétigny.

1370

English ravage countryside from Calais and Aquitaine, but French refuse battle.

1372

Recovery of Poitiers by negotiations of Duguesclin; he and Jean de Berry enter Poitiers together.

1375

Truce requested by the English.

1376

Death of Black Prince.

1377

Death of Edward III. Accession of Richard II.

1378

Beginning of Great Schism.
State visit of Emperor Charles IV to Charles V.

1380

England remains in control only of Bayonne, Bordeaux, Brest, Cherbourg, and Calais.
Death of Charles V.

1381

Movement of revolt also in Languedoc by *Tuchins*. Counter measures by Duke of Berry result in sack of Béziers and heavy taxation.

1382

Battle of Roosebeke. Flemish revolt against French defeated.

1383

Revolt of Maillotins in Paris put down. Enormous fines enrich Dukes of Berry and Burgundy (Froissart).

1384

Death of Louis de Mâle, Count of Flanders. County united with Burgundy.
Death of Louis d'Anjou near Naples, after an Italian campaign of three years.

1385

Marriage of Charles VI with Isabeau de Bavière.

1386

French invasion of England promoted by Philippe le Hardi aborted by delays of his rival, Jean de Berry.

1387

Similar project held up by Duke of Brittany, who feared intrigues of Constable de Clisson.
Period of truce with England.

1388

Royal council at Rheims. In presence of Dukes of Berry and Burgundy, King urged to take Government into his own hands.

1388–1392

Period of administration by Charles VI with own counsellors – government of the lesser men as against government by the princes.

1389

Marriage of Louis, brother of Charles VI, then duc de Touraine (later of Orléans), to Valentina Visconti brings him interest in Northern Italy.

1389–1390

Visit by King to Avignon and Languedoc. Trial of Bétizac.
Duke of Berry deprived of jurisdiction over Languedoc.

1392

First onset of King's madness.

1395

Truce with England, due to expire in 1398, prolonged for a further twenty-eight years. Flemish interests of Duke of Burgundy damaged by continued hostility to England.

1396

Defeat of Crusaders (including Count of Nevers, later Jean sans Peur, and Maréchal de Boucicaut) at Nicopolis.
Marriage of Richard II and Isabelle of France.
Genoa comes under French rule.

1399

Deposition of Richard II neutralizes English truce. Accession of Henry IV.

1400–1404

Minor conflicts with Henry IV. Dukes of Burgundy and Orléans contend for political power.

1404

Death of Philippe le Hardi. Accession of Jean sans Peur.

1404–1407

Jean sans Peur continues Burgundian rivalry with Louis d'Orléans. Duke of Berry acts as mediator, but on December 1, 1405, forms alliance with Orléans and Queen Isabeau.

1407

Assassination of Louis d'Orléans (November 23). Declaration of responsibility by Jean sans Peur (November 25).

1408

Jean sans Peur publicly justifies the assassination. Struggle between Burgundians and Armagnacs approaches civil war.

1411

Burgundians in control of Paris. Berry's Hôtel de Nesle and Château de Bicêtre attacked and looted. Armagnacs in Paris tortured and put to death.

1411–1412

Both sides make overtures to England.
Papers that implicate leading Armagnacs in negotiations with England fall into the hands of the Chancellor of the Dauphin. Duke of Berry involved in ensuing scandal. Jean sans Peur now emerges as defender of the kingdom and his forces joined by those of Charles VI and Dauphin.

March on Bourges and siege. High price demanded by the English for departure has to be paid by Dukes of Orléans and of Berry. The latter withdraws treasures from the Sainte-Chapelle.
Siege of Bourges followed by reconciliation of Berry and Burgundy, and repudiation of English alliance.
August, 1412: Treaty of Auxerre.

1413

Further popular uprisings, particularly by the *Cabochiens*, (pro-Burgundian). Armagnacs compelled to leave Paris, but return in the same year
Death of Henry IV of England and accession of Henry V, intent on taking up English claims to throne of France.

1414

Alliance between Jean sans Peur and Henry V, but the former, concluding Peace of Arras with Charles VI, assures him that he is bound by no pact with enemies of the kingdom.

August. Henry V demands that Charles VI restore to him the kingdom of France. Simultaneously, negotiations for marriage between Catherine, daughter of Charles VI, and Henry V.

December 27. Duke of Burgundy declared enemy of the King.

1415

January 22. Duke of Burgundy declared guilty of high treason.

October. Defeat of French at Agincourt.

1416

June 15. Duke of Berry dies.

June 24. Truce between Burgundian domains and England. Jean sans Peur visits Henry V at Calais on October 6, recognizing the right of Henry and his successors to the throne of France.

Gradual encroachment of English into France. Continued struggle between Burgundians and Armagnacs.

1419

September 10. At meeting between Jean sans Peur and Dauphin on bridge of Montereau, Burgundy is murdered.

1420

Treaty of Troyes. Charles VI and Isabeau de Bavière disclaim the Dauphin.

Henry V accepted as heir to the throne of France and marriage concluded between him and Catherine of France.

1422

August 31. Death of Henry V.

October 22. Death of Charles VI.

JEAN DE BERRY'S CHILDREN

CHARLES DE BERRY. Born in 1371. Comte de Montpensier. Betrothed to Marie de Sully, daughter of Louis de Sully and Isabeau de Craon.
Died before 1383.

BEATRIX. Vaguely mentioned 1373; died before April 1374.

JEANNE. Mentioned 1375.

LOUIS. Living in 1383.

JEAN DE BERRY. Born 1376? Comte de Montpensier after brother's death. Married twice:
(1) 1386. Catherine of France, daughter of Charles V and of Jeanne de Bourbon. +1388.
(2) 1390. Anne de Bourbon, eldest daughter of Jean de Bourbon, Comte de la Marche, and of Catherine de Vendôme.
Died 1397.

BONNE DE BERRY. Born shortly before February, 1367. Married twice:
(1) 1379. Amadée VII, Comte de Savoie. +1391.
(2) 1393. Bernard, Comte d'Armagnac, Constable of France.
Died 1435.

MARIE DE BERRY. Born 1375–1376. Married three times:
(1) 1386. Louis de Chastillon, Comte de Dunois, son of Guy, Comte de Blois, and of Marie de Namur. Died 1391.
(2) 1393. Philippe d'Arthois, Comte d'Eu. Died 1397.
(3) 1400. Jean de Bourbon, Comte de Clermont en Beaugoisis, eldest son and chief heir of Louis II, Duc de Bourbon, Comte de Clermont. House of Bourbon comes from this line.
Died 1434.

Luçon Workshop, 1406: Madonna with Marie de Berry and an Attendant.
Paris, Bibl. nat., fr. 926, fol. 2

GENEALOGICAL TABLE

A list of the children of the Duke of Berry and their spouses precedes the stemma, which includes only those members of other branches of the family important for the text.

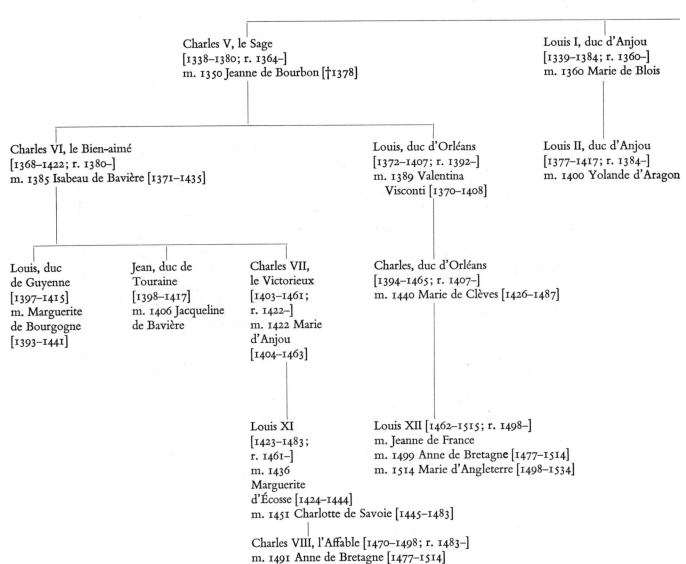

Jean I [1316–1316]

Philippe V, le Long [1293–1322; r. 1316–]
m. 1306 Jeanne I de Bourgogne [†1330]

Charles IV, le Bel [1294–1328; r. 1322–]
m. bef. 1307 Blanche de Bourgogne
m. 1322 Marie de Luxembourg [†1324] no issue
m. 1325 Jeanne II d'Évreux [†1371]

Philippe VI, le Bien-fortuné [1293–1350; r. 1328–]
m. 1313 (?) Jeanne de Bourgogne [†1349]
m. 1349 Blanche de Navarre [1328–1398] no issue

Jean II, le Bon [1319–1364; r. 1350–]
m. 1332 Bonne de Luxembourg [†1349]
m. 1350 Jeanne de Bourgogne [1326–1360]

Charles V, le Sage
[1338–1380; r. 1364–]
m. 1350 Jeanne de Bourbon [†1378]

Louis I, duc d'Anjou
[1339–1384; r. 1360–]
m. 1360 Marie de Blois

Charles VI, le Bien-aimé
[1368–1422; r. 1380–]
m. 1385 Isabeau de Bavière [1371–1435]

Louis, duc d'Orléans
[1372–1407; r. 1392–]
m. 1389 Valentina
Visconti [1370–1408]

Louis II, duc d'Anjou
[1377–1417; r. 1384–]
m. 1400 Yolande d'Aragon

Louis, duc
de Guyenne
[1397–1415]
m. Marguerite
de Bourgogne
[1393–1441]

Jean, duc de
Touraine
[1398–1417]
m. 1406 Jacqueline
de Bavière

Charles VII,
le Victorieux
[1403–1461;
r. 1422–]
m. 1422 Marie
d'Anjou
[1404–1463]

Charles, duc d'Orléans
[1394–1465; r. 1407–]
m. 1440 Marie de Clèves [1426–1487]

Louis XI
[1423–1483;
r. 1461–]
m. 1436
Marguerite
d'Écosse [1424–1444]
m. 1451 Charlotte de Savoie [1445–1483]

Louis XII [1462–1515; r. 1498–]
m. Jeanne de France
m. 1499 Anne de Bretagne [1477–1514]
m. 1514 Marie d'Angleterre [1498–1534]

Charles VIII, l'Affable [1470–1498; r. 1483–]
m. 1491 Anne de Bretagne [1477–1514]

Jean, duc de Berry
[1340–1416; r. 1360–]
m. 1360 Jeanne d'Armagnac
[†1388]
m. 1389 Jeanne de Boulogne
[† ca. 1422]

Philippe le Hardi, duc de Bourgogne
[1342–1404; duc 1363, comte 1384]
m. 1369 Marguerite de Flandre
[1350–1405]

Isabelle de France
[1348–1372]
m. 1360 Gian Galeazzo
Visconti [1351–1402;
r. 1378–]

Jean sans Peur,
duc de Bourgogne
[1371–1419; r. 1404–]
m. 1385 Marguerite
de Bavière [†1423]

Marguerite de
Bourgogne [1374–1441]
m. 1385 Guillaume de
Bavière [1365–1417]

Valentina Visconti
[1370–1408]
m. 1389 Louis,
duc d'Orléans
[1372–1407]

Marguerite [1393–1441]
m. Louis dauphin, duc
de Guyenne [†1415]
m. Arthur, comte de
Richemont [†1458]

Philippe le Bon, duc
de Bourgogne
[1396–1467;
r. 1419–]
m. Michelle de France
[†1422]
m. 1424 Bonne d'Artois
m. 1429 Isabelle de
Portugal [†1472]

Jacqueline, comtesse
de Hollande [1401–1436]
m. 1415 Jean dauphin, duc de Touraine [†1417]
m. Jean IV, duc de Brabant
m. 1423 Humphroy de Gloucester
m. François de Borselle

Charles le Téméraire,
duc de Bourgogne [1433–1477; r. 1467–]
m. 1454 Isabelle de Bourbon [†1465]
m. 1468 Marguerite de York [†1503]

Marie de Bourgogne [1457–1482; r. 1477–]
m. 1477 Maximilien d'Hapsbourg [†1519]

Philippe le Beau [1478–1506; r. 1482–]

XVI

The Valois and Visconti Inventories

1 · JEAN DE BERRY

Published in whole or in part by:

Delisle, *Cabinet*, III, 1881, pp. 170 ff.

Guiffrey, *Inventaires*, 1896, 2 vols.

Delisle, *Charles V*, 1907, II, pp. 223 ff.

Hiver de Beauvoir, 'Trésor', 1857 (Gift to Ste-Chapelle); *idem, Librairie*, 1860 (manuscripts at Mehun in 1416)

Only Guiffrey published the items of even one of the inventories in their entirety, and therefore his book is normally cited in the present publication.

INVENTORY OF 1401–1403. Guiffrey B. Volume II, pp. 1-166 (Delisle A).

Bibl. nat., fr. 11496. Begun by Guillaume de Ruilly, *garde de joyaux*, and finished by Robinet d'Étampes.

It was begun on December 2, 1401, and finished on February 23, 1403, as indicated in the preface signed by Veauce and Sarrebourse. It contains 1317 items (cf. Guiffrey, II, pp. 1-166). The work began in the Château de Dourdan, near Paris. It continued in the Hôtel de Nesle, Paris, in the Château de Mehun-sur-Yèvre, in the Great Tower of the Palace at Bourges, and in the *hôtel* of the Chancellery of the Cathedral.

This inventory contains numerous additional notes indicating objects given by Berry to the Sainte-Chapelle, Bourges, between 1404 and 1407.

At the end of items 1080 and 1187 an affidavit states that the intervening items were not verifiable, having been charged out to Guillaume de Ruilly (all these items are jewels).

INVENTORY OF 1413–1416. Guiffrey A. Volume I, pp. 10-336 (Delisle B).

Archives nationales, KK 258.

Compiled by Robinet d'Étampes. Almost all of the 1251 items listed in this inventory remained in Berry's possession until his death. This inventory is the most methodical of all; it falls into two parts:

Nos. 1-1099 are items inventoried by Robinet

d'Étampes before January 31, 1413 (n.s.).

Nos. 1100-1251 are acquisitions from February 1, 1413, to Berry's death June 16, 1416.

Robinet distinguished carefully between purchases by Berry and gifts to him. This is the only Berry inventory that Guiffrey published in full (I, pp. 1-336).

INVENTORY OF 1416. Guiffrey SG. Volume II, pp. 205-303 (Delisle C).

Bibl. Sainte Geneviève, Lf 54.

Drawn by Jean Lebourne.

Circa 400 items in this inventory are new, but they are not of great value. The other items appeared in the inventory of 1413. The tapestries are listed only in this inventory, because they were not entrusted to the *garde des joyaux*.

INVENTORY OF GIFTS TO SAINTE-CHAPELLE, BOURGES, made by Berry between 1404 and 1407. Guiffrey D. Volume II, pp. 167-186 (Delisle D).

Bibl. nat., nouv. acq. fr. 1363 = copy used by Guiffrey. Bourges, Archives du Cher, liasse 8 G 1452 M = copy used by Hiver de Beauvoir (1856–1860).

These two lists correspond closely, but since Hiver de Beauvoir, in contrast to Guiffrey, occasionally combined several items under one number, the numbers do not agree. Of 346 items in Bibl. nat., nouv. acq. fr. 1363 (numbered 1-343, but including no. 135 bis, ter, and quater), 256 are noted as gifts to Ste-Chapelle in the margins of the inventory of 1401-1403. (Guiffrey listed the 90 additional items in II, pp. 171-186.) Occasional dates that appear in this inventory of gifts to Ste-Chapelle indicate that gifts were made by Berry from 1404–1407.

Nos. 1-174 in the copy in the Bibliothèque nationale are all gifts of 1404; the following items, 175-343, were presented in the next three years (cf. Guiffrey, II, pp. 167 ff.).

Of the 66 books listed by Hiver de Beauvoir[*] 21,

[*] Hiver de Beauvoir, "Trésor," 1857, pp. 96-105.

according to Guiffrey, are not listed in the inventories of 1401–1403, 1413–1416, and 1416. Guiffrey therefore listed these items on pp. 313-316 of Volume II, but he advised caution in accepting them because Hiver de Beauvoir frequently did not indicate his sources (cf. Guiffrey, I, p. v).

2 · OTHER MAJOR COLLECTIONS

CHARLES V

Delisle, L., *Recherches sur la librairie de Charles V*, Paris, 1907

Labarte, J., ed., *Inventaire du mobilier de Charles V, roi de France* (Collection des documents inédits), Paris, 1879.

ANJOU

Laborde, L., *Glossaire français du moyen-âge, à l'usage de l'archéologue et de l'amateur des arts, précédé de l'inventaire des bijoux de Louis, duc d'Anjou, dressé vers 1360*, Paris, 1872.

Moranvillé, H., *Inventaire de l'orfèvrerie et des joyaux de Louis I, duc d'Anjou*, Paris, 1906.

INVENTORY OF THE SAINTE-CHAPELLE, BOURGES.
1552. Bibl. nat., lat. 17173.

List of manuscripts published by Delisle, 1856, pp. 144 ff. Lat. 17173 also contains the list of manuscripts presented to the Bibliothèque nationale in 1752 by 'Messieurs de la Sainte-Chapelle de Bourges' (fols. 234-5).

BURGUNDY

[Barrois, J. B. J.], *Bibliothèque protypographique, ou librairies des fils du roi Jean, Charles V, Jean de Berri, Philippe de Bourgogne et les siens*, Paris, 1830.

Dehaisnes, *Inventaire des biens meubles laissés par Marguerite de Flandre, duchesse de Bourgogne*, in *Histoire de l'art dans la Flandre, l'Artois et le Hainaut avant le XVᵉ siècle*, II, Lille, 1886.

Doutrepont, G., *Inventaire de la 'librairie' de Philippe le Bon (1420)*, Brussels, 1906.

Inventaire de Charles le Téméraire and *Inventaire de joyaux d'or et d'argent de Philippe le Bon, duc de Bourgogne*, in L. Laborde, *Les ducs de Bourgogne*, II, Paris, 1851.

Peignot, G., *Catalogue d'une partie des livres composant la bibliothèque des ducs de Bourgogne, au XVᵉ siècle*, 2nd ed., Dijon, 1841. Peignot, unlike Barrois, gives the complete inventory of the manuscripts of Philippe le Hardi.

ORLEANS

Graves, F. M., *Deux Inventaires de la maison d'Orléans (1389 et 1408)*, Paris, 1926.

VISCONTI

Pellegrin, E., *La Bibliothèque des Visconti et des Sforza ducs de Milan, au XVᵉ siècle*, Paris, 1955.

XVII

Some Reintegrated French Workshops of the Early Fifteenth Century

The reconstructions that appear in the following list have been mentioned in the text above; they will be fully discussed in subsequent volumes of this publication. Most of them were first published by the writer in 1956, but many manuscripts have been added to the earlier list. The precise contribution of a workshop to any given manuscript is not defined here; a manuscript is listed even if the shop painted only one miniature in it.

MASTER OF THE BERRY APOCALYPSE

Ghent, Bibliothèque de l'Université	ms. 141	*Bible moralisée* (attributed by C. Nordenfalk)
Leningrad, State Library	Fr. Q. v. III 4.	*Les dis moraux*
London, Robinson Trust	ms. 832	Jean de Meung, *Œuvres*
Munich, Bayrische Staatsbibliothek	Cod. gall. 26	*Jeu des échecs*
New York, Morgan Library	ms. 133	*Apocalypse* of Jean de Berry
Paris, Bibliothèque nationale	fr. 3	*Bible historiale*
	fr. 25	*Cité de Dieu*
	fr. 964	Commentary on Psalms
	fr. 17183	*Arbre des batailles*
	lat. 14245	Jacques le Grand, *Traité des vices et des vertus*
	Nouv. acq. fr. 14285	*Manuel d'histoire*
Stuttgart, Württembergische Landesbibliothek	Cod. poet. 6	*Roman de la rose*

Related Manuscripts

Besançon, Bibliothèque municipale	ms. 865	Froissart, *Chroniques*
London, British Museum	Roy. 20 B IV	*Méditations de la vie de Christ*
London, Sotheby & Co.	January 2, 1960, lot. 312	*Chroniques de Normandie*
New York, Morgan Library	ms. 723	*Livre des merveilles*
	ms. 804	Froissart, *Chroniques*
Paris, Bibliothèque nationale	fr. 20-21	*Cité de Dieu*
	fr. 1454	*Le Brut d'Angleterre*
	fr. 2663-64	Froissart, *Chroniques*
	fr. 2649	
San Marino, Huntington Library	H. M. 1142	Book of Hours

MASTER OF BERRY'S CLERES FEMMES

Geneva, Bibliothèque publique et universitaire	fr. 77	Tite-Live
Paris, Bibliothèque de l'Arsenal	ms. 5057-58	*Bible historiale*

Paris, Bibliothèque nationale   fr. 117-120   *Lancelot*

fr. 598   Boccaccio, *Des cleres femmes*

Related Manuscripts

Baltimore, Walters Art Gallery	ms. 232	Book of Hours
Cleveland, Museum of Art	62.287	*Gotha Missal*
Cleveland, Museum of Art	64.40	*Hours of Charles le Noble*
London, British Museum	Cotton Domitian A xvii	Book of Hours

MASTER OF THE CORONATION OF THE VIRGIN

Leningrad, State Library	ms. fr. Q.v. xiv 4	*Roman d'Athis*
Paris, Bibliothèque nationale	fr. 159	*Bible historiale*
	fr. 242	*Légende dorée (Coronation of the Virgin)*
	fr. 12201	*Fleur des histoires*
	fr. 12420	Boccaccio, *Des cleres femmes*

Related Manuscripts

Brussels, Bibliothèque royale	ms. 9049-50	Tite-Live
	ms. 10230	Cuvelier, *Livre de Messire Bertrant du Guesclin*
	ms. 11140	*Livre des trésors*
New York, Morgan Library	ms. 515	Book of Hours
New York, Lathrop Harper	Catalogue 13, no. 1	Book of Hours
Vienna, Nationalbibliothek	ms. 2656	Book of Hours

MASTER OF THE BREVIARY OF JEAN SANS PEUR

Baltimore, Walters Art Gallery	ms. 219	Book of Hours
Chantilly, Musée Condé	ms. 65	Book of Hours (*Très Riches Heures* of Jean de Berry)
London, British Museum	Add. 35311	Breviary of Jean sans Peur
	Harley 2897	
Palermo, Biblioteca Nazionale	I. A. 15	Book of Hours
Paris, Bibliothèque nationale	fr. 926	*L'aiguillon d'amour divin*
Vienna, Nationalbibliothek	Ser. nov. 2613	Book of Hours

Related Manuscripts

London, British Museum	Roy. 15 D iii	*Bible historiale*
Paris, Bibliothèque Mazarine	ms. 469	Book of Hours (a few medallions in borders)

MASTER OF THE CITÉ DES DAMES

Barcelona, Biblioteca Central	ms. 1850	Book of Hours
Berlin, Staatsbibliothek	Phillipps 1917	*Grandes chroniques*
Boston, Public Library	ms. 1528	Christine de Pisan, *Livre des trois vertus*
Brussels, Bibliothèque royale	ms. 9024	*Bible historiale*
	ms. 9393	Christine de Pisan, *Cité des Dames*
	ms. 10476	Christine de Pisan, *Livre des faits d'armes*
Chantilly, Musée Condé	ms. 493	Christine de Pisan, *Œuvres*
The Hague, Royal Library	ms. 72 A 24	Vincent of Beauvais, *Miroir historiale*
Lisbon, Gulbenkian Foundation		Boccaccio, *Des cleres femmes*
London, Mr. Martin Breslauer		*Valère Maxime*
London, British Museum	Egerton 2709	*Conquête et les conquérants des Iles Canaries*
	Harley 4431	Christine de Pisan, *Œuvres*
	Roy. 15 D III	*Bible historiale*
	Roy. 19 E VI	William of Burgues, *Chronicle*
Melbourne, National Gallery of Victoria	Felton 3	*Tite-Live*
Munich, Bayrische Staatsbibliothek	Cod. gall. 11	Christine de Pisan, *Mutacion de Fortune*
New York, Morgan Library	ms. 536	*Grandes chroniques*
Paris, Archives nationales	MM 8982	*Abrégé de l'histoire universelle*
Paris, Bibliothèque de l'Arsenal	ms. 3479	*Lancelot*
	ms. 5057-58	*Bible historiale*
Paris, Bibliothèque nationale	fr. 9-10	*Bible historiale*
	fr. 23-24	*Cité de Dieu*
	fr. 131	Boccaccio, *Cas des nobles hommes et femmes*
	fr. 174	*Cité de Dieu*
	fr. 226	Boccaccio, *Cas des nobles hommes et femmes*
	fr. 603	Christine de Pisan, *Œuvres*
	fr. 606	Christine de Pisan, *Épître d'Othéa*
	fr. 607	Christine de Pisan, *Cité des Dames*
	fr. 835-836	Christine de Pisan, *Œuvres*
	fr. 1178	Christine de Pisan, *Cité des Dames*
	fr. 1179	Christine de Pisan, *Cité des Dames*
	fr. 2675	Froissart, *Chroniques*
	fr. 6446	*Antiquités judaïques*
	fr. 12559	Thomas de Saluces, *Chevalier errant*
	fr. 16994	Boccaccio, *Cas des nobles hommes et femmes*
	fr. 23279	*Dialogues de Pierre Salmon*

Pavia, Museo Civico		6 miniatures cut out of a Boccaccio, *Cas des nobles hommes et femmes*
Rome, Biblioteca Vaticana	Pal. lat. 1989	Boccaccio, *Décaméron*,
Turin, Biblioteca Nazionale	R. 1680	*Chevalier errant*
Vienna, Nationalbibliothek	ms. 1855	Book of Hours (drolleries)
	ms. 2569	*Chroniques de Normandie*
	ms. 2615	Geoffroy de la Tour, *Le livre du Chevalier de la Tour*

Related Manuscripts

Oxford, Bodleian Library	ms. 265	Boccaccio, *Cas des nobles hommes et femmes*
Paris, Bibliothèque de l'Arsenal	ms. 664	*Térence des ducs*
	ms. 5060	*Cité de Dieu*
	ms. 5193	Boccaccio, *Cas des nobles hommes et femmes*
Paris, Bibliothèque Mazarine	ms. 2028	*Grandes Chroniques*
Paris, Bibliothèque nationale	fr. 286	*Valère Maxime*
Valencia, Universidad	ms. 1327	*Roman de la rose*
Vienna, Nationalbibliothek	ms. 2653	Boethius, *De consolatione philosophiae*

EGERTON MASTER

Chantilly, Musée Condé	ms. 64	Book of Hours
Cleveland, Museum of Art		*Hours of Charles le Noble*
Florence, Corsini Collection		Book of Hours
London, British Museum	Add. 30899	Book of Hours
	Add. 32454	Book of Hours
	Add. 35311	Breviary of Jean sans Peur
	Cotton Nero E II	*Grandes Chroniques*
	Egerton 1070	Book of Hours
	Harley 2897	Breviary of Jean sans Peur
	Roy. 15 D III	*Bible historiale*
Madrid, Biblioteca Nacional	Vit. 25, no. 1	Book of Hours
Paris, Bibliothèque de l'Arsenal	ms. 650	Book of Hours
Paris, Bibliothèque nationale	fr. 9-10	*Bible historiale*
	fr. 340	*Livre du roy Méliadus*
	fr. 606	Christine de Pisan, *Épître d'Othéa*
	fr. 835-836	Christine de Pisan, *Œuvres*
	Nouv. acq. fr. 4792	*Sept psaumes de pénitence*
Paris, Collection Comte Jean Durrieu		Prayerbook
Paris, Musée de Cluny	ms. 11314	Leaves from a Book of Hours
Seville, Biblioteca Colombina	ms. 1717	Book of Hours

Related Manuscripts

The Hague, Royal Library	ms. 72 A 22	*Cité de Dieu*
London, British Museum	Roy. 19 D III	*Bible historiale*

London, Victoria and Albert Museum	ms. 1646-1902	Book of Hours
Munich, Bayrische Staatsbibliothek	Cod. gall. 3	*Légende dorée*
New York, Mr. H. P. Kraus		Book of Hours
Paris, Bibliothèque nationale	fr. 30	*Tite-Live*
Paris, Charnacé Collection		Book of Hours
Paris, Collection Comte Jean Durrieu		Book of Hours
Philadelphia, Free Library	Widener no. 4	Book of Hours
	Widener no. 6	Book of Hours
Wolfenbüttel, Landesbibliothek	ms. 1.5.3.1 Aug. fol.	*Livre des propriétés*

MASTER OF THE ÉPTÎRE D'OTHÉA

Brussels, Bibliothèque royale	ms. 9508	Christine de Pisan, *Mutacion de Fortune*
Chantilly, Musée Condé	ms. 494	Christine de Pisan, *Mutacion de Fortune*
The Hague, Royal Library	ms. 78 D. 42	Christine de Pisan, *Mutacion de Fortune*
Paris, Bibliothèque Mazarine	ms. 2028	*Grandes Chroniques*
Paris, Bibliothèque nationale	fr. 606	Christine de Pisan, *Épître d'Othéa*
	fr. 835-836	Christine de Pisan, *Œuvres*
Paris, M. Pierre Berès		Christine de Pisan, *Mutacion de Fortune*

LUÇON MASTER

Baltimore, Walters Art Gallery	ms. 231	Book of Hours
	ms. 232	Book of Hours
Barcelona, Biblioteca Central	ms. 1850	Book of Hours
Berlin, Staatsbibliothek (formerly)	Theol. lat. qu. 7	Book of Hours
Brussels, Bibliothèque royale	ms. 9089-9090	Aristotle, *Politiques* and *Éthiques*
Cambridge, Fitzwilliam Museum	Founders 59	Book of Hours
	McClean 80	Book of Hours
Cambridge, Harvard University, Houghton Library	Richardson 45	Book of Hours
Frankfurt-am-Main, Museum für Kunsthandwerk	Linel, L. M. 19	Book of Hours
Geneva, Bibliothèque publique et universitaire	fr. 190	Boccaccio, *Cas des nobles hommes et femmes* (translated by Laurent de Premierfait)
Holkham Hall (Collection Earl of Leicester)	ms. 307	Virgil, *Georgics* and *Bucolics*
Leningrad, State Library	Fr. Q. v. XIV. 3	*Roman de la violette*
London, British Museum	Add. 29433	Book of Hours
	Yates Thompson 37	Book of Hours
London, Sotheby & Co.	Springel Sale, June 28, 1962, lot 49	*Pentecost*
	Northwick Sale, May 21, 1928, lot 17	Book of Hours

Montreal, Collection L. V. Randall		Miniature of the *Coronation of the Virgin*
New York, Mr. H. P. Kraus		Book of Hours ('De Lévis')
Paris, Bibliothèque de l'Arsenal	ms. 5193	Boccaccio, *Cas des nobles hommes et femmes*
Paris, Bibliothèque Mazarine	ms. 491	Book of Hours
Paris, Bibliothèque nationale	fr. 208	Aristotle, *Politiques* and *Éthiques*
	fr. 926	*L'aiguillon d'amour divin*
	fr. 1023	*Livre des bonnes mœurs*
	lat. 1082	Psalter and Hours
	lat. 8886	Pontifical of the Bishop of Luçon
	Nouv. acq. lat. 3108	Book of Hours
Philadelphia, Free Library	Widener no. 4	Book of Hours
Philadelphia, Museum	ms. 45-65-5	Book of Hours
Whereabouts unknown, formerly New York, Mr. Jacob Hirsch		Miniature of the *Ark of the Covenant*
Whereabouts unknown		Book of Hours (Delaissé, 1950)

Related Manuscripts

Baltimore, Walters Art Gallery	ms. 100	Book of Hours
	ms. 103	Book of Hours
Bourges, Musée du Berry		*Hours of Anne de Mathefelon*
Brussels, Bibliothèque royale	ms. 9226	*Légende dorée*
Cambrai, Bibliothèque municipale	ms. 97 (98)	Breviary
Milan, Biblioteca Ambrosiana	I.7. Sup.	Book of Hours
	L.58 Sup.	Book of Hours
New York, Morgan Library	ms. 743	Book of Hours
Paris, Bibliothèque de l'Arsenal	ms. 664	*Térence des ducs*

THE TROYES MASTER

Brussels, Bibliothèque royale	ms. 9125	Missal (initial on fol. 7)
Hamburg-Blankenese, Collection of Mrs. J. Möring Huth		Book of Hours
New York, Morgan Library	ms. 331	Missal
Paris, Bibliothèque nationale	lat. 924	Book of Hours
San Marino, Huntington Library	H M 1179	Book of Hours
Vienna, Nationalbibliothek	Ser. nov. 2613	Book of Hours

Related Manuscripts

Chicago, University of Chicago Library	ms. 250961	Book of Hours
Oxford, Bodleian Library	Douce 102	Book of Hours
Toulouse, Bibliothèque municipale	ms. 512	*Grandes Chroniques*
Whereabouts unknown (formerly Ranshaw Collection)		Book of Hours

MASTER OF WALTERS 219

Baltimore, Walters Art Gallery	ms. 219	Book of Hours
Dublin, Chester Beatty Collection	ms. 84	Book of Hours
London, Collection Arthur Rau		Book of Hours
London, Sotheby & Co.	June 18, 1962, lot. 20	Book of Hours

Related Manuscripts

Baltimore, Walters Art Gallery	ms. 290	Book of Hours
Besançon, Bibliothèque municipale	ms. 123	Book of Hours

VIRGIL MASTER

Brussels, Bibliothèque royale	ms. 9554	Gilles de Rome, *Le livre du gouvernement des roys et des princes*
	ms. 9555-9558	Durand de Champagne, *Le mirouer des dames*
Cambridge, Fitzwilliam Museum	McClean 79	Book of Hours
Chantilly, Musée Condé	ms. 867	*Grandes Chroniques*
Florence, Biblioteca Laurenziana	Plut. xxx. 10	Vitruvius, *De Architectura*
	Med. Pal. 69	Virgil, *Bucolics, Georgics* and *Aeneid*
The Hague, Royal Library	ms. 72 A 25	Froissart, *Chroniques*
The Hague, Museum Meermanno-Westreenianum	ms. 755	*Cité de Dieu*
London, British Museum	Harley 1319	*Fall of Richard II*
	Harley 4381-82	*Bible historiale*
	Roy. 15 D iii	*Bible historiale*
London, Collection Count A. Seilern		Alchandreus, *De Astrologia*; Boethius, *De Arithmetica* and *De Musica*
Paris, Bibliothèque de l'Arsenal	ms. 5057-58	*Bible historiale*
Paris, Bibliothèque nationale	fr. 25	*Cité de Dieu*
	fr. 263	Tite-Live
	fr. 282	Valère Maxime
	fr. 6272	*Cité de Dieu*
	fr. 6445	Tite-Live
Paris, Chambre des Députés	ms. 3	*Bible historiale*
Whereabouts unknown		Book of Hours (Delaissé, 1950)

Related Manuscripts

Chantilly, Musée Condé	ms. 28 (1378)	*Histoire extraite de la Bible* and *Apocalypse*
Paris, Bibliothèque nationale	fr. 414	*Légende dorée*
	fr. 819-820	*Miracles de Notre-Dame*

NOTES TO THE TEXT & BIBLIOGRAPHY

NOTES TO THE TEXT

NOTES TO CHAPTER I

1. *Purgatorio*, XI, 80-81.

2. *Le corps de policie*, pt. 3, chap. IX (Paris, Bibl. de l'Arsenal, ms. 2681, fol. 90).

'Et de ces gens de mestier de tous ovrages a de moult soubtilz à Paris, croy plus que si communément n'a ailleurs, qui moult est belle et notable chose. . . . Mais pour parler un pou au fet de leurs meurs, je vouldroie que il pleust à Dieu, mail à eulx mesmes, car à Dieu plairoit bien, que leur vie fust communément plus sobre et non si délicative comme il ne leur apertiegne: car la lècherie des tavernes et des friandises dont ilz usent à Paris les puet conduire à maints maulx et inconvéniens. . . .'

3. 'à propos de paintrerie, je cognois aujourd'ui une femme que on apelle Anastaise, qui tant est experte et aprise à faire vignetures d'enlumineure en livres et champaignes d'ystoires qu'il n'est mencion d'ouvrier en la ville de Paris, où sont les souverains du monde, qui point l'en passe. . . . Et ce scay-je par experience, car pour moy meismes a ouvré aucunes choses qui sont tenues singulières entre les vignettes des grans ouvriers.'

If 'champaignes d'ystoires' signifies 'landscapes in painted scenes', as Martin believes, it would precede by a century the first known appearance of the concept in another language: *paese* in Italian. The usage has been recorded for actual landscape in 16th-century French by Littré, but in directions for illuminations written *ca.* 1417 by Jean Lebègue the following appears: '. . . et sera ledit varlet . . . en une belle plaine où aura herbe et arbres de diverses façons et au seurplus sera la champaigne de l'istoire en hault faicte graceusement (*sic*)' (Porcher, *Lebègue*, 1962, not paginated). The corresponding miniatures show a plain with a hilly landscape behind. Above the hills there is a diapered background; the current term for that does seem to have been *fond*. See below, p. 266, and Martin, *Miniature française*, 1923, p. 75.

4. 'It is a great miracle that a mere female should do so well' (*Dürers schriftlicher Nachlass*, ed. K. Lange and F. Fuhse, Halle, 1893, p. 166).

5. See below, p. 167.

6. Tr. by H. Rackham (Loeb Classical Library), Cambridge, Mass., 1952, Vol. IX, Book XXXV, Chap. XL, pp. 147 f.

7. In a somewhat later ms., Brit. Mus., Royal 16 G v, fol. 68v., she is at work on this figure, which appears not in medieval dress but nude.

Fr. 12420 was given to Philippe le Hardi by Jacques Raponde for New Year (*étrennes*), 1403 (n.s.). The document giving us this fact was published by Durrieu, 1895, pp. 179 f. Some recent authors erroneously give 1404: see Paris, Bibl. nat. (Porcher), 1955, p. 78. Panofsky (*Netherlandish Painting*, 1953, I, p. 52) says that fr. 598 was executed in the same year as fr. 12420; this is possible, but we can be certain only that the ms. was given to the Duke of Berry in February 1404 (see the List of Manuscripts in the Collection of the Duke). With regard to *étrennes*, the old sense of a new year occurring on January 1 was preserved even though in most French cities at this time the numeration of the year changed on the day of the Annunciation (March 25) that followed.

8. Van Marle, *Italian Schools*, III, fig. 101.

9. In the altarpiece of the chapel of the Bargello. See *De famosis civibus* by Filippo Villani in *Il libro di Antonio Billi*, ed. C. Frey, Berlin, 1892, p. 74.

10. On magnifying lenses in classical antiquity (some actually found in Roman tombs), see H. Blümner, *Technologie und Terminologie der Gewerbe und Künste bei den Griechen und Römern*, III, Leipzig, 1884, p. 300. For spectacles see Rosen, 1956, pp. 13-46, 183-218. Also Disney, *Microscope*, 1928, pp. 28 ff.

11. 'Forgé une platine d'argent doré, pour mettre ez ees (ais) du liure du Duc, pour mettre ses lunettes, afin qu'elles ne fussent cassées' (Peignot, *Bibl. ducs de Bourgogne*, 1841, p. 32).

12. Panofsky, *Netherlandish Painting*, 1953, I, p. 80.

13. *Purgatorio*, XI, 79-87.

14. Bibl. nat., lat. 11935, fol. 642. See Delisle, *Cabinet*, I, 1868, p. 13.

15. For a reproduction of the facing folios see Panofsky, *Netherlandish Painting*, 1953, II, fig. 23.

16. The Petrus Gilberti who inserted his name in the decorative areas of several mss. (Brit. Mus., Royal 15 D III, Royal 19 B xv, and Brussels, Bibl. royale, ms. 9001-9002) was not an *historieur*.

17. Fr. 166. See below, p. 293.

18. See below, p. 297.

19. 1961, pp. 175 f.; Meiss and Eisler, 1960, p. 236, fig.2.

20. 1960, pp. 233-240. Our hypothesis, which has been widely accepted, is that a lost portrait of Jean sans Peur, known through a copy, composes a diptych with the *Madonna*.

21. Actually Jacquemart had some help in executing the miniatures in the *Brussels Hours* but, apart from the first two that are in a very different style, they show a high degree of uniformity.

22. For the documents on both Bibles see Prost, 1891, pp. 342 ff.

23. 1961, pp. 11 ff.

24. Monget, *Chartreuse de Dijon*, I, 1898, p. 133. In one group, working at Argilly, there were three painters, one with an apprentice; another group, at Germolles, consisted of five painters. For records on painters and workshops see Durrieu, in Michel, *Histoire*, III, pt. I, 1907, pp. 102 f.

25. Lespinasse, *Métiers*, III, 1897, pp. 700 f.; M. Crevier, *Histoire de l'Université de Paris*, Paris, 1761, II, p. 337, III, p. 51.

26. Guiffrey, *Journal des savants*, 1915, pp. 145-156, and *idem*, *Archives de l'art français*, 1915, pp. 1-6.

27. Durrieu, *op. cit.*, pp. 102 ff.

28. Lacour, *L'apanage*, 1934, pp. 147 f.

29. *Medieval Miniatures*, [1959], p. 69.

30. See below, p. 47. Also, Prost, 1891, pp. 343 ff.

31. Numerous initials were painted by the workshop of the Master of the Bréviaire de Jean sans Peur (Meiss, *Art Bull.*, 1956, p. 195), who throughout his career was linked with the Limbourgs (see below, p. 355, and Figs. 678, 780.

32. *Merveilles du monde*, Bibl. nat., fr. 2810.

33. Breviary, Châteauroux, Bibl. municipale, ms. 2.

34. *Grandes Heures*, Bibl. nat., lat. 919 and Lectionary, Bourges, Bibl. municipale, ms. 33-36.

35. *Dialogues de Pierre Salmon*, Bibl. nat., fr. 23279.

36. Book of Hours, Musée Jacquemart-André, Paris.

37. See the subsequent volume of this publication.

38. Paris, Bibl. de l'Arsenal, ms. 5077. For a careful examination of the differences from gathering to gathering in a ms. illuminated by followers of the Boucicaut Master see Delaissé, 1948, pp. 78-84.

39. A follower of the Cité des Dames Master painted the *Heautontimorumenos*, while the Luçon Master strongly influenced the miniatures of the frontispiece, the *Phormio*, the *Eunuchus*, and the *Andria*. The painter of the *Adelphoe* resembles the author of the figures in the *Livre de la chasse*, Bibl. nat., fr. 616 (Fig. 439).

40. See the *Hecyra*. For illustrations cf. Martin, *Térence*, 1907.

41. This style is very close to that of the second and third miniatures of Bibl. nat., fr. 247 (Fig. 683).

42. See Martin, *Miniaturistes*, 1906, p. 118.

43. Martin, *Rev. archéol.*, 1904, pp. 17 ff.

44. Martin (*ibid.*, p. 44), counted 95 in the *Trésor des histoires* (Paris, Bibl. de l'Arsenal, ms. 5077).

45. For a similar relationship see Paris, Bibl. de l'Arsenal, ms. 5193, fol. 212.

46. The *Chroniques*, Brussels, Bibl. royale, ms. 3, contains an inferior cycle of around the same time (Brussels, Gaspar and Lyna, I, 1937, pl. CIX).

47. See Brit. Mus., Royal 19 D III, fol. 12v., with a sketch of a ship indicating the Construction of the Ark.

48. U. Procacci, *Sinopie e affreschi*, Florence, 1960.

49. Access to the huge *Crucifixion* by Andrea da Firenze in the Spanish Chapel of S. Maria Novella in Florence, made possible during the cleaning, has disclosed color notes such as *bifo* (mentioned by Cennini) written on the figures.

50. The first ms. is Bibl. nat., fr. 848; those that followed Bibl. nat., fr. 606, and Brit. Mus., Harley 4431 (see Willard, 1963, pp. 149-156).

51. In the Terence each figure was given a label, written just outside the frame (Fig. 300). In Bibl. nat., fr. 340, descriptions were written in the outer margins.

52. Porcher, *Lebègue*, 1962. Instructions for illustrations of a *Somme le roi* were published by Berger and Durrieu, 1893, pp. 24 f.

53. Bibl. nat., lat. 14643, fols. 269-283v. Published by Ouy, in *Mélanges Calot*, 1960, pp. 43 ff.

54. Bibl. royale, ms. 9001, chap. X (see Berger and Durrieu, 1893, p. 11).

55. See below, p. 123.

56. Paris, Bibl. de l'Arsenal, ms. 5077.

57. The ms. is also the earliest copy of the French text. Cf. Durrieu, *Bibl. École des Chartes*, 1910, pp. 58-71; Meiss, 'Remarks on the First Fully Illustrated *Decameron*' (in press).

58. See Winkler, *Flämische Buchmalerei*, 1925, pp. 29, 194.

59. See the printed edition: *Le liure Cameron autremont surnomme le prince Galliot . . . Translate . . . par Laurens du Premierfaict*, Paris, 1521, p. 69. All subsequent extracts are from this edition. I am much indebted to Mr. Lessing Rosenwald for having made accessible to me the copy of this very rare text in his rich library.

60. Wittkower (1957, pp. 155-172) has shown us the consequences of this process in the illustration of the *Merveilles du monde*, painted by the Boucicaut Master and his associates shortly before 1413, where the

fantastic creatures are often those familiar to the illuminator rather than what the text prescribed. For late antique illustration see K. Weitzmann, *Illustrations in Roll and Codex*, Princeton, 1947, pp. 154 ff.

61. 'Et [Gabriel] sans plus dire mot cheut tout plat a terre. Lors Androlla ce voyant bien esbahye se print en son giron et disoit Las mon cher amy quelle maladie avez vous Gabriel. . . .' (*op. cit.*, p. 49).

62. 'Bagno' in Boccaccio's text, 'estuves' according to Laurent (*op. cit.*, p. 36).

63. A well-known Flemish illuminator named after this ms., which was written by Guillebert de Mets at Grammont in Eastern Flanders, according to the colophon.

64. London, Brit. Mus., Millar, 1933, pp. 29 ff.

65. *Art Bull.*, 1956, pp. 194 f.

66. For this ms. see p. 298.

67. Published without comment by Berger and Durrieu, 1893, p. 28 n. 1.

68. *Decameron*, ed. V. Branca, I, 1951, p. 369.

69. *Op. cit.*, p. 36.

70. See E. Verwijs and J. Verdam, *Middelnederlandsch Woordenboek*, and Godefroy, *Dictionnaire de l'ancienne langue française*, s.v. *rivage* and *rivière*. See also Du Cange, s.v. *rivera* and *riveria*. The connotation of river in the Latin *ripa* is retained by most of these derivatives, though there was some ambiguity in *ripa* itself from the time of Augustus on. In medieval Latin *costerium* was used specifically for the seashore.

71. The other three are on fols. 120, 128, 132v. See Paris, Arsenal, Martin and Lauer, 1929, p. 42. None of these has been published.

72. See Winkler, *Flämische Buchmalerei*, 1925, with list of miniatures by him. Also P. Durrieu, *La miniature flamande*, Brussels, 1921, pp. 15 f., and Brussels, Palais des Beaux-Arts (Delaissé), 1959, pp. 17, 21 f. Delaissé was the first to propose a specific date for the Arsenal ms.: between 1434 and *ca.* 1450.

73. Miniature for *nouvelles* 4 (I, 4), 12 (II, 2), 24 (III, 4), 46 (V, 6), 49 (V, 9).

74. For this master see Winkler, *op. cit.*, p. 36, and Delaissé, *op. cit.*, pp. 22, 65.

75. *Nouvelle* 14 (II, 4): Landolfo clings far more effectively to the chest and he is correctly lifted from the water by his hair. *Nouvelle* 15 (II, 5): the latrine, lacking in the Vatican ms., is represented and Andreuccio rightly retains some clothing. *Nouvelle* 77 (VIII, 7): the courtyard is properly closed, not partly open as in the Vatican ms. (Durrieu, *Bibl. École des*

Chartes, 1910, p. 68, overlooks this difference and overstates generally the dependence of the Arsenal ms. on Pal. lat. 1989). *Nouvelle* 81 (IX, 1): the guard with a lantern, important to the story, is represented. *Nouvelle* 86 (IX, 6): five persons are represented, not six. It is true that in the miniature for *Nouvelle* 69 (VIII, 9) the miniature in the Arsenal ms. adds a hedge that is not mentioned by the text, probably to clarify the reclining figures in the Vatican ms. Furthermore *Nouvelles* 69 and 86, both illustrated by him, follow the Vatican ms. rather closely.

76. Panofsky, 'Maître de Rohan', 1939, p. 491 n. 1.

77. See below, p. 162.

78. See below, p.171.

79. For the Byzantine type with two midwives bathing the Child see Duccio's panel from the *Maestà* (van Marle, *Italian Schools*, II, 1924, fig. 17).

80. Panofsky, *Netherlandish Painting*, 1953, II, fig. 211.

81. See below, p. 290.

82. Panofsky, *op. cit.*, I, p. 76, has observed that the mss. acquired by Philippe le Hardi and Jean sans Peur were either produced in Paris, or by the Limbourgs or illuminators connected with them. We may now add that when the Limbourgs were working for the Duke of Burgundy they were resident in *Paris* (see below, p. 293).

83. Lafond, in Lefrançois and Lafond, [1954], p. 224, pointed to the primacy of Paris in the sphere of stained glass.

84. See below, p. 279.

85. *Op. cit.*, I, p. 27.

86. Meiss, 1935, figs. 1, 2.

87. The man on the ground is closest perhaps to the corresponding figure in the great *Crucifixion* at Massa Marittima by Ugolino and perhaps Simone Martini (E. Carli, *Dipinti senesi del contado e della Maremma*, Milan, 1955, pl. 30 – after cleaning).

88. Italian style influenced French stained glass also in the second quarter of the century, especially at St. Ouen, Rouen, but in a less fundamental manner (see Lafond in Lefrançois and Lafond, [1954], pp. 194 ff.).

89. Morand, *Pucelle*, 1962, p. 6, assumes an Italian journey.

90. Meiss, *Gaz. B.-A.*, 1961, p. 291. In the simulated panel the Virgin's right hand, for instance, presses against the Child's body as in Ambrogio's Massa *Madonna* (Fig. 698).

91. Bonne died in 1349. The ms. was probably painted not long before this (cf. Morand, *op. cit.*, p. 40).

92. See below, p. 106.

93. Meiss, *op. cit.*, p. 290.

94. Delisle, *Charles V*, 1907, I, pp. 328 f., 404-410. See below, p. 178.

95. Genesis XXI, 25.

96. London, Brit. Mus., Warner and Gilson, 1921, II, pp. 260 f.

97. Berlin, Staatsbibl. (Kirchner), 1926, pp. 77 ff.

98. I agree with Panofsky, *Netherlandish Painting*, 1953, I, p. 37, and others who have read the inscription in this way. For the view that 'istud opus' refers only to the frontispiece see Delaissé, 1957, p. 111.

99. See Delisle, *Charles V*, 1907, I, pp. 74 ff., who published the long poem in its entirety. Its content has not previously been brought to bear on the problem of the authorship of the illumination.

100. Head. Six lines above 'onques' means never.

101. *Miniature française*, 1923, pp. 44 ff. Panofsky associated this group with Bondol (*Netherlandish Painting*, 1953, I, pp. 36 ff.) while Porcher (Paris, Bibl. nat., 1955, pp. 50 f.; *Medieval Miniatures*, [1959], pp. 56 f.) and Delaissé (1957, p. 111) opposed it.

102. See J. Guiffrey in Michel, *Histoire*, III, pt. I, 1907, p. 352; Lejard, *Apocalypse d'Angers*, 1942.

103. The tapestries of the Duke of Berry in the Metropolitan Museum, New York (Figs. 445, 446) are technically related (see Rorimer and Freeman, 1949, pp. 243 ff.).

104. Prost, 1892, p. 352; Durrieu in Michel, *Histoire*, III, pt. I, 1907, pp. 102, 115 f.; in Thieme-Becker, IV, 1910. In 1379 (n.s.) the Duke of Berry paid Bondol for 'certaines pourtraitures' (Delisle, *Charles V*, 1907, I, p. 81).

105. See especially the *Cité de Dieu* of 1376 (Bibl. nat., fr. 22912-22913), the related ms. of the same text in the Hofer collection, Cambridge (Mass.), (Fig. 535), and the *Grandes Chroniques* of the late 'seventies (Fig. 565).

106. On this entire subject see the fundamental account of Panofsky, *Netherlandish Painting*, 1953, I, pp. 24 ff.

107. Pächt, 1943, p. 51. On England and Italy in the later 14th century see Wormald, 1954, pp. 191 ff.

108. King Louis the Great called Italian illuminators to his court. See M. Harrsen, *The Neckcei-Lipócz Bible*, Washington, 1949, and the bibliography there cited.

109. Coletti, *Tommaso da Modena*, 1933, pls. 67-69. The panels over the altar of the Holy Cross at Karlštejn were not made by Tommaso for their present place; the backgrounds are disproportionately large for Italian taste. Presumably therefore the panels were shipped from Italy. See Chap. XIII, n. 125.

110. The design of the Madonna (but not the donors) over the altar in the Chapel of St. Catherine at Karlštejn is Italian; because of damage and retouching it is difficult to judge the execution (see Dvořáková et al., *Gothic Mural Painting in Bohemia*, 1964, pls. VIII, 73).

111. Meiss, 1941, pp. 54-60.

112. The frescoes represent, in addition to the Coronation, Christ ascending and a bishop saint. They were in the church of Annunziata. F. Bologna, who published them as works by the master of the Bellpuig *Coronation*, ascribed it as well as the Urbino frescoes to the author of a *Madonna* in the Pinacoteca in Urbino (1961, pp. 27 ff.). This panel seems to me entirely unrelated. The face of the Madonna may look 'Spanish' because it is badly damaged and restored, but her hands and the Child, relatively well preserved, show exclusively Simonesque and not Lorenzettian origins. If the frescoes in Urbino are not early works of Bassa himself, their author was at least Bassa's teacher, for the Pedralbes frescoes show resemblances even of small details, such as the unusual cross-hatched pattern on the drapery of the throne of the *Coronation* (Figs. 390, 391). In Bologna's article some extracts or summaries of my text are incorrect; about the important triptych in the Walters Gallery, Baltimore he said (p. 30 n. 15): 'Meiss assegna il trittico alla bottega del Maestro di San Marco'. This is contradicted by my discussion (1941, especially pp. 79-81).

113. For the Master of St. Mark see Meiss, *op. cit.*; Gudiol, *Pintura gótica*, figs. 41-43. Arnau was paid for the panel of St. James in the Museo Diocesano of Barcelona, which is a work of the Master of St. Mark (see Madurell Marimón, 1952, pp. 14-16).

114. Meiss, 1937, p. 281 n. 2.

115. Prof. Lucile Bush kindly called to my attention the similarity between these two compositions. Other scenes in Bibl. nat., fr. 9 (fols. 8v., 13, 16v.) derive in part from Fredi's cycle; this relationship will be discussed in the fourth part of this publication (*Paris 1400–1420*).

116. Meiss, 1937, pp. 275 ff.

117. *Ibid.*, pp. 280 f. In the last line on p. 280, 1321 is incorrectly printed 1311, and in n. 4, 1392 should read 1302.

118. He was paid for his expenses, those of two *valeti*, and for colors 'pro reparatione aule Pictavis . . .' (Moranvillé, 1887, p. 632).

119. See below, p. 37.

120. Durrieu, in Michel, *Histoire*, III, pt. I, 1907, p. 105, said that he worked at St. Denis, without, however, giving a source.

121. 'Trois grans tabliaus et uns petiz ront . . .' (Richard, *Mahaut, comtesse d'Artois*, 1887, p. 359). For Gentilly see Durrieu, *loc cit*. For the meaning of the term. see below, p. 43.

122. *Rituale Armenorum*, Tübingen, Universitätsbibliothek, Phillipps 1398, fol. 91v. [Berlin, Staatsbibl. (Kirchner), 1926, p. 76].

123. We are uncertain of the precise date. Rowlands, 1965, p. 25, has offered evidence to show he was there already in 1336.

124. Énaud, *Les Monuments historiques de la France*, 1963, pp. 115 ff.

125. De Nicola, 1906, pp. 337 f. If the drawing is connected with Bishop Suarez of Vaison it would be datable 1633–1666. See also the full account in Castelnuovo, *Un pittore italiano*, 1962, p. 24 n. 2.

126. While many historians believe the last-mentioned panels were painted late in Simone's career some others date them *ca.* 1320, and point to reflections of them in Italy (see, for instance, Paccagnini, *Simone Martini*, 1955, pp. 111 ff.). On the back of the *Way to Calvary* are the arms of the Orsini, and two prominent members of this family died in Avignon during Simone's visit, Archbishop Matteo in 1341 and Napoleone in 1342. Cardinal Giordano Orsini granted indulgences in 1412 to visitors to Champmol. All the panels first appeared in Dijon in 1826, when they were bought by Van Ertborn. Quarré has argued that they were there already before 1430, because he believes that a retable of Claus de Werwe of that date was influenced by them (*Champmol*, [1960], p. 53). He may be right but the relationship does not seem to me compelling. For their use by Jacquemart *ca.* 1395–1400 see below, p. 215.

127. Laclotte, *Avignon*, 1960, p. 33.

128. *Pétrarque et l'humanisme*, 1907, pp. 271 ff.

129. For the Pliny see the reproductions and the writer's comments in *Illuminated Manuscripts of the Divine Comedy* by P. Brieger, M. Meiss and C. Singleton (in press). For the mediocre drawings in Petrarch's Livy (Bibl. nat., lat. 5690) see Chiovenda, 1933, figs. 13, 15. None of the drawings in his Quintus Curtius (Bibl. nat., lat. 5720) has to my knowledge been reproduced. They are equally mediocre.

130. The records have often been cited; see de Nicola, 1906; Meiss, 1962, pp. 112 f., and Castelnuovo, *op. cit.*, pp. 24–26.

131. The panels of the Infancy and the Passion in the Cathedral of Albi were painted by an itinerant Italian (Meiss, 1962, p. 108, fig. 4). The damaged and repainted but important panel of the *Death of the Virgin* in the Louvre is in my opinion by a good Italian follower of Matteo Giovanetti active in Southern France (*op. cit.*, pp. 105 ff.). Referring to this article but giving it a title supplied by a translator and not approved by me nor adopted, Castelnuovo says the painter had 'seen' Matteo's frescoes but was very probably not Italian, and active somewhat later (*op. cit.*, p. 91 n. 1). A triptych in the Musée Pincé in Angers was executed late in the century for this city by a painter who has been designated as Italian or Tuscan (Dupont, 1935, pp. 370 ff., and Castelnuovo, *op. cit.*, fig. 136) but who was Sienese, as Jacques [Sterling], *Peintres du moyen âge*, [1942], p. 17, recognized. He was, in fact, close to Fei and Andrea di Bartolo, and no connection with Avignon – as proposed by Sterling and others – seems to me evident.

132. Toesca, *Il Trecento*, 1951, p. 545.

133. The claim of Laclotte, *Avignon*, 1960, and Castelnuovo, *op. cit.*, that Matteo influenced not only later French painters and even sculptors but also painters along the Mediterranean coast as far as Bassa in Barcelona and Traini in Pisa seems to me either unsubstantiated or, in the case of Traini, Bassa, and Beauneveu, unsound. Apart from these broad assertions, Kreuter-Eggemann (*Daliwe*, 1964, I, p. 44) sought carefully to demonstrate that a drawing of a male head by Daliwe was based on Matteo but its firm structure seems to me to presuppose a good, late 14th-century Florentine model. For her other suggestions of the influence of Matteo see below, p. 255, n 41. We know that in 1352 Matteo sent drawings for a life of St. Robert to silversmiths in Paris (Labande, *Primitifs*, 1932, I, p. 67).

134. I agree with part of Castelnuovo's eloquent appreciation of Matteo (*op. cit.*); the context of my phrase about his frescoes: 'd'un intérêt restreint' (*Revue des arts*, 1956, p. 140) was his historical importance for French painting, not his personal capacity.

135. Published and ascribed to a Sienese master by Énaud, *Plaisirs de France*, 1963, pp. 12 ff.

136. Brun, 1934, pp. 327–346; Origo, *Merchant*, 1957, pp. 18–20. The records on panels begin in 1371, according to Brun.

137. Origo, *op. cit.*, p. 20.

138. See below, p. 60. For the content of the document

see Brun, *op. cit.*, pp. 338 ff. and Origo, *op. cit.*, p. 18. The Florentine Bernardo di Cino who had placed the order for this *parement* for King Charles VI served as an agent for Jean de Berry (see below, p. 46).

139. Meiss, 1936, p. 449. I see no grounds for the different view of Laclotte, *Avignon*, 1960, pp. 58 f. The normal Simonesque type of the Madonna of Humility was employed in Avignon, ms. 138, fol. 28v., a Neapolitan Missal that was carried to Avignon by 1368 (see n. 148).

140. Its importance for literature, however, and specifically for the diffusion of humanism, was certainly much greater. See Simone, *Rinascimento*, 1961, pp. 3 ff. Simone, however (p. 44), accepts the old and incorrect view that an enthusiasm for Trecento painting in France began with the arrival of Simone Martini in Avignon.

141. *Netherlandish Painting*, 1953, I, p. 24. The entire passage is fundamental. For his account of illumination in Avignon and his summary of the generally mediocre quality of manuscripts painted there see *ibid.*, p. 26 n. 7.

142. See below, p. 34. Louis gave his bride a Milanese *Horae* (Graves, *Inventaires Orléans*, 1926, p. 53).

143. I am most grateful to the Marchesa Guidi di Bagno and to her sons for permission to photograph and reproduce a miniature. The ms. has 317 fols., 345 × 241 mm. The colophon on fol. 316 reads: JACOBUS DE PLACENCIA SCRIPTOR SCRIPSIT MILLO CCCLXXXVI FUIT FINITUM HC LIBRUM NOCTE NATIVITATIS DOMINI. The ms. has three full-pages miniatures (IV., 101V., 191V.) and four initials. It contains the commentary of Jacopo della Lana.

144. Guillibert, 1902, p. 284. For the problem of attribution see Bologna, 1953, p. 52, and Meiss, *Revue des arts*, 1956, p. 142.

145. The first miniature in the Psalter is a bloody scene of David decapitating Goliath, and Saul raising his spear against David. For the Calendar, and the unusual verses at the beginning of each month, see Vienna, Nationalbibl. (Hermann), VIII, part v, 1929, pp. 231 ff.

146. Bibl. nat., fr. 4274 (d'Ancona, *Miniature italienne*, 1925, p. 46, pl. 43).

147. Laborde, *Bible moralisée*, IV, 1921, pp. 5 f.; V, 1927, pp. 114-117, 152; Mâle, *Fin du moyen-âge*, 1925, p. 10; Berenson, *Studies*, 1930, p. 107 n.; Panofsky, 'Maître de Rohan', 1939, p. 491, n. 42; Porcher, 1945, pp. 4-6; Meiss, *Art Bull.*, 1956, p. 192; idem, *Revue des arts*, 1956, pp. 142-145.

148. Avignon, Musée Calvet, ms. 138. See Meiss, *Art Bull.*, 1956, p. 189, and Paris, Bibl. nat. (Porcher), 1955, p. 65, no. 135.

149. De Wald, 1929, fig. 45.

150. The episode is represented only in mss., mainly Byzantine from the 11th century on (for example, Florence, Bibl. Laurenziana, Plut. VI. 23, fol. 96). In these miniatures, as in the Gospels themselves, Joseph appears alone.

151. The *Resurrection* resembles the corresponding scene in the Chapel because it joins the visit of the Maries to the Rising, and because Christ is not shown either standing on the sarcophagus or climbing from it but soaring in the air above (Meiss, *Florence and Siena*, 1951, p. 39, fig. 47). Both miniature and fresco, furthermore, show two angels seated on the sarcophagus, and similar, symmetrical, flat-topped hills on both sides. The scene of *Pentecost* is not limited, as usual earlier, to the reception of the spirit. The Virgin and the Apostles are seated in the open second storey of a house while below people begin to congregate, all as in the corresponding fresco by Bonaiuti (*ibid.*, p. 33, fig. 41). The Oriental in front of the door again carries a large bow, though he lacks Andrea's splendid pigtail.

152. Perkins, 1920, pp. 272 ff.; Paris, Orangerie, *De Giotto à Bellini*, 1956, pp. 27 f.

153. *Revue des arts*, 1956, pp. 142-145.

154. Castelnuovo, *Un pittore italiano*, 1962, p. 142, doubts my tentative proposal – as I now do more also – that the panels are actually by the hand of the chief master of the Bible, but about the close stylistic connections, which are of much greater historical interest, he is silent. He argues that the panels contain star-strewn vaults that are Avignonese, not Neapolitan, but they are common in the *Bible moralisée* and other Neapolitan paintings.

NOTES TO CHAPTER II

1. VII, 1932, chapters X, XII, XIII.

2. Lacour, 1934, pp. 114 ff. The term derives from *ad panem*, and applies to territories given to the sons of a king to permit them to live in appropriate splendor.

Before Jean le Bon's gifts only unimportant lands had been granted for this purpose.

3. Luce, 1889, pp. 275 ff.; Günther, 1963, pp. 79 ff.

4. *Ibid.*, p. 280. He bought four 'romans' in 1371 from

Henri l'Uilier, the largest bookseller in Paris. In 1378 he bought fixtures 'pour tenir chandelle de bougie à lire romanz'.

5. Delachenal, *Charles V*, 1931, I, p. 62; Graves, *Inventaires Orléans*, 1926, pp. 10 f.

6. Luce, *op. cit.*, p. 283; also Guiffrey, *Inventaires*, I, p. CXXVI.

7. Maurice de Bengy-Puyvallée, 1913, pp. 93 ff. See also Lehoux, *Jean de Berri*.

8. Guiffrey, *op. cit.*, I, p. CXXVI.

9. From the *Ménagier de Paris*. See Luce, *op. cit.*, p. 286.

10. Luce, *loc. cit.* Guiffrey (1899, pp. 63 ff.) had believed that the earliest record was of 1397.

11. Guiffrey, *loc. cit.*

12. *Ibid.*

13. *Ibid.*

14. Lacour, *op. cit.*, pp. 115 ff.

15. Froissart, ed. Lettenhove, XIV, pp. 62 f. Froissart was close to these events because in 1388 he was with Berry's enemy, the Comte de Foix, Gaston Phébus. In 1386 he was in Bourges for the marriage of Marie de Berry to Louis, the son of his patron Guy Comte de Blois.

16. *Cent Ballades*, ed. Raynaud, pp. 213 f.

17. Wylie, *Henry the Fifth*, I, 1914, p. 418.

18. Vaughan, *Philip the Bold*, 1962, pp. 42 ff; Lavisse, *Histoire*, IV, 1902, p. 292.

19. See the account of the Monk of St. Denis printed by Hiver de Beauvoir, *Librairie*, 1860, p. 11. Also Froissart (ed. Lettenhove, XIV, pp. 34-39). The Duke of Berry had visited Avignon as early as 1353, and frequently thereafter. See p. 196.

20. Froissart (ed. Lettenhove), XIII, pp. 305 f. To increase the disparity the King or Froissart exaggerated the age of the Duke; he was actually only forty-eight years old.

21. Levesque, V (1800), pp. 418, 422.

22. Lehoux, 1956, p. 54.

23. Vaughan, *loc. cit.*

24. *Le songe véritable*, ed. Moranvillé, pp. 274 f.

25. His lands, for one thing, were surrounded by the royal domain while those of Jean sans Peur were on the margins of it.

26. Chenu, 1931–1933, pp. 147 ff.

27. 'Assistencium vera relacione, qui convencionem cernebant cum cordiali affectu, didici, post singulorum salutacionis affatum, patruum nepotem sic alloqutum non sine lacrimis: "Nepos amantissime, me mala egisse confiteor et vos procul dubio pejora. Nunc resipiscendum est ab inceptis, ut regnum deinceps in transquilitate maneat." ' See *Chronique de St-Denis*, IV, 1842, pp. 691 f.

28. He had earlier named as his chief heir Jean de Touraine, son of his nephew Charles VI and husband of Jacqueline de Bavière. Jean himself had, however, died two months earlier. William of Bavaria, the father of Jacqueline, was related to the Duke of Berry by marriage. These kinships may bear upon the passage of part of the *Très Belles Heures de Notre-Dame* from the Duke's *garde des joyaux*, Robinet d'Estampes, to the house of Bavaria.

29. See the vivid reconstruction by Lehoux, 1956.

30. Champeaux and Gauchery, *Travaux*, 1894, p. 103.

31. Juvenal, *Histoire de Charles VI*, p. 532.

32. Koechlin, *Ivoires*, 1924, I, p. 32. For the movement of tapestry-weavers to the Low Countries see Evans, *Art in France*, 1948, p. 268. For painters see Panofsky, *Netherlandish Painting*, 1953, I, p. 63 n. 3.

33. *Œuvres*, ed. Saint-Hilaire, V, p. 123.

34. For the relation of Charles VII to the Sainte-Chapelle see the *Journal de Glaumeau, 1541–1562*, ed. Hiver de Beauvoir, p. 137.

NOTES TO CHAPTER III

1. See below, p. 148.

2. Philippe le Hardi bought two altarpieces of the same kind for Champmol in 1393 (von Schlosser, 1899, pp. 220 ff.).

3. Nonette was razed in 1633 by Richelieu (Champeaux and Gauchery, *Travaux*, 1894, p. 57).

4. The engraving here reproduced, made by Penot in 1737, is taken from *ibid.*, pl. 2. The stained glass at Riom was installed *ca.* 1470 (Grodecki, 1951, p. 209).

5. Champeaux and Gauchery, *op. cit.*, p. 63.

6. L. Gonse, *L'art gothique*, Paris, 1890, pp. 268-270; Lehoux, *Jean de Berri*, Chapter VIII.

7. The building is usually said to represent Saumur (Durrieu, *Très Riches Heures*, 1904, p. 149), but R. de Beauchamp, 1904, p. 135, proposed Bicêtre, and Lehoux (*op. cit.*, Chapter XI) is inclined to agree.

8. See below, p. 74. Oddly the Hôtel de Nesle was not represented in the Calendar pictures of the *Très Riches Heures*. It is true that *November*, not painted by the Limbourgs, might have shown one of these

buildings, and two views, *June* and *October*, were seen from the site of the Hôtel de Nesle, where the Duke was living while the Calendar was being painted. Two royal castles, Vincennes and the Louvre, were portrayed. Berry was born in the former.

9. Champeaux and Gauchery, *op. cit.*, p. 140. This identification will be discussed in the volume dealing with the Limbourgs.

10. Durrieu identified the château by comparison with a 17th-century print (*Très Riches Heures*, 1904, p. 140).

11. L. Magne, *Palais*, 1904, esp. pp. 6 ff. Also Gonse, *loc. cit.*, and Champeaux and Gauchery, *op. cit.*, pp. 12 ff.

12. For the identification of the château of Poitiers see Durrieu, *op. cit.*, p. 145. For Lusignan and the story of its protectress Mélusine (written in 1387–1394 by Jean d'Arras, the Duke's secretary) see Champeaux and Gauchery, *op. cit.*, p. 17; Wylie, *Henry the Fifth*, II, 1919, pp. 438-447.

13. Bober, 1953, pp. 741 ff.

14. Ed. Lettenhove, XIV, p. 197. See below, p. 148.

15. See below, p. 147.

16. Champeaux and Gauchery, *op. cit.*, p. 5; Bober, *loc. cit.* The Chartreuse at Dijon was projected by Philippe le Hardi in 1377. The cornerstone of the church was laid in 1383, and the building was consecrated in 1388 (Monget, *Chartreuse de Dijon*, I, 1898, pp. 376 ff.).

17. Raynal, *Berry*, I, 1844, pp. 14-38; Champeaux and Gauchery, *op. cit.*, pp. 34 ff. The Duke made payments to sculptors already in 1383 for work on a tomb for the Cathedral of Poitiers. As early as 1371 he bought a base for a Madonna for a chapel he had begun in the Cathedral (*ibid.*, p. 20; Troescher, *Burgundische Plastik*, 1940, p. 177). The significance of the inscription written below a relief in the portal of the Church of the Innocents in Paris allegedly stating the Duke wished to be buried there is not clear (Huizinga, *Waning*, 1924, p. 130).

18. Gauchery, 1919–1920, pp. 51 ff.

19. Lacour, *L'apanage*, 1934, p. 348.

20. Inv. of 1401, no. 996.

21. Lacour, *loc. cit.*; Thaumas de la Thaumassière, *Berry*, II, pp. 230 f.

22. Blanchet, 1919–1920, pp. 78 ff. Some of the coins are preserved in the Musée de Berry at Bourges.

23. Chaumeau, 1566, p. 229.

24. See below, p. 94. After the destructive storm of 1756 the archbishop removed the tomb from the damaged chapel to the Cathedral.

25. P. 35.

26. Hazé, *Berri*, 1834, pp. 53 ff.

27. Monget, *Chartreuse de Dijon*, I, 1898, pp. 293, 296, 301. A retable of Jacques de Baerze was placed in it in 1399 (Quarré, *Champmol*, [1960], p. 14). For the *sedilia* at Morogues see Meiss, *Gaz. B.–A.*, 1963, fig. 22.

28. Translation of the text of the *Chronique de St-Denys*, VI, 1952, pp. 30, 32.

29. Delachenal, *Charles V*, 1931, II, p. 232.

30. See below, p. 60.

31. Inv. of 1413, no. 69. The work bore Greek letters.

32. The gift was mentioned by the chronicler Jean Juvenal des Ursins. See Raynal, *Berry*, II, 1844, p. 418.

33. 34 *livres tournois*. See inv. of 1416, no. 197.

34. Prost, 1895, p. 258; F. de Mély, X, 1903, p. 152, Mater, 1904. See below, p. 129.

35. Inv. of 1413, no. 138. The donor is called 'le duc de Venise'. Several other relics of the Innocents are listed in the inv. of 1401 (nos. 319, 320, 933, 1083).

36. Lasko, 1962, pp. 259-264.

37. Delisle, *Cabinet*, I, 1868, pp. 21 f.; III, 1881, pp. 114 ff.

38. Peignot, *Bibl. ducs de Bourgogne*, 1841, pp. 41-57; [Barrois], *Bibl. protypographique*, 1830, pp. 105-109.

39. Graves, *Inventaires Orléans*, 1926, pp. 83-169.

40. Doutrepont, *Inventaire*, 1906.

41. [Barrois], *op. cit.*, pp. 114-116.

42. Moranvillé, *Inventaire Anjou*, 1906.

43. Delisle, *Cabinet*, I, 1868, p. 21. The royal library was inventoried again on the death of Charles V in 1380, then on the death of Malet in 1411, then again in 1413, and on the death of Charles VI in 1424.

44. Inv. of 1413, nos. 197-200. See also the full transcription of the inscriptions on the remarkable gold relief of the Emperor Philippus (A.D. 244–249), the first Christian emperor, according to Orosius (inv. of 1401, no. 55).

45. Delisle, *Cabinet*, I, 1868, pp. 32 f., notes additional categories of description employed by Robinet.

46. *Ibid.*, II, 1874, p. 142; III, 1881, p. 8.

47. Müntz, *Collections Médicis XVe*, 1888, pp. 11-51.

48. *Ibid.*, pp. 58-96.

49. Müntz, *Collections Médicis XVIe*, 1895, pp. 50-79.

50. Guiffrey, *Inventaires*, I, p. 337.

51. *Ibid.*, II, p. 195.

52. Monget, *Chartreuse de Dijon*, I, 1898, p. 361.

53. Guiffrey, *Inventaires*, II, pp. 198 ff. For the objects in pawn at the time of the Duke's death see *ibid.*, II, p. 255.

54. Toesca, *Lombardia*, 1912, p. 407. Bouchot, *Primitifs*, 1904, pp. 196 ff.; *idem*, 1905, pp. 18 ff.

55. See M. Salmi, 'Ouvraige de Lombardie', in *Actes du XVII*e *Congrès International d'Histoire de l'Art* (1952), The Hague, 1955, pp. 269 ff.; *idem*, in *Storia di Milano*, Milan, VI, 1955, pp. 785 ff. Also Krautheimer, *Ghiberti*, 1956, p. 59; A. van Schendel, *Le dessin en Lombardie jusqu'à la fin du XV*e *siècle*, Brussels, 1938, pp. 49 f.; Toesca, *Trecento*, 1951, p. 775, with the suggestion that 'Lombardie' referred to the whole of Italy.

56. See above, p. 25.

57. Guiffrey, *Inventaires*, II, p. 35 no. 214.

58. *Ibid.*, II, p. 262 no. 791. For other examples of 'ouvrage de Grèce' see below, p. 304.

59. *Ibid.*, II, p. 50 no. 361.

60. *Ibid.*, II, pp. 157 nos. 1286-1288, 161 nos. 1302-1303, 183 no. 296.

61. See below, p. 304.

62. Guiffrey, *Inventaires*, II, p. 311 no. 6.

63. *Ibid.*, II, p. 247 no. 673.

64. *Ibid.*, I, pp. 31 no. 61, 95 no. 318, 176 no. 668, 177 no. 673, 178 no. 677, 179 no. 678, 183 no. 695.

65. See below, p. 62.

66. See below, p. 60. For 'drap de Lucques' see Guiffrey, *Inventaires*, II, pp. 152 no. 1264, 243 no. 565.

67. *Ibid.*, II, pp. 128 no. 1002, p. 177 no. 175, p. 313 (ms. of Galen).

68. *Ibid.*, II, p. 175 no. 171. For a second ms. 'de lettre lombarde' see no. 172.

69. *Ibid.*, I, p. 225 no. 854.

70. *Ibid.*, II, p. 123 no. 957. Other mss. with the same script are *ibid.*, II, pp. 122 no. 951, 175 no. 170. On this script see M. Prou, *Manuel de paléographie*, Paris, 1924, p. 228.

71. Guiffrey, *Inventaires*, II, p. 128 no. 1002.

72. *Ibid.*, I, p. 225 no. 855; II, pp. 126 no. 983, 133 no. 1053.

73. Salmi, *Storia cit.*, refers to Dante (*Inferno* XXVII, 74 ff.; *Purgatorio* XVI, 115, 126, *Paradiso* XVII, 71) and to the *Decameron* (*Giornata* I, *novella* I), where even Tuscany is included.

74. Hiver de Beauvoir, *Librairie*, 1860, p. 9.

75. Mirot, *Études lucquoises*, 1930, p. 2. In Paris the Italian bankers lived on the rue des Lombards.

76. Guiffrey, *Inventaires*, I, p. 39 no. 75. This was sexpartite.

77. *Ibid.*, II, p. 131 no. 1027, now Bibl. nat., lat. 8824. See *The Paris Psalter* (Early English Manuscripts in Facsimile), ed. B. Colgrave, Copenhagen, 1958.

78. Guiffrey, *Inventaires*, I, p. 290 no. 1106.

79. *Ibid.*, I, p. 39 no. 76.

80. *Ibid.*, I, pp. 19 no. 16, 23 no. 31, 31 no. 61; II, p. 58 no. 404.

81. *Ibid.*, I, p. 199 nos. 776, 777. Von Schlosser, 1897, p. 91, thought the contrary.

82. Guiffrey, *Inventaires*, I, p. 70 no. 195. In the descriptions of portraits of the Duke this phrase refers to likeness. No such ancient medal is known, but, the model was no doubt a Roman coin.

The large silver plate representing Constantine on horseback, though clearly Early Christian before the 7th century, is not characterized as *ancien* (*ibid.*, II, p. 182 no. 230).

83. For other objects either antique or *all'antica* see below, pp. 52, 304.

84. See below, p. 302.

85. Champeaux and Gauchery, *Travaux*, 1894, p. 109.

86. Lacour, *L'apanage*, 1934, pp. 144, 147.

87. Champeaux and Gauchery, *loc. cit.*

88. *Ibid.*, pp. 103 ff.; Guiffrey, *Inventaires*, I, p. LXXVII. Jean d'Orléans worked for Charles V as early as 1364, and has sometimes been identified with the Master of the *Parement de Narbonne* (see below, p. 132).

89. Delisle, *Charles V*, 1907, I, p. 81.

90. See p. 148.

91. See p. 227. For Bose, 'peintre du Duc' in 1401, see Champeaux and Gauchery, *op cit.*, p. 113.

92. Champeaux and Gauchery, *op. cit.*, pp. 10 f.

93. See Guiffrey, *Inventaires*, I, pp. LXXX f.; Champeaux and Gauchery, *op. cit.*, p. 110. A certain Richard and Guillemin Deschamps appear in this group.

94. See below, p. 167.

95. See Meiss, *Burl. Mag.*, 1963. See below, p. 84.

96. Champeaux and Gauchery, *op. cit.*, p. 140.

97. *Ibid.*, p. 141.

98. See Chapters VI-VIII.

99. See the following chapters. In 1386 two illuminators were working on a monthly salary, Jean Minèvre and Pierre de Costances (Champeaux and Gauchery, *op. cit.*, p. 118).

100. Champeaux and Gauchery, *op. cit.*, p. 116. Another *verrier*, Berthaud, repaired the windows of the Ste-Chapelle in Bourges after a hurricane in 1408 (*ibid.*, p. 115).

101. See p. 301.

102. Champeaux and Gauchery, *op. cit.*, pp. 179 ff.

103. See below, p. 147. As early as 1372 Philippe le Hardi made a payment to Berry's 'ouvrier de taille' (Prost, 1895, pp. 345 f.).

104. Champeaux and Gauchery, *op. cit.*, pp. 37 f. The account of the sculptor in Thieme-Becker (XVIII,

1925) is misleading with regard to the date when he began to work for Jean de Berry. For other sculptors and architects occasionally employed by the Duke see Guiffrey, *Inventaires*, I, pp. LXXXV ff.

105. See Guiffrey, *op. cit.*, I, p. LXVIII.

106. Inv. of 1413, no. 690.

107. *Ibid.*, nos. 621, 645, 660, 661, 691, 1209.

108. *Ibid.*, no. 646.

109. *Ibid.*, nos. 627–629.

110. *Ibid.*, nos. 296, 336.

111. Ghiberti, *Denkwürdigkeiten*, ed. von Schlosser, p. 43; Krautheimer, *Ghiberti*, 1956, p. 62. The work was destroyed on order of the Duke of Anjou.

112. Guiffrey, *Inventaires*, II, pp. 339 f. See the references to this magnificent object in the inv. of 1413, nos. 339, 359, 360, 363, 364, 366, 371, 467, 1163.

113. Champeaux and Gauchery, *op. cit.*, pp. 164 f., although no specific records for the later years are given.

114. *Ibid.*, pp. 166 f.; Guiffrey, *Inventaires*, I, p. LXVII. See the inv. of 1401–1403, nos. 11, 66, 663, 710, and inv. of 1413, no. 785.

115. Guiffrey, *op. cit.*, I, p. LXIX. Inv. of 1416, no. 1157.

116. Salmon, ed. Crapelet, pp. 86 f. See Champeaux and Gauchery, *op. cit.*, pp. 191 ff.

117. *Ibid.*, pp. 89 f. However, the *Cité de Dieu* that Salmon gave the Duke was distinguished for neither its text nor its miniatures (Bibl. nat., fr. 172–3; see catalogue of Berry's mss.). The adjective *solemnel* employed to characterize the *intarsiatore* meant 'outstanding' (see Du Cange, *s.v. solemnis*, and Godefroy, *Dictionnaire*).

118. E. Carli, *Scultura lignea senese*, Milan, 1951, p. 116; Thieme-Becker, VII, p. 412. P. Bacci, *Francesco di Valdambrino*, Siena, 1936, pp. 119, 131.

119. Inv. of 1413, nos. 29, 30, 50–52, 301, 333, 336.

120. François de Nerly (inv. of 1413, nos. 423, 424, 775); Bureau de Dammartin (*ibid.*, no. 93); Denisot le Breton (Guiffrey, *Inventaires*, II, p. 332); Audebert Catin (*ibid.*, p. 294).

121. Guiffrey, *op. cit.*, II, pp. 198 ff.; Lehoux, *Rev. historique*, 1956, p. 41.

122. Guiffrey, *op. cit.*, II, p. 327.

123. Lehoux, *op. cit.*, p. 54 n. 5 and 6. There are similar records of other members of the family: 'Lonchin', 'Berthe', 'Magne' (*ibid.*, pp. 40 n. 2, 42 n. 4).

124. Guiffrey, *Inventaires*, I, pp. 70 f. See also pp. 66, 89; Lehoux, *op. cit.*, p. 42 n. 1.

125. Guiffrey, *op. cit.*, I, p. 72.

126. *Ibid.*, I, p. 27, no. 54. The Baptist was represented on one side, Saint Eugenia and a miracle on the other. Another Florentine in Paris, 'Forest Corbechi', sold a gold tabernacle to the Duke (inv. of 1413, no. 1112).

127. Champeaux and Gauchery, *op. cit.*, p. 134. In the Duke's accounts of 1413–1416 Baude de Guy is described as 'marchant de Fleurance' (Guiffrey, *Inventaires*, II, p. 336).

128. Guiffrey, *op. cit.*, I, inv. of 1413, nos. 164, 185, 191, 415, 437, 450, 592; II, p. 336.

129. *Ibid.*, I, p. 240 no. 922.

130. *Ibid.*, II, p. 334. See also inv. of 1413, nos. 405, 426, 431, 659, and for gifts from the Duke, nos. 327, 1192.

131. See above, p. 26.

132. In the references to the sources of these embroideries in contemporary records Florentine merchants are named. A Florentine in Toulouse, 'Barthélemy le Bel', sold an embroidered 'dossier d'autel' to the Duke in 1388 (Champeaux and Gauchery, *op. cit.*, p. 184). In 1393 Michele de' Pazzi, then in Avignon, sold three similar objects to Philippe le Hardi (Grönwoldt, 1961, p. 35).

133. Inv. of 1401–1403, nos. 1258, 1262, 1269, 1273, 1277, 1282, 1298, 1299, 1305, 1307, 1309–1313.

134. Guiffrey, *Inventaires*, II, p. 198 ff.; Lehoux, *Rev. historique*, 1956, pp. 46 ff.

135. Vaughan, *Philip the Bold*, 1962, pp. 220 f.

136. Peignot, *Bibl. ducs de Bourgogne*, 1841, p. 29.

137. See also the Lancelot acquired in 1408, now Paris, Bibl. de l'Arsenal, ms. 3479–3480, with miniatures datable around 1405 (and therefore probably the ms. provided by Raponde), and the *Propriété des choses*, acquired in 1403, now Brussels, Bibl. Royale, ms. 9094 (Doutrepont, *Inventaire*, 1906, nos. 68, 81). For other services of the Raponde to the Burgundy library see *ibid.*, nos. 69, 70, 79. The Boccaccio is no. 97 and the *Fleur des histoires* one of the three in no. 108. On Rapondi see Peignot, *Bibl. ducs de Bourgogne*, 1841, pp. 27 ff.

138. Guiffrey, *op. cit.*, II, p. 338.

139. Lehoux, *op. cit.*, 1956, p. 44. Cristoforo De' Mari served as treasurer of the Duke in 1408–1410 (*ibid.*, p. 42 n. 1). See also inv. of 1413, nos. 315, 648, 826. For Giovanni de' Mari see Guiffrey, *Inventaires*, II, p. 329. For Piero Fatinelli see *ibid.*, p. 295 and Lehoux, *op. cit.*, p. 42 n. 3. For 'Hylaire Fatinant' see Guiffrey, *op. cit*, II, p. 320.

140. Inv. of 1413, nos. 70 (an enamelled gold diptych), 162, 425. In 1409 the Duke gave him the enormous sum of 9000 *livres tournois*.

141. Inv. of 1413, nos. 162, 294, 344, 381, 400, 438. See also Nicolas Spinole (Spinola) of Genoa, *ibid.*, nos. 1061, 1064.

142. For acquisitions from the Sac firm see *ibid.*, nos. 162, 343, 344, 381, 468. Also Lehoux, *op. cit.*, p. 42 n. 2. For Jean Picamel of Genoa (Picamilio) see inv. of 1402, no. 1103.

143. Inv. of 1413, nos. 347, 348, 357.

144. Guiffrey, *Inventaires*, I, pp. IX ff., discussed these gifts at some length, and compiled a list on p. LV.

145. Inv. of 1413, no. 994.

146. *Ibid.*, no. 366.

147. See below, p 50.

148. *Ibid.*, nos. 354, 358. See also nos. 12 and 696. The Duke bequeathed Jeanne very little; she did receive a Psalter, which was in the Château des Baux in 1426 (Barthélemy, 1878, p. 32).

149. Inv. of 1413, no. 396.

150. *Ibid.*, nos. 809–813, 823. See also nos. 361, 455, 462.

151. *Ibid.*, nos. 453, 456, 972, 973, 1006, 1152, 1163, 1182. By bequest: nos. 1105, 1106, 1200, 1201, 1250.

152. *Ibid.*, no. 968.

153. See below, p. 388 n. 9.

154. The New Year's gifts of Philippe le Hardi to Berry from 1385 to 1404 were listed by Prost, 1895, pp. 346 ff. For gifts by Jean sans Peur see the inv. of 1413, nos. 10, 391, 831, 1148.

155. See pp. 47, 315. Also Peignot, *Bibl. ducs de Bourgogne*, 1841, p. 32. The third copy was given to Louis d'Orléans.

156. Guiffrey, *Inventaires*, II, p. 132 no. 1050.

157. Prost, 1891, pp. 337 ff. The miniatures were painted by Coene, Stanier, and Haincelin de Haguenau. See *The Boucicaut Master.*

158. Inv. of 1413, no. 340.

159. Bibl. nat., fr. 2810. Inv. of 1413, no. 1005. See *The Boucicaut Master.* See also the facsimile of this ms., Paris, Bibl. nat., *Livre des merveilles* (Omont), [1907].

160. Inv. of 1413, no. 972.

161. Inv. of 1413, nos. 214, 274.

162. Inv. of 1413 (Guiffrey, *op. cit.*, I, p. 56 no. 138).

163. Inv. of 1413, no. 1139. See also nos. 447, 830.

164. *Ibid.*, no. 594.

165. *Ibid.*, nos. 100, 162, 309, 413, 469, 470, 598, 599, 685.

166. See below, p. 243. His Book of Hours is now in Cleveland, Museum of Art (see Chapter x).

167. Guiffrey, *Inventaires*, II, p. 121 no. 949; p. 122 no. 951.

168. Inv. of 1413, no. 958.

169. See below, p. 251.

170. Sidrac, Brussels, Bibl. Royale, ms. 11113, with the signature of Berry. See inv. of 1413, no. 938; see also no. 944, an illuminated Aristotle.

171. The Terence, Bibl. nat., lat. 7907A, is no. 969 in the inv. of 1413. See also no. 993, an illuminated Boccaccio, *Cas des nobles hommes et femmes.*

172. Inv. of 1413, no. 986.

173. *Ibid.*, no. 964.

174. *Ibid.*, no. 1003. See also the ms. of Avicenna, Guiffrey, *Inventaires*, II, p. 94 no. 717.

175. Inv. of 1413, no. 932 (*Chemin de longue estude*, given in 1403, with grisailles); no. 952 (*Mutacion de Fortune*, given in 1404, now in The Hague, Royal Library, ms. 78 D 42); no. 943 (*Faits de Charles V*, given in 1405); no. 977 (*Sept psaumes*, given in 1410); no. 1004 (*Faits d'armes*, given in 1413); no. 1239 (*Livre de la paix*, given in 1414). The date of the gift of the *Épître d'Othéa* (no. 949) is not recorded.

176. *Ibid.*, nos. 943 and 1239.

177. *Ibid.*, no. 959. The identification with this ms. of Bibl. nat., fr. 835–836 (Fig. 324), and of the related Bibl. nat., fr. 606 (Figs. 817, 833, 834) with no. 949, will be discussed in a subsequent volume of this publication.

178. See above, p. 48.

179. Inv. of 1413, no. 1211.

180. *Ibid.*, no. 328: 'une belle pomme de Must . . . paincte par dedans à ymaiges'.

181. See already the earliest inv. of 1402 (Guiffrey, *op. cit.*, II, pp. 80 ff.). Steingräber, *Antique Jewelry*, 1957, p. 53, identified *joyaux* only as jewelry to be worn. In the Duke's inventories objects are usually given specific functional designations, such as chalices, reliquaries, or inkstands, but Robinet's understanding of *joyaux* is indicated by such broader titles as 'tableaux, reliquaires et petits joyaux', or, after listing chalices, paxes, candelabras, and inkstands, he describes the next category as 'autres joyaux de diverses manuaires, pour chapelle. . . .' (Guiffrey, *Inventaires*, I, p. 53; also pp. 17, 27, 35, 70 ff.) Objects as small, on the other hand, as the medals of Augustus and Tiberius were called *joyaux* also (see below, p. 54).

182. Inv. of 1413, no. 14. See Guiffrey, *op. cit.*, I, p. XCVI.

183. No. 7. The resemblance was observed by Durrieu, *Très Riches Heures*, 1904, p. 37.

184. Inv. of 1413, no. 649. Durrieu, *op. cit.*, p. 21, assumes an identity, without question.

185. This is not the place to list even the most splendid

of the Duke's *joyaux*. One of his crucifixes bore no less than 31 *balais* (inv. of 1413, nos. 359, 1086). Another, the *Joyau au mont de Calvaire*, was unusual in so far as it showed the cross and the Duke and Duchess under a sort of vault (*ibid.*, no. 1111).

186. Müller and Steingräber, 1954, p. 32; O. M. Dalton, *Royal Cup*, 1924.

187. Lasko, 1962.

188. Pp. 142 f., 146.

189. See *Mostra d'arte sacra*, Lucca, 1957, p. 20 no. 22. The box measures 17 × 30 × 21 cm. A smaller box in the collection of A. B. Martin is so similar in technique and style that it was probably made in the same workshop. A similar casket is in the Musée de Cluny, Paris. Neither H. Köhlhaussen, (*Minne-kästchen im Mittelalter*, Berlin, 1928, p. 20), who dates the box in Lucca in the third decade, nor G. Gall (*Leder im europäischen Kunsthandwerk*, Braunschweig, 1965, pp. 83 ff.), who dates it *ca.* 1400, is aware that it belonged to Alderigo Antelminelli, as the Lucca catalogue states.

190. For the technique of painting on leather see Merrifield, *Treatises*, 1849, I, pp. CIX ff.

191. Heckscher, 1937–1938, pp. 204 ff.; Panofsky, *Renaissance and Renascences*, 1960, p. 88; Adhémar, *Influences antiques*, 1939, pp. 123 f.; Evans, *Magical Jewels*, 1922, pp. 95 ff.

192. Bibl. nat. (Babelon), 1897, I, p. 2.

193. XXI, II.

194. Sauerländer, 1959, pp. 298 ff.

195. The word appeared in the 13th century. See Du Cange, where as often the distinction between cameos and intaglios is not clear. *Cammaheü* appeared in the inventory of 1246 mentioned in note 213.

196. Wentzel, 1954, pp. 53 ff.

197. Babelon, *Histoire de la gravure sur gemmes*, Paris, 1902, p. 103.

198. See below, p. 73. Guiffrey, *Inventaires*, I, p. 162 no. 606, p. 163 no. 611. The neck of the Duke in the former was composed of a ruby.

199. Guiffrey, *ibid.*, I, p. 148 no. 518, p. 149 no. 536, p. 158 no. 587, p. 159 no. 595, p. 162 no. 604.

200. *Ibid.*, I, p. 34 no. 66, p. 300 no. 1127; II, p. 137 no. 1081.

201. *Ibid.*, II, p. 84 no. 671.

202. *Ibid.*, I, p. 64 no. 176.

203. *Ibid.*, I, p. 64 no. 175. Another cameo (p. 63 no. 167) bore Greek letters.

204. A. Chastel, *Art et humanisme à Florence au temps de Laurent le Magnifique*, Paris, 1959, pls. IV, V.

2 B

205. Guiffrey, *Inventaires*, II, p. 306 art. 127: 'tête d'Aurélien ou de Probus', I, p. 143 no. 481: 'ydole'. See also *ibid.*, II, p. 118 no. 939: 'deux oiseaux qui ont le visage de homme'.

206. *Ibid.*, I, p. 64 no. 172.

207. *Ibid.*, I, p. 44 no. 95. Was the head not a Roman cameo, transformed into a bishop by the addition of a silver miter and bust?

208. *Ibid.*, I, p. 37 no. 72, p. 67 no. 187.

209. Blanchet, 1900, pp. 236-246; Bourges, Bibl. municipale et Musées, *Mécènes berrichons*, 1956, p. 35 no. 49.

210. For the inventory of 1762 (and others) see Blanchet, *op. cit.* On style and subject see Wentzel, 1954, pp. 53 ff., *idem*, 1957, p. 52; and Coche de la Ferté, 1959, p. 174. An almost identical cameo in Munich lacks the halo, and represents a ruler.

211. See cameo no. 18 of the list of 15 *frimaire*, which refers to the break at the top (Blanchet, *op. cit.*). Wentzel, 1954, pp. 53 ff., discussed the style. The treasure of the Ste-Chapelle was enriched in 1447 and 1465 by Charles VII – see *Journal de Glaumeau* (ed. Hiver de Beauvoir), 1867, p. 137 – and later gifts were certainly made to the Cathedral of Bourges.

212. '. . . Una delle più degnie cose, ch'io abbia veduto, ma è anche forse delle più degnie. . . .' (*Trattato*, ed. von Oettingen, p. 659). For the cameo see Eichler and Kris, *Kameen*, 1927, pp. 52 ff.

213. See de Mély, 1886, pp. 244 ff., and 1894, pp. 67 ff. Also Eichler and Kris, *loc. cit.* Possibly the Duke obtained the cameo for a time, and had casts or copies made.

214. In addition to the cameos already mentioned see the following: inv. of 1402, nos. 228, 555; inv. of 1413, nos. 70, 71, 170, 171, 173, 177, 178, 190, 492, 498, 517, 583, 1094. Given to the Ste-Chapelle in 1405: no. 139 (Guiffrey, *Inventaires*, II, p. 308). Inv. of 1416, no. 745.

215. Krautheimer, *Ghiberti*, 1956, p. 300.

216. Guiffrey, *Inventaires*, I, p. 72 no. 199.

217. *Ibid.*, I, p. 72 no. 200.

218. *Ibid.*, I, p. 73 nos. 201, 202.

219. See Weiss, 1963, pp. 134 f., who gives a valuable account of the variations in the extant copies.

220. A good recent review in *ibid.*, pp. 129 ff. To the authorities quoted should be added Panofsky, 1942, p. 54 n. 76, tentatively suggesting an Italian origin because they were bought from an Italian, and Krautheimer, *Ghiberti*, 1956, p. 59, who inclines towards Venice.

221. See Weiss, *op. cit.*, p. 142, approving an earlier proposal by Bode, 1917, p. 316, and Bange, *Bildwerke*, 1923, p. 75. Though referring to the connections of the *Madonna* with Berry, Bange characteristically describes it as 'Burgundian'.

222. Guiffrey, *Inventaires*, II, p. 227 no. 234: '. . . un ymage de Nostre Dame tenant son enfant et quatre angelos portans un paveillon sur ledit ymage. . . .'

223. I feel less certain than Weiss, *loc. cit.*, that Saulmon was the designer of the *Madonna*. The inventory item reads '. . . monseigneur acheta de Michelet Saulmon, son paintre. . . .' This excludes an object made in the service of the Duke, for which the painter received a salary. Saulmon must have ordered it from a gold-smith, and perhaps provided a drawing. For Saulmon see above, p. 44.

224. Guiffrey, *Inventaires*, I, pp. 70-72 nos. 197, 198. The date is given only as March, not March 1 as Weiss states (*op. cit.*, p. 143).

225. 200 *livres tournois* as compared with 400 and 500.

226. Schlosser, 1897, p. 64.

227. *Ibid.*, p. 75; Panofsky, *Netherlandish Painting*, 1953, I, p. 64.

228. See Verdier, 1961, p. 19 n. 24. For the moon see the Madonna of Humility, where it appears below the Virgin's feet (Meiss, *Florence and Siena*, 1951, p. 154).

229. Normally the *pilentum* had four wheels, the *carpentum* only two, but the former was open all around, the latter closed. See Abaecherli, 1935–1936, *passim*.

230. Meiss, *Burl. Mag.*, 1963, p. 53 and figs. 10, 12.

231. J. Strzygowski, 'Der Pinienzapfen als Wasser-speier', *Mitt. des deutschen Arch. Inst.*, XVIII, 1903, pp. 184 ff.; *Bullettino di archeologia cristiana*, VI, 1881, pl. 5; P. Underwood, 'The Fountain of Life in Manuscripts of the Gospels', in *Dumbarton Oaks Papers*, V, 1950, pp. 43 ff.
Both Dr. Viktor Elbern, in conversation, and P. Verdier (in Baltimore, Walters Art Gallery, *International Style*, 1962, p. 146) have suggested that water issues from the *pigna*.

232. Panofsky, *Iconology*, 1939, p. 154; *idem, Netherlandish Painting*, 1951, I, pp. 64, 216 n. 2. Also Schlosser, *loc. cit.*; Habich, *Medaillen*, [1922], pp. 23-26. For a nude Synagogue see Panofsky, *Iconology*, fig. 79.

233. For example, book cover, *ca.* 900 (A. Goldschmidt, *Die Elfenbeinskulpturen aus der Zeit der karolingischen und sächsischen Kaiser*, Berlin, 1914, pl. XXXVI).

234. See *The Book of Beasts*, ed. T. H. White, London, 1955, p. 105.

235. See below, pp. 233, 235. For the medieval inter-pretation of Virgil's Eclogue IV see D. Camparetti, *Virgilio nel medio evo*, Florence, 1955, I, p. 122.

236. Guiffrey, *Inventaires*, I, p. 27 no. 54.

237. *Ibid.*, I, p. 28 no. 55. Philip and Marcus Aurelius were represented kneeling at the opening of the Sixth Seal in illustrations of the commentary on the Apocalypse by Alexander Laicus (see for example Cambridge, University Library, Mm V. 31, fol. 30v.). Robinet's 'face de Dieu' is probably the moon that appeared above. Ernst Kitzinger kindly called these representations to my attention. For a different view see Schlosser, 1897, p. 75. See also above, n. 44.

238. *Ibid.*, II, p. 26 no. 122 (47 gold coins), p. 36 no. 218 (1 gold coin), p. 141 nos. 1108-1110 (35 silver and gold coins). By 1413 he had others: see *ibid.*, I, p. 73 no. 203 (23 coins), p. 74 no. 204 (35 'deniers d'argent').

239. *Ibid.*, I, p. 70 no. 195. Schlosser, 1897, pp. 69 ff., pointed out that copies of Roman coins were pro-duced a little later, from 1404 on, in Venice by the Sesto family, die-cutters employed by the mint.

240. Weiss, 1963, *passim*.

241. G. Schlumberger, *Byzance et Croisades*, Paris, 1927, p. 115, and for the Emperor's visit in general, pp. 106 ff.

242. See Schlosser, 1896.

243. *Ibid.*

244. See W. F. Volbach, *Early Christian Art*, New York, n.d., p. 333.

245. The narrower bands for the walls of churches were known as *lythes*. In the church of the Chartreuse they bore the ducal arms (Monget, *Chartreuse de Dijon*, I, 1898, p. 129).

246. Rorimer and Freeman, 1949, pp. 243 ff.

247. A set of the *Neuf Preux* is listed in the inv. of 1416 (Guiffrey, *Inventaires*, II, p. 209 no. 17). The arms of Berry are not mentioned. The inv. of Charles VI, just before 1422, lists a set of tapestries representing the *Neuf Preuses*, with the arms of Berry (Rorimer and Freeman, *op. cit.*, pp. 252 f.).

248. One set showed 'la Chasse à l'usage de Romme' (Guiffrey, *op. cit.*, II, p. 241 no. 551).

249. Such subjects were common also among the tapestries of Louis d'Orléans (Graves, *Inventaires Orléans*, 1926, pp. 25 f.). For Burgundy see Dehaisnes, *Histoire*, 1886, II, pp. 844 f., 907.

250. Charles VI possessed a tapestry devoted to him (Guiffrey, *Inventaires*, I, p. CVIII).

251. *Ibid.*, II, pp. 207 f. nos. 7-12.

252. *Ibid.*, II, p. 206 nos. 2-4.

253. Huizinga, *Waning*, 1924, pp. 224 f.

254. Dehaisnes, *loc. cit.*, and Graves, *loc. cit.*

255. See for instance Hector in the enamel in the inv. of 1413, no. 702.

256. Guiffrey, *Inventaires*, II, p. 210 no. 26.

257. *Ibid.*, II, p. 241 no. 548.

258. *Ibid.*, II, p. 207 no. 5.

259. Inv. of 1416, nos. 18, 19.

260. *Ibid.*, nos. 550, 553.

261. See also the collection of Louis d'Orléans (Graves, *op. cit.*, p. 27).

262. Guiffrey, *Inventaires*, II, p. 211 nos. 27-43.

263. *Ibid.*, II, p. 213 nos. 44-54.

264. *Ibid.*, II, p. 262 no. 791.

265. *Ibid.*, II, pp. 222 ff. nos. 125-142.

266. See above, p. 42.

267. Salmi, 1931, pp. 385 ff.

268. The first scene represents the Marriage of the Virgin.

269. Guiffrey, *Inventaires*, II, p. 159 no. 1292. '. . . et aux deux coustez dudit Crucifiement est la Vie et Passion Nostre Seigneur'.

270. The resemblance was observed by Kurth, 1931, p. 462, who, however, inferred that both embroidery and painting derived from a lost original, probably a fresco. The embroidery measures 50 × 33 cm.

271. See Meiss, 1936, pp. 22 ff., for a discussion of the original altar in the church.

272. Guiffrey, *op. cit.*, II, p. 164 no. 1317.

273. *Les monumens de la monarchie françoise*, III, Paris, 1731, pp. 181 f. and pl. XXVIII. See Grönwoldt, 1961, fig. 6, for a plausible attempt to reconstruct the entire composition.

274. This role of the embroideries has been observed by *ibid.*, p. 54.

275. Guiffrey, *Inventaires*, II, pp. 58 no. 404, 117 no. 934, 136 no. 1068. On the panels see Durrieu, 1918, pp. 265 ff. Though we have no evidence he assumed that the portraits at Bicêtre were on panel (see below, p. 74).

276. B. Berenson, *Italian Pictures of the Renaissance*, London, 1932, p. 346, as by the Master of the St. George Codex. A. Boschetto, 1953, pp. 155 ff., as by a follower of Simone Martini in Avignon.

277. Hulin de Loo, 1925, p. 125; E. Michel, 1926, pp. 353-356; Hulin de Loo and Michel, *Early Flemish Pictures in the Renders Collection*, London, 1927, pp. 37 ff.; Fry, 1927, p. 262 (French painter in Avignon); Panofsky, *Netherlandish Painting*, 1953, I, p. 81. All these writers emphasized the strong Sienese influence.

278. Letter to me of June 9, 1956, and report of the Laboratoire Central L3/2/77143/PC/RB. This information was mentioned by Meiss and Eisler, 1960, p. 234. According to Fry (*loc. cit.*), the panel was acquired *ca.* 1865 by Désiré de la Rue, in 1894 by Speybrouck, and later by Renders. It entered the Museum in 1952 (Brussels, Musées Royaux, 1956, no. 15).

279. The repainting, on the other hand, is in tempera.

280. Guiffrey, *Inventaires*, I, p. 19 no. 15 (a diptych); II, p. 117 no. 934 (Durrieu, 1918, suggested this might be the panel in Troyes). For a diptych of this type, close to Barna, see Meiss, 1954, p. 308. The quadriptych is Guiffrey, *op. cit.*, I, p. 23 no. 34. For extant representations of the Man of Sorrows see below, p. 63.

281. *Ibid.*, I, p. 21 no. 25. On the Trecento panels of this subject see Meiss, *Florence and Siena*, 1951, pp. 35 ff.

282. Guiffrey, *op. cit.*, I, p. 33 no. 64.

283. Meiss, 'Ovum Struthionis', 1954, p. 98.

284. In his important paper on the diptych that was presented to the Pope in a panel known through a Gaignières copy Otto Pächt ('Avignon Diptych', 1961) maintained that the diptych was Byzantine, partly because of the lack in Trecento painting of comparable busts of the Virgin. There is one, however, from the somewhat later circle of Lorenzo Monaco (Amsterdam, Rijksmuseum). Furthermore the narrow, gabled panels in Gaignières' drawing are not Byzantine in shape but Italian. Miss Janet Backhouse will discuss this question in a forthcoming article.

285. Guiffrey, *Inventaires*, I, p. 39 no. 77. The present participle is normally invariable. *Ibid.*, I, p. 290 no. 1106.

286. *Ibid.*, I, p. 290 no. 1106. Robinet might have intended a Man of Sorrows, but his normal term for this subject was *Pitié de Notre Seigneur*, or more rarely *Pitié* alone (see the inv. of 1402, nos. 53, 934; inv. of 1413, nos. 39, 68, 80, 1119).

287. *Ibid.*, I, p. 25 no. 41.

288. Such figures appear in 14th-century sculpture, especially German: for example, statuette in the Germanisches Nationalmuseum, Nuremberg (H. Wilm, *Die gotische Holzfigur*, Leipzig, 1923, p. 161).

289. See, for instance, the panels in the Walters Art Gallery, Baltimore, and Musée Mayer van den Bergh, Antwerp (Panofsky, *Netherlandish Painting*, 1953, II, figs. 108-109).

290. Guiffrey, *Inventaires*, I, pp. 32 no. 63, 39 nos. 75 and 76, and II, p. 275 no. 1077.

291. *Ibid.*, I, p. 39 no. 75.

292. *Ibid.*, I, p. 24 no. 36.

293. *Ibid.*, II, p. 275 no. 1077.

294. *Ibid.*, I, p. 24 no. 38. The subjects were the Madonna of the Milk and St. John writing.

295. The diptych (*ibid.*, II, p. 285 no. 1266) was, in fact, given to a chapel in Bourges. It was probably larger than the diptych by Jan van Eyck now in the Metropolitan Museum in New York, with which Durrieu tentatively identified it (1918, p. 270).

296. Guiffrey, *Inventaires*, I, p. 19 no. 15.

297. *Ibid.*, I, p. 27 no. 52.

298. As Durrieu, *op. cit.*, p. 268, has proposed. See Guiffrey, *Inventaires*, I, p. 33 no. 65.
Margaret of Austria owned a gilt silver panel with a cameo head set against a background of red enamel. The verso was inscribed 'le duc de Berry' (Michelant, 1870–1871, p. 93).

299. For the portrait see below, p. 68. The other panels are reproduced in Ring, *French Painting*, [1949], pls. 4, 18, 20, and fig. 28.

300. For the panel once in the Ste-Chapelle in Paris see above, n. 293.

301. Meiss and Eisler, 1960, pp. 234 ff., with remarks on painting in color on cloth. Half the summary of this article in the *Répertoire d'art 1960* (1963) is absolutely wrong.

301a. See Thibout, 1952, pp. 85 ff. Panofsky (*op. cit.*, I, p. 42 n. 2) suggests, incorrectly I believe, the influence of Jacquemart.

302. Documents 1, 2. All documents for this section are in an appendix, pp. 66 f.

303. The text of Lebègue, preserved in Bibl. nat., lat. 6741, was published by Merrifield, *Treatises*, 1849, I, pp. 1 ff. Champeaux and Gauchery, *Travaux*, 1894, p. 124, incorrectly date Lebègue's compilation in 1396.

304. Merrifield, *op. cit.*, I, p. 4.

305. *Ibid.*; Lebègue, article 291. This document, and the career of Coene, will be discussed in *The Boucicaut Master*.

306. Merrifield, *op. cit.*, I, p. 281.

307. Document 3.

308. Merrifield, *op. cit.*, I, p. 6.

309. Champeaux and Gauchery, *op. cit.*, p. 122.

310. Merrifield, *loc. cit.*, based on a misreading of G. Moschini, *Della origine e delle vicende della pittura in Padova*, Padua, 1826, pp. 6, 9; cf. also A. Venturi, *Storia dell'arte italiana*, Milan, VII, pt. I, 1911, p. 228; Champeaux and Gauchery, *op. cit.*, pp. 124 ff.;

Prost, 1895, p. 342. Schlosser, too, said Pietro was a painter (1898, p. 352).

311. L. Baer, s.v. 'Pietro da Verona', in Thieme-Becker.

312. Document 4; Guiffrey, *Inventaires*, I, p. 285 no. 1093. Was Pierre producing one of the many volumes that contain a copy of the Calendar of the *Bréviaire de Belleville*? The nearest in date to 1413 is Vienna, Nationalbibl., ms. 1855 by the Bedford Master. 1413 is early for the painting of this ms. but not perhaps for the planning of it.

313. Extensive excerpts from this and other depositions were published by Champeaux and Gauchery, *op. cit.*, pp. 126 ff. For Pierre de Vérone see *ibid.*, pp. 129 ff.

314. '. . . des XXIIII ans a este demourant a Paris' (Paris, Arch. nat. LL85, fol. XI verso). The transcription of the document by Champeaux and Gauchery cited in the preceding note incorrectly gives XXIII.

315. Champeaux and Gauchery, *op. cit.*, p. 129.

316. See, for example, the Lancelot acquired in 1405 (Paris, Bibl. nat., fr. 117-120). See the List of the Extant Illuminated Manuscripts.

317. Champeaux and Gauchery, *op. cit.*, p. 127.

318. This hypothesis, advanced by Durrieu, *La peinture à l'exposition des primitifs français*, Paris, 1904, p. 72, will be discussed in *The Boucicaut Master*.

319. See for example, Bibl. nat., lat. 14863, fol. 117v. Champeaux and Gauchery, *op. cit.*, pp. 125 f.; Delisle, *Cabinet*, II, 1874, p. 217 n. 4.

320. Document 5.

321. Document 6.

322. Document 7.

323. Document 8.

324. Document 9.

325. Document 10.

326. *Histoire littéraire de la France*, Paris, XXIV, 1862, pp. 303 ff.

327. Delalain, *Libraire parisien*, 1891, pp. XVIII-XX.

328. See Gerolamo Zeloni, for example. Canon of the Cathedral of Pistoia, he built a new library for the Chapter, catalogued it, and collected antique inscriptions. He was a friend of several artists, and he himself illuminated some manuscripts that he gave to the library. Of one of these we learn that it was 'di mano propria di detto messer Girolamo come disse e miniato molto degnamente' (P. Bacci, *Documenti e commenti per la storia dell'arte*, Florence, 1944, p. 188). We know that he illuminated also an *Elegantiae* of Lorenzo Valla. I owe this reference to the kindness of Ugo Procacci.

NOTES TO CHAPTER IV

1. *Inventaires*, I, p. CXV.

2. Champeaux and Gauchery, *Travaux*, 1894, p. 20.

3. Guiffrey, *Inventaires*, II, p. 54 no. 380 and p. 143 no. 1159 ('deux images à genolz, l'un pour Monseigneur et l'autre pour Madame'). Also, in the inventory of the collection of Margaret of Austria in 1516, 'ung autre tablaux d'argent doré là où est le visage du duc de Berry' (Le Glay, *Correspondance de l'Empereur Maximilien 1er et de Marguerite d'Autriche* [Société de l'histoire de France], Paris, II, 1839, p. 483).

4. *Ibid.*, II, p. 14 no. 42.

5. *Ibid.*, I, p. 23 no. 35.

6. *Ibid.*, II, p. 117 no. 934.

7. *Ibid.*, II, p. 160 no. 1301, p. 162 no. 1306. See now Grönwoldt, 1961, p. 56.

8. In addition to the late 13th-century panel reproduced (Fig. 515) and the 12th-century relief at Autun mentioned below, see: *Taymouth Hours*, Brit. Mus., Yates Thompson 13, fol. 138v.; painting in the choir of the church at Alken (Clemen, *Die gotischen Monumentalmalereien der Rheinlande*, Düsseldorf, 1930, II, pl. 51); *Queen Mary's Psalter*, fol. 303 (Warner, *Queen Mary's Psalter*, 1912, pl. 298); Dante, *Commedia*, Parma, Bibl. Pal., ms. 3285, fol. 61 (Offner, *Corpus*, III, pt. 7, 1957, pl. III). In Byzantine art Peter usually does not greet the foremost of the elect by grasping his hand or arm but simply walks in front of them towards the gate, as in the frescoes in the Kahrie-Djami, Istanbul, or the church of Panagia, Asinou (Harold, Bishop of Gibraltar, Seymer and Buckler, 1933, p. 335 and pl. XCV, 1).

9. Grivot and Zarnecki, *Gislebertus*, London, 1961, pl. E.

10. Jean sans Peur fingers his pendant jewel in the miniature on fol. IV., Bibl. nat., fr. 23279, but here he is only a bystander in the king's chamber.

11. Kahane, 1957, pp. 423 f.

12. See the French lapidary of the 13th century quoted by Evans, *Magical Jewels*, 1922, p. 74.

13. XXI, 10-11.

14. On this subject see the very penetrating article by Heckscher, 1937–1938; also Lipinsky, 1962, pp. 129 ff.

15. Panofsky, *Abbot Suger*, Princeton, 1946, pp. 21, 63-67.

16. Bibl. nat., fr. 22542, fols. 356 and 356v. This passage has not previously been published. On the text see Bell, *Le songe*, 1955, and *L'idéal éthique*, 1962, pp. 81 f. For Aaron's breastplate see Exodus, XXVIII, 16-22.

17. See pp. 53, 307.

18. *Le chevalier errant*, Paris, Bibl. nat., fr. 12559 (fol. 158v.), written in 1394. See A. Champollion-Figeac, *Documents paléographiques relatifs à l'histoire des beaux-arts*, Paris, 1868, p. 427 n. 1. Also Porcher, *Belles Heures*, 1953, p. 31.

19. '. . . cette question que lui posa Charles VI: "Beaulx oncles, se l'Amourath Bacquin, ou le souldan, ou ung autre roy payen vous envoyoit ung rubis noble et riche, je vous demande se vous le recepvriés?" Le duc de Berry respondy et dist: "Monseigneur, j'en auroye conseil." Or fut il dit et remonstré du Roy, pour tant qu'il n'y avoit pas dix ans que le souldan luy avoit envoyé ung rubis, lequel il avoit acheté vingt mille frans.' (Froissart, ed. Lettenhove, XV, pp. 351 f.)

20. *Paradiso*, IX, 67-69.

21. 30,000 *écus*. See the inv. of 1413, no. 162. Also Guiffrey, *Inventaires*, I, p. CIV.

22. Sterling, 1959, p. 95 notes 26, 37.

23. *Livres d'heures*, II, pp. 37, 39.

24. Rorimer and Freeman (New York, The Cloisters, *Belles Heures*, 1958, pl. 32) say that 'authorities differ' as to whether the Duke is the blue-coated man in the center or the red-coated one at the right.

25. Luce, 1889, p. 281.

26. See p. 51.

27. See p. 45.

28. The figure has been so identified by Durrieu, *Rev. de l'art chrét.*, 1913, p. 313.

29. *Pierre Salmon*, ed. Crapelet, p. 86. For the correspondence of Berry and Salmon see above, p. 46.

30. See the catalogue, *Possible Representations*, no. 1.

31. H. Martin, *Miniaturistes*, 1906, pp. 29 f., lists many of the portraits of Charles V. See the numerous reproductions in Couderc, *Portraits*, [1910], pls. XIX-XL.

32. See Delaissé, *Medieval Illuminations*, 1958, p. 78.

33. Guiffrey, *Inventaires*, I, p. 144 no. 485. The Duke possessed also three 'portraits' of St. Louis, in enamel or composed of precious stones (*ibid.*, II, p. 54 no. 377, p. 144 no. 1160; I, p. 37 no. 71).

34. *Ibid.*, I, p. 141 no. 472: '. . . signet d'or où est le visaige de Monseigneur contrefait au vif'. *Ibid.*, I, p. 162 no. 606: a gold ring with a 'camahieu fait à la semblance du visaige de Mons.'. No. 611 (*ibid.*, I, p. 163) was similar.

35. Steingräber, *Antique Jewelry*, London, 1957, fig. 91.

36. Guiffrey, *Inventaires*, II, p. 227 no. 234. Bought from the painter of the Duke, Michelet Saulmon.

37. See now Chastel, 'Giotto coetaneo di Dante', 1964, pp. 40 ff.

38. Mirot, *Études lucquoises*, Paris, 1930, p. 108. See also J. von Schlosser, 'Geschichte der Porträtbildnerei in Wachs', *Wiener Jahrbuch*, XXIX, 1910, pp. 171-258.

39. Dehaisnes, *Documents*, 1886, Doc. I, p. 336.

40. Monget, *Chartreuse de Dijon*, II, 1901, p. 22; Sterling, 1959, p. 302.

41. The Byzantine Emperor Constantine, interested in a match with Hadwig of Suabia, sent a *pictor eunuchus* to paint her portrait (Westendorp, *Porträttafel*, 1906, p. 57 n. 2).

42. Something like the gallery of kings, a familiar feature of Gothic cathedrals and of public buildings, was also represented in 'private' palaces, as for instance in the castle of the Count of Arras at Hesdin (Richard, *Mahaut, Comtesse d'Artois*, 1887, p. 331).

43. For mural portraits in France and Bohemia in the second half of the 14th century see Sterling, 1959, p. 289 n. 3; Dvořáková et al., *Gothic Mural Painting in Bohemia*, 1964, pp. 53 ff.; Westendorp, *op. cit.*, pp. 42, 68 f.

44. Champeaux and Gauchery, *Travaux*, 1894, p. 20; Aubert, *Sculpture française*, 1946, p. 341.

45. *Chronique de St-Denys*, IV, 1842, p. 522. Durrieu, 1918, p. 268, and others have asserted that these portraits were on panel, but we have no evidence about their technique.

46. Roussel, *La sculpture gothique*, Paris, n.d., pls. 4, 8, 9 (after casts – no cast has been made of the Duke).

47. *Berri*, 1566, p. 229.

48. All the evidence will be set down by Professor Stephen Scher in his forthcoming study of Beauneveu.

49. See Gauchery, 1919–1920, pp. 37 ff. The statue of the Duke is reproduced by Champeaux and Gauchery, *Travaux*, 1894. It resembles the statue of the Duke made for the choir of the Ste-Chapelle, with which, indeed, it has been confused by Weinberger, 1946, p. 9.

50. See [Sterling], *Peintres du moyen âge*, 1941, cat., p. 4.

51. Guiffrey, *Inventaires*, II, p. 275 no. 1077.

52. For the Burgundian portraits see Sterling, 1959, pp. 289 ff., and Meiss and Eisler, 1960, pp. 239 f. To the list of copies of one type of portrait of Philippe le Hardi and Jean sans Peur given by Sterling should be added examples in the Schatzkammer, Vienna.

53. This was in the imperial domain. See Dvořáková et al., *Gothic Mural Painting in Bohemia*, 1964, p. 85.

54. See Vienna, Kunsthist. Mus., *Katalog*, 1962, p. 145, pl. 1.

55. Merrifield, *Treatises*, 1849, I, p. 81.

56. Toesca, *Lombardia*, 1912, fig. 242.

57. The lack of 16th-century copies like those of the Burgundian dukes is in part due to the return of the *apanage* of Berry to the crown after Jean's death.

58. See portrait catalogue, no. 23.

59. Bibl. nat., Cabinet des Estampes, Ob 10, fol. 11. I had not made these observations when I published the portrait of Berry (*Burl. Mag.*, 1963, pp. 51 ff.).

60. For this portrait and its history see Ring, *French Painting* [1949], p. 199 no. 63, or London, Royal Academy of Arts, *Exhibition of French Art*, London, 1932, p. 313 no. 617. On the Gaignières portraits see Grandmaison, 1891, pp. 181 ff.

61. 1961, pp. 265 ff. and *Les primitifs flamands*, Brussels, 1962, pp. 1 ff. The hand of the Duke in the *Merveilles du monde* (Bibl. nat., fr. 2810, fol. 226) assumes the same position, but the ring is not visible. The gesture of the Duke in Bibl. nat., fr. 23279 (dated 1409), fols. 1v., 119, is close to that in the panel (Fig. 506).

62. Panofsky, *Netherlandish Painting*, 1953, I, p. 82.

63. The problem of the date of the original is bound up with this decision. Mme Adhémar's date of 1404–1405, based on the accession of Jean sans Peur to the Duchy at that time, can be accepted only if we assume that the copyist has altered his model radically.

64. In addition to the figures in *May* in the *Très Riches Heures*, see Niobe in the Duke's *Cleres et nobles femmes*, Bibl. nat., fr. 598, fol. 24v.

65. The Duke was insufficiently vain, or too shrewd, to attempt to check the developing baldness by methods offered by contemporary barbers, at least the one tried by his son-in-law Amadée VII de Savoie. According to Froissart the ointments first made this poor man imbecilic, then killed him (*Chroniques*, ed. Lettenhove, XIV, p. 433).

66. See below, p. 248, for this painter.

67. Florentine, about 1410. Vienna, Albertina (Stix and Fröhlich-Bum), 1932, p. 3 no. 3.

68. *Origines*, 1888.

69. See the catalogue of this chapter, no. 66.

70. Ganz, *Die Handzeichnungen Hans Holbeins d. J.*, Berlin, 1937, p. 5. Ganz suggests the drawings were made in preparation for the Darmstadt *Madonna*. I should add that a smiling portrait would not be unique among Holbein's drawings. See the young man in a large hat at Chatsworth.

71. Vitry, *Die gotische Plastik Frankreichs 1226–1270*, Munich, 1929, pls. 71, 74, 81, 83.

72. Panofsky, *Die deutsche Plastik des elften bis dreizehnten Jahrhunderts*, Munich, 1924, II, pls. 84, 89, 102.

See also pls. 120, 124 (*Angel Gabriel*, Regensburg).

73. Beaulieu and Baylé, *Costume*, 1956, p. 61.

74. *Ibid.*, p. 62. Charles V was bearded as the dauphin in Bibl. nat., fr. 5707, dated 1363, but soon thereafter he appeared clean-shaven.

75. *Heures de Milan*, 1911, pp. 5 f.

76. *Très Belles Heures de Notre-Dame*, 1922, pp. 76-78.

77. Bibl. nat., fr. 131, fol. 1.

78. *Sigillographie*, 1912, p. 99, pl. XII.

79. Paris, Arch. nat., J. 382, no. 17.

80. He also ascribes the bearded portraits in the *Petites Heures* to Jacquemart (in our view they are by the Pseudo-Jacquemart) and places them after the marriage contract of 1389, and even towards 1401, the supposed date of the pattern on the seal.

81. A counter-seal is the verso of a seal.

82. Two small crowns set with sapphires, pearls and emeralds are described in the inventories of 1401 (no. 237) and 1413 (no. 146).

83. See p. 125.

84. Lehoux, *Bibl. École des Chartes*, 1956, p. 90.

85. The basic article is von Schlosser, 1899, pp. 220 ff.

86. Rorimer and Freeman, New York, The Cloisters, *Belles Heures*, 1958, pl. 31, refer to a chaplet of flowers. The headdress was much higher and wider than the crown, and there are black strokes at its upper edge. Was it not a fur hat? The Duke wears a green tunic under a blue mantle.

87. *Ibid.* On the other hand Porcher, *Belles Heures*, 1953, p. 42, says the figure of the Duke has been retouched. Reworking of the figure itself is not visible to me.

88. See Durrieu, *Très Belles Heures de Notre-Dame*, 1922, p. 45 and pl. XXVII (from Bastard, *Peintures*). Durrieu says that the pendant jewel on the Duke's breast was described in the inventories as a work of the goldsmith Jean Chenu, but no jewel ascribed to him seems identifiable with the one in the miniature. Bastard reproduced two other miniatures from this ms., the *Adoration of the Magi* and the *Man of Sorrows*.

89. Ganz, *loc. cit.*

90. The figure has been identified as the Duke by Durrieu, *Rev. de l'art a. et m.*, 1906, p. 29, and by Porcher, *op. cit.*, p. 31 n. 60.

NOTES TO CHAPTER V

1. *Dictionarii seu reportorii moralis*, Venice, 1583, I, p. 252.

2. See the *scel secret* of that year; Gandilhon, *Sceaux*, 1933, p. 4 no. 10. Guiffrey, *Inventaires*, I, p. CXXX, dated the appearance of the bear and the swan as late as 1379.

3. *Netherlandish Painting*, 1953, I, pp. 131 ff.

4. See pp. 31, 59. Also the ring with a golden bear (Guiffrey, *op. cit.*, I, p. 117 no. 379), and the head of a bear in a diamond (*ibid.*, p. 130 no. 433).

5. Vienna, Nationalbibliothek, ed. O. Smital and E. Winkler, II, pp. 101 f.

6. Guiffrey, *op. cit.*, I, p. CXXX.

7. Panofsky, *op. cit.*, I, p. 48 n. 2; Hahnloser, *Villard*, 1935, pl. 7.

8. P. Cassel, *Der Schwan*, 1872, pp. 12 ff., 24. I owe this reference to W. S. Heckscher.

9. Prinet, 1911, pp. 469 ff.

10. Miniature on a royal act of 1364 alienating Hôtel St. Pol, exhibited in Paris, Musée, Arch. nat.; Bibl. nat., fr. 22912-3, a copy of *ca.* 1376 of the *Cité de Dieu* for Charles V (Delisle, *Fac-similé*, 1903, pl. IX);

fr. 1792 (Delisle, *Charles V*, 1907, I, p. 55). The *Cité de Dieu*, however, shows *France ancien* also.

11. Prinet, *op. cit.*, pp. 481-484, cites the arms of Charles VI over the portal of the Château de Vincennes, the seals of Isabeau de Bavière (1402-1414), a coin of Charles VI, etc.

12. See Portrait Cat. no. 1, p. 82.

13. See *ibid.*, no. 11, p. 84.

14. Lacour, *L'apanage*, 1934, p. 164. According to the copies of documents and seals of Jean de Berry made for Gaignières the seal with *France moderne* was used already in 1369 (Bibl. nat., fr. 20368, fol. 15).

15. See below, p. 111. The change would have been made in any event before the miniature was copied in the *Grandes Heures* toward 1409 (see p. 261).

16. See below, p. 158.

17. See Portrait Cat. no. 6, p. 83.

18. Some capitals show in addition the arms of Jeanne de Boulogne, whom the Duke married in 1389.

19. For a very different account of the Duke's usage see Porcher, *Belles Heures*, 1953, p. 10 n. 7.

NOTES TO CHAPTER VI

1. Aubert, *Sculpture française*, 1946, p. 338.
2. See above, p. 74.
3. Aubert, *op. cit.*, p. 339, for a reproduction of the Queen. For the commissions of Charles V see especially Pradel, 1951.
4. The church and the right hand of Charles V are unfortunate modern restorations. The same must be said of the right hand and left arm of the Queen.
5. The painter was recorded there still in 1358. We hear of panels and mural paintings by him, as well as a *chapelle* on silk similar to the *Parement de Narbonne*. See Dufour, *Une famille*, 1877, pp. 50 ff.
6. Bouchot, *Primitifs*, 1904, pp. 145 ff.
7. Sterling, 1955, pp. 57 ff.; also Durrieu, in Thieme-Becker, s.v. 'Beaumetz'.
8. Bouchot, 1904, p. 20.
9. See p. 22. Also Durrieu, in Thieme-Becker, s.v. 'Bondol', and Dimier, 1936, p. 222.
10. See p. 27.
11. Smith, 1959, p. 44 and *passim*.
12. Lafond, in Lefrançois-Pillon and Lafond, *XIVe siècle* [1954], pp. 187 f., 225.
13. Sterling, *Primitifs*, 1938, fig. 19; *Peintres du moyen âge*, 1941, rép. no. 3, where its use during Lent is observed, and it is dated 1360–1370.
14. Panofsky, *Netherlandish Painting*, 1953, II, fig. 7. The gesture may be seen in the later Pucellesque tradition: *Entombment* in the *Heures de Yolande de Flandre* by the Passion Master, who also painted the same scene in the *Petites Heures* (Fig. 366; 113).
15. This date is given by most of the authors cited in the catalogue. See especially Sterling, Ring, and Panofsky.
16. See The Hague, Kon. Bibl., Byvanck, 1924, pp. 104 ff.
17. Millar, *La somme le roi*, 1953, pl. XXII. See also the tympanum of the south transept portal of Rouen Cathedral (Lefrançois-Pillon and Lafond, *op. cit.*, pl. V).
18. According to Nordenfalk, 1953, p. 88, the rare scene of the woman actually forging the nails, familiar from Fouquet's miniature in Chantilly, appears first in *Queen Mary's Psalter* (*ibid.*, fig. 16).
19. See van Marle, *Italian Schools*, II, fig. 64.
20. One of the resurrected in the Siena pulpit of Nicola Pisano, for instance, is taken directly from an antique sarcophagus (Swarzenski, *Nicolo Pisano*, 1926, pl. 55). For Reims see Adhémar, *Influences antiques*, 1939, p. 273.

21. This connection was observed by Meiss, 1956–1957, p. 45 n. 12. For the glass in Assisi see G. Marchini, *Le vetrate italiane*, Milan, 1956, fig. 9.
22. For the explicit opinion of Francesco da Barberino, and the view implicit in a legend of St. Catherine of Siena, see Meiss, *Florence and Siena*, 1951, pp. 107 f.
23. Swarzenski, *op. cit.*, pl. 8.
24. E. Carli, *Dipinti senesi del contado e della Maremma*, Milan, 1955, pl. 30.
25. This trend was discussed by Meiss, 1946, pp. 13 f. In France the traditional representation, with an 'earth-bound' Christ, may be seen in miniatures painted around the time of the *Parement*: on the folio of the ms. in Leningrad cited in note 36, and in an initial in the *Très Belles Heures de Notre-Dame* (Fig. 15).
26. Meiss, *Florence and Siena*, 1951, fig. 96.
27. On all of this see Meiss, 1936, pp. 456 ff., and *idem*, *Florence and Siena*, 1951, pp. 149 f.
28. *Idem*, *Gaz. B.-A.*, 1961, pp. 284 ff.
29. Catania, Bibl. Civica, A 72, fol. IV. For this interesting ms., which should be studied, see Rome, Palazzo Venezia, *Mostra della miniatura* [1953], p. 261.
30. Shorr, 1940, pp. 61 ff.
31. Mattingly, *Coins*, II, 1930, pls. 65 nos. 11, 16; 70 no. 8; 72 no. 8; 75 no. 4.
32. The crouching figures in the tympanum of the *Portail de la Calende* of the Cathedral at Rouen, *ca.* 1300, are squeezed by the constricted space of the field and do not seem to belong to this tradition.
33. Cockerell, *Yolande*, 1905, p. 4.
34. For this illuminator see below, p. 160.
35. See the Ducciesque example in Meiss, *Gaz. B.-A.*, 1961, fig. 23.
36. State Library, ms. fr. F. v. 1, vol. II, fol. 1. See Leningrad (St. Pétersbourg), Laborde, I, 1936, pl. IX.
37. *Ibid.*, pp. 284 ff. Years ago Vitzthum inclined to place the ms. in the same region (*Die Pariser Miniaturmalerei*, Leipzig, 1907, pp. 182 f.), and Crowe and Cavalcaselle, *The Early Flemish Painters*, 2nd ed., London, 1872, p. 4, included the ms. for no stated reason. For an ascription to southern France (perhaps Corrèze) see Oxford, Bodleian Library, *An Exchange of Latin Liturgical Manuscripts and Printed Books*, Oxford, 1952, p. 24.
38. Leroquais, *Sacramentaires*, 1924, II, p. 292; Paris, Bibl. nat. (Porcher), 1955, no. 74.
39. Bibl. nat., lat. 765, fol. 14; Meiss, *Gaz. B.-A.*, 1961, fig. 27.

40. The posture appears, for instance, in a Ducciesque panel in Montalcino, but used for a Christ Child in the arms of the Virgin (van Marle, *Italian Schools*, II, fig. 93).

41. For examples, Meiss, *op. cit.*, p. 286. See also a figure of St. John in the Angers Apocalypse tapestries (Lejard, *Apocalypse d'Angers*, 1942, pl. 22).

42. Pp. 103 ff.

43. Guiffrey, *Inventaires*, I, p. 243, no. 931.

44. *Ibid.*, p. 267, no. 997.

45. This construction of Robinet's rather difficult phrases is the same as that of Hulin (*Heures de Milan*, 1911, p. 4) and of Durrieu (*Très Belles Heures de Notre-Dame*, 1922, p. 3).

46. Châtelet, 1956, pp. 199 ff.

47. See p. 317, and Blanchard, *Heures de Savoie*, 1910.

48. Ms. 3-1954, formerly Lord Lee of Fareham. See now Wormald and Giles, 1964.

49. *Très Belles Heures de Notre-Dame*, 1922, p. 8. The Calendar was presumably completed before 1407, when Louis d'Orléans was killed.

50. Delisle, *Gaz. B.-A.*, 1884, pp. 290 f.

50a. Friar Jean Rousseau succeeded Friar Guy d'Aunnelx in that year. For these facts I am once again indebted to Mademoiselle Françoise Lehoux. Precise references to them and probably to the affiliations of later confessors of the Duke will be given in her monograph.

51. See, for instance, fol. 354 of the *Trésor des histoires*, Paris, Bibl. de l'Arsenal 5077.

52. See p. 158. Perhaps the shields were added to the *chapelle* in the *Très Belles Heures de Notre-Dame* in imitation of the shields in the *Brussels Hours* (Fig. 198).

53. The illumination of the *Bible moralisée*, Bibl. nat., fr. 166 (Laborde, *Bible moralisée*, v, 1927, pp. 97 ff.), was interrupted, probably by the death of the patron, Philippe le Hardi. Probably for similar reasons a ms. of the *Antiquités judaïques* (Bibl. nat., fr. 247 – Durrieu, *Antiquités judaïques*, 1908) received only three of its miniatures when it was owned by Jean de Berry; the rest were added by the atelier of Jean Fouquet. The Duke of Berry possessed a copy of the *Cité de Dieu* from before 1402 until his death without having the blank spaces left for initials and miniatures filled (Chantilly, Musée Condé, ms. 122-123; Laborde, *Cité de Dieu*, 1909, II, p. 465).

54. Guiffrey, *Inventaires*, I, p. 253 no. 960.

55. *Heures de Milan*, 1911, pp. 11 ff.

56. Durrieu, *Revue archéol.*, 1910, pp. 48 f. (tentatively to Jacquemart); *Très Belles Heures de Notre-Dame*, 1922, pp. 59 ff.

57. Durrieu's opinion that the earliest miniatures in the *Très Belles Heures de Notre-Dame* were painted by Jacquemart in the early 15th century was maintained by the following historians: Winkler, *Flämische Buchmalerei*, 1925, p. 15; Martens, *Meister Francke*, 1929, fig. 94 (with question); Robb, 1936, p. 496; Bourges, *Musées*, 1951, pp. 32 f.; Porcher in Paris, Bibl. nat., 1955, p. 87 (but dated *ca.* 1390). Panofsky, *Netherlandish Painting*, 1953, I, pp. 45 ff., combined in a sense the judgment of Durrieu with that of Hulin, ascribing the ms. to the workshop of Jacquemart, which, he suggested, the Parement Master had joined after the death of Charles V. Bober, 1953, p. 744, said that the ms. was begun after 1404. Porcher, *Medieval Miniatures*, 1959, p. 60, pl. 66 (but incorrect caption) dates the miniatures *ca.* 1405-1407, and ascribes them to the author of much of the *Grandes Heures*, part of the *Petites Heures*, and the *Parement de Narbonne*. Recently Kreuter-Eggemann, *Daliwe*, 1964, I, pp. 69, 77, dated the *Madonna* in the Parement style towards 1409, and Paris, Louvre (Sterling and Adhémar), 1965, pp. 1 f., dated the early miniatures in Bibl. nat., nouv. acq. lat. 3093 *ca.* 1380 but the O Intemerata leaf in the Louvre early 15th century.

58. Hulin, 1925, pp. 123 ff. This view has influenced the recent opinion of F. Unterkircher, in Vienna, Kunsthist. Mus., *Katalog*, 1962, p. 169, who ascribed the Paris section to Beauneveu and three other masters of the early 15th century.

59. Schilling, 1952, p. 168; Pächt, *Burl. Mag.*, 1956, p. 153; Nordenfalk, in Stockholm, Nationalmuseum, 1958, p. 19 (miniatures dated later, towards 1400). Sterling [1955, p. 80 and Paris, Louvre (Sterling and Adhémar), 1965, p. 1] ascribed the miniatures to a Flemish imitator of the Parement Master, working about 1380-1385.

60. Meiss, *Art Bull.*, 1956, p. 190.

61. See pp. 9 ff., 137, 175, 254.

62. London, Sotheby, July 12, 1948, lot 97, pl. XLII. In the *Crucifixion* in the *Heures de Jeanne de Navarre* vinegar is offered by a Negro (Fig. 544). Negroes appear also in the *Betrayal* (fol. 109) and the *Way to Calvary* (fol. 111) of this ms. [see London, Thompson Collection (Thompson), 1902, p. 173].

63. Perhaps she is the servant involved in Peter's Denial. In the *Heures de Yolande de Flandre*, fol. 44 (Cockerell, *Yolande*, 1905, pl.) she wears a similar head kerchief and bears a lantern.

64. For the 'revival' of the Parement style and

compositions towards 1409 in the *Grandes Heures* see p. 262. For the imitative miniature around the same time in Egerton 1070 see Schilling, 1954, p. 280 (attribution to the Parement Master himself) and Meiss, *Art Bull.*, 1956, p. 190. The only other miniature ascribed to the author of the *Parement* is conservative in style and not closely related. See Paris, Bibl. de l'Arsenal, ms. 2002 (Paris, Arsenal, Martin and Lauer, 1929, pl. xxxv), ascribed by Durrieu, *Rev. de l'art a. et m.*, 1904, p. 247.

65. The fact that preparatory shades in the Virgin's skirt in the *Visitation* (Fig. 7), disclosed by peeling of the piant, do not conform with the final version indicates that a painter of some independence did the final surface.

66. Brit. Mus., Add. 36684, fols. 88v., 89.

67. Brussels, Bibl. royale, ms. 9391, fol. 116. Such integration became widespread in the 14th century. See the Missal of 1343 in Toulouse, Bibl. municipale, ms. 90.

68. Urb. lat. 603. In the border of the Calendar near the water-carrier, for instance, a man balances a jug on his head. When David plays the harp (fol. 13) a nude figure in the border plays a bagpipe.

69. Morand, *Pucelle*, 1962, pp. 11 ff.

70. See the list of mss. owned by Berry, p. 311. He acquired the book between 1380 and 1402.

71. It should be noted that they are lacking in the *Vigils of the Dead* (Fig. 14), as well as in miniatures in the *Heures de Milan*: the *Madonna* (Fig. 50), and the *Adoration of the Child* (Fig. 41). This difference may indicate a somewhat different time of execution, a question already discussed in connection with the *Trinity* (p. 111). Profiled frames simulating stone or wood are common in Flemish mss. from about 1390 to 1420 (Fig. 648).

72. Stange, *Deutsche Malerei*, II, fig. 11.

73. In the Paris section cf. the *Nativity* (Fig. 8), the *Coronation* (Fig. 13), and in the *Heures de Milan* the *Madonna Enthroned* (Fig. 50).

74. See, for example, the juggler on fol. 174 (New York, The Cloisters, *Hours of Jeanne d'Évreux*, 1957, pl.). Similar figures appear on fols. 18, 47v., and in the *Bréviaire de Belleville*, Bibl. nat., lat. 10483, fol. 45v.

75. Florence, Bibl. Laurenziana, Plut. 25.3, fols. 21v., 382 (*ca.* 1300).

76. Bologna, Museo Civico, ms. 85, fol. 1 (Salmi, *Tesori*, 1932, fig. 149).

77. Cf. also one head in the miniature of the *Crucifixion* in Oxford, Bodleian Library, Douce 313 (Meiss, *Gaz. B.-A.*, 1961, fig. 33).

78. Guiffrey, *Inventaires*, II, p. 163, nos. 1311, 1312.

79. *Revue des arts*, 1956, pp. 142 ff.

80. For example, the medallions below the *Stigmatization* in Florence, S. Croce (C. Gnudi, *Giotto*, Milan, 1958, pl. LIII).

81. Robb, 1936, p. 524 n. 158, rightly rejects Labande's identification of this figure as the Christ Child but wrongly suggests it is only a 'decorative adjunct to the architecture'.

82. A chair indicating a room may be seen in a *Visitation* in an initial of 1290 in Baltimore, Walters Art Gallery, ms. 760, fol. 1, Antiphonary of Beaupré [London, Thompson Collection (Thompson), *Illustrations*, VI, 1916, pl. XX].

83. See the polyptych of 1369 by Andrea da Bologna in Fermo (van Marle, *Italian Schools*, IV, fig. 214). Also the initial showing Elizabeth's bed in Copenhagen, Royal Library, Thott 547, fol. 6v. (James and Millar, *Bohun Manuscripts*, 1936, pl. 57).

84. Ed. Ragusa and Green, fig. 16.

85. Cf. the *Heures de Yolande de Flandre* (Cockerell, *Yolande*, 1905, pl. V) and the *Heures de Jeanne de Navarre* (London, Thompson Collection, *Hours of Joan II*, 1899, pl. 19), and still earlier, the *Bréviaire de Belleville*, Bibl. nat., lat. 10484, fol. 290v.

86. Meiss, *Florence and Siena*, 1951, figs. 54-58.

87. *Ibid.*, p. 43.

88. The style of this *Cité de Dieu* may be seen in another ms. of this text, of about 1376, Bibl. nat., fr. 22912-3 and the *Grandes Chroniques*, Bibl. nat., fr. 2813 (Fig. 565).

89. Cambridge, Harvard University, *Exhibition*, 1955, p. 18. See List of Duke's Manuscripts.

90. The mandorla of the *Trinity* has been retouched.

91. Durrieu, *Très Riches Heures*, 1904, pl. XL.

92. The nailing of Christ to a cross laid on the ground, which is represented in the *bas-de-page* below the *Crucifixion* on p. 209 (Fig. 27), will be discussed on p. 180. It too is rather novel and perhaps Italian in origin.

93. *Netherlandish Painting*, 1953, I, p. 46.

94. This observation cannot however be proved by discerning blue angels below the landscape when the folio is held against the light.

95. 'Quando ella parturio
Il gran Figliuol di Dio
Gran luce glie appario
Sopra quel Verbo nato.
Maria s'inginocchiò ne,
E 'l Figliuol adorò ne.
Poi en braccio se 'l recò ne
Stringendolo abbracciato.'
Le poesie spirituali, ed. Venice, 1617, p. 286.

96. Panofsky, *op. cit.*, 1953, I, p. 125, and Meiss, *Florence and Siena*, 1951, p. 149 n. 73. Some earlier Italian Nativities, such as the Lorenzettian one in the Städel Institut in Frankfort (Volpe, 1960, fig. 8) lack only an Infant entirely naked and a cave unencumbered by a shed to conform to the Brigittine vision.

The roof of the shed in the miniature of the *Nativity* (Fig. 8) is intact, whereas in paintings from the later 'eighties on it normally became dilapidated. The state of the roof is thus an indication of date.

97. For example Brit. Mus., Harley 4382, fol. 182v., about 1400. In Tuscany the image served around 1300 as an 'illustration' of St. Bernard on the Passion (Florence, Bibl. Laurenziana, Plut. 25.3, fol. 183v.) – an early example not, we believe, hitherto recorded.

98. Among the panels alone there were Guiffrey, *Inventaires*, I, p. 19 no. 15; p. 23 no. 34; II, p. 117 no. 934.

99. Brit. Mus., Cotton Tiberius B VIII, fols. 59, 64 (J. White, *Space*, 1957, pls. 51, a, c). The image 'invades' the subject of the Trinity, replacing the traditional conception of the Second Person (see the famous tondo of *ca.* 1400 in the Louvre – Fig. 832).

100. Angels rather than the usual Virgin and St. John hold the arms of Christ in the predella of the altarpiece by Tommaso Pisano, Camposanto, Pisa. From such representations were eventually developed the compositions by a follower of Donatello (Victoria and Albert Museum, London) and Castagno (S. Apollonia, Florence).

101. See also the central pinnacle of the altarpiece of the Presentation in the Temple by Jacopino in the Pinacoteca, Bologna.

102. A panel sold by Jean d'Orléans to Philippe le Hardi in 1383 represented 'Nostre Seigneur dedans le sepulcre et l'ange qui le soutenoit'. See Durrieu, 1918–1919, p. 76; Panofsky, 'Imago Pietatis', 1927, p. 278; Mâle, *Fin du moyen âge*, 1908, p. 94 n. 5; G. von der Osten, in *Reallexikon zur deutschen Kunstgeschichte*, s.v. *Engelpietà*.

103. The French type presumably appeared in the predella of the large *Intercessio* of 1402 (?) once in the Cathedral of Florence and now in The Cloisters, New York. See also paintings by the Master of the Bambino Vispo and the workshop of Filippino Lippi (Meiss, 1954, p. 314 and figs.). The Trecento Italian type may, on the other hand, occasionally be found in France in the early 15th century (Bibl. nat., lat. 10528, fol. 20).

104. Meiss, *Andrea Mantegna as Illuminator*, New York and Hamburg, 1957, p. 27.

105. Meiss and Eisler, 1960, p. 235.

106. *Netherlandish Painting*, 1953, I, p. 262.

107. See p. 182.

108. Meiss, *Florence and Siena*, 1951, p. 149.

109. Ed. Ragusa and Green, p. 50.

110. Oxford, Bodleian Library, Douce 313.

111. Joseph holds one of the gifts in Trecento painting (e.g. Bartolo di Fredi, Pinacoteca, Siena). He has a chest for the gifts in later Northern painting (Panofsky, *Netherlandish Painting*, 1953, I, p. 70 n. 3).

112. This action had been introduced by Pucelle (*Heures de Jeanne d'Évreux*), following Italian precedent.

113. Masaccio, *Adoration of the Magi*, Staatl. Museen, Berlin-Dahlem.

114. *Meditations*, ed. Ragusa and Green, p. 51.

115. *Heures de Yolande de Soissons*, New York, Morgan Library, ms. 729, fol. 275v.

116. *Bréviaire de Charles V*, Bibl. nat., lat. 1052, fol. 39v. For the *Bréviaire de Belleville* see Morand, *Pucelle*, 1962, pl. IV b.

117. New York, Morgan Library, ms. 44, fol. 4v.

118. *Meditations, loc. cit.*

119. Also panel in the Vyšši Brod cycle (Matějček and Pešina, *Czech Gothic Painting*, 1950, pl. 9). The kissing of the foot was also represented at this time in Bohemia; see the miniature in the Missal in Prague, Cathedral library, Cim. VI, fol. 32.

120. New York, The Cloisters, *Hours of Jeanne d'Évreux*, 1957, fol. 69 (pl.). This figure persists into the third quarter of the century; see for instance the Missal in Oxford, Bodleian Library, Douce 313, fols. 3v. and 27.

121. Meister Bertram, *Petrialtar*, 1379, Staatl. Kunsthalle, Hamburg (Stange, *Deutsche Malerei*, II, 1936, fig. 167). See also *ibid.*, figs. 160-1, 164, 178, and H. Kehrer, *Die heiligen drei Könige in Literatur und Kunst*, Leipzig, 1909, II, figs. 254, 259 (Lower Rhenish paintings, 1370–1380).

122. For example, Modena, Bibl. Estense, lat. 842 (S. Ludovici, *Le biblioteche dell'Emilia*, Modena, 1959, pl. V).

123. See, however, a drawing on parchment, Styria *ca.* 1325, in the Albertina (Stange, *op. cit.*, I, 1934, fig. 160).

124. Meiss, 1941, p. 74 n. 58. For the identification with Arnau, son of Ferrer Bassa, see Madurell Marimón, 1952, pp. 14-16.

125. Ed. Ragusa and Green, p. 333.

126. *Ibid.*, p. 27.

127. Brit. Mus., Add. 47680, fol. 32; James, 1922–23, pl. xvi. James cites as a textual source the *Dialogues* of Pseudo-Anselm with the Virgin on the Passion.

128. Bibl. nat., lat. 10528, fols. 225v. (*Crucifixion*) and 234v. (*Entombment*). The former has been retouched.

129. See Oberhammer, *Der Altar vom Schloss Tirol*, 1948, p. 59, pl. 52. The nude body had been over-painted at a later period (*ibid.*, figs. 6, 7). De Coo, 1965, p. 165, referred to another instance in an ivory in Darmstadt.

130. Bibl. nat., lat. 757. The ms. was completed before 1395. For a recent notice see Milan, Pal. Reale, *Arte lombarda*, 1959, p. 47. In the *Martyrdom of Catherine* on fol. 362v., the saint is nude.

131. See, for example, the Ducciesque *Madonna* no. 592 in the Pinacoteca, Siena (C. Brandi, *La Regia Pinacoteca di Siena*, Rome, 1933, pl. on p. 175); *La Vierge de Jeanne d'Évreux*, dated 1339, Louvre (Michel, *Histoire de l'art*, ii, p. 2, 1906, pl. xii).

132. J. Rorimer, 1948–1949, p. 221. I am much indebted to Prof. Willibald Sauerländer for pointing out this example.

133. The ms. was in the Dyson-Perrins sale, London, Sotheby, December 1, 1959, lot 67.

134. Fig. 549 is taken from a ms., no. 321 in the *Catalogue of Manuscripts mostly Illuminated. . . . Offered for Sale by J. and J. Leighton*, London, n.d. (*ca.* 1915). The ms. is there classified as 'Anglo-French'. A Metz origin, indicated by the style, is supported by the presence in the Litany of Arnulph and Brice. For another Metz *Madonna of Humility* with a nude Christ see Norden-falk, 1953, fig. 3. The nude Child appeared early in Metz in the Adoration of the Magi also (cf. Bibl. nat., lat. 1403, fol. 51v.).

135. Kraus, *Kunst und Altertum in Elsass-Lothringen*, Strasbourg, iii, 1889, pp. 692–695. The relief was then in Rue St. Gengoulf, and a cast of it in the municipal museum. See also A. Boinet, *Le Vieux Metz*, Paris, 1923, p. 78.

136. Goldschmidt, 'Die Belgische Monumentalplastik des 12. Jahrhunderts', 1923, p. 66 n. 1.

137. Kraus, 1888, p. 78.

138. Matějček and Pešina, *Czech Gothic Painting*, 1950, p. 53.

139. See also the Book of Hours in Modena, Bibl. Estense, R. 7.3, fol. 231.

140. For instance, Giovanni dal Ponte, De Young Museum, San Francisco. See Berti, 1961, p. 87 n. 4.

141. Offner, 'Light on Masaccio's Classicism', 1959, pp. 66 ff., with reference to Dorothy Shorr.

142. *The Nude*, London, 1957, pp. 1 ff.

143. See van Marle, *Italian Schools*, ii, fig. 278.

144. Meiss, *Florence and Siena*, 1951, p. 152.

145. A second *Virgo lactifera* in the *Miracles* may be seen on fol. 84v. See also a crude painting in St. Martin, Laval, reproduced by Lécureux, 1910, p. 236, fig. 18.

146. Panofsky, 'Imago Pietatis', 1927, pp. 292 ff.; Meiss, 1954, pp. 306 ff.

147. Guiffrey, *Inventaires*, i, p. 31 no. 60, p. 292 no. 1111; ii, p. 274 no. 1070. On the general question of Berry's relics and iconography see Chapter iii, p. 39, and Chapter iv.

148. See, however, two *Horae*: Brit. Mus., Add. 15265, fol. 63 (North Italian, 14th century); Milan, Bibl. Trivulziana ms. 445, fol. 108 (Santoro, 1958, pl. 107). The latter, *ca.* 1420, may be French or Lower Rhenish.

149. For the association of the cup with the Marriage at Cana see Ardillots, 1888, col. 572; Prost, 1895, p. 258; Guiffrey, *op. cit.*, i, p. ciii. Mély, 1903, pp. 145 ff., argued rather convincingly against this belief, but the cup cannot, I believe, readily be identified with a chalice of the Last Supper described in the inv. of 1413 (no. 130).

150. Durrieu, *Très Riches Heures*, 1904, pl. lx.

151. The scene at Monreale, known from Gravina's copy, is iconographically almost identical (Demus, *Mosaics of Norman Sicily*, London, 1950, fig. 66a).

152. His technique, different from that of the Parement workshop, deteriorates in a different way. His paint abrades whereas Parement paint scales. The loss of patches of his blue in the arm of Christ at the right in the *Way to Calvary* discloses drawing for folds of a different design than those painted. Loss of some of the blue in the Virgin's mantle in the *Deposition* discloses another blue underneath.

153. Hulin's explicit exclusion of this folio from his stylistic groups (*Heures de Milan*, 1911, pp. 11 ff.) may be explained by the extent of the retouching.

154. A. Friedl, *Magister Theodoricus*, Prague, 1956. Grodecki, *Bull. monumental*, 1957, pp. 207 ff., compared the style of Theodoric with that of the most advanced contemporary painting in France, in the *Bible de Jean de Sy*, begun probably in 1355.

155. Matějček and Pešina, *op. cit.*, pl. 51.

156. *Ibid.*, pls. 4-25.

157. Stange, *Deutsche Malerei*, ii, pls. 1-3.

158. *Grandes Chroniques*, ed. Delachenal, ii, pp. 232 ff. The Emperor, suffering from gout, was borne on a

litter to Ste-Chapelle on Epiphany. In the presence of the French court and the Archbishop three of his knights enacted a sort of Epiphany play, presenting gold, incense, and myrrh, the gifts of the Magi.

159. *Burl. Mag.*, 1956, p. 150 n. 11. See also London, Matthiesen Gallery, *Paintings and Drawings from Christ Church, Oxford*, 1960, no. 21, with reference to Pächt's opinion, and Vienna, Kunsthist. Mus., *Katalog*, 1962, no. 249.

The drawing measures 267 × 160 mm. and bears the number A2 in Christ Church.

160. The *Madonna of Strahov*, for instance, in the National Gallery, Prague, exhibits them, or the angels in the *Madonna of Kladzko*, formerly in the Kaiser-

Friedrich Museum, Berlin, as well as figures in panels by the Master of the Vyšši Brod cycle (Matějček and Pešina, *op. cit.*, pls. 4-25, 27, 28-32).

161. Dufour, *Une famille*, 1877, p. 84.

162. *Ibid.*, p. 151.

163. Champeaux and Gauchery, *Travaux*, 1894, pp. 102 f.

164. *Ibid.*, pp. 102-105. This Jean d'Orléans was still active in 1423.

165. The drawing in Paris, Bibl. de l'Arsenal, ms. 2002 (Paris, Arsenal, Martin and Lauer, 1929, pl. xxxv) ascribed to the Parement Master or a follower by Durrieu (*Rev. de l'art a. et m.*, 1904, pp. 247, 254) is a later and very different work.

NOTES TO CHAPTER VII

1. *Cabinet*, III, 1881, p. 173, item 30. For the item in the inventories see the Catalogue.

2. Mâle, *Fin du moyen âge*, 1908, pp. 259 ff.

3. The twelve apostles are prominent in the *Last Judgment* in the Duke's splendid *Reliquary of the Thorn* in the British Museum (Fig. 571).

4. It is noteworthy that the same concordance is the subject of the late glass installed in the Duke's Ste-Chapelle at Riom by the Duke of Bourbon. See Mâle, *op. cit.*, p. 265.

5. Chaumeau, *Berry*, 1566, p. 229. This writer identifies them as apostles *or* evangelists.

6. Troescher, *Burgundische Plastik*, 1940, II, pl. VI. On the connection of these statues with the Ste-Chapelle see the forthcoming study by Professor Stephen Scher.

7. *Loc. cit.*

8. Panofsky, *Netherlandish Painting*, 1953, I, p. 373 n. 2.

9. Martin, *Miniaturistes*, 1906, p. 61. Troescher, *op. cit.*, p. 38, proposed the collaboration of several assistants.

10. In addition to the remaining folios of the prophets and apostles it appears on fols. 106, 127, 177, 201.

11. Related forms appeared earlier in Bohemian painting, in the *Liber viaticus* of Johann von Neumarkt, fol. 289v.

12. *Le Manuscrit*, 1894, pp. 53 f. His list of prophets was: 7v. Jeremiah; 9v. David; 11v. Isaiah; 13v. Zachariah; 15v. Hosea; 17v. Micah; 19v. Joel; 21v. Zephaniah; 23v. Amos; 25v. Daniel; 27v. Ezekiel; 29v. Malachi. He claimed that three pairs were later exchanged: 17v. and 23v.; 19v. and 21v.; 25v. and 29v.

13. *Fin du moyen âge*, 1908, p. 263. An early example of

the concordance, *ca.* 1300 (*Verger de Soulas*), has the following series of prophets: Jeremiah, David, Isaiah, Daniel, Hosea, Amos, Zephaniah, Joel, Micah, Malachi, Zachariah, Ezekiel (*ibid.*, p. 261).

14. The sequence of prophets in this ms. is: Jeremiah, David, Isaiah, Zachariah, Hosea, Amos, Zephaniah, Joel, Micah, Malachi, Ezekiel, Daniel.

15. Jeremiah, David, Isaiah, Daniel, Hosea, Zephaniah, Micah, Joel, Haggai, Ezekiel, Malachi, Zachariah.

16. See note 12.

17. Leroquais, *Psautiers*, II, 1941, pp. 144 ff. Jeremiah, David, Isaiah, Zachariah, Hosea, Zephaniah, Joel, Malachi, Amos, Daniel, Ezekiel, Micah.

18. 17v. Prophecy: Invocabunt omnes nomen domini et servient ei (Leroquais gives to Zephaniah; Durrieu and Mâle to Micah). Zephaniah III, 9; '. . . invocant omnes in nomine Domini, et serviant ei. . . .'
21v. Prophecy: Accedam contra vos in judicio et ero testis velox (Leroquais gives to Malachi; Mâle and Durrieu to Zephaniah). Malachi III, 5: '. . . Et accedam ad vos in judicio; et ero testis velox maleficis. . . .'
29v. Prophecy: Deponet Dominus omnes iniquitates nostras (Leroquais gives to Micah; Durrieu and Mâle to Malachi). Micah VII, 19: '. . . deponet iniquitates nostras. . . .'

19. Cockerell, *Yolande*, 1905, p. 8, gives the entire text.

20. On fol. 22, opposite 'sophonias', there is a trace of a similar inscription in the same script and ink.

21. For this phase of the Bondol trend see above, p. 23.

22. The basic publication is the excellent article by Müller and Steingräber, 1954. See also Steingräber, *Antique Jewelry*, 1957. These writers maintain the

traditional emphasis upon the production of Burgundy. Actually we do not know where most of the extant objects were made. In this art too Paris was no doubt the great center. The inventories of all the Valois princes contain long lists of *joyaux*, some of them no doubt made by goldsmiths and jewelers attached to the particular courts, but there are records of many artisans in Paris, and even goldsmiths working for one prince might be settled in the capital.

23. *Waning*, 1924 (first published in Dutch 1919), p. 236.

24. Steingräber, *op. cit.*, p. 37.

25. Lasko, 1962, observed that none of the 3906 objects of precious metal in the inventory of Charles V can be identified as enamelled. See also Steingräber, in *Reallexikon zur deutschen Kunstgeschichte*, s.v. *émail*.

26. For a reproduction in color see Milan, Pal. Reale, *Arte lombarda*, 1959, pl. XVI.

27. Visconti di Modrone section, fol. 124v.

28. Only some of the drawings are by Giovannino himself, and many are retouched (see Arslan, 1963, p. 62). Even the drawings on one folio are not always by the same hand. On fol. 4v. the lion at the bottom, freer in draughtsmanship than the other animals, seems to have been added somewhat later. The same might be said of the dog on fol. 2v. The parchment varies in quality and size even within the same gathering. See the facsimile: *Taccuino di disegni. Codice della Biblioteca Civica di Bergamo*, Milan, 1961.

29. Toesca, *Landau-Finaly*, 1951, p. XIII n. 5.

30. Toesca, *Lombardia*, 1912, figs. 234-238.

31. *Ibid.*, fig. 225. Relatively dull also is the *Historia Plantarum* connected with the atelier by Toesca (see Milan, Pal. Reale, *Arte lombarda*, 1959, pl. 44).

32. Gudiol, *Pintura gótica*, p. 105; Domínguez Bordona and Ainaud, *Miniatura*, 1962, p. 182. Thieme-Becker, s.v. 'Martorell'.

33. Domínguez Bordona and Ainaud, *op. cit.*, fig. 222.

34. *Ibid.*, fig. 206.

35. Milan, Pal. Reale, *Arte lombarda*, 1959, pls. 34-39.

36. *Ibid.*, pls. 40, 41.

37. The most firmly dated is also the earliest: the *Horae* of Blanche de Savoie by Giovanni di Benedetto da Como, before 1378 (*ibid.*, p. 47, pls. 28, 29 – Munich, Bayr. Staatsbibl., ms. 23215).

38. Bibl. nat., lat. 757. See *ibid.*, p. 47, pls. 30-33, VIII-XI.

39. *Ibid.*, p. 57, pls. XXII, 65-68.

40. Toesca, *Lombardia*, 1912, pp. 435 f.

41. Meiss, *Arte antica e moderna*, 1961, pp. 125 ff.

42. Graves, *Inventaires Orléans*, 1926, pp. 83 ff.

43. See above, p. 42.

44. Durrieu, [1905]. See the next volume of this publication.

45. Pellegrin, *Bibliothèque des Visconti*, 1955, p. 12.

46. See p. 377 n. 34.

47. Troescher, *Burgundische Plastik*, 1940, p. 30.

48. *Livre de Boucicaut*, ed. Michaud and Poujoulat, p. 255. Whiteness presumably refers to the blamelessness of the good noble ladies that the members of the order obligated themselves to defend. Guillaume de Deguilleville (ed. E. Faral, Paris, 1952) wrote of 'la dame blanche, Virginité'.

49. 1924–1925, p. 268.

50. The document of commission, published by Champeaux and Gauchery, *Travaux*, 1894, p. 93, charges Beauneveu 'a faire faire les tumbes', and refers to the 'ouvriers qui font les tumbes'.

51. For the documents see Troescher, *Burgundische Plastik*, 1940, I, pp. 174 ff.; Pradel, 1951, pp. 273 ff. For the Crucifix in Malines see Roggen, 1936, p. 87. A clarifying review of the documents has been written by Prof. Stephen Scher, in a study that will I hope be published before long.

52. Champeaux and Gauchery, *loc. cit.*

53. Froissart, ed. Lettenhove, XIV, p. 197.

54. Dehaisnes, *Histoire*, 1886, p. 522. Troescher, *op. cit.*, I, p. 178, says the date should be read as 1394. In his study of Beauneveu Prof. Scher demonstrates that Dehaisnes was right. It is not entirely clear that Beauneveu executed the paintings himself.

55. The documents of 1360 at Nieppe (*ibid.*, I, p. 174) do not clearly indicate that the artist was Beauneveu nor that he was doing any painting.

56. Troescher, *op. cit.*, I, p. 47, interpreted the phrase as a reference to authorship, while Martin, *Miniaturistes*, 1906, p. 80, understood ownership.

57. Guiffrey, *Inventaires*, II, p. 119 no. 944. This reference to 'feu maistre Beaunepveu' has been overlooked by those historians who have put the sculptor's death between the two inventories, that is, between 1403 and 1413. This group includes, oddly, Guiffrey himself (*ibid.*, I, p. LXXIV) and Ring, *French Painting*, [1949], p. 244.

58. See above, p. 113.

59. The facial type of a small gilt bronze kneeling prophet in the Louvre is remarkably similar to one of the Bourges prophets (Fig. 593), and the statuette has rightly been loosely connected with Beauneveu (Vienna, Kunsthist. Mus., *Katalog*, 1962, no. 362, pl.

73).The Cleveland Museum of Art has recently acquired a similar, and very beautiful, gilt bronze figure.

60. Aubert, *Sculpture française*, 1946, p. 351, dates them not before 1404, when work on the Ste-Chapelle was pressed forward more rapidly.

61. Troescher, *loc. cit.*, and Bober, 1953, p. 751.

62. In a penetrating study Bober, 1953, pp. 741 ff., rightly rejected the attribution of this head to Jean de Cambrai.

63. I refer the reader to the study by Prof. Stephen Scher mentioned in note 6 of this chapter.

64. Paris, Cabinet des dessins, inv. no. 9832. See Durrieu, *Monuments et mémoires*, 1894, pp. 179 ff.; Lavallée, *Dessin*, 1930, p. 60. The attribution was rejected by [Sterling], *Peintres du moyen âge*, [1941], p. 5. The style of drawing and modelling is connected with the *Parement de Narbonne* in Vienna, Kunsthist. Mus., *Katalog*, 1962, p. 251.

65. The drawing measures 650×327 mm. See Ring, *French Painting*, [1949], p. 192 no. 11.

66. Meiss, *Florence and Siena*, 1951, pp. 43 f.

67. For the early examples of the Virgin kneeling in the Coronation see *ibid.*, p. 149. Formerly the kneeling Virgin in the Coronation was regarded as French in origin (see Durrieu, *Mémoires*, 1911, pp. 381 ff., and Martens, *Meister Francke*, 1929, p. 242 n. 224). In the early 15th century the new form appeared commonly in painting and also in sculpture, especially in the splendid relief at La Ferté-Milon (Aubert, *Sculpture française*, 1946, p. 306). For the appearance of the motive in England at this time see the Lectionary in Brit. Mus., Harley 7026, fol. 4v.

68. *Légende dorée*, Bibl. nat., fr. 242, of about 1402 and the *Boucicaut Hours* a few years later.

69. Meiss, 'Masaccio', 1963, pp. 123 ff.

70. Predella, Stefaneschi Altarpiece, Vatican (Sirén, *Giotto*, 1917, II, pl. 71); Master of the Fogg Pietà, Figline, Collegiata (Offner, *Corpus*, sec. III, vol. VI, 1956, pl. 22).

71. Byzantine, around 1300, Washington, National Gallery (Demus, 1958, pp. 100 ff.). See also Bibl. nat., gr. 54 (Millet, *Recherches*, 1916, fig. 20).

72. See also Ambrogio's frescoed *Madonna* in the Loggia of the Palazzo Pubblico, Siena. The curved throne was not, however, used for the Coronation in the Trecento.

73. Meiss, *Giovanni Bellini's St. Francis in the Frick Collection*, Princeton, 1964, p. 17.

74. See a Tyrolese panel of this date published by G.

Swarzenski, 1944, pp. 41 ff., and the panel by Pedro Nicolau in Cleveland, Museum of Art (Gudiol, *Pintura gótica*, fig. 112). See Denny, 1963, pp. 48 ff.

75. Nuremberg, Germanisches Nationalmuseum, *Die Gemälde des 13. bis 16. Jahrhunderts*, Leipzig, 1937, pl. x.

76. Damage caused by a storm was repaired in that year (Champeaux and Gauchery, *Travaux*, 1894, p. 115). See also Méloizes, *Vitraux de Bourges*, 1891, pp. 21 ff.; Paris, Musée des Arts Décoratifs, *Vitraux de France*, (L. Grodecki), Paris, 1953, p. 76 no. 36; Vienna, Kunsthist. Mus., *Katalog.*, 1962, p. 229. Grodecki gives 1405 as the date *ante quem*.

77. Vienna, Kunsthist. Mus., *Katalog*, 1962, p. 479 no. 534, with bibliography.

78. Prof. Willibald Sauerländer independently observed the resemblances with Beauneveu, and kindly discussed them with me.

79. *Art Bull.*, 1956, pp. 191 ff.

80. See Morand, *Pucelle*, 1962, p. 39.

81. London, Thompson Collection, *Hours of Joan II*, 1899, pl. XIII.

82. *St. Albans Psalter*, fol. 202 (cf. Pächt, Dodwell, and Wormald, *The St. Albans Psalter*, London, 1960, pl. 96).

83. Mid 14th-century German ms. in Lilienfeld, Stiftsbibliothek (Wentzel, 1942, p. 237, fig. 42).

84. See below, p. 314.

85. See Paris, Bibl. nat. (Porcher), 1955, p. 62 no. 128 and Meiss, *Art Bull.*, 1956, p. 191.

86. Meiss, *Giotto and Assisi*, New York, 1960, p. 3.

87. *Idem, Gaz. B.-A.*, 1961, pp. 285 ff.

88. I am grateful to Kathleen Morand for calling this miniature to my attention before I had had the opportunity to see it.

89. Meiss, *loc. cit.*, and Morand, *op. cit.*, p. 29 (though the connection of the miniature with Beauneveu is not correct).

90. See a 13th-century French miniature reproduced in London, Sotheby, sale of February 1, 1960, pl. 15.

91. This figure was copied by the Pseudo-Jacquemart in an initial in a Breviary for St. Ambrose, Bourges (Fig. 607). The paint has flaked off, exposing the drawing. The illumination of this ms., which will be discussed below (p. 320), should be dated 1385–1390.

92. The tree at the left covers part of the capital of the arch.

NOTES TO CHAPTER VIII

1. Some trimming of the ms. is apparent, especially along the side and the bottom, where the ivy leaves sometimes run up to the edge or are cut off.

2. For one of the drawings made for Gaignières while he owned the ms. see Meiss, *Burl. Mag.*, 1963, fig. 2.

3. *Livres d'heures*, 1927, I, pp. 67 ff.

4. See Chapter IV, p. 88, for a discussion of the difficulties of identifying the first group of portraits with Louis I or II of Anjou. The late copy of a portrait of Louis I cited by Delaissé, 1963, n. 28, is scarcely a document to which much significance can be attached.

5. Wormald and Giles, 1964, p. 23.

6. *Op. cit.*, pp. 129-133.

7. Delaissé claims that the portrait on fol. 145v. (Fig. 137) was left unpainted. But if it was intended to represent Berry, why should it have been left incomplete? It would have been, furthermore, the only miniature in this state in the book. Isn't this portrait damaged, accidentally or possibly deliberately? The head of Christ is abraded also.

    Certainly the script and the ink on fol. 97v. are distinctive, as Delaissé observes, but the folio was very probably not added at a significantly later date (see below, p. 163). Other comparable differences of script and ink should be noted: between the instructions for a prince and the Hours of the Virgin. See also the *Grandes Heures*, fols. 18-19.

8. See also fol. 199v. by the Fifth Master. This group includes the portraits cited by Delaissé as portraits of Berry: fols. 97v., 100v., 103v., 196v., 198, 198v., 199v. It is true that the only two portraits by the Pseudo-Jacquemart that show a prince of the Berry type *without* a beard are on fols. 196v., 198, added folios according to Delaissé.

9. Durrieu, *Rev. archéol.*, 1910. For full references to the publications cited in the following paragraphs above see the Catalogue. Since Durrieu dated the *Très Belles Heures de Notre-Dame* in the early 15th century he interpreted the relationship as a dependence of this ms. upon the *Petites Heures*. The text of the *Petites Heures* follows the pattern of the Book of Hours of the Duke's father that likewise had 'enseignemens' after the Calendar (Guiffrey, *Inventaires*, I, p. 257 no. 968).

10. See above, p. 110.

11. Panofsky, *Netherlandish Painting*, 1953, I, pp. 42 ff.; Porcher, *Medieval Miniatures*, [1959], p. 57.

12. *Gaz. B.-A.*, pp. 5 ff.

13. Paris, Bibl. nat., 1955, p. 88 no. 182.

14. *Art Bull.*, 1956, p. 191, and *Gaz. B.-A.*, 1961, p. 284.

15. *Pucelle*, 1962, p. 27.

16. Brit. Mus., Yates Thompson 27. See the facsimile by Cockerell, *Yolande*, 1905.

17. Leroquais, *Bréviaires*, 1934, III, pp. 49 ff. See also the List of the Duke of Berry's Mss. A few miniatures – the *Martyrdom of St. Sebastian* on fol. 321, for example, and also fols. 332, 348v., 350, 391 – are in the Boqueteaux style.

18. The similarity of these two compositions was observed by Panofsky, *op. cit.*, I, p. 44 n. 1.

19. Bibl. nat., lat. 1052, fol. 154; *Petites Heures*, the Virgin in the *Entombment* (Fig. 113).

20. On this ms. see Gagnebin, 1956, pp. 23 ff., and Morand, *op. cit.*, p. 40.

21. For this observation I am indebted to Kathleen Morand.

22. Morand, *op. cit.*, pp. 24 ff.

23. Bibl. nat., fr. 2092, fol. 30.

24. Bibl. nat., fr. 9561, fol. 27. Negroes, of course, may have other connotations. There are Negro saints, such as Maurice (cf. Bibl. nat., lat. 1052, fol. 513). Simone Martini gave him Negroid features in the Chapel of St. Martin in the Lower Church at Assisi.

25. Lehoux, *Jean de Berri*, Chap. I.

26. On the other hand certain figures, such as Malchus, are once again almost identical in the corresponding miniature in the *Heures de Yolande de Flandre*.

27. *Netherlandish Painting*, 1953, I, p. 44. He points out that the covered head is a rare interpretation of Luke XXII, 64. A hood covers the head and part but not all of the face in the comparatively quiet representation of the *Mockery* in an initial of the *Très Belles Heures de Notre-Dame* (Fig. 23). Frequently a cloth binds the eyes of Christ (crucifixes, S. Martino, Pisa, and Uffizi, Florence – E. Sandberg-Vavalà, *La croce dipinta italiana*, Verona, 1929, figs. 209, 210) or a transparent veil covers his head (mid 14th-century triptych, Victoria and Albert Museum, London).

28. E. Gombrich, 'Leonardo's Grotesque Heads. Prolegomena to their Study', in *Leonardo. Saggi e Ricerche*, Rome, 1954, pp. 199 ff.

29. Roger van der Weyden, Uffizi, and Caravaggio, Vatican. See M. A. Graeve, 1958, pp. 225 ff.

30. Delaissé, 1963, pp. 131 f., proposed that the insertion was made at a later date.

31. Pächt, *Burl. Mag.*, 1956, p. 149.

32. See Lavin, 1955, pp. 85 ff., especially p. 85 n. 5, and *idem*, 1961, pp. 319 ff.

33. For instance, the hermits on fols. 113v. and 169v. in Garrett ms. 16 of Princeton University Library, dated 1081 (see J. R. Martin, *Heavenly Ladder*, 1954, fig. 50).

34. 1955, p. 89. Mrs. Lavin refers to French translations of the *Vita* that the illuminator may have known.

35. Probably this fact promoted the usual attribution of this miniature to Jacquemart de Hesdin, recently maintained by Panofsky, *op. cit.*, I, p. 44, and others.

36. Some years ago I ascribed the design of the architecture to Jacquemart alone (*Art Bull.*, 1956, p. 191).

37. As I observed in 1956, *loc. cit.* Panofsky, *loc. cit.*, had already pointed to the *influence* of Pucelle, as did Morand in 1962 (*loc. cit.*). Morand also observed the similarity of Gabriel and St. Michael in the Breviary (Fig. 839).

38. Robb, 1936, fig. 21; Panofsky, *op. cit.*, I, p. 43; Morand, *op. cit.*, 1962, p. 27. Panofsky ascribes the miniature to Jacquemart or his *alter ego*, and believes the motif originated in it.

39. See below, p. 189, and Catalogue of Mss.

40. Brit. Mus., Add. 23145, fol. 44. The pointing gesture has, however, been transferred to the left hand. The *Betrayal* in this manuscript (fol. 162v.) reflects the composition of the Passion Master in the *Petites Heures*.

41. For examples see Panofsky, *loc. cit.*

42. Baltimore, Walters, *International Style*, [1962], p. 46. Dorothy Miner instructively discussed the relationship of the ms. to the *Petites Heures*, and the dependence of the *Annunciation* upon fol. 141v.

43. See for instance, Fra Filippo Lippi, *Adoration of the Child with St. Hilary*, Uffizi.

44. See London, Thompson Collection, *Hours of Joan II*, 1899, pl. XVI.

45. Though reversed, as Morand observed – *op. cit.*, p. 27. The basic ideas for this composition go back, as usual, to the *Heures de Jeanne d'Évreux*.

46. We do not know that the *Breviary* was made for Charles V but it was in his collection in 1380.

47. *Charles V*, 1907, I, pp. 214 ff., 365, 405.

48. Martin, *Miniature française*, 1923, p. 41.

49. *Pucelle*, 1962, p. 28.

50. Delisle, *op. cit.*, p. 214.

51. See p. 300.

52. The Duke possessed a diptych in which the Madonna and the Crucifixion were surrounded by half-length figures of the apostles (Guiffrey, *Inventaires*, I, p. 22 no. 28).

2 C

53. On his scroll is written 'Ecce dies . . . David', perhaps from Jeremiah XXIII, 5.

54. See also the crossed arms in the drawing in Basel, ascribed below to Jean de Beaumetz (Fig. 830).

55. The technique of painting patterns on gold to create drapery, as we see it here, was current in the work of Pucelle as early as the *Bréviaire de Belleville* (Bibl. nat., lat. 10484, fol. 272).

56. This action, which is especially common in the Florentine school in the first half of the Trecento (cf. for instance the Giottesque fresco in the Lower Church in Assisi – van Marle, *Italian Schools*, III, fig. 124), may often be found also in paintings by followers of Pucelle. Cf. the Missal in Lyons, Bibl. municipale, no. 5122. This manuscript is related in other ways also to the *Bréviaire de Charles V*.

57. For these quotations I follow *Meditations*, ed. Ragusa and Green, p. 32.

58. Within the representation of the Nativity, however, I do not recall snow until the second quarter of the 15th century (cf. for instance the *Bedford Hours* in the British Museum, and Baltimore, Walters Art Gallery, ms. 281, by a follower of the Bedford Master).

59. See also a Westphalian panel of *ca.* 1370 (Stange, *Deutsche Malerei*, II, fig. 160).

60. See Panofsky, *op. cit.*, I, p. 278 n. 1.

61. Ed. Ragusa and Green, pp. 32 f.

62. Cf. Panofsky, *op. cit.*, I, pp. 63 n. 3, 95 ff. To the early Northern examples that he cites – the *Très Riches Heures*, the panel formerly in the Deutsches Museum, Berlin, and the shutters in the Mayer van den Bergh Museum, Antwerp, – should be added the *Nativity* in a Book of Hours by a follower of the Boucicaut Master in the Huntington Library, San Marino, HM 1099.

63. Ed. Ragusa and Green, pp. 45-47. 'On the thirteenth day the boy Jesus manifested Himself to the gentiles, that is, to the Magi. . . .' 'On the day of His birth He appeared to the Jews, as personified by the shepherds. . . .' The third King in the miniature is accompanied by a mace-bearer, like the Duke of Berry in the initial on fol. 22. The King is, furthermore, frontal and rather self-important. Is this a reference to a contemporary ruler? The resemblance to Berry is not great; the dress resembles that of Charles V (Fig. 382).

64. For example, fresco by Giotto in the Arena Chapel (van Marle, *Italian Schools*, III, fig. 37).

65. The angel in the border beating a drum is, on the other hand, the work of another collaborator.

66. The *Cité de Dieu* in the Hofer Collection, Harvard

University, is related in style to two exceptionally beautiful copies of this text, Bibl. nat., fr. 22912-3 and Brit. Mus., Add. 15244-5 (see above, p. 141, and Cambridge, Harvard University, *Exhibition*, 1955, p. 18 no. 46). While the *Coronation* was painted by an exceptionally good and advanced painter, I cannot follow Panofsky (*op. cit.*, I, p. 47 n. 4) in discerning the influence of Beauneveu or of Jacquemart.

67. A marked diminution of Christ to represent his ascension may be seen in the *Bible moralisée* by a Neapolitan illuminator of the third quarter of the Trecento that perhaps was acquired by the Anjou before the *Petites Heures* was begun (Figs. 410-412).

68. See the list of illuminators and their works, pp. 354 ff.

69. P. 153.

70. For all these reasons I cannot agree with Pächt (*Burl. Mag.*, 1956, p. 149) that these miniatures in the Hours of the Baptist, though very good, represent a stylistic culmination in the *Petites Heures*, or that they are the most Italianate.

71. Herod (?) brandishing a sword in the margin was painted by Pseudo-Jacquemart.

72. A later example, in the same subject, may be seen in the panel no. 132 in the Pinacoteca, Siena, by Taddeo di Bartolo.

73. Porcher, *Belles Heures*, 1953, pl. LXXVII. See also Focillon, *Le peintre des Miracles Notre-Dame*, 1950, pl. iv.

74. Mâle, *Fin du moyen âge*, 1908, p. 29, and Pächt, 1950, p. 44. The latter referred generally to Italian prototypes.

75. Warner, *Queen Mary's Psalter*, 1912, pl. 257. In Byzantine Psalters the scene may be found as early as the 11th century (Mâle, 1920, p. 134).

76. James, 1922–1923, pl. XIV.

77. See above, p. 27. For a reproduction see Mâle, 1920, p. 89.

78. The earliest dated one is the miniature by Giovanni di Benedetto da Como in Munich (Bayr. Staatsbibl., Cod. 23215 – Cf. Toesca, *Lombardia*, 1912, p. 279, pl. 13). Toesca shows that this ms. must have been made before 1387, and probably *ca.* 1375.

79. See, for instance, the *Flight of Jacob* in the Monreale mosaics or the *Transfiguration* in Florence, Bibl. Laurenziana, Plut. XXV, 3, fol. 371. Italian Trecento examples are so numerous they need scarcely be cited (Master of Codex of St. George; see van Marle, *Italian Schools*, II, fig. 183).

80. See a drawing after Cavallini's fresco in Old St. Paul's, Rome (J. White, 1956, pl. 26c).

81. Vatican, Urb. lat. 603, fol. 127.

82. Cleveland, Museum of Art, *The Gotha Missal*, fol. 16 (New York, Kraus, *Catalogue 100*, pl. 27).

83. In Trecento representations of the *Death of the Virgin* angels sometimes lay their hands on the pillow (see the polyptych by 'Jacopino' in the Pinacoteca, Bologna; van Marle, *Italian Schools*, IV, fig. 212).

84. Koechlin, *Ivoires*, 1924, III, pl. 52; *La collection Spitzer*, 1890–1892, I, pl. 18.

85. Joseph's action was related to the preservation in Aachen of the relic of his stockings (see de Coo, 1965).

86. Panofsky, Netherlandish Painting, 1953, II, fig. 111.

87. Wentzel, 'Jesuskind an der Hand Mariae', 1959, p. 266. Pächt, 1943, p. 53 no. 3, suggest the possibility of the influence of Pucelle on this ms.

88. For example, Crucifix by Coppo di Marcovaldo, Museo Civico, S. Gimignano (E. Sandberg-Vavalà, *La croce dipinta italiana*, Verona, 1929, fig. 479). For the general development cf. G. Swarzenski, 'Italienische Quellen der deutschen Pietà', 1924, pp. 127 ff. For the Byzantine precedents see Weitzmann, 'The Origin of the Threnos', 1961, I, pp. 476 ff.

89. *Op. cit.*, I, p. 44.

90. For this painter, and for the account of the Italian *Vesperbild* that follows above cf. Meiss, 1946, pp. 8-10. Cf. also Swarzenski, *loc. cit.*; H. Kauffmann, *Donatello*, Berlin, 1935, pp. 183-184; Koerte, 1937, pp. 8-18; de Francovich, 1938, pp. 252 ff.; Birkmeyer, 1962, pp. 459 ff. (see especially pp. 461 f. for 'Vesperbild' or *Pietà*); Kalinowski, *Piety*, 1953.

91. Published as Giottesque but under Sienese influence by Swarzenski, *op. cit.*, fig. 5.

92. See the similar type by Lorenzo da Sanseverino, 1400, Pinacoteca, San Severino, and by Simone dei Crocefissi, no. 173, Museo Davia Bargellini, Bologna.

93. Panofsky's term 'pseudo-Vesperbild' (*op. cit.*, p. 262) was partly inspired by his belief that the Italian group was not connected with the Madonna.

94. Pinder, *Deutsche Plastik*, I, 1924, pl. I. The cross, too, sometimes rises behind the Virgin, as in the tympanum of the church of Blaubeuren.

95. *Florence and Siena*, 1951, p. 145.

96. Cf. *ibid.*, fig. 133.

97. The fluent, wavy line of the gilt-edged border of the Madonna's mantle, the delicate limbs and spidery fingers of Christ (though probably not the proportions of his figure, with abnormally short lower limbs) must have been inspired by Simone, and the small roundels with figures of prophets have precedents in the Uffizi *Annunciation*, the Orvieto *Madonna*, and other paintings by Simone or his followers.

98. She appears there already in the late Dugento. Cf. a *Crucifixion* by a follower of Guido da Siena in the Jarves Collection, Yale University (R. Offner, *Italian Primitives at Yale*, New Haven, 1927, fig. 10).

99. Cf. Meiss, *op. cit.*, p. 146.

100. *Crucifixion*, third quarter of the 14th century, formerly in the Deutsches Museum, Berlin (Matějček and Pešina, *Czech Gothic Painting*, 1950, pl. 33).

101. Bibl. nat., lat. 1403. Cf. Leroquais, *Heures*, I, 1927, p. 239.

102. See also the similar form of Lamentation in Bohemian painting (Matějček and Pešina, *Czech Gothic Painting*, 1950, pl. 15).

103. See the Daddesque *Madonna della culla* in Bern, Kunstmuseum (Offner, *Corpus*, sec. III, vol. IV, 1934, add. pl. I), or the French ivory statuette, second half of the 14th century, in the Metropolitan Museum, New York.

104. Nordenfalk, 1953, p. 88.

105. See Chap. VI, p. 126.

106. See Leroquais, *op. cit.*, I, pp. 177 ff., and Panofsky, *Netherlandish Painting*, 1953, I, p. 109.

107. A related group, but with the body of Christ stretched vertically, may be seen in an early Dutch manuscript in Baltimore, Walters Art Gallery, ms. 185, fol. 79v. (Fig. 649).

108. This shadow is not a later addition. The pigments used to define it are employed also for the hair of the angel and in the recesses of the building at the left.

109. It is noteworthy that a partially shaded face was painted by the Passion Master as early as the *Bréviaire de Charles V* (St. Andrew, fol. 285v.).

110. A much more elaborate Throne of Solomon is in the *Miracles de Notre-Dame* by the Pucelle workshop. See Wormald, 'The Throne of Solomon and St. Edward's Chair', 1961, I, pp. 532 ff. and II, p. 176, fig. 4.

111. Meiss, 'The Problem of Francesco Traini', *Art Bull.*, xv, 1933, pp. 168 f. The French type was established by a poem of Baudoin de Condé. The three nobles stand alongside the tombs in the Lombard Book of Hours in Munich (Bayr. Staatsbibl., lat. 23215, fol. 178v.). The *Psalter of Bonne* also contains the deep red and blue grounds with grotesque figures inlaid that appear in the *Petites Heures*.

112. Champeaux and Gauchery, *Travaux*, 1894, p. 35. For this subject see above, p. 20.

113. For the latter two see Morand, *Pucelle*, 1962, pl. XXIII. The *Bréviaire de Belleville* entered the collection of Berry, but only in 1399.

114. See Mâle, *Fin du moyen âge*, 1908, p. 248.

115. 1 Samuel I, 3; II, 12–36; III, 12–13. The story was commonly interpreted in the Middle Ages as an allegory of the eclipse of the Old Testament by the New. See Hugh of St. Victor, *Pat. Lat.*, 175, col. 683. Eli falling over at the news of the victory of the Philitines (1 Samuel IV, 12) is represented sometimes in mss. of the *Cité de Dieu* (Laborde, *Cité de Dieu*, pl. VIIIc).

116. See above, p. 154, and Meiss, *Gaz. B.-A.*, 1961, p. 285.

117. For the prayer in Walters 96 see Baltimore, Walters, *International Style*, [1962], p. 46 (by D. Miner). For the exchanged manuscripts see Chapters III and IX of this volume.

118. The swan floating on water in the border above Christ on fol. 123 is not, like the Duke's emblem, wounded. The borders of this ms. are full of birds.

119. See the list of Berry's mss. This illuminator painted fols. 3v.-16 in Harley 4381 and fols. 150, 172v., 182v., 199 in 4382.

120. See the list of the Duke's mss. The composition of the Trinity on fol. 154 reflects the *Petites Heures*.

121. For this ms. see the Catalogue.

122. Porcher, *Medieval Miniatures*, [1959], p. 60.

123. Panofsky, *Netherlandish Painting*, 1953, I, p. 43.

NOTES TO CHAPTER IX

1. See the Catalogue.

2. *Burl. Mag.*, 1956, pp. 146 ff.

3. Fol. 218. Probably illustrating Nehemiah II, 13.

4. See London, Brit. Mus., *Reproductions*, IV, 1928, p. 13.

5. For the earlier instances in Metz see pp. 126, 186.

6. For a discussion of this ms., Brit. Mus., Yates Thompson 37, see below, p. 276. It is noteworthy that Vat. lat. 50, fol. 1, shows two acanthus leaves of the Trecento Italian type.

7. *Bulletin SFRMP*, I, 1911, p. 87 no. III.

8. Müntz and Fabre, *Bibliothèque du Vatican*, 1887, pp. 48 f. In 1441 Eugenius IV brought some manuscripts from the library at Avignon to Rome.

9. Guiffrey, *Inventaires*, II, p. 121, no. 949. For another gift see *ibid.*, p. 36 no. 222. Items *ibid.*, p. 119 no. 945 and p. 140 no. 1102 had formerly belonged to the Pope.

10. *Ibid.*, p. 122 no. 951. The Duke recovered the Bible after the assassination of Louis (*ibid.*, I, no. 958).

11. *Ibid.*, II, p. 94 no. 717; p. 148 nos. 1199, 1200; p. 149 nos. 1210, 1211.

12. *Ibid.*, I, p. 126 no. 418; p. 269 no. 1003; p. 312 no. 1167; p. 334 no. 1243; II, p. 176 no. 173.

13. William Heckscher has kindly called my attention to a passage in Alanus ab Insulis, *Distinctiones Dictionum*, s.v. 'Canis' (ed. Migne, *Pat. Lat.*, CCX, cols. 728 f.): '*Canis*, proprie, dicitur praedicator vel bonus praelatus. Canis insignes habet proprietates . . . est animal exhibens homini familiaritatem, domini custodiens aedem, furem arcens, latrans contra lupum venientem, fugans latronem, linguam medicinalem habens: secundum has proprietates signat bonum pastorem qui tenetur subditis exhibere compassionis familiaritatem, judicare subditorum infirmitatem, congaudere sanis, compati aegris, regere viantes (?), corrigere deviantes. . . .'

14. Guiffrey, *Inventaires*, I, p. 96 no. 324.

15. The brooch was described as 'French-Burgundian, *ca.* 1400' by Müller and Steingräber, 1954, p. 76 no. 27.

16. See *The Elder Pliny's Chapters on the History of Art*, ed. K. Jex-Blake and E. Sellers, London, 1896, pp. 121 f. For the competition of Clement VII see E. Plon, *Benvenuto Cellini*, Paris, 1883, pp. 143-146.

17. P. M. J. B. Champion, *Vie de Charles d'Orléans*, Paris, 1911, pp. 653 f. Charles' line was: 'Je meurs de soif auprès de la fontaine'.

18. Full references to the numerous publications cited in the paragraphs that follow will be found in the entry for the *Brussels Hours* in the Catalogue.

19. See above, p. 48.

20. The *Fleur des histoires*, now Bibl. nat., fr. 12201, contains beautiful and advanced miniatures by the workshop of the Master of the Coronation and related but weaker illuminators (Fig. 438). The famous *Merveilles du monde*, Bibl. nat., fr. 2810, was illuminated in the workshop of the Boucicaut Master.

20a. The *Brussels Hours* is not the only ms. that disappeared from the Burgundian library. For a *Miroir historiale* that once belonged to Jean sans Peur and Philippe le Bon see London, Thompson Coll., *Illustrations*, 1914, no. 79.

21. *Netherlandish Painting*, 1953, I, pp. 42 f.

22. *Belles Heures*, 1953, p. 11.

23. 1960, p. 239.

24. Brussels, Gaspar and Lyna, I, 1937, pp. 403, 421.

25. *Belles Heures*, 1953, pp. 7 n. 10, 25 f. The three binding instances of dependence upon the *Belles Heures* cited by Porcher seem to me the *Baptism*, *St. Martin and the beggar*, and *Martyrdom of St. Bartholomew*.

26. Meiss, *Art Bull.*, 1956, p. 195.

27. See, for instance, the catalogues of the Paris exhibition of 1955 and of the Vienna exhibition of 1962, both cited below in the bibliography for this ms. in the Catalogue.

28. Panofsky (*Netherlandish Painting*, 1953, I, p. 47 n. 1) cited two 15th-century Netherlandish panels in which small miniatures on vellum hang on the wall. To this evidence I would add an earlier record of a commission given to an illuminator, Hennequin de Virelay, to paint 'un grand tableau d'enluminure' representing the Crucifixion, around which were inscribed moral injunctions on the duties of magistrates, and which was put up in the hall of Parliament (Champeaux and Gauchery, *Travaux*, 1894, p. 206). Delaissé, *Medieval Illuminations*, 1958, p. 42, suggested that the Virgin on the Moon as well as the diptych in the *Brussels Hours* may have been independent, framed miniatures.

29. Similar tendencies can be observed around this time in Lombardy. See Milan, Bibl. Ambrosiana, E 24 inf., illuminated by Pietro da Pavia in 1389.

30. Panofsky, *op. cit.*, I, p. 48 n. 1, suggests that the use of this outmoded perspective is to be explained by the dependence of the Brussels *Madonna* upon an earlier image.

31. Catherine of Valois died in 1346. The ms., the present whereabouts of which is not known to me, was sold in London by Sotheby, June 7, 1932, lot 2. Panofsky (*op. cit.*, I, p. 47) erroneously claimed that uniformity of scale was introduced for the first time in the *Brussels Hours* diptych.

32. It is therefore doubtful that we can judge, as Porcher (1953, p. 122) has done, that the outward turn of the eye in the Brussels miniature is 'less natural' than the glance in Bibl. nat., fr. 926, which is directed at the donor, and that therefore the latter is earlier (Fig. 667).

33. *Op. cit.*, I, p. 47. I should add that the text written on the pages of the book which lies open before the Duke is exactly that of the beginning of Matins of the Hours of the Virgin on p. 19 of the ms.

34. Cf. Parkhurst, 1941, pp. 292 ff.; Panofsky, *op. cit.*, I, p. 48; and Squilbeck, 1950, pp. 127 ff. While Parkhurst and Panofsky believed that the Brussels *Madonna* was the earliest example of the subject, Squilbeck found it in simpler form in sculptures datable before 1380. See the additional evidence for an earlier origin given in the text below.

35. 1953, pp. 121-123. In 1959 he attributed this *Madonna* to Paul de Limbourg (*Enluminure française*, p. 59).

36. Meiss, *Art Bull.*, 1956, p. 193.

37. The folio of the Madonna was attached to a ms. of *Levador del plat de pobres vergonyants*, of the early 14th century. See Ainaud and Gudio-Verrié, *La ciudad Barcelona*, Madrid, 1947, p. 131, fig. 760, and K. G. Boon, *Maandblad voor beeldende Kunsten*, XXVI, 1950, p. 267. A mediocre Swabian drawing that copies the same lost model is in the library of St. Gall (Stange, *Deutsche Malerei*, II, fig. 257).

38. See the *Bible moralisée*, Bibl. nat., fr. 166, and the saints in the *Boucicaut Hours* in Paris, Musée Jacquemart-André.

39. This *Madonna* has almost always been attributed to the Limbourgs themselves. It will be discussed in volume V of this publication.

40. 'Item due tabulle de brodeatura, in quarum una est ymago beate Marie cum filio in brachiis, in altera vero ymagines beati Johannis Baptiste, et sancti Andree, et in medio dictarum duarum ymaginum dux Byturie.' (Fabré, *Trésor*, 1875, p. 60. Fabré takes the Duke to be Charles de Berry, †1472.)

41. See catalogue of portraits, p. 83.

42. The style of this assistant is not unrelated to that of Pseudo-Jacquemart.

43. Because of the lance Méloizes suggested St. Thomas, but Simon too sometimes carries this weapon (Doyé, *Heilige und Selige*, Leipzig, [1930], II, pp. 339 ff.).

44. 'D'azur à trois cigognes d'argent membrés de gueules 2.1.' Cf. Thaumas de la Thaumassière, *Berry*, I, p. 226.

45. The earliest document for the Alegret Chapel is a bull of Pope John XXIII of September 12 (not 17, as given by Méloizes, *Vitraux de Bourges*, 1891, p. 9), 1412, that permits the physician to increase the fund for chaplaincies he had established in the Cathedral. Inasmuch as this document has not, to my knowledge, been published an extract is given here: '. . . quandam capellam de bonis tunc ad eum ratione persone sue spectantibus de novo canonice fundavit et libros necnon aliis paramentis ecclesiasticis ad eundem divinum cultum in prefata capella necessariis congrue adornavit pariter et fulcivit. . . .' (Archives départementales du Cher, 8 G 54 – original). I am indebted for this extract to the great kindness of M. Paul Cravayat, formerly archiviste-en-chef, Bourges. Simon Alegret died at Rouen, September 18, 1415 (Wylie, *Henry the Fifth*, II, 1919, p. 302 n. 3).

46. The intervening pages 12 and 13 are blank. Folios 14, 18, 54, 118, 130, 164, 182, 186, 194, and 198, all containing full-page miniatures, have blank versos.

47. The page opposite it is blank, but all the other pages opposite miniatures contain the beginning of an office.

48. Ghiberti, *Denkwürdigkeiten*, ed. von Schlosser, p. 38.

49. For the cloth and the angels in Siena see Bartolommeo Bulgarini (?), S. Pietro a Ovile, Siena (van Marle, *Italian Schools*, II, fig. 219); Lippo Vanni, SS. Domenico e Sisto, Rome (*ibid.*, fig. 299).

50. The planes of the throne are clearer in the drawing for it, which can still be seen.

51. Van Marle, *ibid.*, fig. 277.

52. Meiss, *Florence and Siena*, 1951, pp. 114 f., fig. 169.

53. For angels on the floor below the throne of the *Coronation* see *ibid.*, fig. 58, and on the throne itself see van Marle, *op. cit.*, IV, fig. 30.

54. Cf., for instance, the frescoes in the Rinuccini Chapel of S. Croce, Florence, by Giovanni da Milano (van Marle, *ibid.*, fig. 111).

55. For the relation of Douce 313 to Italy see above, pp. 20, 106, and Meiss, *Gaz. B.-A.*, 1961, pp. 286 ff. For the kneeling Virgin in the North a few years later see Bibl. nat., lat. 1403, fol. 15 (Metz), and Meister Bertram and his circle (Stange, *Deutsche Malerei*, II, figs. 167, 176, 184).

56. Panofsky, *Netherlandish Painting*, 1953, I, p. 48 n. 5, pointed out also that in previous representations in the North Gabriel had not worn a dalmatic and stole, which, on the other hand, were conventional in Italy.

57. See Fig. 687. Also Meiss, 1941, pp. 55 f., and figs. 11–13. The fresco in Paganico attributed to a follower of Bartolo de Fredi now seems to me by a follower of Ambrogio himself. Cleaning has uncovered the date, 1368.

58. Gabriel folds his arms also in Simone's *Annunciation* in Antwerp, which was part of the complex that Jacquemart seems to have known (Fig. 693).

59. In an *Annunciation* by a follower of Tommaso da Modena in S. Niccolò, Treviso, the angel swoops down through a window (Coletti, 1924–25, fig. 2). There are Byzantine precedents for the flying Gabriel (see the *Homilies of the Monk Jacobus*), and occasionally exigencies of space, as in Taddeo Gaddi's fresco, lead painters to introduce the type. See the 13th-century Tuscan triptych now in the Art Museum, Princeton University (Garrison, *Index*, 1949, p. 300), and the painting in the Emmaus Cloister, Prague, *ca.* 1355 (A. Andersson, 1947, fig. 11).

60. Cf. Panofsky, *op. cit.*, I, pp. 131 f.

61. The pier at the left, in the picture plane at its base and some distance behind it above, is confusing.

62. In Italian representations of the Presentation, and in earlier French representations, the Child is normally

dressed. The miniature in the *Brussels Hours* conforms with the trend towards nudity that has been discussed above (p. 125).

63. In addition to Deodato's panel here reproduced see Pacino di Bonaguida, University of Arizona, Tucson (Offner, *Corpus*, VI, 1956, pl. XLIII).

64. *Meditations*, ed. Ragusa and Green, p. 21 and fig. 15. In the illustration of Bibl. nat., ital. 115 published in that volume Joseph carries a bag on the stick held across his shoulder, much like the scarlet cloth in the miniature.

65. See above, p. 28.

66. Cf. Panofsky, *op. cit.*, I, p. 48 n. 4. The two miniatures cited by Panofsky that follow the rather anomalous Brussels *Nativity* (Baltimore, Walters Art Gallery, ms. 231, fol. 46, and New York, Morgan Library, ms. 743, fol. 58v.) were both painted by illuminators influenced by Jacquemart.

67. See especially the first volume of the *Bréviaire de Belleville*, and Panofsky, *op. cit.*, I, p. 33.

68. But see the *Transfiguration* by Niccolò da Bologna in Munich [Munich, Bayr. Staatsbibl. (Leidinger), 1912, pl. 27].

69. Cf. Meiss, *Florence and Siena*, 1951, pp. 43 f. The composition appeared somewhat later in Lombardy also (cf. Bibl. nat., lat. 757, fol. 245v.).

70. See p. 149.

71. See below, p. 366 n. 126.

72. Recently, for instance, by Panofsky, *op. cit.*, I, p. 48, and by Pächt, *Rev. des arts*, 1956, pp. 149 ff.

73. The predella of the altarpiece in the Museo at Borgo Sansepolcro sometimes ascribed to Niccolo di Segna might also be mentioned.

74. Ambrogio, *Crucifixion*, Fogg Museum, Cambridge (Mass.); Simone, *Crucifixion*, Antwerp (Fig. 674). A more formal fall occurs in the Cavallinesque *Crucifixion* in S. M. di Donna Regina, Naples. In France the Virgin had already been represented *seated* on the ground in the *Heures de Yolande de Flandre* (Fig. 365). The group of St. John supporting the fainting Virgin is rare in Tuscany and more often represented in late 14th-century Bolognese and German painting. For German examples see Stange, *Deutsche Malerei*, II, figs. 64, 100.

75. See also the *Crucifixion* in the predella mentioned in n. 73 in the Museo at Borgo Sansepolcro.

76. For Duccio's *Deposition* see van Marle, *op. cit.*, II, fig. 30.

77. See also Niccolo di Tommaso, Philadelphia, Museum of Art (Johnson Collection).

78. The tunic lies on the floor also in a *Flagellation* represented on a French enamel of around 1425 (Vienna, Kunsthist. Mus., *Katalog*, 1962, pl. 35).

79. Ed. Ragusa and Green, pp. 328-331.

80. Lippo Vanni, fresco dated 1363 in the Palazzo Pubblico, Siena (van Marle, II, fig. 303).

81. See also Bibl. nat., fr. 159, fols. 48 and 397, and Porcher, *Belles Heures*, 1953, pls. CXVII and CXXXV.

82. The little figures of the shepherds in the *Brussels Hours*, standing on a plane just above the shed, may have suggested to Hieronymus Bosch, a known admirer of the art of this time, the placing of the shepherds on the roof of his Prado *Adoration of the Magi*.

83. See above, p. 29, and Meiss, *Rev. des arts*, 1956, pp. 142 ff.

84. Rowley, *Ambrogio Lorenzetti*, 1958, II, pl. 92. The *View of a Town* in the Pinacoteca, Siena, also has a large body of water (*ibid.*, pl. 94). Rowley's attribution of this panel and its companion (Fig. 684) to a 15th-century painter seems to me untenable.

85. For example, Gentile's *Flight into Egypt* in the Uffizi.

86. For this aspect of the development of landscape see Meiss, *Gaz. B.-A.*, 1961, pp. 281 ff.

87. Brandi, *La Regia Pinacoteca di Siena*, Rome, 1933, p. 128. I have been able to study the two landscapes only through the glass that covers them, but I have seen traces of bole and gold along the upper and lower edges of the *City* and along the lower edge of the *Country* – observations kindly confirmed by Elizabeth H. Jones. She believes that a 'beard' is visible also at certain points along the lower edge of both panels. Neither bole nor beard appears along the sides of either panel, and they may therefore have been cut from a strip. All this, however, needs to be confirmed in the laboratory. The small brown and black boats in the *City* have been repainted or added, and likewise the small nude boy in the lower right corner.

88. Brit. Mus., Yates Thompson 37. See below, p. 275.

89. Ambrogio did, however, represent Winter in the Palazzo Pubblico, Siena, as a bust of a man in a heavy snowstorm, holding a snowball (Rowley, *op. cit.*, II, pl. 190).

90. Panofsky, *op. cit.*, I, p. 49. We hear, however, of climatic variations in Trecento painting. Ghiberti described lightning, thunder, hail, and high winds in a fresco by Ambrogio Lorenzetti (Ghiberti, *Denkwürdigkeiten*, ed. von Schlosser, 1912, p. 41).

91. Actually the left and rear walls were painted the same violet and then differentiated by parallel strokes of darker purple.

92. 1963, pp. 124-129. He rightly pointed to Italian pen-work in this and other mss. made for the Duke, but his suggestion that an Italian painter had a share in the main miniatures is untenable.

93. As Pächt, *Rev. des arts*, 1956, has maintained.

94. Around this time Alcherius described several reds used by Parisian and Italian illuminators (Merrifield, *Treatises*, 1849, I, pp. 144, 310 ff.).

95. Cf. Durrieu, *Très Belles Heures de Notre-Dame*, 1922, p. 63; Panofsky, *op. cit.*, I, p. 42 n. 2.

96. Bibl. nat., Mélanges Clairambault, XVI, p. 502. See Delisle, *Cabinet*, I, 1868, p. 62; Champeaux and Gauchery, *Travaux*, 1894, p. 119.

97. This reading seems clear, but Delisle, *loc. cit.*, gave simply 'pour don' and Champeaux and Gauchery, *loc. cit.*, 'pour entier don'.

98. '1399. A Estienne Turpin, chevaucher de mondit seigneur, pour ses fraiz et despens en allant de Paris à Bourges porter lettres de mendit seigneur, à Jacquemart de Hodun et à maistre Dreux de Dampmartin, le Xe jour davril lan mil CCCIIII^{xx} et dix-neuf devant Pasques. IIII l. (Arch. nat., Comptes de l'hôtel, K. K. 254)' (Champeaux and Gauchery, *op. cit.*, p. 119). I have not been able to verify this record. The precise reference to it given by Guiffrey (*Inventaires*, I, p. LXXVI n. 2) – to K. K. 253, fol. 78v. – is incorrect.

99. In 1398–1399 Jean Malouel received some 'papier de Lombardie, de la grant fourme pour pourtraire et faire patrons sur ycellui' (Monget, *Chartreuse de Dijon*, I, 1898, p. 313). In 1396 the same painter's designs for textiles for the Queen were called *patrons* (Gorissen, 1954, p. 197 n. 40). See also Scheller, *Model Books*, 1963, pp. 34 f. For the Flemish *patroen* see Panofsky, *Netherlandish Painting*, 1953, I, p. 291 n. 4.

100. P. Guérin, *Archives historiques du Poitou*, XXIV, 1893, pp. 299-301.

101. Several historians refer tentatively to an unpublished document in the Bibliothèque nationale (not further specified) that is alleged to contain an Aragonese commission to Jacquemart de Hesdin for a painting of St. Martin (C. R. Post, *A History of Spanish Painting*, Cambridge [Mass.], VI, 1935, p. 5; J. de Lozoya, *Historia del arte hispánico*, Barcelona, III, 1940, p. 256; [Sterling], *Peintres du moyen âge*, [1941], p. 80). A document of 1440 published by Caldes (*Revista de ciencias históricas*, 1887, p. 47) refers to the son of a painter named only Jacomart so that the inference of Caldes and later writers that Jacquemart de Hesdin is involved seems unwarranted.

102. Durrieu, *loc. cit.*

103. See p. 256.

104. See p. 8.

105. Champeaux and Gauchery, *Travaux*, 1894, pp. 137 f.

106. See the list of Berry's mss. The earlier version of this style is visible in the *Comedies* of Terence the Duke received for New Year, 1408 (Bibl. nat., lat. 7907A).

107. See p. 300.

NOTES TO CHAPTER X

1. Pächt, *Mary of Burgundy*, [1948], p. 52 n. 19, and *idem*, *Burl. Mag.*, 1956, p. 115 n. 24. Meiss, quoted by Panofsky, *Syllabus of Gothic and Late Medieval Illuminated Manuscripts*, New York University, 1935, p. 74; *idem*, *Art Bull.*, 1956, pp. 193 f.; *idem*, *Gaz. B.-A.*, 1963, p. 159 and n. 36. See the instructive article on the *Heures de Charles le Noble*, now in the Cleveland Museum, by Wixom, 1965, p. 82 n. 14. He wrongly, in my opinion, states that our illuminator worked on several folios of the *Très Riches Heures*. Apart from the Limbourg brothers the chief contribution to the early campaign on this ms. was made, as I proposed earlier (*Art Bull.*, 1956, p. 195), by the workshop of the Master of the Bréviaire de Jean sans Peur. This workshop painted the initials on fols. 44, 45, 46v., 49, 161, 166v., 168, 173, 193v., 194, 195v.

2. To cite only a few instances: Porcher, *Medieval Miniatures*, [1959], p. 58; Schilling, 1957, p. 79 n. 25; Paolini, 1962, p. 36. Wixom, *op. cit.*, pp. 50 ff., as 'Zebo'.

The magnetism of a name is so great that, though I characterized Pächt's proposal as 'very questionable' in 1956, the identification of Zebo was considered established in the very summary of my paper in *Répertoire d'art et d'archéologie*, 1956, published in 1960, p. 219 no. 5858.

3. Malaguzzi Valeri, 1896, pp. 242 ff. Pächt did not refer to a specific place in this publication.

Pächt, *Burl. Mag.*, 1956, p. 115 n. 24, said that the inscription was read as 'Zebo da Firenze' by Porcher, *Manuscrits et livres précieux retrouvés en Allemagne*, Paris [1949], no. 2 – a publication I have not seen.

4. Malaguzzi Valeri, 1896, p. 271.

5. *Ibid.*, p. 291. In publications limited to the 14th century no Zanobi (and of course no Zebo) appears at all. See R. Baldani, 'La pittura a Bologna nel secolo XIV', *Documenti e studi della R. Deputazione di Storia Patria per le Provincie di Romagna*, III, 1909, pp. 373 ff., and F. Filippini and G. Zucchini, *Miniatori e pittori a Bologna, documenti dei secoli XIII e XIV*, Florence, 1947.

6. M. L. d'Ancona, *Miniature e miniatori a Firenze dal secolo XIV al secolo XVI*, Florence, 1962.

7. Prof. Procacci has records only of Zanobi di Giovanni, dipintore, 1346; Zanobi di Filippo, dipintore, 1433; Zanobi di Meriano, miniatore, 1489–1493.

8. I have been given the firmest assurances on this point by Professors Ugo Procacci and Bruno Migliorini, both authorities in such questions. I am grateful to them, and to Professor Procacci for counsel on other aspects of this problem. Pächt gave no reason for his equation of Zebo with Zanobi.

9. Professors Ugo Procacci and Gino Corti both read the word this way.

10. D'Ancona, *op. cit.*

11. oĩ, the bar usually indicating *un*.

12. Admittedly the important *a* in *asino* is lacking. I am indebted to Professor Procacci for this tentative proposal. Perhaps consistent with this jocular interpretation is the fact that the inscription appears on the folio facing the Office of the Dead.

13. For illegible script see pp. 93, 193 of the ms. For monsters in this ms. who read music see now Winternitz, 1965, figs. 69–71. Satire of this kind is frequent in many of the mss. of the workshop. Monsters hold books, for instance, in Brit. Mus., Add. 29433, fols. 14, 18v., 20v., 26, 42, 84, 93, 95v., 108, 113v., 119v., 124, 148, 150v., 168v., 180v., 200.

14. 'ENTOROIS' (?) on fol. 57v., of Brit. Mus., Add. 29433.

15. See above, p. 66, for the doubtful hypothesis of his identity with Pietro da Verona.

16. The arms in the ms. now in Cleveland were identified as those of Charles le Noble by Léopold Delisle, who had written a note in the ms., which I saw for the first time in 1936. I gratefully acknowledge the assistance of M. Pecqueur, Chef du Service Héraldique at the Institut de Recherche et d'Histoire des Textes, Paris, in the attempt to identify the arms in the other mss. Her partial success with the ms. in Madrid is reported in the entry in the Catalogue.

17. The coat of arms on this folio, like all others in the ms., was rather carelessly added, covering the border or even the miniature (fol. 117). Some parts of the litanies were deleted by pasting in line endings. Perhaps these alterations were made when the shields were added. The Calendar is North French.

18. In the *Coronation*, for instance, the Virgin, wearing a crown, is simply seated alongside Christ.

19. See p. 189.

20. Webster, *Labors*, 1938, p. 149.

21. Pruning is the usual subject of this month in France. For a careful review of Calendar illustration with regard to the *Très Riches Heures* see the M.A. dissertation of Alexander Sharp, Institute of Fine Arts, New York University, 1964.

22. For the bath in the Nativity as well as the Book of Hours in Barcelona dated 1401 see p. 18.

23. For the 14th century the Index of Christian Art lists only the following, all non-Italian (except the Veronese altarpiece mentioned below): Gospels of John of Troppau, 1368 (Vienna, Nationalbibl., ms. 1182); window, 13th–14th century, Munich, Bayr. Nat. Mus. (*Meisterwerke*, 1955, fig. 21); Psalter of Humphrey of Bohun, second half 14th century (Oxford, Exeter College Library, ms. 47).

24. It serves the same purpose in Bibl. nat., lat. 924, fol. 19 (Mâle, *Fin du moyen âge*, 1908, fig. 108), a ms. of about the same time, Italianate and perhaps connected with the work of the Brussels Initials Master. See also in this ms. Matthew's angel (fol. 21) and Mark's lion (fol. 24).

25. See the Giottesque *Madonna* in the Stefaneschi altarpiece in Rome, Pinacoteca Vaticana (van Marle, *Italian Schools*, III, fig. 116) and the Byzantine *Madonna* in the National Gallery, Washington (van Marle, *op. cit.*, I, fig. 292).

26. Verdier, 1961; Vayer, 1963; Pächt, *Gaz. B.-A.*, 1963, pp. 113 ff. (with a reference of 1384–1385 to a lost representation of the subject in an Arras tapestry – see p. 121 n. 11); J. Bolten in *Reallexikon zur deutschen Kunstgeschichte*, I, 1937, s.v. 'Augustus'. See also Mâle, *Fin du moyen âge*, 1908, pp. 255 ff., and H. Aurenhammer, in *Lexikon der christlichen Ikonographie*, Vienna, 1962, p. 273.

27. See J. C. Broussolle, *Le Christ de la Légende dorée*, Paris, [1904], pp. 14 ff. Fig. 12 reproduces a crude representation, apparently of the 14th century, in Bibl. nat., fr. 400.

28. *Legenda Aurea*, ed. Graesse, p. 44.

29. Lutz and Perdrizet, *Speculum*, 1907–1909, pp. 193 ff., pl. 16; James and Berenson, *Speculum*, 1926, chap. VIII.

30. Only recently P. Cellini (1962, pp. 180 ff.) published

good photographs of these reliefs. This article was kindly called to my attention by Ronald Malmstrom. The outline of the Virgin at the lower left is curved in an 18th-century engraving, and she appears to be seated (F. Casimiro Romano, *Memorie storiche della chiesa . . . di S. Maria in Araceli di Roma*, Rome, 1736).

31. Bibl. Estense, lat. 461, fol. 92v.

32. F. Hermanin, *L'arte in Roma dal secolo VIII al secolo XIV*, Bologna, 1945, p. 312, mistakenly says the painting was not in the apse.

33. 1962, p. 195.

34. *Vite*, ed. Milanesi, I, p. 539.

35. 1963, pp. 46-48 and fig. 2. The Stuttgart panel includes also miracles contemporary with the vision that are described in the *Golden Legend*: the fountain gushing oil and the collapse of the Temple of Peace. For the inscriptions and a *catena* of opinions about the author of the panel see Vienna, Kunsthist. Mus., *Katalog*, 1962, no. 96.

36. Meiss, *Florence and Siena*, 1951, pp. 132 ff. The Madonna is of the 'Humility type' also in the representation of the vision in the fresco below Raphael's *Disputà*.

37. For example Munich, Bayr. Staatsbibl., Clm. 146, fol. 11 (Lutz and Perdrizet, *op. cit.*, pl. 16). There are Northern representations of the standing Madonna also, such as a late 14th-century triptych in the church at Doberan and a drawing of *ca.* 1410 (not 1400) in the Städel Institut in Frankfurt (Bolten, *op. cit.*, p. 1271, fig. 2). See also the mural painting of the Emmaus church, Prague (Dvořáková et al., *Gothic Mural Painting in Bohemia*, 1964, pp. 72 ff.).

38. Pächt, *Gaz. B.-A.*, pp. 113 ff.

39. James and Berenson, *loc. cit.*

40. Rome, Bibl. Vaticana, lat. 2639, fol. 2v. I owe knowledge of this folio to the kindness of Professor Anthony Melnikas, who will publish the ms. The half-length Virgin as the Ara Coeli occurs also in Princeton University, Kane ms. 44, Lombard, 1433.

41. In this respect also the Venetian panel would not seem to reflect Cavallini's mural.

42. Verdier, 1961, figs. 5, 9.

43. The question of the date of the illumination of this ms. will be discussed in *Paris, 1400-1420*.

44. This transposition had already occurred in the fresco of the third quarter of the 14th century illustrating the *Speculum* in the Emmauskloster in Prague. The half-length Virgin on the moon appeared not infrequently in the 14th century, especially in German art (for instance, Köln, Clarenaltar, cf. Reiners, *Kölner*

Malerschule, 1925, fig. 10) and in France *ca.* 1407 in the *Boucicaut Hours*.

45. See below, p. 294.

46. Guiffrey, *Inventaires*, II, pp. 309 f.

47. Porcher, *op. cit.*, 1953, pp. 18, 39; Verdier, 1961, p. 14; Pächt, *loc. cit.* Verdier cites a Madonna on the sun in a reliquary that Louis d'Orléans possessed in 1403.

48. These resemblances are more significant because of the variety of possible postures for the Emperor and the Sibyl. In a representation, for example, in the church of the Confraternità della Madonna in Siena Augustus raises both hands. Sometimes he is seated (Fig. 816).

49. See above, p. 54. Also Guiffrey, *op. cit.*, I, p. 71 no. 198.

50. *Meditationes Vitae Christi in Sanctae Bonaventurae Opera Omnia*, Venice, XIII, 1756, p. 391.

51. Other examples of Joseph seated on the saddle are Barnaba da Modena, Brera, Milan; Marchigian panel of the second quarter of the 15th century, Pinacoteca Vaticana, no. 242 (Anderson photo 24012); Uccellesque *Adoration of the Magi* in S. Bartolommeo a Quarata (J. Pope-Hennessy, *Paolo Uccello*, London, 1950, pl. 77).

52. For the influence of the vision of St. Bridget on Italian and Netherlandish painting see Panofsky, *Netherlandish Painting*, 1953, I, p. 126. A *Nativity* by Niccolo di Tommaso in the Philadelphia Museum shows a candle on a ledge of the cave (R. Offner, *Studies in Florentine Painting*, New York, 1927, fig. 9).

53. The presence of the figure in this ms. was noted by Pächt, *Burl. Mag.*, 1956, p. 115 n. 24.

54. Panofsky, *op. cit.*, I, p. 126 n. 1.

55. See, for example, Bernardo Daddi, altarpiece in the Uffizi (B. Berenson, *Italian Pictures, Florentine School*, London, 1963, I, fig. 179).

56. The Child in Altichiero's fresco in S. Giorgio, Padua, is similar (Fig. 691), but the Virgin does not clasp her hands.

57. See, for instance, the *Nativity* in the *Bible de Charles V* (Fig. 386), and in general Panofsky, *op. cit.*, I, p. 127.

58. Panofsky, *op. cit.*, II, fig. 110.

59. Baroncelli Chapel, S. Croce, Florence (Berenson, *op. cit.*, I, fig. 121).

60. Meiss, 'Masaccio', 1963, p. 131.

61. Panofsky, *op. cit.*, 1953, II, fig. 60.

62. Meiss, *Gaz. B.-A.*, 1963, pp. 159 ff.

63. See Carlo Crivelli, London, National Gallery (F. Drey, *Carlo Crivelli*, Munich, 1927, pl. 60).

64. For the bird in the cage as a symbol of the soul

'imprisoned in the body' see H. Friedmann, *The Symbolic Goldfinch*, Washington, 1946, p. 55.

65. While the Peacock, as Juno's bird, could be a symbol of pride, the annual renewal of its tail feathers and the resistance of its flesh to decay made it also the symbol of immortality (H. Lother, *Der Pfau in der altchristlichen Kunst*, Leipzig, 1929, pp. 25 ff. and T. H. White, *The Book of Beasts*, London, 1954, p. 149).

66. See, for instance, the *Last Supper* by an assistant of Pietro Lorenzetti in the Lower Church at Assisi (De Wald, 1929, fig. 45).

67. See Meiss, *Florence and Siena*, 1951, p. 124, fig. 121.

68. See p. 123.

69. See p. 123. The inscription is a passage from the Lamentations of Jeremiah (I, 12) that occasionally appeared alongside the Man of Sorrows in Trecento painting (Meiss, *loc. cit.*).

70. *Daliwe*, 1964, I, p. 146 n. 120. Dr. Kreuter-Eggemann also cites a similar composition in the retable of Fray Bonifacio Ferrer in the Museo, Valencia (Gudiol, *Pintura gótica*, fig. 107), and accounts for the relationship by a presumed sojourn of the illuminator at the court of Navarre.

71. See Panofsky, *op. cit.*, I, fig. 43 (New York, Morgan Library, ms. 46, fol. 99v.); *idem*, 'Imago Pietatis', 1927, p. 278.

72. P. Schubring, *Donatello*, Stuttgart, 1917, pl. 46.

73. Brit. Mus., Harley 2979, fol. 54. The colors and the conspicuous *terra verde* in the flesh are Italian.
For the textual source see Pseudo-Matthew, chap. XXIII (James, *Apocrypha*, 1924, p. 75).

74. On this question in general see Meiss, 'Jan van Eyck', 1956, pp. 67 ff.; *idem*, *Gaz. B.-A.*, 1961, pp. 293 ff.

75. See for example Leroquais, *Livres d'heures*, 1927, III, pl. 37.

76. In addition to fol. 205 (Fig. 741), this style appears on fols. 211v. and 212. Folio 195 (The Baptist in the Desert), while basically by the Brussels Initials Master, contains an admixture of French elements. See the Catalogue.

77. Bibl. nat., fr. 835 (fols. 74, 87); fr. 836 (fols. 48, 63, 65, 65v., 66v., 71v., 74v., 76); fr. 606 (fols. 41, 46). See *Paris, 1400–1420*. Also Meiss, *Art Bull.*, 1956, pp. 194 f.

78. The *Mockery*, p. 322, is also influenced by this Netherlandish style.

79. See n. 16.

80. Lehoux, *Jean de Berri*, Chap. XII. Also Michaud, *Biographie universelle*, VII, 1844, pp. 560 f.

81. He gave the Duke precious stones and *joyaux*. See Guiffrey, *Inventaires*, I, nos. 100, 162, 309, 413, 469, 470, 598, 599, 685 (all recorded by Robinet in the inventory of 1413).

82. This initial has not previously been mentioned. Several Bolognese mss. are related to the *Statuti*: Holkham Hall ms. 354, dated 1409; Bologna, Museo Civico, no. 28 and (less closely) no. 93 (Salmi, *Miniatura italiana*, [1955], pl. XI).

83. See Meiss, *Gaz. B.-A.*, 1963, p. 159 n. 36.

84. Modena, Bibl. Estense, lat. 1021. See Fava and Salmi, 1950, p. 32. Another ms. in the Holkham Library, a Livy (ms. 354) written in Bologna in 1409, resembles the Lactantius; it is in fact a Bolognese parallel to it.

85. Maggs, *Bulletin*, no. 1, 1962, no. 6, as 'Zenobi'.

86. Toesca, *Collezione Hoepli*, 1930, p. 57 no. 48, as by a follower of Niccolò da Bologna.

87. Brit. Mus., Add. 34247. See Pächt, *Mary of Burgundy*, [1948], p. 52 n. 19. See also London, Brit. Mus., *Reproductions*, II, 1910, pls. 43, 44. The ms. measures 131 × 100 mm.

88. As examples of the many similar but less closely related mss. see Brit. Mus., Add. 45890, and London, Sotheby, *Springell Sale*, June 28, 1962, no. 50.

89. Vienna, Nationalbibl. (Hermann), VIII, pt. V, 1929, pp. 186 ff. The later miniatures in this ms., like the one on fol, 1, were painted around 1400 or later.

90. See for instance Brit. Mus., Add. 11990, which was written in Ferrara in 1378, though the miniatures are closer to Niccolò. For Bolognese illuminators in Padua see Barzon, *Codici miniati*, *Biblioteca capitolare della cattedrale di Padova*, Padua, 1950, p. XVI.

91. See Fava and Salmi, 1950, p. 32.

92. See the inscription on fol. 172v. of the ms. Cf. Holkham Hall (Dorez), 1908, p. 32.

93. Toesca, *Lombardia*, 1912, fig. 245; Leningrad (Saint-Pétersbourg), Laborde, I, 1936, pl. 35. The rays are in the Calendar of Brit. Mus., Add. 29433; the vines are the work of a French illuminator.

94. For Pietro da Verona see above, p. 64.

95. *Boucicaut Hours*, Musée Jacquemart-André, Paris.

96. For this subject in the Boucicaut workshop see Bibl. nat., lat. 1161, fol. 130v. (Meiss, *Florence and Siena*, 1951, fig. 151), *ca.* 1409, and Bibl. nat., lat. 3107, fol. 232v., *ca.* 1410.

97. See *St. Matthew* by the Brussels Initials Master in the *Heures de Charles le Noble* (Fig. 729).

98. See a Book of Hours from the Rohan workshop, Brit. Mus., Harley 2934, fols. 15, 57.

99. *Gaz. B.-A.*, 1963, p. 159.

100. Fol. 157v. See Porcher, *Belles Heures*, 1953, pl. 86.

NOTES TO CHAPTER XI

1. Châtelet (1956, p. 204) proposed that these miniatures were painted in Liège because of a stylistic relationship – which I cannot see – with the antependium in the museum at Brussels and the Mosan triptych in Rotterdam, both presumably made in that diocese.
2. Ms. HM 1104.
3. Pp. 129 f.
4. Durrieu, *Très Belles Heures de Notre-Dame*, 1922, p. 121, already recognized two different styles in this miniature and also (p. 69) in the *Baptism*.
5. A connection of the Confessors with Hand A in the *Carmelite Missal*, proposed by Rickert (*Carmelite Missal*, 1951, p. 98), does not seem convincing.
6. Durrieu, *op. cit.*, p. 106, noticed the connection of these figures but interpreted it as an indication of the date after 1409 of the *Baptism* in the *Très Belles Heures de Notre-Dame*, the reverse, in other words, of the view advanced above. Kreuter-Eggemann, *Daliwe*, 1964, I, n. 99, seems to understand that Durrieu believed the *Baptism* in the *Très Belles Heures de Notre-Dame* was the predecessor.

   The Baptist Master seems not to have painted the *mantle* of the Baptist; that is, in part at least, the work of the Holy Ghost Master.
7. Panofsky, *Netherlandish Painting*, 1953, II, fig. 443.
8. Meiss, *Gaz. B.-A.*, 1963, figs. 5, 20.
9. Panofsky, *op. cit.*, II, fig. 258.
10. *Ibid.*, I, p. 110, II, figs. 150-152.
11. Bibl. Royale, 10176-8. Panofsky, *op. cit.*, I, p. 108, localized the ms. in the Artois, *ca.* 1390. Delaissé, 1956, pp. 233 ff., argued that the ms. was executed in Paris.
12. New York, Morgan Library, ms. 785, fol. 51v.: 'Aubertus abbas Burgensis predictas ymagines atque figuras ordinavit'. This folio contains also the inscription of Jean de Berry, though his name at the end is now effaced. The ms. was in the inv. of 1413 (Guiffrey, *Inventaires*, I, p. 245 no. 935; Delisle, *Charles V*, 1907, II, pp. 252, 301), which states the date of the gift. Panofsky, *op. cit.*, I, p. 106, erroneously says the ms. was given by the Duke to the Abbot.
13. Weale, 1869–70, pp. 274 ff. This excellent paper, the chief and practically the only source for the great Abbot, is disappointing only because it contains no precise references to the documents. See also Weale, *Gerard David*, London, 1895, p. 58, and Paquot, *Pays-Bas*, V, 1765, p. 362.
14. Guiffrey, *op. cit.*, I, p. 156 no. 578.
15. *Ibid.*, II, p. 128 no. 1001; II, pp. 129-130 no. 1019; II, p. 61 no. 437.
16. *Ibid.*, II, pp. 65 no. 463, 67 no. 484, 41 no. 281.
17. Weale, *loc. cit.*
18. *Ibid.*, Weale suggested that this copy might be no. 7213 in the Bibliothèque du Roi, but the text of this ms. is French (now Bibl. nat., fr. 829), and the illumination a mediocre specimen of the very late Bondol tradition.
19. Weale, *loc. cit.* Lubert was born in Bruges in 1347, became Prior of Eeckhout in 1391, Abbot in 1394.
20. See pp. 45 f.
21. These interesting facts were written by Weale to Delisle, who published them in *Bull. du Bibliophile*, 1896, pp. 106-116.
22. Panofsky, *op. cit.*, I, pp. 52 f. Porcher (Paris, Bibl. nat., 1955, p. 69) refers to the Low Countries, and in his *Medieval Miniatures*, [1959], p. 58, *néerlandais* has been incorrectly translated Dutch (see the French edition, *Enluminure française*, Paris, 1959, p. 58).
23. See especially the *Somme le Roi* dated 1415, Brussels, Bibl. Royale, ms. 11041 and the drawings in a religious treatise in Wiesbaden, Staatsarchiv, written in 1410 (Panofsky, *op. cit.*, I, pp. 107 ff., II, figs. 139-141).
24. The mss. were first grouped by Martens, *Meister Francke*, 1929, pp. 192 ff., as by the 'Master of 1402'. For the present writer's classification see, in addition to the paragraph above, the list of workshops on pp. 354 f.
25. Guiffrey, *Inventaires*, I, p. 225 no. 854.
26. Ms. 5057-8, with Berry's inscription. Cf. Panofsky, *op. cit.*, II, figs. 57, 58; Martin, *Miniature française*, 1923, pl. 75. Thomas, 1952, pp. 81 ff., rightly observed that the best illuminator of this ms. also worked on Paris, Bibl. de l'Arsenal, ms. 3479-80, a Lancelot.
27. Bibl. nat., fr. 159. The words on the scroll of St. John in the *Apocalypse* were identified as perhaps Flemish by Porcher, *Belles Heures*, 1953, p. 14; they had not escaped the eye of Durrieu, 1895, pp. 178 ff., who called them German.
28. Bibl. nat., fr. 12201. Panofsky, *op. cit.*, II, fig. 51. For the *Coronation* see Porcher, *Belles Heures*, 1953, fig. 1, and *The Boucicaut Master*. This workshop was responsible also for the beautiful Book of Hours, Morgan Library, ms. 515 (Fig. 823).
29. Bibl. nat., fr. 598. For the inscription ('hort het

wort'), see Porcher, *op. cit.*, p. 14 (but *wort*, not *merk*, is correct, as G. I. Lieftinck kindly tells me). Guiffrey, *Inventaires*, I, p. 246 no. 940; Martens, *op. cit.*, figs. 42 f., 48 f.

30. Geneva, Bibl. publique, ms. fr. 77 (see Gagnebin, 1959, pp. 193). We should recall that already in 1398 a certain Jean de Hollande was employed as a painter in the Duke's palace at Poitiers (see p. 226).

31. Bibl. nat., fr. 12420. Martens, *op. cit.*, fig. 59.

32. It is hardly necessary to repeat that Jacques Raponde played a role also in introducing these painters to Paris.

33. Porcher (Paris, Bibl. nat., 1955, p. 77) observed that these mss. were the source of the Bedford Master and also (but wrongly I think) of the Limbourgs.

34. The relationship of these two miniatures, and its significance for the date of this group of paintings in the *Hours of the Holy Ghost*, has now been observed by Kreuter-Eggemann, *Daliwe*, 1964, I, p. 67.

35. Bibl. nat., fr. 23279, by the Master of the Cité des Dames, to be discussed in *Paris, 1400–1420*.

36. As pointed out above, p. 92, the iconography of Jean de Berry in the miniature of the Itinerary indicates a date between 1405 and 1409–1410 (Fig. 497).

37. For this master see Chapter XIII, n. 111, and p. 307.

38. Similar flaking may be seen in the two uppermost of the Believers (Fig. 19). In the *Dispersion of the Apostles* the cloud around the Holy Ghost has flaked, exposing the building underneath (Fig. 21).

39. *Très Belles Heures de Notre-Dame*, 1922, p. 106.

40. In the miniatures in this ms. in the Parement style only red lacquer over gold was employed, but green or blue over silver was used in the first decade of the 15th century, especially by the Egerton Master and the Boucicaut Master.

41. It follows from this discussion that I cannot agree with an attribution to Jaques Daliwe proposed by Kreuter-Eggemann (*op. cit.*) in a fundamental, searching study of the pattern-book in Berlin signed by this artist. Dr. Kreuter-Eggemann tentatively discerns the hand of Daliwe also in the miniature of the Madonna enthroned formerly in Turin, ascribed by the present writer to the Baptist Master (Fig. 34). She finds that the painter of the Hours of the Holy Ghost (i.e. 'Daliwe') learned much from the frescoes of Matteo Giovanetti (see her figs. 21-23, 25, 28-30). It would be difficult to disprove the hypothesis that the facial types of the miniaturist were affected to a degree by the varied physiognomies of the Avignon frescoes but if there are Italian elements in the miniatures they do not seem to me important. The Baptist (Fig. 16), likewise derived by Kreuter-Eggemann from Avignon (*op. cit.*, I, p. 64), appears to me wholly in the Northern, even Flemish tradition.

NOTES TO CHAPTER XII

1. At the bottom of the folio, in a different hand: 'Les heures du feu duc de Berry 1416'. In the line below, in a different and later script: 'appartenait au Roy Loux XIIme'.

2. Guiffrey, *Inventaires*, I, p. 253 no. 961.

3. *Ibid.*, no. 960 for the *Belles Heures*, and II, p. 280 no. 1164 for the *Très Riches Heures*.

4. See Catalogue.

5. See Meiss, *Art Bull.*, 1956, pp. 191 ff.

6. See above, p. 98.

7. See the seal used in 1387 (Gandilhon, *Sceaux*, 1933, pl. XII no. 3).

8. Brit. Mus., Eg. 1070. See *The Boucicaut Master*.

9. *Pucelle*, 1962, p. 29 and pl. XXVII.

10. See p. 316.

11. In the *Grandes Heures*, however, a drapery appears behind as well as in front of the Man of Sorrows.

12. The gilt in Christ's mantle, not to be found in the model in the Breviary either, conforms however with the usage of the Boucicaut Master and other painters of the early 15th century.

13. See the list of the Duke's mss., p. 315. The relationship of the two miniatures of the Resurrection was noted by Morand, *op. cit.*, p. 28.

14. See above, p. 186.

15. For examples see Panofsky, *Netherlandish Painting*, 1953, II, figs. 70, 72, 83, 84.

16. See Pächt, *Burl. Mag.*, 1956, pp. 150-153, where, however, the resemblances are considered evidence of a late date for the *Brussels Hours* rather than as an unintelligent imitation of an advanced earlier work.

17. For this opinion and those that follow, see pp. 190 and 381 n. 57.

18. See Chapter VI, p. 128.

19. See above, p. 111.

20. See Chapter IV, no. 24.

21. See p. 381 n. 64. This miniature will be reproduced in *The Boucicaut Master*.

22. The miniatures in the *Grandes Heures* by the Boucicaut Master will be discussed in *The Boucicaut Master*.

23. See above, p. 152.

24. Brit. Mus., Royal 19 B XVII, written in 1382; Breviary, Bourges, Bibl. municipale, ms. 16; Baltimore, Walters Art Gallery, ms. 94. See pp. 188 ff., 387 n. 91. *David* in Walters, ms. 103 (fol. 86) was influenced by the style of Pseudo-Jacquemart.

25. See the *Annunciation* in the Tournai *Horae ca.* 1400 (Panofsky, *Netherlandish Painting*, 1953, I, p. 128, and II, fig. 145).

26. This manuscript contains several miniatures by the Egerton workshop.

27. This initial, the only painting in the manuscript, was called to my attention by Professor Francis Wormald. The acanthus proves that it must have been painted relatively late.

28. Professor Victor Lasareff very kindly sent me photographs of this manuscript, which he had earlier called to my attention.

29. Meiss and Eisler, 1960, pp. 235 f.

30. Porcher, *Belles Heures*, 1953, pp. 7 n. 10, 28.

31. I owe this information about provenance, and indeed knowledge of the glass, to the always generous interest of M. Lafond.

32. See the bibliography in the Catalogue. The same cover was described in Paris, Bibl. nat., *Catalogue manuscrits latins*, I, 1939, p. 327. At the present time the cover has been misplaced in the Bibliothèque nationale.

33. Arch. nat., KK70, fol. 288v.; Delisle, *Charles V*, 1907, II, p. 285.

34. The missing large miniatures might, of course, have needed retouching. *Timpaner* might refer to pressing the miniatures flat. Godefroy, *Dictionnaire*, s.v. *timpaniser*, is not helpful. H iii is a missing folio and not, as Delisle said, h i.

35. Beenken, 1933–1934, p. 216 n. 41, said 'aus Jacquemarts nächster Nähe'; Panofsky, *Netherlandish Painting*, 1953, I, p. 82: '. . . justly associated with Jacquemart de Hesdin'. The painting has also been attributed to the school of Avignon. See Huyghe, 1930, who first published the painting when it was acquired by the Louvre. Also Bazin, *École provençale: XIV-XV siècles*, Geneva, [1944]. Porcher, *Belles Heures*, 1953, p. 17; Bologna, 1953, no. 37, p. 50; Sterling, *Peintres du moyen âge*, 1942, pl. 42, but now in Paris, Louvre (Sterling and Adhémar), 1965, p. 3, tentatively to Jacquemart.

36. See Boutaric, 1864, pp. 38 f. Also Champeaux and

37. Nordenfalk, 1956, p. 185; Pächt, *Rev. des arts*, 1956, pp. 149 ff.

38. In response to my questions in 1956 Professor Charles Sterling of the Louvre kindly undertook to determine by laboratory examination the ground of the painting.

39. Fols. 38, 39, 40, 44, 45, 47, 48, 59, 62, 63, 79.

40. M. Desbrosses thought at first of a press applied when the ms. was trimmed, but that, he believed, would not indent folios within gatherings in the middle of the ms.

41. Brit. Mus., Harley 4431, fol. 3 (Schaefer, 1937, fig. 1).

42. Pächt, *Rev. des arts*, 1956, p. 158. The waistline of the nearer figure seems clearly indicated.

43. Sterling in Paris, Louvre (Sterling and Adhémar), 1965, p. 3, suggests that the dresses are Italian. The cufic pattern is, however, not uncommon in French painting of the time (see the scarf of the waiter in *January*, Fig. 489) and the dress of the Virgin may show horizontal bands (Porcher, *Belles Heures*, 1953, pl. 52).

44. For the 'radiant' haloes see Meiss and Eisler, 1960, p. 235. Another connection between the *Way to Calvary* and French panels, already observed with regard to color, may be observed in the ornaments used on the dress of the old Jew nearest the gate and those that appear on the figure holding ointment in the Louvre *Entombment* (Fig. 695).

45. See Simone's *Annunciation* in the Uffizi.

46. See the haloes of for instance Christ in the *Adoration of the Magi* and the *Presentation in the Temple* (Porcher, *Belles Heures*, 1953, pls. 35, 36).

47. *Meditations*, ed. Ragusa and Green, p. 331.

48. Munich, Bayr. Staatsbibl., lat. 10072, fol. 142. This relationship was observed by Pächt in his careful study of the Italian sources of the French representations in *Revue des arts*, 1956, pp. 149 ff. and fig. 11. The Bolognese miniature is not, however, the first example of this motif; it appeared half a century earlier in the predella of the Sienese altarpiece of the Resurrection, Borgo Sansepolcro (F. M. Perkins, 'Pitture senesi poco conosciute', *La Diana*, v, 1930, pl. 15).

49. See Bibl. nat., fr. 9561, fol. 174.

50. For other, less closely related figures of Judas see Pächt, *op. cit.*, pp. 154 f. Also Offner, *Corpus*, sec. III, vol. VI, 1956, p. 127 n. 22. For the subject in general see Goetz, 'Hie henckt Judas', 1950, pp. 105 ff.

Gauchery, *Travaux*, 1894, p. 206; Panofsky, *op. cit.*, I, p. 47 n. 1.

51. The suicide appeared later in the century in the *Way to Calvary* in the *Heures d'Étienne Chevalier* by Fouquet (*ibid.*, p. 154 n. 10).

52. It may be seen also in a drawing of the same subject in the Crocker Art Gallery, Sacramento; the drawing imitates Bosch.

53. The left arm of the soldier seems to me closer to the man withdrawing nails in Simone's *Deposition* (Fig. 676) than to the figure in the Spanish Chapel, S. Maria Novella, Florence, cited by Pächt (*loc. cit.*). It is true, however, that St. John's clasped hands might have been taken from the Chapel, as Pächt proposed.

54. See p. 215.

55. The group appeared in Sienese painting: fresco by follower of Barna in S. Pietro, S. Gimignano (van Marle, *Italian Schools*, II, fig. 195). Also in Altichiero, S. Antonio, Padua (Pächt, *op. cit.*, fig. 22). The Limbourgs introduced the group into the miniature of Christ leaving the Pretorium, *Très Riches Heures* (Durrieu, *Très Riches Heures*, 1904, pl. LIII).

56. Yates Thompson 37. See the Catalogue.

57. The large building with an external arcade has been questionably identified as the Duke's Château de Nonette, represented with such an arcade in Bibl. nat., fr. 22297 (see Champeaux and Gauchery, *Travaux*, 1894, pl.). More interesting is the resemblance with the building in the Eyckian *Entry* (Durrieu, *Heures de Turin*, 1902, pl. XVIII).

58. The ms. has been tampered with. Four folios between 110 and 111 have been cut out.

59. See Chapter IX, p. 221.

60. This ms., illuminated by the Boucicaut Master, the Master of the Cité des Dames and collaborators, is discussed in *The Boucicaut Master*. For textually motivated clouds in contemporary mss. see the storm clouds in the *Miracle of St. Nicholas* in the *Belles Heures* (Porcher, *Belles Heures*, 1953, pl. CIII).

61. These two figures necessitate an emendation of Panofsky's observation of the complete absence of the type in France (*Netherlandish Painting*, 1953, I, p. 129).

62. Fig. 6. See also Giovanni da Milano, Pinacoteca Vaticana (van Marle, *Italian Schools*, IV, fig. 121).

63. *Nativity* and *Majesty*.

64. His usual long, slant eyes with a blue or gray-blue pupil may be seen in all the heads in Yates Thompson 37.

65. 1936, p. 450. A more distant reflection of the Lorenzetti may be seen earlier in England, in the Grandisson diptych, British Museum (F. Saxl and R. Wittkower, *British Art and the Mediterranean*, London, 1948, pl. 33 no. 11).

66. He seems also to have executed the *Funeral Service* (fol. 83v.) on a design of Pseudo-Jacquemart.

67. London, Thompson Collection (Thompson), VII, 1918, pp. 5 f. See also London, Brit. Mus., *Reproductions*, II, 1910, pl. XXVIII.

68. See above, p. 254.

69. 1936, p. 450.

70. For some examples see Meiss, 1936, p. 450. Panofsky underestimates the interest in the subject in France (*Netherlandish Painting*, 1953, I, p. 128).

71. In addition to the two miniatures reproduced the Madonna of Humility is represented on fol. 86v.

72. See Chapter IX, p. 206. The panels measure 130 × 70 mm.

73. See above, p. 226.

74. See, for instance, the tapestry with wild men listed among the possessions of Charles V (Labarte, *Inventaire*, 1879, no. 3684) and the examples reproduced by Bernheimer, *Wild Men*, 1952, figs. 19, 23, 45.

75. See Kreuter-Eggemann, *Daliwe*, 1964, I, p. 36.

76. Fry, 1906–1907, pp. 31–38. Dimier, 1928–1933, pp. 12 ff., declared that the 'sketch-book' was a forgery, made not long before two folios were reproduced in engravings by Rosini (as utilized by Giotto) in his *Storia della pittura italiana*, Pisa, 1840, II, p. 196.

77. Lavallée, *op. cit.*, pp. 12 f.; Pächt, *Rev. des arts*, 1956, p. 160, tentatively; Kreuter-Eggemann, *op. cit.*, p. 76; Boon, 1950, p. 267 (by assistants); Scheller, *Model Books*, 1963, pp. 104 ff.

78. By Parkhurst, 1941, also, who classifies the two *Madonnas* as Franco-Flemish, the Brussels example *ca.* 1380, the Morgan *ca.* 1390. Fry, *loc. cit.*, and Lavallée, *loc. cit.*, thought a *terminus ante quem* was provided by the masked ball of 1393, to which some courtiers went as wild men, and which ended in a disastrous fire (see Froissart, ed. Lettenhove, XV, pp. 84 ff.). Around this time occurred the first episodes of the 'madness' of King Charles VI.

79. In this respect I agree with Pächt, *loc. cit.*, but not with the inclusion in this group of the Brussels diptych.

80. Panofsky, *Netherlandish Painting*, 1953, II, pl. 48.

81. The attribution of this tondo to Malouel has been greatly strengthened by its deep stylistic connections with the *Madonna* in Berlin that Eisler and the writer (1960, pp. 239 f.) tentatively ascribed to Malouel, chief painter of Jean sans Peur, partly because a portrait of this prince seems originally to have composed a

diptych with the *Madonna*. A few weeks earlier Winkler had connected the *Madonna* with the Limbourgs, Malouel, and Bellechose on stylistic grounds (1959, pp. 182, 189).

82. Meiss, 1935, pp. 65-75; Ring, *French Painting*, [1949], p. 204 no. 90, pl. 36.

83. 210 × 116 mm. Silverpoint heightened in white on pale green paper.

84. Pächt, *Gaz. B.-A.*, 1963, p. 111.

85. Wescher, 1937, p. 16. Earlier Burckhardt (1906,

p. 184) ascribed it to Basel.

86. Ring, *op. cit.*, pp. 193 f. no. 17, connected the drawing with the diptych containing the *Adoration of the Magi* in the Bargello, Florence, and therefore ascribed it to Paris (but the diptych is not French).

87. Sterling, 1955, pp. 57-81. The second panel is in the Chalandon Collection, Lyons.

88. Dimier, 1936, p. 205.

89. Monget, *Chartreuse de Dijon*, I, 1898, p. 348.

90. Meiss and Eisler, 1960, p. 239.

NOTES TO CHAPTER XIII

1. [Barrois], *Bibl. protypographique*, 1830, pp. 105 ff.; Vaughan, *Philip the Bold*, 1962, p. 193. Jean sans Peur had 248 mss. at his death (Doutrepont, *Inventaire*, 1906, *passim*; Thompson, *Medieval Library*, 1939, p. 427). On French libraries of this period in general see *Histoire littéraire de la France*, XXIV, 1862, pp. 304 ff.

2. Delisle, *Charles V*, 1907, II, pp. 3 ff.; Thompson, *op. cit.*, pp. 419 ff.

3. Pellegrin, *Bibliothèque des Visconti*, 1955, *passim*; Vaughan, *op. cit.*, p. 192.

4. Delisle, *Cabinet*, I, 1868, pp. 54 f. See above, p. 27. For Louis d'Orléans, the son of Charles V and nephew of Jean de Berry, see Graves, *Inventaires Orléans*, 1926, pp. 50 ff.; also Delisle, *Cabinet*, III, 1881, p. 98. The Orléans library was installed in the Hôtel de Giac in Paris.

5. Delisle, *Charles V*, 1907, I, pp. 326 ff. Even before his coronation Jean le Bon commissioned the French version of the *Échecs moralisés*, and with his support Bersuire translated Livy.

6. Guiffrey, *Inventaires*, I, p. 257 no. 968. See above, p. 48.

7. This woman of excellent taste set a high standard by commissioning from Pucelle also the Breviary in Chantilly (Figs. 605, 606). The beautiful statuette in the Louvre, dated 1339, was also made for her. Jeanne died as late as 1371.

8. Ed. Saint-Hilaire and Raynaud, IX, pp. 45 f.

9. See above, pp. 21 ff.

10. Delisle, *Charles V*, 1907, I, pp. 82 ff.

11. Guiffrey, *Inventaires*, II, p. 337. In 1374 there is a record of his possession of a Book of Hours, and in 1377 he gave one to his wet nurse.

12. For examples of mediocre illuminations see Bibl. nat., fr. 176, 246, 425, 565, 568, 829, 5631, 9106, 9221.

For mss. without illumination see for example Bibl. nat., lat. 8887, lat. 9328, fr. 2641, and Brussels, Bibl. Royale, ms. 9553.

13. Delisle, *Charles V*, 1907, II, p. 160 no. 975.

14. See Guiffrey, *op. cit.*, I, pp. CXLI f.

15. *Ibid.*, II, p. 124 no. 961.

16. See Bibl. nat., fr. 246.

17. Guiffrey, *op. cit.*, II, p. 127 no. 993. For the Vegetius (Bibl. nat., fr. 1229) see List of the Duke's Mss.

18. Brit. Mus., Burney 275.

19. See Bibl. nat., fr. 373; Lyons, Bibl. municipale, ms. 742.

20. Guiffrey, *op.cit.*, II, p. 130 no. 1020.

21. *Ibid.*, I, p. CXLII. He had medieval encyclopedias also, of Vincent of Beauvais (*ibid.*, II, p. 123 no. 960) and the more recent, 14th-century work of Pierre Bersuire (*ibid.*, II, p. 125 no. 967).

22. *Ibid.*, II, p. 128 no. 996. Given in 1404 to the Ste-Chapelle, perhaps to assure its conservation.

23. Bibl. nat., lat. 7907A, given by his treasurer, and Paris, Bibl. de l'Arsenal, ms. 664, given by the Bishop of Châlons.

24. Guiffrey, *Inventaires*, II, p. 238 no. 524.

25. Bibl. nat., fr. 226, for example. See p. 318, Fig. 503.

26. See Chap. III, n. 175.

27. See the colophon in Bibl. nat., fr. 282, fol. 411v. The ms. was illuminated by the Virgil Master. See also Delisle, *Charles V*, 1907, I, p. 115.

28. Bibl. nat., fr. 190, with dedication to Berry. But this copy must be dated in the late 15th century, and could not have belonged to the Duke (Guiffrey, *Inventaires*, I, p. CLXVII no. 33, is doubtful). The date of the translation, 1372, may be read on fol. 206v.

29. *Charles V*, 1907, II, p. 309.

30. Bibl. nat., nouv. acq. fr. 6194. See E. Roy, 1903 and 1904; Fischer, 1932, pp. 196 ff. The *Vie de Notre*

Seigneur is not identifiable in the Duke of Berry's inventories, and one might be more suspicious of the ascription to him in the printed book if two partly independent mss. did not make the same assertion (see note 31). I might have missed this evidence if Sharon Off Katić, who was exploring this religious literature for me, had not been, as always, very alert. Charles V had a *Passion Nostre-Seigneur rimée par personnages* and a *Passion* was composed in 1398 for Queen Isabeau de Bavière (E. Roy, *op. cit.*, 1903, p. 65).

31. From the copy in the Bibl. nat., Réserve H 155. Brunet, *Manuel, V*, part 2, 1864, col. 1184, refers to another edition by Barthélemy Bruyer, likewise at Lyons, around 1476; I have been unable to find a copy of it. A second copy of Leroy's edition is at Chantilly, III, G. 35.

E. Roy identified two mss. of the same text, Darmstadt, Hessische Landesbibliothek, ms. 1699 (86 fols., not 63) and Carpentras, Bibl. municipale, ms. 28. Both are of the later 15th century (Roy, 1903, p. 20; 1904, p. 250; Roy wrongly dated the Darmstadt ms. in the 14th century). The Carpentras ms. dates the translation made for Jean de Berry in 'mil quatre cens et quarante et uns ans' (see France, *Cat. général des manuscrits*, XXXIV, 1901, p. 12 no. 28). A note in an 18th-century hand at the beginning of the Darmstadt ms. dates the translation for Berry in 1390. A comparative study of these two mss. and of the printed text, which I am undertaking, is beyond the scope of the present publication.

32. Thus the Berry edition omits the speculative chapters 2 and 46–57 in the early Italian ms. published by Ragusa and Green. Many narrative chapters were omitted also.

33. *Sancti Bonaventurae Opera*, 1756, X, p. 290. For the Italian see ed. Ragusa and Green, p. 32 and n. 15.

34. See E. Roy, 1903, pp. 10 ff.

35. See above, pp. 171 f.

36. See above, p. 124.

37. See above, p. 213.

38. See above, p. 217.

39. See, for example, Bibl. nat., fr. 159. The inscription varies slightly from the normal 'ce livre' in one instance to 'cette Bible' in the other.

40. M. Prou, *Manuel de paléographie*, 4th ed., Paris, 1924, p. 241.

41. Guiffrey, *Inventaires*, I, p. CXLII. Guiffrey's total of commissioned mss. is too low.

42. Delisle, *Charles V*, 1907, I, pp. 150 f., 395. If Delisle's hypothesis that this ms. was Bibl. nat., fr. 20090 is right, the Duke put his signature in it also.

43. See the note added to the item in the testamentary inventory (Guiffrey, *op. cit.*, I, p. 335 no. 1249).

44. Guiffrey, *op. cit.* I, p. 258 no. 972.

45. This is the ms. that Berry gave to Jean sans Peur in February, 1413, apparently in return for the *Merveilles du monde* that his nephew had given him a month earlier. See above, p. 49.

46. Guiffrey, *op. cit.*, I, p. 252 no. 958.

47. A traveler's observations published in 1715 describes mss. in the Ste-Chapelle still lying open on the lecterns on which they had been placed three hundred years earlier (D. Martenne, *Voyage littéraire de deux religieux bénédictins*, Paris, 1715, I, p. 29, summarized by Hiver de Beauvoir, *Librairie*, 1860, p. 85).

48. He was at Avignon in 1358, 1359, 1371, 1372, 1391, 1392, 1395. Furthermore, in each of the years 1382, 1384, 1385 he stayed for two or more months. For these facts, and what follows on the Duke's whereabouts see Lehoux, *Jean de Berri*, Itinéraire.

49. See above, p. 226.

50. *Ibid.*

51. Arch. nat., KK 256, fol. 34. See Lehoux, *Jean de Berri*, Chap. IX.

52. Arch. nat., KK 256, fol. 37v.; Lehoux, *loc. cit.*

53. Magne, *Palais*, 1904, pp. 58 f., 159.

54. Lehoux, *Jean de Berri*, Chap. XI.

55. It is true that the inventory of the *joyaux* at Mehun began in May, 1402, apparently before the Duke's arrival. See Guiffrey, *Inventaires*, II, p. 50.

56. See above, p. 199.

57. Petit, *Itinéraires*, 1888, pp. 184–260. He was not at Dijon in 1388, 1392, or 1394.

58. A. Liebreich, *Claus Sluter*, Brussels, 1936, pp. 47 ff.

59. *Ibid.*, pp. 98 ff.

60. See Gorissen, 1954, pp. 197 no. 40 and 198 no. 46.

61. The Duchess Margaret likewise did not visit Dijon after 1397; she resided at Arras (Vaughan, *Philip the Bold*, 1962, p. 152).

62. Gorissen, 1954, p. 203, doc. 69.

63. *Ibid.*, p. 202, doc. 67.

64. *Ibid.*, p. 205, doc. 86.

65. See [Barrois], *Bibl. protypographique*, 1830, p. 105; Vaughan, *op. cit.*, pp. 191 f. At her death the mss. of the Duchess of Burgundy were in chests at her residence in Arras ([Barrois], *op. cit.*, p. 110).

66. It is not certain that this figure was carved before the death of the Duke (see above, p. 94).

67. See above, p. 226.

68. Champeaux and Gauchery, *Travaux*, 1894, pp. 140 f.

69. *Ibid.* See Arch. nat., X^{Ia} 1479, fols. 50v.-51.

70. Gorissen, 1954, p. 210 no. 62.

71. For all the relevant documents, and for information about Jean Durand's *hôtel* in the Cloître Notre-Dame, see Prost, 1891, pp. 342-344; Champeaux and Gauchery, *op. cit.*, pp. 138 f.; and Petit, *Itinéraires*, 1888, pp. 322 f., 328 f., 653.

72. Arch. nat., KK 250, fol. 25v. See Champeaux and Gauchery, *op. cit.*, p. 136.

73. The earliest, 21 gold pieces 'de diverses manières' (Guiffrey, *Inventaires*, II, p. 26 no. 122); then an emerald ring, two diamond rings, and in August 1415 a ruby (*ibid.*, I, p. 125 no. 415; p. 128 no. 421; p. 135 no. 457, after January 1413; and I, p. 102 no. 349).

74. Gorissen (1954, pp. 178 f.), however, assumes that all these payments and gifts establish the presence of the Limbourgs in Bourges. See his *Zeittafel*.

75. Guiffrey, *op. cit.*, I, p. 265 no. 994; p. 323 no. 1211.

76. See p. 309.

77. Guiffrey, *op. cit.*, II, p. 277 no. 1121; I, p. 257 no. 968. The book was given to him in 1407 by his nephew, Louis II d'Anjou.

78. *Ibid.*, II, p. 275 no. 1078.

79. *Ibid.*, II, p. 277 no. 1130.

80. *Ibid.*, II, p. 238 no. 507.

81. *Ibid.*, II, p. 280 no. 1159.

82. *Ibid.*, II, p. 276 no. 1111. The additional mss. in Paris mentioned below are: the Terence (no. 1122); the *Mutacion* of Christine (no. 1116); *Livre d'astrologie* (no. 1107); *Fleur des histoires* (no. 1105). Noteworthy also: *Fais du sage roy Charles*, with its description of the Duke quoted below, p. 308 (no. 1109); *Sept psaumes*, also dedicated to Berry by Christine (no. 1124).

83. For these mss. at Mehun see Guiffrey, *Inventaires*, II, pp. 236-239, and following the sequence of the text above nos. 483, 506, 456, 500, 523, 466, 512.

84. The proposal of Panofsky (*Netherlandish Painting*, 1953, I, p. 64) that a second equestrian Magus derives from the lost Augustus or Tiberius medal (accepted by Krautheimer, *Ghiberti*, 1956, p. 59 no. 28) has been rightly denied by Weiss (1965, p. 143 n. 3) because these medals contained no riders; but the head may have been influential.

85. Guiffrey, *Inventaires*, I, p. 253 no. 961.

86. Panofsky, *op. cit.*, I, p. 38.

87. See also Jean Coste, painter of Jean le Bon, in 1350 (Martin, *Miniaturistes*, 1906, p. 55).

88. Delisle, *Cabinet*, I, 1868, pp. 43 ff.

89. See above, p. 64. At this date one suspects that Pierre wanted to have the famous Calendar illumination copied once more. Vienna, Nationalbibliothek, ms. 1855 (by the Bedford workshop) contains the latest surviving copy of this Calendar, but 1413 seems rather early for a beginning on it.

90. See pp. 260 ff.

91. See p. 259.

92. See Chap. VIII, pp. 170, 180.

93. See *The Boucicaut Master*.

94. Brit. Mus., Harley 4381-4382, illuminated in collaboration with a master close to the *Petites Heures* (Figs. 617, 622).

95. Bibl. nat., fr. 263.

96. Brussels, Bibl. Royale, ms. 9555-8.

97. Florence, Bibl. Laurenziana, Med. Pal. 69. The *Valère Maxime* is Bibl. nat., fr. 282.

98. Bibl. nat., lat. 8886.

99. Bibl. nat., fr. 1023. Given to Berry in 1410.

100. Geneva, Bibl. publique et universitaire, fr. 190.

101. Paris, Bibl. de l'Arsenal, ms. 664.

102. Bibl. nat., lat. 7907A.

103. P. 251.

104. Copies of the *Dialogues*, Bibl. nat., fr. 23279 and Geneva, Bibl. publique et universitaire, fr. 165.

105. Bibl. nat., fr. 2810, and possibly also Bibl. Mazarine, ms. 469.

106. *Croniques de Burgues*, bought in 1407, perhaps largely for its text (Brit. Mus., Royal 19 E vi); *Antiquités judaïques* (Bibl. nat., fr. 6446).

107. Bibl. nat., fr. 607.

108. Barcelona, Biblioteca Central, ms. 1850. By this master are the miniatures on fols. IV. and 2 as well as the last six in the ms., beginning on fol. 183. The other miniatures are all by the Luçon Master (Figs. 334, 705, 810) and this section bears the inscription: 'L'an de grace mil quatre cens et un furent faitez ces heures p Colin le besc'. While the two miniatures at the beginning are on a separate sheet, and fol. 181 begins a new gathering, the miniatures by the Cité des Dames Master are very probably contemporary with the rest, as will be pointed out in *Paris, 1400-1420*. Colin may well be identical with Jean Colin from whom Berry acquired mss. (Guiffrey, *Inventaires*, I, p. 254 no. 962 and II, p. 338). See also Kreuter-Eggemann, 1964, I, fig. 11.

109. The two copies of Christine's *Mutacion* presented in March 1404 to Berry (The Hague, Royal Library, ms. 78 D 42) and in January to Burgundy (Brussels, Bibl. Royale, ms. 9508).

2 D

110. For the text of the ms. in Chantilly see *Mutacion* (ed. Solente), 1959, pp. CIX ff. For the second ms. see Pierre Berès, *Manuscrits et livres* (Catalogue 60), Paris (without date or pagination).

111. Ms. 133. For the reconstruction of this master see Nordenfalk, *Kung praktiks*, 1955, p. 61, and a little later, but independently and with almost identical conclusions, Meiss, *Art Bull.*, 1956, p. 196.

112. See p. 140.

113. Guiffrey, *Inventaires*, I, p. 223 no. 850. The ms. probably appeared in 1380 in the inventory of Charles V.

114. Morand, *Pucelle*, 1962, pl. XXI.

115. Guiffrey, *op. cit.*, I, p. 244 no. 934; II, p. 276 no. 1106.

116. *Ibid.*, I, p. 258 no. 971; II, p. 238 no. 512, p. 298.

117. *Ibid.*, I, pp. 254 f. no. 963.

118. *Ibid.*, I, p. 248 no. 946.

119. *Ibid.*, II, p. 275 no. 1078. The figure is low even in the rather depressed market of 1416.

120. See above, pp. 215 ff.

121. See above, p. 24.

122. See p. 62.

123. See pp. 44 f. For the possibility of Italian painters at Nonette see Champeaux and Gauchery, p. 114.

124. See above, p. 24.

125. As to whether or not the painter himself was there I should observe that the figures in the triptych in the Holy Cross Chapel at Karlštejn are disproportionately small for their spaces, particularly from the point of view of Tommaso's own conventions. It seems more probable that the panels were shipped in and patched out locally. If Tommaso had been on the spot such a reworking could have taken place, of course, after his departure (see Matějček and Pešina, *Czech Gothic Painting*, 1950, pl. 14). The Madonna over the altar in the Chapel of St. Catherine was, on the other hand, painted *in situ* by an Italian master, while the two donors seem Bohemian (see Dvořáková et al., *Gothic Mural Painting in Bohemia*, 1964, pl. VIII).

126. Coville, *Col*, 1934, pp. 15, 19, 73, 142, 146. See also the gift of a book mentioned above, p. 50. For Berry's special support of humanists see Poirion, 1965, p. 33.

127. See above, p. 288. Christine dedicated to the Duke other writings also: *Sept psaumes allégorisés*, presented January, 1410, and *Lamentacion sur les maux de la France*, the same year.

128. Some copies of the *Cas*, completed in 1409, bear dedications to the Duke (see Bibl. nat., fr. 226).

129. For this French group see also Voigt, *Wiederbelebung*, II, 1881, pp. 347–360; Sabbadini, *Scoperte*, 1914, pp. 63–87; Huizinga, *Waning*, 1924, pp. 297 ff.; J. E. Sandys, *A History of Classical Scholarship*, Cambridge, II, 1908, pp. 166 f.

130. Simone, *Coscienza*, 1949, pp. 54 f.

131. *Ibid.*, p. 56.

132. *Ibid.*, p. 36.

133. See Panofsky, *Renaissance and Renascences*, 1960, pp. 8 ff.

134. The passage is quoted by B. L. Ullman, *Studies in the Italian Renaissance*, Rome, 1955, p. 23.

135. Coville, *Col*, 1934, p. 105.

136. *Ibid.*, p. 110.

137. See Pellegrin, *Bibliothèque des Visconti*, 1955, p. 51, for a list of the Roman writers.

138. Guiffrey, *Inventaires*, I, p. 229 no. 872. The ms. had belonged to Louis d'Orléans.

139. Paris, Bibl. nat., fr. 598 and Geneva, Bibliothèque publique et universitaire, fr. 190.

140. Only the Duke's Terence, Bibl. nat., lat. 7907A, might be considered an exception.

141. See on this point Panofsky's 'principle of disjunction' (*op. cit.*, pp. 83 ff.).

142. See above, p. 57.

143. For the Duke's cameos see above, p. 52.

144. We should recall here that subjects drawn from ancient history or mythology were not infrequently represented in murals or tapestries. Thus the young Jean le Bon had a room painted with the life of Julius Caesar, one of the rooms of the royal Hôtel St. Pol in Paris had a *Salle de Thésée* (Evans, *Art in France*, 1948, p. 180) and the Trojan War as well as the Judgment of Paris were represented in tapestries (Adhémar, *Influences antiques*, 1939, p. 293).

145. For the 4th-century plate in Leningrad representing Constantius, son of Constantine, on horseback see L. Matzulewitsch, *Byzantinische Antike, Studien auf Grund der Silbergefässe der Ermitage*, Berlin and Leipzig, 1929, pl. 23. I owe this reference and other facts to the kindness of Ernst Kitzinger. For the inventory item see Guiffrey, *op. cit.*, II, p. 182 no. 230. See also Schlosser, 1897, p. 91, for the identification as Bellerophon.

146. Guiffrey, *op. cit.*, I, p. 199 no. 776. For comments on this extraordinary and puzzling object I feel grateful to Roger Mynors and to A. H. McDonald. To stimulate discussion I append Professor McDonald's translation (tentative at some points) of the inscriptions.
(1) To the prayers of the priests let the gods of the Roman republic give assent, and let the secret defences

of the world, by Apollo's order, with greatest veneration, from this cup of Pallas (Athene) drink the oaths with favour, (those) by whose nod the kingdoms yielded place to the Roman empire. (2) The first class of virtue is to counsel the private minds of men, to control foreigners from the republic in general, first by laws, then by arms [Marcus Aemilius Lepidus]. (3) With how great a treaty, therefore, the elements help the sky, the members assist the structure, and the public state itself (= republic?) is to be defended [Sempronius Gallus]. (4) No despising the stars, therefore, in allegiance, then let the suppliants to the gods hence under the title of 'just war' favour our republic [Publius Claudius]. (5) Nothing profane (unholy) do all the good stars honour, (the stars) which wise nature has brought from the shadows into the sky [Celius Servilius]. (6) To begin these things by the gift of the gods above, with favourable auspices, if towards the refuge of the world, among whatever secret things, we look up to the republic [Lucius Cantulius]. (7) The urn sacrifices unhappy (*litat* usually means 'sacrifice favourably') and dire fates press the springs (*fontes*: perhaps misreading of *sortes* = one's lot), while bad characters make themselves equal with the heavenly [Lucius Simius].

147. *Ibid.*, I, p. 28 no. 55.

148. *Ibid.*, I, p. 27 no. 54.

149. *Ibid.*, I, p. 63 no. 167; I, p. 30 no. 58.

150. *Ibid.*, II, p. 87 no. 683.

151. *Ibid.*, II, p. 274 no. 1061.

152. *Ibid.*, II, p. 262 no. 791.

153. *Ibid.*, I, p. 55 nos. 133-135.

154. See p. 57.

155. See especially Chapter III. But von Schlosser, 1897, p. 64, and Krautheimer, *Ghiberti*, 1956, p. 59, held that the medals of Constantine and Heraclius were 'forgeries' intended to deceive the Duke.

156. See above, p. 74.

157. Von Schlosser, 1897, p. 95, proposed a late antique statue in Aix as the source of this figure; Panofsky, *Netherlandish Painting*, 1953, I, p. 64, suggested an early Renaissance figure seen by the Limbourgs in Florence.

158. For the miniature see Durrieu, *Très Riches Heures*, 1904, pl. 37. Two of the Magi in this scene of the *Meeting* and again in the *Adoration* wear crowns like those of the two Emperors in the medals, to which we have referred above. Augustus in the scene of *Aracoeli* wears it also.

159. *Renaissance and Renascences*, 1960, p. 160.

160. '. . . presertim cum locus iste haud talibus libris (Sanctissimorum Patrum Hieronymi et Augustini insignibus opusculis) abundet, quibus tamen nunc per maxime delector, quibusque totis incumbo praecordiis, satur gentilium lectionum volumine, quae fastidium nunc magis excitant, quam voluptatem pariunt, animumque decerpendi fructus avidum, nec verborum elegantium foliis speciosis, nec suavioris eloquentiae vernantibus flosculis satis pro voto reficiunt. Horum autem patrum libri utilissimi et diserta abunde sunt oratione excultri, et maturos ac solis iustitiae ardore decoctos mihi fructus ferre videntur. Licuit adolescentiae pro legendis aliquamdiu floribus amoenos perambulare hortulos oratorum, sed quomodo florigerum ver non semper durat, verum in aestatem transmutatur, ac deinde in Autumnum vergit . . .' (Nicolai de Clemangiis, *Opera Omnia . . .* primus edidit Iohannes Martini Lydius, Lyon, 1613, p. 320).

161. G. Lanson, *Histoire de la littérature française*, Paris, 1952, pp. 154 ff. The idea of a temporary termination of the humanist movement in France around 1420 has been contested in recent scholarship. See Simone, *Rinascimento*, 1961, pp. 241 ff.

162. See p. 70.

163. See above, p. 70.

164. *Trattato*, ed. von Oettingen, p. 659. See above, p. 53, for discussion of the *Gemma Augustea*.

165. *Livre des fais et bonnes meurs du sage roy Charles*, ed. Michaut and Poujoulat, pp. 17 f.

BIBLIOGRAPHY

The principal entries for all catalogues of exhibitions and of permanent holdings of libraries and museums are listed topographically. For instance *Arte lombarda dai Visconti agli Sforza* appears under Milan, Palazzo Reale.

KEY TO ABBREVIATIONS

Comptes rendus = Paris, *Académie des Inscriptions et Belles-lettres. Comptes rendus.*

Gaz. B.-A. = *Gazette des Beaux-Arts.*

Mémoires = Paris, *Académie des Inscriptions et Belles-Lettres. Mémoires.*

Rev. belge = *Revue belge d'archéologie et d'histoire de l'art.*

Rev. de l'art a. et m. = *Revue de l'art ancien et moderne.*

SFRMP = *Société Française de Reproductions de Manuscrits à Peintures.*

Walters Journal = *Journal of the Walters Art Gallery.*

Abaecherli, A. L., 'Fercula, Carpenta, and Tensae in the Roman Procession', *Boll. dell'Associazione Internazionale Studi Mediterranei*, VI, 1935-1936, pp. 1-20.

Adhémar, H., *Les primitifs flamands. Le musée national du Louvre*, Brussels, I, 1962.

Adhémar, H., 'La date d'un portrait de Jean sans Peur, duc de Bourgogne', *Revue du Louvre*, XI, 1961, pp. 265-268.

Adhémar, H., *see also* Paris, Musée du Louvre.

Adhémar, J., *Influences antiques dans l'art du moyen âge français*, London, 1939.

Aeschlimann, E., and P. d'Ancona, *Dictionnaire des miniaturistes du moyen âge et de la renaissance dans les différentes contrées de l'Europe . . .*, 2nd ed., rev., Milan, 1949.

Ainaud, J., *see* Domínguez Bordona and Ainaud.

Ameisenowa, Z., *see* Cracow, Biblioteka Jagiellónska.

Ameisenowa, Z., *see also* Warsaw, Biblioteka Narodowa.

Ancona, M. L. d', *Miniatura e miniatori a Firenze dal secolo XIV al secolo XVI*, Florence, 1962.

Ancona, P. d', *La miniature italienne du Xᵉ au XVIᵉ siècle*, Paris, 1925.

Andersson, A., 'Till det bóhmiska glasmåleriets historia på Karl IV:s tid', *Konsthistorisk Tidskrift*, XVI, 1947, pp. 72-93.

André-Michel, R., *Avignon, les fresques du Palais des Papes*, Paris, 1920.

Apel, W., *French Secular Music of the Late Fourteenth Century*, Cambridge, Mass., 1950.

Ardillots, Vicomte des, in *L'intermédiare des chercheurs et curieux*, XXI, 1888, cols. 572-573.

Arslan, E., 'Riflessioni sulla pittura gotica "internazionale" in Lombardia nel tardo Trecento', *Arte Lombarda*, VIII, pt. 2, 1963, pp. 25-66.

Arte Lombarda dai Visconti agli Sforza, *see* Milan, Palazzo Reale.

Aubert, H., 'Notices sur les manuscrits Petau, conservés à la Bibliothèque de Genève', *Bibl. École des Chartes*, LXX, 1909, pp. 247-302, 471-522; LXXII, 1911, pp. 279-313, 556-599.

Aubert, H., 'Les principaux manuscrits à peintures de la Bibliothèque publique et universitaire de Genève', *Bulletin de la Société Française de Reproductions de Manuscrits à Peintures*, II, 1912, pp. 55-107.

Aubert, M., *La sculpture française au moyen âge*, Paris, 1946.

Avignon. Musée Calvet. *Catalogue sommaire des manuscrits de la Bibliothèque d'Avignon* (L. H. Labande), Avignon, 1892.

Avignon. Musée Calvet. *Catalogue des tableaux exposés dans les galeries du Musée Calvet d'Avignon* (J. Girard), Avignon, 1909.

Babelon, E., *Histoire de la gravure sur gemmes*, Paris, 1902.

Babelon, E., *see also* Paris, Bibliothèque nationale and Archives nationales.

Bacci, P., *Documenti e commenti per la storia dell'arte*, Florence, 1944.

Bacha, E., *see* Brussels, Bibliothèque Royale de Belgique.

Baldani, R., *La pittura a Bologna nel secolo XIV* (Documenti e Studi della R. Deputazione di Storia Patria per le Provincie di Romagna, III), Bologna, 1909.

Baldass, L., *Jan van Eyck*, London [1952].

Baltimore. Walters Art Gallery. *Illuminated Books of the Middle Ages and Renaissance . . .* (D. Miner), Baltimore, 1949.

Baltimore. Walters Art Gallery. *The International Style* (mss. ed. D. Miner; much else by P. Verdier), [Baltimore, 1962].

Barnes, A. C., and V. de Mazia, *The French Primitives and their Forms, from their Origin to the End of the Fifteenth Century*, Merion, Pa. [1931].

[Barrois, J. B. J.], *Bibliothèque protypographique, ou librairies des fils du roi Jean, Charles V, Jean de Berri, Philippe de Bourgogne et les siens*, Paris, 1830.

Barthélemy, L., 'Inventaire du château des Baux, en 1426' (extract from the *Revue des sociétés savantes*, VI, 1877), Paris, 1878.

Barzon, A., *Codici miniati, Biblioteca capitolare della Cattedrale di Padova*, Padua, 1950.

Basel. Escher, K., *Die Miniaturen in den Basler Bibliotheken, Museen und Archiven*, Basel, 1917.

Bastard, Auguste comte de, *Peintures et ornements des manuscrits . . . depuis le IVe siècle jusqu'à la fin du XVIe*, Paris, 1832–1869.

Bastard, Auguste comte de, *Librairie de Jean de France, duc de Berri*, Paris, 1834. 24 plates – text never published.

Baylé, J., *see* Beaulieu and Baylé.

Bazin, G., *L'école parisienne: XIVe siècle*, Geneva [1942].

Bazin, G., *L'école provençale: XIV-XV siècles*, Geneva [1944].

Beatty Collection, formerly London, *see* Dublin.

Beauchamp, R. de, 'Note sur le château de Bicêtre', *Bull. de la Société des Antiquaires de l'Ouest*, X, 1904, p. 135.

Beaulieu, M. and J. Baylé, *Le costume en Bourgogne de Philippe le Hardi à Charles le Téméraire*, Paris, 1956.

Becker, P. A., 'Christine de Pizan', *Zeitschrift für französische Sprache und Literatur*, LIV, 1931, pp. 129-163.

Beenken, H., 'Zur Entstehungsgeschichte des Genter Altars: Hubert und Jan van Eyck', *Wallraf-Richartz Jahrbuch*, N.S. II-III, 1933-1934, pp. 176-232.

Beer, R., *see* Vienna, Nationalbibliothek.

Behling, L., *Die Pflanze in der mittelalterlichen Tafelmalerei*, Weimar, 1957.

Beissel, S., 'Exposition de l'histoire de l'art à Düsseldorf, 1904', *Arts anciens de Flandre*, I, [1905?], pp. 49-51.

Beissel, S., *see also* Rome, Vatican.

Bell, D., *Le songe du vieil pèlerin de Philippe de Mézières*, Geneva, 1955.

Bell, D., *L'idéal éthique de la royauté en France au moyen âge*, Geneva, 1962.

Bellaguet, M. L., *see Chronique du religieux de Saint-Denys*.

Bengy-Puyvallée, Maurice de, 'Un épisode de la vie du duc Jean de Berry: son mariage avec Jeanne de Boulogne', *Mémoires Société des Antiquaires du Centre*, XXXVI, 1913, pp. 93-116.

Berenson, B., *Italian Pictures of the Renaissance*, London, 1932.

Berenson, B., *Italian Pictures, Florentine School*, London, 1963. 2v.

Berenson, B., *see also* James and Berenson.

Berger, S., *La Bible française au moyen âge. Étude sur les plus anciennes versions de la Bible écrite en prose de langue d'oïl*, Paris, 1884.

Berger, S., and P. Durrieu, 'Les notes pour l'enlumineur dans les manuscrits du moyen âge', *Mémoires Société des Antiquaires de France*, LIII, 1893, pp. 1-30.

Berlin. Staatliche Museen, Gemäldegalerie and Kupferstichkabinett. Winkler, F., 'Die spanischen und französischen Primitiven in der Gemäldegalerie und im Kupferstichkabinett', *Berliner Museen, Berichte*, XLIX, 1928, pp. 6-12.

Berlin. Staatliche Museen. Kupferstichkabinett. *Beschriebendes Verzeichnis der Miniaturen-Handschriften und Einzelblätter des Kupferstichkabinetts der Staatlichen Museen, Berlin* (P. Wescher), Leipzig, 1931.

Berlin. Staatsbibliothek. *Beschreibendes Verzeichnis der Miniaturen und des Initialschmuckes in den Phillipps-Handschriften* (J. Kirchner), Leipzig, 1926.

Berlin. Staatsbibliothek. *Schöne Handschriften aus dem Besitz der Preussischen Staatsbibliothek*, Berlin, 1931.

Bernath, M., 'The Prayer-Book of a Saint', *Burl. Mag.*, XXIV, 1913, pp. 131-134.

Bernheimer, R., *Wild Men in the Middle Ages*, Cambridge, Mass., 1952.

Berthomieu, L., 'Le Parement de Narbonne', *Commission Arch. de Narbonne, Bulletin*, 1912, pp. 291-299.

Berti, L., 'Masaccio 1422', *Commentari*, XII, 1961, pp. 84-107.

Bertrand, G., *see* Leningrad, Publichnaĭa bïblïoteka.

Biagi, G., *see* Florence, Biblioteca Mediceo-Laurenziana.

Bierstadt, O. A., *see* New York, Hoe Library.

Billanovich, G., 'Autografi del Boccaccio nella Biblioteca nazionale di Parigi', *Atti della Accademia Nazionale dei Lincei*, VII, 1952, pp. 376-388.

Birkmeyer, K., 'The Pietà from San Remigio', *Gaz. B.-A.*, LX, 1962, pp. 459-480.

Blanchard, P., *Les Heures de Savoie; Facsimiles of Fifty-two Pages from the Hours Executed for Blanche of Burgundy . . . Burnt at Turin in 1904*, London, 1910.

Blanchet, A., 'Les camées de Bourges', *Congrès archéologique de France* (65th session, Bourges, 1898), Paris, 1900, pp. 236-254.

Blanchet, A., 'Le monnayage du Duc Jean de Berry',

Mémoires Société Antiquaires du Centre, XXXIX, 1919–1920, pp. 78-87.

Blum, A., and P. Lauer, *La miniature française aux XVe et XVIe siècles*, Paris, 1930.

Blum, R., 'Jean Pucelle et la miniature parisienne du XIVe siècle', *Scriptorium*, III, 1949, pp. 211-217.

Blümner, H., *Technologie und Terminologie der Gewerbe und Künste bei den Griechen und Römern*, Leipzig, 1875–1886. 4v.

Bober, H., 'The Zodiacal Miniature of the "Très Riches Heures" of the Duke of Berry – Its Sources and Meaning', *Warburg Journal*, XI, 1948, pp. 1-34.

Bober, H., 'André Beauneveu and Mehun-sur-Yèvre', *Speculum*, XXVIII, 1953, pp. 741-753.

Boccaccio, G., *Le liure Cameron autrement surnomme le prince Galliot . . . Translate de latin en francoys par Laurens du Premierfaict*, Paris, Michel Le Noir, 1521.

Bode, W. von, 'Tonabdrücke von Reliefarbeiten niederländischer Goldschmiede aus dem Kreise der Künstler des Herzogs Johann von Berry', *Amtliche Berichte aus den königlichen Kunstsammlungen*, XXXVIII, 1917, pp. 314-328.

Boeckler, A. and A. A. Schmid, 'Die Buchmalerei', in F. Milkau, *Handbuch der Bibliothekswissenschaft*, 2nd ed., rev. by G. Leyh, Wiesbaden, I, 1952, pp. 249-387.

Boinet, A., *Le vieux Metz*, Paris, 1923.

Boinet, A., *see also* Paris, Bibliothèque de la Chambre des Députés.

Boinet, A., *see also* Paris, Bibliothèque Sainte-Geneviève.

Boinet, A., *see also* Paris, Musée de Cluny.

Bologna, F., 'Les primitifs méditerranéens', *Paragone*, No. 37, 1953, pp. 49-56.

Bologna, F., 'Di alcuni rapporti tra Italia e Spagna nel Trecento e "Antonius Magister"', *Arte antica e moderna*, 1961, pp. 27-48.

Bond, F., *Wood Carvings in English Churches*, London, 1910.

Bonnet, E., 'Une association de peintres montpelliérains et avignonnais au XIVe siècle', *Mémoires Montpellier*, VIII, 1922, pp. 365-372.

Boon, K. G., 'Over Grisaille en Zilverstift', *Maandblad voor beeldende Kunsten*, XXVI, 1950, pp. 263-273.

Bordona, J. Domínguez, *see* Domínguez Bordona, J.

Borenius, T., 'Die französische Ausstellung in London', *Pantheon*, IX, 1932, pp. 82-92.

Borland, C. R., *see* Edinburgh, University Library.

Boschetto, A., 'Dipinti italiani nei Musées Royaux. I. Una "crocifissione" attribuita a "stretto sequace di

Simone Martini ad Avignone"', *Bull. des Musées Royaux des Beaux-Arts*, II, 1953, pp. 155-162.

Bosredon, P. de, *Sigillographie de l'ancienne Auvergne*, Brive, 1895.

Bouchot, H., *Les primitifs français, 1292–1500; complément documentaire au catalogue de l'exposition*, Paris, 1904.

Bouchot, H., 'Jean Foucquet', *Gaz. B.-A.*, IV, 1890, pp. 273-281; 416-426.

Bouchot, H., 'Le "Parement de Narbonne" au Louvre', *Gaz. B.-A.*, XXXI, 1904, pp. 5-26.

Bouchot, H., 'I primitivi francesi: "l'ouvraige de Lombardie"', *L'arte*, VIII, 1905, pp. 18-32.

Bouchot, H., *see also* Paris, Louvre.

Boucicaut, *see* Le livre des faicts du mareschal de Boucicaut.

Bourges. Bibliothèque municipale, Musées, et Comité de la Foire-Exposition. *Mécènes et amateurs d'art berrichons du moyen âge et de la Renaissance*, Exposition, 1956.

Bourges. Musées. *Chefs-d'œuvre des peintres-enlumineurs de Jean de Berry et de l'école de Bourges* [Bourges, 1951].

Boutaric, E., 'Recherches archéologiques sur le Palais de Justice de Paris', *Mémoires Société Antiquaires de France*, XXVII, 1864, pp. 1-70.

Bradley, J. W., *A Dictionary of Miniaturists, Illuminators, Calligraphers, and Copyists . . .*, London, 1887–1889. 3v.

Brandi, C., *La Regia Pinacoteca di Siena*, Rome, 1933.

Braun, J. (Vogelstein), *Von französischer Buchmalerei*, Munich [1914].

Bredt, E. W., *see* Nuremberg, Germanisches Nationalmuseum.

Broussolle, J. C., *Le Christ de la Légende dorée*, Paris [1904].

Brun, R., 'Notes sur le commerce des objets d'art en France et principalement à Avignon à la fin du XIVe siècle', *Bibl. École des Chartes*, XCV, 1934, pp. 327-346.

Brunet, J.-C., *Manuel du libraire et de l'amateur de livres*, 5th ed., Paris, 1860–1865. 6v.

Brussels. Bibliothèque Royale de Belgique. *Catalogue des manuscrits de la Bibliothèque royale de Belgique* (J. van den Gheyn), Brussels, 1901–1936. 12v.

Brussels. Bibliothèque Royale de Belgique. *Un livre d'heures du duc Jean de Berry. Manuscrit de la Bibliothèque royale de Belgique, 11060-61* (K. M. P. de Mont), Haarlem [1904].

Brussels. Bibliothèque Royale de Belgique. *Les très belles miniatures de la Bibliothèque royale de Belgique* (E. Bacha), Brussels and Paris, 1913.

Brussels. Bibliothèque Royale de Belgique. Gaspar, C. and F. Lyna, *Les principaux manuscrits à peintures de la*

Bibliothèque royale de Belgique, SFRMP, Paris, 1937–1947. 2 pts. in 3v.

Brussels. Musées Royaux des Beaux-Arts de Belgique. *Exposition des principales acquisitions récentes (1946–1956)*, Brussels, 1956.

Brussels. Palais des Beaux-Arts. *La miniature flamande. Le mécénat de Philippe le Bon* (L. M. J. Delaissé), Brussels, 1959.

Brutails, A., 'Bible de Charles V et autres manuscrits du chapitre de Girone', *Bibl. École des Chartes*, XLVII, 1886, pp. 637-645.

Bunim, M. S., *Space in Medieval Painting and the Forerunners of Perspective*, New York, 1940.

Burckhardt, D., 'Studien zur Geschichte der altoberrheinischen Malerei', *Jahrbuch der Preussischen Kunstsammlungen*, XXVII, 1906, pp. 179-197.

Byles, A. T. P., see *The Book of Fayttes of Armes and of Chyvalrye*.

Byvanck, A., 'Nord-Nederlandsche miniaturen', *Oudheidkundig Jaarboek*, III, 1923, pp. 188-201.

Byvanck, A., rev. of Bella Martens, '*Meister Francke*', *Oudheidkundig Jaarboek*, X, 1930, pp. 31-34.

Byvanck, A., 'Aanteekeningen over handschriften met miniaturen', *Oudheidkundig Jaarboek*, XI, 1931, pp. 1-18.

Byvanck, A., *see also* The Hague, Koninklijke Bibliotheek.

Byvanck, A., *see also* Netherlands.

Cambridge. Fitzwilliam Museum. *A Descriptive Catalogue of the Manuscripts in the Fitzwilliam Museum* (M. R. James), Cambridge, 1895.

Cambridge. Fitzwilliam Museum. *A Descriptive Catalogue of the McClean Collection of Manuscripts in the Fitzwilliam Museum* (M. R. James), Cambridge, 1912.

Cambridge. Harvard University. *Illuminated and Calligraphic Manuscripts; an Exhibition Held at the Fogg Art Museum and Houghton Library, February 14–April 1, 1955*, Cambridge, 1955.

The Cambridge Medieval History, New York and Cambridge, 1924–1936. 8v.

Campbell, P.-G.-C., *L'Épître d'Othéa. Étude sur les sources de Christine de Pisan*, Paris, 1924.

Camus, 'Notice de deux manuscrits de la Bibliothèque nationale, cotés aujourd'hui 6829 et 6829^2 parmi les manuscrits français; le premier coté ci-devant 250, le second 517 et 1085', *Notices et extraits*, VI [1800], pp. 106-124.

Carli, E., *Dipinti 'senesi' del Contado e della Maremma*, Milan, 1955.

Carta, F., C. Cipolla, and C. Frati, *Atlante paleografico-artistico compilato sui manoscritti esposti in Torino alla mostra d'arte sacra nel MDCCCXCVIII*, Turin, 1899.

Cartellieri, O., *The Court of Burgundy*, New York, 1929.

Cassel, P., *Der Schwan in Sage und Leben*, Berlin, 1872.

Castan, A., 'Les Chroniques de Burgos traduites pour le roi de France Charles V, en partie retrouvées à la bibliothèque de Besançon', *Bibl. École des Chartes*, XLIV, 1883, pp. 265-283.

Castelnuovo, E., *Un pittore italiano alla corte di Avignone. Matteo Giovannetti e la pittura in Provenza nel secolo XIV* [Torino], 1962.

Catalogue général des manuscrits des bibliothèques publiques de France. see France, Ministère de l'Éducation.

Cavalcaselle, G. B., see Crowe and Cavalcaselle.

Cellini, P., 'L'opera di Arnolfo all'Aracoeli', *Boll. d'Arte*, XLVII, 1962, pp. 180-195.

Les cent ballades, ed. G. Raynaud (Société des Anciens Textes Français), Paris, 1905.

Champeaux, A. de, 'Les relations du duc Jean de Berry avec l'art italien', *Gaz. B.-A.*, XXXVIII, 1888, pp. 409-415.

Champeaux, A. de and P. Gauchery, *Les travaux d'art exécutés pour Jean de France, duc de Berry, avec une étude biographique sur les artistes employés par ce prince*, Paris, 1894.

Champion, P. M. J. B., *Vie de Charles d'Orléans*, Paris, 1911.

Champollion-Figeac, A., *Louis et Charles ducs d'Orléans*, Paris, 1844.

Champollion-Figeac, A., *Documents paléographiques relatifs à l'histoire des beaux-arts*, Paris, 1868.

Chantilly. Musée Condé. *Le cabinet des livres: manuscrits*, Paris, 1900–1901. 3v.

Chantilly. Musée Condé. *Les principaux manuscrits à peintures du Musée Condé* (J. Meurgey), SFRMP, Paris, 1930. 2v.

Chartres. Bibliothèque municipale. *Les manuscrits enluminés de la Bibliothèque de Chartres* (Y. Delaporte), Chartres, 1929.

Chastel, A., *Art et humanisme à Florence au temps de Laurent le Magnifique*, Paris, 1959.

Chastel, A., 'Giotto coetaneo di Dante', in *Studien zur toskanischen Kunst. Festschrift für Ludwig Heinrich Heydenreich*, Munich, 1964, pp. 37-44.

Chatelet, A., 'Les étapes de l'enluminure des manuscrits dits de Turin et de Milan-Turin', *Revue des arts*, VI, 1956, pp. 199-206.

Chaumeau, J., *Histoire de Berri*, Lyons, 1566.

Cheltenham, Phillipps Collection (formerly), *see* P. Durrieu.

Cheltenham, Phillipps Collection (formerly), *see also* London, Sotheby & Co.

Chenu, P., 'Au sujet du monnayage du duc Jean de Berry', *Mémoires Société des Antiquaires du Centre*, XLV, 1931–1933, pp. 147-153.

Chichmaref, V., *see* G. de Machaut.

Chiovenda, L., 'Die Zeichnungen Petrarcas', *Archivum Romanicum*, XVII, 1933, pp. 1 ff.

Christ, K., *see* Rome, Vatican.

Christine de Pisan, *Le livre des fais et bonnes meurs du sage roy Charles*, in *Nouvelle collection des mémoires pour servir à l'histoire de France depuis le XIIIᵉ siècle jusqu'à la fin du XVIIIᵉ*, ed. [J. F.]Michaud and [J. J. F.] Poujoulat, ser. I, pt. II, 1850, pp. 1-145.

Christine de Pisan, *Œuvres poétiques de Christine de Pisan*, ed. M. Roy (Société des Anciens Textes Français), Paris, 1886–1896. 3v.

Christine de Pisan, *Le livre de la paix*, ed. C. C. Willard, The Hague, 1958.

Christine de Pisan, *Le livre de la mutacion de fortune* (Société des Anciens Textes Français), I, ed. S. Solente, 1959.

Chronique du religieux de Saint-Denys, contenant le règne de Charles VI, de 1380 à 1422 (Collection de documents inédits sur l'histoire de France), ed. M. L. Bellaguet, Paris, 1839–1852. 6v.

Clark, K., *The Nude*, London, 1957.

Clemen, P., *Die gotischen Monumentalmalereien der Rheinlande*, Düsseldorf, 1930. 2v.

Cleveland. Museum of Art. *Gothic Art 1360–1440* (W. D. Wixom), Cleveland, 1963.

Coche de la Ferté, E., 'Un camée de Bourges et la renaissance paléochrétienne à Venise au XIIIᵉ siècle', *Bull. de la Société Nationale des Antiquaires de France*, 1959, pp. 174-176.

Cockerell, S. C., *The Book of Hours of Yolande of Flanders, a Manuscript of the Fourteenth Century in the Library of Henry Yates Thompson*, London, 1905.

Cockerell, S. C., 'A Primitive Crucifixion', *Burl. Mag.*, L, 1927, pp. 108-111.

Coletti, L., 'Tommaso da Modena', *Boll. d'arte*, IV, 1924–1925, pp. 291-318.

Coletti, L., *L'arte di Tommaso da Modena*, Bologna, 1933.

Colgrave, B., ed., *The Paris Psalter* (Early English Manuscripts in Facsimile), Copenhagen, 1958.

La collection Spitzer, ed. F. Spitzer, Paris, 1890–1892, 2v.

Conway, W. M., *The Van Eycks and their Followers*, New York, 1921.

Conway, W. M., *see also* London, Royal Academy of Arts.

Coo, J. de, 'In Josephs Hosen Jhesus ghewonden wert', *Aachener Kunstblätter*, 1965, pp. 144-184.

Coopland, G. W., *The Tree of Battles of Honoré Bonet*, Cambridge, Mass., 1949.

Cortlandt F. Bishop Library, *see* New York, American Art Association.

Couderc, C., *Album de portraits d'après les collections du Département des manuscrits, Bibliothèque nationale*, Paris [1910].

Couderc, C., *see also* Paris, Bibliothèque nationale.

Courajod, L., *Les origines de la Renaissance en France au XIVᵉ et au XVᵉ siècle*, Paris, 1888.

Courajod, L., *Leçons professées à l'École du Louvre. Vol. II: Origines de la Renaissance*, Paris, 1901.

Coville, A., *Gontier et Pierre Col et l'humanisme en France au temps de Charles VI*, Paris, 1934.

Cracow. Biblioteka Jagiellónska. Ameisenowa, Z., 'Les principaux manuscrits à peintures de la Bibliothèque jagellonienne de Cracovie', *Bulletin de la Société Française de Reproductions de Manuscrits à Peintures*, XVII, 1933.

Cracow. Muzeum Narodowe (formerly Czartoryskich). Gąsiorowska, M. (Jarostawiecka), 'Les principaux manuscrits à peintures de Musée des princes Czartoryski, à Cracovie', *Bulletin de la Société Française de Reproductions de Manuscrits à Peintures*, XVIII, 1935. 2v.

Crapelet, G. A., *see Les demandes faites par le roi Charles VI . . . et les réponses de Pierre Salmon*.

Crevier, M., *Histoire de l'Université de Paris*, Paris, 1761. 7v.

Crowe, J. A., and G. B. Cavalcaselle, *The Early Flemish Painters*, 2nd ed., London, 1872.

Dalton, O. M., *The Royal Gold Cup in the British Museum*, London, 1924.

Dante, *The Divine Comedy*, ed. J. Sinclair, London, 1958. 3v.

Degenhart, B., 'Autonome Zeichnungen bei mittelalterlichen Künstlern', *Münchner Jahrbuch der bildenden Kunst*, I, 1950, pp. 93-158.

Dehaisnes, C., *Documents et extraits divers concernant l'histoire de l'art dans la Flandre, l'Artois et le Hainaut avant le XVᵉ siècle*, Lille, 1886. 2v.

Dehaisnes, C., *Histoire de l'art dans la Flandre, l'Artois et le Hainaut avant le XVᵉ siècle*, Lille, 1886.

Delachenal, R., *Histoire de Charles V*, Paris, 1931. 5v.

Delachenal, R., *see also Les grandes chroniques de France*.

Delaissé, L. M. J., *Medieval Illuminations from the Library of Burgundy in the Department of Manuscripts of the Royal Library of Belgium*, Brussels, 1958. French ed., Geneva, 1959.

Delaissé, L. M. J., 'Une production d'un atelier parisien et le caractère composite de certains livres d'heures', *Scriptorium*, II, 1948, pp. 78-84.

Delaissé, L. M. J., 'Le livre d'heures d'Isabeau de Bavière', *Scriptorium*, IV, 1950, pp. 252-260.

Delaissé, L. M. J., 'Enluminure et peinture dans les Pays-Bas; À propos du livre de E. Panofsky, *Early Netherlandish Painting*', *Scriptorium*, XI, 1957, pp. 109-118.

Delaissé, L. M. J., 'Remaniements dans quelques manuscrits de Jean de Berry', *Gaz. B.-A.*, LXII, 1963, pp. 123-146.

Delaissé, L. M. J., *see also* Brussels, Palais des Beaux-Arts.

Delaissé, L. M. J., *see also* Oberlin, Oberlin College.

Delalain, P., *Étude sur le libraire parisien du XIIIe au XVe siècle*, Paris, 1891.

Delaporte, Y., *see* Chartres, Bibliothèque municipale.

Delisle, L., *Recherches sur l'ancienne Bibliothèque de la cathédrale du Puy*, n.p. [1867?]. See esp. pp. 439-459.

Delisle, L., *Le cabinet des manuscrits de la Bibliothèque impériale*. Paris, 1868-1881. 3v. and atlas. In v. 2-3 and atlas Bibliothèque nationale is substituted for Bibliothèque impériale.

Delisle, L., *Mélanges de paléographie et de bibliographie*, Paris, 1880.

Delisle, L., *Les manuscrits du comte d'Ashburnham . . .*, Paris, 1883.

Delisle, L., *Les collections Bastard d'Estang à la Bibliothèque nationale. Catalogue analytique.* Nogent-le-Rotrou, 1885.

Delisle, L. et P. Meyer, *L'Apocalypse en français au XIIIe siècle*, Paris, 1901.

Delisle, L., *Notice de douze livres royaux du XIIIe et du XIVe siècle*, Paris, 1902.

Delisle, L., *Fac-similé de livres copiés et enluminés pour le roi Charles V*, Nogent-le-Rotrou, 1903.

Delisle, L., *Recherches sur la librairie de Charles V*, Paris, 1907. 2v. and plates.

Delisle, L., *Les heures dites de Jean de Pucelle, manuscrit de la collection de M. le Baron Maurice de Rothschild*, Paris, 1910.

Delisle, L., 'Notes sur la bibliothèque de la Sainte-Chapelle de Bourges', *Bibl. École des Chartes*, II, 1856, pp. 142-159.

Delisle, L., 'Les livres d'heures du duc de Berry', *Gaz. B.-A.*, XXIX, 1884, pp. 97-110, 281-292, 391-405.

Delisle, L., 'Notice sur deux livres ayant appartenu au roi Charles V', *Notices et extraits*, XXXI, 1884, pp. 16-21.

Delisle, L., 'Le missel et pontifical d'Étienne de Loypau évêque de Luçon', *Bibl. École des Chartes*, XLVIII, 1887, pp. 527-534.

Delisle, L., 'Livres d'images destinés à l'instruction religieuse et aux exercises de piété des laïques', in *Histoire littéraire de la France*, XXXI, 1893, pp. 213-285.

Delisle, L., 'Notice sur un livre d'astrologie de Jean duc de Berri', *Bull. du Bibliophile*, 1896, pp. 105-116.

Delisle, L., rev. of P. Margry, *La conquête et les conquérants des îles Canaries . . .*, Paris, 1896, *Journal des savants*, 1896, pp. 644-659.

Delisle, L., 'Notice sur les psaumes allégorisés de Christine de Pisan', *Notices et extraits*, XXXV, pt. 2, 1897, pp. 551-559.

Delisle, L., 'Les heures de l'amiral Prigent de Coëtivy', *Bibl. École des Chartes*, LXI, 1900, pp. 186-200.

Delisle, L., 'Une œuvre nouvelle de peintre Jean Fouquet', *Journal des savants*, I, 1903, pp. 265-275.

Delisle, L., 'La Bible de Robert de Billyng et de Jean Pucelle', *Rev. de l'art chrét.*, LX, 1910, pp. 297-308.

Delisle, L., *see also* Paris, Bibliothèque nationale.

Les demandes faites par le roi Charles VI touchant son état et le gouvernement de sa personne, avec les réponses de Pierre Salmon, son secrétaire et familier, ed. G. A. Crapelet, Paris, 1833.

Demay, G., *Inventaire des sceaux de la collection Clairambault*, Paris, 1885-1886, 2v.

Demus, O., *Mosaics of Norman Sicily*, London, 1950.

Demus, O., 'Zwei konstantinopler Marienikonen des 13. Jahrhunderts', *Jahrbuch der Österreichischen Byzantinischen Gesellschaft*, VII, 1958, pp. 87-104.

Denny, D., 'The Trinity in Enguerrand Quarton's *Coronation of the Virgin*', *Art Bull.*, XLV, 1963, pp. 48-52.

Deschamps, E., *Œuvres*, ed. Q. de Saint-Hilaire and G. Raynaud, Paris, 1878-1903. 11v.

Deshairs, L., *see* Paris, Musée Jacquemart-André.

De Tolnay, C., 'Zur Herkunft des Stiles der van Eyck', *Münchner Jahrbuch der bildenden Kunst*, IX, 1932, pp. 320-338.

De Wald, E. T., 'Pietro Lorenzetti', *Art Studies*, VII, 1929, pp. 131-166.

Dexel, W., *see* Jena, University.

Dijon. Bibliothèque municipale. Oursel, C., 'Les manuscrits à miniatures de la Bibliothèque de Dijon', *Bulletin de la Société Française de Reproductions de Manuscrits à Peintures*, VII, 1923, pp. 5-33.

Dimier, L., *Les primitifs français*, Paris [191-?].

Dimier, L. and L. Réau, *Histoire de la peinture française*, Paris, 1925–27. 5v.

Dimier, L., *L'art d'enluminure; traité du XIVe siècle traduit du latin avec des notes tirées d'autres ouvrages anciens et des commentaires*, Paris, 1927.

Dimier, L., 'Les primitifs français', *Gaz. B.-A.*, LXXVIII, pt. 2, 1936, pp. 35-36, 205-232; LXXIX, pt. 2, 1937, pp. 217-236; LXXX, pt. 1, 1938, pp. 223-232; LXXX, pt. 2, 1938, pp. 81-102, 208-236.

Dimier, L., 'D'un album de dessins supposé du XIVe siècle', *Mémoires Société Antiquaires de France*, LXXVIII, 1928–1933, pp. 12-23.

Diringer, D., *The Illuminated Book*, London, 1958.

Disney, A. N., ed., *Origin and Development of the Microscope*, London, 1928.

Domínguez Bordona, J., *Manuscritos con pinturas*, Madrid, 1933. 2v.

Domínguez Bordona, J. and J. Ainaud, *Miniatura, grabado, encuadernación* (Ars hispaniae, XVIII), Madrid, 1962.

Dorez, L., *see* Holkham Hall.

Douët d'Arcq, L.-C., *Collection de sceaux des archives de l'empire*, Paris, 1863–1868. 3v.

Douët d'Arcq, L.-C., *Inventaire de la bibliothèque du roi Charles VI*, Paris, 1867.

Doutrepont, G., *Inventaire de la 'librairie' de Philippe le Bon (1420)* . . ., Brussels, 1906.

Doutrepont, G., *La littérature française à la cour des ducs de Bourgogne* (Bibl. du XVe siècle, VIII), Paris, 1909.

Doyé, F. von Sales, *Heilige und Selige*, Leipzig [1930]. 2v.

Drobna, Z., *Die gotische Zeichnung in Böhmen*, Prague, 1956.

Dublin. Beatty Collection. Millar, E. G., *The Library of A. Chester Beatty; a Descriptive Catalogue of the Western Manuscripts* . . . [London], 1927–1930. 2v.

Dufour, V., *Une famille de peintres parisiens aux XIVe et XVe siècles*, Paris, 1877.

Dupont, J., *Les primitifs français (1350–1500)* . . ., Paris [1937].

Dupont, J. and C. Gnudi, *Gothic Painting*, Geneva [1954].

Dupont, J., 'Le triptyque d'Angers', *Gaz. B.-A.*, LXXVII, pt. 1, 1935, pp. 370-377.

Durrieu, P., *Heures de Turin; quarante-cinq feuillets à peintures provenant des Très Belles Heures de Jean de France duc de Berry* . . . *d'après les originaux de la Biblioteca nazionale de Turin et du Musée du Louvre*, Paris, 1902.

Durrieu, P., *La peinture à l'exposition des primitifs français*, Paris, 1904.

Durrieu, P., *Les Très Riches Heures de Jean de France, duc de Berry*, Paris, 1904.

Durrieu, P., *Les antiquités judaïques et le peintre Jean Fouquet*, Paris, 1908.

Durrieu, P., *Le Boccace de Munich* . . ., Munich, 1909.

Durrieu, P., *Les heures à l'usage d'Angers de la collection Martin Le Roy*, Paris, 1912.

Durrieu, P., *La miniature flamande*, Brussels, 1921.

Durrieu, P., *Les Très Belles Heures de Notre-Dame du duc Jean de Berry*, Paris, 1922.

Durrieu, P., 'Les manuscrits à peintures de la bibliothèque de Sir Thomas Phillipps à Cheltenham', *Bibl. École des Chartes*, L, 1889, pp. 381-432.

Durrieu, P., 'Manuscrits d'Espagne . . . d'après des notes prises, à Madrid, à l'exposition historique pour le quatrième centenaire de Colomb . . .', *Bibl. École des Chartes*, LIV, 1893, pp. 251-326.

Durrieu, P., 'Un dessin du Musée du Louvre', *Monuments et mémoires*, I, 1894, pp. 179-202.

Durrieu, P., 'Les miniatures d'André Beauneveu', *Le manuscrit*, I, 1894, pp. 51-56, 83-95.

Durrieu, P., 'Manuscrits de luxe exécutés pour des princes et des grands seigneurs français (notes et monographies)', *Le manuscrit*, II, 1895, pp. 1-5, 17-21, 34-35, 49-54, 65-66, 81-87, 97-103, 113-122, 129-135, 145-149, 162-168, 177-181.

Durrieu, P., 'Les débuts des Van Eyck', *Gaz. B.-A.*, XXIX, 1903, pp. 5-18, 107-120.

Durrieu, P., 'L'exposition des primitifs français. III. La peinture en France depuis le commencement du XIVe siècle jusqu'à la fin du règne de Charles VI', *Rev. de l'art a. et m.*, XV, 1904, pp. 241-262.

Durrieu, P., 'Les manuscrits à peintures de la Bibliothèque incendiée de Turin', *Rev. archéol.*, III, 1904, pp. 394-405.

Durrieu, P., 'Les "Belles Heures" de Jean de France duc de Berry', *Gaz. B.-A.*, XXXV, 1906, pp. 265-292.

Durrieu, P., 'Jacques Coene', *Arts anciens de Flandre*, II [1906?], pp. 5-22.

Durrieu, P., 'Le maître des Heures du Maréchal de Boucicaut', *Rev. de l'art a. et m.*, XIX, 1906, pp. 401-415; XX, 1906, pp. 21-35.

Durrieu, P., 'La peinture en France de Jean le Bon à la mort de Charles V (1350–1380)', in A. Michel, *Histoire de l'art*, Paris, III, pt. 1, 1907, pp. 101-137.

Durrieu, P., 'La peinture en France, le règne de Charles VI', in A. Michel, *Histoire de l'art*, Paris, III, pt. 1, 1907, pp. 137-169.

Durrieu, P., 'Les petits chiens du duc Jean de Berry',

Académie des Inscriptions et Belles-Lettres, Comptes rendus, 1909, pp. 866-875.

Durrieu, P., 'Le plus ancien manuscrit de la traduction française du Décaméron', *Académie des Inscriptions et Belles-Lettres, Comptes rendus,* 1909, pp. 342-350.

Durrieu, P., 'Un siècle de l'histoire de la miniature parisienne à partir du règne de Saint Louis', (rev. of Vitzthum, *Pariser Miniaturmalerei*), *Journal des savants,* VII, 1909, pp. 5-19.

Durrieu, P., 'Une vue de l'église du Saint-Sépulcre vers 1436, provenant du bon roi René', in *Florilegium; ... Melchior de Vogüé,* Paris, 1909, pp. 197-207.

Durrieu, P., 'La Bible du duc Jean de Berry conservée au Vatican', *Rev. de l'art a. et m.,* XXVII, 1910, pp. 5-20.

Durrieu, P., 'Découverte de deux importants manuscrits de la "librairie" des ducs de Bourgogne', *Bibl. École des Chartes,* LXXI, 1910, pp. 58-71.

Durrieu, P., 'Les manuscrits à peintures de la "Cité de Dieu"' (rev. of A. de Laborde, *Les manuscrits à peintures de la Cité de Dieu de Saint Augustin*), *Bull. bibliophile,* 1910, pp. 265-272.

Durrieu, P., 'Les "Très Belles Heures de Notre-Dame" du duc Jean de Berry [Fragments de Turin, du Baron M. de Rothschild, du Prince Trivulzio et du Louvre]', *Rev. archéol.,* XVI, 1910, pp. 30-51; 246-279.

Durrieu, P., 'Les aventures de deux splendides livres d'heures ayant appartenu au duc Jean de Berry', *Rev. de l'art a. et m.,* XXX, 1911, pp. 91-103.

Durrieu, P., 'Michelino da Besozzo et les relations entre l'art italien et l'art français à l'époque du règne de Charles VI', *Mémoires de l'Institut National de France. Académie des Inscriptions et Belles-Lettres,* XXXVIII, pt. 2, 1911, pp. 365-393.

Durrieu, P., 'Notes sur quelques manuscrits à peintures d'origine française ou flamande conservés en Italie', *Bulletin de la Société Française de Reproductions de Manuscrits à Peintures,* I, 1911, pp. 85-106.

Durrieu, P., 'La peinture en France depuis l'avènement de Charles VII jusqu'à la fin des Valois (1422-1589)', in A. Michel, *Histoire de l'art,* Paris, IV, pt. 2, 1911, pp. 701-768.

Durrieu, P., 'Le maître des "Grandes Heures de Rohan" et les Lescuier d'Angers', *Rev. de l'art a. et m.,* XXXII, 1912, pp. 81-98; 161-183.

Durrieu, P., 'Les Heures du Maréchal de Boucicaut du Musée Jacquemart-André', *Rev. de l'art chrét.,* LXIII, 1913, pp. 73-81, 145-164, 300-314; LXIV, 1914, pp. 28-35.

Durrieu, P., 'Un mystérieux dessinateur du début du XVIe siècle, le maître du "Monstrelet" de Roche-chouart', *Rev. de l'art a. et m.,* XXXIII, 1913, pp. 241-252, 321-336.

Durrieu, P., 'La provenance d'un des plus beaux manuscrits peints au XIVe siècle par Nicolo di Giacomo da Bologna', in *Bibl. École des Chartes,* LXXVII, 1916, pp. 111-136.

Durrieu, P., 'Les tableaux des collections du duc Jean de Berry', *Bibl. École des Chartes,* LXXIX, 1918, pp. 265-290.

Durrieu, P., 'Une "Pitié de Notre-Seigneur"; tableau français de l'époque du règne de Charles VI donné au Musée du Louvre', *Monuments et mémoires,* XXIII, 1918-1919, pp. 63-111.

Durrieu, P., *see also* Berger and Durrieu.

Durrieu, P., *see also* Paris, Musée Jacquemart-André.

Düsseldorf, Kunsthistorische Ausstellung, 1904. *Katalog,* 2nd ed., Düsseldorf, 1904.

Duverger, J., *Brussel als Kunstcentrum in de XIVe en de XVe Eeuw,* Antwerp, 1935.

Dvořák, M., *Das Rätsel der Kunst der Brüder Van Eyck,* Munich, 1925.

Dvořák, M., 'Die Illuminatoren des Johann von Neumarkt', *Jahrb. Kunsth. Slgn.,* XXII, 1901, pp. 35-126.

Dvořáková, V., J. Krása, A. Merhantová and K. Stejskal, *Gothic Mural Painting in Bohemia and Moravia 1300-1378,* London, 1964.

Edinburgh. University Library. *A Descriptive Catalogue of the Western Mediaeval Manuscripts in Edinburgh University Library* (C. R. Borland), Edinburgh, 1916.

Eichler, F. and E. Kris, *Die Kameen im Kunsthistorischen Museum,* Vienna, 1927, pp. 52-56.

Eisler, C., *see* Meiss and Eisler.

The Elder Pliny's Chapters on the History of Art, ed. K. Jex-Blake and E. Sellers, London, 1896.

Emilia and Romagna. *Emilia e Romagna* (Tesori delle biblioteche d'Italia, I, ed. D. Fava): 'La miniatura' by M. Salmi, Milan, 1932.

Enaud, F., 'L'école de Sienne aux bords du Rhône découverte en Avignon', *Plaisirs de France,* XXIX, 1963, no. 302, pp. 12-21.

Enaud, F., 'Les fresques de Simone Martini à Avignon', *Les monuments historiques de la France,* IX, 1963, pp. 115-181.

Escher, K., *see* Basel.

Evans, J., *Magical Jewels of the Middle Ages and the Renaissance,* Oxford, 1922.

Evans, J., *Art in Mediaeval France, 987-1498,* New York, 1948.

Evans, J., *English Art 1307-1461,* Oxford, 1949.

Evans, J., *Dress in Mediaeval France*, Oxford, 1952.

Evans, J., *Life in Medieval France*, London, 1957.

Fabré, A., *Trésor de la Sainte-Chapelle des ducs de Savoie au château de Chambéry*, Lyon, 1875.

Faucon, M., *La librairie des papes d'Avignon (1316–1420)*, Paris, 1886–1887. 2v.

Fava, D., *see* Emilia and Romagna.

Fava, D., *see also* Modena, Biblioteca Estense, Fava and Salmi.

Ferguson, W. K., *The Renaissance in Historical Thought*, Boston, 1948.

Fierens-Gevaert, H., *La renaissance septentrionale et les premiers maîtres des Flandres*, Brussels, 1905.

Fierens-Gevaert, H., *Les primitifs flamands*, Brussels, 1908–1912. 4v.

Fierens-Gevaert, H., *Les Très Belles Heures de Jean de France, duc de Berry*, Brussels, 1924.

Fierens-Gevaert, H., *Histoire de la peinture flamande des origines à la fin du XVᵉ siècle*, Paris, 1927–1929. 3v.

Filarete, A. A., *Trattato dell'architettura*, ed. and trans. W. von Oettingen (Quellenschriften für Kunstgeschichte und Kunsttechnik des Mittelalters und der Neuzeit), Vienna, 1890.

Filippini, F., and G. Zucchini, *Miniatori e pittori a Bologna, documenti dei secoli XIII e XIV*, Florence, 1947.

Fischer, Columban, O.F.M., 'Die Meditationes Vitae Christi. Ihre handschriftliche Ueberlieferung und die Verfasserfrage', *Archivum Franciscanum Historicum*, XXV, 1932, pp. 1-483.

Florence. Biblioteca Mediceo-Laurenziana. *Riproduzioni di manoscritti miniati* (G. Biagi), Florence, 1914.

Florence. Biblioteca Mediceo-Laurenziana. *Mostra di manoscritti medicei in occasione del V centenario di Lorenzo il Magnifico alla biblioteca Laurenziana di Firenze*, 1949.

Focillon, H., *Art d'Occident, le moyen âge roman et gothique*, Paris, 1938.

Focillon, H., *Le peintre des Miracles Notre Dame*, Paris, 1950.

Fontana, P., 'Osservazioni intorno ai rapporti di Vitruvio colla teorica dell'architettura del Rinascimento', in *Miscellanea di storia dell'arte in onore di Igino Benvenuto Supino*, Florence, 1933, pp. 305-322.

France. Ministère de l'Éducation. *Catalogue général des manuscrits des bibliothèques publiques de France. Départements . . .*, Paris, 1885–1933. 48v.

Francovich, G. de, 'L'origine e la diffusione del crocifisso gotico doloroso', *Römisches Jahrbuch für Kunstgeschichte*, II, 1938, pp. 143-261.

Frantz, M. A. Graeve, 'The Stone of Unction in Caravaggio's Painting for the Chiesa Nuova', *Art Bull.*, XL, 1958, pp. 223-238.

Freeman, M. B., *see* Rorimer and Freeman.

Friedl, A., *Magister Theodoricus*, Prague, 1956.

Friedländer, M. J., 'Die Ausstellung französischer Kunst in London', *Zeitschrift für Kunstgeschichte*, I, 1932, pp. 12-18.

Friedmann, H., *The Symbolic Goldfinch*, Washington, 1946.

Fröhlich-Bum, L., *see* Vienna, Albertina.

Froissart, J., *Œuvres*, ed. K. de Lettenhove, Brussels, 1867–1877.

Fry, R. E., 'On Two Miniatures by de Limbourg', *Burl. Mag.*, VII, 1905, pp. 435-445.

Fry, R. E., 'On a Fourteenth-Century Sketchbook', *Burl. Mag.*, X, 1906–1907, pp. 31-38.

Fry, R. E., 'The Authenticity of the Renders Collection', *Burl. Mag.*, L, 1927, pp. 261-267.

Gagnebin, B., 'Une Bible historiale de l'atelier de Jean Pucelle', *Genava*, IV, 1956, pp. 23-65.

Gagnebin, B., 'Le Boccace du duc de Berry', *Genava*, V, 1957, pp. 129-148.

Gagnebin, B., 'Le Tite-Live du duc de Berry', *Genava*, VII, 1959, pp. 193-214.

Gandilhon, R., *Inventaire des sceaux du Berry antérieurs à 1515, précédé d'une étude de sigillographie et de diplomatique*. Bourges, 1933.

Gandilhon, R., *see also* Hardy and Gandilhon.

Ganz, P., *Die Handzeichnungen Hans Holbeins d. J.*, Berlin, 1911–1937.

Garrison, E., *Italian Romanesque Panel Painting. An Illustrated Index*, Florence, 1949.

Gąsiorowska, M. (Jarostawiecka), *see* Cracow, Muzeum Narodowe.

Gaspar and Lyna, *see* Brussels, Bibliothèque Royale de Belgique.

Gauchery, P., 'Le palais du duc Jean et la Sainte-Chapelle', *Mémoires Société des Antiquaires du Centre*, XXXIX, 1919–1920, pp. 37-77.

Gauchery, P., 'Renseignements complémentaires sur la vie et les travaux de Jean de France duc de Berry', *Mémoires Société des Antiquaires du Centre*, XL, 1921, pp. 195-211.

Gauchery, P., *see also* Champeaux and Gauchery.

Germany. *Manuscrits français à peintures des bibliothèques d'Allemagne* (L. Olschki), Geneva, 1932.

Gheyn, J. van den, *Deux livres d'heures attribués à l'enlumineur Jacques Coene*, Brussels and Paris [1911].

Gheyn, J. van den, *see also* Brussels, Bibliothèque Royale de Belgique.

Lorenzo Ghibertis Denkwürdigkeiten, ed. J. von Schlosser, Berlin, 1912.

Gillet, L., *La peinture française, moyen âge et renaissance*, Paris, 1928.

Gilson, J. P., *see* London, British Museum, Warner and Gilson.

Giovannino de' Grassi, taccuino di disegni, facs. ed., Bergamo, 1961.

Girard, J., *see* Avignon, Musée Calvet.

Girardot, A. de, 'Histoire et inventaire du trésor de la cathédrale de Bourges', *Mémoires Société Antiquaires de France*, XXIV, 1859, pp. 193-272.

Gnudi, C., *Giotto*, Milan, 1958.

Gnudi, C., *see also* Dupont and Gnudi.

Goetz, O., 'Hie hencktt Judas', in *Form und Inhalt, Kunstgeschichtliche Studien O. Schmitt zum 60. Geburtstag*, Stuttgart, 1950, pp. 105-137.

Goldschmidt, A., *Die Elfenbeinskulpturen aus der Zeit der karolingischen und sächsischen Kaiser*, Berlin, 1914.

Goldschmidt, A., 'Die belgische Monumentalplastik des 12. Jahrhunderts', in *Belgische Kunstdenkmäler*, Munich, 1923, I, pp. 51-72.

Gombrich, E., 'Leonardo's Grotesque Heads. Prolegomena to their Study', in *Leonardo. Saggi e ricerche*, Rome, 1954, pp. 197-219.

Gonse, L., *L'art gothique*, Paris, 1890.

Gorissen, F., 'Jan Maelwael und die Brüder Limburg', *Gelre*, LIV, 1954, pp. 153-221.

Graesse, T., *see* Jacobus de Voragine.

Graeve, M. A., *see* Frantz, M. A. Graeve.

Les grandes chroniques de France. Chronique des règnes de Jean II et de Charles V, ed. R. Delachenal, Paris, 1910-1920. 4v.

Grandmaison, C. de, 'Gaignières, ses correspondants et ses collections de portraits', *Bibl. École des Chartes*, III, 1891, pp. 181-219.

Graves, F. M., *Deux inventaires de la maison d'Orléans (1389 et 1408)*, Paris, 1926.

Great Britain. British Manuscripts Project. Born, L. K., comp., *A Checklist of the Microfilms Prepared in England and Wales for the American Council of Learned Societies, 1941-1945*, Washington, 1955.

Green, R. B., *see* Meditations on the Life of Christ.

Greene, B. da Costa, *see* New York, Pierpont Morgan Library.

Grivot, D., and G. Zarnecki, *Gislebertus*, London, 1961.

Grodecki, L., 'Un panneau français au Musée de Princeton et les vitraux de Riom', *Rev. des arts*, 1951, pp. 209-221.

Grodecki, L., 'Les peintures du château de Karlstein et l'art français', *Bulletin monumental*, CXV, 1957, pp. 207-216.

Grodecki, L., 'Les verrières d'Évreux', *L'Œil*, 1957, pp. 18-25.

Groeber, G., *Grundriss der romanischen Philologie*, Strasbourg, 1888-1902. 2v. in 4.

Grönwoldt, R., 'Florentiner Stickereien in den Inventaren des Herzogs von Berry und der Herzöge von Burgund', *Mitteilungen des Kunsthistorischen Institutes in Florenz*, X, 1961, pp. 33-58.

Gudiol, J., S. Alcolea, and J. E. Cirlot, *Historia de la pintura en Cataluña*, Madrid [n.d.].

Gudiol, J., *Pintura gótica* (Ars Hispaniae, IX), Madrid [n.d.].

Guérin, P., *Recueil des documents concernant le Poitou contenus dans les registres de la chancellerie de France* (*Archives historiques du Poitou*), Poitiers, 1881-1909. 11v.

Guiffrey, J., *Inventaires de Jean duc de Berry (1401-1416)*, Paris, 1894-1896. 2v.

Guiffrey, J., 'La ménagerie du duc Jean de Berry, 1370-1403', *Mémoires Société Antiquaires du Centre*, XXIII, 1899, pp. 63-84.

Guiffrey, J., 'Académie de Saint-Luc', in *Archives de l'art français*, IX, 1915, pp. 1-6.

Guiffrey, J., 'La communauté des peintres et sculpteurs parisiens, dite Académie de Saint-Luc (1391-1776)', *Journal des savants*, XIII, 1915, pp. 145-156.

Guiffrey, J., P. Marcel, and C. Terrasse, *La peinture française: Les primitifs*, Paris [1926-1928]. 2v.

Guignard, J., 'Enlumineurs gothiques', *L'information de l'histoire de l'art*, VII, 1962, pp. 104-112.

Guillibert, 'Deux statuettes polychromées de Saint Louis de Provence, évêque de Toulouse, et de Sainte Consorce, conservées à Aix en Provence', *Bull. archéologique*, 1902, pp. 280-289.

Günther, U., 'Die Musiker des Herzogs von Berry', *Musica Disciplina*, XVII, 1963, pp. 79-91.

Guyot de Villeneuve, F. G. A. de, *Notice sur un manuscrit français du XIVe siècle; les heures du maréchal de Boucicaut* (Société des Bibliophiles Français), Paris, 1889.

Habich, G., *Die Medaillen der italienischen Renaissance*, Stuttgart and Berlin [1922].

The Hague. Koninklijke Bibliotheek. Byvanck, A., *Les principaux manuscrits à peintures de la Bibliothèque royale des Pays-Bas et du Musée Meermanno-Westreenianum à la Haye*, SFRMP, Paris, 1924.

The Hague, Museum Meermanno-Westreenianum, *see* The Hague, Koninklijke Bibliotheek.

Hahnloser, H., *Villard de Honnecourt*, Vienna, 1935.

Haller, E., *Analyse einer französischen Handschrift aus dem Anfang des XV. Jahrhunderts* (Diss. Heidelberg), 1932.

Hardy, G. and A. Gandilhon, *Bourges et les abbayes et châteaux du Berry*, Paris, 1912.

Harold, Bishop of Gibraltar, V. Seymer, and W. H. and G. Buckler, 'The Church of Asinou, Cyprus, and its Frescoes', *Archaeologia*, LXXXIII, 1933, pp. 327-350.

Harrsen, M., *The Neckcei-Lipócz Bible*, Washington, 1949.

Haseloff, A., 'La miniature des XIIIᵉ et XIVᵉ siècles', in A. Michel, *Histoire de l'art*, Paris, II, pt. 1, 1906, pp. 329-371.

Haseloff, G., *Die Psalterillustration im 13. Jahrhundert; Studien zur Geschichte der Buchmalerei in England, Frankreich und den Niederlanden* [Kiel], 1938.

Hausenstein, W., *Tafelmalerei der alten Franzosen*, Munich, 1923.

Hazé, M., *Notices pittoresques sur les antiquités et les monumens du Berri*, Bourges, 1834.

Heckscher, W. S., 'Relics of Pagan Antiquity in Mediaeval Settings', *Warburg Journal*, I, 1937-1938, pp. 204-220.

Heimann, A., 'Der Meister der "Grandes Heures de Rohan" und seine Werkstatt', *Städel-Jahrbuch*, VII-VIII, 1932, pp. 1-61.

Heimann, A., 'L'iconographie de la Trinité', *L'art chrét.*, I, 1934, pp. 37-58.

Heimann, A., 'The Giac Book of Hours', *Burl. Mag.*, LXXI, 1937, pp. 83 f.

Heinemann, O. von, *see* Wolfenbüttel, Herzog-August-Bibliothek.

Herbert, J. A., *Illuminated Manuscripts*, New York, 1911.

Hermanin, F., *L'arte in Roma dal secolo VIII al secolo XIV*, Bologna, 1945.

Hermann, H. J., *see* Vienna, Nationalbibliothek.

Hessel, A., *Geschichte der Bibliotheken*, Göttingen, 1925.

Hill, G. F., *Pisanello*, London, 1905.

Histoire littéraire de la France, XXIV (*Quatorzième siècle*), Paris, 1862.

Hiver de Beauvoir, A., *La librairie de Jean duc de Berry au château de Mehun-sur-Yèvre, 1416*, Paris, 1860.

Hiver de Beauvoir, A., 'Description . . . du trésor . . . donné par Jean, duc de Berry, à la Sainte-Chapelle de Bourges', *Mémoires de la Société Historique, Littéraire et Scientifique du Cher*, I, pt. 1, 1857; pp. 1-128; pt. 2, 1860, pp. 255-280.

Hiver de Beauvoir, see also *Journal de Jehan Glaumeau, Bourges, 1541–1562*.

Hoepli Collection, *see* Milan.

Holkham Hall. *Les manuscrits à peintures de la bibliothèque de Lord Leicester à Holkham Hall, Norfolk* (L. Dorez), Paris, 1908.

Homolka, J., *see* Pešina and Homolka.

Hubert, J., 'Quelques vues de la cité au XVᵉ siècle dans un bréviaire parisien conservé à la Bibliothèque municipale de Châteauroux', *Mémoires Société Antiquaires de France*, LXXVII, 1924-1927, pp. 25-42.

Huizinga, J., *The Waning of the Middle Ages*, London, 1924.

Hulin de Loo, G., *Heures de Milan; troisième partie des Très-belles Heures de Notre-Dame, enluminées par les peintres de Jean de France, duc de Berry et par ceux du duc Guillaume de Bavière, comte du Hainaut et de Hollande*, Brussels, 1911.

Hulin de Loo, G., and E. Michel, *Early Flemish Pictures in the Renders Collection*, London, 1927.

Hulin de Loo, G., 'Les Très Riches Heures de Jean de France, duc de Berry, par Pol de Limbourc et ses frères', *Bull. de Gand*, XI, 1903, pp. 178 ff.

Hulin de Loo, G., 'La Bible de Philippe le Hardi historiée par les frères de Limbourc', *Bull. de Gand*, XVI, 1908, pp. 183 ff.

Hulin de Loo, G., 'Rapport', *Académie Royale de Belgique. Bulletins de la classe des beaux-arts*, VII, 1925, pp. 117-127.

Hulin de Loo, see also *Mélanges Hulin de Loo*.

Huth Collection, *see* London, British Museum.

Huyghe, R., 'Un Portement de Croix français de la fin du XIVᵉ siècle', *Bull. Musées de France*, 1930, pp. 99 f.

Jacobus de Voragine, *Legenda Aurea*, ed. T. Graesse, Breslau, 1890.

Jacopone da Todi, *Le poesie spirituali*, Venice, 1617.

James, M. R., *The Apocryphal New Testament*, Oxford, 1926.

James, M. R., and B. Berenson, *Speculum Humanae Salvationis*, Oxford, 1926.

James, M. R., and E. G. Millar, *The Bohun Manuscripts*, Oxford, 1936.

James, M. R., 'An English Bible Picture Book of the Fourteenth Century', *Walpole Society*, XI, 1922-1923, pp. 1-27.

James, M. R., *see also* Cambridge, Fitzwilliam Museum.

James, M. R., *see also* London, Thompson Collection (formerly).

James, M. R., *see also* New York, Pierpont Morgan Library.

Jamot, P., 'French Painting – I', *Burl. Mag.*, LIX, 1931, pp. 257-302.

Jeanroy, A., 'Boccace et Christine de Pisan,' *Romania*, XLVIII, 1922, pp. 93-105.

Jena. University. *Untersuchungen über die französischen illuminierten Handschriften der Jenaer Universitäts-bibliothek vom Ende des 14. bis zur Mitte des 15. Jahrhunderts* (W. Dexel), Strasbourg, 1917.

Journal de Jehan Glaumeau, Bourges, 1541–1562, ed. Hiver de Beauvoir, Bourges, 1867.

Juvenal, J., *Histoire de Charles VI, Roy de France*, in *Nouvelle collection des mémoires pour servir à l'histoire de France depuis le XIIIᵉ jusqu'à la fin du XVIIIᵉ siècle*, ed. [J. F.] Michaud and [J. J. F.] Poujoulat, ser. 1, II, 1850, pp. 333-569.

Kahane, H. and R., 'Pearls before Swine? A Reinterpretation of Matt. 7.6', *Traditio*, XIII, 1957, pp. 421-424.

Kalinowski, L., *Geneza Piety Średniowiecznej*, Cracow, 1953.

Kauffmann, H., *Donatello*, Berlin, 1935.

Kehrer, H., *Die heiligen drei Könige in Literatur und Kunst*, Leipzig, 1908–1909. 2v.

Keller, H., 'Die Entstehung des Bildnisses am Ende des Hochmittelalters', *Römisches Jahrbuch für Kunstgeschichte*, III, 1939, pp. 227-356.

Kirchner, J., *see* Berlin, Staatsbibliothek.

Koechlin, R., *Les ivoires gothiques français*, Paris, 1924. 3v.

Koerte, W., 'Deutsche Vesperbilder in Italien', *Römisches Jahrbuch für Kunstgeschichte*, I, 1937, pp. 1-138.

Kohler, C., *see* Paris, Bibliothèque Sainte-Geneviève.

Kraus, F. X., *Kunst und Alterthum in Elsass-Lothringen*, Strasbourg, 1877–1892. 4v.

Kraus, F. X., 'Karolingisches Madonnenbild in Metz', *Zeitschrift für Christliche Kunst*, I, 1888, p. 77 f.

Krautheimer, R. (in collaboration with T. Krautheimer-Hess), *Lorenzo Ghiberti*, Princeton, 1956.

Kreuter-Eggemann, H., *Das Skizzenbuch des Jaques Daliwe*, Munich, 1964. 2v.

Kris, E., *see* Eichler and Kris.

Krofta, J., 'La peinture monumentale en Bohême à l'époque de Charles IV et la peinture française', in *Actes du Congrès International d'Histoire de l'Art (1958)*, Paris, 1959, pp. 206-209.

Kuhn, A., 'Die Illustration des Rosenromans', *Jahrb. Kunsth. Slgn.*, XXXI, 1912, pp. 1-66.

Kuhn, C. L., 'Herman Scheerre and English Illumina-tion of the Early Fifteenth Century,' *Art Bull.*, XXII, 1940, pp. 138-156.

Kurth, B., 'Ein Freskenzyklus im Adlerturm zu Trient', *Jahrb. des Kunsthistorischen Institutes der K.K. Zentralkommission für Denkmalpflege*, v, 1911, pp. 9-104.

Kurth, B., 'Florentiner Trecento-Stickereien', *Pantheon*, VIII, 1931, pp. 455-462.

Kutal, A., D. Líbal, and A. Matějček, *České Umění Gotické*, Prague, 1949.

Labande, L. H., *Le palais des papes et les monuments d'Avignon au XIVᵉ siècle*, Marseilles, 1925. 2v.

Labande, L. H., *Les primitifs français, peintres et peintres-verriers de la Provence occidentale*, Marseilles, 1932. 2v.

Labande, L. H., 'Les miniaturistes avignonnais et leurs œuvres', *Gaz. B.-A.*, XXXVII, pt. 1, 1907, pp. 213-240, 289-305.

Labande, L. H., *see also* Avignon, Musée Calvet.

Labarte, J., ed., *Inventaire du mobilier de Charles V, roi de France* (Collections des documents inédits), Paris, 1879.

La Batut, G. de, *see* Paris, Bibliothèque Mazarine.

Laborde, A. de, *Les manuscrits à peintures de la Cité de Dieu de Saint Augustin*, Paris, 1909. 3v.

Laborde, A. de, *La Bible moralisée illustrée, conservée à Oxford, Paris et Londres . . .*, Paris, 1911–1927. 5v.

Laborde, A. de, *see also* Leningrad, Publichnaia biblioteka.

Laborde, L., *Les ducs de Bourgogne*, Paris, 1849–1852. 3v.

Laborde, L., *Glossaire français du moyen-âge, à l'usage de l'archéologue et de l'amateur des arts, précédé de l'inventaire des bijoux de Louis, duc d'Anjou, dressé vers 1360*, Paris, 1872.

Lacabane, L., 'Recherches sur les auteurs des grandes chroniques de France, dites de Saint-Denys', *Bibl. École des Chartes*, II, 1840–1841, pp. 57-74.

Laclotte, M., *L'école d'Avignon*, Paris, 1960.

Laclotte, M., 'Tableaux de chevalet français vers 1400', *Art de France*, III, 1963, pp. 220-222.

Lacour, R., *Le gouvernement de l'apanage de Jean, duc de Berry, 1360–1416*, Paris, 1934.

Lafenestre, G., *see* Paris, Musée Jacquemart-André.

Lafond, J., 'Le vitrail du XIVᵉ siècle en France', in L. Lefrançois-Pillon and J. Lafond, *L'art du XIVᵉ siècle en France*, Paris [1954].

Lafond, J., *see also* Lefrançois-Pillon and Lafond.

Lafond, J., *see also* Ritter and Lafond.

Landau-Finaly Collection, *see* London, Sotheby & Co.

Langlois, C., *La connaissance de la nature et du monde*, Paris, 1911.

Langlois, E., *Les manuscrits du Roman de la Rose, description et classement*, Lille, 1910.

Lanson, G., *Histoire de la littérature française*, Paris, 1952.

Lasko, P., 'The Thorn Reliquary', *Apollo*, LXXVI, pt. 1, 1962, pp. 259-264.

Lasteyrie, R. de, 'Les miniatures de André Beauneveu et de Jacquemart de Hesdin', *Monuments et mémoires*, III, 1896, pp. 71-119.

Lauer, P., 'Bibliographie des publications relatives aux manuscrits à peintures, parues de 1923 à 1928', *Bulletin Français de Reproductions de Manuscrits à Peintures*, XI, 1927, pp. 25-44.

Lauer, P., *see also* Blum and Lauer.

Lauer, P., *see also* Paris, Bibliothèque de l'Arsenal, Martin and Lauer.

Laurent de Premierfait, *see* Boccaccio.

Lavallée, P., *Le dessin français du XIIIe au XVIe siècle*, Paris, 1930.

La Vallière, L. C. de la Baume Le Blanc. Library. *Catalogue des livres de la bibliothèque de feu M. le duc de la Vallière*, Paris, 1783. 3v. in 6.

Lavin, M. A., 'Giovannino Battista: A Study in Renaissance Religious Symbolism', *Art Bull.*, XXXVII, 1955, pp. 85-101.

Lavin, M. A., 'Giovannino Battista: A Supplement', *Art Bull.*, XLIII, 1961, pp. 319-326.

Lavisse, E., ed., *Histoire de France depuis les origines jusqu'à la révolution*, Paris, 1900-1911. 9v.

Lecoy, F., 'Note sur quelques ballades de Christine de Pisan', in *Fin du moyen âge et Renaissance. Mélanges de philologie française offerts à Robert Guiette*, Antwerp, 1961, pp. 107-114.

Lécureux, L., 'Les anciennes peintures des églises de Laval', *Revue de l'art chrétien*, LX, 1910, pp. 223-240.

Ledos, G., 'Fragment de l'inventaire des joyaux de Louis Ier, duc d'Anjou', *Bibl. École des Chartes*, L, 1889, pp. 168-179.

Lefrançois-Pillon, L., and J. Lafond, *L'art du XIVe siècle en France*, Paris [1954].

Lehoux, F., *Jean de France, duc de Berri. Sa vie. Son action politique. 1340-1416*, Paris, in the press.

Lehoux, F., 'Le duc de Berri, les Juifs et les Lombards', *Revue historique*, CCXV, 1956, pp. 38-57.

Lehoux, F., 'Mort et funérailles du duc de Berri (juin 1416)', *Bibl. École des Chartes*, CXIV, 1956, pp. 76-96.

Leidinger, G., *see* Munich, Bayrische Staatsbibliothek.

Lejard, A., *Les tapisseries de l'Apocalypse de la Cathédrale d'Angers*, Paris, 1942.

Le Labourer, J., and P. Ménestrier, *Tableaux généalogiques, ou les seize quartiers de nos rois ...*, Paris, 1683.

Lemoisne, P. A., *Gothic Painting in France, Fourteenth and Fifteenth Centuries*, Florence [1931].

Leningrad. Publĭchnaĭa bĭblĭoteka. 'Catalogue des manuscrits français de la Bibliothèque de Saint-Pétersbourg' (G. Bertrand), *Rev. soc. savantes*, VI, 1873, pp. 373-599.

Leningrad. Publĭchnaĭa bĭblĭoteka. Laborde, A. de, *Les principaux manuscrits à peintures conservés dans l'ancienne Bibliothèque impériale publique de Saint-Pétersbourg*, SFRMP, Paris, 1936-1938. 2v.

Leroquais, V., *Les sacramentaires et les missels manuscrits des bibliothèques publiques de France*, Paris, 1924. 3v. and Plates.

Leroquais, V., *Les livres d'heures; manuscrits de la Bibliothèque nationale*, Paris, 1927. 3v. (Text and Plates); *Supplément*, 1943.

Leroquais, V., *Le Bréviaire de Philippe le Bon; bréviaire parisien du XVe siècle; étude du texte et des miniatures*, Brussels, 1929. Text and Plates.

Leroquais, V., *Les bréviaires manuscrits des bibliothèques publiques de France*, Paris, 1934. 5v. and Plates.

Leroquais, V., *Les pontificaux manuscrits des bibliothèques publiques de France*, Paris, 1937. 3v. and Plates.

Leroquais, V., *Les psautiers manuscrits latins des bibliothèques publiques de France*, Mâcon, 1940-1941. 2v. and Plates.

Leroquais, V., *see also* Lyons, Bibliothèque de la ville.

Leroquais, V., *see also* Paris, École des Beaux-Arts.

Le Roux de Lincy, A. J. V., *Paris et ses historiens aux XIVe et XVe siècles*, Paris, 1867.

Lespinasse, R. de, *Histoire générale de Paris: Les métiers et corporations de la ville de Paris*, Paris, 1886-1897. 3v.

Lettenhove, K. de, *see* Froissart.

Levasseur, E., *Histoire des classes ouvrières et de l'industrie en France avant 1789*, 2nd ed., Paris, 1900-1901. 2v.

Levesque, P., 'Notice du livre de Pierre Salmon, présenté par l'auteur à Charles VI', *Notices et extraits*, V [1800], pp. 415-432.

Liebreich, A., *Claus Sluter*, Brussels, 1936.

Lipinsky, A., 'La simbologia delle gemme nella "Divina Commedia" e le sue fonti letterarie', in *Atti del I Congresso di Studi Danteschi*, Florence, 1962, pp. 127-158.

Little, A., *Franciscan History and Legend in English Mediaeval Art*, Manchester, 1937.

Livre de la chasse, par Gaston Phébus, comte de Foix (C. Couderc), Paris [1909].

Le livre des faicts du bon messire Jean le Maingre, dit Boucicaut, in *Nouvelle collection des mémoires pour servir à l'histoire de France depuis le XIIIe jusqu'à la fin du*

XVIIIe siècle, ed. [J. F.] Michaud and [J. J. F.] Pou-joulat, ser. I, II, 1850, pp. 203-332.

Livre du cuer d'amours espris, see Vienna, Nationalbibliothek.

London. Ashburnham Place. *Catalogue of the Manuscripts at Ashburnham Place. Appendix*, London [1861].

London, Beatty Collection, *see* Dublin.

London. British Museum. *A Catalogue of the Harleian Manuscripts in the British Museum*, London, 1808-1812. 4v.

London. British Museum. Warner, G. F., *Illuminated Manuscripts in the British Museum*, Series I-IV, London, 1903.

London. British Museum. *Guide to the Manuscripts Exhibited in the Department of Manuscripts* (G. F. Warner), London, 1906.

London. British Museum. *Reproductions from Illuminated Manuscripts, Ser. I-IV . . .*, London, 1910-1928. 4v.

London. British Museum. *Catalogue of the Fifty Manuscripts and Printed Books Bequeathed to the British Museum by Alfred H. Huth*, London, 1912.

London. British Museum. *Schools of Illumination: Reproductions from Manuscripts in the British Museum*, London, 1914-1930. 6 pts. Part VI: French Mid 14th to 16th centuries.

London. British Museum. Warner, G. F., and J. P. Gilson, *Catalogue of Western Manuscripts in the Old Royal and King's Collections* [London], 1921. 4v.

London. British Museum. *Miniatures from a French Horae, British Museum Add. Ms. 16997, Fifteenth Century. Reproduced in Honour of John Alexander Herbert* [London], 1927.

London. British Museum. Millar, E. G., *Souvenir de l'exposition de manuscrits français à peintures organisée à la Grenville Library (British Museum) en janvier–mars, 1932*, Paris, 1933.

London. Burlington Fine Arts Club. *Exhibition of Illuminated Manuscripts*, London, 1908.

London. Burlington Fine Arts Club. *The Holford Collection*, Oxford, 1924.

London. Lambeth Palace. Millar, E. G., 'Les principaux manuscrits à peintures du Lambeth Palace à Londres', *Bulletin de la Société Française de Reproductions de Manuscrits à Peintures*, VIII-IX, 1924-1925.

London. J. and J. Leighton, *Catalogue of Manuscripts Mostly Illuminated . . . Offered for Sale by J. and J. Leighton*, London, n.d. [1915].

London. Matthiesen Gallery. *Paintings and Drawings from Christ Church, Oxford*, London, 1960.

London. New Palaeographical Society. *Facsimiles of Ancient Manuscripts, etc.*, London, 1903-1912.

London. Palaeographical Society. *Facsimiles of Manuscripts and Inscriptions*, London, 1873-1894. 5v.

London. Royal Academy of Arts. Conway, W. M., ed., *Catalogue of the Loan Exhibition of Flemish and Belgian Art, Burlington House, London, 1927*, London, 1927.

London. Royal Academy of Arts. Exhibition of French Art, 1931, *see* Borenius, 1932; Friedlaender, 1932.

London. Royal Academy of Arts. *Exhibition of French Art*, London, 1932.

London. Royal Academy of Arts. *Commemorative Catalogue of the Exhibition of French Art, 1200–1900*, London, 1933.

London. Sotheby & Co. *Catalogue of Ninety-one Manuscripts on Vellum . . . Chiefly from the Famous Hamilton Collection*, May 23, 1889.

London. Sotheby & Co. *Catalogue of Superb Illuminations from the Collection of the Late John, Lord Northwick, . . .* May 21, 1928.

London. Sotheby & Co. *Bibliotheca Phillippica: Catalogue of a Further Portion of the Renowned Library Formed by the Late Sir Thomas Phillipps*, July 1, 1946.

London. Sotheby & Co. *Catalogue of Very Important Illuminated Manuscripts and Printed Books Selected from the Renowned Library Formed by Baron Horace de Landau (1824–1903), Maintained and Augmented by his Niece Madam Finaly of Florence (d. 1938)*, July 12, 1948.

London. Sotheby & Co. *Catalogue of Western and Oriental Manuscripts and Miniatures*, May 4, 1953.

London. Sotheby & Co. *Catalogue of Fine Western and Oriental Manuscripts and Miniatures*, December 7, 1953.

London. Sotheby & Co. *The Dyson Perrins Collection:* Part I, December 9, 1958. Part II, December 1, 1959.

London. Sotheby & Co. *Catalogue of Important Western and Oriental Manuscripts and Miniatures*, February 1, 1960.

London. Sotheby & Co. *Catalogue of Important Old Master Drawings*, Springell Sale, June 28, 1962.

London. Thompson Collection (formerly). James, M. R., *A Descriptive Catalogue of Fifty Manuscripts from the Collection of Henry Yates Thompson*, Cambridge, 1898.

London. Thompson Collection (formerly). *Thirty-two Miniatures from the Book of Hours of Joan II, Queen of Navarre . . .* (H. Y. Thompson), London, 1899.

London. Thompson Collection (formerly). *A Descriptive Catalogue of the Second Series of Fifty Manuscripts (nos. 51-100) in the Collection of Henry Yates Thompson* (H. Y. Thompson), Cambridge, 1902.

2 E

London. Thompson Collection (formerly). *A Descriptive Catalogue of Twenty Illuminated Manuscripts, nos. LXXV to XCIV. (Replacing Twenty Discarded from the Original Hundred) in the Collection of Henry Yates Thompson* (H. Y. Thompson), Cambridge, 1907.

London. Thompson Collection (formerly). *Illustrations of One Hundred Manuscripts in the Library of Henry Yates Thompson* (H. Y. Thompson), London, 1907–1918. 7v. I. *Ten French MSS. from the XIth to the XVIth Centuries*, 1907. II. *Ten Italian MSS. from the XIth to the XVIth Centuries*, 1908. III. *Ten MSS. of Various Countries from the IXth to the XVIth Centuries*, 1912. IV. *Sixteen MSS. of English Origin from the XIIth to the XVth Centuries*, 1914. V. *Sixteen MSS. Each of which Belonged to Some Individual of Note in France or Italy in the XIVth or XVth Century*, 1915. VI. *Seventeen MSS. with Dates Ranging from the XIIIth to the XVIth Century*, 1916. VII. *The Remaining Twenty-Two MSS.*, 1918.

London. Thompson Collection (formerly). *A Descriptive Catalogue of Fourteen Illuminated Manuscripts, nos. XCV to CVII and 79a, Completing the Hundred in the Library of Henry Yates Thompson* (H. Y. Thompson), Cambridge, 1912.

Longnon, J., 'L'enlumineur Paul de Limbourg et sa famille' (rev. of F. Gorissen, *Jean Maelwael und die Brüder Limburg*, 1954), *Journal des savants*, 1956, pp. 175-188.

Los Angeles. Los Angeles County Museum. *Medieval and Renaissance Illuminated Manuscripts – a Loan Exhibition*, 1953.

Lother, H., *Der Pfau in der altchristlichen Kunst* (Studien über Christliche Denkmäler, N.F., Heft 18), Leipzig, 1929.

Lozoya, J. de Contreras de, *Historia del arte hispánico*, Barcelona, 1931–1949. 5v.

Luce, S., 'Jean, duc de Berry, d'après des documents nouveaux', *Le correspondant*, CLV, 1889, pp. 275-287.

Luchaire, A., *Social France at the Time of Philip Augustus*, trans. E. Krehbiel, London, 1912.

Ludovici, S., *Le biblioteche dell'Emilia*, Modena, 1959.

Lutz, J., and P. Perdrizet, *Speculum Humanae Salvationis*, Mülhausen, 1907–1909. 2v.

Lyna, F., 'Un livre de Prières inconnu de Philippe le Hardi (Bruxelles, ms. 11035-37)', in *Mélanges Hulin de Loo*, 1931, pp. 249-259.

Lyna, F., 'Les miniatures d'un ms. du "Ci nous dit" et le réalisme préeyckien', *Scriptorium*, I, 1946–1947, pp. 106-118.

Lyna, F., *see also* Gaspar and Lyna.

Lyons. Bibliothèque de la ville. *Exposition de manuscrits à peintures du VIe au XVIIe siècle* (V. Leroquais), Lyons, 1920.

Machaut, G. de, *Poésies lyriques*, ed. V. Chichmaref, Paris, 1909. 2v.

M(adan), F., 'Hours of the Virgin Mary', *Bodleian Quarterly Record*, III, 1920, pp. 40-44.

Madan, F., *see also* Oxford, Bodleian.

Madurell Marimón, J. M., 'El pintor Lluís Borrassà', *Anales y Boletín de los Museos de Arte de Barcelona*, X, 1952.

Maeterlinck, L., 'L'école avignonnaise avant les Van Eyck,' *Rev. de l'art a. et m.*, XLI, 1922, pp. 261-272.

Magne, L., *Le Palais de Justice de Poitiers*, Paris, 1904.

Malaguzzi Valeri, F., 'La miniatura in Bologna dal XIII al XVIII secolo', *Archivio storico italiano*, XVII, 1896, pp. 242-315.

Mâle, É., *L'art religieux de la fin du moyen âge en France; étude sur l'iconographie du moyen âge et sur ses sources d'inspiration*, Paris, 1908.

Mâle, É., *L'art religieux du XIIIe siècle en France; étude sur l'iconographie du moyen âge et sur ses sources d'inspiration*, 3rd ed., rev., Paris, 1910.

Mâle, É., *Art et artistes du moyen âge*, Paris, 1927.

Mâle, É., 'L'iconographie française et l'art italien au XIVe siècle et au commencement du XVe', *Rev. de l'art a. et m.*, XXXVII, 1920, pp. 5-16; 79-92; 134-142.

Malo-Rénault, J., 'La lettre ornée au moyen âge (d'après les manuscrits de Montpellier)', *Rev. de l'art a. et m.*, LXV, 1934, pp. 97-110, 145-164.

Marchal, F. J. F., *Catalogue des manuscrits de la Bibliothèque royale des ducs de Bourgogne*, Brussels [1839]–1842. 3v.

Marchal, F. J. F., 'Notice sur un livre d'heures qui appartenait à Jean le Magnifique, duc de Berry, frère de Charles V, roi de France', *Bulletin de l'Académie Royale des Sciences et Belles-Lettres de Bruxelles*, XI, part 1, 1844, pp. 407-424.

Marchini, G., *Le vetrate italiane*, Milan, 1956.

Marinesco, C., 'Deux empereurs byzantins en Occident: Manuel II et Jean VIII Paléologue', in *Comptes rendus de l'Académie des Inscriptions & Belles-Lettres, 1957*, Paris, 1958, pp. 23-35.

Marinesco, C., 'Deux empereurs byzantins', *Bulletin de la Société National des Antiquaires de France*, 1958, pp. 38-40.

Marle, R. van, *The Development of the Italian Schools of Painting*, The Hague, 1923–1936. 18v.

Marle, R. van, *Iconographie de l'art profane au moyen-âge et à la Renaissance et la décoration des demeures*, The Hague, 1931–1932. 2v.

Marle, R. van, 'L'iconographie de la décoration profane des demeures princières en France et en Italie aux XIVᵉ et XVᵉ siècles', *Gaz. B.-A.*, XVIII, pt. 2, 1926, pp. 163-182; 249-274.

Martens, B., *Meister Francke*, Hamburg, 1929. 2v.

Martin, H. M. R., *Les miniaturistes français*, Paris, 1906.

Martin, H. M. R., *Le Térence des ducs*, Paris, 1907.

Martin, H. M. R., *Les peintres de manuscrits et la miniature en France*. Paris [1909?].

Martin, H. M. R., *Le Boccace de Jean sans Peur. Des cas des nobles hommes et femmes*, Brussels, 1911.

Martin, H. M. R., *La miniature française du XIIIᵉ siècle au XVᵉ siècle*, Paris, 1923.

Martin, H. M. R., 'Le Térence des ducs et la mise en scène au moyen âge', *Bull. Soc. Hist. Théâtre*, no. 1, 1902, pp. 15-42.

Martin, H. M. R., 'Les esquisses des miniatures', *Rev. archéol.*, IV, 1904, pp. 17-45.

Martin, H. M. R., 'La Somme le Roi, Bibliothèque Mazarine, no. 870', in *Trésors des bibliothèques de France*, I, 1926, pp. 43-57.

Martin, H. M. R., *see also* Paris, Bibliothèque de l'Arsenal.

Martin, H. M. R., *see also* Paris, Bibliothèque nationale.

Martin, J. R., *The Illustrations of the Heavenly Ladder of John Climacus*, Princeton, 1954.

Masson Collection, *see* Paris, École des Beaux-Arts.

Matějček, A., and J. Pešina, *Czech Gothic Painting, 1350–1450*, Prague, 1950.

Mater, M. D., 'Bassin de jaspe', *Mémoires de la Société des Antiquaires du Centre*, XXVIII, 1904, pp. 201-209.

Mattingly, H., *Coins of the Roman Empire in the British Museum*, London, 1923-1950. 5v.

Meditationes Vitae Christi, Sanctae Bonaventurae Opera Omnia, Venice, XII, 1756.

Meditations on the Life of Christ, ed. I. Ragusa and R. B. Green, Princeton, 1961.

Meditations on the Life of Christ, *see also Smaointe Beatha Chríost*.

Meiss, M., *Painting in Florence and Siena after the Black Death*, Princeton, 1951; New York, 1964 (with revised index).

Meiss, M., *Andrea Mantegna as Illuminator*, New York and Hamburg, 1957.

Meiss, M., *Giotto and Assisi*, New York, 1960.

Meiss, M., *Giovanni Bellini's St. Francis in the Frick Collection*, Princeton, 1964.

Meiss, M., 'Un dessin par le maître des Grandes Heures de Rohan', *Gaz. B.-A.*, LXXVII, pt. 1, 1935, pp. 65-75.

Meiss, M., 'The Madonna of Humility', *Art Bull.*, XVIII, 1936, pp. 434-464.

Meiss, M., 'Fresques italiennes, cavallinesques et autres, à Béziers', *Gaz. B.-A.*, XVIII, 1937, pp. 275-286.

Meiss, M., 'Italian Style in Catalonia and a Fourteenth-Century Catalan Workshop', *Walters Journal*, IV, 1941, pp. 45-87.

Meiss, M., 'Light as Form and Symbol in some Fifteenth-Century Paintings', *Art Bull.*, XXVII, 1945, pp. 175-181.

Meiss, M., 'Italian Primitives at Konopiště', *Art Bull.*, XXVIII, 1946, pp. 1-16.

Meiss, M., 'An Early Altarpiece from the Cathedral of Florence', *Bulletin of the Metropolitan Museum of Art*, XII, 1954, pp. 302-317.

Meiss, M., 'Ovum Struthionis: Symbol and Allusion in Piero della Francesca's Montefeltro Altarpiece', in *Studies in Art and Literature for Belle da Costa Greene*, Princeton, 1954, pp. 92-101.

Meiss, M., 'The Exhibition of French Manuscripts of the XIII-XVI Centuries at the Bibliothèque nationale', *Art Bull.*, XXXVIII, 1956, pp. 187-196.

Meiss, M., 'Jan van Eyck and the Italian Renaissance', in *Venezia e l'Europa, Atti del XVIII Congresso Internazionale di Storia dell'Arte*, Venice, 1956, pp. 58-69.

Meiss, M., 'Primitifs italiens à l'Orangerie', *Rev. des arts*, VI, 1956, pp. 139-148.

Meiss, M., 'The Case of the Frick *Flagellation*', *Walters Journal*, XIX-XX, 1956–1957, pp. 43-63.

Meiss, M., and C. Eisler, 'A New French Primitive', *Burlington Magazine*, CII, 1960, pp. 233-240, 489.

Meiss, M., 'An Early Lombard Altarpiece', *Arte antica e moderna*, 1961, no. 13-16, pp. 125-133.

Meiss, M., ' "Highlands" in the Lowlands: Jan van Eyck, the Master of Flémalle, and the Franco-Italian Tradition', *Gaz. B.-A.*, LVII, 1961, pp. 273-314.

Meiss, M., 'Un fragment rare d'un art honorable', *Revue du Louvre*, XII, 1962, pp. 105-114.

Meiss, M., 'French and Italian Variations on an Early Fifteenth-Century Theme: St. Jerome and His Study', *Gaz. B.-A.*, LXII, 1963, pp. 147-170.

Meiss, M., 'A Lost Portrait of Jean de Berry by the Limbourgs', *Burl. Mag.*, CV, 1963, pp. 51-53.

Meiss, M., 'Masaccio and the Early Renaissance: The Circular Plan', in *Studies in Western Art. Acts of the Twentieth International Congress of the History of Art*, Princeton, 1963, II, pp. 123-145.

Meiss, M., 'The First Fully Illustrated *Decameron*', *Essays in the History of Art Presented to Rudolf Wittkower*, London, 1967.

Meiss, M., *see also* Tintori and Meiss.

Mélanges Hulin de Loo, Brussels, 1931.

Méloizes, A. des, *Les vitraux de Bourges postérieurs au XIIIᵉ siècle*, Lille, 1891.

Mély, F. de, *Les primitifs et leurs signatures. Les miniaturistes*. Paris, 1913.

Mély, F. de, 'Le grand camée de Vienne', *Gazette archéologique*, XI, 1886, pp. 244-253.

Mély, F. de, 'Le "Camayeul" de Saint-Sernin et le Grand Camée de Vienne', *Mémoires de la Société Archéologique du Midi de la France*, XV, 1894–1896, pp. 67-98.

Mély, F. de, 'Vases de Cana', *Académie des Inscriptions et Belles-Lettres. Monuments et mémoires*, X, 1903, pp. 145-170.

Mély, F. de, 'Les Très Riches Heures du duc de Berry et les inscriptions de ses miniatures: Henri Bellechose et Hermann Rust', *Rev. de l'art a. et m.*, XXII, 1907, pp. 41-56.

Mély, F. de, 'Les primitifs et leurs signatures: Jean Fouquet et les "Heures de Laval"', *Gaz. B.-A.*, X, 1913, pp. 1-23.

Menut, A. D., *Maistre Nicole Oresme: Le livre de éthiques d'Aristote*, New York, 1940.

Menut, A. D., 'The French Version of Aristotle's *Economics* in Rouen, Bibl. municipale, MS 927', *Romance Philology*, IV, 1950, pp. 55-62.

Menut, A. D., 'Maistre Nicole Oresme: *Le livre de yconomique d'Aristote*', *Transactions of the American Philosophical Society*, N.S., XLVII, 1957, pp. 785-852.

Merrifield, (Mrs.) M., *Original Treatises, Dating from the XIIth to XVIIIth Centuries on the Arts of Painting . . .*, London, 1849. 2v.

Meurgey, J., *see* Chantilly, Musée Condé.

Michaud, J. F., *see* Christine de Pisan.

Michaud, L.-G., *Biographie universelle, ancienne et moderne*, Paris, 1811-1862.

Michel, A., *Histoire de l'art*, Paris, 1905-1929. 8v. in 17.

Michel, A., *Avignon, les fresques du Palais des Papes*, 2nd ed., Paris, 1926.

Michel, A., *see also* Paris, Musée Jacquemart-André.

Michel, E., *L'école flamande du XVᵉ siècle au Musée du Louvre*, Brussels, 1944.

Michel, E., 'À propos de l'exposition d'art flamand à Londres', *Gaz. B.-A.*, XLVIII, 1926, pp. 345-356.

Michelant, M., 'Inventaire . . . de M. d'Autriche . . . le 9 juillet 1523', *Bulletin de la Commission Royale d'Histoire*, XII, 1870–1871, p. 93.

Middeldorf, U., 'On the Origins of "émail sur rondebosse"', *Gaz. B.-A.*, LV, 1960, pp. 233-244.

Milan. Biblioteca Trivulziana. *I codici miniati della Biblioteca Trivulziana* (C. Santoro), Milan, 1958.

Milan. Hoepli Collection, *see* Toesca.

Milan. Palazzo Reale. *Arte lombarda dai Visconti agli Sforza*, Milan [1958]. 2nd ed., Milan, 1959.

Milanesi, G., *see* Vasari.

Millar, E. G., *English Illuminated Manuscripts of the XIVth and XVth Centuries*, Paris, 1928.

Millar, E. G., *La Somme le Roi*, Oxford, 1953.

Millar, E. G., *see also* Dublin, Beatty Collection.

Millar, E. G., *see also* James and Millar.

Millar, E. G., *see also* London, British Museum.

Millar, E. G., *see also* London, Lambeth Palace.

Millet, G., *Recherches sur l'iconographie de l'Évangile*, Paris, 1916.

Milliken, W. M., 'Illuminated Miniatures in the Cleveland Museum of Art', *Bull. Cleveland Mus.*, XII, 1925, pp. 61-71.

Miner, D., *see* Baltimore, Walters Art Gallery.

Mirot, L., *Études lucquoises*, Paris, 1930.

Mirot, L., 'Notes sur un manuscrit de Froissart et sur Pierre de Fontenay, seigneur de France', *Bibl. École des Chartes*, LXXXIII, 1922, pp. 297-330.

Mirot, L., and E. Lazzareschi, 'Lettere di mercanti lucchesi da Bruges e da Parigi, 1407–1421', *Bollettino storico lucchese*, I, 1929, pp. 165-199.

Modena. Biblioteca Estense. Fava, D., and M. Salmi, *I manoscritti miniati della Biblioteca Estense di Modena*, Florence [1950].

Molinier, A., *see* Paris, Bibliothèque Mazarine.

Monget, C., *La Chartreuse de Dijon d'après les documents des archives de Bourgogne*, Montreuil-sur-Mer, 1898–1905. 3v.

Mont, K. M. P. de, *see* Brussels, Bibliothèque Royale de Belgique.

Montfaucon, Bernard de, *Les monumens de la monarchie françoise*, Paris, 1729-1733. 5v.

Montpellier, Bibliothèque universitaire, *see* Malo-Rénault, J.

Morand, E., 'La ville de Riom et la fête de Mai dans les *Très Riches Heures* du duc de Berry', *Bulletin de l'Académie des Sciences, Belles-Lettres et Arts de Clermont-Ferrand*, 1954, pp. 1-5.

Morand, K., *Jean Pucelle*, Oxford, 1962.

Moranvillé, H., *Chronographia regum Francorum*, Paris, 1891-1897. 3v.

Moranvillé, H., *Inventaire de l'orfèvrerie et des joyaux de Louis I, duc d'Anjou*, Paris, 1906.

Moranvillé, H., 'Peintres romains pensionnaires de Philippe le Bel', *Bibl. École des Chartes*, XLVIII, 1887, pp. 631 f.

Moranvillé, H., 'La chronique du religieux de Saint-Denis. Les mémoires de Salmon et la chronique de la mort de Richard II', *Bibl. École des Chartes*, L, 1889, pp. 5-40.

Moranvillé, H., see also *Le songe véritable; pamphlet politique d'un parisien du XVe siècle*.

Moschini, G., *Della origine e delle vicende della pittura in Padova*, Padua, 1826.

Müller, Th., and E. Steingräber, 'Die französische Gold-emailplastik um 1400', *Münchner Jahrb.*, V, 1954, pp. 29-79.

Munich. Bayrische Staatsbibliothek. *Codices manu scripti . . . gallici, hispani, italici . . .*, ed. J. A. Schmeller and G. M. Thomas (*Catalogus codicum manu scriptorum Bibliothecae regiae monacensis*, VII), Munich, 1858.

Munich. Bayrische Staatsbibliothek. Leidinger, G., *Verzeichnis der wichtigsten Miniaturen-Handschriften der Königlichen Hof- und Staatsbibliothek München*, Munich, 1912.

Müntz, E., and P. Fabre, *La Bibliothèque du Vatican au XVe siècle d'après des documents inédits*, Paris, 1887.

Müntz, E., *Les collections des Médicis au XVe siècle*, Paris, 1888.

Müntz, E., *Les collections d'antiques formées par les Médicis au XVIe siècle*, Paris, 1895.

Müntz, E., 'Les miniatures françaises dans les bibliothèques italiennes', *Bibliofilia*, IV, 1902, pp. 73-83; 219-234.

Netherlands. Byvanck, A., 'Les principaux manuscrits à peintures conservés dans les collections publiques du royaume des Pays-Bas', *Bulletin de la Société Française de Reproductions de Manuscrits à Peintures*, XV, 1931. Texts and Plates.

Neveux, P., and É. Dacier, *Les richesses des bibliothèques provinciales de France*, Paris, 1932. 2v.

New York. American Art Association. *The Cortlandt F. Bishop Library*, part two [I-Q] April 25-27, 1938.

New York. American Art Association – Anderson Galleries. *Illuminated Manuscripts, Incunabula and Americana, from the Libraries of the Marquess of Lothian*, Jan. 27, 1932.

New York. L. C. Harper. *Catalogue 10: Fine Books and Illuminated Manuscripts* [1960].

New York. Hoe Library. *The Library of Robert Hoe* (O. A. Bierstadt). New York, 1895.

New York. Kleinberger Galleries. *Catalogue of a Loan Exhibition of French Primitives and Objects of Art* (E. M. Sperling), New York, 1927.

New York. H. P. Kraus. *Catalogue 100*. New York [1962].

New York. Metropolitan Museum. The Cloisters. *The Hours of Jeanne d'Évreux*, ed. J. J. Rorimer, New York, 1957.

New York. Metropolitan Museum. The Cloisters. *The Belles Heures of Jean, Duke of Berry Prince of France*, ed. J. J. Rorimer and M. B. Freeman, New York, 1958.

New York. Pierpont Morgan Library. *Catalogue of Manuscripts and Early Printed Books from the Libraries of William Morris . . . and other Sources, now Forming Portion of the Library of J. Pierpont Morgan . . .* (M. R. James et al.), London, 1906-1907. 4v.

New York. Pierpont Morgan Library. *The Pierpont Morgan Library: a Review of the Growth, Development and Activities of the Library . . .* (B. da Costa Greene), New York, 1930.

New York. Pierpont Morgan Library. *Exhibition of Illuminated Manuscripts Held at the New York Public Library, November 1933 to April 1934*, New York [1934].

New York. Pierpont Morgan Library. *Illustrated Catalogue of an Exhibition held on the Occasion of the New York World's Fair 1939*, New York, 1939.

New York. Pierpont Morgan Library. *Review of the Activities and Acquisitions of the Library from 1936 through 1940; . . .*, New York, 1941.

New York. Pierpont Morgan Library. *The First Quarter Century of the Pierpont Morgan Library . . .*, New York, 1949.

New York. J. Seligmann & Co. *Illuminated Manuscripts from the Bibliothèque of Their Highnesses the Dukes d'Arenberg*, 1952.

Nicola, G. de, 'L'affresco di Simone Martini ad Avignone', *L'arte*, IX, 1906, pp. 336-344.

Nolhac, P. de, *Pétrarque et l'humanisme*, Paris, 1907.

Nordenfalk, C. A. J., *Kung praktiks och drottning teoris jaktbok. Le livre des deduis du roi Modus et de la reine Ratio*, Stockholm, 1955.

Nordenfalk, C. A. J., 'En Medeltida Bönbok från Metz i Linköpings Stifts- och Landsbibliotek', *Linköpings Biblioteks Handlingar*, N.S., IV, 1953, pp. 65-88.

Nordenfalk, C. A. J., 'Französische Buchmalerei 1200-1500', *Kunstchronik*, IX, 1956, pp. 179-189.

Nouvelle collection des mémoires pour servir à l'histoire de

France, see *Le livre des faicts du mareschal de Boucicaut*, and Juvenal, *Histoire de Charles VI*.

Nuremberg. Germanisches Nationalmuseum. *Katalog der mittelalterlichen Miniaturen des Germanischen Nationalmuseums* (E. W. Bredt), Nuremberg, 1903.

Nuremberg. Germanisches Nationalmuseum. *Die Gemälde des 13. bis 16. Jahrhunderts*, ed. E. Lutze and E. Wiegand, Leipzig, 1937. 2v.

Ó Maonaigh, C., see *Smaointe Beatha Chríost*.

Oberhammer, V., *Der Altar vom Schloss Tirol*, Innsbruck and Vienna, 1948.

Oberlin. Oberlin College. 'An Exhibition of Netherlandish Book Illumination' (L. M. J. Delaissé), *Allen Memorial Art Museum Bulletin*, XVII, 1960, pp. 94-113.

Œuvres complètes du roi René, ed. Théodore comte de Quatrebarbes, Angers, 1843-1846. 4v.

Offner, R., *Italian Primitives at Yale*, New Haven, 1927.

Offner, R., *Studies in Florentine Painting*, New York, 1927.

Offner, R., *A Critical and Historical Corpus of Florentine Painting*, New York, 1930-.

Offner, R., 'Light on Masaccio's Classicism', in *Studies in the History of Art Dedicated to W. E. Suida*, London, 1959, pp. 66-72.

Olschki, L. S., *Manuscrits sur velin avec miniatures du Xe au XVIe siècle . . .*, Florence, 1910.

Olschki, L. S., see also Germany.

Omont, H. A., 'Manuscrits relatifs à l'histoire de France conservés dans la bibliothèque de Sir Thomas Phillipps à Cheltenham', *Bibl. École des Chartes*, L, 1889, pp. 68-96; 180-217.

Omont, H. A., 'Les manuscrits français des rois d'Angleterre au château de Richmond', in *Études romanes dédiées à Gaston Paris*, Paris, 1891, pp. 1-13.

Omont, H. A., see also Paris, Bibliothèque nationale.

Origo, I., *The Merchant of Prato, Francesco di Marco Datini*, New York, 1957.

Osten, Gert von der, 'Engelpietà', in *Reallexikon zur deutschen Kunstgeschichte*, V, 1959, pp. 602-622.

Oursel, C., see Dijon, Bibliothèque municipale.

Ouy, G., 'Une maquette de manuscrit à peinture', in *Mélanges d'histoire du livre et des bibliothèques offerts à Monsieur Frantz Calot*, Paris, 1960.

Oxford. Bodleian Library. *Catalogi codicum manuscriptorum bibliothecae Bodleianae*, Oxford, 1845-1954. 11v. in 18.

Oxford. Bodleian Library. Madan, F., *A Summary Catalogue of Western Manuscripts in the Bodleian Library at Oxford*, Oxford, 1895-1953 .7v.

Oxford. Bodleian Library. *An Exchange of Latin Liturgical Manuscripts and Printed Books*, Oxford, 1952.

Oxford, Christ Church, see London, Matthiesen Gallery.

Paccagnini, G., *Simone Martini*, Milan, 1955.

Pächt, O., *The Master of Mary of Burgundy*, London [1948].

Pächt, O., C. R. Dodwell, and F. Wormald, *The St. Albans Psalter* (Studies of the Warburg Institute, XXV), London, 1960.

Pächt, O., 'A Giottesque Episode in English Mediaeval Art', *Warburg Journal*, VI, 1943, pp. 51-70.

Pächt, O., 'Early Italian Nature Studies and the Early Calendar Landscape', *Warburg Journal*, XIII, 1950, pp. 13-47.

Pächt, O., 'A Forgotten Manuscript from the Library of the Duc de Berry', *Burl. Mag.* XCVIII, 1956, pp. 146-153.

Pächt, O., 'Panofsky's "Early Netherlandish Painting" – I', *Burl. Mag.*, XCVIII, 1956, pp. 110-116.

Pächt, O., 'Un tableau de Jacquemart de Hesdin?', *Rev. des arts*, VI, 1956, pp. 149-160.

Pächt, O., 'The "Avignon Diptych" and Its Eastern Ancestry', in *De Artibus Opuscula XL: Essays in Honor of Erwin Panofsky*, New York, 1961, I, pp. 402-421.

Pächt, O., 'Zur Entstehung des "Hieronymus im Gehäus"', *Pantheon*, XXI, 1963, pp. 131-142.

Pächt, O., 'The Limbourgs and Pisanello', *Gaz. B.-A.*, LXII, 1963, pp. 109-122.

Pajot, S., 'La sculpture en Berry à la fin du moyen âge', *Mémoires Société des Antiquaires du Centre*, XLVIII (1938-1941), 1941, pp. 69-176.

Pannier, L., 'Les joyaux du duc de Guyenne', *Rev. archéologique*, XXVI, 1873, pp. 158-170, 209-225, 306-320, 384-395; XXVII, 1874, pp. 31-42.

Panofsky, E., *Die deutsche Plastik des elften bis dreizehnten Jahrhunderts*, Munich, 1924. 2v.

Panofsky, E., *Studies in Iconology*, New York, 1939.

Panofsky, E., *Abbot Suger on the Abbey Church of St-Denis and its Art Treasures*, Princeton, 1946.

Panofsky, E., *Early Netherlandish Painting: Its Origins and Character*, Cambridge, Mass., 1953. 2v.

Panofsky, E., *Renaissance and Renascences in Western Art*, Stockholm, 1960.

Panofsky, E., 'Die Perspektive als "symbolische Form"', *Vorträge der Bibliothek Warburg*, 1924-1925, pp. 258-330.

Panofsky, E., 'Imago pietatis', in *Festschrift für Max J. Friedländer zum 60. Geburtstage*, Leipzig, 1927, pp. 261-308.

Panofsky, E., 'The Friedsam Annunciation and the Problem of the Ghent Altarpiece', *Art Bull.*, xvii, 1935, pp. 433-473.

Panofsky, E., 'Once more "the Friedsam Annunciation and the Problem of the Ghent Altarpiece" ', *Art Bull.*, xx, 1938, pp. 419-442.

Panofsky, E., 'Reintegration of a Book of Hours Executed in the Workshop of the "Maître des Grandes Heures de Rohan" ', *Medieval Studies in Memory of A. Kingsley Porter*, Cambridge, 1939, ii, pp. 479-499. 2v.

Panofsky, E., 'Conrad Celtes and Kunz von der Rosen: Two Problems in Portrait Identification', *Art Bull.*, xxiv, 1942, pp. 39-54.

Panofsky, E., 'The de Buz Book of Hours', *Harvard Lib. Bull.*, iii, 1949, pp. 163-182.

Pansier, P., *Histoire du livre et de l'imprimerie à Avignon du XIVe au XVIe siècle*, Avignon, 1922.

Paolini, M., 'Il Trionfo della Morte di Palermo e la cultura internazionale', *Rivista dell'Istituto Nazionale d'Archeologia e Storia dell'Arte*, xi, 1962, pp. 1-69.

Paquot, J. N., *Mémoires pour servir à l'histoire littéraire des dix-sept provinces des Pays-Bas*, Louvain, 1763-1770. 18v.

Paris, P., *Les manuscrits françois de la bibliothèque du roi . . .*, Paris, 1836-1846. 7v.

Paris, P., 'Hayton, prince d'Arménie, historien', *Hist. litt.*, xxv, 1869, pp. 479-507.

Paris. Archives nationales. 'Les plus beaux manuscrits à peintures conservés aux Archives nationales' (M. François), in *Trésors des bibliothèques de France*, xxiv, 1938, pp. 3-25.

Paris. Archives nationales. Babelon, J.-P., *Catalogue du Musée de l'histoire de France* (Archives nationales), Paris, ii, 1960.

Paris. Bibliothèque de l'Arsenal. Martin, H. M. R., *Catalogue des manuscrits de la Bibliothèque de l'Arsenal*, Paris, 1885-1899. 9v.

Paris. Bibliothèque de l'Arsenal. *Les principaux manuscrits à peintures de la Bibliothèque de l'Arsenal à Paris; ouvrage posthume de H. Martin, terminé par Ph. Lauer*, SFRMP, Paris, 1929.

Paris. Bibliothèque de la Chambre des Députés. Boinet, A., 'Les principaux manuscrits à peintures de la Bibliothèque de la Chambre des Députés à Paris', *Bulletin de la Société Française de Reproductions de Manuscrits à Peintures*, vi, 1922, pp. 31-61.

Paris. Bibliothèque Mazarine. Molinier, A., *Catalogue des manuscrits de la Bibliothèque Mazarine*, Paris, 1885-1892. 4v.

Paris. Bibliothèque Mazarine. La Batut, G. de, 'Les principaux manuscrits à peintures conservés à la Bibliothèque Mazarine de Paris', *Bulletin de la Société Française de Reproductions de Manuscrits à Peintures*, xvi, 1933.

Paris. Bibliothèque nationale. *Catalogue général des manuscrits français*, 1868-1918. 18v. 2 ser. Ser. i Ancien fonds (mss. 1-6170). Ser. ii Nouveau fonds (mss. 6171-33264 and nouvelles acquisitions, 1-10,000).

Paris. Bibliothèque nationale. *Catalogue des camées antiques et modernes de la Bibliothèque nationale* (E. Babelon), Paris, 1897. 2v.

Paris. Bibliothèque nationale. Omont, H. A., 'Catalogue des manuscrits Ashburnham-Barrois récemment acquis par la Bibliothèque nationale', *Bibl. École des Chartes*, lxii, 1901, pp. 555-610; lxiii, 1902, pp. 10-68.

Paris. Bibliothèque nationale. *Antiquités et Guerre des Juifs de Josèphe; reproduction des 25 miniatures des manuscrits français 247 et nouv. acq. 21013 de la Bibliothèque nationale* (H. A. Omont), Paris [1906].

Paris. Bibliothèque nationale. *Exposition de portraits peints et dessinés du XIIIe au XVIIe siècle*. Paris, 1907.

Paris. Bibliothèque nationale. *Livre des merveilles . . . reproduction des 265 miniatures du manuscrit français 2810 . . .* (H. A. Omont), Paris [1907]. 2v.

Paris. Bibliothèque nationale. *Catalogue de l'exposition du moyen âge: manuscrits, estampes, médailles et objets d'art, imprimés . . .*, Paris, 1926.

Paris. Bibliothèque nationale. *Les enluminures des manuscrits du moyen âge (du VIe au XVe siècle) de la Bibliothèque nationale* (C. Couderc), Paris, 1927.

Paris. Bibliothèque nationale. *Les joyaux de l'enluminure à la Bibliothèque nationale* (H. Martin), Paris and Brussels, 1928.

Paris. Bibliothèque nationale. 'Listes des recueils de facsimilés et des reproductions de manuscrits conservés à la Bibliothèque nationale' (H. Omont and P. Lauer), 3rd ed., Paris, 1935.

Paris. Bibliothèque nationale. *Les plus beaux manuscrits français du VIIIe au XVIe siècle conservés dans les bibliothèques de Paris*, Paris, 1937.

Paris. Bibliothèque nationale. *Catalogue général des manuscrits latins*, Paris, i, 1939.

Paris. Bibliothèque nationale. *Trésors des bibliothèques d'Italie*, Paris, 1950.

Paris. Bibliothèque nationale. *Les manuscrits à peintures en France du XIIIe au XVIe siècle* (J. Porcher,), Paris, 1955.

Paris. Bibliothèque nationale. Exhibition of mss., 1955, *see* Meiss, 1956; Nordenfalk, 1956; Wormald, 1956.

Paris. Bibliothèque nationale. *Les trésors de la Bibliothèque nationale: L'époque de Charles VI* (M. Thomas), Paris, 1958.

Paris. Bibliothèque nationale. Porcher, J., *Manuscrits à peintures offerts à la Bibliothèque nationale par le comte Guy du Boisrouvray*, Paris, 1961.

Paris. Bibl. nationale, *see also* Delisle, *Cabinet.*

Paris, Bibliothèque nationale, *see also* Leroquais, V.

Paris, Bibliothèque nationale, *see also* Paris, Musée du Louvre.

Paris. Bibl. nat., Département des manuscrits, *see* C. Couderc, *Album de portraits . . . du Département des manuscrits.*

Paris. Bibliothèque Sainte-Geneviève. *Catalogue des manuscrits de la Bibliothèque Sainte-Geneviève* (C. Kohler), Paris, 1893–1896. 2v.

Paris. Bibliothèque Sainte-Geneviève. Boinet, A., 'Les manuscrits à peintures de la Bibliothèque Sainte-Geneviève de Paris', *Bulletin de la Société Française de Reproductions de Manuscrits à Peintures*, v, 1921.

Paris. École des Beaux-Arts. 'La donation Jean Masson. Manuscrits' (V. Leroquais), in *Trésors des bibliothèques de France*, II, 1929, pp. 92-97.

Paris. Musée des Art Décoratifs. *Vitraux de France* (L. Grodecki), Paris, 1953.

Paris. Musée de Cluny. Boinet, A., 'Choix de miniatures détachées conservées au Musée de Cluny à Paris', *Bulletin de la Société Française de Reproductions de Manuscrits à Peintures*, VI, 1922, pp. 5-30.

Paris. Musée de l'Orangerie. *De Giotto à Bellini: Les primitifs italiens dans les musées de France* (M. Laclotte), 2nd ed. [Paris], 1956.

Paris. Musée du Louvre. *Exposition des primitifs français au palais du Louvre . . . et à la Bibliothèque nationale*, Paris, 1904.

Paris. Musée du Louvre and Bibliothèque nationale. Bouchot, H., *L'exposition des primitifs français: la peinture en France sous les Valois*, 2nd ed., Paris, 1905.

Paris. Musée du Louvre. *Enluminures et dessins français du XIIIᵉ au XIVᵉ siècles*, Paris, 1957.

Paris. Musée du Louvre. *Peintures, école française, XIVᵉ, XVᵉ, et XVIᵉ siècles* (C. Sterling and H. Adhémar), Paris, 1965.

Paris. Musée Jacquemart-André. Durrieu, P., 'Le Musée Jacquemart-André: Les manuscrits à peintures', *Gaz. B.-A.*, VIII, 1912, pp. 85-96.

Paris. Musée Jacquemart-André. *Le Musée Jacquemart-André* (G. Lafenestre, P. Durrieu, A. Michel, and L. Deshairs), Paris, 1914.

Paris. Palais national des arts. Exhibition. *Chefs-d'œuvre de l'art français* [Paris, 1937].

Parkhurst, C. P., 'The Madonna of the Writing Christ Child', *Art Bull.*, XXIII, 1941, pp. 292-306.

Peignot, G., *Catalogue d'une partie des livres composant la bibliothèque des ducs de Bourgogne au XVᵉ siècle*, 2nd ed., Dijon, 1841.

Pellegrin, E., *La bibliothèque des Visconti et des Sforza ducs de Milan au XVᵉ siècle*, Paris, 1955.

Perdrizet, P., *Le calendrier parisien à la fin du moyen âge d'après le bréviaire et les livres d'heures*, Paris, 1933.

Perdrizet, P., *see also* Lutz and Perdrizet.

Perkins, F. M., 'Some Sienese Paintings in American Collections', *Art in America*, VIII, 1920, pp. 272-292.

Perls, K., 'Le tableau de la famille des Juvénal des Ursins, le "maître du duc de Bedford" et Haincelin de Haguenau', *Rev. de l'art a. et m.*, LXVIII, 1935, pp. 173-180.

Perrins Collection (formerly), *see* London, Sotheby & Co.

Perrins Collection (formerly), *see also* Warner, G.

Pešina, J., and J. Homolka, 'K Problematice Evropského Umění Kolem Roku 1400', *Umění*, XI, 1963, pp. 161-206.

Pešina, J., *see also* Matějček and Pešina.

Petit, E., *Itinéraires de Philippe le Hardi et de Jean sans Peur, ducs de Bourgogne (1363–1419)*, Paris, 1888.

Phillipps Collection (formerly), *see* Durrieu, P.

Phillipps Collection (formerly), *see also* London, Sotheby & Co.

Piaget, A., 'La cour amoureuse dite de Charles VI', *Romania*, XX, 1891, pp. 417-454.

Pinder, W., *Die deutsche Plastik vom ausgehenden Mittelalter bis zum Ende der Renaissance* (Handbuch der Kunstwissenschaft), Wildpark-Potsdam, 1924–1929. 2v.

Pliny, *Natural History*, trans. H. Rackham (Loeb Classical Library), Cambridge, Mass., 1952.

Pliny, see also *The Elder Pliny's Chapters on the History of Art.*

Plon, E., *Benvenuto Cellini*, Paris, 1883.

Poirion, D., *Le poète et le prince: L'évolution du lyrisme courtois de Guillaume de Machaut à Charles d'Orléans*, Paris, 1965.

Pope-Hennessy, J., *Paolo Uccello*, London, 1950.

Porcher, J., *Les Grandes Heures de Rohan* (Les trésors de la peinture française, I, 7, XVI), Geneva, 1943.

Porcher, J., *Les Belles Heures de Jean de France, duc de Berry*, Paris, 1953.

Porcher, J., *Hours of Rohan*, London, 1959; New York [1959].

Porcher, J., *Medieval French Miniatures*, New York [1959]. French ed. *Enluminure française*, Paris, 1959.

Porcher, J., *Jean Lebègue, Les histoires que l'on peu raisonnablement faire sur les livres de Salluste*, Paris, 1962.

Porcher, J., 'Two Models for the "Heures de Rohan" ', *Warburg Journal*, VIII, 1945, pp. 1-6.

Porcher, J., 'Les Très Belles Heures de Jean de Berry et les ateliers parisiens', *Scriptorium*, VII, 1953, pp. 121-123.

Porcher, J., 'Communication sur les *Très Belles Heures de Notre-Dame*', *Bull. de la Société des Antiquaires de France*, 1956, pp. 72-74.

Porcher, J., 'Les *Très Belles Heures de Notre-Dame*', *Revue des arts*, VII, 1937, p. 13 f.

Porcher, J., 'Un amateur de peinture sous Charles VI: Jean Lebègue', in *Mélanges d'histoire du livre et des bibliothèques offerts à Monsieur Frantz Calot*, Paris, 1960.

Porcher, J., *see also* Paris, Bibliothèque nationale.

Portugal. Santos, R. dos, 'Les principaux manuscrits à peintures conservés en Portugal', *Bulletin de la Société Française de Reproductions de Manuscrits à Peintures*, XIV, 1932.

Post, C. R., *A History of Spanish Painting*, Cambridge, Mass., 1930–1941. 8v.

Poujoulat, J. J. F., *see* Christine de Pisan.

Pradel, P., 'Art et politique sous Charles V', *Revue des arts*, 1951, pp. 88-93.

Pradel, P., 'Les tombeaux de Charles V', *Bull. monumental*, CIX, 1951, pp. 273-296.

Pradel, P., 'Le portrait sculpté à la fin du moyen âge', in *Actes du XVIIme Congrès International d'Histoire de l'Art*, The Hague, 1955, pp. 257 f.

Pradel, P., 'Nouveaux documents sur le tombeau de Jean de Berry', *Monuments et mémoires*, XLIX, 1957, pp. 141-157.

Prinet, M., 'Les variations du nombre des fleurs de lis dans les armes de France', *Bull. monumental*, LXXV, 1911, pp. 469-488.

Procacci, U., *Sinopie e affreschi*, Florence, 1960.

Procacci, U., 'Di Jacopo di Antonio e delle compagnie di pittori del Corso degli Adimari nel XV secolo', *Rivista d'arte*, XXXV, 1961, pp. 3-70.

Prost, B., *Inventaires mobiliers et extraits des comptes des ducs de Bourgogne de la maison de Valois (1363-1477)*, Paris, 1902-1913. 2v.

Prost, B., 'Quelques acquisitions de manuscrits par les ducs de Bourgogne Philippe le Hardi et Jean Sans Peur (1396-1415)', *Archives historiques*, II, 1891, pp. 337-353.

Prost, B., 'Un nouveau document sur Jean de Bruges peintre du roi Charles V', *Gaz. B.-A.*, XXXIV, 1892, pt. 1, pp. 349-352.

Prost, B., 'Les arts à la cour du duc de Berry', *Gaz. B.-A.*, XIV, 1895, pp. 254-264, 342-349.

Prou, M., *Manuel de paléographie*, 4th ed., Paris, 1924.

Purkis, G. S., 'Laurent de Premierfait's Translation of the *Decameron*', *Medium Aevum*, XXIV, 1955, pp. 1-15.

Puy, Cathedral, *see* Delisle [1867?].

Quaile, E., *Illuminated Manuscripts: Their Origin, History and Characteristics . . .*, Liverpool, 1897.

Quarré, P., *La Chartreuse de Champmol, foyer d'art au temps des ducs Valois* [Dijon, 1960].

Quarré, P., 'L'influence de Simone Martini sur la sculpture bourguignonne', *Bull. Société des Antiquaires de France*, 1960, pp. 53-55.

Quatrebarbes, Théodore, comte de, *see Œuvres complètes du roi René*.

Ragusa, I., *see Meditations on the Life of Christ*.

Randall, L. M. C., 'Exempla as a Source of Gothic Marginal Illumination', *Art Bull.*, XXXIX, 1957, pp. 97-107.

Randall, L. M. C., 'Fieschi Psalter', *Walters Journal*, XXIII, 1960, pp. 26-47.

Randall, L. M. C., 'A Mediaeval Slander', *Art Bull.*, XLII, 1960, pp. 25-38.

Raynal, L., *Histoire du Berry depuis les temps les plus anciens jusqu'en 1789*, Bourges, 1844-1847. 4v.

Raynaud, G., *see Les cent ballades*.

Raynaud, G., *see also* Deschamps, E.

Réau, L., *French Painting in the XIVth, XVth, and XVIth Centuries*, trans. M. Chamot, London [1939].

Réau, L., *Histoire de la peinture au moyen âge: La miniature*, Melun, 1946.

Réau, L., *see also* Dimier and Réau.

Reinach, S., 'Deux miniatures de la Bibliothèque de Heidelberg attribuées à Jean Malouel', *Gaz. B.-A.*, XXXI, 1904, pp. 55-65.

Reinach, S., 'Manuscrits à miniatures de Genève', *Rev. archéol.*, X, 1907, p. 172 f.

Reiners, H., *Die Kölner Malerschule*, Bonn, 1925.

René of Anjou, *see Œuvres complètes du roi René*.

René of Anjou, *see also* Vienna, Nationalbibliothek.

Reynaud, N., 'A propos du martyre de Saint Denis', *Revue du Louvre*, XI, 1961, pp. 175 f.

de Ricci, S., ed., *Census of Medieval and Renaissance Manuscripts in the United States and Canada*, New York, 1935-1940. 3v. Supplement, 1962.

de Ricci, S., *Les dessins français*, Paris [1938].

Richard, J.-M., *Une petite-nièce de saint Louis, Mahaut, comtesse d'Artois et de Bourgogne (1302–1329)*, Paris, 1887.

Rickert, M., *The Reconstructed English Carmelite Missal in the British Museum*, Chicago, 1951.

Rickert, M., *Painting in Britain: The Middle Ages*, London [1954].

Ring, G., *A Century of French Painting, 1400–1500*, London [1949].

Ring, G., 'Primitifs français', *Gaz. B.-A.*, XIX, pt. I, 1938, pp. 149-168.

Ritter, G., and J. Lafond, *Manuscrits à peintures de l'école de Rouen: Livres d'heures normands*, Paris, 1913.

Robb, D. M., 'The Iconography of the Annunciation in the Fourteenth and Fifteenth Centuries', *Art Bull.*, XVIII, 1936, pp. 480-526.

Roggen, D., 'Het Beeldhouwwerk van het Mechelsche Schepenhuis', in *Gentsche Bijdragen tot de Kunstgeschiedenis*, III, 1936, pp. 86-103.

Rolland, P., 'La Madone italo-byzantine de Frasnes-lez-Buissenal', *Revue belge*, XVII, 1947–1948, pp. 97-106.

Roman, J., *Manuel de sigillographie française*, Paris, 1912.

Rome. Palazzo Venezia. *Mostra storica nazionale della miniatura. Catalogo*, Florence [1953].

Rome. Vatican. Beissel, S., *Vaticanische Miniaturen*, Freiburg, 1893.

Rome. Vatican. *Codices Vaticani latini*, Rome, 1902–1958. 7v. in 9.

Rome. Vatican. Christ, K., *Die altfranzösischen Handschriften der Palatina*, Leipzig, 1916.

Rorimer, J. J., 'The Virgin from Strasbourg Cathedral', *Bull. Metropolitan Museum*, VII, 1948–1949, pp. 220-227.

Rorimer, J. J., and M. B. Freeman, 'The Nine Heroes Tapestries at the Cloisters', *Bull. Metropolitan Museum*, VII, 1949, pp. 243-260.

Rorimer, J. J., *see also* New York, Metropolitan Museum, The Cloisters.

Rosen, E., 'The Invention of Eyeglasses', *Journal of the History of Medicine*, XI, 1956, pp. 13-46; 183-218.

Rosini, G., *Storia della pittura italiana esposta coi monumenti*, Pisa, 1840–1847. 8v.

Roussel, J., *La sculpture gothique*, Paris, n.d.

Rowlands, J., 'The Date of Simone Martini's Arrival in Avignon', *Burl. Mag.*, CVII, 1965, p. 25 f.

Rowley, G., *Ambrogio Lorenzetti*, Princeton, 1958. 2v.

Roy, E., 'Mystère de la Passion en France du XIVe au XVIe siècle', *Revue bourguignonne*, XIII, 1903, pp. 1-189; XIV, 1904, pp. 153-506.

Roy, M., *see* Christine de Pisan.

Sabbadini, R., *Le scoperte dei codici latini e greci ne' secoli XIV e XV* (Bibl. storica del Rinascimento, v), Florence, 1914.

Saint-Hilaire, Q. de, see *Deschamps, E.*

Salmi, M., *La miniatura italiana*, Milan [1955].

Salmi, M., 'Il paliotto di Manresa e l' "opus florentinum" ', *Bollettino d'arte*, X, 1931, pp. 385-406.

Salmi, M., 'La miniatura', in D. Fava, ed., *Emilia e Romagna* (Tesori delle biblioteche d'Italia, I), Milan, 1932, pp. 267-374.

Salmi, M., 'L'Ouvraige de Lombardie e il Primo Rinascimento', in *Actes du XVIIme Congrès International d'Histoire de l'Art (1952)*, The Hague, 1955, pp. 269-274.

Salmi, M., 'La pittura e la miniatura gotica in Lombardia', in *Storia di Milano*, Milan, V, 1955, pp. 815-874.

Salmi, M., *see also* Emilia and Romagna.

Salmi, M., *see also* Modena, Biblioteca Estense, Fava and Salmi.

Salmon, Pierre, see *Les demandes faites par le roi Charles VI . . . avec les réponses de Pierre Salmon.*

Salomon, R., *Opicinus de Canistris. Weltbild und Bekenntnisse eines avignonesischen Klerikers des 14. Jahrhunderts* (Studies of the Warburg Institute), London, 1936. 2v.

Salzer, A., *Die Sinnbilder und Beiworte Mariens in der deutschen Literatur und lateinischen Hymnenpoesie des Mittelalters*, Linz, 1893.

Samek Ludovici, S., *Le biblioteche dell'Emilia*, Modena, 1959.

Sandberg-Vavalà, E., *La croce dipinta italiana*, Verona, 1929.

Sandys, J. E., *A History of Classical Scholarship from the Sixth Century B.C. to the End of the Middle Ages*, Cambridge, 1903–1908. 3v.

Santoro, C., *see* Milan, Biblioteca Trivulziana.

Sauer, J., *Symbolik des Kirchengebäudes*, 2nd ed., Freiburg, 1924.

Sauerländer, W., 'Zu einem unbekannten Fragment im Museum in Chartres', *Kunstchronik*, XII, 1959, pp. 298-304.

Sawicka, S., *see* Warsaw, Biblioteka Narodowa.

Saxl, F., and R. Wittkower, *British Art and the Mediterranean*, Oxford, 1948.

Schaefer, L., 'Die Illustrationen zu den Handschriften der Christine de Pizan', *Marburger Jahrb.*, X, 1937, pp. 119-208.

Scheller, R. W., *A Survey of Medieval Model Books*, Haarlem, 1963.

Schendel, A. van, *Le dessin en Lombardie jusqu'à la fin du XVe siècle*, Brussels, 1938.

Schilling, R., 'A Book of Hours from the Limbourg Atelier', *Burl. Mag.*, LXXX-LXXXI, 1942, pp. 194-197.

Schilling, R., 'An Unknown French Book of Hours (c. 1400)', *Burl. Mag.*, LXXXIV-LXXXV, 1944, pp. 20-24.

Schilling, R., 'The Nativity and Adoration of the Child Christ in French Miniatures of the Early Fifteenth Century', *Connoisseur*, CXXX, 1952, pp. 167-169, 221.

Schilling, R., 'The Master of Egerton 1070 (Hours of René d'Anjou)', *Scriptorium*, VIII, 1954, pp. 272-282.

Schilling, R., 'Ein Gebetbuch des Michelino da Besozzo', *Münchner Jahrbuch der bildenden Kunst*, VIII, 1957, pp. 65-80.

Schlosser, J. von, 'Ein fürstlicher Kunstfreund des XIV. Jahrhunderts in Frankreich', *Beilage zur Münchener Allgemeiner Zeitung*, 1894, nos. 220, 222.

Schlosser, J. von, 'Die höfische Kunst des Abendlandes in byzantinischer Beleuchtung', *Mittheilungen des Institutes für oesterreichische Geschichtsforschung*, XVII, 1896, pp. 441-456.

Schlosser, J. von, 'Die ältesten Medaillen und die Antike', *Jahrb. kunsth. Slgn.*, XVIII, 1897, pp. 64-108.

Schlosser, J. von, 'Die Werkstatt der Embriachi in Venedig', *Jahrb. kunsth. Slgn.*, XX, 1899, pp. 220-282.

Schlosser, J. von, 'Zur Kenntnis der künstlerischen Ueberlieferung im späten Mittelalter', *Jahrb. kunsth. Slgn.*, XXIII, 1903, pp. 279-338.

Schlosser, J. von, see also *Lorenzo Ghibertis Denkwürdigkeiten*.

Schlumberger, G., *Byzance et croisades, pages médiévales*, Paris, 1927.

Schneider, R., *Fin du moyen âge. Renaissance (L'art français*, II), Paris, 1928.

Shorr, D., 'The Mourning Virgin and Saint John', *Art Bull.*, XXII, 1940, pp. 61-69.

Shorr, D., 'The Iconographic Development of the Presentation in the Temple', *Art Bull.*, XXVIII, 1946, pp. 17-32.

Simone, F., *La coscienza della rinascità negli umanisti francesi*, Rome, 1949.

Simone, F., *Il rinascimento francese*, Turin, 1961.

Sirén, O., *Giotto and Some of his Followers*, Cambridge, Mass., 1917. 2v.

Smaointe Beatha Chríost, ed. C. Ó Maonaigh, O.F.M., Dublin, 1944.

Smital, O., see Vienna, Nationalbibliothek.

Smith, M. T., 'The Use of Grisaille as a Lenten Observance', *Marsyas*, VIII, 1959, pp. 43-54.

Smits, K., *Iconographie van de Nederlandsche Primitieven*, Amsterdam, 1933.

Sokolova, J., *Le paysage dans la miniature française à l'époque gothique*, Prague, 1937.

Solente, S., see Christine de Pisan.

Le songe véritable; pamphlet politique d'un parisien du XVe siècle, ed. H. Moranvillé [Mémoires de la Société de l'Histoire de Paris et de l'Île-de-France, XVII (1890)], Paris, 1891.

Spain, see Durrieu, P., *Bibl. École des Chartes*, 1893.

Spencer, E., 'The Master of the Duke of Bedford: The Bedford Hours', *Burl. Mag.*, 1965, pp. 495-502.

Spitzer, F., see *La collection Spitzer*.

Squilbeck, J., 'La Vierge à l'encrier ou à l'enfant écrivant', *Revue belge*, XIX, 1950, pp. 127-140.

Stalter, M., 'La peinture de chevalet dans l'école de Paris à la fin du quatorzième et du début de quinzième siècle', *L'information de l'histoire de l'art*, VIII, 1963, pp. 112-122.

Stange, A., *Deutsche Malerei der Gotik*, Berlin, 1934-1961. 11v.

Steinbart, K., *Konrad von Soest*, Vienna, 1946.

Steingräber, E., *Antique Jewelry*, London, 1957.

Steingräber, E., see also Müller and Steingräber.

Sterling, C., *La peinture française: Les primitifs*, Paris, 1938.

[Sterling, C.], *La peinture française: Les peintres du moyen âge*, par Charles Jacques [pseud.], Paris, 1942.

Sterling, C., 'Les ducs de Bourgogne et la civilisation franco-flamande', *Arts plastiques*, 1951, pp. 163-181.

Sterling, C., 'Œuvres retrouvées de Jean de Beaumetz, peintre de Philippe le Hardi', *Bulletin, Musées Royaux des Beaux-Arts*, IV, 1955, pp. 57-81.

Sterling, C., 'Le style courtois international', in *L'art et l'homme*, ed. R. Huyghe, Paris, 1958, II, pp. 353-364.

Sterling, C., 'La peinture de portrait à la cour de Bourgogne au début du XVe siècle', *Critica d'arte*, VI, 1959, pp. 289-312.

Sterling, C., see also Paris, Musée du Louvre.

Stix, A., see Vienna, Albertina.

Stockholm. Nationalmuseum. *Fem sekler fransk konst; miniatyrer, målningar, teckningar, 1400-1900 . . ., 1958*. [Stockholm, 1958]. 2v. Text and Plates.

Swartwout, R. E., *The Monastic Craftsman*, Cambridge, 1932.

Swarzenski, G., *Nicolo Pisano*, Frankfurt am Main, 1926.

Swarzenski, G., 'Italienische Quellen der deutschen Pietà', in *Festschrift Heinrich Wölfflin*, Munich, 1924, pp. 127-134.

Swarzenski, G., 'A German Primitive', *Bull. Mus. Boston*, XLII, 1944, pp. 41-50.

Swarzenski, G., 'Miniatures from a Lost Manuscript', *Bull. Mus. Boston*, XLII, 1944, pp. 28-33.

Swarzenski, H., *Die lateinischen illuminierten Handschriften des XIII. Jahrhunderts in den Ländern an Rhein, Main und Donau*, Berlin, 1936. 2v.

Swarzenski, H., 'Quellen zum deutschen Andachtsbild', *Zeitschrift für Kunstgeschichte*, IV, 1935, pp. 141-144.

Tesori, see Salmi.

Thaumas de la Thaumassière, G., *Histoire de Berry*, Bourges, 1689. Reprinted 1863–1871. 4v. in 2 and index.

The Book of Fayttes of Armes and of Chyvalrye. Translated and printed by William Caxton from the French original by Christine de Pisan, ed. A. T. P. Byles (Early English Text Society, original series, no. 189), London, 1932. (Reissued with corrections, 1937).

Thibout, M., 'Les peintures murales de l'église d'Ennezat', *Rev. des arts*, II, 1952, pp. 85-90.

Thieme, U., and F. Becker, *Allgemeines Lexikon der bildenden Künstler*, Leipzig, 1910–1950.

Thomas, M., 'Recherches sur un groupe de manuscrits à peintures du début du XVe siècle', *Bulletin bibliographique de la Société Internationale Arthurienne*, no. 4, 1952, pp. 81-89.

Thomas, M., 'Une prétendue signature de peintre dans un manuscrit du début du XVe siècle', *Bulletin de la Société National des Antiquaires de France*, 1958, pp. 114 f.

Thomas, M., *see also* Paris, Bibliothèque nationale.

Thompson, D. V., and G. H. Hamilton, trans., *An Anonymous Fourteenth-Century Treatise, De arte illuminandi, . . .; translated from the Latin of Naples ms. XII. E. 27 . . .*, New Haven and London, 1933.

Thompson, D. V., Jr., *The Materials of Medieval Painting*, New Haven, 1936.

Thompson, H. Y., *A Lecture on some English Illuminated Manuscripts*, London, 1902.

Thompson, H. Y., *see also* London, Thompson Collection (formerly).

Thompson, J. W., *The Medieval Library*, Chicago, 1939.

Tintori, L., and M. Meiss, *The Painting of the Life of St. Francis in Assisi*, New York, 1962; 1967.

Toesca, P., *La pittura e la miniatura nella Lombardia dai più antichi monumenti alla metà del Quattrocento*, Milan, 1912.

Toesca, P., *Monumenti e studi per la storia della miniatura italiana. La collezione di Ulrico Hoepli*, Milan, 1930.

Toesca, P., *Il Trecento*, Turin, 1951.

Toesca, P., *L'ufiziolo visconteo Landau-Finaly*, Florence, 1951.

Toesca, P., 'Manoscritti miniati della Biblioteca del Principe Corsini a Firenze', *Rassegna d'arte*, XVII, 1917, pp. 117-128.

Tovell, R. M., *Flemish Artists of the Valois Courts; a Survey of the Fourteenth and Early Fifteenth-Century Development of Book Illumination and Panel Painting . . .* [Toronto], 1950.

Trenkler, E., *Das Evangeliar des Johannes von Troppau, Handschrift 1182 der Oesterreichischen Nationalbibliothek*, Klagenfurt and Vienna, 1948.

Trenkler, E., *Livre d'heures; Handschrift 1855 der Österreichischen Nationalbibliothek*, Vienna [1948].

Trenkler, E., *see also* Vienna, Nationalbibliothek.

Les Très Riches Heures du duc de Berry, Musée Condé à Chantilly (J. Porcher), Paris [1950?].

Troescher, G., *Claus Sluter und die burgundische Plastik um die Wende des XIV. Jahrhunderts*, Freiburg, 1932.

Troescher, G., *Die burgundische Plastik des ausgehenden Mittelalters und ihre Wirkungen auf die europäische Kunst*, Frankfurt am Main, 1940. 2v.

Turin. Biblioteca Reale. *Codices manuscripti Bibliothecae Regii taurinensis athenaei . . .* (G. Pasini et al.), Turin, 1749. 2v.

Ullman, B. L., *Studies in the Italian Renaissance*, Rome, 1955.

Unterkircher, F., *see* Vienna, Nationalbibliothek.

Vasari, G., *Le vite de' più eccellenti pittori, scultori, et architettori*, ed. G. Milanesi, Florence, 1906. 9v.

Vaughan, R., *Philip the Bold*, Cambridge, Mass., 1962.

Vayer, L., 'L'affresco absidale di Pietro Cavallini nella chiesa di S. Maria in Aracoeli a Roma', *Acta Historiae Artium*, IX, 1963, pp. 39-73.

Venturi, A., *Storia dell'arte italiana*, Milan, 1901–1942. 12v.

Verdier, P., 'A Medallion of the *Ara Coeli* and the Netherlandish Enamels of the Fifteenth Century', *Walters Journal*, XXIV, 1961, pp. 9-37.

Vienna. Albertina. *Die Zeichnungen der toskanischen, umbrischen und römischen Schulen*, ed. A. Stix and L. Fröhlich-Bum (*Beschreibender Katalog der Handzeichnungen in der Graphischen Sammlung Albertina*, III), Vienna, 1932.

Vienna. Kunsthistorisches Museum. *Europäische Kunst um 1400: Ausstellungskatalog*, Vienna, 1962.

Vienna. Nationalbibliothek. *Beschreibendes Verzeichnis der illuminierten Handschriften in Österreich*, ed. F. Wickhoff et al., Leipzig, 1905–1938. N.F. v, pt. v, 2: *Die italienischen Handschriften des Dugento und Trecento*.

Oberitalienische Handschriften der zweiten Hälfte des XIV. Jahrhunderts (H. J. Hermann), Leipzig, 1929. N.F. VII, pt. VII, 2: *Die westeuropäischen Handschriften und Inkunabeln der Gotik und der Renaissance. Englische und französische Handschriften des XIV. Jahrhunderts* (H. J. Hermann), Leipzig, 1936. N.F. VII, pt. VII, 3: *Französische und iberische Handschriften der ersten Hälfte des XV. Jahrhunderts* (H. J. Hermann), Leipzig, 1938.

Vienna. Nationalbibliothek. Beer, R., 'Les principaux manuscrits à peintures de la Bibliothèque impériale de Vienne', *Bulletin de la Société Française de Reproductions de Manuscrits à Peintures*, II, 1912, pp. 5-53; III, 1913, pp. 5-55.

Vienna, Nationalbibliothek. *Livre du cuer d'amours espris*, ed. O. Smital and E. Winkler, Vienna, 1926. 2v.

Vienna. Nationalbibliothek. Trenkler, E., 'Meisterwerke der französischen Buchmalerei in der Oesterreichischen Nationalbibliothek', *Nationalmusei Årsbok*, 1947–1948, pp. 7-38.

Vienna. Nationalbibliothek. *Inventar der illuminierten Handschriften, Inkunabeln und Frühdrucke der Österreichischen Nationalbibliothek: I. Die abendländischen Handschriften* (F. Unterkircher), Vienna, 1957.

Vitry, P., *Die gotische Plastik Frankreichs 1226–1270*, Munich, 1929.

Vitzthum, G., *Die Pariser Miniaturmalerei von der Zeit der Heiligen Ludwig bis zu Philipp von Valois und ihr Verhältnis zur Malerei in Nordwesteuropa*, Leipzig, 1907.

Voigt, G., *Die Wiederbelebung des classischen Alterthums, oder das erste Jahrhundert des Humanismus*, 2nd ed., Berlin, 1880–1881. 2v.

Volbach, W. F., *Early Christian Art*, New York, n.d.

Volpe, C., 'Nuove proposte sui Lorenzetti', *Arte antica e moderna*, no. 11, 1960, pp. 1-15.

Waagen, G. F., *Kunstwerke und Künstler in Paris*, Berlin, 1839.

Waagen, G. F., *Treasures of Art in Great Britain . . .*, London, 1854. 3v.

Wardrop, J., 'Egregius pictor franciscus', *Apollo*, xv, 1932, pp. 76-82.

Warner, G. F., *Queen Mary's Psalter*, London, 1912.

Warner, G. F., *Descriptive Catalogue of Illuminated Manuscripts in the Library of C. W. Dyson Perrins*, Oxford, 1920. 2v.

Warner, G. F., *see also* London, British Museum.

Warsaw. Biblioteka Narodowa. Ameisenowa, Z., 'De quelques précieux manuscrits français à peintures . . .

à la Bibliothèque nationale de Varsovie', *Bull. international de l'Académie Polonaise*, I-II, 1933, pp. 5-10 (as reprint, Cracow, 1934).

Warsaw. Biblioteka Narodowa. Sawicka, S., 'Les principaux manuscrits à peintures de la Bibliothèque nationale de Varsovie, du château royal et des bibliothèques: des Zamoyskie à Varsovie, du séminaire de Płock et du chapitre de Gniezno', *Bulletin de la Société Française de Reproductions de Manuscrits à Peintures*, XIX, 1938.

Watson, A., *The Early Iconography of the Tree of Jesse*, Oxford and London, 1934.

Waugh, W., *A History of Europe from 1378 to 1494*, London [1932].

Weale, W. H. J., *Gerard David*, London, 1895.

Weale, W. H. J., 'Notice sur la fondation de l'abbaye de l'Eeckhout', *La Flandre: Revue des monuments d'histoire et d'antiquités*, 1869–1870, pp. 274 ff.

Weber, L., *Einbanddecken, Elfenbeintafeln, Miniaturen, Schriftproben aus Metzer liturgischen Handschriften*, I, Metz and Frankfurt [1913].

Webster, J. C., *The Labors of the Months in Antique and Mediaeval Art*, Princeton, 1938.

Weese, A., *Skulptur und Malerei in Frankreich im XV. und XVI. Jahrhundert* (Handbuch der Kunstwissenschaft), Wildpark-Potsdam, 1927.

Weinberger, M., 'A French Model of the Fifteenth Century', *Walters Journal*, IX, 1946, pp. 8-21.

Weiss, R., 'The Medieval Medallions of Constantine and Heraclius', *Numismatic Chronicle*, III, 1963, pp. 129-144.

Weitzmann, K., 'The Origin of the Threnos', in *De Artibus Opuscula XL: Essays in Honor of Erwin Panofsky*, New York, 1961, I, pp. 476-490.

Wentzel, H., 'Maria mit dem Jesusknaben an der Hand. Ein seltenes deutsches Bildmotiv', *Zeitschrift des Deutschen Vereins für Kunstwissenschaft*, IX, 1942, pp. 203-250.

Wentzel, H., 'Eine Kamee aus Lothringen in Florenz und andere Kunstkammer-Gemmen', *Jahrb. preuss. Kstslg.*, LXIV, 1943, pp. 1-16.

Wentzel, H., 'Portraits "à l'antique" on French Medieval Gems and Seals', *Warburg Journal*, XVI, 1953, pp. 342-350.

Wentzel, H., 'Die Grosse Kamee mit Poseidon und Athena in Paris', *Wallraf-Richartz Jahrbuch*, XVI, 1954, pp. 53-76.

Wentzel, H., 'Die mittelalterlichen Gemmen der Staatlichen Münzsammlung zu München', *Münchner Jahrbuch der bildenden Kunst*, VIII, 1957, pp. 37-56.

Wentzel, H., 'Das Jesuskind an der Hand Mariae auf dem Siegel des Burkard von Winon 1277', *Festschrift Hahnloser*, Basel and Stuttgart, 1961, pp. 251-270.

Wentzel, H., ' "Staatskameen" im Mittelalter', *Jahrbuch der Berliner Museen*, IV, 1962, pp. 42-77.

Wescher, P., *Jean Fouquet und seine Zeit*, Basel, 1945.

Wescher, P., 'Two Burgundian Drawings of the Fifteenth Century', *Old Master Drawings*, XII, 1937, p. 16.

Wescher, P., 'Eine Modellzeichnung des Paul von Limburg', *Phoebus*, I, 1946, pp. 33 f.

Wescher, P., *see also* Berlin, Staatliche Museen, Kupferstichkabinett.

Westendorp, K., *Die Anfänge der französisch-niederländischen Portraittafel* (Dissertation Strasbourg), Cologne, 1906.

White, J., *The Birth and Rebirth of Pictorial Space*, London, 1957.

White, J., 'Cavallini and the Lost Frescoes in S. Paolo', *Warburg Journal*, XIX, 1956, pp. 84-95.

White, T. H., *The Book of Beasts*, London, 1954.

Wickhoff, F., *see* Vienna, Nationalbibliothek.

Willard, C. C., 'Christine de Pisan's "Clock of Temperance" ', *L'esprit créateur*, II, 1963, pp. 149-156.

Willard, C. C., *see also* Christine de Pisan.

Wilm, H., *Die gotische Holzfigur*, Leipzig, 1923.

Winkler, E., see *Livre du cuer d'amours espris*.

Winkler, E., *see also* Vienna, Nationalbibliothek.

Winkler, F., *Die altniederländische Malerei. Die Malerei in Belgien und Holland von 1400-1600*, Berlin, 1924.

Winkler, F., *Die flämische Buchmalerei des XV. und XVI. Jahrhunderts*, Leipzig, 1925.

Winkler, F., 'Ein neues Werk aus der Werkstatt Pauls von Limburg', *Repertorium für Kunstwissenschaft*, XXXIV, 1911, pp. 536-543.

Winkler, F., 'Zur Pariser Miniaturmalerei im dritten und vierten Jahrzehnt des 15. Jahrhunderts', *Beiträge zur Forschung*, pts. IV-V, 1914, pp. 114-120.

Winkler, F., 'Petrus Gilberti', in Thieme-Becker, XIV, 1921, p. 28.

Winkler, F., 'Jacquemart de Hesdin', in Thieme-Becker, XVI, 1923, pp. 571-573.

Winkler, F., 'Die nordfranzösische Malerei im 15. Jahrhundert und ihr Verhältnis zur altniederländischen Malerei', in *Belgische Kunstdenkmäler*, Munich, 1923, I, pp. 247-268.

Winkler, F., 'Paul de Limbourg in Florence', *Burl. Mag.*, LVI, 1930, pp. 95 f.

Winkler, F., rev. of Erwin Panofsky, 'Early Netherlandish Painting; its Origins and Character', Cambridge, Mass., 1953, *Kunstchronik*, VIII, 1955, pp. 9-26.

Winkler, F., 'Ein frühfranzösisches Marienbild', *Jahrb. Berliner Museen*, I, 1959, pp. 179-189.

Winkler, F., *see also* Berlin, Staatliche Museen (formerly).

Winternitz, E., 'The Hours of Charles the Noble: Musicians and Musical Instruments', *Bull. Cleveland Museum of Art*, LII, 1965, pp. 84-90.

Wittkower, R., 'Marco Polo and the Pictorial Tradition of the Marvels of the East', *Oriente poliano*, 1957, pp. 155-172.

Wixom, W. D., 'The Hours of Charles the Noble', *Bull. Cleveland Museum of Art*, LII, 1965, pp. 50-81.

Wolfenbüttel, Herzog-August-Bibliothek. *Die Handschriften der Herzoglichen Bibliothek zu Wolfenbüttel* (O. von Heinemann), Wolfenbüttel, 1884-1913. 10v.

Wormald, F., 'The Wilton Diptych', *Warburg Journal*, XVII, 1954, pp. 191-203.

Wormald, F., 'French Illuminated Manuscripts in Paris', *Burl. Mag.*, XCVIII, 1956, pp. 323-333.

Wormald, F., 'The Throne of Solomon and St. Edward's Chair', in *De Artibus Opuscula XL: Essays in Honor of Erwin Panofsky*, New York, 1961, I, pp. 532-539.

Wormald, F., and P. M. Giles, 'Description of Fitzwilliam Museum MS. 3-1954', *Transactions of the Cambridge Bibliographical Society*, IV, 1964, pp. 1-28.

Worringer, W., *Die Anfänge der Tafelmalerei*, Leipzig, 1924.

Wylie, J. H., *History of England under Henry IV*, London, 1884-1898. 4v.

Wylie, J. H., *The Reign of Henry the Fifth*, Cambridge, 1914-1919. 3v.

Yates Thompson, H., *see* Thompson, H. Y.

Zarnecki, G., *see* Grivot and Zarnecki.

INDEX

References to reproductions are indexed only topographically.
The Index includes very few of the thousands of objects described in the Duke's inventories
that have not survived. For them the reader is referred to the excellent index of Guiffrey,
Inventaires de Jean duc de Berry.

Adoration of the Magi, 60, 124 ff., 172 ff., 190, 214, 225, 231, 240 f., 246 ff., 290, 379 n. 88, 384 n. 134, 407 n. 158

Agony in the Garden, 121, 178, 260, 273

Aix-en-Provence, Musée Granet
Master of the Angevin Bible – Associate, Annunciation, 29, 120, Nativity, 29, 219, Fig. 414
Neapolitan, St. Louis of Toulouse, 27, Fig. 407

Albi, Cathedral: Italian, altarpiece, *ca.* 1365, 366 n. 131

Alcherius, Johannes, 64; Treatise on technique, 1, 64, 395 n. 94

Alegret, Simon, 50, 195 f., 208; portrait of, 208

Alexander Minorita laicus, Commentary on the Apocalypse, 374 n. 237

Alken, Church: German, Last Judgment, 377 n. 8

Allegory of Salvation, 55 f., 127

Altichiero, 72, 123, 210, 214, 219, 237 f., 240 f., 402 n. 55; influence on Master of the Brussels Initials, 237 f., 245

Altichiero – Follower, 72

Altötting, Pilgrimage Church: French, *Goldenes Rössl*, 51, 142 f., 145 f., Fig. 573

Alvaro Portogallo, 24

Amsterdam, Rijksmuseum
French, triptych with Man of Sorrows (enamel), 123, 142, Fig. 572
Monaco, Lorenzo – Circle, Madonna, 375 n. 284

Anastaise, 3

Anciau de Cens, 6

Andrea da Bologna, 382 n. 83

Andrea da Firenze, *see* Bonaiuti, Andrea

Angel appearing to Joseph, 28

Angers, Bibl. municipale: ms fr. 162 (Cité de Dieu), 298, 309; *see also* Cambridge, Harvard College Library, Hofer Coll.

— Musée des Beaux-Arts (Musée David): Master of the Pietà, Vesperbild, 62, 183 f., Fig. 641

— Musée des Tapisseries, Château: Bondol, Jean, and Nicolas Bataille, Apocalypse of Louis I d'Anjou, 12, 22, 45, 100 f., 381 n. 41, Figs. 380, 381, 387

— Musée Turpin de Crissé (Hôtel de Pincé): Sienese, triptych, 366 n. 131

Anjou, house of: ties with Italy, 27

Annunciation, 19 f., 38, 96, 100, 117, 120, 130, 155, 158, 165 f., 169 f., 194, 211 ff., 231, 237 ff., 248, 264, 275

Annunciation to the Shepherds, 19, 117, 167, 178, 214, 231, 233, 235, 265

Antelminelli, Alderigo, 51 f.

Antonius de Compendio, 64

Antwerp, Musée des Beaux-Arts: Simone Martini, Annunciation, 25, 62, 208, 215, 393 n. 58, Figs. 692, 693, Crucifixion, 25, 62, 105, 208, 215 ff., 280, Fig. 674, Deposition, 25, 62, 215, 217, 402 n. 53, Fig. 676

— Musée Mayer van den Bergh
Broederlam, Melchior – Follower, quadriptych, 182
Guelders (?), panels of quadriptych, 182, 375 n. 289, 389 n. 62, Fig. 629; *see also* Baltimore, Walters Art Gallery

Apocrypha, Protoevangelium of James, 164

Aracoeli, legend of, 57, 233 ff., 407 n. 158

Arbre des batailles, 94, 311, 354

Aristotle: Du ciel et du monde, 313 f., 403 n. 12; Économiques, 73, 288, 314 f., 317, 403 n. 12; Éthiques, 73, 288, 309 f., 317, 358 f.; Politiques, 288, 314 f., 317, 358 f., 403 n. 12

Armagnacs, conflict with Burgundians, 34, 71, 292

Arras, Bibl. municipale: ms 517 (Missal of St. Vaast), 106 f., Fig. 534

Asinou, Church of Panagia: Byzantine, Last Judgment, 377 n. 8

Assisi, San Francesco, Lower Church
Giotto – Followers, Flagellation (glass), 103, Nativity, 389 n. 56
Lorenzetti, Pietro, Deposition, 218, Fig. 688
Lorenzetti, Pietro and associates, Way to Calvary, 216, Fig. 689
Lorenzetti, Pietro – Follower, Last Supper, 28, 398 n. 66

— San Francesco, Lower Church, Chapel of St. Martin: Simone Martini, frescoes, 121, 219, 388 n. 24, Fig. 540

— San Francesco, Upper Church
late 13th cent., Marriage at Cana, 129
Rusuti, Filippo, first scene of creation, 24 f.

Athena, 59

Augustine, St., 307; Cité de Dieu, 14, 122, 174, 288, 298, 309, 312, 314, 354, 356 f., 360, 365 n. 105, 381 n. 53, 382 n. 88, 391 n. 115

Augustus, medal of, 40, 46, 54 ff., 235, 405 n. 84

Aunelx, Friar Guy d', 381 n. 50a

Autun, Cathedral: Gislebertus, Last Judgment, 69, 377 n. 8

Avignon, Musée Calvet
ms 138 (Missal), 27 f., 367 n. 139, Fig. 409
ms 207 (prayer book), 206, Fig. 655

— Notre-Dame-des-Doms: Simone Martini, St. George battling the Dragon, 25; *see also* Avignon, Papal Palace

Avignon, Papal Palace
  Matteo Giovanetti, frescoes, 25 f., Figs. 405, 406
  Simone Martini, Christ Blessing, Madonna of Humility, 25 f., Fig. 397
— Papal Palace, Tour de la Garderobe: frescoes, 59
— St. Didier: Florentine, frescoes, 26, Fig. 404

Bagno a Ripoli, S. Bartolommeo a Quarata: Uccello, Paolo – Follower, Adoration of the Magi, 397 n. 51
Balcarres (Fife), Crawford, Earl of, Coll.: Master of Città di Castello, Crucifixion, 104, 183 f., Fig. 528

Baltimore, Walters Art Gallery
              MANUSCRIPTS
  ms 90 (Horae), 117, Fig. 563
  ms 94 (Horae), 190, 319, 401 n. 24, Figs. 626, 627
  ms 96 (Horae), 166, 189, 194, 231, 242, 319, Figs. 616, 618, 621
  ms 100 (Horae), 184, 186, 359, Fig. 650
  ms 102 (Horae), Fig. 623
  ms 103 (Horae), 359
  ms 125-126 (Bible historiale), 309
  ms 185 (Horae), 391 n. 107, Fig. 649
  ms 219 (Horae), 355, 360
  ms 231 (Horae), 358, 394 n. 66
  ms 232 (Horae), 355, 358
  ms 281 (Horae), 389 n. 58
  ms 287 (Horae), 265, Fig. 262
  ms 290 (Horae), 360
  ms 760 (Antiphonary of Beaupré), 382 n. 82
              PAINTINGS
  Guelders (?), panels of quadriptych, 375 n. 289; see also Antwerp, Musée Mayer van den Bergh
  Niccolo di Tommaso, Coronation of the Virgin, 215, Fig. 702

Bamberg, Cathedral: Abraham with Souls, 79
Baptism of Christ, 22, 180, 249
Barcelona, Archivo Histórico: Horae, 144, Figs. 580, 581
— Bibl. Central: ms 1850 (Horae), 18, 149, 215, 227, 232, 239, 242, 299 f., 356, 358, 405 n. 108, Figs. 334, 705, 706, 810
— Cathedral: Missal of St. Eulalia, 144
— Museo Diocesano: Bassa, Arnau, St. James, 365 n. 113
— Pedralbes: Bassa, Ferrer, frescoes, 24, Fig. 390
— S. María del Mar (formerly): Levador del plat de pobres vergonyants (Madonna with the writing Child), 206 f., 279, Fig. 280
Barna da Siena, 103
Barna da Siena – Follower, 402 n. 55
Barna da Siena – Workshop, 170
Barnaba da Modena, 397 n. 51
Bartolo di Fredi, 24, 365 n. 115, 383 n. 111
Bartolomeus Anglicus, Propriété des choses, 73, 94, 288, 317 f., 371 n. 137
Bartolommeo da Camogli, 171, 277
bas-de-page, development of, 117 f., 203 f.
Basel, Öffentliche Kunstsammlung, Kupferstichkabinett
  Beaumetz, Jean de, Madonnas, 279 f., 389 n. 54, Fig. 830
  Holbein, Hans the Younger, portrait of Jean de Berry (drawing after statue in Ste-Chapelle, Bourges), 45, 68, 78 f., 93,

Basel, Öffentliche Kunstsammlung, Kupferstichkabinett (contd.)
  Fig. 511, portrait of Jeanne de Boulogne (drawing after statue in Ste-Chapelle, Bourges), 45, 78, 93, Fig. 510
Bassa, Arnau, 383 n. 124, see Master of St. Mark
Bassa, Ferrer, 24, 212, 366 n. 133; see also Master of the Bellpuig Coronation
Bataille, Nicolas, 22, 45
Baude de Guy, 46 f.
Beaumetz, Jean de, 7 f., 18, 38, 100, 279 f., 293, 302, 389 n. 54
Beaune, Hôtel-Dieu: Weyden, Roger van der, Last Judgment, 253
Beauneveu, André, 6 f., 10, 36 f., 45, 99 f., 102, 113, 135 ff., 147 ff., 159, 168, 170, 176, 191, 200 f., 207 f., 227 f., 255, 279, 295 ff., 305, 331 f., 366 n. 133; influence on Jacquemart, 191
Beauneveu, André – Workshop, 148
Bedford, John of Lancaster, Duke of, 288
Belbello da Pavia, 143, 145
Belin, Arnoul, 40 f.
Bellechose, Henri, 7, 18, 402 n. 81
Bellini, Giovanni, 185
Bellpuig, Church (formerly): Master of the Bellpuig Coronation, Coronation, 24, Figs. 389, 392; see also Bassa, Ferrer
Benedict XII, 25
Bérenger III, Bishop of Béziers, 24
Bergamo, Accademia Carrara: Pisanello, Antonio, portrait of Lionello d'Este, 75
— Bibl. Civica: Taccuino di disegni, 143
Berlin, Deutsches Museum (formerly)
  Bohemian, Crucifixion, 391 n. 100
  Lower Rhenish, Nativity, 237, 389 n. 62
— Kaiser-Friedrich Museum (formerly)
  Bohemian, Madonna of Kladzko, 385 n. 160
  Caravaggio, St. Matthew, 232
— Preussische Staatsbibliothek (formerly): cod. pict. A 74 (Pattern Book of Jacques Daliwe), 239, 278, Fig. 807

              MANUSCRIPTS
  gr. qu. 66 (Gospel Book), 107, Fig. 543
  Phillipps 1906 (Bible historiale of 1368), 21, 152, Fig. 603
  Phillipps 1917 (Grandes chroniques), 356
  theol. lat. qu. 7 (Horae), 358

Berlin – Dahlem, Staatliche Museen
  French, Madonna (medallion), 54, 74, Fig. 466
              PAINTINGS
  French, Coronation of the Virgin, 279
  Geertgen tot Sint Jans, St. John in the Wilderness, 250
  Malouel, Jean (?), Madonna and Angels, 7, 63, 280, 402 n. 81
  Masaccio, Adoration of the Magi, 383 n. 113
  Orlandi, Deodato, Visitation, 213, Fig. 704
  Simone Martini, Entombment, 25
  Weyden, Roger van der, Lamentation, 186, Fig. 636

Bern, Kunstmuseum: Daddi, Bernardo – Follower, Madonna della culla, 391 n. 103
Bernardo di Cino, 46, 366 n. 138

Berry, Jean duc de
  collections: ancient objects, 303 f. (see also cameos), animals,

Berry, Jean duc de (*contd.*)
31 f., Byzantine objects, 46, 57, 304 f., cameos, 52 f., 303 f., crosses, golden, 45, 48, 52 f., 372 n. 185 (see also *Croix au serpent*; *Joyau au mont de Calvaire*), joyaux, 38 f., 48, 50 f., 196, 235, medals and plaquettes, 36, 40, 43, 46, 53 ff., 295 f., 304 f., 405 n. 84, panel paintings, 61 ff., 389 n. 52, portraits (*see* Bicêtre), precious stones, 47 f., 50, 69 f., relics, 39, rings, 52, 73 f., wall hangings, 58 f.
devotion to Trinity, 87; dress, 79 ff., 82; emblems, 32, 59, 95 f.; and Flemish illumination, 251 ff.; Fr. translations made for, 288 f.; funeral service of, 34 f.; hair styles, 80, 82; inventories, 40 ff., 48, 352; Italianate taste, 66, 301 ff.; manuscripts: access to, 296, 405 n. 89, collaboration in, 9 f., 296 f.; motto, 74; music, 31; painters, competition among, 198, 209, 291, 297; portraits of, 13, 32, 37 f., 45, 50, 54, 68 ff., 95, 111 f., 156 ff., 175, 178, 188, 205, 207, 264, 372 n. 185; sculptors of, 45; seals, 57, 82 ff., 258; signature of, 290; travels, 291 f., 301, 368 n. 19; *verriers* of, 44

Bersuire, Pierre: De proprietatibus rerum, 403 n. 21; Dictionarii seu reportorii moralis, 95; Fr. trans. of Livy, 403 n. 5
Bertrand du Guesclin, 59
Besançon, Bibl. municipale
ms 123 (Horae), 360
ms 865 (Froissart, Chroniques), 354
Bétisac, 32
Betrayal, 113 ff., 162, 214 f., 242, 389 n. 40
Béziers, St. Nazaire: Roman, Legend of St. Stephen, 24, Fig. 395
— St. Nazaire, Chapel of the Holy Ghost: Cavallini – Follower, frescoes, 24, Figs. 398, 399
Bicêtre, 34, 37, 74, Fig. 423; portrait gallery, 37, 74, 305, 375 n. 275
Biondo, Flavio, 74
Birmingham, Barber Institute: Metz, Horae, 126, Fig. 548
Birth of the Virgin, 16, 126, 245, 264
Boccaccio: Cas des nobles hommes et femmes, 80, 93, 295, 298, 303, 310, 318, 356 ff., 372 n. 171 (*see also* Laurent de Premierfait); Decameron, 12, 14 ff., 308, 318, 357 (*see also* Laurent de Premierfait); De mulieribus claris, 4 f., 128, Ulm (Von Etlichen Frauen), 1473, 4, Fig. 288, Venice, 1506, 5, Fig. 293; Des cleres et nobles femmes, 4, 47, 128, 243, 252, 295, 303, 313, 355 f., 378 n. 64; Fr. translations, 4, 14, 288, 295, 302 f., 363 n. 59
Boethius, 64 f., 316, 357, 360
Boisratier, Guillaume, 49
Bologna, Bibl. del Archiginnasio: Statuti della Compagnia dello Spedale di S. Maria della Vita, 230, 243 f., 319 f., Fig. 792
— Museo Civico
ms 28, 398 n. 82
ms 85 (Matricula Societatis Draperiorum), 382 n. 76
ms 93 (Matricula Societatis Draperiorum), 398 n. 82
— Museo Davia Bargellini: Simone dei Crocefissi, Lamentation, 390 n. 92
— Pinacoteca
'Jacopino', polyptych, 383 n. 101, 390 n. 83
Vitale da Bologna, Nativity (fresco from Mezzaratta), 18, Fig. 331
Bonaiuti, Andrea, 28, 105, 363 n. 49
Bondol, Jean, 6, 12, 19 ff., 44, 100, 113 f., 165, 167 f., 177, 205, 218, 287, 296, 298

Bondol, Jean – Followers, 21 ff., 101 f., 118, 122, 160, 188, 204, 287 f., 298, 328, 399 n. 18
Bonn, Rheinisches Landesmuseum: German, Vesperbild, 184, Fig. 637
Bonne de Luxembourg, patron of art, 31, 287
Book of Hours, development of, 14
Book of Hours, and Valois family, 14, 48, 287
Boqueteaux style, 96, 162, 181, 287 f., 298, 388 n. 17; *see also* Bondol, Jean
borders, development of, 203 f., 246, 258
Borgo Sansepolcro, Museo: Sienese, altarpiece of the Resurrection, 394 n. 73, 394 n. 75, 401 n. 48
Bosch, Hieronymus, 103, 394 n. 82, 402 n. 52
Boston, Museum of Fine Arts
Bohemian, Madonna, 131
Tyrolese, Coronation of the Virgin with Trinity, 387 n. 74
— Public Library: ms 1528 (Livre des trois vertus), 356
Botticelli, Sandro, 77
Boucicaut, Jean le Meingre II, Maréchal de, 9, 49, 146, 299
Bourges, Archives du Département du Cher
Seal of Jean de Berry, 1397, 83, Fig. 477
Counter-seal of Jean de Berry, 97, Fig. 522

— Bibliothèque municipale
MANUSCRIPTS
ms 16 (Breviary of St. Ambrose), 320, 387 n. 91, 401 n. 24, Fig. 607
ms 33-36 (Lectionary of Ste-Chapelle), 78 ff., 93, 159, 260, 263 f., 299, 309, 320, Figs. 254, 499
ms 48 (Evangeliary), 91, 93, 159, 263 f., 309, 320 f., Figs. 253, 493

— Cathedral
Beauneveu, André and associates, Apostles (glass from Ste-Chapelle), 39, 135, 150 f., 370 n. 99, Figs. 597-599
French, Simon Alegret and his Nephews presented to the Madonna (glass), 208, Fig. 670
Jean de Cambrai, effigy of Jean de Berry, 38 f., 45, 68, 78 f., 94, 293, Fig. 502, Notre-Dame-la-Blanche, 93
statues of Jean de Berry and Jeanne de Boulogne, 16th cent., 75, 93 f.
— illumination in, 295
— Musée de Berry
Hours of Anne de Mathefelon, 359
yellow agate cup from Ste-Chapelle, Bourges, 36, 39, 51, 129, Fig. 472
— Musée Jacques Cœur
Beauneveu, André, and Workshop, Prophets, 36, 135, 148, Figs. 593-595
French, heads, 148
French, Man of Sorrows (relief), 62, Fig. 433
Jean de Cambrai, head of Jean de Berry, 38, 45, 68, 79, 93, Fig. 501
— Palace of Jean de Berry, 37
— Ste-Chapelle, 34 f., 38 f., 292, Figs. 431, 432; patronage of Charles VII, 35, 94, 373 n. 211; Prophets (*see* Bourges, Musée Jacques Cœur; Paris, Hutinel Coll.); transfer of Duke's manuscripts to, 38, 40, 291, 403 n. 22
— Ste-Chapelle (formerly): Jean de Cambrai, Notre-Dame-la-Blanche with Jean de Berry and Jeanne de Boulogne, 38 f.,

Bourges, Ste-Chapelle (formerly) (*contd.*)
45, 68, 93, 146. *See also* Basel, Öffentliche Kunstsammlung, Holbein, drawings; Bourges: Cathedral *and* Musée Jacques Cœur
— siege in 1412, 38, 45, 292
Bouvet, Somnium super materia scismatis, 13
Braunschweig, Herzog Anton Ulrich Museum: Rohan Master, Miracle of Bethesda (drawing), 279
Breughel, Peter, 241
Bridget, St., 122; Revelationes, 236, 246
Broederlam, Melchior, 213, 279, 293
Broederlam, Melchior – Follower, 182
Bronzino, Angelo, 77

Brussels, Bibliothèque royale
MANUSCRIPTS
ms 3 (Chroniques de France), 363 n. 46
ms 9001 (Bible historiale), 13, 362 n. 16
ms 9024 (Bible historiale), 356
ms 9049-50 (Livy), 355
ms 9089-90 (Politiques and Éthiques), 358
ms 9094 (Propriété des choses), 371 n. 137
ms 9125 (Missal), 359
ms 9226 (Légende dorée), 359
ms 9391 (Horae), 382 n. 67
ms 9393 (Cité des Dames), 356
ms 9505-06 (Éthiques), 73, Fig. 517
ms 9508 (Mutacion de Fortune), 300, 358
ms 9542 (Geoffroi de la Tour-Landry, Livre pour l'enseignement de ses filles), 309
ms 9554 (Gilles de Rome, Le livre du gouvernement des roys), 360
ms 9555-58 (Durand de Champagne, Œuvres), 298, 309
ms 10176-78 (Pèlerinage de l'âme), 251, Fig. 828
ms 10230 (Cuvelier, Livre de Bertrant du Guesclin), 355
ms 10392 (Hours of Philippe le Hardi), 22; *see also* Cambridge, Fitzwilliam Museum, ms 3-1954
ms 10476 (Faits d'armes), 356
ms 11035-37 (Prayer Book of Philippe le Hardi), 201 f., 207, 321, Figs. 666, 668
ms 11041 (Somme le roi), 399 n. 23
ms 11060-61 (Brussels Hours), 7, 9, 35, 49, 77, 79 f., 83 f., 86, 90, 95, 97, 111, 148 ff., 172, 189 ff., 233, 240, 246, 256, 264 ff., 277 ff., 290, 292, 296 f., 309, 321 ff., 363 n. 21, Figs. 179-215, 478, 479, 665; diptych, 82, 113, 199 ff., 210 f., 267, 278 f.; initials, 230, 233 ff., 243; landscapes, 214, 218 ff., 240; Veronica, 201 f.; relationship with other manuscripts: Petites Heures, 224 ff., the Psalter, 207 f., 225, Vat. lat. 50, 208, 224
ms 11113 (Livre de Sydrac), 372 n. 170
ms 11140 (Livre des trésors), 355

— Musées Royaux: French (?), Crucifixion, *ca.* 1380, 61, Fig. 443
Bryn Athyn (Penn.), Pitcairn, Raymond, Coll.: 'Madonna' from S. Gangolf, Metz (relief), 126 f., Fig. 453
Budapest, Museum of Fine Arts: Giotto – Follower, Coronation of the Virgin, 215, Fig. 700
Bulgarini, Bartolommeo, 60, 393 n. 49

Caesar, Julius, medal of, 43, 57
Calendar pictures, iconography of, 72, 117, 139, 171 f., 187, 231 f., 259; *see also* Chantilly, Musée Condé, Très Riches Heures
Cambrai, Bibl. municipale: ms 97 [98] (Breviary), 359

Cambridge (Engl.), Fitzwilliam Museum
MANUSCRIPTS
ms 3-1954 (Hours of Philippe le Hardi), 109, 128, 156, 175, 188, Figs. 564, 608, 609; *see also* Brussels, Bibl. royale, ms 10392
Founders 59 (Horae), 358
McClean 79 (Horae), 360
McClean 80 (Horae), 358

Cambridge (Mass.), Fogg Art Museum
Lorenzetti, Ambrogio, Crucifixion, 394 n. 74
'Ugolino Lorenzetti' (Bartolommeo Bulgarini), Nativity, 60, Fig. 448
— Harvard College Library
Mm V. 31 (Abscander, Commentary on the Apocalypse), 374 n. 237
Richardson 45 (Horae), 358
— Harvard College Library, Hofer, Philip, Coll.: Cité de Dieu, 121 f., 174, 238, 298, 309, 365 n. 105, Fig. 535
Campin, Robert, *see* Master of Flémalle
Caravaggio, 163, 232
Caritas Romana, 128
Carrara, Francesco, medals of, 54, 57, 75, 305, Fig. 468
Cascia, S. Giovenale: Masaccio, Madonna, 127 f., Fig. 554
Caskets, leather, *ca.* 1400, *see* Lucca, Opera del Duomo; New York, Martin Coll.
Castagno, Andrea del, 383 n. 100
Catania, Bibl. Civica: ms A 72 (Bible), 380 n. 29
Catherine de Valois, Bréviaire de, *see* Whereabouts unknown
Cavallini, Pietro, 106, 233 f., 388 n. 80
Cavallini, Pietro – Follower, 24, 394 n. 74
Cecco di Pietro, 183
Cellini, Benvenuto, 198
Châlons, Bishop of, 298
Chambon-sur-Voueize, Church: French, Reliquary of Ste. Valérie, 52, 70, Fig. 509

Chantilly, Musée Condé
MANUSCRIPTS
ms 28 [1378] (Histoire extraite de la Bible and Apocalypse), 360
ms 51 [1887] (Bréviaire de Jeanne d'Évreux), 20, 107, 152 ff., 182, 188, 403 n. 7, Figs. 343, 358, 541, 600, 604-606
ms 64 [1671] (Horae), 357
ms 65 [1284] (Les Très Riches Heures de Jean de Berry), 7, 9, 32, 37 f., 50 f., 78, 95, 97, 109, 122, 127, 129, 202, 235, 256 f., 292 ff., 305 f., 309, 389 n. 62, 395 n. 1, 402 n. 55, 407 n. 158, Figs. 419-424, 442, 489, 844; January, 51, 59, 72 f., 76 ff., 86, 92, 401 n. 43; February, 172; March, 37; April, 37, 76; May, 37, 76; June, 368 n. 8; July, 37; August, 37; September, 37; October, 307, 368 n. 8; November, 368 n. 8.
ms 71 (Heures d'Étienne Chevalier), 380 n. 18, 402 n. 51
ms 277 [1327] (Éthiques), 309 f.

Chantilly, Musée Condé (*contd.*)
  ms 278 [575] (Livres d'Éthique et Yconomique), 317
  ms 279 [320] (Politiques et Yconomiques), 317
  ms 493 [1668] (Christine de Pisan, Œuvres), 356
  ms 494 [567] (Mutacion de Fortune), 300, 358, Figs. 835, 836
  ms 867 [324] (Grandes chroniques), 360

Charles IV, Emperor, 23, 39, 131 f., 302; portraits of, 62, 75
Charles IV, King of France, 287
Charles V, King of France, 51 f., 99 ff., 147, 290, 295 f.; library
  of, 40, 168, 287, 389 n. 46, 403 n. 30; portraits of, 39, 60, 62,
  68, 73, 75, 87, 99 ff., 147; testamentary inventory, 40
Charles VI, King of France, 26, 32 ff., 48, 51, 57 f., 70, 143,
  287 f., 291, 299; portraits of, 13, 37, 74, 91
Charles VII, King of France, 35, 38
Charles le Noble, King of Navarre, 49, 243
Chartres, Cathedral (formerly): *Parement d'autel*, 39, 49, 60, Figs.
  450, 451
Chasteaumorant, Jean de, 304
Châteauroux, Bibl. municipale: ms 2 (Breviary), 39, 299, 363 n.
  33, Fig. 428
Chenu, Jean, 45, 379 n. 88
Chicago, University of Chicago Library: ms 250961 (Horae),
  359
Chrétien de Troyes, *see* Lancelot du Lac
Christ: Before Pilate, 163, 214; Infancy Cycle, 21, 51 (*see also*
  Adoration of the Magi; Flight into Egypt; Nativity; Pre-
  sentation of Christ); in Limbo, 104 f.; in Majesty, 23, 130,
  151, 161, 176, 223; miracles of, 12, 279; Nailed to the Cross,
  180 f., 189, 242, 261; Passion Cycle, 51 f., 60 (*see also*
  Betrayal; Christ before Pilate; Crucifixion; Deposition;
  Way to Calvary, etc.); *see also* Baptism of Christ
Christine de Pisan, 3 f., 14, 50, 299, 308; dedication of works to
  Jean de Berry, 406 n. 127; patronage of Jean de Berry, 288,
  302; works: Chemin de longue estude, 372 n. 175, Cité des
  Dames, 3, 299, 313, 356, Le corps de policie, 3, Épître d'O-
  théa, 12, 235, 313, 356 ff., 372 n. 175, Faits d'armes, 356,
  372 n. 175, Faits de Charles V, 372 n. 175, Lamentation sur
  les maux de la France, 406 n. 127, Livre des fais et bonnes
  meurs, 308, Livre de la paix, 372 n. 175, Livre des trois
  vertus, 356, Mutacion de Fortune, 294, 300, 310, 356, 358,
  372 n. 175, Œuvres, 16, 242, 295, 300, 356 ff., Sept psaumes
  allégorisés, 372 n. 175, 406 n. 127
Christus, Petrus, 250
Chronique de St.-Denys, 39, 74; *see also* Grandes chroniques de
  France
Clamanges, Nicolas de, 302, 307
Clement VI, patron of art, 25
Clement VII, Pope, 38 f., 49, 189, 195 f.

Cleveland, Museum of Art
            MANUSCRIPTS
  ms 62. 287 (Gotha Missal), 80, 102, 355, 390 n. 82, Fig. 519
  ms 64. 40 (Heures de Charles le Noble), 49, 123, 229 f., 232,
    235 ff., 323 f., 355, Figs. 729-731, 734, 745, 749, 758, 759,
    761, 764, 772, 789, 804, 805, 809, 812, 813
            PAINTINGS
  Jean de Beaumetz, Calvary with a Carthusian, 7, 279 f., Fig.
    831
  Nicolau, Pedro, Coronation of the Virgin, 387 n. 74
    2 F 2

Cleveland, Museum of Art (*contd.*)
            OTHER OBJECTS
  Beauneveu, André – Circle, Kneeling Prophet (gilt bronze),
    386 n. 59

clouds, 275
Coene, Jacques, 8, 24, 47, 64, 145, 200, 372 n. 157
Col, Gontier, 50, 302, 307
Col, Pierre, 302, 307
Colin, Jean, 405 n. 108
Cologne, Cathedral: Claren, altarpiece, 397 n. 44
— Wallraf Richartz Museum: Westphalian, altar from Osna-
    brück, 389 n. 59
Constantin de Nicolas, 47
Constantine, medal of, 40, 46, 53 ff., 57 f., 295, 304 ff.; on flying
    horse, 304, 370 n. 82
Copenhagen, Royal Library: Thott 547, 382 n. 83
Coppo di Marcovaldo, 390 n. 88
Coronation of the Virgin, 60, 87, 100, 121 f., 128, 149 f., 174,
    211, 215, 223, 238, 242, 252, 264, 277, 359, 396 n. 18
Courau, Jacques, 298
Courtrai, Notre-Dame: St. Catherine (statue), 208, Fig. 672
Cristoforo de' Mari, 47
Crivelli, Carlo, 397 n. 63
Croix aux camées, 53; *see also* Paris, Musée du Louvre, cameos
Croix au serpent, 51, 295
Croniques de Burgues, 311, 356
Crucifixion, 19 f., 52, 60 ff., 80, 101 f., 104 ff., 126, 129 f., 161,
    163, 178, 180, 185, 189, 202, 215 ff., 221, 273, 275, 381 n. 62,
    389 n. 52, 392 n. 28
Curtius, Quintus, 366 n. 129
Cyriac of Ancona, 64

Daddi, Bernardo, 60, 397 n. 55
Daliwe, Jacques, 239, 278, 366 n. 133, 400 n. 41
Dammartin, Drouet de, 38
Dammartin, Guy de, 37 f.
Dance of Salome, 165, 186 f.
Dante, 3, 6; Divine Comedy, 27, 70, 318, 377 n. 8
Datini company, 26
Death of the Virgin, 181 f., 366 n. 131
Decembrio, Pietro Candido, 75
Deguilleville, Guillaume, Pèlerinage de l'âme, 251
Deposition, 129, 163, 185, 217 f., 242
Deschamps, Eustache, 287
Desmarz, Nicolas, 25
Detroit, Institute of Arts
  Eyck, Jan van, and Petrus Christus, St. Jerome, 250
  Master of the Pietà, Vesperbild, 62, 183 ff., Fig. 640
Dijon, Chartreuse de Champmol, 38, 369 n. 16, 374 n. 245;
    Sluter, Claus: portal, 293, *Puits de Moïse*, 5, 293
— Musée
  Broederlam, Melchior, altar wings, 213, 293, Fig. 711
  Jehan de Marville, Claus Sluter, Claus de Werve, Tomb of
    Philippe le Hardi, 38
  Master of Flémalle, Nativity, 236
Doberan, Church: Westphalian, Legend of Aracoeli, 397 n. 37
Domenico dei Cori, *see* Domenico di Niccolo
Domenico di Niccolo, 44 ff., 301

Domenico Veneziano, 146, 306
Donatello – Follower, 239, 383 n. 100
Dourdan, Château of Jean de Berry, 37, 40, 292, Fig. 420
drawings, marginal, 10 ff.
Dublin, Beatty, Chester A., Coll.
  ms 75 (Mirouer historial), 310
  ms 84 (Horae), 360
Duccio, 104 f., 120, 182, 211, 216 f., 219, 364 n. 79; influence on
    Passion Master, 297; influence on Pucelle, 19 f., 104, 114, 163
Duccio – Follower, 61, 103, 381 n. 40, 384 n. 131
Durand, Jean, 294
Durand de Champagne, Le mirouer des dames, 298, 309
Durandus, Rational, 288, 312, 381 n. 64, 385 n. 165, 403 n. 12
Dürer, Albrecht, 3 f.

Échecs moralisés, 312, 403 n. 5
Edward III, King of England, portrait of, 62, 75
Eeckhout, 49, 251
Embriachi Workshop, 36, 68, 91 f.
embroideries, see Chartres Cathedral (formerly); Florence,
    Museo Nazionale; Manresa Cathedral; New York, Lehman
    Coll.; Whereabouts unknown
Ennezat (near Riom), Church: French, Last Judgment, 63, Fig.
    405a
Entombment, 19, 63, 100 ff., 126, 161, 163, 182, 214 f., 217 ff., 242
Entry into Jerusalem, 248 f., 274 f.
Estampes, Robinet d', 6 f., 40 ff., 108, 296, 304
Étampes, Château of Jean de Berry, 37, Fig. 422
Étienne d'Auxerre, 24
Étrennes, 362, n. 7
Eugenia, relief of, 57, 304
Eyck, Jan van, 63, 105, 123, 146, 205, 221, 240, 250, 307, 376 n.
    295
Eyck, Jan van – Followers, 110

Fama, 59
Fermo, Gallery: Andrea da Bologna, polyptych, 382 n. 83
Ferrara, S. Antonio in Polesina: Ferrarese, frescoes, ca. 1390, 237,
    Fig. 777
Ferrer, Fray Bonifacio, 398 n. 70
Figline Valdarno, Collegiata: Master of the Fogg Pietà, Madonna
    enthroned, 387 n. 70
figures, seated on ground, 105 ff.
Filarete, Antonio Averlino, Treatise on Architecture, 53, 307 f.
Flagellation, 62, 103; 113 ff., 163, 217
Flamel, Jean, signature, 290
Flavius Josephus, Antiquités judaïques, 227, 308, 312, 314, 356,
    381 n. 53, 405 n. 106
Flight into Egypt, 174, 219, 239 f., 277
Florence, Accademia: Jacopo di Cione, Coronation of the Virgin,
    122, 150, Fig. 539
— Bargello, see Museo Nazionale
— Bibl. Laurenziana
  Med. Pal. 69 (Bucolics, Georgics, Aeneid), 189, 298, 360, Fig.
    841
  Plut. VI. 23 (Gospel Book), 367 n. 150
  Plut. XXV. 3 (Supplicationes Variae), 382 n. 75, 383 n. 97,
    390 n. 79
  Plut. XXX. 10 (Vitruvius, De Architectura), 360

Florence, Bibl. Nazionale: Landau-Finaly 22 (Visconti Hours),
    124, 143 f., 182, Figs. 578, 579, 630; see also Milan, Coll.
    Visconti di Modrone
— Corsini Coll.: Horae, 357
— Duomo, Campanile: Painting (relief), 5
— Horne Museum: Barna da Siena – Workshop, Madonna and
    Man of Sorrows, 170, Fig. 631
— Longhi, Roberto, Coll.: Vitale da Bologna, Man of Sorrows,
    62, 123, 239, Fig. 546
— Medici Palace: Benozzo Gozzoli, mural, 306
— Museo Nazionale
  Florentine, antependium, 1325, 60
  French, brooch with camel, ca. 1400, 196, Fig. 664
  French, St. John the Baptist (pin), ca. 1415, 146, Fig. 577
  'Small Bargello Diptych', late 14th cent., 403 n. 86
— Palazzo Pitti: French, Man of Sorrows (onyx), ca. 1400, 17,
    Fig. 326
— S. Apollonia: Castagno, Andrea del, Man of Sorrows, 383 n.
    100
— S. Croce, Bardi Chapel: Giotto, Stigmatization of St.
    Francis, 382 n. 80
— S. Croce, Baroncelli Chapel: Gaddi, Taddeo, frescoes, 173,
    178, 212, 237, Figs. 651, 652
— S. Croce, Chapel of S. Silvestro: Maso di Banco, Christ
    Judging, 69, 205, Fig. 513
— S. Croce, Museo dell'Opera: 'Ugolino Lorenzetti' (Barto-
    lommeo Bulgarini), polyptych, 60
— S. Croce, Rinuccini Chapel: Giovanni da Milano, frescoes,
    208, 393 n. 54, Fig. 671
— S. Maria del Carmine, Brancacci Chapel, 307
— S. Maria Novella, Spanish Chapel: Andrea Bonaiuti, frescoes,
    28, 105, 363 n. 49, 402 n. 53
— Uffizi

PAINTINGS

Botticelli, Sandro, portrait of a Medallist, 77
Bronzino, Angelo, portrait of a sculptor, 77
crucifix, scene on, ca. 1200, 388 n. 27
Daddi, Bernardo, altarpiece, 397 n. 55
Gentile da Fabriano, Flight into Egypt, 394 n. 85
Lippi, Fra Filippo, Adoration of the Child with St. Hilary,
    389 n. 43
Lorenzetti, Ambrogio, Miracle of St. Nicholas, 219, Presenta-
    tion of Christ, 128, 213, Fig. 712
Masaccio, Madonna, 127, Fig. 555
Simone Martini, Annunciation, 212, 390 n. 97, Fig. 708
Weyden, Roger van der, Lamentation, 163

Fons vitae, 18, 55 f., 232
Fool, 11, 20, 153 f., 162, 191
Fouquet, Jean, 380 n. 18, 402 n. 51
Fouquet, Jean – Workshop, 381 n. 53
Francesco da Barberino, Documenti d'Amore, 380 n. 22
Frankfort, Städel Institut
  Legend of the Aracoeli (drawing), ca. 1410, 397 n. 37
  Lorenzetti, Ambrogio – Follower, Nativity and Crucifixion,
    178, 217, 383 n. 96, Fig. 673
Frankfurt-am-Main, Museum für Kunsthandwerk: Linel, L. M.
    19 (Horae), 358
Froissart, Jean, Chroniques, 32 f., 37, 70, 148, 354, 356, 360
Funeral Service, 111, 118, 186 f., 222, 261, 263, 296, 402 n. 66

Gaddi, Taddeo, 173, 178, 212, 237
Gaddi, Taddeo – Workshop, 184
Gauthier de Coincy, Miracles de la Vierge, 19 f., 178, 287, 301, 360, 391 n. 110

Geneva, Bibliothèque publique et universitaire
MANUSCRIPTS
ms fr. 2 (Bible historiale), 161, Fig. 349
ms fr. 77 (Livy), 94, 242, 252, 310, 354, Fig. 825
ms fr. 165 (Dialogues de Pierre Salmon), 405 n. 104
ms fr. 176 (Métamorphoses moralisées), 317
ms fr. 190 (Cas des nobles hommes et femmes), 295, 298, 303, 310, 358

— Bodmer, Martin, Coll.: Psalter of Bonne de Luxembourg, 20, 31, 114, 153 f., 160 ff., 187, 204, 287, 289, Figs. 352-355, 361
Gentile da Fabriano, 123, 219, 236
Geri di Lapo, 60
Gerona, Cathedral: Bible of Jean de Berry, 301, 310, Fig. 837
Gerson, Jean, 13
Ghent, Bibl. de l'Université: ms 141 (Bible moralisée), 354
Ghiberti, Lorenzo, Commentarii, 45, 211, 394 n. 90
Gilbertus, Petrus, 362 n. 16
Giotto, 19, 23, 28, 74, 103, 119 f., 173, 205, 212, 215, 237, 306, 389 n. 64; self portrait, 5
Giotto – Followers, 103, 105, 215, 303
Giovanni di Benedetto da Como, 386 n. 37, 390 n. 78
Giovanni da Milano, 145, 183, 208, 212, 393 n. 54, 402 n. 62
Giovanni dal Ponte, 384 n. 140
Giovannino dei Grassi, 75, 143 ff., 182, 190, 245, 300, 302
Giovannino dei Grassi – Follower, 144
Girard d'Orléans, 100
Giron le Courtois, 144 f.
glazing, see technical innovations
Gouge, Martin, Bishop of Chartres, 49, 108, 189, 298
Gozzoli, Benozzo, 306
Grancher, Jean d'Orléans, 132
Grand Khan, 59
Grandes chroniques de France, 11 f., 14, 141, 291, 314, 318, 356 ff., 363 n. 46, 382 n. 88, 384 n. 158, 400 n. 30
grisaille, 100, 141
Grosseto, Museo Diocesano: St. Peter Master, Last Judgment, 68, Fig. 515
Guido da Siena – Follower, 391 n. 98
Guillaume de Lorris and Jean de Meung, Roman de la rose, 59, 189 f., 313, 315, 317, 354, 357
Guillaume de Machaut, 31; Œuvres, 141; Poésies, 23, 315
Guillaume de Ruilly, 40
Gusmin, 45
Guyenne, Louis, duc de, 290 f., 299

The Hague, Museum Meermanno-Westreenianum
MANUSCRIPTS
ms 10 A 14 (Missal), 172, Fig. 619
ms 10 B 23 (Bible of Charles V), 6, 21 f., 73, 100 ff., 113 f., 124, 165, 177, 182, 204 f., 298, 310, 397 n. 57, Figs. 378, 382, 386
ms 755 (Cité de Dieu), 360

The Hague, Royal Library
MANUSCRIPTS
ms 72 A 22 (Cité de Dieu), 357
ms 72 A 24 (Miroir historiale), 356
ms 72 A 25 (Froissart, Chroniques), 360
ms 78 D 42 (Mutacion de Fortune), 294, 310, 358, 372 n. 175, 405 n. 109

Haincelin de Haguenau, 8, 47, 65, 372 n. 157
Hamburg, Staatliche Kunsthalle: Master Bertram, Petrialtar of 1379, 125
Hamburg-Blankenese, Huth, Mrs. J. Möring, Coll.: Horae, 359
Hautschild, Lubert, 49, 251 ff.; Lat. trans. of Pèlerinage de l'âme, 251
Hayton, Fleur des histoires, 14, 47, 49, 199, 252, 294, 315, 355
Hector, 59
Hell, 241, 245
Hennequin de Virelay, 208
Henri l'Uilier, 367 n. 4
Heraclius, medal of, 40, 46, 53 ff., 57 f., 295, 304 f.; with the Cross, 55
Hildesheim, St. Godehard: St. Albans Psalter, 387 n. 82
Holbein, Hans the Younger, 78 f., 93
Holkham Hall, Leicester, Earl of, Coll.
ms 120 (Lactantius), 230, 244, 324 f., 398 n. 82, Figs. 791, 793, 794
ms 307 (Georgics and Bucolics), 358
ms 354 (Livy), 398 n. 82, 398 n. 84
Homilies of the Monk Jacobus, 56, 393 n. 59
humanists, French, 302 f.

iconography: drollery, satire, 162 ff, 230, 259; Christian adaptation of secular subjects, 52; new subjects, 13 ff.; secular adaptations of religious subjects, 15 f.
illumination: Catalan, 144; Lombard, 143 ff.
Infancy Cycle, see Christ
International Style, 78, 300, 306
inventories, terminology, 41 ff., 50; see also Jean de Berry; Philippe le Hardi, etc.
Irene, Roman painter, 4 f.
Isabeau de Bavière, 48, 51, 142, 293, 296, 403 n. 30; portraits of, 37, 74, 89, 269
Isabelle de France, 287
Istanbul, Kahrie-Djami: Byzantine, Last Judgment, 377 n. 8
Istoire des contes de Flandres, 251
itinerary, prayer, 71 f., 92 f., 156

Jacobus de Voragine, Golden Legend, 93, 188 f., 233, 252, 263, 328, 355, 358 ff., 387 n. 68, 397 n. 35, 400 n. 33
'Jacopino', 390 n. 83
Jacopo di Cione, 26
Jacopone da Todi, Le poesie spirituali, 122
Jacquemart de Hesdin, 6 f., 10, 24, 44, 113 f., 133, 157, 159, 165 f., 169 ff., 176 ff., 179 f., 190 ff., 194, 198, 200 ff., 207, 209 ff., 231, 233, 237, 240, 246, 256 ff., 260 ff., 267, 269 ff., 277 ff., 294, 296 ff., 301, 303, 306, 321 ff., 330 ff., 335 ff., 340 f., 343, 363 n. 21, 379 n. 80, 389 n. 35; color, 172, 224 f.; documents, 198, 226 f.; influence on Boucicaut Master, 240; influence on the Master of the Brussels Initials, 240; Italian

Jacquemart de Hesdin (*contd.*)
tendencies of, 173 f., 190, 210 ff., 226, 272, 301; residence of, 291 ff., 295 ff.
Jacquemart de Hesdin – Followers, 189, 194, 227, 231, 298, 319, 342, 394 n. 66
Jacquemart de Hesdin – Workshop, 194, 223 f., 322 f., 328 f.
Jacques de Baerze, 369 n. 27
Jacques de Chartres, 74
Jacques de Liège, 45
Janus de Grimault (Grimaldi), 47
Jason, 59
Jean d'Arbois, 24, 100, 280, 302
Jean de la Barre, 252
Jean II le Bon, King of France, 20, 48, 162, 290, 405 n. 87, 406 n. 144; Library of, 287; patron of art, 31; portraits of, 62 f., 68, 73, 75, 99, 147; seals of, 52
Jean de Bruges, *see* Bondol, Jean
Jean de Cambrai, 38 f., 45, 68, 78, 93 ff., 293, 305, 387 n. 62
Jean de Gand, 25
Jean de Liège, 99
Jean de Meung, *see* Guillaume de Lorris
Jean de Morselles, 45
Jean de Nogent, 82
Jean le Noir, 44, 167 f.; *see also* Master of the Passion
Jean d'Orléans, 34, 44, 50, 100, 132 f., 159, 383 n. 102; *see also* Master of the Parement de Narbonne
Jean sans Peur, Duke of Burgundy, 9, 15, 34 f., 47 ff., 199, 292, 299, 404 n. 45; library of, 198 f., 403 n. 1; patron of art, 8, 364 n. 82, 402 n. 81; portraits of, 52, 68, 74 ff., 94, 363 n. 20, 377 n. 10; testamentary inventory, 40
Jean de Vaudetar, 21
Jeanne d'Armagnac, 31, 33, 291
Jeanne de Boulogne, 32 f., 48, 291; portraits of, 37 f., 45, 50, 68, 74 f., 83 f., 91 ff., 372 n. 185
Jeanne de Bourbon, Queen of France, portraits of, 60, 91, 99, 101
Jeanne d'Évreux, patron of art, 287, 403 n. 7
Jeanne de Navarre, Hours of, *see* Whereabouts unknown
Jerome, St., 307; in his study, 250
Joanna I of Naples, 27
Johannes Companiosus, 64
John the Baptist, St.: Birth of, 165; in the Desert, 164, 250
John of Bavaria, Bishop of Liège, 109 f.
John of Holland, 226, 278, 400 n. 30
John VIII Paleologus, 58, 306
Joseph of Arimathea before Pilate, 28
Joyau au mont de Calvaire, 372 n. 185
joyaux, 141 ff., 145 f. (*see also* Berry, Jean duc de, collections); connection with painting, 141 ff., 295 f.
Judas, suicide of, 273
Julius II, Pope, Belvedere, collection of antiquities, 38
Juno, 59

Karlštejn, Chapel of St. Catherine: Madonna and two donors, 365 n. 110, 406 n. 125
— Holy Cross Chapel
Master Theodoric, murals, 131
Tommaso da Modena, triptych, 365 n. 109, 406 n. 125
Klosterneuburg, Stiftsmuseum: Austrian, altarpiece of 1324-1329, 23

Lactantius, 230, 245, 264, 324, 328
La Ferté-Milon, Church: French, Coronation of the Virgin (relief), 387 n. 67
Lamentation, 124, 182 f., 185, 243, 261
Lancelot du Lac, 145, 252, 312, 355 f., 371 n. 137, 399 n. 26
landscape, French, 3, 133, 171 f., 214, 218 f., 221; Italian, 219 ff.
Lannelier, Étienne, 43
Last Judgment, 63, 68 f.
Latini, Brunetto, Livre du trésor, 313, 403 n. 12
Laurent de Premierfait, translations of Boccaccio, 288, 302; works dedicated to Jean de Berry, 406 n. 128
Laval, St. Martin: French, Virgo lactifera, 384 n. 145
Lebègue, Jean: Guide to Illustrations of Sallust, 13, 362 n. 3; Technical Treatises, compiled in 1431, 64
Lebourne, Jean, 41
Légende de St. Denis, 162
Legrand, Jacques: Livre des bonnes mœurs, 79 f., 85 f., 92, 298, 314, 359; Traité des vices et des vertus, 354
Leningrad, Hermitage: Master of Flémalle, Madonna at the Fire, 18
— State Library
ms fr. F. v. I (Bible historiale), 380 n. 25, 380 n. 36
ms fr. Q. v. III, 4 (Les dis moraux), 354
ms fr. Q. v. XIV, 3 (Rommant de la violette and Roman de la panthère), 317, 355, 358
ms Q. v. I, 8 (Horae), 264 f., 325, Figs. 255, 256, 259
Leonardo da Vinci, 163
Lilienfeld, Stiftsbibl.: cod. 151 (Concordantia caritatis), 387 n. 83
Limbourg, Paul de, 37, 227, 392 n. 35
Limbourg, Paul and Jean, documented Bible for Jean de Berry, 6, 8, 227
Limbourgs, 6 ff., 24, 32, 43 f., 47, 50 f., 55, 58, 71 f., 75 f., 78, 84, 86, 92 f., 112, 127, 133 f., 142, 156, 172, 178, 193, 202, 206, 218, 234 f., 237 f., 240, 246, 250, 254, 259, 261, 269 f., 273 ff., 295, 297, 299, 303, 305 ff., 334, 337 ff., 400 n. 33, 402 n. 55, 402 n. 81; Italian tendencies of, 246, 301; itinerary, Très Belles Heures de Notre-Dame (copy), 71 f., 76, 80, 92, 108, 110, 254, 337 f., Fig. 497; Jean de Berry investing canons, Charter of Ste-Chapelle, Bourges (copy), 79, 84 f., 96, 246, 301, Fig. 481; place of residence, 292 ff., 364 n. 82; simulated book, 48, 50, 294
Limbourgs – Follower, 207
Lippi, Filippino – Workshop, 383 n. 103
Lippi, Fra Filippo, 389 n. 43
Lisbon, Gulbenkian Foundation: Boccaccio (Des cleres femmes), 356
Liverpool, Walker Art Gallery: Simone Martini, Christ with the Virgin and Joseph, 25
Livy, 14, 64, 288, 310, 313, 355 f., 358, 360, 366 n. 129, 398 n. 84, 403 n. 5
London, Breslauer, Martin: Valère Maxime, 356

— British Museum
MANUSCRIPTS
ms Add. 11990, 398 n. 90
ms Add. 15244-45 (Cité de Dieu), 389 n. 66
ms Add. 15265 (Horae), 384 n. 148
ms Add. 18192 (Horae), 18, Fig. 329
ms Add. 18850 (Bedford Hours), 389 n. 58
ms Add. 23145 (Horae), 166, 194 f., 325, Figs. 620, 660

London, British Museum(*contd.*)

ms Add. 29433 (Horae), 230 ff., 236 ff., 242 ff., 325 ff., 358, 396 n. 13, 396 n. 14, 398 n. 93, Figs. 718, 726, 733, 741, 743, 747, 750, 755, 760, 762, 765, 769, 776, 784, 790, 799, 806, 811

ms Add. 29704-05 (Carmelite Missal), 399 n. 5; *see also* London, Brit. Mus., ms Add. 44892

ms Add. 29986 (Miroir des dames), 310

ms Add. 30899 (Horae), 357

ms Add. 32454 (Horae), 265, 357, Figs. 257, 258

ms Add. 34247 (Horae), 245, 327, Figs. 800, 801

ms Add. 35311 (Breviary of Jean sans Peur), 16, 202, 321, 355, 357, Fig. 678; *see also* London, Brit. Mus., ms Harley 2897

ms Add. 36684 (Horae), 382 n. 66

ms Add. 38119 (Speculum Humanae Salvationis), 234, Fig. 816

ms Add. 44892 (Carmelite Missal), 399 n. 5; *see also* London, Brit. Mus., ms Add. 29704-05

ms Add. 45890, 398 n. 88

ms Add. 47680 (Bible), 126

ms Add. 49622 (Gorleston Psalter), 23

ms Burney 275 (Priscian), 195, 310

ms Cotton Domitian A XVII (Horae), 355

ms Cotton Nero E II (Chroniques de France), 11 f., 357, Figs. 304-311, 314, 315

ms Cotton Tiberius B VIII, 383 n. 99

ms Egerton 1070 (Horae), 357, 381 n. 64

ms Egerton 2709 (Conquête et les conquérants des Îles Canaries), 356

ms Egerton 3266 (Epistles of St. Jerome), 145, Fig. 582

ms Harley 1319 (Fall of Richard II), 360

ms Harley 2891 (Missal), 317

ms Harley 2897 (Bréviaire de Jean sans Peur), 355, 357, Fig. 323; *see also* London, Brit. Mus., ms Add. 35311

ms Harley 2934 (Horae), 398 n. 98

ms Harley 2952 (Horae), 276 f., 327 f., Figs. 270, 273-275

ms Harley 2979 (Horae), 240, Fig. 766

ms Harley 4381-82 (Bible historiale), 189, 265, 298, 310 f., 319, 360, 383 n. 97, Figs. 617, 622

ms Harley 4431 (Christine de Pisan, Œuvres), 89, 356, 363 n. 50, 401 n. 41

ms Harley 4947 (Lactantius), 264, 328, Fig. 248

ms Harley 7026 (Lectionary), 387 n. 67

ms Lansdowne 1175 (Bible), 311

ms Royal 2 B VII (Queen Mary's Psalter), 181, 377 n. 8, 380 n. 18

ms Royal 15 D III (Bible historiale), 11, 355 ff., 362 n. 16, Fig. 317

ms Royal 16 G V (Des cleres femmes), 362 n. 7

ms Royal 17 E VII (Bible historiale, 1357), 20 ff., 204, Figs. 375, 383, 384

ms Royal 19 B XV (Apocalypse), 362 n. 16

ms Royal 19 B XVII (Légende dorée), 93, 188 f., 263, 328, 401 n. 24, Figs. 610, 612, 615

ms Royal 19 D III (Bible historiale of 1411), 12, 357, 360, 363 n. 47, Figs. 312, 313

ms Royal 19 E VI (Croniques de Burgues), 311, 356, 405 n. 106

ms Royal 20 B IV (Méditations de la vie de Christ), 12, 354, Fig. 316

London, British Museum (*contd.*)

ms Royal 20 C VIII (Honoré Bonnet, L'arbre des batailles), 94, 311

ms Yates Thompson 13 (Taymouth Hours), 182, 377 n. 8, Fig. 644

ms Yates Thompson 27 (Heures de Yolande de Flandre), 20, 103, 106, 139, 159 ff., 167 ff., 171, 174, 187, 380 n. 14, 381 n. 63, 382 n. 85, 388 n. 26, 394 n. 74, Figs. 363-366

ms Yates Thompson 37 (Horae), 195, 221, 227, 240, 264, 276 f., 328 f., 358, Figs. 263-267, 269, 271, 272, 276; relationship with the Brussels Hours, 274 f.

OTHER OBJECTS

French, Jean de Berry's Reliquary of the Thorn, 36, 40, 51, 142 f., 146, 385 n. 3, Figs. 571, 842

French, Royal Cup, 36, 51, Figs. 471, 473

Madonna of John Grandisson (ivory), 402 n. 65

Roman, Ulysses and the Sirens, 220, Fig. 681

— Courtauld Institute: Riminese, Adoration of the Magi and Bathing of Christ, 214, Fig. 701

— Maggs Brothers: St. Dominic, *see* Whereabouts unknown

— National Gallery

PAINTINGS

Crivelli, Carlo, Annunciation, 397 n. 63

Masaccio, Madonna, 127

Piero della Francesca, Nativity, 236, Fig. 757

Ugolino da Siena, Way to Calvary, 103

— Rau, Arthur, Coll.: Horae, 360

— Robinson Trust: ms 832 (Œuvres de Jean de Meung), 317, 354

— Seilern, Count A., Coll.

Alchandreus, De Astrologia, 360

Boethius, De Arithmetica and De Musica, 360

— Sotheby

May 21, 1928, lot 17: Horae, 358

Jan. 2, 1960, lot 312: Chroniques de Normandie, 354

Feb. 1, 1960: French, Fool (miniature), 154, 387 n. 90

June 18, 1962, lot 20: Horae, 360

June 28, 1962, lot 49: Pentecost (miniature), 358

June 28, 1962, lot 50: 398 n. 88

— Victoria and Albert Museum

Donatello – Follower, Man of Sorrows, 239, 383 n. 100

French, Madonna (*joyau*), ca. 1412, 145 f.

French, triptych (enamel), mid 14th cent., 388 n. 27

ms 1646-1902 (Horae), 358

Lorenzetti, 103, 113 f., 303

Lorenzetti, Ambrogio, 28, 128, 150, 166, 184, 195, 211 ff., 215 f., 219 ff., 276 f., 306, 364 n. 90, 394 n. 90; influence on Jacquemart, 219 ff.

Lorenzetti, Ambrogio – Followers, 104, 178, 212, 383 n. 96

Lorenzetti, Pietro, 210, 216, 218

Lorenzetti, Pietro – Followers, 221, 398 n. 66

Lorenzo da Sanseverino, 390 n. 92

Louis I, Duke of Anjou, 22, 27, 33, 287, 298, 403 n. 4; inventory, 40; patron of art, 100; portrait of, 74

Louis II, Duke of Anjou, 27, 37, 48, 287; portraits of, 68, 75 f.

Louis, Duke of Guyenne, 9, 48, 290 f.

Louis de Mâle, 147, 227
Louis d'Orléans, 27, 34, 49, 64, 372 n. 155, 397 n. 47, 406 n. 138; library of, 64, 196, 290 f., 403 n. 4; testamentary inventory, 40
Loypeau, Étienne, Bishop of Luçon, 72, 84 f., 276, 298
Lucca, Opera del Duomo: leather casket, 51 f., Figs. 454, 455
Ludwig of Bavaria, 51
Lusignan, Château of Jean de Berry, 36 f., Fig. 419
Lyons, Bibl. municipale
    ms 742 (Métamorphoses), 288, 311
    ms 5122 (Missal), 389 n. 56
— Chalandon Coll.: Beaumetz, Jean de, Calvary with a Carthusian, 7, 279 f.

Maci, Jaquet, 6
Madonna with the Cradle, 186
Madonna on the Crescent, 207
Madonna of Humility, 14, 25 f., 105, 126 ff., 183 f., 195, 234, 276 f.
Madonna with Sleeping Child, 62, 301
Madonna with Writing Child, 201, 205 ff., 265, 278 f., 296
Madonna, see also Virgin Mary
Madrid, Bibl. Nacional: Vit. 25, no. 1 (Horae), 357
— Bibl. del Palacio: ms 2099 (Horae), 230, 232 f., 236 ff., 243, 246, 329, Figs. 748, 752, 754, 763, 768, 770, 775, 786, 787, 798, 808
— Museo Lázaro Galdiano: ms 505 (Propriétés des choses), 317 f.
— Prado: Bosch, Hieronymus, Adoration of the Magi, 394 n. 82
Magdeburg Cathedral: Wise Virgins, 79
Magi, Meeting of the, 306, 407 n. 158; see also Adoration of the Magi
magnifying glass, early use and representations, 5
Mahaut d'Artois, 227
Mainz, Römisch-Germanisches Museum: Roman, Tropeum and Captives, 106, Fig. 531
Malet, Gilles, 40, 287
Malouel, Jean, 7, 18, 63, 74, 279 f., 293, 301 f., 395 n. 99; lost portrait of Jean sans Peur, 363 n. 20
Man of Sorrows, 13 f., 17, 61 ff., 122 f., 169 f., 183, 185, 239, 260, 379 n. 88
Mancini, Antonio, 46, 53, 57
Manresa Cathedral: Geri di Lapo, altar hanging, 60, Fig. 449
Mantegna, Andrea, 123, 145
Manuel II Paleologus, Emperor of Constantinople, 41, 57 ff., 304, 306, 407 n. 152; portrait of, 58, Fig. 45
Marcia, Roman painter, 4
Marco Polo, Le devisement du monde, 314, 403 n. 12
Marguerite de Bavière, Duchess of Burgundy, 198 f., 201, 404 n. 61, 404 n. 65; testamentary inventory, 199
Marguerite d'Orléans, 156
Marie de Berry, 276; portraits of, 201, 269
Marriage at Cana, 111, 128 f., 262, 384 n. 151
Marriage of the Virgin, 375 n. 268
Martorell, Bernardo, 144
Masaccio, 105, 127 f., 303, 381 n. 51
Maso di Banco, 28, 69, 205, 211
Massa Marittima: Ugolino da Siena, Maestà and Crucifixion, 104, 364 n. 87
— Museo: Lorenzetti, Ambrogio, Madonna, 183, 195, 276 f., 364 n. 90, Fig. 698

Massys, Quentin, 77
Master of the Adelphoe, 10, 363 n. 39
Master of the Angevin Bible, 28 f., 390. n. 67
Master of the Angevin Bible – Associate, 29, 120, 219
Master of the Bambino Vispo, 24, 383 n. 103
Master of the Baptist, 78, 86, 129 f., 134, 180, 248 ff., 253, 297, 339 f., 400 n. 41
Master of the Baptist – Workshop, 328 f.
Master of the Bedford Hours, 9 f., 17, 65, 68, 78, 85, 91, 168, 253 f., 265, 297, 299, 332, 334, 376 n. 312, 389 n. 58
Master of the Bedford Hours – Followers, 69, 85, 389 n. 58, 405 n. 89
Master of the Bellpuig Coronation, 24; see also Bassa, Ferrer
Master of the Berry Apocalypse, 254, 277, 300, 307, 354
Master of Berry's Cleres Femmes, 252 f., 354 f.
Master of Berry's Cleres Femmes – Follower, 323
Master Bertram, 125, 393 n. 55
Master of the Boqueteaux, 22; see also Bondol, Jean
Master of the Boucicaut Hours, 9, 20, 39, 49, 73, 78, 94, 142, 200, 206, 221 f., 236 ff., 240, 244, 246, 253, 258 ff., 263 ff., 274 f., 277 f., 295, 297, 299, 306, 320, 332, 341, 363 n. 60, 402 n. 60
Master of the Boucicaut Hours – Associates, 9, 259 ff.
Master of the Boucicaut Hours – Followers, 69, 85, 333 f., 363 n. 38, 389 n. 62
Master of the Boucicaut Hours – Workshop, 11, 86, 93, 259, 297, 320, 332 ff., 398 n. 96
Master of the Bréviaire de Jean sans Peur, 9, 16, 202, 246
Master of the Bréviaire de Jean sans Peur – Workshop, 355, 395 n. 1
Master of the Brussels Initials, 49, 214 f., 218, 229 ff., 278, 320 ff., 324 ff., 342, 344; and the Limbourgs, 234 f., 240, 246
Master of the Brussels Initials – Collaborators, 230, 242
Master of the Chiostro degli Aranci, 24
Master of the Cité des Dames, 9 f., 15, 24, 227, 269, 295, 299 ff., 356 f., 400 n. 35, 402 n. 60
Master of the Cité des Dames – Followers, 93, 357, 363 n. 39
Master of Città di Castello, 104
Master of the Codex of St. George, 25, 390 n. 79
Master of the Comedies of Terence, 10 f.
Master of the Coronation, 218, 252, 274, 300, 355, 400 n. 33
Master of the Coronation – Workshop, 392 n. 20
Master of the De Natura Deorum, 145
Master of Douce 313, 20, 24, 106, 212
Master of Egerton 1070, 9, 16, 142, 235, 242, 246, 300, 323, 332, 357 f.
Master of Egerton 1070 – Workshop, 242, 258, 333, 341, 401 n. 26
Master of the Épître d'Othéa, 274, 295, 299 f., 358
Master of the Épître d'Othéa – Workshop, 294, 300
Master of Flémalle, 18, 63, 236
Master of the Fogg Pietà, 387 n. 70
Master of Guillebert de Mets, 15 ff.
Master of the Holy Ghost, 134, 253 ff., 260, 295, 297, 339
Master Honoré, 3
Master Honoré – Atelier, 103
Master of the Humility Madonnas, 276 f., 327 ff.
Master of Luçon, 10, 18, 149, 215, 239, 242, 276, 295, 298, 358 f.
Master of Luçon – Workshop, 86, 206, 239, 242, 276, 326, 328 f., 331

Master of the Mansel, 15, 17

Master of the Miracles of the Virgin, 24

Master of the Parement de Narbonne, 87, 101 ff., 111 ff., 134, 136, 159 f., 165, 167, 169 f., 173 f., 180, 185, 187, 190, 205, 214 ff., 222, 228, 237 f., 244, 247 ff., 261 ff., 295, 298, 301, 303, 337 ff., 370 n. 88 (*see also* Jean d' Orléans); Italianate tendencies, 104 ff., 120

Master of the Parement de Narbonne – Imitator of, 134, 247 f., 339 f.

Master of the Parement de Narbonne – Workshop, 87, 115 ff., 124, 222, 247 f., 338 ff.

Master of the Passion, 4, 17, 20, 44, 61, 106, 125, 133, 159 ff., 171 f., 174 f., 177, 182, 187, 192, 249 f., 259 f., 273, 295, 297, 301, 335 ff., 380 n. 14; *see also* Jean le Noir

Master, Petites Heures, No. Five, 91, 178, 193, 336 f., 388 n. 8

Master of the Pietà, 183 f.

Master of the Rohan Hours, 8 f., 17 ff., 27, 168, 227, 246, 254, 268, 279, 307

Master of St. Mark, 24, 125; *see also* Bassa, Arnau

Master of the Stefaneschi Altarpiece, 211, 396 n. 25

Master Theodoric, 131

Master of the Trinity, 89, 91, 153, 157, 165 f., 174, 176 ff., 179, 190, 192 ff., 196 ff., 208, 221, 227, 260, 275, 278, 328 f., 335 ff., 343

Master of Troyes, 359

Master of the Virgil texts, 189, 295, 298, 360 f., 403 n. 27

Master of the Vyšši Brod cycle, 383 n. 119, 385 n. 160

Master of Walters 219, 360

Matteo Giovanetti, 25 f., 301, 400 n. 41

Matteo Giovanetti – Follower, 366 n. 131

Medici family, inventories, 40

Meditationes Vitae Christi, 12, 102, 121 f., 124 f., 171, 173, 213, 217, 236 f., 272, 289 f., 354; French trans. made for Jean de Berry, 236, 246, 289 f. (*see also* Vie de nostre bénoit sauveur Jésus Christ); French trans. and Duke's miniatures, 289 f.; Provençal trans., *ca.* 1380, 289

Mehun-sur-Yèvre, Château of Jean de Berry, 32, 35, 37 f., 40, Figs. 424, 425, 430; 'librairie' of Jean de Berry, 291 f., 294 f.; French, head, *see* Paris, Musée du Louvre

Melbourne, National Gallery of Victoria: Felton 3 (Tite-Live), 356

Meran, Schloss Tirol: Austrian, altarpiece, 1370–1372, 126, Fig. 557

merchants, 46 f., 371 n. 132

Merveilles du monde, 14, 49, 59, 199, 299, 314, 363 n. 60, 378 n. 61, 404 n. 45

Michele de' Pazzi, 46, 55, 371 n. 132

Michelino da Besozzo, 75, 145, 302

Mignotus, Johannes, 64

Milan, Bibl. Ambrosiana
  ms E 24 inf., 392 n. 29
  ms I 7 sup. (Horae), 359
  ms L 58 sup. (Horae), 359
  Petrarch's Virgil, 25
— Bibl. Trivulziana
  ms 445 (Horae), 5, 384 n. 148, Fig. 296
  ms 2262 (Beroaldo), 144
— Brera
  Barnaba da Modena, Nativity, 397 n. 51
  Bellini, Giovanni, Man of Sorrows, 185

Milan, Cathedral: Christ and Woman of Samaria, 144
— Coll. Visconti di Modrone: Visconti Hours, 75, 143 f., 386 n. 27; *see also* Florence, Bibl. Nazionale, Landau-Finaly 22

Milet le Cavelier, 44

Mirabilia Urbis Romae, 233

Le miroir des dames, 310

Mockery of Christ, 162 f., 260, 398 n. 78

Modena, Bibl. Estense
  ms lat. 461, 233 f., Fig. 815
  ms lat. 842, 383 n. 122
  ms lat. 1021 (Gradual), 231, 244 f., 330, Fig. 795
  ms R. 7. 3 (Horae), 384 n. 139

Monaco, Lorenzo, 302

Monaco, Lorenzo – Circle, 375 n. 284

Monreale, Byzantine, mosaics, 384 n. 151, 390 n. 79

Montaigu, Jean de, 290 f.

Montalcino, Compagnia di S. Antonio: Duccio – Follower, Madonna and Child, 381 n. 40

Montfaucon, Renaud de, seal, 304

Montreal, Randall, L. V. Coll.: Coronation of the Virgin (miniature), 359

Montreuil, Jean de, 302 f., 305, 307

Morogues, Church: wooden *sedilia* from the Ste-Chapelle, Bourges, 39

Munich, Bayrisches Nationalmuseum
  cameo, Ruler and Angels, 373 n. 210
  copy of a *joyau* of Charles VI and Isabeau de Bavière, 143, 145, Fig. 576
  copy of a Parisian *joyau*, ca. 1404, 296, Fig. 838
  German, St. Mark (glass), 14th cent., 396 n. 23

— Bayrische Staatsbibliothek
  MANUSCRIPTS
  cod. gall. 3 (Légende dorée), 358
  cod. gall. 11 (Mutacion de Fortune), 356
  cod. gall. 26 (Jeu des échecs), 354
  clm. 146 (Speculum Humanae Salvationis), 397 n. 37
  clm. 10072 (Missal), 42, 231, 237, 272, 301, 311, 394 n. 68, Figs. 716, 717, 751
  clm. 23215 (Horae of Blanche de Savoie), 386 n. 37, 390 n. 78, 391 n. 111

Naples, Museo di Capodimonte
  Gaddi, Taddeo – Workshop, Lamentation, 184 f., Fig. 647
  Masaccio, Crucifixion, 105
— S. Chiara: Neapolitan, Vesperbild (fresco), 183
— S. Domenico Maggiore: Roberto di Oderisio, Madonna of Humility, 184
— S. Lorenzo Maggiore, Barresi Chapel: frescoes, 28 f., 219, Fig. 413
— S. M. di Donna Regina: Cavallini – Follower, Crucifixion, 394 n. 74

Nardo di Cione, 211

Nativity, 17 f., 28 f., 60, 117, 122, 126, 162, 171 ff., 178, 182, 218 f., 236 f., 265, 289, 397 n. 56

Nativity, Brigittine, 122, 217, 236

Naumburg Cathedral: Queen Regilindis, 79

Negroes, 114, 162

Neumarkt, Johann von, 131, 302

New Haven, Yale University, Jarves Coll.: Guido da Siena – Follower, Crucifixion, 391 n. 98
— Yale University Library: Roman de Lancelot, 12 f.
New York, Frick Collection: French, Madonna, *ca.* 1400, 170, Fig. 633
— Harper, Lathrop: Horae, 355
— Kraus, H. P.
  Horae, 358
  Horae ('De Lévis'), 359
— Lehman, Robert, Coll.
  Florentine, Adoration of the Magi (embroidery), 60, Fig. 452
  Master of the Angevin Bible – Associate, Adoration of the Magi, 28 f.
— Martin, A. B., Coll.: leather casket, 373 n. 189

— Metropolitan Museum of Art
  Eyck, Jan van, diptych, 376 n. 295
  French, Madonna with a Cradle (ivory), later 14th cent., 391 n. 103
— Metropolitan Museum of Art, Cloisters
  MANUSCRIPTS
  Belles Heures, 44, 55, 71 f., 92 f., 97, 112, 127, 178, 202, 218, 235, 238, 246, 250, 257, 265, 270, 273, 292, 294 f., 297, 311, 402 n. 60, Figs. 261, 495, 496, 518, 746, 779, 785
  Heures de Jeanne d'Évreux, 19 f., 23, 87, 100 ff., 117, 119 f., 125, 141, 163, 165, 171, 174, 182, 190, 204, 211, 287, 294, 300 f., 311, 383 n. 112, 389 n. 45, Figs. 250, 335-338, 342, 360
  Horae, Annunciation from, 1465, 38, Fig. 430
  OTHER OBJECTS
  Florentine, Altarpiece of the Intercessio, 383 n. 103
  Nine Heroes (tapestry), 59, 365 n. 103, Figs. 445, 446

— New York Historical Society
  Duccio – Follower, Crucifixion, 61, Fig. 444
  Nardo di Cione, Madonna, 211, Fig. 699

— Pierpont Morgan Library
  MANUSCRIPTS
  ms 44, 383 n. 117
  ms 46 (Horae), 398 n. 71
  ms 88 (Horae), 126 f., 277, Fig. 550
  ms 90 (Horae), 123, Fig. 545
  ms 133 (Apocalypse), 277, 300, 311, 354, Fig. 843
  ms 331 (Missal), 5, 359, Fig. 297
  ms 515 (Horae), 355, 399 n. 28, Fig. 823
  ms 536 (Grandes chroniques), 356
  ms 723 (Livre des merveilles), 354
  ms 729 (Heures de Yolande de Soissons), 383 n. 115, Fig. 330
  ms 743 (Horae), 359, 394 n. 66
  ms 785 (Livre d'astrologie), 49, 250 f., 294, 311, Figs. 826, 827
  ms 804 (Froissart, Chroniques), 354
  DRAWINGS
  M 346 (pattern book), 206 f., 267, 278 f., 330, Figs. 279, 281-286
  PAINTINGS
  Bohemian, diptych, 125, 131, Fig. 568
  Master of St. Mark, altarpiece, 125, Fig. 559

— Wildenstein and Company: Master of the Stefaneschi Altarpiece, Madonna, Saints and Virtues, 211
Niccolò da Bologna, 6, 42, 231, 234, 237, 272, 301, 394 n. 68

Niccolo Niccoli, 305
Niccolò di Pietro, 302
Niccolò di Tommaso, 122, 215, 217, 394 n. 77, 397 n. 52
Nicola Pisano, 104, 125, 380 n. 20
Nicolau, Pedro, 387 n. 74
night scenes, 178
Nonette, Château of Jean de Berry, 36; representations of, 402 n. 57
Norwich, Bishop of, 65
nude, representations of, 125 ff., 277, 303
Nuremberg, Germanisches Nationalmuseum
  Nuremberg (?), Coronation of St. Clare, 150, Fig. 588
  Swabian, Christ at the Column (statuette), 375 n. 288
— Stadtbibl.: Solger in 4to, No. 4 (Horae), 102

Office of the Dead, 144, 222
Orcagna, Andrea, 28
Ordre de la Dame Blanche, 146
Ordre du St. Esprit, 27, 51
Orlandi, Deodato, 394 n. 63
Orosius, 318
Orvieto, Cathedral: Ugolino di Vieri, Annunciation (enamel), 212, Fig. 709
— Museo Civico: Simone Martini, Madonna, 390 n. 97
Ouvraige d'Angleterre, 41 f.
Ouvraige de Florence, 26, 42, 47, 60
Ouvraige de Grèce, 41 f., 59, 304
Ouvraige de Lombardie, 41 ff.
Ouvraige de Rome, 25, 41 ff.
Ouvraige de Venise, 42
Ovid: Ars Amatoria, Fr. trans., 288; Metamorphoses, Fr. trans., 288, 311, 313, 317

Oxford, Bodleian Library
  MANUSCRIPTS
  ms 265 (Cas des nobles hommes et femmes), 357
  ms D'Orville 141 (Guide to illustrations of Sallust), 13, 362 n. 3
  ms Douce 62 (Horae), 230 f., 238 ff., 330 f., Figs. 724, 725, 739, 740, 742, 753, 767, 771, 782, 783, 788
  ms Douce 102 (Horae), 359
  ms Douce 313 (Missal), 20, 103 f., 106 f., 124, 163, 212, 220, 382 n. 77, 383 n. 120, Figs. 372, 373, 536, 663, 677
  ms Rawl. C. 538 (Secret des secrez), 194, 311, Fig. 654

— Christ Church: Bohemian, Archer (drawing), 132, Fig. 569
— Exeter College Library: ms 47 (Psalter of Humphrey of Bohun), 396 n. 23

Pacino di Bonaguida, 394 n. 63
Padua, Arena Chapel: Giotto, frescoes, 103, 114, 119 f., 129, 173, 212, 215, 237, 389 n. 64, Fig. 653, portrait of Enrico Scrovegni, 205
— Eremitani (formerly): Altichiero, Coronation of the Virgin, 238, Fig. 774
— S. Antonio, Chapel of S. Felice
  Altichiero, Crucifixion, 402 n. 55, Man of Sorrows, 123, 239, Fig. 547
  Altichiero and assistants, St. James Preaching, 214, Fig. 713
  Altichiero – Follower, St. James Led from the City, 72, 240 f., Fig. 514

Padua, S. Giorgio: Altichiero, frescoes, 219, 237 f., 240, 397 n. 56, Figs. 691, 744, 773, 778

Paganico, S. Michele: Lorenzetti, Ambrogio – Follower, Annunciation, 393 n. 57

painters: collaboration of, 8 ff.; female, 3 ff.; French, in Italy, 24; Italian, in France, 24 ff.; positions of, 8, 43 f.

painting: Italian Trecento and Bohemian, 23; Italian Trecento and Catalonian, 23 f.; in reign of Charles V, 100; School of Paris, 295; secular, 14

Paleologus, see John VIII and Manuel II

Palermo, Bibl. Nazionale: ms I. A. 15 (Horae), 355

— Museo Nazionale: Bartolommeo da Camogli, Madonna of Humility, 171, 277, Fig. 634

Parement Master, see Master of the Parement de Narbonne

Paris, Archives nationales

    AE II 393, Initial K (Charles V and Jean de Berry), 38, 82 f., Fig. 475

    AE II 411, Marriage Contract of Jean de Berry and Jeanne de Boulogne, 83, 96, Fig. 476

    AE II 422, Jean de Berry and Order of St. Barthélemy de Bruges, 78, 84, Fig. 480

    J 185 (B), Great Seal of Jean de Berry, 79 ff., 82, 86, 95 f., Fig. 474

    J 211, Secret Seal of Jean de Berry, 96, Fig. 523

    mm 8982 (Abrégé de l'histoire universelle), 356

    Seal of Renaud de Montfaucon, 304, Fig. 469

— Berès, Pierre: Christine de Pisan, Mutacion de Fortune, 358

— Bibliothèque de l'Arsenal

    MANUSCRIPTS

    ms 650 (Horae), 311, 357

    ms 664 (Térence des Ducs), 10, 298, 312, 357, 359, 403 n. 23

    ms 2002 (Rational des divins offices), 381 n. 64, 385 n. 165

    ms 3479-80 (Lancelot), 356, 371 n. 137, 399 n. 26

    ms 5057-58 (Bible historiale), 242, 252, 312, 354, 356, 360, Fig. 829

    ms 5060 (Cité de Dieu), 357

    ms 5070 (Décaméron), 12, 15 ff., Figs. 320, 322

    ms 5077 (Trésor des histoires), 9, 14, 94, 363 n. 44, 381 n. 51

    ms 5107 (Échecs moralisés), 312

    ms 5193 (Cas des nobles hommes et femmes), 357, 359, 363 n. 45

    ms 5212 (Bible historiale), 300 f., 312

— Bibliothèque Mazarine

    MANUSCRIPTS

    ms 469 (Horae), 355, 405 n. 105

    ms 491 (Horae), 359

    ms 2028 (Grandes chroniques), 357 f.

— Bibliothèque nationale

    MANUSCRIPTS

    ms fr. 3 (Bible historiale), 354

    ms fr. 9-10 (Bible historiale), 17, 24, 356 f., 365 n. 115, Figs. 325, 393

    ms fr. 20-21 (Cité de Dieu), 354

    ms fr. 23-24 (Cité de Dieu), 356

    ms fr. 25 (Cité de Dieu), 354, 360

    ms fr. 30 (Livy), 358

Paris, Bibliothèque nationale (contd.)

    ms fr. 117-120 (Lancelot), 242, 252, 312, 355, 376 n. 316, Fig. 824

    ms fr. 129 (Décaméron), 318

    ms fr. 131 (Cas des nobles hommes et femmes), 79 f., 93, 318, 356, Fig. 500

    ms fr. 159 (Bible historiale), 42, 243, 252, 295, 312, 355, 392 n. 20, 394 n. 81, 404 n. 39, Fig. 822

    ms fr. 166 (Bible moralisée), 6, 250, 301, 381 n. 53, 393 n. 38, Fig. 781

    ms fr. 172-173 (Cité de Dieu), 50, 312, 371 n. 117

    ms fr. 174 (Cité de Dieu), 356

    ms fr. 176 (Rationale), 312, 403 n. 12

    ms fr. 190 (Livre des quatre vertus), 403 n. 28

    ms fr. 208 (Politiques and Éthiques), 359

    ms fr. 226 (Cas des nobles hommes et femmes), 93, 318, 356, 403 n. 25, 406 n. 128, Fig. 503

    ms fr. 242 (Légende dorée), 252, 355, 387 n. 68, 400 n. 33

    ms fr. 246 (Livre de Suétoine), 288, 312, 403 n. 12

    ms fr. 247 (Antiquités judaïques), 227, 312, 363 n. 41, 381 n. 53, Fig. 683

    ms fr. 256 (Histoire ancienne), 312

    ms fr. 263 (Livy), 298, 313, 360

    ms fr. 282 (Valère Maxime), 313, 360, 403 n. 27

    ms fr. 286 (Valère Maxime), 357

    ms fr. 290 (Valère Maxime), 318

    ms fr. 301 (Histoires d'Orose), 318

    ms fr. 340 (Livre du roy Méliadus), 357, 363 n. 51

    ms fr. 343 (Lancelot), 145

    ms fr. 373 (Métamorphoses), 288, 313

    ms fr. 380 (Roman de la rose), 189 f., 313, Figs. 624, 845

    ms fr. 400, 396 n. 27

    ms fr. 414 (Légende dorée), 360

    ms fr. 425 (Composition de la Sainte Écriture), 313, 403 n. 12

    ms fr. 565 (Du ciel et du monde), 313, 403 n. 12

    ms fr. 568 (Livre du trésor), 313, 403 n. 12

    ms fr. 574 (Image du monde), 313

    ms fr. 598 (Des cleres femmes), 4 f., 128, 243, 252, 295, 303, 313, 355, 378 n. 64, Figs. 289, 291, 294, 561

    ms fr. 603 (Christine de Pisan, Œuvres), 356

    ms fr. 606 (Épître d'Othéa), 16, 50, 235, 242, 295, 299 f., 313, 356 ff., 363 n. 50, 372 n. 177, Figs. 817, 833, 834; see also Paris, Bibl. nat., ms fr. 835-836

    ms fr. 607 (Cité des Dames), 299, 313, 356

    ms fr. 616 (Livre de la chasse), 59, 218, 363 n. 39, Fig. 439

    ms fr. 819-820 (Miracles de Notre-Dame), 360

    ms fr. 829 (Pèlerinage du corps et de l'âme), 313, 399 n. 18, 403 n. 12

    ms fr. 835-836 (Œuvres de Christine de Pisan), 300, 356 ff., 398 n. 77, Fig. 324; see also Paris, Bibl. nat., ms fr. 606

    ms fr. 848 (Épître d'Othéa), 363 n. 50

    ms fr. 926 (L'Aiguillon d'amour divin), 201, 206, 246, 269, 276, 359, 392 n. 32, Figs. 667, 780

    ms fr. 964 (Commentary on Psalms), 354

    ms fr. 1023 (Livre des bonnes mœurs), 79 f., 85 f., 92, 187, 298, 314, 359, Figs. 486, 643

    ms fr. 1082 (Du ciel et du monde), 314

    ms fr. 1178 (Cité des Dames), 356

    ms fr. 1179 (Cité des Dames), 356

    ms fr. 1210 (Information des rois et des princes), 314

Paris, Bibliothèque nationale (*contd.*)

ms fr. 1229 (Le livre de Vegèce), 314

ms fr. 1454 (Le Brut d'Angleterre), 314, 354

ms fr. 1584 (Œuvres de Guillaume de Machaut), 23, 141, 218, 221, 225, Fig. 385

ms fr. 1792, 379 n. 10

ms fr. 2092 (Légende de St. Denis), 162

ms fr. 2608 (Chroniques de France), 314, 400 n. 30

ms fr. 2649 (Froissart, Chroniques), 354

ms fr. 2663-64 (Froissart, Chroniques), 354

ms fr. 2675 (Froissart, Chroniques), 356

ms fr. 2810 (Merveilles du Monde), 14, 49, 59, 199, 299, 314, 363 n. 32, 363 n. 60, 378 n. 61

ms fr. 2813 (Grandes Chroniques), 132, 141, 318, 365 n. 105, 382 n. 88, Fig. 565

ms fr. 4274 (Statuts, Ordre du St. Esprit), 27

ms fr. 5631 (Devisement du monde), 314, 403 n. 12

ms fr. 5707 (Bible), 290, 314, 379 n. 74

ms fr. 6271 (Cité de Dieu), 314

ms fr. 6272 (Cité de Dieu), 360

ms fr. 6445 (Tite-Live), 360

ms fr. 6446 (Antiquités judaïques), 314, 356, 405 n. 106

ms fr. 9106 (Politiques et Yconomiques), 314 f., 403 n. 12

ms fr. 9141 (Livre de la propriété des choses), 73, 94, 221, Figs. 504, 682

ms fr. 9221 (Poésies de Guillaume de Machaut), 315, 403 n. 12

ms fr. 9561 (Bible moralisée), 27 ff., 100, 181, 213, 219, 388 n. 24, 390 n. 67, 401 n. 49, Figs. 328, 408, 410-412

ms fr. 12201 (Fleur des histoires), 14, 47, 49, 199, 218, 252, 294, 315, 355, Fig. 438

ms fr. 12420 (Des cleres femmes), 4 f., 47, 252, 355

ms fr. 12559 (Chevalier errant), 356

ms fr. 12595 (Roman de la rose), 315

ms fr. 13091 (Psalter of Jean de Berry), 7, 10, 97, 112, 135 ff., 147 f., 151 ff., 170, 191, 196, 218, 225, 228, 255, 291, 295, 297, 315, 331 f., Figs. 51-82; borders, 136; frames, 136

ms fr. 15397 (Bible de Jean de Sy), 11, 20, 31, 141, 152, 168, 172, 178, 298, 315, Figs. 298, 301, 376, 377, 583

ms fr. 15455 (Histoire ancienne), 318

ms fr. 16994 (Cas des nobles hommes et femmes), 356

ms fr. 17183 (Honoré Bonnet, Arbre des batailles), 354

ms fr. 20090 (Bible historiale), 141, 152 f., 167, 177, 180, 315, 404 n. 42, Figs. 602, 611

ms fr. 20412, no. 43 (copies of Berry's seals), 83

ms fr. 22297 (Armorial d'Auvergne), 402 n. 57

ms fr. 22542 (Philippe de Mézières, Songe du vieil pèlerin), 69 f.

ms fr. 22912-13 (Cité de Dieu), 14, 141, 365 n. 105, 379 n. 10, 382 n. 88, 389 n. 66

ms fr. 23279 (Dialogues de Pierre Salmon), 50, 73, 77, 79, 86, 91, 254, 275, 356, 363 n. 35, 377 n. 10, 378 n. 61, 405 n. 104, Fig. 487

ms gr. 54, 387 n. 71

ms ital. 63 (Decameron), 15, Fig. 303

ms ital. 72 (Divina Commedia), 318

ms ital. 115 (Meditationes), 105, 121, 394 n. 64, Fig. 532

ms lat. 248 (Bible de Philippe le Bel), 315

ms lat. 757 (Missal), 127, 144 f., 222, 384 n. 130, 394 n. 69, Figs. 558, 560, 584

ms lat. 765 (Fitzwarin Psalter), 380 n. 39, Fig. 558

Paris, Bibliothèque nationale (*contd.*)

ms lat. 919 (Grandes Heures), 7, 10, 12, 44, 50, 68 ff., 77, 80, 85 ff., 91 f., 95, 111 ff., 129, 136, 139 f., 151, 159, 170, 187 f., 200 f., 228, 248 f., 254, 256 ff., 277 f., 281 ff., 294, 296 f., 299, 315, 332 ff., 379 n. 15, Figs. 217-244, 249, 251, 252, 484, 485 (*see also* Paris, Musée du Louvre, Way to Calvary); borders, 257 ff., 261; relationship with other manuscripts: the Brussels Hours, 257 f., 260, 263, 265 f., 269 f., the Très Belles Heures de Notre-Dame, 12, 248 f., 254, 260, 262 f., 381 n. 64

ms lat. 924 (Horae), 130, 359, 396 n. 24, Fig. 533

ms lat. 1052 (Bréviaire de Charles V), 159 ff., 164 ff., 171, 176, 187, 260, 295 f., 301, 315, 383 n. 116, 388 n. 24, 391 n. 109, Figs. 351, 359, 362, 367-371, 839

ms lat. 1082 (Psalter and Hours), 359

ms lat. 1156 A (Heures de René d'Anjou), 18, Fig. 332

ms lat. 1156 B (Heures de Marguerite d'Orléans), 156

ms lat. 1161 (Horae), 398 n. 96

ms lat. 1364 (Horae), 186, 382 n. 71, 401 n. 71, Fig. 648

ms lat. 1403 (Horae), 185 f., 384 n. 134, 393 n. 55, Figs. 625, 646

ms lat. 3107, 398 n. 96

ms lat. 5690 (Livy), 366 n. 129

ms lat. 5720 (Quintus Curtius), 366 n. 129

ms lat. 5762 (Sallust, Catalina and Jugurtha), 318

ms lat. 6802 (Pliny), 25, Fig. 402

ms lat. 7907 A (Terence, Comedies), 10, 49, 294, 298, 315 f., 395 n. 106, 403 n. 23, 406 n. 140, Fig. 440

ms lat. 8193 (Terence, Comedies), 10 f., 363 n. 51, Figs. 299, 300

ms lat. 8824 (Psalter), 43, 316

ms lat. 8885 (Missal), 316

ms lat. 8886 (Pontifical of Étienne Loypeau), 72, 84 f., 91 f., 242, 276, 295, 298, 316, 359, Figs. 268, 483

ms lat. 8892 (Gospels), 203, Fig. 659

ms lat. 9321 (Boethius, De Consolatione), 316

ms lat. 9471 (Grandes Heures de Rohan), 8, 17, 268, Fig. 327

ms lat. 10426 (Bible de St. Louis), 316

ms lat. 10483-84 (Bréviaire de Belleville), 20, 22, 64, 117, 121 f., 125, 135 f., 139 f., 155, 180, 187, 214, 259, 273, 296, 301, 316, 382 n. 74, 382 n. 85, 389 n. 55, Figs. 260, 344, 374

ms lat. 10525 (Psalter of St. Louis), 3

ms lat. 10528 (Horae), 383 n. 103, 384 n. 128

ms lat. 11935 (Bible de Robert de Billyng), 6, 181, Fig. 357

ms lat. 14245 (Jacques Legrand, Traité des vices et des vertus), 354

ms lat. 14643 (Somnium super materia scismatis), 13

ms lat. 18014 (Petites Heures), 32, 48, 61, 69 ff., 92 f., 96 f., 109 ff., 125, 130, 136, 139 f., 151 ff., 155 ff., 194, 204, 210, 212 ff., 218 f., 222, 224 ff., 231, 237 ff., 243, 275, 291, 297, 316, 334 ff., 380 n. 14, Figs. 83-176, 498; landscapes, 171 f.; portraits, 79 f., 88 ff., 157, 170; relationship with other manuscripts: Grandes Heures, 159, 259 ff., the Psalter, 151 ff., 170, 177, 190 f., the Psalter of Bonne, 160, the Très Belles Heures de Notre-Dame, 108 f., 111, 130, 158, 160, 170 f., 180 ff., 250, 296 f.

ms néerl. 3 (Apocalypse), 250

ms nouv. acq. fr. 4792 (Sept psaumes de pénitence), 357

ms nouv. acq. fr. 5243 (Giron le Courtois), 144 f., Fig. 585

ms nouv. acq. fr. 14285 (Manuel d'histoire), 354

ms nouv. acq. fr. 24541 (Miracles de la Vierge), 19 f., 128, 178, 287, 301, 316, 391 n. 110, Figs. 340, 562

Paris, Bibliothèque nationale (*contd.*)
  ms nouv. acq. lat. 1673 (Tacuinum sanitatis), 145
  ms nouv. acq. lat. 3093 (Très Belles Heures de Notre-Dame),
    12, 48, 94, 96, 108 ff., 134, 148 f., 170 f., 173 f., 180 ff., 185,
    187 ff., 204, 210 f., 213 ff., 222, 237 ff., 244, 247 ff., 252 ff.,
    276, 289 ff., 295 ff., 299, 316, 337 ff., 368 n. 28, 380 n. 25,
    388 n. 27, Figs. 6-28, 570; *bas-de-page* and initials, 117 f.;
    relationship with the Parement de Narbonne, 113 ff.
  ms nouv. acq. lat. 3108 (Horae), 359
  ms suppl. gr. 309 (Manuel II Paleologus), 58, Fig. 441
— Bibl. nationale, Cabinet des Estampes
  'Avignon Diptych', copy for Gaignières, 375 n. 284
  French, Louis II d'Anjou, 68, 75 f., Fig. 505
  French, Palais and Ste-Chapelle, Bourges (drawing), 37, Fig.
    432
  Limbourgs, Portrait of Jean de Berry (copy), 75 ff., 80, 86,
    Fig. 490
— Bibl. nationale, Cabinet des Médailles
  Constantine, medal of (reverse, Allegory of Salvation), 36, 40,
    46, 53 ff., 304 f., 306, Figs. 462, 463
  Heraclius, medal of (reverse, Heraclius with the Cross), 36, 40,
    53 ff., 57 f., 304 f., Figs. 464, 465
  Seal of the Treasurer of Ste-Chapelle, Bourges, 81, 84, 96, Fig.
    482

— Chambre des Députés: ms 3 (Bible historiale), 360
— Charnacé Coll.: Horae, 358
— Durrieu, Comte Jean, Coll.
  Horae, 358
  prayerbook, 264, 275, 341, 357, Figs. 245-247
— Guild of St. Luke, 8
— Hôtel de Nesle, 33 f., 37, 40, 368 n. 8
— Hôtel St. Pol, 31, 379 n. 10; *Salle de Thésée*, 406 n. 1
— Hutinel Coll.: Beauneveu, André – Workshop, Prophet, 36, 135
— Lafond, Jean, Coll.: Pseudo-Jacquemart – Style, Angel (glass),
    265, Fig. 840
— Luart, Comtesse L. du, Coll.: Giovanni da Milano, Vesper-
    bild, 62, 145, 183 f., 208, Fig. 635
— Montesquiou, Comte Blaise de, Coll.: French, Jean sans Peur
    (ring), 52, 68, 74 f., Fig. 512
— Musée de Cluny
  Embriachi Workshop, Altarpieces for Champmol, 92
  French, Entombment (mitre), 100 f., Fig. 526
  ms 11314 (leaves from Horae), 357
— Musée Jacquemart-André
  ms 1 (Heures de Jeanne de Savoie), 187, Fig. 613
  ms 2 (Boucicaut Hours), 20, 238, 240, 275, 279, 297, 387 n. 68,
    393 n. 38, 397 n. 44, 398 n. 95

— Musée du Louvre
            PAINTINGS
  Bellechose, Henri, Martyrdom of St. Denis, 7, 63
  French, Entombment, 1390-1400, 63, 94, 205, 218, 270, 279,
    Fig. 695
  French, Lamentation, 63
  French, portrait of Jean le Bon, 23, 63, 68, 75 f., 99, 102, Fig.
    507
  French, portrait of Jean sans Peur (copy), 68, 75, Fig. 506
  Jacquemart de Hesdin, Way to Calvary, 201, 257, 265, 267 ff.,
    277, 279, 340 f., Figs. 277, 278

Paris, Musée du Louvre (*cont.*)
  Malouel, Jean, Trinity with Man of Sorrows, 63, 270, 279 f.,
    293, 383 n. 99, Fig. 832
  Massys, Quentin, portrait of a Money Changer and Wife, 77
  Matteo Giovanetti – Follower, Death of the Virgin, 366 n. 131
  Parement Master, Parement de Narbonne, 63, 68, 87, 99 ff.,
    107, 113 ff., 130 ff., 148, 216, 248, 340, 387 n. 64, Figs. 1-5
  Pisanello, Antonio, portrait of Margherita Gonzaga (?), 75
  Simone Martini, Way to Calvary, 25, 62, 215 ff., 272 f., 366 n.
    126, Fig. 675
            OTHER OBJECTS
  Beauneveu, André – Circle, Prophet (gilt bronze), 386 n. 59
  cameo from Bourges, Italian (?), Ruler and Angels, 53, 303,
    Fig. 457
  cameo from Bourges, Renaissance, bust of a man, 53, Fig. 460
  cameo from Bourges, Roman, Agrippina Maior as Juno, 53,
    Fig. 456
  cameo from Bourges, Roman, Agrippina Maior as Juno, 53,
    Fig. 461
  cameo from Bourges, Roman, Jupiter, 53, Fig. 458
  cameo from Bourges, Roman, Jupiter, 53, Fig. 459
  Embriachi Workshop, Retable from Poissy, 36, 91 f., Figs.
    427, 494
  French, head from Mehun-sur-Yèvre, 36, 148, Fig. 596
  French, Madonna with the Writing Child (ivory), 206, Fig.
    669
  French, reliquary of the Ordre du St.-Esprit, 51, 146, Fig. 574
  French, St. Louis as Charles V, 99 f., Fig. 524
  French, St. Margaret of Provence as Jeanne de Bourbon, 99 f.
  French, La vierge de Jeanne d'Évreux, 384 n. 131, 403 n. 7
  Jean de Liège, Tomb of Charles le Bel, 99, Tomb of Jeanne
    d'Évreux, 99
— Musée du Louvre, Cabinet des Dessins
  Copy of Beauneveu (?), Death, Assumption, and Coronation
    of the Virgin, 148 ff., 215 f., 255, 264, Fig. 587
  RF 2022-24 (Très Belles Heures de Notre-Dame), 63, 87 f.,
    108, 130, 248, 250, 316, 337, 340, Figs. 32, 33, 36, 37, 492

— Petit Palais: Roman, Venus at her Toilet, 87, Fig. 467
— Sainte-Chapelle, 135; representation of, 39
— Sorbonne, library: Catalogue of 1338, 40
Parler, Peter, 131, 147
Parma, Bibl. Palatina
  ms 56 (Horae), 181, Fig. 614
  ms 3285 (Dante, Commedia), 377 n. 8
  ms lat. 159 (Horae), 215, 230 ff., 242 ff., 341 f., Figs. 714, 715,
    727, 728, 735-738; relationship with Petites Heures, 231, 242
Passeri, Giuseppe, 234
Passion Cycle, *see* Christ
patronage, 8 f.; *see also* Jean de Berry; Philippe le Hardi, etc.
Pavia, Museo Civico
  Cas des nobles hommes et femmes, 6 miniatures from, 357
  Tuscan, Vesperbild, 183
Pedralbes Monastery: Bassa, Ferrer, Annunciation (fresco), 212,
    Fig. 710
Pèlerinage du corps et de l'âme, 313, 403 n. 12
Pentecost, 237 f., 248, 253 f., 276, 358, 367 n. 151
perspective: in Bible de Charles V, 165, 205; Brussels Hours,
    205, 209; Heures de Jeanne d'Évreux, 165; Petites Heures,
    165, 169; Psalter of Jean de Berry, 137 f., 147; Très Belles

perspective (*contd.*)
Heures de Notre-Dame, 113 f., 119; British Museum, ms Yates Thompson, 37, 274 f.
Perugia, Pinacoteca: Master of St. Francis, Lamentation, 183, Fig. 645
Peter, St., Receiving Souls, 68 f.
Petrarch, 25, 31, 131, 302; Remèdes, 288, 303
Petrus de Sacco, see Pierre de Vérone
Phébus, Gaston, Comte de Foix, 32 f., 46; Livre de la Chasse, 59, 218, 363 n. 39
Philadelphia, Free Library
ms Widener no. 4 (Horae), 358 f.
ms Widener no. 6 (Horae), 358
— Museum of Art: ms 45-65-5 (Horae), 359
— Museum of Art, Johnson Coll.: Niccolo di Tommaso, Nativity with St. Bridget, 394 n. 77, 397 n. 52
Philip, relief of emperor, 57, 304
Philippe le Bel, Roman painters of, 24 f.
Philippe le Hardi, Duke of Burgundy, 5 ff., 33, 39, 41, 47 ff., 199, 252, 299; library of, 252, 287, 292, 300 f.; patron, 8, 92, 252, 280, 293, 364 n. 82, 368 n. 2, 383 n. 102; portraits of, 13, 68, 71, 74 f.; testamentary inventory, 40, 353
Philippe de Mézières, Songe du vieil pèlerin, 69 f.
Piero della Francesca, 146, 236, 306
Pierre de Vérone (Petrus de Sacco), 63 ff., 245, 296, 396 n. 15, 405 n. 89
Pietro da Pavia, 392 n. 29
pigna, 56; see also *fons vitae*
Pisa, Baptistery: Nicola Pisano, pulpit, 104
— Camposanto: Tommaso Pisano, altarpiece, 383 n. 100
— Museo Civico
Cecco di Pietro, Vesperbild, 62, 183 f., Fig. 638
Gentile de Fabriano, Madonna, 236, Fig. 821
Pisan, Nativity with St. Bridget, 236, Fig. 756
— S. Martino: crucifix, 388 n. 27
Pisanello, Antonio, 75, 127; medals of, 54
Pliny, Natural History, 4 f., 25, 198, 288
Poitiers, Château de Jean de Berry, 37, 291 f., Fig. 421
— Palais, 24, 36 f.; Cheminée, 37, 74, 91, 97, Figs. 429, 434-437, 520, 521
Polo, Marco, Le Devisement du monde, 314, 403 n. 12
portraiture: cycles of kings, 74; effigies, 74; Flemish, 75, 78; Italo-French, 78; North Italian, 75; Tuscan, 75; see also Jean de Berry; Philippe le Hardi, etc.
Prague, Cathedral: Parler, Peter, and workshop, busts, 147, Fig. 592
— Cathedral, library: ms Cim. VI (Missal), 383 n. 119, Fig. 551
— Emmaus Cloister
Bohemian, Annunciation, 393 n. 59
Bohemian, Legend of Aracoeli, 397 n. 37, 397 n. 44
— Národní Galerie
Bohemian, Madonna of Strahov, 385 n. 160
Bohemian, Votive panel of Jan Očko of Vlašim, 127, Fig. 552
Master of the Vyšší Brod cycle, scenes from Life of Christ, 131, 383 n. 119, 385 n. 160
— Národní Muzeum
ms XVI D. 13 (Laus Mariae), 119, 130 f., 209, Figs. 566, 567
Liber viaticus of Johann von Neumarkt, 131, 138
Prato, Datini House: frescoes, 59

Prato, Galleria Comunale: Giovanni da Milano, Annunciation, 212, Fig. 707
Presentation of Christ, 121, 213 f., 238
Princeton, University Art Museum: Tuscan, triptych, 13th cent., 393 n. 59
— University Library
ms Garrett 16 (Johannes Climacus), 389 n. 33
ms Kane 44 (Suetonius), 397 n. 40
Priscian, 195, 288, 310
prophets and apostles, 135 f.
Pseudo-Anselm, Dialogus Beatae Mariae et Anselmi de Passione Domini, 383 n. 125
Pseudo-Aristotle, Secreta Secretorum, 229
Pseudo-Jacquemart, 12, 77, 85 ff., 93, 130, 151 ff., 157 f., 169, 175, 177, 179 ff., 186 ff., 193, 227, 249, 253 f., 257 ff., 275, 278, 281, 295 ff., 319 ff., 325, 328, 331 ff., 341, 379 n. 80, 390 n. 71
Pseudo-Jacquemart – Followers, 190, 265, 328 f., 341
Pseudo-Jacquemart – Workshop, 90, 212, 254, 259, 276, 332, 334
Pucelle, Jean, 6, 19 f., 23 f., 31, 87, 100 f., 104, 106, 114, 117, 119 f., 125, 128, 133, 141, 162 ff., 167 f., 171, 174, 181, 203 f., 211, 214, 216, 259, 273, 287, 297, 301, 383 n. 112, 389 n. 37, 389 n. 55, 403 n. 7; influence on Jacquemart, 153 f., 191; influence on Parement Master, 101, 119 ff.; influence on the Passion Master, 161 ff., 167 f., 171; manuscripts in Jean de Berry's library, 169, 273, 391 n. 113
Pucelle, Jean, and circle, influence on Pseudo-Jacquemart, 153, 187
Pucelle, Jean – Followers, 106 f., 160, 162, 182, 187, 220, 389 n. 56
Pucelle, Jean – Workshop, 19 f., 100, 106 f., 152 f., 159, 161 f., 178, 391 n. 110

Raoul de Presles: Fr. trans. of Bible, 288; prologue and Fr. trans. of Cité de Dieu, 96
Raoulet d'Auquetonville, 252
Raoulet d'Orléans, 21
Raphael – Follower, 397 n. 36
Raponde, Dino, 47
Raponde, house of the, 47
Raponde, Jacques, 8, 47, 49, 252, 362 n. 7
Raymond du Temple, 99
Regnault du Montet, 65
Reims Cathedral: Angels, 79; Last Judgment, 380 n. 20
René d'Anjou: and Angevin Coll., 29; Livre du cuer d'amour espris, 95 f.
Resurrection of Christ, 100, 187, 260, 367 n. 151
Richard II, King of England, 64 f.
Rince, Herman, 45
Riom, Palais de Jean de Berry, 36 f., 292
— Sainte-Chapelle, 37 ff., Fig. 426; windows, *ca.* 1470, 385 n. 4
Robert d'Anjou, 27
Roberto di Oderisio, 183 f.
Rome, Bibl. Casanatense: ms 459 (Historia Plantarum), 386 n. 31

— Biblioteca Vaticana
MANUSCRIPTS
Barb. lat. 4406 (Old St. Paul's, drawing after Cavallini's fresco), 390 n. 80
Barb. lat. 4426 (St. George and the Dragon, after Simone Martini), 25, Fig. 401

Rome, Biblioteca Vaticana (*contd.*)
  ms grec 1162 (Homilies of the Monk James), 56, Fig. 470
  ms lat. 50-51 (Bible), 49, 166, 194 ff., 201, 208, 224, 226, 228, 269, 291, 295 ff., 316 f., 342 f., Figs. 177, 178, 658, 661, 662
  ms lat. 2639 (Giovanni da Legnano, Trattati), 234, Fig. 818
  ms lat. 3550 (Planisio Bible), 11, Fig. 302
  ms Pal. lat. 1989 (Décaméron), 12, 15 ff., 357, 364 n. 75, Figs. 318, 319, 321
  ms Urb. lat. 603 (Breviary), 117, 164, 181, Fig. 356

— Guidi di Bagno Coll. (Dante, Commedia), 181, Fig. 403
— Musei Vaticani: Etruscan, votive figure, 127, Fig. 556
— Pinacoteca Vaticana
  Caravaggio, Entombment, 163
  Giovanni da Milano, Annunciation, 402 n. 62
  Lorenzetti, Ambrogio – Follower, Crucifixion, 104, Fig. 527
  Marchigian, Nativity, 397 n. 51
  Master of the Stefaneschi Altarpiece, polyptych, 387 n. 70, 396 n. 25
  Niccolo di Tommaso, Nativity with St. Bridget, 122, 217, Fig. 690
  Passeri, Giuseppe, Legend of Aracoeli, 234
  Romanesque, Last Judgment, 233
— S. Maria in Aracoeli
  Roman, Madonna and Two Angels (mosaic), 234, Fig. 819
  Romanesque, Altar of Aracoeli, 233 f., Fig. 814
— S. Maria Maggiore
  Rusuti, Filippo, mosaic façade, 24
  Torriti, Jacopo, Coronation of the Virgin (mosaic), 122, 215
— SS. Domenico e Sisto: Vanni, Lippo, Madonna and Child with Saints, 393 n. 49
— Vatican, Arch. S. Pietro: C. 129 (Codex of St. George), 25, Fig. 400
— Vatican, Stanza della segnatura: Raphael – Follower, Legend of Aracoeli, 397 n. 36
Rotterdam, Boymans Museum
  Florentine, Lamentation, 183, Fig. 642
  Mosan, triptych, *ca.* 1415 (formerly van Beuningen), 399 n. 1
Rouen, Cathedral: Passion of Christ, 380 n. 17, 380 n. 32
— St. Ouen: windows, 364 n. 88
Rousseau, Friar Jean, 381 n. 50a
Rudolph of Hapsburg, Archduke of Austria, portrait of, 75
Rusuti, Filippo, 24 f.
Rusuti, Giovanni, 25

Sacramento, Crocker Art Gallery: Bosch, Hieronymus, Passion scenes (drawing after), 402 n. 52
St. Denis, Cathedral: Beauneveu, André, tomb statues, 99 f., 102, 147, Figs. 589-591
St. Gall, Stiftsbibl.: Cod. 906, Swabian, Madonna with Writing Child, 393 n. 37
St. Sixt, Abbey Church: French, mitre, 100, Fig. 525
Salière du pavillon, 51
Sallust, 318
Salmon, Pierre, 9, 33, 45 f., 50, 73, 251, 299; Dialogues of, 33, 50, 73, 77, 86, 91, 254, 356, 377 n. 10, 405 n. 104
Salomone dei Grassi, 144
San Francisco, De Young Museum: Giovanni dal Ponte, Madonna, 384 n. 140

S. Gimignano, Collegiata
  Barna da Siena, Way to Calvary, 103, Fig. 538
  Bartolo di Fredi, Animals Entering the Ark, 24, 365 n. 115, Fig. 394
— Museo Civico: Coppo di Marcovaldo, Crucifix, 390 n. 88
— S. Pietro: Barna da Siena – Follower, Virgin and Child with Saints, 402 n. 55
San Marino, Huntington Library
  ms HM 1099 (Horae), 389 n. 62
  ms HM 1104 (Horae), 248
  ms HM 1142 (Horae), 354
  ms HM 1179 (Horae), 359
San Severino, Pinacoteca: Lorenzo da Sanseverino, Lamentation, 390 n. 92
Saumon, Michelet, 44, 54, 377 n. 36
sculpture, reign of Charles V, 99 f.
Secret des secrez, 311
Seneca: Epistles, 42; Livre des quatre vertus, 288
Sept psaumes de pénitence, 357
Serra, Pere, 24
Sesto family, 374 n. 239
Seville, Bibl. Colombina: ms 1717 (Horae), 357
Siena, Confraternità della Madonna: Sienese, Legend of Aracoeli, 14th cent., 397 n. 48
— Duomo: Nicola Pisano, pulpit, 125, 380 n. 20
— Duomo, Opera del Duomo: Duccio, Crucifixion, 19, 104 f., 216, 219, Fig. 339, Deposition, 217, Madonna in Majesty, 182
— Palazzo Pubblico
  Lorenzetti, Ambrogio, Good Government, 28, 212, 215, 219 ff., Figs. 686, 687, 703
  Simone Martini, Guidoriccio dei Fogliani, 219 f., Fig. 685, Madonna in Majesty, 119
  Vanni, Lippo, Battle of Val di Chiana, 394 n. 80
— Palazzo Pubblico, Cappella del Popolo: Domenico di Niccolo, Intarsia, 46, Fig. 553
— Palazzo Pubblico, Loggia: Lorenzetti, Ambrogio, Madonna, 387 n. 72
— Pinacoteca
  Bartolo di Fredi, Adoration of the Magi, 380 n. 111
  Duccio, Madonna of the Franciscans, 211
  Duccio – Follower, Madonna, 384 n. 131
  Lorenzetti, Ambrogio, Annunciation, 150, 166, 215, Fig. 628, landscapes, 220, 394 n. 84, Fig. 684
  Lorenzetti, Pietro – Follower, Allegory of Redemption, 221, Fig. 679
  Taddeo di Bartolo, Nativity, 390 n. 72
— S. Agostino: Simone Martini, altarpiece, 219, Fig. 680
— S. Domenico: Lorenzetti, Pietro, Madonna, 210, Fig. 697
— S. Francesco: Lorenzetti, Ambrogio, Madonna del Latte, 277
— S. Pietro a Ovile: Bartolommeo Bulgarini (?), Madonna and Child, 393 n. 49
signatures of artists, 6
Simone dei Crocefissi, 390 n. 92
Simone Martini, 25 f., 62, 103, 119, 121, 184, 205, 208, 215 ff., 219 f., 272, 275, 280, 303, 364 n. 87, 367 n. 140, 388 n. 24, 390 n. 97; influence on Jacquemart, 212, 215 ff., 219, 224, 272 f.
Sixtus IV, Pope, Capitol: collection of antiquities, 38
Sluter, Claus, 5, 18, 38, 45, 99, 280, 293, 305

Somme le roi, 363 n. 52, 399 n. 23

Songe véritable, Le, 34

spectacles, early use and representations, 5

Speculum Humanae Salvationis, 233 f.

Stanier, Imbert, 8, 47, 372 n. 157

Stefaneschi, Cardinal Gaetano, 25

Stimigliano, S. Maria in Vescovio: Roman, Crucifixion, 106, Fig. 529

Strasbourg, Cathedral
  French, Death of the Virgin, 107, Fig. 542
  French, Madonna on the screen, drawing after, 126

Strozzi, Zanobi, 229

Stuttgart, Württembergische Landesbibl.: cod. poet. 6 (Roman de la rose), 354

— Württembergische Staatsgalerie: Venetian, Legend of Aracoeli, 234, 397 n. 41, Fig. 820

Sudarium, 62

Suetonius, 288, 312

Suger, Abbot of St.-Denis, 69

Tacuinum Sanitatis, 50, 145, 386 n. 31

Taddeo di Bartolo, 390 n. 72

technical innovations, 123 f., 142, 225, 254

Temperance, 12

Temptation of Christ, 38

Terence, 10, 14, 49, 288, 294, 298, 303, 312, 315 f., 357, 359

Thamar, 4

Theseus, 59

Thomas de Saluces, Chevalier errant, 70, 307, 356

Three Quick and the Three Dead, 20, 187

Throne of Solomon, 187

Tiberius, medal of, 40, 46, 54 ff., 405 n. 84

Tommaso da Modena, 5, 23, 131, 302, 406 n. 125

Tommaso da Modena – Follower, 393 n. 59

Tommaso Pisano, 383 n. 100

Torriti, Jacopo, 122, 215

Toulouse, Bibl. municipale
  ms 90 (Missal), 382 n. 67
  ms 512 (Grandes chroniques), 359

Traini, Francesco, 366 n. 133

Trapani, Museo: Roberto di Oderisio, Vesperbild, 183 f.

Trento, Torre dell' Aquila: January, 172

Très Belles Heures de Notre-Dame, 107 ff., 155, 158 ff., 180, 247 ff., 252 ff., 256, 262 f. (see also Limbourgs; Paris, Bibl. nationale, ms nouv. acq. lat. 3093; Paris, Musée du Louvre, Cabinet des Dessins, RF 2022-24; Turin: Museo Civico and Royal Library); and Bohemian painting, 130 ff.; documents, 108 ff.; relationship with the Grandes Heures, 248 f.

Trésor des histoires, 9, 14, 94, 363 n. 44, 381 n. 51

Treviso, S. Niccolò
  Tommaso da Modena, frescoes, 5, Fig. 295
  Tommaso da Modena – Follower, Annunciation, 393 n. 59

Trinity, 62 f., 86, 91, 122, 152 f., 176 f., 190 f., 235, 243, 263, 276; see also Coronation of the Virgin

Troyes, Musée: French, Man of Sorrows, 63, 205, 218, 279, 375 n. 280, Fig. 694

Tübingen, Universitätsbibl.: Phillipps 1398 (Rituale Armenorum), 25, Fig. 396

Tucson, University of Arizona, Museum: Pacino di Bonaguida, Visitation, 394 n. 63

Turin, Museo Civico: Heures de Milan (portion of Très Belles Heures de Notre-Dame), 78, 80, 85 ff., 95, 105, 108 f., 122, 205, 214, 221, 236, 240, 247 ff., 317, 337 ff., 382 n. 71, 402 n. 57, Figs. 39, 41-50, 491, 537

— Museo Storico: Roi Modus, 317

— Royal Library (formerly)
  ms EV. 49 (Heures de Savoie), 109, 188, 317
  ms K. IV 29 (Heures de Turin – portion of Très Belles Heures de Notre-Dame), 63, 86, 108 ff., 122, 248, 250, 317, 337 ff., 400 n. 41, Figs. 29-31, 34, 35, 38

Turone, 232, 245

Uccello, Paolo, 306

Uccello, Paolo – Follower, 397 n. 51

'Ugolino Lorenzetti', see Bulgarini, Bartolommeo

Ugolino da Siena, 103, 364 n. 87

Ugolino di Vieri, 212

uomini famosi, 74

Urbino, Church of the Annunziata: Master of the Bellpuig Coronation, Coronation, Ascension of Christ, Bishop Saint, 24, Figs. 388, 391

— Pinacoteca: Simone Martini – Follower, Madonna, 365 n. 112

Valencia, Museo: Ferrer, Fray Bonifacio, retable, 398 n. 70

— Universidad: ms 1327 (Roman de la rose), 357

Valerius Maximus, 14, 288, 298, 303, 313, 318, 356 f., 360

Valois, libraries, 145, 287 ff.

Vanni, Lippo, 393 n. 49, 394 n. 80

Vasari, Giorgio, Lives, 74, 233 f.

Venice, Cini, Giorgio, Fondazione: Prophet (miniature), 231, 245, 344, Fig. 796

— S. Marco: Pala d'Oro, 142, Fig. 575

Venus, 58 f.

Verger de Soulas, 385 n. 13

Verona, Bibl. Capitolare: Corale 5, 245, Fig. 803

— Castelvecchio: Turone, altarpiece, 232, Fig. 732

— S. Anastasia: Altichiero, Madonna with Giorgio Cavalli, 210, Fig. 696

Veronica, see Sudarium

Versailles, Musée: French, copy of portrait of Philippe le Hardi, 68, 71, 75, Fig. 508

Vesperbild, 15, 17, 62, 183 ff., 189, 239

Viaut, Nicolas, 41

Vich, Diocesan Museum: Catalan, Antependium, 151, Fig. 586

Vie de nostre bénoit sauveur Jésus Christ, 289 f.

Vie des Pères, 251

Vienna, Albertina
  Florentine, Portrait of a Monk (drawing), 78
  Styrian, Flight into Egypt and Baptism of Christ (drawing), 383 n. 123

— Diöcesan-Museum: Austrian, portrait of Archduke Rudolf IV, 75

— Kunsthistorisches Museum
  French, Flagellation (enamel), 394 n. 78
  Gemma Augustea, 53

Vienna, Nationalbibliothek
    MANUSCRIPTS
  ms 1182 (Gospels of John of Troppau), 119, 396 n. 23
  ms 1855 (Horae), 357, 376 n. 312, 405 n. 89
  ms 1921 (Prayer Book of Queen Joanna), 27, Figs. 415-418
  ms 2048-49, 245, Fig. 802
  ms 2569 (Chroniques de Normandie), 357
  ms 2615 (Livre du Chevalier de la Tour), 357
  ms 2653 (Boethius, De consolatione philosophiae), 357
  ms 2656 (Horae), 355
  ms ser. nov. 2613 (Horae), 355, 359

Villani, Filippo, Elogium, 308
Villeneuve-lès-Avignon, Chartreuse: Matteo Giovanetti, fres-
    coes, 25, 301
Vincent de Beauvais, Mirouer historial, 49, 291, 294, 310, 356,
    392 n. 20a, 403 n. 21
Virgil: Bucolics, 38, 288, 303; Bucolics, Georgics and Aeneid,
    189, 298, 360; Eclogues, 57; Georgics and Bucolics, 358;
    owned by Petrarch, see Milan, Bibl. Ambrosiana
Virgin Mary: Arrival in Bethlehem, 28; Glikophilousa, 20; life
    of (see Annunciation; Birth of the Virgin; Death of the
    Virgin, etc.); as Virgo lactifera, 128
Virgin Mary, see also Madonna with the Cradle, etc.
Visconti, Gian Galeazzo, 27, 287, 403 n. 3; portraits of, 75
Visconti, library of, 145, 287, 303, 353, 403 n. 3
Visconti, Valentina, Duchess of Orléans, 34, 145, 290, 296, 301
Visitation, 121, 170 f., 179, 213, 231, 237, 265, 275, 289
Vitale da Bologna, 18, 123, 239
Vitruvius, De Architectura, 360
Volterra, Palazzo dei Priori: Tuscan, Vesperbild, 183, Fig. 639

Warsaw, Bibl. Narodowa: ms lat. Q.v.I.111 (Calendar), 230 f.,
    344, Figs. 719-723

Washington, National Gallery
  Byzantine, Madonna, 387 n. 71, 396 n. 25
  Duccio, Nativity, 364 n. 79
Way to Calvary, 102 f., 163, 185, 215 ff., 240, 242, 271 ff., 381
    n. 62
Weyden, Roger van der, 78, 163, 186, 253
Whereabouts unknown
  Ark of the Covenant (miniature), formerly Jacob Hirsch, New
    York, 359
  Bréviaire de Cathérine de Valois, 205, Figs. 656, 657
  Dominic, St. (miniature), formerly Antiquariato Libraio
    Radaeli, Milan, 231, 245, 344, Fig. 797
  Florentine, Nativity (embroidery), 60, Fig. 447
  Giotto – Follower, Crucifixion, 105, Fig. 530
  Heures de Jeanne de Navarre, 20, 87, 104, 106, 120, 139, 152,
    161 ff., 167, 174, 179, 187, 204, 381 n. 62, 382 n. 85, Figs.
    341, 345-348, 350, 544, 601
  Horae, 359 f.
  Horae, Bedford and Boucicaut followers, 69, Fig. 516
  Horae, formerly Ranshaw Coll., 359
  Metz, Madonna of Humility, 126 f., 277, Fig. 549
  See also London, Sotheby
Wiesbaden, Staatsarchiv: Religious treatise of 1410, 399 n. 23
wild men, 278
William IV of Holland and Bavaria, 109
Winchester, Library of the Bishop: Fragment from Heures de
    Savoie, 317; see also Turin, Royal Library, ms E.V. 49
Wolfenbüttel, Landesbibl.: ms 1.5.3.1. Aug. fol. (Livre des
    propriétés), 358
workshop practice, 10 ff.; graphic instructions, 10 ff.; written
    instructions, 12 f.

Zebo (or Zanobi) da Firenze, 229; see also the Master of the
    Brussels Initials
Zeloni, Gerolamo, 376 n. 328